GW00492626

HARRAP

SUPER-MINI
GERMAN
DICTIONARY
English-German/German-English

First published in Great Britain 2001
by Chambers Harrap Publishers Ltd
7 Hopetoun Crescent, Edinburgh EH7 4AY

© Havas Éducation Référence 2001

ISBN 0 245 60688 2

Für diese Ausgabe / For this edition

Patricia Abbou   Karin Albert   Ralf Brockmeier
Marc Chabrier   Monika Hofmann   Frances Illingworth
Volker Lückenkemper   Christina Reinicke   Johannes Schliesser

Für die Erstausgabe / For the first edition

Patrick White   Joaquín Blasco   Monika Hofmann   Louise Richmond
Anne Thompson   Stephanie Geiges   Ulla Knodt
Elke Weiss-Cowen   Roswitha Morris   Neil Morris
Dagmar Förtsch   Hildegard Pesch   Ruth Noble

Printed and bound in Great Britain by Omnia Books Ltd, Glasgow

HARRAP

SUPER-MINI
GERMAN
DICTIONARY
English-German/German-English

HARRAP

LANDESKUNDLICHE EINTRÄGE	CULTURAL NOTES
Abitur	Albert Hall
Autobahn	A level
Bad	April Fools' Day
Bayreuther Festspiele	beer
Berliner Mauer	bingo
Bier	Boxing Day
Brot	Buckingham Palace
Bundesland	Burns' Night
Café	Cajun
Dialekt	ceilidh
Ferienbeginn	Channel Tunnel
Hansestadt	Crown Jewels
Imbissstube	diner
Kaffeehaus	Downing Street
Kanton	Edinburgh Festival
Karneval	Eisteddfod
Kneipe	fete
Krankenkasse	fish and chips
Lebkuchen	Florida Keys
Maibaum	GCSE
Nikolaus	Great Britain
Nummernschild	Guy Fawkes Night
Oktoberfest	Halloween
Osterhase	Highland Games
Passionsspiele	Hollywood
Pension	Houses of Parliament
Prater	jumble sale
Reeperbahn	mall
Reformhaus	Manhattan
Reichstag	Mount Rushmore
Salzburger Festspiele	national park
Schultüte	New Year
Schützenfest	pantomime
Silvester	pub
Stammtisch	royal family
Sylt	Stars and Stripes
Tag der Deutschen Einheit	Statue of Liberty
Trafik	Stratford-upon-Avon
Umweltbewusstsein	Thanksgiving
Universitätsstadt	Tower Bridge
Verein	Westminster
Waldsterben	whisky
Wattenmeer	Windsor Castle
Weihnachten	yellow lines
Weihnachtsmarkt	York Minster
Wein	
Wurst	

Dieses Wörterbuch im praktischen Kleinformat richtet sich vor allem an Anfänger und Reisende.

Über 40 000 Übersetzungen von mehr als 35 000 Stichwörtern und Wendungen geben daher nicht nur Auskunft über den allgemeinen Wortschatz, sondern helfen auch, Schilder und Speisekarten zu verstehen.

Klare typografische Aufmachung und benutzerfreundliches Format erleichtern die Orientierung im Wörterbuch. Zahlreiche Bedeutungsanzeiger ermöglichen ein sicheres Auffinden der gewünschten Übersetzung. Viele Stichwörter werden durch Beispielsätze erläutert.

Das Wörterbuch Englisch-Deutsch ist handlich, zuverlässig und übersichtlich und wird damit zum idealen Ratgeber und Reisebegleiter.

Vorschläge, die zu einer weiteren Verbesserung des Wörterbuchs beitragen können, sind jederzeit willkommen. „Good luck!"

DER HERAUSGEBER

This handy and reliable English-German dictionary has been designed with beginners and travellers in mind.

With over 35,000 references and 40,000 translations, this new dictionary gives thorough coverage of general vocabulary plus extensive treatment of the language found on street signs and menus.

Clear sense markers are provided throughout, while special emphasis has been placed on basic words, with many examples of usage and a particularly user-friendly layout.

Easy to use and comprehensive, this handy book packs a lot of wordpower for users at school, at home and on the move. "Viel Spaß", and don't hesitate to send us your comments.

THE PUBLISHER

ABKÜRZUNGEN

ABBREVIATIONS

Akkusativ	*A*	accusative
Abkürzung	*abk /abbr*	abbreviation
abwertend	*abw*	pejorative
Adjektiv	*adj*	adjective
Adverb	*adv*	adverb
amerikanisches Englisch	*Am*	American English
amtssprachlich, formell	*amt*	administrative, formal
Anatomie	*ANAT*	anatomy
Kfz-Technik	*AUT(O)*	automobile, cars
Hilfsverb	*aux*	auxiliary
britisches Englisch	*Br*	British English
Handel	*COMM*	commerce, business
Komparativ	*compar*	comparative
Datenverarbeitung	*COMPUT*	computers
Konjunktion	*conj*	conjunction
Verlaufsform	*cont*	continuous
Kochkunst	*CULIN*	culinary, cooking
Dativ	*D*	dative
Determinant	*det*	determiner
Datenverarbeitung	*EDV*	computers
etwas	*etw*	
Interjektion	*excl*	exclamation
Femininum	*f*	feminine
umgangssprachlich	*fam*	informal
übertragene Bedeutung	*fig*	figurative
Finanzen	*FIN*	finance, financial
gehoben	*fml*	formal
nicht trennbar	*fus*	inseparable
Genitiv	*G*	genitive
gehoben	*geh*	formal
generell	*gen*	generally
Grammatik	*GRAMM*	grammar
umgangssprachlich	*inf*	informal
Interjektion	*interj*	exclamation
unveränderlich	*inv*	invariable
jemand	*jd*	someone (nominative)

jemandem	*jm*	someone (dative)
jemanden	*jn*	someone (accusative)
jemandes	*js*	someone (genitive)
Rechtswesen	*JUR*	juridical, legal
Komparativ	*komp*	comparative
Konjunktion	*konj*	conjunction
Kochkunst	*KÜCHE*	culinary, cooking
Mathematik	*MATH*	mathematics
Medizin	*MED*	medecine
Militärwesen	*MIL*	military
Musik	*MUS*	music
Schifffahrt	*NAVIG*	nautical, maritime
Norddeutsch	*Norddt*	northern German
Neutrum	*nt*	neuter noun (countries and towns) not used with an article
Zahlwort	*num*	numeral
	o.s.	oneself
Österreichisch	*Österr*	Austrian German
abwertend	*pej*	pejorative
Plural	*pl*	plural
Politik	*POL*	politics
Partizip Perfekt	*pp*	past participle
Präposition	*präp*	preposition
Präsens	*präs*	present
Präteritum	*prät*	preterite
Präposition	*prep*	preposition
Pronomen	*pron*	pronoun
Vergangenheitsform	*pt*	past tense
Warenzeichen	®	registered trademark
reflexives Verb	*ref*	reflexive verb
Religion	*RELIG*	religion
	sb	someone, somebody
Subjekt	*sbj*	subject
Schule	*SCHULE/SCH*	school
Schweizerdeutsch	*Schweiz*	Swiss German
Singular	*sg*	singular
	sthg	something

Süddeutsch	*Süddt*	southern German
Superlativ	*superl*	superlative
Technik, Technologie	*TECH*	technology
Fernsehen	*TV*	television
unregelmäßig	*unr*	irregular
Verb	*v/vb*	verb
intransitives Verb	*vi*	intransitive verb
unpersönliches Verb	*vimp/v impers*	impersonal verb
vor Substantiv	*vor Subst*	before noun
transitives Verb	*vt*	transitive verb
vulgär	*vulg*	vulgar
kulturelle Entsprechung	≈	cultural equivalent
Trennbarkeit des deutschen Verbs			indicates separable German verb

ENGLISCHE KOMPOSITA

Als Komposita werden aus mehreren Wörtern bestehende Einheiten bezeichnet, die eine eigenständige Bedeutung haben, wie z. B. **point of view, kiss of life, virtual reality** und **West Indies.** Sie sind daher in diesem Wörterbuch als eigene Einträge alphabetisch eingeordnet; so folgt das Kompositum **blood test** dem Eintrag **bloodshot,** der seinerseits hinter **blood pressure** steht.

WARENZEICHEN

Als Warenzeichen geschützte Wörter sind in diesem Wörterbuch durch das Zeichen ® gekennzeichnet. Die Markierung mit diesem Symbol, oder sein Fehlen, hat keinen Einfluss auf die Rechtskräftigkeit eines Warenzeichens.

ENGLISH COMPOUNDS

A compound is a word or expression which has a single meaning but is made up of more than one word, e.g. **point of view, kiss of life, virtual reality** and **West Indies.** It is a feature of this dictionary that English compounds appear in the A–Z list in strict alphabetical order. The compound **blood test** will therefore come after **bloodshot** which itself follows **blood pressure**.

TRADEMARKS

Words considered to be trademarks have been designated in this dictionary by the symbol ®. However, neither the presence nor the absence of such designation should be regarded as affecting the legal status of any trademark.

Hinweise zum Deutschen

ATTRIBUTIV GEBRAUCHTE ADJEKTIVE

Adjektive dieser Art werden in ihrer femininen Form angegeben, direkt gefolgt von den Endungen des Maskulinums und des Neutrums; z. B.: **letzte, -r, -s** (eine letzte Zigarette, ein letzter Kuss, ein letztes Mal).

SUBSTANTIVIERTE ADJEKTIVE

Die substantivierten Adjektive sind wie alle anderen Substantive mit dem bestimmten Artikel aufgeführt. In Verbindung mit einem unbestimmten Artikel verändert sich daher die Endung entsprechend dem Genus; z. B.: **Angestellte** der, die wird zu **ein Angestellter** und **eine Angestellte**.

GENUS DER SUBSTANTIVE IN ZUSAMMENGESETZTEN AUSDRÜCKEN (ALS ÜBERSETZUNGEN)

Wenn das Substantiv von einem Adjektiv begleitet wird, trägt dieses das Genus des Substantives; z. B. zeigt die Übersetzung von **first class**, „erste Klasse", durch die feminine Endung des Adjektives an, dass das Wort **Klasse** ein Femininum ist.

RECHTSCHREIBUNG

Dieses Wörterbuch berücksichtigt die Regeln der neuen deutschen Rechtschreibung.

Notes on German

ADJECTIVES ONLY USED ATTRIBUTIVELY

With German adjectives of this type, the feminine form is shown first, followed by the masculine and neuter endings, e.g. **letzte, -r, -s** (eine letzte Zigarette, ein letzter Kuss, ein letztes Mal).

ADJECTIVES USED AS NOUNS

Nominalized German adjectives are, like all other nouns, labelled with the definite article. When used with an indefinite article, the ending of this type of noun changes according to the gender, e.g. **Angestellte** der, die becomes **ein Angestellter** and **eine Angestellte**.

GENDER OF COMPOUND NOUNS IN TRANSLATIONS

When a noun translation is accompanied by an adjective, the adjective ending indicates the gender of the noun. For example, the translation of **first class** is **"erste Klasse"**, where the "e" ending of the adjective shows that **"Klasse"** is feminine.

SPELLING

This dictionary complies with the new rules for German spelling.

LAUTSCHRIFT

Deutsche Vokale

[a]	Affe, Banane
[ɑ:]	Arzt, Antrag
[e]	Beton
[e:]	edel
[ɛ]	echt, Händler
[ɛ:]	Rätsel, Dessert
[ə]	Aktie
[i:]	Vier
[i]	Radio
[ɪ]	Winter
[o]	Melodie
[o:]	apropos
[ɔ]	sollen
[ø]	ökologisch
[ø:]	Öl
[œ]	Köchin, Pumps
[u]	Kuvert, aktuell
[u:]	Kuh
[ʊ]	Kunst
[y]	Büchse, System
[y:]	Tür

Deutsche Diphthonge

[aɪ]	Deichsel
[aʊ]	Auge
[ɔy]	Euro

Deutsche Nasale

[ã]	Chanson
[ã:]	Abonnement
[ɛ̃]	Pointe
[ɔ̃]	Chanson

Halbvokale

Jubiläum	[j]
Hardware	[w]

Konsonanten

Baby	[b]
Chemie	[ç]
Achse, Kaviar	[k]
Duett, Medien	[d]

PHONETIC TRANSCRIPTION

English vowels

[ɑ:]	barn, car, laugh
[æ]	pat, bag, mad
[ɒ]	pot, log
[e]	pet, tend
[ɜ:]	burn, learn, bird
[ə]	mother, suppose
[i:]	bean, weed
[ɪ]	pit, big, rid
[ɔ:]	born, lawn
[u:]	loop, loose
[ʌ]	run, cut
[ʊ]	put, full

English diphthongs

[aɪ]	buy, light, aisle
[aʊ]	now, shout, town
[eɪ]	bay, late, great
[ɔɪ]	boy, foil
[əʊ]	no, road, blow
[ɪə]	peer, fierce, idea
[eə]	pair, bear, share
[ʊə]	poor, sure, tour

Semi-vowels

you, spaniel
wet, why, twin

Consonants

bottle, bib

come, kitchen
dog, did

XI

German	IPA	English
Gin	[dʒ]	jet, fridge
Fantasie, Vier	[f]	fib, physical
Algerien, gut	[g]	gag, great
Hobby	[h]	how, perhaps
alphabetisch, Laser	[l]	little, help
Material, Alarm	[m]	metal, comb
November, Angabe	[n]	night, dinner
singen	[ŋ]	sung, parking
Pony, Pappe	[p]	pop, people
Apfel	[pf]	
Revue, rot	[r]	right, carry
Slalom, Soße	[s]	seal, peace
Stadion, Schule	[ʃ]	sheep, machine
Toast, Volt	[t]	train, tip
Konversation	[ts]	
Chili	[tʃ]	chain, wretched
	[θ]	think, fifth
	[ð]	this, with
Vase, Wagen	[v]	vine, livid
Macht, lachen	[x]	
Soße, Sonne	[z]	zip, his
Etage	[ʒ]	usual, measure

Die Betonung der deutschen Stichwörter wird mit einem Punkt für einen kurzen betonten Vokal (z. B. Berg) und mit einem Strich für einen langen betonten Vokal (z. B. Magen) angegeben.

German headwords have the stress marked either by a dot for a short stressed vowel (e.g. Berg) or by an underscore for a long stressed vowel (e.g. Magen).

Der Hauptton eines englischen Wortes ist durch ein vorangestelltes [ˈ] markiert, der Nebenton durch ein vorangestelltes [ˌ].

The symbol [ˈ] indicates that the following syllable carries primary stress and the symbol [ˌ] that the following syllable carries secondary stress.

Das Zeichen [ʳ] zeigt in der englischen Fonetik an, dass der Endkonsonant "r" ausgesprochen wird, wenn das folgende Wort mit einem Vokal beginnt. Im amerikanischen Englisch wird dieses "r" so gut wie immer mitgesprochen.

The symbol [ʳ] in English phonetics indicates that the final "r" is pronounced only when followed by a word beginning with a vowel. Note that it is nearly always pronounced in American English.

ENGLISH IRREGULAR VERBS
UNREGELMÄSSIGE ENGLISCHE VERBEN

Infinitive	Past Tense	Past Participle	Infinitive	Past Tense	Past Participle
arise	arose	arisen	deal	dealt	dealt
awake	awoke	awoken	dig	dug	dug
be	was/ were	been	do	did	done
			draw	drew	drawn
bear	bore	born(e)	dream	dreamed/ dreamt	dreamed/ dreamt
beat	beat	beaten			
begin	began	begun	drink	drank	drunk
bend	bent	bent	drive	drove	driven
bet	bet/ betted	bet/ betted	eat	ate	eaten
			fall	fell	fallen
bid	bid	bid	feed	fed	fed
bind	bound	bound	feel	felt	felt
bite	bit	bitten	fight	fought	fought
bleed	bled	bled	find	found	found
blow	blew	blown	fling	flung	flung
break	broke	broken	fly	flew	flown
breed	bred	bred	forget	forgot	forgotten
bring	brought	brought	freeze	froze	frozen
build	built	built	get	got	got (Am gotten)
burn	burnt/ burned	burnt/ burned			
burst	burst	burst	give	gave	given
buy	bought	bought	go	went	gone
can	could	–	grind	ground	ground
cast	cast	cast	grow	grew	grown
catch	caught	caught	hang	hung/ hanged	hung/ hanged
choose	chose	chosen	have	had	had
come	came	come	hear	heard	heard
cost	cost	cost	hide	hid	hidden
creep	crept	crept	hit	hit	hit
cut	cut	cut	hold	held	held

Infinitive	Past Tense	Past Participle	Infinitive	Past Tense	Past Participle
hurt	hurt	hurt	ride	rode	ridden
keep	kept	kept	ring	rang	rung
kneel	knelt/ kneeled	knelt/ kneeled	rise	rose	risen
			run	ran	run
know	knew	known	saw	sawed	sawn
lay	laid	laid	say	said	said
lead	led	led	see	saw	seen
lean	leant/ leaned	leant/ leaned	seek	sought	sought
			sell	sold	sold
leap	leapt/ leaped	leapt/ leaped	send	sent	sent
			set	set	set
learn	learnt/ learned	learnt/ learned	shake	shook	shaken
			shall	should	–
leave	left	left	shed	shed	shed
lend	lent	lent	shine	shone	shone
let	let	let	shoot	shot	shot
lie	lay	lain	show	showed	shown
light	lit/ lighted	lit/ lighted	shrink	shrank	shrunk
			shut	shut	shut
lose	lost	lost	sing	sang	sung
make	made	made	sink	sank	sunk
may	might	–	sit	sat	sat
mean	meant	meant	sleep	slept	slept
meet	met	met	slide	slid	slid
mow	mowed	mown/ mowed	sling	slung	slung
			smell	smelt/ smelled	smelt/ smelled
pay	paid	paid			
put	put	put	sow	sowed	sown/ sowed
quit	quit/ quitted	quit/ quitted			
			speak	spoke	spoken
read	read	read	speed	sped/ speeded	sped/ speeded
rid	rid	rid			

Infinitive	Past Tense	Past Participle	Infinitive	Past Tense	Past Participle
spell	spelt/ spelled	spelt/ spelled	swell	swelled	swollen/ swelled
spend	spent	spent	swim	swam	swum
spill	spilt/ spilled	spilt/ spilled	swing	swung	swung
spin	spun	spun	take	took	taken
spit	spat	spat	teach	taught	taught
split	split	split	tear	tore	torn
spoil	spoiled/ spoilt	spoiled/ spoilt	tell	told	told
spread	spread	spread	think	thought	thought
spring	sprang	sprung	throw	threw	thrown
stand	stood	stood	tread	trod	trodden
steal	stole	stolen	wake	woke/ waked	woken/ waked
stick	stuck	stuck	wear	wore	worn
sting	stung	stung	weave	wove/ weaved	woven/ weaved
stink	stank	stunk	weep	wept	wept
strike	struck	struck/ stricken	win	won	won
			wind	wound	wound
swear	swore	sworn	wring	wrung	wrung
sweep	swept	swept	write	wrote	written

EINIGE UNREGELMÄSSIGE DEUTSCHE VERBEN
COMMON GERMAN IRREGULAR VERBS

Infinitiv	Präsens	Präteritum	Perfekt
beginnen	beginnt	begann	hat begonnen
beißen	beißt	biss	hat gebissen
bitten	bittet	bat	hat gebeten
bleiben	bleibt	blieb	ist geblieben
bringen	bringt	brachte	hat gebracht
denken	denkt	dachte	hat gedacht
dürfen	darf	durfte	hat gedurft/dürfen
essen	isst	aß	hat gegessen
fahren	fährt	fuhr	hat/ist gefahren
finden	findet	fand	hat gefunden
fliegen	fliegt	flog	hat/ist geflogen
fließen	fließt	floss	ist geflossen
geben	gibt	gab	hat gegeben
gehen	geht	ging	ist gegangen
gelten	gilt	galt	hat gegolten
geschehen	geschieht	geschah	ist geschehen
gießen	gießt	goss	hat gegossen
greifen	greift	griff	hat gegriffen
haben	hat	hatte	hat gehabt
halten	hält	hielt	hat gehalten
heben	hebt	hob	hat gehoben
heißen	heißt	hieß	hat geheißen
helfen	hilft	half	hat geholfen
kennen	kennt	kannte	hat gekannt
kommen	kommt	kam	ist gekommen
können	kann	konnte	hat können/gekonnt
lassen	lässt	ließ	hat gelassen/lassen
laufen	läuft	lief	hat/ist gelaufen
leihen	leiht	lieh	hat geliehen
lesen	liest	las	hat gelesen
liegen	liegt	lag	hat gelegen
lügen	lügt	log	hat gelogen
messen	misst	maß	hat gemessen
mögen	mag	mochte	hat gemocht/mögen
müssen	muss	musste	hat gemusst/müssen
nehmen	nimmt	nahm	hat genommen
nennen	nennt	nannte	hat genannt

Infinitiv	Präsens	Präteritum	Perfekt
raten	rät	riet	hat geraten
reißen	reißt	riss	hat/ist gerissen
rennen	rennt	rannte	ist gerannt
riechen	riecht	roch	hat gerochen
rufen	ruft	rief	hat gerufen
schieben	schiebt	schob	hat geschoben
schießen	schießt	schoss	hat/ist geschossen
schlafen	schläft	schlief	hat geschlafen
schlagen	schlägt	schlug	hat/ist geschlagen
schließen	schließt	schloss	hat geschlossen
schneiden	schneidet	schnitt	hat geschnitten
schreiben	schreibt	schrieb	hat geschrieben
schreien	schreit	schrie	hat geschrie(e)n
schwimmen	schwimmt	schwamm	hat/ist geschwommen
sehen	sieht	sah	hat gesehen
sein	ist	war	ist gewesen
singen	singt	sang	hat gesungen
sitzen	sitzt	saß	hat gesessen
sprechen	spricht	sprach	hat gesprochen
springen	springt	sprang	hat/ist gesprungen
stehen	steht	stand	hat gestanden
stehlen	stiehlt	stahl	hat gestohlen
sterben	stirbt	starb	ist gestorben
stoßen	stößt	stieß	hat/ist gestoßen
streiten	streitet	stritt	hat gestritten
tragen	trägt	trug	hat getragen
treffen	trifft	traf	hat getroffen
treten	tritt	trat	hat getreten
trinken	trinkt	trank	hat getrunken
tun	tut	tat	hat getan
verlieren	verliert	verlor	hat verloren
waschen	wäscht	wusch	hat gewaschen
werden	wird	wurde	ist geworden/worden
werfen	wirft	warf	hat geworfen
wissen	weiß	wusste	hat gewusst
wollen	will	wollte	hat gewollt/wollen

ENGLISH–GERMAN
ENGLISCH–DEUTSCH

A

a [*stressed* eɪ, *unstressed* ə] *indef art* 1. *(gen)* ein (eine) ; **a woman** eine Frau ; **a restaurant** ein Restaurant ; **a friend** ein Freund ; **an apple** ein Apfel ; **I'm a doctor** ich bin Arzt.

2. *(instead of the number one)* ein (eine) ; **a hundred** hundert ; **a hundred and twenty** einhundertzwanzig ; **for a week** eine Woche lang.

3. *(in prices, ratios)* pro ; **£2 a kilo** 2 Pfund pro Kilo.

AA *n* (*Br* : *abbr of* Automobile Association) Britischer Automobilclub, ≃ ADAC *der*.

aback [ə'bæk] *adv* : **to be taken ~** verblüfft sein.

abandon [ə'bændən] *vt* *(plan)* aufgeben ; *(place, person)* verlassen.

abattoir ['æbətwɑːʳ] *n* Schlachthof *der*.

abbey ['æbɪ] *n* Abtei *die*.

abbreviation [ə,briːvɪ'eɪʃn] *n* Abkürzung *die*.

abdomen ['æbdəmən] *n* Unterleib *der*.

abide [ə'baɪd] *vt* : **I can't ~ him** ich kann ihn nicht ausstehen.

■ **abide by** *vt fus* *(rule, law)* befolgen.

ability [ə'bɪlətɪ] *n* Fähigkeit *die*.

able ['eɪbl] *adj* fähig ; **to be ~ to do sthg** etw tun können.

abnormal [æb'nɔːml] *adj* anormal.

aboard [ə'bɔːd] *adv* & *prep* an Bord (+*G*).

abode [ə'bəʊd] *n* *(fml)* Wohnsitz *der*.

abolish [ə'bɒlɪʃ] *vt* abschaffen.

aborigine [,æbə'rɪdʒənɪ] *n* Ureinwohner *der*.

abort [ə'bɔːt] *vt* *(give up)* abbrechen.

abortion [ə'bɔːʃn] *n* Abtreibung *die*.

about [ə'baʊt] *adv* 1. *(approximately)* ungefähr, etwa ; **~ 50** ungefähr 50 ; **at ~ six o'clock** gegen sechs Uhr.

2. *(referring to place)* herum ; **to walk ~** herumlaufen.

3. *(on the point of)* : **to be ~ to do sthg** im Begriff sein, etw zu tun.

◆ *prep* 1. *(concerning)* um, über ; **a book ~ Scotland** ein Buch über Schottland ; **what's it ~?** worum geht's? ; **what ~ a drink?** wie wär's mit etwas zu trinken?

2. *(referring to place)* herum ; **there are lots of hotels ~ the town** es gibt viele Hotels in der Stadt.

above [ə'bʌv] *prep* *(higher than)* über (+*A,D*) ; *(more than)* über

(+A). ◆ adv oben ; **children aged ten and ~** Kinder ab zehn Jahren ; **~ all** vor allem.

abroad [ə'brɔːd] adv im Ausland ; **to go ~** ins Ausland fahren.

abrupt [ə'brʌpt] adj (sudden) abrupt.

abscess ['æbses] n Abszess der.

absence ['æbsəns] n Abwesenheit die.

absent ['æbsənt] adj abwesend.

absent-minded [-'maɪndɪd] adj zerstreut.

absolute ['æbsəluːt] adj absolut.

absolutely [adv 'æbsəluːtlɪ, excl ‚æbsə'luːtlɪ] adv absolut. ◆ excl genau!

absorb [əb'sɔːb] vt (liquid) aufl saugen.

absorbed [əb'sɔːbd] adj : **to be ~ in sthg** in etw vertieft sein.

absorbent [əb'sɔːbənt] adj saugfähig.

abstain [əb'steɪn] vi : **to ~ (from)** sich enthalten (+G).

absurd [əb'sɜːd] adj absurd.

ABTA ['æbtə] n Verband britischer Reisebüros.

abuse [n ə'bjuːs, vb ə'bjuːz] n (insults) Beschimpfungen pl ; (misuse, maltreatment) Missbrauch der. ◆ vt (insult) beschimpfen ; (misuse, maltreat) missbrauchen.

abusive [ə'bjuːsɪv] adj beleidigend.

AC abbr = **alternating current**.

academic [‚ækə'demɪk] adj akademisch. ◆ n Akademiker der (-in die).

academy [ə'kædəmɪ] n Akademie die.

accelerate [ək'seləreɪt] vi beschleunigen.

accelerator [ək'seləreɪtə'] n Gaspedal das.

accent ['æksent] n Akzent der.

accept [ək'sept] vt (offer, gift, invitation) anlnehmen ; (blame) auf sich nehmen ; (fact, truth) akzeptieren ; (story) glauben ; (responsibility) übernehmen.

acceptable [ək'septəbl] adj akzeptabel.

access ['ækses] n Zugang der.

accessible [ək'sesəbl] adj (place) erreichbar.

accessories [ək'sesərɪz] npl (extras) Zubehör das ; (fashion items) Accessoires pl.

access road n Zufahrtsstraße die.

accident ['æksɪdənt] n Unfall der ; (chance) Zufall der ; **by ~** zufällig.

accidental [‚æksɪ'dentl] adj zufällig.

accident insurance n Unfallversicherung die.

accident-prone adj : **to be ~** ein Pechvogel sein.

acclimatize [ə'klaɪmətaɪz] vi sich akklimatisieren.

accommodate [ə'kɒmədeɪt] vt unterlbringen.

accommodation [ə‚kɒmə'deɪʃn] n Unterkunft die.

accommodations [ə‚kɒmə'deɪʃnz] npl (Am) = **accommodation**.

accompany [ə'kʌmpənɪ] vt begleiten.

accomplish [ə'kʌmplɪʃ] vt erreichen.

accord [ə'kɔːd] n : **of one's own ~** von selbst.

accordance [ə'kɔːdəns] n : in ~ with gemäß (+D).

according to [ə'kɔːdɪŋ-] prep laut (+G,D).

accordion [ə'kɔːdɪən] n Akkordeon das.

account [ə'kaunt] n (at bank, shop) Konto das ; (report) Bericht der ; to take into ~ berücksichtigen ; on no ~ auf keinen Fall ; on ~ of wegen. ▪ **account for** vt fus (explain) erklären ; (constitute) auslmachen.

accountant [ə'kauntənt] n Buchhalter der (-in die).

account number n Kontonummer die.

accumulate [ə'kjuːmjʊleɪt] vt anlsammeln.

accurate ['ækjʊrət] adj genau.

accuse [ə'kjuːz] vt : to ~ sb of sthg jn einer Sache beschuldigen.

accused [ə'kjuːzd] n : the ~ der/die Angeklagte.

ace [eɪs] n As das.

ache [eɪk] vi wehltun. ◆ n Schmerzen pl.

achieve [ə'tʃiːv] vt erreichen.

acid ['æsɪd] adj sauer. ◆ n Säure die ; (inf : drug) Acid das.

acid rain n saurer Regen.

acknowledge [ək'nɒlɪdʒ] vt (accept) anlerkennen ; (admit) einlgestehen ; (letter) den Empfang (+G) bestätigen.

acne ['ækni] n Akne die.

acorn ['eɪkɔːn] n Eichel die.

acoustic [ə'kuːstɪk] adj akustisch.

acquaintance [ə'kweɪntəns] n (person) Bekannte der, die.

acquire [ə'kwaɪə'] vt erwerben.

acre ['eɪkə'] n = 4046,9 m², ≃ 40 Ar.

acrobat ['ækrəbæt] n Akrobat der (-in die).

across [ə'krɒs] prep über (+A,D). ◆ adv hinüber, herüber ; (in crossword) waagerecht ; ~ the street auf der anderen Straßenseite ; 10 miles ~ 10 Meilen breit ; ~ from gegenüber von.

acrylic [ə'krɪlɪk] n Acryl das.

act [ækt] vi (do something) handeln ; (behave) sich benehmen ; (in play, film) spielen. ◆ n (action) Handlung die ; (POL) Gesetz das ; (of play) Akt der ; (performance) Nummer die ; to ~ as (serve as) dienen als.

action ['ækʃn] n Handlung die ; to take ~ Maßnahmen ergreifen ; to put sthg into ~ etw in die Tat umlsetzen ; out of ~ (machine) außer Betrieb ; (person) außer Gefecht.

active ['æktɪv] adj aktiv.

activity [æk'tɪvəti] n Aktivität die. ▪ **activities** npl (leisure events) Veranstaltungen pl.

activity holiday n Aktivurlaub der.

act of God n höhere Gewalt.

actor ['æktə'] n Schauspieler der.

actress ['æktrɪs] n Schauspielerin die.

actual ['æktʃʊəl] adj eigentlich.

actually ['æktʃʊəlɪ] adv (really) wirklich ; (in fact) eigentlich ; (by the way) übrigens.

acupuncture ['ækjʊpʌŋktʃə'] n Akupunktur die.

acute [ə'kjuːt] adj (pain) heftig ; (angle) spitz ; ~ accent Akut der.

ad [æd] n (inf : in newspaper) Annonce die ; (on TV) Werbespot der.

AD (abbr of Anno Domini) n. Chr.

adapt [ə'dæpt] vt anlpassen. ◆ vi sich anlpassen.

adapter [ə'dæptə'] n (for foreign plug) Adapter der ; (for several plugs) Mehrfachsteckdose die.

add [æd] vt (put, say in addition) hinzulfügen ; (numbers) addieren. ■ **add up** vt sep addieren. ■ **add up to** vt fus (total) machen.

adder ['ædə'] n Kreuzotter die.

addict ['ædɪkt] n Süchtige der, die.

addicted [ə'dɪktɪd] adj : to be ~ to sthg nach etw süchtig sein.

addiction [ə'dɪkʃn] n Sucht die.

addition [ə'dɪʃn] n (added thing) Ergänzung die ; (in maths) Addition die ; in ~ außerdem ; in ~ to zusätzlich zu.

additional [ə'dɪʃənl] adj zusätzlich.

additive ['ædɪtɪv] n Zusatz der.

address [ə'dres] n Adresse die. ◆ vt (speak to) anlsprechen ; (letter) adressieren.

address book n Adressbuch das.

addressee [,ædre'siː] n Empfänger der (-in die).

adequate ['ædɪkwət] adj (sufficient) ausreichend ; (satisfactory) angemessen.

adhere [əd'hɪə'] vi : to ~ to (stick to) kleben an (+D) ; (obey) einlhalten.

adhesive [əd'hiːsɪv] adj Klebe-. ◆ n Klebstoff der.

adjacent [ə'dʒeɪsənt] adj angrenzend.

adjective ['ædʒɪktɪv] n Adjektiv das.

adjoining [ə'dʒɔɪnɪŋ] adj Nachbar- ; (room) Neben-.

adjust [ə'dʒʌst] vt (machine) einlstellen. ◆ vi : to ~ to sich anlpassen an (+A).

adjustable [ə'dʒʌstəbl] adj verstellbar.

adjustment [ə'dʒʌstmənt] n (of machine) Einstellung die.

administration [əd,mɪnɪ'streɪʃn] n (organizing) Verwaltung die ; (Am : government) Regierung die.

administrator [əd'mɪnɪstreɪtə'] n Verwalter der (-in die).

admiral ['ædmərəl] n Admiral der.

admire [əd'maɪə'] vt bewundern.

admission [əd'mɪʃn] n (permission to enter) Zutritt der ; (entrance cost) Eintritt der.

admission charge n Eintrittspreis der.

admit [əd'mɪt] vt (confess) zulgeben ; (allow to enter) hereinlassen ; to ~ to sthg etw zulgeben ; '~s one' (on ticket) 'gültig für eine Person'.

adolescent [,ædə'lesnt] n Jugendliche der, die.

adopt [ə'dɒpt] vt (child) adoptieren ; (attitude) anlnehmen ; (plan) übernehmen.

adopted [ə'dɒptɪd] adj adoptiert.

adorable [ə'dɔːrəbl] adj entzückend.

adore [ə'dɔː'] vt über alles lieben.

adult ['ædʌlt] n Erwachsene der, die. ◆ adj (entertainment, *films)* für Erwachsene ; *(animal)* ausgewachsen.

adult education n Erwachsenenbildung *die*.

adultery [ə'dʌltərɪ] n Ehebruch *der*.

advance [əd'vɑːns] n *(money)* Vorschuss *der* ; *(movement)* Vorrücken *das* ; *(progress)* Fortschritt *der*. ◆ vt *(money)* vorlschießen ; *(bring forward)* vorlverlegen. ◆ vi *(move forward)* vorlrücken ; *(improve)* voranlkommen. ◆ adj : ~ **warning** Vorwarnung *die*.

advance booking n Vorbestellung *die*.

advanced [əd'vɑːnst] adj *(student, level)* fortgeschritten.

advantage [əd'vɑːntɪdʒ] n Vorteil *der* ; **to take ~ of** auslnutzen.

adventure [əd'ventʃər] n Abenteuer *das*.

adventurous [əd'ventʃərəs] adj *(person)* abenteuerlustig.

adverb [ˈædvɜːb] n Adverb *das*.

adverse [ˈædvɜːs] adj ungünstig.

advert [ˈædvɜːt] = **advertisement**.

advertise [ˈædvətaɪz] vt *(product)* werben für ; *(event)* bekannt machen.

advertisement [əd'vɜːtɪsmənt] n *(in newspaper)* Anzeige *die* ; *(on TV)* Werbespot *der*.

advice [əd'vaɪs] n Rat *der* ; **a piece of ~** ein Ratschlag.

advisable [əd'vaɪzəbl] adj ratsam.

advise [əd'vaɪz] vt raten *(+D)* ; **to ~ sb to do sthg** jm raten, etw zu

tun ; **to ~ sb against doing sthg** jm von etw ablraten.

advocate [n ˈædvəkət, vb ˈædvəkeɪt] n *(JUR)* Anwalt *der* (Anwältin *die*). ◆ vt befürworten.

aerial [ˈeərɪəl] n Antenne *die*.

aerobics [eəˈrəʊbɪks] n Aerobic *das*.

aerodynamic [ˌeərəʊdaɪˈnæmɪk] adj aerodynamisch.

aeroplane [ˈeərəpleɪn] n Flugzeug *das*.

aerosol [ˈeərəsɒl] n Spray *der*.

affair [əˈfeər] n *(event)* Angelegenheit *die* ; *(love affair)* Verhältnis *das*.

affect [əˈfekt] vt *(influence)* beeinflussen.

affection [əˈfekʃn] n Zuneigung *die*.

affectionate [əˈfekʃnət] adj liebevoll.

affluent [ˈæflʊənt] adj wohlhabend.

afford [əˈfɔːd] vt : **to be able to ~ sthg** *(D)* etw sich leisten können ; **I can't ~ the time** ich habe keine Zeit ; **I can't ~ it** das kann ich mir nicht leisten.

affordable [əˈfɔːdəbl] adj erschwinglich.

afloat [əˈfləʊt] adj über Wasser.

afraid [əˈfreɪd] adj : **to be ~ (of)** Angst haben (vor *(+D)*) ; **I'm ~ so/not** leider ja/nicht.

Africa [ˈæfrɪkə] n Afrika *nt*.

African [ˈæfrɪkən] adj afrikanisch. ◆ n Afrikaner *der* (-in *die*).

after [ˈɑːftər] prep nach. ◆ conj nachdem. ◆ adv danach ; **~ we had eaten** nachdem wir gegessen hatten ; **a quarter ~ ten** *(Am)* Viertel nach zehn ; **to be ~ sb/sthg** *(in* search of) jn/etw suchen; **~ all** (in spite of everything) doch; (it should be remembered) schließlich. ▪ **afters** npl Nachtisch der.

aftercare ['ɑːftəkeə] n Nachbehandlung die.

aftereffects ['ɑːftərɪˌfekts] npl Nachwirkungen pl.

afternoon [ˌɑːftə'nuːn] n Nachmittag der; **good ~!** guten Tag!

afternoon tea n Nachmittagstee der.

aftershave ['ɑːftəʃeɪv] n Aftershave das.

aftersun ['ɑːftəsʌn] n Aftersunlotion die.

afterwards ['ɑːftəwədz] adv danach.

again [ə'gen] adv wieder; **~ and ~** immer wieder; **never ~** nie wieder.

against [ə'genst] prep gegen; **he was leaning ~ the wall** er stand an die Wand gelehnt; **~ the law** rechtswidrig.

age [eɪdʒ] n Alter das; (in history) Zeitalter das; **under ~** minderjährig; **I haven't seen him for ~s** (inf) ich hab' ihn schon ewig nicht mehr gesehen.

aged [eɪdʒd] adj: **to be ~ eight** acht Jahre alt sein; **children ~ eight** achtjährige Kinder.

age group n Altersgruppe die.

age limit n Altersgrenze die.

agency ['eɪdʒənsɪ] n Agentur die.

agenda [ə'dʒendə] n Tagesordnung die.

agent ['eɪdʒənt] n (representative) Vertreter der (-in die).

aggression [ə'greʃn] n Aggression die.

aggressive [ə'gresɪv] adj aggressiv.

agile [(Br) 'ædʒaɪl, (Am) 'ædʒəl] adj beweglich.

agility [ə'dʒɪlətɪ] n Beweglichkeit die.

agitated ['ædʒɪteɪtɪd] adj erregt.

ago [ə'gəʊ] adv: **a month ~** vor einem Monat; **how long ~ was it?** wie lange ist das her?

agonizing ['ægənaɪzɪŋ] adj qualvoll.

agony ['ægənɪ] n Qual die.

agree [ə'griː] vi (be in agreement, correspond) übereinstimmen; (consent) einwilligen; **it doesn't ~ with me** (food) das bekommt mir nicht; **to ~ to sthg** mit etw einverstanden sein; **to ~ to do sthg** bereit sein, etw zu tun. ▪ **agree on** vt fus (time, price) sich einigen auf (+A).

agreed [ə'griːd] adj vereinbart.

agreement [ə'griːmənt] n Zustimmung die; (contract) Vertrag der; **in ~ with** in Übereinstimmung mit.

agriculture ['ægrɪkʌltʃə] n Landwirtschaft die.

ahead [ə'hed] adv: **the road ~** die Straße vor mir/uns etc; **straight ~** geradeaus; **the weeks ~** die kommenden Wochen; **to be ~** (winning) Vorsprung haben; **~ of** (in front of) vor (+D); **~ of the other team** der anderen Mannschaft voraus; **~ of schedule** früher als geplant.

aid [eɪd] n Hilfe die. ◆ vt helfen (+D); **in ~ of** zugunsten (+G); **with the ~ of** mithilfe (+G).

AIDS [eɪdz] n Aids das.

ailment ['eɪlmənt] n (fml) Leiden das.

aim [eɪm] n (purpose) Ziel das. ◆ vt (gun, camera, hose) richten. ◆ vi : to ~ (at) zielen (auf (+A)) ; to ~ to do sthg beabsichtigen, etw zu tun.

air [eəʳ] n Luft die. ◆ vt (room) lüften. ◆ adj (terminal, travel) Flug- ; by ~ (travel) mit dem Flugzeug ; (send) mit Luftpost.

airbed ['eəbed] n Luftmatratze die.

airborne ['eəbɔːn] adj (plane) : whilst we are ~ während des Fluges.

air-conditioned [-kən'dɪʃnd] adj klimatisiert.

air-conditioning [-kən'dɪʃnɪŋ] n Klimaanlage die.

aircraft ['eəkrɑːft] (pl aircraft) n Flugzeug das.

aircraft carrier [-,kærɪəʳ] n Flugzeugträger der.

airfield ['eəfiːld] n Flugplatz der.

airforce ['eəfɔːs] n Luftwaffe die.

air freshener [-,freʃnəʳ] n Raumspray die.

airhostess ['eə,həʊstɪs] n Stewardess die.

airing cupboard ['eərɪŋ-] n Trockenschrank zum Wäschetrocknen.

airletter ['eə,letəʳ] n Luftpostbrief der.

airline ['eəlaɪn] n Fluggesellschaft die.

airliner ['eə,laɪnəʳ] n Verkehrsflugzeug das.

airmail ['eəmeɪl] n Luftpost die ; by ~ mit Luftpost.

airplane ['eəpleɪn] n (Am) Flugzeug das.

airport ['eəpɔːt] n Flughafen der.

air raid n Luftangriff der.

airsick ['eəsɪk] adj luftkrank.

air steward n Steward der.

air stewardess n Stewardess die.

air traffic control n (people) Fluglotsen pl.

airy ['eərɪ] adj luftig.

aisle [aɪl] n (in church) Seitenschiff das ; (in plane, cinema, supermarket) Gang der.

aisle seat n Sitz der am Gang.

ajar [ə'dʒɑːʳ] adj angelehnt.

alarm [ə'lɑːm] n (device) Alarmanlage die. ◆ vt beunruhigen.

alarm clock n Wecker der.

alarmed [ə'lɑːmd] adj (door, car) alarmgesichert.

alarming [ə'lɑːmɪŋ] adj alarmierend.

Albert Hall ['ælbət-] n : the ~ Londoner Konzerthalle.

ALBERT HALL

Diese große Londoner Konzerthalle ist nach Prinz Albert, dem Gemahl von Königin Viktoria, benannt. Neben Konzerten finden hier auch andere Veranstaltungen, wie zum Beispiel aus dem Bereich des Sports, statt.

album ['ælbəm] n Album das.

alcohol ['ælkəhɒl] n Alkohol der.

alcohol-free adj alkoholfrei.

alcoholic [ˌælkə'hɒlɪk] *adj (drink)* alkoholisch. ◆ *n* Alkoholiker *der* (-in *die*).

alcoholism ['ælkəhɒlɪzm] *n* Alkoholismus *der*.

alcove ['ælkəʊv] *n* Nische *die*.

ale [eɪl] *n* Ale *das*.

alert [ə'lɜːt] *adj* wachsam. ◆ *vt (police, authorities)* alarmieren.

A level *n (Br)* einzelne Prüfung des englischen Schulabschlusses.

A LEVEL

Die „A level"-Prüfungen entsprechen in etwa dem deutschen Abitur bzw. der schweizerischen Matura und werden von Schülern im Alter von 18 Jahren abgelegt. Ihr Bestehen ist Voraussetzung für ein Hochschulstudium in Großbritannien. Im britischen Schulsystem wählen die Schüler bis zu vier Fächer, und in jedem Fach wird eine „A level"-Prüfung abgelegt. Die „A level"-Endnoten sind sehr wichtig, da sie mit entscheiden, ob ein Schüler an der Universität der eigenen Wahl angenommen wird.

algebra ['ældʒɪbrə] *n* Algebra *die*.

Algeria [æl'dʒɪərɪə] *n* Algerien *nt*.

alias ['eɪlɪəs] *adv* alias.

alibi ['ælɪbaɪ] *n* Alibi *das*.

alien ['eɪlɪən] *n (foreigner)* Ausländer *der* (-in *die*) ; *(from outer space)* Außerirdische *der, die*.

alight [ə'laɪt] *vi (fml : from train, bus)* auslsteigen (aus). ◆ *adj :* to be ~ brennen.

align [ə'laɪn] *vt* auslrichten.

alike [ə'laɪk] *adj* gleich. ◆ *adv* ähnlich ; to look ~ gleich auslsehen.

alive [ə'laɪv] *adj (living)* lebendig.

all [ɔːl] *adj* 1. *(with singular noun)* ganze ; ~ the money das ganze Geld ; ~ the time immer, die ganze Zeit.
2. *(with plural noun)* alle(-n) (-s) ; ~ the people alle Menschen, alle Leute ; ~ trains stop at Tonbridge alle Züge halten in Tonbridge.
◆ *adv* 1. *(completely)* ganz ; ~ alone ganz allein.
2. *(in scores)* beide ; it's two ~ es steht zwei zu zwei.
3. *(in phrases)* : ~ but empty fast leer ; ~ over *(finished)* zu Ende.
◆ *pron* 1. *(everything)* : ~ of the cake der ganze Kuchen ; is that ~? *(in shop)* ist das alles? ; the best of ~ der/die/das Allerbeste ; the biggest of ~ der/die/das Allergrößte.
2. *(everybody)* alle ; ~ of us went wir sind alle gegangen.
3. *(in phrases)* : in ~ *(in total)* zusammen ; *(in summary)* alles in allem.

Allah ['ælə] *n* Allah *der*.

allege [ə'ledʒ] *vt* behaupten.

allergic [ə'lɜːdʒɪk] *adj :* to be ~ to allergisch sein gegen (+A).

allergy ['ælədʒɪ] *n* Allergie *die*.

alleviate [ə'liːvɪeɪt] *vt* lindern.

alley ['ælɪ] *n* Gasse *die*.

alligator ['ælɪgeɪtə'] *n* Alligator *der*.

all-in *adj (Br : inclusive)* Pauschal-.

all-night *adj (bar, petrol station)* nachts durchgehend geöffnet.

allocate ['æləkeɪt] *vt* zulteilen.

allotment [ə'lɒtmənt] *n (Br : for vegetables)* Schrebergarten *der*.

allow [ə'lau] *vt (permit)* erlauben ; *(time, money)* rechnen ; **to ~ sb to do sthg** jm erlauben, etw zu tun ; **to be ~ed to do sthg** etw tun dürfen. ■ **allow for** *vt fus* einlkalkulieren.

allowance [ə'lauəns] *n (state benefit)* Beihilfe *die* ; *(for expenses)* Spesen *pl* ; *(Am : pocket money)* Taschengeld *das*.

all right *adj (satisfactory, acceptable)* in Ordnung. ◆ *adv (satisfactorily)* ganz gut ; *(yes, okay)* okay ; *(safely)* gut ; **how are you? - I'm ~** wie geht's dir? - mir geht's gut.

ally ['ælaɪ] *n* Verbündete *der, die* ; *(MIL)* Alliierte *der, die*.

almond ['ɑːmənd] *n* Mandel *die*.

almost ['ɔːlməust] *adv* fast.

alone [ə'ləun] *adj & adv* allein ; **to leave sb ~** jn in Ruhe lassen ; **to leave sthg ~** etw in Ruhe lassen.

along [ə'lɒŋ] *adv (forward)* weiter. ◆ *prep* entlang ; **to walk ~** entlanglgehen ; **to bring sthg ~** etw mitlbringen ; **all ~** die

ganze Zeit ; **~ with** zusammen mit.

alongside [ə,lɒŋ'saɪd] *prep* neben. ◆ *adv* : **to come ~** *(boat)* längsseits kommen.

aloof [ə'luːf] *adj* distanziert.

aloud [ə'laud] *adv* laut.

alphabet ['ælfəbet] *n* Alphabet *das*.

Alps [ælps] *npl* : **the ~** die Alpen.

already [ɔːl'redɪ] *adv* schon.

also ['ɔːlsəu] *adv* auch.

altar ['ɔːltə'] *n* Altar *der*.

alter ['ɔːltə'] *vt* ändern.

alteration [,ɔːltə'reɪʃn] *n* Änderung *die* ; *(to house)* Umbau *der*.

alternate [*(Br)* ɔːl'tɜːnət, *(Am)* 'ɔːltərnət] *adj* abwechselnd ; **on ~ days** jeden zweiten Tag.

alternating current ['ɔːltə-neɪtɪŋ-] *n* Wechselstrom *der*.

alternative [ɔːl'tɜːnətɪv] *adj* andere(-r) (-s) ; *(lifestyle, medicine)* alternativ. ◆ *n* Alternative *die*.

alternatively [ɔːl'tɜːnətɪvlɪ] *adv* oder aber.

alternator ['ɔːltəneɪtə'] *n* Wechselstromgenerator *der*.

although [ɔːl'ðəu] *conj* obwohl.

altitude ['æltɪtjuːd] *n* Höhe *die*.

altogether [,ɔːltə'geðə'] *adv (completely)* ganz ; *(in total)* insgesamt.

aluminium [,æljʊ'mɪnɪəm] *n (Br)* Aluminium *das*.

aluminum [ə'luːmɪnəm] *(Am)* = **aluminium**.

always ['ɔːlweɪz] *adv* immer.

am [æm] → **be**.

a.m. *(abbr of ante meridiem)* : at 2 ~ um 2 Uhr morgens.

amateur ['æmətə'] *n* Amateur *der*.

amazed [ə'meɪzd] *adj* erstaunt.

amazing [ə'meɪzɪŋ] *adj* erstaunlich.

Amazon ['æməzn] *n (river)* : the ~ der Amazonas.

ambassador [æm'bæsədə'] *n* Botschafter *der* (-in *die*).

amber ['æmbə'] *adj (traffic lights)* gelb ; *(jewellery)* Bernstein-.

ambiguous [æm'bɪgjʊəs] *adj* zweideutig.

ambition [æm'bɪʃn] *n (desire)* Ehrgeiz *der* ; *(thing desired)* Wunsch *der*.

ambitious [æm'bɪʃəs] *adj* ehrgeizig.

ambulance ['æmbjʊləns] *n* Krankenwagen *der*.

ambush ['æmbʊʃ] *n* Hinterhalt *der*.

amenities [ə'miːnətiz] *npl* Annehmlichkeiten *pl*.

America [ə'merɪkə] *n* Amerika *nt*.

American [ə'merɪkən] *adj* amerikanisch. ◆ *n* Amerikaner *der* (-in *die*).

amiable ['eɪmɪəbl] *adj* freundlich.

ammunition [ˌæmjʊ'nɪʃn] *n* Munition *die*.

amnesia [æm'niːzɪə] *n* Gedächtnisschwund *der*.

among(st) [ə'mʌŋ(st)] *prep* unter (+D).

amount [ə'maʊnt] *n (money)* Betrag *der* ; *(quantity)* Menge

die. ■ **amount to** *vt fus (total)* sich belaufen auf (+A).

amp [æmp] *n* Ampere *das* ; a 13-~ plug ein 13-Ampere Stecker.

ample ['æmpl] *adj* reichlich.

amplifier ['æmplɪfaɪə'] *n* Verstärker *der*.

amputate ['æmpjʊteɪt] *vt* amputieren.

Amtrak ['æmtræk] *n amerikanische Eisenbahngesellschaft.*

amuse [ə'mjuːz] *vt (make laugh)* belustigen ; *(entertain)* unterhalten.

amusement arcade [ə'mjuːzmənt-] *n* Spielhalle *die*.

amusement park [ə'mjuːzmənt-] *n* Vergnügungspark *der*.

amusements [ə'mjuːzmənts] *npl* Vergnügungsmöglichkeiten *pl*.

amusing [ə'mjuːzɪŋ] *adj* lustig.

an [stressed æn, unstressed ən] → **a**.

anaemic [ə'niːmɪk] *adj (Br)* blutarm.

anaesthetic [ˌænɪs'θetɪk] *n (Br)* Narkose *die*.

analgesic [ˌænæl'dʒiːsɪk] *n* Schmerzmittel *das*.

analyse ['ænəlaɪz] *vt* analysieren.

analyst ['ænəlɪst] *n* Analytiker *der* (-in *die*).

analyze ['ænəlaɪz] *(Am)* = **analyse**.

anarchy ['ænəkɪ] *n* Anarchie *die*.

anatomy [ə'nætəmɪ] *n (science)* Anatomie *die* ; *(of person, animal)* Körperbau *der*.

ancestor ['ænsestə'] n Vorfahr der.

anchor ['æŋkə'] n Anker der.

anchovy ['æntʃəvɪ] n Sardine die.

ancient ['eɪnʃənt] adj alt.

and [strong form ænd, weak form ənd, ən] conj und; ~ you? und du/Sie?; a hundred ~ one hunderteins; to try ~ do sthg versuchen, etw zu tun; more ~ more immer mehr.

Andes ['ændiːz] npl: the ~ die Anden.

anecdote ['ænɪkdəʊt] n Anekdote die.

anemic [ə'niːmɪk] (Am) = anaemic.

anesthetic [,ænɪs'θetɪk] (Am) = anaesthetic.

angel ['eɪndʒl] n Engel der.

anger ['æŋgə'] n Ärger der.

angina [æn'dʒaɪnə] n Angina die.

angle ['æŋgl] n Winkel der; at an ~ schräg.

angler ['æŋglə'] n Angler der (-in die).

angling ['æŋglɪŋ] n Angeln das.

angry ['æŋgrɪ] adj böse; to get ~ (with sb) sich (über jn) ärgern.

animal ['ænɪml] n Tier das.

aniseed ['ænɪsiːd] n Anis der.

ankle ['æŋkl] n Knöchel der.

annex ['æneks] n (building) Anbau der.

annihilate [ə'naɪəleɪt] vt vernichten.

anniversary [,ænɪ'vɜːsərɪ] n Jahrestag der.

announce [ə'naʊns] vt (declare) bekannt geben; (delay, departure) durchsagen.

announcement [ə'naʊnsmənt] n Bekanntmachung die; (at airport, station) Durchsage die.

announcer [ə'naʊnsə'] n (on TV, radio) Ansager der (-in die).

annoy [ə'nɔɪ] vt ärgern.

annoyed [ə'nɔɪd] adj ärgerlich; to get ~ (with) sich ärgern (über (+A)).

annoying [ə'nɔɪɪŋ] adj ärgerlich.

annual ['ænjʊəl] adj jährlich.

anonymous [ə'nɒnɪməs] adj anonym.

anorak ['ænəræk] n Anorak der.

another [ə'nʌðə'] adj (additional) noch ein/eine; (different) ein anderer/eine andere/ein anderes. ◆ pron (one more) noch einer/eine/eins; (different one) ein anderer/eine andere/ein anderes; in ~ two weeks in weiteren zwei Wochen; ~ one noch einer/eine/eins; one ~ einander; one after ~ einer nach dem anderen/eine nach der anderen/eins nach dem anderen.

answer ['ɑːnsə'] n Antwort die. ◆ vt (person) antworten (+D); (question, letter) beantworten. ◆ vi antworten; to ~ the door die Tür aufmachen; to ~ the phone ans Telefon gehen. ■ **answer back** vi (child) Widerworte geben.

answering machine ['ɑːnsərɪŋ-] = **answerphone**.

answerphone ['ɑːnsəfəʊn] n Anrufbeantworter der.

ant [ænt] n Ameise die.

Antarctic [æn'tɑːktɪk] n : the ~ die Antarktis.

antenna [æn'tenə] n (Am : aerial) Antenne die.

anthem ['ænθəm] n Hymne die.

antibiotics [ˌæntɪbaɪ'ɒtɪks] npl Antibiotika pl.

anticipate [æn'tɪsɪpeɪt] vt erwarten.

anticlimax [ˌæntɪ'klaɪmæks] n Enttäuschung die.

anticlockwise [ˌæntɪ'klɒkwaɪz] adv (Br) gegen den Uhrzeigersinn.

antidote ['æntɪdəʊt] n Gegenmittel das.

antifreeze ['æntɪfriːz] n Frostschutzmittel das.

antihistamine [ˌæntɪ'hɪstəmɪn] n Antihistamin das.

antiperspirant [ˌæntɪ'pɜːspərənt] n Deodorant das.

antiquarian bookshop [ˌæntɪ'kweərɪən-] n Antiquariat das.

antique [æn'tiːk] n Antiquität die.

antique shop n Antiquitätenladen der.

antiseptic [ˌæntɪ'septɪk] n Antiseptikum das.

antisocial [ˌæntɪ'səʊʃl] adj (person) ungesellig ; (behaviour) asozial.

antlers ['æntləz] npl Geweih das.

anxiety [æŋ'zaɪətɪ] n (worry) Sorge die.

anxious ['æŋkʃəs] adj (worried) besorgt ; (eager) sehnlich.

any ['enɪ] adj 1. (in questions) : have you got ~ money? hast du Geld? ; have you got ~ postcards? haben Sie Postkarten?
2. (in negatives) : I haven't got ~ money ich habe kein Geld ; we don't have ~ rooms wir haben keine Zimmer frei.
3. (no matter which) irgendein(-e) ; take ~ one you like nimm, welches du willst.
◆ pron 1. (in questions) welche ; I'm looking for a hotel - are there ~ nearby? ich suche ein Hotel - gibt es hier welche in der Nähe?
2. (in negatives) : I don't want ~ (of them) ich möchte keinen/keines (von denen).
3. (no matter which one) jede(-r) (-s) ; you can sit at ~ of the tables Sie können sich an jeden beliebigen Tisch setzen.
◆ adv 1. (in questions) : is there ~ more ice cream? ist noch Eis da? ; is that ~ better? ist das besser?
2. (in negatives) : we can't wait ~ longer wir können nicht mehr länger warten.

anybody ['enɪˌbɒdɪ] = anyone.

anyhow ['enɪhaʊ] adv (carelessly) irgendwie ; (in any case) jedenfalls ; (in spite of that) trotzdem.

anyone ['enɪwʌn] pron (any person) jeder ; (in questions) irgendjemand ; there wasn't ~ in niemand war zu Hause.

anything ['enɪθɪŋ] pron (no matter what) alles ; (in questions) irgendetwas ; he didn't tell me ~ er hat mir nichts gesagt.

anyway ['enɪweɪ] adv (in any case) sowieso; (in spite of that) trotzdem; (in conversation) jedenfalls.

anywhere ['enɪweə] adv (any place) überall; (in questions) irgendwo; **I can't find it ~** ich kann es nirgends finden.

apart [ə'pɑːt] adv auseinander; **to come ~** auseinander gehen; **to live ~** getrennt leben; **~ from** (except for) abgesehen von; (as well as) außer (+D).

apartheid [ə'pɑːtheɪt] n Apartheid die.

apartment [ə'pɑːtmənt] n (Am) Wohnung die.

apathetic [ˌæpə'θetɪk] adj apathisch.

ape [eɪp] n Affe der.

aperitif [ə,perə'tiːf] n Aperitif der.

aperture ['æpətʃə] n (of camera) Blende die.

Apex n (plane ticket) reduziertes Flugticket, das im Voraus reserviert werden muss; (Br : train ticket) reduzierte Fahrkarte für Fernstrecken, die nur für bestimmte Züge gilt und im Voraus reserviert werden muss.

apiece [ə'piːs] adv je; **they cost £5 ~** sie kosten je 5 Pfund.

apologetic [ə,pɒlə'dʒetɪk] adj entschuldigend; **to be ~** sich entschuldigen.

apologize [ə'pɒlədʒaɪz] vi : **to ~ (to sb for sthg)** sich (bei jm für etw) entschuldigen.

apology [ə'pɒlədʒɪ] n Entschuldigung die.

apostrophe [ə'pɒstrəfɪ] n Apostroph der.

appal [ə'pɔːl] vt (Br) entsetzen.

appall [ə'pɔːl] (Am) = **appal**.

appalling [ə'pɔːlɪŋ] adj entsetzlich.

apparatus [ˌæpə'reɪtəs] n (device) Gerät das.

apparently [ə'pærəntlɪ] adv (it seems) scheinbar; (evidently) anscheinend.

appeal [ə'piːl] n (JUR) Berufung die; (for money, help) Aufruf der. ◆ vi (JUR) Berufung einlegen; **to ~ to sb (for sthg)** jn (um etw) bitten; **it doesn't ~ to me** das gefällt mir nicht.

appear [ə'pɪə] vi erscheinen; (seem) scheinen; (in play) auftreten; **it ~s that** es scheint, dass.

appearance [ə'pɪərəns] n Erscheinen das; (of performer) Auftritt der; (look) Aussehen das.

appendices [ə'pendɪsiːz] pl → **appendix**.

appendicitis [ə,pendɪ'saɪtɪs] n Blinddarmentzündung die.

appendix [ə'pendɪks] (pl -dices) n (ANAT) Blinddarm der; (of book) Anhang der.

appetite ['æpɪtaɪt] n Appetit der.

appetizer ['æpɪtaɪzə] n Appetithappen der.

appetizing ['æpɪtaɪzɪŋ] adj appetitlich.

applaud [ə'plɔːd] vt & vi applaudieren (+D).

applause [ə'plɔːz] n Applaus der.

apple ['æpl] n Apfel der.

apple charlotte [-'ʃɑːlət] n Apfelauflauf, der in einer mit Brot *ausgelegten und bedeckten Form gebacken wird.*

apple crumble *n* mit Streuseln bestreuter Apfelauflauf.

apple juice *n* Apfelsaft *der.*

apple pie *n* Art gedeckter Apfelkuchen mit dünnen Teigwänden.

apple sauce *n* Apfelmus *das.*

apple strudel *n* Apfelstrudel *der.*

apple tart *n* Apfelkuchen *der.*

apple turnover [-'tɜːn,əʊvə] *n* Apfeltasche *die.*

appliance [ə'plaɪəns] *n* Gerät *das*; **electrical ~** Elektrogerät *das*; **domestic ~** Haushaltsgerät *das.*

applicable [ə'plɪkəbl] *adj*: **to be ~ (to)** zutreffen (auf (+A)); **if ~** falls zutreffend.

applicant ['æplɪkənt] *n* Bewerber *der* (-in *die*).

application [,æplɪ'keɪʃn] *n* (for job) Bewerbung *die*; (for membership) Antrag *der.*

application form *n* (for job) Bewerbungsformular *das*; (for membership) Antragsformular *das.*

apply [ə'plaɪ] *vt* (lotion, paint) auftragen; (brakes) betätigen. ◆ *vi*: **to ~ (to sb for sthg)** (make request) sich (bei jm um etw) bewerben; **to ~ (to sb)** (be applicable) zutreffen (auf jn).

appointment [ə'pɔɪntmənt] *n* (with doctor, hairdresser) Termin *der*; **to have an ~ (with)** einen Termin haben (bei); **to make an ~ (with)** einen Termin vereinbaren (mit); **by ~** nach Vereinbarung.

appreciable [ə'priːʃəbl] *adj* merklich.

appreciate [ə'priːʃɪeɪt] *vt* schätzen; (understand) verstehen.

apprehensive [,æprɪ'hensɪv] *adj* ängstlich.

apprentice [ə'prentɪs] *n* Lehrling *der.*

apprenticeship [ə'prentɪsʃɪp] *n* Lehre *die.*

approach [ə'prəʊtʃ] *n* (road) Zufahrt *die*; (to problem, situation) Ansatz *der.* ◆ *vt* sich nähern (+D); (problem, situation) anlgehen. ◆ *vi* näher kommen.

appropriate [ə'prəʊprɪət] *adj* passend.

approval [ə'pruːvl] *n* Zustimmung *die.*

approve [ə'pruːv] *vi*: **to ~ (of sb/sthg)** (mit jm/etw) einverstanden sein.

approximate [ə'prɒksɪmət] *adj* ungefähr.

approximately [ə'prɒksɪmətlɪ] *adv* ungefähr.

Apr. *abbr* = **April.**

apricot ['eɪprɪkɒt] *n* Aprikose *die*, Marille *die* (Österr).

April ['eɪprəl] *n* April *der*; → **September.**

April Fools' Day *n* der erste April.

APRIL FOOLS' DAY

Der 1. April wird wie im deutschsprachigen Raum auch mit Aprilscherzen begangen: an diesem Tag spielt man anderen gerne Streiche oder treibt sonst allerlei Schabernack. Aprilscherze sind allerdings nur bis zur Mittagszeit erlaubt.

---

apron ['eɪprən] n Schürze die.

apt [æpt] adj (appropriate) passend ; to be ~ to do sthg dazu neigen, etw zu tun.

aquarium [ə'kweərɪəm] (pl -ria [-rɪə]) n Aquarium das.

Aquarius [ə'kweərɪəs] n Wassermann der.

aqueduct ['ækwɪdʌkt] n Aquädukt der.

Arab ['ærəb] adj arabisch. ◆ n Araber der (-in die).

Arabic ['ærəbɪk] adj arabisch. ◆ n Arabisch das.

arbitrary ['ɑːbɪtrərɪ] adj willkürlich.

arc [ɑːk] n Bogen der.

arcade [ɑː'keɪd] n (for shopping) Passage die ; (of video games) Spielhalle die.

arch [ɑːtʃ] n Bogen der.

archaeology [,ɑːkɪ'ɒlədʒɪ] n Archäologie die.

archbishop [,ɑːtʃ'bɪʃəp] n Erzbischof der.

archery ['ɑːtʃərɪ] n Bogenschießen das.

archipelago [,ɑːkɪ'peləgəʊ] n Archipel der.

architect ['ɑːkɪtekt] n Architekt der (-in die).

architecture ['ɑːkɪtektʃəʳ] n Architektur die.

archives ['ɑːkaɪvz] npl Archiv das.

Arctic ['ɑːktɪk] n : the ~ die Arktis.

are [weak form əʳ, strong form ɑːʳ] → be.

area ['eərɪə] n (region) Gegend die ; (space, zone) Bereich der ; (surface size) Fläche die.

area code n (Am) Vorwahl die.

arena [ə'riːnə] n (at circus) Manege die ; (at sportsground) Stadion das.

aren't [ɑːnt] = are not.

Argentina [,ɑːdʒən'tiːnə] n Argentinien nt.

argue ['ɑːgjuː] vi : to ~ (with sb about sthg) sich (mit jm über etw) streiten ; to ~ (that)... die Meinung vertreten, dass...

argument ['ɑːgjʊmənt] n (quarrel) Streit der ; (reason) Argument das.

arid ['ærɪd] adj trocken.

Aries ['eəriːz] n Widder der.

arise [ə'raɪz] (pt arose, pp arisen [ə'rɪzn]) vi : to ~ (from) sich ergeben (aus).

aristocracy [,ærɪ'stɒkrəsɪ] n Adel der.

arithmetic [ə'rɪθmətɪk] n Rechnen das.

arm [ɑːm] n Arm der ; (of chair) Armlehne die ; (of garment) Ärmel der.

arm bands npl (for swimming) Schwimmflügel pl.

armchair ['ɑːmtʃeəʳ] n Sessel der.

armed [ɑːmd] adj bewaffnet.

armed forces npl : the ~ die Streitkräfte.

armor ['ɑːməʳ] (Am) = armour.

armour ['ɑːməʳ] n (Br) Rüstung die.

armpit ['ɑːmpɪt] n Achselhöhle die.

arms [ɑːmz] npl Waffen pl.

army ['ɑːmɪ] n Armee die.

A-road n (Br) ≃ Bundesstraße die.

aroma [ə'rəʊmə] n Aroma das.

aromatic [ˌærə'mætɪk] adj aromatisch.

arose [ə'rəʊz] pt → **arise**.

around [ə'raʊnd] prep um ; (near) ringsherum ; (approximately) ungefähr. ◆ adv herum ; (present) : is she ~? ist sie da? ; ~ here (in the area) hier in der Gegend ; to travel ~ herum|reisen ; to turn ~ sich um|drehen ; to look ~ sich um|sehen.

arouse [ə'raʊz] vt (suspicion, interest) erregen.

arrange [ə'reɪndʒ] vt (objects) ordnen ; (flowers) arrangieren ; (meeting) planen ; to ~ to do sthg (with sb) (mit jm) vereinbaren, etw zu tun.

arrangement [ə'reɪndʒmənt] n (agreement) Vereinbarung die ; (layout) Anordnung die ; by ~ nach Vereinbarung ; to make ~s (to do sthg) Vorkehrungen treffen (, etw zu tun).

arrest [ə'rest] n Verhaftung die. ◆ vt verhaften ; under ~ verhaftet.

arrival [ə'raɪvl] n Ankunft die ; on ~ bei der Ankunft ; new ~ Neuankömmling der.

arrive [ə'raɪv] vi an|kommen.

arrogant ['ærəgənt] adj arrogant.

arrow ['ærəʊ] n Pfeil der.

arson ['ɑːsn] n Brandstiftung die.

art [ɑːt] n Kunst die ; (paintings, sculptures etc) Kunstwerk

das. ▪ **arts** npl (humanities) Geisteswissenschaften pl ; the ~s (fine arts) die schönen Künste pl.

artefact ['ɑːtɪfækt] n Artefakt das.

artery ['ɑːtərɪ] n Arterie die.

art gallery n Kunstgalerie die.

arthritis [ɑː'θraɪtɪs] n Arthritis die.

artichoke ['ɑːtɪtʃəʊk] n Artischocke die.

article ['ɑːtɪkl] n (object) Gegenstand der ; (in newspaper, grammar) Artikel der.

articulate [ɑː'tɪkjʊlət] adj : to be ~ sich gut ausdrücken können.

artificial [ˌɑːtɪ'fɪʃl] adj künstlich.

artist ['ɑːtɪst] n Künstler der (-in die).

artistic [ɑː'tɪstɪk] adj künstlerisch.

arts centre n ≃ Kulturzentrum das.

arty ['ɑːtɪ] adj (pej) pseudokünstlerisch.

as [unstressed əz, stressed æz] adv (in comparisons) : ~... ~ so... wie ; he's ~ tall ~ I am er ist so groß wie ich ; ~ many ~ so viele wie ; ~ much ~ so viel wie. ◆ conj 1. (referring to time) als ; ~ the plane was coming in to land als das Flugzeug beim Landeanflug war. 2. (referring to manner) wie ; ~ expected, ... wie erwartet... 3. (introducing a statement) wie ; ~ I told you... wie ich dir bereits gesagt habe... 4. (because) weil, da.

5. (in phrases) : ~ **for me** was mich betrifft ; ~ **from Monday** ab Montag ; ~ **if** als ob.

◆ prep (referring to function, job) als.

asap (abbr of as soon as possible) baldmöglichst.

ascent [ə'sent] n Aufstieg der.

ascribe [ə'skraɪb] vt : to ~ sthg to sb/sthg jm/einer Sache etw zulschreiben.

ash [æʃ] n (from cigarette, fire) Asche die ; (tree) Esche die.

ashore [ə'ʃɔːʳ] adv an Land.

ashtray ['æʃtreɪ] n Aschenbecher der.

Asia [(Br) 'eɪʃə, (Am) 'eɪʒə] n Asien nt.

Asian [(Br) 'eɪʃn, (Am) 'eɪʒn] adj asiatisch. ◆ n Asiat der (-in die).

aside [ə'saɪd] adv beiseite ; **to move** ~ beiseite treten.

ask [ɑːsk] vt fragen ; (a question) stellen ; (permission) bitten um ; (advice) fragen um ; (invite) einladen. ◆ vi : **to** ~ **after** sich erkundigen nach ; **to** ~ **about sthg** nach etw fragen ; **to** ~ **sb about sthg** jm Fragen über etw stellen ; **to** ~ **sb to do sthg** jn bitten, etw zu tun ; **to** ~ **sb for sthg** jn um etw bitten. ▩ **ask for** vt fus (ask to talk to) verlangen ; (request) bitten um.

asleep [ə'sliːp] adj : **to be** ~ schlafen ; **to fall** ~ einlschlafen.

asparagus [ə'spærəgəs] n Spargel der.

asparagus tips npl Spargelspitzen pl.

aspect ['æspekt] n Aspekt der.

aspirin ['æsprɪn] n Aspirin das.

ass [æs] n (animal) Esel der.

assassinate [ə'sæsɪneɪt] vt erморden.

assault [ə'sɔːlt] n Angriff der. ◆ vt anlgreifen.

assemble [ə'sembl] vt (build) zusammenlbauen. ◆ vi sich versammeln.

assembly [ə'semblɪ] n (at school) Versammlung die.

assembly hall n (at school) Aula die.

assembly point n Treffpunkt der.

assert [ə'sɜːt] vt behaupten ; **to** ~ **o.s.** sich durchlsetzen.

assess [ə'ses] vt (person, situation, effect) bewerten ; (value, damage) schätzen.

assessment [ə'sesmənt] n (of situation, person, effect) Bewertung die ; (of value, damage, cost) Schätzung die.

asset ['æset] n (thing) Vorteil der ; (person) Stütze die.

assign [ə'saɪn] vt : **to** ~ **sthg to sb** jm etw zulteilen ; **to** ~ **sb to sthg** jm etw zulteilen.

assignment [ə'saɪnmənt] n (task) Aufgabe die ; (SCH) Projekt das.

assist [ə'sɪst] vt helfen (+D).

assistance [ə'sɪstəns] n Hilfe die ; **to be of** ~ (to sb) (jm) helfen.

assistant [ə'sɪstənt] n Assistent der (-in die).

associate [n ə'səʊʃɪət, vb ə'səʊʃɪeɪt] n Partner der (-in die). ◆ vt : **to** ~ **sb/sthg with** jn/etw in Verbindung bringen mit.

association [ə,səʊsɪ'eɪʃn] n (group) Verband der.

assorted [əˈsɔːtɪd] *adj* gemischt.

assortment [əˈsɔːtmənt] *n* Auswahl *die*.

assume [əˈsjuːm] *vt (suppose)* annehmen ; *(control, responsibility)* übernehmen.

assurance [əˈʃʊərəns] *n* Versicherung *die*.

assure [əˈʃʊəʳ] *vt* versichern ; **to ~ sb (that)...** jm versichern, dass...

asterisk [ˈæstərɪsk] *n* Sternchen *das*.

asthma [ˈæsmə] *n* Asthma *das*.

asthmatic [æsˈmætɪk] *adj* asthmatisch.

astonished [əˈstɒnɪʃt] *adj* erstaunt.

astonishing [əˈstɒnɪʃɪŋ] *adj* erstaunlich.

astound [əˈstaʊnd] *vt* überraschen.

astray [əˈstreɪ] *adv*: **to go ~** *(person)* sich verlaufen ; *(thing)* verloren gehen.

astrology [əˈstrɒlədʒɪ] *n* Astrologie *die*.

astronomy [əˈstrɒnəmɪ] *n* Astronomie *die*.

asylum [əˈsaɪləm] *n (mental hospital)* psychiatrische Klinik *die*.

at [ət *unstressed*, æt *stressed*] *prep* **1.** *(indicating place, position)* in (+D) ; **~ the end of** am Ende (+G) ; **~ school** in der Schule ; **~ the hotel** *(inside)* im Hotel ; *(outside)* beim Hotel ; **~ my mother's** bei meiner Mutter ; **~ home** zu Hause.
2. *(indicating direction)* an (+A) ; **to look ~ sb/sthg** jn/etw anl-

schauen ; **to smile ~ sb** jn anlächeln.
3. *(indicating time)* um ; **~ nine o'clock** um neun Uhr ; **~ Christmas** zu Weihnachten ; **~ night** nachts.
4. *(indicating rate, level, speed)* mit ; **it works out ~ £5 each** es kommt für jeden auf 5 Pfund ; **~ 60 km/h** mit 60 km/h.
5. *(indicating activity)* : **to be ~ lunch** beim Mittagessen sein ; **to be good/bad ~ sthg** in einer Sache gut/schlecht sein.
6. *(indicating cause)* über (+D) ; **to be pleased ~ sthg** über etw (D) erfreut sein.

ate [*(Br)* et, *(Am)* eɪt] *pt* → **eat**.

atheist [ˈeɪθɪɪst] *n* Atheist *der* (-in *die*).

athlete [ˈæθliːt] *n* Athlet *der* (-in *die*).

athletics [æθˈletɪks] *n* Leichtathletik *die*.

Atlantic [ətˈlæntɪk] *n* : **the ~** **(Ocean)** der Atlantik.

atlas [ˈætləs] *n* Atlas *der*.

atmosphere [ˈætməsfɪəʳ] *n* Atmosphäre *die*.

atom [ˈætəm] *n* Atom *das*.

A to Z *n* Stadtplan *der (im Buchformat)*.

atrocious [əˈtrəʊʃəs] *adj* grauenhaft.

attach [əˈtætʃ] *vt* befestigen ; **to ~ sthg to sthg** etw an etw (D) befestigen.

attachment [əˈtætʃmənt] *n (device)* Zusatzgerät *das*.

attack [əˈtæk] *n* Angriff *der* ; *(of coughing, asthma etc)* Anfall *der*. ◆ *vt* angreifen.

attacker [əˈtækəʳ] *n* Angreifer *der* (-in *die*).

attain [ə'teɪn] *vt (fml)* errei-chen.

attempt [ə'tempt] *n* Versuch *der*. ◆ *vt* versuchen ; **to ~ to do sthg** versuchen, etw zu tun.

attend [ə'tend] *vt (meeting)* teilnehmen an (+D) ; *(Mass, school)* besuchen. ■ **attend to** *vt fus (deal with)* sich kümmern um.

attendance [ə'tendəns] *n* Be-such *der* ; *(number of people)* Be-sucherzahl *die*.

attendant [ə'tendənt] *n (in museum)* Aufsichtsperson *die* ; *(in car park)* Wächter *der* (-in *die*).

attention [ə'tenʃn] *n* Auf-merksamkeit *die* ; **to pay ~** auf-merksam sein ; **to pay ~ to sthg** etw beachten.

attic ['ætɪk] *n* Dachboden *der*.

attitude ['ætɪtjuːd] *n (mental)* Einstellung *die* ; *(behaviour)* Haltung *die*.

attorney [ə'tɜːnɪ] *n (Am)* An-walt *der* (Anwältin *die*).

attract [ə'trækt] *vt* an|ziehen ; *(attention)* erwecken.

attraction [ə'trækʃn] *n (lik-ing)* Anziehung *die* ; *(attractive feature)* Reiz *der* ; *(of town, re-sort)* Attraktion *die*.

attractive [ə'træktɪv] *adj (per-son)* attraktiv ; *(idea, offer)* reiz-voll.

attribute [ə'trɪbjuːt] *vt* : **to ~ sthg to** etw zurück|führen auf (+A).

aubergine ['əʊbəʒiːn] *n (Br)* Aubergine *die*.

auburn ['ɔːbən] *adj* rotbraun.

auction ['ɔːkʃn] *n* Auktion *die*.

audience ['ɔːdɪəns] *n (of play, concert, film)* Publikum *das* ; *(of TV)* Zuschauer *pl* ; *(of radio)* Zuhörer *pl*.

audio ['ɔːdɪəʊ] *adj* Ton-.

audio-visual [-'vɪʒʊəl] *adj* audiovisuell.

auditorium [ˌɔːdɪ'tɔːrɪəm] *n* Zuschauerraum *der*.

Aug. *abbr* = **August**.

August ['ɔːgəst] *n* August *der* ; → **September**.

aunt [ɑːnt] *n* Tante *die*.

au pair [ˌəʊ'peəʳ] *n* Aupair-mädchen *das*.

aural ['ɔːrəl] *adj* : **an ~ exam** ein Hörverständnistest.

Australia [ɒ'streɪlɪə] *n* Aus-tralien *nt*.

Australian [ɒ'streɪlɪən] *adj* australisch. ◆ *n* Australier *der* (-in *die*).

Austria ['ɒstrɪə] *n* Österreich *nt*.

Austrian ['ɒstrɪən] *adj* öster-reichisch. ◆ *n* Österreicher *der* (-in *die*).

authentic [ɔː'θentɪk] *adj* echt.

author ['ɔːθəʳ] *n (of book, art-icle)* Autor *der* (-in *die*) ; *(by pro-fession)* Schriftsteller *der* (-in *die*).

authority [ɔː'θɒrətɪ] *n (power)* Autorität *die* ; *(official organiza-tion)* Behörde *die* ; **the author-ities** die Behörden.

authorization [ˌɔːθəraɪ'zeɪʃn] *n* Genehmigung *die*.

authorize ['ɔːθəraɪz] *vt* ge-nehmigen ; **to ~ sb to do sthg** jn ermächtigen, etw zu tun.

autobiography [ˌɔːtəbaɪ'-ɒgrəfɪ] *n* Autobiografie *die*.

autograph ['ɔːtəgrɑːf] *n* Autogramm *das*.

automatic [,ɔːtə'mætɪk] *adj* automatisch. ◆ *n (car)* Wagen *der* mit Automatikgetriebe.

automatically [,ɔːtə'mætɪklɪ] *adv* automatisch.

automobile ['ɔːtəməbiːl] *n (Am)* Auto *das*.

autumn ['ɔːtəm] *n* Herbst *der*; in (the) ~ im Herbst.

auxiliary (verb) [ɔːg'zɪljərɪ-] *n* Hilfsverb *das*.

available [ə'veɪləbl] *adj* verfügbar; *(product)* lieferbar; to be ~ *(person)* zur Verfügung stehen.

avalanche ['ævəlɑːnʃ] *n* Lawine *die*.

Ave. *abbr* = avenue.

avenue ['ævənjuː] *n (road)* Allee *die*.

average ['ævərɪdʒ] *adj* durchschnittlich. ◆ *n* Durchschnitt *der*; on ~ im Durchschnitt.

aversion [ə'vɜːʃn] *n* Abneigung *die*.

aviation [,eɪvɪ'eɪʃn] *n* Luftfahrt *die*.

avid ['ævɪd] *adj* begeistert.

avocado (pear) [,ævə'kɑːdəʊ-] *n* Avocado *die*.

avoid [ə'vɔɪd] *vt* vermeiden; *(person, place)* meiden; to ~ doing sthg vermeiden, etw zu tun.

await [ə'weɪt] *vt* erwarten.

awake [ə'weɪk] *(pt* awoke, *pp* awoken) *adj* wach. ◆ *vi* erwachen.

award [ə'wɔːd] *n (prize)* Auszeichnung *die*. ◆ *vt* : to ~ sb sthg *(prize)* jm etw verleihen; *(damages, compensation)* jm etw zusprechen.

aware [ə'weəʳ] *adj* : to be ~ of sthg sich *(D)* einer Sache *(G)* bewusst sein.

away [ə'weɪ] *adv* weg; *(not at home, in office)* nicht da; to take sthg ~ (from sb) (jm) etw wegnehmen; far ~ weit entfernt; 10 miles ~ (from here) 10 Meilen (von hier) entfernt; two weeks ~ in zwei Wochen.

awesome ['ɔːsəm] *adj* überwältigend; *(inf* : excellent) toll.

awful ['ɔːfəl] *adj* furchtbar.

awfully ['ɔːflɪ] *adv (very)* furchtbar.

awkward ['ɔːkwəd] *adj (position, shape, situation)* ungünstig; *(movement)* ungeschickt; *(question, task)* schwierig.

awning ['ɔːnɪŋ] *n (on house)* Markise *die*; *(of tent)* Vordach *das*.

awoke [ə'wəʊk] *pt* → awake.

awoken [ə'wəʊkən] *pp* → awake.

axe [æks] *n* Axt *die*.

axle ['æksl] *n* Achse *die*.

B

BA *(abbr of* Bachelor of Arts) Bakkalaureus *der* Geisteswissenschaften.

babble ['bæbl] *vi* plappern.

baby ['beɪbɪ] n Baby das ; **to have a ~** ein Kind bekommen ; **~ sweetcorn** Maiskölbchen pl.

baby carriage n (Am) Kinderwagen der.

baby food n Babynahrung die.

baby-sit vi babysitten.

baby wipe n Babyöltuch das.

bachelor ['bætʃələ] n Junggeselle der.

back [bæk] adv zurück. ◆ n (of person, hand, book) Rücken der ; (of chair) Lehne die ; (inside car) Rücksitz der ; (of room) hintere Teil der ; (of bank note) Rückseite die. ◆ adj (wheels) Hinter-. ◆ vi (car, driver) zurücklsetzen. ◆ vt (support) unterstützen ; **at the ~ of** hinter (+D) ; **in ~ of** (Am) hinter (+D) ; **~ to front** verkehrt herum. ▪ **back up** vt sep (support) unterstützen ; (confirm) bestätigen. ◆ vi (car, driver) zurücklsetzen.

backache ['bækeɪk] n Rückenschmerzen pl.

backbone ['bækbəʊn] n Wirbelsäule die.

back door n Hintertür die.

backfire [ˌbæk'faɪə] vi (car) fehlzünden.

background ['bækgraʊnd] n Hintergrund der ; (of person) Herkunft die.

backlog ['bæklɒg] n Rückstand der.

backpack ['bækpæk] n Rucksack der.

backpacker ['bækpækə] n Rucksacktourist der (-in die).

back seat n Rücksitz der.

backside [ˌbæk'saɪd] n (inf) Hintern der.

back street n Seitenstraße die.

backstroke ['bækstrəʊk] n Rückenschwimmen das.

backwards ['bækwədz] adv rückwärts ; (look) nach hinten.

bacon ['beɪkən] n Schinkenspeck der ; **~ and eggs** Eier pl mit Speck.

bacteria [bæk'tɪərɪə] npl Bakterien pl.

bad [bæd] (compar **worse**, superl **worst**) adj schlecht ; (serious) schwer ; (eyesight, excuse) schwach ; (excuse) schlecht ; (naughty) ungezogen ; (injured) schlimm ; (rotten, off) verdorben ; **not ~** nicht schlecht.

badge [bædʒ] n Sticker der.

badger ['bædʒə] n Dachs der.

badly ['bædlɪ] (compar **worse**, superl **worst**) adv schlecht ; (seriously) schwer ; (very much) sehr ; **to need sthg ~** etw dringend brauchen.

badly paid [-peɪd] adj schlecht bezahlt.

badminton ['bædmɪntən] n Federball der ; (SPORT) Badminton das.

bad-tempered [-'tempəd] adj schlecht gelaunt.

bag [bæg] n (of paper, plastic) Tüte die ; (handbag) Tasche die ; (suitcase) Reisetasche die ; **a ~ of crisps** eine Tüte Chips.

bagel ['beɪgəl] n ringförmiges Brötchen.

baggage ['bægɪdʒ] n Gepäck das.

baggage allowance n Freigepäck das.

baggage reclaim n Gepäckausgabe die.

baggy ['bægɪ] adj weit; (too baggy) ausgeleiert.

bagpipes ['bægpaɪps] npl Dudelsack der.

bail [beɪl] n Kaution die.

bait [beɪt] n Köder der.

bake [beɪk] vt backen. ◆ n Auflauf der.

baked [beɪkt] adj überbacken.

baked Alaska [-ə'læskə] n Dessert aus Eiscreme auf Biskuit, das mit Baiser überzogen ist und kurz überbacken wird.

baked beans npl weiße Bohnen in Tomatensoße.

baked potato n (in der Schale) gebackene Kartoffel.

baker ['beɪkə'] n Bäcker der (-in die); ~'s (shop) Bäckerei die.

Bakewell tart ['beɪkwel-] n Torte, die mit einer Schicht Marmelade zwischen zwei Schichten Mandelmasse gefüllt und mit einer wellenförmigen Glasur überzogen ist.

balance ['bæləns] n (of person) Gleichgewicht das; (of bank account) Kontostand der; (remainder) Rest der. ◆ vt (object) balancieren.

balcony ['bælkənɪ] n Balkon der.

bald [bɔːld] adj kahl; he is bald er hat eine Glatze.

bale [beɪl] n Ballen der.

ball [bɔːl] n Ball der; (in snooker) Kugel die; (of wool, string, paper) Knäuel das; on the ~ (fig) auf Draht.

ballad ['bæləd] n Ballade die.

ballerina [,bælə'riːnə] n Ballerina die.

ballet ['bæleɪ] n Ballett das.

ballet dancer n Balletttänzer der (-in die).

balloon [bə'luːn] n Luftballon der.

ballot ['bælət] n Wahl die.

ballpoint pen ['bɔːlpɔɪnt-] n Kugelschreiber der.

ballroom ['bɔːlrʊm] n Tanzsaal der.

ballroom dancing n Gesellschaftstanz der.

bamboo [bæm'buː] n Bambus der.

bamboo shoots npl Bambussprossen pl.

ban [bæn] n Verbot das. ◆ vt verbieten; to ~ sb from doing sthg jm verbieten, etw zu tun.

banana [bə'nɑːnə] n Banane die.

banana split n Bananensplit das.

band [bænd] n (musical group) Band die; (strip of paper, rubber) Band das.

bandage ['bændɪdʒ] n Verband der. ◆ vt verbinden.

B and B abbr = bed and breakfast.

bandstand ['bændstænd] n Musikpavillon der.

bang [bæŋ] n (noise) Knall der. ◆ vt knallen; (door) zuknallen; to ~ one's head sich (D) den Kopf stoßen.

banger ['bæŋə'] n (Br: inf: sausage) Würstchen das; ~s and mash Würstchen mit Kartoffelbrei.

bangle ['bæŋgl] n Armreif der.

bangs [bæŋz] *npl* *(Am)* Pony *der.*

banister ['bænɪstə'] *n* Treppengeländer *das.*

banjo ['bændʒəʊ] *n* Banjo *das.*

bank [bæŋk] *n (for money)* Bank *die* ; *(of river, lake)* Ufer *das* ; *(slope)* Böschung *die.*

bank account *n* Bankkonto *das.*

bank book *n* Sparbuch *das.*

bank charges *npl* Bankgebühren *pl.*

bank clerk *n* Bankangestellte *der, die.*

bank draft *n* Banküberweisung *die.*

banker ['bæŋkə'] *n* Banker *der.*

banker's card *n* Scheckkarte *die.*

bank holiday *n (Br)* öffentlicher Feiertag.

bank manager *n* Zweigstellenleiter *der* (-in *die*).

bank note *n* Geldschein *der.*

bankrupt ['bæŋkrʌpt] *adj* bankrott.

bank statement *n* Kontoauszug *der.*

banner ['bænə'] *n* Spruchband *das.*

bannister ['bænɪstə'] = **banister.**

banquet ['bæŋkwɪt] *n (formal dinner)* Bankett *das* ; *(at Indian restaurant etc)* Menü für eine bestimmte Anzahl Personen.

bap [bæp] *n (Br)* Brötchen *das.*

baptize [*(Br)* bæp'taɪz, *(Am)* 'bæptaɪz] *vt* taufen.

bar [baː'] *n (pub, in hotel)* Bar *die* ; *(counter in pub)* Theke *die* ; *(of metal, wood)* Stange *die* ; *(of soap)* Stück *das* ; *(of chocolate)* Riegel *der.* ◆ *vt (obstruct)* versperren.

barbecue ['baːbɪkjuː] *n (apparatus)* Grill *der* ; *(party)* Barbecue *das.* ◆ *vt* grillen.

barbecue sauce *n* Barbecuesoße *die.*

barbed wire [baːbd-] *n* Stacheldraht *der.*

barber ['baːbə'] *n* Herrenfriseur *der* ; ~'s *(shop)* Herrenfriseur *der.*

bar code *n* Strichkode *der.*

bare [beə'] *adj* bloß ; *(room, cupboard)* leer.

barefoot [,beə'fʊt] *adv* barfuß.

barely ['beəlɪ] *adv* kaum.

bargain ['baːgɪn] *n (agreement)* Abmachung *die* ; *(cheap buy)* günstiger Kauf. ◆ *vi (haggle)* handeln. ■ **bargain for** *vt fus* rechnen mit.

bargain basement *n* Tiefgeschoss im Kaufhaus mit Sonderangeboten.

barge [baːdʒ] *n* Kahn *der.* ■ **barge in** *vi* : to ~ in *(on sb)* hereinlplatzen (bei jm).

bark [baːk] *n (of tree)* Rinde *die.* ◆ *vi (dog)* bellen.

barley ['baːlɪ] *n* Gerste *die.*

barmaid ['baːmeɪd] *n* Bardame *die.*

barman ['baːmən] *(pl* -men [-mən]) *n* Barkeeper *der.*

bar meal *n* einfaches Essen in einer Kneipe.

barn [baːn] *n* Scheune *die.*

barometer [bə'rɒmɪtə'] *n* Barometer *das.*

baron ['bærən] *n* Baron *der.*

baroque [bə'rɒk] *adj* barock.

barracks ['bærəks] npl Kaserne die.

barrel ['bærəl] n (of beer, wine, oil) Fass das ; (of gun) Lauf der.

barren ['bærən] adj (land, soil) unfruchtbar.

barricade [,bærɪ'keɪd] n Barrikade die.

barrier ['bærɪə'] n (fence, wall etc) Absperrung die ; (problem) Barriere die.

barrister ['bærɪstə'] n (Br) Barrister der, ≃ Rechtsanwalt der (-anwältin die).

bartender ['bɑːtendə'] n (Am) Barkeeper der.

barter ['bɑːtə'] vi tauschen.

base [beɪs] n (of lamp, pillar, mountain) Fuß der ; (MIL) Stützpunkt der. ◆ vt : to ~ sthg on sthg etw auf etw (D) aufbauen.

baseball ['beɪsbɔːl] n Baseball der.

baseball cap n Baseballkappe die.

basement ['beɪsmənt] n (in house) Kellergeschoss das ; (in store) Tiefgeschoss das.

bases ['beɪsiːz] pl → basis.

bash [bæʃ] vt (inf) : to ~ one's head sich (D) den Kopf anhauen.

basic ['beɪsɪk] adj grundlegend ; (accommodation, meal) einfach. ■ **basics** npl : the ~s die Grundlagen.

basically ['beɪsɪklɪ] adv grundsätzlich.

basil ['bæzl] n Basilikum das.

basin ['beɪsn] n (washbasin) Becken das ; (bowl) Schüssel die.

basis ['beɪsɪs] (pl -ses) n Grundlage die ; on a weekly ~ wöchentlich ; on the ~ of auf der Grundlage von.

basket ['bɑːskɪt] n Korb der.

basketball ['bɑːskɪtbɔːl] n Basketball der.

basmati rice [bəz'mæti-] n Basmatireis der.

bass[1] [beɪs] n (singer, instrument) Bass der. ◆ adj : a ~ guitar eine Bassgitarre.

bass[2] [bæs] n (fish) Barsch der.

bassoon [bə'suːn] n Fagott das.

bastard ['bɑːstəd] n (vulg) Scheißkerl der.

bat [bæt] n (in cricket, baseball) Schlagholz das ; (in table tennis) Schläger der ; (animal) Fledermaus die.

batch [bætʃ] n (of letters, books) Stapel der ; (of people) Gruppe die.

bath [bɑːθ] n Bad das ; (tub) Badewanne die. ◆ vt baden ; to have a ~ ein Bad nehmen. ■ **baths** npl (Br : public swimming pool) Schwimmbad das.

bathe [beɪð] vi (Br : swim) baden ; (Am : have bath) ein Bad nehmen.

bathing ['beɪðɪŋ] n (Br) Baden das.

bathrobe ['bɑːθrəub] n Bademantel der.

bathroom ['bɑːθrum] n Badezimmer das ; (Am : toilet) Toilette die.

bathroom cabinet n Badezimmerschrank der.

bathtub ['bɑːθtʌb] n Badewanne die.

baton ['bætən] n (of conductor) Taktstock der ; (truncheon) Schlagstock der.

batter ['bætə'] n (CULIN) Teig der. ◆ vt (wife, child) schlagen.

battered ['bætəd] adj (CULIN) im Teigmantel.

battery ['bætəri] n Batterie die.

battery charger [-,tʃɑːdʒə'] n Batterieladegerät das.

battle ['bætl] n Schlacht die ; (fig : struggle) Kampf der.

battlefield ['bætlfiːld] n Schlachtfeld das.

battlements ['bætlmənts] npl Zinnen pl.

battleship ['bætlʃɪp] n Schlachtschiff das.

Bavaria [bə'veərɪə] n Bayern nt.

bay [beɪ] n Bucht die.

bay leaf n Lorbeerblatt das.

bay window n Erkerfenster das.

B & B abbr = bed and breakfast.

BC (abbr of before Christ) v. Chr.

be [biː] (pt was, were, pp been) vi 1. (exist) sein ; there is/are es ist/sind... da, es gibt ; are there any shops near here? gibt es hier in der Nähe irgendwelche Geschäfte?

2. (referring to location) sein ; the hotel is near the airport das Hotel ist in der Nähe des Flughafens.

3. (referring to movement) sein ; have you ever been to Ireland? warst du/waren Sie schon mal in Irland? ; I'll ~ there in ten minutes ich komme in zehn Minuten.

4. (occur) sein ; my birthday is in June mein Geburtstag ist im Juni.

5. (identifying, describing) sein ; he's a doctor er ist Arzt ; I'm British ich bin Brite ; I'm hot/cold mir ist heiß/kalt.

6. (referring to health) : how are you? wie geht es dir/Ihnen? ; I'm fine mir geht es gut ; she's ill sie ist krank.

7. (referring to age) : how old are you? wie alt bist du/sind Sie? ; I'm 14 (years old) ich bin 14 (Jahre alt).

8. (referring to cost) kosten ; how much is it? wie viel kostet es? ; it's £10 es kostet 10 Pfund.

9. (referring to time, dates) sein ; what time is it? wie viel Uhr ist es? ; it's ten o'clock es ist zehn Uhr.

10. (referring to measurement) sein ; it's 10 metres long/high es ist 10 Meter lang/hoch ; I'm 8 stone ich wiege 50 Kilo.

11. (referring to weather) sein ; it's hot/cold es ist heiß/kalt.

◆ aux vb 1. (forming continuous tense) : I'm learning German ich lerne Deutsch ; we've been visiting the museum wir waren im Museum.

2. (forming passive) werden ; they were defeated sie wurden geschlagen ; the flight was delayed das Flugzeug hatte Verspätung.

3. (with infinitive to express order) : all rooms are to ~ vacated by 10.00 am alle Zimmer müssen bis 10 Uhr geräumt sein.

4. (with infinitive to express future tense) : the race is to start at

noon das Rennen ist für 12 Uhr angesetzt.

5. *(in tag questions)* : it's cold, isn't it? es ist kalt, nicht wahr?

beach [biːtʃ] *n* Strand *der*.

bead [biːd] *n (of glass, wood etc)* Perle *die*.

beak [biːk] *n* Schnabel *der*.

beaker ['biːkə'] *n* Becher *der*.

beam [biːm] *n (of light)* Strahl *der* ; *(of wood, concrete)* Balken *der*. ◆ *vi* strahlen.

bean [biːn] *n* Bohne *die*.

bean curd [-kɜːd] *n* Tofu *der*.

beansprouts ['biːnsprauts] *npl* Sojabohnensprossen *pl*.

bear [beə'] *(pt* bore, *pp* borne) *n (animal)* Bär *der*. ◆ *vt (support)* tragen ; *(endure)* ertragen. ◆ *vi* : to ~ left/right sich links/rechts halten.

bearable ['beərəbl] *adj* erträglich.

beard [biəd] *n* Bart *der*.

bearer ['beərə'] *n (of cheque, passport)* Inhaber *der* (-in *die*).

bearing ['beəriŋ] *n (relevance)* Auswirkung *die* ; to get one's ~s sich orientieren.

beast [biːst] *n (animal)* Tier *das*.

beat [biːt] *(pt* beat, *pp* beaten [biːtn]) *n (of heart, pulse)* Herzschlag *der* ; *(MUS)* Takt *der*. ◆ *vt* schlagen. ▪ **beat down** *vt sep* herunterlhandeln. ◆ *vi (sun)* herunterlbrennen ; *(rain)* herunterlprasseln. ▪ **beat up** *vt sep* verprügeln.

beautiful ['bjuːtiful] *adj* schön.

beauty ['bjuːti] *n* Schönheit *die*.

beauty parlour *n* Schönheitssalon *der*.

beauty spot *n (place)* Ausflugsort *der*.

beaver ['biːvə'] *n* Biber *der*.

became [bi'keim] *pt* → become.

because [bi'kɒz] *conj* weil ; ~ of wegen (+G) or D.

beckon ['bekən] *vi* : to ~ to zulwinken (+D).

become [bi'kʌm] *(pt* became, *pp* become) *vi* werden ; what became of him? was ist aus ihm geworden?

bed [bed] *n* Bett *das* ; *(of sea)* Meeresboden *der* ; *(CULIN)* : served on a ~ of... angerichtet auf (+D)... ; in ~ im Bett ; to get out of ~ auflstehen ; to go to ~ ins Bett gehen ; to go to ~ with sb mit jm ins Bett gehen ; to make the ~ das Bett machen.

bed and breakfast *n (Br)* ≃ Zimmer *das* mit Frühstück.

ℹ️ **BED AND BREAKFAST**

Bei „Bed and Breakfast", meist einfach „B & B" oder auch „guest house" genannt, handelt es sich um eine in Großbritannien sehr verbreitete Unterkunftsmöglichkeit bei Privatleuten, die ein oder mehrere Zimmer für zahlende Gäste bereitstellen. Das Frühstück, ein „English breakfast", besteht aus Würstchen, Eiern, gebratenem Speck, Toast und Tee oder Kaffee und ist im Zimmerpreis inbegriffen.

bedclothes ['bedkləʊðz] *npl* Bettwäsche *die*.

bedding ['bedɪŋ] *n* Bettzeug *das*.

bed linen *n* Bettwäsche *die*.

bedroom ['bedrʊm] *n* Schlafzimmer *das*.

bedside table ['bedsaɪd-] *n* Nachttisch *der*.

bedsit ['bed,sɪt] *n (Br)* ≃ möbliertes Zimmer *das*.

bedspread ['bedspred] *n* Tagesdecke *die*.

bedtime ['bedtaɪm] *n* Schlafenszeit *die*.

bee [biː] *n* Biene *die*.

beech [biːtʃ] *n* Buche *die*.

beef [biːf] *n* Rindfleisch *das* ; ~ Wellington Filet *das* Wellington.

beefburger ['biːf,bɜːgə'] *n* Hamburger *der*.

beehive ['biːhaɪv] *n* Bienenstock *der*.

been [biːn] *pp* → **be**.

beer [bɪə'] *n* Bier *das*.

BEER

Es gibt zweierlei Arten britisches Bier : „bitter" (halbdunkles Bier) und „lager" (helles Bier). In Schottland wird bitter „heavy" genannt. Es ist halbdunkles Bier mit leicht bitterem Geschmack ; „lager" ist das im übrigen Europa verbreitete, helle Bier. Die Bezeichnung „real ale" beschreibt eine spezielle Art von „bitter" und ist meist teurer als gewöhnliches „bitter". Es wird von Hand gezapft und in kleinen Brauereibetrieben nach traditionellen Rezepten und überlieferten Herstellungsverfahren gebraut. In den Vereinigten Staaten ist „lager" die gängige Biersorte.

beer garden *n* Biergarten *der*.

beer mat *n* Bierdeckel *der*.

beetle ['biːtl] *n* Käfer *der*.

beetroot ['biːtruːt] *n* rote Bete *die*.

before [bɪ'fɔː'] *adv* schon einmal. ◆ *prep* vor *(+D)*. ◆ *conj* bevor ; ~ **you leave** bevor du gehst ; **the day** ~ der Tag zuvor ; **the week** ~ **last** vorletzte Woche.

beforehand [bɪ'fɔːhænd] *adv* vorher.

befriend [bɪ'frend] *vt* sich anfreunden mit.

beg [beg] *vi* betteln. ◆ *vt* : to ~ **sb to do sthg** jn bitten, etw zu tun ; **to** ~ **for** *(for money, food)* betteln um.

began [bɪ'gæn] *pt* → **begin**.

beggar ['begə'] *n* Bettler *der* (-in *die*).

begin [bɪ'gɪn] *(pt* began, *pp* begun) *vt* & *vi* anfangen, beginnen ; **to** ~ **doing** OR **to do sthg** anfangen, etw zu tun ; **to** ~ **by doing sthg** etw als Erstes tun ; ~ **with** zunächst.

beginner [bɪ'gɪnə'] *n* Anfänger *der* (-in *die*).

beginning [bɪ'gɪnɪŋ] *n* Anfang *der*.

begun [bɪ'gʌn] *pp* → **begin**.

behalf [bɪ'hɑːf] *n* : **on** ~ **of** im Auftrag *(+G)*.

behave [bɪ'heɪv] vi sich verhalten ; to ~ (o.s.) (be good) sich benehmen.

behavior [bɪ'heɪvjə'] (Am) = behaviour.

behaviour [bɪ'heɪvjə'] n Verhalten das ; good/bad ~ gutes/schlechtes Benehmen.

behind [bɪ'haɪnd] prep hinter (+A,D). ◆ n (inf) Hintern der. ◆ adv hinten ; (late) : to be ~ im Verzug sein ; to leave sthg ~ etw zurücklassen ; to stay ~ dableiben.

beige [beɪʒ] adj beige.

being ['biːɪŋ] n Wesen das ; to come into ~ entstehen.

belated [bɪ'leɪtɪd] adj verspätet.

belch [beltʃ] vi rülpsen.

Belgian ['beldʒən] adj belgisch. ◆ n Belgier der (-in die).

Belgium ['beldʒəm] n Belgien nt.

belief [bɪ'liːf] n Glaube der ; it is my ~ that ich bin davon überzeugt, dass.

believe [bɪ'liːv] vt (story, think) glauben ; (person) glauben (+D). ◆ vi : to ~ in sthg glauben an etw (A) ; to ~ in doing sthg viel von etw halten.

believer [bɪ'liːvə'] n Gläubige der, die.

bell [bel] n Glocke die ; (of phone, door) Klingel die.

bellboy ['belbɔɪ] n Page der.

bellow ['beləʊ] vi brüllen.

belly ['belɪ] n (inf) Bauch der.

belly button n (inf) Bauchnabel der.

belong [bɪ'lɒŋ] vi gehören ; to ~ to (property) gehören (+D) ;

(to club, party) anlgehören (+D).

belongings [bɪ'lɒŋɪŋz] npl Sachen pl.

below [bɪ'ləʊ] adv unten. ◆ prep unter (+A,D).

belt [belt] n (for clothes) Gürtel der ; (TECH) Riemen der.

beltway ['beltweɪ] n (Am) Ringautobahn die.

bench [bentʃ] n Bank die.

bend [bend] (pt & pp bent) n (in road) Kurve die ; (in river, pipe) Biegung die. ◆ vt (leg, knees) beugen ; (pipe, wire) biegen. ◆ vi (road, river, pipe) sich biegen. ■ bend down vi sich bücken. ■ bend over vi sich nach vorn beugen.

beneath [bɪ'niːθ] adv unten. ◆ prep unter (+A,D).

beneficial [ˌbenɪ'fɪʃl] adj nützlich.

benefit ['benɪfɪt] n (advantage) Vorteil der ; (usefulness) Nutzen der ; (money) Unterstützung die. ◆ vt nützen (+D). ◆ vi : to ~ from sthg von etw profitieren ; for the ~ of für.

benign [bɪ'naɪn] adj (MED) gutartig.

bent [bent] pt & pp → bend.

bereaved [bɪ'riːvd] n : the ~ der/die Hinterbliebene.

beret ['bereɪ] n Baskenmütze die.

Berlin [bɜː'lɪn] n Berlin nt.

Bermuda shorts [bə'mjuːdə-] npl Bermudashorts pl.

Bern [bɜːn] n Bern nt.

berry ['berɪ] n Beere die.

berserk [bə'zɜːk] adj : to go ~ vor Wut außer sich geraten.

berth [bɜːθ] *n* (*for ship*) Liegeplatz *der* ; (*in ship*) Koje *die* ; (*in train*) Bett *das*.

beside [bɪ'saɪd] *prep* neben (+*A,D*) ; ~ **the sea/river** am Meer/Fluss ; **to be ~ the point** nichts damit zu tun haben.

besides [bɪ'saɪdz] *adv* außerdem. ◆ *prep* außer (+*D*).

best [best] *adj* beste(-r) (-s). ◆ *adv* am besten. ◆ *n* : **the ~** der/die/das Beste ; **a pint of ~** (*beer*) ein großes Glas 'bitter'-Bier ; **the ~ thing to do is...** am besten wäre es, ... ; **to make the ~ of** sthg das Beste aus einer Sache machen ; **to do one's ~** sein Bestes tun ; **'~ before...'** 'mindestens haltbar bis...' ; **at ~** bestenfalls ; **all the ~!** alles Gute!

best man *n* Trauzeuge *der* (des Bräutigams).

best-seller [-'selə˙] *n* (*book*) Bestseller *der*.

bet [bet] (*pt & pp* bet) *n* Wette *die*. ◆ *vt* wetten. ◆ *vi* : **to ~ on** sthg auf etw (*A*) setzen ; **I ~ (that) you can't do it** ich wette, du kannst das nicht.

betray [bɪ'treɪ] *vt* verraten.

better [betə˙] *adj & adv* besser ; **I'm much ~ now** es geht mir jetzt viel besser ; **you had ~...** du solltest lieber... ; **to get ~** (*in health*) gesund werden ; (*improve*) sich verbessern.

betting [betɪŋ] *n* Wetten *das*.

betting shop *n* (Br) Wettbüro *das*.

between [bɪ'twiːn] *prep* zwischen (+*D*) ; (*in space*) zwischen (+*A,D*) ; (*share*) unter (+*A,D*). ◆ *adv* dazwischen ; **in ~** (*in space*) zwischen (+*A,D*) ;

(*in time*) zwischen (+*D*), dazwischen.

beverage ['bevərɪdʒ] *n* (*fml*) Getränk *das*.

beware [bɪ'weə˙] *vi* : **to ~ of** sich in Acht nehmen vor (+*D*) ; **'~ of the dog'** 'Vorsicht, bissiger Hund'.

bewildered [bɪ'wɪldəd] *adj* verwirrt.

beyond [bɪ'jɒnd] *prep* über... (+*A*) hinaus ; (*responsibility*) außerhalb (+*G*) ; (*doubt, reach*) außer (+*D*). ◆ *adv* darüber hinaus.

biased ['baɪəst] *adj* parteiisch.

bib [bɪb] *n* (*for baby*) Lätzchen *das*.

bible ['baɪbl] *n* Bibel *die*.

biceps ['baɪseps] *n* Bizeps *der*.

bicycle ['baɪsɪkl] *n* Fahrrad *das*.

bicycle path *n* Radweg *der*.

bicycle pump *n* Luftpumpe *die*.

bid [bɪd] (*pt & pp* bid) *n* (*at auction*) Gebot *das* ; (*attempt*) Versuch *der*. ◆ *vt* (*money*) bieten. ◆ *vi* : **to ~ (for)** bieten (auf (+*A*)).

bidet ['biːdeɪ] *n* Bidet *das*.

big [bɪg] *adj* groß ; **my ~ brother** mein großer Bruder ; **how ~ is it?** wie groß ist es?

bike [baɪk] *n* (*inf* : *bicycle*) Rad *das* ; (*motorcycle*) Maschine *die*.

biking [baɪkɪŋ] *n* : **to go ~** eine Radtour machen.

bikini [bɪ'kiːnɪ] *n* Bikini *der*.

bikini bottom *n* Bikinihose *die*.

bikini top *n* Bikinioberteil *das*.

bilingual [baɪ'lɪŋgwəl] *adj* zweisprachig.

bill

bill [bɪl] *n (for meal, hotel room)* Rechnung *die* ; *(Am : bank note)* Geldschein *der* ; *(at cinema, theatre)* Programm *das* ; *(POL)* Gesetzentwurf *der* ; **can I have the ~, please?** die Rechnung, bitte.

billboard ['bɪlbɔːd] *n* Plakatwand *die*.

billfold ['bɪlfəʊld] *n (Am)* Brieftasche *die*.

billiards ['bɪljədz] *n* Billard *das*.

billion ['bɪljən] *n (thousand million)* Milliarde *die* ; *(Br : million million)* Billion *die*.

bin [bɪn] *n (rubbish bin)* Mülleimer *der* ; *(wastepaper bin)* Papierkorb *der* ; *(for bread, flour)* Kasten *der* ; *(on plane)* Ablage *die*.

bind [baɪnd] *(pt & pp bound) vt (tie up)* festlbinden.

binding ['baɪndɪŋ] *n (of book)* Einband *der* ; *(for ski)* Bindung *die*.

bingo ['bɪŋgəʊ] *n* Bingo *das*.

BINGO

Bingo ist ein in Großbritannien weit verbreitetes Glücksspiel, bei dem Geld oder Preise gewonnen werden können. Jeder Spieler erhält eine mit Nummern bedruckte Karte. Ein Zahlenausrufer ruft dann der Reihe nach zufällig gewählte Zahlen aus, und gewonnen hat, wer als Erste(r) eine ganze Reihe bzw. Karte richtig hat. Bingo wird oft in ehemaligen Kinos oder großen Stadt- bzw. Gemeindehal-

len oder in Seebädern gespielt.

---

binoculars [bɪ'nɒkjʊləz] *npl* Fernglas *das*.

biodegradable [ˌbaɪəʊdɪ'greɪdəbl] *adj* biologisch abbaubar.

biography [baɪ'ɒgrəfɪ] *n* Biografie *die*.

biological [ˌbaɪə'lɒdʒɪkl] *adj* biologisch.

biology [baɪ'ɒlədʒɪ] *n* Biologie *die*.

birch [bɜːtʃ] *n* Birke *die*.

bird [bɜːd] *n* Vogel *der* ; *(Br : inf : woman)* Mieze *die*.

bird-watching [-ˌwɒtʃɪŋ] *n* : **to go ~** Vögel beobachten gehen.

Biro® ['baɪərəʊ] *n* Kugelschreiber *der*.

birth [bɜːθ] *n* Geburt *die* ; **by ~** von Geburt ; **to give ~ to** zur Welt bringen.

birth certificate *n* Geburtsurkunde *die*.

birth control *n* Geburtenregelung *die*.

birthday ['bɜːθdeɪ] *n* Geburtstag *der* ; **happy ~!** herzlichen Glückwunsch zum Geburtstag!

birthday card *n* Geburtstagskarte *die*.

birthday party *n* Geburtstagsfeier *die*.

birthplace ['bɜːθpleɪs] *n* Geburtsort *der*.

biscuit ['bɪskɪt] *n (Br)* Plätzchen *das* ; *(Am : scone)* Hefebrötchen, *das üblicherweise mit Bratensaft gegessen wird*.

bishop ['bɪʃəp] n (RELIG) Bischof der (Bischöfin die) ; (in chess) Läufer der.

bistro ['bi:strəʊ] n Bistro das.

bit [bɪt] pt → **bite**. ◆ n (piece) Stück das ; (of drill) Bohrer der (Metallstift) ; (of bridle) Gebiss das ; a ~ ein bisschen ; a ~ of cheese ein bisschen Käse ; not a ~ überhaupt nicht ; ~ by ~ allmählich.

bitch [bɪtʃ] n (vulg : woman) dumme Kuh die ; (dog) Hündin die.

bite [baɪt] (pt bit, pp bitten ['bɪtn]) n (of food) Happen der ; (from insect) Stich der ; (from snake) Biss der. ◆ vt beißen ; (subj : insect) stechen ; to have a ~ to eat eine Kleinigkeit essen.

bitter ['bɪtə'] adj bitter. ◆ n (Br : beer) dem Altbier ähnliches Bier.

bitter lemon n Bitter Lemon das.

bizarre [bɪ'zɑ:'] adj bizarr.

black [blæk] adj schwarz. ◆ n (colour) Schwarz das ; (person) Schwarze der, die. ■ **black out** vi ohnmächtig werden.

black and white adj (film, photo) schwarzweiß.

blackberry ['blækbrɪ] n Brombeere die.

blackbird ['blækbɜ:d] n Amsel die.

blackboard ['blækbɔ:d] n Tafel die.

black cherry n dunkle Kirsche.

blackcurrant [,blæk'kʌrənt] n schwarze Johannisbeere.

black eye n blaues Auge.

Black Forest n Schwarzwald der.

Black Forest gâteau n Schwarzwälder Kirschtorte die.

black ice n Glatteis das.

blackmail ['blækmeɪl] n Erpressung die. ◆ vt erpressen.

blackout ['blækaʊt] n (power cut) Stromausfall der.

black pepper n schwarzer Pfeffer.

black pudding n (Br) Blutwurst die (in Scheiben geschnitten und gebraten).

blacksmith ['blæksmɪθ] n Schmied der.

bladder ['blædə'] n Blase die.

blade [bleɪd] n (of knife, razor) Klinge die ; (of saw, propeller, oar) Blatt das ; (of grass) Halm der.

blame [bleɪm] n Schuld die. ◆ vt beschuldigen ; to ~ sb (for sthg) jm die Schuld (an etw (D)) geben ; to ~ sthg on sb die Schuld an etw (D) auf jn schieben.

bland [blænd] adj fade.

blank [blæŋk] adj leer. ◆ n (empty space) Lücke die.

blank cheque n Blankoscheck der.

blanket ['blæŋkɪt] n Decke die.

blast [blɑ:st] n (explosion) Explosion die ; (of air, wind) Windstoß der. ◆ excl (inf) Mist! ; at full ~ auf Hochtouren.

blaze [bleɪz] n (fire) Feuer das. ◆ vi (fire) brennen ; (sun, light) leuchten.

blazer ['bleɪzə'] n Blazer der.

bleach [bli:tʃ] n Bleichmittel das. ◆ vt bleichen.

bleak [bli:k] adj trostlos.

bleed [bli:d] (pt & pp **bled** [bled]) vi bluten.

blend [blend] n (of coffee, whisky) Mischung die. ◆ vt mischen.

blender ['blendə] n Mixer der.

bless [bles] vt segnen ; ~ you! (said after sneeze) Gesundheit!

blessing ['blesɪŋ] n Segen der.

blew [blu:] pt → blow.

blind [blaɪnd] adj blind. ◆ n (for window) Rouleau das. ◆ npl : the ~ die Blinden.

blind corner n unübersichtliche Kurve.

blindfold ['blaɪndfəʊld] n Augenbinde die. ◆ vt : to ~ sb jm die Augen verbinden.

blind spot n (AUT) toter Winkel.

blink [blɪŋk] vi zwinkern.

blinkers ['blɪŋkəz] npl (Br) Scheuklappen pl.

bliss [blɪs] n vollkommenes Glück.

blister ['blɪstə] n Blase die.

blizzard ['blɪzəd] n Schneesturm der.

bloated ['bləʊtɪd] adj (after eating) vollgegessen.

blob [blɒb] n (of paint) Klecks der ; (of cream) Klacks der.

block [blɒk] n Block der. ◆ vt (obstruct) blockieren ; to have a ~ed (up) nose eine verstopfte Nase haben. ▪ **block up** vt sep (pipe) verstopfen.

blockage ['blɒkɪdʒ] n Verstopfung die.

block capitals npl Druckbuchstaben pl.

block of flats n Wohnblock der.

bloke [bləʊk] n (Br : inf) Typ der.

blond [blɒnd] adj blond. ◆ n Blonde der.

blonde [blɒnd] adj blond. ◆ n Blondine die.

blood [blʌd] n Blut das.

blood donor n Blutspender der (-in die).

blood group n Blutgruppe die.

blood poisoning n Blutvergiftung die.

blood pressure n Blutdruck der.

bloodshot ['blʌdʃɒt] adj blutunterlaufen.

blood test n Blutprobe die.

blood transfusion n Bluttransfusion die.

bloody ['blʌdɪ] adj blutig ; (Br : vulg : damn) verdammt. ◆ adv (Br : vulg) verdammt.

Bloody Mary [-'meərɪ] n Bloody Mary der (Cocktail aus Wodka und Tomatensaft).

bloom [blu:m] n Blüte die. ◆ vi blühen ; to be in ~ in Blüte stehen.

blossom ['blɒsəm] n Blüte die.

blot [blɒt] n (of ink) (Tinten)klecks der.

blotch [blɒtʃ] n Fleck der.

blotting paper ['blɒtɪŋ-] n Löschpapier das.

blouse [blaʊz] n Bluse die.

blow [bləʊ] (pt blew, pp blown) vt blasen ; (subj : wind) wehen. ◆ vi (wind) wehen ; (person) blasen ; (fuse) durchlbrennen. ◆ n Schlag der ; to ~ one's nose sich (D) die Nase putzen.

■ **blow up** vt sep (cause to explode) sprengen; (inflate) auflblasen. ◆ vi (explode) explodieren.

blow-dry n Föhnen das. ◆ vt föhnen.

blown [bləʊn] pp → **blow**.

BLT n (sandwich) Sandwich mit Speck, grünem Salat und Tomaten.

blue [bluː] adj blau; (film) Porno-. ◆ n Blau das. ■ **blues** n (MUS) Blues der.

bluebell ['bluːbel] n Glockenblume die.

blueberry ['bluːbəri] n Blaubeere die.

bluebottle ['bluːˌbɒtl] n Schmeißfliege die.

blue cheese n Blauschimmelkäse der.

bluff [blʌf] n (cliff) Steilhang der. ◆ vi bluffen.

blunder ['blʌndə] n Schnitzer der.

blunt [blʌnt] adj (knife, pencil) stumpf; (fig : person) unverblümt.

blurred [blɜːd] adj unscharf.

blush [blʌʃ] vi erröten.

blusher ['blʌʃə] n Rouge das.

blustery ['blʌstəri] adj stürmisch.

board [bɔːd] n (plank, for games) Brett das; (notice board) schwarzes Brett; (blackboard) Tafel die; (of company) Vorstand der; (hardboard) Pressspan der. ◆ vt (plane, ship) an Bord (+G) gehen; (bus) einlsteigen in (+A); ~ and lodging Unterkunft die und Verpflegung; full ~ Vollpension die

; half ~ Halbpension die; on ~ an Bord; (plane, ship) an Bord (+G); (bus) in (+D).

board game n Brettspiel das.

boarding ['bɔːdɪŋ] n (of plane) Einsteigen das.

boarding card n Bordkarte die.

boardinghouse ['bɔːdɪŋhaʊs, pl -haʊzɪz] n Pension die.

boarding school n Internat das.

board of directors n Vorstand der.

boast [bəʊst] vi : to ~ (about sthg) anlgeben (mit etw).

boat [bəʊt] n Boot das; (large) Schiff das; to go by ~ mit dem Schiff fahren.

bob [bɒb] n (hairstyle) Bob der.

bobby pin ['bɒbɪ-] n (Am) Haarspange die.

bodice ['bɒdɪs] n Oberteil das.

body ['bɒdɪ] n Körper der; (corpse) Leiche die; (garment) Body der; (of car) Karosserie die; (organization) Organisation die.

bodyguard ['bɒdɪgɑːd] n Leibwächter der.

bodywork ['bɒdɪwɜːk] n Karosserie die.

bog [bɒg] n Sumpf der.

bogus ['bəʊgəs] adj (name) falsch.

boil [bɔɪl] vt & vi kochen. ◆ n (on skin) Furunkel der; to ~ the kettle Wasser aufsetzen.

boiled egg [bɔɪld-] n gekochtes Ei.

boiled potatoes [bɔɪld-] npl Salzkartoffeln pl.

boiler ['bɔɪlə] n Boiler der.

boiling (hot) [ˈbɔɪlɪŋ-] *adj* (*inf*: *water*) kochend heiß; (*weather*) wahnsinnig heiß; I'm ~ mir ist fürchterlich heiß.

bold [bəʊld] *adj* (*brave*) mutig.

bollard [ˈbɒlɑːd] *n* (*Br*: *on road*) Poller *der*.

bolt [bəʊlt] *n* (*on door, window*) Riegel *der*; (*screw*) Bolzen *der*. ◆ *vt* (*door, window*) verriegeln.

bomb [bɒm] *n* Bombe *die*. ◆ *vt* bombardieren.

bombard [bɒmˈbɑːd] *vt* bombardieren.

bomb scare *n* Bombenalarm *der*.

bomb shelter *n* Luftschutzkeller *der*.

bond [bɒnd] *n* (*tie, connection*) Verbindung *die*.

bone [bəʊn] *n* Knochen *der*; (*of fish*) Gräte *die*.

boned [bəʊnd] *adj* (*chicken*) ohne Knochen; (*fish*) entgrätet.

boneless [ˈbəʊnləs] *adj* (*chicken, pork*) ohne Knochen.

bonfire [ˈbɒn,faɪə] *n* Feuer *das* (*im Freien*).

bonnet [ˈbɒnɪt] *n* (*Br*: *of car*) Motorhaube *die*.

bonus [ˈbəʊnəs] (*pl* -es) *n* (*extra money*) Prämie *die*; (*additional advantage*) Bonus *der*.

bony [ˈbəʊnɪ] *adj* (*fish*) grätig; (*chicken*) mit viel Knochen.

boo [buː] *vi* buhen.

boogie [ˈbuːgɪ] *vi* (*inf*) schwofen.

book [bʊk] *n* Buch *das*; (*of stamps, matches, tickets*) Heft *das*. ◆ *vt* (*reserve*) buchen.
■ **book in** *vi* (*at hotel*) sich anmelden.

bookable [ˈbʊkəbl] *adj* (*seats, flight*) im Vorverkauf erhältlich.

bookcase [ˈbʊkkeɪs] *n* Bücherschrank *der*.

booking [ˈbʊkɪŋ] *n* (*reservation*) Buchung *die*.

booking office *n* (*in theatre, cinema*) Kasse *die*; (*at train station*) Fahrkartenschalter *der*.

bookkeeping [ˈbʊk,kiːpɪŋ] *n* Buchhaltung *die*.

booklet [ˈbʊklɪt] *n* Broschüre *die*.

bookmaker's [ˈbʊk,meɪkəz] *n* Wettbüro *das*.

bookmark [ˈbʊkmɑːk] *n* Lesezeichen *das*.

bookshelf [ˈbʊkʃelf] (*pl* -shelves [-ʃelvz]) *n* (*shelf*) Bücherregal *das*; (*bookcase*) Bücherschrank *der*.

bookshop [ˈbʊkʃɒp] *n* Buchhandlung *die*.

bookstall [ˈbʊkstɔːl] *n* Bücherstand *der*.

bookstore [ˈbʊkstɔːʳ] = **bookshop**.

book token *n* Büchergutschein *der*.

boom [buːm] *n* (*sudden growth*) Boom *der*. ◆ *vi* dröhnen.

boost [buːst] *vt* (*production*) anIkurbeln; (*profits*) steigern; (*confidence*) stärken.

booster [ˈbuːstəʳ] *n* (*injection*) Wiederholungsimpfung *die*.

boot [buːt] *n* (*shoe*) Stiefel *der*; (*Br*: *of car*) Kofferraum *der*.

booth [buːð] *n* (*for telephone*) Telefonzelle *die*; (*at fairground*) Bude *die*.

booze [buːz] *n* (*inf*) Alkohol *der*. ◆ *vi* (*inf*) saufen.

bop [bɒp] n (inf: dance) : **to have a ~** schwofen.

border ['bɔːdə'] n (of country) Grenze die ; (edge) Rand der ; **the Borders** an England grenzender südlicher Teil Schottlands.

bore [bɔː'] pt → **bear**. ◆ n (inf: boring person) langweiliger Mensch ; (boring thing) langweilige Sache. ◆ vt (person) langweilen ; (hole) bohren.

bored [bɔːd] adj : **to be ~** sich langweilen.

boredom ['bɔːdəm] n Langeweile die.

boring ['bɔːrɪŋ] adj langweilig.

born [bɔːn] adj : **to be ~** geboren werden ; **I was ~ in 1975** ich bin 1975 geboren.

borne [bɔːn] pp → **bear**.

borough ['bʌrə] n Regierungsbezirk, der entweder eine Stadt oder einen Stadtteil umfasst.

borrow ['bɒrəʊ] vt sich (D) borgen, (sich (D)) leihen.

bosom ['bʊzəm] n Busen der.

boss [bɒs] n Chef der (-in die).
▩ **boss around** vt sep herumkommandieren.

bossy ['bɒsɪ] adj herrisch.

botanical garden [bə'tænɪkl-] n botanischer Garten.

both [bəʊθ] adj & pron beide. ◆ adv : **~... and...** sowohl... als auch... ; **~ of them speak German** sie sprechen beide Deutsch ; **~ of us** wir beide.

bother ['bɒðə'] vt stören. ◆ n (trouble) Mühe die. ◆ vi : **don't ~!** das ist nicht nötig! ; **he didn't even ~ to say thank you** er hat sich noch nicht mal bedankt ; **you needn't have ~ed** das wäre

nicht nötig gewesen ; **I can't be ~ed** ich habe keine Lust ; **it's no ~!** kein Problem!

bottle ['bɒtl] n Flasche die.

bottle bank n Altglascontainer der.

bottled ['bɒtld] adj in Flaschen ; **~ beer** Flaschenbier das ; **~ water** Wasser das in der Flasche.

bottle opener [-ˌəʊpnə'] n Flaschenöffner der.

bottom ['bɒtəm] adj (lowest) unterste(-r) (-s) ; (last, worst) schlechteste(-r) (-s). ◆ n (of hill, page, stairs) Fuß der ; (of glass, bin, box) Boden der ; (of sea, river) Grund der ; (buttocks) Hintern der ; **he's ~ of the class** er ist der Schlechteste in der Klasse ; **in ~ gear** im ersten Gang ; **the ~ of** (bag, box) unten in (A,D) ; (page) unten auf (A,D) ; (street, garden) am Ende (+G).

bought [bɔːt] pt & pp → **buy**.

boulder ['bəʊldə'] n Felsblock der.

bounce [baʊns] vi (rebound) ab|prallen ; (jump) springen ; (cheque) nicht gedeckt sein.

bouncer ['baʊnsə'] n (inf) Rausschmeißer der.

bouncy ['baʊnsɪ] adj (person) munter.

bound [baʊnd] pt & pp → **bind**. ◆ vi (leap) springen. ◆ adj : **to be ~ to do sthg** etw ganz bestimmt tun ; **it's ~ to rain** es wird ganz bestimmt regnen ; **to be ~ for** auf dem Weg sein nach/zu ; **this room is out of ~s** dieses Zimmer darf nicht betreten werden.

boundary ['baʊndrɪ] n Grenze die.

bouquet [bʊ'keɪ] n (of flowers) Strauß der ; (of wine) Bukett das.

bourbon ['bɜːbən] n Bourbon der.

bout [baʊt] n (of illness) Anfall der ; (of activity) Drang der.

boutique [buː'tiːk] n Boutique die.

bow¹ [baʊ] n (of head) Verbeugung die ; (of ship) Bug der. ◆ vi sich verbeugen.

bow² [bəʊ] n (knot) Schleife die ; (weapon, for instrument) Bogen der.

bowels ['baʊəlz] npl Darm der.

bowl [bəʊl] n Schüssel die ; (shallower) Schale die ; (for soup) Teller der. ■ **bowls** npl Art Bocciaspiel, bei dem Kugeln über den Rasen gerollt werden.

bowling alley ['bəʊlɪŋ-] n Bowlingbahn die.

bowling green ['bəʊlɪŋ-] n Rasenfläche zum 'Bowls-Spielen.

bow tie [,bəʊ-] n Fliege die.

box [bɒks] n (container) Kiste die ; (smaller) Schachtel die ; (of cardboard) Karton der ; (on form) Kästchen das ; (in theatre) Loge die. ◆ vi boxen ; **a ~ of chocolates** eine Schachtel Pralinen.

boxer ['bɒksə'] n Boxer der.

boxer shorts npl Boxershorts pl.

boxing ['bɒksɪŋ] n Boxen das.

Boxing Day n zweiter Weihnachtsfeiertag.

boxing gloves npl Boxhandschuhe pl.

boxing ring n Boxring der.

box office n Kasse die.

boy [bɔɪ] n Junge der. ◆ excl (inf) : **(oh) ~!** Mensch!

boycott ['bɔɪkɒt] vt boykottieren.

boyfriend ['bɔɪfrend] n Freund der.

boy scout n Pfadfinder der.

BR abbr = **British Rail**.

bra [brɑː] n BH der.

brace [breɪs] n (for teeth) Spange die. ■ **braces** npl (Br) Hosenträger pl.

bracelet ['breɪslɪt] n Armband das.

bracken ['brækn] n Farnkraut das.

bracket ['brækɪt] n (written symbol) Klammer die ; (support) Konsole die.

brag [bræg] vi prahlen.

braid [breɪd] n (hairstyle) Zopf der ; (on clothes) Zopfmuster das.

brain [breɪn] n Gehirn das.

brainy ['breɪnɪ] adj (inf) clever.

braised [breɪzd] adj geschmort.

brake [breɪk] n Bremse die. ◆ vi bremsen.

brake block n Bremsklotz der.

brake fluid n Bremsflüssigkeit die.

brake light n Bremslicht das.

brake pad n Bremsbelag der.

brake pedal n Bremspedal das.

bran [bræn] n Kleie die.

branch [brɑːntʃ] n (of tree) Ast der ; (of bank, company) Filiale die ; (of subject) Zweig der. ■ **branch off** vi ablzweigen.

branch line n Nebenlinie die.

brand [brænd] n (of product) Marke die. ◆ vt : to ~ sb (as) in ablstempeln (als).

brand-new adj nagelneu.

brandy ['brændɪ] n Weinbrand der.

brash [bræʃ] adj (pej) dreist.

brass [brɑːs] n Messing das.

brass band n Blaskapelle die.

brasserie ['bræsərɪ] n Brasserie die.

brassiere [(Br) 'bræsɪə', (Am) brə'zɪr] n Büstenhalter der.

brat [bræt] n (inf) Balg der or das.

brave [breɪv] adj mutig.

bravery ['breɪvərɪ] n Mut der.

bravo [ˌbrɑː'vəʊ] excl bravo!

brawl [brɔːl] n Rauferei die.

Brazil [brə'zɪl] n Brasilien nt.

brazil nut n Paranuss die.

breach [briːtʃ] vt (contract, confidence) brechen.

bread [bred] n Brot das ; ~ and butter Butterbrot das.

bread bin n (Br) Brotkasten der.

breadboard ['bredbɔːd] n Brotbrett das.

bread box (Am) = bread bin.

breadcrumbs ['bredkrʌmz] npl Brotkrumen pl.

breaded ['bredɪd] adj paniert.

bread knife n Brotmesser das.

bread roll n Brötchen das, Semmel die (Süddt, Österr).

breadth [bretθ] n Breite die.

break [breɪk] (pt broke, pp broken) n (interruption) Unterbrechung die ; (rest, playtime) Pause die. ◆ vt (damage) kaputtlmachen ; (smash) zerbrechen ; (law, promise, record) brechen ; (journey) unterbrechen. ◆ vi (object, machine) kaputtlgehen ; (glass) zerbrechen ; (dawn) dämmern ; (voice) im Stimmbruch sein ; to ~ the news melden, dass ; without a ~ ohne Pause ; a lucky ~ ein Glückstreffer ; to ~ one's leg sich (D) das Bein brechen. ■ **break down** vi (car) eine Panne haben ; (machine) versagen ; (person) zusammenlbrechen. ◆ vt sep (door) auflbrechen ; (barrier) niederlreißen. ■ **break in** vi einlbrechen. ■ **break off** vt sep & vi ablbrechen. ■ **break out** vi auslbrechen ; to ~ out in a rash einen Ausschlag bekommen. ■ **break up** vi (with spouse, *partner)* sich trennen ; *(meeting)* zu Ende gehen ; *(marriage)* in die Brüche gehen ; **school ~s up on Friday** am Freitag fangen die Ferien an.

breakage ['breɪkɪdʒ] *n* Bruchschaden *der*.

breakdown ['breɪkdaʊn] *n (of car)* Panne *die* ; *(in communications)* Zusammenbruch *der* ; *(in negotiations)* Scheitern *das* ; *(mental)* Nervenzusammenbruch *der*.

breakdown truck *n* Abschleppwagen *der*.

breakfast ['brekfəst] *n* Frühstück *das* ; **to have ~** frühstücken ; **to have sthg for ~** etw zum Frühstück essen.

breakfast cereal *n* Cornflakes, Müsli *etc*.

break-in *n* Einbruch *der*.

breakwater ['breɪk,wɔːtə'] *n* Wellenbrecher *der*.

breast [brest] *n* Brust *die*.

breastbone ['brestbəʊn] *n* Brustbein *das*.

breast-feed *vt* stillen.

breaststroke ['breststrəʊk] *n* Brustschwimmen *das*.

breath [breθ] *n* Atem *der* ; **out of ~** außer Atem ; **to go for a ~ of fresh air** frische Luft schnappen gehen.

Breathalyser® ['breθəlaɪzə'] *n (Br)* Alkoholtest *der*.

Breathalyzer® ['breθəlaɪzər] *(Am)* = **Breathalyser**®.

breathe [briːð] *vi* atmen.
■ **breathe in** *vi* einlatmen.
■ **breathe out** *vi* auslatmen.

breathtaking ['breθ,teɪkɪŋ] *adj* atemberaubend.

breed [briːd] *(pt & pp* **bred** [bred]) *n (of animal)* Rasse *die* ; *(of plant)* Art *die*. ◆ *vt* züchten. ◆ *vi* sich vermehren.

breeze [briːz] *n* Brise *die*.

breezy ['briːzɪ] *adj (weather, day)* windig.

brew [bruː] *vt (beer)* brauen ; *(tea, coffee)* auflbrühen. ◆ *vi (tea)* ziehen ; *(coffee)* sich setzen.

brewery ['brʊərɪ] *n* Brauerei *die*.

bribe [braɪb] *n* Bestechungsgeld *das*. ◆ *vt* bestechen.

bric-a-brac ['brɪkəbræk] *n* Nippes *pl*.

brick [brɪk] *n* Backstein *der*.

bricklayer ['brɪk,leɪə'] *n* Maurer *der* (-in *die*).

brickwork ['brɪkwɜːk] *n* Mauerwerk *das*.

bride [braɪd] *n* Braut *die*.

bridegroom ['braɪdgrʊm] *n* Bräutigam *der*.

bridesmaid ['braɪdzmeɪd] *n* Brautjungfer *die*.

bridge [brɪdʒ] *n* Brücke *die* ; *(card game)* Bridge *das*.

bridle ['braɪdl] *n* Zaumzeug *das*.

bridle path *n* Reitweg *der*.

brief [briːf] *adj* kurz. ◆ *vt* einlweisen ; **in ~** kurz gesagt. ■ **briefs** *npl (for men)* Slip *der* ; *(for women)* Schlüpfer *der*.

briefcase ['briːfkeɪs] *n* Aktenkoffer *der*.

briefly ['briːflɪ] *adv* kurz.

brigade [brɪ'geɪd] *n* Brigade *die*.

bright [braɪt] *adj* hell ; *(colour)* leuchtend ; *(clever)* aufge-

brow

weckt ; *(lively, cheerful)* fröhlich.

brilliant ['brɪljənt] *adj (colour, light, sunshine)* leuchtend ; *(idea, person)* großartig ; *(inf : wonderful)* toll.

brim [brɪm] *n (of hat)* Krempe *die* ; **full to the ~** bis an den Rand voll.

brine [braɪn] *n* Salzlake *die*.

bring [brɪŋ] *(pt & pp brought) vt (take along)* mitlbringen ; *(move)* bringen ; *(cause)* führen zu. ■ **bring along** *vt sep* mitlbringen. ■ **bring back** *vt sep (return)* zurücklbringen ; *(shopping, gift)* mitlbringen. ■ **bring in** *vt sep (introduce)* einlführen ; *(earn)* einlbringen. ■ **bring out** *vt sep (new product)* herauslbringen. ■ **bring up** *vt sep (child)* erziehen ; *(subject)* zur Sprache bringen ; *(food)* erbrechen.

brink [brɪŋk] *n* : **on the ~ of** am Rande (+G).

brisk [brɪsk] *adj* zügig ; *(wind)* frisch.

bristle ['brɪsl] *n (of brush)* Borste *die* ; *(on chin)* Bartstoppel *die*.

Britain ['brɪtn] *n* Großbritannien *nt*.

British ['brɪtɪʃ] *adj* britisch. ◆ *npl* : **the ~** die Briten.

British Rail *n* ≃ Deutsche Bahn *die*.

British Telecom [-'telɪkɒm] *n* ≃ Deutsche Telekom *die*.

Briton ['brɪtn] *n* Brite *der* (Britin *die*).

brittle ['brɪtl] *adj* zerbrechlich.

broad [brɔːd] *adj* breit ; *(wide-ranging)* weit ; *(description, outline)* allgemein ; *(accent)* stark.

B road *n (Br)* ≃ Landstraße *die*.

broad bean *n* dicke Bohne *die*.

broadcast ['brɔːdkɑːst] *(pt & pp broadcast) n* Sendung *die*. ◆ *vt* senden.

broadly ['brɔːdlɪ] *adv* im Großen und Ganzen ; **~ speaking** allgemein gesagt.

broccoli ['brɒkəlɪ] *n* Brokkoli *der or pl*.

brochure ['brəʊʃə'] *n* Broschüre *die*.

broiled [brɔɪld] *adj (Am)* gegrillt.

broke [brəʊk] *pt* → **break**. ◆ *adj (inf)* pleite.

broken ['brəʊkn] *pp* → **break**. ◆ *adj (machine)* kaputt ; *(window, glass)* zerbrochen ; *(English, German)* gebrochen ; **to have a ~ leg** ein gebrochenes Bein haben.

bronchitis [brɒŋ'kaɪtɪs] *n* Bronchitis *die*.

bronze [brɒnz] *n* Bronze *die*.

brooch [brəʊtʃ] *n* Brosche *die*.

brook [brʊk] *n* Bach *der*.

broom [bruːm] *n* Besen *der*.

broomstick ['bruːmstɪk] *n* Besenstiel *der*.

broth [brɒθ] *n (soup)* Eintopf *der*.

brother ['brʌðə'] *n* Bruder *der*.

brother-in-law *n* Schwager *der*.

brought [brɔːt] *pt & pp* → **bring**.

brow [braʊ] *n (forehead)* Stirn *die* ; *(eyebrow)* Braue *die*.

brown [braʊn] *adj* braun. ◆ *n* Braun *das.*

brown bread *n* Mischbrot *das.*

brownie ['braʊnɪ] *n (CULIN)* Brownie *der.*

Brownie ['braʊnɪ] *n* Pfadfinderin *die (bis 10 Jahren).*

brown rice *n* Naturreis *der.*

brown sauce *n (Br)* aus Gemüseextrakten hergestellte ketschupähnliche Soße.

brown sugar *n* brauner Zucker.

browse [braʊz] *vi (in shop)* sich um|sehen ; **to ~ through sthg** in etw *(D)* blättern.

browser ['braʊzə'] *n (customer)* : '**~s welcome**' 'Bitte sehen Sie sich um' ; *(COMPUT)* Browser *der.*

bruise [bruːz] *n* blauer Fleck.

brunch [brʌntʃ] *n* Brunch *der.*

brunette [bruːˈnet] *n* Brünette *die.*

brush [brʌʃ] *n* Bürste *die* ; *(for painting)* Pinsel *der.* ◆ *vt (floor)* fegen ; *(clothes)* bürsten ; **to ~ one's hair** sich *(D)* die Haare bürsten ; **to ~ one's teeth** sich *(D)* die Zähne putzen.

brussels sprouts [ˌbrʌslz-] *npl* Rosenkohl *der.*

brutal ['bruːtl] *adj* brutal.

BSc *n (abbr of Bachelor of Science)* Bakkalaureus der Naturwissenschaften.

BT *abbr* = **British Telecom.**

bubble ['bʌbl] *n* Blase *die.*

bubble bath *n* Badeschaum *der.*

bubble gum *n* Kaugummi *der.*

bubbly ['bʌblɪ] *n (inf)* Schampus *der.*

buck [bʌk] *n (Am : inf : dollar)* Dollar *der* ; *(male animal)* Bock *der.*

bucket ['bʌkɪt] *n* Eimer *der.*

Buckingham Palace ['bʌkɪŋəm-] *n* Buckinghampalast *der (Residenz der britischen Königin in London).*

ⓘ BUCKINGHAM PALACE

Der im Jahre 1703 für den Duke von Buckingham erbaute Buckingham Palace ist die offizielle Londoner Residenz des britischen Monarchen. Er liegt am Ende von „The Mall", einer von Bäumen eingesäumten Allee zwischen Green Park und St. James Park. Vor dem Palast findet täglich eine Wachablösungszeremonie („Changing of the guard") statt.

buckle ['bʌkl] *n* Schnalle *die.* ◆ *vt (fasten)* zuschnallen. ◆ *vi (warp)* sich verbiegen.

Buck's Fizz *n* Champagner mit Orangensaft.

bud [bʌd] *n* Knospe *die.* ◆ *vi* knospen.

Buddhist ['bʊdɪst] *n* Buddhist *der (-in die).*

buddy ['bʌdɪ] *n (inf)* Kumpel *der.*

budge [bʌdʒ] *vi* sich rühren.

budgerigar ['bʌdʒərɪgɑː'] *n* Wellensittich *der.*

budget ['bʌdʒɪt] *adj (holiday, travel)* Billig-. ◆ *n* Budget *das* ; **the Budget** *(Br)* der Haushaltsplan. ■ **budget for** vt fus einl-planen.

budgie ['bʌdʒɪ] n (Inf) Wellen-sittich der.

buff [bʌf] n (inf) Kenner der (-in die).

buffalo ['bʌfələʊ] (pl -s OR -es) n Büffel der.

buffalo wings npl (Am) frit-tierte und gewürzte Hähnchen-flügel.

buffer ['bʌfə'] n Puffer der.

buffet [(Br) 'bʊfeɪ, (Am) bə'feɪ] n (meal) kalte Büfett das ; (cafe-teria) Imbissstube die.

buffet car ['bʊfeɪ-] n Speise-wagen der.

bug [bʌg] vt (inf : annoy) ner-ven. ◆ n (insect) Ungeziefer das ; (inf : mild illness) : to catch a ~ sich (D) was holen.

buggy ['bʌgɪ] n (pushchair) Sportwagen der ; (Am : pram) Kinderwagen der.

bugle ['bjuːgl] n Bügelhorn das.

build [bɪld] (pt & pp built) n Körperbau der. ◆ vt bauen. ■ **build up** vt sep aufbauen. ◆ vi zulnehmen ; to ~ up speed sich verbessern.

builder ['bɪldə'] n Bauunter-nehmer der (-in die).

building ['bɪldɪŋ] n Gebäude das.

building site n Baustelle die.

building society n (Br) Bau-sparkasse die.

built [bɪlt] pt & pp → build.

built-in adj eingebaut.

built-up area n bebautes Ge-biet.

bulb [bʌlb] n (for lamp) Glüh-birne die ; (of plant) Zwiebel die.

Bulgaria [bʌl'geərɪə] n Bulga-rien nt.

bulge [bʌldʒ] vi (suitcase, box) prall gefüllt sein.

bulk [bʌlk] n : the ~ of der Hauptteil (+G) ; in ~ en gros.

bulky ['bʌlkɪ] adj sperrig.

bull [bʊl] n Bulle der.

bulldog ['bʊldɒg] n Bulldogge die.

bulldozer ['bʊldəʊzə'] n Bull-dozer der.

bullet ['bʊlɪt] n Kugel die.

bulletin ['bʊlətɪn] n (on radio, TV) Kurzmeldung die ; (publi-cation) Bulletin das.

bullfight ['bʊlfaɪt] n Stier-kampf der.

bull's-eye n Schwarze das.

bully ['bʊlɪ] n Schüler, der Schwächere schikaniert. ◆ vt schikanieren.

bum [bʌm] n (inf : bottom) Po der ; (Am : inf : tramp) Penner der.

bum bag n (Br) Gürteltasche die.

bumblebee ['bʌmblbiː] n Hummel die.

bump [bʌmp] n (on surface) Unebenheit die ; (on head, leg) Beule die ; (sound) Bums der ; (minor accident) Zusammen-stoß der. ◆ vt : to ~ one's head sich (D) den Kopf stoßen. ■ **bump into** vt fus (hit) sto-ßen gegen ; (meet) zufällig tref-fen.

bumper ['bʌmpə'] n (on car) Stoßstange die ; (Am : on train) Puffer der.

bumpy ['bʌmpɪ] *adj* (road) un-eben ; *(flight)* unruhig ; *(jour-ney)* holprig.

bun [bʌn] *n* (cake) süßes Brötchen ; *(bread roll)* Brötchen *das*, Semmel *die* (Südd, Österr) ; *(hairstyle)* Knoten *der*.

bunch [bʌntʃ] *n* (of people) Haufen *der* ; *(of flowers)* Strauß *der* ; *(of grapes)* Traube *die* ; *(of bananas)* Staude *die* ; *(of keys)* Bund *der*.

bundle ['bʌndl] *n* Bündel *das*.

bung [bʌŋ] *n* Pfropfen *der*.

bungalow ['bʌŋgələʊ] *n* Bungalow *der*.

bunion ['bʌnjən] *n* Ballen *der*.

bunk [bʌŋk] *n* Koje *die*.

bunk beds *npl* Etagenbett *das*.

bunker ['bʌŋkə'] *n* Bunker *der*.

bunny ['bʌnɪ] *n* Häschen *das*.

buoy [(Br) bɔɪ, (Am) 'buːɪ] *n* Boje *die*.

buoyant ['bɔɪənt] *adj* schwimmend.

BUPA ['buːpə] *n* private britische Krankenkasse.

burden ['bɜːdn] *n* Last *die*.

bureaucracy [bjʊə'rɒkrəsɪ] *n* Bürokratie *die*.

bureau de change [,bjʊərəʊ-də'ʃɒndʒ] *n* Wechselstube *die*.

burger ['bɜːgə'] *n* Hamburger *der* ; *(made with nuts, vegetables etc)* Bratling *der*.

burglar ['bɜːglə'] *n* Einbrecher *der* (-in *die*).

burglar alarm *n* Alarmanlage *die*.

burglarize ['bɜːgləraɪz] *(Am)* = **burgle**.

burglary ['bɜːglərɪ] *n* Einbruch *der*.

burgle ['bɜːgl] *vt* ein|brechen in *(+A)*.

burial ['berɪəl] *n* Beerdigung *die*.

burn [bɜːn] *(pt & pp* **burnt** OR **burned**) *n* Verbrennung *die* ; *(on material)* Brandstelle *die*. ◆ *vt* verbrennen ; *(food)* an|brennen ; *(hand, skin, clothes)* sich *(D)* verbrennen. ◆ *vi* brennen.

burn down *vt sep & vi* ab|brennen.

burning (hot) ['bɜːnɪŋ-] *adj* glühend heiß.

Burns' Night [bɜːnz-] *n* Tag zur Feier des Geburtstags des schottischen Dichters Robert Burns.

BURNS' NIGHT

Am 25. Januar jedes Jahres feiern die Schotten den Geburtstag ihres Nationaldichters Robert Burns (1759-96). Dazu trifft man sich der Tradition gemäß zum Abendessen, den so genannten „Burns' suppers", bei denen die Anwesenden reihum Gedichte von Burns rezitieren. Es werden typische schottische Spezialitäten wie „Haggis" (mit Innereien gefüllter Schafsmagen) serviert. Dazu trinkt man Whisky.

burnt [bɜːnt] *pt & pp* → **burn**.

burp [bɜːp] *vi (inf)* rülpsen.

burrow ['bʌrəʊ] *n* Bau *der*.

burst [bɜːst] *(pt & pp* **burst**) *n* (of gunfire) Hagel *der* ; *(of applause)* Sturm *der*. ◆ *vt* platzen lassen. ◆ *vi* platzen ; **he ~ into the room** er stürzte ins Zimmer ; **to ~ into tears** in Tränen auslbrechen ; **to ~ open** auflspringen.

bury ['berɪ] *vt* (*person*) beerdigen ; (*hide underground*) vergraben.

bus [bʌs] *n* Bus *der* ; **by ~** mit dem Bus.

bus conductor [-,kən'dʌktə*] *n* Busschaffner *der* (-in *die*).

bus driver *n* Busfahrer *der* (-in *die*).

bush [buʃ] *n* Busch *der*.

business ['bɪznɪs] *n* Geschäft *das* ; (*firm*) Betrieb *der* ; (*things to do*) Angelegenheiten *pl* ; (*affair*) Sache *die* ; **mind your own ~!** kümmer' dich um deine eigenen Angelegenheiten! ; '**~ as usual**' 'Wir haben offen'.

business card *n* Visitenkarte *die*.

business class *n* Business Class *die*.

business hours *npl* Geschäftszeit *die*.

businessman ['bɪznɪsmæn] (*pl* **-men** [-men]) *n* Geschäftsmann *der*.

business studies *npl* Betriebswirtschaft *die*.

businesswoman ['bɪznɪs,wʊmən] (*pl* **-women** [-,wɪmɪn]) *n* Geschäftsfrau *die*.

busker ['bʌskə*] *n* (*Br*) Straßenmusikant *der* (-in *die*).

bus lane *n* Busspur *die*.

bus pass *n* Zeitkarte *die*.

bus shelter *n* Wartehäuschen *das*.

bus station *n* Busbahnhof *der*.

bus stop *n* Bushaltestelle *die*.

bust [bʌst] *n* (*of woman*) Busen *der*. ◆ *adj* : **to go ~** (*inf*) Pleite machen.

bustle ['bʌsl] *n* Betrieb *der*.

bus tour *n* Busreise *die* ; (*sightseeing*) Busrundfahrt *die*.

busy ['bɪzɪ] *adj* (*person*) beschäftigt ; (*day, schedule*) hektisch ; (*street, office*) belebt ; (*telephone, line*) besetzt ; **to be ~ doing sthg** mit etw beschäftigt sein.

busy signal *n* (*Am*) Besetztzeichen *das*.

but [bʌt] *conj* aber. ◆ *prep* (*except*) außer ; **the last ~ one** der/die/das vorletzte ; **~ for** außer.

butcher ['butʃə*] *n* Fleischer *der*, Metzger *der* (*Süddt*) ; **~'s** (*shop*) Fleischerei *die*, Metzgerei *die* (*Süddt*).

butt [bʌt] *n* (*of rifle*) Kolben *der* ; (*of cigarette*) Stummel *der*.

butter ['bʌtə*] *n* Butter *die*. ◆ *vt* buttern.

butter bean *n* weiße Bohne *die*.

buttercup ['bʌtəkʌp] *n* Butterblume *die*.

butterfly ['bʌtəflaɪ] *n* Schmetterling *der*.

butterscotch ['bʌtəskɒtʃ] *n* Karamellbonbon *der or das*.

buttocks ['bʌtəks] *npl* Hintern *der*.

button ['bʌtn] *n* Knopf *der* ; (*Am* : *badge*) Button *der*.

buttonhole ['bʌtnhəʊl] *n* Knopfloch *das*.

button mushroom *n* Champignon *der*.

buttress ['bʌtrɪs] n Pfeiler der.

buy [baɪ] (pt & pp **bought**) vt kaufen. ◆ n : a good ~ ein guter Kauf ; to ~ sthg for sb, to ~ sb sthg jm etw kaufen.

buzz [bʌz] vi summen. ◆ n (inf : phone call) : to give sb a ~ jn anrufen.

buzzer ['bʌzə'] n Summer der.

by [baɪ] prep 1. (expressing cause, agent) von ; he was hit ~ a car er ist von einem Auto angefahren worden ; composed ~ Mozart von Mozart komponiert.
2. (expressing method, means) mit ; ~ car/train mit dem Auto/ Zug ; to pay ~ credit card mit Kreditkarte bezahlen.
3. (near to, beside) an (+D) ; ~ the sea am Meer.
4. (past) an (+D)... vorbei ; a car went ~ the house ein Auto fuhr am Haus vorbei.
5. (via) durch ; exit ~ the door on the left Ausgang durch die Tür auf der linken Seite.
6. (with time) : it will be ready ~ tomorrow bis morgen wird es fertig sein ; be there ~ nine sei um neun da ; ~ day tagsüber ; ~ now inzwischen.
7. (expressing quantity) : sold ~ the dozen im Dutzend verkauft ; prices fell ~ 20% die Preise fielen um 20% ; we charge ~ the hour wir berechnen nach Stunde.
8. (expressing meaning) : what do you mean ~ that? was meinst du/meinen Sie damit?
9. (in division) durch ; (in multiplication) mit ; two metres ~ five zwei mal fünf Meter.

10. (according to) nach ; ~ law nach dem Gesetz ; it's fine ~ me ich bin damit einverstanden.
11. (expressing gradual process) : one ~ one eins nach dem anderen ; day ~ day Tag für Tag.
12. (in phrases) : ~ mistake versehentlich ; ~ oneself allein ; ~ profession von Beruf.
◆ adv (past) vorbei ; to go ~ (walk) vorbeigehen ; (drive) vorbeifahren.

bye(-bye) [baɪ(baɪ)] excl (inf) tschüs.

bypass ['baɪpɑːs] n Umgehungsstraße die.

C

C (abbr of Celsius, centigrade) C.

cab [kæb] n (taxi) Taxi das ; (of lorry) Führerhaus das.

cabaret ['kæbəreɪ] n Kabarett das.

cabbage ['kæbɪdʒ] n Kohl der.

cabin ['kæbɪn] n Kabine die ; (wooden house) Hütte die.

cabin crew n Flugpersonal das.

cabinet ['kæbɪnɪt] n (cupboard) Schrank der ; (POL) Kabinett das.

cable ['keɪbl] n (rope) Tau das ; (electrical) Kabel das.

cable car n Seilbahn die.

cable television n Kabelfernsehen das.

cactus ['kæktəs] (pl -tuses OR -ti [-taɪ]) n Kaktus der.

Caesar salad [ˌsiːzə-] *n grüner Salat mit Sardellen, Oliven, Parmesan und Croûtons.*

cafe ['kæfeɪ] *n* Café *das.*

cafeteria [ˌkæfɪ'tɪərɪə] *n* Cafeteria *die.*

cafetière [kæf'tjeəʳ] *n* Kolbenfilter-Kaffeemaschine *die.*

caffeine ['kæfiːn] *n* Koffein *das.*

cage [keɪdʒ] *n* Käfig *der.*

cagoule [kə'guːl] *n (Br)* Regenjacke *die.*

Cajun ['keɪdʒən] *adj* cajun.

ⓘ **CAJUN**

Bezeichnung für die ursprünglich französischen Siedler in Neuschottland/Kanada, die im 18. Jahrhundert nach Louisiana deportiert wurden. Im Laufe der Zeit entwickelte diese Volksgruppe ihren eigenen Dialekt und eine eigene Kultur. Im englischsprachigen Raum ist die scharf gewürzte Cajunsche Küche und die folkloristische Cajun-Musik, bei der die Fiedel und Akkordeon vorherrschen, sehr bekannt.

---

cake [keɪk] *n* Kuchen *der ; (of soap)* Stück *das* ; **fish ~** Fischfrikadelle *die.*

calculate ['kælkjʊleɪt] *vt* berechnen ; *(risks, effect)* kalkulieren.

calculator ['kælkjʊleɪtəʳ] *n* Taschenrechner *der.*

calendar ['kælɪndəʳ] *n* Kalender *der.*

calf [kɑːf] *(pl* **calves)** *n (of cow)* Kalb *das ; (part of leg)* Wade *die.*

call [kɔːl] *n (visit)* Besuch *der ; (phone call)* Anruf *der ; (of bird)* Ruf *der ; (at airport)* Aufruf *der.* ◆ *vt* rufen ; *(name, describe)* nennen ; *(telephone)* anlrufen ; *(meeting)* einlberufen ; *(election)* auslschreiben ; *(flight)* auflrufen. ◆ *vi (visit)* vorbeilkommen ; *(phone)* anlrufen ; **to be ~ed** sich nennen ; **what is he ~ed?** wie heißt er? ; **to be on ~** *(nurse, doctor)* Bereitschaftsdienst haben ; **to pay sb a ~** bei jm vorbeilgehen ; **this train ~s at...** dieser Zug hält in... ; **who's ~ing?** wer spricht da, bitte? ▪ **call back** *vt sep* zurücklrufen. ◆ *vi (phone again)* zurücklrufen ; *(visit again)* zurücklkommen. ▪ **call for** *vt fus (come to fetch)* ablholen ; *(demand)* verlangen ; *(require)* erfordern. ▪ **call on** *vt fus (visit)* vorbeilgehen bei ; **to ~ on sb to do sthg** jn bitten, etw zu tun. ▪ **call out** *vt sep* auslrufen ; *(doctor, fire brigade)* rufen. ◆ *vi* rufen. ▪ **call up** *vt sep (MIL)* einlberufen ; *(telephone)* anlrufen.

call box *n* Telefonzelle *die.*

caller ['kɔːləʳ] *n (visitor)* Besucher *der* (-in *die*) ; *(on phone)* Anrufer *der* (-in *die*).

calm [kɑːm] *adj* ruhig. ◆ *vt* beruhigen. ▪ **calm down** *vt sep* beruhigen. ◆ *vi* sich beruhigen.

Calor gas® ['kælə-] *n* Butangas *das.*

calorie ['kælərɪ] *n* Kalorie *die.*

calves [kɑːvz] *pl* → **calf.**

camcorder ['kæmˌkɔːdəʳ] *n* Camcorder *der.*

came [keɪm] *pt* → **come.**

camel ['kæml] n Kamel das.

camembert ['kæməmbeə'] n Camembert der.

camera ['kæmərə] n Fotoapparat der ; (for filming) Kamera die.

cameraman ['kæmərəmæn] (pl -men [-men]) n Kameramann der.

camera shop n Fotogeschäft das.

camisole ['kæmɪsəul] n Mieder das.

camp [kæmp] n Lager das. ◆ vi zelten.

campaign [kæm'peɪn] n Kampagne die. ◆ vi : to ~ (for/against) kämpfen (für/gegen).

camp bed n Campingliege die.

camper ['kæmpə'] n Camper der (-in die) ; (van) Wohnmobil das.

camping ['kæmpɪŋ] n : to go ~ zelten gehen.

camping stove n Kocher der.

campsite ['kæmpsaɪt] n Campingplatz der.

campus ['kæmpəs] (pl -es) n Universitätsgelände das.

can[1] [kæn] n (of food, drink, paint) Dose die ; (of oil) Kanister der.

can[2] [weak form kən, strong form kæn] (pt & conditional could) aux vb 1. (be able to) können ; ~ you help me? können Sie mir helfen? ; I ~ see you ich kann dich sehen.
2. (know how to) können ; ~ you drive? können Sie/kannst du Auto fahren? ; I ~ speak German ich spreche Deutsch.
3. (be allowed to) können, dür-

fen ; you can't smoke here Sie können OR dürfen hier nicht rauchen.
4. (in polite requests) können ; ~ you tell me the time? können Sie mir sagen, wie viel Uhr es ist?
5. (expressing occasional occurrence) können ; it ~ get cold at night es kann nachts kalt werden.
6. (expressing possibility) können ; they could be lost sie könnten sich verlaufen haben.

Canada ['kænədə] n Kanada nt.

Canadian [kə'neɪdɪən] adj kanadisch. ◆ n Kanadier der (-in die).

canal [kə'næl] n Kanal der.

canapé ['kænəpeɪ] n (food) Partyhäppchen das.

cancel ['kænsl] vt (meeting, visit) absagen ; (booking) rückgängig machen ; (flight, train) streichen ; (cheque) ungültig machen.

cancellation [,kænsə'leɪʃn] n Streichung die ; (booking) Stornierung die ; (cancelled visit) Absage die.

cancer ['kænsə'] n Krebs der.

Cancer ['kænsə'] n Krebs der.

candidate ['kændɪdət] n (for parliament) Kandidat der ; (for job) Bewerber der ; (in exam) Prüfling der.

candle ['kændl] n Kerze die.

candlelight dinner ['kændllɪt-] n Essen das bei Kerzenlicht.

candy ['kændɪ] n (Am : confectionery) Süßigkeiten pl ; (sweet) Bonbon der or das.

candyfloss ['kændıflɒs] n (Br) Zuckerwatte die.

cane [keın] n Stock der; (for furniture, baskets) Rohr das.

canister ['kænıstə'] n (for tea) Dose die; (for gas) Gasflasche die.

cannabis ['kænəbıs] n Cannabis der.

canned [kænd] adj (food, drink) in der Dose.

cannon ['kænən] n Kanone die.

cannot ['kænɒt] = **can not**.

canoe [kə'nuː] n Paddelboot das; (SPORT) Kanu das.

canoeing [kə'nuːıŋ] n Paddeln das; (SPORT) Kanusport der.

canopy ['kænəpı] n Baldachin der.

can't [kɑːnt] = **cannot**.

cantaloup(e) ['kæntəluːp] n Kantalupmelone die.

canteen [kæn'tiːn] n (at work) Kantine die; (at school) Speisesaal der.

canvas ['kænvəs] n (for tent, bag) Segeltuch das.

cap [kæp] n Mütze die; (of pen, bottle) Kappe die; (contraceptive) Spirale die.

capable ['keıpəbl] adj fähig; to be ~ of doing sthg fähig sein, etw zu tun.

capacity [kə'pæsıtı] n (ability) Fähigkeit die; (of stadium, theatre) Fassungsvermögen das.

cape [keıp] n (of land) Kap das; (cloak) Cape das.

capers ['keıpəz] npl Kapern pl.

capital ['kæpıtl] n (of country) Hauptstadt die; (money) Kapital das; (letter) Großbuchstabe der.

capital punishment n Todesstrafe die.

cappuccino [ˌkæpʊ'tʃiːnəʊ] n Cappuccino der.

Capricorn ['kæprıkɔːn] n Steinbock der.

capsicum ['kæpsıkəm] n Paprika der.

capsize [kæp'saız] vi kentern.

capsule ['kæpsjuːl] n Kapsel die.

captain ['kæptın] n Kapitän der; (MIL) Hauptmann der.

caption ['kæpʃn] n (under picture) Unterschrift die; (above picture) Überschrift die.

capture ['kæptʃə'] vt fangen; (town, castle) erobern.

car [kɑː'] n Auto das, Wagen der; (railway wagon) Wagen der.

carafe [kə'ræf] n Karaffe die.

caramel ['kærəmel] n (sweet) Karamellbonbon der or das; (burnt sugar) Karamell der.

carat ['kærət] n Karat das; 24-~ gold 24-karätiges Gold.

caravan ['kærəvæn] n (Br) Wohnwagen der.

caravanning ['kærəvænıŋ] n (Br): to go ~ Urlaub im Wohnwagen machen.

caravan site n (Br) Campingplatz der für Wohnwagen.

carbohydrate [ˌkɑːbəʊ'haıdreıt] n (in foods) Kohlenhydrat das.

carbon ['kɑːbən] n Kohlenstoff der.

carbon copy n Durchschlag der.

carbon dioxide [-daı'ɒksaıd] n Kohlendioxid das.

carbon monoxide [-mɒ'nɒk-saɪd] n Kohlenmonoxid das.

car boot sale n (Br) Basar, bei dem die Waren im Kofferraum ausgelegt werden.

carburetor [,kɑ:bə'retər] (Am) = carburettor.

carburettor [,kɑ:bə'retə'] n (Br) Vergaser der.

car crash n Autounfall der.

card [kɑ:d] n Karte die ; (cardboard) Pappe die, Karton der ; ~s (game) Karten pl.

cardboard ['kɑ:dbɔ:d] n Pappe die, Karton der.

car deck n Fahrzeugdeck das.

cardiac arrest [,kɑ:dɪæk-] n Herzstillstand der.

cardigan ['kɑ:dɪgən] n Strickjacke die.

care [keə'] n (attention) Sorgfalt die. ◆ vi (mind) : I don't ~ es ist mir egal ; to take ~ of sich kümmern um ; would you ~ to...? (fml) würden Sie gerne...? ; to take ~ to do sthg aufpassen, dass man etw tut ; medical ~ ärztliche Betreuung ; take ~! (goodbye) mach's gut! ; with ~ aufmerksam, sorgfältig ; to ~ about sthg (think important) etw wichtig finden ; to ~ about sb jn mögen.

career [kə'rɪə'] n (type of job) Beruf der ; (professional life) Laufbahn die.

carefree ['keəfri:] adj sorglos.

careful ['keəfʊl] adj (cautious) vorsichtig ; (thorough) sorgfältig ; be ~! Vorsicht!

carefully ['keəflɪ] adv (cautiously) vorsichtig ; (thoroughly) sorgfältig.

careless ['keələs] adj (inattentive) unaufmerksam ; (unconcerned) sorglos.

caretaker ['keə,teɪkə'] n (Br : of school, flats) Hausmeister der (-in die).

car ferry n Autofähre die.

cargo ['kɑ:gəʊ] (pl -es OR -s) n Ladung die.

car hire n (Br) Autovermietung die.

Caribbean [(Br) ,kærɪ'bi:ən, (Am) kə'rɪbɪən] n : the ~ die Karibik.

caring ['keərɪŋ] adj fürsorglich.

carnation [kɑ:'neɪʃn] n Nelke die.

carnival ['kɑ:nɪvl] n Karneval der.

carousel [,kærə'sel] n (for luggage) Gepäckförderband das ; (Am : merry-go-round) Karussell das.

carp [kɑ:p] n Karpfen der.

car park n (Br) Parkplatz der ; (building) Parkhaus das ; (underground) Tiefgarage die.

carpenter ['kɑ:pəntə'] n Zimmermann der ; (for furniture) Tischler der (-in die).

carpentry ['kɑ:pəntrɪ] n Zimmerhandwerk das ; (furniture making) Tischlerei die.

carpet ['kɑ:pɪt] n Teppich der.

car rental n (Am) Autovermietung die.

carriage ['kærɪdʒ] n (Br : of train) Abteil das ; (horse-drawn) Kutsche die.

carriageway ['kærɪdʒweɪ] n (Br) Fahrbahn die.

carrier (bag) ['kærɪə'-] n Tragetasche die.

carrot ['kærət] n Karotte die, Möhre die.

carrot cake n Möhrenkuchen der, Rüblitorte die (Schweiz).

carry ['kærɪ] vt tragen; (transport) befördern; (disease) übertragen; (cash, passport, map) bei sich haben. ◆ vi (voice, sound) tragen, reichen.

▓ **carry on** vi (continue) weiter|machen. ◆ vt fus (continue) fortlsetzen; to ~ on doing sthg weiterhin etw tun.

▓ **carry out** vt sep (repairs, order) ausllführen; (plan) durchllführen; (promise) erfüllen.

carrycot ['kærɪkɒt] n (Br) Babytragetasche die.

carryout ['kærɪaʊt] n (Am & Scot) Essen das zum Mitnehmen.

carsick ['kɑːˌsɪk] adj: I get ~ mir wird beim Autofahren schlecht.

cart [kɑːt] n Karren der; (Am : in supermarket) Einkaufswagen der; (inf : video game cartridge) Videospiel das.

carton ['kɑːtn] n Tüte die.

cartoon [kɑː'tuːn] n (drawing) Cartoon der; (film) Zeichentrickfilm der.

cartridge ['kɑːtrɪdʒ] n Patrone die; (for film) Kassette die.

carve [kɑːv] vt (wood) schnitzen; (stone) meißeln; (meat) auflschneiden.

carvery ['kɑːvərɪ] n Büfett mit verschiedenen Fleischgerichten und Bedienung.

car wash n Autowaschanlage die.

case [keɪs] n (Br : suitcase) Koffer der; (container) Etui das; (for jewellery) Schatulle die; (instance) Fall der; (JUR : trial) Fall der; (patient) Fall der; **in any ~** sowieso; **in ~** falls; **in ~ of** im Fall (+G); **just in ~** für alle Fälle; **in that ~** in dem Fall.

cash [kæʃ] n (coins, notes) Bargeld das; (money in general) Geld das. ◆ vt: **to ~ a cheque** einen Scheck einllösen; **to pay ~** bar bezahlen.

cash desk n Kasse die.

cash dispenser [-ˌdɪ'spensə'] n Geldautomat der.

cashew (nut) ['kæʃuː-] n Cashewnuss die.

cashier [kæ'ʃɪə'] n Kassierer der (-in die).

cashmere [kæʃ'mɪə'] n Kaschmir der.

cashpoint ['kæʃpɔɪnt] n (Br) Geldautomat der.

cash register n Kasse die.

casino [kə'siːnəʊ] n (pl -s) n Kasino das.

cask [kɑːsk] n Fass das.

cask-conditioned [-ˌkənˈdɪʃnd] adj (beer) bezeichnet 'real ale'-Bier, das in Fässern gebraut wird.

casserole ['kæsərəʊl] n (stew) Schmorgericht aus Fleisch und Gemüse; ~ **(dish)** Schmortopf der.

cassette [kæ'set] n Kassette die.

cassette recorder n Kassettenrekorder der.

cast [kɑːst] (pt & pp cast) n (actors) Besetzung die; (for broken bone) Gipsverband der. ◆ vt werfen; **to ~ a vote** wählen; **to**

~ **doubt on** in Zweifel ziehen. ■ **cast off** vi (boat, ship) ablegen.

caster ['kɑːstə'] n (wheel) Rolle die.

caster sugar n (Br) Streuzucker der.

castle ['kɑːsl] n Schloss das ; (fortified) Burg die ; (in chess) Turm der.

casual ['kæʒʊəl] adj (relaxed) ungezwungen, lässig ; (remark) beiläufig ; (clothes) leger ; ~ **work** Gelegenheitsarbeit die.

casualty ['kæʒjʊəltı] n (injured) Verletzte der, die ; (dead) Tote der, die ; ~ **(ward)** Unfallstation die.

cat [kæt] n Katze die.

catalog ['kætəlɒg] (Am) = **catalogue**.

catalogue ['kætəlɒg] n Katalog der.

catapult ['kætəpʌlt] n Katapult das.

cataract ['kætərækt] n (in eye) grauer Star.

catarrh [kə'tɑː'] n Katarrh der.

catastrophe [kə'tæstrəfı] n Katastrophe die.

catch [kætʃ] (pt & pp caught) vt fangen ; (bus, train, plane, taxi) nehmen ; (surprise) erwischen ; (illness) bekommen ; (hear) verstehen ; (attention) erregen. ◆ vi (become hooked) sich verfangen. ◆ n (of window, door) Schnappschloss das ; (snag) Haken der. ■ **catch up** vt sep & vi einlholen, auflholen.

catching ['kætʃıŋ] adj (inf) ansteckend.

category ['kætəgərı] n Kategorie die.

cater ['keıtə'] : **cater for** vt fus (Br) eingestellt sein auf (+A).

caterpillar ['kætəpılə'] n Raupe die.

cathedral [kə'θiːdrəl] n Kathedrale die.

Catholic ['kæθlık] adj katholisch. ◆ n Katholik der (-in die).

Catseyes® ['kætsaız] npl (Br) Reflektoren pl (auf der Straße).

cattle ['kætl] npl Vieh das.

cattle grid n Gitter auf Landstraßen, welches Vieh am Überqueren hindert.

caught [kɔːt] pt & pp → catch.

cauliflower ['kɒlı,flaʊə'] n Blumenkohl der, Karfiol der (Österr).

cauliflower cheese n Blumenkohlauflauf der.

cause [kɔːz] n Ursache die, Grund der ; (principle, aim) Sache die. ◆ vt verursachen ; **to ~ sb to do sthg** jn veranlassen, etw zu tun.

causeway ['kɔːzweı] n Damm der.

caustic soda [,kɔːstık-] n Ätznatron das.

caution ['kɔːʃn] n Vorsicht die ; (warning) Verwarnung die.

cautious ['kɔːʃəs] adj vorsichtig.

cave [keıv] n Höhle die. ■ **cave in** vi einlstürzen.

caviar(e) ['kævıɑː'] n Kaviar der.

cavity ['kævətı] n (in tooth) Loch das.

CD n (abbr of compact disc) CD die.

CDI n (abbr of compact disc interactive) CD-Wechsler.

CD player n CD-Player der.

CDW n (abbr of collision damage waiver) Vollkaskoversicherung die.

cease [si:s] vt (fml) auflhören mit. ◆ vi (fml) auflhören.

ceasefire ['si:s,faɪə'] n Waffenstillstand der.

ceilidh ['keɪlɪ] n traditionelle Tanzveranstaltung in Schottland und Irland.

CEILIDH

In Schottland und Irland sind die „ceilidhs" traditionelle gesellige Abende mit Volksmusik, Tanz und Gesang. Ursprünglich traf man sich dazu im Kreise der Familie und Freunde, heute versteht man darunter meist öffentliche Tanzveranstaltungen.

ceiling ['si:lɪŋ] n Decke die.

celebrate ['selɪbreɪt] vt & vi feiern.

celebration [,selɪ'breɪʃn] n (event) Feier die. ■ **celebrations** npl (festivities) Festlichkeiten pl.

celebrity [sɪ'lebrɪtɪ] n (person) Prominente der, die.

celeriac [sɪ'lerɪæk] n Knollensellerie der.

celery ['selərɪ] n Sellerie der.

cell [sel] n Zelle die.

cellar ['selə'] n Keller der.

cello ['tʃeləʊ] n (pl -s) n Cello das.

Cellophane® ['seləfeɪn] n (Br) Cellophan® das.

cellphone ['selfəʊn] n Handy das.

Celsius ['selsɪəs] adj Celsius.

cement [sɪ'ment] n Zement der.

cement mixer n Zementmischer der.

cemetery ['semɪtrɪ] n Friedhof der.

cent [sent] n (Am) Cent der.

center ['sentə'] (Am) = centre.

centigrade ['sentɪgreɪd] adj Celsius.

centimetre ['sentɪ,mi:tə'] n Zentimeter der.

centipede ['sentɪpi:d] n Tausendfüßler der.

central ['sentrəl] adj zentral.

central heating n Zentralheizung die.

central locking [-'lɒkɪŋ] n Zentralverriegelung die.

central reservation n (Br) Mittelstreifen der.

centre ['sentə'] n (Br) Mitte die ; (building) Zentrum das. ◆ adj (Br) mittlere(-r) (-s) ; to be the ~ of attention im Mittelpunkt stehen.

century ['sentʃʊrɪ] n Jahrhundert das.

ceramic [sɪ'ræmɪk] adj Keramik-. ■ **ceramics** npl Keramik die.

cereal ['sɪərɪəl] n (breakfast food) Cornflakes, Müsli etc.

ceremony ['serɪmənɪ] n Zeremonie die.

certain ['sɜ:tn] adj sicher ; (particular) bestimmt, gewiss ; to be ~ to do sthg etw bestimmt tun ; to be ~ of sthg sich (D) einer Sache (G) sicher sein ; to make ~ (that) sich vergewissern, dass.

certainly ['sɜːtnlɪ] *adv* bestimmt; *(of course)* natürlich, sicher.

certificate [sə'tɪfɪkət] *n* Bescheinigung *die*; *(from school)* Zeugnis *das*.

certify ['sɜːtɪfaɪ] *vt* bescheinigen.

chain [tʃeɪn] *n* Kette *die*. ◆ *vt*: to ~ sthg to sthg etw an etw (+A) an|ketten.

chain store *n* zu einer Ladenkette gehörendes Geschäft.

chair [tʃeəʳ] *n* Stuhl *der*; *(armchair)* Sessel *der*.

chair lift *n* Sessellift *der*.

chairman ['tʃeəmən] *(pl* -men [-mən]*) n* Vorsitzende *der*.

chairperson ['tʃeə,pɜːsn] *n* Vorsitzende *der, die*.

chairwoman ['tʃeə,wʊmən] *(pl* -women [-,wɪmɪn]*) n* Vorsitzende *die*.

chalet ['ʃæleɪ] *n* Chalet *das*; *(at holiday camp)* Ferienhaus *das*.

chalk [tʃɔːk] *n* Kreide *die*; a piece of ~ ein Stück Kreide.

chalkboard ['tʃɔːkbɔːd] *n (Am)* Tafel *die*.

challenge ['tʃælɪndʒ] *n* Herausforderung *die*. ◆ *vt (question)* infrage stellen; to ~ sb (to sthg) jn heraus|fordern (zu etw).

chamber ['tʃeɪmbəʳ] *n* Kammer *die*.

chambermaid ['tʃeɪmbəmeɪd] *n* Zimmermädchen *das*.

champagne [,ʃæm'peɪn] *n* Champagner *der*.

champion ['tʃæmpjən] *n* Meister *der* (-in *die*).

championship ['tʃæmpjənʃɪp] *n* Meisterschaft *die*.

chance [tʃɑːns] *n (luck)* Glück *das*; *(possibility)* Chance *die*, Möglichkeit *die*; *(opportunity)* Gelegenheit *die*. ◆ *vt*: to ~ it *(inf)* es riskieren; to take a ~ es darauf an|kommen lassen; by ~ zufällig; on the off ~ auf gut Glück.

Chancellor of the Exchequer [,tʃɑːnsələrəvðɪks'tʃekəʳ] *n (Br)* Schatzkanzler *der*.

chandelier [,ʃændə'lɪəʳ] *n* Kronleuchter *der*.

change [tʃeɪndʒ] *n* Veränderung *die*; *(alteration)* Änderung *die*; *(money received back)* Wechselgeld *das*; *(coins)* Kleingeld *das*. ◆ *vt* ändern; *(switch)* wechseln; *(exchange)* um|tauschen; *(clothes, bedding)* wechseln. ◆ *vi* sich verändern; *(on bus, train)* um|steigen; *(change clothes)* sich um|ziehen; a ~ of clothes Kleidung zum Wechseln; do you have ~ for a pound? können Sie mir ein Pfund wechseln?; for a ~ zur Abwechslung; to get ~d sich um|ziehen; to ~ money Geld wechseln; to ~ a nappy eine Windel wechseln; to ~ a wheel ein Rad wechseln; to ~ trains/planes um|steigen; all ~! *(on train)* alles aussteigen!

changeable ['tʃeɪndʒəbl] *adj (weather)* veränderlich.

change machine *n* Wechselgeldautomat *der*.

changing room ['tʃeɪndʒɪŋ-] n (for sport) Umkleideraum der ; (in shop) Umkleidekabine die.

channel ['tʃænl] n Kanal der ; (on radio) Sender der ; (in sea) Fahrrinne die ; **the (English) Channel** der Ärmelkanal.

Channel Islands npl : **the ~** die Kanalinseln.

Channel Tunnel n : **the ~** der Euro-Tunnel.

ⓘ CHANNEL TUNNEL

Seit 1994 verbindet der Tunnel unter dem Ärmelkanal das englische Dorf Cheriton in der Nähe von Folkestone mit dem französischen Dorf Coquelles in der Nähe von Calais. Dank dieses Tunnels gibt es nun eine direkte Zugverbindung zwischen London und Paris und anderen europäischen Städten. Fahrzeuge können mit dem Autoreisezug, „Le Shuttle" genannt, transportiert werden.

chant [tʃɑːnt] vt (RELIG) singen ; (words, slogan) Sprechchöre anlstimmen.

chaos ['keɪɒs] n Chaos das.

chaotic [keɪ'ɒtɪk] adj chaotisch.

chap [tʃæp] n (Br : inf) Kerl der.

chapel ['tʃæpl] n Kapelle die.

chapped [tʃæpt] adj aufgesprungen.

chapter ['tʃæptə'] n Kapitel das.

character ['kærəktə'] n Charakter der ; (of person) Persön-

lichkeit die ; (in film, book, play) Gestalt die ; (letter) Schriftzeichen das.

characteristic [,kærəktə'rɪstɪk] adj charakteristisch. ◆ n Kennzeichen das.

charcoal ['tʃɑːkəʊl] n (for barbecue) Grillkohle die.

charge [tʃɑːdʒ] n (price) Gebühr die ; (JUR) Anklage die. ◆ vt (money) berechnen ; (JUR) anlklagen ; (battery) auflladen. ◆ vi (ask money) in Rechnung stellen ; (rush) stürmen ; **to be in ~ (of)** verantwortlich sein (für) ; **to take ~ of sthg** die Leitung für etw übernehmen ; **free of ~** gratis ; **there is no ~ for service** es gibt keinen Bedienungszuschlag.

char-grilled ['tʃɑːgrɪld] adj vom Holzkohlengrill.

charity ['tʃærətɪ] n (organization) Wohltätigkeitsverein der ; **to give to ~** für wohltätige Zwecke spenden.

charity shop n Gebrauchtwarenladen, dessen Erlös zugunsten wohltätiger Zwecke geht.

charm [tʃɑːm] n (attractiveness) Reiz der. ◆ vt bezaubern.

charming ['tʃɑːmɪŋ] adj reizend.

chart [tʃɑːt] n (diagram) Diagramm das ; (map) Karte die ; **the ~s** die Hitparade.

chartered accountant [,tʃɑːtəd-] n Wirtschaftsprüfer der (-in die).

charter flight ['tʃɑːtə-] n Charterflug der.

chase [tʃeɪs] n Verfolgungsjagd die. ◆ vt verfolgen, jagen.

chat [tʃæt] n Plauderei die. ◆ vi plaudern ; **to have a ~ (with sb)** plaudern (mit jm). ▪ **chat up** vt sep (Br : inf) anlmachen.

chat show n (Br) Talkshow die.

chatty ['tʃætɪ] adj (person) gesprächig ; (letter) unterhaltsam.

chauffeur ['ʃəʊfəʳ] n Chauffeur der.

cheap [tʃiːp] adj billig.

cheap day return n (Br) reduzierte Rückfahrkarte für bestimmte Züge.

cheaply ['tʃiːplɪ] adv billig.

cheat [tʃiːt] n Betrüger der (-in die) ; (in games) Mogler der (-in die). ◆ vi betrügen ; (in games) mogeln. ◆ vt : **to ~ sb (out of sthg)** in betrügen (um etw).

check [tʃek] n (inspection) Kontrolle die ; (Am : bill) Rechnung die ; (Am : tick) Haken der ; (Am) = **cheque**. ◆ vt kontrollieren. ◆ vi überprüfen ; **to ~ for sthg** auf etw prüfen. ▪ **check in** vt sep & vi einlchecken. ▪ **check off** vt sep ablhaken. ▪ **check out** vi ablreisen, auslchecken. ▪ **check up** vi : **to ~ up (on)** überprüfen.

checked [tʃekt] adj kariert.

checkers ['tʃekəz] n (Am) Damespiel das.

check-in desk n (at airport) Abfertigungsschalter der ; (at hotel) Rezeption die.

checkout ['tʃekaʊt] n Kasse die.

checkpoint ['tʃekpɔɪnt] n Kontrollpunkt der.

checkroom ['tʃekrʊm] n (Am) Gepäckaufbewahrung die.

checkup ['tʃekʌp] n Untersuchung die.

cheddar (cheese) ['tʃedəʳ-] n Cheddarkäse der.

cheek [tʃiːk] n Backe die ; **what a ~!** so eine Frechheit!

cheeky ['tʃiːkɪ] adj frech.

cheer [tʃɪəʳ] n Beifallsruf der. ◆ vi jubeln, applaudieren.

cheerful ['tʃɪəfʊl] adj fröhlich.

cheerio [ˌtʃɪərɪ'əʊ] excl (Br : inf) tschüs!

cheers [tʃɪəz] excl (when drinking) prost! ; (Br : inf : thank you) danke!

cheese [tʃiːz] n Käse der.

cheeseboard ['tʃiːzbɔːd] n Käseplatte die.

cheeseburger ['tʃiːzˌbɜːgəʳ] n Cheeseburger der.

cheesecake ['tʃiːzkeɪk] n Käsekuchen der.

chef [ʃef] n Koch der.

chef's special n Tagesgericht das.

chemical ['kemɪkl] adj chemisch. ◆ n Chemikalie die.

chemist ['kemɪst] n (Br : pharmacist) Apotheker der (-in die) ; (scientist) Chemiker der (-in die) ; **~'s** (Br : shop) Drogerie die ; (dispensing) Apotheke die.

chemistry ['kemɪstrɪ] n Chemie die.

cheque [tʃek] n (Br) Scheck der ; **to pay by ~** mit Scheck bezahlen.

chequebook ['tʃekbʊk] n Scheckbuch das.

cheque card n Scheckkarte die.

cherry ['tʃerɪ] n Kirsche die.

chess [tʃes] n Schach das.

chisel

chest [tʃest] n (of body) Brust die ; (box) Truhe die.

chestnut ['tʃesnʌt] n Kastanie die. ◆ adj (colour) kastanien-braun.

chest of drawers n Kommode die.

chew [tʃuː] vt kauen. ◆ n (sweet) Kaubonbon der or das.

chewing gum ['tʃuːɪŋ-] n Kaugummi der.

chic [ʃiːk] adj schick.

chicken ['tʃɪkɪn] n Huhn das ; (grilled, roasted) Hähnchen das.

chicken breast n Hühner-brust die.

chicken Kiev [-'kiːev] n mit Knoblauchbutter gefülltes, pa-niertes Hähnchenfilet.

chickenpox ['tʃɪkɪnpɒks] n Windpocken pl.

chickpea ['tʃɪkpiː] n Kicher-erbse die.

chicory ['tʃɪkərɪ] n Chicorée der.

chief [tʃiːf] adj (highest-rank-ing) leitend, Ober- ; (main) Haupt-. ◆ n Leiter der (-in die), Chef der (-in die) ; (of tribe) Häuptling der.

chiefly ['tʃiːflɪ] adv (mainly) hauptsächlich ; (especially) vor allem.

child [tʃaɪld] (pl children) n Kind das.

child abuse n Kindesmiss-handlung die.

child benefit n (Br) Kinder-geld das.

childhood ['tʃaɪldhʊd] n Kindheit die.

childish ['tʃaɪldɪʃ] adj (pej : immature) kindisch.

childminder ['tʃaɪld,maɪndə] n (Br) Tagesmutter die.

children ['tʃɪldrən] pl → child.

childrenswear ['tʃɪldrənz-weə'] n Kinderkleidung die.

child seat n Kindersitz der.

Chile ['tʃɪlɪ] n Chile nt.

chill [tʃɪl] n (illness) Erkältung die. ◆ vt kühlen ; **there's a ~ in** the air es ist kühl draußen.

chilled [tʃɪld] adj gekühlt ; 'serve ~' 'gekühlt servieren'.

chilli ['tʃɪlɪ] (pl -ies) n Chili der.

chilli con carne ['tʃɪlɪ-kɒn'kɑːnɪ] n Chili con carne das.

chilly ['tʃɪlɪ] adj kühl.

chimney ['tʃɪmnɪ] n Schorn-stein der.

chimneypot ['tʃɪmnɪpɒt] n Schornsteinaufsatz der.

chimpanzee [,tʃɪmpən'ziː] n Schimpanse der.

chin [tʃɪn] n Kinn das.

china ['tʃaɪnə] n (material) Por-zellan das.

China ['tʃaɪnə] n China nt.

Chinese [,tʃaɪ'niːz] adj chine-sisch. ◆ n (language) Chine-sisch das. ◆ npl : **the ~** die Chi-nesen ; **a ~ restaurant** ein Chi-narestaurant.

chip [tʃɪp] n (small piece) Stückchen das ; (mark) ange-schlagene Stelle ; (for gambling, in computer) Chip der. ◆ vt an-schlagen. ■ **chips** npl (Br : French fries) Pommes frites pl ; (Am : crisps) Chips pl.

chiropodist [kɪ'rɒpədɪst] n Fußpfleger der (-in die).

chisel ['tʃɪzl] n Meißel der ; (for wood) Stemmeisen das.

chives [tʃaɪvz] npl Schnittlauch der.

chlorine ['klɔːriːn] n Chlor
das.

choc-ice ['tʃɒkaɪs] n (Br) Eis-
cremeriegel mit Schokoladen-
überzug.

chocolate ['tʃɒkələt] n Schokolade die ; (sweet) Praline die.
◆ adj Schokoladen-.

chocolate biscuit n Schoko-
ladenkeks der.

choice [tʃɔɪs] n Wahl die ; (variety) Auswahl die. ◆ adj (meat,
ingredients) Qualitäts- ; **with the
topping of your** ~ mit der Garnitur Ihrer Wahl.

choir ['kwaɪə'] n Chor der.

choke [tʃəʊk] n (AUT) Choke
der. ◆ vt verstopfen. ◆ vi (on
fishbone etc) sich verschlucken ; (to death) ersticken.

cholera ['kɒlərə] n Cholera
die.

choose [tʃuːz] (pt chose, pp
chosen) vt wählen, sich (D)
aus|suchen. ◆ vi wählen ; to ~
to do sthg (decide) beschließen,
etw zu tun.

chop [tʃɒp] n (of meat) Kotelett
das. ◆ vt hacken. ▥ **chop
down** vt sep fällen, um|hauen.
▥ **chop up** vt sep klein hacken.

chopper ['tʃɒpə'] n (inf : helicopter) Hubschrauber der.

chopping board ['tʃɒpɪŋ-] n
Hackbrett das.

choppy ['tʃɒpɪ] adj kabbelig.

chopsticks ['tʃɒpstɪks] npl
Stäbchen pl.

chop suey [,tʃɒp'suːɪ] n
Chop-suey das.

chord [kɔːd] n Akkord der.

chore [tʃɔː'] n lästige Pflicht ;
household ~s Hausarbeit die.

chorus ['kɔːrəs] n (of song) Refrain der ; (singers, dancers)
Chor der.

chose [tʃəʊz] pt → choose.

chosen ['tʃəʊzn] pp →
choose.

choux pastry [ʃuː-] n Brand-
teig der.

chowder ['tʃaʊdə'] n Suppe
mit Fisch oder Meeresfrüchten.

chow mein [,tʃaʊ'meɪn] n chi-
nesisches Gericht mit gebratenen
Nudeln.

Christ [kraɪst] n Christus (ohne
Artikel).

christen ['krɪsn] vt taufen.

Christian ['krɪstʃən] adj christlich. ◆ n Christ der (-in die).

Christian name n Vorname
der.

Christmas ['krɪsməs] n Weihnachten das ; Happy ~! Fröhliche Weihnachten!

Christmas card n Weih-
nachtskarte die.

Christmas carol [-'kærəl] n
Weihnachtslied das.

Christmas Day n erster
Weihnachtsfeiertag der.

Christmas Eve n Heiligabend der.

Christmas pudding n Plum-
pudding der.

Christmas tree n Weihnachtsbaum der.

chrome [krəʊm] n Chrom das.

chuck [tʃʌk] vt (inf : throw)
schmeißen ; (boyfriend, girlfriend) Schluss machen mit.
▥ **chuck away** vt sep (inf)
weg|schmeißen.

chunk [tʃʌŋk] n (of meat, cake etc) Stück das.

church [tʃɜːtʃ] n Kirche die ; **to go to** ~ in die Kirche gehen.

churchyard ['tʃɜːtʃjɑːd] n Friedhof der.

chute [ʃuːt] n Rutsche die.

chutney ['tʃʌtnɪ] n Chutney das (Soße aus Früchten und Gewürzen).

cider ['saɪdə'] n ≃ Cidre der.

cigar [sɪ'gɑː'] n Zigarre die.

cigarette [ˌsɪgə'ret] n Zigarette die.

cigarette lighter n Feuerzeug das.

cinema ['sɪnəmə] n Kino das.

cinnamon ['sɪnəmən] n Zimt der.

circle ['sɜːkl] n Kreis der ; (in theatre) Rang der. ◆ vt (draw circle around) einlkreisen ; (move round) umlkreisen. ◆ vi (plane) kreisen.

circuit ['sɜːkɪt] n (track) Rennbahn die ; (lap) Runde die.

circular ['sɜːkjʊlə'] adj rund. ◆ n Rundschreiben das.

circulation [ˌsɜːkjʊ'leɪʃn] n (of blood) Kreislauf der ; (of newspaper, magazine) Auflage die.

circumstances ['sɜːkəmstənsɪz] npl Umstände pl ; **in** OR **under the** ~ unter diesen Umständen.

circus ['sɜːkəs] n Zirkus der.

cistern ['sɪstən] n (of toilet) Wasserbehälter der.

citizen ['sɪtɪzn] n Bürger der (-in die).

city ['sɪtɪ] n größere Stadt ; **the City** Banken- und Börsenviertel in London.

city centre n Stadtzentrum das.

city hall n (Am) Rathaus das.

civilian [sɪ'vɪljən] n Zivilist der (-in die).

civilized ['sɪvɪlaɪzd] adj (society) zivilisiert.

civil rights [ˌsɪvl-] npl Bürgerrechte pl.

civil servant [ˌsɪvl-] n Beamte der (im Staatsdienst) (-in die).

civil service [ˌsɪvl-] n Staatsdienst der.

civil war [ˌsɪvl-] n Bürgerkrieg der.

cl (abbr of centilitre) cl.

claim [kleɪm] n (assertion) Anspruch der ; (demand) Forderung die ; (for insurance) Schadenersatzanspruch der. ◆ vt (allege) behaupten ; (demand) fordern ; (credit) Anspruch erheben auf (+A). ◆ vi (on insurance) Schadenersatz fordern.

claimant ['kleɪmənt] n Antragsteller der (-in die).

claim form n Antragsformular das.

clam [klæm] n Klaffmuschel die.

clamp [klæmp] n (for car) Parkkralle die. ◆ vt (car) eine Parkkralle anllegen.

clap [klæp] vi klatschen.

claret ['klærət] n roter Bordeaux.

clarinet [ˌklærə'net] n Klarinette die.

clash [klæʃ] n (noise) Geklirr das ; (confrontation) Konflikt der. ◆ vi (colours) sich beißen ; (event, date) sich überschneiden.

clasp [klɑːsp] n (fastener)
Schnalle die. ◆ vt festIhalten.
class [klɑːs] n Klasse die ;
(teaching period) Stunde die ;
(type) Art die. ◆ vt : to ~ sb/sthg
as sthg jn/etw als etw einIstu-
fen.
classic ['klæsɪk] adj klassisch.
◆ n Klassiker der.
classical ['klæsɪkl] adj klassisch.
classical music n klassische
Musik.
classification [,klæsɪfɪ'keɪʃn]
n Klassifizierung die ; (category) Kategorie die.
classified ads [,klæsɪfaɪd-]
npl Annoncen pl.
classroom ['klɑːsrʊm] n Klas-
senzimmer das.
claustrophobic [,klɔːstrə-
'fəʊbɪk] adj : to feel ~ Platz-
angst haben.
claw [klɔː] n Kralle die ; (of
crab, lobster) Schere die.
clay [kleɪ] n Ton der.
clean [kliːn] adj sauber. ◆ vt
sauber machen ; (floor) putzen ; to ~ one's teeth sich (D)
die Zähne putzen.
cleaner ['kliːnə] n (person)
Putzfrau die (Putzer der) ; (substance) Putzmittel das.
cleanse [klenz] vt reinigen.
cleanser ['klenzə] n (for skin)
Reinigungsmilch die ; (detergent) Reinigungsmittel das.
clear [klɪə] adj klar ; (image,
sound) deutlich ; (obvious) eindeutig ; (road, view) frei. ◆ vt
(road, path) räumen ; (jump
over) überspringen ; (declare not
guilty) freisprechen ; (authorize) genehmigen ; (cheque)

verrechnen. ◆ vi (weather, fog)
sich aufIklären ; to be ~ (about
sthg) sich (D) im Klaren sein
(über etw (A)) ; to be ~ of sthg
(not touching) etw nicht berühren ; to ~ one's throat sich räuspern ; to ~ the table den Tisch
abIräumen. ▪ **clear up** vt sep
(room, tidy) aufIräumen ; (problem, confusion) klären. ◆ vi
(weather) sich aufIklären ; (tidy
up) aufIräumen.
clearance ['klɪərəns] n (authorization) Genehmigung die ;
(free distance) Spielraum der ;
(for takeoff) Starterlaubnis die.
clearance sale n Ausverkauf
der.
clearing ['klɪərɪŋ] n Lichtung
die.
clearly ['klɪəlɪ] adv (see, speak)
deutlich ; (marked, defined)
klar, deutlich ; (obviously) eindeutig.
clearway ['klɪəweɪ] n (Br)
Straße mit Halteverbot.
clementine ['kleməntaɪn] n
Klementine die.
clerk [(Br) klɑːk, (Am) klɜːrk] n
Büroangestellte der, die ; (Am :
in shop) Verkäufer der (-in die).
clever ['klevə] adj (person)
klug ; (idea, device) clever.
click [klɪk] n Klicken das. ◆ vi
klicken.
client ['klaɪənt] n Kunde der
(Kundin die).
cliff [klɪf] n Klippe die.
climate ['klaɪmɪt] n Klima das.
climax ['klaɪmæks] n Höhepunkt der.
climb [klaɪm] vt (hill, mountain)
besteigen ; (ladder) hinaufI-
steigen ; (tree) hochIklettern ;

◆ vi klettern ; *(plane)* steigen. ▨ **climb down** vt fus herunter|klettern. ◆ vi klein beigeben. ▨ **climb up** vt fus hoch|klettern.

climber ['klaɪmə'] n Bergsteiger *der* (-in *die*).

climbing ['klaɪmɪŋ] n *(mountaineering)* Bergsteigen *das* ; *(rock climbing)* Klettern *das* ; **to go ~** Bergsteigen/Klettern gehen.

climbing frame n *(Br)* Klettergerüst *das*.

clingfilm ['klɪŋfɪlm] n *(Br)* Klarsichtfolie *die*.

clinic ['klɪnɪk] n Klinik *die*.

clip [klɪp] n *(fastener)* Klammer *die* ; *(of film, programme)* Ausschnitt *der*. ◆ vt *(fasten)* zusammen|heften ; *(cut)* schneiden.

cloak [kləʊk] n Umhang *der*.

cloakroom ['kləʊkrʊm] n *(for coats)* Garderobe *die* ; *(Br : toilets)* Toilette *die*.

clock [klɒk] n Uhr *die* ; *(milometer)* Kilometerzähler *der* ; **round the ~** rund um die Uhr.

clockwise ['klɒkwaɪz] adv im Uhrzeigersinn.

clog [klɒg] n Clog *der*. ◆ vt verstopfen.

close[1] [kləʊs] adj nahe ; *(friend, contact, link)* eng ; *(resemblance)* stark ; *(examination)* genau ; *(race, contest)* knapp. ◆ adv nah ; **~ behind** dicht dahinter ; **~ by** in der Nähe ; **~ to** nahe an *(+A,D)*, dicht bei.

close[2] [kləʊz] vt schließen. ◆ vi *(door, eyes)* sich schließen ; *(shop, office)* schließen ; *(deadline, offer)* enden. ▨ **close down** vt sep & vi schließen.

closed [kləʊzd] adj geschlossen.

closely ['kləʊslɪ] adv *(related, involved)* eng ; *(follow)* dicht ; *(examine)* genau.

closet ['klɒzɪt] n *(Am)* Schrank *der*.

close-up ['kləʊs-] n Nahaufnahme *die*.

closing time ['kləʊzɪŋ-] n Ladenschluss *der*.

clot [klɒt] n *(of blood)* Gerinnsel *das*.

cloth [klɒθ] n *(fabric)* Stoff *der* ; *(piece of cloth)* Tuch *das*.

clothes [kləʊðz] npl Kleider *pl*.

clothesline ['kləʊðzlaɪn] n Wäscheleine *die*.

clothes peg n *(Br)* Wäscheklammer *die*.

clothespin ['kləʊðzpɪn] *(Am)* = **clothes peg**.

clothes shop n Bekleidungsgeschäft *das*.

clothing ['kləʊðɪŋ] n Kleidung *die*.

clotted cream [ˌklɒtɪd-] n sehr dicke Sahne, Spezialität Südwestenglands.

cloud [klaʊd] n Wolke *die*.

cloudy ['klaʊdɪ] adj bewölkt ; *(liquid)* trüb.

clove [kləʊv] n *(of garlic)* Zehe *die*. ▨ **cloves** npl *(spice)* Gewürznelken *pl*.

clown [klaʊn] n Clown *der*.

club [klʌb] n Klub *der* ; *(nightclub)* Nachtklub *der* ; *(stick)* Knüppel *der*. ▨ **clubs** npl *(in cards)* Kreuz *das*.

clubbing ['klʌbɪŋ] n : **to go ~** *(inf)* tanzen gehen.

club class n Club Class *die*.

club sandwich n (Am) Club-Sandwich das.

club soda n (Am) Sodawasser das.

clue [kluː] n Hinweis der; (in crossword) Frage die; **I haven't got a ~** ich habe keine Ahnung.

clumsy ['klʌmzɪ] adj (person) ungeschickt.

clutch [klʌtʃ] n Kupplung die. ◆ vt (hold tightly) umklammern.

cm (abbr of centimetre) cm.

c/o (abbr of care of) bei, c/o.

Co. (abbr of company) Co.

coach [kəutʃ] n (bus) Bus der; (of train) Wagen der; (SPORT) Trainer der (-in die).

coach party n (Br) Busreisende pl.

coach station n Busbahnhof der.

coach trip n (Br) Busausflug der.

coal [kəul] n Kohle die.

coal mine n Kohlenbergwerk das.

coarse [kɔːs] adj (rough) grob; (vulgar) vulgär.

coast [kəust] n Küste die.

coaster ['kəustə] n (for glass) Untersetzer der.

coastguard ['kəustgɑːd] n (person) Küstenwächter der (-in die); (organization) Küstenwache die.

coastline ['kəustlaɪn] n Küste die.

coat [kəut] n Mantel der; (of animal) Fell das. ◆ vt: **to ~ sthg (with)** etw überziehen (mit).

coat hanger n Kleiderbügel der.

coating ['kəutɪŋ] n (on surface) Beschichtung die; (on food) Überzug der.

cobbled street ['kɒbld-] n Straße die mit Kopfsteinpflaster.

cobbles ['kɒblz] npl Kopfsteinpflaster das.

cobweb ['kɒbweb] n Spinnennetz das.

Coca-Cola® [,kəukə'kəulə] n Coca-Cola® die or das.

cocaine [kəu'keɪn] n Kokain das.

cock [kɒk] n Hahn der.

cock-a-leekie [,kɒkə'liːkɪ] n Hühnersuppe mit Lauch.

cockerel ['kɒkrəl] n junger Hahn.

cockles ['kɒklz] npl Herzmuscheln pl.

cockpit ['kɒkpɪt] n (of plane) Cockpit das.

cockroach ['kɒkrəutʃ] n Küchenschabe die.

cocktail ['kɒkteɪl] n Cocktail der.

cocktail party n Cocktailparty die.

cock-up n (Br : vulg) : **to make a ~** Scheiße bauen.

cocoa ['kəukəu] n Kakao der.

coconut ['kəukənʌt] n Kokosnuss die.

cod [kɒd] n (pl cod) n Kabeljau der.

code [kəud] n Kode der; (dialling code) Vorwahl die.

cod-liver oil n Lebertran der.

coeducational [,kəuedjuː'keɪʃənl] adj koedukativ.

coffee ['kɒfɪ] n Kaffee der; **black ~** schwarzer Kaffee;

white ~ Kaffee mit Milch; ground ~ gemahlener Kaffee; instant ~ Instantkaffee.

coffee bar n (Br) Café das.

coffee break n Kaffeepause die.

coffeepot ['kɒfɪpɒt] n Kaffeekanne die.

coffee shop n (cafe) Café das.

coffee table n Couchtisch der.

coffin ['kɒfɪn] n Sarg der.

cog(wheel) ['kɒg(wi:l)] n Zahnrad das.

coil [kɔɪl] n Rolle die; (Br : contraceptive) Spirale die. ◆ vt auflrollen.

coin [kɔɪn] n Münze die.

coinbox ['kɔɪnbɒks] n (Br) Münztelefon das.

coincide [ˌkəʊɪn'saɪd] vi : to ~ (with) zusammenlfallen (mit).

coincidence [kəʊ'ɪnsɪdəns] n Zufall der.

Coke® [kəʊk] n Cola® die or das.

colander ['kʌləndə'] n Sieb das.

cold [kəʊld] adj kalt; (unfriendly) kühl. ◆ n (illness) Erkältung die, Schnupfen der; (temperature) Kälte die; to get ~ kalt werden; to catch (a) ~ sich erkälten.

cold cuts (Am) = cold meats.

cold meats npl Aufschnitt der.

coleslaw ['kəʊlslɔ:] n Krautsalat der.

colic ['kɒlɪk] n Kolik die.

collaborate [kə'læbəreɪt] vi zusammenlarbeiten.

collapse [kə'læps] vi (building, tent) einlstürzen; (person) zusammenlbrechen.

collar ['kɒlə'] n Kragen der; (of dog, cat) Halsband das.

collarbone ['kɒləbəʊn] n Schlüsselbein das.

colleague ['kɒli:g] n Kollege der (Kollegin die).

collect [kə'lekt] vt sammeln; (go and get) ablholen. ◆ vi sich sammeln. ◆ adv (Am) : to call (sb) ~ ein R-Gespräch (mit jm) führen.

collection [kə'lekʃn] n Sammlung die; (of mail) Leerung die.

collector [kə'lektə'] n Sammler der (-in die).

college ['kɒlɪdʒ] n (school) Schule die; (Br : of university) College das; (Am : university) Universität die.

collide [kə'laɪd] vi : to ~ (with) zusammenlstoßen (mit).

collision [kə'lɪʒn] n Zusammenstoß der.

cologne [kə'ləʊn] n Kölnischwasser das.

Cologne [kə'ləʊn] n Köln nt.

colon ['kəʊlən] n (GRAMM) Doppelpunkt der.

colonel ['kɜ:nl] n Oberst der.

colony ['kɒlənɪ] n Kolonie die.

color ['kʌlə'] (Am) = colour.

colour ['kʌlə'] n Farbe die. ◆ adj (photograph, film) Farb-. ◆ vt färben. ▪ **colour in** vt sep auslmalen.

colour-blind adj farbenblind.

colourful ['kʌləfʊl] adj bunt; (fig : person, place) schillernd.

colouring ['kʌlərɪŋ] n (of food)
Farbstoff der ; (complexion)
Hautfarbe die.

colouring book n Malbuch
das.

colour supplement n Beilage die.

colour television n Farbfernsehen das.

column ['kɒləm] n Säule die ;
(of figures) Kolumne die ; (of
writing) Spalte die.

coma ['kəʊmə] n Koma das.

comb [kəʊm] n Kamm der. ◆
vt : to ~ one's hair sich (D) die
Haare kämmen.

combination [ˌkɒmbɪ'neɪʃn]
n (mixture) Mischung die ; (of
lock) Kombination die.

combine [kəm'baɪn] vt : to ~
sthg with etw verbinden (mit).

combine harvester ['kɒm-baɪn'hɑːvɪstə'] n Mähdrescher
der.

come [kʌm] (pt came, pp come)
vi 1. (move) kommen ; we came
by taxi wir sind mit dem Taxi
gekommen ; ~ and see! komm
und sieh! ; ~ here! komm her!
2. (arrive) kommen ; to ~ home
nach Hause kommen ; 'coming
soon' 'demnächst'.
3. (in competition) : to ~ first Erster werden ; to ~ last Letzter
werden.
4. (reach) : to ~ up/down to gehen bis.
5. (become) werden ; to ~ true
wahr werden ; to ~ undone
aufgehen.
6. (be sold) : they ~ in packs of six
es gibt sie im Sechserpack.

▨ **come across** vt fus stoßen
auf (+A).

▨ **come along** vi (progress)
voran|kommen ; (arrive) kommen ; ~ along! (as encouragement) komm! ; (hurry up)
komm schon!

▨ **come apart** vi kaputt|gehen.

▨ **come back** vi zurück|kommen.

▨ **come down** vi (price) fallen.

▨ **come down with** vt fus (illness) bekommen.

▨ **come from** vt fus stammen
aus (+D), kommen aus (+D).

▨ **come in** vi herein|kommen ;
(train) ein|fahren ; ~ in! herein!

▨ **come off** vi (button, top) ab|gehen ; (succeed) klappen.

▨ **come on** vi (progress)
voran|kommen ; ~ on! (as encouragement) komm! ; (hurry
up) komm schon!

▨ **come out** vi heraus|kommen ; (stain) heraus|gehen ;
only two photos came out nur
zwei Bilder sind was geworden.

▨ **come over** vi (visit) vorbei|kommen.

▨ **come round** vi (visit)
vorbei|kommen ; (regain consciousness) zu sich kommen.

▨ **come to** vt fus : the bill ~s to
£20 das macht 20 Pfund.

▨ **come up** vi (go upstairs)
hoch|kommen ; (be mentioned)
erwähnt werden ; (happen)
passieren ; (sun, moon) auf|gehen.

▨ **come up with** vt fus (idea)
sich aus|denken.

comedian [kə'miːdjən] n Komiker der.

comedy ['kɒmədɪ] n Komödie
die ; (humour) Komik die.

comfort ['kʌmfət] n Bequemlichkeit die ; (consolation) Trost der. ◆ vt trösten.

comfortable ['kʌmftəbl] adj bequem ; (hotel) komfortabel ; (financially) ohne Sorgen ; **she is ~** (after operation) es geht ihr gut.

comic ['kɒmɪk] adj komisch. ◆ n (person) Komiker der ; (magazine) Comic-Heft das.

comical ['kɒmɪkl] adj ulkig.

comic strip n Comic der.

comma ['kɒmə] n Komma das.

command [kə'mɑ:nd] n Befehl der ; (mastery) Beherrschung die. ◆ vt befehlen (+D) ; (be in charge of) befehligen.

commander [kə'mɑ:ndə'] n Kommandant der.

commemorate [kə'meməreɪt] vt gedenken (+G).

commence [kə'mens] vi (fml) beginnen.

comment ['kɒment] n Kommentar der. ◆ vi bemerken.

commentary ['kɒməntrɪ] n (on TV, radio) Kommentar der.

commentator ['kɒmənteɪtə'] n (on TV, radio) Reporter der (-in die).

commerce ['kɒmɜ:s] n Handel der.

commercial [kə'mɜ:ʃl] adj kommerziell. ◆ n Werbespot der.

commercial break n Werbepause die.

commission [kə'mɪʃn] n (money) Provision die ; (committee) Kommission die.

commit [kə'mɪt] vt (crime, sin, suicide) begehen ; **to ~ o.s. (to sthg)** sich (zu etw) verpflichten.

committee [kə'mɪtɪ] n Ausschuss der.

commodity [kə'mɒdətɪ] n Produkt das.

common ['kɒmən] adj (usual, widespread) häufig ; (shared) gemeinsam ; (pej : vulgar) gewöhnlich. ◆ n (Br : land) Gemeindewiese die ; **in ~** gemeinsam.

commonly ['kɒmənlɪ] adv (generally) allgemein.

Common Market n Gemeinsamer Markt.

common room n Gemeinschaftsraum der.

common sense n gesunder Menschenverstand.

Commonwealth ['kɒmənwelθ] n Commonwealth das.

communal ['kɒmjunl] adj (bathroom, kitchen) Gemeinschafts-.

communicate [kə'mju:nɪkeɪt] vi : **to ~ (with)** sich verständigen (mit).

communication [kə,mju:nɪ'keɪʃn] n Verständigung die.

communication cord n (Br) Notbremse die.

communist ['kɒmjunɪst] n Kommunist der (-in die).

community [kə'mju:nətɪ] n Gemeinschaft die ; (local) ~ Gemeinde die.

community centre n Gemeindezentrum das.

commute [kə'mjuːt] *vi* pendeln.

commuter [kə'mjuːtər] *n* Pendler *der* (-in *die*).

compact [*adj* kəm'pækt, *n* 'kɒmpækt] *adj* kompakt. ◆ *n* (for make-up) Puderdose *die* ; (Am : car) Kleinwagen *der*.

compact disc [ˌkɒmpækt-] *n* Compactdisc *die*.

compact disc player *n* CD-Player *der*.

company ['kʌmpəni] *n* Gesellschaft *die* ; (firm) Firma *die* ; (guests) Besuch *der* ; **to keep sb** ~ jm Gesellschaft leisten.

company car *n* Firmenwagen *der*.

comparatively [kəm'pærətɪvlɪ] *adv* (relatively) relativ.

compare [kəm'peər] *vt* : **to** ~ **sthg** (with) etw vergleichen (mit).

comparison [kəm'pærɪsn] *n* Vergleich *der* ; **in** ~ **with** im Vergleich zu.

compartment [kəm'pɑːtmənt] *n* (of train) Abteil *das* ; (section) Fach *das*.

compass ['kʌmpəs] *n* Kompass *der* ; **(a pair of)** ~**es** ein Zirkel.

compatible [kəm'pætəbl] *adj* : **to be** ~ zusammenlpassen.

compensate ['kɒmpenseɪt] *vt* entschädigen. ◆ *vi* : **to** ~ **for sthg** etw auslgleichen ; **to** ~ **sb for sthg** jn für etw entschädigen.

compensation [ˌkɒmpen-'seɪʃn] *n* (money) Abfindung *die*.

compete [kəm'piːt] *vi* (take

part) teillnehmen ; **to** ~ **with sb for sthg** mit jm um etw konkurrieren.

competent ['kɒmpɪtənt] *adj* fähig.

competition [ˌkɒmpɪ'tɪʃn] *n* (race, contest) Wettbewerb *der* ; (rivalry, rivals) Konkurrenz *die*.

competitive [kəm'petətɪv] *adj* (price) konkurrenzfähig ; (person) wetteifernd.

competitor [kəm'petɪtər] *n* (in race, contest) Teilnehmer *der* (-in *die*) ; (COMM) Konkurrent *der* (-in *die*).

complain [kəm'pleɪn] *vi* : **to** ~ **(about)** sich beschweren (über (+A)).

complaint [kəm'pleɪnt] *n* Beschwerde *die* ; (illness) Beschwerden *pl*.

complement ['kɒmplɪˌment] *vt* ergänzen.

complete [kəm'pliːt] *adj* (whole) vollständig ; (finished) fertig ; (utter) völlig. ◆ *vt* (finish) fertig stellen ; (a form) auslfüllen ; (make whole) vervollständigen ; ~ **with** komplett mit.

completely [kəm'pliːtlɪ] *adv* ganz.

complex ['kɒmpleks] *adj* kompliziert. ◆ *n* Komplex *der*.

complexion [kəm'plekʃn] *n* (of skin) Teint *der*.

complicated ['kɒmplɪkeɪtɪd] *adj* kompliziert.

compliment [*n* 'kɒmplɪmənt, *vb* 'kɒmplɪment] *n* Kompliment *das*. ◆ *vt* : **to** ~ **sb** jm ein Kompliment machen.

complimentary [ˌkɒmplɪ'mentərɪ] *adj (seat, ticket)* Frei-, gratis ; *(words, person)* schmeichelhaft.

compose [kəm'pəʊz] *vt (music)* komponieren ; *(letter, poem)* verfassen ; **to be ~d of** bestehen aus.

composed [kəm'pəʊzd] *adj* gefasst.

composer [kəm'pəʊzə'] *n* Komponist *der* (-in *die*).

composition [ˌkɒmpə'zɪʃn] *n (essay)* Aufsatz *der*.

compound ['kɒmpaʊnd] *n (substance)* Verbindung *die* ; *(word)* Kompositum *das*.

comprehensive [ˌkɒmprɪ'hensɪv] *adj* umfassend.

comprehensive (school) *n (Br)* Gesamtschule *die*.

compressed air [kəm'prest] *n* Pressluft *die*.

comprise [kəm'praɪz] *vt* bestehen aus.

compromise ['kɒmprəmaɪz] *n* Kompromiss *der*.

compulsory [kəm'pʌlsərɪ] *adj* : **to be ~** Pflicht sein.

computer [kəm'pjuːtə'] *n* Computer *der*.

computer game *n* Computerspiel *das*.

computerized [kəm'pjuːtəraɪzd] *adj* computerisiert.

computer operator *n* Anwender *der* (-in *die*).

computer programmer [-'prəʊɡræmə'] *n* Programmierer *der* (-in *die*).

computing [kəm'pjuːtɪŋ] *n* Computertechnik *die*.

con [kɒn] *n (inf : trick)* Schwindel *der* ; **all mod ~s** moderner Komfort.

conceal [kən'siːl] *vt* verbergen.

conceited [kən'siːtɪd] *adj (pej)* eingebildet.

concentrate ['kɒnsəntreɪt] *vt* konzentrieren. ◆ *vi* : **to ~ (on sthg)** sich (auf etw (A)) konzentrieren.

concentrated ['kɒnsəntreɪtɪd] *adj* konzentriert.

concentration [ˌkɒnsən'treɪʃn] *n* Konzentration *die*.

concern [kən'sɜːn] *n (worry)* Sorge *die* ; *(affair)* Angelegenheit *die* ; *(COMM)* Unternehmen *das*. ◆ *vt (be about)* betreffen ; *(worry)* beunruhigen ; *(involve)* anlgehen ; **it's no ~ of mine** das geht mich nichts an ; **to be ~ed about** besorgt sein um ; **to be ~ed with** handeln von ; **to ~ o.s. with sthg** sich um etw kümmern ; **as far as I'm ~ed** was mich betrifft.

concerned [kən'sɜːnd] *adj* besorgt.

concerning [kən'sɜːnɪŋ] *prep* betreffend.

concert ['kɒnsət] *n* Konzert *das*.

concession [kən'seʃn] *n (reduced price)* Ermäßigung *die*.

concise [kən'saɪs] *adj* prägnant.

conclude [kən'kluːd] *vt (deduce)* folgern ; *(fml : end)* ablschließen. ◆ *vi (fml : end)* schließen.

conclusion [kən'kluːʒn] *n* Schluss *der*.

concrete ['kɒŋkri:t] adj (building, path) Beton-; (idea, plan) konkret. ◆ n Beton der.

concussion [kən'kʌʃn] n Gehirnerschütterung die.

condensation [ˌkɒnden'seɪʃn] n Kondensation die.

condensed milk [kən'denst-] n Kondensmilch die.

condition [kən'dɪʃn] n (state) Zustand der; (proviso) Bedingung die; (illness) Leiden das; to be out of ~ keine Kondition haben; on ~ that unter der Bedingung, dass. ■ **conditions** npl (circumstances) Verhältnisse pl.

conditioner [kən'dɪʃnəʳ] n (for hair) Spülung die; (for clothes) Weichspüler der.

condo ['kɒndəʊ] (Am : inf) = condominium.

condom ['kɒndəm] n Kondom das.

condominium [ˌkɒndə'mɪnɪəm] n (Am : apartment) Eigentumswohnung die; (building) Appartmenthaus das (mit Eigentumswohnungen).

conduct [vb kən'dʌkt, n 'kɒndʌkt] vt durchlführen; (MUS) dirigieren. ◆ n (fml : behaviour) Benehmen das; to ~ o.s. (fml) sich verhalten.

conductor [kən'dʌktəʳ] n (MUS) Dirigent der (-in die); (on bus, train) Schaffner der (-in die).

cone [kəʊn] n (shape) Kegel der; (for ice cream) Waffeltüte die; (on roads) Leitkegel der.

confectioner's [kən'fekʃnəz] n (shop) Süßwarenladen der.

confectionery [kən'fekʃnəri] n Süßigkeiten pl.

conference ['kɒnfərəns] n Konferenz die.

confess [kən'fes] vi: to ~ (to) gestehen.

confession [kən'feʃn] n Geständnis das; (RELIG) Beichte die.

confidence ['kɒnfɪdəns] n (self-assurance) Selbstvertrauen das; (trust) Vertrauen das; to have ~ in Vertrauen haben zu.

confident ['kɒnfɪdənt] adj (self-assured) selbstbewusst; (certain) zuversichtlich.

confined [kən'faɪnd] adj begrenzt.

confirm [kən'fɜ:m] vt bestätigen.

confirmation [ˌkɒnfə'meɪʃn] n Bestätigung die; (of Catholic) Firmung die; (of Protestant) Konfirmation die.

conflict [n 'kɒnflɪkt, vb kən'flɪkt] n Konflikt der; (war) Kämpfe pl. ◆ vi: to ~ (with) im Widerspruch stehen (zu).

conform [kən'fɔ:m] vi: to ~ (to) sich anlpassen (an (+A)).

confuse [kən'fju:z] vt verwirren; to ~ sthg with sthg eine Sache mit etw verwechseln.

confused [kən'fju:zd] adj verwirrt; (situation) wirr.

confusing [kən'fju:zɪŋ] adj verwirrend.

confusion [kən'fju:ʒn] n Verwirrung die; (disorder) Durcheinander das; (mix-up) Verwechslung die.

congested [kən'dʒestɪd] adj (street) verstopft.

congestion [kən'dʒestʃn] *n* (*traffic*) Stau *der*.

congratulate [kən'grætʃʊleɪt] *vt* : to ~ sb (on sthg) jm (zu etw) gratulieren.

congratulations [kən,grætʃʊ'leɪʃənz] *excl* herzlichen Glückwunsch.

congregate ['kɒŋgrɪgeɪt] *vi* sich versammeln.

Congress ['kɒŋgres] *n* (*Am*) der Kongress.

conifer ['kɒnɪfə'] *n* Nadelbaum *der*.

conjunction [kən'dʒʌŋkʃn] *n* (GRAMM) Konjunktion *die*.

conjurer ['kʌndʒərə'] *n* Zauberer *der* (Zauberin *die*).

connect [kə'nekt] *vt* verbinden ; (*telephone, machine*) anschließen. ◆ *vi* : to ~ with (*train, plane*) Anschluss haben an (+A).

connecting flight [kə'nektɪŋ-] *n* Anschlussflug *der*.

connection [kə'nekʃn] *n* (*link*) Zusammenhang *der* ; (*train, plane*) Anschluss *der* ; a bad ~ (*on phone*) eine schlechte Verbindung ; a loose ~ (*in machine*) ein Wackelkontakt ; in ~ with in Zusammenhang mit.

conquer ['kɒŋkə'] *vt* erobern.

conscience ['kɒnʃəns] *n* Gewissen *das*.

conscientious [,kɒnʃɪ'enʃəs] *adj* gewissenhaft.

conscious ['kɒnʃəs] *adj* bewusst ; to be ~ (*awake*) bei Bewusstsein sein.

consent [kən'sent] *n* Zustimmung *die*.

consequence ['kɒnsɪkwəns] *n* (*result*) Folge *die*.

consequently ['kɒnsɪkwəntlɪ] *adv* folglich.

conservation [,kɒnsə'veɪʃn] *n* Erhaltung *die*.

conservative [kən'sɜːvətɪv] *adj* konservativ. ▦ **Conservative** *adj* konservativ. ◆ *n* Konservative *der, die*.

conservatory [kən'sɜːvətrɪ] *n* Wintergarten *der*.

consider [kən'sɪdə'] *vt* (*think about*) sich (D) überlegen ; (*take into account*) berücksichtigen ; (*judge*) halten für.

considerable [kən'sɪdrəbl] *adj* beträchtlich.

consideration [kən,sɪdə'reɪʃn] *n* (*careful thought*) Überlegung *die* ; (*factor*) Faktor *der* ; to take sthg into ~ etw berücksichtigen.

considering [kən'sɪdərɪŋ] *prep* in Anbetracht (+G).

consist [kən'sɪst] : consist in *vt fus* bestehen in (+D). ▦ **consist of** *vt fus* bestehen aus.

consistent [kən'sɪstənt] *adj* (*coherent*) übereinstimmend ; (*worker, performance*) konsequent.

consolation [,kɒnsə'leɪʃn] *n* Trost *der*.

console ['kɒnsəʊl] *n* (*for machine*) Steuerpult *das* ; (*for computer game*) Spielkonsole *die*.

consonant ['kɒnsənənt] *n* Konsonant *der*.

conspicuous [kən'spɪkjʊəs] *adj* auffällig.

constable ['kʌnstəbl] *n* (*Br*) Wachtmeister *der* (-in *die*).

constant ['kɒnstənt] *adj (unchanging)* gleichmäßig; *(continuous)* ständig.

constantly ['kɒnstəntlɪ] *adv (all the time)* ständig.

constipated ['kɒnstɪpeɪtɪd] *adj* verstopft.

constitution [ˌkɒnstɪ'tjuːʃn] *n (health)* Konstitution *die*.

construct [kən'strʌkt] *vt* bauen.

construction [kən'strʌkʃn] *n* Bau *der*; **under ~** im Bau.

consul ['kɒnsəl] *n* Konsul *der* (-in *die*).

consulate ['kɒnsjʊlət] *n* Konsulat *das*.

consult [kən'sʌlt] *vt (person)* um Rat fragen; *(doctor)* konsultieren; *(dictionary, map)* nach|sehen.

consultant [kən'sʌltənt] *n (Br : doctor)* Facharzt *der* (-ärztin *die*).

consume [kən'sjuːm] *vt (food)* essen; *(fuel, energy)* verbrauchen.

consumer [kən'sjuːmə] *n* Verbraucher *der* (-in *die*).

contact ['kɒntækt] *n (communication, person)* Kontakt *der*. ◆ *vt* sich in Verbindung setzen mit; **in ~ with** *(touching)* in Berührung mit; *(in communication with)* in Verbindung mit.

contact lens *n* Kontaktlinse *die*.

contagious [kən'teɪdʒəs] *adj* ansteckend.

contain [kən'teɪn] *vt* enthalten; *(control)* zurück|halten.

container [kən'teɪnə] *n* Behälter *der*.

contaminate [kən'tæmɪneɪt] *vt* verunreinigen.

contemporary [kən'tempərərɪ] *adj* zeitgenössisch. ◆ *n* Zeitgenosse *der* (-genossin *die*).

contend [kən'tend] : **contend with** *vt fus* fertig werden mit.

content [*adj* kən'tent, *n* 'kɒntent] *adj* zufrieden. ◆ *n (of vitamins, fibre etc)* Anteil *der*. ▪ **contents** *npl* Inhalt *der*.

contest [*n* 'kɒntest, *vb* kən'test] *n (competition)* Wettbewerb *der*; *(struggle)* Kampf *der*. ◆ *vt (election, seat)* kandidieren; *(decision, will)* an|fechten.

context ['kɒntekst] *n* Zusammenhang *der*.

continent ['kɒntɪnənt] *n* Kontinent *der*; **the Continent** *(Br)* Europa.

continental [ˌkɒntɪ'nentl] *adj (Br : European)* europäisch.

continental breakfast *n* Frühstück mit Kaffee oder Tee, Brötchen und Marmelade.

continental quilt *n (Br)* Federbett *das*.

continual [kən'tɪnjʊəl] *adj* ständig.

continually [kən'tɪnjʊəlɪ] *adv* ständig.

continue [kən'tɪnjuː] *vt* fort|setzen. ◆ *vi* weiter|gehen; *(start again)* weiter|machen; *(carry on speaking)* fort|fahren; *(keep driving)* weiter|fahren; **to ~ doing sthg** etw weiterhin tun; **to ~ with sthg** mit etw fort|fahren.

continuous [kən'tɪnjʊəs] *adj (constant)* gleichmäßig ; *(unbroken)* ununterbrochen.

continuously [kən'tɪnjʊəslɪ] *adv* ununterbrochen.

contraception [ˌkɒntrə'sepʃn] *n* Empfängnisverhütung *die*.

contraceptive [ˌkɒntrə'septɪv] *n* Verhütungsmittel *das*.

contract [*n* 'kɒntrækt, *vb* kən'trækt] *n* Vertrag *der*. ◆ *vt (fml : illness)* sich (D) zulziehen.

contradict [ˌkɒntrə'dɪkt] *vt* widersprechen (+D).

contraflow ['kɒntrəfləʊ] *n (Br)* zeitweilige *Umleitung des Verkehrs auf die Gegenfahrbahn.*

contrary ['kɒntrərɪ] *n* : **on the ~** im Gegenteil.

contrast [*n* 'kɒntrɑːst, *vb* kən'trɑːst] *n* Kontrast *der*. ◆ *vt* vergleichen ; **in ~ to** im Gegensatz zu.

contribute [kən'trɪbjuːt] *vt* & *vi* beiltragen ; **to ~ to** beiltragen zu.

contribution [ˌkɒntrɪ'bjuːʃn] *n* Beitrag *der*.

control [kən'trəʊl] *n (power)* Macht *die* ; *(over emotions)* Kontrolle *die* ; *(operating device)* Steuerung *die*. ◆ *vt (have power over)* beherrschen ; *(car, machine)* steuern ; *(restrict)* beschränken ; **to be in ~** Macht haben ; **out of ~** außer Kontrolle ; **under ~** unter Kontrolle. ▨ **controls** *npl (for TV, video)* Fernbedienung *die* ; *(of aeroplane)* Steuerung *die*.

control tower *n* Kontrollturm *der*.

controversial [ˌkɒntrə'vɜːʃl] *adj* umstritten.

convenience [kən'viːnjəns] *n* Bequemlichkeit *die* ; **at your ~** wann es Ihnen passt.

convenient [kən'viːnjənt] *adj* günstig ; *(well-situated)* in Reichweite ; **to be ~ for sb** jm passen.

convent ['kɒnvənt] *n* Kloster *das*.

conventional [kən'venʃənl] *adj* konventionell.

conversation [ˌkɒnvə'seɪʃn] *n* Gespräch *das*.

conversion [kən'vɜːʃn] *n* Umwandlung *die* ; *(to building)* Umbau *der*.

convert [kən'vɜːt] *vt* umlwandeln ; *(RELIG)* bekehren ; **to ~ sthg into etw** umlwandeln in (+A).

converted [kən'vɜːtɪd] *adj (building, loft)* ausgebaut.

convertible [kən'vɜːtəbl] *n* Kabrio *das*.

convey [kən'veɪ] *vt (fml : transport)* befördern ; *(idea, impression)* vermitteln.

convict [*n* 'kɒnvɪkt, *vb* kən'vɪkt] *n* Strafgefangene *der, die*. ◆ *vt* : **to ~ sb (of)** jn verurteilen (wegen).

convince [kən'vɪns] *vt* : **to ~ sb (of sthg)** jn (von etw) überzeugen ; **to ~ sb to do sthg** jn überreden, etw zu tun.

convoy ['kɒnvɔɪ] *n* Konvoi *der*.

cook [kʊk] *n* Koch *der* (Köchin *die*). ◆ *vt* & *vi* kochen.

cookbook ['kʊk,bʊk] = cookery book.

cooker ['kʊkə] n Herd der.

cookery ['kʊkərɪ] n Kochen
das.

cookery book n Kochbuch
das.

cookie ['kʊkɪ] n (Am) Keks der.

cooking ['kʊkɪŋ] n Kochen
das ; (food) Küche die.

cooking apple n Kochapfel
der.

cooking oil n Öl zum Kochen.

cool [kuːl] adj kühl ; (inf : great)
toll. ◆ vt kühlen. ▪ **cool
down** vi abkühlen ; (become
calmer) sich beruhigen.

cooperate [kəʊ'ɒpəreɪt] vi zu-
sammenarbeiten.

cooperation [kəʊ,ɒpə'reɪʃn]
n Zusammenarbeit die.

cooperative [kəʊ'ɒpərətɪv]
adj hilfsbereit.

coordinates [kəʊ'ɔːdɪnəts]
npl (clothes) Kleidung zum Kombinieren.

cope [kəʊp] vi : to ~ (with) zurechtkommen (mit).

copilot ['kəʊ,paɪlət] n Kopilot
der (-in die).

copper ['kɒpə] n Kupfer das ;
(Br : inf : coin) Penny der.

copy ['kɒpɪ] n Kopie die ; (of
newspaper, book) Exemplar das.
◆ vt kopieren.

cord(uroy) ['kɔːd(ərɔɪ)] n
Kord(samt) der.

core [kɔː] n (of fruit) Kernge-
häuse das.

coriander [,kɒrɪ'ændə] n Ko-
riander der.

cork [kɔːk] n (in bottle) Korken
der.

corkscrew ['kɔːkskruː] n Korkenzieher der.

corn [kɔːn] n (Br : crop) Getreide das ; (Am : maize) Mais
der ; (on foot) Hühnerauge das.

corned beef [,kɔːnd-] n Cor-
nedbeef das.

corner ['kɔːnə] n Ecke die ;
(bend in road) Kurve die ; it's just
around the ~ es ist gleich um die
Ecke.

corner shop n (Br) Tante-
Emma-Laden der.

cornet ['kɔːnɪt] n (Br : ice-
cream cone) Waffeltüte die.

cornflakes ['kɔːnfleɪks] npl
Cornflakes pl.

corn-on-the-cob n (gekochter) Maiskolben.

corporal ['kɔːpərəl] n Unter-
offizier der.

corpse [kɔːps] n Leiche die.

correct [kə'rekt] adj richtig.
◆ vt verbessern.

correction [kə'rekʃn] n Verbesserung die.

correspond [,kɒrɪ'spɒnd] vi :
to ~ (to) (match) entsprechen
(+D) ; to ~ (with) (exchange letters) korrespondieren (mit).

corresponding [,kɒrɪ'spɒn-
dɪŋ] adj entsprechend.

corridor ['kɒrɪdɔː] n Korridor
der.

corrugated iron ['kɒrəgeɪ-
tɪd-] n Wellblech das.

corrupt [kə'rʌpt] adj korrupt.

cosmetics [kɒz'metɪks] npl
Kosmetik die.

cost [kɒst] n (pt & pp cost) n Kosten pl ; (fig : loss) Preis der. ◆ vt
kosten ; how much does it ~?
wie viel kostet es?

costly ['kɒstlɪ] *adj* teuer.

costume ['kɒstjuːm] *n* Kostüm *das*; *(of country, region)* Tracht *die*.

cosy ['kəʊzɪ] *adj (Br : room, house)* gemütlich.

cot [kɒt] *n (Br : for baby)* Kinderbett *das*; *(Am : camp bed)* Feldbett *das*.

cottage ['kɒtɪdʒ] *n* Cottage *das*, Häuschen *das*.

cottage cheese *n* Hüttenkäse *der*.

cottage pie *n (Br) Hackfleischauflauf, bedeckt mit einer Schicht Kartoffelbrei.*

cotton ['kɒtn] *adj (dress, shirt)* Baumwoll-. ◆ *n* Baumwolle *die*; *(thread)* Nähgarn *das*.

cotton candy *n (Am)* Zuckerwatte *die*.

cotton wool *n* Watte *die*.

couch [kaʊtʃ] *n* Couch *die*; *(at doctor's)* Liege *die*.

couchette [kuːˈʃet] *n (on train)* Liegewagen *der*; *(seat on ship)* Liegesessel *der*.

cough [kɒf] *n* Husten *der*. ◆ *vi* husten; **to have a ~** Husten haben.

cough mixture *n* Hustenmittel *das*.

could [kʊd] *pt* → **can**.

couldn't ['kʊdnt] = **could not**.

could've ['kʊdəv] = **could have**.

council ['kaʊnsl] *n (Br : of town)* Stadtrat *der*; *(Br : of county)* Gemeinderat *der*; *(organization)* Rat *der*.

council house *n (Br)* ≃ Sozialwohnung *die*.

councillor ['kaʊnsələ'] *n (Br : of town)* Stadtrat *der* (-rätin *die*); *(of county)* Gemeinderat *der* (-rätin *die*).

council tax *n (Br)* ≃ Gemeindesteuer *die*.

count [kaʊnt] *vt* & *vi* zählen. ◆ *n (nobleman)* Graf *der*. ■ **count on** *vt fus (rely on)* sich verlassen auf (+A); *(expect)* rechnen auf (+A).

counter ['kaʊntə'] *n (in shop)* Ladentisch *der*; *(in bank)* Schalter *der*; *(in board game)* Spielmarke *die*.

counterclockwise [ˌkaʊntə-ˈklɒkwaɪz] *adv (Am)* gegen den Uhrzeigersinn.

counterfoil ['kaʊntəfɔɪl] *n* Beleg *der*.

countess ['kaʊntɪs] *n* Gräfin *die*.

country ['kʌntrɪ] *n* Land *das*; *(scenery)* Landschaft *die*; *(population)* Volk *das*. ◆ *adj* Land-.

country and western *n* Countrymusic *die*.

country house *n* Landhaus *das*.

country road *n* Landstraße *die*.

countryside ['kʌntrɪsaɪd] *n (place)* Land *das*; *(scenery)* Landschaft *die*.

county ['kaʊntɪ] *n (in Britain)* Grafschaft *die*; *(in US)* Verwaltungsbezirk *der*.

couple ['kʌpl] *n* Paar *das*; **a ~ (of) (two)** zwei; *(a few)* ein paar.

coupon ['kuːpɒn] *n (for discount etc)* Gutschein *der*; *(for orders, enquiries)* Kupon *der*.

courage ['kʌrɪdʒ] *n* Mut *der*.

courgette [kɔːˈʒet] n (Br) Zucchini die.

courier [ˈkʊrɪə] n (for holiday-makers) Reiseleiter der (-in die); (for delivering letters) Kurier der.

course [kɔːs] n (of meal) Gang der; (at university, college) Studiengang der; (of evening classes etc) Kurs der; (of treatment, injections) Kur die; (of ship, plane) Kurs der; (of river) Lauf der; (for golf) Platz der; **of ~** natürlich; **of ~ not** natürlich nicht; **in the ~ of** im Laufe (+G).

court [kɔːt] n (JUR: building) Gericht das; (JUR: room) Gerichtssaal der; (SPORT) Platz der; (of king, queen) Hof der.

courtesy coach [ˈkɜːtɪsɪ-] n kostenloser Zubringerbus.

court shoes npl Pumps pl.

courtyard [ˈkɔːtjɑːd] n Hof der.

cousin [ˈkʌzn] n Vetter der (Kusine die).

cover [ˈkʌvə] n (covering) Abdeckung die; (of cushion) Bezug der; (lid) Deckel der; (of book) Einband der; (of magazine) Umschlag der; (blanket) Decke die; (insurance) Versicherung die. ◆ vt bedecken; (travel) zurücklegen; (apply to) gelten für; (discuss) behandeln; (report) berichten über (+A); (be enough for) decken; (subj: insurance) versichern; **to be ~ed in sthg** voller etw sein; **to be ~ed in dust** völlig verstaubt sein; **to ~ sthg with sthg** etw mit etw abdecken; **to take ~** Schutz suchen. ▪ **cover up** vt sep zul-

decken; (facts, truth) vertuschen.

cover charge n Gedeck das.

cover note n (Br) Deckungskarte die.

cow [kaʊ] n Kuh die.

coward [ˈkaʊəd] n Feigling der.

cowboy [ˈkaʊbɔɪ] n Cowboy der.

crab [kræb] n Krabbe die.

crack [kræk] n (in cup, glass) Sprung der; (in wood) Riss der; (gap) Spalt der. ◆ vt (cup, glass) anlschlagen; (wood) anlknacksen; (nut) knacken; (egg) auflschlagen; (whip) knallen. ◆ vi (cup, glass) einen Sprung bekommen; (wood) einen Riss bekommen; **to ~ a joke** (inf) einen Witz reißen.

cracker [ˈkrækə] n (biscuit) Cracker der; (for Christmas) Knallbonbon der or das.

cradle [ˈkreɪdl] n Wiege die.

craft [krɑːft] n (skill) Geschick das; (trade) Handwerk das; (boat: pl inv) Boot das.

craftsman [ˈkrɑːftsmən] (pl -men [-mən]) n Handwerker der.

cram [kræm] vt: **to ~ sthg into** etw stopfen in (+A); **to be crammed with** voll gestopft sein mit.

cramp [kræmp] n Krampf der; **stomach ~s** Magenkrämpfe.

cranberry [ˈkrænbərɪ] n Preiselbeere die.

cranberry sauce n Preiselbeersoße die.

crane [kreɪn] n (machine) Kran der.

crap [kræp] *adj (vulg)* Scheiß-.
◆ *n (vulg : excrement)* Scheiße
die.

crash [kræʃ] *n (accident)* Unfall
der ; (noise) Krachen *das.* ◆ *vt
(car)* einen Unfall bauen mit.
◆ *vi (car, train)* einen Unfall
haben ; *(plane)* ablstürzen.
▦ **crash into** *vt fus* krachen
gegen.

crash helmet *n* Sturzhelm
der.

crash landing *n* Bruchlan-
dung *die.*

crate [kreɪt] *n* Kiste *die.*

crawl [krɔːl] *vi* kriechen ;
(baby) krabbeln. ◆ *n (swimming
stroke)* Kraulen *das.*

crawler lane ['krɔːlə'-] *n (Br)*
Kriechspur *die.*

crayfish ['kreɪfɪʃ] *(pl* **crayfish***)*
n Languste *die.*

crayon ['kreɪɒn] *n (of wax)*
Wachsmalstift *der ; (pencil)*
Buntstift *der.*

craze [kreɪz] *n* Mode *die.*

crazy ['kreɪzɪ] *adj* verrückt ; to
be ~ about verrückt sein nach.

crazy golf *n* Minigolf *das.*

cream [kriːm] *n (food)* Sahne
die ; (for face, burns) Creme *die.*
◆ *adj (in colour)* cremefarben.

cream cake *n (Br)* Sahnetört-
chen *das.*

cream cheese *n* Frischkäse
der.

cream sherry *n* Cream
Sherry *der.*

cream tea *n (Br)* Nachmittagstee mit Gebäck und Sahne.

creamy ['kriːmɪ] *adj (food)*
sahnig ; *(drink)* cremig.

crease [kriːs] *n* Falte *die.*

creased [kriːst] *adj* zerknit-
tert.

create [kriː'eɪt] *vt* schaffen ;
(impression) machen ; *(interest)*
verursachen.

creative [kriː'eɪtɪv] *adj* kreativ.

creature ['kriːtʃə'] *n* Ge-
schöpf *das.*

crèche [kreʃ] *n (Br)* Kinder-
krippe *die.*

credit ['kredɪt] *n (praise)* Anerkennung *die ; (money)* Guthaben *das ; (at school, university)*
Auszeichnung *die ;* to be in ~ im
Haben sein. ▦ **credits** *npl (of
film)* Nachspann *der.*

credit card *n* Kreditkarte *die ;*
'all major ~s accepted' 'wir akzeptieren alle führenden Kre-
ditkarten'.

creek [kriːk] *n (inlet)* Bucht
die ; (Am : river) Bach *der.*

creep [kriːp] *(pt & pp* **crept***) vi*
kriechen. ◆ *n (inf : groveller)*
Schleimer *der.*

cremate [krɪ'meɪt] *vt* einl-
äschern.

crematorium [,kremə'tɔːr-
ɪəm] *n* Krematorium *das.*

crepe [kreɪp] *n (thin pancake)*
Crêpe *der.*

crept [krept] *pt & pp →* **creep.**

cress [kres] *n* Kresse *die.*

crest [krest] *n* Kamm *der ; (emblem)* Wappen *das.*

crew [kruː] *n* Besatzung *die.*

crew neck *n* runder Halsausschnitt.

crib [krɪb] *n (Am : cot)* Kinderbett *das.*

cricket ['krɪkɪt] *n (game)* Kri-
cket *das ; (insect)* Grille *die.*

crime [kraɪm] n Verbrechen das.

criminal ['krɪmɪnl] adj kriminell. ◆ n Kriminelle der, die.

cripple ['krɪpl] n Krüppel der. ◆ vt zum Krüppel machen.

crisis ['kraɪsɪs] (pl crises ['kraɪsiːz]) n Krise die.

crisp [krɪsp] adj (bacon, pastry) knusprig ; (apple) knackig. ■ **crisps** npl (Br) Chips pl.

crispy ['krɪspɪ] adj knusprig.

critic ['krɪtɪk] n Kritiker der (-in die).

critical ['krɪtɪkl] adj kritisch ; (very important) entscheidend.

criticize ['krɪtɪsaɪz] vt kritisieren.

crockery ['krɒkərɪ] n Geschirr das.

crocodile ['krɒkədaɪl] n Krokodil das.

crocus ['krəʊkəs] (pl -es) n Krokus der.

crooked ['krʊkɪd] adj (bent) krumm.

crop [krɒp] n (kind of plant) Feldfrucht die ; (harvest) Ernte die. **crop up** vi auftauchen.

cross [krɒs] adj verärgert. ◆ n Kreuz das. ◆ vt (road, river, ocean) überqueren. ◆ vi (intersect) sich kreuzen ; **to ~ one's arms** die Arme verschränken ; **to ~ one's legs** die Beine übereinander schlagen ; **to ~ a cheque** (Br) einen Scheck zur Verrechnung ausstellen. ■ **cross out** vt sep ausstreichen. ■ **cross over** vt fus (road) überqueren.

crossbar ['krɒsbɑː'] n (of goal) Querlatte die ; (of bicycle) Stange die.

cross-Channel ferry n Fähre die über den Ärmelkanal.

cross-country (running) n Crosscountry das.

crossing ['krɒsɪŋ] n (on road) Überweg der ; (sea, journey) Überfahrt die.

crossroads ['krɒsrəʊdz] (pl crossroads) n Kreuzung die.

crosswalk ['krɒswɔːk] n (Am) Fußgängerüberweg der.

crossword (puzzle) ['krɒsw3ːd-] n Kreuzworträtsel das.

crotch [krɒtʃ] n Schritt der.

crouton ['kruːtɒn] n Croûton der.

crow [krəʊ] n Krähe die.

crowbar ['krəʊbɑː'] n Brechstange die.

crowd [kraʊd] n Menge die (von Personen).

crowded ['kraʊdɪd] adj überfüllt.

crown [kraʊn] n Krone die ; (of head) Scheitel der.

Crown Jewels npl Kronjuwelen pl.

ⓘ **CROWN JEWELS**

Die prachtvollen und kostbaren Kronjuwelen des britischen Monarchen, die bei feierlichen Anlässen getragen werden, sind im Londoner Tower ausgestellt. Die Juwelen der früheren schottischen Krone können im Schloss von Edinburg besichtigt werden.

crucial ['kruːʃl] adj entscheidend.

crude [kru:d] *adj (rough)* grob ; *(rude)* ungeschliffen.

cruel [kruəl] *adj* grausam.

cruelty ['kruəltɪ] *n* Grausamkeit *die*.

cruet (set) ['kru:ɪt-] *n* Menage *die*.

cruise [kru:z] *n* Kreuzfahrt *die*. ◆ *vi (plane)* fliegen ; *(ship)* kreuzen.

cruiser ['kru:zə'] *n (pleasure boat)* Vergnügungsdampfer *der*.

crumb [krʌm] *n* Krümel *der*.

crumble ['krʌmbl] *n* mit Streuseln überbackenes Obstdessert. ◆ *vi (building)* ein|stürzen ; *(cliff)* bröckeln.

crumpet ['krʌmpɪt] *n* Teigküchlein zum Toasten.

crunchy ['krʌntʃɪ] *adj* knusprig.

crush [krʌʃ] *n (drink)* Saftgetränk *das*. ◆ *vt (flatten)* quetschen ; *(garlic, ice)* zerstoßen.

crust [krʌst] *n* Kruste *die*.

crusty ['krʌstɪ] *adj* knusprig.

crutch [krʌtʃ] *n (stick)* Krücke *die* ; *(between legs)* = **crotch**.

cry [kraɪ] *n* Schrei *der*. ◆ *vi (weep)* weinen ; *(shout)* schreien. ■ **cry out** *vi* auf|schreien.

crystal ['krɪstl] *n* Kristall *der* ; *(glass)* Kristallglas *das*.

cub [kʌb] *n (animal)* Junge *das*.

Cub [kʌb] *n* Wölfling *der (junger Pfadfinder)*.

cube [kju:b] *n* Würfel *der*.

cubicle ['kju:bɪkl] *n* Kabine *die*.

Cub Scout = **Cub**.

cuckoo ['kuku:] *n* Kuckuck *der*.

cucumber ['kju:kʌmbə'] *n* Salatgurke *die*.

cuddle ['kʌdl] *n* Liebkosung *die*.

cuddly toy ['kʌdlɪ-] *n* Plüschtier *das*.

cue [kju:] *n (in snooker, pool)* Queue *das*.

cuff [kʌf] *n (of sleeve)* Manschette *die* ; *(Am : of trousers)* Aufschlag *der*.

cuff links *npl* Manschettenknöpfe *pl*.

cuisine [kwɪ'zi:n] *n* Küche *die*.

cul-de-sac ['kʌldəsæk] *n* Sackgasse *die*.

cult [kʌlt] *n* Kult *der*.

cultivate ['kʌltɪveɪt] *vt (grow)* an|bauen.

cultivated ['kʌltɪveɪtɪd] *adj (person)* kultiviert.

cultural ['kʌltʃərəl] *adj* kulturell.

culture ['kʌltʃə'] *n* Kultur *die*.

cumbersome ['kʌmbəsəm] *adj* sperrig.

cumin ['kju:mɪn] *n* Kreuzkümmel *der*.

cunning ['kʌnɪŋ] *adj* schlau.

cup [kʌp] *n* Tasse *die* ; *(trophy, competition)* Pokal *der* ; *(of bra)* Körbchen *das*.

cupboard ['kʌbəd] *n* Schrank *der*.

curator [ˌkjuə'reɪtə'] *n* Direktor *der* (-in *die*).

curb [kɜ:b] *n (Am)* = **kerb**.

curd cheese [ˌkɜ:d-] *n* ≃ Quark *der*.

cure [kjuə'] *n* Heilmittel *das*. ◆ *vt (illness, person)* heilen ; *(with salt)* pökeln ; *(with smoke)* räuchern ; *(by drying)* trocknen.

curious ['kjʊərɪəs] *adj (inquisitive)* neugierig ; *(strange)* seltsam.

curl [kɜ:l] *n* Locke *die*. ◆ *vt* locken.

curler ['kɜ:lə'] *n* Lockenwickler *der*.

curly ['kɜ:lɪ] *adj* lockig.

currant ['kʌrənt] *n* Korinthe *die*.

currency ['kʌrənsɪ] *n (money)* Währung *die*.

current ['kʌrənt] *adj* aktuell. ◆ *n* Strömung *die* ; *(electricity)* Strom *der*.

current account *n (Br)* Girokonto *das*.

current affairs *npl* aktuelle Fragen *pl*.

currently ['kʌrəntlɪ] *adv* zur Zeit.

curriculum [kə'rɪkjələm] *n* Lehrplan *der*.

curriculum vitae [-'vi:taɪ] *n (Br)* Lebenslauf *der*.

curried ['kʌrɪd] *adj* Curry-.

curry ['kʌrɪ] *n* Currygericht *das*.

curse [kɜ:s] *vi* fluchen.

cursor ['kɜ:sə'] *n* Cursor *der*.

curtain ['kɜ:tn] *n* Vorhang *der*.

curve [kɜ:v] *n (shape)* Rundung *die* ; *(in road, river)* Biegung *die*. ◆ *vi* einen Bogen machen.

curved [kɜ:vd] *adj* gebogen.

cushion ['kʊʃn] *n* Kissen *das*.

custard ['kʌstəd] *n* Vanillesoße *die*.

custom ['kʌstəm] *n (tradition)* Brauch *der* ; 'thank you for your ~' 'wir danken Ihnen für Ihre Kundschaft'.

customary ['kʌstəmrɪ] *adj* üblich.

customer ['kʌstəmə'] *n* Kunde *der* (Kundin *die*).

customer services *n (department)* Kundendienst *der*.

customs ['kʌstəmz] *n (place)* Zoll *der* ; **to go through ~** durch den Zoll gehen.

customs duty *n* Zoll *der*.

customs officer *n* Zollbeamte *der* (-beamtin *die*).

cut [kʌt] *(pt & pp* cut) *n* Schnitt *der* ; *(in skin)* Schnittwunde *die* ; *(reduction)* Kürzung *die* ; *(in price)* Senkung *die* ; *(piece of meat)* Stück *das*. ◆ *vi* schneiden. ◆ *vt* schneiden ; *(reduce)* kürzen ; *(price)* senken ; **to ~ one's finger** sich *(D)* in den Finger schneiden ; **~ and blow-dry** schneiden und föhnen ; **to ~ o.s.** sich schneiden ; **to have one's hair ~** sich die Haare schneiden lassen ; **to ~ the grass** den Rasen mähen ; **to ~ sthg open** etw aufⅼschneiden. ■ **cut back** *vi* : **to ~ back on sthg** etw einⅼschränken. ■ **cut down** *vt sep (tree)* fällen. ■ **cut down on** *vt fus* einⅼschränken. ■ **cut off** *vt sep* abⅼschneiden ; *(disconnect)* abstellen ; **I've been ~ off** *(on phone)* ich wurde unterbrochen ; **to be ~ off** *(isolated)* abgeschnitten sein. ■ **cut out** *vt sep* ausⅼschneiden. ◆ *vi (engine)* ausⅼsetzen ; **to ~ out smoking** mit dem Rauchen aufhören ; **~ it out!** *(inf)* lass das! ■ **cut up** *vt sep* zerschneiden.

cute [kju:t] *adj* niedlich.

cut-glass *adj* Kristall-.

cutlery ['kʌtlərɪ] n Besteck das.

cutlet ['kʌtlɪt] n Kotelett das; (of nuts, vegetables) Bratling der.

cut-price adj herabgesetzt.

cutting ['kʌtɪŋ] n (from newspaper) Ausschnitt der.

CV n (Br : abbr of curriculum vitae) Lebenslauf der.

cwt abbr = **hundredweight**.

cybercafé [saɪbə‚kæfeɪ] n Internetcafé das.

cycle ['saɪkl] n Zyklus der; (bicycle) Rad das. ◆ vi mit dem Rad fahren.

cycle hire n Fahrradverleih der.

cycle lane n Fahrradspur die.

cycle path n Radweg der.

cycling ['saɪklɪŋ] n Radfahren das; to go ~ Radfahren gehen.

cycling shorts npl Radlerhose die.

cyclist ['saɪklɪst] n Radfahrer der (-in die).

cylinder ['sɪlɪndə'] n Zylinder der; (for gas) Flasche die.

cynical ['sɪnɪkl] adj zynisch.

Czech [tʃek] adj tschechisch. ◆ n (person) Tscheche der (Tschechin die); (language) Tschechisch das.

Czech Republic n : the ~ die Tschechische Republik.

D

dab [dæb] vt (ointment, cream) auftupfen.

dad [dæd] n (inf) Vati der, Papa der.

daddy ['dædɪ] n (inf) Papa der.

daddy longlegs [-'lɒŋlegz] (pl daddy longlegs) n Weberknecht der.

daffodil ['dæfədɪl] n Osterglocke die.

daft [dɑːft] adj (Br : inf) doof.

daily ['deɪlɪ] adj & adv täglich. ◆ n : a ~ (newspaper) eine Tageszeitung.

dairy ['deərɪ] n (on farm) Molkerei die; (shop) Milchladen der.

dairy product n Milchprodukt das.

daisy ['deɪzɪ] n Gänseblümchen das.

dam [dæm] n Damm der.

damage ['dæmɪdʒ] n Schaden der; (to property) Beschädigung die; (fig : to reputation) Schädigung die; (fig : to chances) Beeinträchtigung die. ◆ vt beschädigen; (fig : reputation) schädigen; (fig : chances) beeinträchtigen.

damn [dæm] excl & adj (inf) verdammt. ◆ n (inf) : I don't give a ~ ist mir total egal.

damp [dæmp] adj feucht. ◆ n Feuchtigkeit die.

damson ['dæmzn] n Haferpflaume die.

dance [dɑːns] n Tanz der; (social event) Tanzveranstaltung die. ◆ vi tanzen; to have a ~ tanzen.

dance floor n Tanzfläche die.

dancer ['dɑːnsə'] n Tänzer der (-in die).

dancing ['dɑːnsɪŋ] n Tanzen das; to go ~ tanzen gehen.

dandelion ['dændɪlaɪən] n Löwenzahn der.

dandruff ['dændrʌf] n Schuppen pl.

Dane [deɪn] n Däne der (Dänin die).

danger ['deɪndʒəʳ] n Gefahr die.

dangerous ['deɪndʒərəs] adj gefährlich.

Danish ['deɪnɪʃ] adj dänisch. ◆ n Dänisch das.

Danish pastry n Plundergebäck das.

Danube ['dænjuːb] n : the ~ die Donau.

dare [deəʳ] vt : to ~ to do sthg wagen, etw zu tun ; to ~ sb to do sthg jn herausfordern, etw zu tun ; how ~ you! was fällt dir ein!

daring ['deərɪŋ] adj kühn.

dark [dɑːk] adj dunkel ; (person with dark hair) dunkelhaarig. ◆ n : after ~ nach Einbruch der Dunkelheit ; in the ~ im Dunkeln.

dark chocolate n bittere Schokolade.

dark glasses npl Sonnenbrille die.

darkness ['dɑːknɪs] n Dunkelheit die.

darling ['dɑːlɪŋ] n Liebling der.

dart [dɑːt] n Pfeil der. ▪ **darts** n (game) Darts das.

dartboard ['dɑːtbɔːd] n Dartscheibe die.

dash [dæʃ] n (of liquid) Schuss der ; (in writing) Gedankenstrich der. ◆ vi flitzen.

dashboard ['dæʃbɔːd] n Armaturenbrett das.

data ['deɪtə] n Daten pl.

database ['deɪtəbeɪs] n Datenbank die.

date [deɪt] n Datum das ; (meeting) Verabredung die ; (Am : person) Freund der (-in die) ; (fruit) Dattel die. ◆ vt (cheque, letter) datieren ; (person) gehen mit. ◆ vi aus der Mode kommen ; what's the ~? der Wievielte ist heute? ; to have a ~ with sb eine Verabredung mit jm haben.

date of birth n Geburtsdatum das.

daughter ['dɔːtəʳ] n Tochter die.

daughter-in-law n Schwiegertochter die.

dawn [dɔːn] n Morgendämmerung die.

day [deɪ] n Tag der ; what ~ is it today? welcher Tag ist heute? ; what a lovely ~! so ein schöner Tag! ; to have a ~ off einen Tag frei haben ; to have a ~ out einen Ausflug machen ; by ~ tagsüber ; the ~ after tomorrow übermorgen ; the ~ before am Tag davor ; the ~ before yesterday vorgestern ; the following ~ am nächsten Tag ; have a nice ~! viel Spaß!

daylight ['deɪlaɪt] n Tageslicht das.

day return n (Br) Tagesrückfahrkarte die.

dayshift ['deɪʃɪft] n Tagschicht die.

daytime ['deɪtaɪm] n Tag der.

day-to-day adj (everyday) tagtäglich.

day trip n Tagesausflug der.

dazzle ['dæzl] vt blenden.

DC (abbr of direct current) GS.

dead [ded] *adj* tot ; *(battery)* leer. ◆ *adv (precisely)* genau ; *(inf : very)* total ; **it's ~ ahead** es ist direkt geradeaus ; **'~ slow'** 'Schrittgeschwindigkeit'.

dead end *n (street)* Sackgasse *die.*

deadline ['dedlaɪn] *n* Termin *der.*

deaf [def] *adj* taub. ◆ *npl* : **the ~** die Tauben *pl.*

deal [diːl] *(pt & pp* dealt) *n (agreement)* Geschäft *das.* ◆ *vt (cards)* geben ; **a good/bad ~** ein gutes/schlechtes Geschäft ; **a great ~ of** viel ; **it's a ~!** abgemacht! ■ **deal in** *vt fus* handeln mit. ■ **deal with** *vt fus* : **to ~ with sthg** *(handle)* sich um etw kümmern ; *(be about)* sich mit etw befassen.

dealer ['diːlə'] *n* Händler *der* (-in *die*) ; *(in drugs)* Dealer *der.*

dealt [delt] *pt & pp* → **deal**.

dear [dɪə'] *adj* lieb ; *(expensive)* teuer. ◆ *n* : **my ~** Schatz ; **Dear Sir** Sehr geehrter Herr ; **Dear Madam** Sehr geehrte gnädige Frau ; **Dear John** Lieber John ; **oh ~!** ach du liebe Güte!

death [deθ] *n* Tod *der.*

debate [dɪ'beɪt] *n* Debatte *die.* ◆ *vt (wonder)* sich fragen.

debit ['debɪt] *n* Soll *das.* ◆ *vt (account)* belasten.

debit card ['debɪtkɑːd] *n* Bankkarte *die.*

debt [det] *n (money owed)* Schulden *pl* ; **to be in ~** Schulden haben.

Dec. *(abbr of December)* Dez.

decaff ['diːkæf] *n (inf)* entkoffeinierter Kaffee.

decaffeinated [dɪ'kæfɪneɪt-ɪd] *adj* koffeinfrei.

decanter [dɪ'kæntə'] *n* Karaffe *die.*

decay [dɪ'keɪ] *n (of building)* Zerfall *der* ; *(of wood)* Verrotten *das* ; *(of tooth)* Fäule *die.* ◆ *vi (rot)* verfaulen.

deceive [dɪ'siːv] *vt* betrügen.

decelerate [ˌdiː'seləreɪt] *vi* langsamer werden.

December [dɪ'sembə'] *n* Dezember *der* ; → **September**.

decent ['diːsnt] *adj* anständig ; *(kind)* nett.

decide [dɪ'saɪd] *vt* entscheiden. ◆ *vi* sich entscheiden ; **to ~ to do sthg** sich entschließen, etw zu tun. ■ **decide on** *vt fus* sich entscheiden für.

decimal ['desɪml] *adj* Dezimal-.

decimal point *n* Komma *das.*

decision [dɪ'sɪʒn] *n* Entscheidung *die* ; **to make a ~** eine Entscheidung treffen.

decisive [dɪ'saɪsɪv] *adj (person)* entschlussfreudig ; *(event, factor)* entscheidend.

deck [dek] *n* Deck *das* ; *(of cards)* Spiel *das.*

deckchair ['dektʃeə'] *n* Liegestuhl *der.*

declare [dɪ'kleə'] *vt* erklären ; **'goods to ~'** 'Waren zu verzollen' ; **'nothing to ~'** 'nichts zu verzollen'.

decline [dɪ'klaɪn] *n* Rückgang *der.* ◆ *vi (get worse)* nachlassen ; *(refuse)* ablehnen.

decorate ['dekəreɪt] *vt (with wallpaper)* tapezieren ; *(with paint)* streichen ; *(make attractive)* schmücken.

decoration [,dekə'reɪʃn] *n (of room)* Innenausstattung *die*; *(decorative object)* Schmuck *der*.

decorator ['dekəreɪtə'] *n* Maler und Tapezierer *der*.

decrease [*n* 'di:kri:s, *vb* di:'kri:s] *n* Abnahme *die*. ◆ *vi* abnehmen.

dedicated ['dedɪkeɪtɪd] *adj (committed)* engagiert.

deduce [dɪ'dju:s] *vt* folgern.

deduct [dɪ'dʌkt] *vt* abziehen.

deduction [dɪ'dʌkʃn] *n (reduction)* Abzug *der*; *(conclusion)* Folgerung *die*.

deep [di:p] *adj & adv* tief.

deep end *n (of swimming pool)* Tiefe *das*.

deep freeze *n* Tiefkühltruhe *die*.

deep-fried [-'fraɪd] *adj* frittiert.

deep-pan *adj*: ~ pizza Pfannenpizza *die*.

deer [dɪə'] *(pl* deer) *n (male)* Hirsch *der*; *(female)* Reh *das*.

defeat [dɪ'fi:t] *n* Niederlage *die*. ◆ *vt* schlagen.

defect ['di:fekt] *n* Fehler *der*.

defective [dɪ'fektɪv] *adj* fehlerhaft.

defence [dɪ'fens] *n* Verteidigung *die*; *(Br: protection)* Schutz *der*.

defend [dɪ'fend] *vt* verteidigen.

defense [dɪ'fens] *(Am)* = **defence**.

deficiency [dɪ'fɪʃnsɪ] *n (lack)* Mangel *der*.

deficit ['defɪsɪt] *n* Defizit *das*.

define [dɪ'faɪn] *vt* definieren.

definite ['defɪnɪt] *adj (clear)* klar; *(certain)* sicher.

definite article *n* bestimmter Artikel.

definitely ['defɪnɪtlɪ] *adv* definitiv; I'm ~ coming ich komme ganz bestimmt.

definition [defɪ'nɪʃn] *n* Definition *die*.

deflate [dɪ'fleɪt] *vt (tyre)* die Luft ablassen aus.

deflect [dɪ'flekt] *vt (ball)* abfälschen.

defogger [,di:'fɒgə'] *n (Am)* Defroster *der*.

deformed [dɪ'fɔ:md] *adj* entstellt.

defrost [,di:'frɒst] *vt (food)* auftauen; *(Am: demist)* freimachen; *(fridge)* abtauen.

degree [dɪ'gri:] *n* Grad *der*; *(amount)* Maß *das*; *(qualification)* akademischer Grad; to have a ~ in sthg einen Hochschulabschluss in etw *(D)* haben.

dehydrated [,di:haɪ'dreɪtɪd] *adj (food)* Trocken-; *(person)* ausgetrocknet.

de-ice [di:'aɪs] *vt* enteisen.

de-icer [di:'aɪsə'] *n* Defroster *der*.

dejected [dɪ'dʒektɪd] *adj* niedergeschlagen.

delay [dɪ'leɪ] *n* Verspätung *die*. ◆ *vt* aufhalten. ◆ *vi* zögern; without ~ ohne Verzögerung.

delayed [dɪ'leɪd] *adj (train, flight)* verspätet.

delegate [*n* 'delɪgət, *vb* 'delɪgeɪt] *n* Delegierte *der, die*. ◆ *vt* delegieren.

delete [dɪ'li:t] *vt* streichen.

deli ['delɪ] *n (inf) (abbr of delicatessen)* Feinkostgeschäft *das*.

deliberate [dɪ'lɪbərət] *adj* absichtlich.

deliberately [dɪ'lɪbərətlɪ] *adv* absichtlich.

delicacy ['delɪkəsɪ] *n (food)* Delikatesse *die.*

delicate ['delɪkət] *adj (situation, question)* heikel ; *(object, china)* zerbrechlich ; *(health, person)* zart ; *(taste, smell)* fein.

delicatessen [,delɪkə'tesn] *n* Feinkostgeschäft *das.*

delicious [dɪ'lɪʃəs] *adj* köstlich.

delight [dɪ'laɪt] *n* Freude *die.*
◆ *vt* erfreuen ; **to take (a) ~ in doing sthg** Freude daran haben, etw zu tun.

delighted [dɪ'laɪtɪd] *adj* hocherfreut.

delightful [dɪ'laɪtfʊl] *adj* reizend.

deliver [dɪ'lɪvə'] *vt (goods)* liefern ; *(letters, newspapers)* zustellen ; *(speech, lecture)* halten ; *(baby)* entbinden.

delivery [dɪ'lɪvərɪ] *n (of goods)* Lieferung *die* ; *(of letters)* Zustellung *die* ; *(birth)* Entbindung *die.*

delude [dɪ'lu:d] *vt* täuschen.

de luxe [də'lʌks] *adj* Luxus-.

demand [dɪ'mɑ:nd] *n* Forderung *die* ; *(COMM)* Nachfrage *die* ; *(requirement)* Anforderung *die.* ◆ *vt* verlangen ; *(require)* erfordern ; **to ~ to do sthg** verlangen, etw zu tun ; **to be in ~** gefragt sein.

demanding [dɪ'mɑ:ndɪŋ] *adj* anspruchsvoll.

demerara sugar [demə'reərə-] *n* brauner Zucker.

demist [,di:'mɪst] *vt (Br)* freimachen.

demister [,di:'mɪstə'] *n (Br)* Defroster *der.*

democracy [dɪ'mɒkrəsɪ] *n* Demokratie *die.*

Democrat ['deməkræt] *n (Am)* Demokrat *der* (-in *die*).

democratic [demə'krætɪk] *adj* demokratisch.

demolish [dɪ'mɒlɪʃ] *vt* abreißen.

demonstrate ['demənstreɪt] *vt (prove)* beweisen ; *(machine, skill)* vorführen. ◆ *vi* demonstrieren.

demonstration [demən'streɪʃn] *n (protest)* Demonstration *die* ; *(proof)* Beweis *der* ; *(of machine, skill)* Vorführung *die.*

denial [dɪ'naɪəl] *n* Leugnen *das.*

denim ['denɪm] *n* Jeansstoff *der.* ▓ **denims** *npl* Jeans *pl.*

denim jacket *n* Jeansjacke *die.*

Denmark ['denmɑːk] *n* Dänemark *nt.*

dense [dens] *adj* dicht.

dent [dent] *n* Delle *die.*

dental ['dentl] *adj* Zahn-.

dental floss [-flɒs] *n* Zahnseide *die.*

dental surgeon *n* Zahnarzt *der* (-ärztin *die*).

dental surgery *n (place)* Zahnarztpraxis *die.*

dentist ['dentɪst] *n* Zahnarzt *der* (-ärztin *die*) ; **to go to the ~'s** zum Zahnarzt gehen.

dentures ['dentʃəz] *npl* Zahnprothese *die.*

deny [dɪˈnaɪ] vt (declare untrue) bestreiten ; (refuse) verweigern.

deodorant [diːˈəʊdərənt] n Deodorant das.

depart [dɪˈpɑːt] vi (person) ablreisen ; (train, bus) ablfahren ; (plane) ablfliegen.

department [dɪˈpɑːtmənt] n (of business, shop) Abteilung die ; (of government) Ministerium das ; (of school) Fachbereich der ; (of university) Seminar das.

department store n Kaufhaus das.

departure [dɪˈpɑːtʃəʳ] n (of person) Abreise die ; (of train, bus) Abfahrt die ; (of plane) Abflug der ; '~s' (at airport) 'Abflug'.

departure lounge n Abflughalle die.

depend [dɪˈpend] vi : it ~s es kommt darauf an. ■ **depend on** vt fus ablhängen von ; (rely on) sich verlassen auf (+A) ; ~ing on je nachdem ; ~ing on the weather je nachdem, wie das Wetter wird.

dependable [dɪˈpendəbl] adj zuverlässig.

deplorable [dɪˈplɔːrəbl] adj bedauerlich.

deport [dɪˈpɔːt] vt auslreisen.

deposit [dɪˈpɒzɪt] n (in bank) Guthaben das ; (part-payment) Anzahlung die ; (against damage) Kaution die ; (on bottle) Pfand das ; (substance) Ablagerung die. ◆ vt (put down) abllegen ; (money in bank) einlzahlen.

deposit account n (Br) Sparkonto das.

depot [ˈdiːpəʊ] n (Am : for buses, trains) Bahnhof der.

depressed [dɪˈprest] adj deprimiert.

depressing [dɪˈpresɪŋ] adj deprimierend.

depression [dɪˈpreʃn] n Depression die.

deprive [dɪˈpraɪv] vt : to ~ sb of sthg jm etw entziehen.

depth [depθ] n Tiefe die ; to be out of one's ~ (when swimming) nicht mehr stehen können ; (fig) überfordert sein ; ~ of field Tiefenschärfe.

deputy [ˈdepjʊtɪ] adj stellvertretend.

derailleur [dəˈreɪljəʳ] n Kettenschaltung die.

derailment [dɪˈreɪlmənt] n Entgleisen das.

derelict [ˈderəlɪkt] adj verfallen.

derv [dɜːv] n (Br) Diesel der.

descend [dɪˈsend] vt & vi (subj : person) herunterlgehen ; (subj : car) herunterlfahren.

descendant [dɪˈsendənt] n Nachkomme der.

descent [dɪˈsent] n Abstieg der ; (slope) Abfall der.

describe [dɪˈskraɪb] vt beschreiben.

description [dɪˈskrɪpʃn] n Beschreibung die.

desert [n ˈdezət, vb dɪˈzɜːt] n Wüste die. ◆ vt verlassen.

deserted [dɪˈzɜːtɪd] adj verlassen.

deserve [dɪˈzɜːv] vt verdienen.

design [dɪ'zaɪn] n (pattern) Muster das ; (art) Design das ; (of machine, building) Konstruktion die. ◆ vt (machine, building) konstruieren ; (dress) entwerfen ; **to be ~ed for** vorgesehen sein für.

designer [dɪ'zaɪnə'] n (of clothes) Designer der (-in die) ; (of machine) Konstrukteur der (-in die). ◆ adj (clothes, sunglasses) Designer-.

desirable [dɪ'zaɪərəbl] adj wünschenswert.

desire [dɪ'zaɪə'] n Wunsch der. ◆ vt wünschen ; **it leaves a lot to be ~d** es lässt viel zu wünschen übrig.

desk [desk] n (in home, office) Schreibtisch der ; (in school) Pult das ; (at airport, station) Schalter der ; (at hotel) Empfang der.

desktop publishing ['desk-ˌtɒp-] n Desktoppublishing das.

despair [dɪ'speə'] n Verzweiflung die.

despatch [dɪ'spætʃ] = **dispatch**.

desperate ['despərət] adj verzweifelt ; **to be ~ for sthg** etw dringend brauchen.

despicable [dɪ'spɪkəbl] adj verachtenswert.

despise [dɪ'spaɪz] vt verachten.

despite [dɪ'spaɪt] prep trotz (+G).

dessert [dɪ'zɜ:t] n Nachtisch der.

dessertspoon [dɪ'zɜ:tspu:n] n Dessertlöffel der.

destination [ˌdestɪ'neɪʃn] n (of person) Reiseziel das ; (of goods) Bestimmungsort der.

destroy [dɪ'strɔɪ] vt zerstören.

destruction [dɪ'strʌkʃn] n Zerstörung die.

detach [dɪ'tætʃ] vt ablnehmen ; (tear off) abltrennen.

detached house [dɪ'tætʃt-] n Einzelhaus das.

detail ['di:teɪl] n Einzelheit die ; **in ~** im Detail. ■ **details** npl (facts) Angaben pl.

detailed ['di:teɪld] adj detailliert.

detect [dɪ'tekt] vt entdecken.

detective [dɪ'tektɪv] n (policeman) Kriminalbeamte der (-beamtin die) ; (private) Detektiv der (-in die) ; **a ~ story** ein Krimi.

detention [dɪ'tenʃn] n (SCH) Nachsitzen das.

detergent [dɪ'tɜ:dʒənt] n (for clothes) Waschmittel das ; (for dishes) Spülmittel das.

deteriorate [dɪ'tɪərɪəreɪt] vi sich verschlechtern.

determination [dɪˌtɜ:mɪ'neɪʃn] n Entschlossenheit die.

determine [dɪ'tɜ:mɪn] vt bestimmen.

determined [dɪ'tɜ:mɪnd] adj entschlossen ; **to be ~ to do sthg** fest entschlossen sein, etw zu tun.

deterrent [dɪ'terənt] n Abschreckungsmittel das.

detest [dɪ'test] vt verabscheuen.

detour ['di:ˌtʊə'] n Umweg der.

detrain [ˌdiː'treɪn] vi (fml) aus dem Zug steigen.

deuce [djuːs] n (in tennis) Einstand der.

devastate ['devəsteɪt] vt (country, town) verwüsten.

develop [dɪ'veləp] vt entwickeln ; (land) erschließen ; (illness) bekommen ; (habit) annehmen. ◆ vi sich entwickeln.

developing country [dɪ'veləpɪŋ-] n Entwicklungsland das.

development [dɪ'veləpmənt] n Entwicklung die ; a housing ~ eine Neubausiedlung.

device [dɪ'vaɪs] n Gerät das.

devil ['devl] n Teufel der ; what the ~...? (inf) was zum Teufel...?

devise [dɪ'vaɪz] vt entwerfen.

devoted [dɪ'vəʊtɪd] adj treu ; to be ~ to sb jm treu lieben.

dew [djuː] n Tau der.

diabetes [ˌdaɪə'biːtiːz] n Zuckerkrankheit die.

diabetic [ˌdaɪə'betɪk] adj zuckerkrank ; (chocolate) Diabetiker-. ◆ n Diabetiker der (-in die).

diagnosis [ˌdaɪəg'nəʊsɪs] (pl -oses [-əʊsiːz]) n Diagnose die.

diagonal [daɪ'ægənl] adj diagonal.

diagram ['daɪəgræm] n schematische Darstellung.

dial ['daɪəl] n (of telephone) Wählscheibe die ; (of clock) Zifferblatt das ; (on radio) Skala die. ◆ vt wählen.

dialling code ['daɪəlɪŋ-] n (Br) Vorwahl die.

dialling tone ['daɪəlɪŋ-] n (Br) Freizeichen das.

dial tone (Am) = dialling tone.

diameter [daɪ'æmɪtə'] n Durchmesser der.

diamond ['daɪəmənd] n Diamant der. ■ **diamonds** npl (in cards) Karo das.

diaper ['daɪpə'] n (Am) Windel die.

diarrhoea [ˌdaɪə'rɪə] n Durchfall der.

diary ['daɪərɪ] n (for appointments) Terminkalender der ; (journal) Tagebuch das.

dice [daɪs] (pl dice) n Würfel der.

diced [daɪst] adj in Würfel geschnitten.

dictate [dɪk'teɪt] vt diktieren.

dictation [dɪk'teɪʃn] n Diktat das.

dictator [dɪk'teɪtə'] n Diktator der (-in die).

dictionary ['dɪkʃnrɪ] n Wörterbuch das.

did [dɪd] pt → do.

die [daɪ] (pt & pp died, cont dying ['daɪɪŋ]) vi sterben ; (animal, plant) eingehen ; to be dying for sthg (inf) etw unbedingt haben wollen ; to be dying to do sthg (inf) darauf brennen, etw zu tun. ■ **die away** vi schwächer werden. ■ **die out** vi aussterben.

diesel ['diːzl] n Diesel der.

diet ['daɪət] n Diät die ; (food eaten) Kost die. ◆ vi eine Diät machen. ◆ adj Diät-.

diet Coke® n Colalight® die.

differ ['dɪfə'] vi sich unterscheiden ; (disagree) anderer Meinung sein.

difference ['dɪfrəns] n Unterschied der ; **it makes no ~** es ist egal ; **a ~ of opinion** eine Meinungsverschiedenheit.

different ['dɪfrənt] adj (not the same) verschieden ; (separate) andere(-r) (-s) ; **to be ~ (from)** anders sein (als).

differently ['dɪfrəntlɪ] adv anders.

difficult ['dɪfɪkəlt] adj schwierig.

difficulty ['dɪfɪkəltɪ] n Schwierigkeit die ; **with ~** mühsam.

dig [dɪg] (pt & pp dug) vt graben ; (garden, land) umlgraben. ◆ vi graben. ▦ **dig out** vt sep (rescue) bergen ; (find) auslgraben. ▦ **dig up** vt sep auslgraben.

digest [dɪ'dʒest] vt verdauen.

digestion [dɪ'dʒestʃn] n Verdauung die.

digestive (biscuit) [dɪ'dʒestɪv-] n (Br) Vollkornkeks der.

digit ['dɪdʒɪt] n (number) Ziffer die ; (finger) Finger der ; (toe) Zehe die.

digital ['dɪdʒɪtl] adj Digital-.

dill [dɪl] n Dill der.

dilute [daɪ'luːt] vt verdünnen.

dim [dɪm] adj (light) trüb ; (room) dämmrig ; (inf : stupid) beschränkt. ◆ vt (light) dämpfen.

dime [daɪm] n (Am) Zehncentstück das.

dimensions [dɪ'menʃnz] npl (measurements) Abmessungen pl ; (aspect) Dimension die.

din [dɪn] n Lärm der.

dine [daɪn] vi speisen. ▦ **dine out** vi auswärts essen.

diner ['daɪnə'] n (Am : restaurant) Lokal das ; (person) Gast der.

 DINER

Ein „diner" ist ein preisgünstiges Restaurant, in dem kleine Mahlzeiten serviert werden. Man findet sie vor allem entlang der Schnellstraßen, aber auch in den Städten. Die Kundschaft besteht meist aus LKW-Fahrern und anderen Durchreisenden. Auf Grund der besonderen Reiseatmosphäre, die sie verkörpern, werden sie in vielen „road movies" verwendet.

dinghy ['dɪŋgɪ] n (with sail) Dingi das ; (with oars) Schlauchboot das.

dingy ['dɪndʒɪ] adj (room) düster.

dining car ['daɪnɪŋ-] n Speisewagen der.

dining hall ['daɪnɪŋ-] n (SCH) Speisesaal der.

dining room ['daɪnɪŋ-] n Esszimmer das ; (in hotel) Speisesaal der.

dinner ['dɪnə'] n (at lunchtime) Mittagessen das ; (in evening) Abendessen das ; **to have ~** (at lunchtime) zu Mittag essen ; (in evening) zu Abend essen.

dinner jacket n Smoking der.

dinner party n Abendgesellschaft die.

dinner set n Tafelgeschirr das.

dinner suit n Smoking der.

dinnertime ['dɪnətaɪm] n Essenszeit die.

dinosaur ['daɪnəsɔːʳ] n Dinosaurier der.

dip [dɪp] n (in road, land) Mulde die ; (food) Dip der. ◆ vt (into liquid) tauchen. ◆ vi sich senken ; **to have a ~** (swim) kurz schwimmen gehen ; **to ~ one's headlights** (Br) abblenden.

diploma [dɪ'pləʊmə] n Diplom das.

dipstick ['dɪpstɪk] n Ölmessstab der.

direct [dɪ'rekt] adj & adv direkt. ◆ vt (aim) richten ; (traffic) regeln ; (control) leiten ; (film, play) Regie führen bei ; (give directions to) : **to ~ sb** jm den Weg beschreiben.

direct current n Gleichstrom der.

direction [dɪ'rekʃn] n Richtung die ; **to ask for ~s** nach dem Weg fragen. ∎ **directions** npl (instructions) Gebrauchsanweisung die.

directly [dɪ'rektlɪ] adv direkt ; (soon) sofort.

director [dɪ'rektəʳ] n (of company) Direktor der (-in die) ; (of film, play) Regisseur der (-in die) ; (organizer) Leiter der (-in die).

directory [dɪ'rektərɪ] n Telefonbuch das.

directory enquiries n (Br) Fernsprechauskunft die.

dirt [dɜːt] n Schmutz der ; (earth) Erde die.

dirty ['dɜːtɪ] adj schmutzig ; (joke) unanständig.

disability [ˌdɪsə'bɪlətɪ] n Behinderung die.

disabled [dɪs'eɪbld] adj behindert. ◆ npl : **the ~** die Behinderten pl ; '~ **toilet**' 'Behindertentoilette'.

disadvantage [ˌdɪsəd'vɑːntɪdʒ] n Nachteil der.

disagree [ˌdɪsə'griː] vi (people) anderer Meinung sein ; **to ~ with sb (about sthg)** mit jm (über etw (+A)) nicht übereinstimmen ; **those mussels ~d with me** diese Muscheln sind mir nicht bekommen.

disagreement [ˌdɪsə'griːmənt] n (argument) Meinungsverschiedenheit die ; (dissimilarity) Diskrepanz die.

disappear [ˌdɪsə'pɪəʳ] vi verschwinden.

disappearance [ˌdɪsə'pɪərəns] n Verschwinden das.

disappoint [ˌdɪsə'pɔɪnt] vt enttäuschen.

disappointed [ˌdɪsə'pɔɪntɪd] adj enttäuscht.

disappointing [ˌdɪsə'pɔɪntɪŋ] adj enttäuschend.

disappointment [ˌdɪsə'pɔɪntmənt] n Enttäuschung die.

disapprove [ˌdɪsə'pruːv] vi : **to ~ of** missbilligen.

disarmament [dɪs'ɑːməmənt] n Abrüstung die.

disaster [dɪ'zɑːstəʳ] n Katastrophe die.

disastrous [dɪ'zɑːstrəs] adj katastrophal.

disc [dɪsk] n (Br) Scheibe die ; (CD) Compactdisc die ; (record) Schallplatte die ; **to slip a ~** einen Bandscheibenvorfall erleiden.

discard [dɪ'skɑːd] *vt* wegwerfen.

discharge [dɪs'tʃɑːdʒ] *vt* (*patient, prisoner*) entlassen ; (*liquid, smoke*) ablassen.

discipline ['dɪsɪplɪn] *n* Disziplin *die*.

disc jockey *n* Diskjockey *der*.

disco ['dɪskəʊ] *n* Disko *die*.

discoloured [dɪs'kʌləd] *adj* verfärbt.

discomfort [dɪs'kʌmfət] *n* (*pain*) Beschwerden *pl*.

disconnect [ˌdɪskə'nekt] *vt* (*unplug*) den Stecker herausziehen (von) ; (*telephone, gas supply*) ablstellen ; (*pipe*) trennen.

discontinued [ˌdɪskən'tɪnjuːd] *adj* (*product*) auslaufend.

discotheque ['dɪskəʊtek] *n* Diskothek *die*.

discount ['dɪskaʊnt] *n* Rabatt *der*.

discover [dɪ'skʌvəʳ] *vt* entdecken.

discovery [dɪ'skʌvərɪ] *n* Entdeckung *die*.

discreet [dɪ'skriːt] *adj* diskret.

discrepancy [dɪ'skrepənsɪ] *n* Diskrepanz *die*.

discriminate [dɪ'skrɪmɪneɪt] *vi* : to ~ against sb jn diskriminieren.

discrimination [dɪ,skrɪmɪ'neɪʃn] *n* (*unfair*) Diskriminierung *die*.

discuss [dɪ'skʌs] *vt* besprechen.

discussion [dɪ'skʌʃn] *n* Gespräch *das*.

disease [dɪ'ziːz] *n* Krankheit *die*.

disembark [ˌdɪsɪm'bɑːk] *vi* von Bord gehen.

disgrace [dɪs'greɪs] *n* Schande *die*.

disgraceful [dɪs'greɪsfʊl] *adj* erbärmlich.

disguise [dɪs'gaɪz] *n* Verkleidung *die*. ◆ *vt* verkleiden ; in ~ verkleidet.

disgust [dɪs'gʌst] *n* Abscheu *der*. ◆ *vt* anlwidern.

disgusting [dɪs'gʌstɪŋ] *adj* widerlich.

dish [dɪʃ] *n* (*container*) Schüssel *die*; (*shallow*) Schale *die*; (*food*) Gericht *das*; (*Am : plate*) Teller *der* ; to do the ~es ablwaschen ; '~ of the day' 'Tagesgericht'. ▪ **dish up** *vt sep* aufltragen.

dishcloth ['dɪʃklɒθ] *n* Spültuch *das*.

disheveled [dɪ'ʃevəld] (*Am*) = **dishevelled**.

dishevelled [dɪ'ʃevəld] *adj* (*Br*) zerzaust.

dishonest [dɪs'ɒnɪst] *adj* unehrlich.

dish towel *n* (*Am*) Geschirrtuch *das*.

dishwasher ['dɪʃ,wɒʃəʳ] *n* (*machine*) Geschirrspülmaschine *die*.

disinfectant [ˌdɪsɪn'fektənt] *n* Desinfektionsmittel *das*.

disintegrate [dɪs'ɪntɪgreɪt] *vi* zerfallen.

disk [dɪsk] *n* (*Am*) = **disc** ; (*COMPUT*) Diskette *die*.

disk drive *n* Diskettenlaufwerk *das*.

dislike [dɪsˈlaɪk] n Abneigung die. ◆ vt nicht mögen ; **to take a ~ to** eine Abneigung haben gegen.

dislocate [ˈdɪsləkeɪt] vt (shoulder, hip) ausrenken.

dismal [ˈdɪzml] adj (weather, place) trostlos ; (terrible) kläglich.

dismantle [dɪsˈmæntl] vt auseinander nehmen.

dismay [dɪsˈmeɪ] n Bestürzung die.

dismiss [dɪsˈmɪs] vt (idea, suggestion) abtun ; (from job, classroom) entlassen.

disobedient [ˌdɪsəˈbiːdjənt] adj ungehorsam.

disobey [ˌdɪsəˈbeɪ] vt nicht gehorchen (+D).

disorder [dɪsˈɔːdəʳ] n (confusion) Unordnung die ; (violence) Unruhen pl ; (illness) Störung die.

disorganized [dɪsˈɔːgənaɪzd] adj chaotisch.

dispatch [dɪˈspætʃ] vt schicken.

dispense [dɪˈspens] : **dispense with** vt fus verzichten auf (+A).

dispenser [dɪˈspensəʳ] n (device) Automat der.

dispensing chemist [dɪˈspensɪŋ-] n (Br) Apotheker der (-in die).

disperse [dɪˈspɜːs] vt zerstreuen. ◆ vi sich zerstreuen.

display [dɪˈspleɪ] n (of goods) Auslage die ; (exhibition) Ausstellung die ; (readout) Anzeige die. ◆ vt (goods) ausstellen ; (feeling, quality) zeigen ; (infor-

mation) aushängen ; **to be on ~** ausgestellt werden.

displeased [dɪsˈpliːzd] adj verärgert.

disposable [dɪˈspəʊzəbl] adj (nappy) Wegwerf- ; (lighter) Einweg-.

dispute [dɪˈspjuːt] n Streit der ; (industrial) Auseinandersetzung die. ◆ vt bestreiten.

disqualify [ˌdɪsˈkwɒlɪfaɪ] vt disqualifizieren ; **to be disqualified from driving** (Br) den Führerschein entzogen bekommen haben.

disregard [ˌdɪsrɪˈgɑːd] vt ignorieren.

disrupt [dɪsˈrʌpt] vt unterbrechen.

disruption [dɪsˈrʌpʃn] n Unterbrechung die.

dissatisfied [ˌdɪsˈsætɪsfaɪd] adj unzufrieden.

dissolve [dɪˈzɒlv] vt auflösen. ◆ vi sich auflösen.

dissuade [dɪˈsweɪd] vt : **to ~ sb from doing sthg** jn davon abbringen, etw zu tun.

distance [ˈdɪstəns] n Entfernung die ; **from a ~** aus der Entfernung ; **in the ~** in der Ferne.

distant [ˈdɪstənt] adj weit entfernt ; (in time) fern ; (reserved) distanziert.

distilled water [dɪˈstɪld-] n destilliertes Wasser.

distillery [dɪˈstɪlərɪ] n Brennerei die.

distinct [dɪˈstɪŋkt] adj (separate) verschieden ; (noticeable) deutlich.

distinction [dɪˈstɪŋkʃn] n Unterschied der ; (mark for work) Auszeichnung die.

do

distinctive [dɪ'stɪŋktɪv] *adj* unverwechselbar.

distinguish [dɪ'stɪŋgwɪʃ] *vt (perceive)* erkennen ; **to ~ sthg from sthg** etw von etw unterscheiden.

distorted [dɪ'stɔːtɪd] *adj* verzerrt.

distract [dɪ'strækt] *vt* ablenken.

distraction [dɪ'strækʃn] *n* Ablenkung die.

distress [dɪ'stres] *n (pain)* Leiden das ; *(anxiety)* Kummer der.

distressing [dɪ'stresɪŋ] *adj* schmerzlich.

distribute [dɪ'strɪbjuːt] *vt* verteilen.

distributor [dɪ'strɪbjutəʳ] *n (COMM)* Vertreiber der (-in die) ; *(AUT)* Verteiler der.

district ['dɪstrɪkt] *n (region)* Gebiet das ; *(of town)* Bezirk der.

district attorney *n (Am)* Bezirksstaatsanwalt der (-anwältin die).

disturb [dɪ'stɜːb] *vt* stören ; *(worry)* beunruhigen ; *(move)* durcheinander bringen ; **'do not ~'** 'bitte nicht stören'.

disturbance [dɪ'stɜːbəns] *n (violence)* Unruhe die.

ditch [dɪtʃ] *n* Graben der.

ditto ['dɪtəʊ] *adv* ebenso.

divan [dɪ'væn] *n* Liege die.

dive [daɪv] *(pt Am* **-d** OR **dove**, *pt Br* **-d)** *n (of swimmer)* Kopfsprung der. ◆ *vi* einen Kopfsprung machen ; *(under sea)* tauchen ; *(bird, plane)* einen Sturzflug machen.

diver ['daɪvəʳ] *n (from divingboard, rock)* Springer der (-in die) ; *(under sea)* Taucher der (-in die).

diversion [daɪ'vɜːʃn] *n (of traffic)* Umleitung die ; *(amusement)* Ablenkung die.

divert [daɪ'vɜːt] *vt* umlleiten ; *(attention)* ablenken.

divide [dɪ'vaɪd] *vt* teilen ; *(share out)* verteilen ; *(into two parts)* zerteilen. ■ **divide up** *vt sep* aufteilen.

diving ['daɪvɪŋ] *n (from divingboard, rock)* Springen das ; *(under sea)* Tauchen das ; **to go ~** tauchen gehen.

divingboard ['daɪvɪŋbɔːd] *n* Sprungbrett das.

division [dɪ'vɪʒn] *n (SPORT)* Liga die ; *(COMM)* Abteilung die ; *(in maths)* Division die ; *(disagreement)* Uneinigkeit die.

divorce [dɪ'vɔːs] *n* Scheidung die. ◆ *vt* sich scheiden lassen von.

divorced [dɪ'vɔːst] *adj* geschieden.

DIY *abbr* = **do-it-yourself**.

dizzy ['dɪzɪ] *adj* schwindlig.

DJ *abbr* = **disc jockey**.

do [duː] *(pt* did, *pp* done, *pl* dos) *aux vb* **1.** *(in negatives)* : **don't do that!** tu das nicht! ; **she didn't listen** sie hat nicht zugehört.

2. *(in questions)* : **did he like it?** hat es ihm gefallen? ; **how ~ you do it?** wie machen Sie/machst du das?

3. *(referring to previous verb)* : **I eat more than you ~** ich esse mehr als du ; **no I didn't!** nein, habe ich nicht! ; **so ~ I** ich auch.

4. *(in question tags)* : **so, you like Scotland, ~ you?** Sie mögen Schottland also, nicht wahr? ;

you come from Ireland, don't you? Sie kommen aus Irland, oder? **5.** *(for emphasis)* : I ~ **like this bedroom** das Schlafzimmer gefällt mir wirklich ; ~ **come in!** kommen Sie doch herein!

◆ *vt* **1.** *(perform)* machen, tun ; **I've a lot to** ~ ich habe viel zu tun ; **to** ~ **one's homework** seine Hausaufgaben machen ; **what is she doing?** was macht sie? ; **what can I** ~ **for you?** was kann ich für Sie tun?

2. *(clean, brush etc)* : **to** ~ **one's make-up** sich schminken ; **to** ~ **one's teeth** sich *(D)* die Zähne putzen.

3. *(cause)* : **to** ~ **damage** Schaden zuIfügen ; **to** ~ **sb good** jm gut tun.

4. *(have as job)* : **what do you** ~? was machen Sie beruflich?

5. *(provide, offer)* anIbieten ; **we** ~ **pizzas for under £4** wir bieten Pizzas für weniger als 4 Pfund an.

6. *(study)* studieren, machen.

7. *(subj: vehicle)* fahren.

8. *(inf : visit)* : **we're doing Switzerland next week** wir fahren nächste Woche in die Schweiz.

◆ *vi* **1.** *(behave, act)* tun ; ~ **as I say** tu, was ich sage.

2. *(progress, get on)* : **to** ~ **badly** schlecht voranIkommen ; *(in exam)* schlecht abIschneiden ; **to** ~ **well** gut voranIkommen ; *(in exam)* gut abIschneiden.

3. *(be sufficient)* reichen, genügen ; **will £5** ~? sind 5 Pfund genug?

4. *(in phrases)* : **how do you** ~? Guten Tag! ; **how are you doing?**

wie geht's? ; **what has that got to** ~ **with it?** was hat das damit zu tun?

◆ *n (party)* Party *die* ; **the ~s and don'ts** was man tun und lassen sollte.

▧ **do out of** *vt sep (inf)* : **to** ~ **sb out of £10** jn um 10 Pfund betrügen.

▧ **do up** *vt sep (fasten)* zuImachen ; *(decorate)* renovieren ; *(wrap up)* einIpacken.

▧ **do with** *vt fus (need)* : **I could** ~ **with a drink** ich könnte einen Drink gebrauchen.

▧ **do without** *vt fus* : **to** ~ **without sthg** ohne etw ausIkommen.

dock [dɒk] *n (for ships)* Dock *das* ; *(JUR)* Anklagebank *die*. ◆ *vi* anIlegen.

doctor ['dɒktə'] *n* Arzt *der* (Ärztin *die*) ; *(academic)* Doktor *der* (-in *die*) ; **to go to the ~'s** zum Arzt gehen.

document ['dɒkjʊmənt] *n* Dokument *das*.

documentary [,dɒkjʊ'mentərɪ] *n* Dokumentarfilm *der*.

Dodgems® ['dɒdʒəmz] *npl (Br)* Autoskooter *pl*.

dodgy ['dɒdʒɪ] *adj (Br : inf) (plan)* gewagt ; *(car, machine)* unzuverlässig.

does [weak form dəz, strong form dʌz] → **do**.

doesn't ['dʌznt] = **does not**.

dog [dɒg] *n* Hund *der*.

dog food *n* Hundefutter *das*.

doggy bag ['dɒgɪ-] *n* Tüte, *in der aus einem Restaurant Essensreste mit nach Hause genommen werden.*

do-it-yourself n Do-it-your-self das.

dole [dəʊl] n : to be on the ~ (Br) stempeln gehen.

doll [dɒl] n Puppe die.

dollar ['dɒlə'] n Dollar der.

dolphin ['dɒlfɪn] n Delphin der.

dome [dəʊm] n Kuppel die.

domestic [də'mestɪk] adj (of house) Haushalts- ; (of family) familiär ; (of country) Innen-.

domestic appliance n Haushaltsgerät das.

domestic flight n Inlandflug der.

domestic science n Hauswirtschaftslehre die.

dominate ['dɒmɪneɪt] vt beherrschen.

dominoes ['dɒmɪnəʊz] n Domino das.

donate [də'neɪt] vt spenden.

donation [də'neɪʃn] n Spende die.

done [dʌn] pp → **do**. ◆ adj (finished), (cooked) gar.

donkey ['dɒŋkɪ] n Esel der.

don't [dəʊnt] = **do not**.

door [dɔ:'] n Tür die.

doorbell ['dɔ:bel] n Türklingel die.

doorknob ['dɔ:nɒb] n Türknauf der.

doorman ['dɔ:mən] (pl -men) n Portier der.

doormat ['dɔ:mæt] n Fußabtreter der.

doormen ['dɔ:mən] pl → **doorman**.

doorstep ['dɔ:step] n Türstufe die ; (Br : piece of bread) dicke Scheibe Brot.

doorway ['dɔ:weɪ] n Eingang der.

dope [dəʊp] n (inf : drug) Stoff der.

dormitory ['dɔ:mətrɪ] n Schlafsaal der.

Dormobile® ['dɔ:mə,bi:l] n Camper der.

dosage ['dəʊsɪdʒ] n Dosis die.

dose [dəʊs] n Dosis die ; (of illness) Anfall der.

dot [dɒt] n Punkt der ; on the ~ (fig) pünktlich.

dotted line ['dɒtɪd-] n gepunktete Linie.

double ['dʌbl] adj doppelt, Doppel-. ◆ adv doppelt. ◆ n (twice the amount) Doppelte das ; (alcohol) Doppelte das. ◆ vt verdoppeln. ◆ vi sich verdoppeln ; it's ~ the size es ist doppelt so groß ; to bend sthg ~ etw zusammenlfalten ; a ~ whisky ein doppelter Whisky ; ~ seven sieben sieben. ▪ **doubles** n (SPORT) Doppel das.

double bed n Doppelbett das.

double-breasted [-'brestɪd] adj zweireihig.

double cream n (Br) Sahne mit hohem Fettgehalt.

double-decker (bus) [-'dekə'-] n Doppeldeckerbus der.

double doors npl Flügeltür die.

double-glazing [-'gleɪzɪŋ] n Doppelverglasung die.

double room n Doppelzimmer das.

doubt [daʊt] n Zweifel der. ◆ vt zweifeln an (+D) ; I ~ it bezweifle ich ; I ~ she'll come ich bezweifle, dass sie kommt ; **in** ~ zweifelhaft ; **no** ~ zweifellos.

doubtful ['dautful] *adj (person)* skeptisch ; *(result)* zweifelhaft ; **it's** ~ **that...** *(unlikely)* es ist fraglich, ob...

dough [dəu] *n* Teig *der.*

doughnut ['dəunʌt] *n* Berliner *der,* Krapfen *der (Süddt, Österr).*

dove[1] [dʌv] *n (bird)* Taube *die.*

dove[2] [dəuv] *pt (Am)* → **dive.**

Dover ['dəuvə'] *n* Dover *nt.*

Dover sole *n* Seezunge *die.*

down [daun] *adv* 1. *(towards the bottom)* nach unten, hinunter/herunter ; ~ **here** hier unten ; ~ **there** dort unten ; **to fall** ~ *(person)* hin|fallen ; *(thing)* herunter|fallen.
2. *(along)* ~ : **I'm going** ~ **to the shops** ich gehe zum Einkaufen.
3. *(downstairs)* herunter, nach unten ; **I'll come** ~ **later** ich komme später herunter.
4. *(southwards)* hinunter/herunter ; **we're going** ~ **to London** wir fahren hinunter nach London ; **they're coming** ~ **from Manchester** sie kommen von Manchester herunter.
5. *(in writing)* : **to write sthg** ~ etw auf|schreiben.
◆ *prep* 1. *(towards the bottom of)* : **they ran** ~ **the hill** sie liefen den Hügel herunter ; **to fall** ~ **the stairs** die Treppe hinunter|fallen.
2. *(along)* entlang ; **I was walking** ~ **the street** ich lief gerade die Straße entlang.
◆ *adj (inf : depressed)* down.
◆ *n (feathers)* Daunen *pl.*

▪ **downs** *npl (Br)* Hügelland *das.*

downhill [,daun'hil] *adv* bergab.

Downing Street ['dauniŋ-] *n* Downing Street *die, Straße, in der sich der offizielle Wohnsitz des britischen Premierministers und Wirtschaftsministers befindet.*

ⓘ **DOWNING STREET**

Diese Straße in London ist berühmt durch den Sitz des britischen Premierministers (Hausnummer 10) und des Schatzkanzlers (Hausnummer 11). Der Begriff kann auch als Bezeichnung für den Premierminister selbst und seine Mitarbeiter verwendet werden.

downpour ['daunpɔː'] *n* Regenguss *der.*

downstairs [,daun'steəz] *adv* unten ; **to go** ~ nach unten gehen.

downtown [,daun'taun] *adj & adv* in der Innenstadt ; **to go** ~ in die Stadt gehen ; ~ **New York** die Innenstadt von New York.

down under *adv (Br : inf)* in Australien.

downwards ['daunwədz] *adv* nach unten.

doz. *abbr* = **dozen.**

doze [dəuz] *vi* dösen.

dozen ['dʌzn] *n* Dutzend *das* ; **a** ~ **eggs** zwölf Eier.

Dr *(abbr of Doctor)* Dr.

drab [dræb] *adj* trist.

draft [drɑːft] n (early version) Entwurf der; (money order) Wechsel der; (Am) = **draught**.

drag [dræg] vt schleppen. ◆ vi (along ground) schleifen; what a ~! (inf) ist das langweilig! ▪ **drag on** vi sich in die Länge ziehen.

dragonfly ['drægnflaɪ] n Libelle die.

drain [dreɪn] n (sewer) Abflussrohr das; (grating in street) Gully der. ◆ vt (tank, radiator) Wasser abllassen von. ◆ vi (vegetables, washing-up) abltropfen.

draining board ['dreɪnɪŋ-] n Abtropffläche die.

drainpipe ['dreɪnpaɪp] n (for rain water) Abflussrohr das; (for waste water) Abwasserleitung die.

drama ['drɑːmə] n Drama das; (art) Dramatik die.

dramatic [drə'mætɪk] adj dramatisch.

drank [dræŋk] pt → **drink**.

drapes [dreɪps] npl (Am) Vorhänge pl.

drastic ['dræstɪk] adj drastisch.

drastically ['dræstɪklɪ] adv drastisch.

draught [drɑːft] n (Br : of air) Luftzug der.

draught beer n Fassbier das.

draughts [drɑːfts] n (Br) Damespiel das.

draughty ['drɑːftɪ] adj zugig.

draw [drɔː] (pt drew, pp drawn) vt ziehen; (picture, map) zeichnen; (attract) anlziehen. ◆ vi (with pen, pencil) zeichnen; (SPORT) unentschie-

den spielen. ◆ n (SPORT : result) Unentschieden das; (lottery) Ziehung die; to ~ the curtains (open) die Vorhänge aufllziehen; (close) die Vorhänge zulziehen. ▪ **draw out** vt sep (money) abllheben. ▪ **draw up** vt sep (list) aufllstellen; (plan) entwerfen. ◆ vi (car, bus) anllhalten.

drawback ['drɔːbæk] n Nachteil der.

drawer [drɔːʳ] n Schublade die.

drawing ['drɔːɪŋ] n (picture) Zeichnung die; (activity) Zeichnen das.

drawing pin n (Br) Reißzwecke die.

drawing room n Wohnzimmer das.

drawn [drɔːn] pp → **draw**.

dreadful ['dredfʊl] adj schrecklich.

dream [driːm] n Traum der. ◆ vt & vi träumen; a ~ house ein Traumhaus.

dress [dres] n Kleid das; (clothes) Kleidung die. ◆ vt anllziehen; (wound) verbinden; (salad) anllmachen. ◆ vi sich anllziehen; he was ~ed in a black suit er trug einen schwarzen Anzug; to get ~ed sich anllziehen. ▪ **dress up** vi (in smart clothes) sich fein machen; (in costume) sich verkleiden.

dress circle n erster Rang.

dresser ['dresəʳ] n (Br : for crockery) Büffet das; (Am : chest of drawers) Kommode die.

dressing ['dresɪŋ] n (for salad) Dressing das; (for wound) Verband der.

dressing gown n Morgenrock der.

dressing room n (for actors) Künstlergarderobe die ; (for players) Umkleidekabine die.

dressing table n Frisierkommode die.

dressmaker ['dres,meɪkə'] n Damenschneider der (-in die).

dress rehearsal n Generalprobe die.

drew [dru:] pt → draw.

dribble ['drɪbl] vi (liquid) tropfen ; (baby) sabbern.

drier ['draɪə'] = dryer.

drift [drɪft] n (of snow) Schneewehe die. ◆ vi treiben.

drill [drɪl] n Bohrer der. ◆ vt (hole) bohren.

drink [drɪŋk] (pt drank, pp drunk) n Getränk das ; (alcoholic) Drink der. ◆ vt & vi trinken ; **to have a ~** (alcoholic) einen trinken.

drinkable ['drɪŋkəbl] adj trinkbar.

drinking water ['drɪŋkɪŋ-] n Trinkwasser das.

drip [drɪp] n Tropfen der. ◆ vi tropfen ; **to be on a ~** am Tropf hängen.

drip-dry adj bügelfrei.

dripping (wet) ['drɪpɪŋ-] adj tropfnass.

drive [draɪv] (pt drove, pp driven) n Fahrt die ; (in front of house) Einfahrt die. ◆ vt fahren ; (operate, power) anltreiben. ◆ vi fahren ; **to ~ sb to do sthg** jn dazu bringen, etw zu tun ; **to go for a ~** spazieren fahren ; **to ~ sb mad** jn verrückt machen.

drivel ['drɪvl] n Blödsinn der.

driven ['drɪvn] pp → drive.

driver ['draɪvə'] n Fahrer der (-in die) ; (of train) Führer der (-in die).

driver's license (Am) = driving licence.

driveshaft ['draɪvʃɑːft] n Antriebswelle die.

driveway ['draɪvweɪ] n Zufahrt die.

driving lesson ['draɪvɪŋ-] n Fahrstunde die.

driving licence ['draɪvɪŋ-] n (Br) Führerschein der.

driving test ['draɪvɪŋ-] n Fahrprüfung die.

drizzle ['drɪzl] n Sprühregen der.

drop [drɒp] n (of liquid) Tropfen der ; (distance down) Höhenunterschied der ; (decrease) Rückgang der ; (in value, wages) Minderung die. ◆ vt fallen lassen ; (reduce) senken ; (from vehicle) ablsetzen ; (omit) wegllassen. ◆ vi fallen ; (decrease) sinken ; **to ~ a hint** eine Anspielung machen ; **to ~ sb a line** jm ein paar Zeilen schreiben. ■ **drop in** vi (inf) vorbeilkommen. ■ **drop off** vt sep (from vehicle) ablsetzen. ◆ vi (fall asleep) einlnicken ; (fall off) abllfallen. ■ **drop out** vi (of college, race) abllbrechen.

drought [draʊt] n Dürre die.

drove [drəʊv] pt → drive.

drown [draʊn] vi ertrinken.

drug [drʌg] n (MED) Medikament das ; (stimulant) Droge die. ◆ vt betäuben.

drug addict n Drogenabhängige der, die.

druggist ['drʌgɪst] n (Am) Drogist der (-in die).

drum [drʌm] n Trommel die.

drummer ['drʌmə'] n Schlagzeuger der (-in die).

drumstick ['drʌmstɪk] n (of chicken) Keule die.

drunk [drʌŋk] pp → **drink**. ◆ adj betrunken. ◆ n Betrunkene der, die ; **to get** ~ sich betrinken.

dry [draɪ] adj trocken. ◆ vt (hands, washing-up) abltrocknen ; (clothes) trocknen. ◆ vi trocknen ; **to** ~ **o.s.** sich abltrocknen ; **to** ~ **one's hair** sich (D) die Haare trocknen. ▪ **dry up** vi ausltrocknen ; (dry the dishes) abltrocknen.

dry-clean vt chemisch reinigen.

dry cleaner's n chemische Reinigung.

dryer ['draɪə'] n (for clothes) Wäschetrockner der ; (for hair) Föhn der.

dry-roasted peanuts [-'rəustɪd-] npl ohne Fett geröstete Erdnüsse pl.

DSS n (Br) Amt für Sozialwesen.

DTP n (abbr of desktop publishing) Desktop-Publishing das.

dual carriageway ['dju:əl-] n (Br) vierspurige Straße.

dubbed [dʌbd] adj (film) synchronisiert.

dubious ['dju:bjəs] adj zweifelhaft.

duchess ['dʌtʃɪs] n Herzogin die.

duck [dʌk] n Ente die. ◆ vi sich ducken.

due [dju:] adj fällig ; (owed) geschuldet ; **in** ~ **course** zu gegebener Zeit ; ~ **to** auf Grund (+G) ; **to be** ~ (train) planmäßig ankommen.

duet [dju:'et] n Duett das.

duffel bag ['dʌfl-] n Seesack der.

duffel coat ['dʌfl-] n Dufflecoat der.

dug [dʌg] pt & pp → **dig**.

duke [dju:k] n Herzog der.

dull [dʌl] adj (boring) langweilig ; (colour) fahl ; (weather) trüb ; (pain) dumpf.

dumb [dʌm] adj (inf : stupid) doof ; (unable to speak) stumm.

dummy ['dʌmɪ] n (Br : for baby) Schnuller der ; (for clothes) Schaufensterpuppe die.

dump [dʌmp] n (for rubbish) Müllkippe die ; (inf : place) Schweinestall der. ◆ vt (drop carelessly) fallen lassen ; (get rid of) losiwerden.

dumpling ['dʌmplɪŋ] n Kloß der, Knödel der.

dune [dju:n] n Düne die.

dungarees [,dʌŋgə'ri:z] npl Latzhose die ; (Am : jeans) Arbeitsjeans pl.

dungeon ['dʌndʒən] n Kerker der.

duplicate ['dju:plɪkət] n Duplikat das.

during ['djuərɪŋ] prep während (+G).

dusk [dʌsk] n Abenddämmerung die.

dust [dʌst] n Staub der. ◆ vt abistauben.

dustbin ['dʌstbɪn] n (Br) Mülltonne die.

dustcart ['dʌstkɑ:t] n (Br) Müllwagen der.

duster ['dʌstə'] n Staubtuch das.

dustman ['dʌstmən] (pl -men [-mən]) n (Br) Müllmann der.

dustpan ['dʌstpæn] n Kehrschaufel die.

dusty ['dʌstɪ] adj staubig.

Dutch [dʌtʃ] adj holländisch. ◆ n Holländisch das. ◆ npl : the ~ die Holländer pl.

Dutchman ['dʌtʃmən] (pl -men [-mən]) n Holländer der.

Dutchwoman ['dʌtʃ,wumən] (pl -women [-,wɪmɪn]) n Holländerin die.

duty ['djuːtɪ] n Pflicht die ; (tax) Zoll der ; to be on ~ Dienst haben ; to be off ~ keinen Dienst haben. ▪ **duties** npl (job) Aufgaben pl.

duty chemist's n Apothekenbereitschaftsdienst der.

duty-free adj zollfrei. ◆ n (shop) Dutyfreeshop der ; (goods) zollfreie Waren pl.

duty-free shop n Dutyfreeshop der.

duvet ['duːveɪ] n Bettdecke die.

dwarf [dwɔːf] (pl dwarves [dwɔːvz]) n Zwerg der.

dwelling ['dwelɪŋ] n (fml) Wohnung die.

dye [daɪ] n Farbe die. ◆ vt färben.

dynamite ['daɪnəmaɪt] n Dynamit das.

dynamo ['daɪnəməʊ] (pl -s) n (on bike) Dynamo der.

dyslexic [dɪs'leksɪk] adj : to be ~ Legastheniker sein.

E

E (abbr of east) O.

E111 n E111 Formular das.

each [iːtʃ] adj jede(-r) (-s). ◆ pron : ~ (one) jede(-r) (-s) ; ~ other einander ; there's one ~ es ist für jeden eins da ; I'd like one of ~ ich möchte von jedem/jeder eins ; they cost £10 ~ sie kosten je 10 Pfund.

eager ['iːgə'] adj eifrig ; to be ~ to do sthg unbedingt etw tun wollen.

eagle ['iːgl] n Adler der.

ear [ɪə'] n Ohr das ; (of corn) Ähre die.

earache ['ɪəreɪk] n : to have ~ Ohrenschmerzen haben.

earl [ɜːl] n Graf der.

early ['ɜːlɪ] adj & adv früh ; at the earliest frühestens ; ~ on schon früh ; to have an ~ night früh zu Bett gehen.

earn [ɜːn] vt verdienen ; to ~ a living seinen Lebensunterhalt verdienen.

earnings ['ɜːnɪŋz] npl Einkommen das.

earphones ['ɪəfəʊnz] npl Kopfhörer pl.

earplugs ['ɪəplʌgz] npl Ohropax® pl.

earrings ['ɪərɪŋz] npl Ohrringe pl.

earth [ɜːθ] n Erde die. ◆ vt (Br : appliance) erden ; how on ~...? wie in aller Welt...?

earthenware ['ɜːθnweə'] adj aus Ton.

earthquake ['ɜːθkweɪk] n Erdbeben das.

ease [i:z] n Leichtigkeit *die*. ◆ vt *(pain)* lindern ; *(problem)* verringern ; **at** ~ unbefangen. ▪ **ease off** vi *(pain, rain)* nachlassen.

easily ['i:zɪlɪ] adv leicht.

east [i:st] n Osten *der*. ◆ adv nach Osten ; *(be situated)* im Osten ; **in the** ~ **of England** im Osten Englands ; **the East** *(Asia)* der Osten.

eastbound ['i:stbaund] adj (in) Richtung Osten.

Easter ['i:stə'] n Ostern *das*.

eastern ['i:stən] adj östlich, Ost- ; **Eastern** *(Asian)* östlich, Ost-.

Eastern Europe n Osteuropa *nt*.

East Germany n Ostdeutschland *nt*.

eastwards ['i:stwədz] adv ostwärts.

easy ['i:zɪ] adj leicht, einfach ; **to take it** ~ etw leicht nehmen.

easygoing [,i:zɪ'gəʊɪŋ] adj gelassen.

eat [i:t] *(pt* **ate**, *pp* **eaten** ['i:tn)] vt & vi essen ; *(subj : animal)* fressen. ▪ **eat out** vi essen gehen.

eating apple ['i:tɪŋ-] n Essapfel *der*.

ebony ['ebənɪ] n Ebenholz *das*.

EC n *(abbr of European Community)* EG *die*.

eccentric [ɪk'sentrɪk] adj exzentrisch.

echo ['ekəʊ] *(pl* **-es**) n Echo *das*. ◆ vi wider|hallen.

ecology [ɪ'kɒlədʒɪ] n Ökologie *die*.

e-commerce [,i:'kɒmɜ:s] n E-Commerce *der*.

economic [,i:kə'nɒmɪk] adj wirtschaftlich. ▪ **economics** n Wirtschaftswissenschaften *pl*.

economical [,i:kə'nɒmɪkl] adj wirtschaftlich ; *(person)* sparsam.

economize [ɪ'kɒnəmaɪz] vi sparen.

economy [ɪ'kɒnəmɪ] n *(of country)* Wirtschaft *die* ; *(saving)* Sparsamkeit *die*.

economy class n Economyklasse *die*.

economy size adj Spar-.

ecotourism ['i:kəʊ,tʊərɪzm] n Ökotourismus *der*.

ecstasy ['ekstəsɪ] n Ekstase *die* ; *(drug)* Ecstasy *das*.

eczema ['eksɪmə] n Ekzem *das*.

edge [edʒ] n Rand *der* ; *(of knife)* Schneide *die*.

edible ['edɪbl] adj essbar.

Edinburgh ['edɪnbrə] n Edinburg *nt*.

Edinburgh Festival n : **the ~** *großes Musik- und Theaterfestival in Edinburg.*

EDINBURGH FESTIVAL

Bei diesem alljährlich im August stattfindenden internationalen Festival in der schottischen Hauptstadt stehen Musik, Theater und Tanz im Mittelpunkt. Parallel zu dem offiziellen, klassischen ausgerichteten Festival findet ein alternatives Festival „Fringe" mit hunderten von unabhängigen Aufführungen auf den kleineren Bühnen der Stadt statt.

---

edition [ɪ'dɪʃn] n Ausgabe die.

editor ['edɪtə] n (of newspaper, magazine) Chefredakteur der (-in die) ; (of book) Redakteur der (-in die) ; (of film, TV programme) Cutter der (-in die).

editorial [,edɪ'tɔːrɪəl] n Leitartikel der.

educate ['edʒʊkeɪt] vt erziehen.

education [,edʒʊ'keɪʃn] n (field) Ausbildung die ; (process) Erziehung die ; (result) Bildung die.

EEC n EWG die.

eel [iːl] n Aal der.

effect [ɪ'fekt] n Wirkung die ; to put sthg into ~ etw in Kraft setzen ; to take ~ in Kraft treten.

effective [ɪ'fektɪv] adj wirksam.

effectively [ɪ'fektɪvlɪ] adv wirksam ; (in fact) effektiv.

efficient [ɪ'fɪʃənt] adj tüchtig ; (machine, organization) leistungsfähig.

effort ['efət] n (exertion) Anstrengung die ; (attempt) Versuch der ; to make an ~ to do sthg sich bemühen, etw zu tun ; it's not worth the ~ es ist nicht der Mühe wert.

e.g. adv z.B.

egg [eg] n Ei das.

egg cup n Eierbecher der.

egg mayonnaise n Brotaufstrich aus gehacktem Ei und Majonäse.

eggplant ['egplɑːnt] n (Am) Aubergine die.

egg white n Eiweiß das.

egg yolk n Eigelb das.

Egypt ['iːdʒɪpt] n Ägypten nt.

eiderdown ['aɪdədaʊn] n Daunendecke die.

eight [eɪt] num acht ; → six.

eighteen [,eɪ'tiːn] num achtzehn ; → six.

eighteenth [,eɪ'tiːnθ] num achtzehnte(-r) (-s) ; → sixth.

eighth [eɪtθ] num achte(-r) (-s) ; → sixth.

eightieth ['eɪtɪθ] num achtzigste(-r) (-s) ; → sixth.

eighty ['eɪtɪ] num achtzig ; → six.

Eire ['eərə] n Irland nt.

Eisteddfod [aɪ'stedfəd] n walisisches Kulturfestival.

ⓘ EISTEDDFOD

Ein walisisches Festival, das alljährlich im August stattfindet und bei dem die walisische Sprache und Kultur im Mittelpunkt stehen. Es geht auf das 12. Jahrhundert, den „Eisteddfod" zurück, einen großen Wettbewerb in Kunst, Dichtung, Schauspiel und Musik.

---

either ['aɪðəʳ, 'iːðəʳ] adj : ~ book will do beide Bücher sind okay. ◆ pron : I'll take ~ (of them) ich nehme einen/eine/eins (von beiden) ; I don't like ~ (of them) ich mag keinen/keine/keins (von beiden). ◆ adv : I can't ~ ich auch nicht ; ~... or entweder... oder ; I don't like ~ him or her ich mag weder ihn noch sie ; **on ~ side** auf beiden Seiten.

eject [ɪ'dʒekt] *vt (cassette)* auswerfen.

elaborate [ɪ'læbrət] *adj* kunstvoll.

elastic [ɪ'læstɪk] *n* Gummi *der or das*.

elastic band *n (Br)* Gummiband *das*.

elbow ['elbəʊ] *n* Ellbogen *der*.

elder ['eldə'] *adj* ältere(-r) (-s).

elderly ['eldəlɪ] *adj* ältere(-r) (-s). ◆ *npl* : **the ~** die ältere Generation.

eldest ['eldɪst] *adj* älteste(-r) (-s).

elect [ɪ'lekt] *vt* wählen ; **to ~ to do sthg** *(fml : choose)* sich entscheiden, etw zu tun.

election [ɪ'lekʃn] *n* Wahl *die*.

electric [ɪ'lektrɪk] *adj* elektrisch.

electrical goods [ɪ'lektrɪkl-] *npl* Elektrowaren *pl*.

electric blanket *n* Heizdecke *die*.

electric drill *n* Bohrmaschine *die*.

electric fence *n* Elektrozaun *der*.

electrician [ˌɪlek'trɪʃn] *n* Elektriker *der* (-in *die*).

electricity [ˌɪlek'trɪsətɪ] *n (supply)* Strom *der* ; *(in physics)* Elektrizität *die*.

electric shock *n* elektrischer Schlag.

electrocute [ɪ'lektrəkjuːt] *vt* durch einen Schlag töten.

electronic [ˌɪlek'trɒnɪk] *adj* elektronisch.

elegant ['elɪgənt] *adj* elegant.

element ['elɪmənt] *n* Element *das* ; *(degree)* Spur *die* ; *(of fire, kettle)* Heizelement *das* ; **the ~s** *(weather)* die Elemente.

elementary [ˌelɪ'mentərɪ] *adj* elementar.

elephant ['elɪfənt] *n* Elefant *der*.

elevator ['elɪveɪtə'] *n (Am)* Aufzug *der*.

eleven [ɪ'levn] *num* elf ; → **six**.

eleventh [ɪ'levnθ] *num* elfte(-r) (-s) ; → **sixth**.

eligible ['elɪdʒəbl] *adj (qualified)* berechtigt.

eliminate [ɪ'lɪmɪneɪt] *vt* ausschalten.

Elizabethan [ɪˌlɪzə'biːθn] *adj* elisabethanisch *(zweite Hälfte des 16. Jh)*.

elm [elm] *n* Ulme *die*.

else [els] *adv* : **I don't want anything ~** ich will nichts mehr ; **anything ~?** sonst noch etwas? ; **everyone ~** alle anderen ; **nobody ~** niemand anders ; **nothing ~** sonst nichts ; **somebody ~** *(additional person)* noch jemand anders ; *(different person)* jemand anders ; **something ~** *(additional thing)* noch etwas ; *(different thing)* etwas anders ; **somewhere ~** woanders ; **to go somewhere ~** woandershin gehen ; **what ~?** was sonst? ; **who ~?** wer sonst? ; **or ~** sonst.

elsewhere [els'weə'] *adv* woanders ; *(go, move)* woandershin.

e-mail ['iːmeɪl] *n* E-Mail *die*. ◆ *vt* : **to ~ sb** jm eine E-Mail schicken ; **to ~ sthg to sb** jm etw mailen, jm etw per E-Mail schicken.

e-mail address ['i:meɪlədres] n E-Mail-Adresse die.

embankment [ɪm'bæŋkmənt] n (next to river, railway) Damm der; (next to road) Böschung die.

embark [ɪm'bɑːk] vi (board ship) an Bord gehen.

embarkation card [‚embɑː-'keɪʃn-] n Bordkarte die.

embarrass [ɪm'bærəs] vt in Verlegenheit bringen.

embarrassed [ɪm'bærəst] adj verlegen.

embarrassing [ɪm'bærəsɪŋ] adj peinlich.

embarrassment [ɪm'bærəsmənt] n Verlegenheit die.

embassy ['embəsɪ] n Botschaft die.

emblem ['embləm] n Emblem das.

embrace [ɪm'breɪs] vt umarmen.

embroidered [ɪm'brɔɪdəd] adj bestickt.

embroidery [ɪm'brɔɪdərɪ] n Stickerei die.

emerald ['emərəld] n Smaragd der.

emerge [ɪ'mɜːdʒ] vi herauslkommen; (fact, truth) sich herauslstellen.

emergency [ɪ'mɜːdʒənsɪ] n Notfall der. ◆ adj Not-; in an ~ im Notfall.

emergency exit n Notausgang der.

emergency landing n Notlandung die.

emergency services npl Notdienst der.

emigrate ['emɪgreɪt] vi auslwandern.

emit [ɪ'mɪt] vt (light) auslstrahlen; (gas) auslströmen.

emotion [ɪ'məʊʃn] n Emotion die.

emotional [ɪ'məʊʃənl] adj (situation) emotionsgeladen; (person) gefühlsbetont.

emphasis ['emfəsɪs] (pl -ases [-əsiːz]) n Betonung die.

emphasize ['emfəsaɪz] vt betonen.

empire ['empaɪə'] n Reich das.

employ [ɪm'plɔɪ] vt (subj : company) beschäftigen; (fml : use) benutzen.

employed [ɪm'plɔɪd] adj angestellt.

employee [ɪm'plɔɪiː] n Angestellte der, die.

employer [ɪm'plɔɪə'] n Arbeitgeber der (-in die).

employment [ɪm'plɔɪmənt] n Arbeit die.

employment agency n Stellenvermittlung die.

empty ['emptɪ] adj leer. ◆ vt leeren.

EMU n EWU die.

emulsion (paint) [ɪ'mʌlʃn-] n Emulsionsfarbe die.

enable [ɪ'neɪbl] vt : to ~ sb to do sthg jm ermöglichen, etw zu tun.

enamel [ɪ'næml] n (decorative) Email das; (on tooth) Zahnschmelz der.

enclose [ɪn'kləʊz] vt (surround) umgeben; (with letter) beillegen.

enclosed [ɪn'kləʊzd] *adj (space)* abgeschlossen.

encounter [ɪn'kaʊntə'] *vt (experience)* stoßen auf *(+A)* ; *(fml : meet)* begegnen *(+D)*.

encourage [ɪn'kʌrɪdʒ] *vt* ermutigen ; **to ~ sb to do sthg** jm Mut machen, etw zu tun.

encouragement [ɪn'kʌrɪdʒmənt] *n* Ermutigung *die*.

encyclopedia [ɪn,saɪklə'piːdjə] *n* Lexikon *das*.

end [end] *n* Ende *das* ; *(of finger, knife)* Spitze *die* ; *(purpose)* Ziel *das*. ◆ *vt* beenden. ◆ *vi* enden ; **at the ~ of April** Ende April ; **to come to an ~** zu Ende gehen ; **to put an ~ to sthg** etw beenden ; **for days on ~** tagelang ; **in the ~** schließlich ; **to make ~s meet** gerade so auslkommen. ■ **end up** *vi* landen ; **to ~ up doing sthg** schließlich etw tun.

endangered species [ɪn'deɪndʒəd-] *n (vom Aussterben)* bedrohte Art.

ending ['endɪŋ] *n* Schluss *der*, Ende *das* ; *(GRAMM)* Endung *die*.

endive ['endaɪv] *n (curly)* Endivie *die* ; *(chicory)* Chicorée *der*.

endless ['endlɪs] *adj* endlos.

endorsement [ɪn'dɔːsmənt] *n (of driving licence)* Strafvermerk *der*.

endurance [ɪn'djʊərəns] *n* Ausdauer *die*.

endure [ɪn'djʊə'] *vt* ertragen.

enemy ['enɪmɪ] *n* Feind *der*.

energy ['enədʒɪ] *n* Energie *die*.

enforce [ɪn'fɔːs] *vt* durch|setzen.

engaged [ɪn'geɪdʒd] *adj (to be married)* verlobt ; *(Br : phone, toilet)* besetzt ; **to get ~** sich verloben.

engaged tone *n (Br)* Besetztzeichen *das*.

engagement [ɪn'geɪdʒmənt] *n (to marry)* Verlobung *die* ; *(appointment)* Verabredung *die*.

engagement ring *n* Verlobungsring *der*.

engine ['endʒɪn] *n* Motor *der* ; *(of train)* Lokomotive *die*.

engineer [,endʒɪ'nɪə'] *n* Ingenieur *der* (-in *die*).

engineering [,endʒɪ'nɪərɪŋ] *n* Technik *die*.

engineering works *npl (on railway line)* technische Bauarbeiten *pl*.

England ['ɪŋglənd] *n* England *nt*.

English ['ɪŋglɪʃ] *adj* englisch. ◆ *n* Englisch *das*. ◆ *npl* : **the ~** die Engländer *pl*.

English breakfast *n* englisches Frühstück *(mit gebratenem Speck, Würstchen, Eiern, Toast und Kaffee oder Tee)*.

English Channel *n* : **the ~** der Ärmelkanal.

Englishman ['ɪŋglɪʃmən] *(pl -men* [-mən]*) n* Engländer *der*.

Englishwoman ['ɪŋglɪʃ,wʊmən] *(pl -women* [-,wɪmɪn]*) n* Engländerin *die*.

engrave [ɪn'greɪv] *vt* gravieren.

engraving [ɪn'greɪvɪŋ] *n* Stich *der*.

enjoy [ɪn'dʒɔɪ] *vt* genießen ; *(film, music, hobby)* mögen ; **to ~ doing sthg** etw gerne tun ; **to ~**

o.s. sich amüsieren ; ~ your meal! guten Appetit!

enjoyable [ɪn'dʒɔɪəbl] *adj* nett.

enjoyment [ɪn'dʒɔɪmənt] *n* Vergnügen *das*.

enlargement [ɪn'lɑːdʒmənt] *n* Vergrößerung *die*.

enormous [ɪ'nɔːməs] *adj* riesig.

enough [ɪ'nʌf] *adj, pron & adv* genug ; ~ **time** Zeit genug ; **is that ~?** reicht das? ; **to have had ~ (of sthg)** genug (von etw) haben.

enquire [ɪn'kwaɪər] *vi* : **to ~ (about)** sich erkundigen (nach).

enquiry [ɪn'kwaɪərɪ] *n (question)* Anfrage *die* ; *(investigation)* Untersuchung *die* ; **'Enquiries'** 'Information', 'Auskunft'.

enquiry desk *n* Informationsschalter *der*.

enrol [ɪn'rəʊl] *vi (Br)* sich einlschreiben.

enroll [ɪn'rəʊl] *(Am)* = **enrol**.

en suite bathroom [ɒn-'swiːt-] *n* Zimmer *das* mit Bad.

ensure [ɪn'ʃʊər] *vt* sicherlstellen ; **to ~ (that)...** dafür sorgen, dass...

entail [ɪn'teɪl] *vt (involve)* mit sich bringen.

enter ['entər] *vt* gehen in (+A) ; *(plane, bus)* einlsteigen in (+A) ; *(college, army)* einltreten in (+A) ; *(competition)* teilInehmen an (+D) ; *(on form)* einltragen. ◆ *vi* hereinIkommen ; *(in competition)* teilInehmen.

enterprise ['entəpraɪz] *n* Unternehmen *das*.

entertain [ˌentə'teɪn] *vt* unterhalten.

entertainer [ˌentə'teɪnər] *n* Entertainer *der*.

entertaining [ˌentə'teɪnɪŋ] *adj* unterhaltsam.

entertainment [ˌentə'teɪnmənt] *n* Unterhaltung *die*.

enthusiasm [ɪn'θjuːzɪæzm] *n* Begeisterung *die*.

enthusiast [ɪn'θjuːzɪæst] *n* Enthusiast *der* (-in *die*).

enthusiastic [ɪn,θjuːzɪ'æstɪk] *adj* enthusiastisch.

entire [ɪn'taɪər] *adj* ganze(-r) (-s).

entirely [ɪn'taɪəlɪ] *adv* völlig.

entitle [ɪn'taɪtl] *vt* : **to ~ sb to sthg** jn zu etw berechtigen ; **to ~ sb to do sthg** jn berechtigen, etw zu tun.

entrance ['entrəns] *n* Eingang *der* ; *(admission)* Zutritt *der*.

entrance fee *n* Eintrittspreis *der*.

entry ['entrɪ] *n* Eingang *der* ; *(admission)* Zutritt *der* ; *(in dictionary)* Eintrag *der* ; *(in competition)* Einsendung *die* ; **'no ~'** 'Eintritt verboten'.

envelope ['envələʊp] *n* Briefumschlag *der*.

envious ['envɪəs] *adj* neidisch.

environment [ɪn'vaɪərənmənt] *n* Umwelt *die*.

environmental [ɪn,vaɪərən'mentl] *adj* Umwelt-.

environmentally friendly [ɪn,vaɪərən'mentəlɪ-] *adj* umweltfreundlich.

envy ['envɪ] *vt* beneiden.

epic ['epɪk] *n* Epos *das*.

epidemic [,epɪ'demɪk] n Epidemie die.

epileptic [,epɪ'leptɪk] adj epileptisch.

episode ['epɪsəʊd] n Episode die ; (of TV programme) Folge die.

equal ['iːkwəl] adj gleich. ◆ vt gleich sein ; **to be ~ to** gleich sein.

equality [ɪ'kwɒlətɪ] n (equal rights) Gleichberechtigung die.

equalize ['iːkwəlaɪz] vi (SPORT) ausǀgleichen.

equally ['iːkwəlɪ] adv gleich ; (share) gleichmäßig ; (at the same time) ebenso.

equation [ɪ'kweɪʒn] n Gleichung die.

equator [ɪ'kweɪtə'] n : **the ~** der Äquator.

equip [ɪ'kwɪp] vt : **to ~ sb/sthg with** jn/etw ausǀrüsten mit.

equipment [ɪ'kwɪpmənt] n Ausǀrüstung die.

equipped [ɪ'kwɪpt] adj : **to be ~ with** ausgerüstet sein mit.

equivalent [ɪ'kwɪvələnt] adj gleichwertig. ◆ n Äquivalent das.

erase [ɪ'reɪz] vt (letter, word) ausǀradieren.

eraser [ɪ'reɪzə'] n Radiergummi der.

erect [ɪ'rekt] adj (person, posture) aufrecht. ◆ vt aufǀstellen.

ERM n Wechselkursmechanismus der.

erotic [ɪ'rɒtɪk] adj erotisch.

errand ['erənd] n Besorgung die.

erratic [ɪ'rætɪk] adj unregelmäßig.

error ['erə'] n Fehler der.

escalator ['eskəleɪtə'] n Rolltreppe die.

escalope ['eskəlɒp] n Schnitzel das.

escape [ɪ'skeɪp] n Flucht die ; (of gas) Ausströmen das. ◆ vi : **to ~ (from)** entkommen (aus) ; (gas) ausǀströmen (aus) ; (water) ausǀlaufen (aus).

escort [n 'eskɔːt, vb ɪ'skɔːt] n (guard) Eskorte die. ◆ vt begleiten.

espadrilles ['espə,drɪlz] npl Espadrilles pl.

especially [ɪ'speʃəlɪ] adv besonders.

esplanade [,esplə'neɪd] n Esplanade die.

essay ['eseɪ] n (at school, university) Aufsatz der.

essential [ɪ'senʃl] adj wesentlich. ■ **essentials** npl Wesentliche das ; **the bare ~s** das Nötigste.

essentially [ɪ'senʃəlɪ] adv im Grunde.

establish [ɪ'stæblɪʃ] vt (set up, create) gründen ; (fact, truth) herausǀfinden.

establishment [ɪ'stæblɪʃmənt] n (business) Unternehmen das.

estate [ɪ'steɪt] n (land in country) Landsitz der ; (for housing) Wohnsiedlung die ; (Br : car) = **estate car**.

estate agent n (Br) Immobilienmakler der.

estate car n (Br) Kombiwagen der.

estimate [n 'estɪmət, vb 'estɪmeɪt] n Schätzung die ; (of cost)

Kostenvoranschlag *der.* ◆ *vt* schätzen.

estuary ['estjʊərɪ] *n* Mündung *die.*

ethnic minority ['eθnɪk-] *n* ethnische Minderheit.

EU *n (abbr of European Union)* EU *die.*

euro ['jʊərəʊ] *n* Euro *der.*

Eurocheque ['jʊərəʊ,tʃek] *n* Euroscheck *der.*

Europe ['jʊərəp] *n* Europa *nt.*

European [,jʊərə'pɪən] *adj* europäisch. ◆ *n* Europäer *der* (-in *die*).

European Community *n* Europäische Gemeinschaft *die.*

Eurostar® ['jʊərəstɑː'] *n* Eurostar® *der.*

evacuate [ɪ'vækjʊeɪt] *vt* evakuieren.

evade [ɪ'veɪd] *vt* vermeiden.

evaporated milk [ɪ'væpəreɪtɪd-] *n* Kondensmilch *die.*

eve [iːv] *n* : on the ~ of am Vorabend (+G).

even ['iːvn] *adj (rate, speed)* gleichmäßig ; *(level, flat)* eben ; *(teams)* gleich stark ; *(number)* gerade. ◆ *adv* sogar ; **to break ~** die Kosten decken ; **~ so** trotzdem ; **~ though** obwohl ; **not ~** nicht einmal.

evening ['iːvnɪŋ] *n* Abend *der* ; **good ~!** guten Abend! ; **in the ~** am Abend, abends.

evening classes *npl* Abendkursus *der.*

evening dress *n (formal clothes)* Abendkleidung *die.*

evening meal *n* Abendessen *das.*

event [ɪ'vent] *n* Ereignis *das* ; *(SPORT)* Wettkampf *der* ; **in the ~ of** *(fml)* im Falle (+G).

eventual [ɪ'ventʃʊəl] *adj* : **the ~ decision was...** schließlich wurde entschieden, dass...

eventually [ɪ'ventʃʊəlɪ] *adv* schließlich.

ever ['evə'] *adv (at any time)* je, jemals ; **he was ~ so angry** er war sehr verärgert ; **for ~** *(eternally)* für immer ; *(for a long time)* seit Ewigkeiten ; **hardly ~** fast nie ; **~ since** seitdem, seit.

every ['evrɪ] *adj* jede(-r) (-s) ; **~ other day** jeden zweiten Tag ; **~ few days** alle paar Tage ; **one in ~ ten** einen/eine/eins von zehn ; **we make ~ effort...** wir geben uns alle Mühe... ; **~ so often** dann und wann.

everybody ['evrɪ,bɒdɪ] = everyone.

everyday ['evrɪdeɪ] *adj* alltäglich.

everyone ['evrɪwʌn] *pron* alle ; *(each person)* jeder.

everyplace ['evrɪ,pleɪs] *(Am)* = everywhere.

everything ['evrɪθɪŋ] *pron* alles.

everywhere ['evrɪweə'] *adv* überall ; *(go)* überallhin.

evidence ['evɪdəns] *n (proof)* Beweis *der* ; *(of witness)* Aussage *die.*

evident ['evɪdənt] *adj* klar.

evidently ['evɪdəntlɪ] *adv* offensichtlich.

evil ['iːvl] *adj* böse. ◆ *n* Böse *das.*

ex [eks] *n (inf)* Ex *der, die.*

exact [ɪg'zækt] adj genau ; '~ fare ready please' 'Bitte das genaue Fahrgeld bereithalten'.

exactly [ɪg'zæktlɪ] adv & excl genau.

exaggerate [ɪg'zædʒəreɪt] vt & vi übertreiben.

exaggeration [ɪg,zædʒə'reɪʃn] n Übertreibung die.

exam [ɪg'zæm] n Prüfung die ; to take an ~ eine Prüfung ablegen.

examination [ɪg,zæmɪ'neɪʃn] n (at school) Prüfung die ; (at university) Examen das ; (MED) Untersuchung die.

examine [ɪg'zæmɪn] vt untersuchen.

example [ɪg'zɑːmpl] n Beispiel das ; for ~ zum Beispiel.

exceed [ɪk'siːd] vt übersteigen.

excellent ['eksələnt] adj ausgezeichnet.

except [ɪk'sept] prep & conj außer ; ~ for abgesehen von ; '~ for access' 'Anlieger frei' ; '~ for loading' 'Be- und Entladen gestattet'.

exception [ɪk'sepʃn] n Ausnahme die.

exceptional [ɪk'sepʃnəl] adj außergewöhnlich.

excerpt ['eksɜːpt] n Auszug der.

excess [ɪk'ses, before noun 'ekses] adj Über-. ◆ n Übermaß das.

excess baggage n Übergewicht das.

excess fare n (Br) Nachlösegebühr die.

excessive [ɪk'sesɪv] adj übermäßig ; (price) übermäßig hoch.

exchange [ɪks'tʃeɪndʒ] n (of telephones) Fernamt das ; (of students) Austausch der. ◆ vt um|tauschen ; to ~ sthg for sthg etw gegen etw ein|tauschen ; to be on an ~ Austauschschüler sein.

exchange rate n Wechselkurs der.

excited [ɪk'saɪtɪd] adj aufgeregt.

excitement [ɪk'saɪtmənt] n Aufregung die.

exciting [ɪk'saɪtɪŋ] adj aufregend.

exclamation mark [,eksklə'meɪʃn-] n (Br) Ausrufezeichen das.

exclamation point [,eksklə'meɪʃn-] (Am) = **exclamation mark**.

exclude [ɪk'skluːd] vt aus|schließen.

excluding [ɪk'skluːdɪŋ] prep ausgenommen (+D).

exclusive [ɪk'skluːsɪv] adj (high-class) exklusiv ; (sole) ausschließlich. ◆ n Exklusivbericht der ; ~ of ausschließlich (+G).

excursion [ɪk'skɜːʃn] n Ausflug der.

excuse [n ɪk'skjuːs, vb ɪk'skjuːz] n Entschuldigung die. ◆ vt entschuldigen ; ~ me! entschuldigen Sie, bitte! ; (as apology) Entschuldigung!

ex-directory adj (Br) : to be ~ nicht im Telefonbuch stehen.

execute ['eksɪkjuːt] vt (kill) hin|richten.

executive [ɪgˈzekjʊtɪv] n (person) leitende Angestellte der, die.

exempt [ɪgˈzempt] adj : ~ (from) befreit (von).

exemption [ɪgˈzempʃn] n Befreiung die.

exercise [ˈeksəsaɪz] n (physical) Bewegung die ; (piece of work) Übung die. ◆ vi sich bewegen ; to do ~s Gymnastik treiben.

exercise book n Heft das.

exert [ɪgˈzɜːt] vt ausüben.

exhaust [ɪgˈzɔːst] vt erschöpfen. ◆ n : ~ (pipe) Auspuff der.

exhausted [ɪgˈzɔːstɪd] adj erschöpft.

exhibit [ɪgˈzɪbɪt] n (in museum, gallery) Ausstellungsstück das. ◆ vt (in exhibition) ausstellen.

exhibition [ˌeksɪˈbɪʃn] n (of art) Ausstellung die.

exist [ɪgˈzɪst] vi existieren.

existence [ɪgˈzɪstəns] n Existenz die ; to be in ~ existieren.

existing [ɪgˈzɪstɪŋ] adj bestehend.

exit [ˈeksɪt] n (door) Ausgang der ; (from motorway) Ausfahrt die ; (act of leaving) Abgang der. ◆ vi hinausgehen.

exotic [ɪgˈzɒtɪk] adj exotisch.

expand [ɪkˈspænd] vi sich ausdehnen ; (in number) sich vermehren.

expect [ɪkˈspekt] vt erwarten ; to ~ to do sthg voraussichtlich etw tun ; to ~ sb to do sthg erwarten, dass jd etw macht ; to be ~ing (be pregnant) in anderen Umständen sein.

expedition [ˌekspɪˈdɪʃn] n Expedition die ; (short outing) Tour die.

expel [ɪkˈspel] vt (from school) von der Schule verweisen.

expense [ɪkˈspens] n Ausgaben pl ; at the ~ of auf Kosten (+G). ◼ **expenses** npl (of businessman) Spesen pl.

expensive [ɪkˈspensɪv] adj teuer.

experience [ɪkˈspɪərɪəns] n Erfahrung die. ◆ vt erfahren.

experienced [ɪkˈspɪərɪənst] adj erfahren.

experiment [ɪkˈsperɪmənt] n Experiment das. ◆ vi experimentieren.

expert [ˈekspɜːt] adj (advice, treatment) fachmännisch. ◆ n Experte der (Expertin die).

expire [ɪkˈspaɪə˞] vi ablaufen.

expiry date [ɪkˈspaɪərɪ-] n : ~ : 15/4/00 gültig bis 15/4/00.

explain [ɪkˈspleɪn] vt erklären.

explanation [ˌekspləˈneɪʃn] n Erklärung die.

explode [ɪkˈspləʊd] vi explodieren.

exploit [ɪkˈsplɔɪt] vt ausbeuten.

explore [ɪkˈsplɔː˞] vt (place) erforschen.

explosion [ɪkˈspləʊʒn] n (of bomb etc) Explosion die.

explosive [ɪkˈspləʊsɪv] n Sprengstoff der.

export [n ˈekspɔːt, vb ɪkˈspɔːt] n Export der, Ausfuhr die. ◆ vt exportieren.

exposed [ɪkˈspəʊzd] adj (place) ungeschützt.

exposure [ɪkˈspəʊʒə˞] n (photograph) Aufnahme die ; (MED)

Unterkühlung *die* ; *(to heat, radiation)* Aussetzung *die.*

express [ɪk'spres] *adj (letter, delivery)* Eil-. ◆ *n (train)* ≃ D-Zug *der.* ◆ *vt (opinion, idea)* ausdrücken. ◆ *adv (send)* per Eilboten.

expression [ɪk'spreʃn] *n* Ausdruck *der.*

expresso [ɪk'spresəʊ] *n* Espresso *der.*

expressway [ɪk'spresweɪ] *n (Am)* Schnellstraße *die.*

extend [ɪk'stend] *vt (visa, permit)* verlängern ; *(road, building)* ausIbauen ; *(hand)* ausIstrecken. ◆ *vi (stretch)* sich erstrecken.

extension [ɪk'stenʃn] *n (of building)* Anbau *der* ; *(for phone)* Nebenanschluss *der* ; *(of deadline)* Verlängerung *die* ; ~ 1263 Apparat 1263.

extension lead *n* Verlängerungskabel *das.*

extensive [ɪk'stensɪv] *adj* umfangreich ; *(damage)* beträchtlich.

extent [ɪk'stent] *n (of knowledge)* Umfang *der* ; *(of damage)* Ausmaß *das* ; **to a certain** ~ in gewissem Maße ; **to what ~...?** inwieweit...?

exterior [ɪk'stɪərɪə] *adj* äußere(-r) (-s). ◆ *n (of car, building)* Außenseite *die.*

external [ɪk'stɜːnl] *adj* äußere(-r) (-s).

extinct [ɪk'stɪŋkt] *adj (species)* ausgestorben ; *(volcano)* erloschen.

extinction [ɪk'stɪŋkʃn] *n* Aussterben *das.*

extinguish [ɪk'stɪŋgwɪʃ] *vt (fire)* löschen ; *(cigarette)* ausImachen.

extinguisher [ɪk'stɪŋgwɪʃə] *n* Feuerlöscher *der.*

extortionate [ɪk'stɔːʃnət] *adj (price)* Wucher-.

extra ['ekstrə] *adj* zusätzlich. ◆ *n (bonus)* Sonderleistung *die* ; *(optional thing)* Extra *das.* ◆ *adv (large, hard)* extra ; ~ **charge** Zuschlag *der* ; ~ **large** übergroß. ▪ **extras** *npl (in price)* zusätzliche Kosten *pl.*

extract [*n* 'ekstrækt, *vb* ɪk-'strækt] *n* Auszug *der.* ◆ *vt (tooth)* ziehen.

extractor fan [ɪk'stræktə-] *n (Br)* Ventilator *der.*

extraordinary [ɪk'strɔːdnrɪ] *adj (wonderful)* außerordentlich ; *(strange)* ungewöhnlich.

extravagant [ɪk'strævəgənt] *adj* extravagant.

extreme [ɪk'striːm] *adj* äußerste(-r) (-s) ; *(radical)* extrem. ◆ *n* Extrem *das.*

extremely [ɪk'striːmlɪ] *adv* äußerst.

extrovert ['ekstrəvɜːt] *n* extrovertierter Mensch.

eye [aɪ] *n* Auge *das* ; *(of needle)* Öhr *das.* ◆ *vt* anIsehen ; **to keep an ~ on** aufIpassen auf (+A).

eyebrow ['aɪbraʊ] *n* Augenbraue *die.*

eye drops *npl* Augentropfen *pl.*

eyeglasses ['aɪglɑːsɪz] *npl (Am)* Brille *die.*

eyelash ['aɪlæʃ] *n* Wimper *die.*

eyelid ['aɪlɪd] *n* Augenlid *das.*

eyeliner ['aɪˌlaɪnə] *n* Eyeliner *der.*

eye shadow n Lidschatten der.

eyesight ['aɪsaɪt] n : to have good/bad ~ gute/schlechte Augen haben.

eye test n Sehtest der.

eyewitness [,aɪ'wɪtnɪs] n Augenzeuge der (-zeugin die).

F

F (abbr of Fahrenheit) F.

fabric ['fæbrɪk] n (cloth) Stoff der.

fabulous ['fæbjʊləs] adj sagenhaft.

facade [fə'sɑːd] n Fassade die.

face [feɪs] n Gesicht das ; (of cliff, mountain) Wand die ; (of clock, watch) Zifferblatt das. ◆ vt : to ~ sb/sthg jm/etw (D) gegenüberIstehen ; to ~ facts sich den Tatsachen stellen ; the hotel ~s the harbour das Hotel geht zum Hafen hinaus ; to be ~d with sthg (problem) etw (D) gegenüberIstehen. ▪ **face up to** vt fus ins Auge sehen (+D).

facecloth ['feɪsklɒθ] n (Br) Waschlappen der.

facial ['feɪʃl] n Gesichtsmassage die.

facilitate [fə'sɪlɪteɪt] vt (fml) erleichtern.

facilities [fə'sɪlɪtiːz] npl Einrichtungen pl.

facsimile [fæk'sɪmɪlɪ] n Faksimile das.

fact [fækt] n Tatsache die ; in ~ (in reality) tatsächlich ; (moreover) sogar.

factor ['fæktə] n Faktor der ; ~ten suntan lotion Sonnenschutzmittel das mit Schutzfaktor zehn.

factory ['fæktərɪ] n Fabrik die.

faculty ['fæklti] n (at university) Fakultät die.

FA Cup n Pokalwettbewerb des britischen Fußballbundes.

fade [feɪd] vi (sound) abklingen ; (flower) verwelken ; (jeans, wallpaper) verbleichen.

faded ['feɪdɪd] adj (jeans) ausgewaschen.

fag [fæg] n (Br : inf : cigarette) Kippe die.

Fahrenheit ['færənhaɪt] adj Fahrenheit.

fail [feɪl] vt (exam) nicht bestehen. ◆ vi (not succeed) scheitern ; (in exam) durchIfallen ; (engine) ausIfallen ; to ~ to do sthg (not do) etw nicht tun.

failing ['feɪlɪŋ] n Fehler der. ◆ prep : ~ that andernfalls.

failure ['feɪljə] n Misserfolg der ; (person) Versager der.

faint [feɪnt] adj schwach. ◆ vi ohnmächtig werden ; I haven't the ~est idea ich habe keinen blassen Schimmer.

fair [feə] adj (just) fair, gerecht ; (quite large) ziemlich groß ; (quite good) ziemlich gut ; (SCH) befriedigend ; (skin) hell ; (hair, person) blond ; (weather) gut. ◆ n (funfair) Jahrmarkt der ; (trade fair) Messe die ; ~ enough! na gut! ; a ~ number of times ziemlich oft.

fairground ['feəgraʊnd] *n* Jahrmarkt *der.*

fair-haired [-'heəd] *adj* blond.

fairly ['feəlɪ] *adv (quite)* ziemlich.

fairy ['feərɪ] *n* Fee *die.*

fairy tale *n* Märchen *das.*

faith [feɪθ] *n* Glaube *der ; (confidence)* Vertrauen *das ;* to have ~ in sb Vertrauen zu jm haben.

faithfully ['feɪθfʊlɪ] *adv :* Yours ~ Hochachtungsvoll.

fake [feɪk] *n (false thing)* Fälschung *die.* ◆ *vt* fälschen.

fall [fɔːl] *(pt* fell, *pp* fallen ['fɔːln]) *vi* fallen. ◆ *n (accident)* Sturz *der ; (decrease)* Sinken *das ; (of snow)* Schneefall *der ; (Am : autumn)* Herbst *der ;* to ~ asleep ein|schlafen ; to ~ ill krank werden ; to ~ in love sich verlieben. ■ **falls** *npl (waterfall)* Fälle *pl.* ■ **fall behind** *vi (with work, rent)* in Rückstand geraten. ■ **fall down** *vi* hin|fallen. ■ **fall off** *vi* herunter|fallen ; *(handle)* ab|fallen ; *(branch)* ab|brechen. ■ **fall out** *vi (hair, teeth)* aus|fallen ; *(argue)* sich streiten. ■ **fall over** *vi* hin|fallen. ■ **fall through** *vi* ins Wasser fallen.

false [fɔːls] *adj* falsch.

false alarm *n* falscher Alarm.

false teeth *npl* Gebiss *das.*

fame [feɪm] *n* Ruhm *der.*

familiar [fə'mɪljə] *adj* bekannt ; *(informal)* vertraulich ; to be ~ with *(know)* sich aus|kennen mit.

family ['fæmlɪ] *n* Familie *die.* ◆ *adj (pack, size)* Familien- ;

(film, holiday) für die ganze Familie.

family planning clinic [-'plænɪŋ-] *n* ≃ Pro Familia-Beratungsstelle *die.*

family room *n (at hotel)* Doppelzimmer mit Kinderbett ; *(at pub, airport)* Raum für Familien mit kleinen Kindern.

famine ['fæmɪn] *n* Hungersnot *die.*

famished ['fæmɪʃt] *adj (inf)* ausgehungert.

famous ['feɪməs] *adj* berühmt.

fan [fæn] *n (electric)* Ventilator *der ; (held in hand)* Fächer *der ; (enthusiast, supporter)* Fan *der.*

fan belt *n* Keilriemen *der.*

fancy ['fænsɪ] *vt (inf : feel like)* Lust haben auf (+A) ; *(be attracted to)* scharf sein auf (+A). ◆ *adj (elaborate)* ausgefallen ; ~ (that)! also so was!

fancy dress *n* Verkleidung *die (Kostüm).*

fan heater *n* Heizlüfter *der.*

fanlight ['fænlaɪt] *n (Br)* Oberlicht *das.*

fantastic [fæn'tæstɪk] *adj* fantastisch.

fantasy ['fæntəsɪ] *n* Fantasie *die.*

far [fɑː] *(compar* further OR farther, *superl* furthest OR farthest) *adv* weit. ◆ *adj :* at the ~ end am anderen Ende ; have you come ~? sind Sie von weit her gekommen? ; how ~ is it (to London)? wie weit ist es (bis London)? ; as ~ as *(town, country)* bis nach ; *(station, school)* bis zu (+D) ; as ~ as I'm concerned was mich betrifft ; as ~ as I know soweit ich weiß ; ~ **better** weit-aus besser ; **by** ~ bei weitem ; **so** ~ *(until now)* bisher.

farce [fɑ:s] *n* Farce *die*.

fare [feəʳ] *n* Fahrpreis *der* ; *(for plane)* Flugpreis *der* ; *(fml : food)* Kost *die*. ◆ *vi* : **she** ~**d well/badly** es ist ihr gut/schlecht ergangen.

Far East *n* : **the** ~ der Ferne Osten.

fare stage *n* *(Br)* Teilstrecke *die*.

farm [fɑ:m] *n* Bauernhof *der*.

farmer ['fɑ:məʳ] *n* Bauer *der* (Bäuerin *die*).

farmhouse ['fɑ:mhaʊs, *pl* -haʊzɪz] *n* Bauernhaus *das*.

farming ['fɑ:mɪŋ] *n* Landwirtschaft *die*.

farmland ['fɑ:mlænd] *n* Ackerland *das*.

farmyard ['fɑ:mjɑ:d] *n* Hof *der*.

farther ['fɑ:ðəʳ] *compar* → **far**.

farthest ['fɑ:ðəst] *superl* → **far**.

fascinating ['fæsɪneɪtɪŋ] *adj* faszinierend.

fascination [ˌfæsɪ'neɪʃn] *n* Faszination *die*.

fashion ['fæʃn] *n* Mode *die* ; *(manner)* Art *die* ; **to be in** ~ in Mode sein ; **to be out of** ~ aus der Mode sein.

fashionable ['fæʃnəbl] *adj* modisch.

fashion show *n* Modenschau *die*.

fast [fɑ:st] *adv* schnell ; *(securely)* fest. ◆ *adj* schnell ; *(clock, watch)* : **to be** ~ vorgehen ; **to be** ~ **asleep** fest schlafen ; **a** ~ **train** ein Schnellzug.

fasten ['fɑ:sn] *vt* *(coat, door, window)* zulmachen ; *(seatbelt)* sich anlschnallen ; *(two things)* festlmachen.

fastener ['fɑ:snəʳ] *n* Verschluss *der*.

fast food *n* Fastfood *der*.

fat [fæt] *adj* dick ; *(meat)* fett. ◆ *n* Fett *das*.

fatal ['feɪtl] *adj* tödlich.

father ['fɑ:ðəʳ] *n* Vater *der*.

Father Christmas *n* *(Br)* Weihnachtsmann *der*.

father-in-law *n* Schwiegervater *der*.

fattening ['fætnɪŋ] *adj* : **to be** ~ dick machen.

fatty ['fætɪ] *adj* fettreich.

faucet ['fɔ:sɪt] *n* *(Am)* Hahn *der*.

fault ['fɔ:lt] *n* *(responsibility)* Schuld *der* ; *(error)* Fehler *der* ; **it's your** ~ du hast Schuld.

faulty ['fɔ:ltɪ] *adj* fehlerhaft.

favor ['feɪvər] *(Am)* = **favour**.

favour ['feɪvəʳ] *n* *(Br : kind act)* Gefallen *der*. ◆ *vt* *(Br : prefer)* vorlziehen ; **to be in** ~ **of sthg** für etw sein ; **to do sb a** ~ jm einen Gefallen tun.

favourable ['feɪvrəbl] *adj* günstig.

favourite ['feɪvrɪt] *adj* Lieblings-. ◆ *n* *(in sport)* Favorit *der* (-in *die*).

fawn [fɔ:n] *adj* hellbraun.

fax [fæks] *n* Fax *das*. ◆ *vt* faxen.

fear [fɪəʳ] *n* Angst *die*. ◆ *vt* fürchten ; **for** ~ **of doing sthg** aus Angst, etw zu tun.

feast [fi:st] *n* Festessen *das*.

feather ['feðəʳ] *n* Feder *die*.

feature ['fiːtʃəʳ] n (characteristic) Merkmal das ; (of face) Gesichtszug der ; (in newspaper, on radio, TV) Feature das. ◆ vt (subj : film) : this film ~s Marlon Brando in diesem Film spielt Marlon Brando mit.

feature film n Spielfilm der.

Feb. (abbr of February) Febr.

February ['februərɪ] n Februar der ; → September.

fed [fed] pt & pp → feed.

fed up adj : to be ~ (with) die Nase voll haben (von etw).

fee [fiː] n Gebühr die.

feeble ['fiːbəl] adj schwach.

feed [fiːd] (pt & pp fed) vt füttern ; (coins) einwerfen.

feel [fiːl] (pt & pp felt) vt fühlen ; (think) glauben. ◆ vi sein ; (ill, old, young) sich fühlen ; (seem) sich anfühlen. ◆ n (of material) : it has a soft ~ es fühlt sich weich an ; I ~ cold mir ist kalt ; I ~ ill ich fühle mich nicht gut ; to ~ like sthg (fancy) Lust haben auf etw (A) ; to ~ up to doing sthg sich einer Sache gewachsen fühlen.

feeling ['fiːlɪŋ] n Gefühl das.

feet [fiːt] pl → foot.

fell [fel] pt → fall. ◆ vt (tree) fällen.

fellow ['feləʊ] adj Mit-. ◆ n (man) Mann der.

felt [felt] pt & pp → feel. ◆ n Filz der.

felt-tip pen n Filzstift der.

female ['fiːmeɪl] adj weiblich. ◆ n (animal) Weibchen das.

feminine ['femɪnɪn] adj feminin.

feminist ['femɪnɪst] n Feministin die.

fence [fens] n Zaun der.

fencing ['fensɪŋ] n (SPORT) Fechten das.

fend [fend] vi : to ~ for o.s. allein zurechtˈkommen.

fender ['fendəʳ] n (for fireplace) Kamingitter das ; (Am : on car) Kotflügel der.

fennel ['fenl] n Fenchel der.

fern [fɜːn] n Farn der.

ferocious [fəˈrəʊʃəs] adj wild.

ferry ['ferɪ] n Fähre die.

fertile ['fɜːtaɪl] adj (land) fruchtbar.

fertilizer ['fɜːtɪlaɪzəʳ] n Dünger der.

festival ['festəvl] n (of music, arts etc) Festspiele pl ; (holiday) Feiertag der.

feta cheese ['fetə-] n Feta der.

fetch [fetʃ] vt holen ; (be sold for) einbringen.

fete [feɪt] n Wohltätigkeitsbazar der.

FETE

Die gewöhnlich in den Sommermonaten abgehaltenen „fetes" sind Wohltätigkeitsbazare im Freien, bei denen Veranstaltungen und Wettbewerbe aller Art stattfinden. An den Ständen wird allerlei Selbstgemachtes verkauft. Der Erlös daraus geht in der Regel als Spende an wohltätige Vereine oder wird zur Finanzierung eines örtlichen Hilfsprojekts verwendet.

fever ['fiːvəʳ] n Fieber das ; to have a ~ Fieber haben.

feverish ['fiːvərɪʃ] adj fiebrig.

few [fju:] *adj* & *pron* wenige ;
the first ~ times die ersten paar
Male ; **a ~** ein paar ; **quite a ~**
eine ganze Menge.

fewer ['fju:ə'] *adj* & *pron* weniger.

fiancé [fɪ'ɒnseɪ] *n* Verlobte
der.

fiancée [fɪ'ɒnseɪ] *n* Verlobte
die.

fib [fɪb] *n* (*inf*) : **to tell a ~** flun-
kern.

fiber ['faɪbər] (*Am*) = **fibre**.

fibre ['faɪbə'] *n* (*Br*) Faser *die* ;
(*in food*) Ballaststoffe *pl*.

fibreglass ['faɪbəglɑːs] *n*
Glasfiber *die*.

fickle ['fɪkl] *adj* launisch.

fiction ['fɪkʃn] *n* Belletristik
die.

fiddle ['fɪdl] *n* (*violin*) Geige
die. ◆ *vi* : **to ~ with sthg** an etw
(*D*) fummeln.

fidget ['fɪdʒɪt] *vi* zappeln.

field [fi:ld] *n* Feld *das* ; (*subject*)
Gebiet *das*.

field glasses *npl* Feldstecher
der.

fierce [fɪəs] *adj* (*animal*) wild ;
(*person, storm*) heftig ; (*heat*)
brütend.

fifteen [,fɪf'tiːn] *num* fünfzehn ; → **six**.

fifteenth [,fɪf'tiːnθ] *num*
fünfzehnte(-r) (-s) ; → **sixth**.

fifth [fɪfθ] *num* fünfte(-r) (-s) ;
→ **sixth**.

fiftieth ['fɪftɪəθ] *num* fünf-
zigste(-r) (-s) ; → **sixth**.

fifty ['fɪftɪ] *num* fünfzig ; →
six.

fig [fɪg] *n* Feige *die*.

fight [faɪt] (*pt* & *pp* **fought**) *n*
Kampf *der* ; (*brawl*) Prügelei

die ; (*argument*) Streit *der*. ◆ *vt*
kämpfen gegen ; (*combat*) bekämpfen. ◆ *vi* kämpfen ;
(*brawl*) sich schlagen ; (*quarrel*)
sich streiten ; **to have a ~ with sb**
sich mit jm schlagen. ■ **fight
back** *vi* zurück|schlagen.
■ **fight off** *vt sep* ab|wehren.

fighting ['faɪtɪŋ] *n* Prügelei
die ; (*military*) Kämpfe *pl*.

figure [(*Br*) 'fɪgə', (*Am*) 'fɪgjər]
n Zahl *die* ; (*shape of body*) Figur
die ; (*outline of person*) Gestalt
die ; (*diagram*) Abbildung *die*.
■ **figure out** *vt sep* heraus|fin-
den.

file [faɪl] *n* Akte *die* ; (*COMPUT*)
Datei *die* ; (*tool*) Feile *die*. ◆ *vt*
(*complaint, petition*) ein|rei-
chen ; **to ~ one's nails** sich (*D*)
die Nägel feilen ; **in single ~** im
Gänsemarsch.

filing cabinet ['faɪlɪŋ-] *n* Ak-
tenschrank *der*.

fill [fɪl] *vt* füllen ; (*role*) aus|
füllen. ■ **fill in** *vt sep* (*form*)
aus|füllen. ■ **fill out** *vt sep* =
fill in. ■ **fill up** *vt sep* füllen ; **~
her up!** (*with petrol*) voll tanken,
bitte!

filled roll ['fɪld-] *n* belegtes
Brötchen.

fillet ['fɪlɪt] *n* Filet *das*.

fillet steak *n* Filetsteak *das*.

filling ['fɪlɪŋ] *n* Füllung *die*. ◆
adj sättigend.

filling station *n* Tankstelle
die.

film [fɪlm] *n* Film *der*. ◆ *vt* filmen.

film star *n* Filmstar *der*.

filter ['fɪltə'] *n* Filter *der*.

filthy ['fɪlθɪ] *adj* dreckig.

fin [fɪn] n Flosse die ; (Am : of swimmer) Schwimmflosse die.

final ['faɪnl] adj letzte(-r) (-s) ; (decision) endgültig. ◆ n Finale das.

finalist ['faɪnəlɪst] n (SPORT) Finalist der (-in die).

finally ['faɪnəlɪ] adv schließlich.

finance [n 'faɪnæns, vb faɪ'næns] n Geldmittel pl ; (management of money) Finanzwesen das. ◆ vt finanzieren.

finances npl Finanzen pl.

financial [fɪ'nænʃl] adj finanziell.

find [faɪnd] (pt & pp found) vt finden ; (find out) herausIfinden. ◆ n Fund der ; **to ~ the time to do sthg** die Zeit finden, etw zu tun. **find out** vt sep herausIfinden. ◆ vi : **to ~ out (about)** herausIfinden (über (+A)).

fine [faɪn] adj (good) herrlich ; (satisfactory) gut, in Ordnung ; (thin) fein. ◆ adv (thinly) fein ; (well) gut. ◆ n Geldstrafe die. ◆ vt zu einer Geldstrafe verurteilen ; **I'm ~** mir geht es gut.

fine art n schöne Künste pl.

finger ['fɪŋgə'] n Finger der.

fingernail ['fɪŋgəneɪl] n Fingernagel der.

fingertip ['fɪŋgətɪp] n Fingerspitze die.

finish ['fɪnɪʃ] n Schluss der ; (SPORT) Finish das ; (on furniture) Oberfläche die, Aspekt der. ◆ vt beenden ; (food, meal) auflessen ; (drink) ausItrinken. ◆ vi (end) zu Ende gehen ; (in race) durchs Ziel gehen ; **to ~ doing sthg** etw zu Ende machen.

finish off vt sep (complete) zu Ende machen ; (food, meal) aufIessen ; (drink) ausItrinken.

finish up vi hinIgelangen ; **to ~ up doing sthg** zum Schluss etw tun.

Finland ['fɪnlənd] n Finnland nt.

Finn [fɪn] n Finne der (Finnin die).

Finnan haddock ['fɪnən-] n schottischer geräucherter Schellfisch.

Finnish ['fɪnɪʃ] adj finnisch. ◆ n Finnisch das.

fir [fɜː'] n Tanne die.

fire ['faɪə'] n Feuer das ; (device) Ofen der. ◆ vt (gun) abIfeuern ; (from job) feuern ; **to be on ~** brennen ; **to catch ~** Feuer fangen.

fire alarm n Feuermelder der.

fire brigade n (Br) Feuerwehr die.

fire department (Am) = **fire brigade**.

fire engine n Feuerwehrauto das.

fire escape n (staircase) Feuertreppe die ; (ladder) Feuerleiter die.

fire exit n Notausgang der.

fire extinguisher n Feuerlöscher der.

fire hazard n : **to be a ~** feuergefährlich sein.

fireman ['faɪəmən] (pl -men [-mən]) n Feuerwehrmann der.

fireplace ['faɪəpleɪs] n Kamin der.

fire regulations npl Brandschutzbestimmungen pl.

fire station n Feuerwache die.

firewood [ˈfaɪəwʊd] n Brennholz das.

firework display [ˈfaɪəwɜːk-] n Feuerwerk das.

fireworks [ˈfaɪəwɜːks] npl Feuerwerkskörper pl.

firm [fɜːm] adj fest ; (mattress) hart. ◆ n Firma die.

first [fɜːst] adj erste(-r) (-s). ◆ adv zuerst ; (in order) als erste ; (for the first time) zum ersten Mal. ◆ pron erste der, die, das. ◆ n (event) erstmaliges Ereignis ; ~ (gear) erster Gang ; ~ thing (in the morning) gleich morgens früh ; for the ~ time zum ersten Mal ; the ~ of January der erste Januar ; at ~ zuerst ; ~ of all zu allererst.

first aid n Erste Hilfe.

first-aid kit n Verbandskasten der.

first class n erste Klasse ; (mail) Post, die schneller befördert werden soll oder in die EU geht.

first-class adj (stamp) für Briefe, die schneller befördert werden sollen oder in die EU gehen ; (ticket) erster Klasse ; (very good) erstklassig.

first floor n (Br) erster Stock ; (Am : ground floor) Erdgeschoss das.

firstly [ˈfɜːstlɪ] adv zuerst.

First World War n : the ~ der Erste Weltkrieg.

fish [fɪʃ] (pl fish) n Fisch der. ◆ vi (with net) fischen ; (with rod) angeln.

fish and chips n ausgebackener Fisch mit Pommes frites.

FISH AND CHIPS

Ein traditionelles englisches Gericht, das aus frittiertem Fisch in Ausbackteig und Pommes frites besteht und das man in den „fish and chip shops" (einer Art Imbissstube) zum Mitnehmen in braunes Packpapier oder Zeitungspapier eingepackt bekommt. „Fish and chip shops" sind in allen Teilen des Landes zu finden und bieten neben „fish and chips" auch eine Auswahl an anderen frittierten Schnellgerichten, zum Beispiel Würstchen, Hähnchen, Blutwurst und „meat pies" (Fleischpasteten) an. „Fish and chips" werden oft auf der Straße direkt aus der Hand gegessen.

fishcake [ˈfɪʃkeɪk] n Fischfrikadelle die.

fisherman [ˈfɪʃəmən] (pl -men [-mən]) n Fischer der.

fish farm n Fischzucht die.

fish fingers npl (Br) Fischstäbchen pl.

fishing [ˈfɪʃɪŋ] n (hobby) Angeln das ; (business) Fischerei die ; to go ~ angeln gehen.

fishing boat n Fischerboot das.

fishing rod n Angel die.

fishmonger's [ˈfɪʃˌmʌŋgəz] n (shop) Fischgeschäft das.

fish sticks (Am) = fish fingers.

fish supper n (Scot) ausgebackener Fisch mit Pommes frites.

fist [fɪst] n Faust die.

fit [fɪt] *adj (healthy)* fit. ◆ *vt passen (+D); (install)* einlbauen; *(insert)* einlstecken. ◆ *vi* passen. ◆ *n (epileptic, of coughing, anger)* Anfall *der; (of clothes, shoes)* **to be a good ~** gut passen; **to be ~ for sthg** *(suitable)* für etw geeignet sein; **~ to eat** essbar sein; **it doesn't ~** es passt nicht; **to get ~** fit werden; **to keep ~** fit bleiben. ■ **fit in** *vt sep (find time for)* einlschieben. ◆ *vi (belong)* sich einlfügen.

fitness ['fɪtnɪs] *n (health)* Fitness *die.*

fitted carpet [ˌfɪtəd-] *n* Teppichboden *der.*

fitted sheet [ˌfɪtəd-] *n* Spannbettlaken *das.*

fitting room ['fɪtɪŋ-] *n* Umkleideraum *der.*

five [faɪv] *num* fünf; → **six.**

fiver ['faɪvə^r] *n (Br : inf : £5)* fünf Pfund *pl; (£5 note)* Fünfpfundschein *der.*

fix [fɪks] *vt (attach)* anlbringen; *(mend)* reparieren; *(decide on, arrange)* festlegen; **to ~ sb a drink/meal** jm einen Drink/etwas zu essen machen. ■ **fix up** *vt sep* : **to ~ sb up with sthg** jm etw besorgen.

fixture ['fɪkstʃə^r] *n (SPORT)* Spiel *das;* **~s and fittings** *zu einer Wohnung gehörende Ausstattung und Installationen.*

fizzy ['fɪzɪ] *adj* kohlensäurehaltig.

flag [flæg] *n* Fahne *die.*

flake [fleɪk] *n* Flocke *die.* ◆ *vi* ablblättern.

flame [fleɪm] *n* Flamme *die.*

flammable ['flæməbl] *adj* feuergefährlich.

flan [flæn] *n (sweet)* Torte *die; (savoury)* Pastete *die.*

flannel ['flænl] *n (material)* Flanell *der; (Br : for washing face)* Waschlappen *der.* ■ **flannels** *npl* Flanellhose *die.*

flap [flæp] *n* Klappe *die.* ◆ *vt (wings)* schlagen mit.

flapjack ['flæpdʒæk] *n (Br)* Haferflockenplätzchen *das.*

flare [fleə^r] *n (signal)* Leuchtrakete *die.*

flared [fleəd] *adj (trousers, skirt)* ausgestellt.

flash [flæʃ] *n* Blitz *der.* ◆ *vi (light)* blinken; **a ~ of lightning** ein Blitz; **to ~ one's headlights** die Lichthupe benutzen.

flashlight ['flæʃlaɪt] *n* Taschenlampe *die.*

flask [flɑːsk] *n (Thermos)* Thermosflasche *die; (hip flask)* Flachmann *der.*

flat [flæt] *adj* flach; *(battery)* leer; *(drink)* abgestanden; *(rate, fee)* Pauschal-. ◆ *adv* flach. ◆ *n (Br : apartment)* Wohnung *die;* **a ~ (tyre)** eine Reifenpanne; **~ out** *(run, work)* mit Volldampf.

flatter ['flætə^r] *vt* schmeicheln *(+D).*

flavor ['fleɪvər] *(Am)* = **flavour.**

flavour ['fleɪvə^r] *n (Br)* Geschmack *der.*

flavoured ['fleɪvəd] *adj* mit Geschmacksstoffen.

flavouring ['fleɪvərɪŋ] *n* Aroma *das.*

flaw [flɔː] *n* Fehler *der.*

flea [fliː] *n* Floh *der.*

flea market n Flohmarkt der.

fleece [fliːs] n (downy material) Fleece der.

fleet [fliːt] n Flotte die.

Flemish ['flemɪʃ] adj flämisch. ◆ n Flämisch das.

flesh [fleʃ] n Fleisch das.

flew [fluː] pt → fly.

flex [fleks] n Schnur die.

flexible ['fleksəbl] adj (bendable) biegsam ; (adaptable) flexibel.

flick [flɪk] vt (a switch) an|knipsen ; (with finger) weg|schnipsen. ■ **flick through** vt fus durch|blättern.

flies [flaɪz] npl (of trousers) Hosenschlitz der.

flight [flaɪt] n Flug der ; a ~ (of stairs) eine Treppe.

flight attendant n Flugbegleiter der (-in die).

flimsy ['flɪmzɪ] adj leicht.

fling [flɪŋ] (pt & pp flung) vt schleudern.

flint [flɪnt] n (of lighter) Feuerstein der.

flip-flop [flɪp-] n (Br) Plastiksandale die.

flipper ['flɪpə'] n (Br : of swimmer) Schwimmflosse die.

flirt [flɜːt] vi : to ~ (with sb) (mit jm) flirten.

float [fləʊt] n (for swimming) Schwimmkork der ; (for fishing) Schwimmer der ; (in procession) Festwagen der ; (drink) Limonade mit einer Kugel Speiseeis. ◆ vi treiben.

flock [flɒk] n (of birds) Schwarm der ; (of sheep) Herde die. ◆ vi (people) strömen.

flood [flʌd] n Überschwemmung die. ◆ vt überschwem-

men. ◆ vi (river) über die Ufer treten.

floodlight ['flʌdlaɪt] n Flutlicht das.

floor [flɔː'] n Boden der ; (storey) Stock der ; (of nightclub) Tanzfläche die.

floorboard ['flɔːbɔːd] n Diele die.

floor show n Revue die.

flop [flɒp] n (inf : failure) Flop der.

floppy disk ['flɒpɪ-] n Diskette die.

floral ['flɔːrəl] adj (pattern) Blumen-, geblümt.

Florida Keys ['flɒrɪdə-] npl Inselkette vor der Küste Floridas.

ℹ️ FLORIDA KEYS

Eine Kette kleiner Inseln vor der Südküste Floridas, die sich über mehr als 150 km hinzieht. Zu der Inselkette gehören auch die beliebten Ferienziele „Key West" und „Key Largo". Die Inseln sind durch den „Overseas Highway", ein Netz von Straßen und Brücken, miteinander verbunden.

---

florist's ['flɒrɪsts] n (shop) Blumenladen der.

flour ['flaʊə'] n Mehl das.

flow [fləʊ] n Fluss der. ◆ vi fließen.

flower ['flaʊə'] n Blume die.

flowerbed ['flaʊəbed] n Blumenbeet das.

flowerpot ['flaʊəpɒt] n Blumentopf der.

flown [fləʊn] pp → fly.

fl oz abbr = fluid ounce.

flu [fluː] n Grippe die.

fluent ['fluːənt] adj fließend ; she speaks ~ German sie spricht fließend Deutsch.

fluff [flʌf] n (on clothes) Fussel die.

fluid ounce ['fluːɪd-] n = 0,0284 Liter.

flume [fluːm] n Wasserbahn die.

flung [flʌŋ] pt & pp → **fling**.

flunk [flʌŋk] vt (Am : inf : exam) verhauen.

fluorescent [fluəˈresənt] adj fluoreszierend.

flush [flʌʃ] vt spülen. ◆ vi : the toilet won't ~ die Spülung funktioniert nicht.

flute [fluːt] n Querflöte die.

fly [flaɪ] (pt flew, pp flown) n (insect) Fliege die ; (of trousers) Hosenschlitz der. ◆ vt fliegen ; (airline) fliegen mit. ◆ vi fliegen ; (flag) wehen.

fly-drive n Fly-drive Urlaub der.

flying ['flaɪɪŋ] n Fliegen das.

flyover ['flaɪˌəʊvə'] n (Br) Flyover der, Straßenüberführung die.

flypaper ['flaɪˌpeɪpə'] n Fliegenfänger der.

flysheet ['flaɪʃiːt] n Überzelt das.

FM n ≃ UKW.

foal [fəʊl] n Fohlen das.

foam [fəʊm] n Schaum der ; (foam rubber) Schaumstoff der.

focus ['fəʊkəs] n Brennpunkt der. ◆ vi : to ~ on sthg (with camera) die Kamera scharf auf etw (A) einstellen ; in ~ scharf ; out of ~ unscharf.

fog [fɒg] n Nebel der.

fogbound ['fɒgbaʊnd] adj (airport) wegen Nebel geschlossen.

foggy ['fɒgɪ] adj neblig.

fog lamp n Nebelscheinwerfer der.

foil [fɔɪl] n (thin metal) Folie die.

fold [fəʊld] n Falte die. ◆ vt falten ; (wrap) einwickeln ; to ~ one's arms die Arme verschränken. ▪ **fold up** vi (chair, bed, bicycle) sich zusammenklappen lassen.

folder ['fəʊldə'] n Mappe die.

foliage ['fəʊlɪɪdʒ] n Laub das.

folk [fəʊk] npl (people) Leute pl. ◆ n : ~ (music) (popular) Folk der ; (traditional) Volksmusik die. ▪ **folks** npl (inf : relatives) Leute pl.

follow ['fɒləʊ] vt folgen (+D) ; (with eyes) mit den Augen folgen (+D) ; (news, fashion) verfolgen. ◆ vi folgen ; as ~s wie folgt. ▪ **follow on** vi (come later) später folgen.

following ['fɒləʊɪŋ] adj folgend. ◆ prep nach.

follow on call n in Telefonzelle, weiterer Anruf, um die eingeworfene Münze zu verbrauchen.

fond [fɒnd] adj : to be ~ of gern haben.

fondue ['fɒnduː] n Fondue das.

food [fuːd] n Essen das ; (for animals) Futter das.

food poisoning [-ˌpɔɪznɪŋ] n Lebensmittelvergiftung die.

food processor [-ˌprəʊsesə'] n Küchenmaschine die.

foodstuffs ['fu:dstʌfs] *npl* Nahrungsmittel *pl.*

fool [fu:l] *n* (*idiot*) Dummkopf *der* ; (*pudding*) Cremespeise aus Sahne und Obst. ◆ *vt* irreführen.

foolish ['fu:lɪʃ] *adj* dumm.

foot [fut] (*pl* feet) *n* Fuß *der* ; by ~ zu Fuß ; on ~ zu Fuß.

football ['futbɔ:l] *n* (*Br*) Fußball *der* ; (*Am* : *American football*) Football *der* ; (*Am* : *in American football*) Ball *der.*

footballer ['futbɔ:lə'] *n* (*Br*) Fußballer *der* (-in *die*).

football pitch *n* (*Br*) Fußballfeld *das.*

footbridge ['futbrɪdʒ] *n* Fußgängerbrücke *die.*

footpath ['futpɑ:θ, *pl* -pɑ:ðz] *n* Fußweg *der.*

footprint ['futprɪnt] *n* Fußabdruck *der.*

footstep ['futstep] *n* Schritt *der.*

footwear ['futweə'] *n* Schuhwerk *das.*

for [fɔ:'] *prep* 1. (*expressing purpose, reason, destination*) für ; this book is ~ you dieses Buch ist für dich/Sie ; a ticket ~ Manchester eine Fahrkarte nach Manchester ; a town famous ~ its wine eine Stadt, die für ihren Wein bekannt ist ; ~ this reason aus diesem Grund ; a cure ~ sore throats ein Mittel gegen Halsschmerzen ; what did you do that ~? wozu hast du das getan? ; what's it ~? wofür ist das? ; to go ~ a walk spazieren gehen ; '~ sale' 'zu verkaufen'.

2. (*during*) seit ; I've lived here ~ ten years ich lebe seit zehn Jahren hier ; we talked ~ hours wir redeten stundenlang.

3. (*by, before*) für ; be there ~ 8 p.m. sei um 8 Uhr abends da ; I'll do it ~ tomorrow ich mache es bis morgen.

4. (*on the occasion of*) zu ; I got socks ~ Christmas ich habe Socken zu Weihnachten bekommen ; what's ~ dinner? was gibt's zum Abendessen?

5. (*on behalf of*) für ; to do sthg ~ sb etw für jn tun.

6. (*with time and space*) für ; there's no room ~ it dafür ist kein Platz ; to have time ~ sthg für etw Zeit haben.

7. (*expressing distance*) : we drove ~ miles wir fuhren meilenweit ; road works ~ 20 miles Straßenarbeiten auf 20 Meilen.

8. (*expressing price*) für ; I bought it ~ five pounds ich kaufte es für fünf Pfund.

9. (*expressing meaning*) : what's the German ~ 'boy'? wie heißt 'Junge' auf Deutsch?

10. (*with regard to*) für ; it's warm ~ November es ist warm für November ; it's easy ~ you es ist leicht für dich ; it's too far ~ us to walk zum Gehen ist es für uns zu weit.

forbid [fə'bɪd] (*pt* -bade [-'beɪd], *pp* -bidden) *vt* verbieten ; to ~ sb to do sthg jm verbieten, etw zu tun.

forbidden [fə'bɪdn] *adj* verboten.

force [fɔ:s] *n* Kraft *die* ; (*violence*) Gewalt *die.* ◆ *vt* (*physically*) zwingen ; (*lock, door*) auflbrechen ; **to ~ sb to do sthg** jn zwingen, etw zu tun ; **to ~ one's way through** sich gewaltsam einen Weg bahnen ; **the ~s** die Streitkräfte.

ford [fɔːd] n Furt *die*.

forecast ['fɔːkɑːst] n Vorhersage *die*.

forecourt ['fɔːkɔːt] n Vorhof *der*.

forefinger ['fɔː,fɪŋgə'] n Zeigefinger *der*.

foreground ['fɔːgraʊnd] n Vordergrund *der*.

forehead ['fɔːhed] n Stirn *die*.

foreign ['fɒrən] adj ausländisch, Auslands- ; **~ country** Ausland *das* ; **~ language** Fremdsprache *die*.

foreign currency n Devisen *pl*.

foreigner ['fɒrənə'] n Ausländer *der* (-in *die*).

foreign exchange n Devisen *pl*.

Foreign Secretary n *(Br)* Außenminister *der* (-in *die*).

foreman ['fɔːmən] *(pl* -men [-mən]*)* n Vorarbeiter *der*.

forename ['fɔːneɪm] n *(fml)* Vorname *der*.

foresee [fɔː'siː] *(pt* -saw [-'sɔː], *pp* -seen [-'siːn]*)* vt voraussehen.

forest ['fɒrɪst] n Wald *der*.

forever [fə'revə'] adv ewig ; *(continually)* ständig.

forgave [fə'geɪv] *pt →* forgive.

forge [fɔːdʒ] vt *(copy)* fälschen.

forgery ['fɔːdʒərɪ] n Fälschung *die*.

forget [fə'get] *(pt* -got, *pp* -gotten*)* vt & vi vergessen ; **to ~ about sthg** etw vergessen ; **to ~ how to do sthg** etw verlernen ; **to ~ to do sthg** vergessen, etw zu tun ; **~ it!** vergiss es!

forgetful [fə'getfʊl] adj vergesslich.

forgive [fə'gɪv] *(pt* -gave, *pp* -given [-'gɪvn]*)* vt vergeben ; **to ~ sb for sthg** jm etw vergeben.

forgot [fə'gɒt] *pt →* forget.

forgotten [fə'gɒtn] *pp →* forget.

fork [fɔːk] n Gabel *die* ; *(of road, path)* Gabelung *die*. ▨ **forks** *npl (of bike, motorbike)* Gabel *die*.

form [fɔːm] n *(type, shape)* Form *die* ; *(piece of paper)* Formular *das* ; *(SCH)* Klasse *die*. ◆ vt bilden. ◆ vi sich bilden ; **off ~** nicht in Form ; **on ~** in Form ; **to ~ part of** einen Teil bilden von.

formal ['fɔːml] adj förmlich ; *(occasion, clothes)* festlich.

formality [fɔː'mælətɪ] n Formalität *die* ; **it's just a ~** das ist eine reine Formalität.

format ['fɔːmæt] n Format *das*.

former ['fɔːmə'] adj ehemalig ; *(first)* früher. ◆ pron : **the ~** der/die/das erstere.

formerly ['fɔːməlɪ] adv früher.

formula ['fɔːmjʊlə] *(pl* -as OR -ae [-iː]*)* n Formel *die*.

fort [fɔːt] n Fort *das*.

forthcoming [fɔːθ'kʌmɪŋ] adj *(future)* bevorstehend.

fortieth ['fɔːtɪɪθ] num vierzigste(-r) (-s) ; *→* sixth.

fortnight ['fɔːtnaɪt] n (Br) vierzehn Tage pl.

fortunate ['fɔːtʃnət] adj glücklich ; **to be ~** Glück haben.

fortunately ['fɔːtʃnətlɪ] adv glücklicherweise.

fortune ['fɔːtʃuːn] n (money) Vermögen das ; (luck) Glück das ; **it costs a ~** (inf) es kostet ein Vermögen.

forty ['fɔːtɪ] num vierzig ; → **six.**

forward ['fɔːwəd] adv (move, lean) nach vorn. ◆ vt (letter, goods) nachlsenden ; **to look ~ to** sich freuen auf (+A).

forwarding address ['fɔːwədɪŋ-] n Nachsendeadresse die.

fought [fɔːt] pt & pp → **fight.**

foul [faul] adj (unpleasant) ekelhaft. ◆ n Foul das.

found [faund] pt & pp → **find.** ◆ vt gründen.

foundation (cream) [faun-'deɪʃn-] n Make-up das.

foundations [faun'deɪʃnz] npl Fundament das.

fountain ['fauntɪn] n Brunnen der.

fountain pen n Füllfederhalter der.

four [fɔː'] num vier ; → **six.**

four-star (petrol) n Super das.

fourteen [,fɔː'tiːn] num vierzehn ; → **six.**

fourteenth [,fɔː'tiːnθ] num vierzehnte(-r) (-s) ; → **sixth.**

fourth [fɔːθ] num vierte(-r) (-s) ; → **sixth.**

four-wheel drive n (car) Geländewagen der.

fowl [faul] (pl fowl) n Geflügel der.

fox [fɒks] n Fuchs der.

foyer ['fɔɪeɪ] n Foyer das.

fraction ['frækʃn] n (small amount) Bruchteil der ; (in maths) Bruch der.

fracture ['fræktʃə'] n Bruch der. ◆ vt brechen.

fragile ['frædʒaɪl] adj zerbrechlich.

fragment ['frægmənt] n Bruchstück das.

fragrance ['freɪgrəns] n Duft der.

frail [freɪl] adj gebrechlich.

frame [freɪm] n Rahmen der ; (of glasses) Gestell das. ◆ vt einlrahmen.

France [frɑːns] n Frankreich nt.

frank [fræŋk] adj offen.

frankfurter ['fræŋkfɜːtə'] n Frankfurter Würstchen das.

frankly ['fræŋklɪ] adv (to be honest) ehrlich gesagt.

frantic ['fræntɪk] adj (person) außer sich ; (activity, pace) hektisch.

fraud [frɔːd] n (crime) Betrug der.

freak [friːk] adj anormal. ◆ n (inf : fanatic) Freak der.

freckles ['freklz] npl Sommersprossen pl.

free [friː] adj frei. ◆ vt (prisoner) befreien. ◆ adv (without paying) umsonst, gratis ; **for ~** umsonst, gratis ; **~ of charge** umsonst, gratis ; **to be ~ to do sthg** etw tun können.

freedom ['friːdəm] n Freiheit die.

freefone ['fri:fəʊn] adj (Br) : a ~ number Anruf der zum Nulltarif.

free gift n Werbegeschenk das.

free house n (Br) brauereiunabhängiges Wirtshaus.

free kick n Freistoß der.

freelance ['fri:lɑ:ns] adj freiberuflich.

freely ['fri:lɪ] adv frei.

free period n (SCH) Freistunde die.

freepost ['fri:pəʊst] n gebührenfreie Sendung ; 'freepost' 'Gebühr zahlt Empfänger'.

free-range adj (eggs) von Hühnern aus Bodenhaltung.

free time n Freizeit die.

freeway ['fri:weɪ] n (Am) Autobahn die.

freeze [fri:z] (pt froze, pp frozen) vt einfrieren. ◆ vi gefrieren. ◆ v impers : it's freezing es friert.

freezer ['fri:zə] n (deep freeze) Tiefkühltruhe die, Gefrierschrank der ; (part of fridge) Gefrierfach das.

freezing ['fri:zɪŋ] adj eiskalt.

freezing point n Gefrierpunkt der.

freight [freɪt] n (goods) Fracht die.

French [frentʃ] adj französisch. ◆ n (language) Französisch das. ◆ npl : the ~ die Franzosen pl.

French bean n grüne Bohne.

French bread n Baguette die.

French dressing n (in UK) Vinaigrette die ; (in US) French Dressing das.

French fries npl Pommes frites pl.

Frenchman ['frentʃmən] (pl -men [-mən]) n Franzose der.

French toast n arme Ritter pl.

French windows npl Verandatür die.

Frenchwoman ['frentʃ,wʊmən] (pl -women [-,wɪmɪn]) n Französin die.

frequency ['fri:kwənsɪ] n Frequenz die.

frequent ['fri:kwənt] adj häufig.

frequently ['fri:kwəntlɪ] adv häufig.

fresh [freʃ] adj frisch ; (new, recent) neu ; ~ **water** Süßwasser das ; **to get some ~ air** an die frische Luft gehen.

fresh cream n Sahne die.

freshen ['freʃn] : **freshen up** vi sich frisch machen.

freshly ['freʃlɪ] adv frisch.

fresh orange (juice) n frischer Orangensaft.

Fri (abbr of Friday) Fr.

Friday ['fraɪdɪ] n Freitag der ; → **Saturday**.

fridge [frɪdʒ] n Kühlschrank der.

fried egg [fraɪd-] n Spiegelei das.

fried rice [fraɪd-] n gebratener Reis.

friend [frend] n Freund der (-in die) ; **to be ~s with sb** mit jm befreundet sein ; **to make ~s with sb** mit jm Freundschaft schließen.

friendly ['frendlɪ] adj freundlich ; **to be ~ with sb** mit jm befreundet sein.

friendship ['frendʃip] *n* Freundschaft *die*.

fries [fraiz] = **French fries**.

fright [frait] *n* Furcht *die* ; **to give sb a ~** jn erschrecken.

frighten ['fraitn] *vt* Angst machen (+D), erschrecken.

frightened ['fraitnd] *adj* : **to be ~ (of)** Angst haben (vor (+D)).

frightening ['fraitnɪŋ] *adj* beängstigend.

frightful ['fraitful] *adj* fürchterlich.

frilly ['frɪlɪ] *adj* mit Rüschen.

fringe [frɪndʒ] *n* (*Br* : *of hair*) Pony *der* ; (*of clothes, curtain etc*) Fransen *pl*.

frisk [frɪsk] *vt* durchsuchen.

fritter ['frɪtə^r] *n* Ausgebackene *das*, *in Pfannkuchenteig getauchtes, frittiertes Obst oder Gemüse*.

fro [frəʊ] *adv* → **to**.

frog [frɒg] *n* Frosch *der*.

from [frɒm] *prep* **1.** (*expressing origin, source*) von ; **where did you get that ~?** woher hast du das? ; **I'm ~ England** ich bin aus England ; **I bought it ~ a supermarket** ich habe es in einem Supermarket gekauft ; **the train ~ Manchester** der Zug aus Manchester.
2. (*expressing removal, deduction*) von ; **away ~ home** weg von zu Hause ; **to take sthg (away) ~ sb** jm etw wegnehmen ; **10% will be deducted ~ the total** es wird 10% von der Gesamtsumme abgezogen.
3. (*expressing distance*) von ; **five miles ~ London** fünf Meilen von London entfernt ; **it's not**

far **~ here** es ist nicht weit von hier.
4. (*expressing position*) von ; **here you can see the valley** von hier aus kann man das Tal sehen.
5. (*expressing starting time*) von... an ; **open ~ nine to five** von neun bis fünf geöffnet ; **~ next year** ab nächstem Jahr.
6. (*expressing change*) von ; **the price has gone up ~ £1 to £2** der Preis ist von 1 auf 2 Pfund gestiegen.
7. (*expressing range*) : **tickets cost ~ £10** Karten gibt es ab 10 Pfund ; **it could take ~ two to six months** es könnte zwischen zwei und sechs Monaten dauern.
8. (*as a result of*) von ; **I'm tired ~ walking** ich bin vom Gehen müde ; **to suffer ~ asthma** an Asthma leiden.
9. (*expressing protection*) vor ; **sheltered ~ the wind** vor dem Wind geschützt.
10. (*in comparisons*) : **different ~** anders als.

fromage frais [,frɒmɑːʒ'frei] *n* Sahnequark *der*.

front [frʌnt] *adj* Vorder-, vordere(-r) (-s). ◆ *n* Vorderteil *das* ; (*of weather*) Front *die* ; (*by the sea*) Promenade *die* ; **in ~** vorne ; **in ~ of** vor (+D).

front door *n* (*of house*) Haustür *die* ; (*of flat*) Wohnungstür *die*.

frontier [frʌn'tɪə^r] *n* Grenze *die*.

front page *n* Titelseite *die*.

front seat *n* Vordersitz *der*.

frost [frɒst] n (on ground) Reif der ; (cold weather) Frost der.

frosty ['frɒstɪ] adj frostig.

froth [frɒθ] n Schaum der.

frown [fraʊn] n Stirnrunzeln das. ◆ vi die Stirn runzeln.

froze [frəʊz] pt → freeze.

frozen ['frəʊzn] pp → freeze. ◆ adj gefroren ; (food) tiefgekühlt, Gefrier- ; I'm ~ mir ist eiskalt.

fruit [fru:t] n Obst das ; (variety of fruit) Frucht die ; ~s of the forest Waldbeeren pl.

fruit cake n englischer Kuchen.

fruiterer ['fru:tərə'] n (Br) Obsthändler der.

fruit juice n Fruchtsaft der.

fruit machine n (Br) Spielautomat der.

fruit salad n Obstsalat der.

frustrating [frʌ'streɪtɪŋ] adj frustrierend.

frustration [frʌ'streɪʃn] n Frustration die.

fry [fraɪ] vt braten.

frying pan ['fraɪɪŋ-] n Bratpfanne die.

ft abbr = foot, feet.

fudge [fʌdʒ] n weiches Bonbon aus Milch, Zucker und Butter.

fuel [fjʊəl] n Kraftstoff der.

fuel pump n Zapfsäule die.

fulfil [fʊl'fɪl] vt (Br) erfüllen ; (role) ausfüllen.

fulfill [fʊl'fɪl] (Am) = fulfil.

full [fʊl] adj & adv voll ; I'm ~ (up) ich bin satt ; ~ of voll von, voller ; in ~ vollständig.

full board n Vollpension die.

full-cream milk n Vollmilch die.

full-length adj (skirt, dress) lang.

full moon n Vollmond der.

full stop n Punkt der.

full-time adj ganztägig, Ganztags-. ◆ adv ganztags.

fully ['fʊlɪ] adv ganz.

fully-licensed adj mit Schankerlaubnis.

fumble ['fʌmbl] vi wühlen.

fun [fʌn] n Spaß der ; it's good - es macht Spaß ; for ~ aus Spaß ; to have ~ sich amüsieren ; to make ~ of sich lustig machen über (+A).

function ['fʌŋkʃn] n Funktion die ; (formal event) Veranstaltung der. ◆ vi funktionieren.

fund [fʌnd] n (of money) Fonds der. ◆ vt finanzieren. ■ funds npl Geldmittel pl.

fundamental [ˌfʌndə'mentl] adj Grund-, grundlegend.

funeral ['fju:nərəl] n Beerdigung die.

funfair ['fʌnfeə'] n Jahrmarkt der.

funky ['fʌŋkɪ] adj (inf: music) funky.

funnel ['fʌnl] n (for pouring) Trichter der ; (on ship) Schornstein der.

funny ['fʌnɪ] adj komisch ; I feel ~ (ill) mir ist (ganz) komisch.

fur [fɜ:'] n Pelz der.

fur coat n Pelzmantel der.

furious ['fjʊərɪəs] adj wütend.

furnished ['fɜ:nɪʃt] adj möbliert.

furnishings ['fɜ:nɪʃɪŋz] npl Einrichtungsgegenstände pl.

furniture ['fɜ:nɪtʃə'] n Möbel pl ; **a piece of** ~ ein Möbelstück.

furry ['fɜ:rɪ] adj (animal) mit dichtem Fell ; (toy, material) Plüsch-.

further ['fɜ:ðə'] compar → **far**. ◆ adv weiter. ◆ adj weitere(-r) (-s) ; **until ~ notice** bis auf weiteres ; **would you like anything ~?** sonst noch etwas?

furthermore [,fɜ:ðə'mɔ:'] adv außerdem.

furthest ['fɜ:ðɪst] superl → **far**. ◆ adj am weitesten entfernt. ◆ adv am weitesten.

fuse [fju:z] n (of plug) Sicherung die ; (on bomb) Zündschnur die. ◆ vi (plug, device) durchlbrennen.

fuse box n Sicherungskasten der.

fuss [fʌs] n Theater das.

fussy ['fʌsɪ] adj (person) pingelig.

future ['fju:tʃə'] n Zukunft die. ◆ adj künftig ; **in ~** in Zukunft.

G

g (abbr of gram) g.

gable ['geɪbl] n Giebel der.

gadget ['gædʒɪt] n Gerät das.

Gaelic ['geɪlɪk] n Gälisch das.

gag [gæg] n (inf : joke) Gag der.

gain [geɪn] vt (get more of) gewinnen ; (achieve) erzielen ; (victory) erringen ; (subj : clock, watch) vorlgehen. ◆ vi (get benefit) profitieren. ◆ n Gewinn der ; **to ~ weight** zulnehmen.

gale [geɪl] n Sturm der.

gallery ['gælərɪ] n (for art etc) Galerie die ; (at theatre) dritter Rang.

gallon ['gælən] n (in UK) = 4,546 l, Gallone die ; (in US) = 3,78 l, Gallone.

gallop ['gæləp] vi galoppieren.

gamble ['gæmbl] n Risiko das. ◆ vi (bet money) (um Geld) spielen.

gambling ['gæmblɪŋ] n Glücksspiel das.

game [geɪm] n Spiel das ; (wild animals, meat) Wild das. ▪ **games** n (SCH) Sport der. ◆ npl (sporting event) Spiele pl.

gammon ['gæmən] n geräucherter Schinken.

gang [gæŋ] n (of criminals) Bande die ; (of friends) Clique die.

gangster ['gæŋstə'] n Gangster der.

gangway ['gæŋweɪ] n (for ship) Gangway die ; (Br : in aeroplane, theatre) Gang der.

gaol [dʒeɪl] (Br) = **jail**.

gap [gæp] n Lücke die ; (of time) Pause die ; (difference) Unterschied der.

garage ['gærɑ:ʒ, 'gærɪdʒ] n (for keeping car) Garage die ; (Br : for petrol) Tankstelle die ; (for repairs) Autowerkstatt die.

garbage ['gɑ:bɪdʒ] n (Am) Müll der.

garbage can n (Am) Mülleimer der.

garbage truck n (Am) Müllwagen der.

garden ['gɑ:dn] n Garten der. ◆ vi im Garten arbeiten.

▓ **gardens** npl *(public park)* Anlagen pl.

garden centre n Gartencenter das.

gardener ['gɑːdnəʳ] n Gärtner der (-in die).

gardening ['gɑːdnɪŋ] n Gartenarbeit die.

garden peas npl Erbsen pl.

garlic ['gɑːlɪk] n Knoblauch der.

garlic bread n Knoblauchbaguette das.

garlic butter n Knoblauchbutter die.

garment ['gɑːmənt] n Kleidungsstück das.

garnish ['gɑːnɪʃ] n *(herbs, vegetables)* Garnierung die ; *(sauce)* Soße die. ◆ vt garnieren.

gas [gæs] n Gas das ; *(Am : petrol)* Benzin das.

gas cooker n *(Br)* Gasherd der.

gas cylinder n Gasflasche die.

gas fire n *(Br)* Gasofen der.

gasket ['gæskɪt] n Dichtung die.

gas mask n Gasmaske die.

gasoline ['gæsəliːn] n *(Am)* Benzin das.

gasp [gɑːsp] vi *(in shock, surprise)* nach Luft schnappen.

gas pedal n *(Am)* Gaspedal das.

gas station n *(Am)* Tankstelle die.

gas stove *(Br)* = **gas cooker**.

gas tank n *(Am)* Benzintank der.

gasworks ['gæswɜːks] *(pl* **gasworks**) n Gaswerk das.

gate [geɪt] n Tor das ; *(at airport)* Flugsteig der.

gâteau ['gætəʊ] *(pl* -x [-z]) n *(Br)* Torte die.

gateway ['geɪtweɪ] n *(entrance)* Tor das.

gather ['gæðəʳ] vt sammeln ; *(understand)* an|nehmen. ◆ vi *(come together)* sich versammeln ; **to ~ speed** schneller werden.

gaudy ['gɔːdɪ] adj grell.

gauge [geɪdʒ] n *(for measuring)* Messgerät das ; *(of railway track)* Spurweite die. ◆ vt *(calculate)* ab|schätzen.

gauze [gɔːz] n Gaze die.

gave [geɪv] pt → **give**.

gay [geɪ] adj *(homosexual)* schwul.

gaze [geɪz] vi : **to ~ at** an|starren (+A).

GB *(abbr of Great Britain)* GB.

GCSE n Abschlussprüfung in der Schule, die meist mit 16 Jahren abgelegt wird.

ⓘ GCSE

Das „GCSE" (kurz für „General Certificate of Secondary Education") wurde 1986 in Großbritannien eingeführt und ersetzt die bis dahin üblichen „O level"-Prüfungen. Es handelt sich um Schulabschlussprüfungen in verschiedenen Fächern, die im Alter von 15 oder 16 Jahren abgelegt werden müssen. Will der Schüler eine weiterführende Schule besuchen und die „A level"-Prüfungen machen, muss er sie in mindestens 5 Schulfächern ablegen. Im Gegensatz zu den „O levels" fließen beim GCSE neben dem Prüfungsergebnis auch die im Laufe des Schuljahres erzielten Ergebnisse in die Endnote mit ein.

gear [gɪə'] n (wheel) Gangschaltung die ; (speed) Gang der ; (equipment, clothes) Sachen pl ; **is the car in ~?** ist der Gang eingelegt? ; **to change ~** schalten.

gearbox ['gɪəbɒks] n Getriebe das.

gear lever n Schalthebel der.

gear shift (Am) = **gear lever**.

gear stick (Br) = **gear lever**.

geese [giːs] pl → **goose**.

gel [dʒel] n Gel das.

gelatine [ˌdʒeləˈtiːn] n Gelatine die.

gem [dʒem] n Juwel das.

Gemini ['dʒemɪnaɪ] n Zwillinge pl.

gender ['dʒendə'] n Geschlecht das.

general ['dʒenərəl] adj allgemein. ◆ n General der ; **in ~** im Allgemeinen.

general anaesthetic n Vollnarkose die.

general election n allgemeine Wahlen.

generally ['dʒenərəlɪ] adv (usually) normalerweise ; (by most people) allgemein.

general practitioner [-præk-ˈtɪʃənə'] n praktischer Arzt (praktische Ärztin).

general store n Gemischtwarenhandlung die.

generate ['dʒenəreɪt] vt erzeugen.

generation [ˌdʒenəˈreɪʃn] n Generation die.

generator ['dʒenəreɪtə'] n Generator der.

generosity [ˌdʒenəˈrɒsətɪ] n Großzügigkeit die.

generous ['dʒenərəs] adj großzügig.

Geneva [dʒɪˈniːvə] n Genf nt.

genitals ['dʒenɪtlz] npl Geschlechtsteile pl.

genius ['dʒiːnjəs] n Genie das.

gentle ['dʒentl] adj sanft.

gentleman ['dʒentlmən] (pl -men [-mən]) n (man) Herr der ; (well-behaved man) Gentleman der ; **'gentlemen'** (men's toilets) 'Herren'.

gently ['dʒentlɪ] adv sanft.

gents [dʒents] n (Br) Herrentoilette die.

genuine ['dʒenjuɪn] adj echt.

geographical [dʒɪəˈgræfɪkl] adj geografisch.

geography [dʒɪˈɒgrəfɪ] n Geografie die ; (terrain) geografische Gegebenheiten pl.

geology [dʒɪˈɒlədʒɪ] n Geologie die.

geometry [dʒɪˈɒmətrɪ] n Geometrie die.

Georgian ['dʒɔːdʒən] adj (architecture etc) georgianisch (1714-1830).

geranium [dʒɪˈreɪnjəm] n Geranie die.

German ['dʒɜːmən] adj deutsch. ◆ n (person) Deutsche der, die ; (language) Deutsch das ; **in ~** auf Deutsch.

German measles n Röteln pl.

Germany ['dʒɜːmənɪ] n Deutschland nt.

germs [dʒɜːmz] *npl* Bazillen *pl.*

gesture ['dʒestʃə'] *n* Geste *die.*

get [get] (*pt & pp* **got**, *Am pp* **gotten**) *vt* 1. (*obtain*) bekommen ; (*buy*) kaufen ; **she got a job** sie hat eine Stelle gefunden.

2. (*receive*) bekommen ; **I got a book for Christmas** ich habe zu Weihnachten ein Buch bekommen.

3. (*train, plane, bus etc*) nehmen ; **let's ~ a taxi** lass uns ein Taxi nehmen.

4. (*fetch*) holen ; **could you ~ me the manager?** (*in shop*) könnten Sie mir den Geschäftsführer holen? ; (*on phone*) könnten Sie mir den Geschäftsführer geben?

5. (*illness*) bekommen ; **I've got a cold** ich habe eine Erkältung.

6. (*cause to become*) : **to ~ sthg done** etw machen lassen ; **can I ~ my car repaired here?** kann ich mein Auto hier reparieren lassen?

7. (*ask, tell*) : **to ~ sb to do sthg** jn bitten, etw zu tun.

8. (*move*) : **I can't ~ it through the door** ich bekomme es nicht durch die Tür.

9. (*understand*) verstehen.

10. (*time, chance*) haben ; **we didn't ~ the chance to see everything** wir hatten nicht die Gelegenheit, uns alles anzuschauen.

11. (*idea, feeling*) haben ; **I ~ a lot of enjoyment from it** ich habe viel Spaß daran.

12. (*phone*) : **could you ~ the phone?** könntest du ans Telefon gehen?

13. (*in phrases*) : **you ~ a lot of rain here in winter** hier regnet es viel im Winter.

◆ *vi* 1. (*become*) werden ; **it's getting late** es wird spät ; **to ~ lost** sich verirren ; **to ~ ready** fertig werden ; **~ lost!** (*inf*) hau ab!, verschwinde!

2. (*into particular state, position*) : **to ~ into trouble** in Schwierigkeiten geraten ; **how do you ~ to Luton from here?** wie kommt man von hier nach Luton? ; **to ~ into the car** ins Auto einsteigen.

3. (*arrive*) an|kommen ; **when does the train ~ here?** wann kommt der Zug hier an?

4. (*in phrases*) : **to ~ to do sthg** die Gelegenheit haben, etw zu tun.

◆ *aux vb* werden ; **to ~ delayed** aufgehalten werden ; **to ~ killed** getötet werden.

▦ **get back** *vi* (*return*) zurück|kommen.

▦ **get in** *vi* (*arrive*) an|kommen ; (*into car, bus*) ein|steigen.

▦ **get off** *vi* (*leave train, bus*) aus|steigen ; (*leave*) los|gehen ; (*in car*) los|fahren.

▦ **get on** *vi* (*enter train, bus*) ein|steigen ; (*in relationship*) sich verstehen ; (*progress*) : **how are you getting on?** wie kommst du voran?

▦ **get out** *vi* (*of car, bus, train*) aus|steigen.

▦ **get through** *vi* (*on phone*) durch|kommen.

▦ **get up** *vi* auf|stehen.

get-together n (inf) Treffen das.

ghastly ['gɑːstlɪ] adj (inf) schrecklich.

gherkin ['gɜːkɪn] n Gewürzgurke die.

ghetto blaster ['getəʊˌblɑːstəʳ] n (inf) Ghettoblaster der.

ghost [gəʊst] n Geist der.

giant ['dʒaɪənt] adj riesig. ◆ n Riese der.

giblets ['dʒɪblɪts] npl Innereien pl.

giddy ['gɪdɪ] adj schwindlig.

gift [gɪft] n (present) Geschenk das ; (talent) Begabung die.

gifted ['gɪftɪd] adj begabt.

gift shop n Laden mit Geschenkartikeln.

gift voucher n (Br) Geschenkgutschein der.

gig [gɪg] n (inf : concert) Gig der.

gigantic [dʒaɪˈgæntɪk] adj riesig.

giggle ['gɪgl] vi kichern.

gill [dʒɪl] n (measurement) = 0,142 l.

gimmick ['gɪmɪk] n Gimmick der.

gin [dʒɪn] n Gin der ; ~ and tonic Gin Tonic der.

ginger ['dʒɪndʒəʳ] n Ingwer der. ◆ adj (colour) rotblond.

ginger ale n Gingerale das.

ginger beer n Ingwerbier das.

gingerbread ['dʒɪndʒəbred] n Pfefferkuchen der.

gipsy ['dʒɪpsɪ] n Zigeuner der (-in die).

giraffe [dʒɪˈrɑːf] n Giraffe die.

girdle ['gɜːdl] n Hüfthalter der.

girl [gɜːl] n Mädchen das.

girlfriend ['gɜːlfrend] n Freundin die.

girl guide n (Br) Pfadfinderin die.

girl scout (Am) = girl guide.

giro ['dʒaɪrəʊ] n (system) Giro das.

give [gɪv] (pt gave, pp given ['gɪvn]) vt geben ; (speech) halten ; (attention, time) widmen ; to ~ sb sthg jm etw geben ; (as present) jm etw schenken ; to ~ sb a look jm ansehen ; to ~ sb a push jm einen Schubs geben ; to ~ sb a kiss jm einen Kuss geben ; ~ or take mehr oder weniger ; '~ way' 'Vorfahrt beachten'. ■ **give away** vt sep (get rid of) weggeben ; (reveal) verraten. ■ **give back** vt sep zurückgeben. ■ **give in** vi nachgeben. ■ **give off** vt fus abgeben. ■ **give out** vt sep (distribute) austeilen. ■ **give up** vt sep & vi aufgeben.

glacier ['glæsjəʳ] n Gletscher der.

glad [glæd] adj froh ; to be ~ to do sthg sich freuen, etw zu tun.

gladly ['glædlɪ] adv (willingly) gern.

glamorous ['glæmərəs] adj glamourös.

glance [glɑːns] n Blick der. ◆ vi : to ~ at einen Blick werfen auf (+A).

gland [glænd] n Drüse die.

glandular fever ['glændjʊlə-] n Drüsenfieber das.

glare [gleəʳ] vi (sun, light) blenden ; (person) : to ~ at böse ansehen.

glass [glɑːs] n Glas das. ◆ adj Glas-. ▨ **glasses** npl Brille die.

glassware ['glɑːsweə'] n Glaswaren pl.

glen [glen] n (Scot) enges Tal.

glider ['glaɪdə'] n Segelflugzeug das.

glimpse [glɪmps] vt flüchtig sehen.

glitter ['glɪtə'] vi glitzern.

global warming [,gləʊbl-'wɔːmɪŋ] n die Erwärmung der Erdatmosphäre.

globe [gləʊb] n Globus der.

gloomy ['gluːmɪ] adj düster.

glorious ['glɔːrɪəs] adj (weather, sight) großartig ; (victory, history) glorreich.

glory ['glɔːrɪ] n Ruhm der.

gloss [glɒs] n (shine) Glanz der ; ~ (paint) Lackfarbe die.

glossary ['glɒsərɪ] n Glossar das.

glossy ['glɒsɪ] adj (magazine, photo) Hochglanz-.

glove [glʌv] n Handschuh der.

glove compartment n Handschuhfach das.

glow [gləʊ] n Glühen das. ◆ vi glühen.

glucose ['gluːkəʊs] n Glukose die.

glue [gluː] n Klebstoff der. ◆ vt kleben.

gnat [næt] n Mücke die.

gnaw [nɔː] vt nagen an (+D).

go [gəʊ] (pt went, pp gone, pl goes) vi 1. (move) gehen ; (travel) fahren ; to ~ for a walk spazieren gehen ; I'll ~ and collect the cases ich gehe die Koffer abholen ; to ~ home nach Hause gehen ; to ~ to Austria nach Österreich fahren ; to ~ by bus mit dem Bus fahren ; to ~ shopping einkaufen gehen. 2. (leave) gehen ; (in vehicle) fahren ; when does the bus ~? wann fährt der Bus ab? ; ~ away! geh weg! 3. (become) werden ; she went pale sie wurde bleich ; the milk has gone sour die Milch ist sauer geworden. 4. (expressing future tense) : to be going to do sthg etw tun werden ; it's going to rain tomorrow morgen wird es regnen ; we're going to go to Switzerland wir fahren in die Schweiz. 5. (function) laufen ; (watch) gehen ; the car won't ~ das Auto springt nicht an. 6. (stop working) kaputtlgehen ; the fuse has gone die Sicherung ist herausgesprungen. 7. (time) vergehen. 8. (progress) gehen, laufen ; to ~ well gut gehen. 9. (alarm) loslgehen. 10. (match) zusammenlpassen ; to ~ with passen zu ; red wine doesn't ~ with fish Rotwein passt nicht zu Fisch. 11. (be sold) verkauft werden ; 'everything must ~' 'alles muss weg'. 12. (fit) passen, gehen. 13. (lead) führen ; where does this path ~? wohin führt dieser Weg? 14. (belong) gehören. 15. (in phrases) : to let ~ of sthg (drop) etw losllassen ; to ~ (Am : to take away) zum Mitnehmen ; how long is there to ~ until Christmas? wie lange ist es noch bis Weihnachten?

◆ n 1. *(turn)* : it's your ~ du bist an der Reihe.

2. *(attempt)* Versuch der ; to have a ~ at sthg etw versuchen, etw probieren ; '50p a ~' *(for game)* 'jede Runde 50p'.

■ **go ahead** vi *(begin)* an|fangen, beginnen ; *(take place)* statt|finden ; ~ ahead! bitte!

■ **go back** vi *(return)* zurück|gehen.

■ **go down** vi *(decrease)* sinken ; *(sun)* unter|gehen ; *(tyre)* platt werden.

■ **go down with** vt fus *(inf : illness)* bekommen.

■ **go in** vi hinein|gehen.

■ **go off** vi *(alarm)* los|gehen ; *(go bad)* schlecht werden ; *(light, heating)* aus|gehen.

■ **go on** vi *(happen)* los sein ; *(light, heating)* an|gehen ; *(continue)* : to ~ on doing sthg etw weiter tun ; ~ on! los!

■ **go out** vi aus|gehen ; *(have relationship)* : to ~ out with sb mit jm gehen ; to ~ out for a meal essen gehen ; to ~ out for a walk einen Spaziergang machen.

■ **go over** vt fus *(check)* über|prüfen.

■ **go round** vi *(revolve)* sich drehen.

■ **go through** vt fus *(experience)* durch|machen ; *(spend)* aus|geben ; *(search)* durchsuchen.

■ **go up** vi *(increase)* steigen.

■ **go without** vt fus : to ~ without sthg ohne etw aus|kommen.

goal [gəʊl] n *(SPORT)* Tor das ; *(aim)* Ziel das.

goalkeeper ['gəʊl,kiːpə'] n Torwart der.

goalpost ['gəʊlpəʊst] n Torpfosten der.

goat [gəʊt] n Ziege die.

gob [gɒb] n *(Br : inf : mouth)* Maul das.

god [gɒd] n Gott der (Göttin die). ■ **God** n Gott.

goddaughter ['gɒd,dɔːtə'] n Patentochter die.

godfather ['gɒd,fɑːðə'] n Pate der.

godmother ['gɒd,mʌðə'] n Patin die.

gods [gɒdz] npl : the ~ *(in theatre : Br : inf)* der Olymp.

godson ['gɒdsʌn] n Patensohn der.

goes [gəʊz] → **go**.

goggles ['gɒglz] npl *(for swimming)* Taucherbrille die ; *(for skiing)* Skibrille die.

going ['gəʊɪŋ] adj *(available)* erhältlich ; the ~ rate der übliche Betrag.

go-kart [-kɑːt] n Gokart der.

gold [gəʊld] n Gold das. ◆ adj *(bracelet, watch)* golden.

goldfish ['gəʊldfɪʃ] *(pl gold-fish)* n Goldfisch der.

gold-plated [-'pleɪtɪd] adj vergoldet.

golf [gɒlf] n Golf das.

golf ball n Golfball der.

golf club n *(place)* Golfklub der ; *(equipment)* Golfschläger der.

golf course n Golfplatz der.

golfer ['gɒlfə'] n Golfspieler der (-in die).

gone [gɒn] pp → **go**. ◆ prep *(Br : past)* nach.

good [gʊd] (compar **better**, superl **best**) adj gut; (well-behaved) artig, brav; (thorough) gründlich. ◆ n (moral correctness) Gute das; to have a ~ time sich gut amüsieren; to be ~ at sthg etw gut können; a ~ ten minutes gute zehn Minuten; in ~ time beizeiten; to make ~ sthg (damage, loss) etw wieder gutmachen; for ~ für immer; for the ~ of zum Wohle (+G); it's no ~ (there's no point) es hat keinen Zweck; that's very ~ of you das ist sehr nett von Ihnen; ~ afternoon! guten Tag!; ~ evening! guten Abend!; ~ morning! guten Morgen!; ~ night! gute Nacht! **goods** npl Waren pl.

goodbye [ˌgʊd'baɪ] excl auf Wiedersehen!

Good Friday n Karfreitag der.

good-looking [-'lʊkɪŋ] adj gut aussehend.

goods train [gʊdz-] n Güterzug der.

goose [guːs] (pl **geese**) n Gans die.

gooseberry ['gʊzbərɪ] n Stachelbeere die.

gorge [gɔːdʒ] n Schlucht die.

gorgeous ['gɔːdʒəs] adj (day, meal, countryside) wunderschön; (inf: good-looking): to be ~ toll aussehen.

gorilla [gə'rɪlə] n Gorilla der.

gossip ['gɒsɪp] n Klatsch der. ◆ vi klatschen.

gossip column n Klatschspalte die.

got [gɒt] pt & pp → get.

gotten ['gɒtn] pp (Am) → get.

goujons ['guːdʒɒnz] npl panierte und frittierte Fisch- oder Fleischstreifen.

goulash ['guːlæʃ] n Gulasch das.

gourmet ['gʊəmeɪ] n Feinschmecker der (-in die). ◆ adj (food, restaurant) Feinschmecker-.

govern ['gʌvən] vt regieren.

government ['gʌvnmənt] n Regierung die.

gown [gaʊn] n (dress) Kleid das.

GP abbr = general practitioner.

grab [græb] vt (take hold of) greifen.

graceful ['greɪsfʊl] adj (elegant) anmutig.

grade [greɪd] n (quality) Klasse die; (in exam) Note die; (Am: year at school) Klasse die.

gradient ['greɪdjənt] n (upward) Steigung die; (downward) Gefälle das.

gradual ['grædʒʊəl] adj allmählich.

gradually ['grædʒʊəlɪ] adv allmählich.

graduate [n 'grædʒʊət, vb 'grædʒʊeɪt] n Akademiker der (-in die); (Am: from high school) Schulabgänger der (-in die). ◆ vi die Universität abschließen; (Am: from high school) die Schule abschließen.

graduation [ˌgrædʒʊ'eɪʃn] n (ceremony) Abschlussfeier einer Universität.

graffiti [grə'fiːtɪ] n Graffiti pl.

grain [greɪn] n (seed) Korn das; (crop) Getreide das; (of sand, salt) Körnchen das.

gram [græm] n Gramm das.

grammar ['græmə'] n Grammatik die.

grammar school n (in UK) ≃ Gymnasium das.

gramme [græm] = gram.

gran [græn] n (Br : inf) Oma die.

grand [grænd] adj (impressive) großartig. ♦ n (inf : thousand pounds) tausend Pfund pl; (thousand dollars) tausend Dollar pl.

grandchild ['græntʃaɪld] (pl -children [-,tʃɪldrən]) n Enkelkind das.

granddad ['grændæd] n (inf) Opa der.

granddaughter ['græn,dɔːtə'] n Enkelin die.

grandfather ['grænd,fɑːðə'] n Großvater der.

grandma ['grænmɑː] n (inf) Oma die.

grandmother ['grænd,mʌðə'] n Großmutter die.

grandpa ['grænpɑː] n (inf) Opa der.

grandparents ['grænd,peərənts] npl Großeltern pl.

grandson ['grænsʌn] n Enkel der.

granite ['grænɪt] n Granit der.

granny ['grænɪ] n (inf) Oma die.

grant [grɑːnt] n (POL) Zuschuss der; (for university) Stipendium das. ♦ vt (fml : give) gewähren; **to take sthg for ~ed** etw als selbstverständlich an|sehen; **he takes his wife for ~ed** er weiß

nicht zu schätzen, was seine Frau alles für ihn tut.

grape [greɪp] n Traube die.

grapefruit ['greɪpfruːt] n Grapefruit die, Pampelmuse die.

grapefruit juice n Grapefruitsaft der.

graph [grɑːf] n Kurvendiagramm das.

graph paper n Millimeterpapier das.

grasp [grɑːsp] vt fest|halten; (understand) begreifen.

grass [grɑːs] n Gras das; (lawn) Rasen der; **'keep off the ~'** 'Betreten der Rasenfläche verboten'.

grasshopper ['grɑːs,hɒpə'] n Heuschrecke die.

grate [greɪt] n (of fire) Rost der.

grated ['greɪtɪd] adj gerieben.

grateful ['greɪtfʊl] adj dankbar.

grater ['greɪtə'] n Reibe die.

gratitude ['grætɪtjuːd] n Dankbarkeit die.

gratuity [grə'tjuːɪtɪ] n (fml) Trinkgeld das.

grave¹ [greɪv] adj (mistake) schwer; (news) schlimm; (situation) ernst. ♦ n Grab das.

grave² [grɑːv] adj (accent) grave.

gravel ['grævl] n Kies der.

graveyard ['greɪvjɑːd] n Friedhof der.

gravity ['grævətɪ] n Schwerkraft die.

gravy ['greɪvɪ] n Soße die.

gray [greɪ] (Am) = grey.

graze [greɪz] vt (injure) auf|schürfen.

grease [griːs] n (for machine, tool) Schmiere die ; (animal fat) Fett das.

greaseproof paper ['griːspruːf-] n (Br) Pergamentpapier das.

greasy ['griːsɪ] adj (tools, clothes) schmierig ; (food, skin, hair) fettig.

great [greɪt] adj (large, famous, important) groß ; (very good) großartig ; (that's) ~! (das ist) toll!

Great Britain n Großbritannien nt.

ⓘ **GREAT BRITAIN**

Großbritannien („Great Britain") ist die Bezeichnung für die aus England, Schottland und Wales bestehende Insel. Im Englischen wird sie verkürzt auch „Britain" genannt. Im Gegensatz dazu umfasst der Begriff „United Kingdom" (Vereinigtes Königreich) zusätzlich Nordirland, während der Begriff „British Isles" (die Britischen Inseln) außer Nordirland auch die Irische Republik, die Isle of Man, Orkney, die Shetlandinseln und die Kanalinseln mit einschließt.

great-grandfather n Urgroßvater der.

great-grandmother n Urgroßmutter die.

greatly ['greɪtlɪ] adv sehr.

Greece [griːs] n Griechenland nt.

greed [griːd] n Gier die.

greedy ['griːdɪ] adj gierig.

Greek [griːk] adj griechisch. ◆ n (person) Grieche der (Griechin die) ; (language) Griechisch das.

Greek salad n griechischer Salat.

green [griːn] adj grün. ◆ n (colour) Grün das ; (in village) Gemeindewiese die ; (on golf course) Green der. ▪ **greens** npl (vegetables) grünes Gemüse das.

green beans npl grüne Bohnen pl.

green card n (Br : for car) grüne Versicherungskarte ; (Am : work permit) Arbeitserlaubnis die.

green channel n Ausgang 'nichts zu verzollen' am Flughafen.

greengage ['griːngeɪdʒ] n Reneklode die.

greengrocer's ['griːnˌgrəʊsəz] n (shop) Obst- und Gemüsegeschäft das.

greenhouse ['griːnhaʊs, pl -haʊzɪz] n Gewächshaus das.

greenhouse effect n Treibhauseffekt der.

green light n (fig) grünes Licht.

green pepper n grüner Paprika.

Greens [griːnz] npl : the ~ die Grünen.

green salad n grüner Salat.

greet [griːt] vt grüßen.

greeting ['griːtɪŋ] n Gruß der.

grenade [grəˈneɪd] n Granate die.

grew [gruː] pt → **grow**.

grey [greɪ] *adj* grau. ◆ *n* Grau *das* ; to go ~ grau werden.

greyhound ['greɪhaʊnd] *n* Windhund *der*.

grid [grɪd] *n* Gitter *das* ; (on map etc) Gitternetz *das*.

grief [griːf] *n* Trauer *die* ; to come to ~ scheitern.

grieve [griːv] *vi* trauern.

grill [grɪl] *n* Grill *der*. ◆ *vt* grillen.

grille [grɪl] *n* (AUT) Kühlergrill *der*.

grilled [grɪld] *adj* gegrillt.

grim [grɪm] *adj* (place, news, reality) düster ; (determined) grimmig.

grimace ['grɪməs] *n* Grimasse *die*.

grimy ['graɪmɪ] *adj* verschmutzt.

grin [grɪn] *n* Grinsen *das*. ◆ *vi* grinsen.

grind [graɪnd] (pt & pp ground) *vt* (pepper, coffee) mahlen.

grip [grɪp] *n* Griff *der* ; (of tyres) Profil *das* ; (bag) Reisetasche *die*. ◆ *vt* (hold) fest|halten.

gristle ['grɪsl] *n* Knorpel *der*.

groan [grəʊn] *n* Stöhnen *das*. ◆ *vi* stöhnen ; (complain) sich beklagen.

groceries ['grəʊsərɪz] *npl* Lebensmittel *pl*.

grocer's ['grəʊsəz] *n* (shop) Lebensmittelgeschäft *das*.

grocery ['grəʊsərɪ] *n* (shop) Lebensmittelgeschäft *das*.

groin [grɔɪn] *n* Leiste *die*.

groove [gruːv] *n* Rille *die*.

grope [grəʊp] *vi* (search) tasten.

gross [grəʊs] *adj* (weight, income) brutto.

grossly ['grəʊslɪ] *adv* (extremely) äußerst.

grotty ['grɒtɪ] *adj* (Br : inf) mies.

ground [graʊnd] *pt* & *pp* → **grind**. ◆ *n* Boden *der* ; (SPORT) Platz *der*. ◆ *adj* (coffee) gemahlen. ◆ *vt* : to be ~ed (plane) keine Starterlaubnis erhalten ; (Am : ELEC) geerdet sein. ▪ **grounds** *npl* (of building) Anlagen *pl* ; (of coffee) Satz *der* ; (reason) Grund *der*.

ground floor *n* Erdgeschoss *das*.

groundsheet ['graʊndʃiːt] *n* Bodenplane *die*.

group [gruːp] *n* Gruppe *die*.

grouse [graʊs] *n* (pl grouse) *n* (bird) Moorschneehuhn *das*.

grovel ['grɒvl] *vi* (be humble) kriechen.

grow [grəʊ] (pt grew, pp grown) *vi* wachsen ; (become) werden. ◆ *vt* (plant, crop) anbauen ; (beard) sich (D) wachsen lassen. ▪ **grow up** *vi* erwachsen werden.

growl [graʊl] *vi* (dog) knurren.

grown [grəʊn] *pp* → **grow**.

grown-up *adj* erwachsen. ◆ *n* Erwachsene *der, die*.

growth [grəʊθ] *n* Wachstum *das* ; (MED) Geschwulst *die*.

grub [grʌb] *n* (inf : food) Futter *das*.

grubby ['grʌbɪ] *adj* (inf) schmuddlig.

grudge [grʌdʒ] *n* Abneigung *die*. ◆ *vt* : to ~ sb sthg jm etw neiden ; to have a ~ against sb etw gegen jn haben.

grueling ['gruəlɪŋ] *(Am)* = **gruelling**.

gruelling ['gruəlɪŋ] *adj (Br)* anstrengend.

gruesome ['gru:səm] *adj* grausig.

grumble ['grʌmbl] *vi (complain)* sich beschweren.

grumpy ['grʌmpɪ] *adj (inf)* grantig.

grunt [grʌnt] *vi* grunzen.

guarantee [,gærən'ti:] *n* Garantie *die*. ◆ *vt* garantieren ; *(product)* Garantie geben.

guard [gɑ:d] *n (of prisoner etc)* Wärter *der* (-in *die*) ; *(Br : on train)* Schaffner *der* (-in *die*) ; *(protective cover)* Schutz *der*. ◆ *vt* bewachen ; to be on one's ~ auf der Hut sein.

guess [ges] *n* Vermutung *die*. ◆ *vt* erraten ; *vi* raten ; **I ~ (so)** ich denke (schon).

guest [gest] *n* Gast *der*.

guesthouse ['gesthaus, *pl* -haʊzɪz] *n* Pension *die*.

guestroom ['gestrʊm] *n* Gästezimmer *das*.

guidance ['gaɪdəns] *n* Beratung *die*.

guide [gaɪd] *n (for tourists)* Fremdenführer *der* (-in *die*) ; *(guidebook)* Reiseführer *der*. ◆ *vt* führen. ▓ **Guide** *n (Br)* Pfadfinderin *die*.

guidebook ['gaɪdbʊk] *n* Reiseführer *der*.

guide dog *n* Blindenhund *der*.

guided tour ['gaɪdɪd-] *n* Führung *die*.

guidelines ['gaɪdlaɪnz] *npl* Richtlinien *pl*.

guilt [gɪlt] *n* Schuld *die*.

guilty ['gɪltɪ] *adj* schuldig ; *(remorseful)* schuldbewusst ; to be ~ of sthg an etw *(D)* schuldig sein ; to feel ~ ein schlechtes Gewissen haben.

guinea pig ['gɪnɪ-] *n* Meerschweinchen *das*.

guitar [gɪ'tɑ:ʳ] *n* Gitarre *die*.

guitarist [gɪ'tɑ:rɪst] *n* Gitarrist *der* (-in *die*).

gulf [gʌlf] *n (of sea)* Golf *der*.

Gulf War *n* : the ~ der Golfkrieg.

gull [gʌl] *n* Möwe *die*.

gullible ['gʌləbl] *adj* leichtgläubig.

gulp [gʌlp] *n (of drink)* Schluck *der*.

gum [gʌm] *n (chewing gum, bubble gum)* Kaugummi *der* ; *(adhesive)* Klebstoff *der*. ▓ **gums** *npl (in mouth)* Zahnfleisch *das*.

gun [gʌn] *n (pistol)* Pistole *die* ; *(rifle)* Gewehr *das* ; *(cannon)* Kanone *die*.

gunfire ['gʌnfaɪəʳ] *n* Geschützfeuer *das*.

gunshot ['gʌnʃɒt] *n* Schuss *der*.

gust [gʌst] *n* Windstoß *der*.

gut [gʌt] *n (inf : stomach)* Bauch *der*. ▓ **guts** *npl (inf : intestines)* Eingeweide *pl* ; *(courage)* Mut *der*.

gutter ['gʌtəʳ] *n (beside road)* Rinnstein *der* ; *(of house)* Regenrinne *die*.

guy [gaɪ] *n (inf : man)* Typ *der*. ▓ **guys** *npl (Am : inf : people)* : you ~s ihr.

Guy Fawkes Night [-'fɔ:ks-] *n* Nacht des 5. November, in der mit Feuerwerk an den Versuch

Guy Fawkes', das Parlament in die Luft zu sprengen, erinnert wird.

 GUY FAWKES NIGHT

An diesem Tag, dem 5. November (auch „Bonfire Night" genannt), wird alljährlich mit Feuerwerken und Freudenfeuern die rechtzeitige Entdeckung des „Gunpowder Plot" gefeiert. Dabei handelte es sich um eine katholische Verschwörung im Jahre 1605, bei der König James I. und die Parlamentsgebäude in die Luft gesprengt werden sollten. Der Brauch will es, dass die Kinder zu dieser Gelegenheit eine Stoff- oder Strohpuppe basteln, die Guy Fawkes, einen der Verschwörer, verkörpert. Diese wird zum Geldsammeln für Feuerwerkskörper benutzt und dann am 5. November im Freudenfeuer verbrannt.

guy rope n Zeltschnur *die.*

gym [dʒɪm] n *(SCH : building)* Turnhalle *die ; (in health club, hotel)* Fitnessraum *der ; (SCH : lesson)* Turnen *das.*

gymnast ['dʒɪmnæst] n Turner *der* (-in *die*).

gymnastics [dʒɪm'næstɪks] n Turnen *das.*

gym shoes npl Turnschuhe *pl.*

gynaecologist [,gaɪnə'kɒlə-dʒɪst] n Frauenarzt *der* (-ärztin *die*).

gypsy ['dʒɪpsɪ] = **gipsy.**

H *abbr* = **hot, hospital.**

habit ['hæbɪt] n Gewohnheit *die.*

hacksaw ['hæksɔː] n Metallsäge *die.*

had [hæd] *pt & pp* → **have.**

haddock ['hædək] *(pl haddock)* n Schellfisch *der.*

hadn't ['hædnt] = **had not.**

haggis ['hægɪs] n *schottische Spezialität, bestehend aus mit Schafsinnereien gefülltem Schafsmagen, üblicherweise serviert mit Kartoffel- und Kohlrabipüree.*

haggle ['hægl] vi feilschen.

hail [heɪl] n Hagel *der.* ◆ v *impers* hageln.

hailstone ['heɪlstəʊn] n Hagelkorn *das.*

hair [heə] n Haare *pl ; (individual hair)* Haar *das ;* **to have one's ~ cut** sich *(D)* die Haare schneiden lassen.

hairband ['heəbænd] n Haarband *das.*

hairbrush ['heəbrʌʃ] n Haarbürste *die.*

hairclip ['heəklɪp] n Haarklip *der.*

haircut ['heəkʌt] n *(style)* Haarschnitt *der ;* **to have a ~** sich *(D)* die Haare schneiden lassen.

hairdo ['heəduː] *(pl -s)* n Frisur *die.*

hairdresser ['heə,dresə] n Friseur *der* (Friseuse *die*) ; **~'s *(salon)*** Friseursalon *der ;* **to go to the ~'s** zum Friseur gehen.

hairdryer ['heə,draɪə'] *n* Föhn *der*.

hair gel *n* Haargel *das*.

hairgrip ['heəgrɪp] *n* (*Br*) Haarklammer *die*.

hairnet ['heənet] *n* Haarnetz *das*.

hairpin bend ['heəpɪn-] *n* Haarnadelkurve *die*.

hair remover [-rɪ,muːvə'] *n* Enthaarungsmittel *das*.

hair rollers [-'rəʊləz] *npl* Lockenwickler *pl*.

hair slide *n* Haarspange *die*.

hairspray ['heəspreɪ] *n* Haarspray *das*.

hairstyle ['heəstaɪl] *n* Frisur *die*.

hairy ['heərɪ] *adj* haarig.

half [(*Br*) hɑːf, (*Am*) hæf] (*pl* **halves**) *n* Hälfte *die* ; (*of match*) Spielhälfte *die* ; (*half pint*) halbes Pint, ≃ kleines Bier ; (*child's ticket*) Kinderfahrkarte *die*. ◆ *adj* & *adv* halb ; **~ of it** die Hälfte davon ; **four and a ~** viereinhalb ; **~ past seven** halb acht ; **~ as big as** halb so groß wie ; **an hour and a ~** anderthalb Stunden ; **~ an hour** eine halbe Stunde ; **~ a dozen** ein halbes Dutzend.

half board *n* Halbpension *die*.

half-day *n* halber Tag.

half fare *n* halber Fahrpreis.

half portion *n* halbe Portion.

half-price *adj* zum halben Preis.

half term *n* (*Br*) Ferien in der Mitte des Trimesters.

half time *n* Halbzeit *die*.

halfway [hɑːf'weɪ] *adv* auf halbem Wege ; **~ through the holiday** mitten im Urlaub.

halibut ['hælɪbət] (*pl* **halibut**) *n* Heilbutt *der*.

hall [hɔːl] *n* (*of house*) Diele *die*, Flur *der* ; (*large room*) Saal *der* ; (*building*) Halle *die* ; (*country house*) Landsitz *der*.

hallmark ['hɔːlmɑːk] *n* (*on silver, gold*) Stempel *der*.

hallo [hə'ləʊ] = **hello**.

hall of residence *n* Studentenwohnheim *das*.

Halloween [,hæləʊ'iːn] *n* *Abend vor Allerheiligen, an dem sich Kinder oft als Gespenster verkleiden.*

HALLOWEEN

Der 31. Oktober, „Halloween", auch „All Hallows Eve" genannt, ist der Tradition zufolge die Nacht, in der Geister und Hexen umgehen. Die Kinder verkleiden sich, machen die Runde in der Nachbarschaft und spielen „trick or treat" (Trick oder Belohnung). Das heißt, sie drohen einen bösen Streich an, wenn sie keine Belohnung in Form von Süßigkeiten oder Geld bekommen. Es ist auch üblich, Laternen zu basteln, indem man einen Kürbis aushöhlt, eine Kerze hineinsteckt und ein Gesicht in eine Seite schnitzt.

halt [hɔːlt] *vi* anⅼhalten. ◆ *n* : **to come to a ~** zum Stillstand kommen.

halve [(Br) hɑːv, (Am) hæv] vt
halbieren.

halves [(Br) hɑːvz, (Am) hævz]
pl → **half**.

ham [hæm] n Schinken der.

hamburger ['hæmbɜːgə'] n
Hamburger der; (Am : mince)
Hackfleisch das.

hamlet ['hæmlɪt] n kleines
Dorf.

hammer ['hæmə'] n Hammer
der. ◆ vt (nail) einschlagen.

hammock ['hæmək] n Hängematte die.

hamper ['hæmpə'] n Picknick-
korb der.

hamster ['hæmstə'] n Hamster der.

hamstring ['hæmstrɪŋ] n
Kniesehne die.

hand [hænd] n Hand die; (of
clock, watch, dial) Zeiger der; **to
give sb a ~** jm helfen; **to get out
of ~** außer Kontrolle geraten;
written by ~ handgeschrieben;
to arrive with an hour in ~ eine
Stunde zu früh ankommen; **on
the one ~** einerseits; **on the
other ~** andererseits. ▨ **hand
in** vt sep einreichen, abgeben.
▨ **hand out** vt sep austeilen.
▨ **hand over** vt sep (give)
übergeben.

handbag ['hændbæg] n Handtasche die.

handbasin ['hændbeɪsn] n
Waschbecken das.

handbook ['hændbʊk] n
Handbuch das.

handbrake ['hændbreɪk] n
Handbremse die.

hand cream n Handcreme
die.

handcuffs ['hændkʌfs] npl
Handschellen pl.

handful ['hændfʊl] n (amount)
Hand voll die.

handicap ['hændɪkæp] n Behinderung die; (disadvantage)
Handikap das.

handicapped ['hændɪkæpt]
adj behindert. ◆ npl : **the ~** die
Behinderten pl.

handkerchief ['hæŋkətʃɪf] (pl
-chiefs OR **-chieves** [-tʃiːvz])
n Taschentuch das.

handle ['hændl] n Griff der. ◆
vt (touch) anfassen; (situation)
bewältigen; '~ **with care**' 'Vorsicht - zerbrechlich'.

handlebars ['hændlbɑːz] npl
Lenkstange die.

hand luggage n Handgepäck das.

handmade [,hænd'meɪd] adj
handgearbeitet.

handout ['hændaʊt] n (leaflet)
Hand-out die.

handrail ['hændreɪl] n Geländer das.

handset ['hændset] n Hörer
der; '**please replace the ~**' 'bitte
den Hörer auflegen'.

handshake ['hændʃeɪk] n
Händedruck der.

handsome ['hænsəm] adj
(man) gut aussehend.

handstand ['hændstænd] n
Handstand der.

handwriting ['hænd,raɪtɪŋ] n
Handschrift die.

handy ['hændɪ] adj praktisch;
(person) geschickt; **to come in ~**
(inf) nützlich sein; **to have sthg
~** (near) etw zur Hand haben.

hang [hæŋ] (pt & pp **hung**) vt
aufhängen; (execute : pt & pp

hanged) hängen. ◆ *vi* hängen. ◆ *n* : to get the ~ of sthg kapieren. ■ **hang about** *vi (Br : inf)* rumlhängen. ■ **hang around** *(inf)* = **hang about**. ■ **hang down** *vi* herunterlhängen. ■ **hang on** *vi (inf : wait)* warten. ■ **hang out** *vt sep (washing)* auflhängen. ◆ *vi (inf : spend time)* sich herumltreiben. ■ **hang up** *vi (on phone)* aufllegen, einlhängen.

hangar ['hæŋə'] *n* Hangar *der.*

hanger ['hæŋə'] *n* Kleiderbügel *der.*

hang-gliding *n* Drachenfliegen *das.*

hangover ['hæŋ,əʊvə'] *n* Kater *der.*

hankie ['hæŋkɪ] *n (inf)* Taschentuch *das.*

happen ['hæpən] *vi* passieren, geschehen ; **to ~ to do sthg** etw zufällig tun.

happily ['hæpɪlɪ] *adv (luckily)* glücklicherweise.

happiness ['hæpɪnɪs] *n* Glück *das.*

happy ['hæpɪ] *adj* glücklich ; **to be ~ about sthg** mit etw zufrieden sein ; **to be ~ to do sthg** *(willing)* etw gern tun ; **to be ~ with sthg** mit etw zufrieden sein ; **Happy Birthday!** Herzlichen Glückwunsch zum Geburtstag! ; **Happy Christmas!** Fröhliche Weihnachten! ; **Happy New Year!** ein gutes neues Jahr!

happy hour *n (inf)* Happy Hour *die.*

harassment ['hærəsmənt] *n* Belästigung *die.*

harbor ['hɑːbər] *(Am)* = **harbour**.

harbour ['hɑːbə'] *n (Br)* Hafen *der.*

hard [hɑːd] *adj* hart ; *(difficult, strenuous)* schwer. ◆ *adv (work)* hart ; *(listen)* gut ; *(hit)* schwer ; *(rain)* heftig ; **to try ~** sich *(D)* Mühe geben.

hardback ['hɑːdbæk] *n* Hardcover *das.*

hardboard ['hɑːdbɔːd] *n* Hartfaserplatte *die.*

hard-boiled egg [-bɔɪld-] *n* hart gekochtes Ei.

hard disk *n* Festplatte *die.*

hardly ['hɑːdlɪ] *adv* kaum ; **~ ever** fast nie.

hardship ['hɑːdʃɪp] *n* Härte *die.*

hard shoulder *n (Br)* Seitenstreifen *der.*

hard up *adj (inf)* : **to be ~** knapp bei Kasse sein.

hardware ['hɑːdweə'] *n (tools, equipment)* Haushaltsgeräte *pl* ; *(COMPUT)* Hardware *die.*

hardwearing [,hɑːd'weərɪŋ] *adj (Br)* strapazierfähig.

hardworking [,hɑːd'wɜːkɪŋ] *adj* fleißig.

hare [heə'] *n* Hase *der.*

harm [hɑːm] *n* Schaden *der.* ◆ *vt* schaden (+D) ; *(person)* verletzen.

harmful ['hɑːmfʊl] *adj* schädlich.

harmless ['hɑːmlɪs] *adj* harmlos.

harmonica [hɑː'mɒnɪkə] *n* Mundharmonika *die.*

harmony ['hɑːmənɪ] *n* Harmonie *die.*

harness ['hɑːnɪs] n (for horse) Geschirr das; (for child) Laufgeschirr das.

harp [hɑːp] n Harfe die.

harsh [hɑːʃ] adj rau; (cruel) hart.

harvest ['hɑːvɪst] n Ernte die.

has [weak form həz, strong form hæz] → have.

hash browns [hæʃ-] npl amerikanische Kartoffelpuffer.

hasn't ['hæznt] = has not.

hassle ['hæsl] n (inf) Ärger der.

hastily ['heɪstɪlɪ] adv (rashly) vorschnell.

hasty ['heɪstɪ] adj (hurried) eilig; (rash) vorschnell.

hat [hæt] n Hut der.

hatch [hætʃ] n (for serving food) Durchreiche die. ◆ vi (chick) ausschlüpfen.

hatchback ['hætʃ,bæk] n Auto das mit Hecktür.

hatchet ['hætʃɪt] n Beil das.

hate [heɪt] n Hass der. ◆ vt hassen; to ~ doing sthg etw ungern tun.

hatred ['heɪtrɪd] n Hass der.

haul [hɔːl] vt ziehen. ◆ n : a long ~ eine weite Strecke.

haunted ['hɔːntɪd] adj : this house is ~ in diesem Haus spukt es.

have [hæv] (pt & pp had) aux vb
1. (to form perfect tenses) haben/sein; ~ you seen the film? hast du den Film gesehen?; I ~ finished ich bin fertig; ~ you been there? - no, I haven't warst du schon mal dort? - nein, noch nie; we had already left wir waren schon gegangen.
2. (must) : to ~ (got) to do sthg

etw tun müssen; do you ~ to pay? muss man bezahlen?

◆ vt **1.** (possess) : to ~ (got) haben; do you ~ OR ~ you got a double room? haben Sie ein Doppelzimmer?; she has (got) brown hair sie hat braunes Haar.
2. (experience) haben; to ~ a cold eine Erkältung haben; to ~ a great time sich großartig amüsieren.
3. (replacing other verbs) : to ~ a bath ein Bad nehmen; to ~ breakfast frühstücken; to ~ a cigarette eine Zigarette rauchen; to ~ a drink etwas trinken; to ~ lunch zu Mittag essen; to ~ a shower duschen; to ~ a swim schwimmen; to ~ a walk spazieren gehen.
4. (feel) haben; I ~ no doubt about it ich habe keine Zweifel daran.
5. (cause to be) : to ~ sthg done etw machen lassen; to ~ one's hair cut sich die Haare schneiden lassen.
6. (be treated in a certain way) : I've had my wallet stolen mir ist mein Geldbeutel gestohlen worden.

haversack ['hævəsæk] n Rucksack der.

havoc ['hævək] n Verwüstung die.

hawk [hɔːk] n Falke der.

hawker ['hɔːkə'] n Hausierer der (-in die).

hay [heɪ] n Heu das.

hay fever n Heuschnupfen der.

haystack ['heɪ,stæk] n Heuhaufen der.

hazard ['hæzəd] n Risiko das.

hazardous ['hæzədəs] adj gefährlich.

hazard warning lights npl (Br) Warnblinkanlage die.

haze [heɪz] n Dunst der.

hazel ['heɪzl] adj nussbraun.

hazelnut ['heɪzl,nʌt] n Haselnuss die.

hazy ['heɪzɪ] adj (misty) dunstig.

he [hi:] pron er ; ~'s tall er ist groß.

head [hed] n Kopf der ; (of table, bed) Kopfende das ; (of company, department) Leiter der (-in die) ; (of school) Schulleiter der (-in die) ; (of beer) Schaumkrone die. ◆ vt (list, procession) anführen ; (organization) leiten. ◆ vi (when walking) gehen ; (in vehicle) fahren ; £10 a ~ 10 Pfund pro Kopf ; ~s or tails? Kopf oder Zahl? □ **head for** vt fus (place) zulsteuern auf (+A).

headache ['hedeɪk] n Kopfschmerzen pl ; to have a ~ Kopfschmerzen haben.

heading ['hedɪŋ] n Überschrift die.

headlamp ['hedlæmp] (Br) = **headlight**.

headlight ['hedlaɪt] n Scheinwerfer der.

headline ['hedlaɪn] n Schlagzeile die.

headmaster [,hed'mɑ:stəʳ] n Schulleiter der.

headmistress [,hed'mɪstrɪs] n Schulleiterin die.

head of state n Staatsoberhaupt das.

headphones ['hedfəʊnz] npl Kopfhörer pl.

headquarters [,hed'kwɔ:təz] npl Hauptquartier das.

headrest ['hedrest] n Kopfstütze die.

headroom ['hedrʊm] n (under bridge) Höhe die.

headscarf ['hedskɑ:f] (pl -scarves [-skɑ:vz]) n Kopftuch das.

head start n Vorsprung der.

head teacher n Schulleiter der (-in die).

head waiter n Oberkellner der.

heal [hi:l] vt & vi heilen.

health [helθ] n Gesundheit die ; to be in good ~ bei guter Gesundheit sein ; to be in poor ~ kränklich sein ; your (very) good ~! auf dein/Ihr Wohl!

health centre n Ärztezentrum das.

health food n Biokost die.

health food shop n Bioladen der.

health insurance n Krankenversicherung die.

healthy ['helθɪ] adj gesund.

heap [hi:p] n Haufen der ; ~s of money (inf) ein Haufen Geld.

hear [hɪəʳ] (pt & pp heard [hɜ:d]) vt & vi hören ; to ~ about sthg von etw hören ; to ~ from sb von jm hören ; to have heard of schon mal gehört haben von.

hearing ['hɪərɪŋ] n (sense) Gehör das ; (at court) Verhandlung die ; to be hard of ~ schwerhörig sein.

hearing aid n Hörgerät das.

heart [hɑ:t] n Herz das ; to know sthg (off) by ~ etw auswendig können ; to lose ~ den

Mut verlieren. ■ **hearts** npl *(in cards)* Herz *das*.

heart attack n Herzinfarkt *der*.

heartbeat ['hɑːtbiːt] n Herzschlag *der*.

heartburn ['hɑːtbɜːn] n Sodbrennen *das*.

heart condition n : to have a ~ herzkrank sein.

hearth [hɑːθ] n Kamin *der*.

hearty ['hɑːtɪ] adj *(meal)* herzhaft.

heat [hiːt] n Hitze *die* ; *(pleasant)* Wärme *die* ; *(of oven)* Temperatur *die*. ■ **heat up** vt sep aufwärmen.

heater ['hiːtə'] n Heizgerät *das*.

heath [hiːθ] n Heide *die*.

heather ['heðə'] n Heidekraut *das*.

heating ['hiːtɪŋ] n Heizung *die*.

heat wave n Hitzewelle *die*.

heave [hiːv] vt wuchten.

Heaven ['hevn] n der Himmel.

heavily ['hevɪlɪ] adv stark.

heavy ['hevɪ] adj schwer ; *(rain, traffic)* stark ; how ~ is it? wie schwer ist es? ; to be a ~ smoker ein starker Raucher sein.

heavy cream n *(Am)* Schlagsahne *die*, Schlagobers *das* *(Österr)*.

heavy goods vehicle n *(Br)* Lastkraftwagen *der*.

heavy industry n Schwerindustrie *die*.

heavy metal n Heavymetal *das*.

heckle ['hekl] vt unterbrechen.

hectic ['hektɪk] adj hektisch.

hedge [hedʒ] n Hecke *die*.

hedgehog ['hedʒhɒg] n Igel *der*.

heel [hiːl] n *(of person)* Ferse *die* ; *(of shoe)* Absatz *der*.

hefty ['heftɪ] adj *(person)* stämmig ; *(fine)* saftig.

height [haɪt] n Höhe *die* ; *(of person)* Körpergröße *die* ; *(peak period)* Höhepunkt *der* ; what ~ is it? wie hoch ist es?

heir [eə'] n Erbe *der*.

heiress ['eərɪs] n Erbin *die*.

held [held] pt & pp → **hold**.

helicopter ['helɪkɒptə'] n Hubschrauber *der*.

he'll [hiːl] = he will.

Hell [hel] n die Hölle.

hello [hə'ləʊ] excl hallo! ; *(on phone)* guten Tag!

helmet ['helmɪt] n Helm *der*.

help [help] n Hilfe *die*. ◆ vt helfen *(+D)*. ◆ vi helfen. ◆ excl Hilfe! ; I can't ~ it ich kann nichts dafür ; to ~ sb (to) do sthg jm helfen, etw zu tun ; to ~ to do sthg *(contribute)* dazu beitragen, etw zu tun ; to ~ o.s. to sthg sich *(D)* etw nehmen ; can I ~ you? *(in shop)* kann ich Ihnen behilflich sein? ■ **help out** vi aushelfen.

helper ['helpə'] n Helfer *der* (-in *die*) ; *(Am : cleaner)* Hausangestellte *der, die*.

helpful ['helpfʊl] adj *(person)* hilfsbereit ; *(useful)* nützlich.

helping ['helpɪŋ] n Portion *die*.

helpless ['helplɪs] adj hilflos.

hem [hem] n Saum *der*.

hemophiliac [,hiːmə'fɪlɪæk] n Bluter *der*.

hemorrhage ['hemərɪdʒ] *n* Blutung *die*.

hen [hen] *n* Henne *die*.

hepatitis [,hepə'taɪtɪs] *n* Hepatitis *die*.

her [hɜːˀ] *adj* ihr. ◆ *pron (accusative)* sie ; *(dative)* ihr ; **I know** ~ ich kenne sie ; **it's** ~ sie ist es ; **send it to** ~ schick es ihr ; **tell** ~ sag ihr ; **he's worse than** ~ er ist schlimmer als sie.

herb [hɜːb] *n* Kraut *das*.

herbal tea ['hɜːbl-] *n* Kräutertee *der*.

herd [hɜːd] *n* Herde *die*.

here [hɪəˀ] *adv* hier ; **come** ~! komm her! ; ~ **you are** hier.

heritage ['herɪtɪdʒ] *n* Erbe *das*.

heritage centre *n* Museum an einem Ort von historischer Bedeutung.

hernia ['hɜːnjə] *n* Bruch *der*.

hero ['hɪərəʊ] *(pl* **-es**) *n* Held *der*.

heroin ['herəʊɪn] *n* Heroin *das*.

heroine ['herəʊɪn] *n* Heldin *die*.

heron ['herən] *n* Reiher *der*.

herring ['herɪŋ] *n* Hering *der*.

hers [hɜːz] *pron* ihre(-r) (-s), ihre *(pl)* ; **a friend of** ~ ein Freund von ihr ; **these shoes are** ~ diese Schuhe gehören ihr.

herself [hɜːˈself] *pron* sich ; *(after prep)* sich selbst ; **she did it** ~ sie hat es selbst getan.

hesitant ['hezɪtənt] *adj* zögernd.

hesitate ['hezɪteɪt] *vi* zögern.

hesitation [,hezɪˈteɪʃn] *n* Zögern *das*.

heterosexual [,hetərəʊ'sekʃʊəl] *adj* heterosexuell. ◆ *n* Heterosexuelle *der, die*.

hey [heɪ] *excl (inf)* he!

HGV *n (abbr of heavy goods vehicle)* Lkw *der*.

hi [haɪ] *excl (inf)* hallo!

hiccup ['hɪkʌp] *n* : **to have (the)** ~**s** (einen) Schluckauf haben.

hide [haɪd] *(pt* hid [hɪd], *pp* hidden ['hɪdn]) *vt* verstecken ; *(truth)* verschweigen ; *(feelings)* verbergen. ◆ *vi* sich verstecken. ◆ *n (of animal)* Haut *die*, Fell *das* ; **to be hidden** *(obscured)* sich verbergen.

hideous ['hɪdɪəs] *adj* scheußlich.

hi-fi ['haɪfaɪ] *n* Hi-Fi-Anlage *die*.

high [haɪ] *adj* hohe(-r) (-s) ; *(inf : from drugs)* high. ◆ *n (weather front)* Hoch *das*. ◆ *adv* hoch ; **to be** ~ *(tall)* hoch sein ; **how** ~ **is it?** wie hoch ist es? ; **it's 10 metres** ~ es ist 10 Meter hoch.

high chair *n* Kinderhochstuhl *der*.

high-class *adj (good-quality)* erstklassig.

Higher ['haɪəˀ] *n (Scot)* schottischer Schulabschluss.

higher education *n* Hochschulbildung *die*.

high heels *npl* hochhackige Schuhe *pl*.

high jump *n* Hochsprung *der*.

Highland Games ['haɪlənd-] *npl* typisches schottisches Sport- und Musikfestival.

ⓘ HIGHLAND GAMES

Dieses schottische Musik- und Sportfest entwickelte sich aus den traditionellen Treffen der schottischen Highland-Clans. Neben Kurz- und Langstreckenlauf, Weitsprung und Hochsprung gehören auch schottische Tänze („Highland dancing") und Dudelsackspielen zu den ausgetragenen Disziplinen. Ein anderer traditioneller Wettkampf ist das Holzmastwerfen („tossing the caber"), eine Kraftprobe, bei der die Teilnehmer schwere Fichtenstämme so weit wie möglich in die Luft schleudern müssen.

Highlands ['haıləndz] *npl* : the ~ das (schottische) Hochland.

highlight ['haılaıt] *n (best part)* Höhepunkt *der*. ◆ *vt* hervorheben. ▪ **highlights** *npl (of football match etc)* Highlights *pl* ; *(in hair)* Strähnchen *pl*.

highly ['haılı] *adv* höchst ; to think ~ of viel halten von ; ~ paid hoch bezahlt.

high-pitched [-'pıtʃt] *adj* hohe(-r) (-s).

high-rise *n (building)* Hochhaus *das*.

high school *n (in UK)* Schule für Elf- bis Achtzehnjährige ; *(in US)* Schule für Fünfzehn- bis Achtzehnjährige.

high season *n* Hochsaison *die*.

high-speed train *n* Hochgeschwindigkeitszug *der*.

high street *n. (Br)* Hauptgeschäftsstraße *die*.

high tide *n* Flut *die*.

highway ['haıweı] *n (Am)* Highway *der* ; *(Br : any main road)* Straße *die*.

Highway Code *n (Br)* Straßenverkehrsordnung *die*.

hijack ['haıdʒæk] *vt* entführen.

hijacker ['haıdʒækə*] *n* Entführer *der*.

hike [haık] *n* Wanderung *die*. ◆ *vi* wandern.

hiking ['haıkıŋ] *n* : to go ~ auf eine Wanderung gehen.

hilarious [hı'leərıəs] *adj* lustig.

hill [hıl] *n* Hügel *der*.

hillwalking ['hılwɔːkıŋ] *n* Bergwandern *das*.

hilly ['hılı] *adj* hügelig.

him [hım] *pron (accusative)* ihn ; *(dative)* ihm ; **I know ~** ich kenne ihn ; **it's ~** er ist es ; **send it to ~** schick es ihm ; **tell ~** sag ihm ; **she's worse than ~** sie ist schlimmer als er.

himself [hım'self] *pron* sich ; *(after prep)* sich selbst ; **he did it ~** er hat es selbst getan.

hinder ['hındə*] *vt (prevent)* behindern ; *(delay)* verzögern.

Hindu ['hınduː] *(pl -s) adj* Hindu-. ◆ *n* Hindu *der*.

hinge [hındʒ] *n* Scharnier *das*.

hint [hınt] *n* Andeutung *die* ; *(piece of advice)* Hinweis *der* ; *(slight amount)* Spur *die*. ◆ *vi* : **to ~ at sthg** etw andeuten.

hip [hıp] *n* Hüfte *die*.

hippopotamus [ˌhıpə'pɒtəməs] *n* Nilpferd *das*.

hippy ['hıpı] *n* Hippie *die*.

hire ['haɪə^r] vt (car, bicycle, television) mieten ; **'for ~'** (taxi) 'frei'. ■ **hire out** vt sep vermieten.

hire car n (Br) Mietwagen der.

hire purchase n (Br) Ratenkauf der.

his [hɪz] adj sein. ◆ pron seine(-r) (-s), seine (pl) ; a friend of ~ ein Freund von ihm ; these shoes are ~ diese Schuhe gehören ihm.

historical [hɪ'stɒrɪkəl] adj historisch.

history ['hɪstərɪ] n Geschichte die.

hit [hɪt] (pt & pp hit) vt schlagen ; (collide with) treffen ; (vehicle) prallen gegen. ◆ n (record, play, film) Hit der ; to one's head sich (D) den Kopfstoßen ; to ~ the target das Ziel treffen.

hit-and-run adj : a ~ accident ein Unfall mit Fahrerflucht.

hitch [hɪtʃ] n (problem) Haken der. ◆ vi per Anhalter fahren, trampen. ◆ vt : to ~ a lift per Anhalter fahren.

hitchhike ['hɪtʃhaɪk] vi per Anhalter fahren, trampen.

hitchhiker ['hɪtʃhaɪkə^r] n Anhalter der (-in die).

hive [haɪv] n Bienenstock der.

HIV-positive adj HIV-positiv.

hoarding ['hɔːdɪŋ] n (Br : for adverts) Plakatwand die.

hoarse [hɔːs] adj heiser.

hoax [həʊks] n Schwindel der.

hob [hɒb] n Kochplatte die.

hobby ['hɒbɪ] n Hobby das.

hock [hɒk] n (wine) Rheinwein der.

hockey ['hɒkɪ] n Hockey das ; (Am : ice hockey) Eishockey das.

hoe [həʊ] n Hacke die.

hold [həʊld] (pt & pp held) vt halten ; (meeting, election) abhalten ; (contain) fassen ; (possess) haben. ◆ vi (offer) gelten ; (weather) sich halten ; (on telephone) warten. ◆ n (grip) Halt der, Griff der ; (of ship, aircraft) Laderaum der ; to ~ sb prisoner jn gefangen halten ; ~ **the line, please** Bleiben Sie dran. ■ **hold back** vt sep zurücklhalten ; (keep secret) vorlenthalten. ■ **hold on** vi (wait) warten ; to ~ on to sthg (grip) etw festlhalten. ■ **hold out** vt sep (extend) auslstrecken. ■ **hold up** vt sep (delay) auflhalten.

holdall ['həʊldɔːl] n (Br) Reisetasche die.

holder ['həʊldə^r] n (of passport, licence) Inhaber der (-in die) ; (container) Halter der.

holdup ['həʊldʌp] n (delay) Verzögerung die.

hole [həʊl] n Loch das.

holiday ['hɒlɪdeɪ] n (period of time) Urlaub der, Ferien pl ; (day off) freier Tag ; (public) Feiertag der. ◆ vi (Br) Ferien machen, urlauben ; to be on ~ im Urlaub sein, in Ferien sein ; to go on ~ in Urlaub fahren, in die Ferien fahren.

holidaymaker ['hɒlɪdɪ,meɪkə^r] n (Br) Urlauber der (-in die).

holiday pay n (Br) Urlaubsgeld das.

Holland ['hɒlənd] n Holland nt.

hollow ['hɒləʊ] *adj* hohl.

holly ['hɒlɪ] *n* Stechpalme *die.*

Hollywood ['hɒlɪwʊd] *n* Hollywood *nt.*

HOLLYWOOD

Dies ist die Bezeichnung für ein weltbekanntes Stadtviertel in Los Angeles, das schon seit 1911 der Mittelpunkt der amerikanischen Filmindustrie ist. Es erlebte seinen Höhepunkt in den 40er und 50er Jahren, als große Filmstudios wie etwa 20th Century Fox, Paramount oder Warner Brothers dort jedes Jahr hunderte von Filmen produzierten. Heute ist „Hollywood" eine der größten Touristenattraktionen in Amerika.

holy ['həʊlɪ] *adj* heilig.

home [həʊm] *n* Zuhause *das ; (own country)* Heimat *die ; (one's family)* Elternhaus *das ; (for old people)* Altersheim *das.* ◆ *adj (not foreign)* einheimisch. ◆ *adv* : **to be ~** zu Hause sein ; **to go ~** nach Hause gehen ; **at ~** zu Hause ; **to make o.s. at ~** es sich *(D)* bequem machen ; **~ address** Heimatanschrift *die ;* **~ number** private Telefonnummer.

home economics *n* Hauswirtschaftslehre *die.*

home help *n (Br)* Haushaltshilfe *die* (meist Sozialarbeiterin).

homeless ['həʊmlɪs] *npl* : **the ~** die Obdachlosen *pl.*

homemade [,həʊm'meɪd] *adj* selbst gemacht.

homeopathic [,həʊmɪəʊ-'pæθɪk] *adj* homöopathisch.

Home Secretary *n (Br)* Innenminister *der.*

homesick ['həʊmsɪk] *adj* : **to be ~** Heimweh haben.

homework ['həʊmwɜːk] *n* Hausaufgaben *pl.*

homosexual [,hɒmə'sekʃʊəl] *adj* homosexuell. ◆ *n* Homosexuelle *der, die.*

honest ['ɒnɪst] *adj* ehrlich.

honestly ['ɒnɪstlɪ] *adv* ehrlich.

honey ['hʌnɪ] *n* Honig *der.*

honeymoon ['hʌnɪmuːn] *n* Flitterwochen *pl.*

honor ['ɒnər] *(Am)* = **honour**.

honour ['ɒnər] *n (Br)* Ehre *die.*

honourable ['ɒnrəbl] *adj* ehrenwert ; *(deed)* ehrenvoll.

hood [hʊd] *n* Kapuze *die ; (on convertible car)* Verdeck *das ; (Am : car bonnet)* Kühlerhaube *die.*

hoof [huːf] *n* Huf *der.*

hook [hʊk] *n* Haken *der ;* **off the ~** *(telephone)* ausgehängt.

hooligan ['huːlɪgən] *n* Hooligan *der.*

hoop [huːp] *n* Reifen *der.*

hoot [huːt] *vi (driver)* hupen.

Hoover® ['huːvə'] *n (Br)* Staubsauger *der.*

hop [hɒp] *vi* hüpfen.

hope [həʊp] *n* Hoffnung *die.* ◆ *vt* hoffen ; **to ~ for sthg** auf etw *(A)* hoffen ; **to ~ to do sthg** hoffen, etw zu tun ; **I ~ so** ich hoffe es.

hopeful ['həʊpfʊl] *adj* hoffnungsvoll.

hopefully ['həupfəlɪ] *adv* hoffentlich.

hopeless ['həuplɪs] *adj (inf: useless)* miserabel ; *(without any hope)* hoffnungslos.

hops [hɒps] *npl* Hopfen *der*.

horizon [hə'raɪzn] *n* Horizont *der*.

horizontal [,hɒrɪ'zɒntl] *adj* horizontal.

horn [hɔːn] *n (of car)* Hupe *die* ; *(on animal)* Horn *das*.

horoscope ['hɒrəskəup] *n* Horoskop *das*.

horrible ['hɒrəbl] *adj* furchtbar.

horrid ['hɒrɪd] *adj* schrecklich.

horrific [hɒ'rɪfɪk] *adj* entsetzlich.

hors d'oeuvre [ɔː'dɜːvrə] *n* Horsd'oeuvre *das*.

horse [hɔːs] *n* Pferd *das*.

horseback ['hɔːsbæk] *n* : on ~ zu Pferd.

horse chestnut *n* Rosskastanie *die*.

horse-drawn carriage *n* Pferdedroschke *die*.

horsepower ['hɔːs,pauə'] *n* Pferdestärke *die*.

horse racing *n* Pferderennen *das*.

horseradish (sauce) ['hɔːs,rædɪʃ] *n* Meerrettich *der (traditionell zu Roastbeef gegessen)*.

horse riding *n* Reiten *das*.

horseshoe ['hɔːsʃuː] *n* Hufeisen *das*.

hose [həuz] *n* Schlauch *der*.

hosepipe ['həuzpaɪp] *n* Schlauch *der*.

hosiery ['həuzɪərɪ] *n* Strumpfwaren *pl*.

hospitable [hɒ'spɪtəbl] *adj* gastfreundlich.

hospital ['hɒspɪtl] *n* Krankenhaus *das* ; in ~ im Krankenhaus.

hospitality [,hɒspɪ'tælətɪ] *n* Gastfreundschaft *die*.

host [həust] *n* Gastgeber *der* ; *(of show, TV programme)* Moderator *der* (-in *die*).

hostage ['hɒstɪdʒ] *n* Geisel *die*.

hostel ['hɒstl] *n (youth hostel)* Jugendherberge *die*.

hostess ['həustes] *n (on aeroplane)* Stewardess *die* ; *(of party, event)* Gastgeberin *die*.

hostile [*(Br)* 'hɒstaɪl, *(Am)* 'hɒstl] *adj* feindselig.

hostility [hɒ'stɪlətɪ] *n* Feindseligkeit *die*.

hot [hɒt] *adj* heiß ; *(water, drink, food)* warm ; *(spicy)* scharf ; I'm ~ mir ist heiß.

hot chocolate *n* heiße Schokolade.

hot-cross bun *n* rundes Rosinenbrötchen mit Gewürzen, das vor allem zu Ostern gegessen wird.

hot dog *n* Hotdog *der* OR *das*.

hotel [həu'tel] *n* Hotel *das*.

hot line *n (between governments)* heißer Draht ; *(public)* Hotline *die*.

hotplate ['hɒtpleɪt] *n* Kochplatte *die*.

hotpot ['hɒtpɒt] *n* Fleischauflauf, bedeckt mit einer Schicht Kartoffelscheiben.

hot-water bottle *n* Wärmflasche *die*.

hour ['auə⁰] n Stunde die ; I've been waiting for ~s ich warte schon seit Stunden.

hourly ['auəlɪ] adj & adv stündlich.

house [n haus, pl 'hauzɪz, vb hauz] n Haus das ; (SCH) traditionelle Schülergemeinschaften innerhalb einer Schule, die untereinander Wettbewerbe veranstalten. ◆ vt unterlbringen.

household ['haushəuld] n Haushalt der.

housekeeping ['haus,ki:pɪŋ] n Haushaltung die.

House of Commons n (Br) britisches Unterhaus.

House of Lords n (Br) britisches Oberhaus.

Houses of Parliament npl (Br) Houses of Parliament pl, Sitz des britischen Parlaments.

 HOUSES OF PARLIAMENT

Die an der Themse gelegenen Parlamentsgebäude („Houses of Parliament") in London, auch „Palace of Westminster" genannt, bestehen aus dem „House of Commons" (Unterhaus) und dem „House of Lords" (Oberhaus). Das heutige Gebäude wurde in der Mitte des 19. Jahrhunderts erbaut und ersetzt den früheren „Palace of Westminster", der 1834 niederbrannte.

housewife ['hauswaif] (pl -wives [-waivz]) n Hausfrau die.

house wine n Hauswein der.

housework ['hauswɜːk] n Hausarbeit die.

housing ['hauzɪŋ] n (houses) Wohnungen pl.

housing estate n (Br) Wohnsiedlung die.

housing project (Am) = **housing estate**.

hovercraft ['hɒvəkrɑːft] n Luftkissenboot das.

hoverport ['hɒvəpɔːt] n Hafen für Luftkissenfahrzeuge.

how [hau] adv 1. (asking about way or manner) wie ; ~ do you get there? wie kommt man dahin? ; tell me ~ to do it sag mir, wie man das macht.
2. (asking about health, quality) wie ; ~ are you? wie geht's dir?, wie geht es Ihnen? ; ~ are you doing? wie geht's dir?, wie geht es Ihnen? ; ~ are things? wie geht's? ; ~ do you do? Guten Tag! ; ~ is your room? wie ist Ihr/dein Zimmer?
3. (asking about degree, amount) wie ; ~ far? wie weit? ; ~ long? wie lang? ; ~ many? wie viele? ; ~ much? wie viel? ; ~ much is it? wie viel kostet es? ; ~ old are you? wie alt bist du/sind Sie?
4. (in phrases) : ~ about a drink? wie wäre es mit etwas zu trinken/einem Drink? ; ~ lovely! wie hübsch!, wie nett!

however [hau'evə⁰] adv jedoch, aber ; ~ long it takes egal, wie lange es dauert.

howl [haul] vi heulen.

HP abbr (Br) = **hire purchase**.

HQ abbr = **headquarters**.

hub airport [hʌb-] n zentraler Flughafen.

hubcap ['hʌbkæp] n Radkappe die.

hug [hʌg] vt umarmen. ◆ n : to give sb a ~ jn umarmen.

huge [hju:dʒ] adj riesig.

hull [hʌl] n Schiffsrumpf der.

hum [hʌm] vi summen.

human ['hju:mən] adj menschlich. ◆ n : ~ (being) Mensch der.

humanities [hju:'mænətɪz] npl Geisteswissenschaften pl.

human rights npl Menschenrechte pl.

humble ['hʌmbl] adj (not proud) demütig ; (of low status) niedrig.

humid ['hju:mɪd] adj feucht.

humidity [hju:'mɪdətɪ] n Feuchtigkeit die.

humiliating [hju:'mɪlɪeɪtɪŋ] adj erniedrigend.

humiliation [hju:,mɪlɪ'eɪʃn] n Erniedrigung die.

hummus ['homəs] n Paste aus pürierten Kichererbsen und Knoblauch.

humor ['hju:mər] (Am) = humour.

humorous ['hju:mərəs] adj lustig.

humour ['hju:mə] n Humor der ; a sense of ~ Sinn für Humor.

hump [hʌmp] n Buckel der ; (of camel) Höcker der.

humpbacked bridge ['hʌmpbækt-] n gewölbte Brücke.

hunch [hʌntʃ] n Gefühl das.

hundred ['hʌndrəd] num hundert ; → six ; a OR one ~ einhundert.

hundredth ['hʌndrətθ] num hundertste(-r) (-s) ; → sixth.

hundredweight ['hʌndrədweɪt] n (in UK) = 50,8 kg, ≃ Zentner der ; (in US) = 45,36 kg, ≃ Zentner der.

hung [hʌŋ] pt & pp → hang.

Hungarian [hʌŋ'geərɪən] adj ungarisch. ◆ n (person) Ungar der (-in die) ; (language) Ungarisch das.

Hungary ['hʌŋgərɪ] n Ungarn nt.

hunger ['hʌŋgə] n Hunger der.

hungry ['hʌŋgrɪ] adj hungrig ; to be ~ Hunger haben.

hunt [hʌnt] n (Br : for foxes) Fuchsjagd die. ◆ vt & vi jagen ; to ~ (for) (search) suchen.

hunting ['hʌntɪŋ] n Jagd die ; (Br : for foxes) Fuchsjagd die.

hurdle ['hɜ:dl] n Hürde die.

hurl [hɜ:l] vt schleudern.

hurricane ['hʌrɪkən] n Orkan der.

hurry ['hʌrɪ] vt (person) hetzen. ◆ vi sich beeilen. ◆ n : to be in a ~ es eilig haben ; to do sthg in a ~ etw hastig tun.
■ **hurry up** vi sich beeilen.

hurt [hɜ:t] (pt & pp hurt) vt verletzen. ◆ vi (be painful) wehtun ; to ~ o.s. sich (D) wehtun ; to ~ one's head sich (D) den Kopf verletzen.

husband ['hʌzbənd] n Ehemann der.

hustle ['hʌsl] n : ~ and bustle geschäftiges Treiben.

hut [hʌt] n Hütte die.

hyacinth ['haɪəsɪnθ] n Hyazinthe die.

hydrofoil ['haɪdrəfoɪl] n Tragflächenboot das.

hygiene ['haɪdʒiːn] n Hygiene
die.

hygienic [haɪ'dʒiːnɪk] adj hygienisch.

hymn [hɪm] n Hymne die.

hypermarket ['haɪpə,mɑːkɪt]
n Großmarkt der.

hyphen ['haɪfn] n Bindestrich
der.

hypocrite ['hɪpəkrɪt] n
Heuchler der (-in die).

hypodermic needle [,haɪpə-
'dɜːmɪk-] n Kanüle die.

hysterical [hɪs'terɪkl] adj hy-
sterisch ; (inf : very funny) lustig.

I

I [aɪ] pron ich ; **I'm tall** ich bin
groß.

ice [aɪs] n Eis das.

iceberg ['aɪsbɜːg] n Eisberg
der.

iceberg lettuce n Eisbergsa-
lat der.

icebox ['aɪsbɒks] n (Am) Kühlschrank der.

ice-cold adj eiskalt.

ice cream n Eis das.

ice cube n Eiswürfel der.

ice hockey n Eishockey das.

Iceland ['aɪslənd] n Island nt.

ice lolly n (Br) Eis das am Stil.

ice rink n Eisbahn die.

ice skates npl Schlittschuhe
pl.

ice-skating n Schlittschuh-
laufen das, Eislaufen das ; **to go
~** Schlittschuh laufen gehen.

icicle ['aɪsɪkl] n Eiszapfen der.

icing ['aɪsɪŋ] n Zuckerguss der.

icing sugar n Puderzucker
der.

icy ['aɪsɪ] adj (road, pavement)
vereist ; (weather) eisig.

I'd [aɪd] = I would, I had.

ID abbr = identification.

ID card n Personalausweis
der.

IDD code n internationale
Vorwahlkennziffer.

idea [aɪ'dɪə] n Idee die ; (opinion) Vorstellung die ; (understanding) Begriff der ; **I've no ~**
ich habe keine Ahnung.

ideal [aɪ'dɪəl] adj ideal. ◆ n
Ideal das.

ideally [aɪ'dɪəlɪ] adv (situated,
suited) ideal ; (preferably) idea-
lerweise.

identical [aɪ'dentɪkl] adj identisch.

identification [aɪ,dentɪfɪ-
'keɪʃn] n (proof of identity) Ausweis der.

identify [aɪ'dentɪfaɪ] vt erkennen.

identity [aɪ'dentətɪ] n Identität die.

idiom ['ɪdɪəm] n Redewendung die.

idiot ['ɪdɪət] n Idiot der.

idle ['aɪdl] adj faul ; (machine)
stillstehend. ◆ vi (engine) leer
laufen.

idol ['aɪdl] n (person) Idol das.

idyllic [ɪ'dɪlɪk] adj idyllisch.

i.e. (abbr of id est) d. h.

if [ɪf] conj wenn, falls ; (in indirect questions, after know, wonder) ob ; **~ I were you** wenn ich
du wäre ; **~ not** (otherwise)
wenn nicht, falls nicht.

ignition [ɪg'nɪʃn] *n (AUT)* Zündung *die.*

ignorant ['ɪgnərənt] *adj* unwissend; *(pej: stupid)* beschränkt.

ignore [ɪg'nɔːʳ] *vt* ignorieren.

ill [ɪl] *adj* krank; *(treatment)* schlecht; ~ **luck** Pech *das.*

I'll [aɪl] = **I will, I shall.**

illegal [ɪ'liːgl] *adj* illegal.

illegible [ɪ'ledʒəbl] *adj* unleserlich.

illegitimate [ˌɪlɪ'dʒɪtɪmət] *adj (child)* unehelich.

illiterate [ɪ'lɪtərət] *adj* : **to be ~** Analphabet sein.

illness ['ɪlnɪs] *n* Krankheit *die.*

illuminate [ɪ'luːmɪneɪt] *vt* beleuchten.

illusion [ɪ'luːʒn] *n* Illusion *die.*

illustration [ˌɪlə'streɪʃn] *n (picture)* Illustration *die*; *(example)* Beispiel *das.*

I'm [aɪm] = **I am.**

image ['ɪmɪdʒ] *n* Bild *das*; *(of company, person)* Image *das.*

imaginary [ɪ'mædʒɪnrɪ] *adj* eingebildet.

imagination [ɪˌmædʒɪ'neɪʃn] *n (ability)* Fantasie *die*; *(mind)* Einbildung *die.*

imagine [ɪ'mædʒɪn] *vt* sich *(D)* vorstellen.

imitate ['ɪmɪteɪt] *vt* nachlahmen.

imitation [ˌɪmɪ'teɪʃn] *n* Nachahmung *die.* ◆ *adj* : ~ **leather** Lederimitation *die.*

immaculate [ɪ'mækjʊlət] *adj* makellos.

immature [ˌɪmə'tjʊəʳ] *adj* unreif.

immediate [ɪ'miːdjət] *adj (without delay)* unmittelbar.

immediately [ɪ'miːdjətlɪ] *adv (at once)* sofort. ◆ *conj (Br)* sobald.

immense [ɪ'mens] *adj* enorm.

immersion heater [ɪ'mɜːʃn-] *n* Heißwasserbereiter *der.*

immigrant ['ɪmɪgrənt] *n* Einwanderer *der* (Einwanderin *die*).

immigration [ˌɪmɪ'greɪʃn] *n* Einwanderung *die*; *(section of airport, port)* Einwanderungskontrolle *die.*

imminent ['ɪmɪnənt] *adj* nahe bevorstehend.

immune [ɪ'mjuːn] *adj* : **to be ~ to sthg** immun sein gegen etw.

immunity [ɪ'mjuːnətɪ] *n* Immunität *die.*

immunize ['ɪmjuːnaɪz] *vt* immunisieren.

impact ['ɪmpækt] *n (effect)* Auswirkung *die*; *(hitting)* Aufprall *der.*

impair [ɪm'peəʳ] *vt* beeinträchtigen.

impatient [ɪm'peɪʃnt] *adj* ungeduldig; **to be ~ to do sthg** es nicht erwarten können, etw zu tun.

imperative [ɪm'perətɪv] *n (GRAMM)* Imperativ *der.*

imperfect [ɪm'pɜːfɪkt] *n (GRAMM)* Imperfekt *das.*

impersonate [ɪm'pɜːsəneɪt] *vt (for amusement)* nachlahmen.

impertinent [ɪm'pɜːtɪnənt] *adj* frech.

implement [*n* 'ɪmplɪmənt, *vb* 'ɪmplɪment] *n* Gerät *das.* ◆ *vt* durchlführen.

implication [ˌɪmplɪ'keɪʃn] *n (consequence)* Konsequenz *die.*

imply [ɪm'plaɪ] *vt* anldeuten.

impolite [,ɪmpə'laɪt] *adj* unhöflich.

import [*n* 'ɪmpɔːt, *vb* ɪm'pɔːt] *n*
Import *der*. ◆ *vt* importieren.

importance [ɪm'pɔːtns] *n*
Wichtigkeit *die*.

important [ɪm'pɔːtnt] *adj*
wichtig; *(person)* einfluss-
reich.

impose [ɪm'pəʊz] *vt* auferlegen. ◆ *vi* zur Last fallen; **to ~
sthg on** etw auferlegen *(+D)*.

impossible [ɪm'pɒsəbl] *adj*
unmöglich.

impractical [ɪm'præktɪkl] *adj*
unpraktisch.

impress [ɪm'pres] *vt* *(person)*
beeindrucken.

impression [ɪm'preʃn] *n* *(opinion)* Eindruck *der*.

impressive [ɪm'presɪv] *adj*
eindrucksvoll.

improbable [ɪm'prɒbəbl] *adj*
unwahrscheinlich.

improper [ɪm'prɒpə] *adj* *(incorrect)* inkorrekt; *(illegal)* un-
lauter; *(rude)* unanständig.

improve [ɪm'pruːv] *vt* verbessern. ◆ *vi* besser werden.
■ **improve on** *vt fus* übertreffen.

improvement [ɪm'pruːv-
mənt] *n* Besserung *die*; *(to
home, to machine)* Verbesserung *die*.

improvise ['ɪmprəvaɪz] *vi* improvisieren.

impulse ['ɪmpʌls] *n* Impuls
der; **on ~** spontan.

impulsive [ɪm'pʌlsɪv] *adj* impulsiv.

in [ɪn] *prep* **1.** *(expressing place,
position)* in *(+A,D)*; **to put sthg ~
sthg** etw in etw *(A)* tun; **it**

comes **~ a box** man bekommt es
in einer Schachtel; **~ the bedroom** im Schlafzimmer; **~ the
street** auf der Straße; **~ California** in Kalifornien; **~ Sheffield**
in Sheffield; **~ here/there** hier/
dort drinnen.

2. *(participating in)* in *(+D)*;
who's ~ the play? war spielt in
dem Stück?

3. *(expressing arrangement)* in
(+D); **~ a circle** in einem Kreis;
they come ~ packs of three es gibt
sie in Dreierpacks.

4. *(during)* in *(+D)*; **~ April** im
April; **~ the afternoon** am
Nachmittag; **~ the morning** am
Morgen; **ten o'clock ~ the morn-
ing** zehn Uhr morgens; **~ 1999**
1999.

5. *(within, after)* in *(+D)*; **it'll be
ready ~ an hour** es ist in einer
Stunde fertig.

6. *(expressing means)*: **write ~
ink** mit Tinte schreiben; **~ writing** schriftlich; **they were talking
~ English** sie sprachen Englisch.

7. *(wearing)* in *(+D)*.

8. *(state)* in *(+D)*; **~ a hurry** in
Eile; **to be ~ pain** Schmerzen
haben; **~ ruins** in Trümmern.

9. *(with regard to)*: **a rise ~ prices**
ein Preisanstieg; **to be 50 me-
tres ~ length** 50 Meter lang sein.

10. *(with numbers)*: **one ~ ten** jeder Zehnte.

11. *(expressing age)*: **she's ~ her
twenties** sie ist in den Zwanzi-
gern.

12. *(with colours)*: **it comes ~
green or blue** es gibt es in grün
oder blau.

13. *(with superlatives)* in *(+D)*;

the best ~ the world der/die/das Beste in der Welt.
◆ adv 1. *(inside)* herein/hinein ; **you can go ~ now** Sie können/du kannst jetzt hineingehen.
2. *(at home, work)* da ; **she's not ~** sie ist nicht da ; **to stay ~** zu Hause bleiben.
3. *(train, bus, plane)* : **to get ~** anlkommen ; **the train's not ~ yet** der Zug ist noch nicht angekommen.
4. *(tide)* : **the tide is ~** es ist Flut.
◆ adj *(inf : fashionable)* in.

inability [ˌɪnəˈbɪlətɪ] n : **~ (to do sthg)** Unfähigkeit *die* (, etw zu tun).

inaccessible [ˌɪnəkˈsesəbl] adj unzugänglich.

inaccurate [ɪnˈækjʊrət] adj ungenau.

inadequate [ɪnˈædɪkwət] adj ungenügend.

inappropriate [ˌɪnəˈprəʊprɪət] adj unpassend.

inauguration [ɪˌnɔːgjʊˈreɪʃn] n *(of person)* Amtseinführung *die* ; *(of institution)* Einweihung *die*.

incapable [ɪnˈkeɪpəbl] adj : **to be ~ of doing sthg** nicht fähig sein, etw zu tun.

incense [ˈɪnsens] n Weihrauch *der*.

incentive [ɪnˈsentɪv] n Anreiz *der*.

inch [ɪntʃ] n = 2,54 cm, Inch *der*.

incident [ˈɪnsɪdənt] n Vorfall *der*.

incidentally [ˌɪnsɪˈdentəlɪ] adv übrigens.

incline [ˈɪnklaɪn] n Abhang *der*.

inclined [ɪnˈklaɪnd] adj *(sloping)* abschüssig ; **to be ~ to do sthg** *(have tendency)* dazu neigen, etw zu tun.

include [ɪnˈkluːd] vt einlschließen ; *(contain)* enthalten.

included [ɪnˈkluːdɪd] adj *(in price)* inbegriffen ; **to be ~ in sthg** in etw (D) eingeschlossen sein.

including [ɪnˈkluːdɪŋ] prep einschließlich (+G).

inclusive [ɪnˈkluːsɪv] adj : **from the 8th to the 16th ~** vom 8. bis einschließlich 16. ; **~ of VAT** inklusive MwSt.

income [ˈɪŋkʌm] n Einkommen *das*.

income support n *(Br)* zusätzliche staatliche Beihilfe zum Lebensunterhalt.

income tax n Einkommensteuer *die*.

incoming [ˈɪnˌkʌmɪŋ] adj *(train)* einfahrend ; *(plane)* landend ; *(phone call)* eingehend.

incompetent [ɪnˈkɒmpɪtənt] adj unfähig.

incomplete [ˌɪnkəmˈpliːt] adj unvollständig.

inconsiderate [ˌɪnkənˈsɪdərət] adj rücksichtslos.

inconsistent [ˌɪnkənˈsɪstənt] adj *(person)* unbeständig ; *(statement)* widersprüchlich.

incontinent [ɪnˈkɒntɪnənt] adj inkontinent.

inconvenient [ˌɪnkənˈviːnjənt] adj ungünstig.

incorporate [ɪnˈkɔːpəreɪt] vt auflnehmen.

incorrect [,ɪnkə'rekt] *adj* unrichtig.

increase [*n* 'ɪnkriːs, *vb* ɪn'kriːs] *n* Anstieg *der* ; *(in wages)* Erhöhung *die*. ◆ *vt* erhöhen. ◆ *vi* steigen ; **an ~ in unemployment** eine Zunahme der Arbeitslosigkeit.

increasingly [ɪn'kriːsɪŋlɪ] *adv* zunehmend.

incredible [ɪn'kredəbl] *adj* unglaublich.

incredibly [ɪn'kredəblɪ] *adv* unglaublich.

incur [ɪn'kɜːʳ] *vt* sich *(D)* zuziehen.

indecisive [,ɪndɪ'saɪsɪv] *adj* unentschlossen.

indeed [ɪn'diːd] *adv* wirklich, tatsächlich ; *(certainly)* natürlich ; **very big ~** wirklich sehr groß.

indefinite [ɪn'defɪnɪt] *adj* unbestimmt ; *(answer, opinion)* unklar.

indefinitely [ɪn'defɪnətlɪ] *adv* *(closed, delayed)* bis auf weiteres.

independence [,ɪndɪ'pendəns] *n* Unabhängigkeit *die*.

independent [,ɪndɪ'pendənt] *adj* unabhängig.

independently [,ɪndɪ'pendəntlɪ] *adv* unabhängig.

independent school *n (Br)* nichtstaatliche Schule.

index ['ɪndeks] *n* Verzeichnis *das*, Register *das*.

index finger *n* Zeigefinger *der*.

India ['ɪndjə] *n* Indien *nt*.

Indian ['ɪndjən] *adj* indisch. ◆ *n* Inder *der* (-in *die*) ; **~ restaurant** indisches Restaurant.

Indian Ocean *n* Indischer Ozean.

indicate ['ɪndɪkeɪt] *vi (AUT)* blinken. ◆ *vt (point to)* zeigen auf *(+A)* ; *(show)* andeuten.

indicator ['ɪndɪkeɪtəʳ] *n (AUT)* Blinker *der*.

indifferent [ɪn'dɪfrənt] *adj* gleichgültig.

indigestion [,ɪndɪ'dʒestʃn] *n* Magenverstimmung *die*.

indigo ['ɪndɪgəʊ] *adj* indigoblau.

indirect [,ɪndɪ'rekt] *adj* indirekt ; **an ~ route** ein Umweg.

individual [,ɪndɪ'vɪdʒʊəl] *adj* einzeln ; *(tuition)* Einzel-. ◆ *n* Einzelne *der, die*.

individually [,ɪndɪ'vɪdʒʊəlɪ] *adv* einzeln.

Indonesia [,ɪndə'niːzjə] *n* Indonesien *nt*.

indoor ['ɪndɔːʳ] *adj (swimming pool, sports)* Hallen-.

indoors [,ɪn'dɔːz] *adv* drinnen, im Haus.

indulge [ɪn'dʌldʒ] *vi* : **to ~ in** sich *(D)* gönnen.

industrial [ɪn'dʌstrɪəl] *adj* industriell ; *(country, town)* Industrie-.

industrial estate *n (Br)* Industriesiedlung *die*.

industry ['ɪndəstrɪ] *n* Industrie *die*.

inedible [ɪn'edɪbl] *adj* ungenießbar.

inefficient [,ɪnɪ'fɪʃnt] *adj* nicht leistungsfähig.

inequality [,ɪnɪ'kwɒlətɪ] *n* Ungleichheit *die*.

inevitable [in'evitəbl] adj unvermeidlich.

inevitably [in'evitəbli] adv zwangsläufig.

inexpensive [ˌinik'spensiv] adj preiswert.

infamous ['infəməs] adj berüchtigt.

infant ['infənt] n (baby) Säugling der ; (young child) Kind das.

infant school n (Br) Vorschule die (für 5- bis 7-Jährige).

infatuated [in'fætjueitid] adj : to be ~ with vernarrt sein in (+A).

infected [in'fektid] adj infiziert.

infectious [in'fekʃəs] adj ansteckend.

inferior [in'fiəriə] adj (person) untergeordnet ; (goods, quality) minderwertig.

infinite ['infinət] adj unendlich.

infinitely ['infinətli] adv unendlich.

infinitive [in'finitiv] n Infinitiv der.

infinity [in'finəti] n Unendlichkeit die.

infirmary [in'fɜːməri] n Krankenhaus das.

inflamed [in'fleimd] adj entzündet.

inflammation [ˌinflə'meiʃn] n Entzündung die.

inflatable [in'fleitəbl] adj aufblasbar.

inflate [in'fleit] vt aufpumpen.

inflation [in'fleiʃn] n (of prices) Inflation die.

inflict [in'flikt] vt (suffering) aufbürden ; (wound) beilbringen.

in-flight adj während des Fluges.

influence ['influəns] vt beeinflussen. ◆ n : ~ (on) Einfluss der (auf (+A)).

inform [in'fɔːm] vt informieren.

informal [in'fɔːml] adj zwanglos.

information [ˌinfə'meiʃn] n Information die ; a piece of ~ eine Information.

information desk n Auskunftsschalter der.

information office n Auskunftsbüro das.

informative [in'fɔːmətiv] adj informativ.

infuriating [in'fjuərieitiŋ] adj ärgerlich.

ingenious [in'dʒiːnjəs] adj raffiniert.

ingredient [in'griːdjənt] n (CULIN) Zutat die.

inhabit [in'hæbit] vt bewohnen.

inhabitant [in'hæbitənt] n Einwohner der (-in die).

inhale [in'heil] vi einlatmen.

inhaler [in'heilə] n Inhaliergerät das.

inherit [in'herit] vt erben.

inhibition [ˌinhi'biʃn] n Hemmung die.

initial [i'niʃl] adj Anfangs-. ◆ vt mit Initialen unterschreiben. ▪ **initials** npl Initialen pl.

initially [i'niʃəli] adv anfangs.

initiative [i'niʃətiv] n Initiative die.

injection [ɪn'dʒekʃn] n (MED)
Spritze die.

injure ['ɪndʒər] vt verletzen ;
to ~ one's arm sich (D) den Arm
verletzen ; to ~ o.s. sich verletzen.

injured ['ɪndʒəd] adj verletzt.

injury ['ɪndʒərɪ] n Verletzung
die.

ink [ɪŋk] n Tinte die.

inland [adj 'ɪnlənd, adv ɪn'lænd]
adj Binnen-. ◆ adv landeinwärts.

inn [ɪn] n Gasthaus das.

inner ['ɪnər] adj innere(-r) (-s).

inner city n Viertel in der Nähe
der Innenstadt, in denen es oft soziale Probleme gibt.

inner tube n Schlauch der.

innocence ['ɪnəsəns] n Unschuld die.

innocent ['ɪnəsənt] adj unschuldig.

inoculate [ɪ'nɒkjʊleɪt] vt : to ~
sb (against sthg) jn (gegen etw)
impfen.

inoculation [ɪ,nɒkjʊ'leɪʃn] n
Impfung die.

input ['ɪnpʊt] vt (COMPUT) einlgeben.

inquire [ɪn'kwaɪər] = enquire.

inquiry [ɪn'kwaɪərɪ] = enquiry.

insane [ɪn'seɪn] adj verrückt.

insect ['ɪnsekt] n Insekt das.

insect repellent [-rə'pelənt]
n Insektenvertreibungsmittel
das.

insensitive [ɪn'sensətɪv] adj
(unkind) gefühllos.

insert [ɪn'sɜːt] vt (coin) einlwerfen ; (ticket) einlführen ;
(key) einlstecken.

inside [ɪn'saɪd] prep (be) in
(+D) ; (go, move) in (+A). ◆ adv
innen. ◆ adj (internal) Innen-.
◆ n : the ~ das Innere ; (AUT : in
UK) die linke Fahrspur ; (AUT :
in Europe, US) die rechte Fahrspur ; ~ out (clothes) links
(herum) ; to be ~ drinnen sein ;
to go ~ hineinlgehen.

inside lane n (AUT : in UK)
linke Fahrspur ; (in Europe, US)
rechte Fahrspur.

inside leg n Schrittlänge die.

insight ['ɪnsaɪt] n Einblick der.

insignificant [,ɪnsɪg'nɪfɪkənt] adj unbedeutend.

insinuate [ɪn'sɪnjʊeɪt] vt anldeuten.

insist [ɪn'sɪst] vi darauf bestehen ; to ~ on doing sthg darauf
bestehen, etw zu tun.

insole ['ɪnsəʊl] n Einlegesohle
die.

insolent ['ɪnsələnt] adj unverschämt.

insomnia [ɪn'sɒmnɪə] n
Schlaflosigkeit die.

inspect [ɪn'spekt] vt (ticket,
passport) kontrollieren ; (look
at closely) genau betrachten.

inspection [ɪn'spekʃn] n (of
ticket, passport) Kontrolle die.

inspector [ɪn'spektər] n (on
bus, train) Kontrolleur der (-in
die) ; (in police force) Kommissar der (-in die).

inspiration [,ɪnspə'reɪʃn] n
Inspiration die.

instal [ɪn'stɔːl] (Am) = install.

install [ɪn'stɔːl] vt (Br) installieren.

installment [ɪn'stɔːlmənt]
(Am) = instalment.

instalment [ɪnˈstɔːlmənt] *n*
(payment) Rate *die* ; *(episode)*
Folge *die*.

instance [ˈɪnstəns] *n* Fall *der* ;
for ~ zum Beispiel.

instant [ˈɪnstənt] *adj* sofortig ;
(food) Instant-. ◆ *n* Moment
der, Augenblick *der*.

instant coffee *n* Instantkaffee *der*, Pulverkaffee *der*.

instead [ɪnˈsted] *adv* stattdessen ; ~ of statt (+G), anstelle
(+G).

instep [ˈɪnstep] *n* Spann *der*.

instinct [ˈɪnstɪŋkt] *n* Instinkt
der.

institute [ˈɪnstɪtjuːt] *n* Institut *das*.

institution [ˌɪnstɪˈtjuːʃn] *n* Institution *die*.

instructions [ɪnˈstrʌkʃnz] *npl*
(for use) Anleitung *die*.

instructor [ɪnˈstrʌktə^r] *n* Lehrer *der* (-in *die*).

instrument [ˈɪnstrʊmənt] *n*
(musical) Instrument *das* ; *(tool)*
Gerät *das*.

insufficient [ˌɪnsəˈfɪʃnt] *adj*
nicht genügend.

insulating tape [ˈɪnsjʊleɪ-
tɪŋ-] *n* Isolierband *das*.

insulation [ˌɪnsjʊˈleɪʃn] *n*
(material) Isoliermaterial *das*.

insulin [ˈɪnsjʊlɪn] *n* Insulin
das.

insult [*n* ˈɪnsʌlt, *vb* ɪnˈsʌlt] *n*
Beleidigung *die*. ◆ *vt* beleidigen.

insurance [ɪnˈʃʊərəns] *n* Versicherung *die*.

insurance certificate *n*
Versicherungsschein *der*.

insurance company *n* Ver-
sicherungsgesellschaft *die*.

insurance policy *n* Versi-
cherungspolice *die*.

insure [ɪnˈʃʊə^r] *vt* versichern.

insured [ɪnˈʃʊəd] *adj* : to be ~
versichert sein.

intact [ɪnˈtækt] *adj* unbeschädigt.

intellectual [ˌɪntəˈlektjʊəl]
adj intellektuell. ◆ *n* Intellek-
tuelle *der, die*.

intelligence [ɪnˈtelɪdʒəns] *n*
Intelligenz *die*.

intelligent [ɪnˈtelɪdʒənt] *adj*
intelligent.

intend [ɪnˈtend] *vt* meinen ; to
~ to do sthg vorⱍhaben, etw zu
tun.

intense [ɪnˈtens] *adj* stark.

intensity [ɪnˈtensəti] *n* Inten-
sität *die*.

intensive [ɪnˈtensɪv] *adj* intensiv.

intensive care *n* Intensivstation *die*.

intent [ɪnˈtent] *adj* : to be ~ on
doing sthg etw unbedingt tun
wollen.

intention [ɪnˈtenʃn] *n* Absicht
die.

intentional [ɪnˈtenʃənl] *adj*
absichtlich.

intentionally [ɪnˈtenʃənəli]
adv absichtlich.

interchange [ˈɪntətʃeɪndʒ] *n*
(on motorway) Autobahnkreuz
das.

Intercity® [ˌɪntəˈsɪti] *n* *(Br)* Intercity *der*.

intercom [ˈɪntəkɒm] *n*
Sprechanlage *die*.

interest [ˈɪntrəst] *n* Interesse
das ; *(on money)* Zinsen *pl*. ◆ *vt*
interessieren ; to take an ~ in
sthg sich für etw interessieren.

interested ['ɪntrəstɪd] adj interessiert ; **to be ~ in** sthg an etw (D) interessiert sein.

interesting ['ɪntrəstɪŋ] adj interessant.

interest rate n Zinssatz der.

interfere [,ɪntə'fɪə'] vi (meddle) sich einlmischen ; **to ~ with** sthg (damage) etw beeinträchtigen.

interference [,ɪntə'fɪərəns] n (on TV, radio) Störung die.

interior [ɪn'tɪərɪə'] adj Innen-. ◆ n Innere die.

intermediate [,ɪntə'miːdjət] adj (stage, level) Zwischen-.

intermission [,ɪntə'mɪʃn] n Pause die.

internal [ɪn'tɜːnl] adj (not foreign) inländisch ; (on the inside) innere(-r) (-s).

internal flight n Inlandflug der.

international [,ɪntə'næʃənl] adj international.

international flight n Auslandsflug der.

Internet ['ɪntənet] n : **the ~** Internet das ; **on the ~** im Internet.

interpret [ɪn'tɜːprɪt] vi dolmetschen.

interpreter [ɪn'tɜːprɪtə'] n Dolmetscher der (-in die).

interrogate [ɪn'terəgeɪt] vt verhören.

interrupt [,ɪntə'rʌpt] vt unterbrechen.

intersection [,ɪntə'sekʃn] n (of roads) Kreuzung die.

interval ['ɪntəvl] n Zeitraum der ; (Br : at cinema, theatre) Pause die.

intervene [,ɪntə'viːn] vi (person) einlgreifen ; (event) dazwischenlkommen.

interview ['ɪntəvjuː] n (on TV, in magazine) Interview das ; (for job) Vorstellungsgespräch das. ◆ vt (on TV, in magazine) interviewen ; (for job) ein Vorstellungsgespräch führen mit.

interviewer ['ɪntəvjuːə'] n Interviewer der (-in die).

intestine [ɪn'testɪn] n Darm der.

intimate ['ɪntɪmət] adj (friends, relationship) eng ; (secrets, thoughts) intim ; (cosy) gemütlich.

intimidate [ɪn'tɪmɪdeɪt] vt einlschüchtern.

into ['ɪntʊ] prep in (+A) ; (crash) gegen ; (research, investigation) über (+A) ; **4 ~ 20 goes 5 (times)** 20 (geteilt) durch 4 ist 5 ; **to translate ~ German** ins Deutsche übersetzen ; **to change ~** sthg (clothes) sich (D) etw anlziehen ; (become) zu etw werden ; **to be ~** sthg (inf : like) auf etw (A) stehen.

intolerable [ɪn'tɒlrəbl] adj unerträglich.

intransitive [ɪn'trænzətɪv] adj intransitiv.

intricate ['ɪntrɪkət] adj kompliziert.

intriguing [ɪn'triːgɪŋ] adj faszinierend.

introduce [,ɪntrə'djuːs] vt (person) vorlstellen ; (new measure) einlführen ; (TV programme) anlkündigen ; **I'd like to ~ you to Fred** ich möchte Ihnen/dir Fred vorstellen.

introduction [,ɪntrə'dʌkʃn] n Einführung die ; (to book) Einleitung die ; (to person) Vorstellung die.

introverted ['ɪntrə,vɜːtɪd] adj introvertiert.

intruder [ɪn'truːdə'] n Eindringling der.

intuition [,ɪntjuː'ɪʃn] n Intuition die.

invade [ɪn'veɪd] vt einǀfallen in.

invalid [adj ɪn'vælɪd, n 'ɪnvəlɪd] adj (ticket, cheque) ungültig. ◆ n Kranke der, die.

invaluable [ɪn'væljuəbl] adj unschätzbar.

invariably [ɪn'veəriəblɪ] adv immer.

invasion [ɪn'veɪʒn] n Invasion die.

invent [ɪn'vent] vt erfinden.

invention [ɪn'venʃn] n Erfindung die.

inventory ['ɪnvəntrɪ] n (list) Bestandsaufnahme die ; (Am : stock) Lagerbestand der.

inverted commas [ɪn'vɜːtɪd-] npl Anführungszeichen pl.

invest [ɪn'vest] vt investieren. ◆ vi : to ~ in sthg in etw (A) investieren.

investigate [ɪn'vestɪgeɪt] vt untersuchen.

investigation [ɪn,vestɪ'geɪʃn] n Untersuchung die.

investment [ɪn'vestmənt] n Anlage die.

invisible [ɪn'vɪzɪbl] adj unsichtbar.

invitation [,ɪnvɪ'teɪʃn] n Einladung die.

invite [ɪn'vaɪt] vt einǀladen ; to ~ sb to do sthg (ask) jn einladen, etw zu tun ; to ~ sb round jn zu sich einladen.

invoice ['ɪnvɔɪs] n Rechnung die.

involve [ɪn'vɒlv] vt (entail) mit sich bringen ; what does it ~? was ist erforderlich? ; to be ~d in sthg (scheme, activity) an etw (D) beteiligt sein ; (accident) in etw (A) verwickelt sein.

involved [ɪn'vɒlvd] adj : what's ~? was ist erforderlich?

inwards ['ɪnwədz] adv nach innen.

IOU n Schuldschein der.

IQ n IQ der.

Iran [ɪ'rɑːn] n Iran der.

Iraq [ɪ'rɑːk] n Irak der.

Ireland ['aɪələnd] n Irland nt.

iris ['aɪərɪs] (pl -es) n (flower) Iris die.

Irish ['aɪrɪʃ] adj irisch. ◆ n (language) Irische das. ◆ npl : the ~ die Iren pl.

Irish coffee n Irishcoffee der (Kaffee mit Whisky und Schlagsahne).

Irishman ['aɪrɪʃmən] (pl -men [-mən]) n Ire der.

Irish stew n Irishstew das (Gericht aus Fleisch, Kartoffeln und Zwiebeln).

Irishwoman ['aɪrɪʃ,womən] (pl -women [-,wɪmɪn]) n Irin die.

iron ['aɪən] n Eisen das ; (for clothes) Bügeleisen das. ◆ vt bügeln.

ironic [aɪ'rɒnɪk] adj ironisch.

ironing board ['aɪənɪŋ-] n Bügelbrett das.

ironmonger's ['aɪən,mʌŋ-gəz] n (Br) Eisenwarengeschäft das.

irrelevant [ɪ'reləvənt] adj belanglos.

irresistible [,ɪrɪ'zɪstəbl] adj unwiderstehlich.

irrespective [,ɪrɪ'spektɪv] : **irrespective of** prep ungeachtet (+G).

irresponsible [,ɪrɪ'spɒnsəbl] adj unverantwortlich.

irrigation [,ɪrɪ'geɪʃn] n Bewässerung die.

irritable ['ɪrɪtəbl] adj reizbar.

irritate ['ɪrɪteɪt] vt (annoy) ärgern ; (skin, eyes) reizen.

irritating ['ɪrɪteɪtɪŋ] adj (annoying) ärgerlich.

IRS n (Am) amerikanisches Finanzamt.

is [ɪz] → be.

Islam ['ɪzlɑːm] n Islam der.

island ['aɪlənd] n Insel die ; (in road) Verkehrsinsel die.

isle [aɪl] n Insel die.

isolated ['aɪsəleɪtɪd] adj (place) isoliert ; (case, error) vereinzelt.

Israel ['ɪzreɪəl] n Israel nt.

issue ['ɪʃuː] n (problem, subject) Thema das ; (of newspaper, magazine) Ausgabe die. ◆ vt (statement) veröffentlichen ; (passport, document) auslstellen ; (banknotes) auslgeben ; (stamps) herauslgeben.

it [ɪt] pron 1. (referring to specific thing : subject) er/sie/es ; (direct object) den/sie/es ; ~'s big er/sie/es ist groß ; she hit ~ sie hat den/sie/es getroffen ; a free book came with ~ es war ein kostenloses Buch dabei.
2. (nonspecific) es ; ~'s easy es ist einfach ; ~'s a difficult question das ist eine schwierige Frage ; tell me about ~! erzähl mir davon! ; ~'s me ich bin's ; who is ~? wer ist da?
3. (used impersonally) es ; ~'s hot es ist heiß ; ~'s six o'clock es ist sechs Uhr ; ~'s Sunday es ist Sonntag.

Italian [ɪ'tæljən] adj italienisch. ◆ n (person) Italiener der (-in die) ; (language) Italienisch das ; an ~ restaurant ein italienisches Restaurant.

Italy ['ɪtəlɪ] n Italien nt.

itch [ɪtʃ] vi jucken.

item ['aɪtəm] n (object) Gegenstand der ; (on agenda) Punkt der ; (of news) Meldung die.

itemized bill ['aɪtəmaɪzd-] n spezifizierte Rechnung.

its [ɪts] adj (masculine or neuter subject) sein ; (feminine subject) ihr.

it's [ɪts] = **it is, it has**.

itself [ɪt'self] pron (reflexive) sich ; (after prep) sich selbst ; **the house ~ is fine** das Haus selbst ist in Ordnung.

I've [aɪv] = **I have**.

ivory ['aɪvərɪ] n Elfenbein das.

ivy ['aɪvɪ] n Efeu der.

J

jab [dʒæb] n (Br : inf : injection) Spritze die.

jack [dʒæk] n *(for car)* Wagenheber der ; *(playing card)* Bube der.

jacket ['dʒækɪt] n *(garment)* Jacke die ; *(of book)* Umschlag der ; *(Am : of record)* Plattenhülle die ; *(of potato)* Schale die.

jacket potato n in der Schale gebackene Kartoffel.

jack-knife vi Klappmesser das.

Jacuzzi® [dʒə'ku:zɪ] n Whirlpool der.

jade [dʒeɪd] n Jade die.

jail [dʒeɪl] n Gefängnis das.

jam [dʒæm] n *(food)* Konfitüre die ; *(of traffic)* Stau der ; *(inf : difficult situation)* Klemme die. ◆ vt *(pack tightly)* hineinⁱquetschen. ◆ vi *(get stuck)* klemmen ; **the roads are jammed** die Straßen sind verstopft.

jam-packed [-'pækt] adj *(inf)* gestopft voll.

Jan. [dʒæn] *(abbr of January)* Jan.

janitor ['dʒænɪtə'] n *(Am & Scot)* Hausmeister der.

January ['dʒænjʊərɪ] n Januar der ; → **September**.

Japan [dʒə'pæn] n Japan nt.

Japanese [,dʒæpə'ni:z] adj japanisch. ◆ n *(language)* Japanisch das. ◆ npl : **the ~** die Japaner pl.

jar [dʒɑ:'] n Glas das.

javelin ['dʒævlɪn] n Speer der.

jaw [dʒɔ:] n Kiefer der.

jazz [dʒæz] n Jazz der.

jealous ['dʒeləs] adj *(envious)* neidisch ; *(possessive)* eifersüchtig.

jeans [dʒi:nz] npl Jeans pl.

Jeep® [dʒi:p] n Jeep® der.

Jello® ['dʒeləʊ] n *(Am)* Wackelpudding der.

jelly ['dʒelɪ] n *(dessert)* Wackelpudding der ; *(Am : jam)* Gelee das.

jellyfish ['dʒelɪfɪʃ] *(pl* **jellyfish)** n Qualle die.

jeopardize ['dʒepədaɪz] vt gefährden.

jerk [dʒɜ:k] n *(movement)* Ruck der ; *(inf : idiot)* Blödmann der.

jersey ['dʒɜ:zɪ] *(pl* **-s)** n *(garment)* Pullover der.

jet [dʒet] n *(aircraft)* Jet der ; *(of liquid, gas)* Strahl der ; *(outlet)* Düse die.

jetfoil ['dʒetfɔɪl] n Tragflächenboot das.

jet lag n Jetlag der.

jet-ski n Jetski der.

jetty ['dʒetɪ] n Bootsanlegestelle die.

Jew [dʒu:] n Jude der (Jüdin die).

jewel ['dʒu:əl] n Edelstein der. ■ **jewels** npl *(jewellery)* Juwelen pl.

jeweler's ['dʒu:ələz] *(Am)* = **jeweller's**.

jeweller's ['dʒu:ələz] n *(Br)* Juweliergeschäft das.

jewellery ['dʒu:əlrɪ] n *(Br)* Schmuck der.

jewelry ['dʒu:əlrɪ] *(Am)* = **jewellery**.

Jewish ['dʒu:ɪʃ] adj jüdisch.

jigsaw (puzzle) ['dʒɪgsɔ:-] n Puzzlespiel das.

jingle ['dʒɪŋgl] n *(of advert)* Jingle der.

job [dʒɒb] n *(regular work)* Stelle die, Job der ; *(task)* Arbeit die ; *(function)* Aufgabe die ; **to lose one's ~** entlassen werden.

job centre n (Br) Arbeitsvermittlungsstelle die.

jockey ['dʒɒkɪ] (pl -s) n Jockei der.

jog [dʒɒg] vt (bump) anlstoßen. ◆ vi joggen. ◆ n : to go for a ~ joggen gehen.

jogging ['dʒɒgɪŋ] n Jogging das ; to go ~ joggen gehen.

join [dʒɔɪn] vt (club, organization) beiltreten (+D) ; (fasten together, link) verbinden ; (other people) sich anlschließen (+D) ; (participate in) teillnehmen an (+D). ■ **join in** vt fus mitlmachen bei (+D). ◆ vi mitlmachen.

joint [dʒɔɪnt] adj gemeinsam. ◆ n (of body) Gelenk das ; (Br : of meat) Braten der ; (in structure) Verbindungsstelle die.

joke [dʒəʊk] n Witz der. ◆ vi scherzen.

joker ['dʒəʊkə'] n (playing card) Joker der.

jolly ['dʒɒlɪ] adj (cheerful) lustig, fröhlich. ◆ adv (Br : inf : very) sehr.

jolt [dʒəʊlt] n Ruck der.

jot [dʒɒt] : **jot down** vt sep notieren.

journal ['dʒɜːnl] n (professional magazine) Zeitschrift die ; (diary) Tagebuch das.

journalist ['dʒɜːnəlɪst] n Journalist der (-in die).

journey ['dʒɜːnɪ] (pl -s) n Reise die.

joy [dʒɔɪ] n Freude die.

joypad ['dʒɔɪpæd] n (of video game) Joypad der.

joyrider ['dʒɔɪraɪdə'] n Autodieb, der mit gestohlenen Autos Spritztouren unternimmt.

joystick ['dʒɔɪstɪk] n (of video game) Joystick der.

judge [dʒʌdʒ] n (JUR) Richter der (-in die) ; (of competition) Preisrichter der (-in die) ; (SPORT) Schiedsrichter der (-in die). ◆ vt (competition) beurteilen ; (evaluate) einlschätzen.

judg(e)ment ['dʒʌdʒmənt] n (JUR) Urteil das ; (opinion) Beurteilung die ; (capacity to judge) Urteilsvermögen das.

judo ['dʒuːdəʊ] n Judo das.

jug [dʒʌg] n Krug der.

juggernaut ['dʒʌgənɔːt] n (Br) Schwerlastzug der.

juggle ['dʒʌgl] vi jonglieren.

juice [dʒuːs] n (from fruit, vegetables) Saft der ; (from meat) Bratensaft der.

juicy ['dʒuːsɪ] adj (food) saftig.

jukebox ['dʒuːkbɒks] n Jukebox die.

July [dʒuːˈlaɪ] n Juli der ; → September.

jumble sale ['dʒʌmbl-] n (Br) Wohltätigkeitsbasar der.

ⓘ **JUMBLE SALE**

Die „Jumble sales" werden gewöhnlich in Pfarrsälen oder Gemeinde- und Stadthallen abgehalten und ähneln den Trödelmärkten im deutschsprachigen Raum. Verkauft werden billige Kleidung, Bücher und Haushaltswaren aus zweiter Hand. Der Erlös kommt meist wohltätigen Vereinen zugute.

jumbo ['dʒʌmbəʊ] adj (inf : big) Riesen-.

jumbo jet n Jumbojet der.

jump [dʒʌmp] n Sprung der. ◆ vi springen ; (with fright) zusammenlfahren ; (increase) rapide anlsteigen. ◆ vt (Am : train, bus) schwarzlfahren in (+D) ; to ~ the queue (Br) sich vorldrängen.

jumper ['dʒʌmpə] n (Br : pullover) Pullover der ; (Am : dress) ärmelloses Kleid.

jump leads npl Starthilfekabel pl.

junction ['dʒʌŋkʃn] n (of roads) Kreuzung die ; (of railway lines) Knotenpunkt der.

June [dʒuːn] n Juni der ; → September.

jungle ['dʒʌŋgl] n Dschungel der.

junior ['dʒuːnjə] adj (of lower rank) untergeordnet ; (Am : after name) junior. ◆ n (younger person) Junior der.

junior school n (Br) Grundschule die (für 7- bis 11-Jährige).

junk [dʒʌŋk] n (inf : unwanted things) Trödel der.

junk food n (inf) ungesundes Essen wie z.B. Fastfood, Chips, Süßigkeiten.

junkie ['dʒʌŋkɪ] n (inf) Junkie der.

junk shop n Trödelladen der.

jury ['dʒʊərɪ] n Geschworenen pl ; (in competition) Jury die.

just [dʒʌst] adv (recently) gerade ; (exactly) genau ; (only) nur ; (simply) einfach. ◆ adj gerecht ; ~ a bit more etwas mehr ; ~ over an hour etwas mehr als eine Stunde ; it's ~ as good es ist genauso gut ; to be ~

about to do sthg dabei sein, etw zu tun ; to have ~ done sthg gerade etw getan haben ; ~ about (almost) fast ; (only) ~ (almost not) gerade (noch) ; ~ a minute! einen Moment!

justice ['dʒʌstɪs] n Gerechtigkeit die.

justify ['dʒʌstɪfaɪ] vt rechtfertigen.

jut [dʒʌt] : jut out vi vorlstehen.

juvenile ['dʒuːvənaɪl] adj (young) jugendlich ; (childish) kindisch.

K

kangaroo [ˌkæŋgə'ruː] n Känguru das.

karate [kə'rɑːtɪ] n Karate das.

kebab [kɪ'bæb] n : doner ~ Gyros der ; shish ~ Kebab der.

keel [kiːl] n Kiel der.

keen [kiːn] adj (enthusiastic) begeistert ; (eyesight, hearing) scharf ; to be ~ on mögen ; to be ~ to do sthg etw unbedingt tun wollen.

keep [kiːp] (pt & pp kept) vt (retain) behalten ; (store) auflbewahren ; (maintain) halten ; (promise, appointment) einlhalten ; (secret) für sich behalten ; (delay) auflhalten ; (record, diary) führen. ◆ vi (food) sich halten ; (remain) bleiben ; to ~ (on) doing sthg (do continuously) etw weiter tun ; (do repeatedly) etw dauernd tun ; to ~ sb from doing sthg jn davon ablhalten, etw zu

tun ; ~ **back!** zurückbleiben! ;
to ~ clear (of) (etw) freilhalten ;
'~ **in lane!**' *Schild, das anzeigt,
dass es verboten ist, die Spur zu
wechseln* ; '~ **left**' 'Links fahren' ; '~ **off the grass!**' 'Betreten
der Rasenfläche verboten!' ; '~
out!' 'Betreten verboten!' ; '~
your distance!' 'Abstand halten!' ■ **keep up** *vt sep*
aufrechterhalten. ◆ *vi* mitlhal-
ten.

keep-fit *n* *(Br)* Fitnessübun-
gen *pl*.

kennel ['kenl] *n* Hundehütte
die.

kept [kept] *pt & pp →* **keep**.

kerb [kɜ:b] *n* *(Br)* Randstein
der.

kerosene ['kerəsi:n] *n* *(Am)*
Petroleum *das*.

ketchup ['ketʃəp] *n* Ketchup
der.

kettle ['ketl] *n* Wasserkessel
der ; **to put the ~ on** Wasser auflsetzen.

key [ki:] *n* Schlüssel *der* ; *(of
piano, typewriter)* Taste *die*.
◆ *adj* Schlüssel-.

keyboard ['ki:bɔ:d] *n* *(of typewriter, piano)* Tastatur *die* ;
(musical instrument) Keyboard
das.

keyhole ['ki:həʊl] *n* Schlüsselloch *das*.

keypad ['ki:pæd] *n* Tastenfeld
das.

key ring *n* Schlüsselring *der*.

kg *(abbr of kilogram)* kg.

kick [kɪk] *n* *(of foot)* Tritt *der*.
◆ *vt* treten.

kickoff ['kɪkɒf] *n* Anstoß *der*.

kid [kɪd] *n* *(inf : child)* Kind *das*.
◆ *vi* *(joke)* scherzen.

kidnap ['kɪdnæp] *vt* entführ-
ren, kidnappen.

kidnaper ['kɪdnæpər] *(Am)* =
kidnapper.

kidnapper ['kɪdnæpəʳ] *n* *(Br)*
Entführer *der*, Kidnapper *der*.

kidney ['kɪdnɪ] *(pl* -s) *n* Niere
die.

kidney bean *n* Kidneybohne
die.

kill [kɪl] *vt* töten ; *(time)* tot-
schlagen ; **my feet are ~ing me!**
meine Füße bringen mich um!

killer ['kɪləʳ] *n* Mörder *der* (-in
die).

kilo ['ki:ləʊ] *(pl* -s) *n* Kilo *das*.

kilogram ['kɪlə,græm] *n* Kilogramm *das*.

kilometre ['kɪlə,mi:təʳ] *n* Kilometer *der*.

kilt [kɪlt] *n* Kilt *der*, Schotten-
rock *der*.

kind [kaɪnd] *adj* nett. ◆ *n* Art
die ; *(of cheese, wine etc)* Sorte
die ; **what ~ of music do you like?**
welche Musik magst du? ; **what
~ of car do you drive?** was für ein
Auto hast du? ; ~ **of** *(Am : inf)* irgendwie.

kindergarten ['kɪndə,gɑːtn]
n Kindergarten *der*.

kindly ['kaɪndlɪ] *adv* : **would
you ~ wait here?** wären Sie so
nett, hier zu warten?

kindness ['kaɪndnɪs] *n*
Freundlichkeit *die*.

king [kɪŋ] *n* König *der*.

kingfisher ['kɪŋ,fɪʃəʳ] *n* Eis-
vogel *der*.

king prawn *n* Riesengarnele
die.

king-size bed *n* Kingsize-
Bett *das*.

knowledge

kiosk ['kiːɒsk] n *(for newspapers etc)* Kiosk der ; *(Br : phone box)* öffentlicher Fernsprecher.

kipper ['kɪpə'] n Räucherhering der.

kiss [kɪs] n Kuss der. ◆ vt küssen.

kiss of life n Mund-zu-Mund-Beatmung die.

kit [kɪt] n *(set)* Ausrüstung die ; *(clothes)* Bekleidung die ; *(for assembly)* Bausatz der.

kitchen ['kɪtʃɪn] n Küche die.

kitchen unit n Einbauküchenelement das.

kite [kaɪt] n *(toy)* Drachen der.

kitten ['kɪtn] n Kätzchen das.

kitty ['kɪtɪ] n *(money)* Gemeinschaftskasse die.

kiwi fruit ['kiːwiː-] n Kiwi die.

Kleenex® ['kliːneks] n Papiertaschentuch das.

km *(abbr of kilometre)* km.

km/h *(abbr of kilometres per hour)* km/h.

knack [næk] n : to get the ~ of doing sthg den Dreh herauskriegen, wie man etw macht.

knackered ['nækəd] adj *(Br : inf)* erledigt.

knapsack ['næpsæk] n Rucksack der.

knee [niː] n Knie das.

kneecap ['niːkæp] n Kniescheibe die.

kneel [niːl] *(pt & pp* knelt [nelt]) vi knien ; *(go down on one's knees)* sich hin|knien.

knew [njuː] pt → **know**.

knickers ['nɪkəz] npl *(Br)* Schlüpfer der.

knife [naɪf] *(pl* knives) n Messer das.

knight [naɪt] n *(in history)* Ritter der ; *(in chess)* Springer der.

knit [nɪt] vt stricken.

knitted ['nɪtɪd] adj gestrickt.

knitting ['nɪtɪŋ] n *(thing being knitted)* Strickzeug das ; *(activity)* Stricken das.

knitting needle n Stricknadel die.

knitwear ['nɪtweə'] n Strickwaren pl.

knives [naɪvz] pl → **knife**.

knob [nɒb] n *(on door etc)* Knauf der ; *(on machine)* Knopf der.

knock [nɒk] n *(at door)* Klopfen das. ◆ vt *(hit)* stoßen. ◆ vi *(at door etc)* klopfen. ■ **knock down** vt sep *(pedestrian)* an|fahren ; *(building)* ab|reißen ; *(price)* reduzieren. ■ **knock out** vt sep bewusstlos schlagen ; *(of competition)* : to be ~ed out aus|scheiden. ■ **knock over** vt sep um|stoßen ; *(pedestrian)* um|fahren.

knocker ['nɒkə'] n *(on door)* Türklopfer der.

knot [nɒt] n Knoten der.

know [nəʊ] *(pt* knew, *pp* known) vt wissen ; *(person, place)* kennen ; *(language)* können ; to get to ~ sb jn kennen lernen ; to ~ about sthg *(understand)* sich mit etw aus|kennen ; *(have heard)* etw wissen ; to ~ how to do sthg etw tun können ; to ~ of kennen ; to be ~n as bekannt sein als ; to let sb ~ sthg jm über etw (A) Bescheid sagen ; you ~ *(for emphasis)* weißt du.

knowledge ['nɒlɪdʒ] n *(facts known)* Kenntnisse pl ; *(aware-*

ness) Wissen *das* ; **to my ~ so-** weit ich weiß.

known [nəʊn] *pp* → **know**.

knuckle ['nʌkl] *n* Knöchel *der* ; *(of pork)* Hachse *die*.

Koran [kɒ'rɑːn] *n* : **the ~** der Koran.

L

l *(abbr of litre)* l.

L *(abbr of large)* L ; *(abbr of learner)* in Großbritannien Schild am Auto, um anzuzeigen, dass der Fahrer noch keinen Führerschein hat und nur in Begleitung fahren darf.

lab [læb] *n (inf)* Labor *das*.

label ['leibl] *n* Etikett *das*.

labor ['leibər] *(Am)* = **labour**.

laboratory [*(Br)* lə'bɒrətrɪ, *(Am)* 'læbrə,tɔːrɪ] *n* Labor *das*.

labour ['leibər] *n* Arbeit *die* ; **to be in ~** *(MED)* in den Wehen liegen.

labourer ['leibərə] *n* Arbeiter *der* (-in *die*).

Labour Party *n (Br)* links ausgerichtete Partei in Großbritannien.

labour-saving *adj* arbeitssparend.

lace [leis] *n (material)* Spitze *die* ; *(for shoe)* Schnürsenkel *der*.

lace-ups *npl* Schnürschuhe *pl*.

lack [læk] *n* Mangel *der*. ◆ *vt* mangeln an (+D). ◆ *vi* : **to be ~ing** fehlen.

lacquer ['lækə'] *n (paint)* Lack *der* ; *(for hair)* Haarspray *der*.

lad [læd] *n (inf : boy)* Junge *der*.

ladder ['lædə'] *n* Leiter *die* ; *(Br : in tights)* Laufmasche *die*.

ladies ['leidiz] *n (Br : toilet)* Damen *n* ⌐

ladies room *(Am)* = **ladies**.

ladieswear ['leidɪz,weə'] *n* Damenbekleidung *die*.

ladle ['leidl] *n* Kelle *die*.

lady ['leidɪ] *n* Dame *die* ; **Lady Diana** Lady Diana.

ladybird ['leidɪbɜːd] *n* Marienkäfer *der*.

lag [læg] *vi* : **to ~ (behind)** zurücklbleiben.

lager ['lɑːgə'] *n* helles Bier, Lagerbier *das*.

lagoon [lə'guːn] *n* Lagune *die*.

laid [leid] *pt & pp* → **lay**.

lain [lein] *pp* → **lie**.

lake [leik] *n* See *der*.

Lake District *n* : **the ~** der Lake District *(Seenlandschaft in Nordwestengland)*.

lamb [læm] *n (animal)* Lamm *das* ; *(meat)* Lammfleisch *das*.

lamb chop *n* Lammkotelett *das*.

lame [leim] *adj* lahm.

lamp [læmp] *n* Lampe *die*.

lamppost ['læmppəʊst] *n* Laternenpfahl *der*.

lampshade ['læmpʃeid] *n* Lampenschirm *der*.

land [lænd] *n* Land *das*. ◆ *vi* landen.

landing ['lændɪŋ] *n (of plane)* Landung *die* ; *(at top of stairs)* Gang *der* ; *(between stairs)* Treppenabsatz *der*.

landlady ['lænd,leɪdɪ] n (of house) Vermieterin die ; (of pub) Gastwirtin die.

landlord ['lændlɔːd] n (of house) Vermieter der ; (of pub) Gastwirt der.

landmark ['lændmɑːk] n Orientierungspunkt der.

landscape ['lændskeɪp] n Landschaft die.

landslide ['lændslaɪd] n Erdrutsch der.

lane [leɪn] n (in country) kleine Landstraße ; (in town) Gasse die ; (on road, motorway) Fahrspur die ; 'get in ~' 'Einordnen'.

language ['læŋgwɪdʒ] n Sprache die ; (words) Ausdrucksweise die ; **bad ~** Kraftausdrücke pl.

lap [læp] n (of person) Schoß der ; (of race) Runde die.

lapel [lə'pel] n Aufschlag der.

lapse [læps] vi (passport, membership) ablaufen.

laptop ['læptɒp] n (COMPUT) Laptop der.

lard [lɑːd] n Schmalz das.

larder ['lɑːdə'] n Vorratskammer die.

large [lɑːdʒ] adj groß.

largely ['lɑːdʒlɪ] adv größtenteils.

large-scale adj Groß-.

lark [lɑːk] n Lerche die.

laryngitis [,lærɪn'dʒaɪtɪs] n Kehlkopfentzündung die.

lasagne [lə'zænjə] n Lasagne die.

laser ['leɪzə'] n Laser der.

lass [læs] n (inf: girl) Mädel das.

last [lɑːst] adj letzte(-r) (-s). ◆ adv zuletzt. ◆ vi dauern ;

(weather) bleiben ; (money, supply) ausreichen. ◆ pron : **the ~ to come** als Letzte(-r) (-s) kommen ; **the ~ but one** der/die/das Vorletzte ; **the day before ~** vorgestern ; **~ year** letztes Jahr ; **the ~ year** das letzte Jahr ; **at ~** endlich.

lastly ['lɑːstlɪ] adv zuletzt.

last-minute adj in letzter Minute.

latch [lætʃ] n Riegel der ; **to be on the ~** nicht abgeschlossen sein.

late [leɪt] adj spät ; (train, flight) verspätet ; (dead) verstorben. ◆ adv spät ; (not on time) zu spät ; **two hours ~** zwei Stunden Verspätung.

lately ['leɪtlɪ] adv in letzter Zeit.

late-night adj (chemist) Nacht- ; (shop) länger geöffnet.

later ['leɪtə'] adj später. ◆ adv : **~ (on)** (afterwards) später ; **at a ~ date** zu einem späteren Zeitpunkt.

latest ['leɪtɪst] adj : **the ~ fashion** die neueste Mode ; **the ~** das Neueste ; **at the ~** spätestens.

lather ['lɑːðə'] n Schaum der.

Latin ['lætɪn] n Latein das.

Latin America n Lateinamerika nt.

Latin American adj lateinamerikanisch. ◆ n Lateinamerikaner der (-in die).

latitude ['lætɪtjuːd] n Breite die.

latter ['lætə'] n : **the ~** der/die/das Letztere.

laugh [lɑːf] n Lachen das. ◆ vi lachen ; **to have a ~** (Br : inf:

have fun) sich amüsieren.
■ **laugh at** *vt fus (mock)* sich lustig machen über *(+A)*.

laughter ['lɑːftə] *n* Gelächter *das.*

launch [lɔːntʃ] *vt (boat)* vom Stapel lassen ; *(new product)* auf den Markt bringen.

laund(e)rette [lɔːn'dret] *n* Waschsalon *der.*

laundry ['lɔːndrɪ] *n (washing)* Wäsche *die* ; *(place)* Wäscherei *die.*

lavatory ['lævtrɪ] *n* Toilette *die.*

lavender ['lævəndə] *n* Lavendel *der.*

lavish ['lævɪʃ] *adj* üppig.

law [lɔː] *n (rule)* Gesetz *das* ; *(system)* Recht *das* ; *(study)* Jura *pl* ; **to be against the ~** gesetzeswidrig sein.

lawn [lɔːn] *n* Rasen *der.*

lawnmower ['lɔːn,məʊə] *n* Rasenmäher *der.*

lawyer ['lɔːjə] *n* Rechtsanwalt *der* (-anwältin *die*).

laxative ['læksətɪv] *n* Abführmittel *das.*

lay [leɪ] *(pt & pp laid) pt → lie.*
◆ *vt* legen ; **to ~ the table** den Tisch decken. ■ **lay off** *vt sep (worker)* Feierschichten machen lassen. ■ **lay on** *vt sep (food etc)* sorgen für ; *(transport)* einsetzen. ■ **lay out** *vt sep* ausllegen.

lay-by *(pl* **lay-bys)** *n* Parkbucht *die.*

layer ['leɪə] *n* Schicht *die.*

layman ['leɪmən] *(pl* **-men** [-mən]) *n* Laie *der* (Laiin *die*).

layout ['leɪaʊt] *n* Plan *der.*

lazy ['leɪzɪ] *adj* faul.

lb *(abbr of pound)* Pfd.

lead¹ [liːd] *(pt & pp led) vt* führen ; *(be in front of)* anlführen. ◆ *vi* führen. ◆ *n (for dog)* Leine *die* ; *(cable)* Schnur *die* ; **to ~ sb to do sthg** jn dazu bringen, etw zu tun ; **to ~ to** führen zu *(+D)* ; **to ~ the way** voranlgehen ; **to be in the ~** *(in race, match)* führen.

lead² [led] *n (metal)* Blei *das* ; *(for pencil)* Mine *die.* ◆ *adj* Blei-.

leaded petrol ['ledɪd-] *n* bleihaltiges Benzin.

leader ['liːdə] *n (person in charge)* Leiter *der* (-in *die*) ; *(in race)* **to be the ~** führen.

leadership ['liːdəʃɪp] *n* Leitung *die.*

lead-free [led-] *adj* bleifrei.

leading ['liːdɪŋ] *adj* leitend.

lead singer [liːd-] *n* Leadsänger *der* (-in *die*).

leaf [liːf] *(pl* **leaves)** *n* Blatt *das.*

leaflet ['liːflɪt] *n* Reklameblatt *das.*

league [liːg] *n* Liga *die.*

leak [liːk] *n (hole)* undichte Stelle *die* ; *(of water)* Leck *das* ; *(of gas)* Gasausfluss *der.* ◆ *vi* undicht sein.

lean [liːn] *(pt & pp leant* [lent] OR **-ed)** *adj (meat, person)* mager. ◆ *vi* sich lehnen. ◆ *vt* **to ~ sthg against sthg** etw gegen etw lehnen ; **to ~ on** sich lehnen an *(+A).* ■ **lean forward** *vi* sich nach vorne lehnen. ■ **lean over** *vi* sich nach vorne beugen.

leap [liːp] *(pt & pp leapt* [lept] OR **-ed)** *vi* springen.

leap year *n* Schaltjahr *das.*

learn [lɜːn] *(pt & pp learnt* OR **-ed)** *vt* lernen ; **to ~ (how) to do**

sthg lernen, etw zu tun ; to ~ about sthg *(hear about)* etw erfahren ; *(study)* etw lernen.

learner (driver) ['lɜːnəʳ-] n Fahrschüler der (-in die).

learnt [lɜːnt] pt & pp → **learn**.

lease [liːs] n Pacht die ; *(contract)* Mietvertrag der. ◆ vt pachten ; to ~ sthg from sb etw von jm pachten ; to ~ sthg to sb jm etw verpachten.

leash [liːʃ] n Leine die.

least [liːst] adv am wenigsten. ◆ adj wenigste(-r) (-s). ◆ pron : (the) ~ das wenigste ; it's the ~ I can do das ist das Mindeste, was ich tun kann ; at ~ wenigstens.

leather ['leðəʳ] n Leder das.
▨ **leathers** npl *(of motorcyclist)* Lederanzug der.

leave [liːv] *(pt & pp left)* vt verlassen ; *(not take away)* lassen ; *(not use, not eat)* übrig lassen ; *(a mark, scar, in will)* hinterlassen ; *(space, gap)* lassen. ◆ vi gehen, fahren ; *(train, bus)* abfahren. ◆ n *(time off work)* Urlaub der ; → **left** ; to ~ a message eine Nachricht hinterlassen.
▨ **leave behind** vt sep lassen.
▨ **leave out** vt sep auslassen.

leaves [liːvz] pl → **leaf**.

Lebanon ['lebənən] n Libanon der.

lecture ['lektʃəʳ] n *(at university, conference)* Vorlesung die.

lecturer ['lektʃərəʳ] n Dozent der (-in die).

lecture theatre n Vorlesungssaal der.

led [led] pt & pp → **lead**.

ledge [ledʒ] n Sims der.

leek [liːk] n Lauch der.

left [left] pt & pp → **leave**. ◆ adj linke(-r) (-s). ◆ adv links. ◆ n linke Seite, Linke die ; on the ~ links ; to be ~ übrig sein ; there are none ~ sie sind alle.

left-hand adj linke(-r) (-s).

left-hand drive n Linkssteuerung die.

left-handed [-'hændɪd] adj *(implement)* für Linkshänder ; to be ~ Linkshänder(-in) sein.

left-luggage locker n (Br) Schließfach das.

left-luggage office n (Br) Gepäckaufbewahrung die.

left-wing adj linke(-r) (-s).

leg [leg] n Bein das ; ~ of lamb Lammkeule die.

legal ['liːgl] adj *(concerning the law)* rechtlich, Rechts- ; *(lawful)* gesetzlich.

legal aid n Prozesskostenhilfe die.

legalize ['liːgəlaɪz] vt legalisieren.

legal system n Rechtswesen das.

legend ['ledʒənd] n Legende die.

leggings ['legɪŋz] npl Leggings pl.

legible ['ledʒɪbl] adj leserlich.

legislation [,ledʒɪs'leɪʃn] n Gesetze pl.

legitimate [lɪ'dʒɪtɪmət] adj legitim.

leisure [(Br) 'leʒəʳ, (Am) 'liːʒəʳ] n Freizeit die.

leisure centre n Freizeitzentrum das.

leisure pool n Freizeitbad das.

lemon ['lemən] n Zitrone die.

lemonade [ˌleməˈneɪd] n Limonade die.

lemon curd [-kɜːd] n (Br) Brotaufstrich aus Zitronensaft, Eiern und Butter.

lemon juice n Zitronensaft der.

lemon sole n Seezunge die.

lemon tea n Zitronentee der.

lend [lend] (pt & pp lent) vt leihen ; **to ~ sb sthg** jm etw leihen.

length [leŋθ] n Länge die ; (of swimming pool) Bahn die.

lengthen [ˈleŋθən] vt verlängern.

lens [lenz] n (of camera) Objektiv das ; (of glasses) Brillenglas das ; (contact lens) Kontaktlinse die.

lent [lent] pt & pp → **lend**.

Lent [lent] n Fastenzeit die.

lentils [ˈlentlz] npl Linsen pl.

Leo [ˈliːəʊ] n Löwe der.

leopard [ˈlepəd] n Leopard der.

leopard-skin adj Leopardenfell-.

leotard [ˈliːətɑːd] n Trikot das.

leper [ˈlepə'] n Leprakranke der, die.

lesbian [ˈlezbɪən] adj lesbisch.
◆ n Lesbierin die.

less [les] adj, adv & pron weniger ; **~ than 20** weniger als 20.

lesson [ˈlesn] n (class) Stunde die.

let [let] (pt & pp let) vt lassen ; (rent out) vermieten ; **to ~ sb do sthg** jn etw tun lassen ; **to ~ go of sthg** etw loslassen ; **to ~ sb have sthg** jm etw überlassen ; **to ~ sb know sthg** jn etw wissen lassen ; **~'s go!** gehen wir! ;

'to ~' (for rent) 'zu vermieten'. ■ **let in** vt sep hereinlassen. ■ **let off** vt sep (excuse) davonkommen lassen ; **can you ~ me off at the station?** kannst du mich am Bahnhof aussteigen lassen? ■ **let out** vt sep hinauslassen.

letdown [ˈletdaʊn] n (inf) Enttäuschung die.

lethargic [ləˈθɑːdʒɪk] adj lethargisch.

letter [ˈletə'] n (written message) Brief der ; (of alphabet) Buchstabe der.

letterbox [ˈletəbɒks] n (Br) Briefkasten der.

lettuce [ˈletɪs] n Kopfsalat der.

leuk(a)emia [luːˈkiːmɪə] n Leukämie die.

level [ˈlevl] adj (flat) eben ; (horizontal) waagerecht ; (at same height) auf gleicher Höhe.
◆ n (height) Höhe die ; (storey) Etage die ; (standard) Niveau das ; **to be ~ with** (in height) sich auf gleicher Höhe befinden wie ; (in standard) auf dem gleichen Niveau sein wie.

level crossing n (Br) Bahnübergang der.

lever [(Br) ˈliːvə', (Am) ˈlevər] n Hebel der.

liability [ˌlaɪəˈbɪlətɪ] n Haftung die.

liable [ˈlaɪəbl] adj : **to be ~ to do sthg** (likely) etw leicht tun können ; **to be ~ for sthg** (responsible) für etw haften.

liaise [lɪˈeɪz] vi : **to ~ with** in ständigem Kontakt stehen mit.

liar [ˈlaɪə'] n Lügner der (-in die).

liberal ['lıbərəl] *adj (tolerant)* tolerant; *(generous)* großzügig.

Liberal Democrat Party *n* britische liberale Partei.

liberate ['lıbəreıt] *vt* befreien.

liberty ['lıbətı] *n* Freiheit *die*.

Libra ['li:brə] *n* Waage *die*.

librarian [laı'breərıən] *n* Bibliothekar *der* (-in *die*).

library ['laıbrərı] *n* Bibliothek *die*.

Libya ['lıbıə] *n* Libyen *nt*.

lice [laıs] *npl* Läuse *pl*.

licence ['laısəns] *n (Br)* Genehmigung *die*; *(for driving)* Führerschein *der*; *(for TV)* Fernsehgebühr *die*. ◆ *vt (Am)* = **license**.

license ['laısəns] *vt (Br)* genehmigen. ◆ *n (Am)* = **licence**.

licensed ['laısənst] *adj (restaurant, bar)* mit Schankkonzession.

licensing hours ['laısənsıŋ-] *npl (Br)* Ausschankzeiten *pl*.

lick [lık] *vt* lecken.

lid [lıd] *n* Deckel *der*.

lie [laı] *(pt* lay, *pp* lain, *cont* lying) *n* Lüge *die*. ◆ *vi (tell lie)* lügen; *(be horizontal, be situated)* liegen; *(lie down)* sich legen; **to ~ to sb** jn anllügen; **to tell ~s** lügen; **to ~ about sthg** etw nicht richtig anlgeben. ▓ **lie down** *vi* sich hinllegen.

lieutenant [(Br) lef'tenənt, (Am) luː'tenənt] *n* Leutnant *der*.

life [laıf] *(pl* lives) *n* Leben *das*.

life assurance *n* Lebensversicherung *die*.

life belt *n* Rettungsring *der*.

lifeboat ['laıfbəʊt] *n* Rettungsboot *das*.

lifeguard ['laıfgɑːd] *n (at swimming pool)* Bademeister *der* (-in *die*); *(at beach)* Rettungsschwimmer *der* (-in *die*).

life jacket *n* Schwimmweste *die*.

lifelike ['laıflaık] *adj* naturgetreu.

life preserver [-prı'zɜːvər] *n (Am : life belt)* Rettungsring *der*; *(life jacket)* Schwimmweste *die*.

life-size *adj* lebensgroß.

lifespan ['laıfspæn] *n* Lebenserwartung *die*.

lifestyle ['laıfstaıl] *n* Lebensstil *der*.

lift [lıft] *n (Br : elevator)* Aufzug *der*. ◆ *vt* heben. ◆ *vi (fog)* sich lichten; **to give sb a ~** jn mitlnehmen. ▓ **lift up** *vt sep* hochlheben.

light [laıt] *(pt & pp* lit OR -ed) *adj (not dark)* hell; *(not heavy)* leicht. ◆ *n* Licht *das*; *(for cigarette)* Feuer *das*. ◆ *vt (fire, cigarette)* anlzünden; *(room, stage)* beleuchten; **have you got a ~?** haben Sie Feuer?; **to set ~ to sthg** etw anlzünden. ▓ **lights** *(traffic lights)* Ampel *die*. ▓ **light up** *vt sep (house, road)* erleuchten. ◆ *vi (inf : light a cigarette)* sich (D) eine anlstecken.

light bulb *n* Glühbirne *die*.

lighter ['laıtə'] *n* Feuerzeug *das*.

light-hearted [-'hɑːtıd] *adj* unbekümmert, leicht.

lighthouse ['laıthaʊs, *pl* -haʊzız] *n* Leuchtturm *der*.

lighting ['laıtıŋ] *n* Beleuchtung *die*.

light meter n Belichtungsmesser der.

lightning ['laɪtnɪŋ] n Blitz der.

lightweight ['laɪtweɪt] adj
leicht.

like [laɪk] prep wie ; (typical of)
typisch für. ◆ vt mögen ; ~ this/
that so ; to ~ doing sthg etw gern
tun ; do you ~ it? gefällt es dir? ;
what's it ~? wie ist es? ; to look ~
sthg jm/etw ähnlich sehen ; I'd
~ to sit down ich würde mich
gern hinlsetzen ; I'd ~ a drink
ich würde gern etwas trinken.

likelihood ['laɪklɪhʊd]nWahr-
scheinlichkeit die.

likely ['laɪklɪ] adj wahrscheinlich.

likeness ['laɪknɪs] n Ähnlichkeit die.

likewise ['laɪkwaɪz] adv
ebenso.

lilac ['laɪlək] adj lila.

Lilo® ['laɪləʊ] (pl -s) n (Br) Luftmatratze die.

lily ['lɪlɪ] n Lilie die.

lily of the valley n Mai-
glöckchen das.

limb [lɪm] n Glied das.

lime [laɪm] n (fruit) Limone
die ; ~ (juice) Limonensaft der.

limestone ['laɪmstəʊn] n
Kalkstein der.

limit ['lɪmɪt] n Grenze die. ◆ vt
begrenzen ; the city ~s die
Stadtgrenze.

limited ['lɪmɪtɪd] adj begrenzt ; (in company name) ≃
GmbH.

limp [lɪmp] adj schlapp. ◆ vi
hinken.

line [laɪn] n Linie die ; (row)
Reihe die ; (Am : queue)
Schlange die ; (of writing, poem,

song) Zeile die ; (rope, for fishing) Leine die ; (for telephone)
Leitung die ; (railway track)
Gleis das ; (of business, work)
Branche die. ◆ vt (coat) füttern ;
(drawers) auslkleiden ; in ~
(aligned) in einer Linie ; in ~
with parallel zu ; it's a bad ~
(on phone) die Verbindung ist
schlecht ; the ~ is engaged (on
phone) der Anschluss ist besetzt ; to drop sb a ~ (inf) jm
schreiben ; to stand in ~ (Am)
Schlange stehen. ▪ **line up** vt
sep (arrange) auflstellen. ◆ vi
sich auflstellen.

lined [laɪnd] adj (paper) liniert.

linen ['lɪnɪn] n (cloth) Leinen
das ; (tablecloths, sheets) Wäsche die.

liner ['laɪnə'] n Passagierschiff
das.

linesman ['laɪnzmən] (pl -men
[-mən]) n Linienrichter der.

linger ['lɪŋgə'] vi verweilen.

lingerie ['lænʒərɪ] n Unterwäsche die.

lining ['laɪnɪŋ] n (of coat, jacket)
Futter das ; (of brake) Bremsbelag der.

link [lɪŋk] n (connection) Verbindung die. ◆ vt verbinden ;
rail ~ Zugverbindung die ; road
~ Straßenverbindung die.

lino ['laɪnəʊ] n (Br) Linoleum
das.

lion ['laɪən] n Löwe der.

lioness ['laɪənes] n Löwin die.

lip [lɪp] n Lippe die.

lip salve [-sælv] n Lippenpo-
made die.

lipstick ['lɪpstɪk] n Lippenstift
der.

liqueur [lɪ'kjʊə'] n Likör der.

liquid ['lɪkwɪd] n Flüssigkeit die.

liquor ['lɪkər] n (Am) Spirituosen pl.

liquorice ['lɪkərɪs] n Lakritze die.

lisp [lɪsp] n : **to have a ~** lispeln.

list [lɪst] n Liste die. ◆ vt auflisten.

listen ['lɪsn] vi : **to ~ (to)** (to person, sound) zulhören (+D) ; (to advice) beherzigen (+A) ; **to ~ to the radio** Radio hören.

listener ['lɪsnə'] n Hörer der (-in die).

lit [lɪt] pt & pp → light.

liter ['liːtər] (Am) = litre.

literally ['lɪtərəlɪ] adv (actually) buchstäblich.

literary ['lɪtərərɪ] adj gehoben.

literature ['lɪtrətʃə] n Literatur die ; (printed information) Informationsmaterial das.

litre ['liːtə'] n (Br) Liter der.

litter ['lɪtə'] n Abfall der.

litterbin ['lɪtəbɪn] n (Br) Abfalleimer der.

little ['lɪtl] adj klein ; (distance, time) kurz ; (not much) wenig. ◆ pron & adv wenig ; **as ~ as possible** so wenig wie möglich ; **~ by ~** nach und nach ; **a ~** (not much) ein bisschen.

little finger n kleiner Finger.

live[1] [lɪv] vi (have home) wohnen ; (be alive) leben ; (survive) überleben ; **to ~ with sb** mit jm zusammenlwohnen. ■ **live together** vi zusammenlwohnen.

live[2] [laɪv] adj (alive) lebendig ; (programme, performance) Live- ; (wire) geladen. ◆ adv live.

lively ['laɪvlɪ] adj lebhaft.

liver ['lɪvə'] n Leber die.

lives [laɪvz] pl → life.

living ['lɪvɪŋ] adj lebend. ◆ n : **to earn a ~** seinen Lebensunterhalt verdienen ; **what do you do for a ~?** was machen Sie beruflich?

living room n Wohnzimmer das.

lizard ['lɪzəd] n Echse die.

load [ləʊd] n Ladung die. ◆ vt laden ; **~s of** (inf) ein Haufen.

loaf [ləʊf] (pl **loaves**) n : **~ (of bread)** Brot das.

loan [ləʊn] n (of money) Kredit der. ◆ vt leihen.

loathe [ləʊð] vt verabscheuen.

loaves [ləʊvz] pl → loaf.

lobby ['lɒbɪ] n (hall) Hotelhalle die.

lobster ['lɒbstə'] n Hummer der.

local ['ləʊkl] adj hiesig. ◆ n (inf : local person) Einheimische der, die ; (Br : pub) Stammkneipe die ; (Am : train) Nahverkehrszug der ; (Am : bus) Nahverkehrsbus der.

local anaesthetic n örtliche Betäubung.

local call n Ortsgespräch das.

local government n Kommunalverwaltung die.

locate [(Br) ləʊ'keɪt, (Am) 'ləʊkeɪt] vt (find) finden ; **to be ~d** sich befinden.

location [ləʊ'keɪʃn] n Lage die.

loch [lɒk] n (Scot) Loch der.

lock [lɒk] n Schloss das ; (on canal) Schleuse die. ◆ vt (door, *house, bicycle)* abl|schließen ; *(valuable object)* ein|schließen. ◆ *vi (door, case)* sich abl|schließen lassen ; *(wheels)* blockieren. ■ **lock in** *vt sep* ein|sperren. ■ **lock out** *vt sep* aus|sperren. ■ **lock up** *vt sep (imprison)* ein|sperren. ◆ *vi* ab|schließen.

locker ['lɒkə'] *n* Schließfach *das.*

locker room *n (Am)* Umkleideraum *der.*

locket ['lɒkɪt] *n* Medaillon *das.*

locomotive [ˌləʊkə'məʊtɪv] *n* Lokomotive *die.*

locum ['ləʊkəm] *n (doctor)* Vertretung *die.*

locust ['ləʊkəst] *n* Heuschrecke *die.*

lodge [lɒdʒ] *n (for hunters, skiers)* Hütte *die.* ◆ *vi (stay)* wohnen ; *(get stuck)* stecken bleiben.

lodger ['lɒdʒə'] *n* Untermieter *der (-in die).*

lodgings ['lɒdʒɪŋz] *npl* möbliertes Zimmer *das.*

loft [lɒft] *n* Dachboden *der.*

log [lɒg] *n* Holzscheit *der.*

logic ['lɒdʒɪk] *n* Logik *die.*

logical ['lɒdʒɪkl] *adj* logisch.

logo ['ləʊgəʊ] *(pl* -s) *n* Logo *das.*

loin [lɔɪn] *n* Lendenstück *das.*

loiter ['lɔɪtə'] *vi* herum|lungern.

lollipop ['lɒlɪpɒp] *n* Lutscher *der.*

lolly ['lɒlɪ] *n (inf : lollipop)* Lutscher *der* ; *(Br : ice lolly)* Eis *das* am Stiel.

London ['lʌndən] *n* London *nt.*

Londoner ['lʌndənə'] *n* Londoner *der (-in die).*

lonely ['ləʊnlɪ] *adj* einsam.

long [lɒŋ] *adj* lang. ◆ *adv* lange ; **it's 2 metres ~** es ist 2 Meter lang ; **it's two hours ~** es dauert zwei Stunden ; **how ~ is it?** *(in distance)* wie lang ist es? ; *(in time)* wie lange dauert es? ; **a ~ time** lange ; **all day ~** den ganzen Tag ; **as ~ as** solange ; **for ~** lange ; **no ~er** nicht mehr ; **so ~!** *(inf)* tschüs! ■ **long for** *vt fus* sich sehnen nach.

long-distance *adj (phone call)* Fern-.

long drink *n* Longdrink *der.*

long-haul *adj* Langstrecken-.

longitude ['lɒndʒɪtjuːd] *n* Länge *die.*

long jump *n* Weitsprung *der.*

long-life *adj (fruit juice)* haltbar gemacht ; *(battery)* mit langer Lebensdauer ; **~ milk** H-Milch *die.*

longsighted [ˌlɒŋ'saɪtɪd] *adj* weitsichtig.

long-term *adj* langfristig.

long wave *n* Langwelle *die.*

longwearing [ˌlɒŋ'weərɪŋ] *adj (Am)* dauerhaft.

loo [luː] *(pl* -s) *n (Br : inf)* Klo *das.*

look [lʊk] *n* Blick *der* ; *(appearance)* Aussehen *das.* ◆ *vi* sehen, schauen ; *(search)* suchen ; *(seem)* aus|sehen ; **to ~ onto** *(building, room)* gehen auf (+A) ; **to have a ~** nach|sehen ; *(search)* suchen ; **to have a ~ at sthg** sich *(D)* etw an|sehen ; **(good) ~s** gutes Aussehen ; **I'm just ~ing** *(in shop)* ich wollte mich nur um|sehen. ■ **look**

after vt fus sich kümmern um.
■ **look at** vt fus an|sehen.
■ **look for** vt fus suchen.
■ **look forward to** vt fus sich freuen auf (+A). ◆ **~ out!** Vorsicht!; **~ out!** Vorsicht!
■ **look out for** vt fus achten auf (+A). ■ **look round** vt fus (city, museum) besichtigen. ◆ vi sich um|sehen; **to ~ round the shops** einen Einkaufsbummel machen. ■ **look up** vt sep (in dictionary) nach|schlagen; (in phone book) heraus|suchen.

loony ['lu:nɪ] n (inf) Spinner der.

loop [lu:p] n (shape) Schleife die.

loose [lu:s] adj lose; **to let sb/sth go ~** jn/etw los|lassen.

loosen ['lu:sn] vt lockern.

lop-sided [-'saɪdɪd] adj schief.

lord [lɔ:d] n Lord der.

lorry ['lɒrɪ] n (Br) Lastwagen der, LKW der.

lorry driver n (Br) Lastwagenfahrer der (-in die).

lose [lu:z] (pt & pp lost) vt verlieren; (subj: watch, clock) nach|gehen. ◆ vi verlieren; **to ~ weight** ab|nehmen.

loser ['lu:zə'] n (in contest) Verlierer der (-in die).

loss [lɒs] n Verlust der.

lost [lɒst] pt & pp → lose. ◆ adj (person): **to be ~** sich verlaufen haben; **to get ~** (lose way) sich verlaufen.

lost-and-found office (Am) = lost property office.

lost property office n (Br) Fundbüro das.

lot [lɒt] n (at auction) Posten der; (Am: car park) Parkplatz

der; (group): **two ~s of books** zwei Stapel Bücher; **two ~s of people** zwei Gruppen; **a ~ (of)** viel, viele pl; **a ~ nicer** viel netter; **the ~ (everything)** alles; **~s (of)** eine Menge.

lotion ['ləʊʃn] n Lotion die.

lottery ['lɒtərɪ] n Lotterie die.

lottery ticket ['lɒtərɪtɪkɪt] n Lottoschein der.

loud [laʊd] adj laut; (colour) grell; (pattern) aufdringlich.

loudspeaker [ˌlaʊd'spi:kə'] n Lautsprecher der.

lounge [laʊndʒ] n Salon der; (at airport) Wartehalle die.

lounge bar n (Br) besser ausgestatteter Teil eines Pubs, wo die Getränke teurer sind.

lousy ['laʊzɪ] adj (inf: poor quality) lausig.

lout [laʊt] n Flegel der.

love [lʌv] n Liebe die; (in tennis) null. ◆ vt lieben; **I would ~ to go to Berlin** ich würde gerne nach Berlin fahren; **I would ~ a drink** ich hätte gern etwas zu trinken; **to ~ doing sth** etw sehr gerne tun; **to be in ~ (with)** verliebt sein (in (+A)); **(with) ~ from** (in letter) alles Liebe.

love affair n Verhältnis das.

lovely ['lʌvlɪ] adj (very beautiful) sehr hübsch; (very nice) nett.

lover ['lʌvə'] n Liebhaber der (-in die).

loving ['lʌvɪŋ] adj liebevoll.

low [ləʊ] adj niedrig; (standard, quality, opinion) schlecht; (level, sound, note) tief; (voice) leise; (depressed) niedergeschlagen. ◆ n (area of low pressure) Tief das; **we're ~ on petrol**

wir haben nicht mehr viel Benzin.

low-alcohol *adj* alkoholarm.

low-calorie *adj* kalorienarm.

low-cut *adj* tief ausgeschnitten.

lower ['ləʊə] *adj* untere(-r) (-s). ◆ *vt* herunterlassen ; *(reduce)* senken.

lower sixth *n (Br)* ≃ elfte Klasse *die*.

low-fat *adj* fettarm.

low tide *n* Ebbe *die*.

loyal ['lɔɪəl] *adj* treu.

loyalty ['lɔɪəltɪ] *n* Loyalität *die*.

lozenge ['lɒzɪndʒ] *n (sweet)* Lutschbonbon *der or das*.

LP *n* LP *die*.

L-plate *n (Br)* Fahrschule-Schild *das*, Schild mit einem L, welches anzeigt, dass der Fahrer des Wagens Anfänger ist.

Ltd *(abbr of limited)* GmbH.

lubricate ['luːbrɪkeɪt] *vt* schmieren.

luck [lʌk] *n* Glück *das* ; bad ~ Pech *das* ; good ~! viel Glück! ; with ~ hoffentlich.

luckily ['lʌkɪlɪ] *adv* glücklicherweise.

lucky ['lʌkɪ] *adj* glücklich ; *(number, colour)* Glücks- ; to be ~ Glück haben.

ludicrous ['luːdɪkrəs] *adj* lächerlich.

lug [lʌg] *vt (inf)* schleppen.

luggage ['lʌgɪdʒ] *n* Gepäck *das*.

luggage compartment *n* Gepäckraum *der*.

luggage locker *n* Schließfach *das*.

luggage rack *n* Gepäckablage *die*.

lukewarm ['luːkwɔːm] *adj* lauwarm.

lull [lʌl] *n* Pause *die*.

lullaby ['lʌləbaɪ] *n* Schlaflied *das*.

lumbago [lʌm'beɪgəʊ] *n* Hexenschuss *der*.

lumber ['lʌmbər] *n (Am : timber)* Bauholz *das*.

luminous ['luːmɪnəs] *adj* leuchtend, Leucht-.

lump [lʌmp] *n (of mud, butter)* Klumpen *der* ; *(of coal)* Stück *das* ; *(of sugar)* Würfel *der* ; *(on body)* Beule *die*.

lump sum *n* Pauschalbetrag *der*.

lumpy ['lʌmpɪ] *adj* klumpig.

lunatic ['luːnətɪk] *n (pej)* Spinner *der*.

lunch [lʌntʃ] *n* Mittagessen *das* ; to have ~ zu Mittag essen.

luncheon ['lʌntʃən] *n (fml)* Mittagessen *das*.

luncheon meat *n* Frühstücksfleisch *das*.

lunch hour *n* Mittagspause *die*.

lunchtime ['lʌntʃtaɪm] *n* Mittagszeit *die*.

lung [lʌŋ] *n* Lunge *die*.

lunge [lʌndʒ] *vi* : to ~ at sb sich auf jn stürzen.

lurch [lɜːtʃ] *vi* torkeln.

lure [ljʊər] *vt* locken.

lurk [lɜːk] *vi* lauern.

lush [lʌʃ] *adj (grass, field)* üppig.

lust [lʌst] *n (sexual desire)* Verlangen *das*.

Luxembourg ['lʌksəmbɜːg] *n* Luxemburg *nt*.

luxurious [lʌg'ʒʊərɪəs] *adj* luxuriös.

luxury ['lʌkʃərɪ] *adj* Luxus-. ◆ *n* Luxus *der*.

lying ['laɪɪŋ] *cont* → **lie**.

lyrics ['lɪrɪks] *npl* (*music*) Text *der*.

M

m (*abbr of metre*) m. ◆ *abbr* = **mile**.

M (*Br* : *abbr of motorway*) A ; (*abbr of medium*) M.

MA *n* (*abbr of Master of Arts*) britischer Hochschulabschluss in einem geisteswissenschaftlichen Fach.

mac [mæk] *n* (*Br* : *inf*) Regenmantel *der*.

macaroni [,mækə'rəʊnɪ] *n* Makkaroni *pl*.

macaroni cheese *n* Auflauf aus Makkaroni und Käsesoße.

machine [mə'ʃiːn] *n* Maschine *die*.

machinegun [mə'ʃiːŋgʌn] *n* Maschinengewehr *das*.

machinery [mə'ʃiːnərɪ] *n* Maschinen *pl*.

machine-washable *adj* waschmaschinenfest.

mackerel ['mækrəl] (*pl* **mackerel**) *n* Makrele *die*.

mackintosh ['mækɪntɒʃ] *n* (*Br*) Regenmantel *der*.

mad [mæd] *adj* verrückt ; (*angry*) wütend ; **to be ~ about** (*inf* : *like a lot*) verrückt sein auf (+A) ; **like ~** wie verrückt.

Madam ['mædəm] *n* (*form of address*) gnädige Frau.

made [meɪd] *pt* & *pp* → **make**.

madeira [mə'dɪərə] *n* Madeira *der*.

made-to-measure *adj* maßgeschneidert.

madness ['mædnɪs] *n* Wahnsinn *der*.

magazine [,mægə'ziːn] *n* Zeitschrift *die*.

maggot ['mægət] *n* Made *die*.

magic ['mædʒɪk] *n* (*supernatural force*) Magie *die* ; (*conjuring*) Zauberei *die* ; (*special quality*) Zauber *der*.

magician [mə'dʒɪʃn] *n* Zauberer *der* (Zauberin *die*).

magistrate ['mædʒɪstreɪt] *n* Friedensrichter *der* (-in *die*).

magnet ['mægnɪt] *n* Magnet *der*.

magnetic [mæg'netɪk] *adj* magnetisch.

magnificent [mæg'nɪfɪsənt] *adj* herrlich.

magnifying glass ['mægnɪfaɪɪŋ-] *n* Lupe *die*.

mahogany [mə'hɒgənɪ] *n* Mahagoni *das*.

maid [meɪd] *n* Dienstmädchen *das*.

maiden name [meɪdn-] *n* Mädchenname *der*.

mail [meɪl] *n* Post *die*. ◆ *vt* (*Am*) schicken.

mailbox ['meɪlbɒks] *n* (*Am*) Briefkasten *der*.

mailman ['meɪlmən] (*pl* -men [-mən]) *n* (*Am*) Briefträger *der*, Postbote *der*.

mail order *n* Versandhandel *der*.

main [meɪn] *adj* Haupt-.

main course n Hauptgericht das.

main deck n Hauptdeck das.

mainland ['meɪnlənd] n : the ~ das Festland.

main line n Hauptstrecke die.

mainly ['meɪnlɪ] adv hauptsächlich.

main road n Hauptstraße die.

mains [meɪnz] npl : the ~ die Hauptleitung.

main street n (Am) Hauptstraße die.

maintain [meɪn'teɪn] vt aufrechterhalten ; (keep in good condition) instand halten.

maintenance ['meɪntənəns] n (of car, machine) Instandhaltung die ; (money) Unterhalt der.

maisonette [ˌmeɪzə'net] n (Br) Maisonette die.

maize [meɪz] n Mais der.

major ['meɪdʒə'] adj (important) groß ; (most important) Haupt-. ◆ n (MIL) Major der. ◆ vi (Am) : to ~ in sthg etw als Hauptfach studieren.

majority [mə'dʒɒrətɪ] n Mehrheit die.

major road n Hauptstraße die.

make [meɪk] (pt & pp made) vt 1. (produce) machen ; (manufacture) herstellen ; to be made of sthg aus etw gemacht sein ; to ~ lunch/supper Mittagessen/Abendessen machen ; made in Japan in Japan hergestellt.
2. (perform, do) machen ; to ~ a decision eine Entscheidung treffen ; to ~ a mistake einen Fehler machen ; to ~ a phone

call telefonieren ; to ~ a speech eine Rede halten.
3. (cause to be) machen ; to ~ sb happy jn glücklich machen.
4. (cause to do, force) : it made her laugh das brachte sie zum Lachen ; to ~ sb do sthg jn etw tun lassen ; (force) jn zwingen etw zu tun.
5. (amount to, total) machen ; that ~s £5 das macht 5 Pfund.
6. (calculate) : I ~ it £4 ich komme auf 4 Pfund ; I ~ it seven o'clock nach meiner Uhr ist es sieben Uhr.
7. (earn) verdienen.
8. (inf : arrive in time for) : we didn't ~ the 10 o'clock train wir haben den 10-Uhr-Zug nicht geschafft.
9. (friend, enemy) machen.
10. (have qualities for) ablgeben ; this would ~ a lovely bedroom das würde ein hübsches Schlafzimmer abgeben.
11. (bed) machen.
12. (in phrases) : to ~ do with auslkommen mit ; to ~ good (damage) wieder gutlmachen ; to ~ it es schaffen.
◆ n (of product) Marke die.

▪ **make out** vt sep (cheque, receipt) auslstellen ; (see) auslmachen ; (hear) verstehen.

▪ **make up** vt sep (invent) erfinden, sich (D) ausldenken ; (comprise) bilden ; (difference) auslgleichen ; to be made up of bestehen aus.

▪ **make up for** vt fus wettlmachen.

makeshift ['meɪkʃɪft] adj behelfsmäßig.

make-up n (cosmetics) Make-up das.

malaria [mə'leərɪə] n Malaria die.

Malaysia [mə'leɪzɪə] n Malaysia nt.

male [meɪl] adj männlich. ◆ n (animal) Männchen das.

malfunction [mæl'fʌŋkʃn] vi (fml) nicht richtig funktionieren.

malignant [mə'lɪgnənt] adj bösartig.

mall [mɔːl] n (shopping centre) Einkaufszentrum das.

THE MALL

In den USA ist „The Mall" ein langer Streifen offenen Parkgeländes im Herzen von Washington D.C. das sich vom Kapitol bis zum Lincoln Memorial erstreckt. Er ist von Museen, Kunstgalerien, dem Weißen Haus und dem Jefferson Memorial umsäumt. Im Westen von „The Mall" liegt „The Wall", auf dem die Namen der im Vietnamkrieg gefallenen Soldaten eingraviert sind. In Großbritannien ist „The Mall" eine lange, von Bäumen eingesäumte Allee im Zentrum von London, die vom Buckingham Palace zum Trafalgar Square führt.

mallet ['mælɪt] n Holzhammer der.

malt [mɔːlt] n Malz das.

maltreat [ˌmæl'triːt] vt misshandeln.

malt whisky n Maltwhisky der.

mammal ['mæml] n Säugetier das.

man [mæn] (pl men) n Mann der; (human being, mankind) Mensch der. ◆ vt (phones, office) besetzen.

manage ['mænɪdʒ] vt (company, business) leiten; (job) bewältigen; (food) schaffen. ◆ vi (cope) zurechtkommen; **can you ~ Friday?** passt dir/Ihnen Freitag?; **to ~ to do sthg** es schaffen, etw zu tun.

management ['mænɪdʒmənt] n Geschäftsführung die.

manager ['mænɪdʒə] n (of business, bank) Direktor der; (of shop) Geschäftsführer der; (of sports team) Trainer der (-in die).

manageress [ˌmænɪdʒə'res] n (of business, bank) Direktorin die; (of shop) Geschäftsführerin die.

managing director ['mænɪdʒɪŋ-] n leitender Direktor (leitende Direktorin).

mandarin ['mændərɪn] n Mandarine die.

mane [meɪn] n Mähne die.

maneuver [mə'nuːvər] (Am) = manoeuvre.

mangetout [ˌmɒnʒ'tuː] n Zuckererbse die.

mangle ['mæŋgl] vt zerquetschen.

mango ['mæŋgəʊ] (pl -es OR -s) n Mango die.

Manhattan [mæn'hætən] n Manhattan nt.

MANHATTAN

Manhattan, Bezeichnung für den Innenbezirk von New York City, ist in „Downtown", „Midtown" und „Upper" eingeteilt. Hier befinden sich die weltberühmten Wolkenkratzer, wie z. B. das Empire State Building und das Chrysler Building, aber auch Sehenswürdigkeiten wie Central Park, Fifth Avenue, Broadway und Greenwich Village.

manhole ['mænhəʊl] n Kanalschacht der.

maniac ['meɪnɪæk] n (inf) Wahnsinniger der.

manicure ['mænɪkjʊəʳ] n Maniküre die.

manifold ['mænɪfəʊld] n (AUT : exhaust) Auspuffrohr das.

manipulate [mə'nɪpjʊleɪt] vt (person) manipulieren ; (machine, controls) handhaben.

mankind [,mæn'kaɪnd] n Menschheit die.

manly ['mænlɪ] adj männlich.

man-made adj künstlich.

manner ['mænəʳ] n (way) Art die. ■ **manners** npl Manieren pl.

manoeuvre [mə'nuːvəʳ] n (Br) Manöver das. ◆ vt (Br) manövrieren.

manor ['mænəʳ] n Gut das.

mansion ['mænʃn] n Villa die.

manslaughter ['mæn,slɔːtəʳ] n Totschlag der.

mantelpiece ['mæntlpiːs] n Kaminsims der.

manual ['mænjʊəl] adj (work) Hand- ; (operated by hand) hand-

betrieben. ◆ n (book) Handbuch das.

manufacture [,mænjʊ'fæktʃəʳ] n Herstellung die. ◆ vt herstellen.

manufacturer [,mænjʊ'fæktʃərəʳ] n Hersteller der.

manure [mə'njʊəʳ] n Mist der.

many ['menɪ] (compar **more**, superl **most**) adj & pron viele.

map [mæp] n Karte die.

Mar. (abbr of March) Mrz.

marathon ['mærəθn] n Marathon der.

marble ['mɑːbl] n (stone) Marmor der ; (glass ball) Murmel die.

march [mɑːtʃ] n Marsch der. ◆ vi marschieren.

March [mɑːtʃ] n März der ; → **September**.

mare [meəʳ] n Stute die.

margarine [,mɑːdʒə'riːn] n Margarine die.

margin ['mɑːdʒɪn] n (of page) Rand der ; (difference) Abstand der.

marina [mə'riːnə] n Jachthafen der.

marinated ['mærɪneɪtɪd] adj mariniert.

marital status ['mærɪtl-] n Familienstand der.

mark [mɑːk] n (spot) Fleck der ; (trace) Spur die ; (on skin) Mal das ; (symbol) Zeichen das ; (SCH) Note die. ◆ vt (blemish) beschädigen ; (put symbol on) kennzeichnen ; (SCH) benoten ; (on map) markieren ; (gas) ~ **five** Stufe fünf.

marker pen ['mɑːkə-] n Marker der.

market ['mɑ:kɪt] n Markt der.

marketing ['mɑ:kɪtɪŋ] n Marketing das.

marketplace ['mɑ:kɪtpleɪs] n Marktplatz der.

markings ['mɑ:kɪŋz] npl (on road) Markierungen pl.

marmalade ['mɑ:məleɪd] n Marmelade die.

marquee [mɑ:'ki:] n Festzelt das.

marriage ['mærɪdʒ] n (event) Hochzeit die ; (time married) Ehe die.

married ['mærɪd] adj verheiratet ; to get ~ heiraten.

marrow ['mærəʊ] n (vegetable) Kürbis der.

marry ['mærɪ] vt & vi heiraten.

marsh [mɑ:ʃ] n Sumpf der.

martial arts [ˌmɑ:ʃl-] npl Kampfsport der.

marvellous ['mɑ:vələs] adj (Br) wunderbar.

marvelous ['mɑ:vələs] (Am) = marvellous.

marzipan ['mɑ:zɪpæn] n Marzipan das.

mascara [mæs'kɑ:rə] n Wimperntusche die, Mascara das.

masculine ['mæskjʊlɪn] adj (typically male) männlich ; (woman, in grammar) maskulin.

mashed potatoes [mæʃt-] npl Kartoffelbrei der.

mask [mɑ:sk] n Maske die.

masonry ['meɪsnrɪ] n Mauerwerk das.

mass [mæs] n Masse die ; (RELIG) Messe die ; ~es of (inf : lots) ein Haufen.

massacre ['mæsəkə^r] n Massaker das.

massage [(Br) 'mæsɑ:ʒ, (Am) mə'sɑ:ʒ] n Massage die. ◆ vt massieren.

masseur [mæ'sɜ:^r] n Masseur der.

masseuse [mæ'sɜ:z] n Masseuse die.

massive ['mæsɪv] adj riesig.

mast [mɑ:st] n Mast der.

master ['mɑ:stə^r] n (at school) Lehrer der ; (of servant) Herr der ; (of dog) Herrchen das. ◆ vt (skill, language) beherrschen.

masterpiece ['mɑ:stəpi:s] n Meisterwerk das.

mat [mæt] n Matte die ; (on table) Untersetzer der.

match [mætʃ] n (for lighting) Streichholz das ; (game) Spiel das. ◆ vt (in colour, design) passen zu ; (be the same as) entsprechen (+G) ; (be as good as) gleichlkommen (+D). ◆ vi (in colour, design) zusammenlpassen.

matchbox ['mætʃbɒks] n Streichholzschachtel die.

matching ['mætʃɪŋ] adj passend.

mate [meɪt] n (inf : friend) Kumpel der ; (Br : inf : form of address) alter Freund. ◆ vi sich paaren.

material [mə'tɪərɪəl] n Stoff der, Material das. ■ **materials** npl Sachen pl.

maternity leave [mə'tɜ:nətɪ-] n Mutterschaftsurlaub der.

maternity ward [mə'tɜ:nətɪ-] n Entbindungsstation die.

math [mæθ] (Am) = maths.

mathematics [ˌmæθəˈmæ-tɪks] *n* Mathematik *die.*

maths [mæθs] *n (Br)* Mathe *die.*

matinée [ˈmætɪneɪ] *n* Nach-mittagsvorstellung *die.*

matt [mæt] *adj* matt.

matter [ˈmætəʳ] *n (issue, situation)* Angelegenheit *die* ; *(physical material)* Materie *die.* ◆ *vi* wichtig sein ; **it doesn't ~** das macht nichts ; **no ~ what happens** egal was passiert ; **there's something the ~ with my car** mit meinem Auto stimmt etwas nicht ; **what's the ~?** was ist los? ; **as a ~ of course** selbstverständlich ; **as a ~ of fact** eigentlich.

mattress [ˈmætrɪs] *n* Ma-tratze *die.*

mature [məˈtjʊəʳ] *adj* reif.

mauve [məʊv] *adj* lila.

max. [mæks] *(abbr of maximum)* max.

maximum [ˈmæksɪməm] *adj* maximal. ◆ *n* Maximum *das.*

may [meɪ] *aux vb* 1. *(expressing possibility)* können ; **it ~ be done as follows** man kann wie folgt vorgehen ; **it ~ rain** es könnte regnen ; **they ~ have got lost** sie haben sich vielleicht verirrt.

2. *(expressing permission)* können ; **~ I smoke?** darf ich rauchen? ; **you ~ sit, if you wish** Sie können sich hinsetzen, wenn Sie wollen.

3. *(when conceding a point)* : **it ~ be a long walk, but it's worth it** es ist vielleicht ein weiter Weg, aber es lohnt sich.

May [meɪ] *n* Mai *der* ; → September.

maybe [ˈmeɪbiː] *adv* vielleicht.

mayonnaise [ˌmeɪəˈneɪz] *n* Majonäse *die.*

mayor [meəʳ] *n* Bürgermeister *der.*

mayoress [ˈmeərɪs] *n (female mayor)* Bürgermeisterin *die* ; *(mayor's wife)* Frau *die* des Bür-germeisters.

maze [meɪz] *n* Irrgarten *der.*

me [miː] *pron (direct object)* mich ; *(indirect object)* mir ; *(after prep : accusative)* mich ; *(after prep : dative)* mir ; **she knows ~** sie kennt mich ; **it's ~** ich bin's ; **send it to ~** schick' es mir ; **tell ~** sagen Sie mal, sag' mal ; **he's worse than ~** er ist schlechter als ich.

meadow [ˈmedəʊ] *n* Wiese *die.*

meal [miːl] *n* Mahlzeit *die.*

mealtime [ˈmiːltaɪm] *n* Es-senszeit *die.*

mean [miːn] *(pt & pp meant) adj (miserly)* geizig ; *(unkind)* gemein. ◆ *vt* bedeuten ; *(intend)* beabsichtigen ; **to ~ to do sthg** vorhaben, etw zu tun ; **the bus was meant to leave at eight** der Bus hätte eigentlich um acht Uhr abfahren sollen ; **it's meant to be good** das soll gut sein ; **I didn't ~ it** ich habe es nicht so gemeint.

meaning [ˈmiːnɪŋ] *n* Bedeu-tung *die.*

meaningless [ˈmiːnɪŋlɪs] *adj* bedeutungslos.

means [miːnz] *(pl means) n (method)* Mittel *das.* ◆ *npl (mon-*

ey) Mittel *pl* ; **by all ~!** auf jeden Fall! ; **by ~ of** mithilfe *(+G)*.

meant [ment] *pt* & *pp* → mean.

meantime ['mi:n,taɪm] : **in the meantime** *adv* in der Zwischenzeit.

meanwhile ['mi:n,waɪl] *adv* inzwischen.

measles ['mi:zlz] *n* Masern *pl*.

measure ['meʒər] *vt* messen. ◆ *n (step, action)* Maßnahme *die* ; *(of alcohol)* Dosis *die* ; **the room ~s 10 m²** das Zimmer misst 10 m².

measurement ['meʒəmənt] *n* Maß *das*.

meat [mi:t] *n* Fleisch *das* ; **red ~** *Lamm- und Rindfleisch* ; **white ~** *Kalbfleisch und Huhn*.

meatball ['mi:tbɔ:l] *n* Fleischklößchen *das*.

mechanic [mɪ'kænɪk] *n* Mechaniker *der (-in die)*.

mechanical [mɪ'kænɪkl] *adj* mechanisch.

mechanism ['mekənɪzm] *n* Mechanismus *der*.

medal ['medl] *n* Medaille *die*.

media ['mi:djə] *n or npl* : **the ~** die Medien *pl*.

medical ['medɪkl] *adj* medizinisch ; *(treatment)* ärztlich. ◆ *n* Untersuchung *die*.

medication [,medɪ'keɪʃn] *n* Medikament *das*.

medicine ['medsɪn] *n* Medikament *das* ; *(science)* Medizin *die*.

medicine cabinet *n* Medizinschrank *der*.

medieval [,medɪ'i:vl] *adj* mittelalterlich.

mediocre [,mi:dɪ'əʊkər] *adj* mittelmäßig.

Mediterranean [,medɪtə'reɪnjən] *n* : **the ~** *(region)* der Mittelmeerraum ; **the ~ (Sea)** das Mittelmeer.

medium ['mi:djəm] *adj* mittelgroß ; *(wine)* halbtrocken.

medium-dry *adj* halbtrocken.

medium-sized [-saɪzd] *adj* mittelgroß.

meet [mi:t] *(pt & pp* met) *vt (by arrangement)* sich treffen mit ; *(by chance)* treffen ; *(get to know)* kennen lernen ; *(go to collect)* abholen ; *(need, requirement)* erfüllen ; *(cost, expenses)* begleichen. ◆ *vi (by arrangement, by chance)* sich treffen ; *(get to know each other)* sich kennen lernen ; *(intersect)* aufeinander treffen. ▓ **meet up** *vi* sich treffen. ▓ **meet with** *vt fus (problems, resistance)* stoßen auf *(+A)* ; *(Am : by arrangement)* sich treffen mit.

meeting ['mi:tɪŋ] *n (for business)* Besprechung *die*.

meeting point *n* Treffpunkt *der*.

melody ['melədɪ] *n* Melodie *die*.

melon ['melən] *n* Melone *die*.

melt [melt] *vi* schmelzen.

member ['membər] *n* Mitglied *das*.

Member of Congress [-'kɒŋgres] *n* Abgeordneter des amerikanischen Kongresses.

Member of Parliament *n* Abgeordneter des britischen Parlaments.

membership ['membəʃɪp] n
Mitgliedschaft die ; (members)
Mitgliederzahl die.

memorial [mɪ'mɔːrɪəl] n
Denkmal das.

memorize ['meməraɪz] vt sich
(D) einlprägen.

memory ['memərɪ] n Erinnerung die ; (of computer) Speicher
der.

men [men] pl → man.

menacing ['menəsɪŋ] adj drohend.

mend [mend] vt reparieren.

menopause ['menəpɔːz] n
Wechseljahre pl.

men's room n (Am) Herrentoilette die.

menstruate ['menstruɛt] vi
menstruieren.

menswear ['menzweə'] n
Herrenbekleidung die.

mental ['mentl] adj geistig ;
(MED) Geistes-.

mental hospital n psychiatrische Klinik.

mentally handicapped
['mentəlɪ-] adj geistig behindert. ◆ npl : the ~ die geistig
Behinderten pl.

mentally ill ['mentəlɪ-] adj
geisteskrank.

mention ['menʃn] vt erwähnen ; don't ~ it! bitte!

menu ['menjuː] n Speisekarte
die ; (COMPUT) Menü das ; children's ~ Kinderspeisekarte die.

merchandise ['mɜːtʃəndaɪz]
n Ware die.

merchant marine [,mɜːtʃənt-
mə'riːn] (Am) = **merchant
navy**.

merchant navy [,mɜːtʃənt-]
n (Br) Handelsmarine die.

mercury ['mɜːkjʊrɪ] n Queck-
silber das.

mercy ['mɜːsɪ] n Gnade die.

mere [mɪə'] adj bloß.

merely ['mɪəlɪ] adv bloß.

merge [mɜːdʒ] vi (combine)
sich zusammenlschließen ;
'merge' (Am) Schild an Auto-
bahnauffahrten, das dazu auffor-
dert, sich in die rechte Spur der
Autobahn einzuordnen.

merger ['mɜːdʒə'] n Fusion
die.

meringue [mə'ræŋ] n Baiser
das.

merit ['merɪt] n (worthiness)
Verdienst der ; (good quality)
Vorzug der ; (in exam) Aus-
zeichnung die.

merry ['merɪ] adj fröhlich ;
(inf : tipsy) angeheitert ; Merry
Christmas! Fröhliche Weihnachten!

merry-go-round n Karussell
das.

mess [mes] n Durcheinander
das ; (difficult situation) Schwierigkeiten pl ; in a ~ (untidy) unordentlich. ▪ mess about vi
(inf) herumlalbern ; to ~ about
with sthg (interfere) mit etw
herumlspielen. ▪ mess up vt
sep (inf : plans) durcheinander
bringen ; (clothes) schmutzig
machen.

message ['mesɪdʒ] n Nachricht die.

messenger ['mesɪndʒə'] n
Bote der (Botin die).

messy ['mesɪ] adj unordentlich.

met [met] pt & pp → meet.

metal ['metl] adj Metall-. ◆ n
Metall das.

might

metalwork ['metəlwɜːk] n (craft) Metallbearbeitung die.

meter ['miːtə] n (device) Zähler der; (Am) = metre.

method ['meθəd] n Methode die.

methodical [mɪ'θɒdɪkl] adj methodisch.

meticulous [mɪ'tɪkjʊləs] adj sorgfältig.

metre ['miːtə] n (Br) Meter der.

metric ['metrɪk] adj metrisch.

mews [mjuːz] (pl mews) n (Br) kleine Seitenstraße mit früheren Stallungen, die oft zu eleganten Wohnungen umgebaut wurden.

Mexican ['meksɪkn] adj mexikanisch. ◆ n Mexikaner der (-in die).

Mexico ['meksɪkəʊ] n Mexiko nt.

mg (abbr of milligram) mg.

miaow [miː'aʊ] vi (Br) miauen.

mice [maɪs] pl → mouse.

microchip ['maɪkrəʊtʃɪp] n Mikrochip der.

microphone ['maɪkrəfəʊn] n Mikrofon das.

microscope ['maɪkrəskəʊp] n Mikroskop das.

microwave (oven) ['maɪkrəʊweɪv-] n Mikrowellenherd der.

midday [,mɪd'deɪ] n Mittag der.

middle ['mɪdl] n Mitte die. ◆ adj (central) mittlere(-r) (-s); in the ~ of the road in der Straßenmitte; in the ~ of April Mitte April; to be in the ~ of doing sthg gerade dabei sein, etw zu tun.

middle-aged adj mittleren Alters; a ~ woman eine Frau mittleren Alters.

middle-class adj (suburb) bürgerlich; a ~ family eine Mittelstandsfamilie.

Middle East n: the ~ der Nahe Osten.

middle name n zweiter Vorname.

middle school n (in UK) staatliche Schule für 9- bis 13-Jährige.

midge [mɪdʒ] n Mücke die.

midget ['mɪdʒɪt] n Zwerg der (-in die).

Midlands ['mɪdləndz] npl: the ~ Mittelengland nt.

midnight ['mɪdnaɪt] n Mitternacht die.

midsummer ['mɪd'sʌmə] n Hochsommer der.

midway [,mɪd'weɪ] adv mitten.

midweek [adj 'mɪdwiːk, adv mɪd'wiːk] adj & adv in der Wochenmitte.

midwife ['mɪdwaɪf] (pl -wives [-waɪvz]) n Hebamme die.

midwinter ['mɪd'wɪntə] n Mittwinter der.

might [maɪt] aux vb 1. (expressing possibility) können; they ~ still come sie könnten noch kommen; they ~ have been killed sie sind vielleicht umgekommen. 2. (fml : expressing permission) können; ~ I have a few words? könnte ich Sie mal sprechen? 3. (when conceding a point): it ~ be expensive, but it's good quality es ist zwar teuer, aber es ist von guter Qualität.

4. *(would)* : **I'd hoped you ~ come too** ich hatte gehofft, du würdest auch mitkommen.

migraine ['miːgreɪn, 'maɪgreɪn] *n* Migräne *die*.

mild [maɪld] *adj* mild ; *(illness, surprise)* leicht. ◆ *n (Br : beer)* Bier, das schwächer und dunkler ist als 'bitter'.

mile [maɪl] *n* Meile *die* ; **it's ~s away** das ist meilenweit entfernt.

mileage ['maɪlɪdʒ] *n* Entfernung *die* in Meilen.

milometer [maɪ'lɒmɪtə'] *n* ≃ Kilometerzähler *der*.

military ['mɪlɪtrɪ] *adj* Militär-, militärisch.

milk [mɪlk] *n* Milch *die*. ◆ *vt* melken.

milk chocolate *n* Milchschokolade *die*.

milkman ['mɪlkmən] *(pl* -men [-mən]) *n* Milchmann *der*.

milk shake *n* Milchmixgetränk *das*.

milky ['mɪlkɪ] *adj (drink)* milchig.

mill [mɪl] *n* Mühle *die* ; *(factory)* Fabrik *die*.

millennium [mɪ'lenɪəm] *n* Jahrtausend *das*.

millennium bug [mɪ'lenɪəmbʌg] *n* Jahr-2000-Computer-Problem *das*.

milligram ['mɪlɪgræm] *n* Milligramm *das*.

millilitre ['mɪlɪ,liːtə'] *n* Milliliter *der*.

millimetre ['mɪlɪ,miːtə'] *n* Millimeter *der*.

million ['mɪljən] *n* Million *die* ; **~s of** *(fig)* tausende von.

millionaire [,mɪljə'neə'] *n* Millionär *der* (-in *die*).

mime [maɪm] *vi* mimen.

min. [mɪn] *(abbr of minute, minimum)* Min.

mince [mɪns] *n (Br)* Hackfleisch *das*.

mincemeat ['mɪnsmiːt] *n (sweet filling)* süße Füllung aus Zitronat, Orangeat, Rosinen, Gewürzen u.a. ; *(Am : mince)* Hackfleisch *das*.

mince pie *n* mit Zitronat, Orangeat, Rosinen, Gewürzen u. a. gefülltes Weihnachtsgebäck.

mind [maɪnd] *n* Verstand *der* ; *(memory)* Gedächtnis *das*. ◆ *vt* aufpassen auf (+A) ; *(be bothered by)* sich stören an (+D). ◆ *vi* : **I don't ~** es ist mir egal ; **it slipped my ~** es ist mir entfallen ; **to my ~** meiner Meinung nach ; **to bear sthg in ~** etw nicht vergessen ; **to change one's ~** seine Meinung ändern ; **to have sthg in ~** etw vorhaben ; **to have sthg on one's ~** sich mit etw beschäftigen ; **to make one's ~ up** sich entscheiden ; **do you ~ if...?** stört es, wenn... ; **I wouldn't ~ a drink** ich würde eigentlich gerne etwas trinken ; **'~ the gap!'** *(on underground)* 'Vorsicht beim Einsteigen und Aussteigen' ; **never ~!** *(don't worry)* macht nichts!

mine[1] [maɪn] *pron* meine(-r) (-s), meine *pl* ; **it's ~** es gehört mir ; **a friend of ~** ein Freund von mir.

mine[2] [maɪn] *n (for coal etc)* Bergwerk *das* ; *(bomb)* Mine *die*.

miner ['maɪnə'] n Bergmann der.

mineral ['mɪnərəl] n Mineral das.

mineral water n Mineralwasser das.

minestrone [,mɪnɪ'strəʊnɪ] n Minestrone die.

mingle ['mɪŋgl] vi sich mischen ; (with other people) Konversation machen.

miniature ['mɪnətʃə'] adj Miniatur-. ◆ n (of alcohol) Miniflasche die.

minibar ['mɪnɪbɑː'] n Hausbar die.

minibus ['mɪnɪbʌs] (pl -es) n Kleinbus der.

minicab ['mɪnɪkæb] n (Br) Kleintaxi das.

minimal ['mɪnɪml] adj minimal.

minimum ['mɪnɪməm] adj Mindest-. ◆ n Minimum das.

miniskirt ['mɪnɪskɜːt] n Minirock der.

minister ['mɪnɪstə'] n (in government) Minister der (-in die) ; (in church) Geistliche der, die.

ministry ['mɪnɪstrɪ] n (of government) Ministerium die.

minor ['maɪnə'] adj kleiner. ◆ n (fml) Minderjährige der, die.

minority [maɪ'nɒrətɪ] n Minderheit die.

minor road n Nebenstraße die.

mint [mɪnt] n (sweet) Pfefferminz das ; (plant) Minze die.

minus ['maɪnəs] prep minus ; it's ~ 10 (degrees C) es ist minus 10 (Grad Celsius).

minuscule ['mɪnəskjuːl] adj winzig.

minute[1] ['mɪnɪt] n Minute die ; any ~ jeden Moment ; just a ~! Moment, bitte!

minute[2] [maɪ'njuːt] adj winzig.

minute steak [,mɪnɪt-] n kurz gebratenes Steak.

miracle ['mɪrəkl] n Wunder das.

miraculous [mɪ'rækjʊləs] adj wunderbar.

mirror ['mɪrə'] n Spiegel der.

misbehave [,mɪsbɪ'heɪv] vi sich schlecht benehmen.

miscarriage [,mɪs'kærɪdʒ] n Fehlgeburt die.

miscellaneous [,mɪsə'leɪnjəs] adj verschieden.

mischievous ['mɪstʃɪvəs] adj ungezogen.

misconduct [,mɪs'kɒndʌkt] n unkorrektes Verhalten.

miser ['maɪzə'] n Geizhals der.

miserable ['mɪzrəbl] adj erbärmlich ; (weather) fürchterlich.

misery ['mɪzərɪ] n (unhappiness) Kummer der ; (poor conditions) Elend das.

misfire [,mɪs'faɪə'] vi (car) fehllzünden.

misfortune [mɪs'fɔːtʃuːn] n (bad luck) Pech das.

mishap ['mɪshæp] n Zwischenfall der.

misjudge [,mɪs'dʒʌdʒ] vt falsch einschätzen.

mislay [,mɪs'leɪ] (pt & pp -laid) vt verlegen.

mislead [,mɪs'liːd] (pt & pp -led) vt irreführen.

miss [mɪs] vt (plane, train, appointment, opportunity) verpassen ; (not notice) übersehen ;

(target) verfehlen ; *(regret absence of)* vermissen. ◆ *vi (fail to hit)* nicht treffen. ▧ **miss out** *vt sep* ausllassen. ◆ *vi* : to ~ **out on** sth sich *(D)* etw entgehen lassen.

Miss [mɪs] *n* Fräulein *das*.

missile *[(Br)* 'mɪsaɪl, *(Am)* 'mɪsl] *n (weapon)* Rakete *die* ; *(thing thrown)* Geschoss *das*.

missing ['mɪsɪŋ] *adj* verschwunden ; to be ~ *(not there)* fehlen.

missing person *n* Vermisste *der, die*.

mission ['mɪʃn] *n* Mission *die*.

missionary ['mɪʃənrɪ] *n* Missionar *der* (-in *die*).

mist [mɪst] *n* Nebel *der*.

mistake [mɪ'steɪk] *(pt* -took, *pp* -taken) *n* Fehler *der*. ◆ *vt (misunderstand)* missverstehen ; by ~ aus Versehen ; to make a ~ einen Fehler machen ; to ~ sb/sthg for jn/etw verwechseln mit.

Mister ['mɪstə'] *n* Herr *der*.

mistook [mɪ'stʊk] *pt* → **mistake**.

mistress ['mɪstrɪs] *n (lover)* Geliebte *die* ; *(Br : teacher)* Lehrerin *die*.

mistrust [,mɪs'trʌst] *vt* misstrauen *(+D)*.

misty ['mɪstɪ] *adj* nebelig.

misunderstanding [,mɪsʌndə'stændɪŋ] *n* Missverständnis *das*.

misuse [,mɪs'juːs] *n* Missbrauch *der*.

mitten ['mɪtn] *n* Fausthandschuh *der*.

mix [mɪks] *vt* mischen ; *(drink)* mixen. ◆ *n (for cake, sauce)* Mi-

schung *die* ; to ~ sthg with sthg etw mit etw vermischen. ▧ **mix up** *vt sep* durcheinander bringen.

mixed [mɪkst] *adj* gemischt.

mixed grill *n* Grillteller *der*.

mixed salad *n* gemischter Salat.

mixed vegetables *npl* Mischgemüse *das*.

mixer ['mɪksə'] *n (for food)* Mixer *der* ; *(drink)* Mixgetränk *das*.

mixture ['mɪkstʃə'] *n* Mischung *die*.

mix-up *n (inf)* Durcheinander *das*.

ml *(abbr of millilitre)* ml.

mm *(abbr of millimetre)* mm.

moan [məʊn] *vi* stöhnen.

moat [məʊt] *n* Burggraben *der*.

mobile ['məʊbaɪl] *adj* mobil.

mobile phone *n* Handy *das*.

mock [mɒk] *adj* Schein-. ◆ *vt* verspotten. ◆ *n (Br : exam)* Vorprüfung *die*.

mode [məʊd] *n* Art *die*.

model ['mɒdl] *n* Modell *das* ; *(fashion model)* Mannequin *das*.

moderate ['mɒdərət] *adj (size, speed, amount)* mittlere(-r) (-s) ; *(views, politician)* gemäßigt ; *(drinker, smoker)* mäßig.

modern ['mɒdən] *adj* modern.

modernized ['mɒdənaɪzd] *adj* modernisiert.

modern languages *npl* moderne Fremdsprachen *pl*.

modest ['mɒdɪst] *adj* bescheiden.

modify ['mɒdɪfaɪ] *vt* abländern.

mohair ['məʊheə'] *n* Mohair *der*.

moist [mɔɪst] *adj* feucht.

moisture ['mɔɪstʃəʳ] *n* Feuchtigkeit *die*.

moisturizer ['mɔɪstʃəraɪzəʳ] *n* Feuchtigkeitscreme *die*.

molar ['məʊləʳ] *n* Backenzahn *der*.

mold [məʊld] *(Am)* = **mould**.

mole [məʊl] *n (animal)* Maulwurf *der ; (spot)* Leberfleck *der*.

molest [mə'lest] *vt (child, woman)* belästigen.

mom [mɒm] *n (Am : inf)* Mutti *die*.

moment ['məʊmənt] *n* Moment *der ;* at the ~ im Moment ; for the ~ momentan.

Mon. *(abbr of Monday)* Mo.

monarchy ['mɒnəkɪ] *n :* the ~ die Monarchie.

monastery ['mɒnəstrɪ] *n* Kloster *das*.

Monday ['mʌndɪ] *n* Montag *der ;* → **Saturday**.

money ['mʌnɪ] *n* Geld *das*.

money belt *n* Gürteltasche mit Geldfächern.

money order *n* Zahlungsanweisung *die*.

mongrel ['mʌŋgrəl] *n* Promenadenmischung *die*.

monitor ['mɒnɪtəʳ] *n (computer screen)* Monitor *der*. ◆ *vt* überwachen.

monk [mʌŋk] *n* Mönch *der*.

monkey ['mʌŋkɪ] *(pl* **monkeys)** *n* Affe *der*.

monkfish ['mʌŋkfɪʃ] *n* Seeteufel *der*.

monopoly [mə'nɒpəlɪ] *n* Monopol *das*.

monorail ['mɒnəʊreɪl] *n* Einschienenbahn *die*.

monotonous [mə'nɒtənəs] *adj* monoton.

monsoon [mɒn'su:n] *n* Monsun *der*.

monster ['mɒnstəʳ] *n* Monster *das*.

month [mʌnθ] *n* Monat *der ;* in a ~'s time in einem Monat.

monthly ['mʌnθlɪ] *adj* & *adv* monatlich.

monument ['mɒnjʊmənt] *n* Denkmal *das*.

mood [mu:d] *n* Laune *die*, Stimmung *die ;* to be in a (bad) ~ schlechte Laune haben ; to be in a good ~ gute Laune haben.

moody ['mu:dɪ] *adj* launisch.

moon [mu:n] *n* Mond *der*.

moonlight ['mu:nlaɪt] *n* Mondlicht *das*.

moor [mɔ:ʳ] *n* Moor *das*. ◆ *vt* festlmachen.

moose [mu:s] *(pl* **moose)** *n* Elch *der*.

mop [mɒp] *n (for floor)* Mop *der*. ◆ *vt (floor)* moppen.
▪ **mop up** *vt sep* aufwischen.

moped ['məʊped] *n* Moped *das*.

moral ['mɒrəl] *adj* moralisch. ◆ *n* Moral *die*.

morality [mə'rælɪtɪ] *n* Moral *die*.

more [mɔ:ʳ] *adj* **1.** *(a larger amount of)* mehr ; there are ~ tourists than usual es sind mehr Touristen als gewöhnlich da. **2.** *(additional)* noch mehr ; are there any ~ cakes? ist noch mehr Kuchen da? ; I'd like two ~ bottles ich möchte zwei Flaschen mehr ; there's no ~ wine es ist kein Wein mehr da.

3. *(in phrases)* : ~ **and more** mehr und mehr.

◆ *adv* **1.** *(in comparatives)* : **it's ~ difficult than before** es ist schwieriger als vorher ; **speak ~ clearly** sprich/sprechen Sie deutlicher.

2. *(to a greater degree)* mehr ; **we ought to go to the cinema ~** wir sollten öfters ins Kino gehen.

3. *(in phrases)* : **I don't go there any ~** ich gehe da nicht mehr hin ; **once ~** noch einmal ; **~ or less** mehr oder weniger ; **we'd be ~ than happy to help** wir würden sehr gerne helfen.

◆ *pron* **1.** *(a larger amount)* mehr ; **I've got ~ than you** ich habe mehr als du ; **~ than 20 types of pizza** mehr als 20 Pizzasorten.

2. *(an additional amount)* noch mehr ; **is there any ~?** ist noch mehr da? ; **there's no ~** es ist nichts mehr da.

moreover [mɔːˈrəʊvəʳ] *adv* *(fml)* außerdem.

morning [ˈmɔːnɪŋ] *n* Morgen *der* ; **two o'clock in the ~** zwei Uhr morgens ; **good ~!** guten Morgen! ; **in the ~** *(early in the day)* morgens, am Morgen ; *(tomorrow morning)* morgen früh.

morning-after pill *n* Pille *die* danach.

morning sickness *n* Schwangerschaftsübelkeit *die*.

Morocco [məˈrɒkəʊ] *n* Marokko *nt*.

moron [ˈmɔːrɒn] *n* *(inf)* Blödian *der*.

Morse (code) [mɔːs-] *n* Morsealphabet *das*.

mortgage [ˈmɔːgɪdʒ] *n* Hypothek *die*.

mosaic [məˈzeɪɪk] *n* Mosaik *das*.

Moslem [ˈmɒzləm] = **Muslim**.

mosque [mɒsk] *n* Moschee *die*.

mosquito [məˈskiːtəʊ] *(pl -es)* *n* Mücke *die* ; *(tropical)* Moskito *der*.

mosquito net *n* Moskitonetz *das*.

moss [mɒs] *n* Moos *das*.

most [məʊst] *adj* **1.** *(the majority of)* die meisten ; **~ people agree** die meisten Leute sind dieser Meinung.

2. *(the largest amount of)* der/die/das meiste ; **I drank (the) ~ beer** ich habe das meiste Bier getrunken.

◆ *adv* **1.** *(in superlatives)* : **she spoke (the) ~ clearly** sie sprach am deutlichsten ; **the ~ expensive hotel in town** das teuerste Hotel in der Stadt.

2. *(to the greatest degree)* am meisten ; **I like this one ~** mir gefällt dieses am besten.

3. *(fml : very)* äußerst, höchst ; **it was a ~ pleasant evening** es war ein äußerst angenehmer Abend.

◆ *pron* **1.** *(the majority)* die meisten ; **~ of the villages** die meisten Dörfer ; **~ of the time** meiste Zeit.

2. *(the largest amount)* das meiste ; **she earns (the) ~** sie verdient am meisten.

3. *(in phrases)* : **at ~** höchstens ; **to make the ~ of sthg** das Beste aus etw machen.

mostly ['məʊstlɪ] *adv* hauptsächlich.

MOT *n* (*Br* : *test*) ≃ TÜV *der*.

motel [məʊ'tel] *n* Motel *das*.

moth [mɒθ] *n* Nachtfalter *der* ; (*in clothes*) Motte *die*.

mother ['mʌðə'] *n* Mutter *die*.

mother-in-law *n* Schwiegermutter *die*.

mother-of-pearl *n* Perlmutt *das*.

motif [məʊ'ti:f] *n* Motiv *das*.

motion ['məʊʃn] *n* Bewegung *die*. ◆ *vi* : **to ~ to sb** jm ein Zeichen geben.

motionless ['məʊʃənlɪs] *adj* unbeweglich.

motivate ['məʊtɪveɪt] *vt* motivieren.

motive ['məʊtɪv] *n* Motiv *das*.

motor ['məʊtə'] *n* Motor *der*.

Motorail® ['məʊtəreɪl] *n* Autoreisezug *der*.

motorbike ['məʊtəbaɪk] *n* Motorrad *das*.

motorboat ['məʊtəbəʊt] *n* Motorboot *das*.

motorcar ['məʊtəkɑ:'] *n* Kraftfahrzeug *das*.

motorcycle ['məʊtə,saɪkl] *n* Motorrad *das*.

motorcyclist ['məʊtə,saɪklɪst] *n* Motorradfahrer *der* (-in *die*).

motorist ['məʊtərɪst] *n* Autofahrer *der* (-in *die*).

motor racing *n* Autorennen *das*.

motorway ['məʊtəweɪ] *n* (*Br*) Autobahn *die*.

motto ['mɒtəʊ] (*pl* -**s**) *n* Motto *das*.

mould [məʊld] *n* (*Br*) : *shape*) Form *die* ; (*substance*) Schim-mel *der*. ◆ *vt* (*Br* : *shape*) formen.

mouldy ['məʊldɪ] *adj* (*Br*) schimmelig.

mound [maʊnd] *n* (*hill*) Hügel *der* ; (*pile*) Haufen *der*.

mount [maʊnt] *n* (*for photo*) Passepartout *das* ; (*mountain*) Berg *der*. ◆ *vt* (*horse*) besteigen ; (*photo*) aufziehen. ◆ *vi* (*increase*) steigen.

mountain ['maʊntɪn] *n* Berg *der*.

mountain bike *n* Mountainbike *das*.

mountaineer [,maʊntɪ'nɪə'] *n* Bergsteiger *der* (-in *die*).

mountaineering [,maʊntɪ'nɪərɪŋ] *n* : **to go ~** bergsteigen gehen.

mountainous ['maʊntɪnəs] *adj* bergig.

Mount Rushmore [-'rʌʃmɔ:'] *n* Mount Rushmore.

 MOUNT RUSHMORE

Die gigantischen Skulpturen der Köpfe der amerikanischen Präsidenten George Washington, Thomas Jefferson, Abraham Lincoln und Theodore Roosevelt sind in die Klippen von Mount Rushmore in Süddakota eingemeißelt. Mount Rushmore ist ein Nationaldenkmal und eine beliebte Touristenattraktion.

mourning ['mɔ:nɪŋ] *n* : **to be in ~** in Trauer sein.

mouse [maʊs] (*pl* **mice**) *n* Maus *die*.

moussaka [muˈsɑːkə] *n* Moussaka *die*.

mousse [muːs] *n* Mousse *die*.

moustache [məˈstɑːʃ] *n* (Br) Schnurrbart *der*.

mouth [maʊθ] *n* Mund *der*; (of cave, tunnel) Öffnung *die*; (of river) Mündung *die*.

mouthful [ˈmaʊθfʊl] *n* (of food) Happen *der*; (of drink) Schluck *der*.

mouthorgan [ˈmaʊθˌɔːgən] *n* Mundharmonika *die*.

mouthpiece [ˈmaʊθpiːs] *n* (of telephone) Sprechmuschel *die*; (of musical instrument) Mundstück *das*.

mouthwash [ˈmaʊθwɒʃ] *n* Mundwasser *das*.

move [muːv] *n* (change of house) Umzug *der*; (movement) Bewegung *die*; (in games) Zug *der*; (course of action) Schritt *der*. ◆ *vt* bewegen; (furniture) rücken; (car) wegfahren; (emotionally) rühren. ◆ *vi* sich bewegen; (vehicle) fahren; **to ~ (house)** umlziehen; **to make a ~ (leave)** auflbrechen. ▪ **move along** *vi* (go away) weiterlgehen. ▪ **move in** *vi* (to house) einlziehen. ▪ **move off** *vi* (train, car) sich in Bewegung setzen. ▪ **move on** *vi* (on foot) weiterlgehen; (car, bus etc) weiterlfahren. ▪ **move out** *vi* (from house) auslziehen. ▪ **move over** *vi* zur Seite rücken. ▪ **move up** *vi* (on seat) auflrücken.

movement [ˈmuːvmənt] *n* Bewegung *die*.

movie [ˈmuːvɪ] *n* Film *der*.

movie theater *n* (Am) Kino *das*.

moving [ˈmuːvɪŋ] *adj* bewegend.

mow [məʊ] *vt*: **to ~ the lawn** den Rasen mähen.

mozzarella [ˌmɒtsəˈrelə] *n* Mozzarella *der*.

MP *abbr* = Member of Parliament.

mph (abbr of miles per hour) Meilen pro Stunde.

Mr [ˈmɪstər] *abbr* Hr.

Mrs [ˈmɪsɪz] *abbr* Fr.

Ms [mɪz] *abbr* Anrede für Frauen, mit der man die Unterscheidung zwischen 'Frau' (verheiratet) und 'Fräulein' (unverheiratet) vermeidet.

MSc *n* (abbr of Master of Science) britischer Hochschulabschluss in einem naturwissenschaftlichen Fach.

much [mʌtʃ] (compar **more**, superl **most**) *adj* viel; **I haven't got ~ money** ich habe nicht viel Geld; **as ~ food as you can eat** so viel du essen kannst/Sie essen können; **how ~ time is left?** wie viel Zeit bleibt noch?; **we have too ~ work** wir haben zu viel Arbeit.
◆ *adv* 1. (to a great extent) viel; **it's ~ better** es ist viel besser; **I like it very ~** es gefällt mir sehr gut; **it's not ~ good** (inf) es ist nicht besonders; **thank you very ~** vielen Dank.
2. (often) oft; **we don't go there ~** wir gehen da nicht oft hin.
◆ *pron* viel; **I haven't got ~ ich** habe nicht viel; **as ~ as you like** so viel Sie wollen/du willst;

how ~ is it? wie viel kostet es? ; you've got too ~ du hast zu viel.

muck [mʌk] n Dreck der. ▪ **muck about** vi (Br : inf) herumalbern. ▪ **muck up** vt sep (Br : inf) vermasseln.

mud [mʌd] n Schlamm der.

muddle ['mʌdl] n : to be in a ~ durcheinander sein.

muddy ['mʌdɪ] adj schlammig.

mudguard ['mʌdgɑːd] n Schutzblech das.

muesli ['mjuːzlɪ] n Müsli das.

muffin ['mʌfɪn] n (roll) Muffin das ; (cake) Kleingebäck aus Mürbeteig.

muffler ['mʌflə] n (Am : silencer) Schalldämpfer der.

mug [mʌg] n (cup) Becher der. ◆ vt (attack) überfallen.

mugging ['mʌgɪŋ] n Überfall der.

muggy ['mʌgɪ] adj schwül.

mule [mjuːl] n Maultier das.

multicoloured ['mʌltɪˌkʌləd] adj bunt.

multiple ['mʌltɪpl] adj mehrfach.

multiplex cinema ['mʌltɪ-pleks-] n Multiplexkino das.

multiplication [ˌmʌltɪplɪ-'keɪʃn] n Multiplikation die.

multiply ['mʌltɪplaɪ] vt multiplizieren. ◆ vi sich vermehren.

multistorey (car park) [ˌmʌltɪ'stɔːrɪ-] n Parkhaus das.

mum [mʌm] n (Br : inf) Mutti die.

mummy ['mʌmɪ] n (Br : inf : mother) Mami die.

mumps [mʌmps] n Mumps der.

munch [mʌntʃ] vt kauen.

Munich ['mjuːnɪk] n München nt.

municipal [mjuː'nɪsɪpl] adj städtisch, Stadt-.

mural ['mjuːərəl] n Wandgemälde das.

murder ['mɜːdə] n Mord der. ◆ vt ermorden.

murderer ['mɜːdərə] n Mörder der (-in die).

muscle ['mʌsl] n Muskel der.

museum [mjuː'ziːəm] n Museum das.

mushroom ['mʌʃrʊm] n Pilz der ; (CULIN) Champignon der.

music ['mjuːzɪk] n Musik die.

musical ['mjuːzɪkl] adj musikalisch. ◆ n Musical das.

musical instrument n Musikinstrument das.

musician [mjuː'zɪʃn] n Musiker der (-in die).

Muslim ['mʊzlɪm] adj moslemisch. ◆ n Moslem der (Moslime die).

mussels ['mʌslz] npl Miesmuscheln pl.

must [mʌst] aux vb müssen ; (with negative) dürfen. ◆ n : it's a ~ (inf) das ist ein Muss ; I ~ go ich muss gehen ; you ~n't be late du darfst nicht zu spät kommen ; the room ~ be vacated by ten das Zimmer ist bis zehn Uhr zu räumen ; you ~ have seen it du musst es doch gesehen haben ; you ~ see that film du musst dir diesen Film ansehen ; you ~ be joking! das kann doch nicht dein Ernst sein!

mustache ['mʌstæʃ] (Am) = moustache.

mustard ['mʌstəd] n Senf der.

mustn't ['mʌsənt] = must
not.
mutter ['mʌtə'] vt murmeln.
mutton ['mʌtn] n Hammelfleisch das.
mutual ['mjuːtʃʊəl] adj (feeling) gegenseitig ; (friend, interest) gemeinsam.
muzzle ['mʌzl] n Maulkorb
der.
my [maɪ] adj mein.
myself [maɪ'self] pron (reflexive : accusative) mich ; (reflexive : dative) mir ; (after prep : accusative) mich selbst ; (after
prep : dative) mir selbst ; I did it
~ ich habe es selbst gemacht.
mysterious [mɪ'stɪərɪəs] adj
rätselhaft.
mystery ['mɪstərɪ] n Rätsel
das.
myth [mɪθ] n (ancient story)
Mythos der ; (false idea) Märchen das.

N

N (abbr of North) N.
nag [næg] vt herum|nörgeln an
(+D).
nail [neɪl] n Nagel der. ◆ vt an|-
nageln.
nailbrush ['neɪlbrʌʃ] n Nagelbürste die.
nail file n Nagelfeile die.
nail scissors npl Nagelschere
die.
nail varnish n Nagellack der.
nail varnish remover [-rə-
'muːvə'] n Nagellackentferner
der.

naive [naɪ'iːv] adj naiv.
naked ['neɪkɪd] adj nackt.
name [neɪm] n Name der ;
(reputation) Ruf der. ◆ vt nennen ; (place) benennen ; first ~
Vorname der ; last ~ Nachname
der ; what's your ~? wie heißen
Sie/heißt du? ; my ~ is... ich
heiße...
namely ['neɪmlɪ] adv nämlich.
nan bread [næn-] n indisches
Fladenbrot, das heiß gegessen
wird.
nanny ['nænɪ] n (childminder)
Kindermädchen das ; (inf :
grandmother) Oma die.
nap [næp] n : to have a ~ ein
Nickerchen machen.
napkin ['næpkɪn] n Serviette
die.
nappy ['næpɪ] n Windel die.
nappy liner n Windeleinlage
die.
narcotic [nɑː'kɒtɪk] n Rauschgift das.
narrow ['nærəʊ] adj schmal,
eng. ◆ vi sich verengen.
narrow-minded [-'maɪndɪd]
adj engstirnig.
nasty ['nɑːstɪ] adj (spiteful) gemein ; (accident, fall) schlimm ;
(smell, taste, weather) scheußlich.
nation ['neɪʃn] n Nation die.
national ['næʃənl] adj national. ◆ n Staatsbürger der (-in
die).
national anthem n Nationalhymne die.
National Health Service n
staatlicher britischer Gesund-
heitsdienst.
National Insurance n (Br)
Sozialversicherung die.

nationality [ˌnæʃə'nælətɪ] n Nationalität die.

National Lottery n : the ~ (Br) die Lotterie.

national park n Nationalpark der.

 NATIONAL PARK

Nationalparks sind ausgedehnte Landschaften, die wegen ihrer natürlichen Schönheit geschützt sind. In Großbritannien und Amerika sind sie für die Öffentlichkeit zugänglich. Zu den britischen Nationalparks zählen Snowdonia, der Lake District und der Peak District. Die bekanntesten amerikanischen Nationalparks sind Yellowstone und Yosemite. In den Nationalparks gibt es immer Campingmöglichkeiten.

nationwide ['neɪʃənwaɪd] adj landesweit.

native ['neɪtɪv] adj (customs, population) einheimisch. ◆ n Einheimische der, die ; ~ country Heimatland das ; he is a ~ speaker of English Englisch ist seine Muttersprache.

NATO ['neɪtəʊ] n NATO die.

natural ['nætʃrəl] adj natürlich ; (swimmer, actor) geboren.

natural gas n Erdgas das.

naturally ['nætʃrəlɪ] adv natürlich.

natural yoghurt n Biojoghurt der.

nature ['neɪtʃə'] n Natur die ; (quality, character) Wesen das.

nature reserve n Naturschutzgebiet das.

naughty ['nɔːtɪ] adj (child) ungezogen.

nausea ['nɔːzɪə] n Übelkeit die.

navigate ['nævɪgeɪt] vi navigieren ; (in car) lotsen.

navy ['neɪvɪ] n (ships) Marine die. ◆ adj : ~ (blue) marineblau.

NB (abbr of nota bene) NB.

near [nɪə'] adj & adv nahe. ◆ prep : ~ (to) nahe an (+D) ; in the ~ future demnächst.

nearby [nɪə'baɪ] adv in der Nähe. ◆ adj nahe gelegen.

nearly ['nɪəlɪ] adv fast.

nearside ['nɪəsaɪd] n (AUT) : (in UK) linke Seite ; (in US, Europe) rechte Seite.

neat [niːt] adj ordentlich ; (writing) sauber ; (whisky, vodka etc) pur.

neatly ['niːtlɪ] adv ordentlich ; (written) sauber.

necessarily [ˌnesə'serɪlɪ, (Br) 'nesəsrəlɪ] adv : not ~ nicht unbedingt.

necessary ['nesəsrɪ] adj nötig, notwendig.

necessity [nɪ'sesətɪ] n Notwendigkeit die. ▪ **necessities** npl Lebensnotwendige das.

neck [nek] n Hals der ; (of jumper, dress, shirt) Kragen der.

necklace ['neklɪs] n Halskette die.

nectarine ['nektərɪn] n Nektarine die.

need [niːd] n Bedürfnis das. ◆ vt brauchen ; to ~ to do sthg etw tun müssen.

needle ['niːdl] n Nadel die.

needlework ['niːdlwɜːk] *n* *(SCH)* Handarbeit *die*.

needn't ['niːdənt] = **need not**.

needy ['niːdɪ] *adj* Not leidend.

negative ['negətɪv] *adj* negativ ; *(person)* ablehnend. ◆ *n (in photography)* Negativ *das* ; *(GRAMM)* Verneinung *die*.

neglect [nɪ'glekt] *vt* vernachlässigen.

negligence ['neglɪdʒəns] *n* Nachlässigkeit *die*.

negotiations [nɪ,gəʊʃɪ'eɪʃnz] *npl* Verhandlungen *pl*.

negro ['niːgrəʊ] *(pl* -es) *n* Neger *der* (-in *die*).

neighbour ['neɪbə'] *n* Nachbar *der* (-in *die*).

neighbourhood ['neɪbəhʊd] *n* Nachbarschaft *die*.

neighbouring ['neɪbərɪŋ] *adj* benachbart.

neither ['naɪðə'] *adj* : ~ **bag is big enough** keine der beiden Taschen ist groß genug. ◆ *pron* : ~ **of us** keiner von uns beiden. ◆ *conj* : ~ **do I** ich auch nicht ; ~... **nor**... weder... noch...

neon light ['niːɒn-] *n* Neonlicht *das*.

nephew ['nefjuː] *n* Neffe *der*.

nerve [nɜːv] *n* Nerv *der* ; *(courage)* Mut *der* ; **what a ~!** so eine Frechheit!

nervous ['nɜːvəs] *adj* nervös.

nervous breakdown *n* Nervenzusammenbruch *der*.

nest [nest] *n* Nest *das*.

net [net] *n* Netz *das*. ◆ *adj* *(profit, result, weight)* netto.

Net [net] *n* : **the ~** das Internet.

netball ['netbɔːl] *n* Sportart, die meist von Frauen gespielt wird und dem Basketball ähnelt.

Netherlands ['neðələndz] *npl* : **the ~** die Niederlande.

nettle ['netl] *n* Nessel *die*.

network ['netwɜːk] *n* Netz *das*.

neurotic [,njʊə'rɒtɪk] *adj* neurotisch.

neutral ['njuːtrəl] *adj* neutral. ◆ *n (AUT)* : **in ~** im Leerlauf.

never ['nevə'] *adv* nie ; *(simple negative)* nicht ; **she's ~ late** sie kommt nie zu spät ; ~ **mind!** macht nichts!

nevertheless [,nevəðə'les] *adv* trotzdem.

new [njuː] *adj* neu.

newly ['njuːlɪ] *adv* frisch.

new potatoes *npl* neue Kartoffeln.

news [njuːz] *n* *(information)* Nachricht *die* ; *(on TV, radio)* Nachrichten *pl* ; **a piece of ~** eine Neuigkeit.

newsagent ['njuːzeɪdʒənt] *n* *(shop)* Zeitungshändler *der*.

newspaper ['njuːz,peɪpə'] *n* Zeitung *die*.

New Year *n* Neujahr *das*.

 NEW YEAR

Der Silvesterabend ("New Year's Eve") wird in Großbritannien mit Parties und Zusammenkünften gefeiert. Wenn die Uhr Mitternacht schlägt, wird traditionsgemäß das Lied "Auld lang Syne" angestimmt. In Schottland, wo dieser Tag eine besondere Bedeutung hat, nennt man ihn

„Hogmanay". Der darauf folgende Neujahrstag („New Year's Day") ist in ganz Großbritannien ein Feiertag.

New Year's Day n Neujahrstag der.

New Year's Eve n Silvester der.

New Zealand [-'zi:lənd] n Neuseeland nt.

next [nekst] adj nächste(-r) (-s). ◆ adv (afterwards) als Nächstes, danach ; (on next occasion) das nächste Mal ; when does the ~ bus leave? wann fährt der nächste Bus ab? ; ~ to neben ; the week after ~ übernächste Woche.

next door adv nebenan.

next of kin [-kɪn] n nächster Angehörige (nächste Angehörige).

NHS abbr = National Health Service.

nib [nɪb] n Feder die.

nibble ['nɪbl] vt knabbern.

nice [naɪs] adj (meal, feeling, taste) gut ; (clothes, house, car, weather) schön ; (kind) nett ; to have a ~ time Spaß haben ; ~ to see you! schön, dich wieder zu sehen!

nickel ['nɪkl] n (metal) Nickel das ; (Am : coin) Fünfcentstück das.

nickname ['nɪkneɪm] n Spitzname der.

niece [ni:s] n Nichte die.

night [naɪt] n Nacht die ; (evening) Abend der ; at ~ nachts ; (in evening) abends ; by ~ nachts.

nightclub ['naɪtklʌb] n Nachtklub der.

nightdress ['naɪtdres] n Nachthemd das.

nightie ['naɪtɪ] n (inf) Nachthemd das.

nightlife ['naɪtlaɪf] n Nachtleben das.

nightly ['naɪtlɪ] adv nächtlich.

nightmare ['naɪtmeə'] n Albtraum der.

night safe n Nachttresor der.

night school n Abendschule die.

nightshift ['naɪtʃɪft] n Nachtschicht die.

nil [nɪl] n (SPORT) null.

Nile [naɪl] n : the ~ der Nil.

nine [naɪn] num neun ; → six.

nineteen [,naɪn'ti:n] num neunzehn ; → six ; ~ ninety-five neunzehnhundertfünfundneunzig.

nineteenth [,naɪn'ti:nθ] num neunzehnte(-r) (-s) ; → sixth.

ninetieth ['naɪntɪəθ] num neunzigste(-r) (-s) ; → sixth.

ninety ['naɪntɪ] num neunzig ; → six.

ninth [naɪnθ] num neunte(-r) (-s) ; → sixth.

nip [nɪp] vt (pinch) zwicken.

nipple ['nɪpl] n (of breast) Brustwarze die ; (of bottle) Sauger der.

nitrogen ['naɪtrədʒən] n Stickstoff der.

no [nəʊ] adv nein. ◆ adj (not any) kein. ◆ n Nein das ; I've got ~ money left ich habe kein Geld übrig.

noble ['nəʊbl] adj (character) edel ; (aristocratic) adlig.

nobody ['nəʊbədɪ] *pron* niemand.

nod [nɒd] *vi* nicken.

noise [nɔɪz] *n* Lärm *der*.

noisy ['nɔɪzɪ] *adj* laut.

nominate ['nɒmɪneɪt] *vt* nennen.

nonalcoholic [ˌnɒnælkə-'hɒlɪk] *adj* alkoholfrei.

none [nʌn] *pron* keine(-r) (-s) ; ~ of us keiner von uns ; ~ of the money nichts von dem Geld.

nonetheless [ˌnʌnðə'les] *adv* nichtsdestoweniger.

nonfiction [ˌnɒn'fɪkʃn] *n* Sachliteratur *die*.

non-iron *adj* bügelfrei.

nonsense ['nɒnsəns] *n* Unsinn *der*.

non-smoker *n* (person) Nichtraucher *der* (-in *die*) ; (railway carriage) Nichtraucherabteil *das*.

nonstick [ˌnɒn'stɪk] *adj* mit Antihaftbeschichtung.

nonstop [ˌnɒn'stɒp] *adj* (flight) Nonstop-. ◆ *adv* (fly, run, rain) ohne Unterbrechung, nonstop.

noodles ['nuːdlz] *npl* Nudeln *pl*.

noon [nuːn] *n* Mittag *der*.

no one = nobody.

nor [nɔːʳ] *conj* auch nicht ; ~ do I ich auch nicht ; → neither.

normal ['nɔːml] *adj* normal.

normally ['nɔːməlɪ] *adv* (usually) normalerweise ; (properly) normal.

north [nɔːθ] *n* Norden *der*. ◆ *adv* nach Norden ; in the ~ of England in Nordengland.

North America *n* Nordamerika *nt*.

northbound ['nɔːθbaʊnd] *adj* in Richtung Norden.

northeast [ˌnɔːθ'iːst] *n* Nordosten *der*.

northern ['nɔːðən] *adj* nördlich.

Northern Ireland *n* Nordirland *nt*.

North Pole *n* Nordpol *der*.

North Sea *n* Nordsee *die*.

northwards ['nɔːθwədz] *adv* nach Norden.

northwest [ˌnɔːθ'west] *n* Nordwesten *der*.

Norway ['nɔːweɪ] *n* Norwegen *nt*.

Norwegian [nɔː'wiːdʒən] *adj* norwegisch. ◆ *n* (person) Norweger *der* (-in *die*) ; (language) Norwegisch *das*.

nose [nəʊz] *n* Nase *die* ; (of animal) Schnauze *die*.

nosebleed ['nəʊzbliːd] *n* Nasenbluten *das*.

no smoking area *n* Nichtraucherecke *die*.

nostril ['nɒstrəl] *n* Nasenloch *das* ; (of animal) Nüster *die*.

nosy ['nəʊzɪ] *adj* neugierig.

not [nɒt] *adv* nicht ; she's ~ there sie ist nicht da ; ~ yet noch nicht ; ~ at all (pleased, interested) überhaupt nicht ; (in reply to thanks) gern geschehen.

notably ['nəʊtəblɪ] *adv* besonders.

note [nəʊt] *n* (message) Nachricht *die* ; (MUS) Note *die* ; (comment) Anmerkung *die* ; (bank note) Geldschein *der*. ◆ *vt* (notice) bemerken ; (write down) notieren ; **to take ~s** Notizen machen.

notebook ['nəʊtbʊk] *n* Notizbuch *das*.

noted ['nəʊtɪd] *adj* bekannt.

notepaper ['nəʊtpeɪpə'] *n* Briefpapier *das*.

nothing ['nʌθɪŋ] *pron* nichts ; **~ new/interesting** nichts Neues/Interessantes ; **for ~** *(for free)* umsonst ; *(in vain)* vergeblich.

notice ['nəʊtɪs] *vt* bemerken. ♦ *n (in newspaper)* Anzeige *die* ; *(on board)* Aushang *der* ; *(warning)* Ankündigung *die* ; **to take ~ of** zur Kenntnis nehmen ; **to hand in one's ~** kündigen.

noticeable ['nəʊtɪsəbl] *adj* bemerkenswert.

notice board *n* Anschlagtafel *die*.

notion ['nəʊʃn] *n* Vorstellung *die*.

notorious [nəʊ'tɔːrɪəs] *adj* berüchtigt.

nougat ['nuːgɑː] *n* Nugat *das*.

nought [nɔːt] *n* Null *die*.

noun [naʊn] *n* Substantiv *das*.

nourishment ['nʌrɪʃmənt] *n* Nahrung *die*.

Nov. *(abbr of November)* Nov.

novel ['nɒvl] *n* Roman *der*. ♦ *adj* neu.

novelist ['nɒvəlɪst] *n* Romanautor *der* (-in *die*).

November [nə'vembə'] *n* November *der* ; → **September**.

now [naʊ] *adv* jetzt. ♦ *conj* : **~ (that)** jetzt, wo... ; **just ~** *(at the moment)* eben ; **right ~** *(at the moment)* im Moment ; *(immediately)* sofort ; **by ~** inzwischen ; **from ~ on** von jetzt an.

nowadays ['naʊədeɪz] *adv* heutzutage.

nowhere ['nəʊweə'] *adv* nirgends.

nozzle ['nɒzl] *n* Düse *die*.

nuclear ['njuːklɪə'] *adj* Atom-.

nude [njuːd] *adj* nackt.

nudge [nʌdʒ] *vt* anstoßen.

nuisance ['njuːsns] *n* : **it's a real ~!** es ist wirklich ärgerlich! ; **he's such a ~!** er ist wirklich lästig!

numb [nʌm] *adj* gefühllos.

number ['nʌmbə'] *n* Nummer *die* ; *(quantity)* Anzahl *die*. ♦ *vt* nummerieren.

numberplate ['nʌmbəpleɪt] *n* Nummernschild *das*.

numeral ['njuːmərəl] *n* Ziffer *die*.

numerous ['njuːmərəs] *adj* zahlreich.

nun [nʌn] *n* Nonne *die*.

nurse [nɜːs] *n* Krankenschwester *die*. ♦ *vt* pflegen ; **male ~** Krankenpfleger *der*.

nursery ['nɜːsərɪ] *n (in house)* Kinderzimmer *das* ; *(for plants)* Gärtnerei *die*.

nursery (school) *n* Kindergarten *der*.

nursery slope *n* Idiotenhügel *der*.

nursing ['nɜːsɪŋ] *n (profession)* Krankenpflege *die*.

nut [nʌt] *n (to eat)* Nuss *die* ; *(of metal)* Mutter *die*.

nutcrackers ['nʌt,krækəz] *npl* Nussknacker *der*.

nutmeg ['nʌtmeg] *n* Muskatnuss *die*.

nylon ['naɪlɒn] *n* Nylon *das*. ♦ *adj* aus Nylon.

O

o' [ə] abbr = **of**.

O n (zero) Null die.

oak [əʊk] n Eiche die. ◆ adj Eichen-.

OAP abbr = **old age pensioner**.

oar [ɔːʳ] n Ruder das.

oatcake ['əʊtkeɪk] n Haferkeks der.

oath [əʊθ] n (promise) Eid der.

oatmeal ['əʊtmiːl] n Hafermehl das.

oats [əʊts] npl Haferflocken pl.

obedient [ə'biːdjənt] adj gehorsam.

obey [ə'beɪ] vt gehorchen (+D).

object [n 'ɒbdʒɪkt, vb ɒb'dʒekt] n Objekt das ; (purpose) Zweck der. ◆ vi : to ~ (to) Einspruch erheben (gegen).

objection [əb'dʒekʃn] n Einwand der.

objective [əb'dʒektɪv] n Ziel das.

obligation [ˌɒblɪ'geɪʃn] n Verpflichtung die.

obligatory [ə'blɪgətrɪ] adj obligatorisch.

oblige [ə'blaɪdʒ] vt : to ~ sb to do sthg jn zwingen, etw zu tun.

oblique [ə'bliːk] adj schief.

oblong ['ɒblɒŋ] adj rechteckig. ◆ n Rechteck das.

obnoxious [əb'nɒkʃəs] adj unausstehlich.

oboe ['əʊbəʊ] n Oboe die.

obscene [əb'siːn] adj obszön.

obscure [əb'skjʊəʳ] adj unklar ; (not well-known) unbekannt.

observant [əb'zɜːvnt] adj aufmerksam.

observation [ˌɒbzə'veɪʃn] n (watching) Beobachtung die ; (comment) Bemerkung die.

observatory [əb'zɜːvətrɪ] n Sternwarte die.

observe [əb'zɜːv] vt (watch, see) beobachten.

obsessed [əb'sest] adj besessen.

obsession [əb'seʃn] n fixe Idee.

obsolete ['ɒbsəliːt] adj veraltet.

obstacle ['ɒbstəkl] n Hindernis das.

obstinate ['ɒbstənət] adj starrsinnig.

obstruct [əb'strʌkt] vt versperren.

obstruction [əb'strʌkʃn] n Blockierung die.

obtain [əb'teɪn] vt erhalten.

obtainable [əb'teɪnəbl] adj erhältlich.

obvious ['ɒbvɪəs] adj eindeutig.

obviously ['ɒbvɪəslɪ] adv offensichtlich.

occasion [ə'keɪʒn] n Gelegenheit die.

occasional [ə'keɪʒənl] adj gelegentlich.

occasionally [ə'keɪʒnəlɪ] adv gelegentlich.

occupant ['ɒkjʊpənt] n (of house) Bewohner der (-in die) ; (of car, plane) Insasse der (Insassin die).

occupation [ˌɒkjʊˈpeɪʃn] n (job) Beruf der ; (pastime) Beschäftigung die.

occupied [ˈɒkjʊpaɪd] adj (toilet) besetzt.

occupy [ˈɒkjʊpaɪ] vt (building) bewohnen ; (seat, country) besetzen ; (keep busy) beschäftigen.

occur [əˈkɜːʳ] vi vor|kommen.

occurrence [əˈkʌrəns] n Ereignis das ; (existence) Auftreten das.

ocean [ˈəʊʃn] n Ozean der ; the ~ (Am : sea) das Meer.

o'clock [əˈklɒk] adv : (at) one ~ (um) ein Uhr.

Oct. (abbr of October) Okt.

October [ɒkˈtəʊbəʳ] n Oktober der ; → **September**.

octopus [ˈɒktəpəs] n Krake der.

odd [ɒd] adj (strange) seltsam ; (number) ungerade ; (not matching) einzeln ; (occasional) gelegentlich ; 60 ~ miles ungefähr 60 Meilen ; some ~ bits of paper irgendwelches Papier ; ~ jobs Gelegenheitsarbeiten pl.

odds [ɒdz] npl Chancen pl ; ~ and ends Kram der.

odor [ˈəʊdəʳ] (Am) = **odour**.

odour [ˈəʊdəʳ] n (Br) Geruch der.

of [ɒv] prep 1. (gen) von, use the genitive case ; the colour ~ the car die Farbe des Autos ; a map ~ Britain eine Karte von Großbritannien ; a group ~ people eine Gruppe Menschen ; a glass ~ beer ein Glas Bier ; the handle ~ the door der Türgriff.

2. (expressing amount) : a pound ~ sweets ein Pfund Bonbons ; a piece ~ cake ein Stück Kuchen ; a fall ~ 20% ein Sinken um 20% ; a town ~ 50 000 people eine Stadt mit 50 000 Einwohnern ; a girl ~ six ein sechsjähriges Mädchen.

3. (made from) aus ; a house ~ stone ein Haus aus Stein ; it's made ~ wood es ist aus Holz.

4. (referring to time) : the summer ~ 1969 der Sommer 1969 ; the 26th ~ August der 26. August.

5. (on the part of) von ; that was very kind ~ you das war sehr nett von Ihnen/dir.

6. (Am : in telling the time) vor ; it's ten ~ four es ist zehn vor vier.

off [ɒf] adv 1. (away) weg ; to get ~ (from bus, train, plane) aus|steigen ; we're ~ to Austria next week wir fahren nächste Woche nach Österreich.

2. (expressing removal) ab ; to take sthg ~ (clothes, shoes) etw aus|ziehen ; (lid, wrapper) etw ab|nehmen.

3. (so as to stop working) : to turn sthg ~ (TV, radio, engine) etw aus|schalten ; (tap) etw zu|drehen.

4. (expressing distance or time away) : it's 10 miles ~ es sind noch 10 Meilen bis dahin ; it's two months ~ yet es sind noch zwei Monate bis dahin ; it's a long way ~ (in distance) es ist noch ein weiter Weg bis dahin ; (in time) bis dahin ist es noch lange hin.

5. (not at work) : I'm taking a week ~ ich nehme mir eine Woche frei.

◆ prep 1. (away from) von ; to

get ~ sthg aus|steigen aus etw ;
~ the coast vor der Küste ; **it's
just ~ the main road** es ist gleich
in der Nähe der Hauptstraße...
2. *(indicating removal)* von...
ab ; **take the lid ~ the jar** mach
den Deckel von dem Glas ab ;
they've taken £20 ~ the price sie
haben es um 20 Pfund billiger
gemacht.
3. *(absent from)* : **to be ~ work**
frei haben.
4. *(inf : from)* von ; **I bought it ~
her** ich habe es von ihr gekauft.
5. *(inf : no longer liking)* : **I'm ~
my food** ich mag mein Essen
nicht mehr.
◆ *adj* **1.** *(meat, cheese, milk,
beer)* schlecht.
2. *(not working)* aus ; *(tap)* zu.
3. *(cancelled)* abgesagt.
4. *(not available)* : **the soup's ~**
es ist keine Suppe mehr da.

offence [əˈfens] *n* [*(Br)* : *crime)*
Straftat *die* ; *(upset)* Beleidigung *die.*

offend [əˈfend] *vt (upset)* beleidigen.

offender [əˈfendər] *n* Täter
der (-in *die*).

offense [əˈfens] *(Am)* = offence.

offensive [əˈfensɪv] *adj (in-
sulting)* beleidigend.

offer [ˈɒfər] *n* Angebot *das.* ◆
vt an|bieten ; *(provide)* bieten ;
on ~ im Angebot ; **to ~ to do sthg**
an|bieten, etw zu tun ; **to ~ sb
sthg** *(gift)* jm etw schenken ;
(food, job, seat, money) jm etw
an|bieten.

office [ˈɒfɪs] *n (room)* Büro *das.*
office block *n* Bürogebäude
das.

officer [ˈɒfɪsər] *n (MIL)* Offizier *der* ; *(policeman)* Beamte
der (Beamtin *die*).

official [əˈfɪʃl] *adj* offiziell.
◆ *n* Repräsentant *der* (-in *die*).

officially [əˈfɪʃəlɪ] *adv* offiziell.

off-licence *n (Br)* Wein- und
Spirituosenhandlung *die.*

off-peak *adj (train, traffic)*
außerhalb der Hauptverkehrs-
zeiten ; *(ticket)* zum Spartarif.

off sales *npl (Br)* Verkauf von
Alkohol in Geschäften oder Pubs
zum Mitnehmen.

off-season *n* Nebensaison
die.

offshore [ˈɒfʃɔːr] *adj (breeze)*
vom Land her ; *(island)* küsten-
nah.

off side *n (AUT)* Fahrerseite *die.*

off-the-peg *adj* von der
Stange.

often [ˈɒfn, ˈɒftn] *adv* oft ; **how
~ do the buses run?** wie oft fährt
der Bus? ; **every so ~** gelegentlich.

oh [əu] *excl* oh!

oil [ɔɪl] *n* Öl *das.*

oilcan [ˈɔɪlkæn] *n* Ölkanister
der.

oil filter *n* Ölfilter *der.*

oil rig *n* Bohrinsel *die.*

oily [ˈɔɪlɪ] *adj* ölig ; *(food)* fettig.

ointment [ˈɔɪntmənt] *n* Salbe
die.

OK [ˌəuˈkeɪ] *adj (inf)* in Ordnung, okay. ◆ *adv (inf : expressing agreement)* in Ordnung, okay ; *(satisfactorily,
well)* gut.

okay [ˌəuˈkeɪ] = **OK.**

old [əʊld] *adj* alt ; **how ~ are you?** wie alt bist du? ; **I'm 36 years ~** ich bin 36 (Jahre alt) ; **to get ~** alt werden.

old age *n* Alter *das*.

old age pensioner *n* Senior *der* (-in *die*).

O level *n ehemaliger britischer Schulabschluss, ersetzt durch das 'GCSE'*.

olive ['ɒlɪv] *n* Olive *die*.

olive oil *n* Olivenöl *das*.

Olympic Games [ə'lɪmpɪk-] *npl* Olympische Spiele *pl*.

omelette ['ɒmlɪt] *n* Omelett *das* ; **mushroom ~** Omelett mit Pilzen.

ominous ['ɒmɪnəs] *adj* unheilvoll.

omit [ə'mɪt] *vt* auslassen.

on [ɒn] *prep* **1.** *(expressing position, location)* auf (+D,A) ; **it's ~ the table** es ist auf dem Tisch ; **put it ~ the table** leg es auf den Tisch ; **a picture ~ the wall** ein Bild an der Wand ; **the exhaust ~ the car** der Auspuff am Auto ; **~ my left** zu meiner Linken ; **~ the right** auf der rechten Seite ; **we stayed ~ a farm** wir übernachteten auf einem Bauernhof ; **~ the Rhine** am Rhein ; **~ the main road** an der Hauptstraße. **2.** *(with forms of transport)* : **~ the train/plane** *(inside)* im Zug/Flugzeug ; *(travel)* mit dem Zug/Flugzeug ; **to get ~ a bus** in einen Bus einsteigen. **3.** *(expressing means, method)* auf (+D) ; **~ foot** zu Fuß ; **~ TV/the radio** im Radio/Fernsehen ; **~ tape** auf Band. **4.** *(using)* : **it runs ~ unleaded petrol** es fährt mit bleifreiem

Benzin ; **to be ~ medication** Medikamente nehmen. **5.** *(about)* über (+A) ; **a book ~ Germany** ein Buch über Deutschland. **6.** *(expressing time)* an (+D) ; **~ arrival** bei Ankunft ; **~ Tuesday** am Dienstag ; **~ 25th August** am 25. August. **7.** *(with regard to)* auf (+D) ; **a tax ~ imports** eine Steuer auf Importe ; **the effect ~ Britain** die Auswirkungen auf Großbritannien. **8.** *(describing activity, state)* : **to be ~ fire** brennen ; **~ holiday** im Urlaub ; **~ offer** im Angebot. **9.** *(in phrases)* : **do you have any money ~ you?** *(inf)* hast du Geld bei dir? ; **the drinks are ~ me** die Drinks gehen auf mich.

◆ *adv* **1.** *(in place, covering)* : **to have sthg ~** *(clothes, hat)* etw anhaben ; **put the lid ~** mach den Deckel drauf ; **to put one's clothes ~** sich (D) seine Kleider anziehen. **2.** *(film, play, programme)* : **the news is ~** die Nachrichten laufen ; **what's ~ at the cinema?** was läuft im Kino? **3.** *(with transport)* : **to get ~** einsteigen. **4.** *(functioning)* an ; **to turn sthg ~** *(TV, radio, engine)* etw einschalten ; *(tap)* etw aufdrehen. **5.** *(taking place)* : **how long is the festival ~?** wie lange geht das Festival? **6.** *(further forward)* weiter ; **to drive ~** weiterfahren. **7.** *(in phrases)* : **to have sthg ~** etw vorhaben.

◆ adj (TV, engine, light) an ; (tap) auf.

once [wʌns] adv einmal. ◆ conj wenn ; **at ~** (immediately) sofort ; (at the same time) gleichzeitig ; **for ~** ausnahmsweise ; **~ more** (one more time) noch einmal ; (again) wieder.

oncoming [ˈɒnˌkʌmɪŋ] adj (traffic) Gegen-.

one [wʌn] num (the number 1) eins ; (with noun) ein/eine/ein. ◆ adj (only) einzige(-r) (-s). ◆ pron eine/einer/eines ; (fml : you) man ; **this ~** diese/dieser/dieses ; **thirty-~** einunddreißig ; **~ fifth** ein Fünftel ; **I like that ~** ich mag den/die/das (da) ; **which ~?** welche/welcher/welches? ; **the ~ I told you about** der/die/das, von dem/der/dem ich dir erzählt habe ; **~ of my friends** einer meiner Freunde ; **~ day** (in past, future) eines Tages.

one-piece (swimsuit) n Einteiler der.

oneself [wʌnˈself] pron (reflexive) sich ; (after prep) sich selbst.

one-way adj (street) Einbahn- ; (ticket) einfach.

onion [ˈʌnjən] n Zwiebel die.

onion bhaji [-ˈbɑːdʒɪ] n indische Vorspeise aus ausgebackenen Teigbällchen mit gehackten Zwiebeln.

onion rings npl frittierte Zwiebelringe pl.

only [ˈəʊnlɪ] adj einzige(-r) (-s). ◆ adv nur ; **an ~ child** ein Einzelkind ; **I ~ want one** ich möchte nur einen/eine/eines ; **we've ~ just arrived** wir sind gerade erst angekommen ; **there's ~ just enough** es ist gerade noch genug da ; **'members ~'** 'nur für Mitglieder' ; **not ~** nicht nur.

onto [ˈɒntuː] prep auf (+A) ; **to get ~ sb** (telephone) jn anrufen.

onward [ˈɒnwəd] adj (journey) Weiter-. ◆ adv = **onwards**.

onwards [ˈɒnwədz] adv (forwards) vorwärts ; **from now ~** von jetzt an ; **from October ~** ab Oktober.

opal [ˈəʊpl] n Opal der.

opaque [əʊˈpeɪk] adj undurchsichtig.

open [ˈəʊpn] adj offen. ◆ vt öffnen ; (door, window, mouth) öffnen, aufmachen ; (bank account, meeting, new building) eröffnen. ◆ vi (door, window, lock) sich öffnen ; (shop, office, bank) öffnen, aufmachen ; (start) beginnen, anfangen ; **are you ~ at the weekend?** haben Sie am Wochenende geöffnet? ; **wide ~** weit offen ; **in the ~** (air) im Freien. ■ **open onto** vt fus führen auf (+A). ■ **open up** vi (unlock the door) aufschließen ; (shop, cinema etc) öffnen.

open-air adj (swimming pool) Frei- ; (theatre, concert) Freilicht-.

opening [ˈəʊpnɪŋ] n (gap) Öffnung die ; (beginning) Eröffnung die ; (opportunity) Möglichkeit die.

opening hours npl Öffnungszeiten pl.

open-minded [-ˈmaɪndɪd] adj aufgeschlossen.

open-plan adj Großraum-.

open sandwich n belegtes Brot.

opera ['ɒpərə] n Oper die.

opera house n Opernhaus das.

operate ['ɒpəreɪt] vt (machine) bedienen. ◆ vi (work) funktionieren ; **to ~ on sb** jn operieren.

operating room ['ɒpəreɪtɪŋ-] (Am) = operating theatre.

operating theatre ['ɒpəreɪtɪŋ-] n (Br) Operationssaal der.

operation [,ɒpə'reɪʃn] n (in hospital) Operation die ; (task) Aktion die ; **to be in ~** (law, system) in Kraft sein ; **to have an ~** sich operieren lassen.

operator ['ɒpəreɪtə] n (on phone) Vermittlung die.

opinion [ə'pɪnjən] n Meinung die ; **in my ~** meiner Meinung nach.

opponent [ə'pəʊnənt] n Gegner der (-in die).

opportunity [,ɒpə'tjuːnətɪ] n Gelegenheit die.

oppose [ə'pəʊz] vt sich wenden gegen ; (argue against) sprechen gegen.

opposed [ə'pəʊzd] adj : **to be ~ to sthg** gegen etw sein.

opposite ['ɒpəzɪt] adj gegenüberliegend ; (totally different) entgegengesetzt. ◆ prep gegenüber (+D). ◆ n : **the ~ (of)** das Gegenteil (von).

opposition [,ɒpə'zɪʃn] n (objections) Opposition die ; (SPORT) Gegner der ; **the Opposition** (POL) die Opposition.

opt [ɒpt] vt : **to ~ to do sthg** sich entscheiden, etw zu tun.

optician's [ɒp'tɪʃns] n (shop) Optiker der.

optimist ['ɒptɪmɪst] n Optimist der (-in die).

optimistic [,ɒptɪ'mɪstɪk] adj optimistisch.

option ['ɒpʃn] n (alternative) Möglichkeit die ; (optional extra) Extra das.

optional ['ɒpʃənl] adj freiwillig ; (subject) wahlfrei.

or [ɔː] conj oder ; (after negative) noch.

oral ['ɔːrəl] adj (spoken) mündlich ; (hygiene) Mund-. ◆ n (exam) mündliche Prüfung.

orange ['ɒrɪndʒ] adj orange. ◆ n (fruit) Orange die, Apfelsine die ; (colour) Orange das.

orange juice n Orangensaft der.

orange squash n (Br) Orangensaftkonzentrat das.

orbit ['ɔːbɪt] n Umlaufbahn die.

orbital (motorway) ['ɔːbɪtl-] n (Br) Ringautobahn die.

orchard ['ɔːtʃəd] n Obstgarten der.

orchestra ['ɔːkɪstrə] n Orchester das.

ordeal [ɔː'diːl] n Tortur die.

order ['ɔːdə] n (sequence) Reihenfolge die ; (command) Befehl der ; (in restaurant) Bestellung die ; (neatness, discipline) Ordnung die ; (COMM) Auftrag der, Bestellung die. ◆ vt (command) befehlen (+D) ; (food, taxi, product) bestellen. ◆ vi (in restaurant) bestellen ; **in ~ to do sthg** um etw zu tun ; **out of ~** außer Betrieb ; **in working ~** in Betrieb ; **to ~ sb to do sthg** jm befehlen, etw zu tun.

order form n Bestellschein
der.

ordinary ['ɔːdənrɪ] adj gewöhnlich.

ore [ɔːʳ] n Erz das.

oregano [ˌɒrɪ'gɑːnəʊ] n Oregano der.

organ ['ɔːgən] n (MUS) Orgel
die ; (in body) Organ das.

organic [ɔː'gænɪk] adj biody-
namisch angebaut.

organization [ˌɔːgənaɪ'zeɪʃn]
n Organisation die.

organize ['ɔːgənaɪz] vt organisieren.

organizer ['ɔːgənaɪzəʳ] n Organisator der (-in die) ; (diary)
Zeitplanbuch das.

oriental [ˌɔːrɪ'entl] adj orien-
talisch.

orientate ['ɔːrɪenteɪt] vt : to ~
o.s. sich orientieren.

origin ['ɒrɪdʒɪn] n Ursprung
der.

original [ə'rɪdʒənl] adj (first)
ursprünglich ; (novel) originell.

originally [ə'rɪdʒənəlɪ] adv
ursprünglich.

originate [ə'rɪdʒəneɪt] vi : to ~
(from) stammen (aus (+D)).

ornament ['ɔːnəmənt] n (object) Schmuckgegenstand der.

ornamental [ˌɔːnə'mentl] adj
Zier-.

ornate [ɔː'neɪt] adj reich ver-
ziert.

orphan ['ɔːfn] n Waise die.

orthodox ['ɔːθədɒks] adj orthodox.

ostentatious [ˌɒstən'teɪʃəs]
adj pompös.

ostrich ['ɒstrɪtʃ] n Strauß der.

other ['ʌðəʳ] adj & pron an-
dere(-r) (-s). ◆ adv : ~ than

außer ; the ~ (one) der/die/das
andere ; the ~ day neulich ; one
after the ~ hintereinander.

otherwise ['ʌðəwaɪz] adv
sonst ; (differently) anders.

otter ['ɒtəʳ] n Otter der.

ought [ɔːt] aux vb : I ~ to go
now ich sollte jetzt gehen ; you
~ not to have said that du hättest
das nicht sagen sollen ; you ~ to
see a doctor du solltest zum
Arzt gehen ; the car ~ to be
ready by Friday das Auto sollte
Freitag fertig sein.

ounce [aʊns] n (unit of measurement) = 28,35 g, Unze die.

our ['aʊəʳ] adj unser.

ours ['aʊəz] pron unsere(-r)
(-s) ; this suitcase is ~ der Koffer
gehört uns ; a friend of ~ ein
Freund von uns.

ourselves [aʊə'selvz] pron
(reflexive, after prep) uns ; we
did it ~ wir haben es selbst gemacht.

out [aʊt] adj (light, cigarette)
aus.
◆ adv 1. (outside) draußen ; to
come ~ (of) heraus|kommen
(aus) ; to get ~ (of) aus|steigen
(aus) ; to go ~ (of) hinaus|gehen
(aus) ; it's cold ~ today es ist kalt
draußen heute.
2. (not at home, work) : she's ~
sie ist nicht da ; to go ~ aus|ge-
hen.
3. (so as to be extinguished) aus ;
put your cigarette ~! mach deine
Zigarette aus!
4. (expressing removal) : to take
sthg ~ (of) etw heraus|nehmen
(aus) ; (money) etw ab|heben
(von).

5. *(outwards)* : **to stick ~** herausstehen.

6. *(expressing distribution)* : **to hand sthg ~** etw austeilen.

7. *(wrong)* : **the bill's £10 ~** die Rechnung stimmt um 10 Pfund nicht.

8. *(in phrases)* : **stay ~ of the sun** bleib aus der Sonne ; **made ~ of wood** aus Holz (gemacht) ; **five ~ of ten women** fünf von zehn Frauen ; **I'm ~ of cigarettes** ich habe keine Zigaretten mehr.

outback ['aʊtbæk] *n* : **the ~** das Hinterland *(in Australien)*.

outboard (motor) ['aʊtbɔːd-] *n* Außenbordmotor *der*.

outbreak ['aʊtbreɪk] *n* Ausbruch *der*.

outburst ['aʊtbɜːst] *n* Ausbruch *der*.

outcome ['aʊtkʌm] *n* Ergebnis *das*.

outcrop ['aʊtkrɒp] *n* Felsvorsprung *der*.

outdated [,aʊt'deɪtɪd] *adj* veraltet.

outdo [,aʊt'duː] *vt* übertreffen.

outdoor ['aʊtdɔːr] *adj (swimming pool)* Frei- ; *(activities)* im Freien.

outdoors [aʊt'dɔːz] *adv* draußen ; **to go ~** nach draußen gehen.

outer ['aʊtər] *adj* äußere(-r) (-s).

outer space *n* Weltraum *der*.

outfit ['aʊtfɪt] *n (clothes)* Kleider *pl*.

outing ['aʊtɪŋ] *n* Ausflug *der*.

outlet ['aʊtlet] *n (pipe)* Abfluss *der* ; **'no ~'** *(Am)* 'Sackgasse'.

outline ['aʊtlaɪn] *n (shape)* Umriss *der* ; *(description)* kurze Beschreibung.

outlook ['aʊtlʊk] *n (for future, of weather)* Aussichten *pl* ; *(attitude)* Einstellung *die*.

out-of-date *adj (old-fashioned)* veraltet ; *(passport, licence)* abgelaufen.

outpatients' (department) ['aʊt,peɪʃnts-] *n* Poliklinik *die*.

output ['aʊtpʊt] *n* Output *der*.

outrage ['aʊtreɪdʒ] *n (cruel act)* Greueltat *die*.

outrageous [aʊt'reɪdʒəs] *adj* empörend.

outright [,aʊt'raɪt] *adv (tell, deny)* unumwunden ; *(own)* ganz.

outside [*adv* ,aʊt'saɪd, *adj*, *prep* & *n* 'aʊtsaɪd] *adv* draußen. ◆ *prep* außerhalb (+G) ; *(in front of)* vor (+A,D). ◆ *adj (exterior)* Außen- ; *(help, advice)* von außen. ◆ *n* : **the ~** of *(building, car, container)* die Außenseite ; *(AUT : in UK)* rechts ; *(AUT : in Europe, US)* links ; **an ~ line** eine Außenlinie ; **to go ~** nach draußen gehen ; **~ the door** vor der Tür ; **~ of** *(Am) (on the outside of)* außerhalb (+G) ; *(apart from)* außer (+D).

outside lane *n (AUT) (in UK)* rechter Fahrstreifen ; *(in Europe, US)* linker Fahrstreifen.

outsize ['aʊtsaɪz] *adj* übergroß.

outskirts ['aʊtskɜːts] *npl* Außenbezirke *pl*.

outstanding [,aʊt'stændɪŋ] *adj (remarkable)* hervorragend ; *(problem)* ungeklärt ; *(debt)* ausstehend.

outward ['aʊtwəd] *adj (external)* Außen- ; **~ journey** Hinreise *die*.

outwards ['aʊtwədz] *adv* nach außen.

oval ['əʊvl] *adj* oval.

ovation [əʊ'veɪʃn] *n* Applaus *der*.

oven ['ʌvn] *n* Ofen *der*.

oven glove *n* Topflappen *der*.

ovenproof ['ʌvnpruːf] *adj* feuerfest.

oven-ready *adj* bratfertig.

over ['əʊvə] *prep* **1.** *(above)* über (+D) ; **a bridge ~ the road** eine Brücke über der Straße.

2. *(across)* über (+A) ; **to walk ~ sthg** über etw laufen ; **it's just ~ the road** es ist gerade gegenüber ; **with a view ~ the gardens** mit Aussicht auf die Gärten.

3. *(covering)* über (+D,A) ; **put a plaster ~ the wound** klebe ein Pflaster auf die Wunde.

4. *(more than)* über (+A) ; **it cost ~ £1,000,** es hat über 1.000 Pfund gekostet.

5. *(during)* : **~ New Year** über Neujahr ; **~ the weekend** übers Wochenende ; **~ the past two years** in den letzten zwei Jahren.

6. *(with regard to)* über (+A) ; **an argument ~ the price** ein Streit über den Preis.

◆ *adv* **1.** *(downwards)* : **to fall ~** umIfallen ; **to lean ~** sich vornüber lehnen.

2. *(referring to position, movement)* herüber/hinüber ; **to drive ~** herüberIfahren ; **~ here** hier drüben ; **~ there** da drüben.

3. *(round to other side)* : **to turn sthg ~** etw umIdrehen.

4. *(more)* : **children aged 12 and ~** Kinder ab 12.

5. *(remaining)* übrig ; **to be (left) ~** übrig bleiben.

6. *(to one's house)* : **to invite sb ~ for dinner** jn zu sich zum Essen einIladen.

7. *(in phrases)* : **all ~** *(finished)* zu Ende ; **all ~ the world** in der ganzen Welt.

◆ *adj (finished)* : **to be ~** fertig sein, zu Ende sein.

overall [*adv* ,əʊvə'rɔːl, *n* 'əʊvərɔːl] *adv (in general)* im Allgemeinen. ◆ *n (Br : coat)* Kittel *der* ; *(Am : boiler suit)* Overall *der* ; **how much does it cost ~?** wie viel kostet das insgesamt? ■ **overalls** *npl (Br : boiler suit)* Overall *der* ; *(Am : dungarees)* Latzhose *die*.

overboard ['əʊvəbɔːd] *adv* über Bord.

overbooked [,əʊvə'bʊkt] *adj* überbucht.

overcame [,əʊvə'keɪm] *pt* → **overcome**.

overcast [,əʊvə'kɑːst] *adj* bedeckt.

overcharge [,əʊvə'tʃɑːdʒ] *vt* : **to ~ sb** jm zu viel berechnen.

overcoat ['əʊvəkəʊt] *n* Wintermantel *der*.

overcome [ˌəʊvəˈkʌm] (*pt* -**came**, *pp* -**come**) *vt* überwältigen.

overcooked [ˌəʊvəˈkʊkt] *adj* verkocht.

overcrowded [ˌəʊvəˈkraʊdɪd] *adj* überfüllt.

overdo [ˌəʊvəˈduː] (*pt* -**did**, *pp* -**done**) *vt* (*exaggerate*) übertreiben ; **to** ~ **it** übertreiben ; (*work too hard*) sich übernehmen.

overdone [ˌəʊvəˈdʌn] *pp* → **overdo.** ◆ *adj* (*food*) verkocht.

overdose [ˈəʊvədəʊs] *n* Überdosis *die*.

overdraft [ˈəʊvədrɑːft] *n* Kontoüberziehung *die* ; **to have an** ~ sein Konto überzogen haben.

overdue [ˌəʊvəˈdjuː] *adj* überfällig.

over easy *adj* (*Am : eggs*) auf beiden Seiten gebraten.

overexposed [ˌəʊvərɪkˈspəʊzd] *adj* (*photograph*) überbelichtet.

overflow [*vb* ˌəʊvəˈfləʊ, *n* ˈəʊvəfləʊ] *vi* (*container, bath*) überlaufen ; (*river*) überschwemmen. ◆ *n* (*pipe*) Überlaufrohr *das*.

overgrown [ˌəʊvəˈɡrəʊn] *adj* überwachsen.

overhaul [ˌəʊvəˈhɔːl] *n* Überholung *die*.

overhead [*adj* ˈəʊvəhed, *adv* ˌəʊvəˈhed] *adj* Ober- ; (*in ceiling*) Decken-. ◆ *adv* oben.

overhead locker *n* (*on plane*) Gepäckfach *das*.

overhear [ˌəʊvəˈhɪə] (*pt & pp* -**heard**) *vt* zufällig (mit)hören.

overheat [ˌəʊvəˈhiːt] *vi* sich überhitzen.

overland [ˈəʊvəlænd] *adv* auf dem Landweg.

overlap [ˌəʊvəˈlæp] *vi* sich überlappen.

overleaf [ˌəʊvəˈliːf] *adv* umseitig.

overload [ˌəʊvəˈləʊd] *vt* überladen.

overlook [*vb* ˌəʊvəˈlʊk, *n* ˈəʊvəlʊk] *vt* (*subj : building, room*) überblicken ; (*miss*) übersehen. ◆ *n* : (*scenic*) ~ (*Am*) Aussichtspunkt *der*.

overnight [*adv* ˌəʊvəˈnaɪt *adj* ˈəʊvənaɪt] *adv* über Nacht. ◆ *adj* (*train, journey*) Nacht-.

overnight bag *n* Reisetasche *die*.

overpass [ˈəʊvəpɑːs] *n* Überführung *die*.

overpowering [ˌəʊvəˈpaʊərɪŋ] *adj* überwältigend.

oversaw [ˌəʊvəˈsɔː] *pt* → **oversee.**

overseas [*adv* ˌəʊvəˈsiːz, *adj* ˈəʊvəsiːz] *adj* Übersee-. ◆ *adv* in Übersee ; **to go** ~ nach Übersee gehen.

oversee [ˌəʊvəˈsiː] (*pt* -**saw**, *pp* -**seen**) *vt* (*supervise*) beaufsichtigen.

overshoot [ˌəʊvəˈʃuːt] (*pt & pp* -**shot**) *vt* (*turning, motorway exit*) vorbeifahren an (+D).

oversight [ˈəʊvəsaɪt] *n* Versehen *das*.

oversleep [ˌəʊvəˈsliːp] (*pt & pp* -**slept**) *vi* verschlafen.

overtake [ˌəʊvəˈteɪk] (*pt* -**took**, *pp* -**taken**) *vt & vi* über-

holen ; 'no overtaking' 'Überholverbot'.

overtime ['əʊvətaɪm] *n* Über-
stunden *pl*.

overtook [,əʊvə'tʊk] *pt* →
overtake.

overture ['əʊvə,tjʊəʳ] *n* Ou-
vertüre *die*.

overturn [,əʊvə'tɜːn] *vi (boat)*
kentern ; *(car)* sich überschlagen.

overweight [,əʊvə'weɪt] *adj*
übergewichtig.

overwhelm [,əʊvə'welm] *vt*
überwältigen.

owe [əʊ] *vt* schulden ; to ~ sb
sthg jm etw schulden ; owing to
wegen (+G).

owl [aʊl] *n* Eule *die*.

own [əʊn] *adj & pron* eigen.
◆ *vt* besitzen ; I have my ~ bedroom ich habe ein eigenes
Zimmer ; on my ~ allein ; to get
one's ~ back sich revanchieren.
■ **own up** *vi* : to ~ up (to sthg)
(etw (A)) zugeben.

owner ['əʊnəʳ] *n* Eigentümer
der (-in *die*).

ownership ['əʊnəʃɪp] *n* Besitz
der.

ox [ɒks] *(pl* oxen ['ɒksən]) *n*
Ochse *der*.

oxtail soup ['ɒksteɪl-] *n* Ochsenschwanzsuppe *die*.

oxygen ['ɒksɪdʒən] *n* Sauerstoff *der*.

oyster ['ɔɪstəʳ] *n* Auster *die*.

oz *abbr* = ounce.

ozone-friendly ['əʊzəʊn-]
adj FCKW-frei, ohne Treibgas.

P

p *(abbr of page)* S. ◆ *abbr* =
penny, pence.

pace [peɪs] *n* Schritt *der*.

pacemaker ['peɪs,meɪkəʳ] *n*
(for heart) Schrittmacher *der*.

Pacific [pə'sɪfɪk] *n* : the ~
(Ocean) der Pazifik.

pacifier ['pæsɪfaɪəʳ] *n (Am : for
baby)* Schnuller *der*.

pacifist ['pæsɪfɪst] *n* Pazifist
der (-in *die*).

pack [pæk] *n (packet)* Packung
die ; *(of crisps)* Tüte *die* ; *(Br : of
cards)* Kartenspiel *das* ; *(rucksack)* Rucksack *der*. ◆ *vt (suitcase, bag)* packen ; *(clothes,
camera etc)* einpacken ; *(product)* verpacken. ◆ *vi (for journey)* packen ; a ~ of lies ein Haufen Lügen ; to ~ sthg into sthg
etw in etw (A) einpacken ; to ~
one's bags sein Bündel schnü-
ren. ■ **pack up** *vi (pack suitcase)* packen ; *(tidy up)* weglräumen ; *(Br : inf : machine, car)*
den Geist aufgeben.

package ['pækɪdʒ] *n (parcel)*
Päckchen *das* ; *(COMPUT)* Paket
das. ◆ *vt* verpacken.

package holiday *n* Pauschalreise *die*.

package tour *n* Pauschalreise *die*.

packaging ['pækɪdʒɪŋ] *n (material)* Verpackung *die*.

packed [pækt] *adj (crowded)*
voll.

packed lunch *n* Lunchpaket
das.

packet ['pækɪt] *n* Päckchen *das* ; **it cost a ~** *(Br : inf)* es hat ein Heidengeld gekostet.

packing ['pækɪŋ] *n* *(for journey)* Packen *das* ; *(material)* Verpackung *die*.

pad [pæd] *n* *(of paper)* Block *der* ; *(of cloth, cotton wool)* Bausch *der* ; *(for protection)* Polster *das*.

padded ['pædɪd] *adj* *(jacket, seat)* gepolstert.

padded envelope *n* gefütterter Briefumschlag.

paddle ['pædl] *n* *(pole)* Paddel *das*. ◆ *vi* paddeln.

paddling pool ['pædlɪŋ-] *n* Planschbecken *das*.

paddock ['pædək] *n* *(at racecourse)* Sattelplatz *der*.

padlock ['pædlɒk] *n* Vorhängeschloss *das*.

page [peɪdʒ] *n* Seite *die*. ◆ *vt* *(call)* ausrufen ; **'paging Mr Hill'** 'Herr Hill, bitte'.

paid [peɪd] *pt & pp* → **pay**. ◆ *adj* *(holiday, work)* bezahlt.

pain [peɪn] *n* Schmerz *der* ; **to be in ~** *(physical)* Schmerzen haben ; **he's such a ~!** *(inf)* er nervt! ▪ **pains** *npl* *(trouble)* Mühe *die*.

painful ['peɪnfʊl] *adj* schmerzhaft.

painkiller ['peɪn,kɪlə'] *n* Schmerzmittel *das*.

paint [peɪnt] *n* Farbe *die*. ◆ *vt* *(wall, room, furniture)* streichen ; *(picture)* malen. ◆ *vi* malen ; **to ~ one's nails** sich *(D)* die Nägel lackieren. ▪ **paints** *npl* *(tubes, pots etc)* Farbe *die*.

paintbrush ['peɪntbrʌʃ] *n* Pinsel *der*.

painter ['peɪntə'] *n* Maler *der* (-in *die*).

painting ['peɪntɪŋ] *n* *(picture)* Gemälde *das* ; *(activity)* Malerei *die* ; *(by decorator)* Malerarbeiten *die*.

pair [peə'] *n* Paar *das* ; **in ~s** paarweise ; **a ~ of pliers** eine Zange ; **a ~ of scissors** eine Schere ; **a ~ of shorts** Shorts *pl* ; **a ~ of tights** eine Strumpfhose ; **a ~ of trousers** eine Hose.

pajamas [pə'dʒɑːməz] *(Am)* = **pyjamas**.

Pakistan [(Br) ,pɑːkɪ'stɑːn, (Am) ,pækɪ'stæn] *n* Pakistan *nt*.

Pakistani [(Br) ,pɑːkɪ'stɑːnɪ, (Am) ,pækɪ'stænɪ] *adj* pakistanisch. ◆ *n* Pakistani *der, die*.

pakora [pə'kɔːrə] *npl* indische Vorspeise aus scharf gewürzten, frittierten Gemüsestückchen.

pal [pæl] *n* *(inf)* Kumpel *der*.

palace ['pælɪs] *n* Palast *der*.

palatable ['pælətəbl] *adj* schmackhaft.

palate ['pælət] *n* *(of mouth)* Gaumen *der* ; *(ability to taste)* Geschmack *der*.

pale [peɪl] *adj* blass.

pale ale *n* Pale Ale *das* *(helles englisches Dunkelbier)*.

palm [pɑːm] *n* *(of hand)* Handfläche *die* ; **~ (tree)** Palme *die*.

palpitations [,pælpɪ'teɪʃnz] *npl* Herzklopfen *pl*.

pamphlet ['pæmflɪt] *n* Broschüre *die*.

pan [pæn] *n* Pfanne *die* ; *(saucepan)* Topf *der*.

pancake ['pænkeɪk] *n* Eierkuchen *der*, Pfannkuchen *der*.

pancake roll *n* Frühlingsrolle *die*.

panda ['pændə] n Panda der.
panda car n (Br) Streifenwagen der.
pane [peɪn] n Scheibe die.
panel ['pænl] n (of wood) Tafel die ; (group of experts) Gremium das ; (on TV, radio) Diskussionsrunde die.
paneling ['pænəlɪŋ] (Am) = **panelling**.
panelling ['pænəlɪŋ] n (Br) Täfelung die.
panic ['pænɪk] (pt & pp **-ked**, cont **-king**) n Panik die. ◆ vi in Panik geraten.
panniers ['pænɪəz] npl (for bicycle) Satteltaschen pl.
panoramic [,pænə'ræmɪk] adj Panorama-.
pant [pænt] vi keuchen.
panties ['pæntɪz] npl (inf) Schlüpfer der.
pantomime ['pæntəmaɪm] n (Br : show) meist um die Weihnachtszeit aufgeführtes Märchenspiel.

PANTOMIME

Die „pantomimes" entsprechen im englischen Sprachraum lustigen Aufführungen für Kinder mit Musikbegleitung. Sie finden um die Weihnachtszeit statt, und es liegt ihnen meist eine Märchenhandlung zugrunde. Um dem Spiel zusätzlichen Witz zu verleihen, übernimmt eine junge Schauspielerin die Rolle des männlichen Helden, während ein junger Schauspieler die Rolle einer alten Frau, auch „dame" genannt, spielt.

pantry ['pæntrɪ] n Speisekammer die.
pants [pænts] npl (Br : for men) Unterhose die ; (Br : for women) Schlüpfer der ; (Am : trousers) Hose die.
panty hose ['pæntɪ-] npl (Am) Strumpfhose die.
papadum ['pæpədəm] n sehr dünnes, knuspriges indisches Brot.
paper ['peɪpə'] n Papier das ; (newspaper) Zeitung die ; (exam) Prüfung die. ◆ adj (cup, plate, hat) Papp-. ◆ vt tapezieren ; **a piece of** ~ (sheet) ein Blatt Papier ; (scrap) ein Papierfetzen. ▓ **papers** npl (documents) Papiere pl.
paperback ['peɪpəbæk] n Taschenbuch das.
paper bag n Papiertüte die.
paperboy ['peɪpəbɔɪ] n Zeitungsjunge der.
paper clip n Büroklammer die.
papergirl ['peɪpəgɜːl] n Zeitungsmädchen das.
paper handkerchief n Papiertaschentuch das.
paper shop n Zeitungshändler der.
paperweight ['peɪpəweɪt] n Briefbeschwerer der.
paprika ['pæprɪkə] n Paprika der.
par [pɑː'] n (in golf) Par das.
paracetamol [,pærə'siːtəmɒl] n Fieber senkende Schmerztablette.
parachute ['pærəʃuːt] n Fallschirm der.

parade [pə'reɪd] n *(procession)* Umzug der ; *(of shops)* Ladenzeile die.

paradise ['pærədaɪs] n Paradies das.

paraffin ['pærəfɪn] n Paraffinöl das.

paragraph ['pærəgrɑ:f] n Absatz der.

parallel ['pærəlel] adj : ~ (to) parallel (zu).

paralysed ['pærəlaɪzd] adj *(Br)* gelähmt.

paralyzed ['pærəlaɪzd] *(Am)* = **paralysed**.

paramedic [,pærə'medɪk] n Rettungssanitäter der (-in die).

paranoid ['pærənɔɪd] adj paranoid.

parasite ['pærəsaɪt] n Schmarotzer der.

parasol ['pærəsɒl] n Sonnenschirm der.

parcel ['pɑ:sl] n Paket das.

parcel post n Paketpost die.

pardon ['pɑ:dn] excl : ~? wie bitte? ; ~ (me)! Entschuldigung! ; I beg your ~! *(apologizing)* Entschuldigung! ; I beg your ~? *(asking for repetition)* bitte?

parent ['peərənt] n *(father)* Vater der ; *(mother)* Mutter die ; ~s Eltern pl.

parish ['pærɪʃ] n Gemeinde die.

park [pɑ:k] n Park der. ◆ vt & vi parken.

park and ride n Park-and-ride-System das.

parking ['pɑ:kɪŋ] n Parken das.

parking brake n *(Am)* Handbremse die.

parking lot n *(Am)* Parkplatz der.

parking meter n Parkuhr die.

parking space n Parkplatz der.

parking ticket n Strafzettel der.

parkway ['pɑ:kweɪ] n *(Am)* breite Straße, deren Mittelstreifen mit Bäumen, Blumen usw. bepflanzt ist.

parliament ['pɑ:ləmənt] n Parlament das.

Parmesan (cheese) [pɑ:mɪ-'zæn-] n Parmesan der.

parrot ['pærət] n Papagei der.

parsley ['pɑ:slɪ] n Petersilie die.

parsnip ['pɑ:snɪp] n Pastinake die.

parson ['pɑ:sn] n Pfarrer der.

part [pɑ:t] n Teil der ; *(in play, film)* Rolle die ; *(Am : in hair)* Scheitel der. ◆ adv *(partly)* teils. ◆ vi *(couple)* sich trennen ; in this ~ of Germany in dieser Gegend Deutschlands ; to form ~ of Teil sein von ; to play a ~ in eine Rolle spielen in (+D) ; to take ~ in teilnehmen an (+D) ; for my ~ was mich betrifft ; for the most ~ größtenteils ; in these ~s in dieser Gegend.

partial ['pɑ:ʃl] adj teilweise ; to be ~ to sthg eine Schwäche für etw haben.

participant [pɑ:'tɪsɪpənt] n Teilnehmer der (-in die).

participate [pɑ:'tɪsɪpeɪt] vi : to ~ (in) teilnehmen (an (+D)).

particular [pə'tɪkjʊlə] adj besondere(-r) (-s) ; *(fussy)* eigen ;

in ~ besonders ; **nothing in ~** nichts Besonderes. ▪ **particulars** npl (details) Einzelheiten pl.

particularly [pə'tıkjʊləlı] adv insbesondere ; (especially) besonders.

parting ['pɑːtıŋ] n (Br : in hair) Scheitel der.

partition [pɑː'tıʃn] n (wall) Trennwand die.

partly ['pɑːtlı] adv teilweise.

partner ['pɑːtnə'] n Partner der (-in die).

partnership ['pɑːtnəʃıp] n Partnerschaft die.

partridge ['pɑːtrıdʒ] n Rebhuhn das.

part-time adj Teilzeit-. ◆ adv halbtags.

party ['pɑːtı] n (for fun) Party die ; (POL) Partei die ; (group of people) Gruppe die ; **to have a ~** eine Party geben.

pass [pɑːs] vt (walk past) vorbeigehen an (+D) ; (drive past) vorbeifahren an (+D) ; (hand over) reichen ; (test, exam) bestehen ; (time, life) verbringen ; (overtake) überholen ; (law) verabschieden. ◆ vi (walk past) vorbeigehen ; (drive past) vorbeifahren ; (road, river, path, pipe) führen ; (overtake) überholen ; (in test, exam) bestehen ; (time, holiday) vergehen. ◆ n (document) Ausweis der ; (in mountain) Pass der ; (SPORT) Pass der ; **to ~ sb sthg** jm etw reichen. ▪ **pass by** vt fus (walk past) vorbeigehen an (+D) ; (drive past) vorbeifahren an (+D). ◆ vi (walk past) vorbeigehen ; (drive past) vorbeifah-

ren. ▪ **pass on** vt sep (message) weiterlgeben. ▪ **pass out** vi (faint) ohnmächtig werden. ▪ **pass up** vt sep (opportunity) vorübergehen lassen.

passable ['pɑːsəbl] adj (road) befahrbar ; (satisfactory) passabel.

passage ['pæsıdʒ] n (corridor) Gang der ; (in book) Passage die ; (sea journey) Überfahrt die.

passageway ['pæsıdʒweı] n Gang der.

passenger ['pæsındʒə'] n Passagier der (-in die).

passerby [,pɑːsə'baı] n Passant der (-in die).

passing place ['pɑːsıŋ-] n Ausweichstelle die.

passion ['pæʃn] n Leidenschaft die.

passionate ['pæʃənət] adj leidenschaftlich.

passive ['pæsıv] n Passiv das.

passport ['pɑːspɔːt] n Reisepass der.

passport control n Passkontrolle die.

passport photo n Passfoto das.

password ['pɑːswɜːd] n Passwort das.

past [pɑːst] adj (earlier) vergangene(-r) (-s) ; (finished) vorbei ; (last) letzte(-r) (-s) ; (former) ehemalig. ◆ prep (in times) nach ; (in front of) an (+D)... vorbei. ◆ adv vorbei. ◆ n (former time) Vergangenheit die ; ~ **(tense)** (GRAMM) Vergangenheit die ; **the ~ month** der letzte Monat ; **he drove ~ the house** er fuhr am Haus vorbei ; **twenty ~ four**

zwanzig nach vier ; **in the ~** früher.

pasta ['pæstə] n Nudeln pl.

paste [peɪst] n (spread) Paste die ; (glue) Kleister der.

pastel ['pæstl] n (for drawing) Pastellstift der ; (colour) Pastellfarbe die.

pasteurized ['pɑːstʃəraɪzd] adj pasteurisiert.

pastille ['pæstɪl] n Pastille die.

pastime ['pɑːstaɪm] n Hobby das.

pastry ['peɪstrɪ] n (for pie) Teig der ; (cake) Gebäck das.

pasture ['pɑːstʃə] n Weide die.

pasty ['pæstɪ] n (Br) Pastete die (Gebäck).

pat [pæt] vt klopfen.

patch [pætʃ] n (for clothes) Flicken der ; (of colour, damp) Fleck der ; (for skin) Pflaster das ; (for eye) Augenklappe die ; **a bad ~** (fig) eine Pechsträhne.

pâté ['pæteɪ] n Pastete die (Leberwurst usw.).

patent [(Br) 'peɪtənt, (Am) 'pætənt] n Patent das.

path [pɑːθ] n Weg der, Pfad der.

pathetic [pə'θetɪk] adj (pej : useless) kläglich.

patience ['peɪʃns] n Geduld die ; (Br : card game) Patience die.

patient ['peɪʃnt] adj geduldig. ◆ n Patient der (-in die).

patio ['pætɪəʊ] n Terrasse die.

patriotic [(Br) ,pætrɪ'ɒtɪk, (Am) ,peɪtrɪ'ɒtɪk] adj patriotisch.

patrol [pə'trəʊl] vt (subj : police) seine Runden machen in (+D) ; (MIL) patrouillieren. ◆ Patrouille die.

patrol car n Streifenwagen der.

patron ['peɪtrən] n (fml : customer) Kunde der (Kundin die) ; **'~s only'** 'nur für Gäste'.

patronizing ['pætrənaɪzɪŋ] adj herablassend.

pattern ['pætn] n (of shapes, colours) Muster das ; (for sewing) Schnitt der.

patterned ['pætənd] adj gemustert.

pause [pɔːz] n Pause die. ◆ vi innehalten.

pavement ['peɪvmənt] n (Br : beside road) Bürgersteig der ; (Am : roadway) Straßenbelag der.

pavilion [pə'vɪljən] n Klubhaus das.

paving stone ['peɪvɪŋ-] n Pflasterstein der.

pavlova n Nachtisch aus zwei Baiserstücken, die mit Sahne und Früchten gefüllt sind.

paw [pɔː] n Pfote die.

pawn [pɔːn] vt verpfänden. ◆ n (in chess) Bauer der.

pay [peɪ] (pt & pp paid) vt (money) zahlen ; (person, bill, fine) bezahlen. ◆ vi zahlen ; (be profitable) sich lohnen. ◆ n (salary) Gehalt das ; **to ~ sb for sthg** jn für etw bezahlen ; **to ~ money into an account** Geld auf ein Konto einlzahlen ; **to ~ attention (to** sthg) achten (auf (+A)) ; **to ~ sb a visit** jn besuchen ; **to ~ by credit card** mit Kreditkarte zahlen. ■ **pay back** vt sep (money) zurücklzahlen ; **to ~ sb back** jm Geld zurücklzahlen. ■ **pay**

for vt fus (purchase) bezahlen. ■ **pay in** vt sep (cheque, money) einlzahlen. ■ **pay out** vt sep (money) auslgeben. ■ **pay up** vi zahlen.

payable ['peɪəbl] adj zahlbar; to make a cheque ~ to sb einen Scheck auslstellen auf jn.

payment ['peɪmənt] n Bezahlung die; (amount) Zahlung die.

payphone ['peɪfəʊn] n Münzfernsprecher der.

PC n (abbr of personal computer) PC der. ◆ abbr (Br) = **police constable**.

PE abbr = **physical education**.

pea [piː] n Erbse die.

peace [piːs] n (no anxiety) Ruhe die; (no war) Frieden der; to leave sb in ~ jn in Ruhe lassen; ~ and quiet Ruhe und Frieden.

peaceful ['piːsfʊl] adj friedlich.

peach [piːtʃ] n Pfirsich der.

peach melba [-'melbə] n Pfirsich Melba das.

peacock ['piːkɒk] n Pfau der.

peak [piːk] n (of mountain) Gipfel der; (of hat) Schirm der; (fig: highest point) Höhepunkt der.

peak hours npl (for electricity) Hauptbelastungszeit die; (for traffic) Hauptverkehrszeit die.

peak rate n Höchsttarif der.

peanut ['piːnʌt] n Erdnuss die.

peanut butter n Erdnussbutter die.

pear [peə'] n Birne die.

pearl [pɜːl] n Perle die.

peasant ['peznt] n Bauer der (Bäuerin die).

pebble ['pebl] n Kieselstein der.

pecan pie ['piːkæn-] n Pekannusskuchen der.

peck [pek] vi picken.

peculiar [pɪ'kjuːljə'] adj (strange) seltsam; to be ~ to (exclusive) eigentümlich sein für; to be ~ to a country nur in einem Land vorlkommen.

peculiarity [pɪ,kjuːlɪ'ærətɪ] n (special feature) Besonderheit die.

pedal ['pedl] n Pedal das. ◆ vi in die Pedale treten.

pedal bin n Treteimer der.

pedalo ['pedələʊ] n Tretboot das.

pedestrian [pɪ'destrɪən] n Fußgänger der (-in die).

pedestrian crossing n Fußgängerüberweg der.

pedestrianized [pɪ'destrɪənaɪzd] adj zur Fußgängerzone gemacht.

pedestrian precinct n (Br) Fußgängerzone die.

pedestrian zone (Am) = **pedestrian precinct**.

pee [piː] vi (inf) pinkeln. ◆ n : to have a ~ (inf) pinkeln.

peel [piːl] n Schale die. ◆ vt (fruit, vegetables) schälen. ◆ vi (paint) ablblättern; (skin) sich schälen.

peep [piːp] n : to have a ~ gucken.

peer [pɪə'] vi angestrengt schauen.

peg [peg] n (for tent) Hering der; (hook) Haken der; (for washing) Klammer die.

pelican crossing ['pelɪkən-] n (Br) Ampelübergang der.

pelvis ['pelvɪs] n Becken das.

pen [pen] n (ballpoint pen) Kugelschreiber der ; (fountain pen) Füller der ; (for animals) Pferch der.

penalty ['penltɪ] n (fine) Geldstrafe die ; (in football) Elfmeter der.

pence [pens] npl Pence pl.
◆ Pence pl : it costs 20 ~ es kostet 20 Pence.

pencil ['pensl] n Bleistift der.

pencil case n Federmäppchen das.

pencil sharpener n Bleistiftspitzer der.

pendant ['pendənt] n (on necklace) Anhänger der.

pending ['pendɪŋ] prep (fml) bis zu.

penetrate ['penɪtreɪt] vt durchdringen.

penfriend ['penfrend] n Brieffreund der (-in die).

penguin ['peŋgwɪn] n Pinguin der.

penicillin [,penɪ'sɪlɪn] n Penizillin das.

peninsula [pə'nɪnsjʊlə] n Halbinsel die.

penis ['piːnɪs] n Penis der.

penknife ['pennaɪf] (pl -knives [-naɪvz]) n Taschenmesser das.

penny ['penɪ] (pl pennies) n (in UK) Penny der ; (in US) Cent der.

pension ['penʃn] n Rente die.

pensioner ['penʃənə'] n Rentner der (-in die).

penthouse ['penthaʊs, pl -haʊzɪz] n Penthouse das.

penultimate [pe'nʌltɪmət] adj vorletzte(-r) (-s).

people ['piːpl] npl Leute pl. ◆ n (nation) Volk das ; the ~ (citizens) die Bevölkerung ; lots of ~ viele Menschen ; German ~ die Deutschen pl.

pepper ['pepə'] n (spice) Pfeffer der ; (vegetable) Paprika der.

peppercorn ['pepəkɔːn] n Pfefferkorn das.

peppermint ['pepəmɪnt] adj Pfefferminz-. ◆ n (sweet) Pfefferminzbonbon der or das.

pepper pot n Pfefferstreuer der.

pepper steak n Pfeffersteak das.

Pepsi® ['pepsɪ] n Pepsi® die OR das.

per [pɜː'] prep pro ; ~ person pro Person ; ~ week pro Woche ; £20 ~ night 20 Pfund pro Nacht.

perceive [pə'siːv] vt wahrnehmen.

per cent adv Prozent.

percentage [pə'sentɪdʒ] n Prozentsatz der.

perch [pɜːtʃ] n (for bird) Stange die.

percolator ['pɜːkəleɪtə'] n Kaffeemaschine die.

perfect [adj & n 'pɜːfɪkt, vb pə'fekt] adj perfekt. ◆ vt perfektionieren. ◆ n : the ~ (tense) das Perfekt.

perfection [pə'fekʃn] n : to do sthg to ~ etw perfekt machen.

perfectly ['pɜːfɪktlɪ] adv perfekt.

perform [pə'fɔːm] vt (task, operation) ausführen ; (play, concert) aufführen. ◆ vi (actor) spielen ; (singer) singen.

performance [pə'fɔ:məns] *n (of play, concert, film)* Aufführung *die* ; *(by actor, musician)* Vorstellung *die* ; *(of car)* Leistung *die*.

performer [pə'fɔ:mə'] *n* Künstler *der* (-in *die*).

perfume ['pɜ:fju:m] *n* Parfüm *das*.

perhaps [pə'hæps] *adv* vielleicht.

perimeter [pə'rɪmɪtə'] *n* Grenze *die*.

period ['pɪərɪəd] *n (of time, history)* Periode *die*, Zeit *die* ; *(SCH)* Stunde *die* ; *(menstruation)* Periode *die* ; *(Am : full stop)* Punkt *der*. ◆ *adj (costume)* zeitgenössisch ; *(furniture)* antik.

periodic [,pɪərɪ'ɒdɪk] *adj* regelmäßig.

period pains *npl* Menstruationsbeschwerden *pl*.

periphery [pə'rɪfərɪ] *n* Rand *der*.

perishable ['perɪʃəbl] *adj (food)* leicht verderblich.

perk [pɜ:k] *n* Vergünstigung *die*.

perm [pɜ:m] *n* Dauerwelle *die*. ◆ *vt* : **to have one's hair ~ed** sich (D) eine Dauerwelle machen lassen.

permanent ['pɜ:mənənt] *adj (lasting)* bleibend ; *(present all the time)* ständig ; *(job)* fest.

permanent address *n* fester Wohnsitz *der*.

permanently ['pɜ:mənəntlɪ] *adv* ständig.

permissible [pə'mɪsəbl] *adj (fml)* zulässig.

permission [pə'mɪʃn] *n* Erlaubnis *die* ; *(official)* Genehmigung *die*.

permit [*vb* pə'mɪt, *n* 'pɜ:mɪt] *vt (allow)* erlauben. ◆ *n* Genehmigung *die* ; **to ~ sb to do sthg** jm erlauben, etw zu tun ; '**~ holders only**' 'nur für Anlieger'.

perpendicular [,pɜ:pən'dɪkjʊlə'] *adj* senkrecht.

persevere [,pɜ:sɪ'vɪə'] *vi* durchhalten.

persist [pə'sɪst] *vi (continue to exist)* fort|dauern ; **to ~ in doing sthg** etw weiterhin tun.

persistent [pə'sɪstənt] *adj* hartnäckig.

person ['pɜ:sn] *(pl* **people**) *n* Mensch *der* ; *(GRAMM)* Person *die* ; **in ~** persönlich.

personal ['pɜ:sənl] *adj* persönlich.

personal assistant *n (of manager)* Assistent *der* in.

personal belongings *npl* persönlicher Besitz *die*.

personal computer *n* Personalcomputer *der*.

personality [,pɜ:sə'nælətɪ] *n* Persönlichkeit *die*.

personally ['pɜ:snəlɪ] *adv* persönlich.

personal property *n* persönliches Eigentum *das*.

personal stereo *n* Walkman® *der*.

personnel [,pɜ:sə'nel] *npl* Personal *das*.

perspective [pə'spektɪv] *n* Perspektive *die*.

Perspex® ['pɜ:speks] *n (Br)* ≃ Plexiglas® *das*.

perspiration [,pɜ:spə'reɪʃn] *n* Schweiß *der*.

persuade [pə'sweɪd] *vt* : to ~ sb (to do sthg) jn überreden (, etw zu tun) ; to ~ sb that... jn davon überzeugen, dass...

persuasive [pə'sweɪsɪv] *adj* überzeugend.

pervert ['pɜːvɜːt] *n* Perverse *der, die*.

pessimist ['pesɪmɪst] *n* Pessimist *der* (-in *die*).

pessimistic [,pesɪ'mɪstɪk] *adj* pessimistisch.

pest [pest] *n* (insect, animal) Schädling *der* ; (inf : person) Nervensäge *die*.

pester ['pestə*] *vt* nerven.

pesticide ['pestɪsaɪd] *n* Schädlingsbekämpfungsmittel *das*.

pet [pet] *n* Haustier *das* ; the teacher's ~ der Liebling des Lehrers.

petal ['petl] *n* Blütenblatt *das*.

pet food *n* Tierfutter *das*.

petition [pɪ'tɪʃn] *n* (letter) Petition *die*.

petits pois [,pətɪ'pwa] *npl* feine Erbsen *pl*.

petrified ['petrɪfaɪd] *adj* (frightened) starr vor Schrecken.

petrol ['petrəl] *n* (Br) Benzin *das*.

petrol can *n* (Br) Benzinkanister *der*.

petrol cap *n* (Br) Tankverschluss *der*.

petrol gauge *n* (Br) Tankanzeige *die*.

petrol pump *n* (Br) Benzinpumpe *die*.

petrol station *n* (Br) Tankstelle *die*.

petrol tank *n* (Br) Benzintank *der*.

pet shop *n* Tierhandlung *die*.

petticoat ['petɪkəʊt] *n* Unterrock *der*.

petty ['petɪ] *adj* (pej : person, rule) kleinlich.

petty cash *n* Portokasse *die*.

pew [pjuː] *n* Bank *die*.

pewter ['pjuːtə*] *adj* Zinn-.

PG (abbr of parental guidance) ≃ bedingt jugendfrei.

pharmacist ['fɑːməsɪst] *n* Apotheker *der* (-in *die*).

pharmacy ['fɑːməsɪ] *n* (shop) Apotheke *die*.

phase [feɪz] *n* Phase *die*.

PhD *n* Dr.phil.

pheasant ['feznt] *n* Fasan *der*.

phenomena [fɪ'nɒmɪnə] *pl* → phenomenon.

phenomenal [fɪ'nɒmɪnl] *adj* phänomenal.

phenomenon [fɪ'nɒmɪnən] (*pl* -mena) *n* Phänomen *das*.

Philippines ['fɪlɪpiːnz] *npl* : the ~ die Philippinen *pl*.

philosophy [fɪ'lɒsəfɪ] *n* Philosophie *die*.

phlegm [flem] *n* Schleim *der*.

phone [fəʊn] *n* Telefon *das*. ◆ *vt* (Br) anlrufen. ◆ *vi* (Br) telefonieren ; to be on the ~ (talking) telefonieren ; (connected) das Telefon haben. ■ **phone up** *vt sep & vi* anlrufen.

phone book *n* Telefonbuch *das*.

phone booth *n* Telefonzelle *die*.

phone box *n* (Br) Telefonzelle *die*.

phone call *n* Telefonanruf *der*.

phonecard ['fəʊnkɑːd] n Telefonkarte die.

phone number n Telefonnummer die.

photo ['fəʊtəʊ] n Foto das ; **to take a ~ of** ein Foto machen von.

photo album n Fotoalbum das.

photocopier [,fəʊtəʊ'kɒpɪə] n Fotokopiergerät das.

photocopy ['fəʊtəʊ,kɒpɪ] n Fotokopie die. ◆ vt fotokopieren.

photograph ['fəʊtəgrɑːf] n Foto das. ◆ vt fotografieren.

photographer [fə'tɒgrəfə] n Fotograf der (-in die).

photography [fə'tɒgrəfɪ] n Fotografie die.

phrase [freɪz] n (expression) Ausdruck der.

phrasebook ['freɪzbʊk] n Sprachführer der.

physical ['fɪzɪkl] adj körperlich. ◆ n Vorsorgeuntersuchung die.

physical education n Sportunterricht der.

physically handicapped ['fɪzɪklɪ-] adj körperbehindert.

physics ['fɪzɪks] n Physik die.

physiotherapy [,fɪzɪəʊ'θerəpɪ] n Physiotherapie die.

pianist ['pɪənɪst] n Pianist der (-in die).

piano [pɪ'ænəʊ] (pl -s) n Klavier das.

pick [pɪk] vt (select) auslsuchen ; (fruit, flowers) pflücken. ◆ n (pickaxe) Spitzhacke die ; **to ~ a fight** einen Streit anlfangen ; **to ~ one's nose** in der Nase bohren ; **to take one's ~** auslsu-

chen. ■ **pick on** vt fus herumlhacken auf (+D). ■ **pick out** vt sep (select) auslsuchen ; (see) entdecken. ■ **pick up** vt sep (lift up) hochlnehmen ; (after dropping) auflheben ; (collect) ablholen ; (acquire) erwerben ; (skill, language) lernen ; (hitchhiker) mitlnehmen ; (inf: woman, man) ablschleppen. ◆ vi (improve) sich bessern.

pickaxe ['pɪkæks] n Spitzhacke die.

pickle ['pɪkl] n (Br : food) Mixed Pickles pl ; (Am : pickled cucumber) Essiggurke die.

pickled onion ['pɪkld-] n eingelegte Zwiebel.

pickpocket ['pɪk,pɒkɪt] n Taschendieb der (-in die).

pick-up (truck) n Pick-up der.

picnic ['pɪknɪk] n Picknick das.

picnic area n Picknickplatz der.

picture ['pɪktʃə] n Bild das ; (film) Film der. ■ **pictures** npl : **the ~s** (Br) das Kino.

picture frame n Bilderrahmen der.

picturesque [,pɪktʃə'resk] adj malerisch.

pie [paɪ] n (savoury) Pastete die ; (sweet) Kuchen der.

piece [piːs] n Stück das ; (component) Teil das ; (in chess) Figur die ; **a 20p ~** ein 20-Pence-Stück ; **a ~ of advice** ein Rat ; **a ~ of furniture** ein Möbelstück ; **to fall to ~s** zerbrechen ; **in one ~** (intact) unbeschädigt ; (unharmed) heil.

pier [pɪə] n Pier der or die.

pierce [pɪəs] *vt* durch|bohren ; **to have one's ears ~d** sich *(D)* Ohrlöcher stechen lassen.

pig [pɪg] *n* Schwein *das* ; *(inf : greedy person)* Vielfraß *der*.

pigeon ['pɪdʒɪn] *n* Taube *die*.

pigeonhole ['pɪdʒɪnhəʊl] *n* Fach *das*.

pigskin ['pɪgskɪn] *adj* Schweinsleder-.

pigtail ['pɪgteɪl] *n* Zopf *der*.

pike [paɪk] *n (fish)* Hecht *der*.

pilau rice ['pɪlaʊ-] *n* Pilaureis *der*, mit Gewürzen gekochter Reis, der dadurch eine bestimmte Farbe annimmt.

pilchard ['pɪltʃəd] *n* Sardine *die*.

pile [paɪl] *n (heap)* Haufen *der* ; *(neat stack)* Stapel *der*. ◆ *vt* sta-peln ; **~s of money** *(inf : a lot)* haufenweise Geld. ▪ **pile up** *vt sep* an|häufen ; *(neatly)* auf|stapeln. ◆ *vi (accumulate)* sich an|sammeln.

piles [paɪlz] *npl (MED)* Hämorrhoiden *pl*.

pileup ['paɪlʌp] *n* Massenkarambolage *die*.

pill [pɪl] *n* Tablette *die* ; **the ~** *(contraceptive)* die Pille.

pillar ['pɪlə'] *n* Säule *die*.

pillar box *n (Br)* Briefkasten *der*.

pillion ['pɪljən] *n* : **to ride ~** auf dem Soziussitz mit|fahren.

pillow ['pɪləʊ] *n* Kissen *das*.

pillowcase ['pɪləʊkeɪs] *n* Kopfkissenbezug *der*.

pilot ['paɪlət] *n* Pilot *der* (-in *die*) ; *(of ship)* Lotse *der*.

pilot light *n* Zündflamme *die*.

pimple ['pɪmpl] *n* Pickel *der*.

pin [pɪn] *n (for sewing)* Stecknadel *die* ; *(drawing pin)* Reißzwecke *die* ; *(safety pin)* Sicherheitsnadel *die* ; *(Am : brooch)* Brosche *die* ; *(Am : badge)* Anstecknadel *die*. ◆ *vt (fasten)* stecken ; **a two-~ plug** ein zweipoliger Stecker ; **I've got ~s and needles in my leg** mein Bein ist eingeschlafen.

pinafore ['pɪnəfɔː'] *n (apron)* Schürze *die* ; *(Br : dress)* Trägerkleid *das*.

pinball ['pɪnbɔːl] *n* Flippern *das*.

pincers ['pɪnsəz] *npl (tool)* Beißzange *die*.

pinch [pɪntʃ] *vt (squeeze)* kneifen ; *(Br : inf : steal)* klauen. ◆ *n (of salt)* Prise *die*.

pine [paɪn] *n* Kiefer *die*. ◆ *adj* Kiefern-.

pineapple ['paɪnæpl] *n* Ananas *die*.

pink [pɪŋk] *adj* rosa. ◆ *n* Rosa *das*.

pinkie ['pɪŋkɪ] *n (Am)* kleiner Finger.

PIN number ['pɪn-] *n* persönliche Geheimzahl.

pint [paɪnt] *n (in UK)* = 0,57 Liter, Pint *das* ; *(in US)* = 0,47 Liter, Pint *das* ; **a ~ (of beer)** *(Br)* ≃ ein (großes) Bier.

pip [pɪp] *n* Kern *der*.

pipe [paɪp] *n (for smoking)* Pfeife *die* ; *(for gas, water)* Rohr *das*.

pipe cleaner *n* Pfeifenreiniger *der*.

pipeline ['paɪplaɪn] *n* Pipeline *die*.

pipe tobacco *n* Pfeifentabak *der*.

pirate ['paɪrət] n Pirat der.

Pisces ['paɪsiːz] n Fische pl.

piss [pɪs] vi (vulg) pissen. ◆ n : to have a ~ (vulg) pissen gehen ; it's ~ing down (vulg) es schifft.

pissed [pɪst] adj (Br : vulg : drunk) besoffen ; (Am : vulg : angry) stocksauer.

pissed off adj (vulg) stocksauer.

pistachio [pɪˈstɑːʃɪəʊ] n Pistazie die. ◆ adj (flavour) Pistazien-.

pistol ['pɪstl] n Pistole die.

piston ['pɪstən] n Kolben der.

pit [pɪt] n (hole, coalmine) Grube die ; (for orchestra) Orchestergraben der ; (Am : in fruit) Stein der.

pitch [pɪtʃ] n (Br : SPORT) Spielfeld das. ◆ vt (throw) werfen ; to ~ a tent ein Zelt aufschlagen.

pitcher ['pɪtʃə] n Krug der.

pitfall ['pɪtfɔːl] n Falle die.

pith [pɪθ] n (of orange) weiße Haut.

pitta (bread) ['pɪtə-] n Pittabrot das.

pitted ['pɪtɪd] adj (olives) entsteint.

pity ['pɪtɪ] n (compassion) Mitleid das ; to have ~ on sb Mitleid mit jm haben ; it's a ~ (that)... schade, dass... ; what a ~! wie schade!

pivot ['pɪvət] n Zapfen der.

pizza ['piːtsə] n Pizza die.

pizzeria [ˌpiːtsəˈriːə] n Pizzeria die.

Pl. (abbr of Place) Platz (als Straßenname).

placard ['plækɑːd] n Plakat das.

place [pleɪs] n (location) Ort der ; (spot) Stelle die ; (house, flat) Haus das ; (seat, position, in race, list) Platz der. ◆ vt (put) setzen ; (put flat) legen ; (put upright) stellen ; (an order) aufgeben ; do you want to come round to my ~? möchtest du zu mir kommen? ; to lay six ~s (at table) für sechs decken ; in the first ~ (firstly) erstens ; to take ~ stattfinden ; to take sb's ~ (replace) js Platz einnehmen ; all over the ~ überall ; in ~ of statt (+G) ; to ~ a bet on Geld setzen auf (+A).

place mat n Platzdeckchen das.

placement ['pleɪsmənt] n (work experience) Praktikum das.

place of birth n Geburtsort der.

plague [pleɪg] n Pest die.

plaice [pleɪs] n Scholle die.

plain [pleɪn] adj (not decorated) schlicht ; (simple) einfach ; (yoghurt) Natur- ; (clear) klar ; (paper) unliniert ; (pej : not attractive) nicht sehr attraktiv. ◆ n Ebene die.

plain chocolate n Zartbitterschokolade die.

plainly ['pleɪnlɪ] adv deutlich.

plait [plæt] n Zopf der. ◆ vt flechten.

plan [plæn] n Plan der. ◆ vt planen ; have you any ~s for tonight? hast du heute Abend etwas vor? ; according to ~ planmäßig ; to ~ to do sthg, to ~ on doing sthg vorhaben, etw zu tun.

plenty

plane [pleɪn] n (aeroplane) Flugzeug das; (tool) Hobel der.

planet ['plænɪt] n Planet der.

plank [plæŋk] n Brett das.

plant [plɑːnt] n Pflanze die; (factory) Werk das. ◆ vt pflanzen; (land) bepflanzen; 'heavy ~ crossing' 'Baustellenverkehr'.

plantation [plæn'teɪʃn] n Plantage die.

plaque [plɑːk] n (plate) Gedenktafel die; (on teeth) Zahnstein der.

plaster ['plɑːstə'] n (Br : for cut) Pflaster das; (for walls) Putz der; in ~ (arm, leg) in Gips.

plaster cast n Gipsverband der.

plastic ['plæstɪk] n Plastik das. ◆ adj Plastik-, Kunststoff-.

plastic bag n Plastiktüte die.

Plasticine® ['plæstɪsiːn] n (Br) Plastilin das.

plate [pleɪt] n Teller der; (of metal, glass) Platte die.

plateau ['plætəʊ] n Hochebene die.

plate-glass adj Flachglas-.

platform ['plætfɔːm] n (at railway station) Bahnsteig der; (raised structure) Podium das; ~ 12 Gleis 12.

platinum ['plætɪnəm] n Platin das.

platter ['plætə'] n (of food) Platte die.

play [pleɪ] vt spielen; (opponent) spielen gegen. ◆ vi spielen. ◆ n (in theatre) Theaterstück das; (on TV) Fernsehspiel das; (button on CD, tape recorder) Playtaste die; to ~ the piano Klavier spielen. ■ **play**

back vt sep abspielen. ■ **play up** vi (machine, car) verrückt spielen.

player ['pleɪə'] n Spieler der (-in die).

playful ['pleɪfʊl] adj verspielt.

playground ['pleɪgraʊnd] n (in school) Schulhof der; (in park etc) Spielplatz der.

playgroup ['pleɪgruːp] n Krabbelgruppe die.

playing card ['pleɪɪŋ-] n Spielkarte die.

playing field ['pleɪɪŋ-] n Sportplatz der.

playroom ['pleɪrʊm] n Spielzimmer das.

playschool ['pleɪskuːl] = playgroup.

playtime ['pleɪtaɪm] n Pause die.

playwright ['pleɪraɪt] n Bühnenautor der (-in die).

plc (Br : abbr of public limited company) ≃ GmbH.

pleasant ['pleznt] adj angenehm.

please [pliːz] adv bitte. ◆ vt (give enjoyment to) gefallen (+D); yes ~! ja, bitte!; whatever you ~ (ganz) wie Sie wollen.

pleased [pliːzd] adj (happy) erfreut; (satisfied) zufrieden; to be ~ with sich freuen über (+A); ~ to meet you! angenehm!

pleasure ['pleʒə'] n Freude die; with ~ gerne; it's a ~! gern geschehen!

pleat [pliːt] n Falte die.

pleated ['pliːtɪd] adj Falten-.

plentiful ['plentɪfʊl] adj reichlich.

plenty ['plentɪ] pron : there are ~ es gibt viele; ~ of viele.

pliers ['plaɪəz] *npl* Zange *die*.

plimsoll ['plɪmsəl] *n (Br)* Turnschuh *der*.

plonk [plɒŋk] *n (Br : inf : wine)* billiger Wein.

plot [plɒt] *n (scheme)* Komplott *das* ; *(of story, film, play)* Handlung *die* ; *(of land)* Stück *das* Land.

plough [plaʊ] *n (Br)* Pflug *der*. ◆ *vt (Br)* pflügen.

ploughman's (lunch) ['plaʊmənz-] *n (Br)* beliebte Pubmahlzeit aus Brot, Käse, Salat und Mixed Pickles.

plow [plaʊ] *(Am)* = **plough**.

ploy [plɔɪ] *n* Taktik *die*.

pluck [plʌk] *vt (eyebrows)* zupfen ; *(chicken)* rupfen.

plug [plʌg] *n (electrical)* Stecker *der* ; *(socket)* Steckdose *die* ; *(for bath, sink)* Stöpsel *der*. ■ **plug in** *vt sep* an|schließen.

plughole ['plʌghəʊl] *n* Abfluss *der*.

plum [plʌm] *n* Pflaume *die*, Zwetschge *die*.

plumber ['plʌmər] *n* Installateur *der*.

plumbing ['plʌmɪŋ] *n (pipes)* Wasserleitungen *pl*.

plump [plʌmp] *adj* rundlich.

plunge [plʌndʒ] *vi* stürzen ; *(dive)* tauchen.

plunge pool *n* Swimmingpool *der*.

plunger ['plʌndʒər] *n (for unblocking pipe)* Sauger *der*.

pluperfect (tense) [,pluː-'pɜːfɪkt-] *n* : the ~ das Plusquamperfekt.

plural ['plʊərəl] *n* Plural *der* ; in the ~ im Plural.

plus [plʌs] *prep* plus ; *(and)* und. ◆ *adj* : 30 ~ über 30.

plush [plʌʃ] *adj* feudal.

plywood ['plaɪwʊd] *n* Sperrholz *das*.

p.m. *(abbr of post meridiem)* nachmittags.

PMT *n (abbr of premenstrual tension)* PMS *das*.

pneumatic drill [njuː'mætɪk-] *n* Pressluftbohrer *der*.

pneumonia [njuː'məʊnjə] *n* Lungenentzündung *die*.

poached egg [pəʊtʃt-] *n* pochiertes Ei, verlorenes Ei.

poached salmon [pəʊtʃt-] *n* Lachs *der* blau.

poacher ['pəʊtʃər] *n* Wilderer *der*.

PO Box *n (abbr of Post Office Box)* Postfach *das*.

pocket ['pɒkɪt] *n* Tasche *die* ; *(on car door)* Seitentasche *die*. ◆ *adj (camera)* Pocket- ; *(calculator)* Taschen-.

pocketbook ['pɒkɪtbʊk] *n (notebook)* Notizbuch *das* ; *(Am : handbag)* Handtasche *die*.

pocket money *n (Br)* Taschengeld *das*.

podiatrist [pə'daɪətrɪst] *n (Am)* Fußpfleger *der* in.

poem ['pəʊɪm] *n* Gedicht *das*.

poet ['pəʊɪt] *n* Dichter *der* (-in *die*).

poetry ['pəʊɪtrɪ] *n* Dichtung *die*.

point [pɔɪnt] *n* Punkt *der* ; *(tip)* Spitze *die* ; *(most important thing)* Sinn *der*, Zweck *der* ; *(Br : electric socket)* Steckdose *die*. ◆ *vi* : to ~ to *(with finger)* zeigen auf (+A) ; *(arrow, sign)* zeigen

polyester

nach ; **five ~ seven** fünf Komma sieben ; **strong ~** Stärke *die* ; **weak ~** Schwäche *die* ; **what's the ~?** wozu? ; **there's no ~** es hat keinen Sinn ; **to be on the ~ of doing sthg** im Begriff sein, etw zu tun ; **to come to the ~** zur Sache kommen. ◼ **points** *npl (Br : on railway)* Weichen *pl*. ◼ **point out** *vt sep* hinlweisen auf *(+A)*.

pointed ['pɔɪntɪd] *adj (in shape)* spitz.

pointless ['pɔɪntlɪs] *adj* sinnlos.

point of view *n* Standpunkt *der*.

poison ['pɔɪzn] *n* Gift *das*. ◆ *vt* vergiften.

poisoning ['pɔɪznɪŋ] *n* Vergiftung *die*.

poisonous ['pɔɪznəs] *adj* giftig, Gift-.

poke [pəʊk] *vt (with stick, elbow)* stoßen ; *(with finger)* stupsen.

poker ['pəʊkə'] *n (card game)* Poker *das*.

Poland ['pəʊlənd] *n* Polen *nt*.

polar bear ['pəʊlə-] *n* Eisbär *der*.

Polaroid® ['pəʊlərɔɪd] *n (photograph)* Polaroidbild *das* ; *(camera)* Polaroidkamera® *die*.

pole [pəʊl] *n (of wood)* Stange *die*.

Pole [pəʊl] *n (person)* Pole *der* (Polin *die*).

police [pə'liːs] *npl* : **the ~** die Polizei.

police car *n* Polizeiwagen *der*.

police force *n* Polizei *die*.

policeman [pə'liːsmən] *(pl -men* [-mən]*) n* Polizist *der*.

police officer *n* Polizeibeamte *der* (-beamtin *die*).

police station *n* Polizeiwache *die*.

policewoman [pə'liːs,wʊmən] *(pl -women* [-,wɪmɪn]*) n* Polizistin *die*.

policy ['pɒləsɪ] *n (approach)* Handlungsweise *die* ; *(for insurance)* Police *die* ; *(in politics)* Politik *die*.

policy-holder *n* Versicherte *der, die*.

polio ['pəʊlɪəʊ] *n* Kinderlähmung *die*.

polish ['pɒlɪʃ] *n (for cleaning)* Politur *die*. ◆ *vt* polieren.

Polish ['pəʊlɪʃ] *adj* polnisch. ◆ *n (language)* Polnisch *das*. ◆ *npl* : **the ~** die Polen *pl*.

polite [pə'laɪt] *adj* höflich.

political [pə'lɪtɪkl] *adj* politisch.

politician [,pɒlɪ'tɪʃn] *n* Politiker *der* (-in *die*).

politics ['pɒlətɪks] *n* Politik *die*.

poll [pəʊl] *n (survey)* Umfrage *die* ; **the ~s** *(election)* die Wahlen *pl*.

pollen ['pɒlən] *n* Pollen *der*.

Poll Tax *n (Br)* Kopfsteuer *die*.

pollute [pə'luːt] *vt* verschmutzen.

pollution [pə'luːʃn] *n* Verschmutzung *die* ; *(substances)* Schmutz *der*.

polo neck ['pəʊləʊ-] *n (Br)* Rollkragen *der*.

polyester [,pɒlɪ'estə'] *n* Polyester *der*.

polystyrene [ˌpɒlɪ'staɪri:n] n Styropor® das.

polytechnic [ˌpɒlɪ'teknɪk] n Hochschule in Großbritannien; seit 1993 haben die meisten Universitätsstatus.

polythene ['pɒlɪθi:n] n Polyäthylen das.

pomegranate ['pɒmɪˌgrænɪt] n Granatapfel der.

pompous ['pɒmpəs] adj wichtigtuerisch.

pond [pɒnd] n Teich der.

pontoon [pɒn'tu:n] n (Br : card game) Siebzehnundvier das.

pony ['pəʊnɪ] n Pony das.

ponytail ['pəʊnɪteɪl] n Pferdeschwanz der.

pony-trekking [-ˌtrekɪŋ] n (Br) Ponyreiten das.

poodle ['pu:dl] n Pudel der.

pool [pu:l] n (for swimming) Schwimmbecken das ; (of water, blood, milk) Lache die ; (small pond) Teich der ; (game) Poolbillard das. ◼ **pools** npl (Br) : the ~s ≃ das Toto.

poor [pɔ:ʳ] adj arm ; (bad) schlecht. ◆ npl : the ~ die Armen pl.

poorly ['pɔ:lɪ] adv schlecht. ◆ adj (Br : ill) : he's ~ es geht ihm schlecht.

pop [pɒp] n (music) Pop der. ◆ vt (inf : put) stecken. ◆ vi (balloon) knallen ; my ears popped ich habe Druck auf den Ohren. ◼ **pop in** vi (Br : visit) vorbeischauen.

popcorn ['pɒpkɔ:n] n Popcorn das.

Pope [pəʊp] n : the ~ der Papst.

pop group n Popgruppe die.

poplar (tree) ['pɒpləʳ-] n Pappel die.

pop music n Popmusik die.

popper ['pɒpəʳ] n (Br) Druckknopf der.

poppy ['pɒpɪ] n Klatschmohn der.

Popsicle® ['pɒpsɪkl] n (Am) Eis das am Stiel.

pop socks npl Kniestrümpfe pl.

pop star n Popstar der.

popular ['pɒpjʊləʳ] adj beliebt ; (opinion, ideas) weit verbreitet.

popularity [ˌpɒpjʊ'lærətɪ] n Beliebtheit die.

populated ['pɒpjʊleɪtɪd] adj bevölkert.

population [ˌpɒpjʊ'leɪʃn] n Bevölkerung die.

porcelain ['pɔ:səlɪn] n Porzellan das.

porch [pɔ:tʃ] n (entrance) Windfang der ; (Am : outside house) Veranda die.

pork [pɔ:k] n Schweinefleisch das.

pork chop n Schweinekotelett das.

pork pie n Schweinepastete die.

pornographic [ˌpɔ:nə'græfɪk] adj pornografisch.

porridge ['pɒrɪdʒ] n Haferbrei der.

port [pɔ:t] n (town) Hafenstadt die ; (harbour area) Hafen der ; (drink) Portwein der.

portable ['pɔ:təbl] adj tragbar.

porter ['pɔːtə^r] n *(at hotel, museum)* Portier der ; *(at station, airport)* Gepäckträger der.

porthole ['pɔːthəʊl] n Bullauge das.

portion ['pɔːʃn] n *(part)* Teil das ; *(of food)* Portion die.

portrait ['pɔːtreɪt] n Porträt das.

Portugal ['pɔːtʃʊgl] n Portugal nt.

Portuguese [,pɔːtʃʊ'gɪːz] adj portugiesisch. ◆ n *(language)* Portugiesisch das. ◆ npl : the ~ die Portugiesen pl.

pose [pəʊz] vt *(problem, threat)* dar|stellen. ◆ vi *(for photo)* sitzen.

posh [pɒʃ] adj *(inf)* piekfein.

position [pə'zɪʃn] n *(place, situation)* Lage die ; *(of plane, ship)* Position die ; *(of body)* Haltung die ; *(setting, rank)* Stellung die ; *(in race, contest)* Platz der ; *(fml : job)* Stelle die ; '~ closed' *(in bank, post office etc)* 'Schalter geschlossen'.

positive ['pɒzətɪv] adj positiv ; *(certain, sure)* sicher.

possess [pə'zes] vt besitzen.

possession [pə'zeʃn] n Besitz der.

possessive [pə'zesɪv] adj *(pej : person)* Besitz ergreifend ; *(GRAMM)* Possessiv-.

possibility [,pɒsə'bɪlətɪ] n Möglichkeit die.

possible ['pɒsəbl] adj möglich ; **it's ~ that we may be late** es kann sein, dass wir zu spät kommen ; **would it be ~ for me to...?** könnte ich vielleicht...? ; **as much as ~** so viel wie möglich ; **if ~** wenn möglich.

possibly ['pɒsəblɪ] adv *(perhaps)* möglicherweise.

post [pəʊst] n *(system, letters, delivery)* Post die ; *(pole)* Pfahl der ; *(fml : job)* Stelle die. ◆ vt *(letter, parcel)* ab|schicken ; **by ~** per Post.

postage ['pəʊstɪdʒ] n Porto das ; **~ and packing** Porto und Verpackung ; **~ paid** Porto zahlt Empfänger.

postage stamp n *(fml)* Briefmarke die.

postal order ['pəʊstl-] n Postanweisung die.

postbox ['pəʊstbɒks] n *(Br)* Briefkasten der.

postcard ['pəʊstkɑːd] n Postkarte die.

postcode ['pəʊstkəʊd] n *(Br)* Postleitzahl die.

poster ['pəʊstə^r] n *(for advertisement)* Plakat das ; *(decoration)* Poster das.

poste restante [,pəʊstres-'tɑːnt] n *(Br)* Schalter der für postlagernde Sendungen.

post-free adv portofrei.

postgraduate [,pəʊst'grædʒʊət] n Student, der auf einen höheren Studienabschluss hinarbeitet.

postman ['pəʊstmən] *(pl* -men [-mən]*)* n Briefträger der.

postmark ['pəʊstmɑːk] n Poststempel der.

post office n *(building)* Post die ; **the Post Office** die Post.

postpone [,pəʊst'pəʊn] vt verschieben.

posture ['pɒstʃə^r] n Haltung die.

postwoman ['pəʊst,wʊmən] (*pl* -**women** [-,wɪmɪn]) *n* Briefträgerin *die*.

pot [pɒt] *n* (*for cooking*) Topf *der*; (*for jam*) Glas *das*; (*for paint*) Dose *die*; (*for coffee, tea*) Kanne *die*; (*inf*: *cannabis*) Hasch *das*; **a ~ of tea** ein Kännchen Tee.

potato [pə'teɪtəʊ] (*pl* -**es**) *n* Kartoffel *die*.

potato salad *n* Kartoffelsalat *der*.

potential [pə'tenʃl] *adj* potenziell. ◆ *n* Potenzial *das*.

pothole ['pɒthəʊl] *n* (*in road*) Schlagloch *das*.

pot plant *n* Topfpflanze *die*.

pot scrubber [-'skrʌbə'] *n* Topfreiniger *der*.

potted ['pɒtɪd] *adj* (*meat, fish*) Dosen-; (*plant*) Topf-.

pottery ['pɒtərɪ] *n* (*clay objects*) Töpferwaren *pl*; (*craft*) Töpferei *die*.

potty ['pɒtɪ] *n* Töpfchen *das*.

pouch [paʊtʃ] *n* (*for money*) Beutel *der*.

poultry ['pəʊltrɪ] *n* OR *npl* Geflügel *das*.

pound [paʊnd] *n* (*unit of money*) ≃ Pfund *das*; (*unit of weight*) = 0,45 Kg. ◆ *vi* (*heart*) pochen; (*head*) dröhnen.

pour [pɔː'] *vt* gießen; (*sugar, sand*) schütten; (*drink*) einlgießen. ◆ *vi* (*flow*) fließen; **it's ~ing** (*with rain*) es gießt. ▪ **pour out** *vt sep* (*drink*) einlgießen.

poverty ['pɒvətɪ] *n* Armut *die*.

powder ['paʊdə'] *n* Pulver *das*.

power ['paʊə'] *n* Macht *die*; (*strength, force*) Kraft *die*; (*en-*

ergy) Energie *die*; (*electricity*) Strom *der*. ◆ *vt* anltreiben; **to be in ~** an der Macht sein.

power cut *n* Stromsperre *die*.

power failure *n* Stromausfall *der*.

powerful ['paʊəfʊl] *adj* stark; (*leader*) mächtig; (*voice*) kräftig.

power point *n* (*Br*) Steckdose *die*.

power station *n* Kraftwerk *das*.

power steering *n* Servolenkung *die*.

practical ['præktɪkl] *adj* praktisch.

practically ['præktɪklɪ] *adv* praktisch.

practice ['præktɪs] *n* (*training*) Übung *die*; (*training session*) Training *das*; (*of doctor, lawyer*) Praxis *die*; (*regular activity*) Gewohnheit *die*; (*custom*) Brauch *der*. ◆ *vt* (*Am*) = **practise**; **out of ~** außer Übung.

practise ['præktɪs] *n* (*Br*) = **practice** (*Am*). ◆ *vt* & *vi* üben; **to ~ as a doctor** als Arzt tätig sein.

praise [preɪz] *n* Lob *das*. ◆ *vt* loben.

pram [præm] *n* (*Br*) Kinderwagen *der*.

prank [præŋk] *n* Streich *der*.

prawn [prɔːn] *n* Garnele *die*.

prawn cocktail *n* Krabbencocktail *der*.

prawn cracker *n* chinesischer Chip mit Krabbengeschmack.

pray [preɪ] *vi* beten; **to ~ for sthg** um etw beten.

prayer [preə'] *n* Gebet *das*.

precarious [prɪˈkeərɪəs] *adj* unsicher.

precaution [prɪˈkɔːʃn] *n* Vorsichtsmaßnahme *die*.

precede [prɪˈsiːd] *vt* (*fml*) voranlgehen (+D).

preceding [prɪˈsiːdɪŋ] *adj* vorhergehend.

precinct [ˈpriːsɪŋkt] *n* (*Br* : *for shopping*) Einkaufsviertel *das* ; (*Am* : *area of town*) Bezirk *der*.

precious [ˈpreʃəs] *adj* kostbar ; (*metal, jewel*) Edel-.

precious stone *n* Edelstein *der*.

precipice [ˈpresɪpɪs] *n* Abgrund *der*.

precise [prɪˈsaɪs] *adj* genau.

precisely [prɪˈsaɪslɪ] *adv* genau.

predecessor [ˈpriːdɪsesəʳ] *n* Vorgänger *der* (-in *die*).

predicament [prɪˈdɪkəmənt] *n* Dilemma *das*.

predict [prɪˈdɪkt] *vt* vorherlsagen.

predictable [prɪˈdɪktəbl] *adj* (*foreseeable*) vorhersehbar ; (*pej* : *unoriginal*) berechenbar.

prediction [prɪˈdɪkʃn] *n* Voraussage *die*.

preface [ˈprefɪs] *n* Vorwort *das*.

prefect [ˈpriːfekt] *n* (*Br* : *at school*) älterer Schüler in britischen Schulen, der den Lehrern bei der Aufsicht hilft.

prefer [prɪˈfɜːʳ] *vt* vorlziehen ; **to ~ to do sthg** etw lieber tun.

preferable [ˈprefrəbl] *adj* : **to be ~ (to)** vorzuziehen sein (+D).

preferably [ˈprefrəblɪ] *adv* vorzugsweise.

preference [ˈprefərəns] *n* Vorzug *der* ; **to have a ~ for sthg** etw bevorzugen.

prefix [ˈpriːfɪks] *n* Vorsilbe *die*.

pregnancy [ˈpregnənsɪ] *n* Schwangerschaft *die*.

pregnant [ˈpregnənt] *adj* schwanger.

prejudice [ˈpredʒʊdɪs] *n* Voreingenommenheit *die* ; **to have a ~ against sb/sthg** ein Vorurteil gegen jn/etw haben.

prejudiced [ˈpredʒʊdɪst] *adj* voreingenommen.

preliminary [prɪˈlɪmɪnərɪ] *adj* Vor-.

premature [ˈpreməˌtjʊəʳ] *adj* vorzeitig ; **a ~ baby** eine Frühgeburt.

premier [ˈpremjəʳ] *adj* bedeutendste(-r) (-s). ◆ *n* Premier *der*.

premiere [ˈpremɪeəʳ] *n* Premiere *die*.

premises [ˈpremɪsɪz] *npl* (*grounds*) Gelände *das* ; (*shop, restaurant*) Räumlichkeiten *pl*.

premium [ˈpriːmjəm] *n* (*for insurance*) Prämie *die*.

premium-quality *adj* (*meat*) Qualitäts-.

preoccupied [priːˈɒkjʊpaɪd] *adj* beschäftigt.

prepacked [ˌpriːˈpækt] *adj* abgepackt.

prepaid [ˈpriːpeɪd] *adj* (*envelope*) frankiert.

preparation [ˌprepəˈreɪʃn] *n* Vorbereitung *die*.

preparatory school [prɪˈpærətrɪ-] *n* (*in UK*) private Grundschule ; (*in US*) private Oberschule.

prepare [prɪ'peəʳ] vt vorbereiten ; *(food)* kochen. ◆ vi sich vorbereiten.

prepared [prɪ'peəd] adj vorbereitet ; **to be ~ to do sthg** bereit sein, etw zu tun.

preposition [ˌprepə'zɪʃn] n Präposition die.

prep school [prep-] = **preparatory school.**

prescribe [prɪ'skraɪb] vt *(medicine, treatment)* verschreiben.

prescription [prɪ'skrɪpʃn] n *(paper)* Rezept das ; *(medicine)* Medikament das.

presence ['prezns] n *(being present)* Anwesenheit die ; **in his ~** in seiner Gegenwart.

present [adj & n 'preznt, vb prɪ'zent] adj *(in attendance)* anwesend ; *(current)* gegenwärtig. ◆ vt *(hand over)* überreichen ; *(represent)* darstellen ; *(TV, radio programme)* moderieren ; *(play)* aufführen. ◆ n *(gift)* Geschenk das ; *(current time)* : **the ~** die Gegenwart ; **the ~ (tense)** *(GRAMM)* das Präsens ; **at ~** zur Zeit ; **to ~ sb with sthg** jm etw überreichen ; **to ~ sb to sb** jn einer Person vorstellen.

presentable [prɪ'zentəbl] adj präsentabel.

presentation [ˌprezn'teɪʃn] n *(way of presenting)* Präsentation die ; *(ceremony)* Verleihung die.

presenter [prɪ'zentəʳ] n *(of TV, radio programme)* Moderator der (-in die).

presently ['prezəntlɪ] adv *(soon)* bald ; *(now)* zur Zeit.

preservation [ˌprezə'veɪʃn] n Erhaltung die.

preservative [prɪ'zɜ:vətɪv] n Konservierungsstoff der.

preserve [prɪ'zɜ:v] n *(jam)* Konfitüre die. ◆ vt erhalten ; *(food)* konservieren.

president ['prezɪdənt] n Präsident der (-in die) ; *(of company)* Vorsitzende der, die.

press [pres] vt drücken ; *(button)* drücken auf (+A) ; *(iron)* plätten. ◆ n : **the ~** *(media)* die Presse ; **to ~ sb to do sthg** jn drängen, etw zu tun.

press conference n Pressekonferenz die.

press-stud n Druckknopf der.

press-up n Liegestütz der.

pressure ['preʃəʳ] n Druck der.

pressure cooker n Schnellkochtopf der.

prestigious [pre'stɪdʒəs] adj renommiert.

presumably [prɪ'zju:məblɪ] adv vermutlich.

presume [prɪ'zju:m] vt annehmen.

pretend [prɪ'tend] vt : **to ~ to do sthg** vorgeben, etw zu tun.

pretentious [prɪ'tenʃəs] adj hochgestochen.

pretty ['prɪtɪ] adj hübsch. ◆ adv *(inf : quite)* ziemlich.

prevent [prɪ'vent] vt verhindern ; **to ~ sb from doing sthg** jn daran hindern, etw zu tun.

prevention [prɪ'venʃn] n Vorbeugung die.

preview ['pri:vju:] n Vorschau die.

previous ['pri:vjəs] adj *(earlier)* früher ; *(preceding)* vorig.

previously ['pri:vjəslɪ] adv vorher.

price [praɪs] n Preis der. ◆ vt auslzeichnen.

priceless ['praɪslɪs] adj unbezahlbar.

price list n Preisliste die.

pricey ['praɪsɪ] adj (inf) teuer.

prick [prɪk] vt stechen.

prickly ['prɪklɪ] adj stachelig.

prickly heat n Hitzepickel pl.

pride [praɪd] n Stolz der. ◆ vt : to ~ o.s. on sthg stolz sein auf etw (A).

priest [priːst] n Priester der.

primarily ['praɪmərɪlɪ] adv hauptsächlich.

primary school ['praɪmərɪ-] n Grundschule die.

prime [praɪm] adj (chief) Haupt-; (quality, beef, cut) erstklassig.

prime minister n Premierminister der (-in die).

primitive ['prɪmɪtɪv] adj primitiv.

primrose ['prɪmrəʊz] n Himmelschlüssel der.

prince [prɪns] n Prinz der.

Prince of Wales n Prinz der von Wales.

princess [prɪn'ses] n Prinzessin die.

principal ['prɪnsəpl] adj Haupt-. ◆ n (of school, university) Rektor der (-in die).

principle ['prɪnsəpl] n Prinzip das; in ~ im Prinzip.

print [prɪnt] n Druck der; (photo) Abzug der; (mark) Abdruck der. ◆ vt drucken; (write) in Druckschrift schreiben; (photo) ablziehen; out of ~ vergriffen. ▪ **print out** vt sep ausldrucken.

printed matter ['prɪntɪd-] n Drucksache die.

printer ['prɪntə'] n Drucker der.

printout ['prɪntaʊt] n Ausdruck der.

prior ['praɪə'] adj (previous) frühere(-r) (-s); ~ to sthg (fml) vor etw ((D)).

priority [praɪ'ɒrətɪ] n Priorität die; to have ~ over Vorrang haben vor (+D).

prison ['prɪzn] n Gefängnis das.

prisoner ['prɪznə'] n Häftling der.

prisoner of war n Kriegsgefangene der, die.

prison officer n Gefängniswärter der (-in die).

privacy ['prɪvəsɪ] n Privatleben das.

private ['praɪvɪt] adj Privat-; (confidential) vertraulich; (quiet) ruhig. ◆ n (MIL) Gefreite der; in ~ privat.

private health care n private Krankenpflege die.

private property n Privatgrundstück das.

private school n Privatschule die.

privilege ['prɪvɪlɪdʒ] n Privileg das; it's a ~! es ist mir eine Ehre!

prize [praɪz] n Preis der.

prize-giving [-,gɪvɪŋ] n Preisverleihung die.

pro [prəʊ] (pl -s) n (inf: professional) Profi der. ▪ **pros** npl : ~s and cons Pro und Kontra das.

probability [,prɒbə'bɪlətɪ] n Wahrscheinlichkeit die.

probable ['prɒbəbl] *adj* wahrscheinlich.

probably ['prɒbəblɪ] *adv* wahrscheinlich.

probation officer [prə-'beɪʃn-] *n* Bewährungshelfer *der* (-in *die*).

problem ['prɒbləm] *n* Problem *das* ; **no ~!** *(inf)* kein Problem!

procedure [prə'si:dʒə'] *n* Verfahren *das*.

proceed [prə'si:d] *vi (fml : continue)* fortlfahren ; *(act)* vorlgehen ; *(walk)* gehen ; *(drive)* fahren ; **~ with caution** Vorsichtig fahren.

proceeds ['prəʊsi:dz] *npl* Erlös *der*.

process ['prəʊses] *n* Prozess *der* ; **to be in the ~ of doing sthg** dabei sein, etw zu tun.

processed cheese ['prəʊsest-] *n* Schmelzkäse *der*.

procession [prə'seʃn] *n* Prozession *die*.

prod [prɒd] *vt (poke)* stupsen.

produce [prə'dju:s] *vt (make, manufacture)* herlstellen ; *(work of art)* schaffen ; *(cause)* hervorlrufen ; *(create naturally)* erzeugen ; *(passport, identification)* vorlzeigen ; *(proof)* liefern ; *(play)* inszenieren ; *(film)* produzieren. ◆ *n* Erzeugnisse *pl*.

producer [prə'dju:sə'] *n (manufacturer)* Produzent *der* (-in *die*) ; *(of film)* Produzent *der* (-in *die*) ; *(of play)* Regisseur *der* (-in *die*).

product ['prɒdʌkt] *n* Produkt *das*.

production [prə'dʌkʃn] *n (manufacture)* Produktion *die* ;

(of film, play) Produktion *die* ; *(play)* Aufführung *die*.

productivity [,prɒdʌk'tɪvətɪ] *n* Produktivität *die*.

profession [prə'feʃn] *n* Beruf *der*.

professional [prə'feʃənl] *adj (relating to work)* Berufs- ; *(expert)* fachmännisch. ◆ *n (not amateur)* Fachmann *der* ; *(SPORT)* Profi *der*.

professor [prə'fesə'] *n (in UK)* Professor *der* (-in *die*) ; *(in US)* Dozent *der* (-in *die*).

profile ['prəʊfaɪl] *n* Profil *das* ; *(description)* Kurzdarstellung *die*.

profit ['prɒfit] *n* Profit *der*, Gewinn *der*. ◆ *vi* : **to ~ (from)** profitieren (von).

profitable ['prɒfitəbl] *adj* Gewinn bringend.

profiteroles [prə'fitərəʊlz] *npl* Profiterolen *pl*.

profound [prə'faʊnd] *adj* tief.

program ['prəʊgræm] *n (COMPUT)* Programm *das* ; *(Am)* = **programme**. ◆ *vt (COMPUT)* programmieren.

programme ['prəʊgræm] *n (Br)* Programm *das* ; *(on TV, radio)* Sendung *die*.

progress [*n* 'prəʊgres, *vb* prə'gres] *n (improvement)* Fortschritt *der* ; *(forward movement)* Vorankommen *das*. ◆ *vi* vorankommen ; *(day, meeting)* vergehen ; **to make ~** *(improve)* Fortschritte machen ; *(in journey)* vorankommen ; **in ~** im Gange.

progressive [prə'gresɪv] *adj (forward-looking)* fortschrittlich.

prohibit [prə'hɪbɪt] vt verbieten ; '**smoking strictly ~ed**' 'Rauchen streng verboten'.

project ['prɒdʒekt] n Projekt das ; (at school) Arbeit die.

projector [prə'dʒektə'] n Projektor der.

prolong [prə'lɒŋ] vt verlängern.

prom [prɒm] n (Am : dance) Schüler-/Studentenball.

promenade [,prɒmə'nɑːd] n (Br : by the sea) Strandpromenade die.

prominent ['prɒmɪnənt] adj (person) prominent ; (noticeable) auffallend.

promise ['prɒmɪs] n Versprechen das. ◆ vt & vi versprechen ; **to show ~** (work, person) viel versprechend sein ; **I ~ (that) I'll come** ich verspreche, dass ich komme ; **to ~ sb sthg** jm etw versprechen ; **to ~ to do sthg** versprechen, etw zu tun.

promising ['prɒmɪsɪŋ] adj viel versprechend.

promote [prə'məʊt] vt befördern.

promotion [prə'məʊʃn] n Beförderung die ; (of product) Sonderangebot das.

prompt [prɒmpt] adj (quick) prompt. ◆ adv : **at six o'clock ~** Punkt sechs Uhr.

prone [prəʊn] adj : **to be ~ to sthg** zu etw neigen ; **to be ~ to do sthg** dazu neigen, etw zu tun.

prong [prɒŋ] n Zinke die.

pronoun ['prəʊnaʊn] n Pronomen das.

pronounce [prə'naʊns] vt (word) aus|sprechen.

pronunciation [prə,nʌnsɪ'eɪʃn] n Aussprache die.

proof [pruːf] n (evidence) Beweis der ; (alcohol) 12% ~ 12% vol.

prop [prɒp] : **prop up** vt sep stützen.

propeller [prə'pelə'] n Propeller der.

proper ['prɒpə'] adj richtig ; (behaviour) anständig.

properly ['prɒpəlɪ] adv richtig.

property ['prɒpətɪ] n (possessions) Eigentum das ; (land) Besitz der ; (fml : building) Immobilien pl ; (quality) Eigenschaft die.

proportion [prə'pɔːʃn] n (part, amount) Teil der ; (ratio) Verhältnis das ; (in art) Proportion die.

proposal [prə'pəʊzl] n Vorschlag der.

propose [prə'pəʊz] vt vor|schlagen. ◆ vi : **to ~ (to sb)** (jm) einen Heiratsantrag machen.

proposition [,prɒpə'zɪʃn] n Vorschlag der.

proprietor [prə'praɪətə'] n (fml) Eigentümer der (-in die).

prose [prəʊz] n (not poetry) Prosa die ; (SCH) Übersetzung die (in die Fremdsprache).

prosecution [,prɒsɪ'kjuːʃn] n (JUR : charge) Anklage die.

prospect ['prɒspekt] n Aussicht die.

prospectus [prə'spektəs] (pl -es) n Broschüre die.

prosperous ['prɒspərəs] adj wohlhabend.

prostitute ['prɒstɪtjuːt] n
Prostituierte die.

protect [prə'tekt] vt schützen ; to ~ sb/sthg from jn/etw
schützen vor (+D) ; to ~ sb/sthg
against jn/etw schützen vor
(+D).

protection [prə'tekʃn] n
Schutz der.

protection factor n (of suntan lotion) Schutzfaktor der.

protective [prə'tektɪv] adj
(person) beschützend ; (clothes)
Schutz-.

protein ['prəʊtiːn] n Protein
das.

protest [n 'prəʊtest, vb
prə'test] n (complaint) Protest
der ; (demonstration) Protest-
marsch der. ◆ vt (Am : protest
against) protestieren gegen.
◆ vi : to ~ (against) protestieren
(gegen).

Protestant ['prɒtɪstənt] n
Protestant der (-in die).

protester [prə'testər] n De-
monstrant der (-in die).

protractor [prə'træktər] n
Winkelmaß das.

protrude [prə'truːd] vi vorlstehen.

proud [praʊd] adj stolz ; to be
~ of stolz sein auf (+A).

prove [pruːv] (pp -d OR proven
[pruːvn]) vt beweisen ; (turn out
to be) sich erweisen als.

proverb ['prɒvɜːb] n Sprichwort das.

provide [prə'vaɪd] vt (supply)
liefern ; to ~ sb with sthg jn mit
etw versorgen. ■ **provide for**

vt fus : to ~ for sb für js Lebensunterhalt sorgen.

provided (that) [prə'vaɪdɪd-]
conj vorausgesetzt (, dass).

providing (that) [prə'vaɪ-
dɪŋ-] = **provided (that)**.

province ['prɒvɪns] n Provinz
die.

provisional [prə'vɪʒənl] adj
provisorisch.

provisions [prə'vɪʒnz] npl
Proviant der.

provocative [prə'vɒkətɪv] adj
provozierend.

provoke [prə'vəʊk] vt (cause)
hervorlrufen ; (annoy) provozieren.

prowl [praʊl] vi herumlstrei-
chen.

prune [pruːn] n Dörrpflaume
die. ◆ vt (tree, bush) beschnei-
den.

PS (abbr of postscript) PS.

psychiatrist [saɪ'kaɪətrɪst] n
Psychiater der (-in die).

psychic ['saɪkɪk] adj : to be ~
übernatürliche Kräfte haben.

psychological [ˌsaɪkə-
'lɒdʒɪkl] adj psychologisch.

psychologist [saɪ'kɒlədʒɪst]
n Psychologe der (Psychologin
die).

psychology [saɪ'kɒlədʒɪ] n
Psychologie die.

psychotherapist [ˌsaɪkəʊ-
'θerəpɪst] n Psychotherapeut
der (-in die).

pt abbr = pint.

PTO (abbr of please turn over)
b.w.

pub [pʌb] n Pub der, Kneipe
die.

pull

ⓘ **PUB**

In Großbritannien spielt sich ein großer Teil des sozialen Lebens, ganz besonders in den ländlichen Gegenden, in den „Pubs" ab, einer Mischung aus Gasthaus und Kneipe. Bis vor einigen Jahren waren die Öffnungszeiten streng reguliert, doch heute sind „Pubs" meist von 11 bis 23 Uhr durchgehend geöffnet. Auch das Pubverbot für Kinder unter 16 gilt heute generell nicht mehr. Dies wird jedoch von Gegend zu Gegend und von Pub zu Pub unterschiedlich gehandhabt. Außer Getränken wird in den meisten Pubs auch eine Auswahl an kleinen Mahlzeiten angeboten.

---

puberty ['pju:bətı] n Pubertät die.

public ['pʌblɪk] adj öffentlich. ◆ n : the ~ die Öffentlichkeit ; in ~ in der Öffentlichkeit.

publican ['pʌblɪkən] n (Br) Gastwirt der (-in die).

publication [ˌpʌblɪ'keɪʃn] n Veröffentlichung die.

public bar n (Br) Raum in einem Pub, der weniger bequem ausgestattet ist als die 'lounge bar' oder 'saloon bar'.

public convenience n (Br) öffentliche Toilette die.

public footpath n (Br) öffentlicher Fußweg.

public holiday n gesetzlicher Feiertag.

public house n (Br : fml) Pub der, Kneipe die.

publicity [pʌb'lɪsɪtɪ] n Publicity die.

public school n (in UK) Privatschule die ; (in US) staatliche Schule.

public telephone n öffentlicher Fernsprecher.

public transport n öffentliche Verkehrsmittel pl.

publish ['pʌblɪʃ] vt veröffentlichen.

publisher ['pʌblɪʃə'] n (person) Verleger der ; (company) Verlag der.

publishing ['pʌblɪʃɪŋ] n (industry) Verlagswesen das.

pub lunch n meist einfaches Mittagessen in einem Pub.

pudding ['pʊdɪŋ] n (sweet dish) Pudding der ; (Br : course) Nachtisch der.

puddle ['pʌdl] n Pfütze die.

puff [pʌf] vi (breathe heavily) keuchen. ◆ n (of air) Stoß der ; (of smoke) Wolke die ; to ~ at (cigarette, pipe) ziehen an (+D).

puff pastry n Blätterteig der.

pull [pʊl] vt ziehen an (+D) ; (tow) ziehen. ◆ vi ziehen. ◆ n : to give sthg a ~ an etw (D) ziehen ; to ~ a face eine Grimasse schneiden ; to ~ a muscle sich (D) einen Muskel zerren ; to ~ the trigger abldrücken ; 'pull' (on door) 'Ziehen'. ▪ **pull apart** vt sep (book) auseinander reißen ; (machine) auseinander nehmen. ▪ **pull down** vt sep (lower) herunterlziehen ; (demolish) ablreißen. ▪ **pull in** vi (train) einlfahren ; (car) anlhalten. ▪ **pull out** vt sep herauslziehen. ◆ vi (train) ablfahren ; (car) auslscheren ; (with-

pulley 236

draw) sich zurück|ziehen.
■ **pull over** *vi (car)* an den
Straßenrand fahren. ■ **pull
up** *vt sep (socks, trousers, sleeve)*
hoch|ziehen. ◆ *vi (stop)* an|halten.

pulley ['pʊlɪ] (*pl* **pulleys**) *n* Flaschenzug *der.*

pull-out *n (Am : beside road)*
Parkbucht *die.*

pullover ['pʊl,əʊvə'] *n* Pullover *der.*

pulpit ['pʊlpɪt] *n* Kanzel *die.*

pulse [pʌls] *n (MED)* Puls *der.*

pump [pʌmp] *n* Pumpe *die.*
■ **pumps** *npl (sports shoes)*
Freizeitschuhe *pl.* ■ **pump up**
vt sep auf|pumpen.

pumpkin ['pʌmpkɪn] *n* Kürbis
der.

pun [pʌn] *n* Wortspiel *das.*

punch [pʌntʃ] *n (blow)* Faustschlag *der ;* *(drink)* Punsch *der.*
◆ *vt (hit)* boxen ; *(ticket)* lochen.

Punch and Judy show
[-'dʒuː-dɪ-] *n* Kasperltheater *das.*

punctual ['pʌŋktʃʊəl] *adj*
pünktlich.

punctuation [,pʌŋktʃʊ'eɪʃn]
n Interpunktion *die.*

puncture ['pʌŋktʃə'] *n (of car
tyre)* Reifenpanne *die ;* *(of bicycle tyre)* Platten *der.* ◆ *vt* stechen in (+A).

punish ['pʌnɪʃ] *vt :* to ~ sb (for
sthg) jn (für etw) bestrafen.

punishment ['pʌnɪʃmənt] *n*
Strafe *die.*

punk [pʌŋk] *n (person)* Punker
der (-in die) ; *(music)* Punk *der.*

punnet ['pʌnɪt] *n (Br)* Körbchen *das.*

pupil ['pjuːpl] *n (student)* Schüler *der (-in die) ;* *(of eye)* Pupille
die.

puppet ['pʌpɪt] *n* Puppe *die.*

puppy ['pʌpɪ] *n* junger Hund.

purchase ['pɜːtʃəs] *vt (fml)*
kaufen. ◆ *n (fml)* Kauf *der.*

pure [pjʊə'] *adj* rein.

puree ['pjʊəreɪ] *n* Püree *das.*

purely ['pjʊəlɪ] *adv* rein.

purity ['pjʊərətɪ] *n* Reinheit
die.

purple ['pɜːpl] *adj* violett.

purpose ['pɜːpəs] *n* Zweck
der ; on ~ absichtlich.

purr [pɜː'] *vi (cat)* schnurren.

purse [pɜːs] *n (Br : for money)*
Portmonee *das ;* *(Am : handbag)* Handtasche *die.*

pursue [pə'sjuː] *vt (follow)* verfolgen ; *(study, inquiry, matter)*
nach|gehen (+D).

pus [pʌs] *n* Eiter *der.*

push [pʊʃ] *vt* schieben ; *(button)* drücken auf (+A) ; *(product)*
puschen. ◆ *vi* schubsen. ◆ *n :*
to give sb/sthg a ~ jm/einer Sache einen Stoß geben ; to ~ sb
into doing sthg jn drängen, etw
zu tun ; 'push' *(on door)* 'Drücken'. ■ **push in** *vi (in queue)*
sich vor|drängen. ■ **push off**
vi (inf : go away) ab|hauen.

push-button telephone *n*
Tastentelefon *das.*

pushchair ['pʊʃtʃeə'] *n (Br)*
Sportwagen *der (für Kinder).*

pushed [pʊʃt] *adj (inf) :* to be ~
(for time) in Eile sein.

push-ups *npl* Liegestütze *pl.*

put [pʊt] *(pt & pp* put) *vt (place)*
tun ; *(place upright)* stellen ;
(lay flat) legen ; *(express)* sa-

gen ; *(write)* schreiben ; *(a question)* stellen ; *(estimate)* : to ~ sthg at etw schätzen auf *(+A)* ; to ~ a child to bed ein Kind ins Bett bringen ; to ~ money into sthg Geld in etw *(A)* investieren ; to ~ sb under pressure jn unter Druck setzen ; to ~ the blame on sb jm die Schuld geben. ■ **put aside** *vt sep (money)* zur Seite legen. ■ **put away** *vt sep (tidy up)* weglräumen. ■ **put back** *vt sep (replace)* zurücklegen ; *(postpone)* verschieben ; *(clock, watch)* zurücklstellen. ■ **put down** *vt sep (place)* setzen ; *(place upright)* (hinl)stellen ; *(lay flat)* (hinl)legen ; *(passenger)* ablsetzen ; *(Br : animal)* einlschläfern ; *(deposit)* anlzahlen. ■ **put forward** *vt sep (clock, watch)* vorlstellen ; *(suggest)* vorlschlagen. ■ **put in** *vt sep (insert)* hineinlstecken ; *(install)* einlbauen. ■ **put off** *vt sep (postpone)* verschieben ; *(distract)* ablenken ; *(repel)* ablstoßen ; *(passenger)* ablsetzen. ■ **put on** *vt sep (clothes)* anlziehen ; *(glasses)* auflsetzen ; *(make-up)* aufllegen ; *(television, light, radio)* anlschalten ; *(record)* aufllegen ; *(CD, tape)* einllegen ; *(play, show)* auflführen ; to ~ on weight zulnehmen ; to ~ the kettle on Wasser auflsetzen. ■ **put out** *vt sep (cigarette, fire, light)* auslmachen ; *(publish)* veröffentllichen ; *(hand, arm, leg)* auslstrecken ; to ~ sb out jm Umstände machen ; to ~ one's back out sich *(D)* den Rücken verrenken. ■ **put together** *vt sep*

(assemble) zusammenlsetzen ; *(combine)* zusammenlstellen. ■ **put up** *vt sep (tent, statue, building)* errichten ; *(umbrella)* auflspannen ; *(a notice)* anlschlagen ; *(sign)* anlbringen ; *(price, rate)* hochltreiben ; *(visitor)* unterlbringen. ◆ *vi (Br : in hotel)* unterlkommen. ■ **put up with** *vt fus* dulden.

putter ['pʌtə'] *n (club)* Putter *der.*

putting green ['pʌtɪŋ-] *n* Platz *der* zum Putten.

putty ['pʌtɪ] *n* Kitt *der.*

puzzle ['pʌzl] *n* Rätsel *das* ; *(jigsaw)* Puzzle *das.* ◆ *vt* verblüffen.

puzzling ['pʌzlɪŋ] *adj* verblüffend.

pyjamas [pə'dʒɑːməz] *npl (Br)* Schlafanzug *der.*

pylon ['paɪlən] *n* Mast *der.*

pyramid ['pɪrəmɪd] *n* Pyramide *die.*

Pyrenees [,pɪrə'niːz] *npl* : the ~ die Pyrenäen *pl.*

Pyrex® ['paɪreks] *n* Jenaer Glas® *das.*

Q

quail [kweɪl] *n* Wachtel *die.*

quail's eggs *npl* Wachteleier *pl.*

quaint [kweɪnt] *adj (village, cottage)* malerisch.

qualification [,kwɒlɪfɪ'keɪʃn] *n (diploma)* Zeugnis *das* ; *(ability)* Qualifikation *die.*

qualified ['kwɒlıfaıd] *adj* qualifiziert.

qualify ['kwɒlıfaı] *vi* sich qualifizieren.

quality ['kwɒlətı] *n* Qualität *die* ; *(feature)* Eigenschaft *die*. ◆ *adj (product)* Qualitäts- ; *(newspaper)* seriös.

quarantine ['kwɒrəntiːn] *n* Quarantäne *die*.

quarrel ['kwɒrəl] *n* Streit *der*. ◆ *vi* sich streiten.

quarry ['kwɒrı] *n (for stone, sand)* Steinbruch *der*.

quart [kwɔːt] *n* = 0,14 Liter, Quart *das*.

quarter ['kwɔːtə'] *n* Viertel *das* ; *(Am : coin)* Vierteldollar *der* ; *(4 ounces)* = 0,1134 kg, Vierteilpfund *das* ; *(three months)* Quartal *das* ; (a) ~ of an hour eine Viertelstunde ; (a) ~ to five *(Br)* Viertel vor fünf ; (a) ~ of five *(Am)* Viertel vor fünf ; (a) ~ past five *(Br)* Viertel nach fünf ; (a) ~ after five *(Am)* Viertel nach fünf.

quarterpounder [,kwɔːtə-'paundə'] *n* Viertelpfünder *der (großer Hamburger)*.

quartet [kwɔː'tet] *n* Quartett *das*.

quartz [kwɔːts] *adj (watch)* Quarz-.

quay [kiː] *n* Kai *der*.

queasy ['kwiːzı] *adj (inf)* unwohl.

queen [kwiːn] *n* Königin *die* ; *(in chess, cards)* Dame *die*.

queer [kwıə'] *adj (strange)* seltsam ; *(inf : ill)* unwohl ; *(inf : homosexual)* schwul.

quench [kwentʃ] *vt* : to ~ one's thirst seinen Durst löschen.

query ['kwıərı] *n* Frage *die*.

question ['kwestʃn] *n* Frage *die*. ◆ *vt (person)* auslfragen ; *(subj : police)* verhören ; it's out of the ~ das kommt nicht in Frage.

question mark *n* Fragezeichen *das*.

questionnaire [,kwestʃə-'neə'] *n* Fragebogen *der*.

queue [kjuː] *n (Br)* Schlange *die*. ◆ *vi (Br)* Schlange stehen.

▪ **queue up** *vi (Br)* Schlange stehen.

quiche [kiːʃ] *n* Quiche *die*.

quick [kwık] *adj & adv* schnell.

quickly ['kwıklı] *adv* schnell.

quid [kwıd] *(pl* quid*) n (Br : inf : pound)* Pfund *das (Geld)*.

quiet ['kwaıət] *adj* ruhig ; *(voice, car)* leise. ◆ *n* Ruhe *die* ; keep ~! Ruhe! ; to keep ~ still sein ; to keep ~ about sthg etw verschweigen.

quieten ['kwaıətn] : **quieten down** *vi* sich beruhigen.

quietly ['kwaıətlı] *adv* ruhig ; *(speak)* leise.

quilt [kwılt] *n (duvet)* Steppdecke *die* ; *(eiderdown)* Bettdecke *die*.

quince [kwıns] *n* Quitte *die*.

quirk [kwɜːk] *n* Schrulle *die*.

quit [kwıt] *(pt & pp* quit*) vi (resign)* kündigen ; *(give up)* auflhören. ◆ *vt (Am : school, job)* auflgeben ; to ~ doing sthg auflhören, etw zu tun.

quite [kwaıt] *adv (fairly)* ziemlich ; *(completely)* ganz ; not ~

nicht ganz ; ~ **a lot (of)** ziemlich viel.

quiz [kwɪz] (*pl* **-zes**) *n* Quiz *das*.

quota ['kwəʊtə] *n* Quote *die*.

quotation [kwəʊ'teɪʃn] *n* (*phrase*) Zitat *das* ; (*estimate*) Kostenvoranschlag *der*.

quotation marks *npl* Anführungszeichen *pl*.

quote [kwəʊt] *vt* (*phrase, writer*) zitieren ; (*price*) nennen. ◆ *n* (*phrase*) Zitat *das* ; (*estimate*) Kostenvoranschlag *der*.

R

rabbit ['ræbɪt] *n* Kaninchen *das*.

rabies ['reɪbiːz] *n* Tollwut *die*.

RAC *n* (*Br : abbr of Royal Automobile Club*) britischer Automobilclub.

race [reɪs] *n* (*competition*) Rennen *das* ; (*ethnic group*) Rasse *die*. ◆ *vi* (*compete*) um die Wette laufen/fahren *etc* ; (*go fast*) rennen ; (*engine*) durch|drehen. ◆ *vt* um die Wette laufen/fahren *etc* mit.

racecourse ['reɪskɔːs] *n* Rennbahn *die*.

racehorse ['reɪshɔːs] *n* Rennpferd *das*.

racetrack ['reɪstræk] *n* (*for horses*) Pferderennbahn *die*.

racial ['reɪʃl] *adj* Rassen-.

racing ['reɪsɪŋ] *n* : (**horse**) ~ Pferderennen *das*.

racing car *n* Rennwagen *der*.

racism ['reɪsɪzm] *n* Rassismus *der*.

racist ['reɪsɪst] *n* Rassist *der* (*-in die*).

rack [ræk] *n* (*for coats, hats*) Ständer *der* ; (*for plates, bottles*) Gestell *das* ; (*luggage*) ~ Gepäckablage *die* ; ~ **of lamb** Lammrücken *der*.

racket ['rækɪt] *n* Schläger *der* ; (*noise*) Lärm *der*.

racquet ['rækɪt] *n* Schläger *der*.

radar ['reɪdɑːʳ] *n* Radar *der*.

radiation [,reɪdɪ'eɪʃn] *n* Strahlung *die*.

radiator ['reɪdɪeɪtəʳ] *n* (*in building*) Heizkörper *der* ; (*of vehicle*) Kühler *der*.

radical ['rædɪkl] *adj* radikal.

radii ['reɪdɪaɪ] *pl* → **radius**.

radio ['reɪdɪəʊ] (*pl* **-s**) *n* (*device*) Radio *das* ; (*system*) Rundfunk *der*. ◆ *vt* (*person*) an|funken ; **on the** ~ im Radio.

radioactive [,reɪdɪəʊ'æktɪv] *adj* radioaktiv.

radio alarm *n* Radiowecker *der*.

radish ['rædɪʃ] *n* Radieschen *das*.

radius ['reɪdɪəs] (*pl* **radii**) *n* Radius *der*.

raffle ['ræfl] *n* Tombola *die*.

raft [rɑːft] *n* (*of wood*) Floß *das* ; (*inflatable*) Schlauchboot *das*.

rafter ['rɑːftəʳ] *n* Sparren *der*.

rag [ræg] *n* (*old cloth*) Lumpen *der*.

rage [reɪdʒ] *n* Wut *die*.

raid [reɪd] *n* (*attack*) Angriff *der* ; (*by police*) Razzia *die* ; (*robbery*) Überfall *der*. ◆ *vt* (*subj: police*) eine Razzia machen in

(+D) ; (subj : thieves) überfallen.

rail [reɪl] n (bar) Stange die ; (on stairs) Geländer das ; (for train, tram) Schiene die. ◆ adj (travel, transport, network) Bahn- ; **by ~** mit der Bahn.

railcard ['reɪlkɑːd] n (Br) ≃ Bahncard die.

railings ['reɪlɪŋz] npl Gitter das.

railroad ['reɪlrəʊd] (Am) = railway.

railway ['reɪlweɪ] n (system) Eisenbahn die ; (track) Eisenbahnstrecke die ; (rails) Gleis das.

railway line n (route) Bahn die ; (track) Eisenbahnstrecke die ; (rails) Gleis das.

railway station n Bahnhof der.

rain [reɪn] n Regen der. ◆ v impers regnen ; **it's ~ing** es regnet.

rainbow ['reɪnbəʊ] n Regenbogen der.

raincoat ['reɪnkəʊt] n Regenmantel der.

raindrop ['reɪndrɒp] n Regentropfen der.

rainfall ['reɪnfɔːl] n Niederschlag der.

rainy ['reɪnɪ] adj regnerisch.

raise [reɪz] vt (lift) heben ; (increase) erhöhen ; (money) beschaffen ; (child) großziehen ; (cattle, sheep etc) aufziehen ; (question, subject) aufwerfen. ◆ n (Am : pay increase) Gehaltserhöhung die.

raisin ['reɪzn] n Rosine die.

rake [reɪk] n Harke die.

rally ['rælɪ] n (public meeting) Kundgebung die ; (motor race)

Rallye die ; (in tennis, badminton, squash) Ballwechsel der.

ram [ræm] n (sheep) Widder der. ◆ vt (bang into) rammen.

Ramadan [ˌræməˈdæn] n Ramadan der.

ramble ['ræmbl] n Wanderung die.

ramp [ræmp] n Rampe die ; 'ramp' (Am : to freeway) Auffahrt die ; (Br : bump) Schild an Baustellen, das auf Straßenschäden hinweist.

ramparts ['ræmpɑːts] npl Wall der.

ran [ræn] pt → run.

ranch [rɑːntʃ] n Ranch die.

ranch dressing n (Am) cremige, würzige Soße.

rancid ['rænsɪd] adj ranzig.

random ['rændəm] adj willkürlich. ◆ n : **at ~** wahllos.

rang [ræŋ] pt → ring.

range [reɪndʒ] n (of radio, aircraft) Reichweite die ; (of prices) Preislage die ; (of temperatures) Temperaturbereich der ; (ages) Altersgruppe die ; (selection of products) Auswahl die ; (of hills, mountains) Kette die ; (for shooting) Schießstand der ; (cooker) Kochherd der. ◆ vi (vary) : **to ~ from X to Y** zwischen X und Y liegen.

ranger ['reɪndʒə'] n (of park, forest) Förster der (-in die).

rank [ræŋk] n Rang der. ◆ adj (smell, taste) übel.

ransom ['rænsəm] n Lösegeld das.

rap [ræp] n (music) Rap der.

rape [reɪp] n Vergewaltigung die. ◆ vt vergewaltigen.

rapid ['ræpɪd] *adj* schnell.
■ **rapids** *npl* Stromschnellen *pl*.

rapidly ['ræpɪdlɪ] *adv* schnell.

rapist ['reɪpɪst] *n* Vergewaltiger *der*.

rare [reəʳ] *adj* selten ; *(meat)* englisch gebraten.

rarely ['reəlɪ] *adv* selten.

rash [ræʃ] *n* Ausschlag *der*. ◆ *adj* unbedacht.

rasher ['ræʃəʳ] *n* Streifen *der*.

raspberry ['rɑːzbərɪ] *n* Himbeere *die*.

rat [ræt] *n* Ratte *die*.

ratatouille [rætə'tuːɪ] *n* Ratatouille *die*.

rate [reɪt] *n (level)* Rate *die* ; *(charge)* Satz *der* ; *(speed)* Tempo *das*. ◆ *vt (consider)* einschätzen ; *(deserve)* verdienen ; ~ **of exchange** Wechselkurs *der* ; **at any ~** auf jeden Fall ; **at this ~** auf diese Weise.

rather ['rɑːðəʳ] *adv (quite)* ziemlich ; *(expressing preference)* lieber ; **I'd ~ not** lieber nicht ; **would you ~...?** möchtest du lieber...? ; **~ than** statt.

ratio ['reɪʃɪəʊ] *(pl* -s) *n* Verhältnis *das*.

ration ['ræʃn] *n* Ration *die*.
■ **rations** *npl (food)* Ration *die*.

rational ['ræʃnl] *adj* rational.

rattle ['rætl] *n (of baby)* Rassel *die*. ◆ *vi* klappern.

rave [reɪv] *n (party)* Rave *der*.

raven ['reɪvn] *n* Rabe *der*.

ravioli [,rævɪ'əʊlɪ] *n* Ravioli *pl*.

raw [rɔː] *adj* roh.

raw material *n* Rohstoff *der*.

ray [reɪ] *n* Strahl *der*.

razor ['reɪzəʳ] *n* Rasierapparat *der*.

razor blade *n* Rasierklinge *die*.

Rd *(abbr of Road)* Str.

re [riː] *prep* betreffs (+G).

RE *n (abbr of religious education)* Religionsunterricht *der*.

reach [riːtʃ] *vt* erreichen ; *(town, country)* ankommen in (+D) ; *(manage to touch)* kommen an (+A) ; *(extend up to)* reichen bis ; *(agreement, decision)* kommen zu. ◆ *n* : **out of ~** außer Reichweite ; **within ~ of the beach** im Strandbereich.
■ **reach out** *vi* : **to ~ out (for)** die Hand aus|strecken (nach).

react [rɪ'ækt] *vi* reagieren.

reaction [rɪ'ækʃn] *n* Reaktion *die*.

read [riːd] *(pt & pp* read [red]) *vt* lesen ; *(say aloud)* vor|lesen ; *(subj : sign, note)* besagen ; *(subj : meter, gauge)* an|zeigen. ◆ *vi* lesen ; **to ~ about sthg** über etw lesen. ■ **read out** *vt sep* laut vor|lesen.

reader ['riːdəʳ] *n* Leser *der* (-in *die*).

readily ['redɪlɪ] *adv (willingly)* gern ; *(easily)* leicht.

reading ['riːdɪŋ] *n* Lesen *das* ; *(of meter, gauge)* Stand *der*.

reading matter *n* Lesestoff *der*.

ready ['redɪ] *adj (prepared)* fertig ; **to be ~ for sthg** *(prepared)* für etw fertig sein ; **to be ~ to do sthg** *(willing)* bereit sein, etw zu tun ; *(likely)* im Begriff sein, etw zu tun ; **to get ~** sich fertig machen ; **to get sthg ~** etw fertig machen.

ready cash *n* Bargeld *das*.

ready-cooked [-kʊkt] *adj* vorgekocht.

ready-to-wear *adj* von der Stange.

real ['rɪəl] *adj (actual)* wirklich; *(genuine, for emphasis)* echt. ◆ *adv (Am)* echt, wirklich.

real ale *n dunkles, nach traditionellem Rezept gebrautes britisches Bier.*

real estate *n* Immobilien *pl.*

realistic [ˌrɪə'lɪstɪk] *adj* realistisch.

reality [rɪ'ælətɪ] *n* Realität *die* ; in ~ in Wirklichkeit.

realize ['rɪəlaɪz] *vt (become aware of)* erkennen ; *(know)* wissen ; *(ambition, goal)* verwirklichen.

really ['rɪəlɪ] *adv* wirklich ; not ~ eigentlich nicht ; ~? *(expressing surprise)* wirklich?

realtor ['rɪəltər] *n (Am)* Immobilienhändler *der* (-in *die*).

rear [rɪər] *adj* hintere(-r) (-s) ; *(window)* Heck-, Hinter-. ◆ *n (back)* Rückseite *die.*

rearrange [ˌriːə'reɪndʒ] *vt (room, furniture)* umlstellen ; *(meeting)* verlegen.

rearview mirror ['rɪəvjuː-] *n* Rückspiegel *der.*

rear-wheel drive *n* Auto *das* mit Hinterradantrieb.

reason ['riːzn] *n* Grund *der* ; for some ~ aus irgendeinem Grund.

reasonable ['riːznəbl] *adj (fair)* angemessen ; *(not too expensive)* preiswert ; *(sensible)* vernünftig ; *(quite big)* annehmbar.

reasonably ['riːznəblɪ] *adv (quite)* ziemlich.

reasoning ['riːznɪŋ] *n* Denken *das.*

reassure [ˌriːə'ʃɔːr] *vt* versichern (+D).

reassuring [ˌriːə'ʃɔːrɪŋ] *adj* beruhigend.

rebate ['riːbeɪt] *n* Rückzahlung *die.*

rebel [*n* 'rebl, *vb* rɪ'bel] *n* Rebell *der* (-in *die*). ◆ *vi* rebellieren.

rebound [rɪ'baʊnd] *vi* ablprallen.

rebuild [ˌriː'bɪld] (*pt & pp* rebuilt [ˌriː'bɪlt]) *vt* wieder aufbauen.

rebuke [rɪ'bjuːk] *vt* tadeln.

recall [rɪ'kɔːl] *vt (remember)* sich erinnern an (+A).

receipt [rɪ'siːt] *n (for goods, money)* Quittung *die* ; on ~ of bei Erhalt von.

receive [rɪ'siːv] *vt* erhalten ; *(guest)* empfangen.

receiver [rɪ'siːvər] *n (of phone)* Hörer *der.*

recent ['riːsnt] *adj* kürzlich, erfolgte(-r) (-s).

recently ['riːsntlɪ] *adv* kürzlich.

receptacle [rɪ'septəkl] *n (fml)* Behälter *der.*

reception [rɪ'sepʃn] *n* Empfang *der* ; *(in hotel)* Rezeption *die* ; *(in hospital)* Aufnahme *die.*

reception desk *n (in hotel)* Rezeption *die.*

receptionist [rɪ'sepʃənɪst] *n (in hotel)* Empfangsdame *die* ; *(man)* Empfangschef *der* ; *(at doctor's)* Sprechstundenhilfe *die.*

recess ['riːses] n (in wall) Nische die ; (Am : SCH) Pause die.

recession [rɪ'seʃn] n Rezession die.

recipe ['resɪpɪ] n Rezept das.

recite [rɪ'saɪt] vt (poem) auflsagen ; (list) auflzählen.

reckless ['reklɪs] adj leichtsinnig.

reckon ['rekn] vt (inf : think) denken. ■ **reckon on** vt fus rechnen mit. ■ **reckon with** vt fus (expect) rechnen mit.

reclaim [rɪ'kleɪm] vt (baggage) ablholen.

reclining seat [rɪ'klaɪnɪŋ-] n Liegesitz der.

recognition [ˌrekəg'nɪʃn] n (recognizing) Erkennen die ; (acceptance) Anerkennung die.

recognize ['rekəgnaɪz] vt erkennen ; (accept) anlerkennen.

recollect [ˌrekə'lekt] vt sich erinnern an (+A).

recommend [ˌrekə'mend] vt empfehlen ; **to ~ sb to do sthg** jm empfehlen, etw zu tun.

recommendation [ˌrekəmen'deɪʃn] n Empfehlung die.

reconsider [ˌriːkən'sɪdə'] vt sich (D) nochmals überlegen.

reconstruct [ˌriːkən'strʌkt] vt wieder auflbauen.

record [n 'rekɔːd, vb rɪ'kɔːd] n (MUS) Schallplatte die ; (best performance, highest level) Rekord der ; (account) Aufzeichnung die. ◆ vt (keep account of) auflzeichnen ; (on tape) auflnehmen.

recorded delivery [rɪ'kɔː-dɪd-] n (Br) Einschreiben das.

recorder [rɪ'kɔːdə'] n (tape recorder) Kassettenrekorder der ; (instrument) Blockflöte die.

recording [rɪ'kɔːdɪŋ] n (tape, record) Aufnahme die.

record player n Plattenspieler der.

record shop n Schallplattengeschäft das.

recover [rɪ'kʌvə'] vt (get back) sicherlstellen. ◆ vi (from illness, shock) sich erholen.

recovery [rɪ'kʌvərɪ] n (from illness) Erholung die.

recovery vehicle n (Br) Abschleppwagen der.

recreation [ˌrekrɪ'eɪʃn] n Erholung die.

recreation ground n Spielplatz der.

recruit [rɪ'kruːt] n (to army) Rekrut der. ◆ vt (staff) anlwerben.

rectangle ['rek,tæŋgl] n Rechteck das.

rectangular [rek'tæŋgjulə'] adj rechteckig.

recycle [ˌriː'saɪkl] vt recyceln.

red [red] adj rot. ◆ n Rot das ; **in the ~** in den roten Zahlen.

red cabbage n Rotkohl der, Blaukraut das (Österr).

Red Cross n Rotes Kreuz.

redcurrant ['redkʌrənt] n rote Johannisbeere.

redecorate [ˌriː'dekəreɪt] vt neu tapezieren/streichen.

redhead ['redhed] n Rothaarige der, die.

red-hot adj (metal) rot glühend.

redial [ˌriː'daɪəl] vi wieder wählen.

redirect [ˌriːdɪˈrekt] vt (letter) nachⵏsenden ; (traffic, plane) umⵏleiten.

red pepper n rote Paprikaschote.

reduce [rɪˈdjuːs] vt reduzieren. ◆ vi (Am : slim) abⵏnehmen.

reduced price [rɪˈdjuːst-] n reduzierter Preis.

reduction [rɪˈdʌkʃn] n (in size) Verkleinerung die ; (in price) Reduzierung die.

redundancy [rɪˈdʌndənsɪ] n (Br) Entlassung die.

redundant [rɪˈdʌndənt] adj (Br) : to be made ~ entlassen werden.

red wine n Rotwein der.

reed [riːd] n (plant) Schilf das.

reef [riːf] n Riff das.

reek [riːk] vi stinken.

reel [riːl] n (of thread) Spule die ; (on fishing rod) Rolle die.

refectory [rɪˈfektərɪ] n Speisesaal der.

refer [rɪˈfɜːʳ] : **refer to** vt fus (speak about) sich beziehen auf (+A) ; (relate to) betreffen ; (dictionary, book) nachschlagen in (+D).

referee [ˌrefəˈriː] n (SPORT) Schiedsrichter der (-in die).

reference [ˈrefrəns] n (mention) Erwähnung die ; (letter for job) Referenz die. ◆ adj (book, library) Nachschlage- ; with ~ to bezüglich (+G).

referendum [ˌrefəˈrendəm] n Volksabstimmung die.

refill [n ˈriːfɪl, vb ˌriːˈfɪl] vt nachⵏfüllen. ◆ n (for ballpoint pen) Mine die ; (for fountain pen) Patrone die ; (inf : drink) : would

you like a ~? darf ich dir nachschenken?

refinery [rɪˈfaɪnərɪ] n Raffinerie die.

reflect [rɪˈflekt] vt (light, heat, image) reflektieren. ◆ vi (think) nachⵏdenken.

reflection [rɪˈflekʃn] n (image) Spiegelbild das.

reflector [rɪˈflektəʳ] n (on bicycle, car) Rückstrahler der.

reflex [ˈriːfleks] n Reflex der.

reflexive [rɪˈfleksɪv] adj reflexiv.

reform [rɪˈfɔːm] n Reform die. ◆ vt reformieren.

refresh [rɪˈfreʃ] vt erfrischen.

refreshing [rɪˈfreʃɪŋ] adj erfrischend.

refreshments [rɪˈfreʃmənts] npl Erfrischungen pl.

refrigerator [rɪˈfrɪdʒəreɪtəʳ] n Kühlschrank der.

refugee [ˌrefjʊˈdʒiː] n Flüchtling der.

refund [n ˈriːfʌnd, vb rɪˈfʌnd] n Rückerstattung die. ◆ vt zurückⵏerstatten.

refundable [rɪˈfʌndəbl] adj rückerstattbar.

refusal [rɪˈfjuːzl] n Weigerung die.

refuse[1] [rɪˈfjuːz] vt (not accept) abⵏlehnen ; (not allow) verweigern. ◆ vi abⵏlehnen ; to ~ to do sthg sich weigern, etw zu tun.

refuse[2] [ˈrefjuːs] n (fml) Abfall der.

refuse collection [ˈrefjuːs-] n (fml) Müllabfuhr die.

regard [rɪˈgɑːd] vt (consider) anⵏsehen. ◆ n : with ~ to in Bezug auf (+A) ; as ~s in Bezug auf (+A). ■ **regards** npl (in greet-

ings) Grüße *pl* ; **give them my ~s** grüße sie von mir.

regarding [rɪ'gɑːdɪŋ] *prep* bezüglich (+G).

regardless [rɪ'gɑːdlɪs] *adv* trotzdem ; **~ of** ohne Rücksicht auf (+A).

reggae ['reɡeɪ] *n* Reggae *der*.

regiment ['redʒɪmənt] *n* Regiment *das*.

region ['riːdʒən] *n* Gebiet *das* ; **in the ~ of** im Bereich von.

regional ['riːdʒənl] *adj* regional.

register ['redʒɪstə'] *n* Register *das*. ◆ *vt* registrieren ; *(subj : machine, gauge)* an|zeigen ; ◆ *vi* sich registrieren lassen ; *(at hotel)* sich ein|tragen.

registered ['redʒɪstəd] *adj* *(letter, parcel)* eingeschrieben.

registration [,redʒɪ'streɪʃn] *n* *(for course)* Einschreibung *die* ; *(at conference)* Anmeldung *die*.

registration (number) *n* polizeiliches Kennzeichen.

registry office ['redʒɪstrɪ-] *n* Standesamt *das*.

regret [rɪ'ɡret] *n* Bedauern *das*. ◆ *vt* bedauern ; **to ~ doing sthg** etw leider tun müssen ; **we ~ any inconvenience caused** eventuelle Unannehmlichkeiten bitten wir zu entschuldigen.

regrettable [rɪ'ɡretəbl] *adj* bedauerlich.

regular ['reɡjʊlə'] *adj* regelmäßig ; *(intervals)* gleichmäßig ; *(time)* üblich ; *(Coke, fries)* normal. ◆ *n* *(customer)* Stammkunde *der* (-kundin *die*).

regularly ['reɡjʊləlɪ] *adv* regelmäßig ; *(spaced, distributed)* gleichmäßig.

regulate ['reɡjʊleɪt] *vt* regulieren.

regulation [,reɡjʊ'leɪʃn] *n* *(rule)* Regelung *die*.

rehearsal [rɪ'hɜːsl] *n* Probe *die*.

rehearse [rɪ'hɜːs] *vt* proben.

reign [reɪn] *n* Herrschaft *die*. ◆ *vi* *(monarch)* regieren.

reimburse [,riːɪm'bɜːs] *vt* *(fml)* zurück|erstatten.

reindeer ['reɪn,dɪə'] *(pl* reindeer) *n* Rentier *das*.

reinforce [,riːɪn'fɔːs] *vt* verstärken ; *(argument, opinion)* bestärken.

reinforcements [,riːɪn'fɔːsmənts] *npl* Verstärkung *die*.

reins [reɪnz] *npl* *(for horse)* Zügel *der* ; *(for child)* Leine *die*.

reject [rɪ'dʒekt] *vt* ab|lehnen ; *(subj : machine)* nicht an|nehmen.

rejection [rɪ'dʒekʃn] *n* Ablehnung *die*.

rejoin [,riː'dʒɔɪn] *vt* *(motorway)* wieder kommen auf (+A).

relapse [rɪ'læps] *n* Rückfall *der*.

relate [rɪ'leɪt] *vt* *(connect)* in Zusammenhang bringen. ◆ *vi* : **to ~ to** *(be connected with)* in Zusammenhang stehen mit ; *(concern)* sich beziehen auf (+A).

related [rɪ'leɪtɪd] *adj* verwandt.

relation [rɪ'leɪʃn] *n* *(member of family)* Verwandte *der*, *die* ; *(connection)* Beziehung *die* ; **in ~**

to in Bezug auf (+A). ▪ **relations** npl (between countries, people) Beziehungen pl.

relationship [rɪ'leɪʃnʃɪp] n Beziehung die.

relative ['relətɪv] adj relativ ; (GRAMM) Relativ-. ◆ n Verwandte der, die.

relatively ['relətɪvlɪ] adv relativ.

relax [rɪ'læks] vi sich entspannen.

relaxation [ˌriːlæk'seɪʃn] n Entspannung die.

relaxed [rɪ'lækst] adj entspannt.

relaxing [rɪ'læksɪŋ] adj entspannend.

relay ['riːleɪ] n (race) Staffel die.

release [rɪ'liːs] vt (set free) freilassen ; (let go of) loslassen ; (record, film) herausbringen ; (brake, catch) lösen. ◆ n : a new ~ (film) ein neuer Film ; (record) eine neue Platte.

relegate ['relɪgeɪt] vt : to be ~d (SPORT) ablsteigen.

relevant ['reləvənt] adj relevant ; (appropriate) entsprechend.

reliable [rɪ'laɪəbl] adj (person, machine) zuverlässig.

relic ['relɪk] n (vestige) Relikt das.

relief [rɪ'liːf] n (gladness) Erleichterung die ; (aid) Hilfe die.

relief road n Entlastungsstraße die.

relieve [rɪ'liːv] vt (pain, headache) lindern.

relieved [rɪ'liːvd] adj erleichtert.

religion [rɪ'lɪdʒn] n Religion die.

religious [rɪ'lɪdʒəs] adj (of religion) Religions- ; (devout) gläubig.

relish ['relɪʃ] n (sauce) dickflüssige Soße.

reluctant [rɪ'lʌktənt] adj widerwillig.

rely [rɪ'laɪ] : **rely on** vt fus (trust) sich verlassen auf (+A) ; (depend on) abhängig sein von.

remain [rɪ'meɪn] vi bleiben ; (be left over) übrig bleiben. ▪ **remains** npl Überreste pl.

remainder [rɪ'meɪndə'] n Rest der.

remaining [rɪ'meɪnɪŋ] adj restlich.

remark [rɪ'mɑːk] n Bemerkung die. ◆ vt bemerken.

remarkable [rɪ'mɑːkəbl] adj bemerkenswert.

remedy ['remədɪ] n (medicine) Heilmittel das ; (solution) Lösung die.

remember [rɪ'membə'] vt sich erinnern an (+A) ; (not forget) denken an (+A). ◆ vi sich erinnern ; to ~ doing sthg sich daran erinnern, etw getan zu haben ; to ~ to do sthg daran denken, etw zu tun.

remind [rɪ'maɪnd] vt : to ~ sb of sthg jn an etw (A) erinnern ; to ~ sb to do sthg jn daran erinnern, etw zu tun.

reminder [rɪ'maɪndə'] n (for bill, library book) Mahnung die.

remittance [rɪ'mɪtns] n (money) Überweisung die.

remnant ['remnənt] n Rest der.

remote [rɪ'məʊt] adj entfernt.

remote control n (device) Fernbedienung die.

removal [rɪ'muːvl] n Entfernung die ; (of furniture) Umzug der.

removal van n Möbelwagen der.

remove [rɪ'muːv] vt entfernen ; (clothes) ausziehen.

renew [rɪ'njuː] vt (licence, membership) verlängern.

renovate ['renəveɪt] vt renovieren.

renowned [rɪ'naund] adj berühmt.

rent [rent] n Miete die. ◆ vt mieten.

rental ['rentl] n (money) Leihgebühr die.

repaid [riː'peɪd] pt & pp → repay.

repair [rɪ'peəʳ] vt reparieren. ◆ n : in good ~ in gutem Zustand. ▪ **repairs** npl Reparatur die.

repair kit n (for bicycle) Flickzeug das.

repay [riː'peɪ] (pt & pp repaid) vt (money) zurücklzahlen ; (favour, kindness) sich revanchieren für.

repayment [riː'peɪmənt] n Rückzahlung die.

repeat [rɪ'piːt] vt wiederholen. ◆ n (on TV, radio) Wiederholung die.

repetition [ˌrepɪ'tɪʃn] n Wiederholung die.

repetitive [rɪ'petɪtɪv] adj eintönig.

replace [rɪ'pleɪs] vt ersetzen ; (put back) zurücklsetzen.

replacement [rɪ'pleɪsmənt] n Ersatz der.

replay ['riːpleɪ] n (rematch) Wiederholungsspiel das ; (on TV) Wiederholung die.

reply [rɪ'plaɪ] n Antwort die. ◆ vt & vi antworten (+D).

report [rɪ'pɔːt] n Bericht der ; (Br : SCH) Zeugnis das. ◆ vt (announce) berichten ; (theft, disappearance, person) melden. ◆ vi : to ~ (on) berichten (über (+A)) ; to ~ sb (go to) sich jm melden.

report card n Zeugnis das.

reporter [rɪ'pɔːtəʳ] n Reporter der (-in die).

represent [ˌreprɪ'zent] vt (act on behalf of) vertreten ; (symbolize) darstellen.

representative [ˌreprɪ'zentətɪv] n Vertreter der (-in die).

repress [rɪ'pres] vt unterdrücken.

reprieve [rɪ'priːv] n (delay) Aufschub der.

reprimand ['reprɪmɑːnd] vt tadeln.

reproach [rɪ'prəutʃ] vt Vorwürfe machen (+D).

reproduction [ˌriːprə'dʌkʃn] n (of painting, furniture) Reproduktion die.

reptile ['reptaɪl] n Reptil das.

republic [rɪ'pʌblɪk] n Republik die.

Republican [rɪ'pʌblɪkən] n (in US) Republikaner der (-in die). ◆ adj (in US) republikanisch.

repulsive [rɪ'pʌlsɪv] adj abstoßend.

reputable ['repjutəbl] adj angesehen.

reputation [ˌrepju'teɪʃn] n Ruf der.

reputedly [rɪ'pjuːtɪdlɪ] adv angeblich.

request [rɪ'kwest] n Bitte die.
◆ vt bitten um ; **to ~ sb to do sthg** jn bitten, etw zu tun ; **available on ~** auf Anfrage erhältlich.

request stop n (Br) Bedarfshaltestelle die.

require [rɪ'kwaɪə'] vt (need) brauchen ; **to be ~d to do sthg** etw tun müssen.

requirement [rɪ'kwaɪəmənt] n (condition) Erfordernis das ; (need) Bedarf der.

resat [,riː'sæt] pt & pp → **resit**.

rescue ['reskjuː] vt retten.

research [,rɪ'sɜːtʃ] n Forschung die.

resemblance [rɪ'zembləns] n Ähnlichkeit die.

resemble [rɪ'zembl] vt ähneln (+D).

resent [rɪ'zent] vt übel nehmen.

reservation [,rezə'veɪʃn] n (booking) Reservierung die ; (doubt) Zweifel der ; **to make a ~** reservieren.

reserve [rɪ'zɜːv] n (SPORT) Reservespieler der (-in die) ; (for wildlife) Reservat das. ◆ vt reservieren.

reserved [rɪ'zɜːvd] adj (booked) reserviert ; (shy) verschlossen.

reservoir ['rezəvwɑː'] n Reservoir das.

reset [,riː'set] (pt & pp **reset**) vt (watch, meter, device) neu stellen.

reside [rɪ'zaɪd] vi (fml : live) wohnhaft sein.

residence ['rezɪdəns] n (fml : house) Wohnsitz der ; **place of ~** Wohnsitz der.

residence permit n Aufenthaltserlaubnis die.

resident ['rezɪdənt] n (of country) Bewohner der (-in die) ; (of hotel) Gast der ; (of area) Anwohner der (-in die) ; (of house) Hausbewohner der (-in die) ; **'~s only'** (for parking) 'Parken nur für Anlieger'.

residential [,rezɪ'denʃl] adj (area) Wohn-.

residue ['rezɪdjuː] n Rest der.

resign [rɪ'zaɪn] vi (from job) kündigen. ◆ vt : **to ~ o.s. to sthg** sich mit etw abfinden.

resignation [,rezɪg'neɪʃn] n (from job) Kündigung die.

resilient [rɪ'zɪlɪənt] adj unverwüstlich.

resist [rɪ'zɪst] vt (temptation) widerstehen (+D) ; (fight against) sich widersetzen (+D) ; **I can't ~ cream cakes** ich kann Sahnetorte nicht widerstehen ; **to ~ doing sthg** etw nicht tun.

resistance [rɪ'zɪstəns] n Widerstand der.

resit [,riː'sɪt] (pt & pp **resat**) vt wiederholen.

resolution [,rezə'luːʃn] n (promise) Vorsatz der.

resolve [rɪ'zɒlv] vt (solve) lösen.

resort [rɪ'zɔːt] n (for holidays) Urlaubsort der ; **as a last ~** als letzter Ausweg. ■ **resort to** vt fus zurück|greifen auf (+A) ; **to ~ to doing sthg** darauf zurückgreifen, etw zu tun.

resourceful [rɪ'sɔːsfʊl] *adj* erfinderisch.

resources [rɪ'sɔːsɪz] *npl* Ressourcen *pl*.

respect [rɪ'spekt] *n* Respekt *der*; *(aspect)* Aspekt *der*. ◆ *vt* respektieren; **in some ~s** in mancher Hinsicht; **with ~ to** in Bezug auf *(+A)*.

respectable [rɪ'spektəbl] *adj* *(person, job etc)* anständig; *(acceptable)* ansehnlich.

respective [rɪ'spektɪv] *adj* jeweilig.

respond [rɪ'spɒnd] *vi* *(reply)* antworten; *(react)* reagieren.

response [rɪ'spɒns] *n* *(reply)* Antwort *die*; *(reaction)* Reaktion *die*.

responsibility [rɪ,spɒnsə-'bɪlətɪ] *n* Verantwortung *die*.

responsible [rɪ'spɒnsəbl] *adj* *(in charge)* verantwortlich; *(sensible)* verantwortungsbewusst; **to be ~ (for)** *(in charge, to blame)* verantwortlich sein (für).

rest [rest] *n* *(break)* Ruhepause *die*; *(support)* Stütze *die*. ◆ *vi* *(relax)* sich ausruhen; **the ~** *(remainder)* der Rest; **to have a ~** sich ausruhen; **to ~ against** lehnen an *(+A)*.

restaurant ['restərɒnt] *n* Restaurant *das*.

restaurant car *n (Br)* Speisewagen *der*.

restful ['restfʊl] *adj* erholsam.

restless ['restlɪs] *adj* *(bored, impatient)* ruhelos; *(fidgety)* unruhig.

restore [rɪ'stɔː'] *vt* *(reintroduce)* wiederherstellen; *(renovate)* renovieren.

restrain [rɪ'streɪn] *vt* zurückhalten.

restrict [rɪ'strɪkt] *vt* beschränken.

restricted [rɪ'strɪktɪd] *adj* beschränkt.

restriction [rɪ'strɪkʃn] *n* Beschränkung *die*.

rest room *n (Am)* Toilette *die*.

result [rɪ'zʌlt] *n* *(outcome)* Ergebnis *das*; *(consequence)* Folge *die*. ◆ *vi*: **to ~ in** zur Folge haben; **as a ~** infolgedessen. ■ **results** *npl* *(of test, exam)* Ergebnisse *pl*.

resume [rɪ'zjuːm] *vi* wieder beginnen.

résumé ['rezjʊmeɪ] *n* *(summary)* Zusammenfassung *die*; *(Am: curriculum vitae)* Lebenslauf *der*.

retail ['riːteɪl] *n* Einzelhandel *der*. ◆ *vt* *(sell)* im Einzelhandel verkaufen. ◆ *vi*: **to ~ at** (im Einzelhandel) kosten.

retailer ['riːteɪlə'] *n* Einzelhändler *der* (-in *die*).

retail price *n* Einzelhandelspreis *der*.

retain [rɪ'teɪn] *vt* *(fml: keep)* bewahren.

retaliate [rɪ'tælɪeɪt] *vi* sich rächen.

retire [rɪ'taɪə'] *vi* *(stop working)* in den Ruhestand treten.

retired [rɪ'taɪəd] *adj* pensioniert.

retirement [rɪ'taɪəmənt] *n* *(leaving job)* Pensionierung *die*; *(period after retiring)* Ruhestand *der*.

retreat [rɪ'triːt] *vi* sich zurück|ziehen. ◆ *n (place)* Zufluchtsort *der*.

retrieve [rɪ'triːv] *vt (get back)* zurück|holen.

return [rɪ'tɜːn] *n (arrival back)* Rückkehr *die*; *(Br: ticket)* Rückfahrkarte *die*; *(Br: for plane)* Rückflugticket *das*. ◆ *vt (put back)* zurück|stellen; *(give back)* zurück|geben; *(ball, serve)* zurück|schlagen. ◆ *vi (come back)* zurück|kommen; *(go back)* zurück|gehen; *(drive back)* zurück|fahren; *(happen again)* wieder auf|treten. ◆ *adj (journey)* Rück-; **to ~ sthg (to sb)** *(give back)* (jm) etw zurück|geben; **by ~ of post** *(Br)* postwendend; **many happy ~s!** herzlichen Glückwunsch zum Geburtstag!; **in ~ (for)** als Gegenleistung (für).

return flight *n* Rückflug *der*.

return ticket *n (Br: for train, bus)* Rückfahrkarte *die*; *(for plane)* Rückflugticket *das*.

reunification [ˌriːjuːnɪfɪ'keɪʃn] *n* Wiedervereinigung *die*.

reunite [ˌriːjuː'naɪt] *vt* wieder|vereinigen.

reveal [rɪ'viːl] *vt* enthüllen.

revelation [ˌrevə'leɪʃn] *n* Enthüllung *die*.

revenge [rɪ'vendʒ] *n* Rache *die*.

reverse [rɪ'vɜːs] *adj* umgekehrt. ◆ *n (AUT)* Rückwärtsgang *der*; *(of coin, document)* Rückseite *die*. ◆ *vt (car)* rückwärts fahren; *(decision)* rückgängig machen. ◆ *vi (car, driver)* rückwärts fahren; **the ~** *(opposite)* das Gegenteil; **in ~ order** in umgekehrter Reihenfolge; **to ~ the charges** *(Br)* ein R-Gespräch führen.

reverse-charge call *n (Br)* R-Gespräch *das*.

review [rɪ'vjuː] *n (of book, record, film)* Kritik *die*; *(examination)* Prüfung *die*. ◆ *vt (Am: for exam)* wiederholen.

revise [rɪ'vaɪz] *vt (reconsider)* revidieren. ◆ *vi (Br: for exam)* wiederholen.

revision [rɪ'vɪʒn] *n (Br: for exam)* Wiederholung *die*.

revive [rɪ'vaɪv] *vt (person)* wieder|beleben; *(economy, custom)* wieder auf|leben lassen.

revolt [rɪ'vəʊlt] *n* Revolte *die*.

revolting [rɪ'vəʊltɪŋ] *adj* scheußlich.

revolution [ˌrevə'luːʃn] *n* Revolution *die*.

revolutionary [revə'luːʃnərɪ] *adj* revolutionär.

revolver [rɪ'vɒlvəʳ] *n* Revolver *der*.

revolving door [rɪ'vɒlvɪŋ-] *n* Drehtür *die*.

revue [rɪ'vjuː] *n* Revue *die*.

reward [rɪ'wɔːd] *n* Belohnung *die*. ◆ *vt* belohnen.

rewind [ˌriː'waɪnd] *(pt & pp* rewound [ˌriː'waʊnd]) *vt* zurück|spulen.

rheumatism ['ruːmətɪzm] *n* Rheuma *das*.

Rhine [raɪn] *n*: **the ~** der Rhein.

rhinoceros [raɪ'nɒsərəs] *(pl* inv OR **-es**) *n* Nashorn *das*.

rhubarb ['ruːbɑːb] *n* Rhabarber *der*.

rhyme [raɪm] n Reim der. ◆ vi sich reimen.

rhythm ['rɪðm] n Rhythmus der.

rib [rɪb] n Rippe die.

ribbon ['rɪbən] n Band das; (for typewriter) Farbband das.

rice [raɪs] n Reis der.

rice pudding n Milchreis der.

rich [rɪtʃ] adj reich; (food) schwer. ◆ npl : the ~ die Reichen pl; to be ~ in sth reich an etw (D) sein.

ricotta cheese [rɪ'kɒtə-] n Ricottakäse der.

rid [rɪd] vt : to get ~ of los|werden.

ridden ['rɪdn] pp → ride.

riddle ['rɪdl] n Rätsel das.

ride [raɪd] (pt rode, pp ridden) n (on horse) Ritt der; (on bike, in vehicle) Fahrt die. ◆ vt (horse) reiten; (bike) fahren mit. ◆ vi (on horse) reiten; (on bike) Rad fahren; (in vehicle) fahren; to go for a ~ (in car) eine Spritztour machen.

rider ['raɪdə'] n (on horse) Reiter der (-in die); (on bike) Fahrer der (-in die).

ridge [rɪdʒ] n (of mountain) Kamm der; (raised surface) Erhebung die.

ridiculous [rɪ'dɪkjʊləs] adj lächerlich.

riding ['raɪdɪŋ] n Reiten das.

riding school n Reitschule die.

rifle ['raɪfl] n Gewehr das.

rig [rɪg] n (offshore) Bohrinsel die. ◆ vt (fix) manipulieren.

right [raɪt] adj 1. (correct) richtig; to be ~ (person) Recht haben; you were ~ to tell me es

war richtig von dir, mir das zu erzählen; have you got the ~ time? haben Sie/hast du die genaue Uhrzeit?; that's ~! das stimmt! das ist richtig! 2. (fair) richtig, gerecht; that's not ~! das ist nicht richtig! 3. (on the right) rechte(-r) (-s); the ~ side of the road die rechte Straßenseite.

◆ n 1. (side) : the ~ die rechte Seite.

2. (entitlement) Recht das; to have the ~ to do sth das Recht haben, etw zu tun.

◆ adv 1. (towards the right) rechts; turn ~ at the post office biegen Sie am Postamt nach rechts ab.

2. (correctly) richtig; am I pronouncing it ~? spreche ich es richtig aus?

3. (for emphasis) genau; ~ here genau hier; I'll be ~ back ich bin gleich zurück; ~ away sofort.

right angle n rechter Winkel.

right-hand adj rechte(-r) (-s).

right-hand drive n Auto das mit Rechtssteuerung.

right-handed [-'hændɪd] adj (person) rechtshändig; (implement) für Rechtshänder.

rightly ['raɪtlɪ] adv (correctly) richtig; (justly) zu Recht.

right of way n (AUT) Vorfahrt die; (path) öffentlicher Weg.

right-wing adj rechte(-r) (-s).

rigid ['rɪdʒɪd] adj starr.

rim [rɪm] n Rand der.

rind [raɪnd] n (of fruit) Schale die; (of bacon) Schwarte die; (of cheese) Rinde die.

ring [rɪŋ] (pt rang, pp rung) n Ring der; (of people) Kreis der;

(sound) Klingeln *das* ; *(on cooker)* Kochplatte *die* ; *(in circus)* Manege *die*. ◆ *vt (Br : make phone call to)* anlrufen ; *(bell)* läuten. ◆ *vi (bell, telephone)* klingeln ; *(Br : make phone call)* telefonieren ; **to give sb a ~** *(phone call)* anlrufen ; **to ~ the bell** *(of house, office)* klingeln, läuten. ▪ **ring back** *vt sep & vi (Br)* zurücklrufen. ▪ **ring off** *vi (Br)* auflegen. ▪ **ring up** *vt sep & vi (Br)* anlrufen.

ringing tone ['rɪŋɪŋ-] *n* Freizeichen *das*.

ring road *n* Ringstraße *die*.

rink [rɪŋk] *n* Eisbahn *die*.

rinse [rɪns] *vt (clothes, hair)* auslspülen ; *(hands)* ablspülen. ▪ **rinse out** *vt sep (clothes, mouth)* auslspülen.

riot ['raɪət] *n* Aufruhr *der* ; **~s** Unruhen *pl*.

rip [rɪp] *n* Riss *der*. ◆ *vt & vi* zerreißen. ▪ **rip up** *vt sep* zerreißen.

ripe [raɪp] *adj* reif.

ripen ['raɪpn] *vi* reifen.

rip-off *n (inf)* Betrug *der*.

rise [raɪz] *(pt* rose, *pp* risen ['rɪzn]) *vi* steigen ; *(sun, moon)* auflgehen ; *(stand up)* auflstehen. ◆ *n (increase)* Anstieg *der* ; *(Br : pay increase)* Gehaltserhöhung *die* ; *(slope)* Anhöhe *die*.

risk [rɪsk] *n* Risiko *das*. ◆ *vt* riskieren ; **to take a ~** ein Risiko einlgehen ; **at your own ~** auf eigenes Risiko ; **to ~ doing sthg** riskieren, etw zu tun ; **to ~ it** es riskieren.

risky ['rɪskɪ] *adj* riskant.

risotto [rɪ'zɒtəʊ] *(pl* -s) *n* Risotto *das*.

ritual ['rɪtʃʊəl] *n* Ritual *das*.

rival ['raɪvl] *adj* gegnerisch. ◆ *n* Rivale *der* (Rivalin *die*).

river ['rɪvə'] *n* Fluss *der*.

river bank *n* Flussufer *das*.

riverside ['rɪvəsaɪd] *n* Flussufer *das*.

Riviera [,rɪvɪ'eərə] *n* : **the (French) ~** die (französische) Riviera.

roach [rəʊtʃ] *n (Am : cockroach)* Kakerlake *die*.

road [rəʊd] *n* Straße *die* ; **by ~** mit dem Auto.

road book *n* Straßenatlas *der*.

road map *n* Straßenkarte *die*.

road safety *n* Straßensicherheit *die*.

roadside ['rəʊdsaɪd] *n* : **the ~** der Straßenrand.

road sign *n* Straßenschild *das*.

road tax *n* Kraftfahrzeugsteuer *die*.

roadway ['rəʊdweɪ] *n* Fahrbahn *die*.

road works *npl* Straßenarbeiten *pl*.

roam [rəʊm] *vi* herumlstreifen.

roar [rɔː'] *n (of crowd)* Gebrüll *das* ; *(of aeroplane)* Dröhnen *das*. ◆ *vi (lion, crowd)* brüllen ; *(traffic)* donnern.

roast [rəʊst] *n* Braten *der*. ◆ *vt (meat)* braten. ◆ *adj* : **~ beef** Rinderbraten *der* ; **~ chicken** Brathähnchen *das*, Broiler *der* (Österr) (Ostdt) ; **~ lamb** Lammbraten *der* ; **~ pork** Schweinebraten *der* ; **~ potatoes** Bratkartoffeln *pl*.

rob [rɒb] vt (house, bank) ausl-
rauben ; (person) berauben ; **to
~ sb of sthg** jm etw stehlen.

robber ['rɒbə'] n Räuber der
(-in die).

robbery ['rɒbərɪ] n Raub der.

robe [rəub] n (Am : bathrobe)
Bademantel der.

robin ['rɒbɪn] n Rotkehlchen
das.

robot ['rəubɒt] n Roboter der.

rock [rɒk] n (boulder) Felsen
der ; (Am : stone) Stein der ;
(substance) Stein der ; (music)
Rock der ; (Br : sweet) Zu-
ckerstange die. ◆ vt schaukeln ;
on the ~s (drink) on the rocks.

rock climbing n Klettern
das ; **to go ~** klettern gehen.

rocket ['rɒkɪt] n Rakete die.

rocking chair ['rɒkɪŋ-] n
Schaukelstuhl der.

rock 'n' roll [,rɒkən'rəul] n
Rock'n'Roll der.

rocky ['rɒkɪ] adj felsig.

rod [rɒd] n (pole) Stange die ;
(for fishing) Angelrute die.

rode [rəud] pt → ride.

roe [rəu] n Fischrogen der.

role [rəul] n Rolle die.

roll [rəul] n (of bread) Brötchen
das, Semmel die (Süddt)
(Österr) ; (of film, paper) Rolle
die. ◆ vi rollen ; (ship) schlin-
gern. ◆ vt rollen ; **to ~ the dice**
würfeln. ▪ **roll over** vi (person,
animal) sich drehen ; (car) sich
überschlagen. ▪ **roll up** vt sep
(map, carpet) aufrollen ;
(sleeves, trousers) hochkrem-
peln.

roller coaster ['rəulə,kəustə']
n Achterbahn die.

roller skate ['rəulə-] n Rollschuh der.

roller-skating ['rəulə-] n
Rollschuhlaufen das.

rolling pin ['rəulɪŋ-] n Nudel-
holz das.

Roman ['rəumən] adj römisch.
◆ n Römer der (-in die).

Roman Catholic n Katholik
der (-in die).

romance [rəu'mæns] n (love)
Romantik die ; (love affair) Ro-
manze die ; (novel) Liebesro-
man der.

Romania [ru:'meɪnjə] n Ru-
mänien nt.

romantic [rəu'mæntɪk] adj romantisch.

romper suit ['rɒmpə-] n
Strampelanzug der.

roof [ru:f] n Dach das.

roof rack n Dachgepäckträger der.

room [rum, ru:m] n Zimmer
das ; (space) Platz der.

room number n Zimmer-
nummer die.

room service n Zimmerservice der.

room temperature n Zim-
mertemperatur die.

roomy ['ru:mɪ] adj geräumig.

root [ru:t] n Wurzel die.

rope [rəup] n Seil das. ◆ vt
festbinden.

rose [rəuz] pt → rise. ◆ n Rose
die.

rosé ['rəuzeɪ] n Roséwein der.

rosemary ['rəuzmərɪ] n Ros-
marin der.

rot [rɒt] vi verfaulen.

rota ['rəutə] n Dienstplan der.

rotate [rəu'teɪt] vi rotieren.

rotten ['rɒtn] adj (food, wood) verfault ; (inf : not good) mies ; I feel ~ (ill) ich fühle mich lausig.

rouge [ru:ʒ] n Rouge das.

rough [rʌf] adj (road, ground) uneben ; (surface, skin, cloth, conditions) rau ; (sea, crossing) stürmisch ; (person, estimate) grob ; (area, town) unsicher ; (wine) sauer. ◆ n (on golf course) Rough das ; at a ~ guess grob geschätzt ; to have a ~ time es schwer haben.

roughly ['rʌflɪ] adv (approximately) ungefähr ; (push, handle) grob.

roulade [ru:'lɑ:d] n (savoury) Roulade die ; (sweet) Rolle die.

roulette [ru:'let] n Roulette das.

round [raʊnd] adj rund.
◆ n 1. (gen) Runde die.
2. (of sandwiches) belegtes Brot mit zwei Scheiben Brot.
3. (of toast) Scheibe die.
◆ adv 1. (in a circle) : to go ~ sich drehen ; to spin ~ sich im Kreis drehen.
2. (surrounding) herum ; it had a fence all (the way) ~ es hatte einen Zaun rundherum.
3. (near) : ~ about in der Nähe.
4. (to someone's house) : why don't you come ~? warum kommst du nicht vorbei? ; to ask some friends ~ ein paar Freunde zu sich einladen.
5. (continuously) : all year ~ das ganze Jahr über.
◆ prep 1. (surrounding, circling) um... herum ; to go ~ the corner um die Ecke gehen ; we walked ~ the lake wir gingen um den See herum.

2. (visiting) : to go ~ a museum ein Museum besuchen ; to go ~ a town sich eine Stadt ansehen ; to show sb ~ sthg jn in etw (D) herumführen.
3. (approximately) rund ; ~ (about) 100 rund 100 ; ~ ten o'clock gegen zehn Uhr.
4. (near) : ~ here hier in der Nähe.
5. (in phrases) : it's just ~ the corner (nearby) es ist gerade um die Ecke ; ~ the clock rund um die Uhr.

■ **round off** vt sep (meal, day, visit) ablrunden.

roundabout ['raʊndəbaʊt] n (Br : in road) Kreisverkehr der ; (at fairground, in playground) Karussell das.

rounders ['raʊndəz] n dem Baseball ähnliches britisches Ballspiel.

round trip n Hin- und Rückfahrt die.

route [ru:t] n Route die ; (of bus) Linie die. ◆ vt (flight, plane) die Route festlegen für.

routine [ru:'ti:n] n Routine die ; (pej : drudgery) Trott der. ◆ adj Routine-.

row[1] [rəʊ] n (line) Reihe die. ◆ vt & vi rudern ; in a ~ (in succession) nacheinander.

row[2] [raʊ] n (argument) Streit der ; (inf : noise) Krach der ; to have a ~ sich streiten.

rowboat ['rəʊbəʊt] (Am) = rowing boat.

rowdy ['raʊdɪ] adj rowdyhaft.

rowing ['rəʊɪŋ] n Rudern das.

rowing boat n (Br) Ruderboot das.

royal ['rɔɪəl] adj königlich.

royal family *n* königliche Familie.

ⓘ ROYAL FAMILY

Die britische königliche Familie besteht aus dem Monarchen und seiner Familie. Ihr derzeitiges Oberhaupt ist Königin Elizabeth. Weitere direkte Mitglieder der königlichen Familie sind der Gatte der Königin, Prinz Philip (auch Duke of Edinburgh genannt), ihre Söhne Prinz Charles (auch Prince of Wales genannt), Prinz Andrew und Prinz Edward und ihre Tochter Prinzessin Anne. Wenn Mitglieder der königlichen Familie einer offiziellen Zeremonie beiwohnen, wird die Nationalhymne gespielt. Immer dann, wenn sie sich in einem ihrer Paläste in Residenz befinden, weht dort die britische Flagge, der Union Jack.

royalty ['rɔɪəltɪ] *n* Mitglieder *pl* der königlichen Familie.

RRP *(abbr of recommended retail price)* unverbindliche Preisempfehlung.

rub [rʌb] *vt* reiben ; *(polish)* polieren. ◆ *vi (with hand, cloth)* reiben ; *(shoes)* scheuern. ▣ **rub in** *vt sep (lotion, oil)* einlreiben. ▣ **rub out** *vt sep (erase)* auslradieren.

rubber ['rʌbəʳ] *adj* Gummi-. ◆ *n* Gummi *das* ; *(Br : eraser)* Radiergummi *der* ; *(Am : inf : condom)* Gummi *der*.

rubber band *n* Gummiband *das*.

rubber gloves *npl* Gummihandschuhe *pl*.

rubber ring *n* Gummiring *der*.

rubbish ['rʌbɪʃ] *n (refuse)* Müll *der* ; *(inf : worthless thing)* Schund *der* ; *(inf : nonsense)* Quatsch *der*.

rubbish bin *n (Br)* Mülleimer *der*.

rubbish dump *n (Br)* Müllhalde *die*.

rubble ['rʌbl] *n* Schutt *der*.

ruby ['ru:bɪ] *n* Rubin *der*.

rucksack ['rʌksæk] *n* Rucksack *der*.

rudder ['rʌdəʳ] *n* Ruder *das*.

rude [ru:d] *adj* unhöflich ; *(joke, picture)* unanständig.

rug [rʌg] *n* Läufer *der* ; *(large)* Teppich *der* ; *(Br : blanket)* Wolldecke *die*.

rugby ['rʌgbɪ] *n* Rugby *das*.

ruin ['ru:ɪn] *vt* ruinieren. ▣ **ruins** *npl* Ruinen *pl*.

ruined ['ru:ɪnd] *adj (building)* zerstört ; *(clothes, meal, holiday)* ruiniert.

rule [ru:l] *n* Regel *die*. ◆ *vt (country)* regieren ; **against the ~s** gegen die Regeln ; **as a ~** in der Regel. ▣ **rule out** *vt sep* auslschließen.

ruler ['ru:ləʳ] *n (of country)* Herrscher *der* (-in *die*) ; *(for measuring)* Lineal *das*.

rum [rʌm] *n* Rum *der*.

rumor ['ru:məʳ] *(Am)* = **rumour**.

rumour ['ruːmə] n (Br) Gerücht das.

rump steak [,rʌmp-] n Rumpsteak das.

run [rʌn] (pt ran, pp run) vi 1. (on foot) rennen, laufen; we had to ~ for the bus wir mussten rennen, um den Bus zu erwischen.
2. (train, bus) fahren; the bus ~s every hour jede Stunde; the train is running an hour late der Zug hat eine Stunde Verspätung.
3. (operate) laufen; to ~ on unleaded petrol mit bleifreiem Benzin fahren.
4. (tears, liquid) laufen.
5. (road, track) führen, verlaufen; (river) fließen; the path ~s along the coast der Weg verläuft entlang der Küste.
6. (play, event) laufen; 'now running at the Palladium' 'jetzt im Palladium'.
7. (tap) laufen.
8. (nose) laufen; (eyes) tränen; my nose is running mir läuft die Nase.
9. (colour) ausllaufen; (clothes) ablfärben.
10. (remain valid) gültig sein, laufen; the offer ~s until July das Angebot gilt bis Juli.
◆ vt 1. (on foot) rennen, laufen.
2. (compete in): to ~ a race ein Rennen laufen.
3. (business, hotel) führen; (course) leiten.
4. (bus, train): we're running a special bus to the airport wir betreiben einen Sonderbus zum Flughafen.
5. (take in car) fahren; I'll ~ you home ich fahre dich nach Hause.
6. (bath): to ~ a bath ein Bad einllassen.
◆ n 1. (on foot) Lauf der; to go for a ~ laufen gehen.
2. (in car) Fahrt die; to go for a ~ eine Fahrt machen.
3. (of play, show) Laufzeit die.
4. (for skiing) Piste die.
5. (Am: in tights) Laufmasche die.
6. (in phrases): in the long ~ auf lange Sicht (gesehen).

▨ **run away** vi weglrennen, weglaufen.

▨ **run down** vt sep (run over) überlfahren; (criticize) herunterlmachen.
◆ vi (battery) leer werden.

▨ **run into** vt fus (meet) zufällig treffen; (subj: car) laufen gegen, fahren gegen; (problem, difficulty) stoßen auf (A).

▨ **run out** vi (supply) auslgehen.

▨ **run out of** vt fus: we've out of petrol/money wir haben kein Benzin/Geld mehr.

▨ **run over** vt sep (hit) überlfahren.

runaway ['rʌnəweɪ] n Ausreißer der (-in die).

rung [rʌŋ] pp → ring. ◆ n (of ladder) Sprosse die.

runner ['rʌnə] n (person) Läufer der (-in die); (for door, drawer) Laufschiene die; (of sledge) Kufe die.

runner bean n Stangenbohne die.

runner-up (pl runners-up) n Zweite der, die.

running ['rʌnɪŋ] n (SPORT) Laufen das; (management) Leitung die. ◆ adj: three days ~ drei Tage hintereinander; to go ~ joggen gehen.

running water n fließendes Wasser.

runny ['rʌnɪ] adj (sauce, egg, omelette) dünnflüssig; (eye) tränend; (nose) laufend.

runway ['rʌnweɪ] n Landebahn die.

rural ['rʊərəl] adj ländlich.

rush [rʌʃ] n Eile die; (of crowd) Andrang der. ◆ vi (move quickly) rasen; (hurry) sich beeilen. ◆ vt (food) hastig essen; (work) hastig erledigen; (transport quickly) schnell transportieren; to be in a ~ in Eile sein; there's no ~! keine Eile!; don't ~ me! hetz mich nicht!

rush hour n Hauptverkehrszeit die, Stoßzeit die.

Russia ['rʌʃə] n Russland nt.

Russian ['rʌʃn] adj russisch. ◆ n (person) Russe der (Russin die); (language) Russisch das.

rust [rʌst] n Rost der. ◆ vi rosten.

rustic ['rʌstɪk] adj rustikal.

rustle ['rʌsl] vi rascheln.

rustproof ['rʌstpruːf] adj rostfrei.

rusty ['rʌstɪ] adj rostig; (fig: language, person) eingerostet.

RV n (Am: abbr of recreational vehicle) Wohnmobil das.

rye [raɪ] n Roggen der.

rye bread n Roggenbrot das.

S

S (abbr of south, small) S.

saccharin ['sækərɪn] n Saccharin das.

sachet ['sæʃeɪ] n (of shampoo, cream) Briefchen das, (of sugar, coffee) Tütchen das.

sack [sæk] n (bag) Sack der. ◆ vt entlassen; to get the ~ entlassen werden.

sacrifice ['sækrɪfaɪs] n (fig) Opfer das.

sad [sæd] adj traurig; (unfortunate) bedauerlich.

saddle ['sædl] n Sattel der.

saddlebag ['sædlbæg] n Satteltasche die.

sadly ['sædlɪ] adv (unfortunately) leider; (unhappily) traurig.

sadness ['sædnɪs] n Traurigkeit die.

s.a.e. n (Br: abbr of stamped addressed envelope) adressierter Freiumschlag.

safari park [sə'fɑːrɪ-] n Safaripark der.

safe [seɪf] adj sicher; (out of harm) in Sicherheit. ◆ n Safe der; a ~ place ein sicherer Platz; (have a) ~ journey! gute Fahrt!; ~ and sound gesund und wohlbehalten.

safe-deposit box n Tresorfach das.

safely ['seɪflɪ] adv sicher; (arrive) gut.

safety ['seɪftɪ] n Sicherheit die.

safety belt n Sicherheitsgurt der.

safety pin n Sicherheitsnadel die.

sag [sæg] vi (hang down) durchhängen; (sink) absacken, einsinken.

sage [seɪdʒ] n (herb) Salbei der.

Sagittarius [,sædʒɪˈteərɪəs] n
Schütze der.

said [sed] pt & pp → say.

sail [seɪl] n Segel das. ◆ vi segeln ; (ship) fahren ; (depart)
abfahren. ◆ vt : to ~ a boat
segeln ; to set ~ auslaufen.

sailboat['seɪlbəʊt] (Am) = sailing boat.

sailing ['seɪlɪŋ] n Segeln das ;
(departure) Abfahrt die ; to go ~
segeln gehen.

sailing boat n Segelboot das.

sailor ['seɪlə'] n (on ferry, cargo
ship etc) Seemann der ; (in navy)
Matrose der.

saint [seɪnt] n Heilige der, die.

sake [seɪk] n : for my/their ~ um
meinetwillen/ihretwillen ; for
God's ~! um Gottes willen!

salad ['sæləd] n Salat der.

salad bar n Salatbar die.

salad bowl n Salatschüssel
die.

salad cream n (Br) Salatma-
jonäse die.

salad dressing n Salatsoße
die.

salami [səˈlɑːmɪ] n Salami die.

salary ['sælərɪ] n Gehalt das.

sale [seɪl] n Verkauf der ; (at reduced prices) Ausverkauf der ;
'for ~' 'zu verkaufen' ; on ~ im
Handel ; on ~ at erhältlich bei.
■ **sales** npl(COMM) Absatz der ;
the ~s (at reduced prices) der
Ausverkauf.

sales assistant ['seɪlz-] n
Verkäufer der (-in die).

salesclerk ['seɪlzklɜːrk] (Am)
= sales assistant.

salesman ['seɪlzmən] n (pl -men
[-mən]) n (in shop) Verkäufer
der ; (rep) Vertreter der.

sales rep(resentative) n
Vertreter der (-in die).

saleswoman ['seɪlz,wʊmən]
(pl -women [-,wɪmɪn]) n Ver-
käuferin die.

saliva [səˈlaɪvə] n Speichel der.

salmon ['sæmən] n (pl salmon)
Lachs der.

salon ['sælɒn] n (hairdresser's)
Salon der.

saloon [səˈluːn] n (Br : car) Li-
mousine die ; (Am : bar) Saloon
der ; ~ (bar) (Br) Nebenraum eines Pubs mit mehr Komfort.

salopettes [,sælə'pets] npl
Skihose die.

salt [sɔːlt, sɒlt] n Salz das.

saltcellar ['sɔːlt,selə'] n (Br)
Salzstreuer der.

salted peanuts ['sɔːltɪd-] npl
gesalzene Erdnüsse pl.

salt shaker [-,ʃeɪkə'] (Am) =
saltcellar.

salty ['sɔːltɪ] adj salzig.

salute [səˈluːt] n Salut der. ◆ vi
salutieren.

same [seɪm] adj : the ~ (un-
changed) der/die/das Gleiche,
die Gleichen (pl) ; (identical)
derselbe/dieselbe/dasselbe,
dieselben (pl).
◆ pron : the ~ derselbe/die-
selbe/dasselbe, dieselben (pl) ;
they look the ~ sie sehen gleich
aus ; I'll have the ~ as her ich
möchte das Gleiche wie sie ;
you've got the ~ book as me du
hast das gleiche Buch wie ich ;
it's all the ~ to me es ist mir
gleich ; all the ~ trotzdem ; the
~ to you gleichfalls.

samosa [səˈməʊsə] n gefüllte
und frittierte dreieckige indische
Teigtasche.

sample ['sɑːmpl] n (of work, product) Muster das ; (of blood, urine) Probe die. ◆ vt (food, drink) probieren.

sanctions ['sæŋkʃnz] npl Sanktionen pl.

sanctuary ['sæŋktʃʊərɪ] n (for birds, animals) Tierschutzgebiet das.

sand [sænd] n Sand der. ◆ vt (wood) abschmirgeln. ▪ **sands** npl (beach) Strand der.

sandal ['sændl] n Sandale die.

sandcastle ['sænd,kɑːsl] n Sandburg die.

sandpaper ['sænd,peɪpə'] n Sandpapier das.

sandwich ['sænwɪdʒ] n Sandwich das.

sandwich bar n ≃ Imbissbar die.

sandy ['sændɪ] adj (beach) sandig ; (hair) dunkelblond.

sang [sæŋ] pt → **sing**.

sanitary ['sænɪtrɪ] adj (conditions, measures) Hygiene- ; (hygienic) Hygiene-.

sanitary napkin (Am) = **sanitary towel**.

sanitary towel n (Br) Monatsbinde die.

sank [sæŋk] pt → **sink**.

sapphire ['sæfaɪə'] n Saphir der.

sarcastic [sɑːˈkæstɪk] adj sarkastisch.

sardine [sɑːˈdiːn] n Sardine die.

SASE n (Am : abbr of self-addressed stamped envelope) adressierter Freiumschlag.

sat [sæt] pt & pp → **sit**.

Sat. (abbr of Saturday) Sa.

satchel ['sætʃəl] n Ranzen der.

satellite ['sætəlaɪt] n (in space) Satellit der ; (at airport) Einsteigestation die.

satellite dish n Parabolantenne die.

satellite TV n Satellitenfernsehen das.

satin ['sætɪn] n Satin der.

satisfaction [,sætɪsˈfækʃn] n (pleasure) Befriedigung die.

satisfactory [,sætɪsˈfæktərɪ] adj befriedigend.

satisfied ['sætɪsfaɪd] adj zufrieden.

satisfy ['sætɪsfaɪ] vt (please) zufrieden stellen ; (need, requirement, conditions) erfüllen.

satsuma [,sætˈsuːmə] n (Br) Satsuma die.

saturate ['sætʃəreɪt] vt (with liquid) tränken.

Saturday ['sætədɪ] n Samstag der, Sonnabend der ; it's ~ es ist Samstag ; ~ morning Samstagmorgen ; on ~ am Samstag ; on ~s samstags ; last ~ letzten Samstag ; this ~ diesen Samstag ; next ~ nächsten Samstag ; ~ week, a week on ~ Samstag in einer Woche.

sauce [sɔːs] n Soße die.

saucepan ['sɔːspən] n Kochtopf der.

saucer ['sɔːsə'] n Untertasse die.

Saudi Arabia [,saʊdɪəˈreɪbjə] n Saudi-Arabien nt.

sauna ['sɔːnə] n Sauna die.

sausage ['sɒsɪdʒ] n Wurst die.

sausage roll n Blätterteig mit Wurstfüllung.

sauté [(Br) 'saʊteɪ, (Am) saʊ'teɪ] adj sautiert.

savage ['sævɪdʒ] adj brutal.

save [seɪv] vt (rescue) retten; (money, time, space) sparen; (reserve) auflheben; (SPORT) ablwehren; (COMPUT) speichern. ◆ n (SPORT) Parade die; **to ~ a seat for sb** jm einen Platz freilhalten. ▪ **save up** vi : **to ~ up (for sthg)** (auf etw (A)) sparen.

saver ['seɪvə'] n (Br : ticket) verbilligte Fahrkarte.

savings ['seɪvɪŋz] npl Ersparnisse pl.

savings and loan association n (Am) Bausparkasse die.

savings bank n Sparkasse die.

savory ['seɪvərɪ] (Am) = **savoury**.

savoury ['seɪvərɪ] adj (Br : not sweet) pikant.

saw [sɔː] (Br pt -ed, pp sawn, Am & pt & pp -ed) pt → **see**. ◆ n (tool) Säge die. ◆ vt sägen.

sawdust ['sɔːdʌst] n Sägemehl das.

sawn [sɔːn] pp → **saw**.

Saxony ['sæksənɪ] n Sachsen nt.

saxophone ['sæksəfəʊn] n Saxophon das.

say [seɪ] (pt & pp said) vt sagen; (subj : clock, meter) anlzeigen; (subj : sign) besagen. ◆ n : **to have a ~ in sthg** etw zu sagen haben bei etw; **could you ~ that again?** könntest du das nochmal sagen?; **~ we met at nine?** könnten wir uns um neun treffen?; **that is to ~** das heißt; **what did you ~?** was hast du gesagt?; **the letter ~s...** in dem Brief steht...

saying ['seɪɪŋ] n Redensart die.

scab [skæb] n Schorf der.

scaffolding ['skæfəldɪŋ] n Gerüst das.

scald [skɔːld] vt verbrühen.

scale [skeɪl] n (for measurement) Skala die; (of map, drawing, model) Maßstab der; (extent) Umfang der; (MUS) Tonleiter die; (of fish, snake) Schuppe die; (in kettle) Kalk der. ▪ **scales** npl (for weighing) Waage die.

scallion ['skæljən] n (Am) Schalotte die.

scallop ['skɒləp] n Jakobsmuschel die.

scalp [skælp] n Kopfhaut die.

scampi ['skæmpɪ] n Scampi pl.

scan [skæn] vt (consult quickly) überfliegen. ◆ n (MED) Scan der, Computertomografie die.

scandal ['skændl] n (disgrace) Skandal der; (gossip) Klatsch der.

Scandinavia [,skændɪ'neɪvjə] n Skandinavien nt.

scar [skɑː'] n Narbe die.

scarce ['skeəs] adj knapp.

scarcely ['skeəslɪ] adv (hardly) kaum.

scare [skeə'] vt erschrecken.

scarecrow ['skeəkrəʊ] n Vogelscheuche die.

scared ['skeəd] adj : **to be ~ (of)** Angst haben (vor (+D)).

scarf ['skɑːf] (pl **scarves**) n (woollen) Schal der; (for women) Tuch das.

scarlet ['skɑːlət] adj scharlachrot.

scarves [skɑːvz] pl → **scarf**.

scary ['skeərɪ] adj (inf) unheimlich.

scatter ['skætə*] *vt* verstreuen. ◆ *vi* sich zerstreuen.

scene [si:n] *n (in play, film, book)* Szene *die*; *(of crime, accident)* Schauplatz *der*; *(view)* Anblick *der*; **the music ~** die Musikszene; **to make a ~** eine Szene machen.

scenery ['si:nəri] *n (countryside)* Landschaft *die*; *(in theatre)* Bühnenbild *das*.

scenic ['si:nik] *adj* malerisch.

scent [sent] *n (smell)* Duft *der*; *(of animal)* Fährte *die*; *(perfume)* Parfüm *das*.

sceptical ['skeptikl] *adj (Br)* skeptisch.

schedule [(Br) 'ʃedjuːl, (Am) 'skedʒul] *n (of things to do)* Programm *das*; *(of work)* Arbeitsplan *der*; *(timetable)* Fahrplan *der*; *(list)* Tabelle *die*. ◆ *vt (plan)* planen; **according to ~** planmäßig; **behind ~** im Verzug; **on ~** planmäßig; **to arrive on ~** pünktlich ankommen.

scheduled flight [(Br) 'ʃedjuːld-, (Am) 'skedʒuld-] *n* Linienflug *der*.

scheme [ski:m] *n (plan)* Programm *das*; *(pej: dishonest plan)* Komplott *das*.

scholarship ['skɒləʃip] *n (award)* Stipendium *das*.

school [skuːl] *n* Schule *die*; *(university department)* Fakultät *die*; *(Am: university)* Hochschule *die*. ◆ *adj (age, holiday, report)* Schul-; **at ~** in der Schule; **to go to ~** in die Schule gehen.

schoolbag ['skuːlbæg] *n* Schultasche *die*.

schoolbook ['skuːlbʊk] *n* Schulbuch *das*.

schoolboy ['skuːlbɔi] *n* Schuljunge *der*.

school bus *n* Schulbus *der*.

schoolchild ['skuːltʃaild] *(pl* -**children** [-tʃildrən]*) n* Schulkind *das*.

schoolgirl ['skuːlgɜːl] *n* Schulmädchen *das*.

schoolmaster ['skuːl,mɑːstə*] *n (Br)* Schullehrer *der*.

schoolmistress ['skuːl,mistris] *n (Br)* Schullehrerin *die*.

schoolteacher ['skuːl,tiːtʃə*] *n* Lehrer *der* (-in *die*).

school uniform *n* Schuluniform *die*.

science ['saiəns] *n* Wissenschaft *die*; *(SCH)* Physik, Chemie und Biologie *die*.

science fiction *n* Sciencefiction *die*.

scientific [,saiən'tifik] *adj* wissenschaftlich.

scientist ['saiəntist] *n* Wissenschaftler *der* (-in *die*).

scissors ['sizəz] *npl* : **(pair of) ~** Schere *die*.

scold [skəuld] *vt* aus|schimpfen.

scone [skɒn] *n* britisches Teegebäck.

scoop [skuːp] *n (for ice cream)* Portionierer *der*; *(of ice cream)* Kugel *die*; *(in media)* Exklusivmeldung *die*.

scooter ['skuːtə*] *n (motor vehicle)* Roller *der*.

scope [skəup] *n (possibility)* Spielraum *der*; *(range)* Rahmen *der*.

scorch [skɔːtʃ] vt (clothes) versengen.

score [skɔːʳ] n (total, final result) Ergebnis das ; (current position) Stand der. ◆ vt (goal) schießen ; (point, try, in test) erzielen. ◆ vi (get goal) ein Tor schießen ; (get point) einen Punkt erzielen.

scorn [skɔːn] n Verachtung die.

Scorpio ['skɔːpɪəʊ] n Skorpion der.

scorpion ['skɔːpjən] n Skorpion der.

Scot [skɒt] n Schotte der (Schottin die).

scotch [skɒtʃ] n Scotch der.

Scotch broth n Eintopf aus Fleischbrühe, Gemüse und Graupen.

Scotch tape® n (Am) Tesafilm® der.

Scotland ['skɒtlənd] n Schottland nt.

Scotsman ['skɒtsmən] (pl -men [-mən]) n Schotte der.

Scotswoman ['skɒtswʊmən] (pl -women [-,wɪmɪn]) n Schottin die.

Scottish ['skɒtɪʃ] adj schottisch.

scout [skaʊt] n (boy scout) Pfadfinder der.

scowl [skaʊl] vi ein böses Gesicht machen.

scrambled eggs [,skræmbld-] npl Rührei das.

scrap [skræp] n (of paper, cloth) Fetzen der ; (old metal) Schrott der.

scrapbook ['skræpbʊk] n Sammelalbum das.

scrape [skreɪp] vt (rub) reiben ; (scratch) kratzen.

scrap paper n (Br) Schmierzettel der.

scratch [skrætʃ] n Kratzer der. ◆ vt kratzen ; (mark) zerkratzen ; to be up to ~ gut genug sein ; to start from ~ von vorne anfangen.

scratch paper (Am) = scrap paper.

scream [skriːm] n Schrei der. ◆ vi schreien.

screen [skriːn] n (of TV, computer) Bildschirm der ; (for cinema film) Leinwand die ; (hall in cinema) Kinosaal der ; (panel) Trennwand die. ◆ vt (film, programme) vorführen.

screening ['skriːnɪŋ] n (of film) Vorführung die.

screen wash n Scheibenwaschmittel das.

screw [skruː] n Schraube die. ◆ vt (fasten) anlschrauben ; (twist) schrauben.

screwdriver ['skruː,draɪvəʳ] n Schraubenzieher der.

scribble ['skrɪbl] vi kritzeln.

script [skrɪpt] n (of play, film) Drehbuch das.

scrub [skrʌb] vt schrubben.

scruffy ['skrʌfɪ] adj vergammelt.

scrumpy ['skrʌmpɪ] n stark alkoholischer Apfelwein aus dem Südwesten Englands.

scuba diving ['skuːbə-] n Sporttauchen das.

sculptor ['skʌlptəʳ] n Bildhauer der (-in die).

sculpture ['skʌlptʃəʳ] n (statue) Skulptur die.

sea [si:] n Meer das, See die ; **by ~** auf dem Seeweg ; **by the ~** am Meer.

seafood ['si:fu:d] n Meeresfrüchte pl.

seafront ['si:frʌnt] n Uferpromenade die (am Meer gelegene Straße eines Küstenortes).

seagull ['si:gʌl] n Seemöwe die.

seal [si:l] n (animal) Seehund der ; (on bottle, container) Verschluss der ; (official mark) Siegel das. ◆ vt versiegeln.

seam [si:m] n (in clothes) Saum der.

search [sɜ:tʃ] n Suche die. ◆ vt durchsuchen. ◆ vi : **to ~ for** suchen nach.

seashell ['si:ʃel] n Muschel die.

seashore ['si:ʃɔ:r] n Meeresküste die.

seasick ['si:sɪk] adj seekrank.

seaside ['si:saɪd] n : **the ~** die Küste.

seaside resort n Urlaubsort der an der Küste.

season ['si:zn] n (of year) Jahreszeit die ; (period) Saison, Zeit die. ◆ vt (food) würzen ; **in ~** (holiday) in der Hochsaison ; **out of ~** (holiday) in der Nebensaison ; **strawberries are in/out of ~** es ist Erdbeerzeit/keine Erdbeerzeit.

seasoning ['si:znɪŋ] n Gewürz das.

season ticket n (for train) Dauerkarte die ; (for theatre) Abonnement das.

seat [si:t] n (place) Platz der ; (chair) (Sitz)platz der ; (in parliament) Sitz der. ◆ vt (subj :

building, vehicle) Sitzplatz haben für ; **'please wait to be ~ed'** 'bitte warten Sie hier, bis Sie zu Ihrem Platz geleitet werden'.

seat belt n Sicherheitsgurt der.

seaweed ['si:wi:d] n Seetang der.

secluded [sɪ'klu:dɪd] adj abgeschieden.

second ['sekənd] n Sekunde die. ◆ num zweite(-r) (-s) ; **~ gear** zweiter Gang ; → **sixth**.

■ **seconds** npl (goods) Waren pl zweiter Wahl ; (inf : of food) Nachschlag.

secondary school ['sekəndrɪ-] n höhere Schule.

second-class adj (ticket) zweiter Klasse ; (inferior) zweitklassig ; **~ stamp** billigere Briefmarke für Post, die weniger schnell befördert wird.

second-hand adj gebraucht.

Second World War n : **the ~** der Zweite Weltkrieg.

secret ['si:krɪt] adj geheim. ◆ n Geheimnis das.

secretary [(Br) 'sekrətrɪ, (Am) 'sekrə,terɪ] n Sekretär der (-in die).

Secretary of State n (Am : foreign minister) Außenminister der (-in die) ; (Br : government minister) Minister der (-in die).

section ['sekʃn] n (part) Teil der.

sector ['sektə'] n Sektor der.

secure [sɪ'kjʊə'] adj sicher ; (firmly fixed) fest. ◆ vt (fix) sichern ; (fml : obtain) sich (D) sichern.

security [sɪ'kjʊərətɪ] n Sicherheit die.

security guard n Sicherheitsbeamter der (-beamtin die).

sedative ['sedətɪv] n Beruhigungsmittel das.

seduce [sɪ'djuːs] vt verführen.

see [siː] (pt saw, pp seen) vt sehen ; (visit) besuchen ; (doctor, solicitor) gehen zu ; (understand) einlsehen ; (accompany) begleiten. ◆ vi sehen ; I ~ (understand) ich verstehe ; to ~ if one can do sthg sehen, ob man etw tun kann ; to ~ to sthg (deal with) sich um etw kümmern ; (repair) etw reparieren ; ~ you! tschüs! ; ~ you later! bis bald! ; ~ you soon! bis bald! ; ~ p 14 siehe S. 14. ▪ **see off** vt sep (say goodbye to) verabschieden.

seed [siːd] n Samen der.

seedy ['siːdɪ] adj heruntergekommen.

seeing (as) ['siːɪŋ-] conj in Anbetracht dessen, dass.

seek [siːk] (pt & pp sought) vt (fml) (look for) suchen ; (request) erbitten.

seem [siːm] vi scheinen. ◆ v impers : it ~ (that)... anscheinend.

seen [siːn] pp → see.

seesaw ['siːsɔː] n Wippe die.

segment ['segmənt] n (of fruit) Scheibe die, Schnitz der (Süddt).

seize [siːz] vt (grab) ergreifen ; (drugs, arms) beschlagnahmen. ▪ **seize up** vi (machine) sich festlfressen ; (leg, back) sich versteifen.

seldom ['seldəm] adv selten.

select [sɪ'lekt] vt auslwählen. ◆ adj (exclusive) ausgesucht.

selection [sɪ'lekʃn] n (selecting) Wahl die ; (range) Auswahl die.

self-assured [ˌselfə'ʃʊəd] adj selbstsicher.

self-catering [ˌself'keɪtərɪŋ] adj mit Selbstversorgung.

self-confident [ˌself-] adj selbstbewusst.

self-conscious [ˌself-] adj gehemmt.

self-contained [ˌselfkən'teɪnd] adj (flat) abgeschlossen.

self-defence [ˌself-] n Selbstverteidigung die.

self-employed [ˌself-] adj selbstständig.

selfish ['selfɪʃ] adj egoistisch.

self-raising flour [ˌself'reɪzɪŋ-] n (Br) Mehl das mit Backpulverzusatz.

self-rising flour [ˌself'raɪzɪŋ-] (Am) = self-raising flour.

self-service [ˌself-] adj mit Selbstbedienung.

sell [sel] (pt & pp sold) vt & vi verkaufen ; to ~ for £20 20 Pfund kosten ; to ~ sb sthg jm etw verkaufen.

sell-by date n Mindesthaltbarkeitsdatum das.

seller ['selə'] n Verkäufer der (-in die).

Sellotape® ['seləteɪp] n (Br) ≃ Tesafilm® der.

semester [sɪ'mestə'] n Semester das.

semicircle ['semɪˌsɜːkl] n Halbkreis der.

semicolon [ˌsemɪ'kəʊlən] *n* Strichpunkt *der*.

semidetached [ˌsemɪdɪ'tætʃt] *adj* : a ~ house eine Doppelhaushälfte.

semifinal [ˌsemɪ'faɪnl] *n* Halbfinale *das*.

seminar ['seminɑː'] *n* Seminar *das*.

semolina [ˌseməˈliːnə] *n* Grieß *der*.

send [send] (*pt* & *pp* sent) *vt* schicken; *(TV or radio signal)* senden; to ~ sthg to sb jm etw schicken. ■ **send back** *vt sep* zurückschicken. ■ **send off** *vt sep (letter, parcel)* abschicken; *(SPORT)* vom Platz stellen. ◆ *vi* : to ~ off for sthg sich (D) etw schicken lassen.

sender ['sendə'] *n* Absender *der*.

senile ['siːnaɪl] *adj* senil.

senior ['siːnjə'] *adj (high-ranking)* leitend; *(higher-ranking)* höher. ◆ *n (Br : SCH)* Schüler der höheren Klassen; *(Am : SCH)* amerikanischer Student im letzten Studienjahr.

senior citizen *n* Senior *der* (-in *die*).

sensation [sen'seɪʃn] *n* Gefühl *das*; *(cause of excitement)* Sensation *die*.

sensational [sen'seɪʃənl] *adj (very good)* sensationell.

sense [sens] *n* Sinn *der*; *(common sense)* Verstand *der*; *(of word, expression)* Bedeutung *die*. ◆ *vt* spüren; to make ~ Sinn ergeben; ~ of direction Orientierungssinn *der*; ~ of humour Sinn für Humor.

sensible ['sensəbl] *adj (person)* vernünftig; *(clothes, shoes)* praktisch.

sensitive ['sensɪtɪv] *adj* empfindlich; *(emotionally)* sensibel; *(subject, issue)* heikel.

sent [sent] *pt* & *pp* → send.

sentence ['sentəns] *n (GRAMM)* Satz *der*; *(for crime)* Strafe *die*. ◆ *vt* verurteilen.

sentimental [ˌsentɪ'mentl] *adj* sentimental.

Sep. *(abbr of September)* Sept.

separate [*adj* 'seprət, *vb* 'sepəreɪt] *adj* getrennt; *(different)* verschieden. ◆ *vt* trennen. ◆ *vi* sich trennen. ■ **separates** *npl (Br)* Kleidungsstücke wie Röcke, Hosen, Blusen, die mit mit einem Ober- oder Unterteil kombiniert werden müssen; im Gegensatz zu Kleidern oder Anzügen.

separately [ˈseprətlɪ] *adv (individually)* einzeln; *(alone)* getrennt.

separation [ˌsepə'reɪʃn] *n* Trennung *die*.

September [sep'tembə'] *n* September *der*; at the beginning of ~ Anfang September; at the end of ~ Ende September; during ~ im September; every ~ jeden September; in ~ im September; last ~ letzten September; next ~ nächsten September; this ~ diesen September; 2 ~ 1999 *(in letters etc)* 2. September 1999.

septic ['septɪk] *adj* vereitert.

septic tank *n* Faulgrube *die*.

sequel ['siːkwəl] *n* Fortsetzung *die*.

sequence ['si:kwəns] n (series) Reihe die ; (order) Reihenfolge die.

sequin ['si:kwɪn] n Paillette die.

sergeant ['sɑːdʒənt] n (in police force) Wachtmeister der ; (in army) Feldwebel der.

serial ['sɪərɪəl] n Serie die.

series ['sɪəriːz] (pl series) n (sequence) Reihe die ; (on TV, radio) Serie die.

serious ['sɪərɪəs] adj ernst ; (injury, problem) schwer ; **are you ~?** ist das dein Ernst? ; **to be ~ about sthg** etw ernst nehmen.

seriously ['sɪərɪəslɪ] adv ernsthaft.

sermon ['sɜːmən] n Predigt die.

servant ['sɜːvənt] n Diener der (-in die).

serve [sɜːv] vt (food) servieren ; (drink) aus|schenken ; (customer) bedienen. ◆ vi (SPORT) aufschlagen ; (work) dienen. ◆ n (SPORT) Aufschlag der ; **to ~ as** (be used for) dienen als ; **the town is ~d by two airports** die Stadt hat zwei Flughäfen ; **'~s two'** (on packaging, menu) 'für zwei Personen' ; **it ~s you right** geschieht dir recht!

service ['sɜːvɪs] n (in shop, restaurant etc) Bedienung die ; (job, organization) Dienst der ; (at church) Gottesdienst der ; (SPORT) Aufschlag der ; (of car) Wartung die. ◆ vt (car) warten. **'out of ~'** 'außer Betrieb' ; **'~ included'** 'Bedienung inbegriffen' ; **'~ not included'** 'Bedienung nicht inbegriffen' ; **to be of ~ to sb** (fml) jm behilflich

sein. ■ **services** npl (on motorway) Raststätte die ; (of person) Dienste pl.

service area n Tankstelle die und Raststätte.

service charge n Bedienungszuschlag der.

service department n Kundendienst der.

service station n Tankstelle die.

serviette [,sɜːvɪ'et] n Serviette die.

serving ['sɜːvɪŋ] n (helping) Portion die.

serving spoon n Servierlöffel der.

sesame seeds ['sesəmɪ-] npl Sesam der.

session ['seʃn] n (of activity) Runde die ; (formal meeting) Sitzung die.

set [set] (pt & pp set) adj 1. (fixed) fest ; (date) festgesetzt ; **a ~ lunch** ein Mittagsmenü. 2. (text, book) Pflicht-. ◆ n 1. (collection) Satz der ; **a chess ~** ein Schachspiel. 2. (TV) : **a (TV) ~** ein Fernsehgerät. 3. (in tennis) Satz der. 4. (SCH) Gruppe von Schülern mit gleichem Niveau innerhalb eines Faches. 5. (of play) Bühnenbild das. 6. (at hairdresser's) : **a shampoo and ~** Waschen und Legen. ◆ vt 1. (put) setzen ; (put upright) stellen ; (put flat) legen. 2. (cause to be) : **to ~ a machine going** eine Maschine in Gang bringen ; **to ~ fire to sthg** etw in Brand setzen. 3. (controls) ein|stellen ; (clock)

stellen ; ~ **the alarm for 7 a.m.** stell den Wecker für 7 Uhr früh.
4. *(price, time)* festlegen.
5. *(the table)* decken.
6. *(a record)* auflstellen.
7. *(broken bone)* richten.
8. *(homework, essay)* auflgeben ; *(exam)* zusammenlstellen.
9. *(play, film, story)* : **to be ~** spielen.
◆ *vi* **1.** *(sun)* unterlgehen.
2. *(glue, jelly)* fest werden.
■ **set down** *vt sep (Br : passengers)* ablsetzen.
■ **set off** *vt sep (alarm)* ausllösen.
◆ *vi (on journey)* auflbrechen.
■ **set out** *vt sep (arrange)* herlrichten.
◆ *vi (on journey)* auflbrechen.
■ **set up** *vt sep (barrier)* auflstellen ; *(equipment)* auflbauen ; *(meeting, interview)* organisieren.
set meal *n* Menü *das.*
set menu *n* Menü *das.*
settee [se'ti:] *n* Sofa *das.*
setting ['setɪŋ] *n (on machine)* Einstellung *die* ; *(surroundings)* Lage *die.*
settle ['setl] *vt (argument)* beillegen ; *(bill)* bezahlen ; *(stomach, nerves)* beruhigen ; *(arrange, decide on)* entscheiden.
◆ *vi (start to live)* sich niederllassen ; *(come to rest)* sich hinlsetzen ; *(sediment, dust)* sich setzen. ■ **settle down** *vi (calm down)* sich beruhigen ; *(sit comfortably)* sich gemütlich hinlsetzen. ■ **settle up** *vi (pay bill)* bezahlen.

settlement ['setlmənt] *n (agreement)* Einigung *die* ; *(place)* Siedlung *die.*
seven ['sevn] *num* sieben ; → **six.**
seventeen [,sevn'ti:n] *num* siebzehn ; → **six.**
seventeenth [,sevn'ti:nθ] *num* siebzehnte(-r) (-s) ; → **sixth.**
seventh ['sevnθ] *num* siebte(-r) (-s) ; → **sixth.**
seventieth ['sevntjəθ] *num* siebzigste(-r) (-s) ; → **sixth.**
seventy ['sevntɪ] *num* siebzig ; → **six.**
several ['sevrəl] *adj & pron* mehrere, einige.
severe [sɪ'vɪəʳ] *adj (conditions, illness)* schwer ; *(criticism, person, punishment)* hart ; *(pain)* heftig.
sew [səʊ] *(pp* **sewn***) vt & vi* nähen.
sewage ['su:ɪdʒ] *n* Abwasser *das.*
sewing ['səʊɪŋ] *n (activity)* Nähen *das* ; *(things sewn)* Nähzeug *das.*
sewing machine *n* Nähmaschine *die.*
sewn [səʊn] *pp* → **sew.**
sex [seks] *n (gender)* Geschlecht *das* ; *(sexual intercourse)* Sex *der* ; **to have ~ (with)** Sex haben (mit).
sexist ['seksɪst] *n* Sexist *der.*
sexual ['sekʃʊəl] *adj* sexuell.
sexy ['seksɪ] *adj* sexy.
shabby ['ʃæbɪ] *adj (clothes, room)* schäbig ; *(person)* heruntergekommen.
shade [ʃeɪd] *n (shadow)* Schatten *der* ; *(lampshade)* Schirm

der ; (of colour) Ton der. ◆ vt (protect) schützen. ■ **shades** npl (inf : sunglasses) Sonnenbrille die.

shadow ['ʃædəʊ] n Schatten der.

shady ['ʃeɪdɪ] adj schattig ; (inf : person, deal) zwielichtig.

shaft [ʃɑːft] n (of machine) Welle die ; (of lift) Schacht der.

shake [ʃeɪk] (pt shook, pp shaken ['ʃeɪkn]) vt schütteln ; (shock) erschüttern. ◆ vi (person) zittern ; (building, earth) beben ; to ~ hands with sb jm die Hand geben ; to ~ one's head den Kopf schütteln.

shall [weak form ʃəl, strong form ʃæl] aux vb 1. (expressing future) werden ; I ~ be late tomorrow morgen werde ich später kommen ; I ~ be ready soon ich bin bald fertig.
2. (in questions) sollen ; ~ I buy some wine? soll ich Wein kaufen? ; where ~ we go? wo sollen wir hingehen?
3. (fml : expressing order) : payment ~ be made within a week die Zahlung muss innerhalb einer Woche erfolgen.

shallot [ʃəˈlɒt] n Schalotte die.

shallow ['ʃæləʊ] adj (pond, water) seicht.

shallow end n (of swimming pool) flaches Ende.

shambles ['ʃæmblz] n wildes Durcheinander.

shame [ʃeɪm] n (remorse) Scham die ; (disgrace) Schande die ; it's a ~ that schade, dass ; what a ~! wie schade!

shampoo [ʃæmˈpuː] (pl -s) n (liquid) Shampoo das ; (wash) Shampoonieren das.

shandy ['ʃændɪ] n Radler der.

shape [ʃeɪp] n Form die ; (person) Gestalt die ; to be in good/bad ~ in guter/schlechter Form sein.

share [ʃeəʳ] n (part) Anteil der ; (in company) Aktie die. ◆ vt (room, work, cost, responsibility) teilen ; (divide) aufteilen. ■ **share out** vt sep aufteilen.

shark [ʃɑːk] n Hai der.

sharp [ʃɑːp] adj scharf ; (pencil, needle, teeth) spitz ; (change) groß ; (bend) scharf ; (rise) steil ; (quick, intelligent) aufgeweckt ; (painful) stechend ; (food, taste) säuerlich. ◆ adv (exactly) : at one o'clock ~ Punkt eins.

sharpen ['ʃɑːpn] vt (knife) schärfen ; (pencil) spitzen.

shatter ['ʃætəʳ] vt (break) zerschmettern. ◆ vi zerbrechen.

shattered ['ʃætəd] adj (Br : inf : tired) erschlagen.

shave [ʃeɪv] vt rasieren. ◆ vi sich rasieren. ◆ n : to have a ~ sich rasieren ; to ~ one's legs sich (D) die Beine rasieren.

shaver ['ʃeɪvəʳ] n Rasierapparat der.

shaver point n Steckdose für einen Rasierapparat.

shaving brush ['ʃeɪvɪŋ-] n Rasierpinsel der.

shaving cream ['ʃeɪvɪŋ-] n Rasiercreme die.

shaving foam ['ʃeɪvɪŋ-] n Rasierschaum der.

shawl [ʃɔːl] n Schultertuch das.

she [ʃiː] *pron* sie ; ~'s tall sie ist groß.

sheaf [ʃiːf] (*pl* **sheaves**) *n* (*of paper, notes*) Bündel *das*.

shears [ʃɪəz] *npl* Gartenschere *die*.

sheaves [ʃiːvz] *pl* → **sheaf**.

shed [ʃed] (*pt* & *pp* **shed**) *n* Schuppen *der*. ◆ *vt* (*tears, blood*) vergießen.

she'd [*weak form* ʃɪd, *strong form* ʃiːd] = **she had, she would.**

sheep [ʃiːp] (*pl* **sheep**) *n* Schaf *das*.

sheepdog ['ʃiːpdɒg] *n* Hirtenhund *der*.

sheepskin ['ʃiːpskɪn] *adj* Schaffell *das*.

sheer [ʃɪəʳ] *adj* (*pure, utter*) rein ; (*cliff*) steil ; (*stockings*) hauchdünn.

sheet [ʃiːt] *n* (*for bed*) Laken *das* ; (*of paper*) Blatt *das* ; (*of glass, metal, wood*) Platte *die*.

shelf [ʃelf] (*pl* **shelves**) *n* Regal *das*.

shell [ʃel] *n* (*of egg, nut*) Schale *die* ; (*on beach*) Muschel *die* ; (*of tortoise*) Panzer *der* ; (*of snail*) Haus *das* ; (*bomb*) Granate *die*.

she'll [ʃiːl] = **she will, she shall.**

shellfish ['ʃelfɪʃ] *n* Schalentiere *pl* ; (*food*) Meeresfrüchte *pl*.

shell suit *n* (*Br*) Jogginganzug aus Nylonaußenmaterial und Baumwollfutter.

shelter ['ʃeltəʳ] *n* Schutz *der* ; (*structure*) Schutzdach *das*. ◆ *vt* (*protect*) schützen. ◆ *vi* sich unterǀstellen ; **to take ~** sich unterǀstellen.

sheltered ['ʃeltəd] *adj* (*place*) geschützt.

shelves [ʃelvz] *pl* → **shelf**.

shepherd ['ʃepəd] *n* Schafhirtin die).

shepherd's pie ['ʃepədz-] *n* Auflauf aus Hackfleisch, bedeckt mit einer Schicht Kartoffelbrei.

sheriff ['ʃerɪf] *n* (*in US*) Sheriff *der*.

sherry ['ʃerɪ] *n* Sherry *der*.

she's [ʃiːz] = **she is, she has.**

shield [ʃiːld] *n* Schild *der*. ◆ *vt* schützen.

shift [ʃɪft] *n* (*change*) Veränderung *die* ; (*period of work*) Schicht *die*. ◆ *vt* (*move*) rücken ; (*rearrange*) umǀstellen. ◆ *vi* (*move*) sich verschieben ; (*change*) sich verändern.

shin [ʃɪn] *n* Schienbein *das*.

shine [ʃaɪn] (*pt* & *pp* **shone**) *vi* scheinen ; (*surface, glass*) glänzen. ◆ *vt* (*shoes*) polieren ; (*torch*) leuchten.

shiny ['ʃaɪnɪ] *adj* glänzend.

ship [ʃɪp] *n* Schiff *das* ; **by ~** mit dem Schiff.

shipwreck ['ʃɪprek] *n* (*accident*) Schiffbruch *der* ; (*wrecked ship*) Wrack *das*.

shirt [ʃɜːt] *n* Hemd *das*.

shit [ʃɪt] *n* (*vulg*) Scheiße *die*.

shiver ['ʃɪvəʳ] *vi* zittern.

shock [ʃɒk] *n* (*surprise*) Schock *der* ; (*force*) Wucht *die*. ◆ *vt* (*surprise*) einen Schock versetzen (+D) ; (*horrify*) schockieren ; **to be in ~** (*MED*) unter Schock stehen.

shock absorber [-əb,zɔːbəʳ] *n* Stoßdämpfer *der*.

shocking ['ʃɒkɪŋ] *adj (very bad)* entsetzlich.

shoe [ʃuː] *n* Schuh *der*.

shoelace ['ʃuːleɪs] *n* Schnürsenkel *der*.

shoe polish *n* Schuhcreme *die*.

shoe repairer's [-rɪ,peərəz] *n* Schuhmacher *der*.

shoe shop *n* Schuhgeschäft *das*.

shone [ʃɒn] *pt & pp* → **shine**.

shook [ʃʊk] *pt* → **shake**.

shoot [ʃuːt] (*pt & pp* shot) *vt (kill)* erschießen ; *(injure)* anschießen ; *(gun)* abfeuern ; *(arrow)* abschießen ; *(film)* drehen. ◆ *vi* schießen. ◆ *n (of plant)* Trieb *der*.

shop [ʃɒp] *n* Geschäft *das*, Laden *der*. ◆ *vi* einkaufen.

shop assistant *n (Br)* Verkäufer *der* (-in *die*).

shop floor *n* Produktionsabteilung *die*.

shopkeeper ['ʃɒp,kiːpə'] *n* Geschäftsinhaber *der* (-in *die*).

shoplifter ['ʃɒp,lɪftə'] *n* Ladendieb *der* (-in *die*).

shopper ['ʃɒpə'] *n* Käufer *der* (-in *die*).

shopping ['ʃɒpɪŋ] *n (things bought)* Einkäufe *pl* ; *(activity)* Einkaufen *das* ; **to do the ~** den Einkauf erledigen ; **to go ~** einkaufen gehen.

shopping bag *n* Einkaufstüte *die*.

shopping basket *n* Einkaufskorb *der*.

shopping centre *n* Einkaufszentrum *das*.

shopping list *n* Einkaufsliste *die*.

shopping mall *n* Einkaufszentrum *das*.

shop steward *n* gewerkschaftlicher Vertrauensmann.

shop window *n* Schaufenster *das*.

shore [ʃɔː'] *n (of sea, river, lake)* Ufer *das* ; **on ~** *(on land)* an Land.

short [ʃɔːt] *adj* kurz ; *(not tall)* klein. ◆ *adv (cut)* kurz. ◆ *n (Br : drink)* Kurze *der* ; *(film)* Kurzfilm *der* ; **to be ~ of sthg** *(time, money)* zu wenig von etw haben ; **to be ~ of breath** außer Atem sein ; **in ~** kurz (gesagt). ▪ **shorts** *npl (short trousers)* Shorts *pl* ; *(Am : underpants)* Unterhose *die*.

shortage ['ʃɔːtɪdʒ] *n* Mangel *der*.

shortbread ['ʃɔːtbred] *n* Buttergebäck *das*.

short-circuit *vi* einen Kurzschluss haben.

shortcrust pastry ['ʃɔːtkrʌst-] *n* Mürbeteig *der*.

short cut *n* Abkürzung *die*.

shorten ['ʃɔːtn] *vt (in time)* verkürzen ; *(in length)* kürzen.

shorthand ['ʃɔːthænd] *n* Stenografie *die*.

shortly ['ʃɔːtlɪ] *adv (soon)* in Kürze ; **~ before** kurz bevor.

shortsighted [,ʃɔːt'saɪtɪd] *adj* kurzsichtig.

short-sleeved [-,sliːvd] *adj* kurzärmelig.

short-stay car park *n* Parkplatz *der* für Kurzparker.

short story *n* Kurzgeschichte *die*.

short wave *n* Kurzwelle *die*.

shot [ʃɒt] *pt* & *pp* → **shoot**. ◆ *n* (*of gun, in football*) Schuss *der* ; (*in tennis, golf*) Schlag *der* ; (*photo*) Aufnahme *die* ; (*in film*) Einstellung *die* ; (*inf : attempt*) Versuch *der* ; (*of alcohol*) Schuss *der*.

shotgun [ˈʃɒtgʌn] *n* Schrotflinte *die*.

should [ʃʊd] *aux vb* 1. (*expressing desirability*) : **we ~ leave now** wir sollten jetzt gehen. 2. (*asking for advice*) : **~ I go too?** soll ich auch gehen? 3. (*expressing probability*) : **she ~ be home soon** sie müsste bald zu Hause sein. 4. (*ought to*) : **they ~ have won the match** sie hätten das Spiel gewinnen sollen. 5. (*fml : in conditionals*) : **~ you need anything, call reception** sollten Sie irgendetwas brauchen, rufen Sie die Rezeption an. 6. (*fml : expressing wish*) : **I ~ like to come with you** ich würde gerne mit dir mitkommen.

shoulder [ˈʃəʊldəʳ] *n* Schulter *die* ; (*of meat*) Schulterstück *das* ; (*Am : of road*) Seitenstreifen *der*.

shoulder pad *n* Schulterpolster *das*.

shouldn't [ˈʃʊdnt] = **should not**.

should've [ˈʃʊdəv] = **should have**.

shout [ʃaʊt] *n* Schrei *der*. ◆ *vt* & *vi* schreien. ■ **shout out** *vt sep* heraus|schreien.

shove [ʃʌv] *vt* stoßen ; (*put carelessly*) stopfen.

shovel [ˈʃʌvl] *n* Schaufel *die*.

show [ʃəʊ] (*pp* -ed OR shown) *n* (*at theatre, on TV, radio*) Show *die* ; (*exhibition*) Schau *die*. ◆ *vt* zeigen ; (*accompany*) begleiten. ◆ *vi* (*be visible*) sichtbar sein ; (*film*) laufen ; **to ~ sthg to sb** jm etw zeigen ; **to ~ sb how to do sthg** jm zeigen, wie man etw tut. ■ **show off** *vi* an|geben. ■ **show up** *vi* (*come along*) kommen ; (*be visible*) zu sehen sein.

shower [ˈʃaʊəʳ] *n* (*for washing*) Dusche *die* ; (*of rain*) Guss *der*. ◆ *vi* (*wash*) duschen ; **to have a ~** duschen.

shower gel *n* Duschgel *das*.

shower unit *n* Dusche *die*.

showing [ˈʃəʊɪŋ] *n* (*of film*) Vorführung *die*.

shown [ʃəʊn] *pp* → **show**.

showroom [ˈʃəʊrʊm] *n* Ausstellungsraum *der*.

shrank [ʃræŋk] *pt* → **shrink**.

shrimp [ʃrɪmp] *n* Krabbe *die*.

shrine [ʃraɪn] *n* Schrein *der*.

shrink [ʃrɪŋk] (*pt* shrank, *pp* shrunk) *n* (*inf : psychoanalyst*) Psychiater *der*. ◆ *vi* (*become smaller*) schrumpfen ; (*clothes*) ein|laufen ; (*diminish*) ab|nehmen.

shrub [ʃrʌb] *n* Strauch *der*.

shrug [ʃrʌg] *n* Achselzucken *das*. ◆ *vi* die Achseln zucken.

shrunk [ʃrʌŋk] *pp* → **shrink**.

shuffle [ˈʃʌfl] *vt* (*cards*) mischen. ◆ *vi* schlurfen.

shut [ʃʌt] (*pt* & *pp* shut) *adj* zu, geschlossen. ◆ *vt* schließen, zu|machen. ◆ *vi* (*door, mouth, eyes*) schließen ; (*shop, restaurant*) schließen, zu|machen. ■ **shut down** *vt sep* schließen. ■ **shut up** vi (inf : stop talking) den Mund halten.

shutter ['ʃʌtə'] n (on window) Fensterladen der ; (on camera) Verschluss der.

shuttle ['ʃʌtl] n (plane) Pendelmaschine die ; (bus) Pendelbus der.

shuttlecock ['ʃʌtlkɒk] n Federball der.

shy [ʃaɪ] adj schüchtern.

sick [sɪk] adj (ill) krank ; to be ~ (vomit) sich übergeben ; I feel ~ mir ist schlecht ; to be ~ of (fed up with) die Nase voll haben von.

sick bag n Tüte die.

sickness ['sɪknɪs] n Krankheit die.

sick pay n Krankengeld das.

side [saɪd] n Seite die ; (Br : TV channel) Kanal der. ◆ adj (door, pocket) Seiten- ; at the ~ of neben (+D) ; on the other ~ auf der anderen Seite ; on this ~ auf dieser Seite ; ~ by ~ Seite an Seite.

sideboard ['saɪdbɔːd] n Anrichte die.

sidecar ['saɪdkɑː'] n Beiwagen der.

side dish n Beilage die.

side effect n Nebenwirkung die.

sidelight ['saɪdlaɪt] n (Br : of car) Begrenzungsleuchte die.

side order n Beilage die.

side salad n Salatbeilage die.

side street n Seitenstraße die.

sidewalk ['saɪdwɔːk] n (Am) Bürgersteig der.

sideways ['saɪdweɪz] adv seitwärts.

sieve [sɪv] n Sieb das.

sigh [saɪ] n Seufzer der. ◆ vi seufzen.

sight [saɪt] n (eyesight) Sehvermögen das ; (thing seen) Anblick der ; at first ~ auf den ersten Blick ; to catch ~ of erblicken ; in ~ in Sicht ; to lose ~ of aus den Augen verlieren ; out of ~ außer Sicht. ■ **sights** npl (of city, country) Sehenswürdigkeiten pl.

sightseeing ['saɪt‚siːɪŋ] n : to go ~ Sehenswürdigkeiten besichtigen.

sign [saɪn] n Zeichen das ; (next to road, in shop, station) Schild das. ◆ vt & vi unterschreiben ; there's no ~ of her von ihr ist nichts zu sehen. ■ **sign in** vi (at hotel, club) sich einItragen.

signal ['sɪgnl] n Signal das ; (Am : traffic lights) Ampel die. ◆ vi (in car, on bike) die Fahrtrichtung anIzeigen.

signature ['sɪgnətʃə'] n Unterschrift die.

significant [sɪg'nɪfɪkənt] adj (large) beträchtlich ; (important) bedeutend.

signpost ['saɪnpəʊst] n Wegweiser der.

Sikh [siːk] n Sikh der, die.

silence ['saɪləns] n Stille die.

silencer ['saɪlənsə'] n (Br : AUT) Auspufftopf der.

silent ['saɪlənt] adj still.

silk [sɪlk] n Seide die.

sill [sɪl] n Sims der.

silly ['sɪlɪ] adj albern.

silver ['sɪlvə'] n Silber das ; (coins) Silbergeld das. ◆ adj (made of silver) Silber-.

silver foil n Alufolie die.

silver-plated [-'pleɪtɪd] adj versilbert.

similar ['sɪmɪlə'] adj ähnlich; **to be ~ to** ähnlich sein *(+D)*.

similarity [ˌsɪmɪ'lærətɪ] n Ähnlichkeit die.

simmer ['sɪmə'] vi leicht kochen.

simple ['sɪmpl] adj einfach.

simplify ['sɪmplɪfaɪ] vt vereinfachen.

simply ['sɪmplɪ] adv einfach.

simulate ['sɪmjʊleɪt] vt simulieren.

simultaneous [(Br) ˌsɪmǝl'teɪnjǝs, (Am) ˌsaɪmǝl'teɪnjǝs] adj gleichzeitig.

simultaneously [(Br) ˌsɪmǝl'teɪnjǝslɪ, (Am) ˌsaɪmǝl'teɪnjǝslɪ] adv gleichzeitig.

sin [sɪn] n Sünde die. ◆ vi sündigen.

since [sɪns] adv seitdem. ◆ prep seit. ◆ conj (in time) seit; (as) da; **I've been here ~ six o'clock** ich bin hier seit sechs Uhr; **ever ~** seitdem, seit.

sincere [sɪn'sɪə'] adj aufrichtig.

sincerely [sɪn'sɪəlɪ] adv aufrichtig; **Yours ~** mit freundlichen Grüßen.

sing [sɪŋ] (pt sang, pp sung) vt & vi singen.

singer ['sɪŋə'] n Sänger der (-in die).

single ['sɪŋgl] adj (just one) einzig, einzig; (not married) ledig. ◆ n (Br: ticket) einfache Fahrkarte

; (record) Single die; **every ~** jede(-r) (-s) einzelne. ■ **singles** n (SPORT) Einzel das. ◆ adj Singles-.

single bed n Einzelbett das.

single cream n (Br) Sahne mit niedrigem Fettgehalt.

single currency n Einheitswährung die.

single parent n Alleinerziehende der, die.

single room n Einzelzimmer das.

single track road n einspurige Straße.

singular ['sɪŋgjʊlə'] n Singular der; **in the ~** im Singular.

sinister ['sɪnɪstə'] adj finster.

sink [sɪŋk] (pt sank, pp sunk) n (in kitchen) Spülbecken das; (washbasin) Waschbecken das. ◆ vi sinken.

sink unit n Spüle die.

sinuses ['saɪnǝsɪz] npl Nebenhöhlen pl.

sip [sɪp] n Schlückchen das. ◆ vt in kleinen Schlucken trinken.

siphon ['saɪfn] n (tube) Saugheber der. ◆ vt (liquid) absaugen.

sir [sɜː'] n mein Herr; **Dear Sir/Sirs** Sehr geehrte Herren; **Sir Richard Blair** Sir Richard Blair.

siren ['saɪǝrǝn] n Sirene die.

sirloin steak [ˌsɜːlɔɪn-] n Lendensteak das.

sister ['sɪstə'] n Schwester die.

sister-in-law n Schwägerin die.

sit [sɪt] (pt & pp sat) vi (be seated) sitzen; (sit down) sich setzen; (be situated) liegen. ◆ vt *(place)* setzen ; *(Br : exam)* machen ; **to be sitting** sitzen. ◼ **sit down** *vi* sich hinlsetzen ; **to be sitting down** sitzen. ◼ **sit up** *vi (after lying down)* sich auflsetzen ; *(stay up late)* auflbleiben.

site [saɪt] *n* Stelle *die* ; *(building site)* Baustelle *die*.

sitting room ['sɪtɪŋ-] *n* Wohnzimmer *das*.

situated ['sɪtjʊeɪtɪd] *adj* : **to be ~** liegen.

situation [ˌsɪtjʊ'eɪʃn] *n* Lage *die* ; **'~s vacant'** 'Stellenangebote'.

six [sɪks] *num adj* sechs. ◆ *num n* Sechs *die* ; **to be ~ (years old)** sechs (Jahre. alt) sein ; **it's ~ (o'clock)** es ist sechs Uhr ; **a hundred and ~** hundertsechs ; **~ Hill St** Hill St Nummer sechs ; **it's minus ~ (degrees)** es sind minus sechs (Grad).

sixteen [sɪks'tiːn] *num* sechzehn ; → **six**.

sixteenth [sɪks'tiːnθ] *num* sechzehnte(-e) (-s) ; → **sixth**.

sixth [sɪksθ] *num adj & adv* sechste(-r) (-s). ◆ *num pron* Sechste *der, die, das*. ◆ *num n (fraction)* Sechstel *das* ; **the ~ (of September)** der sechste (September).

sixth form *n (Br)* die letzten beiden Klassen vor den 'A-level'-Prüfungen.

sixth-form college *n (Br)* College für Schüler, die ihre 'A-level'-Prüfungen machen.

sixtieth ['sɪkstɪəθ] *num* sechzigste(-r) (-s) ; → **sixth**.

sixty ['sɪkstɪ] *num* sechzig ; → **six**.

size [saɪz] *n* Größe *die* ; **what ~ do you take?** welche Größe haben Sie? ; **what ~ is this?** welche Größe ist das?

sizeable ['saɪzəbl] *adj* beträchtlich.

skate [skeɪt] *n (ice skate)* Schlittschuh *der* ; *(roller skate)* Rollschuh *der* ; *(fish)* Rochen *der*. ◆ *vi (ice-skate)* Schlittschuh laufen ; *(roller-skate)* Rollschuh laufen.

skateboard ['skeɪtbɔːd] *n* Skateboard *das*.

skater ['skeɪtə'] *n (ice-skater)* Schlittschuhläufer *der* (-in *die*) ; *(roller-skater)* Rollschuhläufer *der* (-in *die*).

skating ['skeɪtɪŋ] *n* : **to go ~** *(ice-skating)* Schlittschuh laufen gehen ; *(roller-skating)* Rollschuh laufen gehen.

skeleton ['skelɪtn] *n* Skelett *das*.

skeptical ['skeptɪkl] *(Am)* = **sceptical**.

sketch [sketʃ] *n (drawing)* Skizze *die* ; *(humorous)* Sketch *der*. ◆ *vt* skizzieren.

skewer ['skjʊə'] *n* Spieß *der*.

ski [skiː] *(pt & pp* **skied**, *cont* **skiing)** *n* Ski *der*. ◆ *vi* Ski laufen.

ski boots *npl* Skistiefel *pl*.

skid [skɪd] *n* Schleudern *das*. ◆ *vi* schleudern.

skier ['skiːə'] *n* Skiläufer *der* (-in *die*).

skiing ['skiːɪŋ] *n* Skilaufen *das* ; **to go ~** Ski laufen gehen ; **a ~ holiday** ein Skiurlaub.

skilful ['skɪlfʊl] *adj (Br)* geschickt.

ski lift *n* Skilift *der*.

skill [skɪl] n (ability) Geschick das ; (technique) Fertigkeit die.

skilled [skɪld] adj (worker, job) qualifiziert, Fach- ; (driver, chef) erfahren.

skillful ['skɪlfʊl] (Am) = **skilful**.

skimmed milk ['skɪmd-] n entrahmte Milch.

skin [skɪn] n Haut die ; (on fruit, vegetable) Schale die ; (from animal) Fell das.

skin freshener [-,freʃnə'] n Gesichtswasser das.

skinny ['skɪnɪ] adj mager.

skip [skɪp] vi (with rope) seillspringen ; (jump) hüpfen. ◆ vt (omit) ausllassen. ◆ n (container) Container der.

ski pants npl Skihose die.

ski pass n Skipass der.

ski pole n Skistock der.

skipping rope ['skɪpɪŋ-] n Sprungseil das.

skirt [skɜːt] n Rock der.

ski slope n Skipiste die.

ski tow n Schlepplift der.

skittles ['skɪtlz] n (game) Kegeln das.

skull [skʌl] n Schädel der.

sky [skaɪ] n Himmel der.

skylight ['skaɪlaɪt] n Dachfenster das.

skyscraper ['skaɪ,skreɪpə'] n Wolkenkratzer der.

slab [slæb] n Platte die.

slack [slæk] adj (rope) locker ; (careless) nachlässig ; (not busy) ruhig.

slacks [slæks] npl Hose die.

slam [slæm] vt zulschlagen.

slander ['slɑːndə'] n Verleumdung die.

slang [slæŋ] n Slang der.

slant [slɑːnt] n (slope) Schräge die. ◆ vi sich neigen.

slap [slæp] n (smack) Schlag der. ◆ vt schlagen.

slash [slæʃ] vt (cut) auflschlitzen ; (fig : prices) reduzieren. ◆ n (written symbol) Schrägstrich der.

slate [sleɪt] n (rock) Schiefer der ; (on roof) Schieferplatte die.

slaughter ['slɔːtə'] vt (animal) schlachten ; (fig : defeat) fertig machen.

slave [sleɪv] n Sklave der (Sklavin die).

sled [sled] = **sledge**.

sledge [sledʒ] n Schlitten der.

sleep [sliːp] (pt & pp **slept**) n Schlaf der ; (nap) Schläfchen das. ◆ vi schlafen. ◆ vt : the house ~s six in dem Haus können sechs Leute übernachten ; did you ~ well? hast du gut geschlafen? ; I couldn't get to ~ ich konnte nicht einschlafen ; to go to ~ einlschlafen ; to ~ with sb mit jm schlafen.

sleeper ['sliːpə'] n (train) Schlafwagenzug der ; (sleeping car) Schlafwagen der ; (Br : on railway track) Schwelle die ; (Br : earring) Ohrstecker der.

sleeping bag ['sliːpɪŋ-] n Schlafsack der.

sleeping car ['sliːpɪŋ-] n Schlafwagen der.

sleeping pill ['sliːpɪŋ-] n Schlaftablette die.

sleeping policeman ['sliːpɪŋ-] n (Br) Geschwindigkeitsschwelle die.

sleepy ['sliːpɪ] adj schläfrig.

sleet [sliːt] n Schneeregen der.
◆ v impers : it's ~ing es fällt
Schneeregen.

sleeve [sliːv] n Ärmel der ; (of
record) Hülle die.

sleeveless ['sliːvlɪs] adj är-
mellos.

slept [slept] pt & pp → sleep.

slice [slaɪs] n (of bread, meat)
Scheibe die ; (of cake, pizza)
Stück das. ◆ vt (bread, meat) in
Scheiben schneiden ; (cake,
vegetables) in Stücke schnei-
den.

sliced bread [ˌslaɪst-] n Brot
das in Scheiben.

slide [slaɪd] (pt & pp slid [slɪd])
n (in playground) Rutsche die ;
(of photograph) Dia das ; (Br :
hair slide) Haarspange die. ◆ vi
(slip) rutschen.

sliding door [ˌslaɪdɪŋ-] n
Schiebetür die.

slight [slaɪt] adj (minor) leicht ;
the ~est der/die/das Gerings-
te ; not in the ~est nicht im Geringsten.

slightly ['slaɪtlɪ] adv leicht.

slim [slɪm] adj (person, waist)
schlank ; (book) schmal. ◆ vi
abnehmen.

slimming ['slɪmɪŋ] n Abnehmen das.

sling [slɪŋ] (pt & pp slung) n (for
arm) Schlinge die. ◆ vt (inf :
throw) schmeißen.

slip [slɪp] vi rutschen. ◆ n (mistake) Ausrutscher der ; (of paper) Zettel der ; (petticoat) Unterrock der. ■ slip up vi (make
a mistake) einen Schnitzer machen.

slipper ['slɪpəʳ] n Hausschuh
der.

slippery ['slɪpərɪ] adj (surface)
glatt ; (object) schlüpfrig.

slip road n (Br) (onto motorway) Auffahrt die ; (leaving
motorway) Ausfahrt die.

slit [slɪt] n Schlitz der.

slob [slɒb] n (inf) Schwein das.

slogan ['sləʊgən] n Slogan der.

slope [sləʊp] n (incline) Neigung die ; (hill) Hang der ; (in
skiing) Piste die. ◆ vi sich neigen.

sloping ['sləʊpɪŋ] adj (upwards) ansteigend ; (downwards) abfallend.

slot [slɒt] n (for coin) Schlitz
der ; (groove) Nut die.

slot machine n (vending machine) Automat der ; (for gambling) Spielautomat der.

Slovakia [sləˈvækɪə] n Slowakei die.

slow [sləʊ] adj langsam ; (business) flau. ◆ adv langsam ; to be
~ (clock, watch) nachgehen ;
'slow' (sign on road) 'langsam
fahren' ; a ~ train ein Nahverkehrszug. ■ slow down vt
sep verlangsamen. ◆ vi langsamer werden.

slowly ['sləʊlɪ] adv langsam.

slug [slʌg] n (animal) Nackt-
schnecke die.

slum [slʌm] n (building)
Elendsquartier das. ■ slums
npl (district) Elendsviertel das.

slung [slʌŋ] pt & pp → sling.

slush [slʌʃ] n (snow) Schnee-
matsch der.

sly [slaɪ] adj (cunning) schlau ;
(deceitful) verschlagen.

smack [smæk] n (slap) Schlag
der ; (on bottom) Klaps der. ◆ vt
(slap) schlagen.

small [smɔ:l] *adj* klein.

small change *n* Kleingeld *das*.

smallpox ['smɔ:lpɒks] *n* Pocken *pl*.

smart [smɑ:t] *adj* (*elegant*) elegant; (*clever*) clever; (*posh*) fein.

smart card *n* Chipkarte *die*.

smash [smæʃ] *n* (SPORT) Schmetterball *der*; (*inf* : *car crash*) Zusammenstoß *der*. ◆ *vt* (*plate*) zerschlagen; (*window*) einⅼschlagen. ◆ *vi* (*plate, vase etc*) zerbrechen.

smashing ['smæʃɪŋ] *adj* (*Br* : *inf*) toll.

smear test ['smɪə-] *n* Abstrich *der*.

smell [smel] (*pt* & *pp* -ed OR smelt) *n* (*smell*) Geruch *der*; (*bad odour*) Gestank *der*. ◆ *vt* (*sniff at*) riechen an (+D); (*detect*) riechen. ◆ *vi* (*have odour*) riechen; (*have bad odour*) stinken; **to ~ of sthg** nach etw riechen.

smelly ['smelɪ] *adj* stinkend.

smelt [smelt] *pt* & *pp* → **smell**.

smile [smaɪl] *n* Lächeln *das*. ◆ *vi* lächeln.

smoke [sməʊk] *n* Rauch *der*. ◆ *vt* & *vi* rauchen; **to have a ~** eine rauchen.

smoked [sməʊkt] *adj* geräuchert.

smoked salmon *n* Räucherlachs *der*.

smoker ['sməʊkə'] *n* Raucher *der* (-in *die*).

smoking ['sməʊkɪŋ] *n* Rauchen *das*; '**no ~**' 'Rauchen verboten'.

smoking area *n* Raucherzone *die*.

smoking compartment *n* Raucherabteil *das*.

smoky ['sməʊkɪ] *adj* (*room*) verräuchert.

smooth [smu:ð] *adj* (*surface, road, mixture*) glatt; (*skin*) weich; (*wine, beer*) süffig; (*flight, journey*) ruhig; (*takeoff, landing*) weich. ▨ **smooth down** *vt sep* glatt streichen.

smother ['smʌðə'] *vt* (*cover*) bedecken.

smudge [smʌdʒ] *n* Fleck *der*.

smuggle ['smʌgl] *vt* schmuggeln.

snack [snæk] *n* Imbiss *der*.

snack bar *n* Schnellimbiss *der*.

snail [sneɪl] *n* Schnecke *die*.

snake [sneɪk] *n* Schlange *die*.

snap [snæp] *vt* (*break*) zerbrechen. ◆ *vi* (*break*) brechen. ◆ *n* (*inf* : *photo*) Schnappschuss *der*; (*Br* : *card game*) Schnippschnapp *das*.

snare [sneə'] *n* (*trap*) Schlinge *die*.

snatch [snætʃ] *vt* (*grab*) schnappen; (*steal*) klauen.

sneakers ['sni:kəz] *npl* (*Am*) Turnschuhe *pl*.

sneeze [sni:z] *n* Niesen *das*. ◆ *vi* niesen.

sniff [snɪf] *vi* (*from cold, crying*) schniefen. ◆ *vt* (*smell*) schnuppern an (+D).

snip [snɪp] *vt* schnippeln.

snob [snɒb] *n* Snob *der*.

snog [snɒg] *vi* (*Br* : *inf*) knutschen.

snooker ['snu:kə'] *n* Snooker *das*.

snooze [snuːz] *n* Nickerchen *das*.

snore [snɔːʳ] *vi* schnarchen.

snorkel ['snɔːkl] *n* Schnorchel *der*.

snout [snaʊt] *n* Schnauze *die*.

snow [snəʊ] *n* Schnee *der*. ◆ *v impers* : it's ~ing es schneit.

snowball ['snəʊbɔːl] *n* Schneeball *der*.

snowdrift ['snəʊdrɪft] *n* Schneewehe *die*.

snowflake ['snəʊfleɪk] *n* Schneeflocke *die*.

snowman ['snəʊmæn] (*pl* -men [-men]) *n* Schneemann *der*.

snowplough ['snəʊplaʊ] *n* Schneepflug *der*.

snowstorm ['snəʊstɔːm] *n* Schneesturm *der*.

snug [snʌg] *adj* (*place*) gemütlich ; (*person*) behaglich.

so [səʊ] *adv* 1. (*emphasizing degree*) so ; it's ~ difficult (that...) es ist so schwierig (, dass...).
2. (*referring back*) : ~ you knew already du hast es also schon gewusst ; I don't think ~ ich glaube nicht ; I'm afraid ~ leider ja ; if ~ falls ja.
3. (*also*) : ~ do I ich auch.
4. (*in this way*) so.
5. (*expressing agreement*) : ~ there is ja, das stimmt.
6. (*in phrases*) : or ~ oder so, etwa ; ~ as um ; ~ that sodass.
◆ *conj* 1. (*therefore*) deshalb ; I'm away next week ~ I won't be there ich bin nächste Woche weg, also werde ich nicht kommen.
2. (*summarizing*) also ; ~ what

have you been up to? na, was treibst du so?
3. (*in phrases*) : ~ what? (*inf*) na und? ; ~ there! (*inf*) das war's!

soak [səʊk] *vt* (*leave in water*) einlweichen ; (*make very wet*) nass machen. ◆ *vi* : to ~ through sthg etw durchnässen. ■ **soak up** *vt sep* auflsaugen.

soaked [səʊkt] *adj* (*very wet*) patschnass.

soaking ['səʊkɪŋ] *adj* (*very wet*) patschnass.

soap [səʊp] *n* Seife *die*.

soap opera *n* Seifenoper *die*.

soap powder *n* Seifenpulver *das*.

sob [sɒb] *n* Schluchzer *der*. ◆ *vi* schluchzen.

sober ['səʊbəʳ] *adj* (*not drunk*) nüchtern.

soccer ['sɒkəʳ] *n* Fußball *der*.

sociable ['səʊʃəbl] *adj* gesellig.

social ['səʊʃl] *adj* (*problem, conditions*) gesellschaftlich ; (*acquaintance, function*) privat.

social club *n* Klub *der*.

socialist ['səʊʃəlɪst] *adj* sozialistisch. ◆ *n* Sozialist *der* (-in *die*).

social life *n* gesellschaftliches Leben.

social security *n* (*money*) Sozialhilfe *die*.

social worker *n* Sozialarbeiter *der* (-in *die*).

society [sə'saɪətɪ] *n* Gesellschaft *die* ; (*organization, club*) Verein *der*.

sociology [,səʊsɪ'ɒlədʒɪ] *n* Soziologie *die*.

sock [sɒk] *n* Socke *die*.

socket ['sɒkɪt] *n* (*for plug*) Steckdose *die* ; (*for light bulb*) Fassung *die*.

sod [sɒd] *n* (*Br* : *vulg*) Sau *die*.

soda ['səʊdə] *n* (*soda water*) Soda *das* ; (*Am* : *fizzy drink*) Brause *die*.

soda water *n* Sodawasser *das*.

sofa ['səʊfə] *n* Sofa *das*.

sofa bed *n* Schlafcouch *die*.

soft [sɒft] *adj* weich ; (*touch, breeze*) sanft ; (*not loud*) leise.

soft cheese *n* Weichkäse *der*.

soft drink *n* alkoholfreies Getränk.

software ['sɒftweə'] *n* Software *die*.

soil [sɔɪl] *n* (*earth*) Erde *die*.

solarium [sə'leərɪəm] *n* Solarium *das*.

solar panel ['səʊlə-] *n* Sonnenkollektor *der*.

sold [səʊld] *pt & pp* → **sell**.

soldier ['səʊldʒə'] *n* Soldat *der*.

sold out *adj* ausverkauft.

sole [səʊl] *adj* (*only*) einzig ; (*exclusive*) alleinig. ◆ *n* (*of shoe, foot*) Sohle *die* ; (*fish* : *pl inv*) Seezunge *die*.

solemn ['sɒləm] *adj* (*person*) ernst ; (*occasion*) feierlich.

solicitor [sə'lɪsɪtə'] *n* (*Br*) Rechtsanwalt *der* (-anwältin *die*).

solid ['sɒlɪd] *adj* (*not liquid or gas*) fest ; (*strong*) stabil ; (*gold, silver, rock, oak*) massiv.

solo ['səʊləʊ] (*pl* -s) *n* (*MUS*) Solo *das* ; '~ m/cs' (*traffic sign*) 'Parken nur für Motorräder'.

soluble ['sɒljʊbl] *adj* löslich.

solution [sə'luːʃn] *n* Lösung *die*.

solve [sɒlv] *vt* lösen.

some [sʌm] *adj* 1. (*certain amount of*) etwas ; ~ **meat** ein bisschen Fleisch ; ~ **money** etwas Geld ; **I had** ~ **difficulty getting here** es war ziemlich schwierig für mich, hierher zu kommen ; **do you want** ~ **more tea?** möchten Sie noch Tee? 2. (*certain number of*) einige ; ~ **people** einige Leute ; **I've known him for** ~ **years** ich kenne ihn schon seit einigen Jahren ; **can I have** ~ **sweets?** Kann ich Bonbons haben? 3. (*not all*) manche ; ~ **jobs are better paid than others** manche Jobs sind besser bezahlt als andere. 4. (*in imprecise statements*) irgendein(-e) ; **she married** ~ **Italian (or other)** sie hat irgend so einen Italiener geheiratet.

◆ *pron* 1. (*certain amount*) etwas ; **can I have** ~? kann ich etwas davon haben?

2. (*certain number*) einige ; **can I have** ~? kann ich welche haben? ; ~ **(of them) left early** einige (von ihnen) gingen vorher.

◆ *adv* (*approximately*) ungefähr ; **there were** ~ **7,000 people there** es waren um die 7.000 Leute da.

somebody ['sʌmbədɪ] = **someone**.

somehow ['sʌmhaʊ] *adv* irgendwie.

someone ['sʌmwʌn] *pron* jemand ; ~ **or other** irgendjemand.

someplace ['sʌmpleɪs] (*Am*) = **somewhere**.

somersault ['sʌməsɔːlt] *n* Purzelbaum *der*.

something ['sʌmθɪŋ] *pron* etwas ; **it's really ~** es ist ganz toll ; **or ~** *(inf)* oder so etwas ; **like** ungefähr ; **~ or other** irgend etwas.

sometime ['sʌmtaɪm] *adv* irgendwann.

sometimes ['sʌmtaɪmz] *adv* manchmal.

somewhere ['sʌmweə'] *adv* irgendwo ; *(go, travel)* irgendwohin ; *(approximately)* ungefähr.

son [sʌn] *n* Sohn *der*.

song [sɒŋ] *n* Lied *das*.

son-in-law *n* Schwiegersohn *der*.

soon [suːn] *adv* bald ; *(quickly)* schnell ; **too ~** zu früh ; **as ~ as** sobald ; **as ~ as possible** so bald wie möglich ; **~ after** kurz danach ; **~er or later** früher oder später.

soot [sʊt] *n* Ruß *der*.

soothe [suːð] *vt (pain, sunburn)* lindern ; *(person, anger)* beruhigen.

sophisticated [sə'fɪstɪkeɪtɪd] *adj (chic)* gepflegt ; *(complex)* hoch entwickelt.

sorbet ['sɔːbeɪ] *n* Sorbet *das*.

sore [sɔː'] *adj (painful)* schmerzhaft ; *(inflamed)* wund ; *(Am : inf : angry)* sauer. ◆ *n* wunde Stelle ; **to have a ~ throat** Halsschmerzen haben.

sorry ['sɒrɪ] *adj (sad, upset)* traurig ; *(in apologies)* : **I'm ~!** Entschuldigung ; **I'm ~ I'm late** es tut mir Leid, dass ich zu spät komme ; **~?** *(pardon)* wie bitte? ; **to feel ~ for sb** jn bemit-

leiden ; **I'm ~ about yesterday** es tut mir Leid wegen gestern.

sort [sɔːt] *n (type)* Sorte *die*. ◆ *vt* sortieren ; **what ~ of car?** was für ein Auto? ; **a ~ of** eine Art von ; **~ of** irgendwie. ▪ **sort out** *vt sep (classify)* sortieren ; *(resolve)* klären.

so-so *adj* & *adv (inf)* so lala.

soufflé ['suːfleɪ] *n* Soufflé *das*.

sought [sɔːt] *pt* & *pp* → **seek**.

soul [səʊl] *n (spirit)* Seele *die* ; *(soul music)* Soul *der*.

sound [saʊnd] *n* Geräusch *das* ; *(volume)* Ton *der*. ◆ *vt (horn)* hupen ; *(bell)* klingeln. ◆ *vi* klingen. ◆ *adj (structure)* solide ; *(reliable)* vernünftig ; **to ~ like** *(make a noise like)* sich anhören wie ; *(seem to be)* sich anhören.

soundproof ['saʊndpruːf] *adj* schalldicht.

soup [suːp] *n* Suppe *die*.

soup spoon *n* Suppenlöffel *der*.

sour ['saʊə'] *adj* sauer ; **to go ~** sauer werden.

source [sɔːs] *n* Quelle *die* ; *(cause)* Ursache *die*.

sour cream *n* saure Sahne.

south [saʊθ] *n* Süden *der*. ◆ *adj* Süd-. ◆ *adv (fly, walk)* nach Süden ; *(be situated)* im Süden ; **in the ~ of England** in Südengland.

South Africa *n* Südafrika *nt*.

South America *n* Südamerika *nt*.

southbound ['saʊθbaʊnd] *adj* in Richtung Süden.

southeast [ˌsaʊθ'iːst] *n* Südosten *der*.

southern ['sʌðən] *adj* südlich, Süd-.

South Pole n Südpol der.

southwards ['sauθwədz] adv südwärts.

southwest [,sauθ'west] n Südwesten der.

souvenir [,su:və'nɪə'] n Souvenir das, Andenken das.

Soviet Union [,səuvɪət-] n : the ~ die Sowjetunion.

sow¹ [səu] (pp **sown**) vt (seeds) säen.

sow² [sau] n (pig) Sau die.

soya ['sɔɪə] n Soja die.

soya bean n Sojabohne die.

soy sauce [,sɔɪ-] n Sojasoße die.

spa [spa:] n Bad das.

space [speɪs] n Platz der; (in astronomy etc) Weltraum der; (period) Zeitraum der. ◆ vt in Abständen verteilen.

spaceship ['speɪsʃɪp] n Raumschiff das.

space shuttle n Raumtransporter der.

spacious ['speɪʃəs] adj geräumig.

spade [speɪd] n (tool) Spaten der. ▓ **spades** npl (in cards) Pik das.

spaghetti [spə'getɪ] n Spaghetti pl.

Spain [speɪn] n Spanien nt.

span [spæn] pt → **spin**. ◆ n (of time) Spanne die.

Spaniard ['spænjəd] n Spanier der (-in die).

spaniel ['spænjəl] n Spaniel der.

Spanish ['spænɪʃ] adj spanisch. ◆ n (language) Spanisch nt.

spank [spæŋk] vt verhauen.

spanner ['spænə'] n Schraubenschlüssel der.

spare [speə'] adj (kept in reserve) zusätzlich, Extra-; (not in use) übrig. ◆ n (spare part) Ersatzteil das; (spare wheel) Ersatzreifen der. ◆ vt : to ~ sb sthg (time, money) jm etw geben; with ten minutes to ~ mit noch zehn Minuten übrig.

spare part n Ersatzteil das.

spare ribs npl Spare Ribs pl.

spare room n Gästezimmer das.

spare time n Freizeit die.

spare wheel n Ersatzreifen der.

spark [spa:k] n Funken der.

sparkling ['spa:klɪŋ-] adj (mineral water, soft drink) sprudelnd.

sparkling wine n Schaumwein der.

spark plug n Zündkerze die.

sparrow ['spærəu] n Spatz der.

spat [spæt] pt & pp → **spit**.

speak [spi:k] (pt **spoke**, pp **spoken**) vt & vi sprechen; who's ~ing? (on phone) mit wem spreche ich?; can I ~ to Sarah? - ~ing! (on phone) kann ich bitte Sarah sprechen? - Am Apparat!; to ~ to sb about sthg mit jm über etw (A) sprechen. ▓ **speak up** vi (more loudly) lauter sprechen.

speaker ['spi:kə'] n (person) Redner der (-in die); (loudspeaker, of stereo) Lautsprecher der; to be an English ~ Englisch sprechen.

spear [spɪə'] n Speer der.

special ['speʃl] adj (not ordinary) besondere(-r) (-s); (particu-

lar) speziell. ◆ *n (dish)* Spezialität *die* ; 'today's ~' 'Tagesgericht'.

special delivery *n (Br)* Eilzustellung *die.*

special effects *npl* Special effects *pl.*

specialist ['speʃəlɪst] *n (doctor)* Facharzt *der* (-ärztin *die*).

speciality [ˌspeʃɪ'ælətɪ] *n* Spezialität *die.*

specialize ['speʃəlaɪz] *vi* : to ~ (in) sich spezialisieren (auf (+A)).

specially ['speʃəlɪ] *adv* speziell.

special offer *n* Sonderangebot *das.*

special school *n (Br)* Sonderschule *die.*

specialty ['speʃltɪ] *(Am)* = **speciality.**

species ['spiːʃiːz] *n* Art *die.*

specific [spə'sɪfɪk] *adj (particular)* bestimmt ; *(exact)* genau.

specification [ˌspesɪfɪ'keɪʃn] *n (of machine, building etc)* genaue Angaben *pl.*

specimen ['spesɪmən] *n (MED)* Probe *die* ; *(example)* Exemplar *das.*

specs [speks] *npl (inf)* Brille *die.*

spectacle ['spektəkl] *n (sight)* Anblick *der.*

spectacles ['spektəklz] *npl* Brille *die.*

spectacular [spek'tækjʊləʳ] *adj* spektakulär.

spectator [spek'teɪtəʳ] *n* Zuschauer *der* (-in *die*).

sped [sped] *pt & pp* → **speed.**

speech [spiːtʃ] *n* Sprache *die* ; *(talk)* Rede *die.*

speech impediment [-ɪm-ˌpedɪmənt] *n* Sprachbehinderung *die.*

speed [spiːd] *(pt & pp* **-ed** OR **sped)** *n* Geschwindigkeit *die* ; *(of film)* Lichtempfindlichkeit *die* ; *(bicycle gear)* Gang *der.* ◆ *vi (move quickly)* rasen ; *(drive too fast)* zu schnell fahren ; **at ~** mit hoher Geschwindigkeit ; 'reduce ~ now' 'Geschwindigkeit senken'. ▪ **speed up** *vi* beschleunigen.

speedboat ['spiːdbəʊt] *n* Rennboot *das.*

speeding ['spiːdɪŋ] *n* Geschwindigkeitsüberschreitung *die.*

speed limit *n* Geschwindigkeitsbeschränkung *die.*

speedometer [spɪ'dɒmɪtəʳ] *n* Tachometer *der.*

spell [spel] *(Br pt & pp* **-ed** OR **spelt,** *Am pt & pp* **-ed)** *vt* buchstabieren ; *(subj : letters)* schreiben. ◆ *n (period)* Weile *die* ; *(of weather)* Periode *die* ; *(magic)* Zauberformel *die.*

spelling ['spelɪŋ] *n (correct order)* Schreibweise *die* ; *(ability)* Rechtschreibung *die.*

spelt [spelt] *pt & pp (Br)* → **spell.**

spend [spend] *(pt & pp* **spent** [spent]) *vt (money)* ausgeben ; *(time)* verbringen.

sphere [sfɪəʳ] *n (round shape)* Kugel *die.*

spice [spaɪs] *n* Gewürz *das.* ◆ *vt* würzen.

spicy ['spaɪsɪ] *adj* pikant.

spider ['spaɪdəʳ] *n* Spinne *die.*

spider's web *n* Spinnennetz *das.*

spike [spaɪk] n Spitze die.

spill [spɪl] (Br pt & pp -ed OR spilt [spɪlt], Am pt & pp -ed) vt verschütten. ◆ vi (liquid) überlaufen ; (sugar, salt) verschüttet werden.

spin [spɪn] (pt span OR spun, pp spun) vt (wheel) drehen ; (coin) werfen ; (washing) schleudern. ◆ n (on ball) Drall der ; **to go for a ~** (inf : in car) eine Spritztour machen.

spinach [ˈspɪnɪdʒ] n Spinat der.

spine [spaɪn] n Wirbelsäule die ; (of book) Buchrücken der.

spinster [ˈspɪnstəʳ] n ledige Frau.

spiral [ˈspaɪərəl] n Spirale die.

spiral staircase n Wendeltreppe die.

spire [ˈspaɪəʳ] n Turmspitze die.

spirit [ˈspɪrɪt] n (soul) Geist der ; (energy) Schwung der ; (courage) Mut der ; (mood) Stimmung die. ▨ **spirits** npl (Br : alcohol) Spirituosen pl.

spit [spɪt] (Br pt & pp spat, Am pt & pp spit) vi (person) spucken ; (fire) zischen ; (food) spritzen. ◆ n (saliva) Spucke die ; (for cooking) Spieß der. ◆ v impers : **it's spitting** es tröpfelt.

spite [spaɪt] : **in spite of** prep trotz (+G).

spiteful [ˈspaɪtfʊl] adj boshaft.

splash [splæʃ] n (sound) Platschen das. ◆ vt spritzen.

splendid [ˈsplendɪd] adj (beautiful) herrlich ; (very good) großartig.

splint [splɪnt] n Schiene die.

splinter [ˈsplɪntəʳ] n Splitter der.

split [splɪt] (pt & pp split) n (tear) Riss der ; (crack) Spalt der. ◆ vt (tear) zerreißen ; (wood) spalten ; (stone) zerbrechen ; (bill, cost, profits, work) teilen. ◆ vi (tear) reißen ; (wood) splittern ; (stone) brechen. ▨ **split up** vi (group, couple) sich trennen.

spoil [spɔɪl] (pt & pp -ed OR spoilt) vt (ruin) verderben ; (child) verziehen.

spoke [spəʊk] pt → **speak**. ◆ n (of wheel) Speiche die.

spoken [ˈspəʊkn] pp → **speak**.

spokesman [ˈspəʊksmən] (pl -men [-mən]) n Sprecher der.

spokeswoman [ˈspəʊks,wʊmən] (pl -women [-,wɪmɪn]) n Sprecherin die.

sponge [spʌndʒ] n (for cleaning, washing) Schwamm der.

sponge bag n (Br) Kulturbeutel der.

sponge cake n Biskuitkuchen der.

sponsor [ˈspɒnsəʳ] n (of event, TV programme) Sponsor der.

sponsored walk [,spɒnsəd-] n Wanderung mit gesponserten Teilnehmern.

spontaneous [spɒnˈteɪnjəs] adj spontan.

spoon [spuːn] n Löffel der.

spoonful [ˈspuːnfʊl] n Löffel der.

sport [spɔːt] n Sport der.

sports car [spɔːts-] n Sportwagen der.

sports centre [spɔːts-] n Sportzentrum das.

sports jacket [spɔːts-] *n* sportlicher Sakko.

sportsman ['spɔːtsmən] (*pl* -men [-mən]) *n* Sportler *der*.

sports shop [spɔːts-] *n* Sportgeschäft *das*.

sportswoman ['spɔːts,wumən] (*pl* -women [-,wɪmɪn]) *n* Sportlerin *die*.

spot [spɒt] *n* (*stain*) Fleck *der*; (*dot*) Punkt *der*; (*of rain*) Tropfen *der*; (*on skin*) Pickel *der*; (*place*) Stelle *die*. ◆ *vt* entdecken; **on the ~** (*at once*) auf der Stelle; (*at the scene*) an Ort und Stelle.

spotless ['spɒtlɪs] *adj* makellos sauber.

spotlight ['spɒtlaɪt] *n* Scheinwerfer *der*.

spotty ['spɒtɪ] *adj* pickelig.

spouse [spaʊs] *n* (*fml*) Gatte *der* (Gattin *die*).

spout [spaʊt] *n* Schnabel *der*.

sprain [spreɪn] *vt* verstauchen; **to ~ one's wrist** sich (D) das Handgelenk verstauchen.

sprang [spræŋ] *pt* → spring.

spray [spreɪ] *n* (*of aerosol, perfume*) Spray *der*; (*droplets*) Sprühnebel *der*; (*from sea*) Gischt *die*. ◆ *vt* (*surface, wall*) sprühen; (*car, crops, paint, water*) spritzen.

spread [spred] (*pt* & *pp* spread) *vt* (*butter, jam, glue*) streichen; (*map, tablecloth, blanket*) ausbreiten; (*legs, fingers, arms*) ausstrecken; (*disease, news, rumour*) verbreiten. ◆ *vi* (*disease, news, rumour*) sich verbreiten; (*fire*) sich ausbreiten. ◆ *n* (*food*) Aufstrich

der. ▪ **spread out** *vi* (*disperse*) sich verteilen.

spring [sprɪŋ] (*pt* sprang, *pp* sprung) *n* (*season*) Frühling *der*; (*coil*) Feder *die*; (*in ground*) Quelle *die*. ◆ *vi* (*leap*) springen; **in (the) ~** im Frühling.

springboard ['sprɪŋbɔːd] *n* Sprungbrett *das*.

spring-cleaning [-'kliːnɪŋ] *n* Frühlingsputz *der*.

spring onion *n* Frühlingszwiebel *die*.

spring roll *n* Frühlingsrolle *die*.

sprinkle ['sprɪŋkl] *vt* (*liquid*) sprengen; (*salt, sugar*) streuen.

sprinkler ['sprɪŋklə^r] *n* Sprinkler *der*.

sprint [sprɪnt] *n* Sprint *der*. ◆ *vi* rennen; (*SPORT*) sprinten.

Sprinter® ['sprɪntə^r] *n* (*Br : train*) Nahverkehrszug *der*.

sprout [spraʊt] *n* (*vegetable*) Rosenkohl *der*.

spruce [spruːs] *n* Fichte *die*.

sprung [sprʌŋ] *pp* → spring. ◆ *adj* (*mattress*) gefedert.

spud [spʌd] *n* (*inf*) Kartoffel *die*.

spun [spʌn] *pt* & *pp* → spin.

spur [spɜː^r] *n* (*for horse rider*) Sporn *der*; **on the ~ of the moment** ganz spontan.

spurt [spɜːt] *vi* spritzen.

spy [spaɪ] *n* Spion *der* (-in *die*).

squall [skwɔːl] *n* Bö *die*.

squalor ['skwɒlə^r] *n* Schmutz *der*.

square [skweə^r] *adj* (*in shape*) quadratisch. ◆ *n* (*shape*) Quadrat *das*; (*in town*) Platz *der*; (*of chocolate*) Stück *das*; (*on chess-*

board) Feld *das*; **2 ~ metres** 2 Quadratmeter; **it's 2 metres ~** es ist 2 Meter im Quadrat; **we're (all) ~ now** *(not owing money)* jetzt sind wir quitt.

squash [skwɒʃ] *n (game)* Squash *das*; *(Br : drink)* Fruchtsaftgetränk *das*; *(Am : vegetable)* Kürbis *der*. ◆ *vt* zerquetschen.

squat [skwɒt] *adj* gedrungen. ◆ *vi (crouch)* hocken.

squeak [skwiːk] *vi* quietschen.

squeeze [skwiːz] *vt (hand)* drücken; *(tube)* ausldrücken; *(orange)* auslpressen. ▪ **squeeze in** *vi* sich hineinzwängen.

squid [skwɪd] *n* Tintenfisch *der*.

squint [skwɪnt] *n* Schielen *das*. ◆ *vi* blinzeln.

squirrel [*(Br)* 'skwɪrəl, *(Am)* 'skwɜːrəl] *n* Eichhörnchen *das*.

squirt [skwɜːt] *vi* spritzen.

St *(abbr of Street)* Str.; *(abbr of Saint)* St.

stab [stæb] *vt* stechen.

stable ['steɪbl] *adj* stabil. ◆ *n* Stall *der*.

stack [stæk] *n (pile)* Stapel *der*; **~s of money** *(inf)* haufenweise Geld.

stadium ['steɪdjəm] *n* Stadion *das*.

staff [stɑːf] *n (workers)* Personal *das*.

stage [steɪdʒ] *n (phase)* Phase *die*; *(in theatre)* Bühne *die*.

stagger ['stægə] *vt (arrange in stages)* staffeln. ◆ *vi* schwanken.

stagnant ['stægnənt] *adj (water)* stehend.

stain [steɪn] *n* Fleck *der*. ◆ *vt* beflecken.

stained glass [,steɪnd-] *n* farbiges Glas.

stainless steel ['steɪnlɪs-] *n* Edelstahl *der*.

staircase ['steəkeɪs] *n* Treppe *die*.

stairs [steəz] *npl* Treppe *die*.

stairwell ['steəwel] *n* Treppenhaus *das*.

stake [steɪk] *n (share)* Anteil *der*; *(in gambling)* Einsatz *der*; *(post)* Pfahl *der*; **to be at ~** auf dem Spiel stehen.

stale [steɪl] *adj (food)* trocken.

stalk [stɔːk] *n* Stiel *der*.

stall [stɔːl] *n (in market, at exhibition)* Stand *der*. ◆ *vi (car, engine)* ablsterben. ▪ **stalls** *npl (Br : in theatre)* Parkett *das*.

stamina ['stæmɪnə] *n* Ausdauer *die*.

stammer ['stæmə] *vi* stottern.

stamp [stæmp] *n (for letter)* Briefmarke *die*; *(in passport, on document)* Stempel *der*. ◆ *vt (passport, document)* stempeln. ◆ *vi* : **to ~ on sthg** auf etw *(A)* treten; **to ~ one's foot** mit dem Fuß stampfen.

stamp-collecting [-kə,lektɪŋ] *n* Briefmarkensammeln *das*.

stamp machine *n* Briefmarkenautomat *der*.

stand [stænd] *(pt & pp* **stood**) *vi* stehen; *(get to one's feet)* auflstehen. ◆ *vt (place)* stellen; *(put up with)* ertragen; *(withstand)* auslhalten. ◆ *n (stall)* Stand *der*; *(for umbrellas, coats, motorbike)* Ständer *der*; *(at*

sports stadium) Tribüne die ; **I
can't ~ him** ich kann ihn nicht
ausstehen ; **to be ~ing** stehen ;
to ~ sb a drink jm ein Getränk
spendieren ; **'no ~ing'** *(Am : AUT)*
'Halten verboten'. ■ **stand
back** *vi* zurücktreten. ■
stand for *vt fus (mean)* bedeuten ; *(tolerate)* hinnehmen. ■
stand in *vi* : **to ~ in for sb** für
jn einspringen. ■ **stand out**
vi (be conspicuous) auffallen ;
(be superior) hervorstechen. ■
stand up *vi (be on feet)* stehen ; *(get to one's feet)* aufstehen. ◆ *vt sep (inf : boyfriend,
girlfriend etc)* versetzen. ■
stand up for *vt fus* eintreten für.

standard ['stændəd] *adj (normal)* Standard-. ◆ *n (level)* Niveau das ; *(point of comparison)*
Maßstab der ; **up to ~** der Norm
entsprechend. ■ **standards**
npl (principles) Maßstäbe *pl*.

standard-class *adj (Br : on
train)* zweiter Klasse.

standby ['stændbaɪ] *adj (ticket)* Standby-.

stank [stæŋk] *pt → **stink**.

staple ['steɪpl] *n (for paper)*
Heftklammer die.

stapler ['steɪplə'] *n* Hefter der.

star [staː'] *n* Stern der ; *(famous
person)* Star der. ◆ *vt (subj : film,
play etc)* : **the film ~s** Cary Grant
Cary Grant spielt die Hauptrolle in diesem Film. ■ **stars**
npl (horoscope) Sterne *pl*.

starboard ['staːbəd] *adj* Steuerbord-.

starch [staːtʃ] *n* Stärke die.

stare [steə'] *vi* starren ; **to ~ at**
jn anstarren.

starfish ['staːfɪʃ] *(pl starfish)*
n Seestern der.

starling ['staːlɪŋ] *n* Star der.

Stars and Stripes *n* : **the ~**
das Sternenbanner.

 STARS AND STRIPES

Dies ist eine der vielen landläufigen Bezeichnungen für
die Nationalflagge der Vereinigten Staaten, auch „Old
Glory", „The Star-Spangled
Banner" und „The Stars and
Bars" genannt. Die Flagge
weist 50 Sterne auf, einen für
jeden der 50 amerikanischen
Bundesstaaten, sowie 13 rote
und weiße Streifen, die die 13
Gründerstaaten Amerikas
symbolisieren. Die Amerikaner sind sehr stolz auf ihre
Flagge, und viele stellen sie
deshalb vor ihrem Haus auf.

start [staːt] *n* Anfang der, Beginn der ; *(SPORT)* Start der. ◆ *vt*
anfangen, beginnen ; *(car, engine)* anlassen ; *(business, club)*
gründen. ◆ *vi* anfangen, beginnen ; *(car, engine)* anspringen ; *(begin journey)* aufbrechen ; **prices ~ at** OR **from £5**
Preise ab 5 Pfund ; **to ~ doing
sthg** OR **to do sthg** beginnen,
etw zu tun ; **to ~ with** *(in the first
place)* erstens ; *(when ordering
meal)* als Vorspeise. ■ **start
out** *vi (on journey)* aufbrechen ; **to ~ out as sthg** ursprünglich etw sein. ■ **start up** *vt
sep (car, engine)* anlassen ;
(business) gründen ; *(shop)* eröffnen.

starter ['stɑːtə'] n (Br : of meal) Vorspeise die ; (of car) Anlasser der ; for ~s (in meal) als Vorspeise.

starter motor n Anlasser der.

starting point ['stɑːtɪŋ-] n Ausgangspunkt der.

startle ['stɑːtl] vt erschrecken.

starvation [stɑːˈveɪʃn] n Verhungern das.

starve [stɑːv] vi (have no food) hungern ; I'm starving! ich habe einen Mordshunger.

state [steɪt] n (condition) Zustand der ; (country, region) Staat der. ◆ vt (declare) erklären ; (specify) anlgeben ; the State der Staat ; the States die Vereinigten Staaten.

statement ['steɪtmənt] n (declaration) Erklärung die ; (from bank) Kontoauszug der.

state school n staatliche Schule.

statesman ['steɪtsmən] (pl -men [-mən]) n Staatsmann der.

static ['stætɪk] n (on radio, TV) atmosphärische Störungen pl.

station ['steɪʃn] n Bahnhof der ; (on radio) Sender der.

stationary ['steɪʃnərɪ] adj stehend.

stationer's ['steɪʃnəz] n (shop) Schreibwarengeschäft das.

stationery ['steɪʃnərɪ] n Schreibwaren pl.

station wagon n (Am) Kombiwagen der.

statistics [stəˈtɪstɪks] npl Statistik die.

statue ['stætʃuː] n Statue die.

Statue of Liberty n : the ~ die Freiheitsstatue.

ⓘ **STATUE OF LIBERTY**

Die „Statue of Liberty", die amerikanische Freiheitsstatue, stellt eine Frau dar, die eine Fackel emporhält. Sie steht auf einer winzigen Insel an der Einfahrt zum New Yorker Hafen. Sie wurde den USA 1884 von Frankreich als Geschenk überreicht und kann besichtigt werden.

status ['steɪtəs] n Status der.

stay [steɪ] n (time spent) Aufenthalt der. ◆ vi (remain) bleiben ; (as guest) übernachten ; (Scot : reside) wohnen ; to ~ the night übernachten. ▪ stay away vi weglbleiben. ▪ stay in vi zu Hause bleiben. ▪ stay out vi (from home) weglbleiben. ▪ stay up vi auflbleiben.

STD code n Vorwahl die.

steady ['stedɪ] adj (firm, stable) stabil ; (hand) ruhig ; (gradual) stetig ; (job) fest. ◆ vt festlhalten.

steak [steɪk] n Steak das ; (of fish) Fischscheibe die.

steak and kidney pie n mit Rindfleisch und Nieren gefüllte Pastete.

steakhouse ['steɪkhaʊs, pl -haʊzɪz] n Steakhaus das.

steal [stiːl] (pt stole, pp stolen) vt stehlen ; to ~ sthg from sb jm etw stehlen.

steam [stiːm] n Dampf der. ◆ vt (food) dünsten.

steamboat ['sti:mbəʊt] n Dampfschiff das.

steam engine n Dampflokomotive die.

steam iron n Dampfbügeleisen das.

steel [sti:l] n Stahl der. ◆ adj Stahl-.

steep [sti:p] adj steil.

steeple ['sti:pl] n Kirchturm der.

steer ['stɪər] vt (car) lenken ; (boat, plane) steuern.

steering ['stɪərɪŋ] n Lenkung die.

steering wheel n Lenkrad das.

stem [stem] n Stiel der.

step [step] n (of staircase, ladder) Stufe die ; (pace) Schritt der ; (measure) Maßnahme die ; (stage) Schritt der. ◆ vi : to ~ on sthg auf etw (A) treten ; 'mind the ~' 'Vorsicht, Stufe'.
▪ **steps** npl (stairs) Treppe die.
▪ **step aside** vi (move aside) zur Seite treten. ▪ **step back** vi (move back) zurücktreten.

step aerobics n Step-Aerobic das.

stepbrother ['step,brʌðər] n Stiefbruder der.

stepdaughter ['step,dɔ:tər] n Stieftochter die.

stepfather ['step,fɑ:ðər] n Stiefvater der.

stepladder ['step,lædər] n Trittleiter die.

stepmother ['step,mʌðər] n Stiefmutter die.

stepsister ['step,sɪstər] n Stiefschwester die.

stepson ['stepsʌn] n Stiefsohn der.

stereo ['steriəʊ] (pl -s) adj Stereo-. ◆ n (hi-fi) Stereoanlage die ; (stereo sound) Stereo das.

sterile ['sterail] adj (germ-free) steril.

sterilize ['sterəlaiz] vt (container, milk, utensil) sterilisieren.

sterling ['stɜ:lɪŋ] adj (pound) Sterling-. ◆ n Sterling der.

sterling silver n Sterlingsilber das.

stern [stɜ:n] adj (strict) streng. ◆ n (of boat) Heck das.

stew [stju:] n Eintopf der.

steward ['stjʊəd] n (on plane, ship) Steward der ; (at public event) Ordner der (-in die).

stewardess ['stjʊədɪs] n Stewardess die.

stewed [stju:d] adj : ~ fruit Kompott das.

stick [stɪk] (pt & pp stuck) n (of wood) Stock der ; (for sport) Schläger der ; (of chalk) Stück das ; (of celery, cinnamon) Stange die. ◆ vt (glue) kleben ; (push, insert) stecken ; (inf : put) tun. ◆ vi kleben ; (jam) klemmen. ▪ **stick out** vi (protrude) vorlstehen ; (be noticeable) sich ablheben. ▪ **stick to** vt fus (decision) bleiben bei ; (promise) halten. ▪ **stick up** vt sep (poster, notice) anlschlagen. ◆ vi hochlstehen. ▪ **stick up for** vt fus einltreten für.

sticker ['stɪkər] n Aufkleber der.

sticking plaster ['stɪkɪŋ-] n Heftpflaster das.

stick shift n (Am : car) Handschaltgetriebe das.

sticky ['stɪkɪ] *adj* klebrig ; *(label, tape)* Klebe- ; *(weather)* schwül.

stiff [stɪf] *adj* steif. ◆ *adv* : **to be bored ~** *(inf)* sich zu Tode langweilen.

stile [staɪl] *n* Zauntritt *der*.

stiletto heels [stɪ'letəʊ-] *npl (shoes)* Stöckelschuhe *pl*.

still [stɪl] *adv* noch ; *(even now)* immer noch ; *(despite that)* trotzdem. ◆ *adj (motionless)* bewegungslos ; *(quiet, calm)* ruhig ; *(not fizzy)* ohne Kohlensäure ; **we've ~ got 10 minutes** wir haben noch 10 Minuten ; **~ more** noch mehr ; **to stand ~** still stehen.

Stilton ['stɪltn] *n* Stilton *der (britische, starke Blauschimmelkäse)*.

stimulate ['stɪmjʊleɪt] *vt* anregen.

sting [stɪŋ] *(pt & pp* **stung)** *vt (subj: bee, wasp)* stechen ; *(subj: nettle)* brennen. ◆ *vi (skin, eyes)* brennen.

stingy ['stɪndʒɪ] *adj (inf)* geizig.

stink [stɪŋk] *(pt* **stank** OR **stunk**, *pp* **stunk)** *vi* stinken.

stipulate ['stɪpjʊleɪt] *vt* festlegen.

stir [stɜːʳ] *vt* umrühren.

stir-fry *n* auf chinesische Art in einer Pfanne gebratenes Gemüse oder Fleisch. ◆ *vt* schnell braten.

stirrup ['stɪrəp] *n* Steigbügel *der*.

stitch [stɪtʃ] *n (in sewing)* Stich *der* ; *(in knitting)* Masche *die* ; **to have a ~** *(stomach pain)* Seiten-

stechen haben. ▮ **stitches** *npl (for wound)* Stiche *pl*.

stock [stɒk] *n (of shop, business)* Warenbestand *der* ; *(supply)* Vorrat *der* ; *(FIN)* Aktienkapital *das* ; *(in cooking)* Brühe *die*. ◆ *vt (have in stock)* auf Lager haben ; **in ~** vorrätig ; **out of ~** nicht vorrätig.

stock cube *n* Brühwürfel *der*.

Stock Exchange *n* Börse *die*.

stocking ['stɒkɪŋ] *n* Strumpf *der*.

stock market *n* Börse *die*.

stodgy ['stɒdʒɪ] *adj (food)* pappig.

stole [stəʊl] *pt* → **steal**.

stolen ['stəʊln] *pp* → **steal**.

stomach ['stʌmək] *n (organ)* Magen *der* ; *(belly)* Bauch *der*.

stomachache ['stʌməkeɪk] *n* Bauchschmerzen *pl*.

stomach upset [-'ʌpset] *n* Magenverstimmung *die*.

stone [stəʊn] *n* Stein *der* ; *(measurement : pl inv)* = 6,35 kg ; *(gem)* Edelstein *der*. ◆ *adj* Stein-.

stonewashed ['stəʊnwɒʃt] *adj* stonewashed.

stood [stʊd] *pt & pp* → **stand**.

stool [stuːl] *n (for sitting on)* Hocker *der*.

stop [stɒp] *n (for bus)* Haltestelle *die* ; *(for train)* Station *die* ; *(in journey)* Aufenthalt *der*. ◆ *vt* anhalten ; *(machine)* abstellen ; *(prevent)* verhindern. ◆ *vi* aufhören ; *(vehicle)* halten ; *(walker, machine, clock)* stehen bleiben ; *(on journey)* einen Halt machen ; *(stay)* bleiben ; **to ~ sb from doing sthg** jn daran hindern, etw zu tun ; **to**

~ sthg from happening verhindern, dass etw geschieht; to ~ doing sthg aufhören, etw zu tun; to put a ~ to sthg etw abstellen; 'stop' *(road sign)* 'Stop'; 'stopping at...' *(train, bus)* 'Haltestellen...' ■ **stop off** *vi* Zwischenstation machen.

stopover ['stɒp,əʊvə^r] *n (on flight)* Zwischenlandung die; *(on journey)* Zwischenaufenthalt der.

stopper ['stɒpə^r] *n* Stöpsel der.

stopwatch ['stɒpwɒtʃ] *n* Stoppuhr die.

storage ['stɔːrɪdʒ] *n* Lagerung die.

store [stɔː^r] *n (shop)* Laden der; *(department store)* Kaufhaus das; *(supply)* Vorrat der. ◆ *vt* lagern.

storehouse [,stɔːhaʊs, *pl* -haʊzɪz] *n* Lagerhaus das.

storeroom ['stɔːrʊm] *n* Lagerraum der.

storey ['stɔːrɪ] *(pl -s)* *n (Br)* Stockwerk das.

stork [stɔːk] *n* Storch der.

storm [stɔːm] *n* Sturm der.

stormy ['stɔːmɪ] *adj* stürmisch.

story ['stɔːrɪ] *n* Geschichte die; *(Am)* = **storey**.

stout [staʊt] *adj (fat)* beleibt. ◆ *n (drink)* Art britisches Dunkelbier.

stove [stəʊv] *n (for heating)* Ofen der; *(for cooking)* Herd der.

straight [streɪt] *adj* gerade; *(hair)* glatt; *(consecutive)* ununterbrochen; *(drink)* pur. ◆ *adv* *(in a straight line)* gerade; *(upright)* aufrecht; *(directly)* direkt; ~ **ahead** geradeaus; ~ **away** sofort.

straightforward [,streɪt-ˈfɔːwəd] *adj (easy)* einfach.

strain [streɪn] *n* Belastung die; *(tension)* Spannung die; *(injury)* Zerrung die. ◆ *vt (muscle)* zerren; *(eyes)* überanstrengen; *(food)* abgießen; *(tea)* abseihen.

strainer ['streɪnə^r] *n* Sieb das.

strait [streɪt] *n* Meerenge die.

strange [streɪndʒ] *adj (odd)* seltsam; *(unfamiliar)* fremd.

stranger ['streɪndʒə^r] *n* Fremde der, die.

strangle ['stræŋgl] *vt* erwürgen.

strap [stræp] *n (of bag, camera, shoe)* Riemen der; *(of dress)* Träger der; *(of watch)* Armband das.

strapless ['stræplɪs] *adj* trägerlos.

strategy ['strætɪdʒɪ] *n* Strategie die.

Stratford - upon - Avon [,strætfədəpɒnˈeɪvn] *n* Stratford-upon-Avon.

ⓘ **STRATFORD-UPON-AVON**

Dieses Städtchen in der englischen Grafschaft Warwickshire ist der berühmte Geburtsort des Bühnenschriftstellers und Dichters William Shakespeare (1564-1616). Heute ist Stratford-upon-Avon ein Zentrum der britischen Schauspielkunst, und die hier ansässige „Royal Shakespeare Company" führt Stücke von Shakespeare und anderen Bühnenschriftstellern auf.

straw [strɔː] n (substance) Stroh das ; (for drinking) Strohhalm der.

strawberry ['strɔːbərɪ] n Erdbeere die.

stray [streɪ] adj (animal) streunend. ◆ vi streunen.

streak [striːk] n Streifen der ; lucky/unlucky ~ Glücks-/Pechsträhne die.

stream [striːm] n Strom der ; (small river) Bach der.

street [striːt] n Straße die.

streetcar ['striːtkɑːʳ] n (Am) Straßenbahn die.

street light n Straßenlampe die.

street plan n Stadtplan der.

strength [streŋθ] n Stärke die ; (of person, animal) Kraft die ; (of structure) Stabilität die.

strengthen ['streŋθn] vt (structure) verstärken ; (argument) unterstützen.

stress [stres] n (tension) Stress der ; (on word, syllable) Betonung die. ◆ vt betonen.

stretch [stretʃ] n (of land) Stück das ; (of water) Teil der ; (of time) Zeitraum der. ◆ vt (rope, material) spannen ; (body) strecken ; (elastic, clothes) dehnen. ◆ vi (land, sea) sich erstrecken ; (person, animal) sich strecken ; to ~ one's legs (fig) sich (D) die Beine vertreten. ▨ **stretch out** vt sep

(hand) auslstrecken. ◆ vi (lie down) sich hinllegen.

stretcher ['stretʃəʳ] n Tragbahre die.

strict [strɪkt] adj streng ; (exact) genau.

strictly ['strɪktlɪ] adv streng ; (exclusively) ausschließlich ; ~ speaking genau genommen.

stride [straɪd] n Schritt der.

strike [straɪk] (pt & pp **struck**) n (of employees) Streik der. ◆ vt (fml : hit) schlagen ; (fml : collide with) treffen ; (a match) anlzünden. ◆ vi (refuse to work) streiken ; (happen suddenly) auslbrechen ; the clock struck eight es schlug acht Uhr.

striking ['straɪkɪŋ] adj auffallend.

string [strɪŋ] n Schnur die ; (thinner) Bindfaden der ; (of pearls, beads) Kette die ; (of musical instrument, tennis racket) Saite die ; (series) Reihe die ; a piece of ~ eine Schnur.

strip [strɪp] n Streifen der. ◆ vt (paint, wallpaper) entfernen. ◆ vi (undress) sich auslziehen.

stripe [straɪp] n Streifen der.

striped [straɪpt] adj gestreift.

strip-search vt Kleider zum Zweck einer Leibesvisitation auslziehen.

strip show n Stripshow die.

stroke [strəʊk] n (MED) Schlaganfall der ; (in tennis, golf) Schlag der ; (swimming style) Stil der. ◆ vt streicheln ; a ~ of luck ein Glücksfall.

stroll [strəʊl] n Spaziergang der.

stroller ['strəʊlər] n (Am : pushchair) Sportwagen der (für Kinder).

strong [strɒŋ] adj stark ; (structure, bridge, chair) stabil ; (possibility, subject) gut.

struck [strʌk] pt & pp → **strike**.

structure ['strʌktʃər] n Struktur die ; (building) Bau der.

struggle ['strʌgl] n (great effort) Anstrengung die. ◆ vi (fight) kämpfen ; **to ~ to do sthg** sich abmühen, etw zu tun.

stub [stʌb] n (of cigarette) Kippe die ; (of cheque, ticket) Abschnitt der.

stubble ['stʌbl] n (on face) Stoppeln pl.

stubborn ['stʌbən] adj (person) stur.

stuck [stʌk] pt & pp → **stick**. ◆ adj (jammed) eingeklemmt ; **to be ~** nicht weiterlkönnen.

stud [stʌd] n (on boots) Stollen der ; (fastener) Niete die ; (earring) Ohrstecker der.

student ['stju:dnt] n (at university, college) Student der (-in die) ; (at school) Schüler der (-in die).

student card n Studentenausweis der.

students' union [,stju:dnts-] n Studentenvereinigung die.

studio ['stju:diəʊ] n (pl -s) n (for filming, broadcasting) Studio das ; (of artist) Atelier das.

studio apartment (Am) = **studio flat**.

studio flat n (Br) Einzimmerwohnung die.

study ['stʌdi] n (learning) Studium das ; (piece of research) Studie die ; (room) Arbeitszimmer das. ◆ vt (learn about) studieren ; (examine) untersuchen. ◆ vi studieren.

stuff [stʌf] n (inf : substance) Stoff der ; (things, possessions) Zeug das. ◆ vt stopfen.

stuffed [stʌft] adj (food) gefüllt ; (inf : full up) voll ; (dead animal) ausgestopft.

stuffing ['stʌfɪŋ] n (food) Füllung die ; (of pillow, cushion) Füllmaterial das.

stuffy ['stʌfɪ] adj (room, atmosphere) stickig.

stumble ['stʌmbl] vi stolpern.

stump [stʌmp] n Stumpf der.

stun [stʌn] vt (astound) fassungslos machen.

stung [stʌŋ] pt & pp → **sting**.

stunk [stʌŋk] pt & pp → **stink**.

stunning ['stʌnɪŋ] adj (very beautiful) hinreißend ; (very surprising) sensationell.

stupid ['stju:pɪd] adj dumm.

sturdy ['stɜ:dɪ] adj stabil.

stutter ['stʌtər] vi stottern.

sty [staɪ] n Schweinestall der.

style [staɪl] n Stil der. ◆ vt (hair) frisieren.

stylish ['staɪlɪʃ] adj elegant.

stylist ['staɪlɪst] n (hairdresser) Haarstylist der (-in die).

sub [sʌb] n (SPORT : inf) Ersatzspieler der (-in die) ; (Br : subscription) Abo das.

subdued [səb'dju:d] adj (person) still ; (lighting, colour) gedämpft.

subject [n 'sʌbdʒekt, vb səb-'dʒekt] n (topic) Thema das ; (at school, university) Fach das ; (GRAMM) Subjekt das ; (fml : of country) Staatsbürger der (-in

suggest

die). ◆ vt : **to ~ sth to sb** to sthg jn etw (D) unterwerfen ; **~ to availability** solange der Vorrat reicht ; **~ to an additional charge** vorbehaltlich eines Aufschlages.

subjunctive [səb'dʒʌŋktɪv] n Konjunktiv der.

submarine [ˌsʌbmə'riːn] n Unterseeboot das.

submit [səb'mɪt] vt (present) vorlegen. ◆ vi (give in) sich fügen.

subordinate [sə'bɔːdɪnət] adj (GRAMM) untergeordnet.

subscribe [səb'skraɪb] vi : **to ~ to sthg** (to magazine, newspaper) etw abonnieren.

subscription [səb'skrɪpʃn] n Abonnement das.

subsequent ['sʌbsɪkwənt] adj später.

subside [səb'saɪd] vi (ground) sich senken ; (noise, feeling) abklingen.

substance ['sʌbstəns] n Stoff der.

substantial [səb'stænʃl] adj (large) erheblich.

substitute ['sʌbstɪtjuːt] n (replacement) Ersatz der ; (SPORT) Ersatzspieler der (-in die).

subtitles ['sʌbˌtaɪtlz] npl Untertitel pl.

subtle ['sʌtl] adj (difference, change) fein ; (person) feinfühlig ; (plan) raffiniert.

subtract [səb'trækt] vt abziehen.

subtraction [səb'trækʃn] n Subtraktion die.

suburb ['sʌbɜːb] n Vorort der ; **the ~s** der Stadtrand.

subway ['sʌbweɪ] n (Br : for pedestrians) Unterführung die ;

(Am : underground railway) U-Bahn die.

succeed [sək'siːd] vi (person) Erfolg haben ; (plan) gelingen. ◆ vt (fml : follow) folgen (+D) ; **I ~ed in doing it** es ist mir gelungen.

success [sək'ses] n Erfolg der.

successful [sək'sesfʊl] adj erfolgreich.

succulent ['sʌkjʊlənt] adj saftig.

such [sʌtʃ] adj solche(-r) (-s). ◆ adv : **~ a lot** so viel ; **it's ~ a lovely day** es ist so ein schöner Tag ; **~ a thing should never have happened** so etwas hätte nie passieren dürfen ; **~ people** solche Leute ; **~ as** wie.

suck [sʌk] vt (teat) saugen ; (sweet, thumb) lutschen.

sudden ['sʌdn] adj plötzlich ; **all of a ~** plötzlich.

suddenly ['sʌdnlɪ] adv plötzlich.

sue [suː] vt verklagen.

suede [sweɪd] n Wildleder das.

suffer ['sʌfə'] vt erleiden. ◆ vi leiden ; **to ~ from** (illness) leiden an (+D).

suffering ['sʌfrɪŋ] n (mental) Leid das ; (physical) Leiden das.

sufficient [sə'fɪʃnt] adj (fml) genug.

sufficiently [sə'fɪʃntlɪ] adv (fml) genug.

suffix ['sʌfɪks] n Nachsilbe die.

suffocate ['sʌfəkeɪt] vi ersticken.

sugar ['ʃʊgə'] n Zucker der.

suggest [sə'dʒest] vt (propose) vorschlagen ; **to ~ doing sthg** vorschlagen, etw zu tun.

suggestion [sə'dʒestʃn] n (proposal) Vorschlag der ; (hint) Andeutung die.

suicide ['suisaid] n Selbstmord der ; **to commit ~** Selbstmord begehen.

suit [suːt] n (man's clothes) Anzug der ; (woman's clothes) Kostüm das ; (in cards) Farbe die ; (JUR) Prozess der. ◆ vt (subj : clothes, colour, shoes) stehen (+D) ; (be convenient for) passen (+D) ; (be appropriate for) passen zu ; **to be ~ed to** geeignet sein für ; **pink doesn't ~ me** Rosa steht mir nicht ; **does 10 o'clock ~ you?** passt dir/Ihnen 10 Uhr?

suitable ['suːtəbl] adj geeignet ; **to be ~ for** geeignet sein für.

suitcase ['suːtkeis] n Koffer der.

suite [swiːt] n (set of rooms) Suite die ; (furniture) Garnitur die.

sulk [sʌlk] vi schmollen.

sultana [səl'tɑːnə] n (Br) Sultanine die.

sultry ['sʌltri] adj (weather, climate) schwül.

sum [sʌm] n Summe die ; (calculation) Rechnung die. ▪ **sum up** vt sep (summarize) zusammenǀfassen.

summarize ['sʌməraiz] vt zusammenǀfassen.

summary ['sʌməri] n Zusammenfassung die.

summer ['sʌmə] n Sommer der ; **in (the) ~** im Sommer ; **~ holidays** Sommerferien pl.

summertime ['sʌmətaim] n Sommer der.

summit ['sʌmit] n Gipfel der.

summon ['sʌmən] vt (send for) kommen lassen ; (JUR) vorǀladen.

sumptuous ['sʌmptʃuəs] adj luxuriös.

sun [sʌn] n Sonne die. ◆ vt : **to ~ o.s.** sich sonnen ; **to catch the ~** viel Sonne abǀbekommen ; **in the ~** in der Sonne ; **out of the ~** im Schatten.

Sun. (abbr of Sunday) So.

sunbathe ['sʌnbeið] vi sonnenbaden.

sunbed ['sʌnbed] n Sonnenbank die.

sun block n Sonnencreme die.

sunburn ['sʌnbɜːn] n Sonnenbrand der.

sunburnt ['sʌnbɜːnt] adj : **to be ~** einen Sonnenbrand haben.

sundae ['sʌndei] n Eisbecher der.

Sunday ['sʌndi] n Sonntag der ; → **Saturday**.

Sunday school n Sonntagsschule die.

sundress ['sʌndres] n Strandkleid das.

sundries ['sʌndriz] npl (on bill) Verschiedenes.

sunflower ['sʌn,flauə] n Sonnenblume die.

sunflower oil n Sonnenblumenöl das.

sung [sʌŋ] pt → **sing**.

sunglasses ['sʌn,glɑːsiz] npl Sonnenbrille die.

sunhat ['sʌnhæt] n Sonnenhut der.

sunk [sʌŋk] pp → **sink**.

sunlight ['sʌnlait] n Sonnenlicht das.

sun lounger [-ˌlaʊndʒəʳ] *n* Liegestuhl *der*.

sunny ['sʌnɪ] *adj* sonnig.

sunrise ['sʌnraɪz] *n* Sonnenaufgang *der*.

sunroof ['sʌnruːf] *n* Schiebedach *das*.

sunset ['sʌnset] *n* Sonnenuntergang *der*.

sunshine ['sʌnʃaɪn] *n* Sonnenschein *der* ; **in the ~** in der Sonne.

sunstroke ['sʌnstrəʊk] *n* Sonnenstich *der*.

suntan ['sʌntæn] *n* Bräune *die*.

suntan cream *n* Sonnencreme *die*.

suntan lotion *n* Sonnenmilch *die*.

super ['suːpəʳ] *adj (wonderful)* super. ◆ *n (petrol)* Super *das*.

superb [suːˈpɜːb] *adj* erstklassig.

superficial [ˌsuːpəˈfɪʃl] *adj (pej : person)* oberflächlich ; *(wound)* äußerlich.

superfluous [suːˈpɜːfluəs] *adj* überflüssig.

Superglue® ['suːpəgluː] *n* Sekundenkleber *der*.

superior [suːˈpɪərɪəʳ] *adj (in quality)* überlegen ; *(in rank)* höher. ◆ *n* Vorgesetzte *der*, *die*.

supermarket ['suːpəˌmɑːkɪt] *n* Supermarkt *der*.

supernatural [ˌsuːpəˈnætʃrəl] *adj* übernatürlich.

Super Saver® *n (Br : rail ticket)* Sparpreisticket oder -angebot.

superstitious [ˌsuːpəˈstɪʃəs] *adj* abergläubisch.

superstore ['suːpəstɔːʳ] *n* Verbrauchermarkt *der*.

supervise ['suːpəvaɪz] *vt* beaufsichtigen.

supervisor ['suːpəvaɪzəʳ] *n (of workers)* Vorarbeiter *der* (-in *die*).

supper ['sʌpəʳ] *n* Abendessen *das*.

supple ['sʌpl] *adj (person)* gelenkig ; *(material)* geschmeidig.

supplement [*n* 'sʌplɪmənt, *vb* 'sʌplɪment] *n (of magazine)* Beilage *die* ; *(extra charge)* Zuschlag *der* ; *(of diet)* Zusatz *der*. ◆ *vt* ergänzen.

supplementary [ˌsʌplɪˈmentərɪ] *adj* zusätzlich, Zusatz-.

supply [səˈplaɪ] *n (store)* Vorrat *der* ; *(providing)* Versorgung *die*. ◆ *vt* liefern ; **to ~ sb with sthg** jn mit etw versorgen. ◼ **supplies** *npl* Vorräte *pl*.

support [səˈpɔːt] *n (aid, encouragement)* Unterstützung *die* ; *(object)* Stütze *die*. ◆ *vt* unterstützen ; *(hold up)* tragen ; **to ~ a football team** ein Fan von einem Fußballverein sein.

supporter [səˈpɔːtəʳ] *n (SPORT)* Fan *der* ; *(of cause, political party)* Anhänger *der* (-in *die*).

suppose [səˈpəʊz] *vt* annehmen. ◆ *conj* = **supposing** ; **I ~ so** vermutlich ; **to be ~d to do sthg** etw tun sollen.

supposing [səˈpəʊzɪŋ] *conj* angenommen.

supreme [sʊˈpriːm] *adj* größte(-r) (-s).

surcharge ['sɜːtʃɑːdʒ] *n* Zuschlag *der*.

sure [ʃʊəʳ] *adj* sicher. ◆ *adv* (*inf* : *yes*) klar ; (*Am* : *inf* : *certainly*) wirklich ; **to be ~ of o.s.** selbstsicher sein ; **for ~** auf jeden Fall ; **to make ~ that...** sich vergewissern, dass...

surely [ˈʃʊəlɪ] *adv* sicherlich.

surf [sɜːf] *n* Brandung *die*. ◆ *vi* surfen.

surface [ˈsɜːfɪs] *n* Oberfläche *die*.

surface area *n* Oberfläche *die*.

surface mail *n* Post auf dem Land-/Seeweg.

surfboard [ˈsɜːfbɔːd] *n* Surfbrett *das*.

surfing [ˈsɜːfɪŋ] *n* Surfen *das* ; **to go ~** Surfen gehen.

surgeon [ˈsɜːdʒən] *n* Chirurg *der* (-in *die*).

surgery [ˈsɜːdʒərɪ] *n* (*treatment*) Chirurgie *die* ; (*Br* : *building*) Praxis *die* ; (*Br* : *period*) Sprechstunde *die* ; **to have ~** operiert werden.

surname [ˈsɜːneɪm] *n* Nachname *der*.

surplus [ˈsɜːpləs] *n* Überschuss *der*.

surprise [səˈpraɪz] *n* Überraschung *die*. ◆ *vt* überraschen.

surprised [səˈpraɪzd] *adj* überrascht.

surprising [səˈpraɪzɪŋ] *adj* überraschend.

surrender [səˈrendəʳ] *vi* kapitulieren. ◆ *vt* (*fml* : *hand over*) übergeben.

surround [səˈraʊnd] *vt* umgeben.

surrounding [səˈraʊndɪŋ] *adj* umliegend. ■ **surroundings** *npl* Umgebung *die*.

survey [ˈsɜːveɪ] *n* (*investigation*) Untersuchung *die* ; (*poll*) Umfrage *die* ; (*of land*) Vermessung *die* ; (*Br* : *of house*) Begutachtung *die*.

surveyor [səˈveɪəʳ] *n* (*Br* : *of houses*) Gutachter *der* (-in *die*) ; (*of land*) Vermesser *der* (-in *die*).

survival [səˈvaɪvl] *n* Überleben *das*.

survive [səˈvaɪv] *vt & vi* überleben.

survivor [səˈvaɪvəʳ] *n* Überlebende *der, die*.

suspect [*vb* səˈspekt, *n & adj* ˈsʌspekt] *vt* (*believe*) vermuten ; (*mistrust*) verdächtigen. ◆ *n* Verdächtige *der, die*. ◆ *adj* verdächtig ; **to ~ sb of sthg** jn einer Sache verdächtigen.

suspend [səˈspend] *vt* (*delay*) vorläufig einIstellen ; (*from team, school, work*) ausIschließen ; (*hang*) aufIhängen.

suspender belt [səˈspendə-] *n* Strumpfhalter *der*.

suspenders [səˈspendəz] *npl* (*Br* : *for stockings*) Strumpfhalter *pl* ; (*Am* : *for trousers*) Hosenträger *pl*.

suspense [səˈspens] *n* Spannung *die*.

suspension [səˈspenʃn] *n* (*of vehicle*) Federung *die* ; (*from team*) Sperrung *die* ; (*from school, work*) Ausschluss *der*.

suspicion [səˈspɪʃn] *n* (*mistrust*) Misstrauen *das* ; (*idea*) Ahnung *die* ; (*trace*) Spur *die*.

suspicious [səˈspɪʃəs] *adj* (*behaviour, situation*) verdächtig ; **to be ~ of sb/sthg** jm/etw (*D*) misstrauen.

swipe

swallow ['swɒləʊ] n (bird) Schwalbe die. ◆ vt & vi schlucken.

swam [swæm] pt → swim.

swamp [swɒmp] n Sumpf der.

swan [swɒn] n Schwan der.

swap [swɒp] vt tauschen; (ideas, stories) ausltauschen; to ~ sthg for sthg etw gegen etw einltauschen.

swarm [swɔːm] n (of bees) Schwarm der.

swear [sweə'] (pt swore, pp sworn) vi (use rude language) fluchen; (promise) schwören. ◆ vt : to ~ to do sthg schwören, etw zu tun.

swearword ['sweəwɜːd] n Kraftausdruck der.

sweat [swet] n Schweiß der. ◆ vi schwitzen.

sweater ['swetə'] n Pullover der.

sweatshirt ['swetʃɜːt] n Sweatshirt das.

swede [swiːd] n (Br) Kohlrübe die.

Swede [swiːd] n Schwede der (Schwedin die).

Sweden ['swiːdn] n Schweden nt.

Swedish ['swiːdɪʃ] adj schwedisch. ◆ n (language) Schwedisch das. ◆ npl : the ~ die Schweden pl.

sweep [swiːp] (pt & pp swept) vt (with brush, broom) kehren, fegen.

sweet [swiːt] adj (food, drink, smell) süß; (person, nature) lieb. ◆ n (br : candy) Bonbon der or das; (dessert) Nachtisch der.

sweet-and-sour adj süßsauer.

sweet corn n Zuckermais der.

sweetener ['swiːtnə'] n (for drink) Süßstoff der.

sweet potato n Batate die.

sweet shop n (br) Süßwarengeschäft das.

swell [swel] (pp swollen) vi anlschwellen.

swelling ['swelɪŋ] n Schwellung die.

swept [swept] pt & pp → sweep.

swerve [swɜːv] vi auslscheren.

swig [swɪg] n (inf) Schluck der.

swim [swɪm] (pt swam, pp swum) vi schwimmen. ◆ n : to have a ~ schwimmen; to go for a ~ schwimmen gehen.

swimmer ['swɪmə'] n Schwimmer der (-in die).

swimming ['swɪmɪŋ] n Schwimmen das; to go ~ schwimmen gehen.

swimming baths npl (Br) Schwimmbad das.

swimming cap n Bademütze die.

swimming costume n (Br) Badeanzug der.

swimming pool n Schwimmbecken das.

swimming trunks npl Badehose die.

swimsuit ['swɪmsuːt] n Badeanzug der.

swindle ['swɪndl] n Betrug der.

swing [swɪŋ] (pt & pp swung) n (for children) Schaukel die. ◆ vt & vi (from side to side) schwingen.

swipe [swaɪp] vt (credit card etc) ablziehen.

Swiss [swɪs] *adj* schweizerisch. ◆ *n (person)* Schweizer *der* (-in *die*). ◆ *npl* : **the ~** die Schweizer *pl.*

Swiss cheese *n* Schweizer Käse.

swiss roll *n* ≃ Biskuitrolle *die.*

switch [swɪtʃ] *n (for light, power, television)* Schalter *der.* ◆ *vt (change)* ändern ; *(exchange)* tauschen. ◆ *vi* wechseln. ▪ **switch off** *vt sep (light)* aus|schalten ; *(radio, engine)* ab|schalten. ▪ **switch on** *vt sep (light, radio, engine)* ein|schalten.

Switch® *n (Br)* ≃ EC-Karte *die.*

switchboard ['swɪtʃbɔːd] *n* Telefonzentrale *die.*

Switzerland ['swɪtsələnd] *n* die Schweiz.

swivel ['swɪvl] *vi* sich drehen.

swollen ['swəʊln] *pp* → **swell**. ◆ *adj (ankle, arm etc)* geschwollen.

swop [swɒp] = **swap**.

sword [sɔːd] *n* Schwert *das.*

swordfish ['sɔːdfɪʃ] (*pl* **swordfish**) *n* Schwertfisch *der.*

swore [swɔːʳ] *pt* → **swear**.

sworn [swɔːn] *pp* → **swear**.

swum [swʌm] *pp* → **swim**.

swung [swʌŋ] *pt & pp* → **swing**.

syllable ['sɪləbl] *n* Silbe *die.*

syllabus ['sɪləbəs] *n* Lehrplan *der.*

symbol ['sɪmbl] *n* Symbol *das.*

sympathetic [,sɪmpə'θetɪk] *adj (understanding)* verständnisvoll.

sympathize ['sɪmpəθaɪz] *vi* : **to ~ (with sb)** *(feel sorry)* Mitleid haben (mit jm) ; *(understand)* Verständnis haben (für jn).

sympathy ['sɪmpəθɪ] *n (understanding)* Verständnis *das.*

symphony ['simfənɪ] *n* Sinfonie *die.*

symptom ['sɪmptəm] *n* Symptom *das.*

synagogue ['sɪnəgɒg] *n* Synagoge *die.*

synthesizer ['sɪnθəsaɪzəʳ] *n* Synthesizer *der.*

synthetic [sɪn'θetɪk] *adj* synthetisch.

syringe [sɪ'rɪndʒ] *n* Spritze *die.*

syrup ['sɪrəp] *n* Sirup *der.*

system ['sɪstəm] *n* System *das* ; *(hi-fi)* Anlage *die.*

T

ta [tɑː] *excl (Br : inf)* danke!

tab [tæb] *n (of cloth, paper etc)* Etikett *das* ; *(bill)* Rechnung *die* ; **put it on my ~** setzen Sie es auf meine Rechnung.

table ['teɪbl] *n* Tisch *der* ; *(of figures etc)* Tabelle *die.*

tablecloth ['teɪblklɒθ] *n* Tischtuch *das.*

tablemat ['teɪblmæt] *n* Untersetzer *der.*

tablespoon ['teɪblspuːn] *n* Servierlöffel *der.*

tablet ['tæblɪt] *n (pill)* Tablette *die* ; *(of soap)* Stück *das* ; *(of chocolate)* Tafel *die.*

table tennis n Tischtennis der.

table wine n Tafelwein der.

tabloid ['tæbloɪd] n Boulevardzeitung die.

tack [tæk] n (nail) kleiner Nagel.

tackle ['tækl] n (SPORT) Angriff der; (◆ for fishing) Ausrüstung die. ◆ vt (SPORT) an|greifen; (deal with) an|gehen.

tacky ['tækı] adj (inf) geschmacklos.

taco ['tækəʊ] (pl -s) n mit Hackfleisch oder Bohnen gefüllter, sehr dünner knuspriger Maisfladen, mexikanische Spezialität.

tact [tækt] n Takt der.

tactful ['tæktfʊl] adj taktvoll.

tactics ['tæktɪks] npl Taktik die.

tag [tæg] n (label) Schild das.

tagliatelle [,tæglɪə'telɪ] n Bandnudeln pl.

tail [teɪl] n Schwanz der. ◆ **tails** n (of coin) Zahl die. ◆ npl (formal dress) Frack der.

tailgate ['teɪlgeɪt] n (of car) Heckklappe die.

tailor ['teɪlə'] n Schneider der (-in die).

Taiwan [,taɪ'wɑːn] n Taiwan nt.

take [teɪk] vt 1. (gen) nehmen; **to ~ the bus** den Bus nehmen.
2. (carry) mit|nehmen.
3. (do, make): **to ~ a bath/shower** ein Bad/eine Dusche nehmen; **to ~ an exam** eine Prüfung ab|legen; **to ~ a photo** ein Foto machen.
4. (drive) bringen.
5. (require) brauchen; **how long**

will it ~? wie lange wird es dauern?
6. (steal): **to ~ sthg from sb** jm etw weg|nehmen.
7. (size in clothes, shoes) haben; **what size do you ~?** welche Größe hast du/haben Sie?
8. (subtract): **to ~ sthg from sthg** etw von etw ab|ziehen.
9. (accept) an|nehmen; **do you ~ traveller's cheques?** nehmen Sie Travellerschecks? ; **to ~ sb's advice** js Rat folgen.
10. (contain) fassen.
11. (react to) auf|nehmen.
12. (control, power) übernehmen; **to ~ charge of** die Leitung übernehmen.
13. (tolerate) aus|halten, ertragen.
14. (attitude, interest) haben.
15. (assume): **I ~ it that...** ich gehe davon aus, dass...
16. (temperature, pulse) messen.
17. (rent) mieten.

▥ **take apart** vt sep auseinander nehmen.

▥ **take away** vt sep (remove) weg|nehmen; (subtract) ab|ziehen.

▥ **take back** vt sep (return) zurück|bringen; (faulty goods, statement) zurück|nehmen.

▥ **take down** vt sep (picture, curtains) ab|nehmen.

▥ **take in** vt sep (include) ein|schließen; (understand) verstehen; (deceive) herein|legen; (clothes) enger machen.

▥ **take off** vt sep (remove) ab|nehmen; (clothes) aus|ziehen; (as holiday) sich (D) frei|nehmen.

◆ vi (plane) ab|heben.

▨ **take out** vt sep (from container, pocket) heraus|nehmen ; (library book) aus|leihen ; (loan) auf|nehmen ; (insurance policy) ab|schließen ; (go out with) aus|führen.

▨ **take over** vi : to ~ over from sb jn ablösen.

▨ **take up** vt sep (use up) in Anspruch nehmen ; (trousers, skirt, dress) kürzen ; (begin) : to ~ up the clarinet an|fangen, Klarinette zu spielen.

takeaway ['teɪkə,weɪ] n (Br : shop) Restaurant das mit Straßenverkauf ; (food) Essen das zum Mitnehmen.

taken ['teɪkn] pp → **take**.

takeoff ['teɪkɒf] n (of plane) Start der.

takeout ['teɪkaʊt] (Am) = **takeaway**.

takings ['teɪkɪŋz] npl Einnahmen pl.

talcum powder ['tælkəm-] n Körperpuder der.

tale [teɪl] n Geschichte die.

talent ['tælənt] n Talent das.

talk [tɔːk] n (conversation) Gespräch das ; (speech) Vortrag der. ◆ vi reden, sprechen ; to ~ to sb (about sthg) mit jm (über etw (A)) sprechen ; to ~ with sb mit jm reden. ▨ **talks** npl Gespräche pl.

talkative ['tɔːkətɪv] adj gesprächig.

tall [tɔːl] adj groß ; (building, tree) hoch ; **how ~ are you?** wie groß bist du? ; **I'm five and a half feet ~** ich bin 1,65 Meter groß.

tame [teɪm] adj (animal) zahm.

tampon ['tæmpɒn] n Tampon der.

tan [tæn] n (suntan) Bräune die. ◆ vi braun werden. ◆ adj (colour) gelbbraun.

tangerine [,tændʒə'riːn] n Tangerine die.

tank [tæŋk] n (container) Tank der ; (vehicle) Panzer der.

tanker ['tæŋkəʳ] n (truck) Tankwagen der.

tanned [tænd] adj braun gebrannt.

tap [tæp] n (for water) Hahn der. ◆ vt (hit) klopfen.

tape [teɪp] n (cassette, video) Kassette die ; (in cassette) Tonband das ; (adhesive material) Klebeband das ; (strip of material) Band das. ◆ vt (record) auf|nehmen ; (stick) kleben.

tape measure n Metermaß das.

tape recorder n Tonbandgerät das.

tapestry ['tæpɪstrɪ] n Wandteppich der.

tap water n Leitungswasser das.

tar [tɑːʳ] n Teer der.

target ['tɑːgɪt] n Ziel das ; (board) Zielscheibe die.

tariff ['tærɪf] n (price list) Preisliste die ; (Br : menu) Speisekarte die ; (at customs) Zoll der.

tarmac ['tɑːmæk] n (at airport) Rollfeld die. ▨ **Tarmac**® n (on road) Makadam der.

tarpaulin [tɑː'pɔːlɪn] n Plane die.

tart [tɑːt] n Törtchen das.

tartan ['tɑːtn] n (design) Schottenkaro das ; (cloth) Schottenstoff der.

tartare sauce [ˌtɑːtə-] n Remouladensoße die.

task [tɑːsk] n Aufgabe die.

taste [teɪst] n Geschmack der. ◆ vt (sample) kosten ; (detect) schmecken. ◆ vi : to ~ of sthg nach etw schmecken ; it ~s bad es schmeckt schlecht ; it ~s good es schmeckt gut ; to have a ~ of sthg (food, drink) etw probieren ; (fig : experience) etw kennen lernen.

tasteful ['teɪstfʊl] adj geschmackvoll.

tasteless ['teɪstlɪs] adj geschmacklos.

tasty ['teɪstɪ] adj lecker.

tattoo [tə'tuː] (pl -s) n (on skin) Tätowierung die ; (military display) Zapfenstreich der.

taught [tɔːt] pt & pp → teach.

Taurus ['tɔːrəs] n Stier der.

taut [tɔːt] adj straff.

tax [tæks] n Steuer die. ◆ vt (goods, person) besteuern ; (income) versteuern.

tax disc n (Br) Steuerplakette die.

tax-free adj steuerfrei.

taxi ['tæksɪ] n Taxi das. ◆ vi (plane) rollen.

taxi driver n Taxifahrer der (-in die).

taxi rank n (Br) Taxistand der.

taxi stand (Am) = **taxi rank**.

T-bone steak n T-Bone-Steak das.

tea [tiː] n Tee der ; (evening meal) Abendessen das.

tea bag n Teebeutel der.

teacake ['tiːkeɪk] n flaches Rosinenbrötchen, das getoastet und mit Butter gegessen wird.

teach [tiːtʃ] (pt & pp taught) vt & vi unterrichten ; to ~ sb sthg, to ~ sthg to sb jm Unterricht in etw (D) geben ; to ~ sb (how) to do sthg jm etw beibringen.

teacher ['tiːtʃə'] n Lehrer der (-in die).

teaching ['tiːtʃɪŋ] n (profession) Lehrberuf der ; (of subject) Unterrichten das.

tea cloth = **tea towel**.

teacup ['tiːkʌp] n Teetasse die.

team [tiːm] n (SPORT) Mannschaft die ; (group) Team das.

teapot ['tiːpɒt] n Teekanne die.

tear[1] [teə'] (pt tore, pp torn) (rip) zerreißen. ◆ vi (move quickly) rasen. ◆ n Riss der. ▣ **tear up** vt sep zerreißen.

tear[2] [tɪə'] n Träne die.

tearoom ['tiːrʊm] n Teestube die.

tease [tiːz] vt necken.

tea set n Teeservice das.

teaspoon ['tiːspuːn] n Teelöffel der.

teaspoonful ['tiːspuːnˌfʊl] n Teelöffel der.

teat [tiːt] n (of animal) Zitze die ; (Br : of bottle) Sauger der.

teatime ['tiːtaɪm] n Abendessenszeit die.

tea towel n Geschirrtuch das.

technical ['teknɪkl] adj technisch ; (point, reason) fachlich.

technical drawing n technische Zeichnung.

technicality [ˌteknɪ'kælətɪ] n (detail) technisches Detail.

technician [tek'nɪʃn] n Techniker der (-in die).

technique [tek'ni:k] n *(method)* Methode *die ; (skill)* Technik *die.*

technological [,teknə'lɒdʒɪkl] *adj* technisch.

technology [tek'nɒlədʒɪ] n Technik *die.*

teddy (bear) ['tedɪ-] n Teddy *der.*

tedious ['ti:djəs] *adj* langweilig.

tee [ti:] n Tee *das.*

teenager ['ti:n,eɪdʒəʳ] n Teenager *der.*

teeth [ti:θ] *pl* → tooth.

teethe [ti:ð] *vi* : to be teething zahnen.

teetotal [ti:'təʊtl] *adj* abstinent.

telebanking ['telɪbæŋkɪŋ] n Telefonbanking *das,* Homebanking *das.*

telegram ['telɪgræm] n Telegramm *das.*

telegraph ['telɪgrɑːf] n Telegraf *der.* ◆ *vt* telegrafieren.

telegraph pole n Telegrafenmast *der.*

telephone ['telɪfəʊn] n Telefon *das.* ◆ *vt & vi* anrufen ; to be on the ~ *(talking)* telefonieren ; *(connected)* ein Telefon haben.

telephone booth n Telefonzelle *die.*

telephone box n Telefonzelle *die.*

telephone call n Telefonanruf *der.*

telephone directory n Telefonbuch *das.*

telephone number n Telefonnummer *die.*

telephonist [tɪ'lefənɪst] n *(Br)* Telefonist *der* (-in *die*).

telephoto lens [,telɪ'fəʊtəʊ-] n Teleobjektiv *das.*

telescope ['telɪskəʊp] n Teleskop *das.*

television ['telɪ,vɪʒn] n Fernsehen *das ; (set)* Fernseher *der ;* on (the) ~ *(broadcast)* im Fernsehen ; to watch ~ fernsehen.

telex ['teleks] n Telex *das.*

tell [tel] *(pt & pp* told) *vt (inform)* sagen (+D) ; *(story, joke, lie)* erzählen ; *(truth)* sagen ; *(distinguish)* erkennen. ◆ *vi (know)* wissen ; can you ~ me the time? kannst du mir sagen, wie spät es ist? ; to ~ sb sthg jm etw sagen ; to ~ sb about sthg jm etw erzählen ; to ~ sb how to do sthg jm sagen, wie man etw tut ; to ~ sb to do sthg jm sagen, etw zu tun. ▪ **tell off** *vt sep* schimpfen.

teller ['teləʳ] n *(in bank)* Kassierer *der* (-in *die*).

telly ['telɪ] n *(Br : inf)* Fernseher *der.*

temp [temp] n Zeitarbeitskraft *die.* ◆ *vi* Zeitarbeit machen.

temper ['tempəʳ] n : to be in a ~ wütend sein ; to lose one's ~ wütend werden.

temperature ['temprətʃəʳ] n Temperatur *die ; (MED)* Fieber *das ;* to have a ~ Fieber haben.

temple ['templ] n *(building)* Tempel *der ; (of forehead)* Schläfe *die.*

temporary ['tempərərɪ] *adj* vorübergehend.

tempt [tempt] *vt* verleiten ; to be ~ed to do sthg versucht sein, etw zu tun.

temptation [temp'teɪʃn] *n* Verlockung *die*.

tempting ['temptɪŋ] *adj* verlockend.

ten [ten] *num* zehn ; → **six**.

tenant ['tenənt] *n (of house, flat)* Mieter *der* (-in *die*) ; *(of land)* Pächter *der* (-in *die*).

tend [tend] *vi* : to ~ to do sthg dazu neigen, etw zu tun.

tendency ['tendənsɪ] *n (trend)* Trend *der* ; *(inclination)* Neigung *die*.

tender ['tendə'] *adj (affectionate)* zärtlich ; *(sore)* empfindlich ; *(meat)* zart. ◆ *vt (fml : pay)* anlbieten.

tendon ['tendən] *n* Sehne *die*.

tenement ['tenəmənt] *n* Mietshaus *das*.

tennis ['tenɪs] *n* Tennis *das*.

tennis ball *n* Tennisball *der*.

tennis court *n* Tennisplatz *der*.

tennis racket *n* Tennisschläger *der*.

tenpin bowling ['tenpɪn-] *n (Br)* Bowling *das*.

tenpins ['tenpɪnz] *(Am)* = **tenpin bowling**.

tense [tens] *adj* angespannt ; *(situation)* spannungsgeladen. ◆ *n (GRAMM)* Zeit *die*.

tension ['tenʃn] *n (of person)* Anspannung *die* ; *(of situation)* Spannung *die*.

tent [tent] *n* Zelt *das*.

tenth [tenθ] *num* zehnte(-r) (-s) ; → **sixth**.

tent peg *n* Hering *der*.

tepid ['tepɪd] *adj (water)* lauwarm.

tequila [tɪ'kiːlə] *n* Tequila *der*.

term [tɜːm] *n (word, expression)* Ausdruck *der* ; *(at school)* Halbjahr *das* ; *(at university)* Semester *das* ; in the long ~ langfristig ; in the short ~ kurzfristig ; in ~s of im Hinblick auf (+A) ; in business ~s geschäftlich. ◆ **terms** *npl (of contract)* Bedingungen *pl* ; *(price)* Zahlungsbedingungen *pl*.

terminal ['tɜːmɪnl] *adj (illness)* unheilbar. ◆ *n (for buses)* Endhaltestelle *die* ; *(at airport, of computer)* Terminal *das*.

terminate ['tɜːmɪneɪt] *vi (train, bus)* enden.

terminus ['tɜːmɪnəs] *n* Endstation *die*.

terrace ['terəs] *n (patio)* Terrasse *die* ; the ~s *(at football ground)* die Ränge.

terraced house ['terəst-] *n (Br)* Reihenhaus *das*.

terrible ['terəbl] *adj* schrecklich.

terribly ['terəblɪ] *adv* furchtbar.

terrier ['terɪə'] *n* Terrier *der*.

terrific [tə'rɪfɪk] *adj (inf : very good)* toll ; *(very great)* irrsinnig.

terrified ['terɪfaɪd] *adj* verängstigt.

territory ['terətrɪ] *n (political area)* Staatsgebiet *das* ; *(terrain)* Gebiet *das*.

terror ['terə'] *n (fear)* panische Angst.

terrorism ['terərɪzm] *n* Terrorismus *der*.

terrorist ['terərɪst] *n* Terrorist *der* (-in *die*).

terrorize ['terəraɪz] vt terrorisieren.

test [test] n Test der; (at school) Klassenarbeit die. ◆ vt (check) testen, überprüfen; (give exam to) prüfen; (dish, drink) probieren.

testicles ['testɪklz] npl Hoden pl.

tetanus ['tetənəs] n Wundstarrkrampf der.

text [tekst] n Text der.

textbook ['tekstbʊk] n Lehrbuch das.

textile ['tekstaɪl] n Stoff der.

texture ['tekstʃə'] n Beschaffenheit die; (of fabric) Struktur die.

Thai [taɪ] adj thailändisch.

Thailand ['taɪlænd] n Thailand nt.

Thames [temz] n : the ~ die Themse.

than [weak form ðən, strong form ðæn] prep & conj als; **you're better ~ me** du bist besser als ich; **I'd rather stay in ~ go out** ich bleibe lieber zu Hause (, als auszugehen); **more ~ ten** mehr als zehn.

thank [θæŋk] vt : **to ~ sb (for sthg)** jm (für etw) danken. ▪ **thanks** npl Dank der. ◆ excl danke!; **~ to** dank (+D) or G; **many ~s!** vielen Dank!

Thanksgiving ['θæŋks,gɪvɪŋ] n amerikanisches Erntedankfest.

THANKSGIVING

In den USA ist „Thanksgiving" (Erntedankfest) ein Feiertag, der an jedem vierten Donnerstag im November zum Dank für die Ernte, aber auch für alle anderen Segnungen des vergangenen Jahres gefeiert wird. Das Fest geht auf das Jahr 1621 zurück, als die ersten Siedler aus Großbritannien, die „Pilgrims", ihre erste Ernte einbrachten. Das traditionelle Thanksgiving-Essen besteht aus Truthahnbraten und „pumpkin pie", einem Kürbisgericht.

thank you excl danke (schön)!; **~ very much!** vielen Dank!; **no ~!** nein danke!

that [ðæt, weak form of pron senses 3, 4, 5 & conj ðət] (pl **those**) adj 1. (referring to thing, person mentioned) der/die/das, die (pl), jene(-r) (-s), jene (pl); **~ film was good** der Film war gut; **those chocolates are delicious** die Pralinen da schmecken köstlich.
2. (referring to thing, person further away) jene(-r) (-s), jene (pl); **I prefer ~ book** ich bevorzuge das Buch da; **I'll have ~ one** ich nehme das da.
◆ pron 1. (referring to thing, person mentioned) das; **what's ~?** was ist das?; **~'s interesting** das ist interessant; **who's ~?** wer ist das?; **is ~ Lucy?** (on telephone) bist du das, Lucy?; (pointing) ist das Lucy?; **after ~** danach.
2. (referring to thing, person further away) jene(-r) (-s), jene (pl); **I want those there** ich möchte die da.
3. (introducing relative clause: subject) der/die/das, die (pl)

a shop ~ sells antiques ein Geschäft, das Antiquitäten verkauft.
4. *(introducing relative clause : object)* den/die/das, die *(pl)* ; **the film ~ I saw** den Film, den ich gesehen habe.
5. *(introducing relative clause : after prep +D)* dem/der/dem, denen *(pl)* ; *(after prep +A)* den/die/das, die *(pl)* ; **the place ~ I'm looking for** der Ort, nach dem ich suche.
◆ *adv* so ; **it wasn't ~ bad/good** es war nicht so schlecht/gut.
◆ *conj* dass ; **tell him ~ I'm going to be late** sag ihm, dass ich später komme.

thatched [θætʃt] *adj* strohgedeckt.

that's [ðæts] = **that is**.

thaw [θɔː] *vi (snow, ice)* tauen.
◆ *vt (frozen food)* auftauen.

the [*weak form* ðə, *before vowel* ðɪ, *strong form* ðiː] *definite article* **1.** *(gen)* der/die/das, die *(pl)* ; **~ book** das Buch ; **~ man** der Mann ; **~ woman** die Frau ; **~ girls** die Mädchen ; **~ Wilsons** die Wilsons ; **to play ~ piano** Klavier spielen.
2. *(with an adjective to form a noun)* : **~ British** die Briten ; **~ impossible** das Unmögliche.
3. *(in dates)* der ; **~ twelfth (of May)** der Zwölfte (Mai) ; **~ forties** die Vierziger.
4. *(in titles)* der ; **Elizabeth ~ Second** Elizabeth die Zweite.

theater ['θɪətər] *n (Am : for plays, drama)* = **theatre** ; *(for films)* Kino *das*.

theatre ['θɪətər] *n (Br)* Theater *das*.

theft [θeft] *n* Diebstahl *der*.

their [ðeər] *adj* ihr.

theirs [ðeəz] *pron* ihre(-r) (-s) ; **a friend of ~** ein Freund von ihnen.

them [*weak form* ðəm, *strong form* ðem] *pron (accusative)* sie ; *(dative)* ihnen ; **I know ~** ich kenne sie ; **it's ~** sie sind es ; **send it to ~** schicke es ihnen ; **tell ~** sage ihnen ; **he's worse than ~** er ist schlimmer als sie.

theme [θiːm] *n* Thema *das*.

theme park *n* Freizeitpark *der (mit themabezogenen Attraktionen)*.

theme pub *n* Themenkneipe *die*.

themselves [ðəm'selvz] *pron (reflexive)* sich ; *(after prep)* sich (selbst) ; **they did it ~** sie machten es selbst.

then [ðen] *adv* dann ; *(at time in past)* damals ; **from ~ on** von da an ; **until ~** bis dahin.

theory ['θɪərɪ] *n* Theorie *die* ; **in ~** theoretisch.

therapist ['θerəpɪst] *n* Therapeut *der* (-in *die*).

therapy ['θerəpɪ] *n* Therapie *die*.

there [ðeər] *adv (existing, present)* da ; *(at, in that place)* dort ; *(to that place)* dorthin. ◆ *pron* **~ is** ist es, es gibt ; **~ are** da sind, es gibt ; **is Bob ~, please?** *(on phone)* ist Bob da? ; **over ~** da drüben ; **~ you are** *(when giving)* bitte schön.

thereabouts [,ðeərə'baʊts] *adv* : **or ~** so ungefähr.

therefore ['ðeəfɔːr] *adv* deshalb.

there's [ðeəz] = **there is**.

thermal underwear [ˌθɜː-ml-] *n* Thermounterwäsche *die*.

thermometer [θəˈmɒmɪtəʳ] *n* Thermometer *das*.

Thermos (flask)® [ˈθɜːməs-] *n* Thermosflasche® *die*.

thermostat [ˈθɜːməstæt] *n* Thermostat *der*.

these [ðiːz] *pl* → this.

they [ðeɪ] *pron* sie ; *(people in general)* man.

thick [θɪk] *adj* dick ; *(fog, hair)* dicht ; *(inf : stupid)* dumm ; it's 1 metre ~ es ist 1 Meter dick.

thicken [ˈθɪkn] *vt (sauce, soup)* eindicken. ◆ *vi (mist, fog)* dichter werden.

thickness [ˈθɪknɪs] *n* Dicke *die*.

thief [θiːf] *(pl* thieves [θiːvz]*) n* Dieb *der* (-in *die*).

thigh [θaɪ] *n* Oberschenkel *der*.

thimble [ˈθɪmbl] *n* Fingerhut *der*.

thin [θɪn] *adj* dünn.

thing [θɪŋ] *n (object)* Ding *das* ; *(event, action, subject)* Sache *die* ; the ~ is die Sache ist die, dass... ; for one ~ erstens. ■ **things** *npl (clothes, possessions)* Sachen *pl* ; how are ~s? *(inf)* wie geht's?

thingummyjig [ˈθɪŋəmɪdʒɪg] *n (inf)* Dingsbums *der/die/das*.

think [θɪŋk] *(pt & pp* thought*) vt* denken ; *(believe)* meinen. ◆ *vi (reflect)* nachdenken ; to ~ about *(have in mind)* nachdenken über (+A) ; *(consider)* denken an (+A) ; to ~ of denken an (+A) ; *(invent)* sich (D) ausdenken ; *(remember)* sich erinnern

an (+A) ; what do you ~ of it? was hältst du davon? ; to ~ of doing sthg daran denken, etw zu tun ; I ~ so ich glaube schon ; I don't ~ so ich glaube nicht ; do you ~ you could...? meinst du, du könntest...? ; to ~ highly of sb jn sehr schätzen. ■ **think over** *vt sep* nachdenken über (+A). ■ **think up** *vt sep* ausdenken.

third [θɜːd] *num* dritte(-r) (-s) ; → sixth.

third party insurance *n* Haftpflichtversicherung *die*.

Third World *n* : the ~ die Dritte Welt.

thirst [θɜːst] *n* Durst *der*.

thirsty [ˈθɜːstɪ] *adj* durstig.

thirteen [ˌθɜːˈtiːn] *num* dreizehn ; → six.

thirteenth [ˌθɜːˈtiːnθ] *num* dreizehnte(-r) (-s) ; → sixth.

thirtieth [ˈθɜːtɪəθ] *num* dreißigste(-r) (-s) ; → sixth.

thirty [ˈθɜːtɪ] *num* dreißig ; → six.

this [ðɪs] *(pl* these*) adj* diese(-r) (-s), diese *(pl)* ; I prefer ~ book ich bevorzuge dieses Buch ; these chocolates are delicious diese Pralinen schmecken köstlich ; ~ morning heute Morgen ; ~ week diese Woche ; I'll have ~ one ich nehme dieses ; there was ~ man... da war dieser Mann...

◆ *pron* 1. *(referring to thing, person mentioned)* dies ; ~ is for you das ist für dich ; what are these? was ist das? ; ~ is David Gregory *(introducing someone)* das ist David Gregory ; *(on telephone)* hier ist David Gregory.

2. *(referring to thing, person nearer)* diese(-r) (-s), diese *(pl)* ; **I want these here** ich möchte diese hier.

◆ *adv* so ; **it was ~ big** es war so groß.

thistle ['θɪsl] *n* Distel *die*.

thorn [θɔːn] *n* Dorn *der*.

thorough ['θʌrə] *adj* gründlich.

thoroughly ['θʌrəlɪ] *adv (completely)* völlig.

those [ðəʊz] *pl* → **that**.

though [ðəʊ] *conj* obwohl.
◆ *adv* doch ; **even ~** obwohl.

thought [θɔːt] *pt & pp* → **think**. ◆ *n (idea)* Gedanke *der* ; *(thinking)* Überlegung *die*.
▓ **thoughts** *npl (opinion)* Gedanken *pl*.

thoughtful ['θɔːtfʊl] *adj (serious)* nachdenklich ; *(considerate)* rücksichtsvoll.

thoughtless ['θɔːtlɪs] *adj* gedankenlos.

thousand ['θaʊznd] *num* tausend ; **a** OR **one ~** eintausend ; **~s of** tausende von ; *see also* **six**.

thrash [θræʃ] *vt (inf: defeat)* vernichtend schlagen.

thread [θred] *n (of cotton etc)* Faden *der*. ◆ *vt (needle)* einfädeln.

threadbare ['θredbeə'] *adj* abgenutzt.

threat [θret] *n* Drohung *die* ; *(possibility)* Gefahr *die*.

threaten ['θretn] *vt* bedrohen ; **to ~ to do sthg** drohen, etw zu tun.

threatening ['θretnɪŋ] *adj* drohend.

three [θriː] *num* drei ; → **six**.

three-D *adj* drei-D-.

three-piece suite *n* Polstergarnitur *die*.

three-quarters [-'kwɔːtəz] *n* drei Viertel *pl* ; **~ of an hour** eine Dreiviertelstunde.

threshold ['θreʃhəʊld] *n (fml)* Schwelle *die*.

threw [θruː] *pt* → **throw**.

thrifty ['θrɪftɪ] *adj* sparsam.

thrilled [θrɪld] *adj* begeistert.

thriller ['θrɪlə'] *n* Thriller *der*.

thrive [θraɪv] *vi (plant, animal)* gedeihen ; *(person)* aufblühen ; *(business, tourism)* florieren.

throat [θrəʊt] *n* Hals *der*.

throb [θrɒb] *vi (head, pain)* pochen ; *(noise, engine)* dröhnen.

throne [θrəʊn] *n* Thron *der*.

throttle ['θrɒtl] *n (of motorbike)* Gasgriff *der*.

through [θruː] *prep* durch ; *(during)* während (+G). ◆ *adv* durch. ◆ *adj* : **to be ~ (with sthg) (finished)** (mit etw) fertig sein ; **you're ~** *(on phone)* Sie sind jetzt verbunden ; **Monday ~ Thursday** *(Am)* Montag bis Donnerstag ; **to let sb ~** jn durchllassen ; **~ traffic** Durchgangsverkehr *der* ; **a ~ train** ein durchgehender Zug ; **'no ~ road'** *(Br)* 'Keine Durchfahrt'.

throughout [θruː'aʊt] *adv (all the time)* die ganze Zeit ; *(everywhere)* überall. ◆ *prep* : **~ the day/morning** den ganzen Tag/Morgen über ; **~ the year** das ganze Jahr hindurch ; **~ the country** im ganzen Land.

throw [θrəʊ] *(pt* threw, *pp* thrown [θrəʊn]) *vt* werfen ; *(a switch)* betätigen ; **to ~ the dice**

würfeln; **to ~ sthg in the bin** etw in den Mülleimer werfen. ■ **throw away** vt sep weglwerfen. ■ **throw out** vt sep (get rid of) weglwerfen; (person) hinauslwerfen. ■ **throw up** vi (inf : vomit) sich übergeben.

thru [θru:] (Am) = **through**.

thrush [θrʌʃ] n (bird) Drossel die.

thud [θʌd] n dumpfes Geräusch.

thug [θʌg] n Schläger der.

thumb [θʌm] n Daumen der. ◆ vt : **to ~ a lift** trampen.

thumbtack ['θʌmtæk] n (Am) Reißzwecke die.

thump [θʌmp] n (punch) Schlag der; (sound) dumpfer Schlag. ◆ vt schlagen.

thunder ['θʌndər] n Donner der.

thunderstorm ['θʌndəstɔ:m] n Gewitter das.

Thurs. (abbr of Thursday) Do.

Thursday ['θɜ:zdɪ] n Donnerstag der; → **Saturday**.

thyme [taɪm] n Thymian der.

tick [tɪk] n (written mark) Haken der; (insect) Zecke die. ◆ vt ablhaken. ◆ vi (clock, watch) ticken. ■ **tick off** vt sep (mark off) ablhaken.

ticket ['tɪkɪt] n (for cinema, theatre, match) Eintrittskarte die; (for plane) Flugschein der, Ticket das; (for bus, tube) Fahrschein der; (for train) Fahrkarte die; (for car park) Parkschein der; (label) Etikett das; (for lottery) Los das; (for speeding, parking) Strafzettel der.

ticket collector n (at barrier) Fahrkartenkontrolleur der (-in die).

ticket inspector n (on train) Schaffner der (-in die).

ticket machine n Fahrscheinautomat der.

ticket office n (in cinema, theatre) Kasse die; (in station) Fahrkartenschalter der.

tickle ['tɪkl] vt & vi kitzeln.

ticklish ['tɪklɪʃ] adj kitzlig.

tick-tack-toe n (Am) Spiel, bei dem Dreierreihen von Kreisen und Kreuzen zu erzielen sind.

tide [taɪd] n (of sea) Gezeiten pl.

tidy ['taɪdɪ] adj ordentlich. ■ **tidy up** vt sep auflräumen.

tie [taɪ] (pt & pp **tied**, cont **tying**) n (around neck) Krawatte die; (draw) Unentschieden das; (Am : on railway track) Schwelle die. ◆ vt binden; (knot) machen. ◆ vi (game) unentschieden spielen; (competition) gleich stehen. ■ **tie up** vt sep (fasten) festlbinden; (parcel) verschnüren; (laces) binden; (delay) auflhalten.

tiepin ['taɪpɪn] n Krawattennadel die.

tier [tɪər] n (of seats) Rang der.

tiger ['taɪgər] n Tiger der.

tight [taɪt] adj (drawer, tap) fest; (nut, knot) fest angezogen; (clothes, shoes, bend) eng; (rope, material) straff; (schedule) knapp; (chest) beengt; (inf : drunk) blau. ◆ adv (hold) fest.

tighten ['taɪtn] vt (nut, knot) fest anlziehen; (rope) straffen.

tightrope ['taɪtrəʊp] n Hochseil das.

tights [taɪts] npl Strumpfhose die ; **a pair of ~** eine Strumpfhose.

tile ['taɪl] n (for roof) Ziegel der ; (for floor) Fliese die ; (for wall) Kachel die.

till [tɪl] n (for money) Kasse die. ◆ prep & conj bis.

tiller ['tɪlə'] n Ruderpinne die.

tilt [tɪlt] vt & vi kippen.

timber ['tɪmbə'] n (wood) Holz das ; (of roof) Balken der.

time [taɪm] n Zeit die ; (occasion) Mal das. ◆ vt (measure) stoppen ; (arrange) zeitlich abstimmen ; **to be well ~d** gut abgepasst sein ; **I haven't got the ~** mir fehlt die Zeit ; **it's ~ to go** es ist Zeit zu gehen ; **what's the ~?** wie spät ist es?, wie viel Uhr ist es? ; **two at a ~** zwei auf einmal ; **two ~s two** zwei mal zwei ; **five ~s as much** fünfmal so viel ; **in a month's ~** in einem Monat ; **to have a good ~** sich amüsieren ; **all the ~** die ganze Zeit ; **every ~** jedesmal ; **from ~ to ~** von Zeit zu Zeit ; **for the ~ being** vorläufig ; **in ~** (arrive) rechtzeitig ; **in good ~** früh ; **last ~** letztes Mal ; **most of the ~** meistens ; **on ~** pünktlich ; **some of the ~** manchmal ; **this ~** diesmal.

time difference n Zeitunterschied der.

time limit n Frist die.

timer ['taɪmə'] n (machine) Schaltuhr die.

time share n Ferienwohnung, an der man einen Besitzanteil hat.

timetable ['taɪmˌteɪbl] n (of trains, buses, boats etc) Fahrplan der ; (SCH) Stundenplan der ; (of events) Programm das.

time zone n Zeitzone die.

timid ['tɪmɪd] adj scheu.

tin [tɪn] n (metal) Blech das ; (container) Dose die. ◆ adj Blech-.

tinfoil ['tɪnfɔɪl] n Alufolie die.

tinned food [tɪnd-] n (Br) Konserven pl.

tin opener [-ˌəʊpnə'] n (Br) Dosenöffner der.

tinsel ['tɪnsl] n Lametta das.

tint [tɪnt] n (colour) Ton der.

tinted glass [ˌtɪntɪd-] n getöntes Glas.

tiny ['taɪnɪ] adj winzig.

tip [tɪp] n (point, end) Spitze die ; (of cigarette) Filter der ; (to waiter, taxi driver etc) Trinkgeld das ; (piece of advice) Tipp der ; (rubbish dump) Müllhalde die. ◆ vt (waiter, taxi driver etc) Trinkgeld geben (+D) ; (tilt) kippen ; (pour) schütten. ■ **tip over** vt sep & vi umkippen.

tire ['taɪə'] vi ermüden. ◆ n (Am) = **tyre.**

tired ['taɪəd] adj müde ; **to be ~ of sthg** (fed up with) etw satt haben.

tired out adj müde.

tiring ['taɪərɪŋ] adj ermüdend.

tissue ['tɪʃuː] n (handkerchief) Taschentuch das.

tissue paper n Seidenpapier das.

tit [tɪt] n (vulg : breast) Titte die.

title ['taɪtl] n Titel der.

T-junction n Einmündung die (in eine Vorfahrtsstraße).

to [*unstressed before consonant* tə, *unstressed before vowel* tʊ, *stressed* tu:] *prep* **1.** *(indicating direction)* nach ; **to go ~ France** nach Frankreich fahren ; **to go ~ school** in die Schule gehen ; **to go ~ work** zur Arbeit gehen.
2. *(indicating position)* : **~ one side** auf der einen Seite ; **~ the left/right** *(move)* nach links/rechts.
3. *(expressing indirect object)* : **to give sthg ~ sb** jm etw geben ; **to listen ~ the radio** Radio hören ; **we added milk ~ the mixture** wir fügten Milch zu der Mischung hinzu.
4. *(indicating reaction, effect)* zu ; **~ my surprise** zu meiner Überraschung.
5. *(until)* bis ; **to count ~ ten** bis zehn zählen ; **we work from 9 ~ 5** wir arbeiten von 9 bis 5.
6. *(indicating change of state)* : **to turn ~ sthg** zu etw werden ; **it could lead ~ trouble** das könnte Ärger geben.
7. *(Br : in expressions of time)* vor ; **it's ten ~ three** es ist zehn vor drei.
8. *(in ratios, rates)* : **10 kilometres ~ the litre** 10 Kilometer pro Liter.
9. *(of, for)* : **the key ~ the car** der Schlüssel für das Auto ; **a letter ~ my daughter** ein Brief an meine Tochter.
10. *(indicating attitude)* zu ; **to be rude ~ sb** frech zu jm sein.
◆ *with infinitive* **1.** *(forming simple infinitive)* : **~ laugh** lachen ; **~ walk** gehen.
2. *(following another verb)* : **begin ~ do sthg** anfangen, etw

zu tun ; **to want ~ do sthg** etw tun wollen.
3. *(following an adjective)* zu ; **difficult ~ do** schwer zu tun ; **ready ~ go** bereit zu gehen.
4. *(indicating purpose)* um zu ; **we came here ~ look at the castle** wir sind hierher gekommen, um das Schloss anzuschauen.

toad [təʊd] *n* Kröte *die*.

toadstool ['təʊdstu:l] *n* Giftpilz *der*.

toast [təʊst] *n* Toast *der*. ◆ *vt* *(bread)* toasten ; **a piece OR slice of ~** eine Scheibe Toast.

toasted sandwich ['təʊstɪd-] *n* getoastetes Sandwich *das*.

toaster ['təʊstə'] *n* Toaster *der*.

toastie ['təʊstɪ] = **toasted sandwich**.

tobacco [tə'bækəʊ] *n* Tabak *der*.

tobacconist's [tə'bækənɪsts] *n* Tabakladen *der*.

toboggan [tə'bɒgən] *n* Schlitten *der*.

today [tə'deɪ] *n & adv* heute.

toddler ['tɒdlə'] *n* Kleinkind *das*.

toe [təʊ] *n* Zeh *der*.

toe clip *n* Rennhaken *der*.

toenail ['təʊneɪl] *n* Zehennagel *der*.

toffee ['tɒfɪ] *n* *(sweet)* Karamellbonbon *der* ; *(substance)* Karamell *der*.

together [tə'geðə'] *adv* zusammen ; *(at the same time)* gleichzeitig ; **~ with** zusammen mit.

toilet ['tɔɪlɪt] *n* Toilette *die* ; **to go to the ~** auf die Toilette gehen ; where's the ~? wo ist die Toilette?

toilet bag n Kulturbeutel der.

toilet paper n Toilettenpapier das.

toiletries ['tɔɪlɪtrɪz] npl Toilettenartikel pl.

toilet roll n Rolle die Toilettenpapier.

toilet water n Eau de Toilette das.

token ['təʊkn] n (metal disc) Marke die.

told [təʊld] pt & pp → **tell**.

tolerable ['tɒlərəbl] adj leidlich.

tolerant ['tɒlərənt] adj tolerant.

tolerate ['tɒləreɪt] vt (put up with) ertragen ; (permit) dulden.

toll [təʊl] n (for road, bridge) Gebühr die, Maut die (Österr).

tollbooth ['təʊlbu:θ] n Kabine, an der Straßengebühr gezahlt wird.

toll-free adj (Am) gebührenfrei.

tomato [(Br) tə'mɑ:təʊ, (Am) tə'meɪtəʊ] (pl -es) n Tomate die.

tomato juice n Tomatensaft der.

tomato ketchup n Tomatenketschup der.

tomato puree n Tomatenmark das.

tomato sauce n Tomatensoße die.

tomb [tu:m] n Grab das.

tomorrow [tə'mɒrəʊ] n & adv morgen ; the day after ~ übermorgen ; ~ afternoon morgen Nachmittag ; ~ morning mor-

gen früh ; ~ night morgen Abend.

ton [tʌn] n (in UK) = 1.016 kg, Tonne die ; (in US) = 907 kg, Tonne ; (metric tonne) Tonne ; ~s of (inf) haufenweise.

tone [təʊn] n Ton der.

tongs [tɒŋz] npl (for hair) Lockenstab der ; (for sugar) Zuckerzange die.

tongue [tʌŋ] n Zunge die.

tonic ['tɒnɪk] n (tonic water) Tonic das ; (medicine) Tonikum das.

tonic water n Tonic das.

tonight [tə'naɪt] n & adv heute Abend ; (later) heute Nacht.

tonne [tʌn] n Tonne die.

tonsillitis [ˌtɒnsɪ'laɪtɪs] n Mandelentzündung die.

too [tu:] adv zu ; (also) auch ; it's not ~ good es ist nicht besonders gut ; it's ~ late to go out es ist zu spät zum Ausgehen ; ~ many zu viele ; ~ much zu viel.

took [tʊk] pt → **take**.

tool [tu:l] n Werkzeug das.

tool kit n Werkzeug das.

tooth [tu:θ] (pl teeth) n Zahn der.

toothache ['tu:θeɪk] n Zahnschmerzen pl.

toothbrush ['tu:θbrʌʃ] n Zahnbürste die.

toothpaste ['tu:θpeɪst] n Zahnpasta die.

toothpick ['tu:θpɪk] n Zahnstocher der.

top [tɒp] adj (highest) oberste(-r) (-s) ; (best, most important) beste(-r) (-s). ◆ n (of hill, tree) Spitze die ; (of table) Platte die ; (of class, league) Erste die, der ; (of bottle, jar) Deckel der ; (of *pen, tube)* Kappe *die* ; *(garment)* Oberteil *das* ; *(of street, road)* Ende *das* ; **at the ~ (of)** oben (auf (+A)) ; **on ~ of** *(on highest part of)* oben auf (+A) ; **on ~ of that** obendrein ; **at ~ speed** mit Höchstgeschwindigkeit ; **~ gear** höchster Gang. ▓ **top up** *vt sep* *(glass)* nachlfüllen. ◆ *vi (with petrol)* voll tanken.

top floor *n* oberstes Stockwerk.

topic ['tɒpɪk] *n* Thema *das*.

topical ['tɒpɪkl] *adj* aktuell.

topless ['tɒplɪs] *adj* oben ohne.

topped [tɒpt] *adj* : **~ with** *(food)* mit.

topping ['tɒpɪŋ] *n* Garnierung *eines Gerichts.*

torch [tɔ:tʃ] *n (Br : electric light)* Taschenlampe *die.*

tore [tɔ:ʳ] *pt → tear¹.*

torment [tɔ:'ment] *vt (annoy)* plagen.

torn [tɔ:n] *pp → tear¹.* ◆ *adj (ripped)* zerrissen.

tornado [tɔ:'neɪdəʊ] *(pl -es* OR *-s) n* Wirbelsturm *der.*

torrential rain [tə,renʃl-] *n* strömender Regen.

tortoise ['tɔ:təs] *n* Schildkröte *die.*

tortoiseshell ['tɔ:təʃel] *n* Schildpatt *das.*

torture ['tɔ:tʃəʳ] *n (punishment)* Folter *die.* ◆ *vt (punish)* foltern.

Tory ['tɔ:rɪ] *n* Tory *der.*

toss [tɒs] *vt (throw)* werfen ; *(salad)* mischen ; *(pancake)* wenden ; **to ~ a coin** eine Münze werfen.

total ['təʊtl] *adj (number, amount)* gesamt ; *(complete)* völlig. ◆ *n* Gesamtzahl *die* ; *(sum)* Gesamtsumme *die* ; **in ~** insgesamt.

touch [tʌtʃ] *n* Berührung *die* ; *(sense of touch)* Tastsinn *der* ; *(small amount)* Spur *die* ; *(detail)* Detail *das.* ◆ *vt* berühren. ◆ *vi* sich berühren ; **to get in ~ (with sb)** sich (mit jm) in Verbindung setzen ; **to keep in ~ (with sb)** (mit jm) in Kontakt bleiben. ▓ **touch down** *vi (plane)* auflsetzen.

touching ['tʌtʃɪŋ] *adj (moving)* rührend.

tough [tʌf] *adj (resilient)* widerstandsfähig ; *(meat)* zäh ; *(difficult)* schwierig ; *(harsh, strict)* hart.

tour [tʊəʳ] *n (journey)* Tour *die* ; *(of city, castle etc)* Besichtigung *die* ; *(of pop group, theatre company)* Tournee *die.* ◆ *vt* reisen durch ; **on ~** auf Tournee.

tourism ['tʊərɪzm] *n* Tourismus *der.*

tourist ['tʊərɪst] *n* Tourist *der* (-in *die*).

tourist class *n* Touristclass *die.*

tourist information office *n* Fremdenverkehrsbüro *das.*

tournament ['tɔ:nəmənt] *n* Turnier *das.*

tour operator *n* Reiseveranstalter *der.*

tout [taʊt] *n* Schwarzhändler *der.*

tow [təʊ] *vt* ablschleppen.

toward [tə'wɔ:d] *(Am)* = **towards**.

towards [tə'wɔːdz] *prep (Br : in the direction of)* zu ; *(facing)* nach ; *(with regard to)* gegenüber (+D) ; *(with time)* gegen ; *(to help pay for)* für ; **to run ~ sb** auf jn zullaufen ; **to sit ~ the front/back** vorne/hinten sitzen.

towaway zone ['təʊəweɪ-] *n (Am)* Abschleppzone *die*.

towel ['taʊəl] *n* Handtuch *das*.

toweling ['taʊəlɪŋ] *(Am)* = **towelling**.

towelling ['taʊəlɪŋ] *n (Br)* Frottee *das*.

towel rail *n* Handtuchhalter *der*.

tower ['taʊəʳ] *n* Turm *der*.

tower block *n (Br)* Hochhaus *das*.

Tower Bridge *n Zwillingszugbrücke über die Themse, in der Nähe des Londoner Tower.*

TOWER BRIDGE

Diese im 19. Jahrhundert erbaute Brücke im neugotischen Stil führt in Höhe des Londoner Tower über die Themse. Es handelt sich um sehr markante Zwillingszugbrücke, die bei der Durchfahrt hoher Schiffe hochgezogen werden kann.

Tower of London *n* : **the ~** der Londoner Tower.

TOWER OF LONDON

Am nördlichen Ufer der Themse liegt der „Tower of London", eine Festung, die auf das 11. Jahrhundert zurückgeht und bis zum 17. Jahrhun-

dert ein königlicher Palast war. Heute ist der Tower eine beliebte Touristenattraktion, die zur Besichtigung offen steht und ein Museum beherbergt.

town [taʊn] *n* Stadt *die*.

town centre *n* Stadtzentrum *das*.

town hall *n* Rathaus *das*.

towpath ['taʊpɑːθ, *pl* -pɑːðz] *n* Treidelpfad *der*.

towrope ['təʊrəʊp] *n* Abschleppseil *das*.

tow truck *n (Am)* Abschleppwagen *der*.

toxic ['tɒksɪk] *adj* giftig.

toy [tɔɪ] *n* Spielzeug *das*.

toy shop *n* Spielwarengeschäft *das*.

trace [treɪs] *n* Spur *die*. ◆ *vt (find)* finden.

tracing paper ['treɪsɪŋ-] *n* Pauspapier *das*.

track [træk] *n (path)* Weg *der* ; *(of railway)* Gleis *das* ; *(SPORT)* Bahn *die* ; *(song)* Stück *das*.
■ **track down** *vt sep* ausfindig machen.

tracksuit ['træksuːt] *n* Trainingsanzug *der*.

tractor ['træktə] *n* Traktor *der*.

trade [treɪd] *n (COMM)* Handel *der* ; *(job)* Handwerk *das*. ◆ *vt (exchange)* tauschen. ◆ *vi (COMM)* handeln.

trade-in *n (action)* Inzahlungnahme *die*.

trademark ['treɪdmɑːk] *n* Warenzeichen *das*.

trader ['treɪdəʳ] *n* Händler *der* (-in *die*).

tradesman ['treɪdzmən] (*pl* -men [-mən]) *n (deliveryman)* Lieferant *der* ; *(shopkeeper)* Einzelhändler *der*.

trade union *n* Gewerkschaft *die*.

tradition [trə'dɪʃn] *n* Tradition *die*.

traditional [trə'dɪʃənl] *adj* traditionell.

traffic ['træfɪk] (*pt & pp* -ked) *n (cars etc)* Verkehr *der*. ◆ *vi* : **to ~ in** handeln mit.

traffic circle *n (Am)* Kreisverkehr *der*.

traffic island *n* Verkehrsinsel *die*.

traffic jam *n* Stau *der*.

traffic lights *npl* Ampel *die*.

traffic warden *n (Br)* ≃ Hilfspolizist *der* (Politesse *die*).

tragedy ['trædʒədɪ] *n* Tragödie *die*.

tragic ['trædʒɪk] *adj* tragisch.

trail [treɪl] *n (path)* Weg *der* ; *(marks)* Spur *die*. ◆ *vi (be losing)* zurückliegen.

trailer ['treɪlə'] *n (for boat, luggage)* Anhänger *der* ; *(Am : caravan)* Wohnwagen *der* ; *(for film, programme)* Trailer *der*.

train [treɪn] *n (on railway)* Zug *der*. ◆ *vt (teach)* auslbilden. ◆ *vi (SPORT)* trainieren ; **by ~** mit dem Zug.

train driver *n* Zugführer *der* (-in *die*).

trainee [treɪ'niː] *n* Auszubildende, die ; *(in management)* Trainee *der, die*.

trainer ['treɪnə'] *n (of athlete etc)* Trainer *der* (-in *die*).

▓ **trainers** *npl (Br : shoes)* Turnschuhe *pl*.

training ['treɪnɪŋ] *n (instruction)* Ausbildung *die* ; *(exercises)* Training *das*.

training shoes *npl (Br)* Turnschuhe *pl*.

tram [træm] *n (Br)* Straßenbahn *die*.

tramp [træmp] *n* Tramp *der*.

trampoline ['træmpəliːn] *n* Trampolin *das*.

trance [trɑːns] *n* Trance *die*.

tranquilizer ['træŋkwɪlaɪzər] *(Am)* = **tranquillizer**.

tranquillizer ['træŋkwɪlaɪzə'] *n (Br)* Beruhigungsmittel *das*.

transaction [træn'zækʃn] *n* Geschäft *das*.

transatlantic [,trænzət'læntɪk] *adj* transatlantisch.

transfer [*n* 'trænsfɜː', *vb* træns'fɜː'] *n (of money)* Überweisung *die* ; *(of power)* Übertragung *die* ; *(SPORT)* Transfer *der* ; *(picture)* Abziehbild *das* ; *(Am : ticket)* Fahrkarte mit Umsteigeerlaubnis. ◆ *vt* übertragen ; *(money)* überweisen. ◆ *vi (change bus, plane etc)* umsteigen ; '**~s**' *(in airport)* 'Transitpassagiere'.

transfer desk *n (in airport)* Transitschalter *der*.

transform [træns'fɔːm] *vt* verändern.

transfusion [træns'fjuːʒn] *n* Transfusion *die*.

transistor radio [træn'zɪstə-] *n* Transistorradio *das*.

transit ['trænzɪt] : **in transit** *adv* im Transit.

transitive ['trænzɪtɪv] *adj* transitiv.

transit lounge n Transit Lounge die.

translate [træns'leɪt] vt übersetzen.

translation [træns'leɪʃn] n Übersetzung die.

translator [træns'leɪtə'] n Übersetzer der (-in die).

transmission [trænz'mɪʃn] n Übertragung die.

transmit [trænz'mɪt] vt übertragen.

transparent [træns'pærənt] adj (see-through) durchsichtig.

transplant ['trænsplɑːnt] n Transplantation die.

transport [n 'trænspɔːt, vb træn'spɔːt] n (cars, trains, planes etc) Verkehrsmittel pl ; (moving) Transport der, Beförderung die. ◆ vt transportieren, befördern.

transportation [ˌtrænspɔː'teɪʃn] n (Am) (cars, trains, planes etc) Verkehrsmittel pl ; (moving) Transport der, Beförderung die.

trap [træp] n Falle die. ◆ vt : to be trapped (stuck) festsitzen.

trapdoor [ˌtræp'dɔːr] n Falltür die.

trash [træʃ] n (Am : waste material) Müll der.

trashcan ['træʃkæn] n (Am) Mülleimer die.

trauma ['trɔːmə] n Trauma das.

traumatic [trɔː'mætɪk] adj traumatisch.

travel ['trævl] n Reisen das. ◆ vt (distance) fahren. ◆ vi reisen ; (in vehicle) fahren.

travel agency n Reisebüro das.

travel agent n Reiseverkehrskaufmann der (-kauffrau die) ; ~'s (shop) Reisebüro das.

Travelcard ['trævlkɑːd] n (Br) Zeitkarte im Londoner Nahverkehrssystem.

travel centre n (in railway, bus station) Reiseinformation die.

travel documents npl Reisedokumente pl.

traveler ['trævlər] (Am) = **traveller.**

travel insurance n Reiseversicherung die.

traveller ['trævlə'] n (Br) Reisende der, die.

traveller's cheque n Travellerscheck der.

travelsick ['trævəlsɪk] adj reisekrank.

trawler ['trɔːlə'] n Trawler der.

tray [treɪ] n Tablett das.

treacherous ['tretʃərəs] adj (person) verräterisch ; (roads, conditions) gefährlich.

treacle ['triːkl] n (Br) Sirup der.

tread [tred] (pt trod, pp trodden) n (of tyre) Profil das. ◆ vi : to ~ on sthg auf etw (A) treten.

treasure ['treʒə'] n Schatz der.

treat [triːt] vt behandeln. ◆ n (special thing) Freude die ; to ~ sb to sthg jm etw spendieren.

treatment ['triːtmənt] n Behandlung die.

treble ['trebl] adj dreifach ; ~ the amount dreimal so viel.

tree [triː] n Baum der.

trek [trek] n Wanderung die.

tremble ['trembl] vi zittern.

tremendous [trɪ'mendəs] *adj*
enorm ; *(inf : very good)* toll.

trench [trentʃ] *n* Graben *der.*

trend [trend] *n (tendency)* Tendenz *die* ; *(fashion)* Trend *der.*

trendy ['trendɪ] *adj (inf)*
trendy.

trespasser ['trespəsə'] *n* Unbefugte *der, die* ; '~s will be prosecuted' 'Betreten verboten'.

trial ['traɪəl] *n (JUR)* Prozess
der ; *(test)* Test *der* ; a ~ period
eine Probezeit.

triangle ['traɪæŋgl] *n* Dreieck
das.

triangular [traɪ'æŋgjʊlə'] *adj*
dreieckig.

tribe [traɪb] *n* Stamm *der.*

tributary ['trɪbjʊtrɪ] *n* Nebenfluss *der.*

trick [trɪk] *n* Trick *der.* ◆ *vt*
überlisten ; to play a ~ on sb jm
einen Streich spielen.

trickle ['trɪkl] *vi (liquid)* tropfen.

tricky ['trɪkɪ] *adj* kniffelig.

tricycle ['traɪsɪkl] *n* Dreirad
das.

trifle ['traɪfl] *n (dessert)* Nachtisch aus mit Sherry getränktem
Biskuit, Früchten, Vanillecreme
und Sahne in Schichten.

trigger ['trɪgə'] *n* Abzug *der.*

trim [trɪm] *n (haircut)* Nachschneiden *das.* ◆ *vt (hair,
beard, hedge)* nachschneiden.

trinket ['trɪŋkɪt] *n* Schnickschnack *der.*

trio ['tri:əʊ] *(pl* -s) *n* Trio *das.*

trip [trɪp] *n (voyage)* Reise *die* ;
(short) Ausflug *der.* ◆ *vi* stolpern. ■ **trip up** *vi* stolpern.

triple ['trɪpl] *adj* dreifach.

tripod ['traɪpɒd] *n* Stativ *das.*

triumph ['traɪəmf] *n* Triumph
der.

trivial ['trɪvɪəl] *adj (pej)* trivial.

trod [trɒd] *pt* → **tread.**

trodden ['trɒdn] *pp* → **tread.**

trolley ['trɒlɪ] *(pl* -s) *n (Br : at
airport etc)* Gepäckwagen *der* ;
(Br : in supermarket) Einkaufswagen *der* ; *(Br : for food,
drinks)* Wagen *der* ; *(Am : tram)*
Straßenbahn *die.*

trombone [trɒm'bəʊn] *n* Posaune *die.*

troops [tru:ps] *npl* Truppen
pl.

trophy ['trəʊfɪ] *n* Trophäe *die.*

tropical ['trɒpɪkl] *adj* tropisch ; ~ **fruit** Südfrucht *die.*

trot [trɒt] *vi (horse)* traben. ◆
n : on the ~ *(inf)* hintereinander.

trouble ['trʌbl] *n (problems)*
Ärger *der* ; *(difficulty)* Schwierigkeiten *pl* ; *(inconvenience)*
Mühe *die* ; *(pain, illness)* Beschwerden *pl.* ◆ *vt (worry)* beunruhigen ; *(bother)* stören ; to
be in ~ *(having problems)* in
Schwierigkeiten sein ; *(with
police, parents)* Ärger haben ; to
get into ~ Ärger bekommen ; to
take the ~ to do sthg sich die
Mühe machen, etw zu tun ; it's
no ~ das macht keine Umstände.

trough [trɒf] *n (for animals)*
Trog *der.*

trouser press ['traʊzə-] *n* Hosenspanner *der.*

trousers ['traʊzəz] *npl* Hose
die ; a pair of ~ eine Hose.

trout [traʊt] *(pl* trout) *n* Forelle
die.

trowel ['traʊəl] *n (for gardening)* Schaufel *die.*

truant ['tru:ənt] *n* : to play ~ die Schule schwänzen.

truce [tru:s] *n* Waffenstillstand *der*.

truck [trʌk] *n* Lastwagen *der*, LKW *der*.

true [tru:] *adj (not false, actual)* wahr ; *(genuine, sincere)* echt.

truly ['tru:lɪ] *adv* : yours ~ mit freundlichen Grüßen.

trumpet ['trʌmpɪt] *n* Trompete *die*.

trumps [trʌmps] *npl* Trumpf *der*.

truncheon ['trʌntʃən] *n* Schlagstock *der*.

trunk [trʌŋk] *n (of tree)* Stamm *der* ; *(Am : of car)* Kofferraum *der* ; *(case, box)* Truhe *die* ; *(of elephant)* Rüssel *der*.

trunk call *n (Br)* Ferngespräch *das*.

trunk road *n (Br)* Landstraße *die*.

trunks [trʌŋks] *npl (for swimming)* Badehose *die*.

trust [trʌst] *n (confidence)* Vertrauen *das*. ◆ *vt* vertrauen (+D) ; *(fml : hope)* hoffen.

trustworthy ['trʌst,wɜ:ðɪ] *adj* vertrauenswürdig.

truth [tru:θ] *n* Wahrheit *die*.

truthful ['tru:θfʊl] *adj (statement, account)* wahr ; *(person)* ehrlich.

try [traɪ] *n (attempt)* Versuch *der*. ◆ *vi* versuchen ; *(make effort)* sich bemühen. ◆ *vt* versuchen ; *(food)* probieren ; *(JUR)* : to ~ sb jn vor Gericht bringen ; to ~ to do sthg versuchen, etw zu tun. ▨ **try on** *vt sep (clothes)* an|probieren. ▨ **try out** *vt sep* aus|probieren.

T-shirt *n* T-Shirt *das*.

tub [tʌb] *n (of margarine etc)* Becher *der* ; *(inf : bath)* Wanne *die*.

tube [tju:b] *n (container)* Tube *die* ; *(Br : inf : underground)* U-Bahn *die* ; *(pipe)* Rohr *das* ; by ~ mit der U-Bahn.

tube station *n (Br : inf)* U-Bahn-Station *die*.

tuck [tʌk] : **tuck in** *vt sep (shirt)* hinein|stecken ; *(child, person)* zu|decken. ◆ *vi (inf)* rein|hauen.

tuck shop *n (Br)* ≃ Süßwarenladen *der (in einer Schule)*.

Tudor ['tju:dər] *adj (architecture)* Tudor- *(16. Jahrhundert)*.

Tues. *(abbr of Tuesday)* Di.

Tuesday ['tju:zdɪ] *n* Dienstag *der* ; → **Saturday**.

tuft [tʌft] *n (of hair, grass)* Büschel *das*.

tug [tʌg] *vt* ziehen. ◆ *n (boat)* Schlepper *der*.

tuition [tju:'ɪʃn] *n* Unterricht *der*.

tulip ['tju:lɪp] *n* Tulpe *die*.

tumble-dryer ['tʌmbldraɪə*] *n* Wäschetrockner *der*.

tumbler ['tʌmblə*] *n (glass)* Glas *das*.

tummy ['tʌmɪ] *n (inf)* Bauch *der*.

tummy upset *n (inf)* Bauchschmerzen *pl*.

tumor ['tu:mər] *(Am)* = **tumour**.

tumour ['tju:mə*] *n (Br)* Tumor *der*.

tuna [(Br) 'tju:nə-, (Am) 'tu:nə-] *n* Thunfisch *der*.

tuna melt n (Am) mit Thunfisch und Käse überbackener Toast.

tune [tjuːn] n Melodie die. ◆ vt (radio, TV, engine) einlstellen ; (instrument) stimmen ; **in ~** (instrument) richtig gestimmt ; **out of ~** (instrument) verstimmt ; **to sing in/out of ~** richtig/falsch singen.

tunic ['tjuːnɪk] n (SCH) Trägerkleid das.

Tunisia [tjuːˈnɪzɪə] n Tunesien nt.

tunnel ['tʌnl] n Tunnel der.

turban ['tɜːbən] n Turban der.

turbo ['tɜːbəʊ] (pl -s) n Turbo der.

turbulence ['tɜːbjʊləns] n (when flying) Turbulenz die.

turf [tɜːf] n (grass) Rasen der.

Turk [tɜːk] n Türke der (Türkin die).

turkey ['tɜːkɪ] (pl -s) n Truthahn der, Pute die.

Turkey ['tɜːkɪ] n Türkei die.

Turkish ['tɜːkɪʃ] adj türkisch. ◆ n (language) Türkisch das. ◆ npl : **the ~** die Türken pl.

Turkish delight n Lokum das.

turn [tɜːn] n (in road) Abzweigung die ; (of knob, key, switch) Drehung die. ◆ vi (person) sich wenden ; (turn round) sich umldrehen ; (car) ablbiegen ; (rotate) sich drehen ; (milk) sauer werden. ◆ vt (head, car) wenden ; (table, chair, knob, key) drehen ; (page) umlblättern ; (a switch) stellen ; (become) werden ; **to ~ sthg black** etw schwarz machen ; **to ~ into sthg**

(become) sich in etw (A) verwandeln ; **to ~ sthg into sthg** etw in etw (A) verwandeln ; **to ~ left/right** links/rechts ablbiegen ; **to ~ the corner** um die Ecke biegen ; **it's your ~** du bist an der Reihe ; **at the ~ of the century** um die Jahrhundertwende ; **to take it in ~s to do sthg** sich ablwechseln, etw zu tun ; **to ~ sthg inside out** etw umkehren. ▪ **turn back** vt sep (person, car) zurücklweisen. ◆ vi umlkehren. ▪ **turn down** vt sep (heating) herunterlstellen ; (radio) leiser stellen ; (offer, request) ablehnen. ▪ **turn off** vt sep (engine, water, gas) ablstellen ; (light, TV) auslschalten ; (tap) zuldrehen. ◆ vi (leave road) ablfahren. ▪ **turn on** vt sep (light, TV) einlschalten ; (engine, water, gas, tap) anlstellen. ▪ **turn out** vt sep (light) auslmachen. ◆ vi (come, attend) erscheinen. ◆ vt fus : **to ~ out well/badly** gut/schlecht auslgehen ; **to ~ out to be sthg** sich als etw herauslstellen. ▪ **turn over** vt sep (page) umlblättern ; (card, omelette) umldrehen. ◆ vi (in bed) sich umldrehen ; (Br : change channels) umlstellen. ▪ **turn round** vt sep (car, table etc) umldrehen. ◆ vi (person) sich umldrehen. ▪ **turn up** vt sep (heating) aufldrehen ; (radio, volume) lauter stellen. ◆ vi (come, attend) erscheinen.

turning ['tɜːnɪŋ] n (off road) Abzweigung die.

turnip ['tɜːnɪp] n weiße Rübe.

turn-up n (Br : on trousers) Aufschlag der.

turps [tɜːps] n (Br : inf) Terpentin das.

turquoise ['tɜːkwɔɪz] adj türkis.

turtle ['tɜːtl] n Schildkröte die.

turtleneck ['tɜːtlnek] n Rollkragenpullover der.

tutor ['tjuːtə'] n (private teacher) Privatlehrer der.

tuxedo [tʌk'siːdəʊ] (pl -s) n (Am) Smoking der.

TV n Fernsehen das ; (television set) Fernseher der ; **on** ~ im Fernsehen.

tweed [twiːd] n Tweed der.

tweezers ['twiːzəz] npl Pinzette die.

twelfth [twelfθ] num zwölfte(-r) (-s) ; → **sixth**.

twelve [twelv] num zwölf ; → **six**.

twentieth ['twentɪəθ] num zwanzigste(-r) (-s) ; **the** ~ **century** das zwanzigste Jahrhundert ; see also **sixth**.

twenty ['twentɪ] num zwanzig ; → **six**.

twice [twaɪs] adv zweimal ; **it's** ~ **as good** das ist doppelt so gut.

twig [twɪg] n Zweig der.

twilight ['twaɪlaɪt] n Dämmerung die.

twin [twɪn] n Zwilling der.

twin beds npl zwei Einzelbetten pl.

twine [twaɪn] n Bindfaden der.

twin room n Zweibettzimmer das.

twist [twɪst] vt drehen ; **to** ~ **one's ankle** sich (D) den Fuß verrenken.

twisting ['twɪstɪŋ] adj (road, river) sich windend.

two [tuː] num zwei ; → **six**.

two-piece adj (swimsuit, suit) zweiteilig.

type [taɪp] n (kind) Art die. ◆ vt & vi tippen.

typewriter ['taɪp,raɪtə'] n Schreibmaschine die.

typhoid ['taɪfɔɪd] n Typhus der.

typical ['tɪpɪkl] adj typisch.

typist ['taɪpɪst] n Schreibkraft die.

tyre ['taɪə'] n (Br) Reifen der.

Tyrol [tɪ'rəʊl] n : **the** ~ Tirol nt.

U

U adj (Br : film) jugendfrei.

UFO n (abbr of unidentified flying object) Ufo das.

ugly ['ʌglɪ] adj (unattractive) hässlich.

UHT adj (abbr of ultra heat treated) : ~ **milk** H-Milch die.

UK n : **the** ~ das Vereinigte Königreich.

ulcer ['ʌlsə'] n Geschwür das.

ultimate ['ʌltɪmət] adj (final) endgültig ; (best, greatest) größte(-r) (-s).

ultraviolet [,ʌltrə'vaɪələt] adj ultraviolett.

umbrella [ʌm'brelə] n Regenschirm der.

umpire ['ʌmpaɪə'] n Schiedsrichter der.

UN n (abbr of United Nations) : **the** ~ die UNO.

unable [ʌn'eɪbl] *adj* : to be ~ to do sthg etw nicht tun können.

unacceptable [ˌʌnək'septəbl] *adj* unannehmbar.

unaccustomed [ˌʌnə'kʌstəmd] *adj* : to be ~ to sthg an etw (A) nicht gewöhnt sein.

unanimous [ju:'nænɪməs] *adj* einstimmig.

unattended [ˌʌnə'tendɪd] *adj* (baggage) unbeaufsichtigt.

unattractive [ˌʌnə'træktɪv] *adj* unattraktiv.

unauthorized [ˌʌn'ɔ:θəraɪzd] *adj* unbefugt.

unavailable [ˌʌnə'veɪləbl] *adj* nicht erhältlich.

unavoidable [ˌʌnə'vɔɪdəbl] *adj* unvermeidlich.

unaware [ˌʌnə'weəʳ] *adj* : to be ~ of sthg sich (D) einer Sache (G) nicht bewusst sein.

unbearable [ʌn'beərəbl] *adj* unerträglich.

unbelievable [ˌʌnbɪ'li:vəbl] *adj* unglaublich.

unbutton [ˌʌn'bʌtn] *vt* aufknöpfen.

uncertain [ʌn'sɜ:tn] *adj* unsicher.

uncertainty [ˌʌn'sɜ:tntɪ] *n* Unsicherheit *die*.

uncle ['ʌŋkl] *n* Onkel *der*.

unclean [ˌʌn'kli:n] *adj* unsauber.

unclear [ˌʌn'klɪəʳ] *adj* unklar.

uncomfortable [ˌʌn'kʌmftəbl] *adj* (chair, bed) unbequem ; to feel ~ (person) sich nicht wohl fühlen.

uncommon [ʌn'kɒmən] *adj* (rare) ungewöhnlich.

unconscious [ʌn'kɒnʃəs] *adj* (after accident) bewusstlos ; (unaware) unbewusst ; to be ~ of sthg sich (D) einer Sache (G) nicht bewusst sein.

unconvincing [ˌʌnkən'vɪnsɪŋ] *adj* nicht überzeugend.

uncooperative [ˌʌnkəʊ'ɒpərətɪv] *adj* nicht entgegenkommend.

uncork [ˌʌn'kɔ:k] *vt* entkorken.

uncouth [ʌn'ku:θ] *adj* ungehobelt.

uncover [ʌn'kʌvəʳ] *vt* (discover) entdecken ; (car, swimming pool etc) abdecken.

under ['ʌndəʳ] *prep* unter (+A, D) ; (according to) nach ; children ~ ten Kinder unter zehn ; ~ the circumstances unter diesen Umständen ; to be ~ pressure unter Druck sein.

underage [ˌʌndər'eɪdʒ] *adj* minderjährig.

undercarriage ['ʌndəˌkærɪdʒ] *n* Fahrwerk *das*.

underdone [ˌʌndə'dʌn] *adj* (food) nicht gar ; (rare) nicht durchgebraten.

underestimate [ˌʌndər'estɪmeɪt] *vt* unterschätzen.

underexposed [ˌʌndərɪk'spəʊzd] *adj* (photograph) unterbelichtet.

undergo [ˌʌndə'gəʊ] (pt -went, pp -gone) *vt* sich unterziehen (+D).

undergraduate [ˌʌndə'grædjʊət] *n* Student *der* (-in *die*).

underground ['ʌndəgraʊnd] *adj* unterirdisch ; (secret) Untergrund-. ◆ *n (Br : railway)* U-Bahn *die*.

undergrowth ['ʌndəɡrəʊθ] *n* Gestrüpp *das*.

underline [,ʌndə'laın] *vt* unterstreichen.

underneath [,ʌndə'ni:θ] *prep* unter *(+A,D)*. ◆ *adv* darunter. ◆ *n* Unterseite *die*.

underpants ['ʌndəpænts] *npl* Unterhose *die*.

underpass ['ʌndəpɑːs] *n* Unterführung *die*.

undershirt ['ʌndəʃɜːt] *n (Am)* Unterhemd *das*.

underskirt ['ʌndəskɜːt] *n* Unterrock *der*.

understand [,ʌndə'stænd] *(pt & pp -stood) vt & vi* verstehen ; **I don't ~** ich verstehe das nicht ; **to make o.s. understood** sich verständlich machen ; **I ~ that...** *(believe)* ich habe gehört, dass...

understanding [,ʌndə'stændɪŋ] *adj* verständnisvoll. ◆ *n (agreement)* Vereinbarung *die* ; *(knowledge)* Kenntnis *die* ; *(interpretation)* Annahme *die* ; *(sympathy)* Verständnis *das*.

understatement [,ʌndə'steɪtmənt] *n* : **that's an ~** das ist untertrieben.

understood [,ʌndə'stʊd] *pt & pp* → **understand**.

undertake [,ʌndə'teɪk] *(pt -took, pp -taken) vt (job, task)* übernehmen ; **to ~ to do sthg** sich verpflichten, etw zu tun.

undertaker ['ʌndə,teɪkəʳ] *n (firm)* Bestattungsinstitut *das* ; *(person)* Leichenbestatter *der*.

undertaking [,ʌndə'teɪkɪŋ] *n (promise)* Versprechen *das* ; *(task)* Unternehmen *das*.

undertook [,ʌndə'tʊk] *pt* → **undertake**.

underwater [,ʌndə'wɔːtəʳ] *adj* Unterwasser-. ◆ *adv* unter Wasser.

underwear ['ʌndəweəʳ] *n* Unterwäsche *die*.

underwent [,ʌndə'went] *pt* → **undergo**.

undesirable [,ʌndɪ'zaɪərəbl] *adj* unerwünscht.

undo [,ʌn'duː] *(pt -did, pp -done) vt* auflmachen ; *(tie)* lösen.

undone [,ʌn'dʌn] *adj (coat, shirt, shoelaces)* offen.

undress [,ʌn'dres] *vi* sich auslziehen. ◆ *vt* auslziehen.

undressed [,ʌn'drest] *adj* ausgezogen ; **to get ~** sich auslziehen.

uneasy [ʌn'iːzɪ] *adj* unbehaglich.

uneducated [,ʌn'edjʊkeɪtɪd] *adj* ungebildet.

unemployed [,ʌnɪm'plɔɪd] *adj* arbeitslos. ◆ *npl* : **the ~** die Arbeitslosen *pl*.

unemployment [,ʌnɪm'plɔɪmənt] *n* Arbeitslosigkeit *die*.

unemployment benefit *n* Arbeitslosenunterstützung *die*.

unequal [,ʌn'iːkwəl] *adj* ungleich.

uneven [,ʌn'iːvn] *adj (surface)* uneben ; *(speed, beat)* ungleichmäßig ; *(share, competition, race)* ungleich.

uneventful [ˌʌnɪˈventfʊl] *adj* ereignislos.

unexpected [ˌʌnɪkˈspektɪd] *adj* unerwartet.

unexpectedly [ˌʌnɪkˈspektɪd-lɪ] *adv* unerwartet.

unfair [ˌʌnˈfeəʳ] *adj* ungerecht.

unfairly [ˌʌnˈfeəlɪ] *adv* ungerecht.

unfaithful [ˌʌnˈfeɪθfʊl] *adj* untreu.

unfamiliar [ˌʌnfəˈmɪljəʳ] *adj* ungewohnt ; to be ~ with sthg sich mit etw nicht aus|kennen.

unfashionable [ˌʌnˈfæʃnəbl] *adj* unmodern.

unfasten [ˌʌnˈfɑːsn] *vt* auf|machen.

unfavourable [ˌʌnˈfeɪvrəbl] *adj* ungünstig.

unfinished [ˌʌnˈfɪnɪʃt] *adj* unvollendet ; *(work)* unerledigt.

unfit [ˌʌnˈfɪt] *adj (not healthy)* nicht fit ; to be ~ for sthg für etw ungeeignet sein ; to be ~ for work arbeitsunfähig sein.

unfold [ʌnˈfəʊld] *vt (map, sheet)* auseinander falten.

unforgettable [ˌʌnfəˈgetəbl] *adj* unvergesslich.

unforgivable [ˌʌnfəˈgɪvəbl] *adj* unverzeihlich.

unfortunate [ʌnˈfɔːtʃnət] *adj* bedauerlich.

unfortunately [ʌnˈfɔːtʃnətlɪ] *adv* leider.

unfriendly [ˌʌnˈfrendlɪ] *adj* unfreundlich.

unfurnished [ˌʌnˈfɜːnɪʃt] *adj* unmöbliert.

ungrateful [ʌnˈgreɪtfʊl] *adj* undankbar.

unhappy [ʌnˈhæpɪ] *adj (sad)* unglücklich ; *(not pleased)* unzufrieden ; to be ~ about sthg mit etw unzufrieden sein.

unharmed [ʌnˈhɑːmd] *adj* unverletzt.

unhealthy [ʌnˈhelθɪ] *adj* ungesund.

unhelpful [ʌnˈhelpfʊl] *adj* : to be ~ *(person)* nicht hilfsbereit sein ; *(information)* nicht hilfreich sein.

unhurt [ʌnˈhɜːt] *adj* unverletzt.

unhygienic [ˌʌnhaɪˈdʒiːnɪk] *adj* unhygienisch.

unification [ˌjuːnɪfɪˈkeɪʃn] *n* Vereinigung *die*.

uniform [ˈjuːnɪfɔːm] *n* Uniform *die*.

unimportant [ˌʌnɪmˈpɔːtənt] *adj* unwichtig.

unintelligent [ˌʌnɪnˈtelɪdʒənt] *adj* nicht intelligent.

unintentional [ˌʌnɪnˈtenʃənl] *adj* unbeabsichtigt.

uninterested [ˌʌnˈɪntrəstɪd] *adj* desinteressiert.

uninteresting [ˌʌnˈɪntrəstɪŋ] *adj* uninteressant.

union [ˈjuːnjən] *n (of workers)* Gewerkschaft *die*.

Union Jack *n* : the ~ der Union Jack *(die britische Fahne)*.

unique [juːˈniːk] *adj* einmalig ; to be ~ to beschränkt sein auf (+A).

unisex [ˈjuːnɪseks] *adj* Unisex-.

unit [ˈjuːnɪt] *n* Einheit *die* ; *(department)* Abteilung *die* ; *(piece of furniture)* Element *das* ; *(machine)* Anlage *die*.

unite [juːˈnaɪt] *vt* vereinigen. ◆ *vi* sich zusammenschließen.

United Kingdom [juːˈnaɪtɪd-] *n* : **the ~** das Vereinigte Königreich.

United Nations [juːˈnaɪtɪd-] *npl* : **the ~** die Vereinten Nationen *pl*.

United States (of America) [juːˈnaɪtɪd-] *npl* : **the ~** die Vereinigten Staaten *pl* (von Amerika).

unity [ˈjuːnətɪ] *n* Einigkeit *die*.

universal [ˌjuːnɪˈvɜːsl] *adj* allgemein.

universe [ˈjuːnɪvɜːs] *n* Universum *das*.

university [ˌjuːnɪˈvɜːsətɪ] *n* Universität *die*.

unjust [ˌʌnˈdʒʌst] *adj* ungerecht.

unkind [ʌnˈkaɪnd] *adj (person)* unfreundlich ; *(remark)* spitz.

unknown [ˌʌnˈnəʊn] *adj* unbekannt.

unleaded (petrol) [ˌʌnˈledɪd-] *n* Bleifrei *das*.

unless [ənˈles] *conj* es sei denn.

unlike [ˌʌnˈlaɪk] *prep (different to)* nicht ähnlich (+D) ; *(in contrast to)* im Gegensatz zu ; it's ~ him es ist nicht seine Art.

unlikely [ʌnˈlaɪklɪ] *adj (not probable)* unwahrscheinlich ; **to be ~ to do sthg** etw wahrscheinlich nicht tun.

unlimited [ʌnˈlɪmɪtɪd] *adj* unbegrenzt ; **~ mileage** unbegrenzte Meilenzahl.

unlisted [ʌnˈlɪstɪd] *adj (Am : phone number)* : **to be ~** nicht im Telefonbuch stehen.

unload [ˌʌnˈləʊd] *vt* entladen.

unlock [ˌʌnˈlɒk] *vt* aufschließen.

unlucky [ʌnˈlʌkɪ] *adj* unglücklich.

unmarried [ˌʌnˈmærɪd] *adj* unverheiratet.

unnatural [ʌnˈnætʃrəl] *adj* unnatürlich.

unnecessary [ʌnˈnesəsərɪ] *adj* unnötig.

unobtainable [ˌʌnəbˈteɪnəbl] *adj (product)* nicht erhältlich ; *(phone number)* nicht erreichbar.

unoccupied [ˌʌnˈɒkjʊpaɪd] *adj (place, seat)* frei.

unofficial [ˌʌnəˈfɪʃl] *adj* inoffiziell.

unpack [ˌʌnˈpæk] *vt & vi* auspacken.

unpleasant [ʌnˈpleznt] *adj* unangenehm.

unplug [ʌnˈplʌg] *vt* den Stecker herauslziehen von.

unpopular [ˌʌnˈpɒpjʊlə] *adj* unbeliebt.

unpredictable [ˌʌnprɪˈdɪktəbl] *adj* unberechenbar.

unprepared [ˌʌnprɪˈpeəd] *adj* unvorbereitet.

unprotected [ˌʌnprəˈtektɪd] *adj* ungeschützt.

unqualified [ˌʌnˈkwɒlɪfaɪd] *adj (person)* unqualifiziert.

unreal [ˌʌnˈrɪəl] *adj* unwirklich.

unreasonable [ʌnˈriːznəbl] *adj* unangemessen.

unrecognizable [ˌʌnrekəgˈnaɪzəbl] *adj* unkenntlich.

unreliable [ˌʌnrɪˈlaɪəbl] *adj* unzuverlässig.

unrest [ˌʌnˈrest] *n* Unruhen *pl*.

unroll [ˌʌnˈrəʊl] *vt* auf|rollen.

unsafe [ˌʌnˈseɪf] *adj* unsicher.

unsatisfactory [ˌʌnsætɪsˈfæktərɪ] *adj* unbefriedigend.

unscrew [ˌʌnˈskruː] *vt (lid, top)* ab|schrauben.

unsightly [ʌnˈsaɪtlɪ] *adj* unansehnlich.

unskilled [ˌʌnˈskɪld] *adj (worker)* ungelernt.

unsociable [ʌnˈsəʊʃəbl] *adj* ungesellig.

unsound [ˌʌnˈsaʊnd] *adj (building, structure)* nicht sicher; *(argument, method)* nicht stichhaltig.

unspoiled [ˌʌnˈspɔɪld] *adj (place, beach)* unberührt.

unsteady [ˌʌnˈstedɪ] *adj (pile, person)* wackelig; *(structure)* unsicher; *(hand)* zitterig.

unstuck [ˌʌnˈstʌk] *adj* : to come ~ *(label, poster etc)* sich lösen.

unsuccessful [ˌʌnsəkˈsesfʊl] *adj* erfolglos.

unsuitable [ˌʌnˈsuːtəbl] *adj* unpassend.

unsure [ˌʌnˈʃɔː] *adj* : to be ~ of sthg sich *(D)* einer Sache *(G)* nicht sicher sein; to be ~ about sb sich *(D)* über jn nicht im Klaren sein.

unsweetened [ˌʌnˈswiːtnd] *adj* ungesüßt.

untidy [ʌnˈtaɪdɪ] *adj* unordentlich.

untie [ˌʌnˈtaɪ] *(cont* **untying** [ˌʌnˈtaɪɪŋ]*) vt (person)* los|binden; *(knot)* auf|binden.

until [ənˈtɪl] *prep & conj* bis; ~ the evening/end bis zum Abend/Ende; not ~ erst.

untrue [ˌʌnˈtruː] *adj (false)* unwahr; to be ~ nicht wahr sein.

untrustworthy [ˌʌnˈtrʌstˌwɜːðɪ] *adj* nicht vertrauenswürdig.

unusual [ʌnˈjuːʒl] *adj* ungewöhnlich.

unusually [ʌnˈjuːʒəlɪ] *adv* ungewöhnlich.

unwell [ˌʌnˈwel] *adj* unwohl; to feel ~ sich nicht wohl fühlen.

unwilling [ˌʌnˈwɪlɪŋ] *adj* : to be ~ to do sthg etw nicht tun wollen.

unwind [ˌʌnˈwaɪnd] *(pt & pp* **unwound** [ˌʌnˈwaʊnd]*) vt* ab|wickeln. ◆ *vi (relax)* sich entspannen.

unwrap [ˌʌnˈræp] *vt* aus|packen.

unzip [ˌʌnˈzɪp] *vt* : to ~ sthg den Reißverschluss von etw auf|machen.

up [ʌp] *adv* **1.** *(towards higher position, level)* hoch; we walked ~ to the top wir sind zum Gipfel hoch gelaufen; to pick sthg ~ etw auf|heben; prices are going ~ die Preise steigen. **2.** *(in higher position)* oben; she's ~ in her bedroom sie ist oben in ihrem Zimmer; ~ there da oben. **3.** *(into upright position)* : to stand ~ auf|stehen; to sit ~ *(from lying position)* sich auf|setzen; *(sit straight)* sich gerade hin|setzen. **4.** *(northwards)* : I'm coming ~ to Edinburgh ich komme hoch nach Edinburgh.

5. *(in phrases)* : to walk/jump ~ and down auf und ab gehen/ springen ; ~ to six weeks/ten people bis zu sechs Wochen/ zehn Personen ; are you ~ to travelling? bist du reisefähig? ; what are you ~ to? was treibst du so? ; it's ~ to you das liegt ganz bei dir ; ~ until ten o'clock bis um zehn Uhr.
◆ *prep* **1.** *(towards higher position)* : to walk ~ a hill einen Hügel hinaufgehen ; I went ~ the stairs ich ging die Treppe hinauf.
2. *(in higher position)* : ~ a hill oben auf einem Hügel.
3. *(at end of)* : they live ~ the road from us sie wohnen weiter oben in der gleichen Straße wie wir.
◆ *adj* **1.** *(out of bed)* auf ; I was ~ at six today ich war heute um sechs auf.
2. *(at an end)* um, zu Ende ; time's ~ die Zeit ist um.
3. *(rising)* : the ~ escalator die Rolltreppe nach oben.
◆ *n* : ~s and downs Höhen und Tiefen.

update [ˌʌp'deɪt] *vt* auf den neusten Stand bringen.

uphill [ˌʌp'hɪl] *adv* bergauf.

upholstery [ʌp'həʊlstərɪ] *n* Polsterung *die.*

upkeep [ˈʌpkiːp] *n* Instandhaltung *die.*

up-market *adj* anspruchsvoll.

upon [ə'pɒn] *prep (fml* : *on)* auf (+A, D) ; ~ hearing the news, we... als wir die Nachricht hörten...

upper [ˈʌpəʳ] *adj* obere(-r) (-s).
◆ *n (of shoe)* Obermaterial *das.*

upper class *n* Oberschicht *die.*

uppermost [ˈʌpəməʊst] *adj (highest)* oberste(-r) (-s).

upper sixth *n (Br* : *SCH)* ≃ dreizehnte Klasse.

upright [ˈʌpraɪt] *adj & adv* aufrecht.

upset [ʌp'set] *(pt & pp* upset) *adj (distressed)* bestürzt. ◆ *vt (distress)* erschüttern ; *(plans)* durcheinander bringen ; *(knock over)* umlstoßen ; to have an ~ stomach sich *(D)* den Magen verdorben haben ; to be ~ about sthg über etw *(A)* bestürzt sein ; to get ~ about sthg sich über etw *(A)* aufregen.

upside down [ˌʌpsaɪd-] *adj* auf dem Kopf stehend. ◆ *adv* verkehrt herum.

upstairs [ˌʌp'steəz] *adj* im Obergeschoss. ◆ *adv (on a higher floor)* oben ; to go ~ nach oben gehen.

up-to-date *adj* up to date.

upwards [ˈʌpwədz] *adv* nach oben ; ~ of 100 people mehr als 100 Leute.

urban [ˈɜːbən] *adj* städtisch, Stadt-.

urban clearway [-ˈklɪəweɪ] *n (Br)* ≃ Stadtautobahn *die.*

Urdu [ˈʊəduː] *n* Urdu *das.*

urge [ɜːdʒ] *vt* : to ~ sb to do sthg jn drängen, etw zu tun.

urgent [ˈɜːdʒənt] *adj* dringend.

urgently [ˈɜːdʒəntlɪ] *adv* dringend.

urinal [ˌjʊəˈraɪnl] n ([fml] : *place*) Pissoir *das* ; *(bowl)* Urinal *das*.

urinate [ˈjʊərɪneɪt] vi *(fml)* urinieren.

urine [ˈjʊərɪn] n Urin *der*.

us [ʌs] pron uns ; **they know ~** sie kennen uns ; **it's ~** wir sind's ; **send it to ~** schicke es uns ; **tell ~** sage uns ; **they're worse than ~** sie sind schlimmer als wir.

US n *(abbr of United States)* : **the ~** die USA *pl*.

USA n *(abbr of United States of America)* : **the ~** die USA *pl*.

usable [ˈjuːzəbl] adj brauchbar.

use [n juːs, vb juːz] n *(using)* Benutzung *die* ; *(purpose)* Verwendung *die*. ◆ vt benutzen, verwenden ; *(exploit)* auslnutzen ; *(run on)* brauchen ; **to be of ~** nützlich sein ; **to have the ~ of sthg** etw benutzen können ; **to make ~ of sthg** Gebrauch machen von etw ; *(opportunity)* etw auslnutzen ; **'out of ~'** 'außer Betrieb' ; **to be in ~** in Gebrauch sein ; **it's no ~** es hat keinen Zweck ; **what's the ~?** wozu? ; **to ~ sthg as sthg** etw als etw gebrauchen ; **'~ before...'** *(food, drink)* 'mindestens haltbar bis...' ▪ **use up** vt sep verbrauchen.

used [adj juːzd, aux vb juːst] adj *(towel, glass etc)* benutzt ; *(car)* Gebrauchs-. ◆ aux vb : **I ~ to live near here** ich habe früher hier in der Nähe gewohnt ; **I ~ to go there every day** ich bin früher jeden Tag dorthin gegangen ; **to be ~ to sthg** an etw *(A)* gewöhnt

sein ; **to get ~ to sthg** sich an etw *(A)* gewöhnen.

useful [ˈjuːsfʊl] adj nützlich.

useless [ˈjuːslɪs] adj *(not useful)* nutzlos ; *(pointless)* zwecklos ; *(inf : very bad)* : **to be ~** zu nichts zu gebrauchen sein.

user [ˈjuːzə] n Benutzer *der* (-in *die*).

usher [ˈʌʃə] n *(at cinema, theatre)* Platzanweiser *der*.

usherette [ˌʌʃəˈret] n Platzanweiserin *die*.

USSR n : **the (former) ~** die (ehemalige) UdSSR.

usual [ˈjuːʒəl] adj üblich ; **as ~** wie gewöhnlich.

usually [ˈjuːʒəlɪ] adv normalerweise.

utensil [juːˈtensl] n Gerät *das*.

utilize [ˈjuːtəlaɪz] vt *(fml)* nutzen.

utmost [ˈʌtməʊst] adj äußerste(-r) (-s). ◆ n : **to do one's ~** sein Möglichstes tun.

utter [ˈʌtə] adj völlig. ◆ vt von sich geben.

utterly [ˈʌtəlɪ] adv völlig.

U-turn n *(in vehicle)* Wenden *das*.

V

vacancy [ˈveɪkənsɪ] n *(job)* freie Stelle ; **'vacancies'** 'Zimmer frei' ; **'no vacancies'** 'belegt'.

vacant [ˈveɪkənt] adj *(room, seat)* frei ; **'vacant'** *(toilet)* 'frei'.

vacate [vəˈkeɪt] vt *(fml : room, house)* räumen.

vacation [vəˈkeɪʃn] *n (Am : holiday)* Urlaub *der.* ◆ *vi (Am)* Urlaub machen ; **to go on ~ in** Urlaub gehen.

vacationer [vəˈkeɪʃənər] *n (Am)* Urlauber *der (-in die).*

vaccination [ˌvæksɪˈneɪʃn] *n* Impfung *die.*

vaccine [*(Br)* ˈvæksiːn, *(Am)* vækˈsiːn] *n* Impfstoff *der.*

vacuum [ˈvækjʊəm] *vt* Staub saugen.

vacuum cleaner *n* Staubsauger *der.*

vague [veɪg] *adj* vage ; *(shape, outline)* verschwommen ; *(person)* geistesabwesend.

vain [veɪn] *adj (pej : conceited)* eitel ; **in ~** vergeblich.

Valentine card [ˈvæləntaɪn-] *n* Karte *die* zum Valentinstag.

Valentine's Day [ˈvæləntaɪnz-] *n* Valentinstag *der.*

valet [ˈvæleɪ, ˈvælɪt] *n (in hotel) für* *die Reinigungsservice der Gäste zuständiger Hotelangestellter.*

valet service *n (in hotel, for car)* Reinigungsservice *der.*

valid [ˈvælɪd] *adj (ticket, passport)* gültig.

validate [ˈvælɪdeɪt] *vt (ticket)* bestätigen.

Valium® [ˈvælɪəm] *n* Valium *das.*

valley [ˈvælɪ] *n* Tal *das.*

valuable [ˈvæljʊəbl] *adj* wertvoll. ■ **valuables** *npl* Wertsachen *pl.*

value [ˈvæljuː] *n (financial)* Wert *der* ; *(usefulness)* Nutzen *der* ; **a ~ pack** = ein Sonderangebot ; **to be good ~ (for money)**

(das Geld) wert sein. ■ **values** *npl (principles)* Werte *pl.*

valve [vælv] *n* Ventil *das.*

van [væn] *n* Lieferwagen *der.*

vandal [ˈvændl] *n* Rowdy *der.*

vandalize [ˈvændəlaɪz] *vt* mutwillig zerstören.

vanilla [vəˈnɪlə] *n* Vanille *die.*

vanish [ˈvænɪʃ] *vi* verschwinden.

vapor [ˈveɪpər] *(Am)* = **vapour.**

vapour [ˈveɪpəʳ] *n (Br)* Dampf *der.*

variable [ˈveərɪəbl] *adj* unbeständig.

varicose veins [ˈværɪkəʊs-] *npl* Krampfadern *pl.*

varied [ˈveərɪd] *adj* unterschiedlich.

variety [vəˈraɪətɪ] *n (collection)* Vielfalt *die* ; *(of products)* Auswahl *die* ; *(type)* Sorte *die.*

various [ˈveərɪəs] *adj* verschiedene(-r) (-s).

varnish [ˈvɑːnɪʃ] *n (for wood)* Lack *der.* ◆ *vt (wood)* lackieren.

vary [ˈveərɪ] *vi & vt* ändern ; **to ~ from sthg to sthg** zwischen etw (D) und etw (D) schwanken ; **prices ~** ≃ unterschiedliche Preise.

vase [*(Br)* vɑːz, *(Am)* veɪz] *n* Vase *die.*

Vaseline® [ˈvæsəliːn] *n* Vaseline *die.*

vast [vɑːst] *adj* riesig.

vat [væt] *n* Bottich *der.*

VAT [væt, ˌviːeɪˈtiː] *n (abbr of value added tax)* MwSt.

vault [vɔːlt] *n (in bank)* Tresorraum *der* ; *(in church)* Gewölbe *das.*

VCR n (abbr of video cassette recorder) Videorekorder der.

VDU n (abbr of visual display unit) Bildschirmgerät das.

veal [vi:l] n Kalbfleisch das.

veg [vedʒ] abbr = **vegetable**.

vegan ['vi:gən] adj streng vegetarisch. ◆ n Veganer der (-in die).

vegetable ['vedʒtəbl] n Gemüse das.

vegetable oil n Pflanzenöl das.

vegetarian [‚vedʒɪ'teərɪən] adj vegetarisch. ◆ n Vegetarier der (-in die).

vegetation [‚vedʒɪ'teɪʃn] n Vegetation die.

vehicle ['vi:əkl] n Fahrzeug das.

veil [veɪl] n Schleier der.

vein [veɪn] n Vene die.

Velcro® ['velkrəʊ] n Klettverschluss der.

velvet ['velvɪt] n Samt der.

vending machine ['vendɪŋ-] n Automat der.

venetian blind [vɪ‚ni:ʃn-] n Jalousie die.

venison ['venɪzn] n Wild das.

vent [vent] n (for air, smoke etc) Abzug der.

ventilation [‚ventɪ'leɪʃn] n Belüftung die.

ventilator ['ventɪleɪtə'] n (fan) Ventilator der.

venture ['ventʃə'] n Unternehmung die. ◆ vi (go) sich wagen.

venue ['venju:] n Veranstaltungsort der.

veranda [və'rændə] n Veranda die.

verb [vɜ:b] n Verb das.

verdict ['vɜ:dɪkt] n Urteil das.

verge [vɜ:dʒ] n (of lawn, path) Rand der ; (of road) Bankette die ; 'soft ~s' 'Bankette nicht befahrbar!'

verify ['verɪfaɪ] vt überprüfen.

vermin ['vɜ:mɪn] n Ungeziefer das.

vermouth ['vɜ:məθ] n Wermut der.

versa→ **vice versa**.

versatile ['vɜ:sətaɪl] adj (person) flexibel ; (machine, food) vielseitig.

verse [vɜ:s] n (of song, poem) Vers der ; (poetry) Lyrik die.

version ['vɜ:ʃn] n Version die ; (of book, film, play) Fassung die.

versus ['vɜ:səs] prep gegen.

vertical ['vɜ:tɪkl] adj senkrecht.

vertigo ['vɜ:tɪgəʊ] n Schwindel der.

very ['verɪ] adv sehr. ◆ adj genau ; ~ much sehr ; not ~ nicht sehr ; my ~ own room mein eigenes Zimmer ; the ~ person genau derjenige/diejenige.

vessel ['vesl] n (fml : ship) Schiff das.

vest [vest] n (br : underwear) Unterhemd das ; (Am : waistcoat) Weste die.

vet [vet] n (Br) Tierarzt der (-ärztin die).

veteran ['vetrən] n (of war) Veteran der.

veterinarian [‚vetərɪ'neərɪən] (Am) = **vet**.

veterinary surgeon ['vetərɪnrɪ-] (Br : fml) = **vet**.

VHF n (abbr of very high frequency) UKW.

VHS n (abbr of video home system) VHS.

via ['vaɪə] prep (place) über (+A) ; (by means of) durch.

viaduct ['vaɪədʌkt] n Viadukt der.

vibrate [vaɪ'breɪt] vi vibrieren.

vibration [vaɪ'breɪʃn] n Vibration die.

vicar ['vɪkə'] n Pfarrer der.

vicarage ['vɪkərɪdʒ] n Pfarrhaus das.

vice [vaɪs] n (fault) Laster das.

vice-president n Vizepräsident der (-in die).

vice versa [,vaɪsɪ'vɜːsə] adv umgekehrt.

vicinity [vɪ'sɪnətɪ] n : in the ~ in der Nähe.

vicious ['vɪʃəs] adj (attack, animal) bösartig ; (comment) boshaft.

victim ['vɪktɪm] n Opfer das.

Victorian [vɪk'tɔːrɪən] adj viktorianisch (zweite Hälfte des 19. Jahrhunderts).

victory ['vɪktərɪ] n Sieg der.

video ['vɪdɪəʊ] (pl -s) n (recording, tape) Video das ; (video recorder) Videorekorder der. ◆ vt (using video recorder) aufnehmen ; (using camera) (mit einer Videokamera) filmen ; on ~ auf Video.

video camera n Videokamera die.

video game n Videospiel das.

video recorder n Videorekorder der.

video shop n Videothek die.

videotape ['vɪdɪəʊteɪp] n Videokassette die.

Vienna ['vɪenə] n Wien nt.

Vietnam [(Br) ,vjet'næm, (Am) ,vjet'nɑːm] n Vietnam nt.

view [vjuː] n (scene) Aussicht die ; (line of sight) Sicht die ; (opinion) Ansicht die ; (attitude) Betrachtung die. ◆ vt (look at) betrachten ; in my ~ meiner Ansicht nach ; in ~ of (considering) angesichts (+G) ; to come into ~ in Sicht kommen.

viewer ['vjuːə'] n (of TV) Zuschauer der (-in die).

viewfinder ['vjuː,faɪndə'] n Sucher der.

viewpoint ['vjuːpɔɪnt] n (opinion) Standpunkt der ; (place) Aussichtspunkt der.

vigilant ['vɪdʒɪlənt] adj (fml) wachsam.

villa ['vɪlə] n Villa die.

village ['vɪlɪdʒ] n Dorf das.

villager ['vɪlɪdʒə'] n Dorfbewohner der (-in die).

villain ['vɪlən] n (of book, film) Bösewicht der ; (criminal) Verbrecher der.

vinaigrette [,vɪnɪ'gret] n Vinaigrette die.

vine [vaɪn] n (grapevine) Rebe die ; (climbing plant) Kletterpflanze die.

vinegar ['vɪnɪgə'] n Essig der.

vineyard ['vɪnjəd] n Weinberg der.

vintage ['vɪntɪdʒ] adj (wine) erlesen. ◆ n (year) Jahrgang der.

vinyl ['vaɪnɪl] n Vinyl das.

viola [vɪ'əʊlə] n Bratsche die.

violence ['vaɪələns] n (violent behaviour) Gewalt die.

violent ['vaɪələnt] adj (person, behaviour) gewalttätig ; (storm, row) heftig.

violet ['vaɪələt] adj violett. ◆ n (flower) Veilchen das.

violin [ˌvaɪə'lɪn] n Geige die.

VIP n (abbr of very important person) Prominente der, die.

virgin ['vɜːdʒɪn] n Jungfrau die.

Virgo ['vɜːgəʊ] n (pl -s) n Jungfrau die.

virtually ['vɜːtʃʊəlɪ] adv praktisch.

virtual reality ['vɜːtʃʊəl-] n virtuelle Realität.

virus ['vaɪrəs] n Virus das.

visa ['viːzə] n Visum das.

viscose ['vɪskəʊs] n Viskose die.

visibility [ˌvɪzɪ'bɪlətɪ] n Sicht die.

visible ['vɪzəbl] adj (that can be seen) sichtbar ; (noticeable) offensichtlich.

visit ['vɪzɪt] vt besuchen. ◆ n Besuch der.

visiting hours ['vɪzɪtɪŋ-] npl Besuchszeit die.

visitor ['vɪzɪtə'] n Besucher der (-in die).

visitor centre n (at tourist attraction) Touristeninformation die.

visitors' book n Gästebuch das.

visitor's passport n (Br) Reisepass der.

visor ['vaɪzə'] n (of hat) Schirm der ; (of helmet) Visier das.

vital ['vaɪtl] adj (essential) wesentlich.

vitamin [(Br) 'vɪtəmɪn, (Am) 'vaɪtəmɪn] n Vitamin das.

vivid ['vɪvɪd] adj (colour) leuchtend ; (description, memory) lebhaft.

V-neck n (design) V-Ausschnitt der.

vocabulary [və'kæbjʊlərɪ] n Wortschatz der.

vodka ['vɒdkə] n Wodka der.

voice [vɔɪs] n Stimme die.

voice mail n Anrufbeantworter der ; to check one's ~ seinen Anrufbeantworter abhören.

volcano [vɒl'keɪnəʊ] (pl -es OR -s) n Vulkan der.

volleyball ['vɒlɪbɔːl] n Volleyball das.

volt [vəʊlt] n Volt das.

voltage ['vəʊltɪdʒ] n Spannung die.

volume ['vɒljuːm] n (sound level) Lautstärke die ; (space occupied) Rauminhalt der ; (amount) Menge die ; (book) Band der.

voluntary ['vɒləntrɪ] adj freiwillig ; (work) ehrenamtlich.

volunteer [ˌvɒlən'tɪə'] n Freiwillige der, die. ◆ vt : to ~ to do sthg sich anlbieten, etw zu tun.

vomit ['vɒmɪt] n Erbrochene das. ◆ vi sich übergeben.

vote [vəʊt] n (choice) Stimme die ; (process) Abstimmung die ; (number of votes) Stimmen pl. ◆ vi : to ~ (for) wählen.

voter ['vəʊtə'] n Wähler der (-in die).

voucher ['vaʊtʃə'] n Gutschein der.

vowel ['vaʊəl] n Vokal der.

voyage ['vɔɪɪdʒ] n Reise die.

vulgar ['vʌlgə'] adj (rude) vulgär ; (in bad taste) ordinär.

vulture ['vʌltʃə'] n Geier der.

W

W (abbr of west) W.

wad [wɒd] n (of paper, bank-notes) Bündel das ; (of cotton) Bausch der.

waddle ['wɒdl] vi watscheln.

wade [weɪd] vi waten.

wading pool ['weɪdɪŋ-] n (Am) Planschbecken das.

wafer ['weɪfə'] n (biscuit) Waffel die.

waffle ['wɒfl] n (pancake) Waffel die. ◆ vi (inf) schwafeln.

wag [wæg] vt wedeln mit.

wage [weɪdʒ] n Lohn der. ▪ **wages** npl Lohn der.

wagon ['wægən] n (vehicle) Wagen der ; (Br : of train) Waggon der.

waist [weɪst] n Taille die.

waistcoat ['weɪskəʊt] n Weste die.

wait [weɪt] n Wartezeit die. ◆ vi warten ; I can't ~! ich kann es nicht erwarten! ▪ **wait for** vt fus warten auf (+A) ; to ~ for sb to do sthg darauf warten, dass jd etw tut.

waiter ['weɪtə'] n Kellner der ; ~! Herr Ober!

waiting room ['weɪtɪŋ-] n Warteraum der ; (at doctor's) Wartezimmer das.

waitress ['weɪtrɪs] n Bedienung die.

wake [weɪk] (pt woke, pp woken) vt wecken. ◆ vi aufwachen. ▪ **wake up** vt sep auflwecken. ◆ vi (wake) auflwachen.

Waldorf salad ['wɔ:ldɔ:f-] n Waldorfsalat der.

Wales [weɪlz] n Wales nt.

walk [wɔ:k] n Spaziergang der ; (hike) Wanderung die ; (path) Fußweg der. ◆ vi zu Fuß gehen ; (as hobby) wandern. ◆ vt (distance) gehen ; (dog) Gassi gehen mit ; to go for a ~ spazieren gehen ; it's a short ~ es ist ein kurzes Stück zu Fuß ; to take the dog for a ~ mit dem Hund Gassi gehen ; 'walk' (Am) 'gehen' ; 'don't ~' (Am) 'warten'. ▪ **walk away** vi weglgehen. ▪ **walk in** vi reinlkommen/reinlgehen. ▪ **walk out** vi gehen.

walker ['wɔ:kə'] n Spaziergänger der (-in die) ; (hiker) Wanderer der (Wanderin die).

walking boots ['wɔ:kɪŋ-] npl Wanderschuhe pl.

walking stick ['wɔ:kɪŋ-] n Spazierstock der.

Walkman® ['wɔ:kmən] n Walkman der.

wall [wɔ:l] n (inside) Wand die ; (outside) Mauer die.

wallet ['wɒlɪt] n Brieftasche die.

wallpaper ['wɔ:l,peɪpə'] n Tapete die.

wally ['wɒlɪ] n (Br : inf) Trottel der.

walnut ['wɔ:lnʌt] n (nut) Walnuss die.

waltz [wɔ:ls] n Walzer der.

wander ['wɒndə'] vi herumlwandern.

want [wɒnt] vt wollen ; (need) brauchen ; to ~ to do sthg etw tun wollen ; to ~ sb to do sthg wollen, dass jd etw tut.

war [wɔːʳ] n Krieg der.

ward [wɔːd] n (in hospital) Station die.

warden [ˈwɔːdn] n (of park) Aufseher der (-in die) ; (of youth hostel) Herbergsvater der (-mutter die).

wardrobe [ˈwɔːdrəʊb] n Kleiderschrank der.

warehouse [ˈweəhaʊs, pl -haʊzɪz] n Lagerhalle die.

warm [wɔːm] adj warm. ◆ vt wärmen. ▪ **warm up** vt sep auflwärmen. ◆ vi (get warmer) wärmer werden ; (do exercises) sich auflwärmen ; (machine, engine) warm laufen.

war memorial n Kriegerdenkmal das.

warmth [wɔːmθ] n (heat) Wärme die.

warn [wɔːn] vt warnen ; to ~ sb about sthg jn vor etw warnen ; to ~ sb not to do sthg jn davor warnen, etw zu tun.

warning [ˈwɔːnɪŋ] n (of danger) Warnung die ; (advance notice) Vorwarnung die.

warranty [ˈwɒrəntɪ] n (fml) Garantie die.

warship [ˈwɔːʃɪp] n Kriegsschiff das.

wart [wɔːt] n Warze die.

was [wɒz] pt → be.

wash [wɒʃ] vt waschen ; (dishes) ablwaschen. ◆ vi sich waschen. ◆ n : to give sthg a ~ etw waschen ; to have a ~ sich waschen ; to ~ one's hands sich (D) die Hände waschen. ▪ **wash up** vi (Br : do washing-up) ablwaschen ; (Am : clean oneself) sich waschen.

washable [ˈwɒʃəbl] adj waschbar.

washbasin [ˈwɒʃˌbeɪsn] n Waschbecken das.

washbowl [ˈwɒʃbəʊl] n (Am) Waschbecken das.

washer [ˈwɒʃəʳ] n (ring) Dichtungsring der.

washing [ˈwɒʃɪŋ] n (activity) Waschen das ; (clothes) Wäsche die.

washing line n Wäscheleine die.

washing machine n Waschmaschine die.

washing powder n Waschpulver das.

washing-up n (Br) : to do the ~ ablwaschen.

washing-up bowl n (Br) Abwaschschüssel die.

washing-up liquid n (Br) Geschirrspülmittel das.

washroom [ˈwɒʃrʊm] n (Am) Toilette die.

wasn't [wɒznt] = was not.

wasp [wɒsp] n Wespe die.

waste [weɪst] n (rubbish) Abfall der. ◆ vt verschwenden ; it's a ~ of money das ist Geldverschwendung ; it's a ~ of time das ist Zeitverschwendung.

wastebin [ˈweɪstbɪn] n Abfalleimer der.

waste ground n Ödland das.

wastepaper basket [ˌweɪstˈpeɪpə-] n Papierkorb der.

watch [wɒtʃ] n (wristwatch) (Armband)uhr die. ◆ vt beobachten ; (film) sich (D) anlsehen ; (be careful with) achten auf (+A) ; to ~ television fernlsehen. ▪ **watch out** vi (be careful) auflpassen ; to ~ out for *(look for)* Ausschau halten nach.

watchstrap ['wɒtʃstræp] n Uhrarmband das.

water ['wɔːtə'] n Wasser das. ◆ vt *(plants, garden)* gießen. ◆ vi *(eyes)* tränen; **my mouth was ~ing** mir lief das Wasser im Mund zusammen.

water bottle n Wasserflasche die.

watercolour ['wɔːtə,kʌlə'] n *(picture)* Aquarell das.

watercress ['wɔːtəkres] n Brunnenkresse die.

waterfall ['wɔːtəfɔːl] n Wasserfall der.

watering can ['wɔːtərɪŋ-] n Gießkanne die.

watermelon ['wɔːtə,melən] n Wassermelone die.

waterproof ['wɔːtəpruːf] adj wasserdicht.

water purification tablets [-pjʊərɪfɪ'keɪʃn-] npl Wasser aufbereitende Tabletten pl.

water skiing n Wasserskilaufen das.

watersports ['wɔːtəspɔːts] npl Wassersport der.

water tank n Wassertank der.

watertight ['wɔːtətaɪt] adj wasserdicht.

watt [wɒt] n Watt das; **a 60-~ bulb** eine 60-Watt-Glühbirne.

wave [weɪv] n Welle die. ◆ vt *(hand)* winken mit; *(flag)* schwenken. ◆ vi *(move hand)* winken.

wavelength ['weɪvleŋθ] n Wellenlänge die.

wavy ['weɪvɪ] adj *(hair)* gewellt.

wax [wæks] n Wachs das; *(in ears)* Schmalz das.

way [weɪ] n *(manner)* Art die; *(method)* Art und Weise die; *(route, distance)* Weg der; *(direction)* Richtung die; **which ~ is the station?** wie kommt man zum Bahnhof?; **the town is out of our ~** die Stadt liegt nicht auf unserem Weg; **to be in the ~** im Weg sein; **to be on the ~** auf dem Weg sein; **to get out of the ~** aus dem Weg gehen; **to get under ~** in Gang kommen; **a long ~** ein weiter Weg; **a long ~ away** weit entfernt; **to lose one's ~** sich verlaufen; *(in car)* sich verfahren; **on the ~ back** auf dem Rückweg; **on the ~ there** auf dem Hinweg; **that ~** *(like that)* so; *(in that direction)* dort entlang; **this ~** *(like this)* so; *(in this direction)* hier entlang; **'give ~'** 'Vorfahrt beachten'; **'~ in'** 'Eingang'; **'~ out'** 'Ausgang'; **no ~!** *(inf)* auf keinen Fall!

WC n *(abbr of water closet)* WC das.

we [wiː] pron wir.

weak [wiːk] adj schwach; *(drink, soup)* dünn.

weaken ['wiːkn] vt schwächen.

weakness ['wiːknɪs] n Schwäche die.

wealth [welθ] n Reichtum der.

wealthy ['welθɪ] adj reich.

weapon ['wepən] n Waffe die.

wear [weə'] *(pt wore, pp worn)* vt tragen. ◆ n *(clothes)* Kleidung die; **~ and tear** Verschleiß der. ▧ **wear off** vi nachlassen. ▧ **wear out** vi sich ablnutzen.

weary ['wɪərɪ] *adj* müde.

weasel ['wiːzl] *n* Wiesel *das*.

weather ['weðəʳ] *n* Wetter *das*; **what's the ~ like?** wie ist das Wetter?; **to be under the ~** *(inf)* nicht auf dem Posten sein.

weather forecast *n* Wettervorhersage *die*.

weather forecaster [-fɔːkɑːstəʳ] *n* Meteorologe *der* (Meteorologin *die*).

weather report *n* Wetterbericht *der*.

weather vane [-veɪn] *n* Wetterfahne *die*.

weave [wiːv] *(pt* wove, *pp* woven) *vt (material)* weben; *(basket)* flechten.

web [web] *n (of spider)* Netz *das*.

Web *n*: **the ~** das Web; **on the ~** im Web.

web site *n* Webseite *die*.

Wed. *(abbr of Wednesday)* Mi.

wedding ['wedɪŋ] *n* Hochzeit *die*.

wedding anniversary *n* Hochzeitstag *der*.

wedding dress *n* Hochzeitskleid *das*.

wedding ring *n* Ehering *der*.

wedge [wedʒ] *n (of cake)* Stück *das*; *(of wood etc)* Keil *der*.

Wednesday ['wenzdɪ] *n* Mittwoch *der*; → **Saturday**.

wee [wiː] *adj (Scot)* klein. ◆ *n (inf)* Pipi *das*.

weed [wiːd] *n* Unkraut *das*.

week [wiːk] *n* Woche *die*; **a ~ today** heute in einer Woche; **in a ~'s time** in einer Woche.

weekday ['wiːkdeɪ] *n* Wochentag *der*.

weekend [ˌwiːk'end] *n* Wochenende *das*.

weekly ['wiːklɪ] *adj* & *adv* wöchentlich. ◆ *n* Wochenzeitschrift *die*.

weep [wiːp] *(pt* & *pp* wept) *vi* weinen.

weigh [weɪ] *vt* wiegen; **how much does it ~?** wie viel wiegt es?

weight [weɪt] *n* Gewicht *das*; **to lose ~** abnehmen; **to put on ~** zunehmen. ■ **weights** *npl (for weight training)* Hanteln *pl*.

weightlifting ['weɪtˌlɪftɪŋ] *n* Gewichtheben *das*.

weight training *n* Hanteltraining *das*.

weir [wɪəʳ] *n* Wehr *das*.

weird [wɪəd] *adj* sonderbar.

welcome ['welkəm] *adj* willkommen. ◆ *n* Willkommen *das*. ◆ *vt* begrüßen. ◆ *excl* willkommen!; **to make sb feel ~** jn freundlich aufnehmen; **you're ~!** bitte, gern geschehen!; **to be ~ to do sthg** etw gerne tun können; **you're ~ to stay** Sie sind bei uns herzlich willkommen.

weld [weld] *vt* schweißen.

welfare ['welfeəʳ] *n* Wohl *das*; *(Am: money)* Sozialhilfe *die*.

well [wel] *(compar* better, *superl* best) *adj (healthy)* gesund. ◆ *adv* gut. ◆ *n (for water)* Brunnen *der*; **to get ~** gesund werden; **get ~ soon!** gute Besserung!; **to go ~** gut gehen; **~ done!** gut gemacht!; **it may ~ happen** es kann durchaus passieren; **it's ~ worth it** es lohnt sich unbedingt; **as ~ (in addi-**

tion) auch ; **as ~ as** *(in addition to)* sowohl... als auch.

we'll [wi:l] = **we shall, we will**.

well-behaved [-bɪ'heɪvd] *adj* artig.

well-built *adj* : **to be ~** gut gebaut sein.

well-done *adj (meat)* gut durchgebraten.

well-dressed [-'drest] *adj* gut gekleidet.

wellington (boot) ['welɪŋtən-] *n* Gummistiefel *der.*

well-known *adj* bekannt.

well-off *adj (rich)* wohlhabend.

well-paid *adj* gut bezahlt.

welly ['welɪ] *n (Br : inf)* Gummistiefel *der.*

Welsh [welʃ] *adj* walisisch. ◆ *n (language)* Walisisch *das.* ◆ *npl* : **the ~** die Waliser *pl.*

Welshman ['welʃmən] *(pl -men* [-mən]*) n* Waliser *der.*

Welsh rarebit [-'reəbɪt] *n* Toast mit geschmolzenem Käse.

Welshwoman ['welʃ,wʊmən] *(pl -women* [-,wɪmɪn]*) n* Waliserin *die.*

went [went] *pt →* **go**.

wept [wept] *pt & pp →* **weep**.

were [wɜːr] *pt →* **be**.

we're [wɪər] = **we are**.

weren't [wɜːnt] = **were not**.

west [west] *n* Westen *der.* ◆ *adj* West-, westlich. ◆ *adv (fly, walk, be situated)* nach Westen ; **in the ~ of England** im Westen Englands.

westbound ['westbaʊnd] *adj* in Richtung Westen.

West Country *n* : **the ~** *der*

Südwesten Englands, mit den Grafschaften Cornwall, Devon und Somerset.

West End *n* : **the ~** *(of London)* Londoner Viertel mit Theatern und großen Kaufhäusern.

western ['westən] *adj* westlich. ◆ *n (film)* Western *der.*

West Germany *n* Westdeutschland *nt.*

West Indies [-'ɪndiːz] *npl* Westindische Inseln *pl.*

Westminster ['westmɪnstər] *n* Westminster *nt (Sitz des britischen Parlaments).*

WESTMINSTER

Mit „Westminster" bezeichnet man ein an der Themse gelegenes Viertel in London. Hier befinden sich die Parlamentsgebäude („Houses of Parliament") sowie Westminster Abbey. Oft wird der Ausdruck auch als Umschreibung für das britische Parlament verwendet.

Westminster Abbey *n* die Abtei von Westminster.

WESTMINSTER ABBEY

In dieser großen Kirche im Londoner Viertel Westminster werden der Tradition gemäß die britischen Monarchen gekrönt. Sie ist gleichzeitig Grabstätte einer Reihe von berühmten Männern und Frauen : in einer Ecke, dem „Poet's Corner", sind bekannte Dichter und Schriftsteller des Landes, wie Geoffrey Chaucer, Charles Dickens und Thomas Hardy, begraben.

westwards ['westwədz] *adv* westwärts.

wet [wet] (*pt & pp* **wet** OR **-ted**) *adj* nass ; *(rainy)* regnerisch. ◆ *vt* nass machen ; **to get ~** nass werden ; **'~ paint'** 'frisch gestrichen'.

wet suit *n* Tauchanzug *der* ; *(for surfing)* Surfanzug *der*.

we've [wiːv] = we have.

whale [weɪl] *n* Wal *der*.

wharf [wɔːf] (*pl* **-s** OR **wharves** [wɔːvz]) *n* Kai *der*.

what [wɒt] *adj* 1. *(in questions)* welche(-r) (-s) ; **~ colour is it?** welche Farbe hat es? ; **he asked me ~ colour it was** er fragte mich, welche Farbe es hatte. 2. *(in exclamations)* was für ; **~ a surprise!** was für eine Überraschung! ; **~ a beautiful day!** was für ein schöner Tag!
◆ *pron* 1. *(in questions)* was ; **~ is going on?** was ist los? ; **~ are they doing?** was tun sie da? ; **~'s your name?** wie heißt du? ; **she asked me ~ happened** sie fragte mich, was passiert war ; **~ is it for?** wofür ist das?
2. *(introducing relative clause)* was ; **I didn't see ~ happened** ich habe nicht gesehen, was passiert ist ; **you can't have ~ you want** du kannst nicht das haben, was du willst.
3. *(in phrases)* : **~ for?** wozu? ; **~ about going out for a meal?** wie wäre es mit Essen gehen?
◆ *excl* was!

whatever [wɒt'evər] *pron* : **take ~ you want** nimm, was du willst ; **~ I do, I'll lose** was ich auch tue, ich verliere ; **~ that may be** was auch immer das sein mag.

wheat [wiːt] *n* Weizen *der*.

wheel [wiːl] *n* Rad *das* ; *(steering wheel)* Lenkrad *das*.

wheelbarrow ['wiːl,bærəʊ] *n* Schubkarre *die*.

wheelchair ['wiːl,tʃeər] *n* Rollstuhl *der*.

wheelclamp [,wiːl'klæmp] *n* Parkkralle *die*.

wheezy ['wiːzɪ] *adj* keuchend.

when [wen] *adv* *(in questions)* wann. ◆ *conj* *(specifying time)* wenn ; *(in the past)* als ; *(although, seeing as)* wo ... doch.

whenever [wen'evər] *conj* (immer) wenn ; **~ you like** wann immer du willst.

where [weər] *adv & conj* wo ; **~ do you come from?** woher kommst du? ; **~ are you going?** wohin gehst du?

whereabouts ['weərəbaʊts] *adv* wo. ◆ *npl* Aufenthaltsort *der*.

whereas [weər'æz] *conj* während.

wherever [weər'evər] *conj* wo immer ; *(from any place)* woher auch immer ; *(to any place)* wohin auch immer ; *(everywhere)* überall wo ; **~ that may be** wo immer das sein mag.

whether ['weðər] *conj* ob.

which [wɪtʃ] *adj* *(in questions)* welche(-r) (-s) ; **~ room do you want?** welches Zimmer willst du? ; **~ one?** welches? ; **she asked me ~ room I wanted** sie fragte mich, welches Zimmer ich möchte.

◆ *pron* **1.** *(in questions : subject)* welche(-r) (-s) ; **~ is the cheapest?** welches ist das Billigste ? ; **he asked me ~ was the best** er fragte mich, welcher der Beste sei.

2. *(in questions : object)* welche(-n) (-s) ; **~ do you prefer?** welches gefällt dir besser? ; **he asked me ~ I preferred** er fragte mich, welchen ich bevorzuge.

3. *(in questions : after prep +A)* welche(-n) (-s) ; **~ should I put the vase on?** auf welchen soll ich die Vase stellen?

4. *(in questions : after prep +D)* welcher/welchem/welchem ; **he asked me ~ I was talking about** er fragte mich, von welchem ich gesprochen hatte.

5. *(introducing relative clause : subject)* der/die/das, die *(pl)* ; **the house ~ is on the corner** das Haus, das an der Ecke steht.

6. *(introducing relative clause : object, after prep +A)* den/die/das, die *(pl)* ; **the television ~ I bought** der Fernseher, den ich gekauft habe.

7. *(introducing relative clause : after prep +D)* dem/der/dem, denen *(pl)* ; **the settee on ~ I'm sitting** das Sofa, auf dem ich sitze.

8. *(referring back)* was ; **he's late, ~ annoys me** er ist spät dran, was mich ärgert ; **he's always late, ~ I don't like** er verspätet sich immer, was ich nicht leiden kann.

whichever [wɪtʃˈevəʳ] *adj* *(any)* welche(-r) (-s) ; *(no matter*

which) egal welche. ◆ *pron* welche(-r) (-s).

while [waɪl] *conj* während ; *(although)* obgleich. ◆ *n* : **a ~** eine Weile ; **for a ~** eine Weile ; **in a ~** bald ; **a short ~ ago** vor kurzem.

whim [wɪm] *n* Laune *die.*

whine [waɪn] *vi (make noise)* winseln ; *(complain)* jammern.

whip [wɪp] *n* Peitsche *die.* ◆ *vt* peitschen.

whipped cream [wɪpt-] *n* Schlagsahne *die,* Schlagobers *das (Österr).*

whirlpool ['wɜːlpuːl] *n (Jacuzzi)* Whirlpool *der.*

whisk [wɪsk] *n (utensil)* Quirl *der.* ◆ *vt (eggs, cream)* schlagen.

whiskers ['wɪskəz] *npl (of person)* Backenbart *der* ; *(of animal)* Schnurrhaar *das.*

whiskey ['wɪskɪ] *(pl* **-s)** *n* Whiskey *der.*

whisky ['wɪskɪ] *n* Whisky *der.*

WHISKY

Das schottische Nationalgetränk, der Whisky, wird aus Malzgerste hergestellt und reift in hölzernen Fässern heran. Sein Geschmack variiert je nach Herstellungsmethode und Art des verwendeten Wassers. Der reine Malzwhisky („malt whisky"), der oftmals in kleinen Lokaldistillerien hergestellt wird, gilt als qualitativ hochwertiger als die preisgünstigeren „blended whiskies", die aus mehreren Gerstensorten hergestellt werden.

whisper ['wɪspə'] *vt* & *vi* flüstern.

whistle ['wɪsl] *n (instrument)* Pfeife *die* ; *(sound)* Pfiff *der*. ◆ *vi* pfeifen.

white [waɪt] *adj* weiß ; *(coffee, tea)* mit Milch. ◆ *n (colour)* Weiß *das* ; *(of egg)* Eiweiß *das* ; *(person)* Weiße *der, die*.

white bread *n* Weißbrot *das*.

White House *n* : the ~ das Weiße Haus *(Amtssitz des US-Präsidenten)*.

white sauce *n* Béchamelsoße *die*.

white spirit *n* Verdünner *der*.

whitewash ['waɪtwɒʃ] *vt* tünchen.

white wine *n* Weißwein *der*.

whiting ['waɪtɪŋ] *(pl* whiting) *n* Wittling *der*.

Whitsun ['wɪtsn] *n* Pfingsten *das*.

who [huː] *pron (in questions)* wer ; *(accusative)* wen ; *(dative)* wem ; *(in relative clauses)* der/die/das, die *(pl)*.

whoever [huːˈevər] *pron (whichever person)* wer immer ; ~ it is wer es auch ist.

whole [həʊl] *adj* ganz. ◆ *n* : the ~ of the money das ganze Geld ; on the ~ im Großen und Ganzen.

wholefoods ['həʊlfuːdz] *npl* Vollwertkost *die*.

wholemeal bread ['həʊlmiːl-] *n (Br)* Vollkornbrot *das*.

wholesale ['həʊlseɪl] *adv (COMM)* en gros.

wholewheat bread ['həʊl-wiːt-] *(Am)* = **wholemeal bread**.

whom [huːm] *pron (fml* : *in questions)* wen ; *(dative)* wem ; *(in relative clauses)* den/die/das, die *(pl)* ; *(dative)* dem/der/dem, denen *(pl)* ; to ~ *(in questions)* wem ; *(in relative clauses)* dem/der/dem, denen *(pl)*.

whooping cough ['huːpɪŋ-] *n* Keuchhusten *der*.

whose [huːz] *adj (in questions)* wessen ; *(in relative clauses)* dessen/deren/dessen, deren *(pl)*. ◆ *pron (in questions)* wessen ; ~ jumper is this? wessen Pullover ist das? ; the woman ~ daughter I know die Frau, deren Tochter ich kenne ; ~ is this? wem gehört das?

why [waɪ] *adv* & *conj* warum ; ~ not? warum nicht?

wick [wɪk] *n (of candle, lighter)* Docht *der*.

wicked ['wɪkɪd] *adj (evil)* böse, schlecht ; *(mischievous)* schelmisch.

wicker ['wɪkə'] *adj* Korb-.

wide [waɪd] *adj* breit ; *(opening)* weit ; *(range, difference, gap)* groß. ◆ *adv* : to open sthg ~ etw weit öffnen ; how ~ is the road? wie breit ist die Straße? ; it's 12 metres ~ er/sie/es ist 12 Meter breit ; ~ open weit offen.

widely ['waɪdlɪ] *adv* weit.

widen ['waɪdn] *vt* verbreitern. ◆ *vi (gap, difference)* größer werden.

widespread ['waɪdspred] *adj* weit verbreitet.

widow ['wɪdəʊ] *n* Witwe *die*.

widower ['wɪdəʊə'] *n* Witwer *der*.

width [wɪdθ] *n* Breite *die*.

wife [waɪf] (*pl* **wives**) *n* Ehefrau *die*.

wig [wɪg] *n* Perücke *die*.

wild [waɪld] *adj* wild ; (*crazy*) verrückt ; **to be ~ about** (*inf*) verrückt sein auf (+A).

wild flower *n* wilde Blume.

wildlife ['waɪldlaɪf] *n* Tierwelt *die*.

will¹ [wɪl] *aux vb* **1.** (*expressing future tense*) werden ; **I ~ see you next week** wir sehen uns nächste Woche ; **~ you be here next Friday?** wirst du nächsten Freitag hier sein? ; **yes I ~** ja, werde ich ; **no I won't** nein, werde ich nicht.
2. (*expressing willingness*) wollen, werden ; **I won't do it** ich werde das nicht tun ; **no one ~ do it** niemand will das machen.
3. (*expressing polite question*) : **~ you have some more tea?** möchten Sie noch mehr Tee?
4. (*in commands, requests*) : **~ you please be quiet!** sei bitte ruhig! ; **close that window, ~ you?** mach doch das Fenster zu, bitte.

will² [wɪl] *n* (*document*) Testament *das* ; **against his ~** gegen seinen Willen.

willing ['wɪlɪŋ] *adj* : **to be ~ (to do sthg)** bereit sein (, etw zu tun).

willingly ['wɪlɪŋlɪ] *adv* bereitwillig, gern.

willow [ˈwɪləʊ] *n* Weide *die*.

win [wɪn] (*pt & pp* **won**) *n* Sieg *der*. ◆ *vt* gewinnen. ◆ *vi* gewinnen ; (*in battle*) siegen ; (*be ahead*) in Führung liegen.

wind¹ [wɪnd] *n* Wind *der* ; (*in stomach*) Blähungen *pl*.

wind² [waɪnd] (*pt & pp* **wound**) *vi* (*road, river*) sich winden. ◆ *vt* : **to ~ sthg round sthg** etw um etw wickeln. ▨ **wind up** *vt sep* (*Br* : *inf* : *annoy*) ärgern ; (*car window*) hochkurbeln ; (*clock, watch*) aufziehen.

windbreak ['wɪndbreɪk] *n* Windschutz *der*.

windmill ['wɪndmɪl] *n* Windmühle *die*.

window ['wɪndəʊ] *n* Fenster *das*.

window box *n* Blumenkasten *der*.

window cleaner *n* Fensterputzer *der* (*-in die*).

windowpane ['wɪndəʊ,peɪn] *n* Fensterscheibe *die*.

window seat *n* Fensterplatz *der*.

window-shopping *n* Schaufensterbummel *der*.

windowsill ['wɪndəʊsɪl] *n* Fenstersims *der* OR *das*.

windscreen ['wɪndskriːn] *n* (*Br*) Windschutzscheibe *die*.

windscreen wipers *npl* (*Br*) Scheibenwischer *pl*.

windshield ['wɪndʃiːld] (*Am*) = **windscreen**.

Windsor Castle ['wɪnzə-] *n* Schloss Windsor.

(i)   **WINDSOR CASTLE**

Schloss Windsor, in der englischen Grafschaft Berkshire, geht auf das 11. Jahrhundert zurück. Es wurde von Wilhelm dem Eroberer („William the Conqueror") begründet. Heute ist es eine der ofiziellen Residenzen des britischen

Monarchen, Teile davon sind jedoch der Öffentlichkeit zugänglich. 1992 brannte ein großer Teil des Schlosses ab. Seitdem ist Windsor Castle mit öffentlichen Geldern wieder aufgebaut worden.

windsurfing ['wɪnd,sɜːfɪŋ] n Windsurfen das ; **to go ~** windsurfen gehen.

windy ['wɪndɪ] adj windig.

wine [waɪn] n Wein der.

wine bar n (Br) Weinstube die.

wineglass ['waɪnɡlɑːs] n Weinglas das.

wine list n Weinkarte die.

wine tasting [-'teɪstɪŋ] n Weinprobe die.

wine waiter n Weinkellner der.

wing [wɪŋ] n Flügel der ; (of plane) Tragfläche die ; (of car) Kotflügel der. ■ **wings** npl : **the ~s** (in theatre) die Kulissen.

wink [wɪŋk] vi zwinkern.

winner ['wɪnəʳ] n Gewinner der (-in die) ; (SPORT) Sieger der (-in die).

winning ['wɪnɪŋ] adj (person, team) siegreich ; (ticket, number) Gewinn-.

winter ['wɪntəʳ] n Winter der ; **in (the) ~** Winter-.

wintertime ['wɪntətaɪm] n Winterzeit die.

wipe [waɪp] vt abwischen ; (floor) aufwischen ; **to ~ one's feet** sich (D) die Füße abtreten ; **to ~ one's hands** sich (D) die Hände abwischen. ■ **wipe up** vt sep (liquid, dirt)

auflwischen. ◆ vi (dry the dishes) abltrocknen.

wiper ['waɪpəʳ] n (AUT) Scheibenwischer der.

wire ['waɪəʳ] n Draht der ; (electrical wire) Kabel das. ◆ vt (plug) anlschließen.

wireless ['waɪəlɪs] n Radio das.

wiring ['waɪərɪŋ] n Leitungen pl.

wisdom tooth ['wɪzdəm-] n Weisheitszahn der.

wise [waɪz] adj weise.

wish [wɪʃ] n Wunsch der. ◆ vt wünschen ; **best ~es** alles Gute ; **to ~ for sthg** sich (D) etw wünschen ; **to ~ to do sthg** (fml) etw zu tun wünschen ; **to ~ sb luck/happy birthday** jm Glück/ alles Gute zum Geburtstag wünschen ; **if you ~** (fml) wenn Sie es wünschen.

witch [wɪtʃ] n Hexe die.

with [wɪð] prep 1. (gen) mit ; **come ~ me** komm mit mir ; **a man ~ a beard** ein Mann mit Bart ; **a room ~ a bathroom** ein Zimmer mit Bad ; **he hit me ~ a stick** er hat mich mit einem Stock geschlagen ; **be careful ~ that!** sei vorsichtig damit! ; **to argue ~ sb** mit jm streiten ; **topped ~ cream** mit Sahne. 2. (at house of) bei ; **we stayed ~ friends** wir haben bei Freunden übernachtet. 3. (indicating emotion) vor (+ D) ; **to tremble ~ fear** vor Angst zittern.

withdraw [wɪð'drɔː] (pt -drew, pp -drawn) vt (take out) herauslnehmen ; (money) ablheben. ◆ vi *(from race, contest)* zurück|ziehen.

withdrawal [wɪð'drɔːəl] n *(from bank account)* Abheben das.

withdrawn [wɪð'drɔːn] pp → **withdraw**.

withdrew [wɪð'druː] pt → **withdraw**.

wither ['wɪðə'] vi verwelken.

within [wɪ'ðɪn] prep innerhalb *(+G)*. ◆ adv innen ; ~ walking distance zu Fuß erreichbar ; ~ the next week innerhalb der nächsten Woche ; ~ 10 miles im Umkreis von 10 Meilen.

without [wɪð'aut] prep ohne ; ~ doing sthg ohne etw zu tun.

withstand [wɪð'stænd] *(pt & pp* **-stood)** vt stand|halten *(+D)*.

witness ['wɪtnɪs] n Zeuge der (Zeugin die). ◆ vt *(see)* Zeuge sein *(+G)*.

witty ['wɪtɪ] adj geistreich.

wives [waɪvz] pl → **wife**.

wobbly ['wɒblɪ] adj wackelig.

wok [wɒk] n Wok der.

woke [wəuk] pt → **wake**.

woken ['wəukn] pp → **wake**.

wolf [wulf] *(pl* wolves [wulvz]) n Wolf der.

woman ['wumən] *(pl* women) n Frau die.

womb [wuːm] n Gebärmutter die.

women ['wɪmɪn] pl → **woman**.

won [wʌn] pt & pp → **win**.

wonder ['wʌndə'] vi *(ask oneself)* sich fragen. ◆ n *(amazement)* Staunen das, Verwunderung die ; I ~ if I could ask you a favour? könnte ich Sie/dich

vielleicht um einen Gefallen bitten?

wonderful ['wʌndəful] adj wunderbar.

won't [wəunt] = will not.

wood [wud] n Holz das ; *(small forest)* Wald der.

wooden ['wudn] adj Holz-, hölzern.

woodland ['wudlənd] n Waldung die.

woodpecker ['wud,pekə'] n Specht der.

woodwork ['wudwɜːk] n *(SCH)* Werkunterricht der.

wool [wul] n Wolle die.

woolen ['wulən] *(Am)* = **woollen**.

woollen ['wulən] adj *(Br)* Woll-.

woolly ['wulɪ] adj wollen.

wooly ['wulɪ] *(Am)* = **woolly**.

Worcester sauce ['wustə-] n Worcestersoße die.

word [wɜːd] n Wort das ; in other ~s mit anderen Worten ; to have a ~ with sb mit jm sprechen.

wording ['wɜːdɪŋ] n Wortlaut der.

word processing [-'prəusesɪŋ] n Textverarbeitung die.

word processor [-'prəusesə'] n Textverarbeitungssystem das.

wore [wɔː'] pt → **wear**.

work [wɜːk] n Arbeit die ; *(painting, novel etc)* Werk das. ◆ vi arbeiten ; *(operate)* funktionieren ; *(have desired effect)* klappen ; *(take effect)* wirken. ◆ vt *(machine, controls)* bedienen ; out of ~ arbeitslos ; to be at ~ *(at workplace)* auf der Ar-

beit sein ; *(working)* arbeiten ;
to be off ~ nicht arbeiten ; **the
~s** *(inf : everything)* alles ; **how
does it ~?** wie funktioniert
das?, wie geht das? ; **it's not
~ing** es funktioniert nicht, es
geht nicht. ■ **work out** *vt sep*
(price, total) auslrechnen ; *(solution)* herauslfinden ; *(method,
plan)* auslarbeiten. ◆ *vi (result)*
laufen ; *(be successful)* klappen ; *(do exercise)* trainieren ; **it
~s out at £20 each** *(bill, total)* es
kommt für jeden auf 20 Pfund.
worker ['wɜːkə] *n* Arbeiter
der (-in *die*).
working class ['wɜːkɪŋ-] *n* :
the ~ die Arbeiterklasse.
working hours ['wɜːkɪŋ-] *npl*
Arbeitszeit *die*.
workman ['wɜːkmən] *(pl* -men
[-mən]) *n* Handwerker *der*.
work of art *n* Kunstwerk *das*.
workout ['wɜːkaʊt] *n* Fitness-
training *das*.
work permit *n* Arbeitserlaubnis *die*.
workplace ['wɜːkpleɪs] *n* Arbeitsplatz *der*.
workshop ['wɜːkʃɒp] *n (for repairs)* Werkstatt *die*.
work surface *n* Arbeitsflä-
che *die*.
world [wɜːld] *n* Welt *die*. ◆ *adj*
Welt-.
worldwide [,wɜːld'waɪd] *adv*
weltweit.
World Wide Web *n* : **the ~**
World Wide Web *das*.
worm [wɜːm] *n* Wurm *der*.
worn [wɔːn] *pp* → **wear**. ◆ *adj*
(clothes) abgetragen ; *(carpet)*
abgenutzt.

worn-out *adj (clothes, shoes
etc)* abgetragen ; *(tired)* erschöpft.
worried ['wʌrɪd] *adj* besorgt.
worry ['wʌrɪ] *n* Sorge *die*. ◆ *vt*
beunruhigen. ◆ *vi* : **to ~ (about)**
sich *(D)* Sorgen machen (über
(+A)).
worrying ['wʌrɪɪŋ] *adj* beun-
ruhigend.
worse [wɜːs] *adj* & *adv*
schlechter, schlimmer ; **to get
~** schlechter werden ; **he's getting ~** *(more ill)* es geht ihm
schlechter ; **to be ~ off** *(in worse
position)* schlechter dran sein ;
(poorer) schlechter dalstehen.
worsen ['wɜːsn] *vi* sich verschlechtern.
worship ['wɜːʃɪp] *n (church
service)* Gottesdienst *der*. ◆ *vt
(god)* preisen ; *(fig : person)* anbeten.
worst [wɜːst] *adj* schlechtes-
te(-r) (-s), schlimmste(-r) (-s).
◆ *adv* am schlechtesten, am
schlimmsten. ◆ *n* : **the ~** der/
die/das Schlechteste, der/die/
das Schlimmste.
worth [wɜːθ] *prep* : **how much
is it ~?** wie viel ist das wert? ;
it's ~ £50 es ist 50 Pfund wert ;
it's ~ seeing es ist sehenswert ;
it's not ~ it es lohnt sich nicht ;
£50 ~ of traveller's cheques Tra-
vellerschecks im Wert von 50
Pfund.
worthless ['wɜːθlɪs] *adj* wertlos.
worthwhile [,wɜːθ'waɪl] *adj*
lohnenswert.
worthy ['wɜːðɪ] *adj (winner,
cause)* würdig ; **to be ~ of sthg**
etw verdienen.

would [wʊd] *aux vb* 1. *(in reported speech)* : **she said she ~ come** sie sagte, sie würde kommen.

2. *(indicating condition)* : **what ~ you do?** was würdest du tun? ; **what ~ you have done?** was hättest du getan? ; **I ~ be most grateful** ich wäre äußerst dankbar.

3. *(indicating willingness)* : **she ~n't go** sie wollte einfach nicht gehen ; **he ~ do anything for her** er würde alles für sie tun.

4. *(in polite questions)* : **~ you like a drink?** möchtest du etwas trinken? ; **~ you mind closing the window?** könntest du das Fenster zu machen?

5. *(indicating inevitability)* : **he ~ say that** er musste das sagen.

6. *(giving advice)* : **I ~ report it if I were you** ich würde es melden, wenn ich du wäre.

7. *(expressing opinions)* : **I ~ prefer coffee** ich hätte lieber Kaffee ; **I ~ prefer to go by bus** ich würde lieber mit dem Bus fahren ; **I ~ have thought (that)...** ich hätte gedacht, (dass)...

wound¹ [wuːnd] *n* Wunde *die.* ◆ *vt* verwunden.

wound² [waʊnd] *pt & pp* → **wind²**.

wove [wəʊv] *pt* → **weave**.

woven ['wəʊvn] *pp* → **weave**.

wrap [ræp] *vt (package)* einlwickeln ; **to ~ sthg round sthg** etw um etw wickeln. ■ **wrap up** *vt sep (package)* einlwickeln. ◆ *vi (dress warmly)* sich warm einlpacken.

wrapper ['ræpə'] *n* Hülle *die* ; *(for sweets)* Bonbonpapier *das.*

wrapping ['ræpɪŋ] *n (material)* Verpackung *die.*

wrapping paper *n* Geschenkpapier *das.*

wreath [riːθ] *n* Kranz *der.*

wreck [rek] *n* Wrack *das.* ◆ *vt (destroy)* kaputtlmachen ; *(spoil)* ruinieren ; **to be ~ed** *(ship)* schiffbrüchig sein.

wreckage ['rekɪdʒ] *n* Trümmer *pl.*

wrench [rentʃ] *n (Br : monkey wrench)* Engländer *der* ; *(Am : spanner)* Schraubenschlüssel *der.*

wrestler ['reslə'] *n* Ringer *der* (-in *die*).

wrestling ['reslɪŋ] *n* Ringen *das.*

wretched ['retʃɪd] *adj (miserable)* unglücklich ; *(very bad)* erbärmlich.

wring [rɪŋ] *(pt & pp* wrung) *vt (clothes, cloth)* auslwringen.

wrinkle ['rɪŋkl] *n* Falte *die.*

wrist [rɪst] *n* Handgelenk *das.*

wristwatch ['rɪstwɒtʃ] *n* Armbanduhr *die.*

write [raɪt] *(pt* wrote, *pp* written) *vt* schreiben ; *(Am : send letter to)* schreiben (+D). ◆ *vi* schreiben ; **to ~ to sb** *(Br)* jm schreiben. ■ **write back** *vi* zurücklschreiben. ■ **write down** *vt sep* auflschreiben. ■ **write off** *vt sep (Br : inf : car)* zu Schrott fahren. ◆ *vi* : **to ~ off for sthg** etw bestellen. ■ **write out** *vt sep (list)* auflstellen ; *(essay)* ins Reine schreiben ; *(cheque, receipt)* aus1stellen ;

write-off n (vehicle) Total-schaden der.

writer ['raɪtə] n (author) Schriftsteller der (-in die).

writing ['raɪtɪŋ] n (handwriting) Schrift die ; (activity, words) Schreiben das.

writing desk n Schreibtisch der.

writing pad n Schreibblock der.

writing paper n Schreibpapier das.

written ['rɪtn] pp → write. ◆ adj (exam, notice) schriftlich.

wrong [rɒŋ] adj falsch ; (bad, immoral) unrecht. ◆ adv falsch ; what's ~? was ist los? ; something's ~ with the car mit dem Auto stimmt etwas nicht ; to be in the ~ im Unrecht sein ; to get sthg ~ etw falsch verstehen ; to go ~ (machine) kaputtgehen ; '~ way' (Am) Schild, das anzeigt, dass man nicht in eine Straße einbiegen darf.

wrongly ['rɒŋlɪ] adv fälschlicherweise.

wrong number n : you've got the ~ Sie sind falsch verbunden.

wrote [rəʊt] pt → write.

wrought iron [rɔːt-] n Schmiedeeisen das.

wrung [rʌŋ] pt & pp → wring.

WWW n (abbr of World Wide Web) WWW.

xing (Am : abbr of crossing) : 'ped ~' Schild für einen Fußgängerüberweg.

XL (abbr of extra-large) XL.

Xmas ['eksməs] n (inf) Weihnachten das.

X-ray n (picture) Röntgenbild das. ◆ vt röntgen ; to have an ~ sich röntgen lassen.

Y

yacht [jɒt] n (for pleasure) Jacht die ; (for racing) Segelboot das.

yard [jɑːd] n (unit of measurement) = 91,44 cm, Yard das ; (enclosed area) Hof der ; (Am : behind house) Hinterhof der.

yard sale n (Am) Verkauf von gebrauchten Gegenständen vor einem Haus.

yarn [jɑːn] n (thread) Garn das.

yawn [jɔːn] vi (person) gähnen.

yd abbr = yard.

yeah [jeə] adv (inf) ja.

year [jɪə] n Jahr das ; (at school, of wine) Jahrgang der ; next ~ nächstes Jahr ; this ~ dieses Jahr ; I'm 15 ~s old ich bin 15 Jahre alt ; I haven't seen her for ~s (inf) ich hab' sie seit Jahren nicht mehr gesehen ; which ~ are you in? (at school) in welche Klasse gehst du?

yearly ['jɪəlɪ] adj jährlich ; (every year) Jahres-.

yeast [ji:st] *n* Hefe *die.*

yell [jel] *vi* schreien.

yellow ['jeləʊ] *adj* gelb. ◆ *n* Gelb *das.*

yellow lines *npl* gelbe Linie am Straßenrand, die Parkverbot anzeigt.

YELLOW LINES

In Großbritannien wird Parkverbot mit einer einfachen bzw. doppelten Linie am Straßenrand angezeigt. Eine einfache Linie bedeutet, dass zwischen 8 Uhr und 16 Uhr 30 an Werktagen Parkverbot besteht ; außerhalb dieser Zeiten ist das Parken erlaubt. Eine doppelte Linie bedeutet, dass zu keiner Zeit geparkt werden darf.

Yellow Pages® *n* : the ~ die gelben Seiten *pl.*

yes [jes] *adv* ja ; *(contradicting)* doch.

yesterday ['jestədɪ] *n* Gestern *das.* ◆ *adv* gestern ; **the day before ~** vorgestern ; **~ afternoon** gestern Nachmittag ; **~ morning** gestern Morgen.

yet [jet] *adv* noch ; *(in questions)* schon. ◆ *conj* doch ; **not ~** noch nicht ; **I've ~ to do it** ich muss es noch tun ; **~ again** schon wieder ; **~ another delay** noch eine Verspätung ; **are you ready ~?** bist du schon fertig?

yew [ju:] *n* Eibe *die.*

yield [ji:ld] *vt (profit, interest)* ab!werfen. ◆ *vi (break, give way)* nach!geben ; **'yield'** *(Am : AUT)* 'Vorfahrt beachten'.

YMCA *n* CVJM.

yob [jɒb] *n (Br : inf)* Rowdy *der.*

yoga ['jəʊgə] *n* Yoga *der.*

yoghurt ['jɒgət] *n* Joghurt *der.*

yolk [jəʊk] *n* Dotter *der,* Eigelb *das.*

York Minster [jɔ:k'mɪnstəʳ] *n* die Kathedrale von York.

YORK MINSTER

Die Kathedrale York Minster in der befestigten, ehemaligen Römerstadt York im Norden Englands wurde im 12. Jahrhundert erbaut. Sie ist wegen ihres hellen Mauerwerks und ihrer Fensterrosette berühmt. 1984 wurde die Kathedrale durch Blitzschlag schwer beschädigt, ist aber inzwischen wieder in Stand gesetzt worden.

Yorkshire pudding ['jɔ:kʃə-] *n souffléartige kleine Pfannkuchen, die zu Roastbeef gegessen werden.*

you [ju:] *pron* 1. *(subject : singular)* du ; *(plural)* ihr ; *(polite form)* Sie ; **~ Germans** ihr Deutschen.
2. *(direct object, after prep +A : singular)* dich ; *(plural)* euch ; *(polite form)* Sie ; **I hate ~!** ich hasse dich/Sie/euch! ; **I did it for ~** ich habe es für dich/Sie/euch getan.
3. *(indirect object, after prep +D : singular)* dir ; *(plural)* euch ; *(polite form)* Ihnen ; **I told ~** ich habe es dir/Ihnen/euch gesagt ; **after ~!** nach Ihnen!

4. *(indefinite use : subject)* man ; *(object)* einen ; ~ **never know** man kann nie wissen.

young [jʌŋ] *adj* jung. ◆ *npl* : **the** ~ die Jugend.

younger ['jʌŋgə'] *adj* jüngere(-r) (-s).

youngest ['jʌŋgəst] *adj* jüngste(-r) (-s).

youngster ['jʌŋstə'] *n* Jugendliche *der, die* ; *(child)* Kleine *der, die.*

your [jɔː'] *adj* **1.** *(singular subject)* dein/deine, deine *(pl)* ; *(plural subject)* euer/eure, eure *(pl)* ; *(polite form)* Ihr/Ihre, Ihre *(pl)* ; ~ **dog** dein/euer/Ihr Hund ; ~ **house** dein/euer/Ihr Haus ; ~ **children** deine/eure/Ihre Kinder. **2.** *(indefinite subject)* : **it's good for** ~ **teeth** es ist gut für die Zähne.

yours [jɔːz] *pron (singular subject)* dein/deines, deine *(pl)* ; *(plural subject)* euer/eure/eures, eure *(pl)* ; *(polite form)* Ihr/Ihre/Ihres, Ihre *(pl)* ; **a friend of** ~ ein Freund von dir.

yourself [jɔː'self] *pron (pl -selves) (reflexive, after prep +A : singular)* dich ; *(reflexive, after prep +D : singular)* dir ; *(plural)* euch ; *(polite form)* sich ; **did you do it** ~? hast du/haben Sie das selbst gemacht? ; **did you do it yourselves?** habt ihr das selbst gemacht?

youth [juːθ] *n* Jugend *die* ; *(young man)* Jugendliche *der.*

youth club *n* Jugendklub *der.*

youth hostel *n* Jugendherberge *die.*

Yugoslavia [ˌjuːgə'slɑːviə] *n* Jugoslawien *nt.*

yuppie ['jʌpɪ] *n* Yuppie *der.*

YWCA *n* CVJF.

Z

zebra [*(Br)* 'zebrə, *(Am)* 'ziːbrə] *n* Zebra *das.*

zebra crossing *n (Br)* Zebrastreifen *der.*

zero ['zɪərəʊ] *(pl -es) n* Null *die* ; **five degrees below** ~ fünf Grad unter Null.

zest [zest] *n (of lemon, orange)* Schale *die.*

zigzag ['zɪgzæg] *vi* im Zickzack laufen.

zinc [zɪŋk] *n* Zink *das.*

zip [zɪp] *n (Br)* Reißverschluss *der.* ◆ *vt* den Reißverschluss zulziehen an (+D). ■ **zip up** *vt sep* den Reißverschluss zulziehen an (+D).

zip code *n (Am)* Postleitzahl *die.*

zipper ['zɪpə'] *n (Am)* Reißverschluss *der.*

zit [zɪt] *n (inf)* Pickel *der.*

zodiac ['zəʊdɪæk] *n* Tierkreis *der.*

zone [zəʊn] *n* Zone *die.*

zoo [zuː] *(pl -s) n* Zoo *der.*

zoom (lens) [zuːm-] *n* Zoom *das.*

zucchini [zuː'kiːnɪ] *(pl zucchini) n (Am)* Zucchini *die.*

DEUTSCH-ENGLISCH
GERMAN-ENGLISH

A

à *präp (+A)* at ; **15 Stück ~ 2,95 DM** 15, at 2.95 marks each.

A *(pl -)* die *(abk für Autobahn)* M *(Br)*, I *(Am)*.

ab *präp (+D)* **1.** *(zeitlich)* from ; **~ 8 Uhr** from 8 o'clock ; **~ 18 (Jahren)** over (the age of) 18. **2.** *(räumlich)* from ; **~ Dortmund 12.35 Uhr** leaving Dortmund at 12.35. ◆ *adv (los, weg)* off ; **~ ins Bett!** off you go to bed!

■ **ab und zu** *adv* now and then.

Abb. *abk* = **Abbildung**.

ab|bestellen *vt* to cancel.

ab|biegen *vi unr ist (mit Auto)* to turn off ; **nach rechts/links ~** to turn right/left.

Abbiegespur *(pl -en)* die filter lane.

ab|bilden *vt* to illustrate.

Abbildung *(pl -en)* die illustration.

ab|blenden *vi* to dip one's headlights *(Br)*, to dim one's headlights *(Am)*.

Abblendlicht *das* dipped headlights *(Br) (pl)*, dimmed headlights *(Am) (pl)*.

ab|brechen *vt unr hat* to break off. ◆ *vi unr ist* to break off ; *(aufhören)* to stop.

ab|buchen *vt* to debit.

ab|dichten *vt (gegen kalte Luft)* to insulate ; *(gegen Wasser)* to waterproof.

Abdichtung die *(gegen kalte Luft)* insulation ; *(gegen Wasser)* waterproofing.

Abend *(pl -e)* der evening ; **Guten ~!** good evening! ; **am ~** in the evening ; **heute/gestern/morgen ~** this/yesterday/tomorrow evening ; **zu ~ essen** to have one's evening meal.

Abendessen *(pl -)* das evening meal.

Abendgarderobe *(pl -n)* die evening dress.

Abendkasse *(pl -n)* die box office *(open just before performance)*.

Abendmahl *(pl -e)* das Holy Communion.

abends *adv* in the evening ; **spät ~** late in the evening.

Abenteuer *(pl -)* das adventure.

Abenteuerurlaub *(pl -e)* der adventure holiday.

aber *konj* but. ◆ *adv* : **jetzt ist ~ Schluss!** that's enough now! ; **das ist ~ nett!** how nice! ; **~ gerne!** of course! ; **du kommst ~ spät!** you're a bit late, aren't you? ; **~ bitte!** go ahead!

Aberglaube *der* superstition.

abergläubisch *adj* superstitious.

ab|fahren *vi unr ist* to leave; *(von Autobahn)* to turn off. ◆ *vt unr hat (Reifen)* to wear down; *(Weg, Strecke)* to drive along.

Abfahrt *(pl -en) die (von Zug, Bus)* departure; *(von Autobahn)* exit; *(von Skifahrer)* descent.

Abfall *(pl Abfälle) der (Müll)* rubbish *(Br)*, garbage *(Am)*.

Abfalleimer *(pl -) der* rubbish bin *(Br)*, garbage can *(Am)*.

ab|fallen *vi unr ist (Straße)* to dip; *(Obst, Blätter)* to fall.

ab|färben *vi (Material)* to run.

Abfertigungsschalter *(pl -) der* check-in desk.

ab|fliegen *vi unr ist (Flugzeug)* to depart; *(Person)* to fly.

Abflug *(pl -flüge) der* departure.

Abflughalle *(pl -n) die* departure lounge.

Abflugzeit *(pl -en) die* departure time.

Abfluss *(pl -flüsse) der (im Waschbecken)* plughole.

Abführmittel *(pl -) das* laxative.

Abgase *pl* exhaust fumes.

ab|geben *vt unr (einreichen)* to hand in; *(übergeben)* to hand over; *(an der Garderobe)* to leave; *(verkaufen)* to sell; *(Wärme, Feuchtigkeit)* to give off; *(Erklärung, Urteil)* to make; **jm etw ~** to give sb sthg.

abgebildet *adj*: **wie ~** as illustrated.

abgekocht *adj* boiled.

abgelaufen *adj (Pass)* expired; *(Zeit)* up, over.

abgemacht *adj* fixed.

abgenutzt *adj* worn out.

abgepackt *adj* packed.

abgeschlossen *pp* → **ab|schließen**. ◆ *adj*: **~e Berufsausbildung** German vocational qualification obtained after three years' study on a day-release basis.

ab|gewöhnen *vt*: **sich (D) etw ~** to give sthg up.

abgezählt *adj (Kleingeld)* correct, exact.

ab|haken *vt* to tick off.

Abhang *(pl -hänge) der* slope.

ab|hängen *vt (Anhänger)* to unhitch; *(Verfolger)* to shake off. ◆ *vi*: **~ von** to depend on; **das hängt davon ab, ob...** that depends on whether...

abhängig *adj (süchtig)* addicted; **~ sein von** *(von Hilfe)* to be dependent on; *(von Bedingungen)* to depend on.

ab|heben *vt unr (Hörer)* to pick up; *(Geld)* to withdraw. ◆ *vi unr (Flugzeug)* to take off.

ab|heften *vt* to file.

ab|holen *vt* to collect.

Abitur *das* ≃ A levels *(Br)*, ≃ SATs *(Am)*.

ⓘ **ABITUR**

The "Abitur" is the series of exams taken by approximately a third of German pupils at the end of their school career and is a requirement if they wish to go on to university. Pupils select one main subject and a number of optional subjects. Each of the "Bundesländer" administers its own examinations.

ab|klappern *vt* to search.

Abkommen (*pl* -) *das* agreement.

ab|kühlen *vi ist* to cool down. ◆ *vimp* : **es kühlt ab** (*Wetter*) it's getting cooler.

ab|kürzen *vt* (*Wort*) to abbreviate ; **den Weg ~** to take a short cut.

Abkürzung (*pl* -en) *die* (*von Strecke*) short cut ; (*von Wort*) abbreviation.

ab|legen *vt* (*Mantel*) to take off ; (*Gewohnheit, Charakterzug*) to get rid of ; (*Prüfung*) to take ; (*Akten*) to file. ◆ *vi* (*Schiff*) to cast off ; (*Person*) to take off one's coat/jacket.

ab|lehnen *vt* (*Vorschlag, Bitte*) to reject ; (*Geschenk, Einladung*) to refuse ; (*Person, Ansicht*) to disapprove of.

ab|lenken *vt* to distract.

ab|lesen *vt* (*Temperatur, Kilometerstand*) to read ; (*Text*) to read out.

ab|liefern *vt* to deliver.

ab|lösen *vt* (*Etikett, Pflaster*) to peel off ; (*Person*) to take over from. ▨ **sich ablösen** *ref* (*Personen*) to take turns ; (*Tapete, Etikett*) to come off.

ab|machen *vt* (*entfernen*) to remove ; (*vereinbaren*) to agree on, to fix ; **mit jm einen Termin ~** to make an appointment with sb.

ab|melden *vt* (*Telefon*) to have disconnected ; (*Auto*) to take off the road ; (*Person*) to cancel the membership of. ▨ **sich abmelden** *ref* (*bei der Polizei*) to give notice that one is moving away.

ab|nehmen *vt unr* (*Bild, Wäsche*) to take down ; (*Brille, Hut*) to take off ; (*Hörer*) to pick up ; (*Fahrzeug, Maschine*) to inspect ; (*amputieren*) to amputate ; (*Blut*) to take. ◆ *vi unr* (*Anzahl*) to decrease ; (*an Gewicht*) to lose weight ; **jm etw ~** (*Arbeit, Last*) to relieve sb of sthg ; (*fam : glauben*) to buy sthg from sb ; (*abkaufen*) to buy sthg from sb ; **fünf Kilo ~** to lose five kilos.

Abonnement (*pl* -s) *das* (*für Zeitung*) subscription ; (*im Theater*) season ticket.

abonnieren *vt* to subscribe to.

ab|raten *vi unr* (+D) : (*jm*) **von etw ~** to advise (sb) against sthg.

ab|räumen *vt* (*Tisch*) to clear ; (*Geschirr*) to clear away.

ab|reagieren *vt* (*Wut*) to take out. ▨ **sich abreagieren** *ref* : **sich an jm ~** to take it out on sb.

ab|rechnen *vi* (*mit Rechnung*) to settle up ; (*fam : sich rächen*) to get even. ◆ *vt* (*subtrahieren*) to deduct.

Abrechnung (*pl* -en) *die* : **~ machen** to do the accounts.

ab|reiben *vt unr* (*Fläche, Gegenstand*) to rub clean ; (*Schmutz*) to rub off.

Abreise *die* departure.

ab|reisen *vi* to depart.

ab|reißen vt unr hat (Pflaster, Zettel) to tear off; (Haus) to tear down. ◆ vi unr ist (Seil) to break; (Verbindung) to end.

ab|richten vt to train (an animal).

ab|runden vt (Zahl) to round down; (Kante, Ecke) to round off.

abrupt adj abrupt. ◆ adv abruptly.

Abs. abk = Absender, Absatz.

ab|sagen vt & vi to cancel; jm ~ to tell sb one can't come.

Absatz der (vom Schuh) heel; (im Text) paragraph.

ab|schalten vt & vi to switch off.

abscheulich adj disgusting.

ab|schicken vt to post.

ab|schieben vt unr (Flüchtling) to deport.

Abschied (pl -e) der parting.

Abschleppdienst (pl -e) der (vehicle) recovery service.

ab|schleppen vt (Auto) to tow away; (fam : aus Disco, von Party) to pick up.

Abschleppseil (pl -e) das towrope.

Abschleppwagen (pl -) der recovery vehicle.

abschließbar adj (Schrank) lockable.

ab|schließen vt unr (Tür, Wohnung) to lock; (beenden) to complete; (Vertrag) to conclude; (von Außenwelt) to cut off. ◆ vi to lock up.

ab|schmecken vt to season (according to taste).

ab|schminken vt to remove the make-up from. ▪ **sich abschminken** ref to remove one's make-up.

ab|schneiden vt unr to cut off. ◆ vi unr : gut/schlecht ~ to do well/badly; jm/sich (D) etw ~ to cut sthg off for sb/o.s.

Abschnitt (pl -e) der (von Eintrittskarte, Ticket) stub; (im Text; von Strecke) section; (Zeitraum) period.

ab|schrauben vt to unscrew.

absehbar adj foreseeable; in ~er Zeit in the foreseeable future.

abseits adv (SPORT) offside; ~ stehen (entfernt) to stand a little way away.

Absender (pl -) der (auf Brief) sender's name and address; (Person) sender.

ab|setzen vt (Hut, Brille, Theaterstück) to take off; (Tasche, Glas) to put down; (Mitfahrer) to drop off; (Medikament) to come off; (von der Steuer) to deduct. ▪ **sich absetzen** ref (Kalk, Schlamm) to be deposited, to build up; (fam : fliehen) to take off.

ab|sichern vt to make safe. ▪ **sich absichern** ref to cover o.s.

Absicht (pl -en) die intention; mit ~ intentionally, on purpose.

absichtlich adj intentional. ◆ adv intentionally, on purpose.

absolut adj absolute. ◆ adv completely.

ab|sperren *vt (Straße)* to block off ; *(Tür, Wohnung)* to lock. ◆ *vi* to lock up.

Absperrung *(pl -en) die* barrier.

ab|sprechen *vt unr* to agree on ; ~ **mit** to arrange with. ▓ **sich absprechen** *ref* to come to an agreement.

Abstand *(pl -stände) der (räumlich)* distance ; *(zeitlich)* interval ; *(innere Distanz)* reserve ; **mit** ~ by far ; ~ **halten** to keep one's distance.

Abstecher *(pl -) der* detour ; **einen** ~ **machen** to make a detour.

ab|stellen *vt (Gerät)* to turn off ; *(Fahrrad, Auto)* to put ; *(Tasche, Tablett)* to put down ; *(Missstand, Problem)* to put an end to.

Abstellraum *(pl -räume) der* storage room.

Abstieg *der (ins Tal)* descent ; *(SPORT)* relegation.

ab|stimmen *vi* to vote. ◆ *vt* : **etw auf etw** (+A) ~ to adapt sthg to sthg ; ~ **über** (+A) to vote on.

Abstimmung *(pl -en) die (Wahl)* ballot.

abstrakt *adj* abstract.

ab|streiten *vt unr* to deny.

ab|stürzen *vi ist* to crash.

absurd *adj* absurd.

Abt. *(abk für Abteilung)* dept.

Abtei *(pl -en) die* abbey.

Abteil *(pl -e) das (im Zug)* compartment.

Abteilung *(pl -en) die (in Firma, Kaufhaus)* department.

Abtreibung *(pl -en) die* abortion.

ab|trocknen *vt* to dry ; **sich** (D) **die Hände** ~ to dry one's hands. ▓ **sich abtrocknen** *ref* to dry o.s.

abwärts *adv* downwards.

Abwasch *der* washing-up.

ab|waschen *vt unr (Geschirr, Kacheln)* to wash ; *(Schmutz)* to wash off. ◆ *vi unr* to wash up (Br), to wash the dishes (Am).

Abwasser *(pl -wässer) das (häuslich)* sewage ; *(industriell)* effluent.

ab|wechseln : **sich abwechseln** *ref (Personen)* to take turns ; *(Zustände, Landschaften)* to alternate.

abwechselnd *adv* alternately.

Abwechslung *die* change.

abweisend *adj* unfriendly.

ab|werten *vt (Person, Idee)* to belittle ; *(Währung)* to devalue.

Abwertung *(pl -en) die (von Währung)* devaluation.

abwesend *adj* absent. ◆ *adv* absently.

ab|wickeln *vt (Schnur)* to unwind.

ab|wischen *vt (Tisch)* to wipe ; *(Schmutz)* to wipe off.

Abzeichen *(pl -) das* badge.

ab|ziehen *vt unr (Hülle)* to take off ; *(Bett)* to strip ; *(Stimme, Anzahl)* to take away ; *(kopieren)* to copy ; *(Foto)* to print. ◆ *vi unr (Rauch)* to clear ; *(fam : weggehen)* to clear off.

Abzug *(pl -züge) der (Foto)* print.

abzüglich *präp* (+G) minus ; ~ **15% Skonto** less a 15% discount.

Abzweigung (*pl* -en) *die* turning.

ach *interj* oh! ; **ach ja!** oh, yes! ; **ach so!** (oh,) I see!

Achse (*pl* -n) *die* (AUTO) axle.

Achsel (*pl* -n) *die* armpit.

acht *num* eight ; → **sechs**.

Acht : **~ geben** to take care.

achte, r, s *adj* eighth ; → **sechste**.

Achtel (*pl* -) *das* eighth.

achten *vt* to respect. ◆ *vi* : **~ auf** (+A) (*sich konzentrieren auf*) to pay attention to ; (*aufpassen auf*) to look after.

Achterbahn (*pl* -en) *die* roller coaster.

Achtung *die* (*Respekt*) respect. ◆ *interj* look out! ; **alle ~!** well done!

achtzehn *num* eighteen ; → **sechs**.

achtzig *num* eighty ; → **sechs**.

Acker (*pl* Äcker) *der* field.

ADAC *der* ≃ AA (*Br*), ≃ AAA (*Am*).

Adapter (*pl* -) *der* adapter.

addieren *vt* & *vi* to add.

ade *interj* cheerio!

Ader (*pl* -n) *die* vein.

Adler (*pl* -) *der* eagle.

adoptieren *vt* to adopt.

Adoptivkind (*pl* -er) *das* adopted child.

Adressbuch (*pl* -bücher) *das* (*persönlich*) address book ; (*von Stadt*) (local) address directory.

Adresse (*pl* -n) *die* address.

Advent *der* Advent.

ADVENT

Advent, the four weeks preceding Christmas, has a special significance in Germany and many traditions are associated with this time of year. Streets and houses are decorated and Christmas fairs are held. In the home it is traditional to hang up Advent wreaths with four candles, one of which is lit each Sunday of Advent, and to bake special Christmas biscuits.

Adventskranz (*pl* -kränze) *der* Advent wreath.

Aerobic *das* aerobics (*sg*).

Affäre (*pl* -n) *die* affair.

Affe (*pl* -n) *der* (*klein*) monkey ; (*groß*) ape.

Afrika *nt* Africa.

Afrikaner, in (*mpl* -) *der, die* African.

afrikanisch *adj* African.

After (*pl* -) *der* anus.

AG (*pl* -s) *die* ≃ plc (*Br*), ≃ corp. (*Am*).

aggressiv *adj* aggressive. ◆ *adv* aggressively.

Ägypten *nt* Egypt.

ah *interj* oh! ; **~ so!** (oh,) I see! ; **~ ja!** (oh,) I see!

ähneln *vi* (+D) to be similar to, to be like.

ähnlich *adj* similar. ◆ *adv* similarly ; **jm/etw ~ sein** to be similar to sb/sthg ; **jm/etw ~ sehen** to look like sb/sthg.

Ähnlichkeit (*pl* -en) *die* similarity.

Ahnung (*pl* -en) *die* (*Vorgefühl*) feeling ; **keine ~!** no idea!

ahnungslos adj unsuspecting. ◆ adv unsuspectingly.

Aids nt AIDS.

Aids-Handschuh (pl -e) der surgical glove.

Airbag (pl -s) der airbag.

Akkordeon (pl -s) das accordion.

Akku (pl -s) der (rechargeable) battery.

Akkusativ (pl -e) der accusative.

Akne die acne.

Akt (pl -e) der (Handlung, von Drama) act ; (Bild) nude ; (Zeremonie) ceremony.

Akte (pl -n) die file.

Aktenkoffer (pl -) der attaché case.

Aktie (pl -n) die share.

Aktiengesellschaft (pl -en) die public limited company (Br), corporation (Am).

aktiv adj active. ◆ adv actively.

aktuell adj (modisch) fashionable ; (Thema, Problem) current ; (Theaterstück, Buch) topical.

Akustik die acoustics (pl).

Akzent (pl -e) der accent.

Alarm der alarm ; ~ schlagen to raise the alarm.

Alarmanlage (pl -n) die (von Gebäude) burglar alarm ; (von Auto) car alarm.

albern adj silly. ◆ adv in a silly way.

Albtraum (pl -träume) der nightmare.

alias adv alias.

Alkohol der alcohol.

alkoholarm adj low-alcohol.

alkoholfrei adj alcohol-free.

Alkoholiker, in (mpl -) der, die alcoholic.

alkoholisch adj alcoholic.

alkoholkrank adj alcoholic.

all det all (of) ; ~ das Warten hat mich müde gemacht all this waiting has made me tired.

All das space.

alle, r, s det 1. (sämtliche) all ; ~ Kleider all the clothes ; ~ beide both ; ~s Gute! all the best! 2. (völlig) all ; in ~r Ruhe in peace. 3. (jede) all ; Getränke ~r Art all kinds of drinks. 4. (im Abstand von) every ; ~ 50 Meter every 50 metres ; ~ zwei Wochen every two weeks. ◆ pron all ; das ist ~s that's all ; ~ sind da everyone's here ; trotz ~m in spite of everything ; vor ~m above all. ◆ adj (fam) : die Butter ist ~ there's no more butter.

Allee (pl -n) die avenue.

allein adj (ohne andere) alone ; (einsam) lonely. ◆ adv (ohne andere) alone ; (einsam) alone ; (selbstständig) on one's own ; (nur) only ; von ~ by oneself/itself etc.

allein erziehend adj single (parent).

Alleingang (pl -gänge) der single-handed effort ; im ~ single-handedly.

allein stehend adj (Person) single ; (Haus) detached.

allemal *adv (sicher)* definitely.

allenfalls *adv* at most.

allerdings *adv (aber)* though ; *(ja)* certainly.

allererste, r, s *adj* very first.

Allergie *(pl -n) die (MED)* allergy.

allergisch *adj* allergic. ◆ *adv* allergically ; ~ **gegen** *(+A)* allergic to.

allerhand *pron* all sorts of things.

Allerheiligen *nt* All Saints' Day.

alles *pron* → **alle.**

Alleskleber *(pl -) der* all-purpose glue.

allgemein *adj (allen gemeinsam, unspezifisch)* general ; *(alle betreffend)* universal. ◆ *adv* generally ; **im Allgemeinen** in general.

alljährlich *adj* annual. ◆ *adv* annually.

allmählich *adj* gradual. ◆ *adv* gradually.

Alltag *der (Normalität)* everyday life.

alltäglich *adj* everyday.

allzu *adv* far too ; ~ **sehr** far too much.

Allzweckreiniger *(pl -) der* multi-purpose cleaner.

Alm *(pl -en) die* mountain pasture.

Alpen *pl* : **die** ~ the Alps.

Alpenverein *der organization which promotes study of the Alps and organizes mountain hikes etc.*

Alpenvorland *das* foothills of the Alps.

alphabetisch *adj* alphabetical. ◆ *adv* alphabetically.

alpin *adj* alpine.

Alptraum *der* → **Albtraum.**

als *konj* 1. *(zeitlich)* when ; *(während)* as ; ~ **es dunkel wurde** when it got dark ; **erst** ~ only when.

2. *(vergleichend)* than ; **sie ist besser** ~ **ihr Bruder** she is better than her brother ; **der Wein ist besser,** ~ **ich dachte** the wine is better than I thought it would be ; **mehr** ~ more than.

3. *(Angabe von Vermutung)* as if ; ~ **ob** as if ; **es sieht so aus,** ~ **würde es bald regnen** it looks like it's going to rain soon.

4. *(Angabe von Urteil, Zweck)* as ; **ich verstehe es** ~ **Kompliment** I take it as a compliment.

5. *(Angabe von Identität)* as ; ~ **Kind** as a child.

also *interj* well. ◆ *konj (das heißt)* in other words ; *(demnach)* so. ◆ *adv (demnach)* so ; ~ **dann** all right then ; ~ **nein!** no!

Alsterwasser *(pl -) das* shandy.

alt *(komp* **älter,** *superl* **am ältesten)** *adj* old ; **wie** ~ **bist du?** how old are you? ; **zwei Jahre älter** two years older ; **12 Jahre** ~ 12 years old.

Alt[1] *(pl -) das (Bier)* type of dark, German beer.

Alt[2] *(pl -e) der (MUS)* alto.

Altar *(pl* **Altäre)** *der* altar.

Altbier *(pl -) das* type of dark, German beer.

Altenheim *(pl -e) das* old people's home.

Alter das (Lebensalter) age ; (hohes Alter) old age ; **im ~ von** at the age of.

alternativ adj alternative.

Alternative (pl -n) die alternative.

Altersgrenze (pl -n) die (allgemein) age limit ; (für Rente) retirement age.

Altglas das glass for recycling.

altmodisch adj old-fashioned.

Altpapier das paper for recycling ; **aus ~** made from recycled paper.

Altstadt die old town.

Alufolie die tinfoil.

Aluminium das aluminium.

am präp = an dem ; **~ besten gehen wir zu Fuß** it would be best if we walked ; **das gefällt mir ~ besten** I like this one best ; **wie kommt man ~ besten nach Köln?** what's the best way of getting to Cologne? ; **~ Abend** in the evening ; **~ Flughafen** at the airport ; **~ Freitag** on Friday ; **~ Meer** by the sea.

Amateur, in (mpl -e) der, die amateur.

Ambulanz (pl -en) die (Krankenwagen) ambulance ; (im Krankenhaus) outpatients' (department).

Ameise (pl -n) die ant.

amen interj amen.

Amerika nt America.

Amerikaner, in (mpl -) der, die American.

amerikanisch adj American.

Ampel (pl -n) die (im Verkehr) traffic lights (pl).

Amphitheater (pl -) das amphitheatre.

Amt (pl Ämter) das (Behörde) department ; (Gebäude, Posten) office.

amtlich adj official.

amüsieren vt to amuse. ▨ **sich amüsieren** ref to amuse o.s.

Amüsierviertel (pl -) das area with a lot of bars, restaurants etc.

an präp (+A) 1. (räumlich) to ; **sich ~ den Tisch setzen** to sit down at the table ; **etw ~ die Wand lehnen** to lean sthg against the wall ; **~ Münster 13.45 Uhr** arriving at Münster at 13.45. 2. (mit Verb) : **~ jn/etw denken** to think about sb/sthg ; **sich ~ jn/ etw erinnern** to remember sb/ sthg. 3. (fast) : **~ die 30 Grad** nearly 30 degrees.

◆ präp (+D) 1. (räumlich) at ; **am Tisch sitzen** to be sitting at the table ; **am See** by the lake ; **~ der Wand** on the wall ; **~ der Hauptstraße** on the main road ; **der Ort, ~ dem wir gepicknickt haben** the place where we had a picnic. 2. (zeitlich) on ; **am Freitag** on Friday ; **~ diesem Tag** on that day. 3. (mit Hilfe von) with ; **am Stock gehen** to walk with a stick ; **jn ~ der Stimme erkennen** to recognize sb by their voice. 4. (an einer Institution) at ; **Lehrer**

~ **einem Gymnasium** teacher at a grammar school.
5. *(von)* : **genug ~ Beweisen haben** to have enough proof.
◆ *adv* **1.** *(ein)* on ; **Licht ~!** turn the light on! ; **~ - aus** on-off ; *siehe auch* **an sein**.
2. *(ab)* : **von jetzt ~** from now on ; **von heute ~** from today.
Analyse *(pl* -n*)* die analysis.
analysieren *vt* to analyse.
Ananas *(pl* -*)* die pineapple.
Anbau[1] *der (von Pflanzen)* cultivation.
Anbau[2] *(pl* -ten*)* der *(Gebäude)* extension.
an|bieten *vt unr* to offer ; **darf ich Ihnen etwas ~?** may I offer you something to eat/drink?
an|braten *vt unr* to brown.
an|brechen *vt unr (Packung)* to open. ◆ *vi unr (Tag)* to dawn ; *(Nacht)* to fall.
an|brennen *vi unr (Speisen)* to burn ; **etw ~ lassen** to burn sthg.
an|bringen *vt unr (Schild, Regal)* to fix, to attach ; *(fam : mitbringen)* to bring home.
an|dauern *vi* to continue, to go on.
Andenken *(pl* -*)* das *(Souvenir)* souvenir ; *(Erinnerung)* memory.
andere, r, s *adj (unterschiedlich)* different ; *(weitere)* other.
◆ *pron* : **der/die/das ~** the other one ; **die ~n** the others ; **eine ~/ein ~r** *(Ding)* a different one ; *(Person)* someone else ; **etwas ~s** something else ; **niemand ~s** nobody else ; **ich habe noch zwei**

~ **I have two others** ; **unter ~m** among other things.
ändern *vt* to change ; *(Kleid)* to alter. ▧ **sich ändern** *ref* to change.
anders *adj* different. ◆ *adv (andersartig)* differently ; **wer/wo ~?** who/where else? ; **~ als** differently from ; **irgendwo ~** somewhere else ; **jemand ~** someone else.
andersherum *adv* the other way round.
anderswo *adv (fam)* somewhere else.
anderthalb *num* one and a half.
Änderung *(pl* -en*)* die change ; **~en vorbehalten** subject to alteration.
Änderungsschneiderei *(pl* -en*)* die tailor's shop that does alterations.
an|deuten *vt* to hint at.
Andorra *nt* Andorra.
aneinander *adv (drücken, befestigen)* together ; *(grenzen, stoßen)* one another ; **~ denken** to think about one another ; **sich ~ gewöhnen** to get used to each other.
Anfahrt *(pl* -en*)* die journey there.
Anfang *(pl* -fänge*)* der beginning, start ; **am ~** at the beginning ; **~ Oktober** at the beginning of October.
an|fangen *vi unr* to begin, to start ; **mit etw ~** to start sthg, to begin sthg.
Anfänger, in *(mpl* -*)* der, die beginner.
anfangs *adv* at first.

an|fassen vt (berühren) to touch.

Anflug (pl -flüge) der (von Flugzeug) descent, approach.

an|fordern vt (Hilfe, Gutachten) to ask for ; (per Post) to send off for.

Anforderung (pl -en) die (Erwartung) requirement ; hohe ~en heavy demands.

Anfrage (pl -n) die (amt) enquiry.

an|fühlen : sich anfühlen ref : sich weich/gut ~ to feel soft/good.

an|führen vt (leiten) to lead.

Anführungszeichen pl inverted commas ; in ~ in inverted commas.

Angabe (pl -n) die (Information) detail ; nähere ~n further details ; technische ~n specifications.

an|geben vt unr (Namen, Quellen) to give ; (Tempo, Ton) to set.

angeblich adj alleged. ◆ adv allegedly.

angeboren adj innate.

Angebot (pl -e) das (Anbieten) offer ; (an Waren) selection ; (Sonderangebot) special offer.

an|gehen vt unr : jn nichts ~ to be none of sb's business.

Angehörige (pl -n) der, die (in Familie) relative ; (von Firma, Gruppe) member.

Angel (pl -n) die (zum Fischen) fishing rod.

Angelegenheit (pl -en) die matter, affair.

angeln vt (fischen) to catch. ◆ vi to fish.

Angelschein (pl -e) der fishing permit.

angenehm adj pleasant. ◆ adv pleasantly. ◆ interj pleased to meet you!

angesichts präp (+G) in view of.

angespannt adj (Aufmerksamkeit) close ; (konfliktgeladen) tense.

Angestellte (pl -n) der, die employee.

angestrengt adv (nachdenken) intently. ◆ adj (Gesichtsausdruck) intent.

angetrunken adj slightly drunk.

an|gewöhnen vt : sich (D) etw ~ to get into the habit of sthg.

Angewohnheit (pl -en) die habit.

Angora nt angora.

an|greifen vt & vi unr to attack.

Angst (pl Ängste) die fear ; ~ haben vor (+D) to be afraid of ; jm ~ machen to scare sb.

ängstlich adj (Mensch, Tier) easily frightened ; (Verhalten, Blick) frightened. ◆ adv (blicken, reagieren) frightenedly.

an|haben vt unr (Hose, Schuhe) to be wearing ; jm nichts ~ können to be unable to harm sb.

an|halten vi unr (stoppen) to stop ; (andauern) to last. ◆ vt unr to stop.

Anhalter, in (mpl -) der, die hitchhiker ; per ~ fahren ODER reisen to hitchhike.

Anhaltspunkt (*pl* -e) *der* clue.

an|hängen *vt* (*Anhänger*) to hook up ; (*hinzufügen*) to add ; (*unterschieben*) : jm etw ~ to pin sthg on sb.

Anhänger (*pl* -) *der* (*Wagen*) trailer ; (*Schmuck*) pendant ; (*von Partei, Ideologie*) supporter.

Anhängerkupplung (*pl* -en) *die* tow hook.

anhänglich *adj* affectionate.

Anhieb *der* : auf ~ first time, straight off.

an|hören *vt* (*Musikstück, Kassette*) to listen to. ▪ **sich anhören** *ref* to sound ; sich gut/ schlecht ~ to sound good/bad.

Anker (*pl* -) *der* anchor.

an|kleben *vt* to stick.

Ankleidekabine (*pl* -n) *die* (changing) cubicle.

an|kommen *vi unr ist* (*Zug, Reisende, Brief*) to arrive ; (*gefallen*) to go down well ; ~ auf (+A) to depend on ; das kommt darauf an it depends.

an|kreuzen *vt* to mark with a cross.

an|kündigen *vt* (*Kursus, Vortrag*) to announce. ▪ **sich ankündigen** *ref* to announce itself ; es hat sich Besuch angekündigt we're expecting visitors.

Ankunft *die* arrival.

Anlage (*pl* -n) *die* (*Gelände*) park ; (*TECH*) (production) line.

an|lassen *vt unr* (*Motor*) to start up ; (*Kleidung, Licht, Apparat*) to leave on.

Anlasser (*pl* -) *der* starter.

Anlauf (*pl* -läufe) *der* (*SPORT*) run-up ; (*Versuch*) attempt.

an|laufen *vi unr ist* (*Motor, Aktion*) to start ; (*Brille, Spiegel*) to mist up. ◆ *vt unr hat* (*Hafen*) to call at.

an|legen *vt* (*Liste, Register*) to draw up ; (*Geld*) to invest ; (*Schmuck, Verband*) to put on ; (*Garten*) to lay out. ◆ *vi* (*Schiff*) to dock ; es darauf anlegen, etw zu tun to intend to do sthg. ▪ **sich anlegen** *ref* : sich mit jm ~ to pick a fight with sb.

Anlegestelle (*pl* -n) *die* mooring.

Anleitung (*pl* -en) *die* (*Hinweis*) instruction ; (*Text*) instructions (*pl*).

Anlieger, in (*mpl* -) *der, die* : '~ frei' 'residents only'.

an|machen *vt* (*Licht, Gerät*) to turn on ; (*fam* : *Person*) to chat up (*Br*), to hit on (*Am*) ; (*Salat*) to dress.

an|melden *vt* (*beim Arzt usw*) to make an appointment for ; (*Fernseher, Auto*) to register. ▪ **sich anmelden** *ref* to register ; sich ~ zu to enrol for.

Anmeldung (*pl* -en) *die* (*amtlich*) registration ; (*beim Arzt*) appointment ; (*Rezeption*) reception.

Anmietung *die* hire (*Br*), rental (*Am*).

an|nähen *vt* to sew on.

annähernd *adv* nearly.

Annahme (*pl* -n) *die* (*von Brief, Paket*) receipt ; (*Vermutung*) assumption ; 'keine ~ von 50-Pfennig-Stücken' 'this machine does not accept 50 Pfennig coins'.

an|nehmen *vt unr (vermuten)* to assume ; *(entgegennehmen, akzeptieren)* to accept ; *(Form)* to assume ; ~, **dass** to assume (that).

Annonce *(pl -n) die* classified advertisement.

Anorak *(pl -s) der* anorak.

an|packen *vt (berühren)* to seize ; *(fam : bewältigen)* to tackle.

an|passen *vt :* **etw an etw** *(A)* ~ to adapt sthg to sthg. ▪ **sich anpassen** *ref* to adapt.

Anpassung *die* adaptation.

an|probieren *vt* to try on.

Anrede *die* form of address.

an|regen *vt (Aktion)* to initiate ; *(Verdauung, Fantasie)* to stimulate. ◆ *vi (Tee, Kaffee)* to act as a stimulant.

Anregung *(pl -en) die (Hinweis)* suggestion ; *(Aktivierung)* stimulation.

an|richten *vt (Salat, Büfett)* to arrange ; *(Chaos, Schaden)* to cause.

Anruf *(pl -e) der* (phone) call.

Anrufbeantworter *(pl -) der* answerphone.

an|rufen *vt & vi unr (per Telefon)* to ring, to call.

Ansage *(pl -n) die* announcement.

an|schaffen *vt (kaufen)* to buy.

an|schauen *vt* to look at ; **sich** *(D)* **etw** ~ to look at sthg.

Anschein *der* appearance ; **es hat den** ~, **dass** it appears that.

anscheinend *adv* apparently.

an|schieben *vt unr* to push start.

Anschlag *(pl -schläge) der (Bekanntmachung)* notice ; *(Attentat)* assassination attempt.

an|schließen *vt unr (Elektrogerät)* to plug in ; *(Telefon)* to connect ; *(mit Schlüssel)* to lock. ▪ **sich anschließen** *ref unr (mit Meinung)* to agree ; **sich jm** ~ *(Gruppe)* to join sb.

anschließend *adv* afterwards.

Anschluss *(pl -schlüsse) der* connection ; *(Telefonapparat)* extension ; *(zu Personen)* **finden** to make friends ; **kein** ~ **unter dieser Nummer!** the number you have dialled has not been recognized ; **Sie haben** ~ **nach Basel, 15.39 Uhr** there is a connection to Basel at 15:39.

Anschlussflug *(pl -flüge) der* connecting flight.

an|schnallen *vt* to put on. ▪ **sich anschnallen** *ref* to fasten one's seatbelt.

Anschrift *(pl -en) die* address.

an|schwellen *vi unr ist (Körperteil)* to swell ; *(Gewässer)* to rise.

an|sehen *vt unr* to look at ; **sich** *(D)* **etw** ~ *(Film, Programm)* to watch sthg ; *(Stadt, Gebäude)* to look round sthg ; *(prüfend)* to look at sthg.

an|sein *vi unr ist* to be on.

an|setzen *vt (Bowle, Teig)* to prepare ; *(Kalk, Grünspan)* to become covered with ; *(Termin)* to fix ; **Rost ~** to rust.

Ansicht *(pl -en) die (von Stadt)* view ; *(Meinung)* opinion ; **meiner ~ nach** in my opinion.

Ansichtskarte *(pl -n) die* postcard.

ansonsten *adv* otherwise.

an|spielen *vi* : **~ auf** *(+A)* to allude to.

Anspielung *(pl -en) die* allusion.

Ansprache *(pl -n) die* speech.

an|springen *vt unr (angreifen)* to pounce on. ◆ *vi unr (Motor)* to start ; *(fam : auf Vorschlag, Angebot)* : **auf etw** *(A)* **~** to jump at sthg.

Anspruch *(pl -sprüche) der (Recht)* claim ; **~ auf etw** *(A)* **haben** to be entitled to sthg. ■ **Ansprüche** *pl (Forderungen)* demands.

anspruchslos *adj (bescheiden)* unpretentious.

anspruchsvoll *adj* demanding.

anstatt *präp (+G)* konj instead of.

an|stecken *vt (mit Krankheit)* to infect. ■ **sich anstecken** *ref* : sich mit etw **~** to catch sthg.

ansteckend *adj* infectious.

an|stehen *vi unr (in Warteschlange)* to queue *(Br)*, to stand in line *(Am)* ; *(Termin)* to be set ; *(Problem)* to need to be dealt with.

anstelle *präp (+G)* instead of.

an|stellen *vt (Gerät)* to turn on ; *(Mitarbeiter)* to employ ; *(Dummheiten)* to get up to. ■ **sich anstellen** *ref (War-*

tende) to queue *(Br)*, to stand in line *(Am)* ; **sich dumm bei etw ~** to make a mess of sthg ; **sich geschickt bei etw ~** to get the hang of sthg.

an|streichen *vt unr* to paint.

an|strengen *vt* to strain. ■ **sich anstrengen** *ref* to try (hard).

anstrengend *adj* tiring.

Antarktis *die* Antarctic.

Anteil *(pl -e) der* share.

Antenne *(pl -n) die* aerial.

Antibabypille *(pl -n) die* (contraceptive) pill.

Antibiotikum *(pl -ka) das* antibiotic.

Antihistamin *(pl -e) das* antihistamine.

antik *adj* antique.

Antillen *pl* West Indies.

Antiquariat *(pl -e) das* second-hand bookshop ; **modernes ~** remainder bookshop.

Antiquität *(pl -en) die* antique.

Antiquitätenhändler, in *(mpl -) der, die* antique dealer.

Antrag *(pl -träge) der* application ; **einen ~ auf etw** *(A)* **stellen** to apply for sthg.

an|treffen *vt unr* to find.

an|treiben *vt unr (zur Eile)* to urge ; *(Maschine)* to drive.

an|treten *vt* to start.

Antrieb *der (von Maschine)* drive ; *(Motivation)* impetus ; **aus eigenem ~** on one's own initiative.

Antritt *der* beginning ; **vor ~ der Reise** before setting off.

Antwort *(pl -en) die* answer.

antworten *vi* to answer ; auf etw *(A)* ~ to answer sthg ; jm ~ to answer sb.

An- und Verkauf *der* : '~ von Antiquitäten' 'antiques bought and sold'.

Anweisung (*pl* -en) *die (Befehl)* instruction ; *(von Geld)* money order.

an|wenden *vt unr* to use.

anwesend *adj* present.

Anwohner, in (*mpl* -) *der, die* resident.

Anwohnerparkplatz (*pl* -plätze) *der* residents' car park.

Anzahl *die* number.

Anzahlung (*pl* -en) *die* down payment.

Anzeichen (*pl* -) *das* sign.

Anzeige (*pl* -n) *die (in Zeitung)* advertisement ; *(bei Polizei)* report.

an|zeigen *vt (Delikt)* to report ; *(Temperatur, Zeit)* to show.

an|ziehen *vt unr (Kleidung, Schuhe)* to put on ; *(anlocken)* to attract ; *(Schraube, Knoten)* to tighten. ■ **sich anziehen** *ref unr* to get dressed.

Anzug (*pl* -züge) *der (Bekleidung)* suit.

anzüglich *adj* offensive.

an|zünden *vt* to light.

an|zweifeln *vt* to doubt.

AOK *die health insurance scheme for German workers, students etc not covered by private insurance policies.*

Apfel (*pl* Äpfel) *der* apple.

Apfelbaum (*pl* -bäume) *der* apple tree.

Apfelkorn *der* apple schnapps.

Apfelkuchen (*pl* -) *der* apple cake.

Apfelkücherl (*pl* -) *das (Süddt)* ring-shaped apple fritter, sprinkled with icing sugar.

Apfelmus *das* apple sauce.

Apfelsaft *der* apple juice.

Apfelsine (*pl* -n) *die* orange.

Apfelstrudel (*pl* -) *der* apple strudel.

Apfelwein *der* cider.

Apostroph (*pl* -e) *der* apostrophe.

Apotheke (*pl* -n) *die* chemist's shop *(Br)*, pharmacy *(Am)*.

apothekenpflichtig *adj* only available through a chemist.

Apotheker, in (*mpl* -) *der, die* pharmacist.

App. *abk* = Appartement.

Apparat (*pl* -e) *der (Gerät)* appliance ; *(Telefon)* telephone ; am ~! speaking!

Appartement (*pl* -s) *das (Wohnung)* flat *(Br)*, apartment *(Am)* ; *(im Hotel)* suite.

Appetit *der* appetite ; guten ~ enjoy your meal!

appetitlich *adj* appetizing.

Applaus *der* applause.

Aprikose (*pl* -n) *die* apricot.

April *der* April ; → September.

Aprilscherz (*pl* -e) *der* April Fool's trick.

apropos *adv* by the way.

Aquarell (*pl* -e) *das* watercolour.

Aquarium (*pl* -rien) *das* aquarium.

Äquator *der* equator.

Arbeit *(pl -en) die (Tätigkeit, Mühe)* work ; *(Arbeitsstelle, Aufgabe)* job ; *(in Schule)* test.

arbeiten *vi* to work.

Arbeiter, in *(mpl -) der, die* worker.

Arbeitgeber, in *(mpl -) der, die* employer.

Arbeitnehmer, in *(mpl -) der, die* employee.

Arbeitsamt *(pl -ämter) das* job centre.

Arbeitserlaubnis *(pl -se) die* work permit.

arbeitslos *adj* unemployed.

Arbeitslose *(pl -n) der, die* unemployed person.

Arbeitsplatz *(pl -plätze) der (Anstellung)* job ; *(Ort)* workplace.

Arbeitsteilung *die* division of labour.

Arbeitszeit *(pl -en) die* working hours *(pl)*.

Arbeitszimmer *(pl -) das* study.

Architekt, in *(mpl -en) der, die* architect.

Archiv *(pl -e) das* archive.

arg *(komp* ärger, *superl* am ärgsten) *adj* bad.

Ärger *der (Probleme)* trouble ; *(Zorn)* anger.

ärgerlich *adj (wütend)* annoyed ; *(unangenehm)* annoying.

ärgern *vt* to annoy. ■ **sich ärgern** *ref* to get annoyed ; sich ~ über *(+A)* to get annoyed at.

Argument *(pl -e) das* argument.

Arktis *die* Arctic.

arm *adj* poor.

Arm *(pl -e) der* arm.

Armaturenbrett *(pl -er) das* dashboard.

Armband *(pl -bänder) das (Schmuck)* bracelet ; *(von Uhr)* strap.

Armbanduhr *(pl -en) die* watch.

Armbruch *(pl -brüche) der* broken arm.

Armee *(pl -n) die* army.

Ärmel *(pl -) der* sleeve.

Ärmelkanal *der* (English) Channel.

Armlehne *(pl -n) die* armrest.

Aroma *(pl* Aromen) *das (Duft)* aroma ; *(Geschmacksrichtung)* flavour ; *(zum Backen)* flavouring.

arrogant *adj* arrogant.

Arsch *(pl* Ärsche) *der (vulg)* arse *(Br)*, ass *(Am)*.

Art *(pl -en) die (Weise)* way ; *(Wesen)* nature ; *(Sorte)* sort ; *(von Lebewesen)* species ; ~ **und Weise** way ; **auf seine ~** in his own way ; **eine ~ (von)** a kind of ; **Gulasch nach ~ des Hauses** chef's special goulash.

Arterie *(pl -n) die* artery.

artig *adj* good, well-behaved.

Artikel *(pl -) der* article.

Artischocke *(pl -n) die* artichoke.

Artist, in *(mpl -en) der, die (circus)* performer.

artistisch *adj* acrobatic.

Arznei *(pl -en) die* medicine.

Arzt *(pl* Ärzte) *der* doctor.

Arztausfahrt *(pl -en) der*: 'Arztausfahrt' sign indicating that *driveway should be kept clear as it is used by a doctor.*

Ạrzthelferin (pl -nen) die (doctor's) receptionist.

Ạrztin (pl -nen) die doctor.

ärztlich adj medical.

Ạsche die ash; 'keine heiße ~ einfüllen' 'no hot ashes'.

Ạschenbecher (pl -) der ashtray.

Ạschermittwoch der Ash Wednesday.

Asien nt Asia.

Aspẹkt (pl -e) der aspect.

Asphạlt (pl -e) der asphalt.

Aspirịn® das aspirin.

aß prät → **essen**.

Ạst (pl Äste) der branch.

Ạsthma das (MED) asthma.

Astrologie die astrology.

astrologisch adj astrological.

Astronomie die astronomy.

Asyl (pl -e) das (Schutz) asylum; (Unterkunft) hostel, home.

Ạtem der breath; außer ~ out of breath.

atemlos adj breathless. ◆ adv breathlessly.

Ạtemnot die difficulty in breathing.

Athlẹt, in (mpl -en) der, die athlete.

Atlạntik der Atlantic.

Atlạntische Ozean der Atlantic Ocean.

ạtmen vi & vt to breathe.

Ạtom (pl -e) das atom.

Atomkraft die nuclear power.

Atomkraftwerk (pl -e) das nuclear power station.

Atomwaffe (pl -n) die nuclear weapon.

Attentat (pl -e) das (erfolglos) assassination attempt; (erfolgreich) assassination.

Attẹst (pl -e) das doctor's certificate.

Attraktion (pl -en) die attraction.

attraktiv adj attractive.

Attrạppe (pl -n) die dummy.

ätzend adj (Chemikalie) corrosive; (fam: unangenehm) grim, gruesome.

au interj (Ausdruck von Schmerz) ow!; ~ ja! great!

AU (abk für Abgassonderuntersuchung) test of exhaust emissions.

Aubergine (pl -n) die aubergine (Br), eggplant (Am).

auch adv (ebenfalls) also, too; (sogar) even; wo ~ immer wherever; was ~ immer whatever; wer ~ immer whoever; ich ~ me too; ich ~ nicht me neither; hast du die Tür ~ wirklich zugemacht? are you sure you closed the door?

audiovisuẹll adj audiovisual.

auf präp (+D) 1. (räumlich) on; ~ dem Tisch on the table; ~ dem Land in the country; ~ der Post at the post office. 2. (während): ~ der Reise on the journey; ~ der Hochzeit/Party at the wedding/party.

◆ präp (+A) 1. (räumlich) on; ~ den Tisch on the table; ~s Land to the country; ~ eine Party gehen to go to a party. 2. (Angabe der Art und Weise): ~

diese Art in this way ; ~ Deutsch in German.

3. *(Angabe einer Beschäftigung)* : ~ Reisen gehen to go on a tour ; ~ die Uni gehen to go to university.

4. *(Angabe des Anlasses)* : ~ js Rat hin on sb's advice.

5. *(Angabe einer Folge)* : von heute ~ morgen overnight.

6. *(Angabe eines Wunsches)* : ~ Ihr Wohl! your good health!

◆ *adv (offen)* open ; Tür ~! open the door! ; *siehe auch* **auf sein**.

■ **auf einmal** *adv (plötzlich)* suddenly.

■ **auf und ab** *adv* up and down.

auf|atmen *vi* to breathe a sigh of relief.

Aufbau *der (Bauen)* building ; *(Struktur)* structure.

auf|bauen *vt (Zelt, Gerüst)* to put up ; *(Organisation)* to build up.

auf|bewahren *vt (Gepäck)* to leave ; *(Lebensmittel)* to store.

aufblasbar *adj* inflatable.

auf|bleiben *vi unr ist (Person)* to stay up ; *(Tür, Fenster)* to stay open.

auf|blenden *vi* to put one's headlights on full beam.

auf|brechen *vt unr hat* to force open. ◆ *vi unr ist (abreisen)* to set off.

auf|bringen *vt unr (Geld)* to raise.

Aufbruch *der* departure.

auf|decken *vt (Plane, Laken)* to turn back ; *(Geheimnis)* to uncover.

auf|drängen *vt : jm etw ~ to* force sthg on sb.

auf|drehen *vt (Wasserhahn)* to turn on.

aufdringlich *adj* pushy.

aufeinander *adv (einer auf dem anderen)* one on top of the other ; *(nacheinander)* one after the other ; *(aufpassen)* one another ; ~ eifersüchtig sein to be jealous of one another.

Aufenthalt *(pl -e) der (von Person)* stay ; *(Unterbrechung)* stop ; der Zug hat 10 Minuten ~ the train will stop for 10 minutes ; ständiger ~ place of residence ; schönen ~! have a nice stay!

Aufenthaltsgenehmigung *(pl -en) die* residence permit.

Aufenthaltsraum *(pl -räume) der* common room.

auf|essen *vt unr* to eat up.

auf|fahren *vi unr ist : dicht ~* to tailgate.

Auffahrt *(pl -en) die (zu Haus)* drive ; *(zu Autobahn)* slip road *(Br)*, ramp *(Am)*.

Auffahrunfall *(pl -unfälle) der* rear-end collision.

auf|fallen *vi unr ist* to stand out ; jm ~ to strike sb.

auffallend *adj* striking.

auffällig *adj (Benehmen)* odd ; *(Kleidung, Auto)* ostentatious. ◆ *adv (sich kleiden)* ostentatiously.

auf|fangen *vt unr (Ball)* to catch ; *(Funkspruch)* to pick up.

auf|fordern vt (bitten) to ask ; (befehlen) to require.

auf|frischen vt (Kenntnisse) to brush up on ; (Farbe) to brighten up.

auf|führen vt (auf Bühne) to perform ; (auf Liste) to list.

Aufführung (pl -en) die performance.

Aufgabe (pl -n) die (Arbeit) task ; (Verpflichtung) responsibility ; (bei Wettkampf) retirement ; (von Paket) posting ; (von Koffer) checking in ; (in der Schule) exercise.

Aufgang (pl -gänge) der (von Treppe) stairs (pl) ; (von Sonne) rising.

auf|geben vt unr (Gewohnheit, Stelle, Geschäft) to give up ; (Schularbeiten) to set ; (Paket, Brief) to post (Br), to mail (Am) ; (Koffer) to check in. ◆ vi (resignieren) to give up.

auf|gehen vi unr ist (Sonne, Mond) to rise ; (Knoten) to come undone.

aufgehoben pp → auf|heben. ◆ adj : gut/schlecht ~ sein to be/not to be in good hands.

aufgelegt adj : gut/schlecht ~ sein to be in a good/bad mood.

aufgrund präp (+G) because of.

auf|halten vt unr (Tür) to hold open ; (Person) to hold up.
■ **sich aufhalten** ref to stay.

auf|hängen vt to hang up.

auf|heben vt unr (aufbewahren) to keep ; (vom Boden) to pick up.

auf|hetzen vt to incite.

auf|holen vt to make up. ◆ vi to catch up.

auf|horchen vi to prick up one's ears.

auf|hören vi to stop ; ~, etw zu machen to stop doing sthg ; mit etw ~ to stop sthg.

auf|klappen vt to open.

auf|klären vt (Missverständnis) to clear up ; jn über etw (A) ~ to tell sb sthg.

Aufklärung die (von Missverständnis) clearing up ; (Information) information.

Aufkleber (pl -) der sticker.

auf|kommen vi unr ist (entstehen) to arise ; ~ für (zahlen) to pay for.

auf|krempeln vt : die Ärmel/Hosenbeine ~ to roll up one's sleeves/trouser legs.

auf|kriegen vt (fam) to get open.

Auflage (pl -n) die (von Buch) edition ; (von Zeitung) circulation ; (Bedingung) condition.

auf|lassen vt unr (Tür) to leave open ; (Mütze, Hut) to keep on.

Auflauf (pl -läufe) der (von Menschen) crowd ; (KÜCHE) bake.

auf|legen vt (Schallplatte, Tischdecke) to put on ; (Buch, Zeitschrift) to publish ; (Telefonhörer) to hang up.

auf|leuchten vi to light up.

auf|listen vt to list.

auf|lösen vt (Vertrag) to cancel ; (Tablette) to dissolve ; (Knoten) to undo.

Auflösung (*pl* -en) *die* (*von Rätsel*) solution; (*von Organisation, Verein*) disbanding.

auf|machen *vt* to open; jm ~ to let sb in. ▨ **sich aufmachen** *ref* (*abreisen*) to set off.

aufmerksam *adj* attentive; jn ~ machen auf (+A) to draw sb's attention to.

Aufmerksamkeit (*pl* -en) *die* (*Interesse*) attention; (*Geschenk*) gift.

Aufnahme (*pl* -n) *die* (*Foto*) photograph; (*von Musik*) recording; (*von Protokoll, Aussage*) taking down; (*in Krankenhaus, Verein*) admission.

auf|nehmen *vt unr* (*Gast*) to receive; (*Foto*) to take; (*Musik*) to record; (*Protokoll, Aussage*) to take down; mit jm Kontakt ~ to contact sb.

Aufnehmer (*pl* -) *der* (floor) cloth.

auf|passen *vi* to pay attention; ~ auf (+A) to look after; pass auf! be careful!

auf|pumpen *vt* to pump up.

auf|räumen *vt* (*Raum*) to tidy up; (*Gegenstand*) to put away. ◆ *vi* to tidy up.

auf|regen *vt* to excite. ▨ **sich aufregen** *ref* to get worked up.

Aufregung (*pl* -en) *die* excitement.

auf|rollen *vt* (*Leine, Schnur*) to roll up.

Aufruf *der* call; letzter ~ last call; 'dringender ~ für Flug LH 404' 'last call for passengers on flight LH 404'.

auf|rufen *vt unr* to call.

auf|runden *vt* to round up.

Aufsatz (*pl* -sätze) *der* (SCHULE) essay.

auf|schieben *vt unr* to put off.

Aufschlag (*pl* -schläge) *der* (SPORT) serve; (*auf Preis*) extra charge.

auf|schließen *vt unr* to unlock.

Aufschnitt *der* sliced cold meat and cheese.

auf|schreiben *vt unr* to write down.

Aufsehen *das* : ~ erregen to cause a stir.

auf sein *vi unr* ist (*fam* : *offen sein*) to be open; (*Person*) to be up.

Aufsicht *die* (*Person*) supervisor; (*Kontrolle*) supervision.

auf|spannen *vt* (*Regenschirm*) to open.

Aufstand (*pl* -stände) *der* rebellion.

auf|stehen *vi unr* ist to get up. ◆ *vt unr* hat (*Tür, Fenster*) to be open.

auf|stellen *vt* (*Zelt*) to put up; (*Behauptung*) to put forward.

Aufstellung (*pl* -en) *die* (*von Mannschaft*) line-up; (*von Behauptung*) putting forward.

Aufstieg *der* (*auf Berg*) climb; (*in Sport, Arbeit*) promotion.

auf|stocken *vt* (*erhöhen*) to increase.

Auftakt (*pl* -e) *der* (MUS) upbeat; (*Beginn*) start.

auf|tanken *vi* to fill up.

aus

auf|tauchen vi ist (erscheinen, auftreten) to appear ; (aus dem Wasser) to surface.

auf|tauen vt (Gefrorenes) to thaw.

auf|teilen vt to share out.

Auftrag (pl -träge) der (Aufgabe) job ; (Bestellung) order.

auf|tragen vt unr (Farbe) to apply ; (befehlen) : jm ~, etw zu tun to tell sb to do sthg.

auf|treten vi unr ist (sich benehmen) to behave ; (auf Bühne) to appear ; (Problem) to come up.

Auftritt (pl -e) der (Theater) entrance.

auf|wachen vi ist to wake up.

Aufwand der (Geld) expenditure ; (Anstrengung) effort.

auf|wärmen vt (Essen) to warm up.

aufwärts adv upwards.

auf|wecken vt to wake (up).

auf|werten vt (Ansehen) to enhance.

auf|wischen vt to wipe up.

auf|zählen vt to list.

auf|zeichnen vt (mit Skizze) to draw ; (Film, Musik) to record.

auf|ziehen vt unr (Uhr) to wind up ; (Kind) to bring up ; (Tier) to raise.

Aufzug (pl -züge) der (Fahrstuhl) lift (Br), elevator (Am).

Auge (pl -n) das eye ; unter vier ~n in private ; ein blaues ~ a black eye ; etw im ~ behalten to keep sthg in mind.

Augenblick (pl -e) der moment ; einen ~, bitte! just a moment, please! ; im ~ at the moment.

augenblicklich adv (sofort) immediately.

Augenbraue (pl -n) die eyebrow.

Augenbrauenstift (pl -e) der eyebrow pencil.

Augencreme (pl -s) die eye cream.

Augenfarbe (pl -n) die : welche ~ hat sie? what colour are her eyes?

Augenoptiker, in (mpl -) der, die optician.

Augentropfen pl eyedrops.

August der August ; → September.

Auktion (pl -en) die auction.

aus präp (+D) 1. (zur Angabe der Richtung) out of ; ~ dem Haus gehen to go out of the house. 2. (zur Angabe der Herkunft) from ; ~ Amerika from America. 3. (zur Angabe des Materials) made of ; ~ Plastik made of plastic. 4. (zur Angabe des Grundes) for ; ~ welchem Grund...? for what reason...?, why...? ; ~ Spaß for fun ; ~ Wut in anger. 5. (zur Angabe der Entfernung) from ; ~ 50 m Entfernung from 50 m away. 6. (zur Angabe eines Teils) of ; einer ~ der Gruppe a member of the group.

◆ adv 1. (außer Funktion) off ; hier schaltet man die Maschine an und ~ this is where you switch the machine on and off ; Licht ~! lights out! ; siehe auch **aus sein.**

2. *(zu Ende)* over ; ~ **und vorbei** all over.

Aus *das* : **ins ~ gehen** *(SPORT)* to go out of play.

aus|arbeiten *vt (Entwurf)* to draw up ; *(Projekt)* to work on.

aus|baden *vt* : **etw ~ müssen** to take the blame for sthg.

aus|bauen *vt (Straße, Haus)* to extend ; *(Dach)* to convert ; *(Kenntnisse)* to expand ; *(Motor, Teil)* to remove.

aus|bessern *vt* to mend.

aus|beulen *vt* to beat out.

Ausbildung *(pl -en) die (schulisch)* education ; *(beruflich, fachlich)* training.

aus|brechen *vi unr ist* to break out.

aus|breiten *vt* to spread out.
■ **sich ausbreiten** *ref* to spread ; *(Landschaft)* to stretch out.

ausdauernd *adj* persevering.

aus|denken *vt unr* : **sich** *(D)* **etw ~** to think sthg up.

Ausdruck[1] *(pl -drücke) der* expression.

Ausdruck[2] *(pl -e) der (EDV)* printout.

aus|drücken *vt (sagen)* to express. ■ **sich ausdrücken** *ref* to express o.s.

auseinander *adv* apart.

auseinander gehen *vi unr ist (Personen)* to break up ; *(Wege)* to fork ; *(Vorhang)* to open ; *(Meinungen)* to differ.

auseinander nehmen *vt unr* to dismantle.

Auseinandersetzung *(pl -en) die* argument.

aus|fahren *vt unr hat (Ware)* to deliver ; *(spazieren fahren)* to take for a drive. ◆ *vi unr ist (Person)* to go for a drive.

Ausfahrt *(pl -en) die* exit ; '~ **freihalten!**' 'keep clear!'

aus|fallen *vi unr ist (Aufführung, Konzert)* to be cancelled ; *(Gerät)* to break down ; *(Strom)* to be cut off ; *(Haare, Zähne)* to fall out ; **gut/schlecht ~** to turn out well/badly ; **die Schule fällt heute aus** there's no school today.

ausfindig *adv* : **jn/etw ~ machen** to locate sb/sthg.

Ausflug *(pl -flüge) der* trip.

Ausflugsboot *(pl -e) das* pleasure boat.

Ausflugslokal *(pl -e) das* cafe or pub in the countryside, to which you can drive or walk out.

Ausflugsziel *(pl -e) das* destination *(of a trip)*.

Ausfluss *(pl -flüsse) der (MED)* discharge ; *(von Wanne, Becken)* plughole.

aus|fragen *vt* to interrogate.

aus|führen *vt (ins Ausland)* to export ; *(zum Essen, Tanzen)* to take out ; *(Arbeit, Plan, Befehl)* to carry out ; *(Hund)* to walk.

ausführlich *adj* detailed. ◆ *adv* in detail.

aus|füllen *vt (Formular)* to fill out ; *(Raum)* to fill.

Ausgabe *(pl -n) die (von Geld)* expenditure ; *(von Essen)* serving ; *(von Buch)* edition. ■ **Ausgaben** *pl* expenditure *(sg)*.

Ausgang (pl -gänge) der (von Haus, Raum) exit; (von Dorf, Wald) end.

aus|geben vt unr (Geld) to spend; (verteilen) to give out; jm etw ~ (fam) to buy sb sthg. ▦ **sich ausgeben** ref: sich als etw ~ to pretend to be sthg.

ausgebucht adj fully-booked.

ausgefallen adj (Geschmack, Idee) unusual.

aus|gehen vi unr (Licht, Person) to go out; (Heizung) to go off; (Motor) to stop; (Film, Roman) to end; mir ist das Geld ausgegangen my money has run out; davon ~, dass to assume (that).

ausgelastet adj: voll ~ sein to have one's hands full; nicht ~ sein not to be stretched.

ausgeleiert adj baggy.

ausgenommen konj except.

ausgerechnet adv precisely; ~ du! you of all people!; ~ heute! today of all days!

ausgeschaltet adj (switched) off.

ausgeschildert adj signposted.

ausgeschlossen adj (unmöglich): ~ sein to be impossible.

ausgestellt adj: auf jn ~ (Scheck) made out to sb; (Pass) issued to sb.

ausgewiesen adj: ~ durch den Reisepass passport used as proof of identity.

ausgewogen adj balanced.

ausgezeichnet adj (sehr gut) excellent; (mit Preis) priced. ◆ adv (sehr gut) extremely well.

ausgiebig adj (Frühstück) large.

aus|gießen vt unr (Flüssigkeit) to pour out; (Gefäß) to empty.

aus|gleichen vt unr (Differenzen) to even out; (Mangel) to make up for.

Ausguss (pl -güsse) der drain.

aus|halten vt unr to stand.

Aushang (pl -hänge) der notice.

aus|helfen vi unr to help out.

Aushilfe (pl -n) die (im Büro) temp.

aus|holen vi (mit Arm) to move one's arm back.

aus|kennen ▦ sich auskennen refunr (in Stadt) to know one's way around; (in Fach) to be an expert.

aus|kommen vi unr ist: mit etw ~ to make sthg last; mit jm gut/schlecht ~ to get on well/badly with sb; mit jm nicht ~ not to get on with sb.

Auskunft (pl -künfte) die (Information) information; (am Telefon) directory enquiries (pl) (Br), information (Am); (Schalter) information office.

aus|lachen vt to laugh at.

aus|laden vt unr (Gepäck, Fahrzeug) to unload; (Gäste): jn ~ to tell sb not to come.

Auslage (pl -n) die display. ▦ **Auslagen** pl (Spesen) expenses.

Ausland das: im ~ abroad; ins ~ abroad.

Ausländer, in (*mpl* -) *der, die* foreigner.

ausländisch *adj* foreign.

Auslandsgespräch (*pl* -e) *das* international call.

Auslandsschutzbrief (*pl* -e) *der motor insurance document for travel abroad*, ≃ green card (*Br*).

aus|lassen *vt unr* (*überspringen*) to leave out ; (*Gelegenheit*) to miss ; etw an jm ~ (*Ärger, Wut*) to take sthg out on sb.

Auslauf *der* : ~ haben/brauchen to have/need plenty of room (to run about).

aus|laufen *vi unr ist* (*Flüssigkeit*) to run out ; (*Gefäß, Tank*) to leak.

aus|legen *vt* (*Ware*) to display ; (*Geld*) to lend ; ein Zimmer mit Teppichen ~ to carpet a room.

aus|leihen *vt unr* : jm etw ~ to lend sb sthg ; sich (*D*) etw ~ to borrow sthg.

Auslese (*pl* -n) *die* (*Auswahl*) selection ; (*Wein*) quality wine made from specially-selected grapes.

aus|löschen *vt* to extinguish.

Auslöser (*pl* -) *der* (*am Fotoapparat*) (shutter release) button.

aus|machen *vt* (*Feuer, Zigarette*) to put out ; (*Licht, Gerät*) to turn off ; (*absprechen*) to agree on ; (*Termin*) to make ; mit jm ~, dass etw gemacht wird to arrange with sb to have sthg done ; das macht mir nichts aus I don't mind ; macht es Ihnen

etwas aus, wenn ich rauche? do you mind if I smoke?

Ausmaß (*pl* -e) *das* extent.

Ausnahme (*pl* -n) *die* exception ; eine ~ machen to make an exception.

ausnahmsweise *adv* just this once.

aus|nutzen *vt* (*Gelegenheit, Zeit*) to use ; (*Person*) to exploit.

aus|packen *vt* to unpack.

Auspuff (*pl* -e) *der* exhaust.

aus|rangieren *vt* (*Auto*) to scrap ; (*Kleider*) to throw out.

aus|rechnen *vt* to calculate ; sich (*D*) gute Chancen ~ to fancy one's chances.

Ausrede (*pl* -n) *die* excuse.

aus|reichen *vi* to be enough ; es muss bis März ~ it has to last until March.

Ausreise *die* : bei der ~ on leaving the country.

Ausreisegenehmigung (*pl* -en) *die* exit visa.

aus|reißen *vi unr ist* to run away. ♦ *vt unr hat* to pull out.

aus|renken *vt* : sich (*D*) die Schulter ~ to dislocate one's shoulder.

aus|richten *vt* : jm etw ~ to tell sb sthg.

aus|rufen *vt unr* (*über Lautsprecher*) to announce ; jn ~ lassen to page sb.

Ausrufezeichen (*pl* -) *das* exclamation mark.

aus|ruhen : sich ausruhen *ref* to rest.

Ausrüstung (*pl* -en) *die* (*für Sport*) equipment.

aus|rutschen *vi ist* to slip.

aus|sagen *vt* to state.

aus|schalten *vt* to switch off.

Ausschank *der (von Getränken)* serving.

Ausschau *die* : ~ halten nach to look out for.

aus|schlafen *vi unr* to lie in ; **bist du ausgeschlafen?** did you get enough sleep?

Ausschlag *(pl* -schläge) *der (MED)* rash ; **den ~ geben** to be the decisive factor.

aus|schließen *vt unr* to exclude.

ausschließlich *adv* exclusively. ◆ *präp (+G)* excluding.

aus|schneiden *vt unr* to cut out.

Ausschreitungen *pl* violent clashes.

aus|schütteln *vt* to shake out.

aus|schütten *vt (Gefäß)* to empty ; *(Flüssigkeit)* to pour out.

aus|schwenken *vi ist* to swing out.

aus|sehen *vi unr* to look ; **gut/schlecht ~** *(Person, Gegenstand)* to look nice/horrible ; *(Situation)* to look good/bad ; **wie sieht es aus?** *(Situation)* how are you getting on? ; **es sieht nach Regen aus** it looks like rain.

aus sein *vi unr ist (zu Ende sein)* to be over ; *(Gerät, Heizung)* to be off ; *(Feuer)* to be out ; **~ auf** *(+A)* to be after.

außen *adv* outside ; **von ~** from the outside ; **nach ~** outwards.

Außenbordmotor *(pl* -en) *der* outboard motor.

Außenrückspiegel *(pl* -) *der* door mirror.

Außenseite *(pl* -n) *die* outside.

Außenseiter, in *(mpl* -) *der, die* outsider.

Außenspiegel *(pl* -) *der* door mirror.

Außentemperatur *(pl* -en) *die* outside temperature.

außer *präp (+D) (ausgenommen)* except (for) ; *(neben)* as well as. ◆ *konj* except ; **ich komme, ~ es regnet** I'll come, unless it rains ; **alle, ~ ihm** everyone except (for) him ; **nichts, ~...** nothing but... ; **~ sich sein** *(vor (+D))* to be beside o.s. (with) ; **~ Betrieb** out of order.

außerdem *adv* also, moreover.

außergewöhnlich *adj* unusual. ◆ *adv* exceptionally.

außerhalb *präp (+G)* outside. ◆ *adv* out of town.

äußerlich *adj* external. ◆ *adv* externally.

äußern *vt* to express. ■ **sich äußern** *ref (erkennbar werden)* to show (itself) ; *(sprechen)* to speak ; **sich ~ zu** to comment on.

außerordentlich *adj* extraordinary. ◆ *adv* exceptionally.

außerplanmäßig *adj (Zug)* extra, special.

äußerst *adv* extremely.

aus|setzen *vt (Hund, Kind)* to abandon ; *(Preis, Belohnung)* to offer. ◆ *vi (Herz, Musik)* to stop ; *(bei Spiel)* to miss one's turn ; **an allem etwas auszusetzen**

haben to constantly find fault with everything.

Aussicht (*pl* -en) die (*Blick*) view ; (*Chance*) prospect.

aussichtslos *adj* hopeless.

Aussichtsplattform (*pl* -en) die viewing platform.

Aussichtspunkt (*pl* -e) der viewpoint.

Aussichtsterrasse (*pl* -n) die cafe terrace with a view.

Aussichtsturm (*pl* -türme) der lookout tower.

aus|spannen *vi* (*sich erholen*) to relax.

aus|sperren *vt* (*aus Raum*) to lock out.

Aussprache (*pl* -n) die (*von Wörtern*) pronunciation ; (*Gespräch*) discussion (*to resolve a dispute*).

aus|sprechen *vt unr* (*Wort, Satz*) to pronounce ; (*Gedanke, Verdacht*) to express. ◆ *vi unr* (*zu Ende reden*) to finish (speaking). ▨ **sich aussprechen** *ref unr* to pour one's heart out ; **sich mit jm ~** to talk things through with sb.

aus|spucken *vt* to spit out. ◆ *vi* to spit.

aus|spülen *vt* (*Glas, Mund*) to rinse out ; (*Wunde*) to wash ; (*Haare*) to rinse.

Ausstattung (*pl* -en) die (*Ausrüstung*) equipment ; (*von Zimmer*) furnishings (*pl*) ; (*von Auto*) fittings (*pl*).

aus|steigen *vi unr ist* (*aus Fahrzeug*) to get out ; '~ bitte Knopf drücken' 'press to open'.

aus|stellen *vt* (*Gerät*) to turn off ; (*in Museum, Ausstellung*) to display ; (*Pass*) to issue ; (*Quittung*) to write out.

Ausstellung (*pl* -en) die (*in Museum*) exhibition.

aus|sterben *vi unr ist* to die out.

aus|strahlen *vt* (*Programm*) to broadcast. ◆ *vi* (*Freude, Ruhe*) to radiate.

Ausstrahlung die (*von Programm*) broadcasting ; (*von Person*) charisma.

aus|strecken *vt* to stretch out. ▨ **sich ausstrecken** *ref* to stretch.

aus|streichen *vt unr* (*Satz*) to cross out.

aus|suchen *vt* to choose ; **sich** (D) **etw ~** to choose sthg.

aus|teilen *vt* to distribute.

Auster (*pl* -n) die oyster.

Australien *nt* Australia.

aus|trinken *vt unr* (*Glas*) to empty ; (*Bier*) to finish.

aus|trocknen *vt hat* (*Erde, Haut*) to dry out. ◆ *vi ist* to dry out.

Ausverkauf der clearance sale.

ausverkauft *adj* sold out.

Auswahl die selection, choice.

aus|wandern *vi ist* to emigrate.

auswärts *adv* : **~ essen** to eat out ; **~ spielen** to play away (from home).

aus|wechseln *vt* (*ersetzen*) to replace ; (*Fußballspieler*) to substitute.

aus|weichen *vi unr ist* (+D) (*vor Auto, Frage*) to avoid.

Ausweis (*pl* -e) *der (Personalausweis)* identity card ; *(für Bibliothek, Studenten)* card.

Ausweiskontrolle (*pl* -n) *die* identity card check.

Ausweisnummer (*pl* -n) *die* identity card number.

Ausweispapiere *pl* identification *(sg)*.

auswendig *adv* by heart.

aus|wringen *vt unr* to wring out.

aus|wuchten *vt* to balance.

aus|zahlen *vt (Lohn, Zinsen)* to pay. ■ **sich auszahlen** *ref* to pay.

Auszahlungsbetrag (*pl* -beträge) *der* total payment.

aus|zeichnen *vt (ehren)* to honour ; *(mit Preisschild)* to price.

aus|ziehen *vt unr* hat *(Kleidung, Schuhe)* to take off ; *(Antenne, Tisch)* to extend ; *(Person)* to undress. ◆ *vi unr* ist *(aus Wohnung)* to move out. ■ **sich ausziehen** *ref* to undress ; **sich die Schuhe ~** to take one's shoes off.

Auszubildende (*pl* -n) *der*, *die* trainee.

Auto (*pl* -s) *das* car ; **mit dem ~ fahren** to go by car, to drive.

Autoatlas (*pl* -atlanten) *der* road atlas.

Autobahn (*pl* -en) *die* motorway *(Br)*, freeway *(Am)*.

ⓘ **AUTOBAHN**

At over 11,000 km, the German motorway network is the second longest in the world after the United States. There is no speed limit on German motorways, although there is a recommended limit of 130 km/h. No toll is charged for using the motorway.

Autobahngebühr (*pl* -en) *die* toll.

Autobahnkreuz (*pl* -e) *das* interchange.

Autobahnmeisterei (*pl* -en) *die* motorway maintenance department.

Autobahnring (*pl* -e) *der* motorway ring road *(Br)*, beltway *(Am)*.

Autobus (*pl* -se) *der* bus.

Autofähre (*pl* -n) *die* car ferry.

Autofahrer, in (*mpl* -) *der*, *die* (car) driver.

Autogramm (*pl* -e) *das* autograph.

Automat (*pl* -en) *der (für Zigaretten, Fahrkarten usw.)* vending machine.

Automatik *die (AUTO)* automatic transmission.

Automatikgetriebe (*pl* -) *das (AUTO)* automatic transmission.

Automatikwagen (*pl* -) *der* automatic (car).

automatisch *adj* automatic. ◆ *adv* automatically.

Autor (*pl* Autoren) *der* author.

Autoradio (*pl* -s) *das* car radio.

Autoreifen (*pl* -) *der* car tyre.

Autoreisezug (*pl* -züge) *der* ~ motorail train.

Autoreparatur (pl -en) die car repairs (pl).

Autorin (pl -nen) die author.

Autoschlange (pl -n) die tailback.

Autostopp der hitchhiking ; per ~ fahren to hitch-hike.

Autounfall (pl -unfälle) der car accident.

Autovermietung (pl -en) die (Firma) car hire firm (Br), car rental firm (Am).

Autowaschanlage (pl -n) die car wash.

Autowäsche (pl -n) die car wash.

Autowaschstraße (pl -n) die drive-through car wash.

Autozubehör das car accessories (pl).

Avocado (pl -s) die avocado.

Axt (pl Äxte) die axe.

B

B (pl -) abk = **Bundesstraße**.

Baby (pl -s) das baby.

Babybett (pl -en) das cot (Br), crib (Am).

Babyfläschchen (pl -) das baby's bottle.

Babynahrung die baby food.

Babysitter, in (mpl -) der, die babysitter.

Babysitz (pl -e) der child seat.

Baby-Wickelraum (pl -räume) der parent and baby room.

Bach (pl Bäche) der stream.

Backbord das port.

Backe (pl -n) die (Wange) cheek.

backen vt & vi unr to bake.

Bäcker, in (mpl -) der, die baker.

Bäckerei (pl -en) die bakery.

Backmischung (pl -en) die cake mix.

Backofen (pl -öfen) der oven.

Backpflaume (pl -n) die prune.

Backpulver das baking powder.

bäckt präs → backen.

Backwaren pl bread, cakes and pastries.

Bad (pl Bäder) das (Badezimmer) bathroom ; (Baden) bath ; (Kurort) spa ; mit ~ und WC with en suite bathroom ; ein ~ nehmen to have a bath.

BAD

When a place name begins with the word "Bad", as for example in "Bad Ems" or "Bad Tölz", this indicates that it is a spa town with a medicinal spring, or a health resort with a beneficial climate. A stay in one of these places may be prescribed by a doctor for people who are ill or convalescing, and the costs are covered by the "Krankenkasse".

Badeanzug (pl -anzüge) der swimming costume, swimsuit.

Badegast (pl -gäste) der (im Badeort) visitor ; (im Schwimmbad) bather.

Badehose (*pl* -n) *die* swimming trunks (*pl*).

Badekappe (*pl* -n) *die* swimming cap.

Bademeister, in (*mpl* -) *der, die* pool attendant.

Bademütze (*pl* -n) *die* swimming cap.

baden *vi* (*in Badewanne*) to have a bath ; (*schwimmen*) to swim. ◆ *vt* to bath ; ~ **gehen** to go for a swim.

Baden-Würtemberg *nt* Baden-Würtemberg.

Badeort (*pl* -e) *der* (seaside) resort.

Badesachen *pl* swimming things.

Badetuch (*pl* -tücher) *das* bath towel.

Badewanne (*pl* -n) *die* bath (tub).

Badezimmer (*pl* -) *das* bathroom.

Badminton *das* badminton.

baff *adj* : ~ **sein** (*fam*) to be gobsmacked.

BAFöG *das* maintenance grant awarded to students and apprentices by the state.

Bagger (*pl* -) *der* mechanical digger.

Baggersee (*pl* -n) *der* artificial lake where people go to have picnics, swim etc.

Bahn (*pl* -en) *die* (*Zug*) train ; (*Straßenbahn*) tram (*Br*), streetcar (*Am*) ; (*von Rakete, Planet*) path ; (*in Schwimmbad, Stadion*) lane ; (*von Stoff, Tapete*) strip ; **die** ~ (*Bundesbahn*) German rail company ; **drei ~en schwimmen** to swim three lengths ; **jn zur ~**

bringen to take sb to the station ; **mit der** ~ by train, by rail.

Bahnbus (*pl* -se) *der* bus run by railway company.

Bahncard (*pl* -s) *die* railcard.

Bahnfracht *die* : **per** ~ by rail (freight).

Bahngesellschaft *die* one of the rail companies that make up the German Bundesbahn.

Bahnhof (*pl* -höfe) *der* (railway) station.

Bahnhofsmission (*pl* -en) *die* room at a station where charitable organizations provide care for rail travellers.

Bahnlinie (*pl* -n) *die* (*Strecke*) railway line (*Br*), railroad line (*Am*).

Bahnpolizei *die* railway police (*Br*), railroad police (*Am*).

Bahnsteig (*pl* -e) *der* platform ; **am selben** ~ **gegenüber** on the opposite side of the platform.

Bahnübergang (*pl* -übergänge) *der* level crossing (*Br*), grade crossing (*Am*) ; **unbeschrankter** ~ level crossing with no barrier.

Bahnverbindung (*pl* -en) *die* (train) connection.

Bakterie (*pl* -n) *die* germ.

balancieren *vt* & *vi* to balance.

bald *adv* soon ; (*fam : fast*) almost ; **bis** ~! see you soon!

Baldrian *der* valerian.

Balken (*pl* -) *der* beam.

Balkon (*pl* -e) *der* balcony.

Ball (*pl* Bälle) *der* ball.

Ballett (*pl* -e) *das* ballet.

Ballon (*pl* -s) *der* balloon.

Ballspiel (*pl* -e) *das* ball game.

Ballungsgebiet (*pl* -e) *das* conurbation.

banal *adj* (*abw* : geistlos) banal ; (einfach) everyday.

Banane (*pl* -n) *die* banana.

band *prät* → **binden**.

Band¹ (*pl* Bänder) *das* (Schnur) ribbon ; (Tonband) tape.

Band² (*pl* Bände) *der* (Buch) volume.

Band³ (*pl* -s) *die* (MUS) band.

Bandage (*pl* -n) *die* bandage.

bandagieren *vt* to bandage.

Bandscheibe (*pl* -n) *die* disc (in spine).

Bank¹ (*pl* -en) *die* bank.

Bank² (*pl* Bänke) *die* bench.

Bankanweisung (*pl* -en) *die* standing order.

Bankett (*pl* -e) *das* banquet.

Bankkonto (*pl* -konten) *das* bank account.

Bankleitzahl (*pl* -en) *die* bank sort code.

Banknote (*pl* -n) *die* banknote.

bankrott *adj* bankrupt.

Bankverbindung (*pl* -en) *die* account details (*pl*).

bar *adv* (in) cash. ◆ *adj* : ~es Geld cash ; in ~ in cash.

Bar (*pl* -s) *die* bar.

Bär (*pl* -en) *der* bear.

barfuß *adv* barefoot. ◆ *adj* : ~ sein to be barefoot.

barg *prät* → **bergen**.

Bargeld *das* cash.

bargeldlos *adj* cash-free. ◆ *adv* without using cash.

Bariton (*pl* -e) *der* baritone.

Barkeeper (*pl* -) *der* barman.

barock *adj* baroque.

Barometer (*pl* -) *das* barometer.

Barriere (*pl* -n) *die* barrier.

barsch *adj* curt.

Barscheck (*pl* -s) *der* uncrossed cheque.

Bart (*pl* Bärte) *der* beard.

Barzahlung (*pl* -en) *die* payment in cash ; Verkauf nur gegen ~ cash sales only.

Basar (*pl* -e) *der* bazaar.

Basel *nt* Basel, Basle.

Basilikum *das* basil.

Basis *die* (Grundlage) basis.

Basketball *der* basketball.

Bass (*pl* Bässe) *der* bass.

basteln *vt* to make. ◆ *vi* : er bastelt gerne he likes making things himself.

bat *prät* → **bitten**.

Batterie (*pl* -n) *die* battery ; wieder aufladbare ~ rechargeable battery.

batteriebetrieben *adj* battery-powered.

Bau¹ (*pl* -ten) *der* (Vorgang, Gebäude) building ; (Baustelle) building site.

Bau² (*pl* -e) *der* (von Tier) hole.

Bauarbeiten *pl* construction work (*sg*) ; 'wegen ~ gesperrt' 'road closed due to construction work'.

Bauarbeiter, **in** (*mpl* -) *der*, *die* builder.

Bauch (*pl* Bäuche) *der* stomach.

Bauchschmerzen *pl* stomach-ache (*sg*) ; ~ haben to have stomach-ache.

Bauchspeck *der* belly pork.

Bauchspeicheldrüse (pl -n) die pancreas.

Baudenkmal (pl -mäler) das monument.

bauen vt (Haus, Straße, Auto) to build ; (Möbel, Maschine) to make. ◆ vi to build ; **an etw** (D) ~ to be building sthg ; ~ **auf** (+A) to rely on.

Bauer (pl -n) der (Beruf) farmer ; (Schachfigur) pawn ; (Spielkarte) jack.

Bäuerin (pl -nen) die farmer's wife.

Bauernbrot (pl -e) das farmhouse loaf.

Bauernfrühstück (pl -e) das fried potatoes with scrambled egg and pieces of bacon.

Bauernhof (pl -höfe) der farm. ◆

baufällig adj dilapidated.

Baum (pl Bäume) der tree.

Baumarkt (pl -märkte) der DIY store.

Baumwolle die cotton.

Baustelle (pl -n) die building site ; 'Vorsicht ~!' 'men at work'.

Baustellenausfahrt(pl -en) die works exit.

Bauwerk (pl -e) das building.

Bayern nt Bavaria.

Bayreuther Festspiele pl Wagner festival held annually in the town of Bayreuth.

ⓘ **BAYREUTHER FESTSPIELE**

Every August, a Wagner Festival is held in Bayreuth (Bavaria), commemorating the town's most famous son, Richard Wagner. Events are staged in the "Festspielhaus" (festival theatre), which was built without an orchestra pit, in accordance with Wagner's wishes. The Bayreuth Festival has become world-famous and attracts thousands of visitors each year.

Bazillus (pl Bazillen) der germ.

Bd. (abk für Band) vol.

beabsichtigen vt to intend.

beachten vt (Verbot) to observe ; (Person) to notice.

Beamte (pl -n) der (bei Finanzamt, Botschaft) civil servant ; (Polizist, beim Zoll) officer.

Beamtin (pl -nen) die (bei Finanzamt, Botschaft) civil servant ; (Polizist, beim Zoll) officer.

beanspruchen vt (strapazieren) to wear out ; (Zeit, Platz) to take up ; **jn stark** ~ to keep sb very busy.

beanstanden vt to complain about ; **es gibt nichts zu** ~ there's no cause for complaint.

Beanstandung (pl -en) die complaint.

beantragen vt to apply for.

beantworten vt to answer.

bearbeiten vt (Antrag) to deal with ; (Feld, Stein, Holz) to work.

Bearbeitungsgebühr (pl -en) die handling charge.

beatmen vt : **jn künstlich** ~ (MED) to put sb on a respirator.

beaufsichtigen *vt* to supervise.

beauftragen *vt* : jn mit etw ~ to entrust sthg to sb ; jn ~, etw zu tun to instruct sb to do sthg.

Becher (*pl* -) der (*zum Trinken*) cup (*without handles*) ; (*aus Plastik*) beaker ; (*für Eis*) dish ; (*für Joghurt*) pot.

Becken (*pl* -) das (*Waschbecken*) basin ; (*Spülbecken*) sink ; (*Schwimmbecken*) pool ; (*Körperteil*) pelvis ; (MUS) cymbal.

Beckenrand der edge of the pool ; 'Springen vom ~ nicht erlaubt!' 'no diving!'

bedanken : sich bedanken *ref* : sich (bei jm) ~ to say thank you (to sb).

Bedarf der need ; bei ~ if necessary.

Bedarfshaltestelle (*pl* -n) die request stop.

bedauerlich *adj* unfortunate.

bedauern *vt* (*bemitleiden*) to feel sorry for ; (*schade finden*) to regret. ◆ *vi* to be sorry ; bedaure! I'm sorry!

bedecken *vt* (*Boden, Schultern*) to cover.

bedeckt *adj* overcast.

bedeuten *vt* (*meinen*) to mean ; das hat nichts zu ~ that doesn't matter.

bedeutend *adj* important.

Bedeutung (*pl* -en) die (*Sinn, Inhalt*) meaning ; (*Wichtigkeit*) importance.

bedienen *vt* (*Gast, Kunde*) to serve ; (*Maschine*) to operate. ◆ *vi* (*Kellner*) to serve. ▓ **sich**

bedienen *ref* to help o.s. ; ~ Sie sich! help yourself!

Bedienung (*pl* -en) die (*von Gast, Kunde*) service ; (*von Maschine*) operation ; (*Kellner*) waiter (waitress) ; inklusive ~ including service.

Bedienungsanleitung (*pl* -en) die operating instructions (*pl*).

Bedienungshandbuch (*pl* -bücher) das (operating) manual.

Bedingung (*pl* -en) die condition ; unter einer ~ on one condition.

bedrohen *vt* to threaten.

Bedürfnis (*pl* -se) das need.

beeilen : sich beeilen *ref* to hurry.

beeindrucken *vt* to impress.

beeinflussen *vt* to influence.

beenden *vt* to end.

Beerdigung (*pl* -en) die funeral.

Beere (*pl* -n) die berry.

Beet (*pl* -e) das (*mit Blumen*) flower bed ; (*mit Gemüse*) patch.

Beete die : rote ~ beetroot.

befahl *prät* → befehlen.

befahrbar *adj* passable.

befahren (*präs* befährt, *prät* befuhr, *pp* befahren) *vt* to use.

Befehl (*pl* -e) der order.

befehlen (*präs* befiehlt, *prät* befahl, *pp* befohlen) *vt* to order.

befestigen *vt* (*anbringen*) to fasten ; (*Straße*) to surface.

befiehlt *präs* → befehlen.

befinden : sich befinden (*prät* befand, *pp* befunden) *ref* to be ; 'Sie ~ sich hier' 'you are here'.

befohlen *pp* → befehlen.

befolgen *vt* to obey.

befördern *vt (mit Auto, Zug)* to transport ; *(beruflich)* to promote.

Beförderung (*pl* -en) *die (Transport)* transport ; *(beruflich)* promotion.

Beförderungsbedingungen *pl (amt)* conditions of carriage.

Beförderungsentgelt *das (amt)* fare.

befragen *vt* to question.

befreien *vt* to free. ■ sich befreien *ref* to escape.

befreundet *adj* : mit jm ~ sein to be friends with sb.

befriedigend *adj (zufrieden stellend)* satisfactory.

befristet *adj* temporary.

Befund (*pl* -e) *der* results (*pl*) ; ohne ~ negative.

befürchten *vt* to fear.

begabt *adj* talented.

begann *prät* → beginnen.

begegnen *vi* ist (+D) to meet. ■ sich begegnen *ref* to meet.

begehrt *adj* coveted.

begeistert *adj* enthusiastic. ◆ *adv* enthusiastically.

Beginn *der* beginning ; zu ~ at the beginning.

beginnen (*prät* begann, *pp* begonnen) *vt* & *vi* to begin, to start ; ~ mit (+D) to begin with, to start with.

beglaubigen *vt* to certify.

Beglaubigung (*pl* -en) *die* certification.

begleiten *vt* to accompany.

Begleitperson (*pl* -en) *die* escort.

Begleitung *die* company ; in ~ von accompanied by.

beglückwünschen *vt* to congratulate.

begonnen *pp* → beginnen.

Begräbnis (*pl* -se) *das* funeral.

begreifen (*prät* begriff, *pp* begriffen) *vt* & *vi* to understand.

Begrenzung (*pl* -en) *die (zeitlich)* restriction ; *(Grenze)* boundary.

Begriff (*pl* -e) *der (Wort)* term.

begründen *vt* to justify ; *(gründen)* to establish.

Begründer, in (*mpl* -) *der, die* founder.

Begründung (*pl* -en) *die* reason ; *(Gründung)* establishment.

begrüßen *vt (Person)* to greet.

Begrüßung (*pl* -en) *die* greeting.

behalten (*präs* behält, *prät* behielt, *pp* behalten) *vt (nicht abgeben)* to keep ; *(in Erinnerung)* to remember ; etw für sich ~ *(nicht erzählen)* to keep sthg to o.s.

Behälter (*pl* -) *der* container.

behandeln *vt* to treat ; *(Thema)* to deal with ; jn gut/ schlecht ~ to treat sb well/ badly ; mit Antibiotika ~ to treat with antibiotics.

Behandlung (*pl* -en) *die* treatment.

behaupten *vt* (*versichern*) to claim. ▪ **sich behaupten** *ref* to assert o.s.

beheimatet *adj* (*geh*): **in Deutschland ~ sein** to come from Germany.

beheizt *adj* heated.

behelfen: **sich behelfen** (*präs* **behilft**, *prät* **behalf**, *pp* **beholfen**) *ref* to manage.

behelfsmäßig *adj* makeshift.

beherbergen *vt* to put up, to accommodate.

beherrschen *vt* (*bestimmen*) to rule; (*Sprache*) to have a command of. ▪ **sich beherrschen** *ref* to control o.s.

behilflich *adj*: **jm ~ sein** to help sb.

behindern *vt* (*Sicht, Verkehr*) to obstruct; (*Person*) to hinder.

behindert *adj* handicapped.

Behinderte (*pl* -n) *der, die* handicapped person.

Behindertenaufzug (*pl* -aufzüge) *der* disabled lift (*Br*), disabled elevator (*Am*).

Behinderung (*pl* -en) *die* (*körperlich, geistig*) handicap; (*im Verkehr*) delay; **mit ~en muss gerechnet werden** delays are likely.

Behörde (*pl* -n) *die* authority.

bei *präp* (+*D*) **1.** (*an einem Ort*) at; **~ der Post** at the post office; **~m Arzt** at the doctor's; **~ meiner Tante** at my aunt's; **~ mir** at my house; **hast du Geld ~ dir?** have you got any money on you?; **sie arbeitet ~ einem Verlag**

she works for a publishing company.

2. (*in der Nähe von*) near; **das Hotel ist gleich ~m Bahnhof** the hotel is right next to the station.

3. (*Angabe von Umständen*): **~ Regen vorsichtig fahren** drive carefully in the rain; **~ Regen fällt der Ausflug aus** if it rains the trip will be cancelled; **kannst du das Buch ~ Gelegenheit vorbeibringen?** could you bring the book round next time you get the chance?; **~ Tag/Nacht** by day/night.

4. (*Angabe von Zeit*) at; **~ Beginn** at the beginning; **~ der Arbeit** at work; **~m Sport brach er sich den Arm** he broke his arm (while) playing sport.

5. (*Angabe von Ursache, Grund*) with; **~ deinem Benehmen muss er ja verärgert sein** it's hardly surprising he's angry, after the way you behaved.

6. (*trotz*): **~ aller Liebe, aber so nicht!** however much I love you, you can't do that.

beibringen *vt* (*lehren*) to teach.

beichten *vt* & *vi* to confess.

beide *pron* & *adj* both; **meine ~n Töchter** both (of) my daughters; **ihr ~** you two; **jeder der ~n** each of them.

beidseitig *adj* (*Einverständnis*) mutual. ♦ *adv* (*beschrieben*) on both sides.

Beifahrer, in (*mpl* -) *der, die* (*im PKW*) front-seat passenger.

Beifahrersitz (*pl* -e) *der* passenger seat.

Beifall *der* applause; ~ spenden ODER **klatschen** to applaud.

beige *adj* beige.

Beilage (*pl* -n) *die* : mit Reis als ~ (served) with rice.

Beileid *das* condolences (*pl*); herzliches ODER **aufrichtiges** ~ my sincere condolences.

beiliegend *adj* (*amt*) enclosed.

beim *präp* = bei + dem.

Bein (*pl* -e) *das* leg.

beinahe *adv* almost.

Beinbruch (*pl* -brüche) *der* broken leg.

beinhalten *vt* (*enthalten*) to contain.

Beipackzettel (*pl* -) *der* instructions (*pl*).

Beisammensein *das* gettogether.

Beispiel (*pl* -e) *das* example; zum ~ for example.

beispielsweise *adv* for example.

beißen (*prät* **biss**, *pp* **gebissen**) *vt & vi* to bite; in etw (A) ~ to bite into sthg.

Beitrag (*pl* -träge) *der* (*Geld, Mitarbeit*) contribution; (*für Verein*) subscription.

bekämpfen *vt* to fight.

bekannt *adj* (*allgemein*) wellknown; (*individuell*) familiar; mit jm ~ sein to know sb.

Bekannte (*pl* -n) *der, die* (*flüchtig*) acquaintance; (*Freund*) friend.

bekannt geben *vt unr* to announce.

bekannt machen *vt* to announce; jn mit jm ~ to introduce sb to sb.

Bekanntschaft (*pl* -en) *die* (*Kontakt*) acquaintance; (*Gruppe*) acquaintances (*pl*).

beklagen : sich beklagen *ref* to complain.

bekleckern *vt* : etw mit etw ~ to spill sthg on sthg. ◼ **sich bekleckern** *ref* : sich mit etw ~ to spill sthg on o.s.

Bekleidung *die* clothes (*pl*).

bekommen (*prät* **bekam**, *pp* **bekommen**) *vt* hat ~ to get; (*Kind, Besuch*) to expect; (*Zug, Bus*) to catch. ◆ *vi* ist : jm gut ~ (*Klima, Luft*) to be good for sb; (*Essen*) to agree with sb; jm schlecht ~ to disagree with sb; etw geschenkt/geliehen ~ to be given/lent sthg; ich bekomme noch 100 DM von dir you owe me 100 marks; was ~ Sie? what would you like?; was ~ Sie dafür? how much is it?; etw zu essen/trinken ~ to get sthg to eat/drink.

bekömmlich *adj* easy to digest.

beladen (*präs* **belädt**, *prät* **belud**, *pp* **beladen**) *vt* to load.

Belag (*pl* **Beläge**) *der* (*auf Brot*) topping; (*auf Bremse*) lining; (*auf Straße*) surface.

belangen *vt* (*amt* : verklagen) to prosecute.

belasten *vt* (*deprimieren*) to put a strain on; (*Umwelt, Luft*) to pollute; (*mit Gewicht*) to weigh down.

belästigen *vt* (*sexuell*) to harass; (*stören*) to bother.

Belastung *(pl -en)* die *(psychisch, körperlich)* strain ; *(von Umwelt)* pollution ; *(Last)* load.

belaufen : sich belaufen *(präs* beläuft, *prät* belief, *pp* belaufen) *ref* : die Rechnung beläuft sich auf 120 DM the bill comes to 120 marks.

belebt *adj* busy.

Beleg *(pl -e)* der *(Quittung)* receipt.

belegt *adj (Sitzplatz)* occupied ; *(Hotel)* full ; *(Telefonanschluss)* engaged ; *(Zunge)* furred ; *(Stimme)* hoarse ; ~es Brötchen/Brot open roll/sandwich ; **voll** ~ no vacancies.

belehren *vt* to inform.

beleidigen *vt* to insult.

Beleidigung *(pl -en)* die *(Bemerkung, Handlung)* insult.

Beleuchtung die *(Scheinwerfer, Lampen)* lights *(pl)*.

Belgien *nt* Belgium.

Belgier, in *(mpl -)* der, die Belgian.

belgisch *adj* Belgian.

belichten *vt* to expose.

Belichtung *(pl -en)* die exposure.

Belichtungsmesser *(pl -)* der light meter.

Belichtungszeit *(pl -en)* die exposure time.

Belieben das : nach ~ as you like.

beliebig *adj* any. ◆ *adv* : ~ viel as much as you like ; in ~er Reihenfolge in any order ; zu jeder ~en Zeit whenever you like.

beliebt *adj* popular.

beliefern *vt* to supply.

bellen *vi* to bark.

belohnen *vt* to reward.

Belohnung *(pl -en)* die *(Geld, Geschenk)* reward.

Belüftung die ventilation.

belügen *(prät* belog, *pp* belogen) *vt* to lie to. ■ sich belügen *ref* to deceive o.s.

bemerkbar *adj* noticeable ; sich ~ machen *(durch Rufen, Klopfen)* to attract attention ; *(sich zeigen)* to become apparent.

bemerken *vt (wahrnehmen)* to notice ; *(geh : sagen)* to remark ; nebenbei bemerkt by the way.

Bemerkung *(pl -en)* die remark ; eine ~ machen to make a remark.

bemühen : sich bemühen *ref* : sich ~, etw zu tun to try to do sthg.

Bemühungen *pl* efforts.

benachrichtigen *vt* to inform.

Benachrichtigung *(pl -en)* die notification.

benehmen : sich benehmen *(präs* benimmt, *prät* benahm, *pp* benommen) *ref* : sich gut/schlecht ~ to behave well/badly.

beneiden *vt* to envy.

benötigen *vt* to need.

benutzen *vt* to use.

benützen = benutzen.

Benutzer, in *(mpl -)* der, die user.

Benzin das petrol *(Br)*, gas *(Am)* ; bleifreies ~ unleaded petrol *(Br)*, unleaded gas *(Am)* ; ~ tanken to fill up with petrol *(Br)*, to fill up with gas *(Am)*.

Benzingutschein (*pl* -e) *der* petrol coupon (*Br*), gas coupon (*Am*).

Benzinkanister (*pl* -) *der* petrol can (*Br*), gas can (*Am*).

Benzin-Öl-Gemisch *das* petrol-oil mixture (*Br*), gas-oil mixture (*Am*).

Benzinpumpe (*pl* -n) *die* petrol pump (*Br*), gas pump (*Am*).

beobachten *vt* (*betrachten*) to observe ; (*bemerken*) to notice ; (*überwachen*) to watch.

Beobachter, in (*mpl* -) *der, die* observer.

bequem *adj* (*Hose, Sitz, Größe*) comfortable ; (*faul*) lazy ; (*Lösung*) easy. ◆ *adv* comfortably ; machen Sie es sich ~! make yourself at home!

Bequemlichkeit *die* (*Komfort*) comfort ; (*Faulheit*) laziness.

beraten (*präs* berät, *prät* beriet, *pp* beraten) *vt* (*Kunde*) to advise ; (*Vorhaben*) to discuss. ◆ *vi* (*diskutieren*) : über etw (A) ~ to discuss sthg. ■ **sich beraten** *ref* : sich über etw (A) ~ to discuss sthg.

Beratungsstelle (*pl* -n) *die* advice centre.

berechnen *vt* (*ausrechnen*) to calculate ; (*verlangen*) to charge ; jm für eine Konsultation 120 DM ~ to charge sb 120 marks for a consultation.

berechtigt *adj* (*Zweifel*) justified ; ~ sein zu etw to be entitled to sthg.

Bereich (*pl* -e) *der* area.

bereisen *vt* to travel.

bereit *adj* ready ; ~ sein (*fertig sein*) to be ready ; ~ sein, etw zu tun (*willens sein*) to be willing to do sthg.

bereit|halten *vt unr* to have ready. ■ **sich bereithalten** *ref* to be ready.

bereit|machen : sich bereitmachen *ref* to get ready.

bereits *adv* already ; (*nur, allein*) even ; ~ um 6 Uhr as early as 6 o'clock.

Bereitschaft *die* readiness.

Bereitschaftsdienst (*pl* -e) *der* emergency service.

bereit|stehen *vi unr* to be ready.

bereuen *vt* to regret.

Berg (*pl* -e) *der* mountain ; (*kleiner*) hill ; in die ~e fahren to go to the mountains.

bergab *adv* downhill ; ~ fahren/laufen to drive/run downhill.

bergauf *adv* uphill ; ~ fahren/laufen to drive/run uphill.

Bergbahn (*pl* -en) *die* funicular railway.

Bergbau *der* mining.

bergen (*präs* birgt, *prät* barg, *pp* geborgen) *vt* (*retten*) to rescue.

Bergführer, in (*mpl* -) *der, die* mountain guide.

Berghütte (*pl* -n) *die* mountain hut.

bergig *adj* mountainous.

Bergnot *die* : in ~ geraten to get into trouble while climbing a mountain.

Bergschuh (*pl* -e) *der* climbing boot.

bergsteigen (*pp* **berggestiegen**) *vi* to go (mountain) climbing.

Bergsteigen *das* (mountain) climbing.

Bergsteiger, in (*mpl* -) *der, die* (mountain) climber.

Bergtour (*pl* -en) *die* (mountain) hike.

Bergung (*pl* -en) *die* rescue.

Bergwacht *die* mountain rescue.

Bergwanderung (*pl* -en) *die* hillwalking.

Bergwerk (*pl* -e) *das* mine.

Bericht (*pl* -e) *der* report.

berichten *vi* to report.

berichtigen *vt* to correct. ■ **sich berichtigen** *ref* to correct o.s.

Berichtigung (*pl* -en) *die* correction.

Berlin *nt* Berlin.

Berliner (*pl* -) *der* (*Gebäck*) doughnut.

Berliner Mauer *die* : die ~ the Berlin Wall.

DIE BERLINER MAUER

The Berlin Wall, sometimes also known as "die Mauer" (the Wall), was built on 13 August 1961 in order to stem the growing tide of people leaving East Berlin for the West. It encircled West Berlin, cutting it off from the surrounding GDR, and came to be a potent symbol of the post-war division of Germany. Some 80 people died while attempting to escape over the Wall to West Berlin. The fall of the Wall on 9 November 1989 marked the beginning of the process of German reunification. Today, little of the Wall remains, although a few sections have been left standing as a memorial and others can be found in museums.

Bern *nt* Bern, Berne.

berüchtigt *adj* notorious.

berücksichtigen *vt* (*bei Überlegung*) to take into account ; (*Bewerber, Wunsch*) to consider.

Beruf (*pl* -e) *der* profession ; Tischler von ~ sein to be a carpenter ; was sind Sie von ~? what do you do for a living?

beruflich *adj* professional. ◆ *adv* : ~ unterwegs away on business.

Berufsschule (*pl* -n) *die* vocational school attended part-time by apprentices.

berufstätig *adj* employed.

Berufstätige (*pl* -n) *der, die* working person.

Berufsverkehr *der* rush-hour traffic.

beruhigen *vt* to calm (down). ■ **sich beruhigen** *ref* (*Person*) to calm down ; (*Wetter, See*) to become calm.

Beruhigungsmittel (*pl* -) *das* sedative.

berühmt *adj* famous ; ~ sein wegen ODER für to be famous for.

berühren *vt* & *vi* to touch ; bitte nicht ~! please don't touch! ■ **sich berühren** *ref* to touch.

beschädigen *vt* to damage.

beschädigt *adj* damaged.

beschäftigen *vt (Angestellte)* to employ ; *(gedanklich)* to occupy. ■ **sich beschäftigen** *ref : sich ~ mit (mit Person)* to devote a lot of attention to ; *(mit Thema)* to deal with ; *(mit Gedanken)* to think about.

Beschäftigung *(pl -en) die (Arbeit)* occupation ; *(Hobby)* activity ; *(gedanklich)* preoccupation.

Bescheid *(pl -e) der (Nachricht)* answer ; **jm ~ geben** ODER **sagen** to let sb know ; **~ wissen (über** (+A)**)** to know (about).

bescheiden *adj* modest.

bescheinigen *vt (mit Zeugnis)* to certify ; *(Erhalt von Sendung)* to sign for.

Bescheinigung *(pl -en) die* certificate.

beschimpfen *vt* to swear at.

beschissen *adj (vulg)* shitty.

Beschlag *der :* **in ~ nehmen** to monopolize.

beschlagnahmen *vt (Beute)* to confiscate.

beschleunigen *vt (Tempo, Verfahren, Ablauf)* to speed up. ◆ *vi (Auto)* to accelerate. ■ **sich beschleunigen** *ref* to speed up.

Beschleunigung *die (von Verfahren)* speeding up ; *(von Auto)* acceleration.

beschließen *(prät beschloss, pp beschlossen) vt (entscheiden)* to decide on ; *(Gesetz)* to pass ; *(beenden)* to end ; **~, etw zu tun** to decide to do sthg.

Beschluss *(pl Beschlüsse) der* decision.

beschränken *vt* to limit.

Beschränkung *(pl -en) die* limit.

beschreiben *(prät beschrieb, pp beschrieben) vt (schildern)* describe ; **jm den Weg ~** to tell sb the way.

Beschreibung *(pl -en) die* description.

beschriften *vt* to label.

beschuldigen *vt* to accuse.

Beschuldigung *(pl -en) die* accusation.

beschützen *vt* to protect.

Beschwerde *(pl -n) die* complaint. ■ **Beschwerden** *pl (Gesundheitsprobleme)* trouble *(sg)*.

beschweren : **sich beschweren** *ref* to complain.

beschwipst *adj* tipsy.

beseitigen *vt (Abfall)* to get rid of ; *(Problem)* to deal with.

Besen *(pl -) der* broom.

besetzt *adj :* **~ sein** *(Telefonanschluss, Toilette)* to be engaged ; *(Sitzplatz)* to be taken ; **das Büro ist zur Zeit nicht ~** the office is currently closed.

Besetztzeichen *das* engaged tone *(Br)*, busy signal *(Am)*.

Besetzung *(pl -en) die (am Theater)* cast.

besichtigen *vt* to look round.

Besichtigung *(pl -en) die* tour ; '**zur ~ freigegeben**' 'open to the public'.

besiegen *vt* to defeat.

Besitz der (Eigentum) property.

besitzen (prät **besaß**, pp **besessen**) vt (Eigentum) to own; (Qualität, Ausrüstungsgegenstand) to have.

Besitzer, in (mpl -) der, die owner.

besoffen adj (fam) sloshed.

besondere, r, s adj (speziell) special; (außergewöhnlich) particular.

besonders adv particularly; nicht ~ (fam : nicht gut) not very well; nicht ~ sein (fam : nicht gut) to be not very good.

besorgen vt (holen, kaufen) to get.

besorgt adj worried. ◆ adv worriedly.

besprechen (präs **bespricht**, prät **besprach**, pp **besprochen**) vt (diskutieren) to discuss.

besser komp & adv better. ◆ adj (sehr gut) good; (abw : kaum besser) : das Hotel ist eine ~e Absteige the hotel is just a glorified dosshouse.

bessern : sich bessern ref (Erkältung) to get better; (Chancen, Wetter) to improve.

Besserung die : gute ~! get well soon!

beständig adj (Wetter) settled.

Bestandteil (pl -e) der component, part.

bestätigen vt to confirm. ◼ **sich bestätigen** ref to prove true.

Bestätigung (pl -en) die confirmation.

beste, r, s superl best. ◆ adj ideal. ◆ adv : am ~n best; ich gehe jetzt am ~n I'd better go now; sie spricht am ~n Deutsch von allen she speaks the best German of everyone.

Beste (pl -n) der, die, das best.

Bestechung (pl -en) die bribery.

Besteck (pl -e) das (zum Essen) cutlery.

bestehen (prät **bestand**, pp **bestanden**) vt (Prüfung) to pass. ◆ vi (existieren) to exist; (bei Prüfung) to pass; ~ auf (+D) to insist on; ~ aus to consist of.

besteigen (prät **bestieg**, pp **bestiegen**) vt to climb.

bestellen vi (im Lokal) to order. ◆ vt (Ware) to order; (Eintrittskarte, Hotelzimmer) to reserve; (Nachricht) : jm schöne Grüße ~ to give sb one's regards.

Bestellformular (pl -e) das order form.

Bestellkarte (pl -n) die order form.

Bestellnummer (pl -n) die order number.

Bestellung (pl -en) die (von Waren) ordering; (von Eintrittskarte, Hotelzimmer) reservation; (Ware) order; auf ~ to order.

bestens adv very well.

bestimmen vt (ermitteln) to determine; (festlegen) to fix; (klassifizieren) to classify. ◆ vi (befehlen) to decide; bestimmt sein für to be meant for.

bestimmt adv (sehr wahrscheinlich) no doubt; (sicher)

certainly ; *(wissen)* for certain ; *(entschlossen)* decisively. ◆ *adj (gewiss)* certain ; *(Betrag, Anzahl)* fixed ; *(Auftreten)* decisive.

Bestimmung *(pl -en) die (Vorschrift)* regulation ; *(ermitteln)* determining.

Bestimmungsland *(pl -länder) das (amt)* (country of) destination.

Bestimmungsort *(pl -e) der (amt)* (place of) destination.

bestmöglich *adj* best possible. ◆ *adv* as well as possible.

bestrafen *vt* to punish.

bestrahlen *vt (MED : Patienten, Haut)* to treat with radiotherapy.

bestreiten *(prät bestritt, pp bestritten) vt (leugnen)* to deny.

bestürzt *adj* : ~ sein to be dismayed.

Besuch *(pl -e) der* visit ; *(Gast)* visitor ; *(von Schule)* attendance ; bei jm zu ~ sein to be visiting sb.

besuchen *vt (Person, Veranstaltung)* to visit ; *(Schule)* to attend.

Besucher, in *(mpl -) der, die* visitor ; 'nur für ~' 'visitors only'.

Besuchszeit *(pl -en) die* visiting hours *(pl).*

besucht *adj* : gut/schlecht ~ sein to be well/poorly attended.

betätigen *vt (Hebel)* to operate.

betäuben *vt* to anaesthetize.

Betäubung *die* : unter ~ stehen to be under anaesthetic.

beteiligen *vt (teilnehmen lassen)* to include ; *(finanziell)* to give a share. ▦ **sich beteiligen** *ref* : sich ~ an *(+D) (teilnehmen)* to take part (in) ; *(finanziell)* to have a share (in).

Beteiligung *(pl -en) die (Teilnahme)* participation ; *(finanziell)* share.

beten *vi* to pray.

Beton *der* concrete.

betonen *vt* to stress.

Betonung *(pl -en) die (von Wort)* stress.

betrachten *vt* to look at ; jn als etw ~ to consider sb to be sthg.

Betrachter, in *(mpl -) der, die* observer.

beträchtlich *adj* considerable. ◆ *adv* considerably.

Betrag *(pl Beträge) der* amount ; bitte angezeigten ~ bezahlen please pay the amount displayed ; ~ dankend erhalten *(amt)* received with thanks.

betragen *(präs beträgt, prät betrug, pp betragen) vt* to come to. ▦ **sich betragen** *ref (sich benehmen)* to behave.

betreffen *(präs betrifft, prät betraf, pp betroffen) vt (angehen)* to concern ; *(bestürzen)* to affect ; was mich betrifft as far as I'm concerned.

betreiben *(prät betrieb, pp betrieben) vt (Handel)* to carry on ; betrieben werden mit to be driven by.

betreten *(präs betritt, prät betrat, pp betreten) vt* to enter ; 'Betreten verboten!' 'no entry!'

betreuen vt to look after.

Betreuer, in (mpl -) der, die (von Patient) nurse ; (von Kind) childminder ; (von Touristen) groupleader.

Betrieb (pl -e) der (Firma) firm ; (Aktivität, Verkehr) hustle and bustle ; außer ~ out of order ; in ~ in operation.

betrieben pp → betreiben.

betriebsbereit adj operational.

Betriebsrat (pl -räte) der works council.

betrifft präs → betreffen.

betrinken : sich betrinken (prät betrank, pp betrunken) ref to get drunk.

betroffen pp → betreffen. ◆ adj (nicht verschont) affected ; (bestürzt) upset. ◆ adv (bestürzt) : jn ~ ansehen to look at sb in consternation.

betrügen (prät betrog, pp betrogen) vt (finanziell) to cheat ; (sexuell) to be unfaithful to. ▪ sich betrügen ref to deceive o.s.

Betrüger, in (mpl -) der, die cheat.

betrunken adj drunk.

Bett (pl -en) das (Möbel) bed ; das ~ machen to make the bed ; zu ODER ins ~ gehen to go to bed ; französisches ~ double bed.

Bettdecke (pl -n) die (continental) quilt.

Bettler, in (mpl -) der, die beggar.

Bettsofa (pl -s) das sofa bed.

Betttuch (pl -tücher) das sheet.

Bettwäsche die bed linen.

Bettzeug das bedding.

beugen vt (Kopf, Knie) to bend ; (Substantiv, Adjektiv) to decline ; (Verb) to conjugate.

Beule (pl -n) die (am Kopf) swelling ; (am Auto) dent.

beunruhigt adj : ~ sein to be worried.

beurteilen vt to judge.

Beutel (pl -) der bag.

Bevölkerung (pl -en) die population.

bevollmächtigt adj authorized.

bevor konj before.

bevorzugen vt to prefer.

bewacht adj guarded.

bewährt adj tried and tested.

bewegen vt to move. ▪ sich bewegen ref to move ; (sportlich) to exercise.

Bewegung (pl -en) die movement ; (Sport) exercise ; (Rührung) emotion ; sich in ~ setzen to start moving.

Beweis (pl -e) der (für Theorie, Annahme) proof.

beweisen (prät bewies, pp bewiesen) vt (Theorie, Annahme) to prove ; (Mut, Geduld) to show.

bewerben : sich bewerben (präs bewirbt, prät bewarb, pp beworben) ref : sich ~ (um) to apply (for).

Bewerbung (pl -en) die application.

bewilligen vt to approve.

Bewohner, in (mpl -) der, die inhabitant.

bewohnt adj inhabited.

bewölkt adj cloudy.

Bewölkung *die (Wolken)* cloud ; *(Bewölken)* clouding over.

bewundern *vt* to admire.

bewusst *adj (Handlung)* deliberate ; *(Entscheidung)* conscious ; *(bekannt)* in question. ◆ *adv (handeln)* deliberately ; *(entscheiden)* consciously ; **sich** *(D)* **einer Sache ~ sein** to be aware of sthg.

bewusstlos *adj* unconscious.

bezahlen *vt (Person)* to pay ; *(Ware, Leistung)* to pay for. ◆ *vi (für Ware, Leistung)* to pay.

bezahlt *adj* paid.

Bezahlung *die* payment.

Bezeichnung *(pl -en) die (Wort)* name ; 'genaue ~ des Inhalts' 'exact description of the contents'.

beziehen *(prät bezog, pp bezogen) vt (Kissen, Sofa)* to cover ; *(Haus)* to move into ; *(Ware, Zeitung, Einkünfte)* to get ; **das Bett frisch ~** to change the bed. ▮ **sich beziehen** *ref (Himmel, Wetter)* to cloud over ; **sich ~ auf** *(+A)* to refer to.

Beziehung *(pl -en) die* connection ; *(erotisch)* relationship. ▮ **Beziehungen** *pl (politisch)* relations.

beziehungsweise *konj (genauer gesagt)* that is ; *(und)* and ; *(oder)* or.

Bezirk *(pl -e) der (amt)* district.

bezweifeln *vt* to doubt.

BH *(pl -s) der (abk für Büstenhalter)* bra.

Bhf. *abk* = **Bahnhof**.

Bibel *(pl -n) die* Bible.

Bibliothek *(pl -en) die* library.

biegen *(prät bog, pp gebogen) vt hat* to bend. ◆ *vi ist (Auto, Fahrer)* : **~ (in** *(+A)***)** to turn (into) ; **nach links ~** to turn left ; **um die Ecke ~** to turn the corner. ▮ **sich biegen** *ref* to bend.

Biegung *(pl -en) die* bend.

Biene *(pl -n) die* bee.

Bienenstich *(pl -e) der (Insektenstich)* bee sting ; *(Kuchen)* cake coated with sugar and almonds and filled with custard or cream.

Bier *(pl -e) das* beer ; **ein Glas ~** a glass of beer ; **vom Fass** draught beer ; **ein großes ~** a half-litre glass of beer ; **ein kleines ~** a 30cl glass of beer.

BIER

There are over 1,000 breweries in Germany and each region boasts several different kinds of local beer. The most common kinds are the pale lager beers, either strong, hoppy "Pils" or the milder "Export" which in Bavaria is often drunk in a litre glass called a "Maßkrug". Another popular beer in Bavaria is "Weizenbier", a fizzy beer made from wheat which is slightly cloudy because of the yeast sediment that it contains. "Berliner Weiße" is similar but weaker and is often drunk with a dash of raspberry cordial ("mit Schuss"). In the Rhineland, light "Kölsch" and dark "Altbier" are both common. The brewing of beer in Germany is governed by strict laws regulating its purity (the 1516 "Reinheitsgebot").

Biergarten (*pl* -gärten) *der* beer garden.

BIERGARTEN

Beer gardens are a common sight in summer, especially in Bavaria. Customers sit outdoors at tables with long, wooden benches and drink a "Maß" (litre measure) of beer. Beer gardens are usually found in parks or outside the major breweries and most of them serve snacks as well as beer, although customers are often allowed to bring their own food with them. Some of the monasteries where beer is brewed, such as "Andechs" and "Weihenstephan", have beer gardens which are particularly worth visiting.

Bierglas (*pl* -gläser) *das* beer glass.

Bierzelt (*pl* -e) *das* beer tent.

bieten (*prät* **bot**, *pp* **geboten**) *vi (bei Auktion)* to bid. ◆ *vt* to offer ; **einen schönen Anblick ~** to be pretty. ▪ **sich bieten** *ref (Chance)* to present itself ; **es bietet sich ein wunderbarer Anblick** there is a wonderful view.

Bild (*pl* -er) *das* picture ; *(Vorstellung)* idea ; *(Abbild)* image.

bilden *vt* to form ; *(unterrichten)* to educate. ◆ *vi* to be educational. ▪ **sich bilden** *ref (sich formen)* to form ; *(sich informieren)* to educate o.s.

Bilderbuch (*pl* -bücher) *das* picture book.

Bildhauer, in (*mpl* -) *der, die* sculptor (sculptress).

Bildschirm (*pl* -e) *der* screen ; '**~ berühren!**' *sign on information point indicating that the system is operated by touching the screen.*

Bildschirmtext *der German teletext service offering information, home banking etc via a computer and telephone line.*

Bildung *die (Wissen)* education ; *(Entstehung)* formation.

Billard *das* billiards *(sg)*.

billig *adj* cheap ; *(abw : Ausrede)* feeble. ◆ *adv (preisgünstig)* cheaply.

bin *präs* → **sein**.

Binde (*pl* -n) *die (Monatsbinde)* sanitary towel ; *(Verband)* bandage.

Bindehautentzündung (*pl* -en) *die* conjunctivitis *(sg)*.

binden (*prät* **band**, *pp* **gebunden**) *vt* to tie ; *(Buch)* to bind ; *(KÜCHE : Soße)* to thicken.

Bindestrich (*pl* -e) *der* hyphen.

Bindfaden (*pl* -fäden) *der* string.

Bindung (*pl* -en) *die (Verpflichtung)* commitment ; *(Zuneigung)* attachment ; *(für Ski)* binding.

Biokost *die* health food.

Bioladen (*pl* -läden) *der* health food shop.

Biologie *die* biology.

birgt *präs* → **bergen**.

Birne (*pl* -n) *die* (*Obst*) pear; (*Glühbirne*) light bulb; (*fam*: *Kopf*) nut.

bis *präp* (+A) **1.** (*zeitlich*) until; **wir bleiben ~ morgen** we're staying until tomorrow; **das muss ~ Mittwoch fertig sein** it must be ready by Wednesday; **von Montag ~ Freitag** from Monday to Friday; **~ auf weiteres** until further notice; **~ bald!** see you soon! **; ~ dahin!** until then. **2.** (*örtlich*) to; **es sind noch 200 km ~ Berlin** there are still 200 km to go to Berlin. **3.** (*zwischen*) to; **zwei ~ drei Tage** two to three days. **4.** (*Angabe von Grenze*): **~ zu** up to; **~ zu 20 Personen** up to 20 people. **5.** (*außer*): **~ auf** (+A) except for.
◆ *konj* until.

Bischof (*pl* Bischöfe) *der* bishop.

bisher *adv* (*bis jetzt*) until now.

bisherig *adj* previous.

Biskuit (*pl* -s) *das* sponge.

biss *prät* → **beißen**.

Biss (*pl* -e) *der* bite.

bisschen *pron*: **das ~ Regen macht nichts!** that little bit of rain won't harm you! **; ein ~ a** bit, a bit of; **ein ~ Salz** a bit of salt; **kein ~** not at all; **kein ~ Schnee** no snow at all.

bissig *adj* (*Tier*) vicious; 'Vorsicht, **~er Hund**' 'beware of the dog'.

bist *präs* → **sein**.

bitte *adv* please. ◆ *interj* (*Ausdruck von Zustimmung*) of course! **; (*Antwort auf Dank*) you're welcome! **; (*Ausdruck von Angebot*) please; aber ~! of course! **; ach ~** please; **~ schön** ODER **sehr** you're welcome! **; ~? (*in Geschäft*) can I help you? **; ja ~? (*am Telefon*) hello? **; wie ~? sorry?

Bitte (*pl* -n) *die* request; **eine ~ haben** to have a favour to ask.

bitten (*prät* bat, *pp* gebeten) *vt* (*Person*) to ask; **~ um** to ask for.

bitter *adj* & *adv* bitter.

Blähung (*pl* -en) *die* wind.

blamieren *vt* to disgrace.
■ **sich blamieren** *ref* to disgrace o.s.

Blankoscheck (*pl* -s) *der* blank cheque.

Blase (*pl* -n) *die* (*auf der Haut*) blister; (*Harnblase*) bladder; (*Luftblase*) bubble.

blasen (*präs* bläst, *prät* blies, *pp* geblasen) *vi* (*pusten*) to blow.

Blasenentzündung (*pl* -en) *die* cystitis (*sg*).

blass *adj* (*Haut, Person*) pale.

bläst *prät* → **blasen**.

Blatt (*pl* Blätter) *das* (*Papier*) sheet; (*von Pflanze*) leaf; (*Zeitung*) paper; (*bei Kartenspiel*) hand.

Blätterteig *der* puff pastry.

Blattspinat *der* spinach.

blau *adj* blue; **~ sein** (*fam*) to be sloshed.

Blau *das* blue.

Blaubeere (*pl* -n) *die* blueberry.

Blaulicht das flashing blue light (on ambulance etc).

blaumachen vi (fam) to skip work.

Blazer (pl -) der blazer.

Blech (pl -e) das (Metall) tin ; (Kuchenblech) baking tray.

Blechschaden der body-work damage.

Bleibe die place to stay.

bleiben (prät blieb, pp geblieben) vi ist to stay ; (als Rest) to remain. ◆ vimp ist : es bleibt dabei we'll leave it at that.

bleifrei adj unleaded.

Bleistift (pl -e) der pencil.

Blende (pl -n) die (FOTO) aperture.

blenden vt (anstrahlen) to dazzle. ◆ vi (Licht, Sonne) to be dazzling.

Blick (pl -e) der (Schauen) look ; (Aussicht) view ; (Urteil) eye.

blieb prät → bleiben.

blind adj blind. ◆ adv blindly.

Blinddarmentzündung (pl -en) die appendicitis (sg).

Blinde (pl -n) der, die blind person.

Blindenschrift die braille.

blinken vi (Autofahrer, Auto) to indicate.

Blinker (pl -) der indicator.

Blinklicht (pl -er) das flashing light.

Blitz (pl -e) der (bei Gewitter) (flash of) lightning ; (von Kamera) flash ; wie der ~ as quick as lightning.

blitzen vt (Autofahrer) to photograph with a speed camera. ◆ vi (mit Blitzlicht) to use a flash. ◆ vimp : es blitzt there is lightning.

Blitzlicht (pl -er) das flash.

Block (pl Blöcke) der (Schreibblock) pad ; (Gebäude, Stück) block.

Blockhaus (pl -häuser) das log cabin.

blockieren vt to block. ◆ vi (Räder) to lock.

Blockschrift die block capitals (pl).

blöd adj (fam) stupid. ◆ adv (fam) stupidly.

Blödsinn der nonsense.

blond adj blond.

bloß adv only, just ; ~ noch zwei Wochen only two more weeks left ; was ist ~ los? so what's wrong, then? ; was hast du ~ wieder angestellt? what have you gone and done now? ; pass ~ auf! just watch out!

blühen vi (Pflanze) to bloom.

Blume (pl -n) die flower.

Blumenkasten (pl -kästen) der window box.

Blumenkohl der cauliflower.

Blumenstand (pl -stände) der flower stall.

Blumenstrauß (pl -sträuße) der bunch of flowers.

Blumentopf (pl -töpfe) der flowerpot.

Blumentopferde die potting compost.

Bluse (pl -n) die blouse.

Blut das blood ; ~ spenden to give blood.

Blutbild (pl -er) das blood test results (pl).

Blutdruck der blood pressure ; hoher/niedriger ~ high/low blood pressure.

bluten vi to bleed.

Bluter (pl -) der haemophiliac.

Bluterguss (pl -güsse) der bruise.

Blutgruppe (pl -n) die blood group.

Blutprobe (pl -n) die blood test.

Blutspende (pl -n) die giving blood.

blutstillend adj styptic.

Blutübertragung (pl -en) die blood transfusion.

Blutung (pl -en) die bleeding.

Blutvergiftung (pl -en) die blood-poisoning.

Blutwurst (pl -würste) die black pudding (Br), blood sausage (Am).

BLZ abk = Bankleitzahl.

Bockbier das bock (strong dark beer).

Bocksbeutel (pl -) der wide, round bottle containing 'Frankenwein'.

Bockwurst (pl -würste) die type of pork sausage, usually boiled and eaten in a bread roll with mustard.

Boden (pl Böden) der (im Raum) floor ; (Erde) ground ; (Speicher) loft ; (von Gefäß, Koffer) bottom.

Bodennebel der ground mist.

Bodenpersonal das ground staff.

Bodensee der Lake Constance.

Bodybuilding das bodybuilding.

Böe (pl -n) die gust.

bog prät → biegen.

Bogen (pl Bögen) der (Form) curve ; (SPORT : Waffe) bow.

Bohne (pl -n) die bean.

bohren vt & vi to drill.

Bohrer (pl -) der drill.

Bohrmaschine (pl -n) die drill.

böig adj gusty.

Boiler (pl -) der boiler.

Boje (pl -n) die buoy.

Bombe (pl -n) die bomb.

Bon (pl -s) der (Kassenzettel) receipt ; (Gutschein) voucher.

Bonbon (pl -s) der ODER das sweet.

Bonn nt Bonn.

Boot (pl -e) das boat ; ~ fahren to go boating.

Bootsverleih der boat hire.

Bord der : an ~ on board ; von ~ gehen to disembark.

Bordkarte (pl -n) die boarding card.

Bordstein der kerb.

Bordsteinkante die kerb.

borgen vt : jm etw ~ to lend sb sthg ; sich (D) etw ~ to borrow sthg.

Börse (pl -n) die (ECO) stock market ; (Gebäude) stock exchange ; (Geldbeutel) purse.

Böschung (pl -en) die bank.

böse adj (bösartig, schlecht) bad ; (fam : wütend) angry. ◆ adv (schlimm, bösartig) badly ; (wütend) angrily ; ~ sein auf (+A) to be angry with ; jm ~ sein to be angry with sb.

bot prät → bieten.

botanische Gärten (*pl -n Gärten*) *der* botanical gardens (*pl*).

Botschaft (*pl -en*) *die* (*diplomatische Vertretung*) embassy ; (*Gebäude*) embassy ; (*Nachricht*) message.

Botschafter, in (*mpl -*) *der, die* ambassador.

Boutique (*pl -n*) *die* boutique.

Bowle (*pl -n*) *die* punch.

Bowling *das* tenpin bowling.

Box (*pl -en*) *die* (*Dose, Kiste*) box ; (*Lautsprecher*) speaker.

boxen *vi* to box. ◆ *vt* to punch.

Boykott (*pl -s*) *der* boycott.

brach *prät* → **brechen**.

brachte *prät* → **bringen**.

Branchenverzeichnis (*pl -se*) *das* ≃ yellow pages (*pl*).

Brandenburg *nt* Brandenburg.

Brandung *die* surf.

Brandwunde (*pl -n*) *die* burn.

brannte *prät* → **brennen**.

braten (*präs* **brät**, *prät* **briet**, *pp* **gebraten**) *vt & vi* (*in der Pfanne*) to fry ; (*im Ofen*) to roast.

Braten (*pl -*) *der* roast.

Brathähnchen (*pl -*) *das* roast chicken.

Bratkartoffeln *pl* fried potatoes.

Bratpfanne (*pl -n*) *die* frying pan.

Bratwurst (*pl -würste*) *die* (fried) sausage.

Brauch (*pl* **Bräuche**) *der* custom.

brauchen *vt* (*benötigen*) to need ; (*verwenden, verbrauchen*) to use. ◆ *aux* to need ; **du brauchst nur auf den Knopf zu drücken** all you need (to) do is press the button ; **etw ~ für** to need sthg for ; **etw ~ zu** to need sthg for.

brauen *vt* (*Bier*) to brew.

Brauerei (*pl -en*) *die* brewery.

braun *adj* brown.

Braun *das* brown.

Bräune *die* suntan.

bräunen *vt* (*Braten*) to brown ; (*Haut*) to tan. ■ **sich bräunen** *ref* to sunbathe.

braun gebrannt *adj* tanned.

Bräunungsstudio (*pl -s*) *das* tanning studio.

Brause (*pl -n*) *die* (*Dusche*) shower.

brausen *vi* (*duschen*) to have a shower ; (*sausen*) to roar.

Braut (*pl* **Bräute**) *die* bride.

Bräutigam (*pl -e*) *der* bridegroom.

brav *adj* (*Kind*) good.

bravo *interj* bravo!

BRD (*abk für Bundesrepublik Deutschland*) FRG.

brechen (*präs* **bricht**, *prät* **brach**, *pp* **gebrochen**) *vt* hat to break ; (*erbrechen*) to vomit. ◆ *vi ist* (*zerbrechen*) to break. ◆ *vi* hat (*erbrechen*) to vomit ; **sich** (*D*) **das Bein ~** to break one's leg.

Brechreiz *der* nausea.

Brei *der* (*aus Haferflocken*) porridge ; (*aus Kartoffeln*) mashed potatoes (*pl*).

breit adj wide ; (Rücken, Hände) broad ; (allgemein) general.

Breite (pl -n) die width.

Bremen nt Bremen.

Bremsbelag (pl -beläge) der brake lining.

Bremse (pl -n) die (von Auto, Fahrrad) brake ; (Insekt) horsefly.

bremsen vt (Auto, Fahrrad) to brake ; (Person, Fortschritt) to slow down. ◆ vi to brake.

Bremsflüssigkeit die brake fluid.

Bremskraftverstärker der brake booster.

Bremslicht (pl -er) das brake light.

Bremspedal (pl -e) das brake pedal.

brennbar adj flammable.

brennen (prät brannte, pp gebrannt) vi (Feuer, Kerze, Haus) to burn ; (Licht) to be on ; (Haut, Augen) to sting. ◆ vt (Loch) to burn ; (Schnaps) to distil ; (Ton, Ziegel) to fire. ◆ vimp : es brennt! fire!

Brennholz das firewood.

Brennnessel (pl -n) die stinging nettle.

Brennspiritus der methylated spirits (sg).

Brennstoff (pl -e) der (zum Heizen) fuel.

Brett (pl -er) das (aus Holz) plank ; (zum Spielen) board ; schwarzes ~ noticeboard.

Brettspiel (pl -e) das board game.

Brezel (pl -n) die pretzel.

bricht präs → brechen.

Brief (pl -e) der letter ; eingeschriebener ~ ≃ letter sent by recorded delivery.

Briefdrucksache die letter comprising an order form, questionnaire etc, which costs less to send than an ordinary letter.

Brieffreund, in (mpl -e) der, die penfriend.

Briefkasten (pl -kästen) der (öffentlich) postbox ; (am Haus) letterbox.

Briefmarke (pl -n) die stamp.

Briefmarkenautomat (pl -en) der stamp machine.

Briefpapier das notepaper.

Brieftasche (pl -n) die wallet.

Briefträger, in (mpl -) der, die postman (postwoman).

Briefumschlag (pl -umschläge) der envelope.

Briefwaage (pl -n) die letter scales (pl).

briet prät → braten.

Brille (pl -n) die (für Augen) glasses (pl).

Brillenetui (pl -s) das glasses case.

bringen (prät brachte, pp gebracht) vt (wegbringen) to take ; (holen) to bring ; (Ergebnis) to cause ; (finanziell) to make ; (im Fernsehen) to broadcast ; (in Zeitung) to publish ; jm etw ~ to bring sb sthg ; jn nach Hause ~ to take sb home.

Brise (pl -n) die breeze.

Brite (pl -n) der Briton ; die ~n the British.

Britin (pl -nen) die Briton.

britisch adj British.

Britischen Inseln pl : die ~ the British Isles.

Broccoli der broccoli.

Brombeere (pl -n) die blackberry.

Bronchitis die bronchitis (sg).

Bronze die bronze.

Broschüre (pl -n) die brochure.

Brot (pl -e) das bread ; (Brotlaib) loaf (of bread) ; (Brotscheibe) slice of bread.

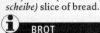

BROT

In Germany there are hundreds of different types of bread, the most common being "Graubrot", which is made from a mixture of rye and wheat flour, although wholemeal and multigrain breads are also popular. At breakfast, instead of sliced bread, Germans usually eat bread rolls (known as "Brötchen" or "Semmel" depending on the region) and these too come in a wide variety.

Brotaufstrich (pl -e) der spread.

Brötchen (pl -) das (bread) roll ; **belegtes ~** filled roll.

Brotmesser (pl -) das bread knife.

Bruch (pl Brüche) der (Knochenbruch) fracture ; (mit Partner, Vergangenheit) break ; (Leistenbruch) hernia ; (Bruchteil) fraction.

Bruchteil (pl -e) der fraction.

Brücke (pl -n) die bridge.

Brückenschäden pl damaged bridge.

Bruder (pl Brüder) der brother.

Brüderschaft die : ~ trinken to agree to use the familiar 'du' form and celebrate with a drink.

Brühe (pl -n) die (Suppe) broth ; (zum Kochen) stock.

Brühwürfel (pl -) der stock cube.

brüllen vi to shout.

brummen vi (Tier) to growl ; (Motor, Maschine) to drone.

Brunnen (pl -) der (zum Wasserholen) well ; (Springbrunnen) fountain.

Brüssel nt Brussels.

Brust (pl Brüste) die breast ; (Thorax) chest.

Brustschwimmen das breaststroke.

Brüstung (pl -en) die parapet.

brutal adj brutal.

brutto adv gross.

brutzeln vt & vi to fry.

Btx abk = Bildschirmtext.

Buch (pl Bücher) das book ; **~ führen** to keep a record.

buchen vt (reservieren) to book ; (auf Konto) to enter. ◆ vi (reservieren) to book.

Bücherei (pl -en) die library.

Buchhalter, in (mpl -) der, die bookkeeper.

Buchhandlung (pl -en) die bookshop.

Buchmesse (pl -n) die book fair.

Büchse (pl -n) die tin, can.

Büchsenmilch die tinned milk.

Büchsenöffner (*pl* -) *der* tin opener, can opener.

Buchstabe (*pl* -n) *der* letter ; **kleiner/großer** ~ small/capital letter.

buchstabieren *vt* to spell.

Bucht (*pl* -en) *die* bay.

Buchung (*pl* -en) *die* booking.

bücken : **sich bücken** *ref* to bend down.

Bude (*pl* -n) *die* (*Kiosk*) stall ; (*fam* : *Wohnung*) place.

Büfett (*pl* -s) *das* buffet ; **kaltes** ~ cold buffet.

Bügel (*pl* -) *der* (*Kleiderbügel*) (coat) hanger ; (*von Brille*) arm.

Bügeleisen (*pl* -) *das* iron.

bügelfrei *adj* non-iron.

bügeln *vt* & *vi* to iron.

Bügelspray *das* spray used to make clothes easier to iron.

Bühne (*pl* -n) *die* stage.

Bulgarien *nt* Bulgaria.

bummeln *vi* ist (*langsam gehen*) to stroll ; (*langsam sein*) to dawdle.

Bummelzug (*pl* -züge) *der* slow train.

Bund[1] (*pl* Bünde) *der* (*Zusammenschluss*) association ; (*fam* : *Bundeswehr*) armed forces (*pl*).

Bund[2] (*pl* Bunde) *das* (*von Gemüse, Blumen*) bunch.

Bundesbahn *die* German state railway company.

Bundesbürger, in (*mpl* -) *der, die* German citizen.

Bundeskanzler, in (*mpl* -) *der, die* German chancellor.

Bundesland (*pl* -länder) *das* Land (*German state*).

ⓘ **BUNDESLAND**

Germany is a federal republic which consists of 16 states known as "Bundesländer", each with its own parliament and constitution. The states enjoy autonomy from central government in certain areas such as education and culture. Each state is represented in the upper house of the German parliament, the "Bundesrat", which has the right to reject legislation put forward by the central government.

Bundesliga *die* division of German football league.

Bundesregierung (*pl* -en) *die* German government.

Bundesrepublik *die* Federal Republic of Germany.

Bundesstraße (*pl* -n) *die* ≃ A road (*Br*), ≃ state highway (*Am*).

Bundestag *der* German parliament.

Bundeswehr *die* German army.

bundesweit *adj* nationwide (*in Germany*). ◆ *adv* across Germany.

Bündnis (*pl* -se) *das* alliance.

Bungalow (*pl* -s) *der* bungalow.

bunt *adj* (*vielfarbig*) colourful. ◆ *adv* (*vielfarbig*) colourfully ; ~er Abend social evening.

Buntstift (*pl* -e) *der* coloured pencil.

Burg (*pl* -en) *die* castle.

bürgen *vi* : **für jn/etw** ~ to vouch for sb/sthg.

Burgenland nt Burgenland.

Bürger, in (mpl -) der, die (Einwohner) citizen ; (aus dem Mittelstand) middle-class person.

bürgerlich adj (Küche) plain ; (Hotel) respectable.

Bürgermeister, in (mpl -) der, die mayor.

Bürgersteig (pl -e) der pavement (Br), sidewalk (Am).

Büro (pl -s) das office.

Büroklammer (pl -n) die paper clip.

Bürste (pl -n) die brush.

bürsten vt to brush.

Bus (pl -se) der bus ; mit dem ~ fahren to go by bus.

Busbahnhof (pl -bahnhöfe) der bus station.

Busen (pl -) der bosom.

Busfahrer, in (mpl -) der, die bus driver ; 'Fahrscheine beim ~' 'tickets from the driver'.

Bushaltestelle (pl -n) die bus stop.

Business Class die (ohne pl) business class.

Buslinie (pl -n) die bus route.

Busreise (pl -n) die coach trip (Br), bus trip (Am).

Bußgeld (pl -er) das fine.

Bußgeldbescheid (pl -e) der notification of a fine.

Buß- und Bettag der Day of Prayer and Repentance, German public holiday in November.

Büstenhalter (pl -) der bra.

Busverbindung (pl -en) die bus connection, bus service.

Butangas das butane.

Butter die butter.

Butterbrot (pl -e) das slice of bread and butter.

Butterfahrt (pl -en) die short ferry trip outside German waters to allow passengers to buy duty-free goods.

Butterkäse (pl -) der full-fat cheese.

Buttermilch die buttermilk.

Butterschmalz das clarified butter.

bzw. abk = beziehungsweise.

C

ca. (abk für circa) approx.

Cabaret (pl -s) das cabaret.

Cabrio (pl -s) das convertible.

Café (pl -s) das café.

ℹ️ CAFÉ

Most German cafés serve cakes and gateaux with coffee or tea, although there are also "Eiscafés" which specialize in ice cream. You normally select your cake at the counter and it is then brought to your table. Two popular types of cake are Black Forest gateau ("Schwarzwälder Kirschtorte") and a type of cheesecake known as "Käsekuchen". Many cafés have a terrace where you can sit outside in summer, but if you do this coffee may only be ordered by the pot.

Cafeteria (*pl* -ien ODER -s) *die* cafeteria.

campen *vi* to camp.

Camping *das* camping.

Campingführer (*pl* -) *der* camping guidebook.

Campingplatz (*pl* -plätze) *der* campsite.

Campingwagen (*pl* -) *der* camper van.

Cashewnuss (*pl* -nüsse) *die* cashew nut.

CB-Funker, in (*mpl* -) *der, die* CB ham.

CD (*pl* -s) *die* CD.

CD-Spieler (*pl* -) *der* CD player.

Cello (*pl* -s) *das* cello.

Celsius *nt* celsius ; 10 Grad ~ 10 degrees centigrade.

Champagner *der* champagne.

Champignon (*pl* -s) *der* mushroom.

Chance (*pl* -n) *die* chance, opportunity.

Change *der* (*Geldwechsel*) bureau de change.

Chanson (*pl* -s) *das* satirical song.

chaotisch *adj* chaotic.

Charakter (*pl* -tere) *der* character.

charakteristisch *adj* characteristic.

charmant *adj* charming. ◆ *adv* charmingly.

Charterflug (*pl* -flüge) *der* charter flight.

Chartermaschine (*pl* -n) *die* charter plane.

chartern *vt* to charter.

chauvinistisch *adj* chauvinist.

Chef, in (*mpl* -s) *der, die* boss.

Chefarzt (*pl* -ärzte) *der* (senior) consultant.

Chefärztin (*pl* -nen) *die* (senior) consultant.

Chemie *die* chemistry.

chemisch *adj* chemical ; ~e Reinigung (*Laden*) dry cleaner's.

chic *adj* chic.

Chicorée *der, die* chicory.

Chiffre (*pl* -n) *die* (*von Zeitungsanzeige*) box number.

Chili *der* chilli.

China *nt* China.

Chinarestaurant (*pl* -s) *das* Chinese restaurant.

Chinese (*pl* -n) *der* Chinese (man) ; die ~n the Chinese.

Chinesin (*pl* -nen) *die* Chinese (woman).

chinesisch *adj* Chinese.

Chinesisch(e) *das* Chinese.

Chip (*pl* -s) *der* chip.

Chipkarte (*pl* -n) *die* (*EDV*) smart card.

Chips *pl* (*KÜCHE*) crisps (Br), chips (Am).

Chirurg, in (*mpl* -en) *der, die* surgeon.

chlorfrei *adj* chlorine-free ; '~ gebleicht' 'produced using chlorine-free bleaching processes'.

Choke (*pl* -s) *der* choke.

Cholesterin *das* cholesterol.

Chor (*pl* Chöre) *der* choir.

Choreografie, Choreographie (*pl* -n) *die* choreography.

Christ, in (*mpl* -en) *der, die* Christian.

Christi Himmelfahrt *nt* Ascension Day.

Chronik (*pl* -en) *die* chronicle.

chronisch *adj* chronic.

chronologisch *adj* chronological.

circa *adv* approximately.

City (*pl* -s) *die* city centre.

clever *adj* clever, smart.

Clique (*pl* -n) *die* clique.

Clown (*pl* -s) *der* clown.

Club (*pl* -s) *der* club.

Cluburlaub (*pl* -e) *der* club holiday.

Cocktail (*pl* -s) *der* cocktail.

Cognac® (*pl* -s) *der* cognac.

Cola (*pl* -s) *die* ODER *das* Coke®.

Comic (*pl* -s) *der* cartoon.

Computer (*pl* -) *der* computer.

Container (*pl* -) *der* container.

Cord *der* corduroy.

Couch (*pl* -en) *die* couch.

Cousin (*pl* -s) *der* cousin.

Cousine *die* → Kusine.

Creme (*pl* -s) *die* cream.

Curry (*pl* -s) *das* curry.

Currywurst (*pl* -würste) *die* sausage with curry sauce.

D

da *adv* 1. (*dort*) there ; ~, wo wir uns das letzte Mal getroffen haben where we met (the) last time ; ~ lang along there. 2. (*hier*) here ; ist Herr Müller ~? (*am Telefon*) is Mr Müller

there? ; sind alle ~? is everyone here? ; ~ und dort here and there ; *siehe auch* **da sein**. 3. (*übrig*) : ist noch Butter ~? is there any butter left? 4. (*zeitlich*) : gestern, ~ hat es geregnet it rained yesterday. 5. (*in diesem Fall*) there ; ~ hat er Recht he's right there. 6. (*plötzlich*) : ~ fällt mir ein... I've just thought... ◆ *konj* (*weil*) as, since.

dabei *adv* (*räumlich*) next to it ; (*gleichzeitig*) at the same time ; (*doch*) and (what is more) ; jm ~ helfen, etw zu tun to help sb do sthg ; nahe ~ nearby.

dabeibleiben *vi unr ist* (*an Ort*) to stay on ; (*bei Meinung*) to stick with it.

dabeihaben *vt unr* (*Person*) to have with one ; (*Gegenstand, Werkzeug*) to have on one.

dabei sein *vi unr ist* (*anwesend sein*) to be there ; nicht ~ sein to be missing ; ich bin ~, die Koffer zu packen I'm just packing the cases.

Dach (*pl* Dächer) *das* roof.

Dachboden (*pl* -böden) *der* loft.

Dachgepäckträger (*pl* -) *der* roofrack.

dachte *prät* → denken.

dadurch *adv* (*räumlich*) through it ; (*deshalb*) for that reason. ◆ *konj* : ~, dass... because...

dafür *adv* (*trotzdem*) nonetheless. ◆ *konj* : ~, dass considering ; ich habe 200 DM ~ bekommen I got 200 marks for it.

dafür können *vt unr* : sie kann nichts ~ it's not her fault.

dagegen *adv (als Gegensatz)* in comparison ; **das Auto fuhr ~** the car drove into it ; **etwas ~haben, dass** to mind that ; **nichts ~haben, dass** not to mind that.

dagegen sein *vi unr* to be against it.

daheim *adv* at home.

daher *adv (Herkunft)* from there ; *(deshalb)* that's why.

dahin *adv (räumlich)* there ; *(zeitlich)* : **bis ~** until then.

dahinten *adv* over there.

dahinter *adv* behind it.

dahinter kommen *vi unr ist* to find out.

damals *adv* then, in those days.

Dame *(pl -n) die (Person)* lady ; *(Spiel)* draughts *(sg)* ; *(in Schach, Kartenspiel)* queen ; **meine ~n und Herren** ladies and gentlemen! ▪ **Damen** *pl (Damentoilette)* ladies *(sg)*.

Damenbinde *(pl -n) die* sanitary towel.

Damenschuh *(pl -e) der* ladies' shoe.

Damentoilette *(pl -n) die* ladies (toilet).

damit *konj* so that. ◆ *adv (dadurch)* therefore ; **ich will ~ spielen** I want to play with it ; **was meinst du ~?** what do you mean by that?

Damm *(pl Dämme) der (gegen Überschwemmung)* dam ; *(für Straße, Schienen)* embankment.

dämmern *vimp* : **es dämmert** *(morgens)* it's getting light ; *(abends)* it's getting dark.

Dämmerung *(pl -en) die (morgens)* dawn ; *(abends)* dusk.

dämmrig *adj* dim.

Dampf *(pl Dämpfe) der* steam. ▪ **Dämpfe** *pl (chemisch)* fumes.

Dampfbad *(pl -bäder) das* Turkish bath.

dampfen *vi* to steam.

dämpfen *vt (Licht)* to dim ; *(Geräusch)* to muffle ; *(Wut)* to calm ; *(Begeisterung)* to dampen ; *(kochen)* to steam.

Dampfer *(pl -) der* steamship.

Dampfnudel *(pl -n) die (Süddt)* sweet dumpling made with yeast dough.

danach *adv (zeitlich)* afterwards ; **sie sehnt sich ~** she longs for it ; **kurz ~** shortly afterwards.

Däne *(pl -n) der* Dane.

daneben *adv (räumlich)* next to it ; *(vergleichend)* in comparison.

Dänemark *nt* Denmark.

Dänin *(pl -nen) die* Dane.

dänisch *adj* Danish.

Dänisch(e) *das* Danish.

Dank *der* thanks *(pl)* ; **vielen ~!** thank you! ; **besten ~!** thank you! ; **herzlichen ~!** thank you! ; **schönen ~!** thank you! ; **vielen ~ im Voraus** thanking you in advance.

dankbar *adj (Person)* grateful ; **jm für etw ~ sein** to be grateful to sb for sthg.

danke *interj* thanks!; ~, gleichfalls! thanks, you too!; ~ schön ODER sehr! thanks!

danken *vi* to say thank you; jm ~ to thank sb; für etw ~ to say thank you for sthg; nichts zu ~! don't mention it!

dann *adv* then; bis ~! see you then!; also ~ all right, then.

daran *adv (räumlich)* on/to/ against/next to it; es liegt ~, dass... it is because of the fact that...

darauf *adv (räumlich)* on it; *(zeitlich)* afterwards; ~ warten, dass... to wait for...; am Tag ~ the next day; die Tage ~ the next few days.

daraus *adv (aus Gefäß, Behälter)* out of it; *(aus Material)* from it; mach dir nichts ~! don't let it bother you!

darf *präs* → dürfen.

darin *adv (räumlich)* in it; ~ liegt ein Widerspruch that's a contradiction.

Darlehen *(pl -)* das loan.

Darm *(pl Därme)* der intestine.

Darmgrippe *die* gastric flu.

Darsteller, in *(mpl -)* der, die actor (actress).

Darstellung *(pl -en)* die representation.

darüber *adv (räumlich)* over it; *(sprechen, diskutieren)* about it.

darum *adv (deshalb)* that's why; ~ geht es nicht that's not the point; es geht ~, zu gewinnen the main thing is to win.

darunter *adv (räumlich)* under it; *(weniger)* : 30 Meter oder etwas ~ 30 metres or a little less; viele Besucher, ~ auch einige aus dem Ausland many visitors, including some foreigners; was verstehst du ~? what do you understand by that?

das *det* the. ◆ *pron (Demonstrativpronomen)* that; *(Relativpronomen)* that, which; ~ Rauchen smoking; ~ da! that one there!

da sein *vi unr ist* to be there; ist noch Bier da? is there any beer left?

dass *konj (im Objektsatz)* that; *(im Subjektsatz)* the fact that; ~ das bloß klappt! let it work!; sich so freuen, ~... to be so happy that...

dasselbe *det* the same. ◆ *pron* the same one; ~ tun to do the same (thing).

Datei *(pl -en)* die file.

Datenschutz *der* data protection.

Dativ *der* dative.

Dattel *(pl -n)* die date.

Datum *(pl Daten)* das date.

Dauer *die* duration; auf (die) ~ in the long term; für die ~ von vier Jahren for (a period of) four years.

Dauerauftrag *(pl -aufträge)* der standing order.

Dauerkarte *(pl -n)* die season ticket.

Dauerlauf *der* jog.

dauern *vi* to last; es dauerte drei Wochen, bis ich den Brief bekam it took three weeks for the letter to reach me.

dauernd *adj* constant. ◆ *adv* constantly.

Dauerparkplatz (*pl* -plätze) *der* long-stay car park.

Dauerwelle (*pl* -n) *die* perm.

Daumen (*pl* -) *der* thumb ; jm die ~ drücken to keep one's fingers crossed for sb.

Daunendecke (*pl* -n) *die* eiderdown.

davon *adv* (*räumlich*) from it ; (*von Thema*) about it ; (*von Menge*) of it.

davor *adv* (*räumlich*) in front of it ; (*zeitlich*) beforehand ; **ich habe Angst ~** I'm scared of it ; **kurz ~ sein, etw zu tun** to be on the point of doing sthg.

dazu *adv* (*außerdem*) in addition ; **es schneit, ~ ist es kalt** it's snowing and it's cold too ; **ich habe keine Lust ~** I don't feel like it ; **ich bin nicht ~ gekommen** I didn't get round to it.

dazu|geben *vt unr* to add.

dazu|gehören *vi* (*Person*) to belong ; (*Zubehör*) to go with it.

dazu|kommen *vi unr ist* (*zu Gruppe*) to come along ; **kommt noch etwas dazu?** would you like anything else? ; **es kommt noch Mehrwertsteuer ~** it doesn't include VAT.

dazwischen *adv* in between.

dazwischen|kommen *vi unr ist* : **mir ist etwas dazwischengekommen** something has cropped up.

Deck (*pl* -s) *das* deck ; **an ~** on deck.

Decke (*pl* -n) *die* (*von Bett*) blanket ; (*von Tisch*) tablecloth ; (*von Raum*) ceiling.

Deckel (*pl* -) *der* lid.

decken *vt* to cover ; **etw über jn/etw ~** to cover sb/sthg with sthg.

Deckfarbe (*pl* -n) *die* gouache.

Decoder (*pl* -) *der* (*für Pay-TV*) decoder.

defekt *adj* faulty.

definieren *vt* to define.

Defizit (*pl* -e) *das* deficit.

deftig *adj* (*Speise*) substantial.

dehnbar *adj* elastic.

Deich (*pl* -e) *der* dike.

dein, e *det* your.

deine, r, s ODER **deins** *pron* yours.

Deklination (*pl* -en) *die* declension.

deklinieren *vt* to decline.

Dekolletee, Dekolleté (*pl* -s) *das* low neckline.

Dekoration (*pl* -en) *die* decoration.

Delfin *der* → Delphin.

delikat *adj* (*Angelegenheit*) delicate ; (*Speise*) delicious.

Delikatesse (*pl* -n) *die* delicacy.

Delle (*pl* -n) *die* (*an Auto*) dent.

Delphin (*pl* -e) *der* dolphin.

dem *det* (to) the. ◆ *pron* (*Demonstrativpronomen : Person*) to him ; (*Sache*) to that one ; (*Relativpronomen : Person*) to whom ; (*Sache*) to which.

demnächst *adv* shortly.

Demokratie (*pl* -n) *die* democracy.

demokratisch *adj* democratic.

demolieren *vt* to demolish.

Demonstration (pl -en) die demonstration.

demonstrieren vi : ~ gegen/für to demonstrate against/for.

den det the. ◆ pron (Demonstrativpronomen : Person) him ; (Sache) that (one) ; (Relativpronomen : Person) whom ; (Sache) to which.

denen pron (Demonstrativpronomen) (to) them ; (Relativpronomen : Person) to whom ; (Sache) to which.

denken (prät dachte, pp gedacht) vi & vt to think ; ~ an (+A) (planen) to think about ; (sich erinnern an, berücksichtigen) to think of ; denk an den Kaffee! don't forget the coffee! ; ~ über (+A) to think about ; ~ von to think of ; sich (D) etw ~ to imagine sthg ; das hätte ich mir ~ können I might have known.

Denkmal (pl -mäler) das monument.

Denkmalschutz der : unter ~ stehen to be classified as a historical monument.

denn konj (weil) because. ◆ adv then ; was hast du ~? so what's wrong?

Deo (pl -s) das deodorant.

Deodorant (pl -s) das deodorant.

Deponie (pl -n) die dump.

deponieren vt (Gepäck, Paket) to deposit.

Depression (pl -en) die depression.

der det (Nominativ) the ; (Genitiv) of the ; (Dativ) (to) the. ◆ pron (Demonstrativpronomen : Person) him ; (Sache) that (one) ; (Relativpronomen : Person) who ; (Sache) which ; der Hut ~ Frau the woman's hat ; der Fußball ~ Jungen the boys' football.

deren det their. ◆ pron (bei Person) whose ; (bei Sache) of which.

derselbe det the same. ◆ pron the same one.

derzeit adv at the moment.

des det of the ; der Hut ~ Mannes the man's hat.

deshalb adv therefore.

Desinfektionsmittel (pl -) das disinfectant.

desinfizieren vt to disinfect.

dessen det (bei Person) his ; (bei Sache) its. ◆ pron (bei Person) whose ; (bei Sache) of which.

Dessert (pl -s) das dessert ; zum ~ for dessert.

desto konj → je.

deswegen adv therefore.

Detail (pl -s) das detail.

Detektiv, in (mpl -e) der, die detective.

deutlich adj clear. ◆ adv clearly ; ~ sprechen to speak clearly.

deutsch adj German. ◆ adv : auf Deutsch in German.

Deutsch das German.

Deutsche[1] (pl -n) der, die (Person) German.

Deutsche[2] das (Sprache) German.

Deutsche Bundesbahn die German state railway company.

Deutsche Bundesbank *die German federal bank.*

Deutsche Bundespost *die German postal service.*

Deutschland *nt* Germany.

deutschsprachig *adj* German-speaking.

Devisen *pl* foreign currency *(sg).*

Dezember *der* December ; → September.

d. h. *(abk für das heißt)* i.e.

Dia *(pl -s) das* slide.

Diabetes *der* diabetes *(sg).*

Diabetiker, in *(mpl -) der, die* diabetic ; **für ~ geeignet** diabetic *(vor Subst).*

Diafilm *(pl -e) der* slide film.

Diagnose *(pl -n) die (MED)* diagnosis.

Dialekt *(pl -e) der* dialect.

ⓘ **DIALEKT**

Although all countries have regional dialects, some of those in the German-speaking world are particularly strong and often even German speakers from other regions are unable to understand them. The main dialects are the following : "Plattdeutsch", spoken in the north of Germany, "Kölsch", spoken around Cologne, "Berlinerisch" in Berlin, "Sächsisch" in Saxony, "Bayrisch" in Bavaria and the dialects of Switzerland and Austria. Standard "high German" is usually used when writing and for official purposes.

Dialog *(pl -e) der* dialogue.

Diaprojektor *(pl -en) der* slide projector.

Diarahmen *(pl -) der* slide frame.

Diät *(pl -en) die* diet ; **eine ~ machen** to go on a diet.

Diavortrag *(pl -vorträge) der* slide presentation.

dich *pron* you ; *(Reflexivpronomen)* yourself.

dicht *adj* thick ; *(gegen Wasser)* watertight ; *(gegen Luft)* airtight ; *(Dach, Fenster)* weatherproof ; *(Verkehr)* heavy. ◆ *adv* tightly ; **~ neben etw (D) stehen** to stand right next to sthg ; **~ davor, etw zu tun** to be on the verge of doing sthg.

Dichter, in *(mpl -) der, die (von Gedichten)* poet ; *(von Dramen, Theaterstücken)* writer.

Dichtung *(pl -en) die (Gedichte)* poetry ; *(Literatur)* literature ; *(Dichtungsring)* washer.

Dichtungsring *(pl -e) der* washer.

dick *adj* thick ; *(Person, Körperteil)* fat ; *(geschwollen)* swollen. ◆ *adv* thickly.

Dickmilch *die* sour milk.

die *det* the. ◆ *pron (Demonstrativpronomen : Person)* her, them *(pl)* ; *(Sache)* that one, those ones *(pl)* ; *(Relativpronomen : Person)* who ; *(Sache)* which.

Dieb, in *(mpl -e) der, die* thief.

Diebstahl *(pl -stähle) der* theft ; **einen ~ anzeigen** to report a theft.

Diebstahlversicherung (*pl* -en) *die* insurance against theft.

Diele (*pl* -n) *die (Flur)* hall.

dienen *vi* (+D) to serve ; *(fördern)* to be to the benefit of.

Dienst (*pl* -e) *der* service ; hast du morgen ~? do you have to go to work tomorrow? ; im ~ on duty ; der öffentliche ~ the civil service ; ~ habend on duty.

Dienstag (*pl* -e) *der* Tuesday ; → **Samstag**.

dienstags *adv* on Tuesdays.

Dienstbereitschaft *die* : die Apotheke hat heute Nacht ~ the chemist's is open all night tonight.

Dienstfahrt (*pl* -en) *die* business trip.

Dienstleistung (*pl* -en) *die* service.

dienstlich *adj* business (vor *Subst*). ◆ *adv* on business.

Dienstreise (*pl* -n) *die* business trip.

Dienststelle (*pl* -n) *die (amt)* office.

Dienstzeit (*pl* -en) *die* working hours (*pl*).

diese, r, s ODER **dies** *det* this, these (*pl*). ◆ *pron* this one, these ones (*pl*).

Diesel (*pl* -) *der* diesel.

dieselbe *det* the same. ◆ *pron* the same one.

Dieselkraftstoff (*pl* -e) *der* diesel fuel.

Dieselmotor (*pl*-en) *der* diesel engine.

Dieselöl *das* diesel.

dieser *det* → **diese**.

dieses *det* → **diese**.

diesig *adj* misty.

diesmal *adv* this time.

diesseits *adv* on this side. ◆ *präp* (+G) on this side of.

Differenz (*pl* -en) *die* difference.

Digitalanzeige (*pl* -n) *die* digital display.

Diktat (*pl* -e) *das (in Schule)* dictation.

Diktatur (*pl* -en) *die* dictatorship.

diktieren *vt* to dictate.

Dill *der* dill.

DIN *(abk für Deutsche Industrienorm)* ≃ BS *(Br)*, ≃ ASA *(Am)*.

Ding (*pl* -e) *das* thing.

Dings *der, die, das (fam)* thingamajig.

Dingsbums *der, die, das (fam)* = **Dings**.

Dingsda *der, die, das (fam)* = **Dings**.

DIN-Norm (*pl* -en) *die (amt)* German standard.

Dinosaurier (*pl* -) *der* dinosaur.

Diphterie *die* diphtheria.

Diplom (*pl* -e) *das (Titel)* degree.

Diplomat, in (*mpl* -en) *der, die* diplomat.

dir *pron* (to) you.

direkt *adj* direct. ◆ *adv* directly ; *(ohne Zwischenzeit)* straight ; ~ neben right next to.

Direktflug (*pl*-flüge) *der* direct flight.

Direktor (*pl* -toren) *der (von Hotel)* manager ; *(von Firma)* director ; *(von Schule)* headmaster.

Direktorin (*pl* -nen) *die (von Hotel)* manageress ; *(von Firma)* director ; *(von Schule)* headmistress.

Direktübertragung (*pl*-en) *die* live broadcast.

Dirigent, in (*mpl* -en) *der, die* conductor.

dirigieren *vt & vi (MUS)* to conduct.

Diskette (*pl* -n) *die (EDV)* (floppy) disk.

Disko (*pl* -s) *die (fam)* disco, (night) club ; **in die ~ gehen** to go clubbing.

Diskothek (*pl* -en) *die* disco(theque).

diskret *adj* discreet. ◆ *adv* discreetly.

diskriminieren *vt (benachteiligen)* to discriminate against.

Diskriminierung (*pl*-en) *die* discrimination.

Diskussion (*pl* -en) *die* discussion.

diskutieren *vt* to discuss. ◆ *vi* to have a discussion ; **~ mit** to have a discussion with ; **~ über** (+A) to have a discussion about.

Distanz (*pl* -en) *die* distance.

Distel (*pl* -n) *die* thistle.

diverse *adj* various.

dividieren *vt & vi* to divide.

DLRG *die German life-savers society.*

DM *(abk für Deutsche Mark)* DM.

D-Mark (*pl* -) *die* Deutschmark, German mark.

doch *interj* yes. ◆ *konj* yet, but. ◆ *adv (konzessiv)* anyway ;

er wollte erst nicht, aber dann hat er es ~ gemacht at first he didn't want to, but then he did it anyway ; **setzen Sie sich ~!** do sit down! ; **nicht ~, so war das nicht gemeint!** okay, okay, I didn't mean it that way ; **das kann ~ nicht wahr sein!** but surely that can't be true! ; **willst du nicht? -~, ich will** don't you want to? - yes, I do ; **~ noch** after all.

Doktor (*pl* Doktoren) *der (fam : Arzt)* doctor ; *(Titel)* doctorate.

Doktorin (*pl* -nen) *die (fam : Ärztin)* doctor.

Dokument (*pl* -e) *das (Urkunde)* document.

Dokumentation (*pl* -en) *die (schriftlich)* documentation ; *(filmisch)* documentary.

dolmetschen *vi* to interpret.

Dolmetscher, in (*mpl* -) *der, die* interpreter.

Dom (*pl* -e) *der* cathedral.

dominieren *vt* to dominate. ◆ *vi* to predominate.

Domino *das (Spiel)* dominoes (*sg*).

Donau *die* : **die ~** the Danube.

Donner *der* thunder.

donnern *vimp* : **es donnert** it's thundering.

Donnerstag (*pl* -e) *der* Thursday ; → **Samstag**.

donnerstags *adv* on Thursdays.

doof *adj (fam)* stupid. ◆ *adv (fam)* stupidly.

Doppelbett (*pl*-en) *das* double bed.

Doppeldecker (*pl* -) *der (Bus)* double decker.

Doppelname (*pl* -n) *der* (*Nachname*) double-barrelled name.

Doppelpunkt (*pl* -e) *der* co-lon.

Doppelstecker (*pl* -) *der* two-way adapter.

doppelt *adj* double. ◆ *adv* twice ; **so viel** twice as much.

Doppelzimmer (*pl* -) *das* double room.

Dorf (*pl* Dörfer) *das* village.

Dorn (*pl* -en) *der* thorn.

Dörrobst *das* dried fruit.

dort *adv* there ; ~ **drüben** over there.

dorther *adv* from there.

dorthin *adv* there.

Dose (*pl* -n) *die* (*aus Holz, Plastik*) box ; (*aus Porzellan*) pot ; (*Konservendose*) tin, can ; **Erbsen aus der** ~ tinned ODER canned peas.

dösen *vi* to snooze.

Dosenmilch *die* tinned milk, canned milk.

Dosenöffner (*pl* -) *der* tin opener, can opener.

dosieren *vt* to measure out.

Dosierung (*pl* -en) *die* dosage.

Dosierungsanleitung (*pl* -en) *die* directions for use (*pl*).

Dosis (*pl* Dosen) *die* dose.

Dozent, in (*mpl* -en) *der, die* lecturer.

Dr. (*abk für Doktor*) Dr.

Drachen (*pl* -) *der* (*aus Papier*) kite ; (*SPORT*) hang-glider.

Drachenfliegen *das* hang-gliding.

Dragee (*pl* -s) *das* (*Medikament*) pill ; (*Bonbon*) sweet.

Draht (*pl* Drähte) *der* wire.

Drahtseilbahn (*pl* -en) *die* cable railway.

Drama (*pl* Dramen) *das* drama.

dramatisch *adj* (*spannend*) dramatic.

Dramaturg, in (*mpl* -en) *der, die* person who selects and adapts plays for the stage.

dran *adv* (*fam*) = **daran** ; ~ **sein** (*an der Reihe sein*) to be next.

dran|bleiben *vi unr ist* (*am Telefon*) to hold (the line).

drängeln *vi* (*durch Schieben*) to push. ▣ **sich drängeln** *ref* : **sich nach vorn** ~ to push one's way forward.

drängen *vt* (*schieben*) to push ; (*überreden*) to press.

dran|kommen *vi unr ist* (*an die Reihe kommen*) to have one's turn ; (*heranreichen*) to reach.

drauf *adv* (*fam*) = **darauf** ; **gut/schlecht** ~ **sein** to be in a good/bad mood.

draus *adv* (*fam*) = **daraus**.

draußen *adv* outside ; **nach** ~ outside ; **von** ~ from outside.

Dreck *der* (*fam : Schmutz*) dirt.

dreckig *adj* (*fam : schmutzig*) dirty ; **etw** ~ **machen** to get sthg dirty.

drehen *vt* (*Kurbel, Schraube*) to turn ; (*Film*) to film ; (*Zigarette*) to roll. ◆ *vi* (*Fahrzeug, Wind*) to turn ; **an etw** (*D*) ~ to turn sthg ; **etw laut/leise** ~ to turn sthg up/down. ▣ **sich drehen** *ref* to turn over ; **sich** ~ **um** (*thematisch*) to be about.

Drehtür (*pl* -en) *die* revolving door.

Drehzahlmesser (*pl* -) *der* rev counter.

drei *num* three ; → **sechs**.

Dreieck (*pl* -e) *das* triangle.

Dreieckstuch (*pl* -tücher) *das* headscarf.

dreifach *num* triple.

dreihundert *num* three hundred.

Dreikönigstag *der* Epiphany.

dreimal *adv* three times.

dreispurig *adj* three-lane.

dreißig *num* thirty ; → **sechs**.

drei Viertel *adv* three quarters ; *(Süddt : in Uhrzeit)* : **es ist ~ acht** it's a quarter to eight *(Br)*, it's a quarter of eight *(Am)*.

dreizehn *num* thirteen ; → **sechs**.

dressieren *vt* to train.

Dressing (*pl* -s) *das* dressing.

Dressur (*pl* -en) *die* dressage.

drin *adv* = darin ; **das ist nicht ~** that's out.

dringen (*prät* **drang**, *pp* **gedrungen**) *vi* **ist : in** ODER **durch etw** (*A*) **~** to penetrate sthg.

dringend *adj* urgent. ◆ *adv* urgently.

drinnen *adv* inside.

dritt *num* : **wir sind zu ~** there are three of us.

dritte, r, s *adj* third ; → **sechste**.

Drittel (*pl* -) *das* third ; → **Sechstel**.

drittens *adv* thirdly.

Dritte Reich *das* Third Reich.

Dritte Welt *die* Third World.

DRK *das* (*abk für* Deutsches Rotes Kreuz) German Red Cross.

Droge (*pl* -n) *die* (*Rauschgift*) drug.

drogenabhängig *adj* : **~ sein** to be a drug addict.

Drogenberatungsstelle (*pl* -n) *die* drug advice centre.

Drogerie (*pl* -n) *die* ≃ chemist's (shop) *(Br)*, drugstore *(Am)*.

Drogeriemarkt (*pl* -märkte) *der* discount chemist's *(Br)*, discount drugstore *(Am)*.

drohen *vi* to threaten.

drosseln *vt* (*Tempo*) to reduce.

drüben *adv* over there.

drüber *adv* (*fam*) = darüber.

Druck[1] *der* (*Kraft*) pressure ; *(von Finger)* touch ; *(von Hand)* shake ; *(von Büchern)* printing.

Druck[2] (*pl* -e) *der* (*Gravur*) print.

Druckbuchstabe (*pl* -n) *der* printed letter ; **'bitte in ~n schreiben!'** 'please write in block capitals'.

drucken *vt* to print.

drücken *vi* (*pressen*) to press ; *(Schuhe)* to pinch. ◆ *vt* (*Knopf, Schalter*) to press ; **auf etw** (*A*) **~** to press sthg ; **'drücken'** 'push' ; **jn ~** (*fam : umarmen*) to hug sb. ▪ **sich drücken** *ref* (*fam : sich entziehen*) : **sich ~ vor** (+ *D*) to get out of.

drückend *adj* (*Hitze*) oppressive.

Druckknopf (*pl* -knöpfe) *der* (*an Kleidung*) press stud.

Drucksache (*pl* -n) *die* printed matter.

Druckschrift *die* block capitals *(pl)*.

drum *adv (fam)* = **darum**.

■ **Drum** *das* : **mit allem Drum und Dran** *(fam)* with all the trappings.

drunter *adv (fam)* = **darunter** ; **es geht ~ und drüber** *(fam)* everything's all over the place.

dt. *abk* = **deutsch**.

du *pron* you ; **Du sagen** *to use the 'du' form of address* ; **mit jm per Du sein** ≃ to be on first name terms with sb.

Dübel *(pl -)* der Rawlplug®.

Duett *(pl -e) das* duet.

duften *vi* to smell nice. ◆ *vimp* : **es duftet nach...** there's a smell of...

dumm *(komp* dümmer, *superl* am dümmsten) *adj* stupid. ◆ *adv* stupidly ; **~es Zeug** *(abw)* rubbish.

Dummkopf *(pl -köpfe) der* idiot.

dumpf *adj (Klang)* muffled.

Düne *(pl -n) die* dune.

Dünger *der* fertilizer.

dunkel *(komp* dunkler, *superl* am dunkelsten) *adj* dark ; *(Klang)* deep. ◆ *adv (färben)* dark ; **seine Stimme klingt ~** his voice is deep ; **es wird ~** it's getting dark.

dunkelblond *adj* light brown.

dunkelhaarig *adj* darkhaired.

Dunkelheit *die (nächtlich)* darkness.

dünn *adj* thin ; *(Getränk)* weak. ◆ *adv* thinly ; **etw ~ auftragen** to apply sthg sparingly.

dünsten *vt* to steam.

dunstig *adj (Wetter)* hazy.

Duo *(pl -s) das (Musikstück)* duet ; *(zwei Musiker)* duo.

Dur *das* major.

durch *präp (+A)* through ; *(mithilfe von)* by (means of) ; *(wegen)* as a result of. ◆ *adv* through ; **die ganze Nacht ~** throughout the night ; **darf ich mal bitte ~?** excuse me, please! ; **~ und ~** through and through ; **~ die Schweiz reisen** to travel across Switzerland.

durch|atmen *vi* to breathe deeply.

durchaus *adv* absolutely ; **~ nicht** not at all.

Durchblutung *die* circulation.

durch|brechen *vt unr hat (Stock)* to snap. ◆ *vi unr ist (Stock, Brett)* to snap.

durch|brennen *vi unr ist (Sicherung)* to blow.

durch|drehen *vi ist (Räder)* to spin ; *(fig : Person)* to crack up.

durcheinander *adv* all over the place. ◆ *adj* : **~ sein** *(Zimmer, Haus)* to be in a mess ; *(Person)* to be confused.

Durcheinander *das* chaos.

durch|fahren *vi unr ist (mit Auto)* to drive through ; *(Zug)* to go through.

Durchfahrt *die* : **auf der ~ sein** to be travelling through ; **'~ verboten!'** 'no through road' *(Br)*, 'no outlet' *(Am)*.

Durchfall *(pl -fälle) der* diarrhoea.

durch|fragen : sich durch-**fragen** *ref* to ask the way ; **sich zum Bahnhof ~** to ask the way to the station.

durch|führen *vt* to carry out.

Durchgang (*pl* -gänge) *der (zwischen Gebäuden)* passage ; 'kein ~!' 'keep out'.

Durchgangsverkehr *der* through traffic.

durchgebrannt *pp* → **durchbrennen**. ◆ *adj (Sicherung)* blown.

durchgebraten *adj* well-done.

durchgefroren *adj* frozen.

durch|gehen *vi unr ist* to go through ; **bitte ~!** *(in Bus)* please move to the back of the bus!

durchgehend *adj (Zug)* through *(vor Subst)*. ◆ *adv* : '~ geöffnet' 'open all day'.

durch|halten *vi unr* to hold out. ◆ *vt unr* to withstand.

durch|kommen *vi unr ist* to get through.

durch|lassen *vt unr (Person)* to let through ; *(Wasser)* to let in.

durchlässig *adj* leaky.

Durchlauferhitzer (*pl* -) *der* water heater.

durch|machen *vt (ertragen)* to go through ; **die Nacht ~** *(fam : feiern)* to party all night.

Durchmesser (*pl* -) *der* diameter.

Durchreise *die* : **auf der ~ (sein)** (to be) travelling through.

Durchreisevisum (*pl* -visa) *das* transit visa.

durch|reißen *vt unr hat* to snap. ◆ *vi unr ist* to snap.

Durchsage (*pl* -n) *die* announcement ; **Achtung, eine ~!** attention, please, here is an announcement.

durch|sagen *vt* to announce.

durchschauen *vt* to see through.

Durchschlag (*pl* -schläge) *der* carbon copy.

durch|schlagen : sich **durchschlagen** *ref (zur Grenze)* to make it ; *(finanziell)* to get by.

durch|schneiden *vt unr* to cut through.

Durchschnitt *der* average ; **im ~** on average.

durchschnittlich *adj* average. ◆ *adv (im Durchschnitt)* on average ; *(mittelmäßig)* averagely.

Durchschnittsgeschwindigkeit *die* average speed.

durch sein *vi unr ist (fam : Zug)* to have gone through ; *(Fleisch)* to be done ; *(Kleidung, Schuhe)* to have worn through.

durch|setzen *vt* to push through. ▣ **sich durchsetzen** *ref (Person)* to get one's way.

durchsichtig *adj (Material)* transparent.

durch|stellen *vt (an Telefon)* to put through.

durch|streichen *vt unr* to cross out.

durchsuchen *vt* to search.

Durchwahl *die* extension.

durch|wählen *vi* to dial direct.

durch|zählen *vt* to count up.

durch|ziehen *vt unr (durch Öffnung)* to pull through ; *(Plan)* to see through.

Durchzug *der (Luftzug)* draught.

dürfen *(präs* **darf**, *prät* **durfte**, *pp* **dürfen**) *aux* 1. *(als Erlaubnis)* : **etw tun** ~ to be allowed to do sthg ; **sie** ~ **gerne hineinkommen** please, come in!

2. *(in Fragen)* : **darf ich mich setzen?** may I sit down? ; **darf ich fragen...** may I ask...

3. *(als Aufforderung)* : **das** ~ **wir nicht vergessen** we mustn't forget that ; **so etwas darf einfach nicht passieren** such a thing simply should not happen.

4. *(als Annahme)* : **das dürfte genügen** that should be enough.

◆ *vi (als Erlaubnis : pp gedurft)* : **sie darf nicht ins Schwimmbad** she's not allowed to go swimming.

◆ *vt (als Erlaubnis : pp gedurft)* : **das darf man nicht!** you're not allowed to do that! ; **was darf es sein?** what can I get you?

Durst *der* thirst ; ~ **auf ein Bier haben** to fancy a beer ; ~ **haben** to be thirsty.

durstig *adj* thirsty ; ~ **sein** to be thirsty.

Dusche *(pl* -n) *die* shower.

duschen *vi* to have a shower. ▪ **sich duschen** *ref* to have a shower.

Duschgel *das* shower gel.

Duschkabine *(pl* -n) *die* shower (cubicle).

Duschvorhang *(pl* -hänge) *der* shower curtain.

Düsenflugzeug *(pl* -e) *das* jet.

düster *adj (dunkel)* gloomy.

Dutzend *(pl* -) *das* dozen. ▪ **Dutzende** *pl* dozens.

duzen *vt to use the 'du' form of address.* ▪ **sich duzen** *ref to use the 'du' form of address* ; **sich** ~ **mit jm** ≃ to be on first name terms with sb.

DVD *(abk für Digital Video* ODER *Versatile Disc)* DVD.

Dynamo *(pl* -s) *der* dynamo.

DZ *abk* = **Doppelzimmer**.

E

Ebbe *(pl* -n) *die (an Meer)* low tide ; ~ **und Flut** tides *(pl)*.

eben *adj (Boden)* flat. ◆ *adv* just. ◆ *interj (genau)* exactly! ; ~ **nicht!** that's not true! ; **sie war** ~ **nicht hier** she was just here ; **komm mal** ~ **her!** come here a minute!

Ebene *(pl* -n) *die (Flachland)* plain ; *(Niveau)* level.

ebenfalls *adv (auch)* as well ; *(gleichfalls)* you too.

ebenso *adv* just as.

EC *(pl* -s) *abk* = **EuroCity**.

Echo *(pl* -s) *das* echo.

echt adj (Gold, Leder) genuine ; (Freund, Gefühl) real. ◆ adv really.

Ecke (pl -n) die corner ; um die ~ round the corner.

eckig adj (quadratisch) square ; (rechteckig) rectangular.

Economyklasse die economy class.

Edelstahl der stainless steel.

Edelstein (pl -e) der precious stone.

Edelweiß (pl -e) das edelweiss.

Edinburg nt Edinburgh.

EDV die data processing.

Efeu (pl -s) das ivy.

Effekt (pl -e) der effect.

EG die (abk für Europäische Gemeinschaft) EC.

egal adj (gleichgültig) all the same ; das ist ~ it doesn't matter ; ~, wie groß no matter how big ; ~ ob no matter whether ; es ist mir ~ I don't mind.

egoistisch adj selfish.

ehe konj before.

Ehe (pl -n) die marriage.

Ehefrau (pl -en) die wife.

Eheleute pl married couple (sg).

ehemalig adj former.

Ehemann (pl -männer) der husband.

Ehepaar (pl -e) das married couple.

eher adv sooner ; es ist ~ grün als blau it's more green than blue.

Ehering (pl -e) der wedding ring.

Ehre (pl -n) die (Würde) honour.

ehrenamtlich adj honorary.

Ehrengast (pl -gäste) der guest of honour.

ehrgeizig adj ambitious.

ehrlich adj (Person, Antwort) honest. ◆ adv (antworten) honestly.

Ei (pl -er) das egg ; ein weiches/hart gekochtes ~ a soft-boiled/hard-boiled egg.

Eiche (pl -n) die (Baum) oak.

Eichhörnchen (pl -) das squirrel.

Eid (pl -e) der oath.

Eidechse (pl -n) die lizard.

eidesstattlich adj sworn. ◆ adv solemnly.

Eierbecher (pl -) der egg cup.

Eierstock (pl -stöcke) der ovary.

eifersüchtig adj jealous.

eifrig adj eager. ◆ adv eagerly.

Eigelb (pl -e) das egg yolk.

eigen adj own.

eigenartig adj strange. ◆ adv strangely.

Eigenbedarf der : für den ~ for one's own use.

Eigenschaft (pl -en) die (Charakteristikum) characteristic.

eigentlich adj (wirklich) actual. ◆ adv (im Grunde) actually ; kennst du ~ meinen Bruder? do you know my brother? ; wer sind Sie ~? who might you be? ; was denkst du dir ~? what on earth do you think you're doing?

Eigentum *das* property.

Eigentümer, in *(mpl -) der, die* owner.

Eigentumswohnung *(pl -en) die* owner-occupied flat *(Br)*, owner-occupied apartment *(Am)*.

eignen : **sich eignen** *ref* to be suitable.

Eilbrief *(pl -e) der* express letter.

Eile *die* hurry ; **in ~ sein** to be in a hurry.

eilen *vi ist* to hurry ; **eilt!** urgent!

eilig *adj (dringend)* urgent ; *(schnell)* hurried. ◆ *adv (schnell)* hurriedly ; **es ~ haben** to be in a hurry.

Eilsendung *(pl -en) die* express letter/parcel.

Eilzug *(pl -züge) der* fast stopping train.

Eilzustellung *(pl -en) die* express delivery.

Eimer *(pl -) der* bucket.

ein, e *det* a, an *(vor Vokal)* ; **~ Hund** a dog ; **~e Idee** an idea ; **~ Mädchen** a girl ; **~es Tages** one day.
◆ *adj* **1.** *(als Zahl)* one ; **~e einzelne Rose** a single rose ; **~ Uhr** one o'clock.
2. *(gleich)* : **~er Meinung sein** to have the same opinion.
◆ *pron* **1.** *(Teil aus Menge)* one ; **hier ist noch ~s/~e** here's another one.
2. *(fam : man)* one ; **das kann ~em schon mal passieren** these things can happen to you.
◆ *adv* : **'~ - aus'** 'on-off' ; **~ und aus gehen** to come and go.

einander *pron* each other.

ein|arbeiten *vt (Person)* : **jn ~** to show sb the ropes.

ein|atmen *vi* to breathe in.

Einbahnstraße *(pl -n) die* one-way street.

ein|bauen *vt (Kamin, Bad)* to fit.

Einbauküche *(pl -n) die* fitted kitchen.

Einbettzimmer *(pl -) das* single room.

ein|biegen *vi unr ist* to turn.

ein|bilden *vt* : **sich** *(D)* **etw ~** to imagine sthg.

ein|brechen *vi unr ist (als Einbrecher)* to break in ; *(in Eis)* to fall through.

Einbrecher, in *(mpl -) der, die* burglar.

Einbruch *(pl -brüche) der (von Einbrecher)* break-in ; **nach ~ der Dunkelheit** after dark.

Einbürgerung *die (von Person)* naturalization.

ein|checken *vi* to check in.

ein|cremen *vt* to put cream on. ■ **sich eincremen** *ref* to put cream on.

eindeutig *adj* clear. ◆ *adv* clearly.

ein|dringen *vi unr ist (Wasser)* to get in ; *(Einbrecher)* to break in.

Eindruck *(pl -drücke) der (von Person)* impression ; **den ~ haben, dass** to have the impression that.

eindrucksvoll *adj* impressive.

eine → **ein**.

eineinhalb *num* one and a half.

einerseits *adv* : ~... anderer-seits on the one hand... on the other hand.

einfach *adj* simple ; *(Fahrt, Fahrkarte)* single. ◆ *adv* : ~ **oder hin und zurück?** would you like a single or a return? ; ~ **klasse!** just brilliant!

ein|fahren *vi unr* ist *(Zug)* to arrive.

Einfahrt *(pl* -en) *die (Tor, Weg)* entrance ; *(von Zug)* arrival ; '~ **freihalten!**' 'keep clear' ; ~ **haben** to arrive.

Einfall *(pl* -fälle) *der (Idee)* idea.

ein|fallen *vi unr* ist *(+D)* : **jm** ~ to occur to sb ; **mir fällt gerade ein...** I've just remembered...

Einfamilienhaus *(pl* -häu-ser) *das* detached house.

einfarbig *adj* all one colour.

Einfluss *(pl* -flüsse) *der* influ-ence ; ~ **auf jn/etw haben** *(Effekt)* to influence sb/sthg ; *(Macht)* to have influence over sb/sthg.

ein|frieren *vt unr* hat *(Lebens-mittel)* to freeze. ◆ *vi unr* ist to freeze.

Einfuhr *(pl* -en) *die (von Ware)* importation.

Einfuhrbeschränkung *(pl* -en) *die* import tariff.

Einfuhrbestimmungen *pl* import regulations.

ein|führen *vt (Waren)* to im-port ; *(Zäpfchen, Sonde)* to in-sert ; *(Neuerung)* to introduce ; **jn in etw** *(A)* ~ to introduce sb to sthg.

Einführung *(pl* -en) *die* in-troduction ; *(von Sonde)* inser-tion.

ein|füllen *vt* to pour in.

Eingang *(pl* -gänge) *der (von Haus)* entrance ; *(von Post)* re-ceipt.

Eingangshalle *(pl* -n) *die* entrance hall.

ein|geben *vt unr* (EDV : *Daten)* to input.

eingebildet *adj (arrogant)* arrogant ; *(ausgedacht)* imagin-ary. ◆ *adv (arrogant)* arro-gantly.

ein|gehen *vi unr* ist *(Klei-dung)* to shrink ; *(Pflanze, Tier)* to perish ; ~ **auf** *(+A) (auf Vor-schlag)* to agree to.

eingeschaltet *adj* (switched) on.

eingeschlossen *pp* → **ein-schließen**.

eingetragen *adj* : ~**es Waren-zeichen** registered trademark.

ein|gewöhnen : **sich ein-gewöhnen** *ref* to settle in.

eingezogen *pp* → **einzie-hen** ; '**warten, bis der Geldschein vollständig ~ ist**' 'please wait until the note has been accept-ed by the machine'.

ein|gießen *vt unr* to pour. ◆ *vi unr* : **darf ich ~?** shall I fill your glass up?

ein|greifen *vi unr* to inter-vene.

Eingriff *(pl* -e) *der (Operation)* operation.

ein|hängen *vt* & *vi* to hang up.

einheimisch *adj* local.

Einheit (*pl* -en) *die* (*auf Skala*) unit ; (*Ganzes*) unity.

einheitlich *adj* (*Vorschriften*) uniform. ◆ *adv* (*regeln*) uniformly.

einhundert *num* a ODER one hundred.

einig *adj* : sich ~ sein to agree.

einige, r, s *det* & *pron* (*ein paar*) a few ; (*reichlich*) quite a few ; nach ~r Zeit after some time ; ~ Probleme (*ein paar*) a few problems ; (*viele*) quite a lot of problems ; nur ~ waren da (*ein paar*) there were only a few people there ; ~ waren da (*viele*) there were quite a lot of people there.

einigen : sich einigen *ref* : sich über/auf etw (A) ~ to agree on sthg.

einigermaßen *adv* (*relativ*) fairly.

Einkauf (*pl* -käufe) *der* (*in Laden*) shopping ; (*ECO*) purchase. ■ **Einkäufe** *pl* (*Gegenstände*) shopping (*sg*).

ein|kaufen *vt* (*Ware*) to buy. ◆ *vi* to shop ; ~ gehen to go shopping.

Einkaufsbummel (*pl* -) *der* : einen ~ machen to go round the shops.

Einkaufstasche (*pl* -n) *die* shopping bag.

Einkaufstüte (*pl* -n) *die* carrier bag.

Einkaufszentrum (*pl* -zentren) *das* shopping centre (*Br*), mall (*Am*).

ein|kehren *vi* ist (*in einem Gasthaus*) to stop off.

ein|kleiden *vt* (*Kind*) to kit out. ■ **sich einkleiden** *ref* : sich neu ~ to buy a whole new wardrobe.

ein|klemmen *vt* to trap.

Einkommen (*pl* -) *das* income.

ein|laden *vt unr* (*Gepäck*) to load ; (*nach Hause*) to invite ; darf ich Sie zu einem Kaffee ~? may I buy you a coffee? ; jn in ein Restaurant ~ to take sb out for a meal.

Einladung (*pl* -en) *die* invitation.

Einlage (*pl* -n) *die* (*in Programm*) interlude ; (*in Schuh*) insole ; (*in Suppe*) noodles, meat etc in a soup.

Einlass *der* admission.

ein|laufen *vi unr* ist (*Wasser*) to run in ; (*Kleidung*) to shrink.

ein|leben : sich einleben *ref* to settle in.

ein|legen *vt* (*Film*) to put in ; (*Gang*) to engage.

Einleitung (*pl* -en) *die* (*Text*) introduction.

ein|liefern *vt* (*in Krankenhaus*) to admit.

Einlieferungsschein (*pl* -e) *der* proof of delivery.

ein|lösen *vt* (*Scheck*) to cash ; (*Gutschein*) to redeem.

einmal *adv* once ; (*in der Zukunft*) sometime ; auf ~ (*plötzlich*) all of a sudden ; (*gleichzeitig*) at once ; nicht ~ not even ; noch ~ once again, once more.

einmalig *adj* (*einzig*) unique ; (*hervorragend*) excellent.

ein|mischen : sich einmischen *ref* to interfere.

Einnahme (*pl* -n) die (*Geld*) takings (*pl*) ; (*von Medikament*) taking.

ein|nehmen *vt unr* to take.

ein|ölen *vt* to rub oil in. ■ **sich einölen** *ref* to rub oil on o.s.

ein|ordnen *vt* (*in Regal, Kartei*) to put in its place. ■ **sich einordnen** *ref* (*in Autoschlange*) to get in lane.

ein|packen *vt* (*in Koffer, Tasche*) to pack ; (*in Geschenkpapier*) to wrap ; ~ **oder zum Hieressen?** to eat in or take away?

ein|parken *vi & vt* (*Fahrer*) to park.

ein|prägen *vt* : sich (D) etw ~ to memorize sthg.

ein|räumen *vt* (*Bücher, Kleidung*) to put away ; (*Schrank, Regal*) to fill up.

ein|reiben *vt unr* (*Salbe, Creme*) to rub in ; jn mit etw ~ to rub sthg into sb ; sich (D) das Gesicht mit etw ~ to rub sthg into one's face.

ein|reichen *vt* (*Antrag*) to hand in.

Einreise (*pl* -n) die entry.

ein|reisen *vi ist* to enter.

Einreisevisum (*pl* -visa) das entry visa.

ein|richten *vt* (*Wohnung, Zimmer*) to furnish.

Einrichtung (*pl* -en) die (*Möbel*) furnishings (*pl*) ; (*Institution*) institution.

eins *num* one ; → **sechs**. ◆ *pron* → **ein**.

einsam *adj* lonely. ◆ *adv* alone.

ein|sammeln *vt* (*von Boden*) to gather ; (*bei Personen*) to collect.

Einsatz (*pl* -sätze) der (*Verwendung*) use ; (*Geld*) stake ; (*Engagement*) commitment.

ein|schalten *vt* (*Gerät*) to switch on.

ein|schenken *vt* : jm etw ~ to pour sb sthg.

ein|schicken *vt* to send in.

ein|schieben *vt unr* to fit in.

ein|schiffen : sich einschiffen *ref* to set sail.

ein|schlafen *vi unr ist* (*Person*) to fall asleep ; (*Körperteil*) to go to sleep ; (*fig : Kontakt*) to drop off.

ein|schließen *vt unr* (*Person, Gegenstand*) to lock up ; (*enthalten*) to include.

einschließlich *präp* (+G) including, inclusive of. ◆ *adv* inclusive ; bis Montag ~ up to and including Monday.

ein|schränken *vt* (*Person*) to restrict ; (*Trinken, Rauchen*) to cut down on. ■ **sich einschränken** *ref* to tighten one's belt.

ein|schreiben : sich einschreiben *ref* to register.

Einschreiben (*pl* -) das recorded delivery letter/parcel.

ein|sehen *vt unr* (*Fehler*) to recognize.

einseitig *adj* (*Argumentation*) one-sided ; (*Beschriftung*) on one side of the page.

ein|senden *vt unr* to send in.

ein|setzen vt (Hilfsmittel) to use ; (Polizei, Personal) to employ ; (Leben) to risk ; (Geld) to stake. ◆ vi (beginnen) to begin. ▩ **sich einsetzen** ref : sich für etw ~ to support sthg.

Einsicht (pl -en) die (Erkenntnis) insight.

ein|sinken vi unr ist to sink.

Einspänner (pl -) der (Österr) glass of black coffee topped with whipped cream.

ein|springen vi unr ist to stand in.

Einspruch (pl -sprüche) der (amt) objection.

einspurig adj (Straße) single-lane. ◆ adv : 'nur ~ befahrbar' 'single-lane traffic only'.

ein|stecken vt (mitnehmen) to take ; (in Briefkasten) to post ; (Stecker) to plug in ; vergiss nicht, Geld einzustecken! don't forget to take some money with you!

ein|steigen vi unr ist (in Auto) to get in ; (in Bus, Zug) to get on ; 'bitte ~!' 'please get on, the bus/train is about to depart!'

einstellbar adj adjustable.

ein|stellen vt (regulieren) to adjust ; (neu festsetzen) to set ; (Programm, Sender) to tune into ; (in Firma) to take on ; (beenden) to stop ; die Entfernung ~ to focus (the camera). ▩ **sich einstellen** ref : sich ~ auf (+A) to prepare o.s. for.

Einstellung (pl -en) die (von Arbeitskräften) appointment ; (von Blende) setting ; (Meinung) attitude ; (von Sender) tuning.

Einstieg der : '~ nur mit Fahrausweis' 'do not board without a ticket' ; '~ nur vorne' 'entry at the front of the vehicle only'.

ein|stürzen vi ist to collapse.

Einsturzgefahr die : 'Vorsicht, ~!' 'danger, building unsafe!'

eintägig adj one-day.

ein|tauschen vt to exchange.

eintausend num a ODER one thousand ; → **sechs**.

ein|teilen vt to divide up.

einteilig adj one-piece.

Einteilung (pl -en) die (von Zeit) organization ; (von Geld, Vorrat) management.

Eintopf (pl -töpfe) der stew.

ein|tragen vt unr (in Liste) to put down. ▩ **sich eintragen** ref to register.

ein|treten vt unr hat (Tür, Eis) to kick down. ◆ vi unr ist (in Raum) to enter ; (in Verein) : in etw (A) ~ to join sthg.

Eintritt (pl -e) der admission ; '~ frei' 'admission free' ; '~ verboten!' 'no entry'.

Eintrittsgeld (pl -er) das admission charge.

Eintrittskarte (pl -n) die ticket.

Eintrittspreis (pl -e) der admission charge.

einverstanden adj agreed. ◆ interj OK! ; mit etw ~ sein to agree with sthg.

ein|wandern vi ist to immigrate.

einwandfrei adj perfect. ◆ adv perfectly.

Einwegflasche (*pl* -n) *die* disposable bottle.

ein|weichen *vt* to soak.

Einweihung (*pl* -en) *die* (*von Gebäude*) opening.

Einweihungsparty (*pl* -s) *die* housewarming party.

ein|weisen *vt unr* (*in Krankenhaus*) to admit.

ein|werfen *vt unr* (*Brief*) to post (*Br*), to mail (*Am*); (*Münze*) to insert; (*Ball, Bemerkung*) to throw in.

ein|wickeln *vt* (*Gegenstand*) to wrap up; (*fam* : *Person*) to take in.

Einwohner, **in** (*mpl* -) *der*, *die* inhabitant.

Einwurf (*pl* -würfe) *der* (*Frage, Bemerkung*) comment; (*an Automaten*) slot; (*SPORT*) throw-in.

ein|zahlen *vt* & *vi* to pay in.

Einzahlung (*pl* -en) *die* (*Geld*) deposit.

Einzahlungsschein (*pl* -e) *der* paying-in slip.

ein|zeichnen *vt* to mark.

Einzelbett (*pl* -en) *das* single bed.

Einzelfahrschein (*pl* -e) *der* single (ticket) (*Br*), one-way ticket (*Am*).

Einzelgänger, **in** (*mpl* -) *der*, *die* loner.

Einzelhandel *der* retail trade.

Einzelheit (*pl* -en) *die* detail.

Einzelkabine (*pl* -n) *die* single cabin.

Einzelkind (*pl* -er) *das* only child.

einzeln *adj* (*speziell*) individual; (*isoliert*) single; (*ohne Gegenstück*) odd. ◆ *adv* (*nacheinander*) separately; (*extra*) individually. ◆ *det* : ~e Personen/Fragen a few.

einzelne, **r**, **s** *pron* (*Personen*) some people; (*Sachen*) some things; jeder/jede/jedes Einzelne (*Individuum*) every single one.

Einzelperson (*pl* -en) *die* single person.

Einzelreisende (*pl* -n) *der*, *die* person travelling alone.

Einzelteil (*pl* -e) *das* component.

Einzelticket (*pl* -s) *das* single (ticket).

Einzelzimmer (*pl* -) *das* single room.

Einzelzimmerzuschlag(*pl* -zuschläge) *der* single room supplement.

ein|ziehen *vi unr ist* (*in Wohnung*) to move in; (*in Haut*) to be absorbed. ◆ *vt unr hat* (*von Konto*) to collect; (*in Automaten*) to take in.

einzig *adj* & *adv* only; der/die/ das ~e... the only...; das Einzige, was... the only thing that...; ich habe keinen Einzigen gesehen I didn't see a single one.

Eis *das* ice; (*Speiseeis*) ice cream; ~ am Stiel ice lolly (*Br*), Popsicle® (*Am*).

Eisbecher (*pl* -) *der* sundae.

Eiscafé (*pl* -s) *das* ice-cream parlour.

Eiscreme (*pl* -s) *die* ice cream.

Eisen *das* (*Metall*) iron.

Eisenbahn (*pl* -en) *die (Zug)* train ; *(Institution)* railway *(Br)*, railroad *(Am)*.

Eisenbahnbrücke (*pl* -n) *die* railway bridge.

Eisenbahnnetz (*pl* -e) *das* rail network.

eisgekühlt *adj* chilled.

Eishockey *das* ice hockey.

eisig *adj (Wetter, Kälte)* freezing. ◆ *adv* : ~ **kalt** freezing cold.

Eiskaffee (*pl* -s) *der chilled coffee containing vanilla ice cream and whipped cream.*

eiskalt *adj (Getränk, Wind)* ice-cold ; *(fig : skrupellos)* cold-blooded.

Eiskugel (*pl* -n) *die* scoop of ice cream.

Eiskunstlauf *der* figure skating.

Eismann (*pl* -männer) *der* ice cream man.

Eisschokolade (*pl* -n) *die chilled drinking chocolate containing ice cream and whipped cream.*

Eiswaffel (*pl* -n) *die* wafer *(in an ice cream).*

Eiswürfel (*pl* -) *der* ice cube.

Eiszapfen (*pl* -) *der* icicle.

eitel (*komp* eitler, *superl* am eitelsten) *adj (Person)* vain.

Eiter *der* pus.

eitern *vi* to fester.

Eiweiß (*pl* -e) *das (in Ei)* egg white ; *(Protein)* protein.

ekeln : sich ekeln *ref :* sich ~ (vor (+ D)) to be disgusted (by).

Ekzem (*pl* -e) *das* eczema.

Elastikbinde (*pl* -n) *die* elastic bandage.

elastisch *adj (Material)* elastic.

Elefant (*pl* -en) *der* elephant.

elegant *adj* elegant. ◆ *adv* elegantly.

Elektriker, in (*mpl* -) *der, die* electrician.

elektrisch *adj* electrical. ◆ *adv* electrically.

Elektrizität *die* electricity.

Elektrogerät (*pl* -e) *das* electrical appliance.

Elektrogeschäft (*pl* -e) *das* electrical goods store.

Elektroherd (*pl* -e) *der* electric oven.

Elektronik *die (Fachgebiet)* electronics *(sg)* ; *(System)* electronics *(pl).*

elektronisch *adj* electronic. ◆ *adv* electronically.

Element (*pl* -e) *das* element.

Elend *das* misery.

elf *num* eleven ; → **sechs**.

elfhundert *num* one thousand one hundred.

Elfmeter (*pl* -) *der* penalty.

elfte *adj* eleventh ; → **sechste**.

Ellbogen (*pl* -) *der (Gelenk)* elbow.

Eltern *pl* parents.

EM *die (abk für Europameisterschaft)* European Championships *(pl).*

E-Mail (*pl* -s) *die (EDV)* e-mail ; **jm eine E-Mail schicken** to send someone an e-mail, to e-mail someone.

E-Mail-Adresse *die (EDV)* e-mail address.

Emanzipation *die* emancipation.

emanzipieren : sich emanzipieren ref to become emancipated.

emotional adj emotional.

empfahl prät → empfehlen.

empfand prät → empfinden.

Empfang (pl Empfänge) der reception ; (von Post) receipt ; etw in ~ nehmen to receive sthg.

empfangen (präs empfängt, prät empfing, pp empfangen) vt to receive.

Empfänger, in (mpl -) der, die (Adressat) addressee.

Empfängerabschnitt (pl -e) der (von Einschreiben) part of a recorded delivery form given to the addressee.

Empfängnisverhütung die contraception.

Empfangsbescheinigung (pl -en) die proof of receipt.

empfängt präs → empfangen.

empfehlen (präs empfiehlt, prät empfahl, pp empfohlen) vt to recommend ; jm etw ~ ommend sthg to sb. ▪ sich empfehlen ref (ratsam sein) to be recommended.

empfehlenswert adj recommendable.

Empfehlung (pl -en) die recommendation.

empfiehlt präs → empfehlen.

empfinden (prät empfand, pp empfunden) vt to feel.

empfindlich adj (Person, Haut) sensitive ; (Material) delicate.

empfing prät → empfangen.

empfohlen pp → empfehlen.

empfunden pp → empfinden.

empört adj indignant. ◆ adv indignantly.

Ende (pl -n) das end ; am ~ at the end ; ~ März at the end of March ; zu ~ sein to be over.

enden vi to end.

endgültig adj final. ◆ adv finally.

Endivie (pl -n) die endive.

endlich adv at last.

Endstation (pl -en) die (von Straßenbahn, Bus, U-Bahn) terminus.

Endung (pl -en) die (GRAMM) ending.

Energie (pl -n) die energy.

Energiebedarf der energy requirements (pl).

Energieverbrauch der energy consumption.

energisch adj energetic.

eng adj (schmal) narrow ; (Kleidung) tight ; (Kontakt) close. ◆ adv (dicht gedrängt) closely ; (anliegen) tightly ; (nah) close ; ~ befreundet sein to be close friends.

Engagement (pl -s) das (Einsatz) commitment ; (Auftrag, Stelle) engagement.

engagieren vt to engage. ▪ sich engagieren ref : sich ~ für to show commitment to.

England nt England.

Engländer, in (mpl -) der, die Englishman (Englishwoman) ; die ~ the English.

englisch adj English.

Englisch(e) das English.

Enkel, **in** (mpl -) der, die grandson (granddaughter). ▨ **Enkel** pl grandchildren.

enorm adj enormous. ◆ adv enormously.

Ensemble (pl -s) das (Musiker) ensemble ; (Tänzer) company.

entdecken vt to discover.

Ente (pl -n) die duck.

entfernen vt (Schmutz) to remove.

entfernt adj distant ; (abgelegen) remote. ◆ adv (verwandt) distantly ; 50 km von München = 50 km (away) from Munich ; **weit** ~ a long way away.

Entfernung (pl -en) die (Distanz) distance ; (Beseitigung) removal.

entführen vt (Person) to kidnap ; (Flugzeug) to hijack.

Entführung (pl -en) die (von Person) kidnapping ; (von Flugzeug) hijacking.

entgegen präp (+D) contrary to.

entgegengesetzt adj opposite ; (Ansichten) opposing. ◆ adv (liegen) opposite.

entgegen|kommen vi unr ist : **jm** ~ (räumlich) to approach sb ; (mit Angebot) to make concessions to sb.

entgegenkommend adj (Auto) oncoming ; (Angebot, Person) accommodating. ◆ adv (sich verhalten) accommodatingly.

entgegnen vt to retort.

Entgelt das remuneration ; '~ für Platzreservierung im Zuschlag enthalten' 'seat reservation included in supplement'.

enthaaren vt to remove hair from.

Enthaarungscreme (pl -s) die hair-remover.

enthalten (präs enthält, prät enthielt, pp enthalten) vt (subj : Behälter) to contain ; (in Preis) to include. ▨ **sich enthalten** ref to abstain.

entkommen (prät entkam, pp entkommen) vi ist to escape.

entlang präp (+A, G) along. ◆ adv : **am Strand** ~ **gehen** to walk along the beach ; **die Straße** ~ along the road.

entlang|gehen vt unr ist to walk along.

entlassen (präs entlässt, prät entließ, pp entlassen) vt (Mitarbeiter) to sack ; (aus Krankenhaus) to discharge ; **aus der Schule** ~ **werden** to leave school.

Entlassung (pl -en) die (Kündigung) dismissal ; (aus Krankenhaus) discharge ; (aus Schule) leaving.

Entlastungszug (pl -züge) der extra train.

entlaufen (präs entläuft, prät entlief, pp entlaufen) vi ist to escape.

entlegen adj isolated.

Entnahme die (von Wechselgeld, Blut) taking.

entnehmen (präs entnimmt, prät entnahm, pp entnommen) vt (Wechselgeld, Blut) to take.

entrahmt adj : ~**e Milch** skimmed milk.

Entschädigung (*pl* -en) *die* (*Geldsumme, Gegenstand*) compensation.

entscheiden (*prät* entschied, *pp* entschieden) *vt* to decide.
■ **sich entscheiden** *ref* to decide ; sich ~ für/gegen to decide on/against ; sich ~, etw zu tun to decide to do sthg.

Entscheidung (*pl* -en) *die* decision.

entschließen : **sich entschließen** (*prät* entschloss, *pp* entschlossen) *ref* to decide.

entschlossen *pp* → entschließen.

Entschluss (*pl* -schlüsse) *der* decision.

entschuldigen *vt* to excuse.
■ **sich entschuldigen** *ref* to apologize ; sich ~ für to apologize for ; sich bei jm ~ to apologize to sb ; ~ Sie bitte! excuse me!

Entschuldigung (*pl* -en) *die* (*Rechtfertigung*) excuse ; (*Brief, Worte*) apology. ◆ *interj* sorry!

entsetzlich *adj* terrible. ◆ *adv* terribly.

entsorgen *vt* (*Müll*) to dispose of.

entspannen *vi* & *vt* to relax.
■ **sich entspannen** *ref* to relax.

Entspannung *die* relaxation.

entsprechend *adj* (*äquivalent*) corresponding ; (*geeignet*) appropriate. ◆ *präp* (+D) according to.

entstehen (*prät* entstand, *pp* entstanden) *vi* ist (*sich entwi-* ckeln) to arise ; (*Gebäude*) to be built ; (*Schaden*) to result.

enttäuschen *vt* to disappoint. ◆ *vi* to be disappointing.
enttäuscht *adj* disappointed.
Enttäuschung (*pl* -en) *die* disappointment.

entweder *konj* : ~... oder either... or.

entwerfen (*präs* entwirft, *prät* entwarf, *pp* entworfen) *vt* (*Zeichnung*) to sketch ; (*Gebäude*) to design.

entwerten *vt* (*Fahrkarte*) to validate.

Entwerter (*pl* -) *der* (*für Fahrkarten*) ticket validating machine.

entwickeln *vt* to develop.
■ **sich entwickeln** *ref* to develop ; (*Gase*) to be produced.

Entwicklung (*pl* -en) *die* development ; (*von Film*) developing ; (*von Gasen*) production.

Entwicklungshilfe *die* development aid.

Entziehungskur (*pl* -en) *die* rehabilitation course.

Entzug *der* (*von Konzession*) withdrawal ; (*fam* : *Entziehungskur*) rehabilitation course.

entzünden *vt* (*Feuer*) to light.
■ **sich entzünden** *ref* (*Wunde, Blinddarm*) to become inflamed ; (*Feuer*) to catch fire.

Entzündung (*pl* -en) *die* (*MED*) inflammation.

Enzian (*pl* -e) *der* (*Pflanze*) gentian.

Epilepsie (*pl* -n) *die* epilepsy.
er *pron* (*bei Personen*) he ; (*bei Sachen*) it.

Erbauer, in (*mpl* -) *der, die* constructor.

Erbe (*pl* -n) *der* heir. ◆ *das* inheritance.

erben *vt* to inherit. ◆ *vi* to come into one's inheritance.

Erbin (*pl* -nen) *die* heiress.

erblich *adj* hereditary.

erbrechen (*präs* erbricht, *prät* erbrach, *pp* erbrochen) *vt* to bring up. ◆ *vi* to be sick, to vomit. ■ **sich erbrechen** *ref* to be sick, to vomit.

Erbse (*pl* -n) *die* pea.

Erdbeben (*pl* -) *das* earthquake.

Erdbeere (*pl* -n) *die* strawberry.

Erde (*pl* -n) *die* earth ; (*Erdreich*) soil ; (*TECH* : *Draht*) earth (*Br*), ground (*Am*).

erden *vt* to earth (*Br*), to ground (*Am*).

Erdgas *das* natural gas.

Erdgeschoss (*pl* -e) *das* ground floor.

Erdnuss (*pl* -nüsse) *die* peanut.

Erdöl *das* oil.

Erdteil (*pl* -e) *der* continent.

ereignen : **sich ereignen** *ref* to happen.

Ereignis (*pl* -se) *das* event.

ereignisreich *adj* eventful.

erfahren (*präs* erfährt, *prät* erfuhr, *pp* erfahren) *adj* experienced. ◆ *vt* (*aus mündlicher Quelle*) to hear ; (*aus schriftlicher Quelle*) to read ; **etw von jm ~** to learn sthg from sb.

Erfahrung (*pl* -en) *die* experience.

erfinden (*prät* erfand, *pp* erfunden) *vt* to invent.

Erfolg (*pl* -e) *der* success ; **~ haben** to be successful ; **viel ~!** good luck!

erfolglos *adj* unsuccessful. ◆ *adv* without success.

erfolgreich *adj* successful. ◆ *adv* successfully.

erforderlich *adj* necessary.

erforschen *vt* (*Land, Natur*) to explore.

erfreulich *adj* pleasing. ◆ *adv* pleasingly.

erfrieren (*prät* erfror, *pp* erfroren) *vi ist* to freeze to death.

erfrischen *vt* to refresh. ■ **sich erfrischen** *ref* to refresh o.s.

erfrischend *adj* refreshing.

Erfrischung (*pl* -en) *die* refreshment.

erfüllen *vt* to fulfil. ■ **sich erfüllen** *ref* to come true.

ergänzen *vt* (*vervollständigen*) to complete ; (*erweitern*) to expand ; (*Bemerkung*) to add.

Ergebnis (*pl* -se) *das* result.

ergebnislos *adj* unsuccessful.

ergiebig *adj* long-lasting.

erhalten (*präs* erhält, *prät* erhielt, *pp* erhalten) *vt* to receive ; (*bewahren*) to preserve. ■ **sich erhalten** *ref* (*sich bewahren*) to endure.

erhältlich *adj* available ; **hier ~** available here.

erheben (*prät* erhob, *pp* erhoben) *vt* : **Gebühren ~** to levy a charge.

erheblich *adj* considerable. ◆ *adv* considerably.

erhitzen vt *(Fett, Wasser)* to heat.

erhöhen vt *(Zaun, Mauer)* to raise ; *(anheben)* to raise, to increase. ■ **sich erhöhen** ref to rise, to increase.

erholen : **sich erholen** ref to rest ; sich ~ von to recover from.

erholsam adj relaxing.

Erholung die recovery ; gute ~! have a relaxing time!

erinnern vt to remind ; jn ~ an *(+A)* to remind sb of. ■ **sich erinnern** ref to remember ; sich ~ an *(+A)* to remember.

Erinnerung *(pl* -en) die *(Gedanke)* memory ; *(Souvenir)* memento.

erkälten : **sich erkälten** ref to catch a cold.

erkältet adj :.~ sein to have a cold.

Erkältung *(pl* -en) die cold.

erkennen *(prät* erkannte, *pp* erkannt) vt *(sehen)* to make out ; *(Trick, Ursache)* to realize ; *(wiedererkennen)* to recognize.

Erker *(pl* -) der bay window.

erklären vt *(erläutern)* to explain ; *(verkünden)* to declare ; sich *(D)* etw ~ to understand sthg ; jm etw ~ to explain sthg to sb. ■ **sich erklären** ref : sich zu etw bereit ~ to agree to sthg.

Erklärung *(pl* -en) die *(Erläuterung)* explanation.

erkundigen : **sich erkundigen** ref : sich (nach jm/etw) ~ to enquire (about sb/sthg).

erlassen *(präs* erlässt, *prät* erließ, *pp* erlassen) vt *(Gebühren)* to waive ; *(Schulden)* to write off.

erlauben vt *(nicht verbieten)* to allow ; jm etw ~ to allow sb sthg ; jm ~, etw zu tun to allow sb to do sthg.

Erlaubnis die *(Erlauben)* permission ; *(Schriftstück)* permit.

Erläuterung *(pl* -en) die explanation ; '~ siehe Rückseite' 'see reverse for explanation'.

erleben vt *(erfahren)* to experience.

Erlebnis *(pl* -se) das *(Erfahrung)* experience.

erledigen vt *(Arbeit)* to see to ; *(Auftrag)* to fulfil.

erledigt adj : ~ sein *(müde sein . fam)* to be shattered ; *(beendet sein)* to be finished ; der Fall ist für mich ~ as far as I'm concerned, the matter is closed.

erleichtert adj relieved.

erlesen adj choice.

erlischt präs → **erlöschen**.

Erlös der proceeds *(pl)*.

erlöschen *(präs* erlischt, *prät* erlosch, *pp* erloschen) vi ist *(Feuer, Licht)* to go out.

ermahnen vt to warn.

ermäßigt adj reduced.

Ermäßigung *(pl* -en) die reduction.

ermöglichen vt to make possible.

ermorden vt to murder.

ermutigen vt to encourage.

ernähren : **sich ernähren** ref *(essen)* to eat.

Ernährung die *(Nahrung)* food.

erneuern vt (Fensterscheibe, Schloss) to replace.

erneut adj renewed.

ẹrnst adj serious. ◆ adv seriously ; jn/etw ~ nehmen to take sb/sthg seriously.

Ẹrnst der seriousness.

Ẹrnstfall der emergency.

ẹrnsthaft adj serious. ◆ adv seriously.

Ẹrnte (pl -n) die harvest.

Ẹrntedạnkfest (pl -e) das Harvest Festival.

ẹrnten vt (Heu, Äpfel, Mais) to harvest.

erọ̈ffnen vt (Geschäft) to open ; ein Konto ~ to open an account.

Erọ̈ffnung (pl -en) die opening.

erọtisch adj erotic.

Erprẹssung (pl -en) die blackmail.

errạten (präs errạ̈t, prät errịet, pp errạten) vt to guess.

Errẹger (pl -) der (MED) cause (of illness).

errẹichbar adj reachable.

errẹichen vt to reach ; (Zweck, Ziel) to achieve.

Ersạtz der (Stellvertreter) substitute ; (Entschädigung) replacement.

Ersạtzreifen (pl -) der spare tyre.

Ersạtzteil (pl -e) das spare part.

erschẹinen (prät erschiẹn, pp erschiẹnen) vi ist to appear ; (wirken) to seem, to appear ; gut/wichtig ~ to seem good/important.

erschọ̈pft adj (müde) exhausted. ◆ adv wearily.

Erschọ̈pfung die exhaustion.

erschrẹcken[1] vt hat to startle. ▪ **sich erschrecken** ref to be startled.

erschrẹcken[2] (präs erschrịckt, prät erschrạk, pp erschrọcken) vi ist to be startled.

ersẹtzen vt (auswechseln) to replace ; (Schaden) to make good ; jm etw (voll) ~ (Schaden) to compensate sb (fully) for sthg.

erst adv (relativ spät) not until ; (noch relativ früh, relativ wenig) only ; (vor kurzem) (only) just ; (zuerst) first ; der erste Roman war gut, aber der zweite ~! the first novel was good, but the second one was even better ; er kommt ~ um 10 Uhr he won't be here until ten o'clock ; sie war ~ gestern hier she was here only yesterday ; ~ einmal (nur einmal) only once.

erstạtten vt (Kosten) to refund.

Erstạttung die (von Kosten) refund.

Erstaufführung (pl -en) die premiere.

erstaunt adj amazed.

ẹrste, r, s adj first ; (vorläufig) preliminary ; als ~s first of all ; ~ Klasse first class ; → sechste.

Ẹrste (pl -n) der, die, das first (one).

Ẹrste Hịlfe die → Hilfe.

ẹrstens adv firstly.

ẹrstklassig adj first-class.

erstrecken : sich erstrecken *ref* to stretch.

erteilen *vt (amt)* to give.

Ertrag *(pl* Erträge*) der (an Gemüse, Getreide)* yield ; *(finanziell)* profits *(pl)*.

ertrinken *(prät* ertrank*, pp* ertrunken*) vi ist* to drown.

Erw. *abk* = Erwachsene.

erwachen *vi ist (Person)* to wake up.

erwachsen *adj* adult, grown-up.

Erwachsene *(pl* -n*) der, die* adult ; ein ~r, zwei Kinder, bitte! one adult and two children, please!

erwähnen *vt* to mention.

erwarten *vt (warten auf)* to wait for ; *(rechnen mit)* to expect ; einen Anruf ~ to be expecting a phone call ; ein Kind ~ to be expecting a baby ; erwartet werden to be expected.

erweitern *vt (Raum)* to extend. ■ sich erweitern *ref* to expand ; *(Pupillen)* to dilate.

erwerbstätig *adj* employed.

erwidern *vt (auf Frage)* to reply ; *(Besuch)* to return.

erwünscht *adj (willkommen)* welcome.

erzählen *vt* to tell.

Erzählung *(pl* -en*) die* story.

erzeugen *vt (produzieren)* to produce.

Erzeugnis *(pl* -se*) das (Produkt)* product.

erziehen *(prät* erzog*, pp* erzogen*) vt* to bring up ; *(in Schule)* to educate.

Erzieher, in *(mpl* -*) der, die* teacher.

Erziehung *die (in Schule)* education ; *(durch Eltern)* upbringing.

erzogen *pp* → erziehen. ◆ *adj* : gut/schlecht ~ well/badly brought up.

es *pron* it ; *(bei Person : im Nominativ)* he (she) ; *(bei Person : im Akkusativ)* him (her) ; ~ freut mich, dass... I'm pleased that... ; ~ ist drei Uhr it's three o'clock ; ~ regnet/schneit it's raining/snowing ; wer war ~? who was it? ; ~ geht mir gut I'm fine.

Esel *(pl* -*) der* donkey.

Espresso *(pl* -s*) der* espresso.

essbar *adj* edible.

essen *(präs* isst*, prät* aß*, pp* gegessen*) vt & vi* to eat ; ~ gehen to go out for a meal.

Essen *(pl* -*) das (Mahlzeit)* meal ; *(fam : Nahrung)* food ; beim ~ while eating ; ~ machen/kochen to make/cook a meal ; vor dem ~ before the meal.

Essig *der* vinegar.

Esslöffel *(pl* -*) der* dessertspoon.

Esszimmer *(pl* -*) das* dining room.

Etage *(pl* -n*) die* floor, storey.

Etagenbett *(pl* -en*) das* bunk bed.

Etappe *(pl* -n*) die* stage.

Etikett *(pl* -en*) das* label.

etliche, r, s *det & pron* several.

Etui *(pl* -s*) das* case.

etwa *adv (ungefähr)* about ; *(zum Beispiel)* for example ; ist

es ~ schon 10 Uhr? oh no, is it 10 o'clock already? ; **hast du das ~ vergessen?** you haven't gone and forgotten it, have you?

etwas *pron* something ; *(in Fragen)* anything ; *(ein wenig)* some. ◆ *det (irgendetwas)* something ; *(in Fragen)* anything ; *(ein wenig)* a little. ◆ *adv (ein wenig)* rather ; **~ anderes** something else ; **so ~** such a thing.

EU *(abk für Europäische Union)* die EU.

euch *pron (im Akkusativ)* you ; *(im Dativ)* (to) you ; *(Reflexivpronomen)* yourselves.

euer, e ODER **eure** *det* your.

eure, r, s *pron* yours. ◆ *det →* **euer.**

Euro *(pl -)* der euro.

Eurocard *(pl -s)* die Eurocard.

Eurocheque *(pl -s)* der = **Euroscheck.**

EuroCity *(pl -s)* der *international train linking two or more major European cities.*

Europa *nt* Europe.

Europäer, in *(mpl -)* der, die European.

europäisch *adj* European.

Europaparlament *das* European Parliament.

Euroscheck *(pl -s)* der Eurocheque.

ev. *abk* = **evangelisch.**

e.V. *abk* = **eingetragener Verein.**

evangelisch *adj* Protestant.

eventuell *adv* maybe, perhaps. ◆ *adj* possible ; **er übernimmt alle ~en Schäden** he'll pay for any damages.

ewig *adj (nie endend)* eternal ; *(fam : ständig)* constant. ◆ *adv (nie endend)* eternally ; *(fam : ständig)* constantly.

exakt *adj* exact. ◆ *adv* exactly.

Examen *(pl -)* das examination.

Exemplar *(pl -e)* das example ; *(von Buch)* copy.

Exil *das* exile.

Existenz *(pl -en)* die existence.

existieren *vi* to exist.

exklusiv *adj* exclusive. ◆ *adv* exclusively.

Exkursion *(pl -en)* die *(in Schule)* school trip.

exotisch *adj* exotic.

Expedition *(pl -en)* die expedition.

Experte *(pl -n)* der expert.

Expertin *(pl -nen)* die expert.

explodieren *vi ist* to explode.

Explosion *(pl -en)* die explosion.

Export[1] *(pl -e)* der *(Ausfuhr, Ware)* export.

Export[2] *(pl -)* das *(Bier)* export.

extra *adv (fam : absichtlich)* on purpose ; *(separat)* separately ; *(speziell)* specially ; *(zusätzlich)* extra. ◆ *adj (zusätzlich)* extra.

Extraausgabe *(pl -n)* die special edition.

Extrablatt *das* extra.

extrem *adj* extreme.

exzellent *adj* excellent.

EZ *abk* = **Einzelzimmer.**

F

fabelhaft *adj* fantastic.

Fabrik (*pl* -en) *die* factory.

fabrikneu *adj* brand new.

Fach (*pl* Fächer) *das* (*in Schrank*) compartment ; (*Schulfach, Fachgebiet*) subject.

Facharzt (*pl* -ärzte) *der* specialist.

Fachärztin (*pl* -nen) *die* specialist.

Fachausdruck (*pl* -drücke) *der* specialist term.

Fachgeschäft (*pl* -e) *das* specialist store.

Fachmann (*pl* -leute ODER -männer) *der* expert.

fachmännisch *adj* expert. ◆ *adv* expertly.

Fachnummer (*pl* -n) *die* locker number.

Fachwerkhaus (*pl* -häuser) *das* timbered building.

fade *adj* & *adv* bland.

Faden (*pl* Fäden) *der* (*zum Nähen*) thread.

fähig *adj* capable ; ~ sein, etw zu tun to be capable of doing sthg.

Fahne (*pl* -n) *die* (*Flagge*) flag ; er hat eine ~ (*fam*) his breath smells of alcohol.

Fahrausweis (*pl* -e) *der* ticket.

Fahrausweisautomat (*pl* -en) *der* ticket machine.

Fahrausweisentwerter (*pl* -) *der* ticket validating machine.

Fahrausweiskontrolle (*pl* -n) *die* ticket inspection.

Fahrausweisverkauf *der* ticket sales (*pl*).

Fahrbahn (*pl* -en) *die* road.

Fahrbahnschäden *pl* damage to road surface.

Fahrbahnverschmutzung *die* : 'Fahrbahnverschmutzung' sign indicating that there is rubble, oil etc on road ahead.

Fähre (*pl* -n) *die* ferry.

fahren (*präs* fährt, *prät* fuhr, *pp* gefahren) *vi* ist 1. (*mit Auto*) to drive ; (*mit Fahrrad*) to ride ; durch Wien ~ to drive/ride through Vienna ; langsam ~ to drive slowly ; zu schnell ~ to drive too fast ; mit dem Zug/Bus ~ to go by train/bus ; ins Gebirge ~ to go to the mountains ; wir ~ nach England we're going to England.
2. (*Fahrzeug*) to go.
3. (*abfahren*) to leave.
◆ *vt* hat to drive.
◆ *vt* ist 1. (*Entfernung, Route*) to drive ; 120 km/h ~ to drive at 120 km/h.
2. (*SPORT*) : Rollschuh ~ to rollerskate ; Ski ~ to ski.

Fahrer, in (*mpl* -) *der, die* driver.

Fahrerflucht *die* hit-and-run.

Fahrersitz (*pl* -e) *der* driver's seat.

Fahrgast (*pl* -gäste) *der* passenger.

Fahrgeld *das* fare.

Fahrgelderstattung *die* refund (*of fare*).

Fahrgestell (*pl* -e) *das* chassis.

Fahrkarte (*pl* -n) *die* ticket.

Fahrkartenausgabe *die* ticket desk.

Fahrkartenautomat (*pl* -en) *der* ticket machine.

Fahrkartenschalter (*pl* -) *der* ticket desk.

Fahrkosten *pl* travelling expenses.

Fahrplan (*pl* -pläne) *der* timetable.

Fahrplanauszug (*pl* -züge) *der* timetable (*for specific route*).

Fahrplanhinweise *pl* details concerning the timetable.

fahrplanmäßig *adj* scheduled. ◆ *adv* on time.

Fahrpreis (*pl* -e) *der* fare.

Fahrrad (*pl* -räder) *das* bicycle, cycle ; **mit dem ~** by bicycle.

Fahrradflickzeug *das* bicycle repair kit.

Fahrrad-Mitnahme *die* possibility of taking bicycles on a railway or underground train.

Fahrradreparatur (*pl* -en) *die* cycle repair shop.

Fahrradschlauch (*pl* -schläuche) *der* inner tube.

Fahrradschloss (*pl* -schlösser) *das* bicycle lock.

Fahrradverleih (*pl* -e) *der* cycle hire (*Br*), cycle rental (*Am*).

Fahrradweg (*pl* -e) *der* cycle path.

Fahrschein (*pl* -e) *der* ticket ; '**~e hier entwerten**' 'validate your ticket here'.

Fahrscheinentwerter (*pl* -) *der* ticket validating machine.

Fahrschule (*pl* -n) *die* driving school.

Fahrspur (*pl* -en) *die* lane ; **die ~ wechseln** to change lane ; **die linke/rechte ~** the left-hand/right-hand lane.

Fahrstreifen (*pl* -) *der* lane ; **verengte ~** road narrows.

Fahrstuhl (*pl* -stühle) *der* lift (*Br*), elevator (*Am*).

Fahrt (*pl* -en) *die* (*Reise*) journey ; (*kurzer Ausflug*) trip ; (*in Auto*) drive ; '**den Fahrer während der ~ nicht ansprechen**' 'do not speak to the driver while the vehicle is in motion' ; **auf der ~ nach Berlin** on the way to Berlin ; **nach sechs Stunden ~** after travelling for six hours ; **nun wieder freie ~ auf der A3** traffic is moving freely again on the A3 ; **gute ~!** have a good journey! ; **eine ~ ins Blaue machen** to go for a drive.

fährt *präs* → **fahren**.

Fahrtantritt *der* beginning of the journey ; '**Fahrscheine vor ~ entwerten**' 'please validate your ticket before beginning your journey'.

Fahrtenschreiber (*pl* -) *der* tachograph.

Fahrtrichtung (*pl* -en) *die* (*im Zug*) direction of travel.

fahrtüchtig *adj* (*Person*) fit to drive ; (*Fahrzeug*) roadworthy.

Fahrtunterbrechung (*pl* -en) *die* stop.

Fahrtziel (*pl* -e) *das* destination.

Fahrverbot (*pl* -e) *das (Führerscheinentzug)* driving ban ; ~ für Traktoren no tractors.

Fahrzeit (*pl* -en) *die* journey time.

Fahrzeug (*pl* -e) *das* vehicle.

Fahrzeugbrief (*pl* -e) *der* registration document.

Fahrzeughalter, in (*mpl* -) *der, die* registered owner.

Fahrzeugpapiere *pl* vehicle documents.

Fahrzeugschein (*pl* -e) *der* vehicle documents (*pl*).

Fahrziel (*pl* -e) *das* destination.

fair *adj* fair.

Fall (*pl* Fälle) *der* case ; *(Sturz)* fall ; auf jeden ~ in any case ; auf keinen ~ on no account ; für den ~, dass in case... ; in diesem ~ in this case.

fallen (*präs* fällt, *prät* fiel, *pp* gefallen) *vi* ist to fall.

fallen lassen (*pp* fallen lassen ODER fallen gelassen) *vt (Gegenstand)* to drop ; *(Bemerkung)* to let drop.

fällig *adj* due ; am 1.10. ~ due on 1 October.

falls *konj* if.

Fallschirm (*pl* -e) *der* parachute.

Fallschirmspringer, in (*mpl* -) *der, die* parachutist.

fällt *präs* → fallen.

falsch *adj (inkorrekt)* wrong ; *(Name, Versprechung, Person)* false ; *(Schmuck)* fake ; *(Pass)* forged. ◆ *adv (inkorrekt)* wrongly ; *(hinterhältig)* falsely ;

~ fahren to drive in the wrong direction.

fälschen *vt* to forge.

Falschfahrer, in (*mpl* -) *der, die person driving on the wrong side of the road.*

Falschgeld *das* forged money.

Fälschung (*pl* -en) *die (Falschgeld, Bild)* forgery.

Falte (*pl* -n) *die (Hautfalte)* wrinkle ; *(Knitterfalte)* crease ; *(gebügelt)* pleat.

falten *vt (Pullover, Papier)* to fold.

Familie (*pl* -n) *die* family.

Familienbesitz *der* : in ~ family-owned.

Familienname (*pl* -n) *der* surname.

Familienstand *der* marital status.

Fan (*pl* -s) *der* fan.

fand *prät* → finden.

fangen (*präs* fängt, *prät* fing, *pp* gefangen) *vt* to catch. ■ **Fangen** *das* : Fangen spielen to play tag.

Fantasie (*pl* -n) *die* imagination.

fantastisch *adj* fantastic. ◆ *adv (großartig)* fantastically.

Farbband (*pl* -bänder) *das* typewriter ribbon.

Farbbild (*pl* -er) *das* colour photograph ; ~er in 24 Stunden 24-hour colour photos.

Farbe (*pl* -n) *die (Eigenschaft)* colour ; *(zum Malen, Streichen)* paint ; welche ~ hat das Auto? what colour is the car?

farbecht *adj* colourfast.

färben vt (Stoff, Haare) to dye.

Farbfernseher (pl -) der colour television.

Farbfestiger (pl -) der colour set.

Farbfilm (pl -e) der colour film.

Farbfoto (pl -s) das colour photo.

farbig adj (mehrfarbig) colourful; (einfarbig, Person) coloured. ◆ adv (mehrfarbig) colourfully.

Farbige (pl -n) der, die coloured person.

Farbposter (pl -) das colour poster.

Farbstoff (pl -e) der colouring; mit/ohne ~ with/without colouring.

Fasan (pl -e) der pheasant.

Fasching der (Süddt & Österr) carnival before Lent; → Karneval.

Faschismus der fascism.

Faschist, in (mpl -en) der, die fascist.

faschistisch adj fascist.

Fass (pl Fässer) das barrel; Bier vom ~ draught beer.

Fassbier das draught beer.

fassen vt (mit den Händen) to take, to hold; (Verbrecher) to catch; (Inhalt) to hold; (begreifen) to grasp. ◆ vi (mit den Händen): an etw (A) ~ to feel sthg; etw nicht ~ können to be unable to understand sthg. ■ **sich fassen** ref to pull o.s. together.

Fassung (pl -en) die (für Glühbirne) fitting; (Selbstbeherrschung) composure.

fast adv nearly, almost.

fasten vi to fast.

Fastenzeit (pl -en) die (christlich) Lent; (mohammedanisch) Ramadan.

Fastnacht die (Süddt & Österr) carnival period before Lent; → **Karneval**.

faul adj (Obst) rotten; (Person) lazy.

faulen vi hat & ist to rot.

faulenzen vi to laze about.

Faust (pl Fäuste) die fist; auf eigene ~ off one's own bat.

Fax (pl -e) das fax.

faxen vt to fax.

Faxgerät (pl -e) das fax machine.

Faxnummer (pl -n) die fax number.

Faxpapier das fax paper.

FCKW der CFC.

Februar der February; → September.

fechten (präs ficht, prät focht, pp gefochten) vi to fence.

Feder (pl -n) die (vom Vogel) feather; (aus Metall) spring; (zum Schreiben) nib.

Federball (pl -bälle) der (Ball) shuttlecock; (Spiel) badminton.

Federbett (pl -en) das quilt.

Federhalter (pl -) der fountain pen.

Federung (pl -en) die (von Auto) suspension; (von Sofa) springs (pl).

Federweiße der young, cloudy white wine.

fegen vt (Boden, Raum) to sweep. ◆ vi (sauber machen) to sweep up.

Fehlbetrag (*pl* -beträge) *der* shortfall.

fehlen *vi* to be missing. ◆ *vi* (+D) : **sie fehlt mir** I miss her ; **was fehlt Ihnen/dir?** what's the matter? ; **im Unterricht ~** to miss school.

Fehler (*pl* -) *der* mistake ; (*von Charakter*) fault.

Fehlzündung (*pl* -en) *die* : **eine ~ haben** to misfire.

Feier (*pl* -n) *die* party.

Feierabend (*pl* -e) *der* : **~ machen** to finish work.

Feierlichkeiten *pl* celebrations.

feiern *vt & vi* (*Fest*) to celebrate ; **jn ~** to fête sb ; **eine Party ~** to throw ODER have a party.

Feiertag (*pl* -e) *der* holiday ; **schöne ~!** have a good holiday!

feiertags *adv* on public holidays.

feige *adj* (*Person*) cowardly.

Feige (*pl* -n) *die* (*Frucht*) fig.

Feile (*pl* -n) *die* file.

feilen *vt* to file.

fein *adj* (*dünn, pulverförmig*) fine ; (*vornehm*) refined ; (*erfreulich*) great. ◆ *adv* (*dünn, pulverförmig*) finely ; (*fam : gut*) well ; (*vornehm*) elegantly ; (*fam : brav*) : **~ hier bleiben!** be a good boy/girl and stay here! ; **~ gemacht!** (*fam*) well done! ▪ **Feinste** *der, die, das* : **vom Feinsten** first-class.

Feind, in (*mpl* -e) *der, die* (*von Person*) enemy ; **ein ~ des Rauchens sein** to be against smoking.

feindlich *adj* hostile.

Feinkost *die* delicacies (*pl*).

Feinkostgeschäft (*pl* -e) *das* delicatessen.

Feinschmecker, in (*mpl* -) *der, die* gourmet.

Feinwaschmittel (*pl* -) *das* mild detergent.

Feld (*pl* -er) *das* (*Acker, Thema, im Sport*) field ; (*von Brettspiel*) square ; (*von Formular*) box.

Feldsalat *der* lamb's lettuce.

Feldweg (*pl* -e) *der* footpath.

Felge (*pl* -n) *die* wheel rim.

Felgenbremse (*pl* -n) *die* wheel rim brake.

Fell (*pl* -e) *das* (*von Tier*) fur ; (*verarbeitet*) skin.

Fels (*pl* -en) *der* (*Felsblock*) rock.

Felsen (*pl* -) *der* cliff.

felsig *adj* rocky.

feminin *adj* feminine.

Feminismus *der* feminism.

feministisch *adj* feminist.

Fenchel *der* fennel.

Fenster (*pl* -) *das* window.

Fensterbrett (*pl* -er) *das* windowsill.

Fensterladen (*pl* -läden) *der* shutter.

Fensterplatz (*pl* -plätze) *der* window seat.

Fensterscheibe (*pl* -n) *die* windowpane.

Ferien *pl* holiday (*sg*) (*Br*), vacation (*sg*) (*Am*) ; **~ machen** to go on holiday (*Br*), to go on vacation (*Am*) ; **große ~** summer holidays (*Br*), summer vacation (*Am*) ; **schöne ~!** have a good holiday! ; **in ~ sein** to be on holiday (*Br*), to be on vacation (*Am*).

Ferienbeginn *der* beginning of the school summer holidays.

ⓘ FERIENBEGINN

In Germany, each state sets its own date for the beginning of the school summer holidays. This is often done years in advance, the only restriction being that they must fall between 15 June and 15 September. The sequence in which the states begin their holidays varies from year to year, with the exception of Bavaria which is always last.

Ferienbungalow (pl -s) der holiday bungalow.

Feriengast (pl -gäste) der holidaymaker (Br), vacationer (Am).

Ferienhaus (pl -häuser) das holiday home.

Ferienlager (pl -) das holiday camp.

Ferienort (pl -e) der holiday resort.

Ferienwohnung (pl -en) die holiday flat (Br), holiday apartment (Am).

fern adj (Land) far-off, distant.

Fernbedienung (pl -en) die remote control.

Ferne die : in der ~ in the distance.

Ferngespräch (pl -e) das long-distance call.

ferngesteuert adj remote-controlled. ◆ adv by remote control.

Fernglas (pl -gläser) das binoculars (pl).

fern|halten vt unr to keep away. ■ **sich fernhalten** ref to keep away.

Fernlicht das full beam (Br), high beam (Am).

Fernmeldeamt (pl -ämter) das telephone exchange.

Fernschreiben (pl -) das telex.

Fernschreiber (pl -) der teleprinter.

Fernsehapparat (pl -e) der television (set).

fern|sehen vi unr to watch television.

Fernsehen das television ; im ~ on television.

Fernseher (pl -) der television.

Fernsehprogramm (pl -e) das (Kanal) channel ; (Sendung) (television) programme.

Fernsehsendung (pl -en) die (television) programme.

Fernsehturm (pl -türme) der television tower.

Fernsehzeitschrift (pl -en) die TV magazine.

Fernsprechamt (pl -ämter) das (amt) telephone exchange.

Fernsprechauskunft die (amt) directory enquiries (sg).

Fernsteuerung (pl -en) die remote control.

Fernstraße (pl -n) die trunk road (Br), highway (Am).

Fernverkehr der long-distance traffic.

Ferse (pl -n) die heel.

fertig adj (vollendet) finished ; (fam : erschöpft) worn out ; ~ sein (vollendet, bereit sein) to be ready ; (fam : erschöpft sein) to be worn out ; *(fam : niederge-schlagen sein)* to be shattered ; **mit etw ~ sein** to have finished sthg.

Fertiggericht *(pl -e)* das ready-made meal.

fertig machen vt *(beenden)* to finish ; *(bereitmachen)* to get ready ; *(fam : zurechtweisen)* to lay into ; *(fam : erschöpfen)* to wear out.

fest adj *(Knoten, Verband)* tight ; *(Händedruck, Griff)* firm ; *(Material, Kleidung)* strong ; *(Vertrag, Gehalt, Wohnsitz)* fixed ; *(Pläne, Termin)* definite. ◆ adv *(straff)* tightly ; *(kräftig)* hard ; *(verbindlich)* firmly.

Fest *(pl -e)* das *(Feier)* party ; *(religiös)* festival ; **frohes ~!** *(frohe Weihnachten)* Happy Christmas!

Festbetrag *(pl -beträge)* der fixed amount.

fest|binden vt unr to tie up.

Festessen *(pl -)* das banquet.

fest|halten vt unr *(mit der Hand)* to hold (on to) ; *(doku-mentieren)* to record. ▪ **sich fest halten** ref : **sich ~ (an (+D)** to hold on (to).

Festiger *(pl -)* der setting lotion.

Festival *(pl -s)* das festival.

Festland das mainland.

fest|legen vt *(Treffpunkt, Route)* to fix.

festlich adj festive.

fest|machen vt to fasten ; *(Boot)* to moor ; *(Termin, Treffpunkt)* to arrange.

fest|nehmen vt unr to arrest.

Festpreis *(pl -e)* der fixed price.

fest|setzen vt *(Termin)* to arrange.

Festspiele pl festival *(sg)*.

fest|stehen vi unr to have been decided.

fest|stellen vt *(durch Ermittlung)* to find out ; *(beobachten)* to notice.

Feststellung *(pl -en)* die *(An-merkung)* remark.

Festwochen pl festival *(sg)*.

Fete *(pl -n)* die *(fam)* party.

fett adj *(Fleisch, Gericht)* fatty ; *(abw : Person, Körperteil)* fat.

Fett *(pl -e)* das fat.

fettarm adj low-fat.

fettig adj greasy.

Fettstift *(pl -e)* der lip salve.

feucht adj damp.

Feuchtigkeitscreme *(pl -s)* die moisturizer.

Feuer *(pl -)* das fire ; *(fig : Temperament)* passion ; **(ein) ~ ma-chen** to light a fire ; **'~ und offenes Licht verboten!'** 'no naked flames!' ; **haben Sie ~, bitte?** have you got a light, please? ; **jm ~ geben** to give sb a light.

Feueralarm der fire alarm.

feuerfest adj fireproof.

feuergefährlich adj flammable.

Feuerlöscher *(pl -)* der fire extinguisher.

Feuermelder *(pl -)* der fire alarm.

Feuertreppe *(pl -n)* die fire escape.

Feuerwehr (*pl* -en) *die* fire brigade.

Feuerwehrmann (*pl* -männer) *der* fireman.

Feuerwehr-Zufahrt (*pl* -en) *die* fire lane.

Feuerwerk (*pl* -e) *das* fireworks (*pl*).

Feuerzeug (*pl* -e) *das* lighter.

ficht *präs* → **fechten**.

Fieber *das* (*Körpertemperatur*) temperature ; **~ haben** to have a temperature ; **bei jm ~ messen** to take sb's temperature.

Fieberthermometer (*pl* -) *das* thermometer.

fiebrig *adj* (*Erkältung*) feverish. ◆ *adv* (*glänzen, sich anfühlen*) feverishly.

fiel *prät* → **fallen**.

Figur (*pl* -en) *die* (*Körperform, Person*) figure ; (*in Schach*) piece ; (*Plastik*) sculpture ; **eine gute ~ haben** to have a good figure.

Filet (*pl* -s) *das* fillet.

Filetsteak (*pl* -s) *das* fillet steak.

Filiale (*pl* -n) *die* branch.

Film (*pl* -e) *der* film.

filmen *vt* to film.

Filmkamera (*pl* -s) *die* (*Camcorder*) camcorder.

Filter (*pl* -) *der* filter ; **mit ~** filter-tipped ; **ohne ~** plain.

Filtertüte (*pl* -n) *die* filter.

Filterzigarette (*pl* -n) *die* filter-tipped cigarette.

Filzstift (*pl* -e) *der* felt-tip pen.

Finale (*pl* -) *das* (*in Sport*) final.

finanziell *adj* financial. ◆ *adv* financially.

finanzieren *vt* to finance.

finden (*prät* **fand**, *pp* **gefunden**) *vi* to find one's way. ◆ *vt* to find ; **ich finde, dass...** I think (that)... ; **ich finde sie nett** I think she's nice ; **wie findest du...?** what do you think of...? ; **wo finde ich die Post, bitte?** where is the post office, please? ▪ **sich finden** *ref* : der Schlüssel hat sich gefunden I/we found the key again.

Finderlohn *der* reward (*for finding something*).

fing *prät* → **fangen**.

Finger (*pl* -) *der* finger.

Fingernagel (*pl* -nägel) *der* fingernail.

Finne (*pl* -n) *der* Finn.

Finnin (*pl* -nen) *die* Finn.

finnisch *adj* Finnish.

Finnisch(e) *das* Finnish.

Finnland *nt* Finland.

finster *adj* (*dunkel*) dark ; (*unheimlich*) sinister.

Firma (*pl* **Firmen**) *die* firm, company.

First Class *die* (*ohne pl*) first class.

Fisch (*pl* -e) *der* fish. ▪ **Fische** *pl* (*Sternzeichen*) Pisces (*sg*).

Fischbesteck (*pl* -e) *das* fish knife and fork.

fischen *vt* (*Fische*) to fish for. ◆ *vi* (*angeln*) to fish.

Fischer (*pl* -) *der* fisherman.

Fischerboot (*pl* -e) *das* fishing boat.

Fischgericht (*pl* -e) *das* fish dish.

Fischhändler, in (*mpl* -) *der, die* fishmonger.

Fischstäbchen *(pl -)* das fish finger *(Br)*, fish stick *(Am)*.

Fischsuppe *(pl -n)* die fish soup.

fit *adj* fit.

fix *adj (fam : schnell)* quick ; *(Kosten)* fixed ; **~ und fertig** *(vollendet)* finished ; *(müde)* worn-out.

FKK die *(abk für Freikörperkultur)* nudism.

FKK-Strand *(pl -Strände)* der nudist beach.

flach *adj* flat ; *(Wasser, Teller)* shallow.

Fläche *(pl -n)* die *(Oberfläche)* surface ; *(Gebiet)* area.

Flagge *(pl -n)* die flag.

flambiert *adj* flambé.

Flamme *(pl -n)* die *(von Feuer)* flame.

Flanell das flannel.

Flasche *(pl -n)* die bottle.

Flaschenbier das bottled beer.

Flaschenöffner *(pl -)* der bottle opener.

Flaschenpfand das deposit *(on a bottle)*.

Flaschenweine *pl* bottled wines.

Flaute *(pl -n)* die *(Windstille)* calm.

flechten *(präs* **flicht**, *prät* **flocht**, *pp* **geflochten)** *vt (Haar)* to plait *(Br)*, to braid *(Am)* ; *(Korb)* to weave.

Fleck *(pl -e)* der spot ; **blauer ~** bruise.

Fleckentferner *(pl -)* der stain remover.

Fledermaus *(pl -mäuse)* die bat.

Fleisch das *(Muskel)* flesh ; *(Nahrung)* meat.

Fleischbrühe *(pl -n)* die bouillon.

Fleischer *(pl -)* der butcher.

Fleischerei *(pl -en)* die butcher's (shop).

Fleischsalat der salad made from strips of meat and vegetables with mayonnaise.

Fleisch- und Wurstwaren *pl* meat and sausages.

Fleischvergiftung *(pl -en)* die food poisoning from meat.

fleißig *adj* hard-working. ◆ *adv (arbeiten)* hard.

flicht *präs* → **flechten**.

flicken *vt (Kleidung)* to mend ; *(Reifen)* to patch.

Flickzeug das *(für Reifen)* puncture repair kit ; *(für Kleidung)* sewing kit.

Fliege *(pl -n)* die *(Insekt)* fly ; *(Schleife)* bow tie.

fliegen *(prät* **flog**, *pp* **geflogen)** *vt & vi ist* to fly ; **nach Paris ~** to fly to Paris ; **über Paris ~** to fly via Paris.

fliehen *(prät* **floh**, *pp* **geflohen)** *vi ist* to flee.

Fliese *(pl -n)* die tile.

Fließband *(pl -bänder)* das conveyor belt.

fließen *(prät* **floss**, *pp* **geflossen)** *vi ist* to flow.

fließend *adj (Verkehr)* moving. ◆ *adv :* **~ Englisch sprechen** to speak fluent English ; **~es Wasser** running water.

Flipper *(pl -)* der pinball machine.

flippern *vi* to play pinball.

Flirt *(pl -s)* der flirtation.

flirten *vi* to flirt.

Flitterwochen *pl* honeymoon *(sg)*.

flocht *prät* → flechten.

flog *prät* → fliegen.

floh *prät* → fliehen.

Floh *(pl* Flöhe*) der* flea.

Flohmarkt *(pl* -märkte*) der* flea market.

floss *prät* → fließen.

Floß *(pl* Flöße*) das* raft.

Flosse *(pl* -n*) die (Schwimmflosse)* flipper *(Br)*, fin *(Am)* ; *(von Tieren)* fin.

Flöte *(pl* -n*) die (Blockflöte)* recorder ; *(Querflöte)* flute.

fluchen *vi* to swear.

Flucht *die* flight.

flüchten *vi ist* to flee.

Flüchtling *(pl* -e*) der* refugee.

Flug *(pl* Flüge*) der (Flugreise)* flight ; ein ~ nach Berlin a flight to Berlin ; ein ~ über London a flight via London ; guten ~! have a good flight! ; 'zu den Flügen' ≃ 'passengers only beyond this point'.

Flugblatt *(pl* -blätter*) das* leaflet.

Flügel *(pl* -*) der* wing ; *(Instrument)* grand piano.

Fluggast *(pl* -gäste*) der* passenger *(on plane)*.

Fluggepäck *das* luggage.

Fluggesellschaft *(pl* -en*) die* airline.

Flughafen *(pl* -häfen*) der* airport.

Fluginformation *(pl* -en*) die* flight information.

Flugnummer *(pl* -n*) die* flight number.

Flugplan *(pl* -pläne*) der* flight schedule.

Flugplatz *(pl* -plätze*) der* airfield.

Flugschein *(pl* -e*) der (Ticket)* plane ticket.

Flugscheinkontrolle *(pl* -n*) die* ticket control.

Flugsteig *(pl* -e*) der* gate.

Flugstrecke *(pl* -n*) die* flight distance.

Flugticket *(pl* -s*) das* plane ticket.

Flugverbindung *(pl* -en*) die* (flight) connection.

Flugverkehr *der* air traffic.

Flugzeug *(pl* -e*) das* (aero)plane, airplane *(Am)* ; mit dem ~ fliegen to go by air, to fly.

Flur *(pl* -e*) der (Diele)* hall.

Fluss *(pl* Flüsse*) der (Wasserlauf)* river.

flüssig *adj (Material)* liquid. ◆ *adv (sprechen)* fluently.

Flüssigkeit *(pl* -en*) die* liquid.

flüstern *vi & vt* to whisper.

Flut *(pl* -en*) die (von Gezeiten)* tide ; *(von Beschwerden, Anträgen)* flood. ▨ **Fluten** *pl (Wassermassen)* floods.

Flutlicht *das* floodlight.

focht *prät* → fechten.

Fohlen *(pl* -*) das* foal.

Föhn *der (Haartrockner)* hairdryer ; *(Wind)* hot, dry wind typical of the Alps.

föhnen *vt* to blow-dry ; sich *(D)* die Haare ~ to dry one's hair.

Folge *(pl* -n*) die (Konsequenz)* result, consequence ; *(von*

Fernsehserie) episode ; **etw zur ~ haben** to result in sthg.

folgen *vi ist (+D)* to follow ; **~ auf** *(+A)* to follow ; **~ aus** to follow from ; **bitte ~!** please follow me!

folgend *adj* following ; *(Konsequenz)* resulting ; **~e Punkte** the following points.

folgendermaßen *adv* as follows.

Folie *(pl -n) die (aus Metall)* foil ; *(aus Kunststoff)* film.

Folklore *die* folklore.

folkloristisch *adj* folkloric.

Fondue *(pl -s) die* ODER *das* fondue.

fordern *vt (verlangen)* to demand ; *(Preis)* to ask ; *(beanspruchen)* to make demands on.

fördern *vt (finanziell)* to support ; *(mit Engagement)* to promote.

Forderung *(pl -en) die (Verlangen)* demand ; *(finanzieller Anspruch)* claim.

Forelle *(pl -n) die* trout ; **~ blau** poached trout ; **~ Müllerinnen Art** trout fried in butter and served with lemon juice and parsley.

Form *(pl -en) die (räumlich)* shape, form ; *(für Kuchen)* baking tin ; **in ~ sein** to be in good form ; **in ~ von** in the form of.

Formalität *(pl -en) die (Regel)* formality.

Format *(pl -e) das (Größe)* format.

Formblatt *(pl -blätter) das* form.

formen *vt (Ton, Teig)* to shape.

formlos *adj* shapeless.

Formular *(pl -e) das* form ; **ein ~ ausfüllen** to fill in a form.

formulieren *vt* to word.

Forschung *(pl -en) die* research.

Forst *(pl -e) der* forest.

fort *adv* away ; **~ sein** to be gone.

fort|bewegen *vt* to move away. ■ **sich fortbewegen** *ref* to move.

fort|fahren *vi unr ist (mit Auto, Zug)* to leave ; *(weitermachen)* to continue. ◆ *vt unr hat (Auto, Bus)* to drive away.

fort|gehen *vi unr ist (weggehen)* to leave.

Fortgeschrittene *(pl -n) der, die* advanced student.

Fortschritt *(pl -e) der* progress ; **~e machen** to make progress.

fort|setzen *vt* to continue.

Fortsetzung *(pl -en) die (von Streik, Verhandlungen)* continuation ; *(von Serie)* episode.

Foto *(pl -s) das* photo.

Fotoapparat *(pl -e) der* camera.

Fotogeschäft *(pl -e) das* camera shop.

Fotograf, in *(mpl -en) der, die* photographer.

Fotografie *(pl -n) die (Bild)* photograph.

fotografieren *vt* to photograph. ◆ *vi* to take photographs.

Fotokopie *(pl -n) die* photocopy.

fotokopieren *vt* & *vi* to photocopy.

Foyer *(pl -s) das* foyer.

Fr. *(abk für Frau)* Mrs.

Fracht *(pl -en)* die *(mit Zug)* freight ; *(mit Schiff)* cargo.

Frachter *(pl -)* der freighter.

Frack *(pl Fräcke)* der tails *(pl)*.

Frackzwang der : es besteht ~ please wear tails.

Frage *(pl -n)* die *(Fragesatz)* question ; *(Problem)* issue ; **eine** ~ **haben** to have a question ; **eine** ~ **(an jn) stellen** to ask (sb) a question ; **die** ~ **nach** the question of ; **noch** ~n? any more questions? ; **etw in** ~ **stellen** to call sthg into question ; **nicht in** ~ **kommen** to be out of the question.

Fragebogen *(pl -bögen)* der questionnaire.

fragen vt & vi to ask ; ~ **nach** to ask about. ■ **sich fragen** ref to wonder. ◆ vimp : **es fragt sich, ob...** it is debatable whether...

Fragezeichen *(pl -)* das question mark.

Fraktion *(pl -en)* die *(POL)* (parliamentary) party.

Frankenwein *(pl -e)* der white wine from northern Bavaria.

frankieren vt to stamp.

Frankreich nt France.

Franzose *(pl -n)* der Frenchman.

Französin *(pl -n en)* die Frenchwoman.

französisch adj French.

Französisch(e) das French.

fraß prät → fressen.

Frau *(pl -en)* die *(Erwachsene)* woman ; *(Ehefrau)* wife ; *(als Anrede)* Mrs *(verheiratet)*, Ms *(neutral)*.

Frauenarzt, ärztin *(mpl -ärzte)* der, die gynaecologist.

Frauenberatungsstelle *(pl -n)* die women's advice centre.

Frauenbewegung die women's movement.

Frauenbuchladen *(pl -läden)* der feminist bookshop.

Frauencafé *(pl -s)* das café for women only.

frauenfeindlich adj misogynistic.

Frauenhaus *(pl -häuser)* das women's refuge.

Frauenlokal *(pl -e)* das bar for women only.

Fräulein das *(Anrede)* Miss.

frech adj cheeky. ◆ adv cheekily.

Frechheit *(pl -en)* die *(Bemerkung, Handlung)* cheeky thing.

Freeclimbing das free climbing.

frei adj free ; *(Mitarbeiter)* freelance ; *(nackt)* bare. ◆ adv freely ; *(gratis)* for free ; ~ **von** free of ; **drei Wochen** ~ **haben** to have three weeks off ; **etw** ~ **Haus liefern** to deliver sthg free ; **machen Sie sich bitte** ~ please take your clothes off ; **im Freien** in the open air.

Freibad *(pl -bäder)* das open-air swimming pool.

freiberuflich adj self-employed.

Freibier das free beer.

freigegeben adv : '~ **ab 18 Jahren'** indicates that a film can *only be watched by people over eighteen.*

Freiheit (*pl* -en) die (*Unabhängigkeit*) freedom ; (*Vorrecht*) liberty.

Freikarte (*pl* -n) die free ticket.

frei|lassen vt unr to set free.

freilich adv (*allerdings*) admittedly ; (*Südt : sicher*) of course.

Freilichtbühne (*pl* -n) die open-air theatre.

frei|machen vi (*fam : Urlaub nehmen*) to take time off. ◆ vt (*Brief*) to stamp. ■ **sich freimachen** ref (*Urlaub machen*) to take time off ; (*sich ausziehen*) to take one's clothes off.

Freistoß (*pl* -stöße) der free kick.

Freitag (*pl* -e) der Friday ; → Samstag.

freitags adv on Fridays.

freiwillig adj voluntary. ◆ adv of one's own free will.

Freizeichen (*pl* -) das ringing tone.

Freizeit die free time.

Freizeitbad (*pl* -bäder) das leisure pool.

Freizeitkleidung die casual clothes (*pl*).

Freizeitpark (*pl* -s) der park (*with recreational facilities*).

fremd adj (*ausländisch*) foreign ; (*unbekannt*) strange ; **~e Angelegenheiten** other people's business ; **ich bin hier ~** I'm a stranger here.

Fremde (*pl* -n) der, die (*Unbekannter*) stranger.

Fremdenführer, in (*mpl* -) der, die tourist guide.

Fremdenverkehrsamt (*pl* -ämter) das tourist board.

Fremdenverkehrsbüro (*pl* -s) das tourist information centre.

Fremdenzimmer (*pl* -) das (guest) room.

Fremdkörper (*pl* -) der foreign body.

Fremdsprache (*pl* -n) die foreign language.

Fremdsprachenkenntnisse pl knowledge of foreign languages.

Fremdwort (*pl* -e) das foreign word.

Frequenz (*pl* -en) die (*von Radiosender*) frequency.

fressen (*präs* frisst, *prät* fraß, *pp* gefressen) vt (*Futter*) to eat ; (*Benzin, Strom*) to eat up. ◆ vi (*Tier*) to feed ; (*abw : Mensch*) to stuff o.s.

Freude (*pl* -n) die pleasure, joy ; **jm eine ~ machen** to make sb happy. ■ **Freuden** pl pleasures.

freuen vt to please ; **freut mich sehr!** pleased to meet you! ■ **sich freuen** ref to be pleased ; **sich ~ auf** (+A) to look forward to ; **sich ~ über** (+A) to be pleased about.

Freund, in (*mpl* -e) der, die friend ; (*Geliebter*) boyfriend (girlfriend) ; **~e und Bekannte** friends and acquaintances.

freundlich adj (*Person*) friendly ; (*Umgebung, Wetter*) nice. ◆ adv (*grüßen*) in a friendly way.

Freundschaft (*pl* -en) *die* (*vertraute Beziehung*) friendship.

Frieden *der* peace.

Friedhof (*pl* -höfe) *der* cemetery.

frieren (*prät* fror, *pp* gefroren) *vi* hatliat (*Person*) to be cold ; (*Wasser*) to freeze. ◆ *vimp* hat : **es friert** it's freezing.

Frikadelle (*pl* -n) *die* rissole.

frisch *adj* fresh ; (*Temperatur*) cool ; (*Farbe*) wet. ◆ *adv* freshly ; **sich ~ machen** to freshen up ; 'Vorsicht, ~ gestrichen!' 'wet paint'.

Frischfleisch *das* fresh meat.

Frischhaltebeutel (*pl* -) *der* airtight bag.

Frischhaltefolie (*pl* -n) *die* clingfilm (*Br*), Saran wrap® (*Am*).

Frischkäse (*pl* -) *der* soft cream cheese.

Friseur (*pl* -e) *der* hairdresser.

Friseuse (*pl* -n) *die* hairdresser.

Frisiercreme (*pl* -s) *die* styling cream.

frisieren *vt* : **jn ~** to do sb's hair. ▓ **sich frisieren** *ref* to do one's hair.

frisst *präs* → fressen.

Frist (*pl* -en) *die* period ; **eine ~ einhalten** to stick to a deadline.

fristgerecht *adj* within the time allowed.

Frisur (*pl* -en) *die* hairstyle.

frittieren *vt* to deep-fry.

Frl. (*abk für Fräulein*) Miss.

froh *adj* happy ; **~ sein über** (+A) to be pleased about.

fröhlich *adj* cheerful. ◆ *adv* cheerfully.

Fronleichnam *nt* Corpus Christi (*Catholic festival*).

fror *prät* → frieren.

Frost (*pl* Fröste) *der* frost.

Frostgefahr *die* : **es besteht ~** there's a danger of frost.

Frostschutzmittel (*pl* -) *das* antifreeze.

Frottee (*pl* -s) *der* ODER *das* towelling.

Frucht (*pl* Früchte) *die* fruit.

Fruchteis *das* fruit-flavoured ice-cream.

Früchtetee (*pl* -s) *der* fruit tea.

fruchtig *adj* fruity.

Fruchtsaft (*pl* -säfte) *der* fruit juice.

Fruchtsaftkonzentrat (*pl* -e) *das* squash (*Br*), juice concentrate (*Am*).

Fruchtsalat (*pl* -e) *der* fruit salad.

früh *adj* & *adv* early ; **~ am Abend** early in the evening ; **gestern/heute/morgen ~** yesterday/this/tomorrow morning.

früher *adj* (*ehemalig*) former. ◆ *adv* formerly.

frühestens *adv* at the earliest.

Frühjahr (*pl* -e) *das* spring.

Frühling (*pl* -e) *der* spring ; **im ~** in spring.

Frühlingsrolle (*pl* -n) *die* spring roll.

Frühschicht (*pl* -en) *die* early shift.

Frühstück (*pl* -e) *das* breakfast ; **zum ~** for breakfast.

frühstücken *vi* to have breakfast.

Frühstücksbüfett (*pl* -s) *das* breakfast bar.

Frühstücksraum(*pl*-räume) *der* breakfast room.

Fuchs (*pl* Füchse) *der* fox.

fühlen *vt* & *vi* to feel ; nach etw ~ to feel for sthg. ▪ **sich fühlen** *ref* to feel.

fuhr *prät* → **fahren**.

führen *vt* (*Person, Leben*) to lead ; (*Touristen*) to show round ; (*Geschäft*) to run ; (*Buch, Konto*) to keep ; (*Ware*) to stock ; (*Gespräch*) to hold. ◆ *vi* to lead ; **England führt mit 1 : 0** England are one-nil ahead ; ~ **zu** (*an ein Ziel*) to lead to.

Führer (*pl* -) *der* (*Person, Buch*) guide.

Führerin (*pl* -ne n) *die* guide.

Führerschein (*pl* -e) *der* driving licence (*Br*), driver's license (*Am*).

Führung (*pl* -en) *die* (*Besichtigung*) (guided) tour ; **nächste** ~ **: 12.30 Uhr** the next tour is at 12.30 ; **in** ~ **liegen** to be in the lead.

füllen *vt* (*Gefäß*) to fill ; (*Teig, Fleisch*) to stuff ; (*Flüssigkeit*) to put.

Füller (*pl* -) *der* fountain pen.

Füllung (*pl* -en) *die* filling.

Fund (*pl* -e) *der* (*Vorgang*) discovery ; (*Gegenstand*) find.

Fundbüro (*pl* -s) *das* lost property office (*Br*), lost-and-found office (*Am*).

Fundsachen *pl* lost property (*sg*).

fünf *num* five ; → **sechs**.

fünfhundert *num* five hundred.

fünfmal *adv* five times.

Fünfmarkstück (*pl* -e) *das* five-mark coin.

fünfte *adj* fifth. → **sechste**.

Fünftel (*pl* -) *das* fifth.

fünfzehn *num* fifteen ; → **sechs**.

fünfzig *num* fifty ; → **sechs**.

Fünfzigmarkschein (*pl* -e) *der* fifty-mark note.

Funk *der* radio.

funken *vi* to radio.

Funkgerät (*pl* -e) *das* radio set.

Funktelefon (*pl* -e) *das* (*Handy*) mobile phone ; (*kabelloses Telefon*) cordless phone.

Funktion (*pl* -en) *die* function ; (*Funktionieren*) functioning.

funktionieren *vi* to work.

für *präp* (+A) for ; **Wort** ~ **Wort** word by word ; **Tag** ~ **Tag** day after day ; **was** ~ **ein Auto hast du?** what kind of car do you have? ; **jn** ~ **dumm halten** to think sb is stupid.

Furcht *die* fear.

furchtbar *adj* terrible. ◆ *adv* terribly.

fürchten *vt* to fear. ▪ **sich fürchten** *ref* to be afraid ; **sich** ~ **vor** (+D) to be afraid of.

fürchterlich *adj* terrible. ◆ *adv* terribly.

füreinander *adv* for each other.

fürs *präp* & *det* = **für das**.

Fuß (*pl* Füße) *der* foot ; (*von Möbel*) leg ; (*von Lampe*) base ; **zu** ~ on foot.

Fußball (pl -bälle) der (Ball) football (Br), soccer ball (Am) ; (Sport) football (Br), soccer (Am).

Fußballmannschaft (pl -en) die football team (Br), soccer team (Am).

Fußballplatz (pl -plätze) der football pitch (Br), soccer pitch (Am).

Fußballspiel (pl -e) das football match (Br), soccer match (Am).

Fußballspieler, in (mpl -) der, die footballer (Br), soccer player (Am).

Fußbank (pl -bänke) die footstool.

Fußboden (pl -böden) der floor.

Fußbremse (pl -n) die footbrake.

Fußgänger, in (mpl -) der, die pedestrian.

Fußgängerbrücke (pl -n) die footbridge.

Fußgängertunnel (pl -) der subway, underpass.

Fußgängerüberweg (pl -e) der pedestrian crossing.

Fußgängerzone (pl -n) die pedestrian precinct.

Fußgelenk (pl -e) das ankle.

Fußnagel (pl -nägel) der toenail.

Fußweg (pl -e) der footpath.

Futter das (für Tiere) food ; (von Mantel, Tasche) lining.

füttern vt to feed ; 'bitte nicht ~!' 'please do not feed the animals'.

Futur (pl -e) das future (tense).

G

gab prät → geben.

Gabel (pl -n) die (Besteck) fork.

gabeln : sich gabeln ref to fork.

Gabelung (pl -en) die fork.

Gag (pl -s) der gag.

gähnen vi to yawn.

Gala (pl -s) die (Veranstaltung) gala ; (Kleidung) formal dress.

Galerie (pl -n) die gallery.

Galle (pl -n) die bile.

galoppieren vi ist to gallop.

Galopprennen (pl -) das horse racing.

galt prät → gelten.

gammeln vi (fam : Person) to loaf around.

Gang (pl Gänge) der (Flur) corridor ; (in Flugzeug) aisle ; (von Menü) course ; (von Fahrzeug) gear ; (Gangart) gait ; (Spaziergang) walk ; etw in ~ setzen to get sthg going ; im ersten ~ in first gear.

Gangschaltung (pl -en) die gears (pl).

Gangway (pl -s) die (von Schiff) gangway ; (von Flugzeug) steps (pl).

Gans (pl Gänse) die goose.

Gänsehaut die goose pimples (pl).

Gänseleberpastete (pl -n) die foie gras, pâté made from goose liver.

ganz adj (komplett, heil) whole ; (alle) all. ◆ adv (sehr) really ; (völlig) completely ; (ziemlich) quite ; der ~e Kaffee all the coffee ; ~ Paris the whole of Paris ; ~ **bleiben** to stay in one piece ; ~ **bestimmt** quite certainly ; ~ **und gar** completely ; ~ **und gar nicht** not at all ; ~ **gut** quite well/good.

ganztägig *adj (Beschäftigung)* full-time. ◆ *adv* all day.

ganztags *adv* all day.

gar *adj (Speise)* done. ◆ *adv* : es war ~ keiner da there was no one there at all ; ~ **nicht** not at all ; ~ **nichts** nothing at all ; auf ~ **keinen Fall** under no circumstances.

Garage *(pl -n) die* garage.

Garagenanlage *(pl -n) die* row of garages.

Garantie *(pl -n) die* guarantee.

garantieren *vt* to guarantee. ◆ *vi* : ~ **für** to guarantee.

garantiert *adv* : er hat es ~ **vergessen** he's bound to have forgotten it.

Garderobe *(pl -n) die (Kleidung)* coat, scarf, hat etc ; *(Raum)* cloakroom.

Gardine *(pl -n) die* curtain.

Garn *(pl -e) das* thread.

Garten *(pl Gärten) der* garden.

Gartenlokal *(pl -e) das* beer garden.

Gartenstuhl *(pl -stühle) der* garden chair.

Gärtner, in *(mpl -) der, die* gardener.

Gärtnerei *(pl -en) die* nursery.

Garzeit *(pl -en) die* cooking time.

Gas *(pl -e) das* gas ; *(Gaspedal)* accelerator ; ~ **geben** to accelerate.

Gasflasche *(pl -n) die* gas cylinder.

Gasheizung *(pl -en) die* gas heating.

Gaskocher *(pl -) der* camping stove.

Gaspedal *(pl -e) das* accelerator.

Gaspistole *(pl -n) die* pistol that fires gas cartridges.

Gasse *(pl -n) die (Straße)* lane.

Gast *(pl Gäste) der* guest ; **zu** ~ **sein bei jm** to be sb's guest.

Gastarbeiter, in *(mpl -) der, die* foreign worker.

Gästebett *(pl -en) das* spare bed.

Gästebuch *(pl -bücher) das* visitor's book.

Gästehaus *(pl -häuser) das* guest house.

Gästezimmer *(pl -) das* guest room.

gastfreundlich *adj* hospitable.

Gastgeber, in *(mpl -) der, die* host.

Gasthaus *(pl -häuser) das* inn.

Gasthof *(pl -höfe) der* inn.

Gastland *(pl -länder) das* foreign country *(where someone is staying)*.

Gastronomie *die* catering.

Gaststätte *(pl -n) die* pub *(also offering a full menu of local food)*.

Gaststube *(pl -n) die* restaurant *(in a hotel or inn)*.

Gạstwirt, in (mpl -e) der, die landlord (landlady).

Gaze die gauze.

geändert adj : ~e Abfahrtszeiten revised departure times ; ~e Öffnungszeiten new opening hours ; 'Vorfahrt ~' sign indicating altered right of way.

geb. abk = geboren.

Gebäck das pastries (pl).

gebạcken adj baked.

Gebärmutter die womb.

Gebäude (pl -) das building.

gebeizt adj (Holz) stained.

geben (präs gibt, prät gab, pp gegeben) vt 1. (reichen, schenken) : jm etw ~ to give sb sthg, to give sthg to sb. 2. (bezahlen) to give ; er hat mir 20 DM dafür gegeben he gave me 20 marks for it. 3. (sagen, erteilen) to give ; Unterricht ~ to teach. 4. (in Reparatur) : etw in Reparatur ~ to have sthg repaired. 5. (am Telefon) : jm jn ~ to put sb through to sb. ◆ vimp : es gibt there is/are ; hier gibt es viele Studenten there are a lot of students here ; was gibt es? what's up? ; was gibt es im Fernsehen? what's on television? ■ **sich geben** ref to act ; sich cool ~ to act cool.

gebeten pp → bitten.

Gebiet (pl -e) das (Gegend) area.

Gebirge (pl -) das mountains (pl).

gebịrgig adj mountainous.

Gebịss (pl -e) das (Zähne) teeth (pl) ; (künstlich) dentures (pl).

gebịssen pp beißen.

Gebịssreiniger (pl -) der denture tablets (pl).

Gebläse (pl -) das fan.

geblasen pp → blasen.

geblieben pp bleiben.

gebogen pp → biegen. ◆ adj bent.

gebohnert adj polished ; 'frisch ~' 'slippery floor'.

geboren adj : ~e Maier née Maier.

geborgen pp → bergen.

geboten pp → bieten.

gebracht pp → bringen.

gebrannt pp → brennen.

gebraten pp → braten. ◆ adj (in der Pfanne) fried ; (im Backofen) roast.

gebrauchen vt to use ; deine Hilfe könnte ich gut ~ I could use your help.

Gebrauchsanweisung (pl -en) die instructions (pl).

gebrauchsfertig adj ready-to-use.

Gebrauchsgegenstand (pl -stände) der utensil.

gebraucht adj used, secondhand.

Gebrauchtwagen (pl -) der used car.

gebrochen pp → brechen. ◆ adj broken. ◆ adv : ~ Englisch sprechen to speak broken English.

Gebühr (pl -en) die (für Telefon, Rundfunk) charge ; (für Arzt, Anwalt) fee ; '~ bezahlt

Empfänger' 'postage to be paid by the addressee'.

Gebühreneinheit (*pl* -en) *die* unit (*on phone*).

gebührenfrei *adj* free of charge.

Gebührenordnung (*pl* -en) *die* tariff.

gebührenpflichtig *adj* subject to a charge.

gebunden *pp* → binden.

Geburt (*pl* -en) *die* birth.

Geburtsdatum *das* date of birth.

Geburtsjahr *das* year of birth.

Geburtsname *der* maiden name.

Geburtsort *der* place of birth.

Geburtstag (*pl* -e) *der* birthday ; alles Gute zum ~ happy birthday.

Geburtstagsfeier (*pl* -n) *die* birthday party.

Geburtsurkunde (*pl* -n) *die* birth certificate.

gedacht *pp* → denken.

Gedächtnis (*pl* -se) *das* memory.

Gedanke (*pl* -n) *der* thought.

Gedeck (*pl* -e) *das* place setting.

Gedenkfeier (*pl* -n) *die* memorial service.

Gedenkstätte (*pl* -n) *die* memorial.

Gedenktafel (*pl* -n) *die* (memorial) plaque.

Gedicht (*pl* -e) *das* poem.

Geduld *die* patience ; bitte haben Sie etwas ~ (*am Telefon*) please hold the line.

gedulden : sich gedulden *ref* to wait (patiently) ; bitte ~ Sie sich einen Augenblick please wait a moment.

geduldig *adj* patient. ◆ *adv* patiently.

gedünstet *adj* steamed.

gedurft *pp* → dürfen.

geehrt *adj* : Sehr ~e Frau Müller Dear Mrs Müller ; Sehr ~er Herr Braun Dear Mr Braun.

geeignet *adj* suitable ; ~ für suitable for ; er ist zum Lehrer ~ he'd make a good teacher ; nicht ~ unsuitable.

Gefahr (*pl* -en) *die* danger ; auf eigene ~ at one's own risk ; 'bei ~ Scheibe einschlagen' 'break the glass in case of emergency'.

gefahren *pp* → fahren.

Gefahrenfall *der* : 'nur im ~ benutzen' 'for emergency use only'.

gefährlich *adj* dangerous.

Gefälle (*pl* -) *das* incline.

gefallen *vi* : es gefällt mir I like it ; es gefällt ihm he likes it ; sich (D) etw ~ lassen to put up with sthg ; sich (D) nichts ~ lassen not to put up with any nonsense.

Gefallen (*pl* -) *der* favour ; jm einen ~ tun to do sb a favour ; jm um einen ~ bitten to ask sb a favour.

gefälligst *adv* : komm ~ her! will you please come here!

gefangen *pp* → fangen.

Gefängnis (*pl* -se) *das* prison.

Gefäß (*pl* -e) *das* container, receptacle.

geflochten *pp* → flechten.

geflogen *pp* → fliegen.

geflohen pp fliehen.

geflossen pp fließen.

Geflügel das poultry.

gefochten pp → fechten.

gefressen pp → fressen.

Gefrierbeutel (pl -) der freezer bag.

gefrieren (präs gefriert, prät gefror, pp gefroren) vi ist/hat to freeze.

Gefrierfach (pl -fächer) das freezer (compartment).

Gefriertruhe (pl -n) die freezer.

gefroren pp → frieren, gefrieren. ◆ adj frozen.

Gefühl (pl -e) das feeling.

gefüllt adj (Speisen) stuffed.

gefunden pp → finden.

gegangen pp → gehen.

gegeben pp → geben.

gegebenenfalls adv if necessary.

gegen präp (+A) against ; (Angabe eines Vergleichs) in comparison to ; ~ fünf Uhr at about five o'clock ; ~ etw sein to be opposed to sthg ; Leipzig ~ Dresden Leipzig versus Dresden ; ein Mittel ~ Grippe a medicine for flu, a flu remedy ; etwas ~ jm haben to have something against sb ; ~ bar for cash.

Gegend (pl -en) die area ; in der ~ nearby ; in der ~ von near.

gegeneinander adv against each other.

Gegenfahrbahn (pl -en) die opposite carriageway.

Gegenlicht das : bei ~ with the light in one's eyes.

Gegenmittel (pl -) das antidote.

Gegenrichtung die opposite direction.

Gegensatz (pl -sätze) der contrast ; im ~ zu in contrast to.

gegenseitig adj mutual. ◆ adv : sich ~ beeinflussen to influence each other.

Gegensprechanlage (pl -n) die intercom.

Gegenstand (pl -stände) der object.

Gegenteil (pl -e) das opposite ; im ~ on the contrary.

gegenüber präp (+D) (räumlich) opposite ; (Angabe eines Vergleichs) in comparison to ; (Angabe einer Beziehung) : jm ~ towards sb.

Gegenverkehr der oncoming traffic.

Gegenwart die (GRAMM) present (tense) ; (jetzt) present ; in ~ von in the presence of.

Gegenwind der headwind.

gegessen pp → essen.

geglichen pp → gleichen.

geglitten pp → gleiten.

Gegner, in (mpl -) der, die opponent.

gegolten pp → gelten.

gegossen pp → gießen.

gegriffen pp → greifen.

gegrillt adj grilled.

Gehackte das mince (Br), mincemeat (Am).

Gehalt (pl Gehälter) das (von Angestellten) salary.

gehbehindert adj disabled (used of people who have difficulty walking).

geheim adj secret.

Geheimnis (*pl* -se) *das* secret.

geheimnisvoll *adj* mysterious.

Geheimnummer (*pl* -n) *die* (*von Scheckkarte*) PIN (number) ; (*von Telefon*) ex-directory number (*Br*), unlisted number (*Am*).

geheißen *pp* → heißen.

gehen (*präs* **geht**, *prät* **ging**, *pp* **gegangen**) *vi* ist 1. (*gen*) to go ; **einkaufen ~** to go shopping ; **zu Fuß ~** to walk.

2. (*weggehen, abfahren*) to go ; **mein Zug geht um acht Uhr** my train goes at eight o'clock.

3. (*funktionieren*) to work.

4. (*erlaubt sein*) to be allowed ; **das geht nicht** you can't do that.

5. (*möglich sein*) to be possible ; **heute geht es nicht** it's not possible today.

6. (*reichen*) : **~ bis** to come up to, to go as far as.

7. (*passen*) : **in/durch etw ~** to go in/through sthg.

8. (*berühren*) : **an etw** (*A*) **~** to touch sthg.

9. (*sich richten*) : **es kann nicht immer nach dir ~** you can't always have things your own way.

10. (*Belastung*) : **das geht über unsere Mittel** that's beyond our means.

11. (*kündigen*) to leave.

12. (*Teig*) to rise.

13. (*Post*) to go.

◆ *vimp* 1. (*sich befinden*) : **wie geht's?** how are you? ; **wie geht es Ihnen?** how are you? ; **es geht mir gut/schlecht** I'm well/not very well ; **wie gefällt es dir? - es**

geht how do you like it? - it's O.K.

2. (*sich handeln um*) : **es geht um deine Mutter** it's about your mother ; **es geht darum, als Erster anzukommen** you have to try and arrive first ; **worum geht es in diesem Buch?** what's this book about?

Gehirn (*pl* -e) *das* brain.

Gehirnerschütterung (*pl* -en) *die* concussion.

gehoben *pp* → heben. ◆ *adj* (*Position*) senior.

geholfen *pp* → helfen.

gehorchen *vi* to obey ; **jm ~** to obey sb.

gehören *vi* : **jm ~** to belong to sb ; **~ zu** (*als Teil*) to belong to ; **~ in** (+*A*) (*an Platz*) to belong in.

■ **sich gehören** *ref* : **das gehört sich nicht!** that's not the done thing!

Gehörlose (*pl* -n) *der, die* deaf person.

gehorsam *adj* obedient.

Gehweg (*pl* -e) *der* pavement (*Br*), sidewalk (*Am*).

Geige (*pl* -n) *die* violin.

Geisel (*pl* -n) *die* hostage.

Geist (*pl* -er) *der* (*Verstand*) mind ; (*Gespenst*) ghost.

Geisterbahn (*pl* -en) *die* ghost train.

Geisterfahrer, in (*mpl* -) *der, die* person who drives in the wrong direction on a motorway.

geizig *adj* mean, miserly.

gekannt *pp* → kennen.

geklungen *pp* → klingen.

gekniffen *pp* → kneifen.

gekocht *adj* cooked.

gekommen *pp* → kommen.

gekonnt pp → können.

gekrochen pp → kriechen.

gekühlt adj (Getränk) chilled ; '~ mindestens haltbar bis...' 'if refrigerated best before...'

Gel (pl -s) das gel.

geladen pp → laden.

gelähmt adj paralysed.

Gelände (pl -) das (Grundstück) site ; (Gebiet) terrain.

Geländer (pl -) das (von Treppe) banister ; (von Brücke) parapet ; (von Balkon) railing.

gelang prät → gelingen.

gelassen adj calm, cool.

Gelatine die gelatine.

gelaunt adj : gut ~ good-tempered ; schlecht ~ bad-tempered.

gelb adj (Farbe) yellow ; (Ampel) amber.

Gelb das (Farbe) yellow ; (von Ampel) amber.

Gelbsucht die jaundice.

Geld (pl -er) das money. ▪ **Gelder** pl funds.

Geldautomat (pl -en) der cash dispenser.

Geldbörse (pl -n) die (Brieftasche) wallet ; (für Münzen) purse.

Geldeinwurf der coin slot.

Geld|karte die smart card.

Geldrückgabe die coin return (button).

Geldschein (pl -e) der banknote.

Geldstrafe (pl -n) die fine.

Geldtasche (pl -n) die money bag.

Geldwechsel der exchange ; 'kein ~' 'currency not exchanged here'.

Geldwechselautomat (pl -en) der change machine.

Gelee (pl -s) das jelly.

gelegen pp → leihen.

Gelegenheit (pl -en) die (Möglichkeit, Anlass) opportunity ; (Angebot) bargain ; bei ~ some time.

Gelenk (pl -e) das (von Knochen) joint.

Geliebte (pl -n) der, die lover.

geliehen pp → leihen.

gelingen vi unr ist to be a success ; jm ~ to turn out well for sb ; es ist mir gelungen, ihn zu überreden I managed to convince him.

gelitten pp → leiden.

gelockt adj curly.

gelogen pp → lügen.

gelten (präs gilt, prät galt, pp gegolten) vt to be valid for. ◆ vi to be valid ; ~ bis to be valid until.

Geltungsbereich (pl -e) der (von Fahrkarte) zone or zones for which a ticket is valid.

Geltungsdauer die (von Fahrkarte, Ausweis) period for which a ticket, passport etc is valid.

gelungen pp → gelingen.

gemahlen adj (Kaffee) ground.

Gemälde (pl -) das painting.

gemein adj (böse) nasty, mean.

Gemeinde (pl -n) die (Verwaltungseinheit) municipality ; (Menschen) community ; (kirchlich) parish.

gemeinsam adj common. ◆ adv together.

Gemeinschaft (pl -en) die (Gruppe) community ; (Zusammensein) company.

gemeint adj : das war nicht so ~ I didn't mean it like that.

gemieden pp → meiden.

gemischt adj mixed ; ~er Salat mixed salad.

gemocht pp → mögen.

gemolken pp → melken.

Gemüse das vegetables (pl).

Gemüsehändler, in (mpl -) der, die greengrocer.

gemusst pp → müssen.

gemütlich adj (bequem) cosy ; (Abend) pleasant ; (langsam) leisurely ; es sich ~ machen to make o.s. at home.

genannt pp → nennen.

genau adj exact. ◆ adv (aufmerksam) carefully ; (exakt) precisely, exactly ; ~! (richtig) exactly!

genauso adv just as ; ~ gut/ schlecht/schnell just as good/ bad/fast.

genehmigen vt to authorize.

Genehmigung (pl -en) die (Genehmigen) authorization ; (Schein) permit.

generalüberholen vt to service.

Generation (pl -en) die generation.

generell adj general.

Genf nt Geneva.

Genfer See der Lake Geneva.

Genick (pl -e) das (back of the) neck.

genießbar adj (Speise) edible ; das Fleisch ist nicht mehr ~ the meat has gone off.

genießen (prät genoss, pp genossen) vt to enjoy.

Genitiv (pl -e) der genitive.

genommen pp → nehmen.

genormt adj standardized.

genoss prät → genießen.

genossen pp → genießen.

genug adv enough ; ~ haben (bei Überdruss) to have had enough.

genügen vi to be enough ; jm ~ to be enough for sb ; das genügt! that's enough!

Genuss (pl Genüsse) der (Freude) pleasure ; (Verzehr, Verbrauch) consumption.

geöffnet adj (Geschäft, Schalter) open.

geografisch, geographisch adj geographical.

geordnet adj orderly.

Gepäck das luggage.

Gepäckabfertigung die (luggage) check-in.

Gepäckablage (pl -n) die luggage rack.

Gepäckannahme die (zur Aufbewahrung) = Gepäckaufbewahrung ; (Abfertigung am Bahnhof) office where large items of luggage sent by rail have to be registered.

Gepäckaufbewahrung die left-luggage office (Br), baggage room (Am).

Gepäckaufgabe die (Abfertigung am Bahnhof) = Gepäckannahme ; (zur Aufbewahrung) = Gepäckaufbewahrung.

Gepäckaufsicht *die* left-luggage office *(Br)*, baggage room *(Am)*.

Gepäckausgabe *die (aus Aufbewahrung)* = **Gepäckaufbewahrung**; *(Abfertigung am Bahnhof)* office where large items of luggage sent by rail can be collected.

Gepäckkarren *(pl -)* der luggage trolley.

Gepäckkontrolle *(pl -n) die* luggage search.

Gepäcknetz *(pl -e) das* luggage rack.

Gepäckrückgabe *die (aus Aufbewahrung)* = **Gepäckaufbewahrung**; *(Abfertigung am Flughafen)* baggage reclaim.

Gepäckschein *(pl -e) der* luggage ticket.

Gepäckschließfach *(pl -fächer) das* left-luggage locker *(Br)*, baggage locker *(Am)*.

Gepäckstück *(pl -e) das* item of luggage.

Gepäckträger *(pl -) der (von Fahrrad)* carrier.

Gepäckversicherung *(pl -en) die* luggage insurance.

Gepäckwagen *(pl -) der* luggage van *(Br)*, luggage car *(Am)*.

gepfiffen *pp* → **pfeifen**.

gequollen *pp* → **quellen**.

gerade *adv* just; *(jetzt)* just now; ~ er he of all people; ~ deshalb precisely for that reason; ~ erst only just; ~ noch only just; er wollte ~ gehen he was just about to go; nicht ~ not exactly.

geradeaus *adv* straight ahead; immer ~ straight ahead.

gerannt *pp* → **rennen**.

geraspelt *adj* grated.

gerät *präs* → **geraten**.

Gerät *(pl -e) das (Vorrichtung, Maschine)* device; *(Werkzeug)* tool; *(Kochlöffel, Dosenöffner usw.)* utensil; *(Radio, Fernseher)* set.

geraten *(präs gerät, prät geriet, pp geraten) vi ist (gelangen)* to get; auf die falsche Fahrbahn ~ to get into the wrong lane; in Schwierigkeiten ~ to get into difficulties.

geräuchert *adj* smoked.

geräumig *adj* roomy.

Geräusch *(pl -e) das* noise.

gerecht *adj* just, fair.

Gerechtigkeit *die* justice.

Gericht *(pl -e) das (Institution)* court; *(Speise)* dish.

gerieben *pp* → **reiben**. ◆ *adj* grated.

gerieten *prät* → **geraten**.

gering *adj (Menge, Preis, Temperatur)* low; *(Zeit, Abstand)* short; *(Bedeutung)* minor; *(Chance)* slight; nicht im Geringsten not in the least.

geringfügig *adj* slight, minor.

gerinnen *(prät gerann, pp geronnen) vi ist (Milch)* to curdle; *(Blut)* to clot.

gerissen *pp* → **reißen**. ◆ *adj (abw: Person)* cunning.

geritten *pp* → **reiten**.

gern(e) : **gerne** *(komp lieber, superl am liebsten) adv* : jn/etw ~ haben to like sb/sthg; jn/etw ~ mögen to like sb/sthg; etw ~ tun to like doing sthg; aber ~! I'd love to! ; ~ geschehen! don't mention it! ; ich möchte ~... I'd like to... ; ja ~! of course!

gerochen pp → riechen.

geronnen pp → gerinnen, rinnen. ◆ adj (Milch) curdled.

geröstet adj roasted.

Geruch (pl Gerüche) der smell.

gerufen pp → rufen.

gerungen pp → ringen.

gesalzen adj (Speise) salted ; (fam : Preis) steep.

gesamt adj (Familie, Inhalt) whole ; (Einkommen, Kosten) total.

gesamtdeutsch adj united German ; ~e Beziehungen relations between the two Germanys.

Gesamtschule (pl -n) die ≃ comprehensive school.

gesandt pp → senden[1].

Geschädigte (pl -n) der, die injured party.

Geschäft (pl -e) das (Laden) shop ; (Betrieb) business ; (Handel) deal.

Geschäftsbedingungen pl terms.

Geschäftsfrau (pl -en) die businesswoman.

Geschäftsführer, in (mpl -) der, die manager (f manageress).

Geschäftsleute pl businessmen.

Geschäftsmann (pl -männer) der businessman.

Geschäftsreise (pl -n) die business trip.

Geschäftsschluss der closing time.

Geschäftsstelle (pl -n) die office.

Geschäftsstraße (pl -n) die high street (Br), main street (Am).

Geschäftszeiten pl business hours.

geschah prät → geschehen.

geschehen (präs geschieht, prät geschah, pp geschehen) vi ist to happen ; jm ~ to happen to sb ; ~ mit to happen to.

Geschenk (pl -e) das present, gift ; soll ich es als ~ einpacken? would you like it gift-wrapped?

Geschenkartikel (pl -) der gift.

Geschenkgutschein (pl -e) der gift token.

Geschenkpapier (pl -e) das gift wrap.

Geschichte (pl -n) die (Text) story ; (Vergangenheit) history.

geschickt adj skilful.

geschieden pp → scheiden. ◆ adj (Mann, Frau) divorced.

geschieht präs → geschehen.

geschienen pp → scheinen.

Geschirr das (zum Essen) crockery ; (das) ~ spülen to wash up ; das ~ abtrocknen to dry up.

Geschirrspülmaschine (pl -n) die dishwasher.

Geschirrspülmittel (pl -) das washing-up liquid.

Geschirrtuch (pl -tücher) das tea towel (Br), dish towel (Am).

geschissen pp → scheißen.

Geschlecht das (biologisch) sex ; (GRAMM) gender.

Geschlechtskrankheit (*pl* -en) *die* sexually transmitted disease.

Geschlechtsverkehr *der* sexual intercourse.

geschlichen *pp* → schleichen.

geschliffen *pp* → schleifen.

geschlossen *pp* → schließen. ◆ *adj* closed ; (*Ortschaft*) built-up.

geschlungen *pp* → schlingen.

Geschmack (*pl* Geschmäcker) *der* taste ; **guten ~ haben** to have good taste ; **schlechten ~ haben** to have bad taste.

geschmacklos *adj* tasteless.

geschmackvoll *adj* tasteful.

geschmissen *pp* → schmeißen.

geschmolzen *pp* → schmelzen.

geschmort *adj* braised.

Geschnetzelte *das* small pieces of veal or chicken cooked in a sauce.

geschnitten *pp* → schneiden. ◆ *adj* (*Wurst, Käse*) sliced ; **~ oder am Stück?** would you like it sliced or unsliced?

geschoben *pp* → schieben.

gescholten *pp* → schelten.

geschoren *pp* → scheren.

Geschoss (*pl* -e) *das* (*Etage*) floor.

geschossen *pp* → schießen.

Geschrei *das* shouting.

geschrieben *pp* → schreiben.

geschrien *pp* → schreien.

geschritten *pp* → schreiten.

geschwiegen *pp* → schweigen.

Geschwindigkeit (*pl* -en) *die* speed.

Geschwindigkeitsbeschränkung (*pl* -en) *die* speed limit.

Geschwindigkeitsübertretung (*pl* -en) *die* speeding.

Geschwister *pl* brothers and sisters.

geschwollen *pp* → schwellen. ◆ *adj* (*Finger, Bein*) swollen.

geschwommen *pp* → schwimmen.

geschworen *pp* → schwören.

geschwungen *pp* → schwingen.

Geschwür (*pl* -e) *das* ulcer.

gesellig *adj* (*Person*) sociable ; (*Abend*) social.

Gesellschaft (*pl* -en) *die* (*System*) society ; (*Gruppe*) group (of people) ; (*Touristen*) party ; (*Begleitung*) company ; **jm ~ leisten** to keep sb company.

Gesellschaftsraum (*pl* -räume) *der* function suite.

gesessen *pp* → sitzen.

Gesetz (*pl* -e) *das* law.

gesetzlich *adj* legal ; **~er Feiertag** public holiday.

gesetzwidrig *adj* illegal.

Gesicht (*pl* -er) *das* face.

Gesichtcreme (*pl* -s) *die* face cream.

Gesichtswasser *das* toner.

gesoffen *pp* → saufen.

gesogen *pp* → saugen.

gespannt adj (Atmosphäre) tense. ◆ adv (warten) eagerly ; auf etw (A) ~ sein (Person) to be looking forward to sthg.

gesperrt adj (Straße) closed off.

gesponnen pp → spinnen.

Gespräch (pl -e) das (Konversation) conversation ; (per Telefon) call.

Gesprächspartner, in (mpl -) der, die person one is talking to.

gesprochen pp → sprechen.

gesprungen pp → springen. ◆ adj (Glas) cracked.

Gestalt (pl -en) die (Person, Figur) figure ; (Form) shape.

gestanden pp → stehen.

Gestank der stench.

gestärkt adj (Wäsche) starched.

gestatten vt (geh : erlauben) to permit, to allow. ◆ vi (geh) : ~ Meier allow me to introduce myself - my name is Meier ; ~ Sie? may I? ; jm etw ~ to allow sb sthg.

gestattet adj (amt) : ~ sein to be allowed ; nicht ~ prohibited.

Geste (pl -n) die (mit Händen, mit Kopf) gesture.

gestern adv yesterday ; ~ Morgen/Mittag/Abend yesterday morning/lunchtime/evening ; ~ früh early yesterday.

gestiegen pp → steigen.

gestochen pp → stechen. ◆ adv : ~ scharf sharp.

gestohlen pp → stehlen ; etw als ~ melden to report the theft of sthg.

gestorben pp → sterben.

gestreift adj striped, stripy.

gestrichen pp → streichen. ◆ adj (Löffel) level.

gestrig adj (von Vortag) : die ~e Zeitung yesterday's paper.

gestritten pp → streiten.

gestunken pp → stinken.

gesund (komp gesünder, superl am gesündesten) adj healthy. ◆ adv healthily ; wieder ~ werden to get better.

Gesundheit die health ; ~! bless you!

gesundheitsschädlich adj (Inhaltsstoff) damaging to one's health.

gesungen pp → singen.

gesunken pp → sinken.

getan pp → tun.

Getränk (pl -e) das drink ; alkoholische ~e alcoholic beverages ; nichtalkoholische ~e soft drinks.

Getränkeautomat (pl -en) der drinks machine.

Getränkekarte (pl -n) die wine list.

Getränkemarkt (pl -märkte) der discount drink store.

Getreide das cereal, grain.

getrennt adj (Zimmer, Rechnung) separate. ◆ adv separately ; ~ leben to live apart ; ~ zahlen to pay separately.

Getriebe (pl -) das (von Auto, in Technik) gearbox.

getrieben pp → treiben.

Getriebeschaden (pl -schäden) der gearbox damage.

getrocknet adj dried.

getroffen pp → treffen.

getrunken pp → trinken.

gewachsen pp → wachsen.

Gewähr die guarantee ; ohne ~ (auf Fahrplan) subject to alteration.

Gewalt die (Brutalität) violence ; (Kraft) force ; (Macht) power.

gewandt pp → wenden.

gewann prät → gewinnen.

gewaschen pp → waschen.

Gewebe (pl -) das (Stoff) fabric ; (Körpergewebe) tissue.

Gewehr (pl -e) das gun.

gewellt adj (Haare) wavy.

Gewerbegebiet (pl -e) das business park.

gewerblich adj (Nutzung) commercial.

Gewerkschaft (pl -en) die trade union.

gewesen pp → sein.

Gewicht (pl -e) das weight.

gewiesen pp → weisen.

Gewinn (pl -e) der (Preis) prize ; (Profit) profit ; (bei Glücksspiel, beim Wetten) winnings (pl).

gewinnen (prät gewann, pp gewonnen) vi to win ; (besser werden) to gain. ◆ vt to win ; (produzieren) to obtain.

Gewinner, in (mpl -) der, die winner.

Gewinnspiel (pl -e) das game show.

gewiss adj certain.

Gewissen das conscience.

Gewitter (pl -) das (Wetter) storm.

gewittrig adj (Gewitter ankündigend) stormy.

gewogen pp → wiegen.

gewöhnen : jn an etw (A) ~ to accustom sb to sthg. ■ sich gewöhnen ref : sich ~ an (+A) to get used to.

Gewohnheit (pl -en) die habit.

gewöhnlich adj (normal) usual ; (primitiv) common. ◆ adv (normalerweise) usually ; wie ~ as usual.

gewohnt adj usual ; etw ~ sein to be used to sthg.

Gewölbe (pl -) das (Deckengewölbe) vault.

gewonnen pp → gewinnen.

geworben pp → werben.

geworden pp → werden.

geworfen pp → werfen.

Gewürz (pl -e) das spice.

Gewürzgurke (pl -n) die pickled gherkin.

gewürzt adj seasoned ; scharf ~ hot.

gewusst pp → wissen.

Gezeiten pl tides.

gezogen pp → ziehen.

gezwungen pp → zwingen.

gibt präs → geben.

Gicht die gout.

gierig adj greedy.

gießen (prät goss, pp gegossen) vt (schütten) to pour ; (Pflanzen) to water. ◆ vimp : es gießt it's pouring (down).

Gießkanne (pl -n) die watering can.

Gift (pl -e) das poison.

giftig adj (Substanz, Pflanze) poisonous ; (fig : Person, Bemerkung) venomous.

gilt präs → gelten.

Gin der gin.

ging prät → gehen.

Gipfel (*pl* -) *der (von Berg)* summit, peak.

Gips *der (Gipspulver)* plaster ; *(Gipsverband)* plaster cast.

Gipsbein (*pl* -e) *das* : **ein ~ haben** to have one's leg in plaster.

Gipsverband (*pl* -verbände) *der* plaster cast.

Giraffe (*pl* -n) *die* giraffe.

Girokonto (*pl* -konten) *das* current account *(Br)*, checking account *(Am)*.

Gischt *der* spray.

Gitarre (*pl* -n) *die* guitar.

Gitter (*pl* -) *das* bars *(pl)*.

Gitterbett (*pl* -en) *das* cot *(Br)*, crib *(Am)*.

glänzen *vi (Metall, Wasser)* to shine.

glänzend *adj (leuchtend)* shining ; *(ausgezeichnet)* brilliant.

Glas (*pl* Gläser) *das* glass ; *(Einmachglas)* jar ; **aus ~** glass ; **ein ~ Wein** a glass of wine.

Gläschen (*pl* -) *das* little glass.

Glasscheibe (*pl* -n) *die* pane (of glass).

Glastür (*pl* -en) *die* glass door.

glatt *adj (eben)* smooth ; *(rutschig)* slippery ; *(fam : problemlos)* smooth. ◆ *adv (fam : problemlos)* smoothly.

Glätte *die (Eisglätte)* (patch of) black ice.

Glatteis *das* black ice.

Glatteisgefahr *die* : **Vorsicht, ~!** watch out for black ice!

Glatze (*pl* -n) *die* : **eine ~ haben** to be bald.

glauben *vt (meinen, denken)* to think ; *(für wahr halten)* to believe. ◆ *vi (meinen, denken)*

to think ; **~ an** (+A) to believe in ; **jm ~** to believe sb.

gleich *adj* same. ◆ *adv (identisch)* equally ; *(ähnlich)* the same ; *(egal)* no matter ; *(sofort, bald)* straight away ; *(ebenso gut)* just as well ; **zwei ~ Tassen** two identical cups ; **bis ~!** see you soon! ; **~ groß sein** to be the same size ; **das ist mir ~** I don't care ; **ich komme ~** I'm just coming.

gleichaltrig *adj* : **~ sein** to be the same age.

gleichberechtigt *adj (Mann und Frau)* : **~ sein** to have equal rights.

gleiche, r ODER **s** *pron* : **der/ die/das ~** the same (one).

gleichen (*prät* glich, *pp* geglichen) *vi* (+D) to resemble.

gleichfalls *adv* also, as well ; **danke ~!** thanks, you too!

gleichgültig *adj* : **es ist mir ~** it's all the same to me.

gleichmäßig *adj (Tempo)* even. ◆ *adv (ziehen)* steadily ; *(auftragen)* evenly.

Gleichstrom *der* direct current.

gleichzeitig *adj* simultaneous. ◆ *adv* at the same time.

Gleis (*pl* -e) *das (Bahnsteig)* platform.

gleiten (*prät* glitt, *pp* geglitten) *vi* ist *(rutschen)* to glide.

Gleitschirm (*pl* -e) *der* paraglider.

Gletscher (*pl* -) *der* glacier.

glich *prät* → gleichen.

Glied (*pl* -er) *das (Einzelteil)* link ; *(Arm, Bein)* limb ; *(Penis)* member.

glitschig *adj* slippery.

glitt *prät* → **gleiten**.

glitzern *vi* sparkle.

Glocke (*pl* -n) die bell.

Glück das (*Ereignis*) luck ; (*Gefühl*) happiness ; ~ **haben** to be lucky ; **viel** ~! good luck! ; **zum** ~ luckily.

glücklich *adj* (*froh*) happy ; (*Zufall, Zusammentreffen*) fortunate. ◆ *adv* (*froh*) happily ; (*günstig*) fortunately.

glücklicherweise *adv* luckily.

Glücksspiel (*pl* -e) das (*um Geld*) game of chance.

Glückwunsch (*pl* -wünsche) der congratulations (*pl*) ; **herzlichen** ~! congratulations!

Glückwunschtelegramm (*pl* -e) das telegram sent to congratulate someone.

Glühbirne (*pl* -n) die light bulb.

glühen *vi* (*Kohle*) to glow ; (*Gesicht, Wangen*) to burn.

Glühwein der mulled wine.

Glut die (*im Feuer*) embers (*pl*).

Gnagi das (*Schweiz*) boiled knuckle of pork.

Gold das gold ; **aus** ~ gold.

golden *adj* (*aus Gold*) gold ; (*goldfarben*) golden.

Goldschmied, in (*mpl* -e) der, die goldsmith.

Golf das (*Sportart*) golf.

Golfplatz (*pl* -plätze) der golf course.

Golfschläger (*pl* -) der golf club.

gönnen *vt* (+D) : **jm etw** ~ not to begrudge sb sthg ; **sich** (*D*) **etw** ~ to allow o.s. sthg.

goss *prät* → **gießen**.

gotisch *adj* Gothic.

Gott (*pl* Götter) der (*christlich*) God ; (*Gottheit*) god ; ~ **sei Dank!** thank God! ; **Grüß** ~! (*Südt & Österr*) hello! ; **um** ~**es Willen!** for God's sake!

Gottesdienst (*pl* -e) der service.

Grab (*pl* Gräber) das grave.

graben (*präs* gräbt, *prät* grub, *pp* gegraben) *vt & vi* to dig.

Graben (*pl* Gräben) der (*Vertiefung*) ditch.

Grabstein (*pl* -e) der gravestone.

gräbt *präs* → **graben**.

Grad (*pl* -e) der degree ; **drei** ~ **unter/über Null** three degrees below/above zero ; **im höchsten** ~ highly.

Graffiti *pl* (*an Haus, U-Bahn*) graffiti.

Grafik (*pl* -en), **Graphik** die (*Technik*) graphics (*sg*) ; (*Bild, Schema*) diagram.

Gramm (*pl* -) das (*Gewichtseinheit*) gram.

Grammatik (*pl* -en) die grammar.

Grapefruit (*pl* -s) die grapefruit.

Grapefruitsaft (*pl* -säfte) der grapefruit juice.

Graphik die → **Grafik**.

Gras (*pl* Gräser) das grass.

grässlich *adj* horrible. ◆ *adv* (*sehr*) terribly ; (*Schrecken erregend*) terrifyingly.

Gräte (*pl* -n) die (*fish*) bone.

gratis *adv & adj* free.

Gratulation (pl -en) die (Glückwunsch) congratulations (pl).

gratulieren vi : jm (zu etw) ~ to congratulate sb (on sthg).

grau adj (Farbe, Haare) grey ; (trist) gloomy.

Graubrot (pl -e) das bread made with mixed wholemeal, rye and wheat flour.

grauhaarig adj grey-haired.

Graupelschauer (pl -) der sleet.

grausam adj (Mensch, Tat) cruel ; (Schmerzen, Hitze) terrible.

greifen (prät griff, pp gegriffen) vt to take hold of. ◆ vi (Räder) to grip ; nach etw ~ to reach for sthg.

grell adj (Licht) glaring ; (Ton) harsh ; (Farbe) loud. ◆ adv (leuchten) glaringly ; (klingen) harshly.

Grenzbeamte (pl -n) der customs and immigration officer.

Grenzbeamtin (pl -nen) die customs and immigration officer.

Grenze (pl -n) die (von Land) border ; (von Stadt, Grundstück) boundary ; (begrifflich, ideell) borderline ; (Beschränkung) limit ; grüne ~ border area without major road or border patrols.

grenzen vi : ~ an (+A) (räumlich) to border.

Grenzkontrolle (pl -n) die border checkpoint.

Grenzübergang (pl -gänge) der (Ort) border crossing.

Grenzverkehr der cross-border traffic.

Grenzwert (pl -e) der (für Schadstoffe) limit.

Griebenschmalz das spread made from animal fat, similar to dripping.

Grieche (pl -n) der Greek.

Griechenland nt Greece.

Griechin (pl -nen) die Greek.

griechisch adj Greek.

Griechisch(e) das Greek.

Grieß der semolina.

Griff (pl -e) der (mit der Hand) grip ; (zum Halten) handle.

griff prät → greifen.

Grill (pl -e) der grill.

grillen vt & vi to grill.

Grillfest (pl -e) das barbecue.

Grillspieß (pl -e) der (mit Fleisch) (shish) kebab.

Grillstube (pl -n) die grill (restaurant).

Grillteller (pl -) der mixed grill.

grinsen vi to grin.

Grippe (pl -n) die flu.

Grippewelle (pl -n) die flu epidemic.

grob (komp gröber, superl am gröbsten) adj (Zucker, Salz) coarse ; (Person, Verhalten) crude ; (Leder, Stoff) rough.

Grog (pl -s) der hot toddy.

Groschen (pl -) der (deutsche Münze) ten pfennig coin ; (österreichische Münze) one hundredth of an Austrian schilling.

groß (komp größer, superl am größten) adj (räumlich) big, large ; (Person) tall ; (Buchstabe) capital ; (Gefühl, Lärm, Künstler) great ; (Vermögen) large ;

(Angebot) wide ; *(erwachsen)* grown-up. ◆ *adv (räumlich)* on a large scale ; *(glanzvoll)* in style.

großartig *adj* brilliant.

Großaufnahme *(pl -n) die* close-up.

Großbritannien *nt* Great Britain.

Großbuchstabe *(pl -n) der* capital letter.

Größe *(pl -n) die* size ; *(Höhe)* height.

Großeltern *pl* grandparents.

Großhandel *der* wholesale.

Großmarkt *(pl -märkte) der* cash-and-carry.

Großmutter *(pl -mütter) die* grandmother.

Großraumwagen *(pl -) der (in Zug)* open carriage *(not divided into compartments)*.

großschreiben *(unreg)* to write with a capital letter.

Großschreibung *die* capitalization.

Großstadt *(pl -städte) die* city.

Großvater *(pl -väter) der* grandfather.

großzügig *adj (freigiebig)* generous. ◆ *adv (freigiebig)* generously.

Grotte *(pl -n) die* cave, grotto.

grub *prät →* **graben**.

Gruft *(pl Grüfte) die* crypt.

grün *adj* green ; ~er Pfeil filter arrow ; ~e Versicherungskarte green card *(Br)*, insurance card for travel abroad ; Grüner Punkt *(auf Verpackung)* symbol placed on product to indicate that it meets certain recycling standards.

Grün *das* green.

Grünanlage *(pl -n) die* park.

Grund *(pl Gründe) der (Ursache, Motiv)* reason ; *(von Gewässer)* bed ; *(Erdboden)* ground ; auf ~ von *(wegen)* because of ; aus diesem ~ for this reason ; im ~e basically.

gründen *vt (Verein, Betrieb)* to found.

Gründer, in *(mpl Gründer) der, die* founder.

Grundgebühr *(pl -en) die (für Telefon)* line rental.

Grundgesetz *das* German constitution.

Grundkurs *(pl -e) der* foundation course.

Grundlage *(pl -n) die* basis ; die ~n der Theorie the basic principles of the theory.

gründlich *adj* thorough. ◆ *adv* thoroughly.

Grundnahrungsmittel *(pl -) das* staple (food).

Gründonnerstag *(pl -e) der* Maundy Thursday.

Grundrecht *(pl -e) das* basic right.

Grundschule *(pl -n) die* ≃ primary school *(attended by pupils aged 6 to 10)*.

Grundstück *(pl -e) das* plot (of land).

Gründung *(pl -en) die* foundation.

Grüne[1] *(pl -n) der, die* Green ; die ~n the Greens.

Grüne[2] *das :* im ~n in the country.

Grünfläche *(pl -n) die* park.

Grünkohl der kale.

Gruppe (pl -n) die group.

Gruppenermäßigung (pl -en) die group reduction.

Gruppenkarte (pl -n) die group ticket.

Gruppenreise (pl -n) die group tour.

Gruß (pl Grüße) der greeting; **herzliche Grüße an...** greetings to...; **mit freundlichen Grüßen** yours sincerely; **viele Grüße!** best wishes!

grüßen vi to say hello. ◆ vt (begrüßen) to greet; (grüßen lassen) to say hello to; **Michaela lässt dich ~** Michaela says hello; **jn von jm ~** to say hello to sb from sb.

gucken vi to look.

Gulasch (pl -s) der ODER das goulash.

Gulaschkanone (pl -n) die large tureen used to serve hot food at outdoor public events.

gültig adj (Ticket, Vertrag) valid.

Gültigkeit die validity.

Gummi (pl -s) das (Material) rubber; (Gummiring) rubber band.

Gummiband (pl -bänder) das rubber band.

Gummistiefel (pl -) der wellington (boot).

Gunst die : **zu ~en von** → **zugunsten**.

günstig adj (vorteilhaft) favourable; (preisgünstig) cheap; (Moment) convenient.

gurgeln vi to gargle.

Gurke (pl -n) die (Salatgurke) cucumber; **saure ~** pickled gherkin.

Gurt (pl -e) der (an Tasche, Sattel) strap; (Sicherheitsgurt) seat belt.

Gürtel (pl -) der (an Hose) belt.

Gürtelreifen (pl -) der radial (tyre).

Gürtelrose die shingles (sg).

Gürteltasche (pl -n) die bumbag (Br), fanny pack (Am).

Gurtpflicht die compulsory wearing of seat belts.

gut (komp besser, superl am besten) adj good. ◆ adv well; (leicht) easily; **~ befreundet sein** to be good friends; **mit jm auskommen** to get on well with sb; **~ schmecken** to taste good; **ihr ist nicht ~** she's not well; **~ wie** as good as. ■ **Gute** das good; **alles Gute!** all the best!

Gutachter, in (mpl -) der, die expert.

gutbürgerlich adj : **~e Küche** good, plain food.

Güteklasse (pl -n) die grade.

Güterbahnhof (pl -höfe) der goods depot.

Güterzug (pl -züge) der goods train.

gut gehen vi unr ist to go well. ◆ vimp unr ist : **es geht ihm gut** he's doing well.

gut gelaunt adj in a good mood.

Guthaben (pl -) das balance (positive).

Gutschein (pl -e) der voucher.

gut|schreiben vt unr to credit.

Gutschrift (*pl* -en) *die (Quittung)* credit slip.

gut tun *vi unr (+D)* : jm ~ to do sb good.

Gymnasium (*pl* -sien) *das* ≃ grammar school *(Br)*, secondary school attended by 10- to 19-year-olds.

Gymnastik *die* keep-fit.

Gynäkologe (*pl* -n) *der* gynaecologist.

Gynäkologin (*pl* -nen) *die* gynaecologist.

Gyros *das* doner kebab.

H

Haar (*pl* -e) *das* hair ; sich die ~e schneiden lassen to have one's hair cut.

Haarbürste (*pl* -n) *die* hairbrush.

Haarfärbemittel (*pl* -) *das* hair dye.

Haarfestiger (*pl* -) *der* setting lotion.

Haargel (*pl* -s) *das* hair gel.

Haarklammer (*pl* -n) *die* hair grip.

Haarkur (*pl* -en) *die* hair treatment cream.

Haarnadel (*pl* -n) *die* hairpin.

Haarnadelkurve (*pl* -n) *die* hairpin bend.

haarscharf *adv (sehr nah)* only just ; *(fig : sehr genau)* precisely.

Haarschnitt (*pl* -e) *der* haircut.

Haarshampoo (*pl* -s) *das* shampoo.

Haarspange (*pl* -n) *die* hair clip.

Haarspray (*pl* -s) *das* hairspray.

Haartrockner (*pl* -) *der* hairdryer.

Haarwasser (*pl* -wässer) *das* hair tonic.

haben (*präs* hat, *prät* hatte, *pp* gehabt) *aux* to have ; sie hat gegessen she has eaten.

◆ *vt* **1.** *(gen)* to have ; sie hat blaue Augen she has (got) blue eyes ; hast du Geld bei dir? have you got any money on you? **2.** *(mit Zeitangabe)* : wie spät ~ wir? what's the time? ; wir ~ zehn Uhr it's ten o'clock ; heute ~ wir Dienstag it's Tuesday today. **3.** *(Unterricht, Dienst)* to have ; einen Tag frei ~ to have a day off. **4.** *(Erlebnis)* to have. **5.** *(im Restaurant, Geschäft)* : ich hätte gerne... I'd like... **6.** *(zur Verfügung)* to have ; es eilig ~ to be in a hurry. **7.** *(Krankheit, Problem)* to have ; Kopfschmerzen ~ to have a headache ; was hast du denn? what's wrong? **8.** *(Gefühl)* : Angst ~ to be afraid ; Durst ~ to be thirsty ; Hunger ~ to be hungry ; ~ Sie etwas dagegen, wenn...? do you mind if...? **9.** *(Angabe von Zwang)* : etw zu tun ~ to have to do sthg.

Haben *das* credit.

Hackbraten (*pl* -) *der* meatloaf.

hacken *vt* (*Holz*) to chop.

Hackfleisch *das* mince (*Br*), mincemeat (*Am*).

Hafen (*pl* Häfen) *der* (*klein*) harbour ; (*groß*) port.

Hafenrundfahrt (*pl* -en) *die* boat trip round the harbour.

Hafenstadt (*pl* -städte) *die* port.

Haferflocken *pl* rolled oats.

Haft *die* custody.

haftbar *adj* liable.

haften *vi* (*für Schaden*) to be liable.

Haftpflichtversicherung (*pl* -en) *die* third party insurance.

Haftpulver *das* (*für Gebiss*) denture fixative.

Haftung *die* liability.

Haftungsbeschränkung (*pl* -en) *die* limited liability.

Hagebuttentee *der* rosehip tea.

Hagel *der* (*Eisregen*) hail.

hageln *vimp* : es hagelt it's hailing.

Hahn (*pl* Hähne) *der* (*Tier*) cock ; (*Wasserhahn*) tap (*Br*), faucet (*Am*).

Hähnchen (*pl* -) *das* (*Brathähnchen*) chicken ; ein halbes ~ half a (roast) chicken.

Hai (*pl* -e) *der* shark.

häkeln *vt* & *vi* to crochet.

Häkelnadel (*pl* -n) *die* crochet hook.

Haken (*pl* -) *der* (*an der Wand*) hook ; (*Zeichen*) tick ; einen ~ haben (*fam*) to have a catch.

halb *adj* & *adv* half ; ein ~es Kilo half a kilo ; eine ~e Stunde half an hour ; die ~e Stadt half the town ; ~ und ~ (*fast*) more or less ; ~ sechs half past five ; ~ so... wie half as... as ; ~ durch (*KÜCHE*) undercooked.

halbautomatisch *adj* (*Getriebe, Kamera*) semi-automatic.

Halbe (*pl* -n) *der, die* (*Bier*) half a litre.

halbfett *adj* (*Margarine, Käse*) low-fat.

halbieren *vt* (*teilen*) to halve.

Halbinsel (*pl* -n) *die* peninsula.

Halbjahr (*pl* -e) *das* six months (*pl*).

Halbmond *der* half moon.

Halbpension *die* half board ; ein Zimmer mit ~ a room with half board.

Halbschuh (*pl* -e) *der* shoe.

halbtags *adv* part-time.

Halbtagsarbeit *die* part-time work.

halb voll *adj* half-full.

halbwegs *adv* halfway.

Halbzeit (*pl* -en) *die* halftime.

half *prät* → **helfen**.

Hälfte (*pl* -n) *die* half ; die ~ (der Flasche) half (the bottle) ; etw zur ~ tun to half-do sthg ; er hat es erst zur ~ bezahlt he only paid for half of it.

Halle (*pl* -n) *die* hall.

Hallenbad (*pl* -bäder) *das* (indoor) swimming pool.

hallo *interj* hello!

Halogenlampe (*pl* -n) *die* halogen lamp.

Hals (*pl* **Hälse**) *der* (*Körperteil*) neck ; (*Rachen*) throat.

Halsausschnitt (*pl* -e) *der* neckline.

Halsband (*pl* -bänder) *das* (*von Hund*) collar.

Halsentzündung (*pl* -en) *die* throat infection.

Halskette (*pl* -n) *die* necklace.

Hals-Nasen-Ohren-Arzt, **-Ärztin** (*mpl* -Ärzte) *der, die* ear, nose and throat specialist.

Halsschmerzen *pl* : ~ haben to have a sore throat.

Halstuch (*pl* -tücher) *das* scarf.

halt *interj* stop! ◆ *adv* (*Süddt* : *nun einmal*) : so ist das ~ that's just the way it is.

Halt *der* : ~ machen to stop.

haltbar *adj* (*Lebensmittel*) : lange ~ sein to keep well ; 'mindestens ~ bis' 'best before'.

Haltbarkeitsdatum (*pl* -daten) *das* best before date.

halten (*präs* **hält**, *prät* **hielt**, *pp* **gehalten**) *vt* 1. (*fest halten*) to hold ; sie hielt die Tasse in der Hand she held the cup in her hand. 2. (*einhalten, behalten*) to keep. 3. (*Haustier*) to keep. 4. (*SPORT*) to save. 5. (*Vortrag, Rede*) to give. 6. (*einschätzen, denken*) : jn für etw halten to take sb for sthg ; was hältst du von ihm? what do you think of him/it? ; ich habe ihn für klüger gehalten I thought he was cleverer than that ; viel/wenig von jm/etw ~ to think a lot/not much of sb/sthg.

◆ *vi* 1. (*Fahrzeug*) to stop. 2. (*Beziehung*) to last. 3. (*Lebensmittel*) : ~ bis to keep until. 4. (*zur Unterstützung*) : zu jm ~ to stand by sb.

■ **sich halten** *ref* 1. (*sich fest halten*) to hold on. 2. (*Lebensmittel*) : sich ~ bis to keep until. 3. (*Person*) : für sein Alter hält er sich gut he's keeping well for his age. 4. (*in eine Richtung*) : sich rechts/links ~ to keep right/left.

Haltepunkt (*pl* -e) *der* stop.

Halterung (*pl* -en) *die* holder.

Haltestelle (*pl* -n) *die* stop.

Halteverbot *das* (*Stelle*) no waiting zone, clearway (*Br*) ; hier herrscht ~ there is no waiting here.

Halteverbotsschild (*pl* -er) *das* no waiting sign.

haltmachen *vi* → Halt.

Hamburg *nt* Hamburg.

Hammelfleisch *das* mutton.

Hammer (*pl* **Hämmer**) *der* hammer.

hämmern *vi* to hammer.

Hammerwerfen *das* (throwing the) hammer.

Hand (*pl* **Hände**) *die* hand ; aus erster/zweiter ~ second-hand (with one/two previous owners) ; rechter/linker ~ on the right/left.

Handarbeit (*pl* -en) *die* needlework ; (*Gegenstand*) handmade article.

Handball *der* handball.

Handbremse (*pl* -n) *die* handbrake *(Br)*, parking brake *(Am)*.

Handbuch (*pl* -bücher) *das* handbook.

Handel *der* (*An- und Verkauf*) trade ; (*Geschäftsleute, Geschäftswelt*) business.

handeln *vi* (*Handel treiben*) to trade ; (*agieren*) to act ; (*feilschen*) to haggle. ◆ *vimp* : bei diesem Buch handelt es sich um einen Roman this book is a novel ; ~ von (*von Thema*) to be about.

Handelskammer (*pl* -n) *die* chamber of commerce.

Handelspartner (*pl* -) *der* trading partner.

Handelsschule (*pl* -n) *die* business school.

Handfeger (*pl* -) *der* brush.

Handfläche (*pl* -n) *die* palm.

Handgelenk (*pl* -e) *das* wrist.

handgemacht *adj* handmade.

Handgepäck *das* hand luggage.

handgeschrieben *adj* hand-written.

Handgriff (*pl* -e) *der* movement (of the hand).

Handkoffer (*pl* -) *der* (small) suitcase.

Händler, in (*mpl* -) *der, die* dealer.

handlich *adj* handy.

Handlung (*pl* -en) *die* (*von Roman, Film*) plot ; (*Tat, Aktion*) act.

Handschlag *der* : etw per ~ besiegeln to shake on sthg.

Handschrift (*pl* -en) *die* (*Schrift*) handwriting ; (*Text*) manuscript.

Handschuh (*pl* -e) *der* glove.

Handschuhfach (*pl* -fächer) *das* glove compartment.

Handtasche (*pl* -n) *die* handbag.

Handtuch (*pl* -tücher) *das* towel.

Handwaschbecken (*pl* -) *das* handbasin.

Handwerker, in (*mpl* -) *der, die* craftsman.

Handwerkszeug *das* tools (*pl*).

Handy (*mpl* -s) *das* mobile (phone) ; er nahm sein Handy mit he took his mobile with him.

Handzeichen (*pl* -) *das* hand signal.

Hang (*pl* Hänge) *der* (*Abhang*) slope.

Hängebrücke (*pl* -n) *die* suspension bridge.

Hängematte (*pl* -n) *die* hammock.

hängen[1] (*prät* hängte, *pp* gehängt) *vt* (*anbringen*) to hang ; etw an etw (*A*) ~ to hang sthg on sthg.

hängen[2] (*prät* hing, *pp* gehangen) *vi* (*angebracht sein*) to hang ; ~ an (+*D*) (*örtlich*) to hang on ; (*emotional*) to be attached to.

hängen bleiben *vi unr ist* : mit dem Ärmel an der Türklinke ~ to catch one's sleeve on the door handle.

hängen lassen *vt unr* (*vergessen*) to leave behind.

Hannover *nt* Hanover.

Hạnsestadt (*pl* **-städte**) *die* town which formerly belonged to the Hanseatic League.

 HANSESTADT

The Hanseatic League was originally a guild of merchants which grew into an association of merchant towns, formed to protect trade. It existed from the 12th-17th century and had a major influence on economic and cultural life. Most of the German towns that were members of the League are in the north of the country, on the North Sea and Baltic coasts. They include Lübeck, Hamburg, Bremen and Rostock.

Hạntel (*pl* **-n**) *die* dumbbell.
Hạ̈ppchen (*pl* **-**) *das* (*kleine Speise*) canapé.
Hạrdware (*pl* **-s**) *die* hardware.
Hạrke (*pl* **-n**) *die* rake.
hạrmlos *adj* harmless.
harmonisch *adj* harmonious.
Hạrn *der* urine.
Hạrnblase (*pl* **-n**) *die* bladder.
Harpune (*pl* **-n**) *die* harpoon.
hạrt (*komp* **härter**, *superl* **am härtesten**) *adj* hard ; (*Urteil, Strafe*) harsh. ◆ *adv* (*arbeiten, zuschlagen*) hard ; (*urteilen, bestrafen*) harshly ; (*sitzen, liegen*) on a hard surface ; **~ an** (+D) right next to.
Hạ̈rte *die* (*von Material*) hardness ; (*Strenge*) harshness.

hạrt gekọcht *adj* : **~es Ei** hard-boiled egg.
hạrtnạ̈ckig *adj* stubborn.
Hạschisch *das* hashish.
Hase (*pl* **-n**) *der* hare.
Hạselnuss (*pl* **-nüsse**) *die* hazelnut.
Hạss *der* hatred.
hạssen *vt* to hate.
hạ̈sslich *adj* (*Aussehen*) ugly.
hạst *präs* → **haben**.
hạstig *adj* hasty.
hạt *präs* → **haben**.
hạtte *prät* → **haben**.
Haube (*pl* **-n**) *die* (*von Auto*) bonnet (*Br*), hood (*Am*) ; (*Trockenhaube*) hairdryer.
hauchdụ̈nn *adj* wafer-thin.
hauchen *vi* (*blasen*) to breathe.
hauen *vt* (*Person*) to hit ; (*Statue, Figur*) to carve ; (*Loch*) to knock. ◆ *vi* (*mit der Hand*) to hit out.
Haufen (*pl* **-**) *der* (*kleiner Berg*) pile ; (*fam : größere Menge*) : **ein ~ Freunde** loads of friends.
häufig *adj* frequent. ◆ *adv* often.
Hauptbahnhof (*pl* **-höfe**) *der* main station.
hauptberuflich *adj* & *adv* full-time.
Haupteingang (*pl* **-gänge**) *der* main entrance.
Hauptfach (*pl* **-fächer**) *das* main subject.
Hauptgericht (*pl* **-e**) *das* main course.
Hauptgeschäftszeit (*pl* **-en**) *die* peak shopping hours (*pl*).

Hauptpost *die* main post office.

Hauptproblem (*pl* -e) *das* main problem.

Hauptreisezeit (*pl* -en) *die* peak travelling times (*pl*).

Hauptrolle (*pl* -n) *die (im Film)* main role.

Hauptsache (*pl* -n) *die* main thing.

hauptsächlich *adv* principally.

Hauptsaison *die* high season.

Hauptschule (*pl* -n) *die* secondary school attended by pupils aged 10 - 15.

Hauptstadt (*pl* -städte) *die* capital.

Hauptstraße (*pl* -n) *die* main road.

Hauptverkehrsstraße (*pl* -n) *die* major road.

Hauptverkehrszeit (*pl* -en) *die* rush hour.

Haus (*pl* Häuser) *das* house ; nach ~e home ; zu ~e at home.

Hausapotheke (*pl* -n) *die* medicine cabinet.

Hausarbeit (*pl* -en) *die (im Haushalt)* housework ; (*Hausaufgabe*) homework.

Hausarzt (*mpl* -ärzte) *der* family doctor.

Hausärztin (*pl* -nen) *die* family doctor.

Hausbar (*pl* -s) *die (Raum)* bar ; (*Schrank*) drinks cabinet.

Hausbewohner, in (*mpl* -) *der, die* occupier.

hauseigen *adj* : die Firma hat einen ~en Parkplatz the firm has its own car park.

Hausflur (*pl* -e) *der* hall.

Hausfrau (*pl* -en) *die* housewife.

hausgemacht *adj* home-made.

Haushalt (*pl* -e) *der (Hausarbeit)* housework ; (*Wohnung*) household ; (*Etat*) budget.

Haushälter, in (*mpl* -) *der, die* housekeeper.

Haushaltsreiniger (*pl* -) *der* household cleaner.

Haushaltswaren *pl* household goods.

Hausmannskost *die* plain food.

Hausmarke (*pl* -n) *die (Wein)* house wine.

Hausmeister, in (*mpl* -) *der, die* caretaker (Br), janitor (Am).

Hausnummer (*pl* -n) *die* house number.

Hausordnung (*pl* -en) *die* house rules (*pl*).

Hausschlüssel (*pl* -) *der* house key.

Hausschuh (*pl* -e) *der* slipper.

Haustier (*pl* -e) *das* pet.

Haustür (*pl* -en) *die* front door.

Hausverbot *das* : ~ haben to be barred.

Hauszelt (*pl* -e) *das* family tent.

Haut (*pl* Häute) *die* skin.

Hautarzt, ärztin (*mpl* -ärzte) *der, die* dermatologist.

Hautausschlag (*pl* -schläge) *der* skin rash.

Hautcreme (*pl* -s) *die* skin cream.

hauteng *adj* skintight.

Hautfarbe (pl -n) die skin colour.

Hbf. abk = Hauptbahnhof.

Hebamme (pl -n) die midwife.

Hebel (pl -) der lever.

heben (prät hob, pp gehoben) vt (hochnehmen) to lift. ▨ sich heben ref (Vorhang, Schranke) to rise.

Heck (pl -s) das (von Auto) rear ; (von Schiff) stern.

Hecke (pl -n) die hedge.

Heckklappe (pl -n) die tailgate.

Heckscheibe (pl -n) die rear window.

Heckscheibenheizung (pl -en) die heated rear window.

Hecktür (pl -en) die tailgate.

Hefe die yeast.

Hefeteig der dough.

hefetrüb adj cloudy.

Heft (pl -e) das (Schulheft) exercise book ; (Zeitschrift) issue.

Hefter (pl -) der binder.

heftig adj violent. ◆ adv violently.

Heftklammer (pl -n) die staple.

Heftpflaster (pl -) das plaster (Br), Bandaid (Am).

Heftzwecke (pl -n) die drawing pin (Br), thumbtack (Am).

Heide die (Landschaft) heath, moor.

Heidelbeere (pl -n) die bilberry.

heikel (komp heikler, superl am heikelsten) adj (Problem) tricky.

heil adj intact.

Heilbad (pl -bäder) das spa.

heilbar adj curable.

heilen vt to cure. ◆ vi to heal.

heilig adj (Person, Ort) holy.

Heiligabend der Christmas Eve.

Heilkräuter pl medicinal herbs.

Heilmittel (pl -) das treatment.

Heilpflanze (pl -n) die medicinal plant.

Heilpraktiker, in (mpl -) der, die alternative practitioner.

Heilquelle (pl -n) die medicinal spring.

Heilung (pl -en) die (durch Arzt) curing ; (von Wunde) healing.

Heim (pl -e) das home.

Heimat die (von Person) home (town, country).

Heimatadresse (pl -n) die home address.

Heimathafen (pl -häfen) der home port.

Heimatland (pl -länder) das home country.

Heimatmuseum (pl -museen) das heritage museum.

Heimfahrt die return journey, journey home.

heimlich adj secret. ◆ adv secretly.

Heimreise die return journey, journey home.

Heimspiel (pl -e) das home game.

Heimweg der way home.

Heimweh das homesickness ; ~ haben to be homesick.

Heimwerker (pl -) der handyman.

Heimwerkermarkt (*pl -märkte*) *der* DIY store.

Heirat (*pl -en*) *die* marriage.

heiraten *vt & vi* to marry.

heiser *adj* hoarse. ◆ *adv* hoarsely.

Heiserkeit *die* hoarseness.

heiß *adj* hot ; (*Diskussion*) heated ; (*fam : toll*) brilliant. ◆ *adv* (*lieben*) passionately ; (*fam : toll*) brilliantly ; ~ **baden** to have a hot bath ; **es ist** ~ it's hot ; **mir ist** ~ I'm hot.

heißen (*prät* **hieß**, *pp* **geheißen**) *vi* (*mit Namen*) to be called ; (*bedeuten*) mean ; **wie heißt das auf Deutsch?** how do you say that in German? ; **wie heißt du?** what's your name? ; **das heißt** (*erklärend*) so ; (*einschränkend*) that is.

heiß laufen *vi unr ist* (*Motor*) to overheat.

Heißluftballon (*pl -s*) *der* hot air balloon.

Heißwassergerät (*pl -e*) *das* water heater.

heiter *adj* (*Person, Stimmung*) cheerful ; (*Wetter*) fine.

heizbar *adj* heated.

Heizdecke (*pl -n*) *die* electric blanket.

heizen *vt* (*Raum*) to heat. ◆ *vi* to have the heating on.

Heizgerät (*pl -e*) *das* (*elektrisch*) heater.

Heizkissen (*pl -*) *das* heated pad (*for back etc*).

Heizkörper (*pl -*) *der* radiator.

Heizung (*pl -en*) *die* (*Heizungsanlage*) heating ; (*Heizkörper*) radiator.

hektisch *adj* hectic.

helfen (*präs* **hilft**, *prät* **half**, *pp* **geholfen**) *vi* to help ; **jm** ~ to help sb ; **jm** ~ **bei** to help sb with ; **sich** (*D*) **zu** ~ **wissen** to know what to do.

Helfer, in (*mpl -*) *der, die* helper.

hell *adj* (*Licht*) bright ; (*Farbe*) light ; (*Ton*) high. ◆ *adv* (*leuchten*) brightly ; **ihre Stimme klingt** ~ she has a high-pitched voice ; **es wird** ~ it's getting light.

hellblau *adj* light blue.

hellblond *adj* very blonde.

Hellseher, in (*mpl -*) *der, die* clairvoyant.

Helm (*pl -e*) *der* helmet.

Hemd (*pl -en*) *das* (*Oberhemd*) shirt ; (*Unterhemd*) vest.

Hendl (*pl -n*) *das* (*Süddt & Österr*) roast chicken.

Hengst (*pl -e*) *der* stallion.

Henkel (*pl -*) *der* handle.

her *adv* : **komm** ~! come here! ; **von Norden** ~ from the North ; **von weit** ~ from a long way away ; **ich kenne sie von früher** ~ I know her from before ; **das ist 10 Jahre** ~ that was 10 years ago ; *siehe auch* **her sein** ; **von der Größe** ~ as far as its size is concerned ; ~ **damit!** give me that!

herab *adv* down.

herab|setzen *vt* (*Preis, Tempo*) to reduce.

heran *adv* : **etwas rechts** ~ a bit further to the right.

heran|kommen *vi unr ist* (*sich nähern*) to approach.

Heranwachsende (*pl* -n) *der, die* adolescent.

herauf *adv* up.

herauf|kommen *vi unr ist* (*Person, Fahrzeug*) to come up. ◆ *vt unr ist* (*Treppe, Berg*) to climb (up).

herauf|setzen *vt* (*Preis*) to raise.

heraus *adv* out.

heraus|bekommen *vt unr* (*Geheimnis*) to find out ; (*Lösung*) to work out ; (*Fleck*) to get out ; (*Wechselgeld*) : noch 10 Pfennig ~ to get 10 pfennigs change.

heraus|bringen *vt unr* (*Buch, Platte*) to bring out.

heraus|finden *vt unr* (*entdecken*) to find out.

heraus|fordern *vt* (*provozieren*) to provoke.

Herausforderung (*pl* -en) *die* (*Provokation*) provocation ; (*Aufgabe*) challenge.

heraus|geben *vt unr* (*Buch, Zeitung*) to publish ; (*Geisel, Beute*) to hand over ; (*Wechselgeld*) to give in change ; auf 100 DM ~ to give change for 100 Marks ; jm 2 DM ~ to give sb 2 Marks in change.

Herausgeber, in (*mpl* -) *der, die* publisher.

heraus|gehen *vi unr ist* (*nach draußen*) to get out.

heraus|halten *vt unr* to put out. ▧ **sich heraushalten** *ref* to stay out of it.

heraus|holen *vt* (*nach draußen*) to bring out.

heraus|kommen *vi unr ist* to come out.

heraus|nehmen *vt unr* to take out.

heraus|stellen *vt* (*nach draußen*) to put out ; (*hervorheben*) to emphasize. ▧ **sich herausstellen** *ref* to become clear.

heraus|suchen *vt* to pick out.

heraus|ziehen *vt unr* to pull out.

herb *adj* (*Geschmack*) sharp ; (*Wein*) dry ; (*Enttäuschung*) bitter. ◆ *adv* (*bitter*) bitterly ; (*schlimm*) badly.

herbei *adv* : komm ~! come here!

Herberge (*pl* -n) *die* (*Jugendherberge*) hostel.

her|bringen *vt unr* to bring.

Herbst (*pl* -e) *der* autumn (*Br*), fall (*Am*) ; im ~ in (the) autumn (*Br*), in (the) fall (*Am*).

herbstlich *adj* autumn (*vor Subst*).

Herd (*pl* -e) *der* (*Küchenherd*) cooker.

Herde (*pl* -n) *die* (*von Tieren*) herd ; (*von Schafen*) flock.

herein *adv* in ; ~! come in!

herein|fallen *vi unr ist* (*fallen*) to fall in ; (*getäuscht werden*) to be taken in.

herein|holen *vt* to bring in.

herein|kommen *vi unr ist* (*von draußen*) to come in.

herein|lassen *vt unr* to let in.

herein|legen *vt* (*fam* : *täuschen*) to take for a ride.

Herfahrt *die* journey here.

her|geben *vt unr* (*geben*) to give.

her|gehen *vi unr ist* : ~ **vor/hinter/neben** (+D) to walk in front of/behind/next to.

her|haben *vt unr (fam)* : **wo hast du das her?** where did you get that from?

Hering (*pl* -e) *der (Fisch)* herring ; *(am Zelt)* tent peg.

Heringstopf (*pl* -töpfe) *der* salad of marinated herring, onion, mayonnaise and beetroot.

her|kommen *vi unr ist* to come ; **wo kommst du her?** where are you from?

Herkunft *die (von Person)* origins *(pl)* ; *(von Sache)* origin.

Herkunftsland (*pl* -länder) *das* country of origin.

Herkunftsort (*pl* -e) *der* place of origin.

Heroin *das* heroin.

Herr (*pl* -en) *der (Mann)* gentleman ; *(als Anrede)* Mr ; **an ~n Müller** to Mr Müller. ■ **Herren** *pl (Herrentoilette)* : 'Herren' 'gentlemen'.

Herrenbekleidung *die* menswear.

Herrenfriseur (*pl* -e) *der* barber, men's hairdresser.

Herrenschuh (*pl* -e) *der* man's shoe.

Herrentoilette (*pl* -n) *die* men's toilet.

herrlich *adj* wonderful. ◆ *adv* wonderfully ; **es schmeckt ~** it tastes wonderful.

herrschen *vi (regieren)* to rule ; *(bestehen)* to be.

her sein *vi unr ist* : **wo bist du her?** where are you from? ; **es ist erst drei Tage her** it was only three days ago.

her|stellen *vt (produzieren)* to make, to produce.

Hersteller, in (*mpl* Hersteller) *der, die* manufacturer.

Herstellung *die (Produktion)* production.

herüber *adv* over.

herum *adv* round ; **um... ~** around ; **um den Tisch ~** around the table ; **um die 50 DM ~** around 50 Marks.

herum|drehen *vt (auf die andere Seite)* to turn over ; *(Schlüssel, Hebel)* to turn. ■ **sich herumdrehen** *ref* to turn round.

herum|fahren *vi unr ist & vt unr hat* to drive around.

herum|führen *vt* to show around. ◆ *vi* to go around.

herum|gehen *vi unr ist* to walk around.

herum|kommen *vi unr ist (reisen)* to travel around ; **~ um** *(fam : sich drücken)* to get out of.

herum|liegen *vi unr* to lie around.

herunter *adv* down.

herunter|fallen *vi unr ist* to fall down.

herunter|gehen *vi unr ist (Person)* to go down ; **mit dem Preis ~** to lower the price.

herunter|handeln *vt* to beat down.

herunter|holen *vt* to bring down.

herunter|lassen *vt unr (Jalousie)* to lower.

herunter|schlucken *vt (Essen)* to swallow.

hervor *adv* : komm ~! come out!

hervorragend *adj* excellent. ◆ *adv* excellently.

hervor|rufen *vt unr (verursachen)* to cause.

Herz *(pl -en) das* heart ; *(Spielfarbe)* hearts *(pl)* ; **von ganzem ~en** wholeheartedly.

Herzbeschwerden *pl* heart trouble *(sg)*.

herzhaft *adj (Essen)* hearty.

Herzinfarkt *(pl -e) der* heart attack.

Herzklopfen *das* : **ich habe ~** my heart is pounding.

herzlich *adj (freundlich)* warm ; *(aufrichtig)* sincere. ◆ *adv (freundlich)* warmly ; *(aufrichtig)* sincerely.

Herzschrittmacher *(pl -) der* pacemaker.

Herzstillstand *(pl -stände) der* cardiac arrest.

Hessen *nt* Hesse.

hetzen *vt & vi* to rush. ▨ **sich hetzen** *ref* to rush.

Heu *das* hay.

heuer *adv (Süddt & Österr)* this year.

heulen *vi* to howl.

Heurige *(pl -n) der (Österr : Wein)* new wine *(from most recent harvest)* ; *(Lokal)* bar, particularly in the region of Vienna, that serves new wine from the local vineyards.

Heuschnupfen *der* hay fever.

heute *adv* today ; ~ **früh** (early) this morning ; ~**Morgen/Mittag/Abend** this morning/ lunchtime/evening ; ~ **in einer Woche** a week today.

heutig *adj* today's.

hielt *prät →* **halten**.

hier *adv* here ; *(zeitlich)* now ; **das** ~ this one here ; ~, **nimm!** here, take it! ; ~ **und da** here and there ; **von** ~ **aus** from here ; ~! here!, present!

hierauf *adv (auf diese Sache)* (on) here.

hier behalten *vt unr (fam : Person, Sache)* to keep here.

hier bleiben *vi unr ist* to stay here.

hierher *adv* here.

hierhin *adv* here.

hiermit *adv* with this.

hier sein *vi unr ist* to be here.

hiervon *adv (von Sache, Menge)* of this.

hiesig *adj* local.

hieß *prät →* **heißen**.

Hilfe *(pl -n) die (Helfen)* help ; *(Person)* assistant ; **mit** ~ **von** with the help of ; ~! help! ; **um** ~ **rufen** to call for help ; **erste** ~ first aid.

hilflos *adj* helpless. ◆ *adv* helplessly.

hilfsbereit *adj* helpful.

hilft *präs →* **helfen**.

Himbeere *(pl -n) die (Frucht)* raspberry.

Himbeergeist *der* raspberry brandy.

Himmel *der (Luftraum)* sky ; *(RELIG)* heaven.

Himmelfahrt *(Feiertag)* Ascension Day.

Himmelsrichtung *(pl -en) die* direction.

hịn adv : bis zum Baum ~ up to the tree ; **der Weg ~** the way there ; **zweimal nach München, ~ und zurück** two returns to Munich ; **~ und her** back and forth ; **~ und wieder** now and again.

hinạb adv down.

hinạuf adv up.

hinạuf|gehen vi & vt unr ist to go up.

hinạuf|steigen vi & vt unr ist to climb.

hinạus adv (nach draußen) out.

hinạus|gehen vi unr ist (nach draußen) to go out ; **zur Straße ~** to look out onto the street.

hinạus|laufen vi unr ist (nach draußen) to run out.

Hịnblick der : **in** ODER **im ~ auf** (+A) with regard to.

hịndern vt to hinder ; **jn (daran) ~, etw zu tun** to prevent sb from doing sthg.

Hịndernis (pl -se) das obstacle.

hindụrch adv (räumlich) through ; (zeitlich) throughout.

hinẹin adv (räumlich) in.

hinẹin|gehen vi unr ist to go in.

hinẹin|stecken vt to put in.

hịn|fahren vi unr ist to go there. ◆ vt unr hat (Passagiere) to drive there.

Hịnfahrt (pl -en) die (mit Auto) journey there ; (mit Zug) outward journey.

hịn|fallen vi unr ist to fall down.

Hịnflug (pl -flüge) die der outward flight.

hịng prät → hängen.

hịn|gehen vi unr ist (gehen) to go.

hịnken vi to limp.

hịn|knien : **sich hinknien** to kneel down.

hịn|kommen vi unr ist (ankommen) to get there ; (hingehören) to belong ; **mit etw ~** to make sthg last.

hịn|legen vt (Kind, Besteck, Tasche) to put down. ▪ **sich hinlegen** ref to lie down.

Hịnreise (pl -n) die journey there.

hịn|setzen vt (Person) to seat. ▪ **sich hinsetzen** ref to sit down.

hịn|stellen vt (Gegenstand) to put down. ▪ **sich hinstellen** ref to stand.

hịnten adv (am Ende) at the back ; (an der Rückseite) on the back ; (zur Richtungsangabe) back ; **~ im Buch** at the back of the book ; **~ am Radio** on the back of the radio ; **~ sitzen** (im Auto) to sit in the back ; **da dort ~** back there ; **weit ~** a long way behind ; **bitte nach ~ durchgehen!** please move down to the back!

hịnter präp (+D,A) behind.

Hịnterachse (pl -n) die rear axle.

Hịnterausgang (pl -ausgänge) der rear exit.

hịntere, r, s adj back, rear.

hintereinạnder adv (räumlich) one behind the other ; (zeitlich) one after the other.

Hịntereingang (pl -eingänge) der rear entrance.

Hintergrund (*pl* -gründe) *der* background.

hinterher *adv* (*räumlich*) behind ; (*zeitlich*) afterwards.

hinterher|fahren *vi unr ist* to drive behind ; jm ~ to follow sb.

hinterher|gehen *vi unr ist* to walk behind ; jm ~ to follow sb.

hinterlassen (*präs* hinterlässt, *prät* hinterließ, *pp* hinterlassen) *vt* to leave.

hinterlegen *vt* to leave.

Hintern (*pl* -) *der* (*fam*) bottom.

Hinterrad (*pl* -räder) *das* rear wheel.

Hinterradantrieb *der* rear wheel drive.

Hintertür (*pl* -en) *die* back door.

Hinterzimmer (*pl* -) *das* back room.

hinüber *adv* over, across.

Hin- und Rückfahrt *die* round trip.

hinunter *adv* down.

Hinweg (*pl* -e) *der* : auf dem ~ on the way there.

Hinweis (*pl* -e) *der* (*Tipp, Fingerzeig*) tip ; (*für Polizei*) lead ; (*Anleitung*) instruction ; (*Indiz*) sign ; **nähere ~e** detailed instructions.

hin|weisen *vt unr* : jn auf etw (A) ~ to point sthg out to sb. ◆ *vi unr* (*zeigen*) : auf jn/etw ~ to point to sb/sthg.

Hinweisschild (*pl* -er) *das* sign.

hin|werfen *vt unr* (*Gegenstand*) to throw down.

hinzu *adv* in addition.

hinzu|fügen *vt* (*Gewürz, Zutat*) to add.

hinzu|kommen *vi unr ist* (*Person*) to arrive ; (*Tatsache*) hinzukommt, dass... moreover... ; **kommt noch etwas hinzu?** (*im Geschäft*) would you like anything else?

Hirn (*pl* -e) *das* (*Organ*) brain ; (*Gericht*) brains (*pl*).

Hirsch (*pl* -e) *der* (*Tier*) deer ; (*Fleisch*) venison.

Hirse *die* millet.

historisch *adj* (*geschichtlich*) historical. ◆ *adv* (*geschichtlich*) historically.

Hit (*pl* -s) *der* (*Lied*) hit.

Hitparade (*pl* -n) *die* charts (*pl*).

Hitze *die* heat.

hitzebeständig *adj* heat-resistant.

Hitzewelle (*pl* -n) *die* heatwave.

Hitzschlag *der* heatstroke.

HIV-positiv *adj* HIV-positive.

H-Milch *die* long-life milk.

hob *prät* → heben.

Hobby (*pl* -s) *das* hobby.

hoch (*komp* höher, *superl* am höchsten) *adj* high ; (*Baum*) tall ; (*Alter, Gewicht*) great ; (*Anzahl, Summe*) large. ◆ *adv* high ; (*sehr*) highly.

Hoch (*pl* -s) *das* (*Wetterlage*) high.

hochachtungsvoll *adv* Yours faithfully (*nach Dear Sir/Madam*), Yours sincerely (*nach Dear Mr/Mrs X*).

Hochbetrieb der : es herrscht ~ it's the busiest time.

hochdeutsch adj standard German.

Hochdruck der (technisch) high pressure.

Hochdruckgebiet (pl -e) das area of high pressure.

Hochdruckzone (pl -n) die area of high pressure.

Hochebene (pl -n) die plateau.

hocherfreut adj delighted.

hoch|fliegen vi unr ist to fly up.

Hochgebirge (pl -) das high mountains (pl).

hoch|gehen vi unr ist to go up ; (Bombe) to go off.

hoch|halten vt unr (Gegenstand) to hold up.

Hochhaus (pl -häuser) das high-rise building.

hoch|heben vt unr to lift.

hoch|klappen vt to fold up.

hoch|klettern vi & vt ist to climb (up).

hoch|kommen vi & vt unr ist to come up.

hoch|krempeln vt to roll up.

hochnäsig adj (abw) conceited.

hochprozentig adj (Getränk) strong.

Hochsaison die (in Ferienort) high season.

Hochschule (pl -n) die college ; (Universität) university.

Hochschulreife die qualification needed for university entrance.

hochschwanger adj heavily pregnant.

Hochsommer (pl -) der midsummer.

Hochspannung die (Strom) high voltage ; 'Vorsicht, ~ : Lebensgefahr!' 'danger, high voltage!'

Hochsprung der high jump.

höchste superl → hoch.

höchstens adv (mit Zahlenangabe) at (the) most ; (allenfalls) at best.

Höchstgeschwindigkeit (pl -en) die (auf Straße) speed limit ; (von Auto) top speed.

Höchstparkdauer die maximum stay (when parking).

Hochwasser das : ~ haben to be in spate.

hochwertig adj high-quality.

Hochzeit (pl -en) die wedding.

Hochzeitsreise (pl -n) die honeymoon.

Hochzeitstag (pl -e) der wedding day.

hoch|ziehen vt unr (Strumpf) to pull up ; (Jalousie) to raise. ◼ **sich hochziehen** ref (sich nach oben ziehen) to pull o.s. up.

hocken vi (kauern) to crouch. ◼ **sich hocken** ref (sich kauern) to crouch down.

Hocker (pl -) der stool.

Hockey das hockey.

Hof (pl Höfe) der (Innenhof, Hinterhof) yard ; (Bauernhof) farm.

hoffen vt to hope.

hoffentlich adv hopefully.

Hoffnung (*pl* -en) *die* (*Wunsch*) hope.

höflich *adj* polite. ◆ *adv* politely.

Höflichkeit *die* politeness.

Höhe (*pl* -n) *die* height ; (*von Summe*) amount ; (*von Klang*) pitch ; **ein Betrag in ~ von 200 DM** the sum of 200 Marks ; **in ~ der ersten Querstraße** level with the first turning.

Höhenlage *die* altitude.

Höhensonne (*pl* -n) *die* (*Gerät*) sunlamp.

Höhepunkt (*pl* -e) *der* (*von Entwicklung, Fest*) high point ; (*Orgasmus*) climax.

höher *komp* → **hoch.**

hohl *adj* (*Baum*) hollow ; (*abw : Gerede*) empty.

Höhle (*pl* -n) *die* (*im Felsen*) cave ; (*von Tieren*) den.

holen *vt* (*heranholen*) to fetch, to collect ; (*entnehmen*) to take ; (*Polizei, Arzt, Handwerker*) to fetch ; (*fam : einkaufen*) to get ; **etw ~ kommen** to come for sthg ; **sich** (*D*) **etw ~** (*Gegenstand*) to get sthg ; (*Krankheit*) to catch sthg.

Holland *nt* Holland.

Holländer, in (*mpl* -) *der, die* Dutchman (Dutchwoman).

holländisch *adj* Dutch.

holprig *adj* bumpy.

Holunder (*pl* -) *der* (*Baum*) elder.

Holz (*pl* Hölzer) *das* wood.

holzig *adj* (*Spargel*) woody.

Holzkohle (*pl* -n) *die* charcoal.

Homepage (*fpl* -s) *die* homepage.

homöopathisch *adj* homeopathic.

homosexuell *adj* homosexual.

Homosexuelle (*mpl* -n) *der, die* homosexual.

Honig *der* honey.

Honigmelone (*pl* -n) *die* honeydew melon.

Honorar (*pl* -e) *das* fee.

Hopfen *der* hops (*pl*).

horchen *vi* (*angestrengt hören*) to listen.

hören *vt* (*Laut, Geräusch, Information*) to hear ; (*anhören*) to listen to. ◆ *vi* (*als Hörfähigkeit*) to hear ; (*zuhören, gehorchen*) to listen ; **~ auf** (+A) to listen to ; **hör mal!** listen! ; **schwer ~** to be hard of hearing.

Hörer (*pl* -) *der* (*von Telefon*) receiver ; (*Person*) listener.

Hörerin (*pl* -nen) *die* listener.

Hörfunk *der* radio.

Hörgerät (*pl* -e) *das* hearing aid.

hörgeschädigt *adj* hard of hearing.

Horizont (*pl* -e) *der* horizon.

horizontal *adj* horizontal.

Hormon (*pl* -e) *das* hormone.

Horn (*pl* Hörner) *das* horn.

Hörnchen (*pl* -) *das* (*Gebäck*) croissant.

Hornhaut (*pl* -häute) *die* (*auf Haut*) patch of hard skin ; (*von Augen*) cornea.

Hornisse (*pl* -n) *die* hornet.

Horoskop (*pl* -e) *das* horoscope.

horrend *adj* horrendous.

Hörspiel (*pl* -e) *das* radio play.

Höschenwindel (*pl* -n) *die* nappy *(Br)*, diaper *(Am)*.

Hose (*pl* -n) *die* (*Kleidungsstück*) (pair of) trousers *(Br)*, (pair of) pants *(Am)* ; (*Unterhose*) underpants *(pl)* ; **kurze ~** shorts *(pl)*.

Hosentasche (*pl* -n) *die* trouser pocket.

Hosenträger (*pl* -) *der* braces *(pl)* *(Br)*, suspenders *(pl)* *(Am)*.

Hospital (*pl* -täler) *das* hospital.

Hotdog (*pl* -s) *der* ODER *das* hot dog.

Hotel (*pl* -s) *das* hotel ; **~ Garni** ≃ bed and breakfast.

Hotelbar (*pl* -s) *die* hotel bar.

Hotelführer (*pl* -) *der* hotel guide.

Hotelhalle (*pl* -n) *die* hotel foyer.

Hotelverzeichnis (*pl* -se) *das* hotel register.

Hotelzimmer (*pl* -) *das* hotel room.

Hr. (*abk für Herr*) Mr.

Hubraum *der* (*beim Auto*) cubic capacity.

hübsch *adj* (*schön*) pretty, beautiful.

Hubschrauber (*pl* -) *der* helicopter.

huckepack *adv* (*fam*) : **jn ~ nehmen** to give sb a piggy-back.

Huf (*pl* -e) *der* hoof.

Hüfte (*pl* -n) *die* hip.

Hügel (*pl* -) *der* (*kleiner Berg*) hill.

hügelig *adj* hilly.

Huhn (*pl* Hühner) *das* chicken.

Hühnchen (*pl* -) *das* chicken.

Hühnerauge (*pl* -n) *das* corn.

Hühnerbrühe (*pl* -n) *die* chicken broth.

Hülle (*pl* -n) *die* (*Schutzhülle*) cover ; (*von Schallplatte*) sleeve.

human *adj* humane.

Hummel (*pl* -n) *die* bumblebee.

Hummer (*pl* -) *der* lobster.

Humor *der* humour.

humpeln *vi* to limp.

Hund (*pl* -e) *der* (*Tier*) dog ; '**Vorsicht, bissiger ~**' 'beware of the dog'.

Hundeleine (*pl* -n) *die* dog lead.

hundert *num* a hundred ; → **sechs**.

Hunderter (*pl* -) *der* (*Hundertmarkschein*) hundred-mark note.

Hundertmarkschein (*pl* -e) *der* hundred-mark note.

Hundertmeterlauf (*pl* -läufe) *der* hundred metres *(sg)*.

hundertprozentig *adj* (*Alkohol, Lösung*) pure ; (*völlig*) complete.

hunderttausend *num* one hundred thousand.

Hundesteuer (*pl* -n) *die* dog licence fee.

Hunger *der* (*nach Nahrung*) hunger ; **~ haben auf** (+A) to feel like (eating) sthg ; **~ haben** to be hungry.

Hungerstreik (*pl* -s) *der* hunger strike.

hungrig *adj* hungry ; **~ sein** to be hungry.

Hupe (*pl* -n) *die* horn.

hupen vi to sound one's horn.

hüpfen vi ist to hop.

Hürdenlauf (pl -läufe) der hurdles (sg).

hurra interj hurray!

husten vi to cough.

Husten der cough ; ~ haben to have a cough.

Hustenbonbon (pl -s) das cough sweet.

Hustensaft (p -säfte) der cough mixture.

Hustentee (pl -s) der tea which is good for a cough.

Hut (pl Hüte) der (Kleidungsstück) hat.

Hütte (pl -n) die (kleines Haus) cottage ; (Berghütte) hut.

Hüttenkäse der cottage cheese.

hygienisch adj hygienic.

hypnotisieren vt to hypnotize.

I

IC abk = Intercity.

ICE abk = Intercity Express.

ich pron I ; ~ bin's it's me.

IC-Zuschlag (pl -Zuschläge) der intercity supplement.

ideal adj ideal.

Idealgewicht das ideal weight.

Idee (pl -n) die idea ; (ein bisschen) bit, touch.

identifizieren vt (erkennen) to identify. ■ **sich identifizieren** ref (sich gleichsetzen) : sich ~ mit to identify with.

identisch adj identical ; ~ sein to be exactly the same.

Identität die identity.

Ideologie (pl -n) die ideology.

Idiot (pl -en) der idiot.

idiotisch adj idiotic.

idyllisch adj idyllic. ◆ adv : ~ gelegen in an idyllic location.

Igel (pl -) der hedgehog.

ignorieren vt to ignore.

ihm pron (Dativ von er : Person) (to) him ; (: Ding) (to) it.

ihn pron (Akkusativ von er : Person) him ; (Ding) it.

ihnen pron (Dativ Plural von sie) (to) them.

Ihnen pron (Dativ von Sie) (to) you.

ihr[1] pron (Nominativ) you ; (Dativ von sie : Person) (to) her ; (Ding) (to) it.

ihr[2], **e** det (Singular : von Person) her ; (von Ding) its ; (Plural) their.

Ihr (pl -e) det your.

ihre, **r**, **s** pron (Singular : von Person) hers ; (von Ding) its ; (Plural) their.

Ihre, **r**, **s** pron yours.

illegal adj illegal. ◆ adv illegally.

Illusion (pl -en) die illusion.

Illustrierte (pl -n) die magazine.

im präp = in + dem.

Image (pl -s) das (von Person) image.

Imbiss (pl -e) der (Mahlzeit) snack ; (Imbissbude) snack bar.

Imbissbude (pl -n) die snack bar.

Imbissstube (pl -n) die snack bar.

IMBISSSTUBE

An "Imbissstube", usually to be found either in city centres or at the side of main roads, is a stall or small snack bar where you can get a drink and something quick and simple to eat, typically a fried sausage in a bread roll ("Bratwurst"), chips, a doner kebab or a pizza. Customers usually eat standing up at tall tables. It is very common for Germans to eat this type of snack between meals.

imitieren vt to imitate.

imitiert adj (Material) imitation (vor Subst).

Immatrikulation (pl -en) die matriculation.

immer adv always ; ~ schwieriger more and more difficult ; ~ stärker stronger and stronger ; ~ noch still ; ~ wenn whenever ; ~ wieder again and again.

immerhin adv (dennoch, trotzdem) nevertheless ; (wenigstens) at least ; (schließlich) after all, still.

Immigrant, in (mpl -en) der, die immigrant.

Immobilien pl property (sg).

Immobilienmakler, in (mpl -) der, die estate agent (Br), realtor (Am).

immun adj (gegen Krankheit) immune.

impfen vt to vaccinate.

Impfschein (pl -e) der vaccination certificate.

Impfstoff (pl -e) der vaccine.

Impfung (pl -en) die vaccination.

Import der (Einfuhr) import.

importieren vt to import.

imprägnieren vt (Kleidung) to waterproof.

imprägniert adj (Holz) waterproofed ; (Kleidung) waterproof.

impressionistisch adj (Kunstwerk) Impressionist.

improvisieren vt & vi to improvise.

impulsiv adj impulsive. ◆ adv impulsively.

imstande adj : ~ sein, etw zu tun to be capable of doing sthg.

in präp (+A) (räumlich) into ; ~s Wasser fallen to fall into the water ; ~ die Stadt fahren to go to town ; ~ die Schule gehen to go to school.
◆ präp (+D) 1. (räumlich) in ; im Bett liegen to be in bed ; ~ der Schule at school.
2. (zeitlich) in ; ~ dieser Woche this week ; im Moment at the moment ; wir fahren ~ einer Stunde we're going in an hour ; das schaffe ich ~ einer Stunde I can do that in an hour.
3. (zur Angabe von Umständen) in ; ~ Betrieb sein to be working.
4. (zur Angabe von Mengen) in.
◆ adj (fam) : ~ sein to be in.

inbegriffen adj included.

Inbetriebnahme die (amt : von Anlage) start-up.

indem konj by ; er startete die Maschine, ~ er auf den Knopf drückte he started the machine by pressing the button.

Inder, in (*mpl* -) *der, die* Indian.

Indien *nt* India.

indirekt *adj* indirect.

indisch *adj* Indian.

indiskret *adj* indiscreet.

indiskutabel *adj* out of the question.

Individualist, in (*mpl* -en) *der, die* individualist.

individuell *adj (persönlich)* individual. ◆ *adv (persönlich)* individually.

Individuum (*pl* -duen) *das (Einzelperson)* individual.

Industrie (*pl* -n) *die* industry.

Industriegebiet (*pl* -e) *das* industrial area.

industriell *adj* industrial.

Industriepark (*pl* -s) *der* industrial estate (*Br*), industrial park (*Am*).

Industrie- und Handelskammer (*pl* -n) *die* chamber of commerce.

Infarkt (*pl* -e) *der* heart attack.

Infektion (*pl* -en) *die* infection.

infizieren *vt* to infect. ▓ **sich infizieren** *ref* to get infected.

Inflation (*pl* -en) *die* inflation.

infolge *präp* (+G) (*amt*) owing to.

Information (*pl* -en) *die* information ; (*Informationsstelle*) information desk ; **eine ~** a piece of information ; **~en über** (+A) information about ; **wünschen Sie weitere ~en?** would you like any further information?

Informationsmaterial (*pl* -ien) *das* information.

Informationsstand (*pl* -stände) *der* information point.

Informationszentrum (*pl* -zentren) *das* information centre.

informieren *vt* to inform ; **jn ~ über** (+A) to inform sb about. ▓ **sich informieren** *ref* to find out.

Infusion (*pl* -en) *die* : **eine ~ bekommen** to be on a drip.

Ingenieur, in (*mpl* -e) *der, die* engineer.

Inh. *abk* = Inhaber.

Inhaber, in (*mpl* -) *der, die (Besitzer)* owner ; (*von Pass, Genehmigung*) holder.

inhalieren *vt (Rauch)* to inhale. ◆ *vi (bei Erkältung)* to use an inhalant.

Inhalt (*pl* -e) *der (von Behälter)* contents (*pl*) ; (*von Buch, von Film*) content.

Inhaltsverzeichnis (*pl* -se) *das* list of contents.

Initiative (*pl* -n) *die* initiative.

Injektion (*pl* -en) *die* injection.

inkl. (*abk für inklusive*) incl.

inklusive *präp* (+G) including.

Inklusivpreis (*pl* -e) *der* inclusive price.

inkonsequent *adj* inconsistent.

Inland *das* : **im ~** at home.

Inlandsflug (*pl* -flüge) *der* domestic flight.

Inlandsgespräch (*pl* -e) *das* national call.

Inlineskates *pl* in-line skates, roller-blades ; **auf/mitfahren** to go rollerblading.

innen *adv* inside ; **nach ~** inwards.

Innenhof (*pl* -höfe) *der* inner courtyard.

Innenpolitik *die* (*Maßnahmen*) domestic policy.

Innenraum (*pl* -räume) *der* inner room.

Innenseite (*pl* -n) *die* inside.

Innenspiegel (*pl* -) *der* rearview mirror.

Innenstadt (*pl* -städte) *die* town centre.

innere, r, s *adj* (*Schicht, Wand, Gefühl*) inner ; (*Verletzung, Organe*) internal ; (*Jackentasche*) inside.

innerhalb *präp* (+G) within. ◆ *adv* : ~ **von** within.

innerlich *adj* (*körperlich*) internal.◆*adv*(*psychisch*)inwardly.

Innung (*pl* -en) *die* guild.

inoffiziell *adj* unofficial.

ins *präp* = in + das.

Insassen(unfall)versicherung (*pl* -en) *die* passenger insurance.

insbesondere *adv* especially.

Insekt (*pl* -en) *das* insect.

Insektenschutzmittel(*pl*-) *das* insect repellent.

Insektenstich (*pl* -e) *der* insect bite.

Insel (*pl* -n) *die* (*geografisch*) island.

Inserat (*pl* -e) *das* advertisement.

inserieren *vi* to advertise.

insgesamt *adv* altogether.

Inspektion (*pl* -en) *die* (*von Autos*) service.

inspizieren *vt* to inspect.

Installateur, in (*mpl* -e) *der, die* (*für Wasser*) plumber ; (*für Strom*) electrician.

installieren *vt* to install.

Instantgetränk (*pl* -e) *das* instant drink.

Instinkt (*pl* -e) *der* instinct.

Institut (*pl* -e) *das* (*Einrichtung*) institute.

Institution (*pl* -en) *die* institution.

Instrument (*pl* -e) *das* instrument.

Inszenierung (*pl* -en) *die* (*am Theater*) production.

intakt *adj* (*Apparat*) intact.

integrieren *vt* to integrate.

intellektuell *adj* intellectual.

intelligent *adj* intelligent.

Intelligenz *die* intelligence.

Intendant, in (*mpl* -en) *der, die* director.

intensiv *adj* (*Schulung, Arbeit*) intensive ; (*Geschmack, Gefühl*) strong. ◆ *adv* (*schmecken*) strong ; (*sich einarbeiten, vorbereiten*) intensively.

Intensivkurs (*pl* -e) *der* crash course.

Intensivstation (*pl* -en) *die* intensive care unit.

Intercity (*pl* -s) *der* intercity train.

Intercity Express (*pl* -) *der* high-speed train connecting two or more large cities.

Intercity-Zuschlag (*pl* -Zuschläge) *der* intercity supplement.

interessant *adj* interesting.

Interesse (*pl* -n) *das* interest.

interessieren *vt* to interest. ■ **sich interessieren** *ref* : sich ~ für to be interested in.

Internat (*pl* -e) *das* boarding school.

international *adj* international.

Internet *das* (*ohne pl*) Internet ; im ~ on the Internet ; im ~ surfen to surf the Net.

Internet|café *das* Internet café.

Internetnutzer, in (*mpl* -) *der, die* Internet user.

interpretieren *vt* to interpret.

Interrail-Karte (*pl* -n) *die* interrail ticket.

Interregio (*pl* -s) *der* train covering medium distances, stopping frequently.

Interview (*pl* -s) *das* interview.

interviewen *vt* to interview.

intim *adj* intimate.

intolerant *adj* intolerant.

intransitiv *adj* intransitive.

intuitiv *adj* intuitive.

Invalide (*pl* -n) *der, die* disabled person.

Inventur (*pl* -en) *die* stocktaking ; 'wegen ~ geschlossen' 'closed for stocktaking'.

investieren *vt* (*Geld*) to invest.

inzwischen *adv* (*gleichzeitig*) in the meantime ; (*jetzt*) now.

Ire (*pl* -n) *der* Irishman ; die ~n the Irish.

irgendein, e *det* (*unbekannt*) some ; (*beliebig, in Fragen*) any.

irgendeine, r, s *pron* (*unbekannte Person*) someone ; (*beliebige Person, in Fragen*) anyone ; (*beliebige Sache*) any.

irgendetwas *pron* something ; (*beliebige Sache, in Fragen*) anything.

irgendjemand *pron* someone ; (*beliebige Person, in Fragen*) anyone.

irgendwann *adv* (*zu unbekannter Zeit*) sometime ; (*zu beliebiger Zeit*) any time.

irgendwas *pron* = **irgendetwas**.

irgendwer *pron* = **irgendjemand**.

irgendwie *adv* (*auf unbekannte Weise*) somehow ; (*auf beliebige Weise*) anyhow.

irgendwo *adv* (*an unbekanntem Ort*) somewhere ; (*an beliebigem Ort*) anywhere.

Irin (*pl* -nen) *die* Irishwoman.

irisch *adj* Irish.

Irland *nt* Ireland.

ironisch *adj* ironic.

irre *adj* (*verrückt*) mad ; (*fam : gut*) fantastic.

irren *vi* ist (*herumlaufen*) to wander. ■ **sich irren** *ref* hat to be wrong.

Irrtum (*pl* -tümer) *der* mistake.

irrtümlich *adj* wrong.

Ischias der (Nerv) sciatic nerve ; (Schmerz) sciatica.

Islam der Islam.

Isolierband (pl -bänder) das (für elektrische Leitungen) insulating tape.

isolieren vt to insulate ; (Person) to isolate. ◆ vi to insulate. ▨ **sich isolieren** ref to isolate o.s.

Isolierung (pl -en) die insulation ; (von Person) isolation.

Israel nt Israel.

isst präs → essen.

ist präs → sein.

Italien nt Italy.

Italiener, in (mpl -) der, die Italian.

italienisch adj Italian.

Italienisch(e) das Italian.

J

ja interj yes ; (selbstverständlich) of course ; das ist ~ toll! that's really great! ; ~, bitte (selbstverständlich) please do ; da bist du ~! there you are! ; ich komme ~ schon I'm coming.

Jacht (pl -en) die yacht.

Jacke (pl -n) die (Mantel, Jackett) jacket ; (Strickjacke) cardigan.

Jackett (pl -s) das jacket.

Jagd (pl -en) die (auf Tiere) hunt ; auf die ~ gehen to go hunting.

jagen vt (Tier) to hunt.

Jäger, in (mpl -) der, die (Person) hunter.

Jägerschnitzel (pl -) das escalope of pork with mushroom sauce.

Jahr (pl -e) das year ; die 90er ~e the nineties ; ein gutes Neues ~! Happy New Year!

jahrelang adv for years. ◆ adj : ~es Warten years of waiting.

Jahresabonnement (pl -s) das annual subscription.

Jahreseinkommen (pl -) das annual income.

Jahrestag (pl -e) der anniversary.

Jahresurlaub der annual leave.

Jahreszeit (pl -en) die season.

Jahrgang (pl -gänge) der (von Wein) year, vintage.

Jahrhundert (pl -e) das century.

jährlich adj & adv yearly.

Jahrmarkt (pl -märkte) der fair.

Jahrzehnt (pl -e) das decade.

jähzornig adj bad-tempered.

Jalousie (pl -n) die venetian blind.

jammern vi to moan.

Jänner der (Österr) January ; → September.

Januar der January, September.

Japan nt Japan.

Japaner, in (mpl -) der, die Japanese.

japanisch adj Japanese.

Japanisch(e) das Japanese.

jaulen vi to howl.

Jause (pl -n) die (Österr) snack.

Jausenstation (*pl* -en) *die* (*Österr*) *mountain refuge where food and drink are served.*

jawohl *interj* (*ja*) yes.

Jazz *der* jazz.

je *adv* (*jeweils*) each ; (*pro*) per ; (*jemals*) ever. ◆ *konj* : ~ schneller, desto besser the quicker the better ; drei Gruppen mit ~ fünf Personen three groups, each of five people ; 30 DM ~ Stunde 30 Marks per hour ; bist du ~ mit ihm zusammengetroffen? have you ever met him? ; ~ nachdem it depends ; oh ~! oh no!

Jeans (*pl* -) *die* (pair of) jeans (*pl*).

jede, r, s *det* every, each. ◆ *pron* (*Person*) everyone ; (*Gegenstand*) each (one) ; ~r dritte every third one.

jedenfalls *adv* (*wenigstens*) at least ; (*auf jeden Fall*) in any case.

jederzeit *adv* at any time.

jedesmal *adv* every time.

jedoch *adv* however.

jemand *pron* (*unbekannte Person*) someone ; (*in Fragen*) anyone.

jene, r, s *det* (*geh*) that. ◆ *pron* (*geh*) that one.

jenseits *präp* (+G) (*räumlich*) on the other side of.

Jetlag (*pl* -s) *der* jet lag.

jetzig *adj* current.

jetzt *adv* (*momentan*) now ; (*heutzutage*) nowadays ; (*bald, gleich*) soon ; (*damals*) then ; bis ~ until now ; ~ gleich right now.

jeweils *adv* (*jeder*) each ; (*jedesmal*) each time ; ~ vier Punkte four points each ; ~ am Monatsersten on the first of each month.

Jh. (*abk für Jahrhundert*) C.

JH *abk* = Jugendherberge.

Job (*pl* -s) *der* job.

jobben *vi* to work.

Jod *das* iodine.

jodeln *vi* to yodel.

joggen *vi ist* to jog.

Jogging *das* jogging.

Jogginganzug (*pl* -anzüge) *der* tracksuit.

Joghurt (*pl* -s), **Jogurt** *der* ODER *das* yoghurt.

Johannisbeere (*pl* -n) *die* : rote ~ redcurrant ; schwarze ~ blackcurrant.

Jolle (*pl* -n) *die* (*Segelboot*) dinghy.

Journal (*pl* -e) *das* magazine.

Journalist, in (*mpl* -en) *der, die* journalist.

jubeln *vi* to cheer.

Jubiläum (*pl* -läen) *das* jubilee.

jucken *vi* (*Haut*) to itch ; (*Material*) to be itchy.

Juckreiz *der* itch.

Jude (*pl* -n) *der* Jew.

Jüdin (*pl* -nen) *die* Jew.

jüdisch *adj* Jewish.

Jugend *die* youth.

jugendfrei *adj* : nicht ~ not suitable for children.

Jugendherberge (*pl* -n) *die* youth hostel.

Jugendherbergsausweis (*pl* -e) *der* youth hostel card.

Jugendherbergsschlafsack (*pl* -säcke) *der* sheet sleeping bag.

jugendlich *adj (jung)* young ; *(jung wirkend)* youthful. ◆ *adv (jung wirkend)* youthfully.

Jugendliche *(pl -n)* der, die young person.

Jugendstil der Art Nouveau.

Jugendzentrum *(pl -zentren)* das youth centre.

Jugoslawien *nt* Yugoslavia.

Juli der July ; → **September**.

jung *(komp* **jünger**, *superl* am jüngsten) *adj* young.

Junge *(pl -n)* der *(Knabe)* boy. ◆ das *(von Tieren)* young animal ; **die ~n** the young ; **die Katze hat ~** the cat has got kittens.

Jungfrau die *(Sternzeichen)* Virgo ; *(Mädchen)* virgin.

Junggeselle *(pl -n)* der bachelor.

Juni der June ; → **September**.

Jura ohne Artikel law.

Jurist, in *(mpl -en)* der, die lawyer.

juristisch *adj* legal.

Jury *(pl -s)* die jury.

Justiz die *(Rechtsbehörden)* judiciary.

Juwelier, in *(mpl -e)* der, die jeweller.

K

Kabarett *(pl -s)* das cabaret.

Kabel *(pl -)* das *(elektrische Leitung)* cable.

Kabelanschluss *(pl -anschlüsse)* der : **~ haben** to have cable television.

Kabelfernsehen das cable television.

Kabeljau *(pl -s)* der cod.

Kabelkanal *(pl -kanäle)* der cable TV channel.

Kabine *(pl -n)* die *(Umkleidekabine)* cubicle ; *(im Schiff)* cabin.

Kabinenbahn *(pl -en)* die cable railway.

Kabinett *(pl -e)* das *(von Ministern)* cabinet. ◆ der *(Wein)* term designating a high-quality German wine.

Kabrio *(pl -s)* das convertible.

Kachel *(pl -n)* die tile.

Kachelofen *(pl -öfen)* der tiled wood-burning stove used for heating.

Käfer *(pl -)* der beetle.

Kaffee *(pl -s)* der coffee ; *(Mahlzeit)* light afternoon meal of coffee and cakes, biscuits etc ; **eine Tasse ~** a cup of coffee ; **~ trinken** to drink coffee.

Kaffeebar *(pl -s)* die coffee bar.

Kaffeefahrt *(pl -en)* die day trip organized by a company on which its products are promoted and sold.

Kaffeefilter *(pl -)* der coffee filter.

Kaffeehaus *(pl -häuser)* das coffee shop.

 KAFFEEHAUS

The "Kaffeehaus" is one of the most typical sights of the city of Vienna. Customers come here to drink coffee in a friendly atmosphere, to talk, read the newspapers provided on the premises or to play cards and billiards. A wide variety of different types of coffee is available, including "Brauner" (white coffee), "Schwarzer" (black coffee), "Melange" (milky coffee) and "Einspänner" (mocha topped with cream).

Kaffeekanne (pl -n) die coffeepot.

Kaffeeklatsch (pl -e) der ≃ coffee morning.

Kaffeelöffel (pl -) der teaspoon.

Kaffeemaschine (pl -n) die coffee machine.

Kaffeepause (pl -n) die coffee break.

Kaffeesahne die coffee cream.

Kaffeetasse (pl -n) die coffee cup.

Käfig (pl -e) der cage.

Kahn (pl Kähne) der (Ruderboot) rowing boat (Br), rowboat (Am) ; (Stechkahn) punt.

Kai (pl -s) der quay.

Kaiser, in (mpl -) der, die emperor, (f empress).

Kaiserschmarrn (pl -) der (Südot & Österr) pancake cut into thin strips.

Kajak (pl -s) das kayak.

Kajüte (pl -n) die cabin.

Kakao der cocoa ; eine Tasse ~ a cup of cocoa.

Kaktus (pl Kakteen) der cactus.

Kalb (pl Kälber) das (von Kuh) calf ; (Fleisch) veal.

Kalbfleisch das veal.

Kalender (pl -) der (Wandkalender) calendar ; (Taschenkalender) diary.

Kalifornien nt California.

Kalk der (im Wasser) lime.

Kalorie (pl -n) die calorie.

kalorienarm adj low-calorie.

kalt (komp kälter, superl am kältesten) adj cold. ◆ adv (gefühllos) coldly ; ~ duschen to have a cold shower ; es ist ~ it's cold ; mir ist ~ I'm cold.

Kälte die (Temperatur) cold ; (von Person) coldness.

Kälteeinbruch (pl -einbrüche) der cold snap.

Kaltfront (pl -en) die cold front.

Kaltmiete (pl -n) die rent not including bills.

Kaltstartautomatik die automatic choke.

kam prät → kommen.

Kamel (pl -e) das (Tier) camel.

Kamera (pl -s) die camera.

Kamillentee (pl -s) der camomile tea.

Kamin (pl -e) der (im Raum) fireplace ; (Schornstein) chimney.

Kamm (pl Kämme) der (für Haare) comb.

kämmen vt to comb. ◼ **sich kämmen** ref to comb one's hair.

Kammermusik die chamber music.

Kampf (pl Kämpfe) der (Streit) fight ; (in Sport) contest ; (politisch, sozial) struggle ; (im Krieg) battle.

kämpfen *vi* to fight; *(in Sport)* to compete; **~ für** to fight for; **~ gegen** to fight; **~ um** to fight for; *(in Sport)* to compete for.

Kämpfer, in *(mpl -)* der, die fighter.

Kampfrichter, in *(mpl -)* der, die referee.

kampieren *vi* to camp.

Kanada *nt* Canada.

Kanal *(pl Kanäle)* der *(Wasserweg)* canal; *(im Radio, Fernsehen)* channel; *(Abwasserkanal)* sewer.

Kanaldeckel *(pl -)* der manhole cover.

Kanalinseln *pl* Channel Islands.

Kanalisation *(pl -en)* die sewers *(pl).*

Kandidat, in *(mpl -en)* der, die *(für Amt)* candidate.

kandiert *adj* candied.

Kandiszucker der candy sugar.

Kaninchen *(pl -)* das rabbit.

Kanister *(pl -)* der can.

kann *präs* → **können.**

Kännchen *(pl -)* das pot; **ein ~ Kaffee** a pot of coffee.

Kanne *(pl -)* die *(für Kaffee, Tee)* pot; *(für Milch)* jug; *(für Öl, zum Gießen)* can.

kannte *prät* → **kennen.**

Kante *(pl -n)* die edge.

Kantine *(pl -n)* die canteen.

Kanton *(pl -e)* der canton.

Kanu *(pl -s)* das *(Paddelboot)* canoe.

Kanzel *(pl -n)* die *(in Kirche)* pulpit.

Kanzler, in *(mpl -)* der, die *(Bundeskanzler)* chancellor.

Kapelle *(pl -n)* die *(in Kirche)* chapel; *(MUS)* band.

Kapern *pl* capers.

kapieren *vt & vi* to understand.

Kapital das *(Vermögen)* capital.

Kapitän *(pl -e)* der captain.

Kapitel *(pl -)* das chapter.

kapitulieren *vi (resignieren)* to give up.

Kaplan *(pl Kapläne)* der chaplain.

Kappe *(pl -n)* die cap.

Kapsel *(pl -n)* die *(Medikament)* capsule.

kaputt *adj* broken; *(fam: erschöpft)* exhausted; **~ sein** *(fam: erschöpft)* to be exhausted; **mein Auto ist ~** my car has broken down.

kaputt|gehen *vi unr ist (Gegenstand)* to break; *(Auto)* to break down; **an etw** *(D)* **~** *(Person)* to go to pieces because of sthg.

Kapuze *(pl -n)* die hood.

Kapuziner (*pl* -) *der (Österr)* *coffee with just a drop of milk.*

Karabinerhaken (*pl* -) *der* karabiner.

Karaffe (*pl* -n) *die* decanter.

Karamellbonbon (*pl* -s) *das* toffee.

Karat (*pl* -) *das* carat.

Karate *das* karate.

Kardinal (*pl* -äle) *der* cardinal.

Karfreitag (*pl* -e) *der* Good Friday.

kariert *adj* (*Hose, Stoff*) checked ; (*Papier*) squared.

Karies *die* tooth decay.

Karikatur (*pl* -en) *die* (*Bild*) caricature.

Karneval *der* carnival.

ⓘ **KARNEVAL**

The biggest "Karneval" celebrations take place in the Rhineland (Cologne, Düsseldorf and Mainz), although the tradition is also associated with Bavaria (where it is known as "Fasching") and Swabia (where it is known as "Fasenacht" or "Fasnet"). The "Karneval" period officially begins at eleven minutes past eleven on 11 November and ends on Ash Wednesday. On the Monday before Ash Wednesday ("Rosenmontag"), there are processions with floats carrying figures that caricature social and political life.

Karnevalskostüm (*pl* -e) *das* carnival costume.

Karnevalssitzung (*pl* -en) *die* evening entertainment at carnival time where satirical sketches are performed.

Karnevalszug (*pl* -züge) *der* carnival procession.

Kärnten *nt* Carinthia.

Karo *das* (*Spielfarbe*) diamonds (*pl*).

Karosserie (*pl* -n) *die* (AUTO) bodywork.

Karotte (*pl* -n) *die* carrot.

Karpfen (*pl* -) *der* carp.

Karte (*pl* -n) *die* card ; (*Eintrittskarte, Fahrkarte*) ticket ; (*Postkarte*) postcard ; (*Speisekarte*) menu ; (*Landkarte*) map ; 'folgende ~n werden akzeptiert' 'the following credit cards are accepted' ; '~ einführen!' 'please insert your card' ; '~ entnehmen!' 'please take your card' ; '~ fehlerhaft' 'this card is faulty' ; '~ ungültig' 'this card is invalid' ; mit der ~ bezahlen to pay by credit card ; ~n spielen to play cards.

Kartei (*pl* -en) *die* card index.

Karteikarte (*pl* -n) *die* index card.

Kartenspiel (*pl* -e) *das* (*Karten*) pack of cards (*Br*), deck of cards (*Am*) ; (*Spielen*) card game.

Kartentelefon (*pl* -e) *das* card phone.

Kartenvorverkauf (*pl*-käufe) *der* advance booking.

Kartoffel (*pl* -n) *die* potato.

Kartoffelchips *pl* crisps (*Br*), chips (*Am*).

Kartoffelkloß (*pl* -klöße) *der* potato dumpling.

Kartoffelknödel (pl -) der potato dumpling.

Kartoffelpuffer (pl -) die ODER der potato fritter.

Kartoffelpüree das mashed potato.

Kartoffelsalat der potato salad.

Karton (pl -s) der (Schachtel) cardboard box.

Karussell (pl -s) das merry-go-round ; ~ fahren to have a ride on a merry-go-round.

Karwoche (pl -n) die Holy Week.

Kaschmir der (Material) cashmere.

Käse der cheese ; ~ am Stück unsliced cheese ; ~ in Scheiben sliced cheese.

Käsefondue (pl -s) das cheese fondue.

Käsekuchen (pl -) der cheesecake.

Käseplatte (pl -n) die cheeseboard.

Käse-Sahne-Torte (pl -n) die type of cheesecake made with cream.

Kasino (pl -s) das (Spielkasino) casino ; (Gemeinschaftsraum) common room ; (für Offiziere) mess.

Kaskoversicherung (pl -en) die fully comprehensive insurance.

Kasperletheater (pl -) das (Vorstellung) Punch and Judy show ; (Gebäude) Punch and Judy theatre.

Kasse (pl -n) die (Apparat) till ; (in Supermarkt) checkout ; (in Theater, Kino) box office ; (in Bank) counter ; '~ beim Fahrer' 'please pay the driver'.

Kassenarzt, ärztin (mpl -ärzte) der, die doctor who treats patients who have health insurance.

Kassenbereich der (im Supermarkt) checkout area.

Kassenbon (pl -s) der receipt ; gegen Vorlage des ~s on production of a receipt.

Kassenpatient, in (mpl -en) der, die patient with health insurance policy.

Kassenzettel (pl -) der receipt.

Kassette (pl -n) die (für Musik, Video) tape, cassette ; (Behälter) box.

Kassettenrekorder (pl -) der tape recorder.

kassieren vt (Eintrittsgeld, Fahrgeld) to collect. ◆ vi (Kellner, Busfahrer) to collect the money.

Kassierer, in (mpl -) der, die cashier.

Kastanie (pl -n) die (Baum) chestnut (tree) ; (essbare Frucht) chestnut ; (nicht essbare Frucht) horse chestnut.

Kasten (pl Kästen) der (Kiste, Dose) box ; (Getränkekasten) crate.

Kat (pl -s) der catalytic converter.

Katalog (pl -e) der catalogue.

Katalysator (pl -satoren) der (am Auto) catalytic converter.

Katarrh (pl -e), **Katarr** der catarrh.

katastrophal adj disastrous.

Katastrophe (*pl* -n) *die* disaster.

Kategorie (*pl* -n) *die* category.

Kater (*pl* -) *der* (*Tier*) tomcat ; einen ~ haben (*von Alkohol*) to have a hangover.

kath. *abk* = **katholisch**.

Kathedrale (*pl* -n) *die* cathedral.

Katholik, in (*mpl* -en) *der, die* Catholic.

Katholikentag (*pl* -e) *der* biannual congress of German Catholics.

katholisch *adj* Catholic.

Kat-Motor (*pl* -en) *der* engine of a car fitted with a catalytic converter.

Katze (*pl* -n) *die* cat.

kauen *vt & vi* to chew.

Kauf (*pl* Käufe) *der* (*Handlung*) purchase.

kaufen *vt* to buy ; sich (*D*) etw ~ to buy o.s. sthg.

Käufer, in (*mpl* -) *der, die* buyer.

Kauffrau (*pl* -en) *die* businesswoman.

Kaufhaus (*pl* -häuser) *das* department store.

Kaufhausdieb, in (*mpl* -e) *der, die* shoplifter (*from department stores*).

Kaufhausdiebstahl (*pl* -stähle) *der* shoplifting (*from department stores*).

Kaufleute *pl* (*Händler*) shopkeepers.

Kaufmann (*pl* -leute) *der* (*im Betrieb*) businessman.

Kaufpreis (*pl* -e) *der* purchase price.

Kaufvertrag (*pl* -träge) *der* bill of sale.

Kaugummi (*pl* -s) *der* ODER *das* chewing gum.

kaum *adv* hardly, barely ; es regnet ~ noch it's almost stopped raining.

Kaution (*pl* -en) *die* (*für Wohnung*) deposit.

Kaviar *der* caviar.

Kefir *der* sour-tasting fermented milk.

Kegelbahn (*pl* -en) *die* bowling alley.

Kegelklub (*pl* -s) *der* bowling club.

kegeln *vi* to go bowling.

Kehlkopf (*pl* -köpfe) *der* larynx.

Kehrblech (*pl* -e) *das* dustpan.

kehren *vt & vi* (*fegen*) to sweep.

kehrt|machen *vi* to turn round.

Keilriemen (*pl* -) *der* (*AUTO*) fan belt.

kein, e *det* no ; ich habe ~ Geld/~e Zeit I haven't got any money/time ; ~ Mensch no one ; ~e einzige Mark not a single mark ; ~e Stunde less than an hour.

keine, r, s *pron* (*Person*) no one ; (*Gegenstand*) none ; ~s der Kinder none of the children ; ~r von den beiden neither of them ; von diesen Gerichten mag ich ~s I don't like any of these dishes.

keinerlei *det* : das hat ~ Wirkung gehabt it had no effect at all.

keinesfalls *adv* on no account.

keineswegs *adv* not at all.

Keks (*pl* -e) *der* biscuit (*Br*), cookie (*Am*).

Keller (*pl* -) *der* cellar.

Kellerei (*pl* -en) *die* wine cellars (*pl*).

Kellner, in (*mpl* -) *der, die* waiter (waitress).

kennen (*prät* **kannte**, *pp* **gekannt**) *vt* to know ; **jn/etw gut ~ to** know sb/sthg well. ■ **sich kennen** *ref* to know each other.

kennen lernen *vt* to get to know ; **freut mich, Sie kennen zu lernen!** pleased to meet you!

Kenner, in (*mpl* -) *der, die* expert.

Kenntnisse *pl* knowledge (*sg*).

Kennwort (*pl* -e) *das* (*für Sparbuch*) password.

Kennzahl (*pl* -en) *die* (*für Telefon*) dialling code (*Br*), area code (*Am*).

Kennzeichen (*pl* -) *das* (*am Auto*) registration (number) (*Br*), license (number) (*Am*) ; (*Merkmal*) characteristic ; **amtliches ~** registration number (*Br*), license number (*Am*) ; **'besondere ~'** 'distinguishing features'.

Kennziffer (*pl* -n) *die* reference number.

Keramik (*pl* -en) *die* (*Gegenstand*) (piece of) pottery.

Kerl (*pl* -e) *der* guy.

Kern (*pl* -e) *der* (*von Apfel, Birne*) pip ; (*von Pfirsich, Aprikose*) stone ; (*von Nuss*) kernel.

Kernenergie *die* nuclear power.

Kernforschung *die* nuclear research.

kerngesund *adj* as fit as a fiddle.

Kernkraft *die* nuclear power.

Kernkraftwerk (*pl* -e) *das* nuclear power station.

kernlos *adj* (*Weintraube*) seedless.

Kernwaffe (*pl* -n) *die* nuclear weapon.

Kerze (*pl* -n) *die* (*aus Wachs*) candle ; (*AUTO* : *Zündkerze*) spark plug.

Kerzenlicht *das* candlelight.

Kessel (*pl* -) *der* (*Wasserkessel*) kettle.

Ketschup, Ketchup *der* ODER *das* ketchup.

Kette (*pl* -n) *die* chain.

keuchen *vi* to pant.

Keuchhusten *der* whooping cough.

Keule (*pl* -n) *die* (*Fleisch*) leg.

Keyboard (*pl* -s) *das* keyboard.

Kfz (*pl* -) *abk* = Kraftfahrzeug.

Kfz-Brief (*pl* -e) *der* ≃ logbook (*Br*), *document of ownership of a motor vehicle*.

Kfz-Schein (*pl* -e) *der* vehicle registration document.

Kfz-Steuer (*pl* -n) *die* road tax.

Kfz-Werkstatt (*pl* -stätten) *die* garage.

kichern *vi* to giggle.

Kiefer[1] (*pl* -) *der* (*Knochen*) jaw.

Kiefer² (*pl* -n) *die (Baum)* pine (tree).

Kies *der (Steine)* gravel.

Kieselstein (*pl* -e) *der* pebble.

Kilo (*pl* -s ODER **Kilo**) *das* kilo.

Kilogramm (*pl* -) *das* kilogram.

Kilokalorie (*pl* -n) *die* kilocalorie.

Kilometer (*pl* -) *der* kilometre ; 50 ~ pro Stunde 50 kilometres an hour.

kilometerlang *adj* several kilometres long.

Kilometerstand *der* ≃ mileage.

Kilometerzähler (*pl* -) *der* ≃ milometer.

Kind (*pl* -er) *das* child ; ein ~ erwarten to be expecting (a baby).

Kinderarzt, ärztin (*mpl* -ärzte) *der, die* paediatrician.

Kinderbetreuung *die* child care.

Kinderbett (*pl* -en) *das* cot (*Br*), crib (*Am*).

Kinderbuch (*pl* -bücher) *das* children's book.

Kinderfahrkarte (*pl* -n) *die* child's ticket.

Kinderfrau (*pl* -en) *die* nanny.

Kindergarten (*pl* -gärten) *der* nursery school.

Kindergärtner, in (*mpl* -) *der, die* nursery school teacher.

Kinderheim (*pl* -e) *das* children's home.

Kinderkrankheit (*pl* -en) *die* children's illness.

Kinderlähmung *die* polio.

kinderlieb *adj* : ~ sein to be fond of children.

Kinderlied (*pl* -er) *das* nursery rhyme.

Kindernahrung *die* baby food.

Kinderprogramm (*pl* -e) *das (im Fernsehen)* children's programme.

Kinderschuh (*pl* -e) *der* child's shoe.

kindersicher *adj* childproof.

Kindersicherung (*pl* -en) *die (an Tür)* childproof lock.

Kindersitz (*pl* -e) *der* child seat.

Kinderteller (*pl* -) *der* children's portion.

Kindertragesitz (*pl* -e) *der* baby sling.

Kinderwagen (*pl* -) *der* pram (*Br*), baby carriage (*Am*).

Kinderzimmer (*pl* -) *das* child's bedroom.

Kindheit *die* childhood.

kindisch *adj* childish.

Kinn (*pl* -e) *das* chin.

Kino (*pl* -s) *das* cinema (*Br*), movie theater (*Am*) ; ins ~ gehen to go to the cinema (*Br*), to go to the movies (*Am*) ; was läuft im ~? what's on at the cinema? (*Br*), what's on at the movies? (*Am*).

Kinobesucher, in (*mpl* -) *der, die* cinemagoer (*Br*), moviegoer (*Am*).

Kinoprogramm (*pl* -e) *das (in Zeitung)* cinema guide (*Br*), movie guide (*Am*).

Kiosk (*pl* -e) *der* kiosk.

kippen *vt hat (lehnen)* to tip. ◆ *vi ist (umfallen)* to tip over.

Kirche *(pl -n) die* church.

Kirchenchor *(pl -chöre) der* church choir.

Kirchenmusik *die* church music.

Kirchenschiff *(pl -e) das* nave.

Kirchentag *(pl -e) der German church congress.*

Kirchturm *(pl -türme) der* church steeple.

Kirmes *(pl -sen) die* fair.

Kirsche *(pl -n) die* cherry.

Kirschkuchen *(pl -) der* cherry tart.

Kissen *(pl -) das (in Bett)* pillow; *(auf Stuhl, Sofa)* cushion.

Kiste *(pl -n) die* box; **eine ~ Wein** a case of wine.

kitschig *adj* kitschy.

Kittel *(pl -) der* overalls *(pl)*; *(für Arzt, Laborant)* white coat; *(für Hausfrau)* housecoat.

kitzelig *adj* ticklish.

kitzeln *vt & vi* to tickle.

Kiwi *(pl -s) die* kiwi fruit.

Klage *(pl -n) die (Beschwerde)* complaint; *(vor Gericht)* suit.

klagen *vi (jammern)* to moan; *(vor Gericht)* to sue; **~ über** *(+A)* to complain about.

klamm *adj (Finger)* numb; *(Wäsche)* damp.

Klammer *(pl -n) die (für Wäsche)* clothes peg; *(für Zähne)* brace; *(geschrieben)* bracket.

klammern *vt (mit Klammer)* to peg. ■ **sich klammern** *ref (fest halten)*: **sich ~ an** *(+A)* to cling to.

Klamotten *pl (fam : Kleider)* clothes.

klang *prät →* **klingen**.

Klang *(pl Klänge) der* sound.

Klappbett *(pl -en) das* folding bed.

Klappe *(pl -n) die (am Briefkasten)* flap; '**~ hochschieben**' *(an Verkaufsautomat)* 'lift door'.

klappen *vi (gelingen)* to work. ◆ *vt*: **etw nach oben/hinten ~** *(Kragen)* to turn sthg up/down; **gut ~** to go well.

klappern *vi* to rattle.

Klapprad *(pl -räder) das* folding bicycle.

Klappsitz *(pl -e) der* folding seat.

klar *adj* clear. ◆ *adv (deutlich)* clearly; **mir ist nicht ~, wie das funktioniert** I don't understand how it works; **alles ~?** is everything clear? ; **alles ~!** OK!

Kläranlage *(pl -n) die* sewage works *(sg)*.

Klare *(pl -n) der* schnapps.

klären *vt (Problem, Frage)* to settle. ■ **sich klären** *ref (Problem, Frage)* to be settled.

Klarinette *(pl -n) die* clarinet.

klar|kommen *vi unr ist (fam)*: **mit jm ~** to get on well with sb; **mit etw ~** to be able to cope with sthg.

klar machen *vt*: **jm etw ~** to explain sthg to sb.

Klarsichtfolie *(pl -n) die* clingfilm *(Br)*, Saran wrap® *(Am)*.

Klarsichthülle *(pl -n) die* clear plastic cover.

klar stellen *vt* to make clear ; *(Missverständnis)* to clear up.

Klärung *(pl -en)* die *(von Problem, Frage)* settling.

klar werden *vi unr ist* : jm ~ to become clear to sb ; sich *(D)* ~ über etw *(A)* *(erkennen)* to realize sthg.

klasse *adj (fam)* great.

Klasse *(pl -n)* die class ; *(Raum)* classroom ; **erster/zweiter ~** *(in Zug)* first/second class.

Klassenkamerad, in *(mpl -en)* der, die classmate.

Klassik die *(Epoche)* classical period.

klassisch *adj (typisch)* classic ; *(Musik)* classical.

klatschen *vi (Wasser)* to splash ; *(in Hände)* to clap ; *(tratschen)* to gossip.

klauen *vt (fam)* to pinch ; jm etw ~ to pinch sthg from sb.

Klavier *(pl -e)* das piano.

Klavierkonzert *(pl -e)* das *(Komposition)* piano concerto.

kleben *vt (reparieren)* to stick together ; *(ankleben)* to stick. ◆ *vi (klebrig sein)* to be sticky ; *(haften)* to stick.

Klebestreifen *(pl -)* der sticky tape.

klebrig *adj* sticky.

Klebstoff *(pl -e)* der glue.

kleckern *vi (Person)* to make a mess.

Kleid *(pl -er)* das *(für Frauen)* dress. ▨ **Kleider** *pl (Bekleidung)* clothes.

Kleiderbügel *(pl -)* der *(clothes)* hanger.

Kleiderschrank *(pl -schränke)* der wardrobe.

Kleidung die clothes *(pl)*.

Kleidungsstück *(pl -e)* das garment.

klein *adj* small, little ; *(Pause, Weile)* short. ◆ *adv* : mein ~er Bruder my little brother ; ein ~ wenig a little bit ; bis ins Kleinste to the last detail ; haben Sie es ~? do you have the right change?

Kleinanzeige *(pl -n)* die classified advertisement.

Kleinbus *(pl -s e)* der minibus.

Kleingedruckte das small print.

Kleingeld das change ; '~ bitte bereithalten' 'please have the right change ready'.

Kleinigkeit *(pl -en)* die *(Unwichtiges)* trifle ; *(Geschenk)* little gift ; *(Zwischenmahlzeit)* snack.

Kleinkind *(pl -er)* das small child.

Kleinkunstbühne *(pl -n)* die cabaret.

kleinlich *adj* petty.

klein machen *vt (fam : Geldschein)* to change.

klein schneiden *vt unr* to chop finely.

klein|schreiben *vt unr* : ein Wort ~ to write a word with a small initial letter.

Kleinschreibung die writing with small initial letters.

Kleinstadt *(pl -städte)* die small town.

Kleister *(pl -)* der paste.

klemmen vt & vi to jam ; sich (D) den Finger in etw ~ to get one's finger caught in sthg.

Klempner, in (mpl -) der, die plumber.

klettern vi ist (Person) to climb ; (Preis, Temperatur) to rise.

Klient, in (mpl -en) der, die client.

Klima das (Wetter) climate ; (Stimmung) atmosphere.

Klimaanlage (pl -n) die air conditioning.

klimatisiert adj air-conditioned.

Klinge (pl -n) die (von Messer) blade.

Klingel (pl -n) die bell.

klingeln vi to ring ; (Radfahrer) to ring one's bell. ◆ vimp : es klingelt there's someone at the door ; bitte ~ bei... please ring at...

klingen (prät klang, pp geklungen) vi (Person, Äußerung) to sound ; (Glocke) to ring.

Klinik (pl -en) die clinic.

Klinke (pl -n) die handle.

Klippe (pl -n) die (am Meer) cliff.

Klischee (pl -s) das stereotype.

Klo (pl -s) das (fam) loo (Br), john (Am) ; aufs ~ müssen to need the loo (Br), to need the john (Am).

Klopapier das (fam) toilet paper.

klopfen vi (Herz) to beat ; (auf Schulter) to tap ; (an Tür) to knock. ◆ vimp : es klopft (an

Tür) there's someone at the door.

Klosett (pl -s) das toilet.

Kloß (pl Klöße) der dumpling.

Kloster (pl Klöster) das (für Mönche) monastery ; (für Nonnen) convent.

Klotz (pl Klötze) der (von Baum) log.

Klub (pl -s) der club.

klug adj clever.

knabbern vt & vi to nibble ; an etw (D) ~ to nibble sthg.

Knäckebrot (pl -e) das crispbread.

knacken vt (Nuss) to crack ; (fam : Auto) to break into ; (fam : Schloss) to force. ◆ vi (Holz) to crack.

knackig adj (Obst, Gemüse) crisp ; (fam : Körper) sexy.

Knall (pl -e) der bang.

knapp adj (Vorrat, Angebot) short ; (Kleidung) tight ; (Mehrheit) narrow. ◆ adv (verlieren, gewinnen) narrowly ; (fast) not quite ; ~ werden (Vorrat) to be running short ; ~ 10 Meter not quite 10 metres ; das war ~ that was close.

knarren vi to creak.

Knast (pl Knäste) der (fam) clink, prison.

Knäuel (pl -) das ball (of wool).

knautschen vt to crumple.

kneifen (prät kniff, pp gekniffen) vt to pinch.

Kneifzange (pl -n) die pincers (pl).

Kneipe (pl -n) die pub.

KNEIPE

Unlike in most British pubs, in a German "Kneipe" light meals are served not only throughout the day but also in the evening. There is usually a waiter or waitress who brings the beer to the tables, and customers pay when they are ready to leave, rather than a round at a time. A feature of many German pubs is the "Stammtisch" which is a table reserved for regular customers. In Austria, "Kneipen" are called "Beisel".

knicken vt (Papier) to fold.

Knie (pl -) das knee.

Kniegelenk (pl -e) das knee-(joint).

knien vi to be kneeling. ■ **sich knien** ref to kneel down.

Kniescheibe (pl -n) die knee-cap.

Kniestrumpf (pl -strümpfe) der knee-length sock.

kniff prät → kneifen.

knipsen vt (fam : fotografieren) to snap.

knistern vi (Feuer) to crackle ; (Papier) to rustle.

knitterfrei adj crease-resistant.

Knoblauch der garlic.

Knöchel (pl -) der (von Fuß) ankle ; (von Finger) knuckle.

Knochen (pl -) der bone.

Knochenbruch (pl -brüche) der fracture.

Knödel (pl -) der dumpling.

Knopf (pl Knöpfe) der button ; '~ drücken' 'press the button'.

Knopfdruck der : durch ~ by pressing the button.

knöpfen vt to button.

Knopfloch (pl -löcher) das buttonhole.

Knorpel (pl -) der cartilage.

knoten vt to tie.

Knoten (pl -) der knot.

knurren vi (Hund) to growl ; (Magen) to rumble.

knusprig adj crusty.

knutschen vi (fam) to neck.

Koalition (pl -en) die coalition.

Koch (pl Köche) der cook, chef.

Kochbeutel (pl -) der (KÜCHE) bag containing food, for boiling.

kochen vi (für Mahlzeit) to cook ; (Wasser) to boil. ◆ vt (Mahlzeit) to cook ; (Tee, Kaffee) to make ; (Eier) to boil ; jm etw ~ to cook sb sthg.

Kocher (pl -) der cooker.

Kochgelegenheit (pl -en) die cooking facilities (pl).

Köchin (pl -nen) die cook.

Kochlöffel (pl -) der wooden spoon.

Kochrezept (pl -e) das recipe.

Kochsalz das cooking salt.

Kochtopf (pl -töpfe) der saucepan.

Kochwäsche die washing that needs to be boiled.

Koffein das caffeine.

koffeinfrei adj decaffeinated.

Koffer (pl -) der suitcase ; die ~ packen to pack (one's bags).

Kofferkuli (*pl* -s) *der* (luggage) trolley ; '~ **nur gegen Pfand**' *sign indicating that a deposit is required for the use of a luggage trolley.*

Kofferradio (*pl* -s) *das* portable radio.

Kofferraum (*pl* -räume) *der* boot (*Br*), trunk (*Am*).

Kognac *der* = Cognac.

Kohl *der* cabbage.

Kohle *die* (*Material*) coal ; (*fam* : *Geld*) cash.

Kohlenhydrat (*pl* -e) *das* carbohydrate.

Kohlensäure *die* carbon dioxide ; Mineralwasser mit/ohne ~ sparkling/still mineral water.

Kohlrabi (*pl* -s) *der* kohlrabi.

Kohlroulade (*pl* -n) *die* cabbage leaves stuffed usually with meat.

Koje (*pl* -n) *die* berth.

Kokosnuss (*pl* -nüsse) *die* coconut.

Kolben (*pl* -) *der* (AUTO) piston ; (*von Mais*) cob.

Kolik (*pl* -en) *die* colic.

Kollaps (*pl* -e) *der* (MED) collapse.

Kollege (*pl* -n) *der* colleague.

Kollegin (*pl* -nen) *die* colleague.

Kollision (*pl* -en) *die* collision.

Köln *nt* Cologne.

Kölnisch Wasser *das* eau de Cologne.

Kolonne (*pl* -n) *die* column ; (*von Fahrzeugen*) queue.

Kölsch *das* strong lager brewed in Cologne.

Kombi (*pl* -s) *der* (*Auto*) estate car (*Br*), station wagon (*Am*).

Kombination (*pl* -en) *die* combination.

kombinieren *vt* to combine ; etw mit etw ~ to combine sthg with sthg.

Kombi-Ticket (*pl* -s) *das* ticket valid for travel on train, bus, metro etc.

Kombiwagen (*pl* -) *der* estate car (*Br*), station wagon (*Am*).

Komfort *der* luxury ; mit allem ~ (*Haus, Hotelzimmer*) with all mod cons.

komfortabel *adj* with all mod cons.

komisch *adj* funny. ◆ *adv* funnily.

Komma (*pl* -ta) *das* (*in Satz*) comma ; (*in Zahl*) decimal point ; null ~ fünf Prozent nought point five per cent.

kommandieren *vi* to give orders.

kommen (*prät* kam, *pp* gekommen) *vi* 1. (*an einen Ort*) to come ; wie komme ich zum Markt? how do I get to the market? ; jn/etw ~ lassen to send for sb/sthg ; nach Hause ~ to get home.

2. (*aus einem Ort*) to come ; aus Deutschland ~ to come from Germany.

3. (*erscheinen*) to come out ; rechts kommt der Bahnhof the station's coming up on the right.

4. (*eintreten*) to come.

5. (*in Reihenfolge*) : wer kommt zuerst? who's first?

6. *(Gefühl, Gedanke)* : **mir kam eine Idee** I had an idea ; **auf etw** *(A)* **~** to think of sthg.

7. *(gehören)* to belong, to go.

8. *(zum Ziel, Ergebnis)* : **zu etw ~** to reach sthg ; **hinter etw** *(A)* **~** *(erraten)* to find sthg out ; **an die Macht ~** to come to power.

9. *(Zeit haben)* : **dazu ~, etw zu tun** to get round to doing sthg.

10. *(um Besitz)* : **um etw ~** to lose sthg.

11. *(als Folge)* : **von etw ~** to result from sthg ; **das kommt davon!** see what happens!

12. *(zu Bewusstsein)* : **zu sich ~** to come round.

13. *(bei Institution)* : **in die/aus der Schule ~** to start/leave school ; **ins/aus dem Krankenhaus ~** to go to/leave hospital.

14. *(Film, Programm)* : **im Fernsehen ~** to be on (the) television ; **im Kino ~** to be on at the cinema *(Br)*, to be on at the movies *(Am)*.

15. *(anfangen)* : **ins Rutschen/Stocken ~** to slip/falter.

◆ *vimp* : **es kam zu einem Streit** it ended in a quarrel.

kommend *adj* coming.

Kommentar *(pl -e) der (in Zeitung, Fernsehen)* commentary ; *(Bemerkung)* comment.

kommerziell *adj* commercial.

Kommode *(pl -n) die* chest of drawers.

kommunal *adj* local.

Kommunikation *die* communication.

Kommunion *(pl -en) die* Communion.

Kommunismus *der* communism.

Komödie *(pl -n) die* comedy.

kompakt *adj* compact.

Komparativ *(pl -e) der* comparative.

Kompass *(pl -e) der* compass.

kompatibel *adj* compatible.

kompetent *adj* competent.

komplett *adj* complete ; **wir sind ~** we are all here.

Kompliment *(pl -e) das* compliment.

kompliziert *adj* complicated.

Komponist, in *(mpl -en) der, die* composer.

Kompott *(pl -e) das* stewed fruit.

Kompresse *(pl -n) die* compress.

Kompromiss *(pl -e) der* compromise.

Kondensmilch *die* condensed milk.

Kondenswasser *das* condensation.

Kondition *(pl -en) die* condition.

Konditionstraining *das* fitness training.

Konditor *(pl Konditoren) der* pastry cook.

Konditorei *(pl -en) die* cake shop.

Konditorin *(pl -nen) die* pastry cook.

Kondom *(pl -e) das* condom.

Konfekt *das* sweets *(pl) (Br)*, candy *(Am)*.

Konfektionsgröße *(pl -n) die* size.

Konferenz (*pl* -en) *die* conference.

Konferenzraum (*pl* -räume) *der* conference room.

Konfession (*pl* -en) *die* denomination.

Konfetti *das* confetti.

Konfirmation (*pl* -en) *die* confirmation.

Konfitüre (*pl* -n) *die* jam.

Konflikt (*pl* -e) *der* conflict.

Kongress (*pl* -e) *der* (*Treffen*) conference.

Kongresshalle (*pl* -n) *die* conference centre.

Kongressleitung (*pl* -en) *die* conference organizers (*pl*).

König (*pl* -e) *der* king.

Königin (*pl* -nen) *die* queen.

Konjugation (*pl* -en) *die* (*GRAMM*) conjugation.

konjugieren *vt* (*GRAMM*) to conjugate.

konkret *adj* concrete.

Konkurrenz *die* competition ; **jm ~ machen** to compete with sb.

können (*präs* **kann**, *prät* **konnte**, *pp* **können** ODER **gekonnt**) *aux* **1.** (*gen*) can ; **etw tun** ~ to be able to do sthg ; **er kann Klavier spielen** he can play the piano ; **sie kann nicht kommen** she can't come ; **das kann sein** that's quite possible ; **wenn ich wollte, könnte ich ein Auto kaufen** I could buy a car if I wanted to ; **es kann sein, dass ich mich geirrt habe** I may have been wrong ; **man kann nie wissen** you never know. **2.** (*dürfen, sollen*) can ; **kann ich noch ein Eis haben?** can I have

another ice cream? ; **könnte ich mal telefonieren?** could I use the telephone? ; **du kannst gehen** you can go.
◆ *vt* (*pp* **gekonnt**) **1.** (*Sprache*) to (be able to) speak ; ~ **Sie Deutsch?** can ODER do you speak German? **2.** (*fam* : *auswendig*) to know. **3.** (*Angabe von Verantwortung*) : **ich kann nichts dafür** I can't help it ; **er kann nichts dafür, dass...** it's not his fault that... ◆ *vi* (*pp* **gekonnt**) **1.** (*fähig sein*) can ; **fahren, so schnell man kann** to drive as fast as you can ; **ich kann nicht mehr** (*fam*) I've had it, I'm exhausted. **2.** (*dürfen*) can ; **kann ich ins Kino?** can I go to the cinema?

konnte *prät* → können.

konsequent *adj* consistent. ◆ *adv* consistently.

Konsequenz (*pl* -en) *die* consequence.

konservativ *adj* conservative.

Konserve (*pl* -n) *die* tinned food, canned food.

Konservendose (*pl* -n) *die* tin, can.

Konservierungsmittel(*pl*-) *das* preservative.

Konservierungsstoff(*pl*-e) *der* preservative.

Konsonant (*pl* -en) *der* consonant.

konstruieren *vt* to construct.

Konsulat (*pl* -e) *das* consulate.

Konsum *der* consumption.

Kontakt (*pl* -e) *der* contact ; ~ **haben zu** ODER **mit** to be in contact with.

Kontaktlinse (*pl* -n) *die* contact lens ; **weiche/harte** ~ soft/hard contact lens.

Kontinent (*pl* -e) *der* continent.

Konto (*pl* **Konten**) *das* account ; **ein** ~ **eröffnen** to open an account ; **ein** ~ **auflösen** to close an account.

Kontoauszug (*pl* -züge) *der* bank statement.

Kontostand *der* bank balance.

Kontrabass (*pl* -bässe) *der* double-bass.

Kontrast (*pl* -e) *der* contrast.

Kontrollabschnitt (*pl* -e) *der* stub.

Kontrolle (*pl* -n) *die* (*von Fahrkarte, Gepäck*) inspection, check ; (*Aufsicht, Beherrschung*) control ; **die** ~ **über ein Fahrzeug verlieren** to lose control of a vehicle.

Kontrolleur, in (*mpl* -e) *der, die* (*in Bus, Straßenbahn*) ticket inspector.

kontrollieren *vt* (*prüfen*) to check.

Kontrollleuchte (*pl* -n) *die* warning light.

Konversation (*pl* -en) *die* conversation.

Konzentrationslager (*pl* -) *das* concentration camp.

konzentrieren : **sich konzentrieren** *ref* to concentrate ; **sich** ~ **auf** (+A) to concentrate on.

konzentriert *adj* concentrated ; ~ **sein** (*Person*) to be concentrating.

Konzern (*pl* -e) *der* group (of companies).

Konzert (*pl* -e) *das* (*Veranstaltung*) concert.

Konzertsaal (*pl* -säle) *der* concert hall.

kooperativ *adj* cooperative.

koordinieren *vt* to coordinate.

Kopf (*pl* **Köpfe**) *der* head ; **den** ~ **schütteln** to shake one's head ; **pro** ~ per person.

Kopfhörer (*pl* -) *der* headphone.

Kopfkissen (*pl* -) *das* pillow.

Kopfsalat (*pl* -e) *der* lettuce.

Kopfschmerzen *pl* headache (*sg*) ; ~ **haben** to have a headache.

Kopfsprung (*pl* -sprünge) *der* dive.

Kopfstand (*pl* -stände) *der* headstand.

Kopfstütze (*pl* -n) *die* headrest.

Kopftuch (*pl* -tücher) *das* headscarf.

Kopie (*pl* -n) *die* copy.

kopieren *vt & vi* to copy.

Kopierer (*pl* -) *der* photocopier.

Kopiergerät (*pl* -e) *das* photocopier.

Korb (*pl* **Körbe**) *der* basket ; (*Material*) wicker.

Kordel (*pl* -n) *die* cord.

Kordsamt *der* corduroy.

Korinthe (*pl* -n) *die* currant.

Korken (*pl* -) *der* cork.

Korkenzieher (*pl -*) *der* corkscrew.

Korn[1] (*pl* Körner) *das* grain ; (*Getreide*) grain, corn.

Korn[2] (*pl -*) *der* (*Schnaps*) schnapps.

Körper (*pl -*) *der* body ; (*Figur*) figure.

körperbehindert *adj* disabled.

Körpergewicht *das* weight.

Körpergröße (*pl -n*) *die* height.

körperlich *adj* physical. ◆ *adv* physically.

Körperlotion (*pl -en*) *die* body lotion.

Körperpflege *die* personal hygiene.

Körperverletzung *die* physical injury.

korpulent *adj* corpulent.

korrekt *adj* correct. ◆ *adv* correctly.

Korrektur (*pl -en*) *die* correction.

Korridor (*pl -e*) *der* corridor.

korrigieren *vt* to correct. ▨ **sich korrigieren** *ref* to correct o.s.

Kosmetik *die* (*Pflege*) beauty care.

Kosmetika *pl* cosmetics.

Kosmetikerin (*pl -nen*) *die* beautician.

Kosmetiksalon (*pl -s*) *der* beauty salon.

Kosmetiktücher *pl* paper tissues.

Kost *die* food.

kostbar *adj* valuable.

kosten *vt* to cost ; (*Wein, Speise*) to taste. ◆ *vi* (*Wein, Speise*) to have a taste ; **was kostet das?** how much does it cost?

Kosten *pl* costs ; **auf js ~** at sb's expense ; **~ rückerstatten** to refund expenses.

kostenlos *adj & adv* free.

kostenpflichtig *adj* (*amt*) liable to pay costs. ◆ *adv* : **~ abgeschleppt werden** to be towed away at the owner's expense.

Kostenvoranschlag (*pl -schläge*) *der* estimate.

köstlich *adj* (*Speise, Getränk*) delicious ; (*amüsant*) funny.

Kostprobe (*pl -n*) *die* (*von Speise, Getränk*) taste.

Kostüm (*pl -e*) *das* (*Damenkleidung*) suit ; (*Verkleidung*) costume.

Kot *der* excrement.

Kotelett (*pl -s*) *das* chop, cutlet.

Kotflügel (*pl -*) *der* wing.

kotzen *vi* (*vulg*) to puke.

Krabbe (*pl -n*) *die* (*Krebs*) crab ; (*Garnele*) shrimp.

krabbeln *vi ist* to crawl.

Krabbencocktail (*pl -s*) *der* prawn cocktail.

Krach *der* (*Lärm*) noise ; (*fam* : *Streit*) row ; **~ haben mit** to row with.

Kräcker (*pl -*) *der* cracker.

Kraft (*pl* Kräfte) *die* (*körperlich, psychisch*) strength ; (*physikalisch*) force ; (*Wirkung*) power ; (*Person*) worker ; **etw außer ~ setzen** to cancel ; **in ~** in force.

Kraftbrühe (*pl -n*) *die* strong meat broth.

Kraftfahrer, in (*mpl -*) *der, die* driver.

Kraftfahrzeug (*pl* -e) *das* motor vehicle.

Kraftfahrzeugbrief (*pl* -e) *der* ≃ logbook *(Br)*, *document of ownership of a motor vehicle.*

Kraftfahrzeugkennzeichen (*pl* -) *das* registration number *(Br)*, license number *(Am)*.

Kraftfahrzeugschein (*pl* -e) *der* vehicle registration document.

Kraftfahrzeugsteuer (*pl* -n) *die* road tax.

kräftig *adj* (*Person, Muskeln*) strong ; (*Mahlzeit*) nourishing. ◆ *adv* (*stark*) hard.

Kraftstoff (*pl* -e) *der* fuel.

Kraftstoffverbrauch *der* fuel consumption.

Kraftwerk (*pl* -e) *das* power station.

Kragen (*pl* -) *der* collar.

Kralle (*pl* -n) *die* claw.

Kram *der* stuff.

kramen *vi* (*herumsuchen*) to rummage about.

Krampf (*pl* Krämpfe) *der* (*von Muskeln*) cramp.

Krampfader (*pl* -n) *die* varicose vein.

Kran (*pl* Kräne) *der* crane.

krank (*komp* kränker, *superl* am kränksten) *adj* ill, sick ; ~ werden to be taken ill.

Kranke (*pl* -n) *der, die* sick person ; (*im Krankenhaus*) patient.

Krankenhaus (*pl* -häuser) *das* hospital.

Krankenkasse (*pl* -n) *die* health insurance association.

i **KRANKENKASSE**

A "Krankenkasse" is a medical insurance organization that is responsible for national health insurance in Germany. People from different professions belong to different "Krankenkassen", for example there are ones for miners and seamen, individual firms and guilds, as well as private health insurance schemes. Most people are covered by the "Allgemeine Ortskrankenkasse" (AOK) which operates at a regional level.

Krankenpfleger (*pl* -) *der* (male) nurse.

Krankenschwester (*pl* -n) *die* nurse.

Krankenversichertenkarte (*pl* -n) *die* smart card *which must be shown at the doctor's for health insurance purposes.*

Krankenversicherung (*pl* -en) *die* health insurance.

Krankenwagen (*pl* -) *der* ambulance.

Krankheit (*pl* -en) *die* illness ; (*schwer*) disease.

Krapfen (*pl* -) *der* doughnut.

Krater (*pl* -) *der* crater.

kratzen *vt* to scratch ; (*Reste, Farbe*) to scrape. ■ **sich kratzen** *ref* to scratch o.s.

Kratzer (*pl* -) *der* scratch.

kraulen *vi* ist (SPORT : *schwimmen*) to do the crawl. ◆ *vt haf* (*Tier*) to tickle.

Kraut (*pl* **Kräuter**) *das* (*Heilpflanze, Gewürzpflanze*) herb ; (*Süddt : Kohl*) cabbage.

Kräuterbutter *die* herb butter.

Kräuterlikör (*pl* -e) *der bitter liqueur made from herbs.*

Kräutersauce (*pl* -n) *die* herb sauce.

Kräutertee (*pl* -s) *der* herbal tea.

Krautsalat *der* ~ coleslaw.

Krawatte (*pl* -n) *die* tie.

Krawattenzwang *der* : es besteht ~ ties must be worn.

kreativ *adj* creative.

Krebs (*pl* -e) *der* (*Tier*) crab ; (*Krankheit*) cancer ; (*Sternzeichen*) Cancer ; ~ haben to have cancer.

Kredit (*pl* -e) *der* (*Darlehen*) loan ; einen ~ aufnehmen to take out a loan.

Kreditinstitut (*pl* -e) *das* bank.

Kreditkarte (*pl* -n) *die* credit card ; kann ich mit ~ bezahlen? can I pay by credit card?

Kreide (*pl* -n) *die* (*Tafelkreide*) chalk.

Kreis (*pl* -e) *der* circle ; (*Landkreis*) district ; im ~ in a circle.

Kreislaufstörungen *pl* circulatory disorder (*sg*).

Kreisstadt (*pl* -städte) *die* district capital.

Kreisverkehr *der* roundabout (*Br*), traffic circle (*Am*).

Krempel *der* (*fam*) stuff.

Kren *der* (*Österr*) horseradish.

Kresse *die* cress.

kreuz *adv* : ~ und quer all over.

Kreuz (*pl* -e) *das* cross ; (*fam : Rücken*) small of the back ; (*Autobahnkreuz*) intersection ; (*Spielfarbe*) clubs (*pl*).

Kreuzfahrt (*pl* -en) *die* cruise.

Kreuzgang (*pl* -gänge) *der* cloister.

Kreuzigung (*pl* -en) *die* crucifixion.

Kreuzschlüssel (*pl* -) *der* wheel nut cross brace.

Kreuzung (*pl* -en) *die* (*Straßenkreuzung*) crossroads (*sg*).

Kreuzworträtsel (*pl* -) *das* crossword (puzzle).

kriechen (*prät* **kroch**, *pp* **gekrochen**) *vi* ist to crawl.

Kriechspur (*pl* -en) *die* crawler lane.

Krieg (*pl* -e) *der* war.

kriegen *vt* (*fam : bekommen*) to get.

Krimi (*pl* -s) *der* (*fam*) thriller.

Kriminalität *die* (*Handlungen*) crime.

Kriminalpolizei *die* ≃ Criminal Investigation Department (*Br*), ≃ Federal Bureau of Investigation (*Am*).

kriminell *adj* criminal.

Kripo *die* = Kriminalpolizei.

Krise (*pl* -n) *die* crisis.

Kritik (*pl* -en) *die* (*Beurteilung*) criticism ; (*von Buch, Film usw.*) review.

kritisch *adj* critical. ◆ *adv* critically.

kritisieren *vt* (*Person, Verhalten*) to criticize ; (*Buch, Film usw.*) to review. ◆ *vi* (*beurteilen*) to criticize.

kroch

kroch *prät →* kriechen.

Krokant *das* brittle *(crunchy sweet made with nuts)*.

Krokette *(pl -n) die* croquette.

Krokodil *(pl -e) das* crocodile.

Krone *(pl -n) die (von König)* crown ; *(von Baum)* top.

Kronleuchter *(pl -) der* chandelier.

Kröte *(pl -n) die (Tier)* toad.

Krücke *(pl -n) die* crutch.

Krug *(pl* Krüge) *der* jug ; *(für Bier)* stein, mug.

Krümel *(pl -) der* crumb.

krumm *(komp* krümmer, *superl am* krümmsten) *adj* crooked.

Kruste *(pl -n) die (von Brot)* crust ; *(auf Wunde)* scab.

Kruzifix *(pl -e) das* crucifix.

Krypta *(pl* Krypten) *die* crypt.

Kt. *abk =* Kanton.

Kto. *(abk von Konto)* a/c.

Kubikmeter *(pl -) der* cubic metre.

Küche *(pl -n) die* kitchen ; *(Art zu kochen)* cooking, cuisine.

Kuchen *(pl -) der* cake.

Küchenecke *(pl -n) die* kitchenette.

Kuchenform *(pl -en) die* cake tin.

Kuchengabel *(pl -n) die* cake fork.

Küchenrolle *(pl -n) die* kitchen roll.

Küchenwaage *(pl -n) die* kitchen scales *(pl)*.

Kugel *(pl -n) die (Gegenstand)* ball ; *(Form)* sphere ; *(Geschoss)* bullet.

Kugellager *(pl -) das* ball bearing.

Kugelschreiber *(pl -) der* ballpoint pen, Biro®.

Kugelstoßen *das* shot put.

Kuh *(pl* Kühe) *die* cow.

kühl *adj* cool. ◆ *adv* coolly.

kühlen *vt* to cool.

Kühler *(pl -) der (AUTO)* radiator.

Kühlerhaube *(pl -n) die (AUTO)* bonnet *(Br)*, hood *(Am)*.

Kühlschrank *(pl -schränke) der* fridge.

Kühltasche *(pl -n) die* cool bag.

Kühltruhe *(pl -n) die* freezer.

Kühlung *(pl -en) die (Kühlen)* cooling ; *(TECH)* cooling system.

Kühlwasser *das (AUTO)* radiator water.

Küken *(pl -) das (Tier)* chick.

kulant *adj* obliging.

Kuli *(pl -s) der (fam)* Biro®.

kultiviert *adj* cultivated.

Kultur *(pl -en) die* culture.

Kulturbeutel *(pl -) der* toilet bag.

kulturell *adj* cultural.

Kümmel *der (Gewürz)* caraway seed.

Kummer *der (Ärger)* trouble ; *(Leiden)* grief, sorrow ; jm ~ machen to cause sb trouble.

kümmern *vt (Person)* to concern ; jn nicht ~ not to bother sb. ■ **sich kümmern** *ref* : sich ~ um *(um Person)* to look after ; *(um Arbeit, Gegenstand)* to see to ; *(um Klatsch, Angelegenheit)* to worry about.

Kunde *(pl -n) der* customer ; 'nur für ~n' 'patrons only'.

Kundendienst *der* customer service.

Kundendienststelle *(pl* -n*)* die customer service point.

Kundenkarte *(pl* -n*)* die *(von Bank)* bank card ; *(von Geschäft)* discount card *(for regular customers).*

Kundennummer *(pl* -n*)* die customer number.

Kundenparkplatz *(pl* -plätze*)* der customer car park.

Kundenservice *der* customer service.

kündigen *vt (Vertrag)* to terminate. ◆ *vi* to give notice ; jm ~ to give sb his notice ; die Arbeitsstelle ~ to hand in one's notice ; jm die Wohnung ~ to give sb notice to leave.

Kündigung *(pl* -en*)* die *(von Vertrag, Kredit)* cancellation ; *(von Wohnung, Arbeitsstelle)* notice.

Kündigungsfrist *(pl* -en*)* die period of notice.

Kündigungsschutz *der (für Mieter)* protection against wrongful eviction ; *(für Arbeitnehmer)* protection against wrongful dismissal.

Kundin *(pl* -nen*)* die customer.

Kunst *(pl* Künste*)* die art.

Kunstausstellung *(pl* -en*)* die art exhibition.

Kunstfaser *(pl* -n*)* die synthetic fibre.

Kunstgalerie *(pl* -n*)* die art gallery.

Kunstgewerbe *das* arts and crafts *(pl).*

Kunsthalle *(pl* -n*)* die art gallery.

Kunsthandwerk *(pl* -e*)* das craft.

Künstler, in *(mpl* -*)* der, die artist.

künstlerisch *adj* artistic.

Künstlername *(pl* -n*)* der *(von Schauspieler, Sänger)* stage name.

künstlich *adj* artificial.

Kunstmuseum *(pl* -museen*)* das art gallery.

Kunststoff *(pl* -e*)* der *(Plastik)* plastic.

Kunststück *(pl* -e*)* das trick.

Kunstwerk *(pl* -e*)* das work of art.

Kupfer *das* copper.

Kuppel *(pl* -n*)* die dome.

Kupplung *(pl* -en*)* die clutch ; die ~ treten to depress the clutch.

Kupplungspedal *(pl* -e*)* das clutch pedal.

Kur *(pl* -en*)* die cure *(at a health resort)* ; in ODER zur ~ sein to take a cure *(at a health resort).*

Kurbel *(pl* -n*)* die crank ; *(an Fenster)* winder.

Kürbis *(pl* -se*)* der pumpkin.

Kurfestiger *(pl* -*)* der setting lotion.

Kurgast *(pl* -gäste*)* der visitor at a health resort.

kurieren *vt (Krankheit)* to cure.

Kurkonzert *(pl* -e*)* das concert at a spa.

Kurort *(pl* -e*)* der *(Badeort)* spa ; *(in den Bergen)* health resort.

Kurpackung (pl -en) die hair conditioner.

Kurpark (pl -s) der spa gardens (pl).

Kurs (pl -e) der (Unterricht, Richtung) course ; (von Aktie) price ; (von Devise) exchange rate.

Kursbuch (pl -bücher) das timetable.

Kurschatten (pl -) der person with whom one has a fling whilst at a health resort.

Kursus (pl Kurse) der course.

Kurswagen (pl -) der through carriage.

Kurtaxe (pl -n) die tax paid by visitors to health resorts, in exchange for which they receive reductions on certain services.

Kurve (pl -n) die (Linie) curve ; (von Straße) bend ; **scharfe ~** sharp bend.

kurvenreich adj winding.

Kurverwaltung (pl -en) die spa administration.

kurz (komp kürzer, superl am kürzesten) adj short. ◆ adv (zeitlich) briefly ; (schnell) quickly ; ~ vor/hinter just in front of/behind ; ~ vor dem Konzert shortly before the concert ; vor ~em recently ; sich ~ fassen to be brief ; ~ und bündig concisely.

kurzärmelig adj short-sleeved.

kürzen vt (Kleidung) to shorten ; (Haare, Nägel, Zahlungen) to cut.

kurzfristig adj (Absage, Kündigung) sudden ; (Vertrag) short-term ; (Entscheidung, Abreise) quick. ◆ adv at short notice.

Kurzgeschichte (pl -n) die short story.

kurzhaarig adj short-haired.

kürzlich adv recently.

Kurznachrichten pl news in brief (sg).

Kurzparken das short-stay parking.

Kurzparker (pl -) der driver who parks for a short period of time.

Kurzparkzone (pl -n) die short-stay parking zone.

Kurzschluss (pl -schlüsse) der short-circuit.

kurzsichtig adj short-sighted.

Kurzstrecke (pl -n) die short journey on public transport, within city centre.

Kurzstreckenkarte (pl -n) die ticket valid for a 'Kurzstrecke'.

Kurzstreckentarif (pl -e) der rate for 'Kurzstrecke' tickets.

Kurzurlaub (pl -e) der short break.

Kurzwelle die short wave.

Kurzzeitparken das short-stay parking.

Kurzzeitparkplatz (pl -plätze) der short-stay car park.

Kusine (pl -n) die cousin.

Kuss (pl Küsse) der kiss.

küssen vt to kiss. ■ **sich küssen** ref to kiss.

Küste (pl -n) die coast ; **an der ~** at the seaside.

Küstenwache (pl -n) die coastguard.

Kutsche (*pl* -n) *die* coach.

Kuvert (*pl* -s) *das* envelope.

Kuvertüre (*pl* -n) *die* chocolate icing.

L

Labor (*pl* -s) *das* laboratory.

Labyrinth (*pl* -e) *das* labyrinth.

lächeln *vi* to smile ; ~ über (+A) to smile at.

lachen *vi* to laugh ; ~ über (+A) to laugh at.

lächerlich *adj* ridiculous.

Lachs (*pl* -e) *der* salmon.

Lack (*pl* -e) *der (farbig)* paint ; *(farblos)* varnish.

lackieren *vt (Holz)* to varnish ; *(Auto)* to spray ; **sich** (D) **die Nägel ~** to paint one's nails.

Lackierung (*pl* -en) *die (farbig)* paint ; *(farblos)* varnish.

Ladefläche (*pl* -n) *die* capacity *(of lorry)*.

laden (*präs* **lädt**, *prät* **lud**, *pp* **geladen**) *vt* to load ; **auf sich ~** *(Verantwortung)* to take on.

Laden (*pl* **Läden**) *der (Geschäft)* shop ; *(am Fenster)* shutter.

Ladendieb, in (*mpl* -e) *der, die* shoplifter.

Ladendiebstahl (*pl* -stähle) *der* shoplifting ; 'gegen ~ gesichert' 'security cameras in operation'.

Ladenpreis (*pl* -e) *der* shop price.

Ladenschluss *der* (shop) closing time.

lädt *präs* → **laden**.

Ladung (*pl* -en) *die (Fracht)* cargo ; *(Munition)* charge.

lag *prät* → **liegen**.

Lage (*pl* -n) *die* situation, position ; *(Schicht)* layer ; **in der ~ sein, etw zu tun** to be in a position to do sthg.

Lageplan (*pl* -pläne) *der* map.

Lager (*pl* -) *das (für Waren)* warehouse ; *(Camp)* camp.

Lagerfeuer (*pl* -) *das* campfire.

lagern *vt (Lebensmittel, Waren)* to store.

Lähmung (*pl* -en) *die (Krankheit)* paralysis.

Laib (*pl* -e) *der* loaf.

Laie (*pl* -n) *der* layman (laywoman).

Laken (*pl* -) *das* sheet.

Lakritz (*pl* -en) *die* liquorice.

Lamm (*pl* **Lämmer**) *das* lamb.

Lammfleisch *das* lamb.

Lammkeule (*pl* -n) *die* leg of lamb.

Lammrücken (*pl* -) *der* saddle of lamb.

Lampe (*pl* -n) *die (in Raum)* lamp ; *(an Fahrrad)* light.

Lampenschirm (*pl* -e) *der* lampshade.

Lampion (*pl* -s) *der* Chinese lantern.

Land (*pl* **Länder**) *das (Nation, nicht Stadt)* country ; *(Bundesland)* state ; *(Festland)* land ; **auf dem ~** in the country.

Landbrot (*pl* -e) *das* brown rye bread with a hard crust.

Landebahn (*pl* -en) *die* runway.

Landeerlaubnis *die* clearance to land.

landen *vi ist* to land.

Landeplatz (*pl* -plätze) *der* landing strip.

Landesfarben *pl* national colours.

Landesinnere *das* interior *(of a country)*.

Landesregierung (*pl* -en) *die* state government.

Landessprache (*pl* -n) *die* national language.

landesüblich *adj (Tracht, Gericht)* national, typical of the country.

Landeswährung (*pl* -en) *die* national currency.

Landhaus (*pl* -häuser) *das* country house.

Landkarte (*pl* -n) *die* map.

Landkreis (*pl* -e) *der* district.

ländlich *adj* rural.

Landschaft (*pl* -en) *die* countryside ; *(in Kunst)* landscape.

landschaftlich *adj (regional)* regional.

Landschaftsschutzgebiet (*pl* -e) *das* nature reserve.

Landsleute *pl* compatriots.

Landstraße (*pl* -n) *die* country road.

Landtag (*pl* -e) *der* state parliament.

Landung (*pl* -en) *die (von Flugzeug)* landing.

Landwein (*pl* -e) *der* table wine.

Landwirt, in (*mpl* -e) *der, die* farmer.

Landwirtschaft *die* agriculture.

lang (*komp* längere, *superl* längste) *adj* long ; *(Person)* tall. ◆ *adv (fam : entlang)* along ; *(groß)* tall ; **den ganzen Tag** ~ all day ; **drei Meter** ~ three metres long ; **es dauerte drei Tage** ~ it lasted for three days ; **hier/dort** ~ this/that way.

langärmelig *adj* long-sleeved.

lange (*komp* länger, *superl* am längsten) *adv (während langer Zeit)* a long time ; *(seit langer Zeit)* for a long time ; **es hat** ~ **gedauert** it lasted a long time ; **das Wetter war** ~ **nicht so gut** the weather hasn't been so good for a long time ; **es ist** ~ **her** it was a long time ago ; **wie** ~? how long?

Länge (*pl* -n) *die* length ; *(von Person)* height ; **der** ~ **nach** lengthways ; **von drei km/sechs Stunden** ~ three km/six hours long.

Längenmaß (*pl* -e) *das* unit of length.

Langeweile *die* boredom.

langfristig *adj* long-term. ◆ *adv (planen)* for the long term.

Langlauf *der* cross-country skiing.

Langlaufski (*pl* -er) *der* cross-country ski.

langsam *adj* slow. ◆ *adv* slowly.

Langschläfer, in (*mpl* -) *der, die* late riser.

längst *adv* for a long time ; ~ **nicht so gut** nowhere near as good.

Lạngstreckenlauf *der* long-distance running.

Langụste (*pl* -n) *die* crayfish.

lạngweilen *vt* to bore. ▓ **sich langweilen** *ref* to be bored.

lạngweilig *adj* boring.

Lạngwelle *die* long wave.

lạngwierig *adj* lengthy.

Lạngzeitparker (*pl* -) *der* long-stay parker.

Lạppen (*pl* -) *der* (*zum Wischen*) cloth.

Lärche (*pl* -n) *die* (*Baum*) larch.

Lärm *der* noise.

lärmen *vi* to be noisy.

Lärmschutz *der* (*Vorrichtung*) soundproof barrier.

Lärmschutzmauer (*pl* -n) *die* soundproof wall.

las *prät* → **lesen**.

Lạsche (*pl* -n) *die* loop.

Laser (*pl* -) *der* laser.

lạssen (*präs* **lässt**, *prät* **ließ**, *pp* **gelassen** ODER **lassen**) *aux* 1. (*veranlassen*) : **etw machen** ODER **tun** ~ to have sthg done ; **jn etw tun** ~ to have sb do sthg ; **sich** (*D*) **einen Anzug machen** ~ to have a suit made ; **sich** (*D*) **die Haare schneiden** ~ to have one's hair cut.
2. (*zulassen*) : **jn etw tun** ~ to let sb do sthg ; ~ **wir uns überraschen** we'll see ; **es lässt sich machen** it can be done ; **es lässt sich trinken** it's drinkable ; **etw mit sich machen** ~ to put up with sthg ; **etw nicht mit sich machen** ~ not to stand for sthg.
3. (*geschehen lassen*) : **die Milch kochen** ~ to leave the milk to boil ; **die Vase fallen** ~ to drop the vase ; **jn warten** ~ to keep sb waiting.

◆ *vt* (*pp* **gelassen**) 1. (*unterlassen*) to stop ; **das Rauchen sein** ~ to stop smoking ; **lass das!** stop it!
2. (*belassen*) to leave ; **lass bitte alles so, wie es ist** leave everything as it is ; **jn (in Ruhe)** ~ to leave sb alone.
3. (*gehen lassen*) to let ; **jn nicht ins Haus** ~ not to let sb in the house.
4. (*überlassen*) : **jm etw** ~ to let sb have sthg.
5. (*zurücklassen*) to leave ; **das habe ich zu Hause gelassen** I left it at home.
6. (*loslassen*) to let go ; **lass mich!** let me go!
7. (*strömen lassen*) to let ; **Wasser in die Badewanne** ~ to run a bath ; **die Luft aus den Reifen** ~ to let the tyres down.

◆ *vi* (*pp* **gelassen**) 1. (*aufgeben*) : **von jm/etw** ~ (*geh*) to drop sb/sthg ; **er ließ schnell von dem Projekt** he quickly dropped the project.
2. (*sein lassen*) : **lass mal, ich mach das schon** leave it, I'll do it ; **lass mal, du bist heute eingeladen** no, I'm paying today.

lässig *adj* casual.

lässt *präs* → **lassen**.

Lạst (*pl* -en) *die* (*Traglast*) load ; (*psychisch*) burden.

Lạstenaufzug (*pl* -aufzüge) *der* goods lift (*Br*), goods elevator (*Am*).

Lạster (*pl* -) *der* (*LKW*) lorry.

lästern vi to make nasty remarks.

lästig adj annoying.

Lastkraftwagen (pl -) der (amt) heavy goods vehicle.

Last-Minute-|Angebot das last-minute offer.

Last-Minute-|Flug der last-minute flight.

Lastschiff (pl -e) das freighter.

Lastschrift (pl -en) die debit.

Lastwagen (pl -) der lorry.

Latein das Latin.

Laterne (pl -n) die (Straßenlaterne) streetlight; (Lampion) Chinese lantern.

Lätzchen (pl -) das bib.

Latzhose (pl -n) die dungarees (pl).

lau adj (Wasser) lukewarm; (Abend) mild.

Laub das (auf Baum) foliage; (auf Erde) dead leaves (pl).

Lauch der leek.

lauern vi : ~ auf (+A) (im Hinterhalt) to lie in wait for; (auf Chance, Vorteil) to wait for.

Lauf (pl Läufe) der (Verlauf) course; (SPORT) race; **im ~e des Tages** in the course of the day.

laufen (präs **läuft**, prät **lief**, pp **gelaufen**) vi ist 1. (schnell) to run.

2. (gehen) to walk.

3. (Motor, Maschine) to run.

4. (funktionieren) to work.

5. (fließen) to run; **mir läuft die Nase** my nose is running.

6. (andauern) to go on.

7. (Film, Drama) to run; **der Film läuft schon seit zehn Minuten** the film started ten minutes ago;

was läuft im Kino? what's on at the cinema?

◆ vt ist 1. (schnell) to run; **den Marathon ~** to run the marathon.

2. (gehen) to walk.

3. (SPORT) : **Ski ~** to ski; **Schlittschuh ~** to skate.

laufend adj (Wechsel) constant; (Kosten, Motor, Gerät) running; (Monat, Jahr) current. ◆ adv (ständig) regularly.

Läufer (pl -) der (Sportler) runner; (Teppich) rug.

Läuferin (pl -nen) die runner.

Laufmasche (pl -n) die ladder (Br), run (Am).

läuft präs → laufen.

Laufzeit (pl -en) die (von Film) running time.

Lauge (pl -n) die (zum Waschen) soapy water.

Laugenbrezel (pl -n) die pretzel.

Laune (pl -n) die (Stimmung) mood; **gute/schlechte ~ haben** to be in a good/bad mood.

launisch adj moody.

Laus (pl **Läuse**) die louse.

lauschen vi (konzentriert) to listen; (heimlich) to eavesdrop.

laut adj loud. ◆ adv loudly. ◆ prep (+G or +D) (amt) according to.

läuten vi to ring. ◆ vimp : **es läutet** the bell is ringing.

lauter det nothing but; **aus ~ Dankbarkeit** out of sheer gratitude.

Lautsprecher (pl -) der loudspeaker.

Lautsprecherdurchsage (*pl* -n) *die* announcement over the loudspeaker.

Lautstärke *die* volume.

lauwarm *adj* lukewarm.

Lawine (*pl* -n) *die* avalanche.

Lawinengefahr *die* danger of an avalanche.

Leasing (*pl* -s) *das* leasing.

leben *vi* to live; ~ **von** *(Nahrungsmittel)* to live on; *(Tätigkeit)* to make one's living from.

Leben (*pl* -) *das* life; **am ~ sein/bleiben** to be/stay alive; **sich das ~ nehmen** to take one's (own) life; **ums ~ kommen** to die.

lebendig *adj (lebhaft)* lively; *(lebend)* alive.

Lebensalter *das* age.

Lebensbedingungen *pl* living conditions.

Lebensgefahr *die*: 'Lebensgefahr!' 'danger'; **außer ~ sein** to be out of danger; **er ist in ~** his life is at risk.

lebensgefährlich *adj (Unternehmen)* very dangerous; *(Krankheit)* critical.

Lebensgefährte, gefährtin (*mpl* -n) *der, die* companion.

Lebensjahr (*pl* -e) *das*: **im vierten ~** four years old.

lebenslänglich *adj* life *(vor Subst)*.

Lebenslauf (*pl* -läufe) *der* curriculum vitae.

lebenslustig *adj* full of life.

Lebensmittel *pl* food *(sg)*.

Lebensmittelgeschäft (*pl* -e) *das* grocer's (shop).

Lebensmittelvergiftung (*pl* -en) *die* food poisoning.

lebensnotwendig *adj* essential to life.

Lebensretter, in (*mpl* -) *der, die* lifesaver.

Lebensunterhalt *der* living, livelihood.

Lebensversicherung (*pl* -en) *die* life assurance.

lebenswichtig *adj* essential.

Lebenszeichen (*pl* -) *das* sign of life.

Leber (*pl* -n) *die* liver.

Leberfleck (*pl* -en) *der* liver spot.

Leberknödel (*pl* -) *der* liver dumpling.

Leberpastete (*pl* -n) *die* liver pâté.

Leberwurst (*pl* -würste) *die* liver sausage.

Lebewesen (*pl* -) *das* living thing.

lebhaft *adj* lively.

Lebkuchen (*pl* -) *der* gingerbread.

 LEBKUCHEN

A type of gingerbread, "Lebkuchen" is made with honey and a mixture of spices including cinnamon, cloves, nutmeg and aniseed. The most famous "Lebkuchen" is a spongy variety from Nuremberg which is usually eaten at Christmas. "Lebkuchen" normally comes in the form of small hearts, stars or round biscuits but, particularly at funfairs, it is also

sold as large hearts decorated
with icing.

---

leck *adj (Schiff)* leaky.

Leck *(pl -s) das* leak.

lecken *vi* to leak. ◆ *vt* to lick.

lecker *adj* delicious.

Leckerbissen *(pl -) der (Speise)* delicacy.

Leder *das* leather.

Lederhose *(pl -n) die* lederhosen *(pl)*, short leather trousers
with braces.

Lederwaren *pl* leather
goods.

ledig *adj (unverheiratet)* single.

lediglich *adv* only.

leer *adj* empty ; *(Blatt, Heft)*
blank ; **etw ~ machen** *(Behälter, Raum)* to empty sthg.

Leergut *das* empties *(pl)*.

Leerlauf *der (von Auto, Fahrrad)* neutral ; **im ~** in neutral.

Leerung *(pl -en) die (von Briefkästen)* collection ; '**nächste ~ 17 Uhr'** 'next collection at
5 pm'.

legal *adj* legal.

legen *vt* 1. *(ablegen)* to put ;
leg den Schlüssel auf den Tisch
put the key on the table.
2. *(waagerecht hinlegen)* to lay ;
**du musst die Flaschen ins Regal ~,
nicht stellen** you should lay the
bottles flat in the rack rather
than upright.
3. *(installieren)* to lay.
4. *(Termin)* to arrange ; **den Urlaub auf Juli ~** to arrange one's
holidays for July.
5. *(Haare)* to set ; **sich** *(D)* **die**

Haare ~ lassen to have one's
hair set.
6. *(Eier)* to lay.
■ **sich legen** *ref* 1. *(sich hinlegen)* to lie down.
2. *(aufhören)* to die down.

Legende *(pl -n) die* legend.

legitim *adj (Forderungen, Interesse)* legitimate.

Lehm *der* clay.

Lehne *(pl -n) die (Rückenlehne)*
back *(of chair)*.

lehnen *vt & vi* to lean. ■ **sich
lehnen** *ref* to lean ; **sich ~ an**
(+A) to lean against.

Lehrbuch *(pl -bücher) das*
textbook.

Lehre *(pl -n) die (Ausbildung)*
apprenticeship ; *(Erfahrung)*
lesson ; *(religiös, politisch)* doctrine.

lehren *vt* to teach.

Lehrer, in *(mpl -) der, die*
teacher.

Lehrgang *(pl -gänge) der*
course.

Lehrling *(pl -e) der* apprentice.

Leib *(pl -er) der* body.

Leibgericht *(pl -e) das* favourite meal.

Leiche *(pl -n) die* corpse.

leicht *adj* light ; *(Aufgabe, Arbeit)* easy ; *(Erkrankung)* slight ;
(Zigaretten) mild. ◆ *adv (einfach, schnell)* easily ; *(regnen, erkältet)* slightly ; **~ bekleidet**
wearing summer clothes.

Leichtathletik *die* athletics
(sg).

leicht fallen *vi unr ist* to be
easy ; **jm ~** to be easy for sb.

leichtsinnig *adj* careless.

leid adj : es ~ sein, etw zu tun to be tired of doing sthg.

Leid das sorrow ; er tut mir ~ I feel sorry for him ; es tut mir ~! I'm sorry!

leiden (prät litt, pp gelitten) vt & vi to suffer ; ~ an (+D) to suffer from ; ich kann ihn/es nicht ~ I can't stand him/it.

leidenschaftlich adj passionate.

leider adv unfortunately.

Leihbücherei (pl -en) die (lending) library.

leihen (prät lieh, pp geliehen) vt (ausleihen) to borrow ; jm etw ~ to lend sb sthg ; sich (D) etw ~ to borrow sthg.

Leihfrist (pl -en) die hire period.

Leihgebühr (pl -en) die hire charge.

Leihwagen (pl -) der hire car.

Leim der glue.

Leine (pl -n) die (Seil) cord ; (für Wäsche) (washing) line ; (Hundeleine) lead.

Leinen das linen.

Leinsamen der linseed.

Leinwand (pl -wände) die (im Kino) screen ; (zum Malen) canvas.

Leipziger Allerlei das mixed vegetables including peas, carrots and green beans.

leise adj (Geräusch) quiet. ◆ adv quietly.

leisten vt (vollbringen) to achieve ; (Beitrag, Zahlung) to make ; sich (D) etw ~ (sich kaufen) to treat o.s. to sthg ; sich (D) etw ~ können to be able to afford sthg.

Leistung (pl -en) die (Arbeit) performance ; (Zahlung) payment.

leistungsfähig adj efficient.

Leistungskurs (pl -e) der (SCHULE) one of the subjects which pupils choose to specialize in for their 'Abitur'.

Leitartikel (pl -) der leader.

leiten vt (Team) to lead ; (Firma) to run ; (Strom) to conduct ; (Wasser, Verkehr) to divert.

Leiter[1] (pl -n) die (mit Sprossen) ladder.

Leiter[2] (pl -) der (von Gruppe) leader ; (von Firma) manager.

Leiterin (pl -nen) die (von Gruppe) leader ; (von Firma) manager.

Leitfaden (pl -fäden) der introductory guide.

Leitplanke (pl -n) die crash barrier.

Leitung (pl -en) die (von Firma) management ; (Telefonleitung) line ; (Stromleitung) wire ; (Wasserleitung) pipe ; unter der ~ von (Orchester) conducted by.

Leitungsrohr (pl -e) das (water)pipe.

Leitungswasser das tap water.

Lektion (pl -en) die (Kapitel) lesson.

Lektüre (pl -n) die reading.

lenken vt & vi to steer.

Lenker (pl -) der (Lenkrad) steering wheel ; (Lenkstange) handlebars (pl).

Lenkrad (*pl* -räder) *das* steering wheel.

Lenkradschloss (*pl* -schlösser) *das* steering lock.

Lenkstange (*pl* -n) *die* handlebars (*pl*).

Lenkung (*pl* -en) *die (am Fahrzeug)* steering.

lernen *vt* to learn ; *(Beruf)* to train as. ◆ *vi (für Prüfung)* to study ; *(in Lehre)* to train ; *(aus Erfahrung)* to learn.

lesbisch *adj* lesbian.

Lesebuch (*pl* -bücher) *das* reader.

lesen (*präs* **liest**, *prät* **las**, *pp* **gelesen**) *vt* & *vi* to read.

Leser, in (*mpl* -) *der, die* reader.

letzte¹ *adj* last.

letzte², r, s *det* last ; **~s Jahr** last year.

Letzte (*pl* -n) *der, die (Person)* : **der/die ~** the last ; **~ werden** to come last.

letztemal → **Mal**.

letztenmal → **Mal**.

letztens *adv (vor kurzem)* recently.

leuchten *vi* to shine.

Leuchter (*pl* -) *der (für Kerzen)* candlestick.

Leuchtstift (*pl* -e) *der* highlighter.

Leuchtstoffröhre (*pl* -n) *die* strip light.

Leuchtturm (*pl* -türme) *der* lighthouse.

leugnen *vt (Tat, Schuld)* to deny. ◆ *vi (Angeklagter)* to deny everything.

Leukämie *die* leukaemia.

Leute *pl* people.

Lexikon (*pl* -ka) *das (Enzyklopädie)* encyclopaedia ; *(Wörterbuch)* dictionary.

liberal *adj* liberal.

Licht (*pl* -er) *das* light ; **~ machen** to put the light on ; **das ~ ausmachen** to turn the light off ; **offenes ~** naked flame.

lichtempfindlich *adj (film)* photosensitive.

Lichthupe *die* : **die ~ betätigen** to flash one's headlights.

Lichtmaschine (*pl* -n) *die* alternator.

Lichtschalter (*pl* -) *der* light switch.

Lichtschranke (*pl* -n) *die* photoelectric beam.

Lichtschutzfaktor (*pl* -en) *der* factor *(of suntan lotion)*.

Lichtstrahl (*pl* -en) *der* ray of light.

Lichtung (*pl* -en) *die* clearing.

Lid (*pl* -er) *das* eyelid.

Lidschatten (*pl* -) *der* eyeshadow.

lieb *adj (nett)* kind ; *(als Anrede)* dear ; **jn ~ haben** to be fond of sb ; **~er Karl-Heinz!** *(in Brief)* Dear Karl-Heinz.

Liebe *die* love.

lieben *vt* to love ; *(sexuell)* to make love to. ■ **sich lieben** *ref. (lieb haben)* to be in love ; *(sexuell)* to make love.

liebenswürdig *adj* kind. ◆ *adv* kindly.

lieber *komp* rather, → **gern**. ◆ *adv (besser)* better. ◆ *adj (angenehmer)* : **ein warmes Essen wäre mir ~** I'd prefer a hot meal ; **das hättest du ~ nicht sa-**

gen **sollen** it would have been better if you hadn't said that.

Liebesbrief (*pl* -e) *der* love letter.

Liebespaar (*pl* -e) *das* couple (of lovers).

liebevoll *adj* loving.

lieb haben *vt unr* to love.
▩ **sich lieb haben** *ref* (*sich gern haben*) to be in love ; (*erotisch*) to make love.

Liebhaber (*pl* -) *der* lover.

Liebhaberin (*pl* -nen) *die* lover.

lieblich *adj* (*Wein*) sweet.

Liebling (*pl* -e) *der* (*Anrede*) darling.

Lieblingsgericht (*pl* -e) *das* favourite meal.

lieblos *adj* unloving.

liebsten *superl* → **gern** ; **am ~** best of all ; **das ist mir am ~** I like it best of all.

Liechtenstein *nt* Liechtenstein.

Lied (*pl* -er) *das* song ; (*RELIG*) hymn.

lief *prät* → **laufen**.

Lieferant (*pl* -en) *der* (*Person*) deliveryman ; (*Firma*) supplier ; "~en frei" "except for loading".

lieferbar *adj* available.

Lieferfrist (*pl* -en) *die* delivery time.

liefern *vt* (*Ware*) to deliver ; (*Beispiel, Argument*) to provide.
◆ *vi* (*Geschäft*) to deliver ; **wir ~ frei Haus** we deliver free to your home.

Lieferung (*pl* -en) *die* delivery.

Lieferwagen (*pl* -) *der* van.

Liege (*pl* -n) *die* camp bed ; (*für Garten*) sun lounger.

liegen (*präs* **liegt**, *prät* **lag**, *pp* **gelegen**) *vi* 1. (*Person, Gegenstand*) to lie.
2. (*sich befinden*) to be ; **Bonn liegt am Rhein** Bonn is on the Rhine.
3. (*zeitlich*) to be ; **das liegt lange zurück** that was a long time ago.
4. (*in Reihenfolge*) to lie ; **sie liegt auf dem vierten Platz** she's lying in fourth place.
5. (*Grund, Ursache*) : **sein Asthma liegt an der schlechten Luft** his asthma is caused by the poor air ; **der Fehler liegt an dir** the mistake is your fault.
6. (*abhängen*) : **das liegt bei dir** it's up to you.
7. (*wichtig sein*) : **es liegt mir viel daran** it matters a lot to me.
8. (*begabt sein für*) : **Physik liegt mir nicht** physics isn't my subject.

liegen bleiben *vi unr ist* (*nicht aufstehen*) to stay in bed ; (*vergessen werden*) to be left behind ; (*Arbeit*) to be left undone ; (*fam* : *mit Auto, Bus*) to break down.

liegen lassen *vt unr* to leave.

Liegesitz (*pl* -e) *der* reclining seat.

Liegestuhl (*pl* -stühle) *der* (*am Strand*) deck chair ; (*im Garten*) sun lounger.

Liegestütz (*pl* -e) *die* press-up.

Liegewagen (*pl* -) *der* couchette car.

Liegewagenplatz (*pl* -plätze) *der* couchette.

Liegewiese (*pl* -n) *die* lawn.

lieh *prät* → **leihen**.

ließ *prät* → **lassen**.

liest *präs* → **lesen**.

Lift (*pl* -e) *der* (*Aufzug*) lift (*Br*), elevator (*Am*) ; (*Skilift*) ski lift.

light *adj* (*Nahrungsmittel*) low-calorie ; (*Cola*) diet (*vor Subst*) ; (*Zigaretten*) mild.

Likör (*pl* -e) *der* liqueur.

lila *adj* light purple, lilac.

Limo (*pl* -s) *die* (*fam*) fizzy drink.

Limonade (*pl* -n) *die* fizzy drink.

Linde (*pl* -n) *die* (*Baum*) lime tree.

lindern *vt* to relieve.

Lineal (*pl* -e) *das* ruler.

Linie (*pl* -n) *die* line ; (*Bus, Straßenbahn*) number ; **in erster ~** first and foremost.

Linienbus (*pl* -se) *der* regular bus.

Linienflug (*pl* -flüge) *der* scheduled flight.

Linienmaschine (*pl* -n) *die* scheduled plane.

Linienverkehr *der* (*Flugverkehr*) scheduled flights (*pl*).

link *adj* (*abw*) sly.

linke, r, s *adj* (*Seite*) left ; (*Politik*) left-wing.

links *adv* (*Seitenangabe*) on the left ; (*Richtungsangabe*) left ; (*wählen*) for the left ; **~ von jm/etw** on sb's/sthg's left ; **nach ~** left ; **von ~** from the left.

Linksabbieger (*pl* -) *der* car turning left.

linksherum *adv* (*nach links*) round to the left ; (*verkehrt herum*) the wrong way round.

Linkskurve (*pl* -n) *die* left-hand bend.

Linkssteuerung (*pl* -en) *die* left-hand drive.

Linksverkehr *der* driving on the left.

Linse (*pl* -n) *die* (*Gemüse*) lentil ; (*in Kamera*) lens.

Linsensuppe (*pl* -n) *die* lentil soup.

Linzer Torte *die* fruit tart with lattice pastry covering.

Lippe (*pl* -n) *die* lip.

Lippenstift (*pl* -e) *der* lipstick.

List (*pl* -en) *die* (*Trick*) trick.

Liste (*pl* -n) *die* list.

Liter (*pl* -) *der* litre.

Literatur (*pl* -en) *die* literature.

Literflasche (*pl* -n) *die* litre bottle.

Litfasssäule (*pl* -n) *die* advertising column.

litt *prät* → **leiden**.

Lizenz (*pl* -en) *die* (*Erlaubnis*) licence.

LKW (*pl* -s) *der* HGV.

Lob *das* (*von Person*) praise.

loben *vt* to praise.

Loch (*pl* Löcher) *das* hole.

lochen *vt* to punch a hole/holes in.

Locher (*pl* -) *der* hole punch.

Locke (*pl* -n) *die* curl.

Lockenschere (*pl* -n) *die* curling tongs (*pl*).

Lockenwickler (*pl* -) *der* curler.

locker *adj* loose ; (*Haltung*) laid-back ; (*Beziehung*) casual. ◆ *adv* (*knoten*) loosely ; (*fam* : *leicht, einfach*) easily.

lockern *vt* (*Knoten*) to loosen. ▨ **sich lockern** *ref* (*Knoten, Schraube*) to work itself loose.

lockig *adj* curly.

Löffel (*pl* -) *der* spoon.

Löffelbisquit (*pl* -s) *der* sponge finger.

löffeln *vt* to spoon.

log *prät* → **lügen**.

Loge (*pl* -n) *die* box (*at theatre*).

logisch *adj* logical.

Lohn (*pl* **Löhne**) *der* (*Bezahlung*) wages (*pl*), pay ; (*Belohnung*) reward.

lohnen : **sich lohnen** *ref* to be worth it.

Lohnsteuer *die* income tax.

Lohnsteuerkarte (*pl* -n) *die* form filled in by employer stating annual income and tax paid, ≃ P60 (*Br*).

Loipe (*pl* -n) *die* cross-country ski run.

Lok (*pl* -s) *die* = **Lokomotive**.

lokal *adj* local.

Lokal (*pl* -e) *das* pub.

Lokalnachrichten *pl* local news (*sg*).

Lokomotive (*pl* -n) *die* locomotive.

London *nt* London.

Los (*pl* -e) *das* (*von Lotterie*) ticket.

los *adj* (*lose*) loose. ◆ *interj* come on! ; es ist viel/wenig/ nichts ~ there is a lot/not

much/nothing going on ; **jn/ etw ~ sein** to have got rid of sb/ sthg ; **was ist ~?** what's the matter?

löschen *vt* (*Feuer*) to put out, to extinguish ; (*Aufnahme*) to erase ; (*Daten*) to delete.

Löschpapier *das* blotting paper.

lose *adj* loose. ◆ *adv* loosely.

losen *vi* to draw lots.

lösen *vt* (*Fahrkarte, Eintrittskarte*) to buy ; (*Aufgabe, Rätsel*) to solve ; (*Knoten*) to undo ; (*Bremse*) to take off ; (*auflösen*) to dissolve. ▨ **sich lösen** *ref* (*sich lockern*) to become loose ; (*Problem*) to be solved ; (*sich auflösen*) to dissolve.

los|fahren *vi unr ist* to set off.

los|gehen *vi unr ist* (*Person*) to set off ; (*Veranstaltung*) to start.

los|lassen *vt unr* (*Person, Gegenstand*) to let go of.

löslich *adj* (*Kaffee*) instant.

los|machen *vt* to untie.

Lösung (*pl* -en) *die* solution.

los|werden *vt unr ist* (*Person, Grippe*) to get rid of ; (*Geld*) to lose.

Lotion (*pl* -en) *die* lotion.

lotsen *vt* to guide.

Lotterie (*pl* -n) *die* lottery.

Lotto *das* national lottery.

Lottoschein (*pl* -e) *der* national lottery ticket.

Löwe (*pl* -n) *der* (*Tier*) lion ; (*Sternzeichen*) Leo.

Löwenzahn *der* dandelion.

Lücke (*pl* -n) *die* gap.

lud *prät* → **laden**.

Luft *die* air ; frische ~ fresh air.

Luftballon (*pl* -s) *der* balloon.

luftdicht *adj* airtight.

Luftdruck *der* air pressure.

lüften *vt* (*Zimmer*) to air. ◆ *vi* (*im Zimmer*) to let some air in.

Luftfahrtgesellschaft (*pl* -en) *die* airline.

Luftfeuchtigkeit *die* humidity.

Luftfilter (*pl* -) *der* air filter.

Luftfracht *die* air freight.

Luftkissenboot (*pl* -e) *das* hovercraft.

Luftkurort (*pl* -e) *der* health resort.

Luftlinie *die* : (es sind) 100 km ~ (it's) 100 km as the crow flies.

Luftmatratze (*pl* -n) *die* airbed.

Luftpost *die* airmail ; **per ~** (by) airmail.

Luftpumpe (*pl* -n) *die* air pump.

Luftröhre (*pl* -n) *die* windpipe.

Luftschlange (*pl* -n) *die* streamer.

Lüftung (*pl* -en) *die* (*Gerät*) ventilation (system).

Luftverkehr *der* air traffic.

Luftverschmutzung *die* air pollution.

Luftzug *der* draught.

Lüge (*pl* -n) *die* lie.

lügen (*prät* **log**, *pp* **gelogen**) *vi* to lie.

Lügner, in (*mpl* -) *der, die* liar.

Lunchpaket (*pl* -e) *das* packed lunch.

Lunge (*pl* -n) *die* lungs (*pl*).

Lungenentzündung (*pl* -en) *die* pneumonia.

Lüngerl *das* (*Süddt*) finely-chopped calf's lights boiled in vinegar and usually eaten with 'Semmelknödel'.

Lupe (*pl* -n) *die* magnifying glass.

Lust (*pl* **Lüste**) *die* (*Bedürfnis*) desire ; (*Freude*) pleasure ; (*sexuell*) lust ; **(keine) ~ haben auf** (+A) (not) to feel like ; **~ haben, etw zu tun** to feel like doing sthg.

lustig *adj* (*komisch*) funny ; (*unterhaltsam*) entertaining ; **sich ~ machen über** (+A) to make fun of.

lutschen *vt* to suck.

Lutscher (*pl* -) *der* lollipop.

Luxemburg *nt* Luxembourg.

Luxemburger, in (*mpl* -) *der, die* Luxemburger.

luxemburgisch *adj* of/from Luxembourg.

luxuriös *adj* luxurious.

Luxus *der* luxury.

Luzern *nt* Lucerne.

M

machen *vt* **1.** (*tun*) to do ; **da kann man nichts ~** there's nothing we can do about it ; **mach die Musik leiser** turn the music down ; **mach's gut!** take care! **2.** (*herstellen*) to make ; (*Foto*) to take ; **jm etw ~** to make sthg for sb ; **etw aus etw ~** to make sthg

out of sthg ; **mach keine Dumm-heiten!** don't do anything silly!
3. *(verändern, bewirken)* to make ; **jn krank/glücklich ~** to make sb ill/happy ; **etw sauber ~** to clean sthg.
4. *(Urlaub)* to go on ; **eine Pause ~** to have a break.
5. *(Reise, Wanderung)* to go on ; *(Spaziergang)* to go for ; **einen Besuch bei jm ~** to pay sb a visit.
6. *(Arbeit, Hausaufgaben)* to do ; *(Reparatur, Korrektur)* to make.
7. *(Gefühl)* : **jm Angst/Freude ~** to make sb afraid/happy.
8. *(Kurs, Lehrgang)* to do.
9. *(Prüfung)* to do, to take.
10. *(Summe, Ergebnis)* to be ; **fünf mal drei macht fünfzehn** five times three is fifteen ; **das macht 5 Mark!** that comes to 5 marks.
11. *(ausmachen)* : **die Hitze macht mir nichts** I don't mind the heat ; **das macht nichts!** it doesn't matter!
12. *(mögen)* : **sich** *(D)* **nichts ~ aus** not to be keen on.
◆ *vi* : **mach schnell!** hurry up! ; **mach schon!** *(fam)* get a move on!
▓ **sich machen** *ref* : **sich gut ~** *(wirken)* to look good ; *(fam : entwickeln)* to make good progress.

Macht *(pl* Mächte*)* die power ; **an der ~ sein** to be in power.

mächtig *adj (König, Land)* powerful.

machtlos *adj* powerless.

Macke *(pl* -n*)* die *(fam : Spleen)* quirk ; *(an Tasse, Tisch)* chip.

Mädchen *(pl* -*)* das girl.

Mädchenname *(pl* -n*)* der maiden name.

Made *(pl* -n*)* die maggot.

Madonna *(pl* Madonnen*)* die Madonna.

mag *präs →* **mögen**.

Magazin *(pl* -e*)* das magazine ; *(Lager)* storeroom.

Magen *(pl* Mägen*)* der stomach ; **sich** *(D)* **den ~ verderben** to get an upset stomach.

Magenbeschwerden *pl* stomach trouble *(sg)*.

Magenbitter *(pl* -*)* der bitters *(sg)*.

Magengeschwür *(pl* -e*)* das stomach ulcer.

Magenschmerzen *pl* stomach-ache *(sg)*.

mager *adj (Person, Tier)* thin ; *(Käse)* low-fat ; *(Fleisch)* lean.

Magermilch die skimmed milk.

Maggi® das type of brown, liquid seasoning.

Magnet *(pl* -e*)* der *(Metall)* magnet.

mähen *vt (Gras, Feld)* to mow.

Mahl *(pl* -e*)* das meal.

mahlen *vt* to grind.

Mahlzeit *(pl* -en*)* die meal ; **~!** *(Gruß)* hello! *(said around mealtimes)*.

Mähne *(pl* -n*)* die mane.

mahnen *vt (erinnern)* to remind.

Mahngebühr *(pl* -en*)* die charge for failure to pay a bill or fine.

Mahnmal *(pl* -e*)* das memorial.

Mahnung (*pl* -en) *die* re-minder.

Mai *der* May ; **der erste ~** May Day ; → **September**.

Maibaum (*pl* -bäume) *der* maypole.

 MAIBAUM

The maypole is an old spring tradition. In many areas it is customary to fell a tree, usually a birch, on the day before 1 May. The trunk is decorated with ribbons and erected on the village square. A campfire is then built and the maypole is guarded all night to prevent the young people from neighbouring villages from attempting to steal it. The pole is also used in other festivals throughout the year.

Maifeiertag (*pl* -e) *der* May Day.

Mais *der* (*Körner*) sweetcorn ; (*Pflanze*) maize.

Maiskolben (*pl* -) *der* corn on the cob.

Majonäse (*pl* -n) *die* mayonnaise.

Majoran *der* marjoram.

Make-up (*pl* -s) *das* (*Schminke*) make-up ; (*Creme*) foundation.

Makkaroni *pl* macaroni (*sg*).

Makler, in (*mpl* -) *der, die* estate agent.

Makrele (*pl* -n) *die* mackerel.

Makrone (*pl* -n) *die* macaroon.

mal *adv* (*fam* : in Zukunft) sometime ; (*in Vergangenheit*) once.

◆ *konj* (*zur Multiplikation*) times ; **bald ~** sometime soon ; **komm ~ her** come here ; **ich muss dir ~ was sagen** there's something I need to tell you ; **hör ~!** (*fam*) listen ; **sag ~!** (*fam*) tell me ; **er redet ~ so, ~ so** (*fam*) he says one thing one minute and another the next.

Mal (*pl* -e) *das* (*Zeitpunkt*) time ; **letztes ~** last time ; **nächstes ~** next time ; **zum ersten/letzten ~** for the first/last time ; **das letzte ~** the last time ; **ein paar ~** a few times.

Malaria *die* malaria.

Malbuch (*pl* -bücher) *das* colouring book.

malen *vt & vi* to paint.

Maler, in (*mpl* -) *der, die* (*Künstler*) artist ; (*Anstreicher*) painter.

malerisch *adj* (*Ort*) picturesque.

Malteser Hilfsdienst *der* voluntary paramedic service, ≃ St John's Ambulance (*Br*).

Malventee *der* mallow tea.

Malzbier *das* malt beer.

Mama (*pl* -s) *die* (*fam*) mummy.

man *pron* (*jeder, ich*) you ; (*irgendjemand*) they ; **wie sagt ~ das auf Deutsch?** how do you say that in German? ; **dieses Jahr trägt ~ Miniröcke** miniskirts are in this year.

Manager, in (*mpl* -) *der, die* manager.

manche, r, s *pron* (*einige Dinge*) some ; (*einige Leute*) some people ; (*viele, viel*) many things. ◆ det *(einige)* some; *(viele)* many.

manchmal *adv* sometimes.

Mandarine *(pl -n)* die mandarin.

Mandel *(pl -n)* die almond. ▨ **Mandeln** *pl (im Hals)* tonsils.

Mandelentzündung *(pl -en)* die tonsilitis.

Manege *(pl -n)* die (circus) ring.

Mangel *(pl Mängel)* der *(Zustand)* lack; *(Fehler)* fault; ~ an *(+D)* shortage of.

mangelhaft *adj (nicht ausreichend)* poor; *(Schulnote)* unsatisfactory, poor.

mangels *präp (+G) (amt)* owing to lack of.

Mango *(pl -s)* die mango.

Manieren *pl* manners.

Maniküre *die* manicure.

manipulieren *vt (Person)* to manipulate; *(Stimmzettel, Motor)* to rig.

Mann *(pl Männer)* der *(Erwachsener)* man; *(Ehemann)* husband. ◆ *interj (fam)* my God!

Mannequin *(pl -s)* das model.

männlich *adj* male; *(GRAMM)* masculine.

Mannschaft *(pl -en)* die *(beim Sport)* team; *(von Schiff, Flugzeug)* crew.

Manöver *(pl -)* das manoeuvre.

manövrieren *vt (Fahrzeug)* to manoeuvre.

Manschettenknopf *(pl -knöpfe)* der cufflink.

Mantel *(pl Mäntel)* der *(Kleidungsstück)* coat; *(von Reifen)* outer casing.

manuell *adj* manual.

Manuskript *(pl -e)* das manuscript.

Mappe *(pl -n)* die *(Hülle)* folder; *(Tasche)* briefcase; *(von Schüler)* schoolbag.

Maracuja *(pl -s)* die passion fruit.

Marathon *(pl -s)* der marathon.

Märchen *(pl -)* das fairy tale.

Margarine *die* margarine.

Mariä Himmelfahrt *nt* Assumption.

Marienkäfer *(pl -)* der ladybird *(Br)*, ladybug *(Am)*.

Marille *(pl -n)* die *(Österr)* apricot.

Marillenknödel *(pl -)* der *(Österr)* dessert consisting of a potato dumpling with an apricot in the middle.

Marinade *(pl -n)* die marinade.

marinieren *vt* to marinate.

Marionette *(pl -n)* die puppet.

Marionettentheater *(pl -)* das *(Veranstaltung)* puppet show; *(Gebäude)* puppet theatre.

Mark *(pl -)* die *(Währung)* mark; *(Knochenmark)* marrow; *(aus Obst, Gemüse)* puree.

Marke *(pl -n)* die *(von Hersteller)* make, brand; *(Briefmarke)* stamp; *(von Polizist)* badge; *(für Garderobe)* (metal) token.

Markenartikel *(pl -)* der brand-name article.

Markenzeichen (*pl* -) *das* trademark.

markieren *vt (kennzeichnen)* to mark.

Markierung (*pl* -en) *die* marking ; 'fehlende ~' 'no road markings'.

Markise (*pl* -n) *die* awning.

Markklößchen (*pl* -) *das* small dumpling made from marrow and breadcrumbs eaten in soup.

Markstück (*pl* -e) *das* one-mark coin.

Markt (*pl* Märkte) *der* market ; *(Marktplatz)* marketplace ; **auf den** ODER **zum ~ gehen** to go to (the) market.

Marktforschung *die* market research.

Marktfrau (*pl* -en) *die* market woman.

Markthalle (*pl* -n) *die* covered market.

Marktplatz (*pl* -plätze) *der* marketplace.

Marktwirtschaft *die* market economy.

Marmelade (*pl* -n) *die* jam.

Marmor *der* marble.

Marmorkuchen (*pl* -) *der* marble cake, *sponge cake with a pattern made in darker (often chocolate) sponge on the inside.*

Marone (*pl* -n) *die (Kastanie)* chestnut ; *(Pilz)* chestnut mushroom.

Marsch¹ (*pl* Märsche) *der* march.

Marsch² (*pl* -en) *die (an Küste)* marsh *(on coast)*.

marschieren *vi ist* to march.

Marschmusik *die* marches *(pl)*.

Marxismus *der* Marxism.

März *der* March ; → **September**.

Marzipan *das* marzipan.

Maschine (*pl* -n) *die (Gerät)* machine ; *(fam : Flugzeug)* plane ; **~ schreiben** to type.

maschinell *adj* machine *(vor Subst).* ◆ *adv* by machine.

Masern *pl* measles *(sg).*

Maske (*pl* -n) *die* mask.

Maskenball (*pl* -bälle) *der (Kostümball)* fancy dress party.

maskieren *vt (Person)* to disguise. ■ **sich maskieren** *ref (Einbrecher, sich verkleiden)* to disguise o.s.

Maskottchen (*pl* -) *das* mascot.

maskulin *adj* masculine.

maß *prät* → **messen**.

Maß (*pl* -e) *das (von Raum, Größe)* measurement ; *(Einheit)* measure ; **in hohem/geringem ~** to a great/small extent ; **nach ~** to measure.

Maß (*pl* Mass) *die (Süddt : Liter)* litre (glass).

Massage (*pl* -n) *die* massage.

Massageöl (*pl* -e) *das* massage oil.

Masse (*pl* -n) *die (Brei)* mixture ; *(von Personen)* crowd ; *(von Dingen)* mass ; **in ~n** in great numbers ; **die breite ~** the masses *(pl).*

Maßeinheit (*pl* -en) *die* unit of measurement.

massenhaft *adj* great numbers of.

Massenmedien *pl* mass media.

Massentourismus *der* mass tourism.

Masseur, in (*mpl* -e) *der, die* masseur (masseuse).

maßgeschneidert *adj* (*Kleidung*) made-to-measure.

massieren *vt* to massage.

mäßig *adj* (*Leistung, Wetter*) average ; (*moderat*) moderate. ◆ *adv* (*moderat*) moderately.

massiv *adj* solid ; (*Kritik*) strong.

Maßkrug (*pl* -krüge) *der* (*Süddt*) litre beer mug.

Maßnahme (*pl* -n) *die* measure.

Maßstab (*pl* -stäbe) *der* (*auf Landkarten*) scale ; (*Richtlinie*) standard ; **im ~ 1 : 25 000** to a scale of 1 : 25,000.

Mast (*pl* -en) *der* (*für Segel, Fahne*) mast.

Material (*pl* -ien) *das* material.

materialistisch *adj* (*Person, Einstellung*) materialistic.

materiell *adj* (*Bedürfnis, Schaden*) material ; (*Schwierigkeiten*) financial ; (*materialistisch*) materialistic.

Mathematik *die* mathematics (*sg*).

Matinee (*pl* -n) *die* matinee.

Matjes (*pl* -) *der* salted herring.

Matratze (*pl* -n) *die* mattress.

Matrose (*pl* -n) *der* sailor.

Matsch *der* (*Schlamm*) mud.

matt *adj* (*glanzlos*) matt ; (*müde*) weak.

Matte (*pl* -n) *die* mat.

Mauer (*pl* -n) *die* wall.

Mauerwerk *das* masonry.

Maul (*pl* Mäuler) *das* (*von Tieren*) mouth.

Maulwurf (*pl* -würfe) *der* mole.

Maurer, in (*mpl* -) *der, die* bricklayer.

Maus (*pl* Mäuse) *die* mouse.

Mausefalle (*pl* -n) *die* mousetrap.

Mautgebühr (*pl* -en) *die* (*Österr*) toll.

Mautstelle (*pl* -n) *die* (*Österr*) tollgate.

Mautstraße (*pl* -n) *die* (*Österr*) toll road.

maximal *adj* maximum. ◆ *adv* at most.

Maximum (*pl* Maxima) *das* maximum.

Mayo *die* (*fam*) mayonnaise.

Mayonnaise *die* → **Majonäse**.

Mechaniker, in (*mpl* -) *der, die* mechanic.

mechanisch *adj* mechanical. ◆ *adv* mechanically.

Mechanismus (*pl* -men) *der* mechanism.

meckern *vi* (*fam : Person*) to moan.

Mecklenburg-Vorpommern *nt* Mecklenburg-West Pomerania.

Medaille (*pl* -n) *die* medal.

Medien *pl* media.

Medikament (*pl* -e) *das* medicine ; **ein ~ gegen** a medicine for.

Meditation (*pl* -en) *die* meditation.

meditieren *vi* to meditate.

Medizin die medicine.
medizinisch adj (Bäder, Anwendungen) medicinal.
Meer (pl -e) das sea ; am ~ by the sea ; ans ~ fahren to go to the seaside.
Meerenge (pl -n) die straits (pl).
Meeresfrüchte pl seafood (sg).
Meeresspiegel der sea level ; 50 m über/unter dem ~ 50 m above/below sea level.
Meerrettich der horseradish.
Meerschweinchen (pl -) das guinea pig.
Meerwasser das seawater.
Mehl das (aus Getreide) flour.
Mehlschwitze (pl -n) die roux.
Mehlspeise (pl -n) die dish made from flour, eggs and milk, such as pasta, dumplings or pastries.
mehr komp → viel. ◆ det, pron, adv more ; es ist keiner ~ da there is no one left there ; vom Käse ist nichts ~ da there's nothing left of the cheese ; nie ~ never again.
mehrere adj & pron several.
mehrfach adv several times. ◆ adj multiple.
Mehrfahrten-Ausweis (pl -e) der multiple journey ticket.
Mehrheit (pl -en) die majority.
mehrmals adv several times.
mehrsprachig adj multilingual.
Mehrwertsteuer die VAT (Br), sales tax (Am).

Mehrzahl die (GRAMM) plural ; (Mehrheit) majority.
meiden (prät mied, pp gemieden) vt to avoid. ■ sich meiden ref to avoid each other.
Meile (pl -n) die mile.
mein, e det my.
meine, r, s ODER **meins** pron mine. ◆ det → mein.
meinen vt (denken, glauben) to think ; (sagen) to say ; (sich beziehen auf) to mean ; etw ironisch/wörtlich ~ to mean sthg ironically/literally ; das war nicht so gemeint it wasn't meant like that.
meinetwegen adv (wegen mir) because of me ; (von mir aus) as far as I'm concerned.
Meinung (pl -en) die opinion.
Meinungsumfrage (pl -n) die opinion poll.
Meise (pl -n) die tit.
Meißel (pl -) der chisel.
meist adv usually, mostly.
meiste superl → viel. ◆ adj & pron most ; die ~n (Leute) most people ; er hat das ~ Geld he has got the most money.
meistens adv usually, mostly.
Meister, in (mpl -) der, die (Titel) master ; (SPORT) champion.
Meisterschaft (pl -en) die (SPORT) championship.
Meisterwerk (pl -e) das masterpiece.
Meldefrist (pl -en) die (für Wettbewerb) period within which entries must be made.
melden vt to report. ■ sich melden ref (sich bemerkbar ma-

chen) to make itself felt ; *(am Telefon)* to answer ; **es meldet sich niemand** there's no answer.

Meldeschluss *der* closing date.

melken *(prät* **molk**, *pp* **gemolken)** *vt* to milk.

Melodie *(pl -n) die* melody.

Melone *(pl -n) die* melon.

Memoiren *pl* memoirs.

Menge *(pl -n) die (Anzahl)* quantity ; *(Vielzahl)* lot ; *(Menschenmenge)* crowd ; **eine (ganze) ~ Geld** *(relativ viel)* (quite) a lot of money ; **jede ~** *(fam : sehr viel)* loads of.

Mengenrabatt *(pl -e) der* bulk discount.

Mensa *(pl* **Mensen)** *die* university canteen.

Mensch *(pl -en) der (Lebewesen)* human (being) ; *(Person)* person ; **kein ~** no one ; **Mensch!** *(fam : wütend)* for heaven's sake! ; *(begeistert)* wow!

Menschenkenntnis *die* knowledge of human nature.

menschenleer *adj* deserted.

Menschenmenge *(pl -n) die* crowd.

Menschenrechte *pl* human rights.

Menschenwürde *die* human dignity.

Menschheit *die* humanity, mankind.

menschlich *adj (Körper, Irrtum)* human ; *(human)* humane.

Menstruation *(pl -en) die* menstruation.

Mentalität *(pl -en) die* mentality.

Menthol *das* menthol.

Menü *(pl -s) das (Essen)* set menu.

Merkblatt *(pl -blätter) das* leaflet.

merken *vt (erkennen)* to realize ; **sich** *(D)* **etw ~** *(sich einprägen)* to remember sthg.

Merkmal *(pl -e) das* feature.

merkwürdig *adj* strange.

Messbecher *(pl -) der* measuring jug.

Messe *(pl -n) die (Gottesdienst)* mass ; *(Ausstellung)* (trade) fair.

Messegast *(pl -gäste) der* visitor at a trade fair.

Messegelände *(pl -) das* exhibition centre.

messen *(präs* **misst**, *prät* **maß**, *pp* **gemessen)** *vt (Temperatur, Größe)* to measure ; *(in Maßangaben)* to be ; **sie misst 1,80 m** she's 1.80m tall.

Messer *(pl -) das* knife.

Messestadt *(pl -städte) die* town that hosts a major trade fair.

Messgerät *(pl -e) das* gauge.

Messing *das* brass.

Messung *(pl -en) die (Handlung)* measurement.

Metall *(pl -e) das* metal.

Meteorologe, in *(mpl -n) der, die* weather forecaster.

Meter *(pl -) der* metre ; **ein ~ achtundzwanzig** one metre twenty-eight ; **zwei ~ hoch/breit sein** to be two metres high/wide.

Metermaß *(pl -e) das* tape measure.

Methode *(pl -n) die* method.

Mettwurst *(pl -würste) die* soft, smoked pork and beef sausage, usually spread on bread.

Metzger, in (*mpl* -) *der, die* butcher.

Metzgerei (*pl* -en) *die* butcher's (shop).

MEZ (*abk für mitteleuropäische Zeit*) CET.

Mezzosopran *der* mezzosoprano.

MFG *abk* = **Mitfahrgelegenheit**.

mich *pron* (*Personalpronomen*) me ; (*Reflexivpronomen*) myself.

mied *prät* → **meiden**.

Miederwaren *pl* corsetry (*sg*).

Miene (*pl* -n) *die* expression.

mies *adj* (*fam*) awful ; **sich ~ fühlen** to feel awful.

Mietdauer *die* lease period.

Miete (*pl* -n) *die* (*für Wohnung*) rent ; (*für Auto*) rental.

mieten *vt* (*Wohnung*) to rent ; (*Auto*) to hire ; **sich** (*D*) **etw ~** to rent/hire sthg.

Mieter, in (*mpl* -) *der, die* tenant.

Mietfahrzeug (*pl* -e) *das* hire car.

Mietkauf (*pl* -käufe) *der* hire purchase.

Mietshaus (*pl* -häuser) *das* block of flats (*Br*), apartment building (*Am*).

Mietvertrag (*pl* -verträge) *der* lease.

Mietwagen (*pl* -) *der* hire car.

Mietwohnung (*pl* -en) *die* rented flat (*Br*), rented apartment (*Am*).

Migräne (*pl* -n) *die* migraine.

Mikrofon, Mikrophon (*pl* -e) *das* microphone.

Mikrowellenherd (*pl* -e) *der* microwave oven.

Milch *die* milk ; **fettarme ~** skimmed milk.

Milchbrötchen (*pl* -) *das* bread roll made with milk.

Milcheis *das* ice cream (*made with milk*).

Milchkaffee (*pl* -s) *der* milky coffee.

Milchmixgetränk (*pl* -e) *das* milk shake.

Milchprodukt (*pl* -e) *das* dairy product.

Milchpulver *das* powdered milk.

Milchreis *der* rice pudding.

Milchschokolade *die* milk chocolate.

mild *adj* mild. ◆ *adv* mildly.

Militär *das* military.

Milliarde (*pl* -n) *die* thousand million (*Br*), billion (*Am*).

Milligramm (*pl* -) *das* milligramme.

Milliliter (*pl* -) *der* millilitre.

Millimeter (*pl* -) *der* millimetre.

Million (*pl* -en) *die* million.

Millionär, in (*mpl* -e) *der, die* millionaire.

Milz (*pl* -en) *die* spleen.

Mimik *die* facial expression.

Minderheit (*pl* -en) *die* minority.

minderjährig *adj* minor, underage.

Minderjährige (*pl* -n) *der, die* minor.

minderwertig *adj* (*Qualität*) inferior.

Mindestalter *das* minimum age.

Mindestbetrag (*pl* -beträge) *der* minimum amount.

mindeste *adj* least.

mindestens *adv* (*wenigstens*) at least.

Mindesthaltbarkeitsdatum *das* best-before date.

Mindestpreis (*pl* -e) *der* minimum price.

Mine (*pl* -n) *die* (*von Bleistift*) lead ; (*von Kugelschreiber*) refill ; (*Bergwerk*) mine.

Mineral (*pl* -ien) *das* mineral.

Mineralbad (*pl* -bäder) *das* (*Kurort*) spa.

Mineralölsteuer *die* tax on oil.

Mineralwasser (*pl* -wässer) *das* mineral water.

Mini (*pl* -s) *der* (*fam : Rock*) miniskirt.

Minigolf *das* crazy golf.

Minigolfanlage (*pl* -n) *die* crazy golf course.

minimal *adj* minimal.

Minimum (*pl* Minima) *das* minimum.

Minirock (*pl* -röcke) *der* miniskirt.

Minister, in (*mpl* -) *der, die* minister.

Ministerium (*pl* Ministerien) *das* ministry.

Ministerpräsident, in (*mpl* -en) *der, die* (*von Bundesland*) title given to leader of government in the German federal states ; (*Premierminister*) prime minister.

minus *konj* & *adv* minus ; 10 Grad ~ minus 10 degrees.

Minus *das* (*Fehlbetrag*) deficit.

Minute (*pl* -n) *die* minute.

minutenlang *adv* for minutes.

Minze (*pl* -n) *die* mint.

Mio. *abk* = **Million.**

mir *pron* (*Personalpronomen*) me ; (*Reflexivpronomen*) : **ich habe es ~ so vorgestellt** I imagined it like this.

Mirabelle (*pl* -n) *die* mirabelle plum.

Mischbrot (*pl* -e) *das* bread made from a mixture of rye and wheat flour.

mischen *vt* (*Futtermischung, Salat*) to mix ; (*Karten*) to shuffle.

Mischung (*pl* -en) *die* mixture ; (*von Tee, Kaffee*) blend.

missachten *vt* (*Vorschrift, Regel*) to disregard.

Missachtung *die* (*von Vorschrift*) disregard.

Missbrauch (*pl* -bräuche) *der* abuse ; **'vor ~ wird gewarnt'** ≃ 'do not exceed the stated dose'.

missbrauchen *vt* to abuse.

Misserfolg (*pl* -e) *der* failure.

Missgeschick (*pl* -e) *das* mishap ; **mir ist ein kleines ~ passiert** I had a slight mishap.

Misshandlung (*pl* -en) *die* mistreatment.

misslingen (*prät* misslang, *pp* misslungen) *vt* to fail ; **das ist mir misslungen** I failed.

misst *präs* → **messen.**

misstrauen *vi* (+*D*) to mistrust.

Misstrauen *das* mistrust.

mi̱sstrauisch *adj* mistrustful.

Mi̱ssverständnis (*pl* -se) *das* misunderstanding.

mi̱ssverstehen (*prät* mi̱ssverstand, *pp* mi̱ssverstanden) *vt* to misunderstand.

Mi̱st *der* (*Dung*) dung, manure ; (*fam : Plunder, Blödsinn*) rubbish.

mi̱t *präp* (+D) **1.** (*zusammen*) with ; **er kommt ~ seiner Frau** he's coming with his wife ; **Kaffee ~ Zucker** coffee with sugar. **2.** (*Angabe von Instrument, Mittel*) with ; **~ dem Zug/Bus/Flugzeug** by train/bus/plane. **3.** (*Angabe von Umstand*) : **~ Verspätung eintreffen** to arrive late ; **~ Absicht** intentionally, on purpose. **4.** (*Angabe von Zeitpunkt*) at ; **~ 16 Jahren** at the age of 16.
◆ *adv* (*zusammen mit anderen*) too ; **sie war nicht ~ dabei** she wasn't there.

mi̱t|arbeiten *vi* to collaborate.

Mi̱tarbeiter, in (*mpl* -) *der, die* colleague.

mi̱t|bekommen *vt unr* (*verstehen*) to follow ; (*aufschnappen*) to hear.

mi̱t|bestimmen *vi* to have a say.

Mi̱tbestimmung *die* say.

Mi̱tbewohner, in (*mpl* -) *der, die* flatmate.

mi̱t|bringen *vt unr* to bring ; (*von Reise*) to bring back ; **jm etw ~** to bring sthg for sb.

Mi̱tbringsel (*pl* -) *das* souvenir.

mi̱teinander *adv* (*zusammen*) with each other.

mi̱t|erleben *vt* : **er hat den Krieg noch miterlebt** he lived through the war.

Mi̱tesser (*pl* -) *der* blackhead.

mi̱t|fahren *vi unr* ist to get a lift.

Mi̱tfahrgelegenheit (*pl* -en) *die* lift.

Mi̱tfahrzentrale (*pl* -n) *die agency which organizes lifts, passengers contributing to petrol costs.*

mi̱t|geben *vt unr* to give ; **jm etw ~** to give sb sthg.

Mi̱tgefühl *das* sympathy.

mi̱t|gehen *vi unr* ist (*mitkommen*) to go along.

Mi̱tglied (*pl* -er) *das* member.

Mi̱tgliedsausweis (*pl* -e) *der* membership card.

Mi̱tgliedsbeitrag (*pl* -beiträge) *der* membership fee.

mithi̱lfe *adv* (+G) → **Hilfe**.

mi̱t|kommen *vi unr* ist (*gemeinsam kommen*) to come along ; (*fam : folgen können*) to follow ; **kommst du mit?** are you coming?

Mi̱tleid *das* pity.

mi̱t|machen *vt* (*Kurs, Tätigkeit*) to take part in ; (*Schwierigkeiten*) to go through. ◆ *vi* (*sich beteiligen*) to take part.

mi̱t|nehmen *vt unr* to take ; **sich** (D) **etw ~** (*kaufen*) to get o.s. sthg ; **zum Mitnehmen** take away (*Br*), to go (*Am*).

Mi̱treisende (*pl* -n) *der, die* fellow traveller.

Mi̱tschüler, in (*mpl* -) *der, die* classmate.

mit|spielen *vi & vt* to play.

Mitspieler, in *(mpl -)* der, die *(bei Spiel)* player.

Mittag *(pl -e)* der *(Tageszeit)* midday ; *(12 Uhr)* noon ; **am ~** at midday ; **gegen ~** around midday ; **heute/gestern/morgen ~** at midday today/yesterday/tomorrow ; **zu ~ essen** to have lunch.

Mittagessen *(pl -)* das lunch.

mittags *adv* at midday.

Mittagspause *(pl -n)* die lunch break.

Mittagstisch der lunch.

Mitte *(pl -n)* die middle ; *(politisch)* centre ; **in der ~** in the middle ; **~ nächster Woche** the middle of next week ; **~ vierzig sein** to be in one's mid-forties.

mit|teilen *vt* : **jm etw ~** to inform sb of sthg. ▓ **sich mitteilen** *ref* to communicate.

Mitteilung *(pl -en)* die announcement.

Mittel *(pl -)* das *(Hilfsmittel)* aid ; *(zum Reinigen)* agent ; *(Medikament)* medicine ; **ein ~ gegen Grippe** a flu remedy.

Mittelalter das Middle Ages.

mittelalterlich *adj* medieval.

Mittelamerika *nt* Central America.

Mitteleuropa *nt* Central Europe.

Mittelgebirge *(pl -)* das low mountain range.

mittelmäßig *adj* (Spiel, Wetter) average. ◆ *adv* (spielen) averagely.

Mittelmeer das : **das ~** the Mediterranean (Sea).

Mittelohrentzündung *(pl -en)* die infection of the middle ear.

Mittelpunkt *(pl -e)* der centre ; **im ~ stehen** to be the centre of attention.

mittels *präp* (+G) *(amt)* by means of.

Mittelstreifen *(pl -)* der *(von Straße)* central reservation *(Br)*, median *(Am)*.

Mittelwelle die medium wave.

mitten *adv* in the middle ; **~ durch** through the middle of ; **~ in etw** *(A, D)* in the middle of sthg ; **~ in der Nacht** in the middle of the night.

Mitternacht die midnight ; **um ~** at midnight.

mittlere, r, s *adj* *(durchschnittlich)* average ; *(in der Mitte)* central.

mittlerweile *adv* *(inzwischen)* in the meantime.

Mittwoch *(pl -e)* der Wednesday ; → **Samstag**.

mittwochs *adv* on Wednesdays.

mixen *vt* *(Cocktail, Salatsoße)* to mix.

Mixer *(pl -)* der *(Gerät)* food mixer.

Möbel *pl* furniture *(sg)*.

Möbelwagen *(pl -)* der removal van *(Br)*, moving van *(Am)*.

mobil *adj* *(beweglich)* mobile.

Mobiliar das furniture.

Mobiltelefon *(pl -e)* das mobile phone.

möbliert *adj* furnished.

mochte *prät* → mögen.

möchte *präs* → mögen.

Mode (*pl* -n) *die* fashion.

Modehaus (*pl* -häuser) *das* fashion house.

Modell (*pl* -e) *das* model.

Modenschau (*pl* -en) *die* fashion show.

Moderator, torin (*mpl* -to- ren) *der, die* presenter.

modern *adj* (*modisch*) fashion- able ; (*jetzig*) modern.

modernisieren *vt* (*Haus, Be- trieb*) to modernize.

Modeschmuck *der* fashion jewellery.

Modezeitschrift (*pl* -en) *die* fashion magazine.

modisch *adj* fashionable.

Mofa (*pl* -s) *das* moped.

mögen (*präs* **mag**, *prät* **mochte**, *pp* **gemocht** ODER **mö- gen**) *vt* (*pp gemocht*) 1. (*gern ha- ben*) to like ; jn/etw gern ~ to like sb/sthg ; jn/etw nicht ~ not to like sb/sthg.
2. (*wollen*) : ich möchte ein Eis I would like an ice cream ; was möchten Sie, bitte? what would you like?
◆ *vi* (*pp mögen*) (*wollen*) : er möchte nach Hause he wants to go home.
◆ *aux* (*pp mögen*) 1. (*wollen*) : möchtest du mitkommen? would you like to come? ; sie mag nicht ins Kino gehen she doesn't want to go to the cinema.
2. (*hypothetisch*) : mag sein that may well be ; mag sein, dass sie noch anruft she may still call.

möglich *adj* & *adv* possible ; alles Mögliche everything pos- sible.

möglicherweise *adv* pos- sibly.

Möglichkeit (*pl* -en) *die* pos- sibility ; (*Gelegenheit*) oppor- tunity.

möglichst *adv* if possible ; kommt ~ schnell come as quickly as possible ; ~ viel as much as possible.

Mohammedaner, in (*mpl* -) *der, die* Muslim.

Mohn *der* (*Blume*) poppy ; (*Körner*) poppy seeds (*pl*).

Möhre (*pl* -n) *die* carrot.

Mohrenkopf (*pl* -köpfe) *der* *chocolate-covered marshmallow*.

Mokka (*pl* -s) *der* mocha, *strong coffee drunk in small cups*.

molk *prät* → melken.

Molkerei (*pl* -en) *die* dairy.

Moll *das* (MUS) minor.

mollig *adj* (*Person*) plump.

Moment (*pl* -e) *der* (*Augen- blick*) moment ; einen ~, bitte just a moment, please ; im ~ at the moment ; ~ mal! wait a mo- ment!

momentan *adj* present. ◆ *adv* at the moment.

Monarchie (*pl* -n) *die* mon- archy.

Monat (*pl* -e) *der* month ; die- sen ~ this month.

monatelang *adj* & *adv* for several months.

monatlich *adj* & *adv* monthly.

Monatsbinde (*pl* -n) *die* sani- tary towel.

Monatsgehalt (*pl* -gehälter) *das* monthly salary.

Monatskarte (*pl* -n) *die* monthly season ticket.

Monatsrate (*pl* -n) *die* monthly instalment.

Mönch (*pl* -e) *der* monk.

Mond (*pl* -e) *der* moon.

Mondfinsternis (*pl* -se) *die* eclipse of the moon.

Monitor (*pl* -e) *der* (*von Computer*) monitor.

monoton *adj* monotonous.

Montag (*pl* -e) *der* Monday ; → **Samstag.**

Montage (*pl* -n) *die* (*von Apparaten*) installation.

montags *adv* on Mondays.

Monteur, in (*mpl* -e) *der, die* engineer.

montieren *vt* (*anbringen*) to install.

Monument (*pl* -e) *das* monument.

Moor (*pl* -e) *das* bog.

Moos (*pl* -e) *das* (*Pflanze*) moss.

Moped (*pl* -s) *das* moped.

Moral *die* (*Ethik*) morals (*pl*).

moralisch *adj* moral.

Morast *der* quagmire.

Mord (*pl* -e) *der* murder.

Mörder, in (*mpl* -) *der, die* murderer.

morgen *adv* (*Tag nach heute*) tomorrow ; ~ **früh** tomorrow morning ; **bis ~!** see you tomorrow!

Morgen (*pl* -) *der* (*Tageszeit*) morning ; **am ~** in the morning ; **guten ~!** good morning! ; (*Vormittag*) : **gestern/heute ~** yesterday/this morning.

Morgengrauen *das* dawn.

morgens *adv* in the morning ; **früh ~** early in the morning ; **von ~ bis abends** from dawn till dusk.

morgig *adj* tomorrow's ; **der ~e Tag** tomorrow.

Morphium *das* morphine.

morsch *adj* rotten.

Mosaik (*pl* -en) *das* mosaic.

Moschee (*pl* -n) *die* mosque.

Mosel *die* Moselle.

Moselwein (*pl* -e) *der* white wine from the Moselle valley.

Moskau *nt* Moscow.

Moskito (*pl* -s) *der* mosquito.

Moskitonetz (*pl* -e) *das* mosquito net.

Moslem (*pl* -s) *der* Muslim.

Moslime (*pl* -n) *die* Muslim.

Mostrich *der* (*Norddt*) mustard.

Motel (*pl* -s) *das* motel.

Motiv (*pl* -e) *das* (*von Bild*) subject ; (*von Handlung*) motive.

motivieren *vt* (*Person*) to motivate.

Motor (*pl* -en) *der* engine ; **~ abstellen!** switch off engine!

Motorboot (*pl* -e) *das* motorboat.

Motorhaube (*pl* -n) *die* bonnet (*Br*), hood (*Am*).

Motoröl *das* engine oil.

Motorpanne (*pl* -n) *die* engine failure.

Motorrad (*pl* -räder) *das* motorcycle, motorbike.

Motorradfahrer, in (*mpl* -) *der, die* motorcyclist.

Motorradhelm (*pl* -e) *der* motorcycle helmet.

Motorroller (pl -) der (motor)scooter.

Motorschaden (pl -schäden) der engine trouble.

Motorsport der motor sport.

Motoryacht (pl -en) die motor yacht.

Motte (pl -n) die moth.

Motto (pl -s) das motto.

Möwe (pl -n) die seagull.

Mrd. abk = Milliarde.

Mücke (pl -n) die midge.

Mückenstich (pl -e) der midge bite.

müde adj (schläfrig) tired.

Müdigkeit die tiredness.

Mühe (pl -n) die effort ; sich (D) ~ geben to make an effort.

Mühle (pl -n) die (Gerät) grinder ; (Gebäude) mill ; (Spiel) board game for two players.

mühsam adj laborious.

Mull der (Material) muslin.

Müll der (Abfall) rubbish (Br), trash (Am) ; etw in den ~ werfen to throw sthg away.

Müllabfuhr die (Institution) cleansing department.

Mullbinde (pl -n) die gauze bandage.

Müllcontainer (pl -) der rubbish skip.

Mülldeponie (pl -n) die refuse disposal site.

Mülleimer (pl -) der bin.

Müllplatz (pl -plätze) der tip.

Müllschlucker (pl -) der refuse chute.

Mülltonne (pl -n) die dustbin (Br), garbage can (Am).

Müllwagen (pl -) der dustbin lorry (Br), garbage truck (Am).

multiplizieren vt to multiply.

Mumie (pl -n) die mummy.

Mumps der mumps.

München nt Munich.

Mund (pl Münder) der mouth ; halt den ~! (fam) shut up!

Mundart (pl -en) die dialect.

münden vi (Fluss) to flow ; der Rhein mündet in die Nordsee the Rhine flows into the North Sea.

Mundharmonika (pl -s) die mouthorgan.

mündlich adj oral. ◆ adv orally.

Mündung (pl -en) die mouth.

Mundwasser das mouthwash.

Münster (pl -) das minster.

munter adj (wach) wide awake ; (fröhlich) cheerful.

Münzautomat (pl -en) der slot machine.

Münze (pl -n) die coin ; 'nur mit ~n zahlen' 'coins only'.

Münzeinwurf (pl -würfe) der coin slot.

Münzfernsprecher (pl -) der payphone.

Münzgeld das : '~ einwerfen' 'insert coins'.

Münzrückgabe (pl -n) die coin return ; 'keine ~' 'no change given'.

Münz-Wäscherei (pl -en) die launderette.

Münzwechsler (pl -) der change machine.

murmeln vt & vi to murmur.

mürrisch adj surly.

Mus das puree.

Muschel (*pl* -n) *die* (*Schale*) shell ; (*Schalentier*) mussel.

Museum (*pl* Mus**ee**n) *das* museum.

Musical (*pl* -s) *das* musical.

Musik *die* music.

musikalisch *adj* musical.

Musikbox (*pl* -en) *die* (*Automat*) musical box.

Musiker, in (*mpl* -) *der, die* musician.

Musikinstrument (*pl* -e) *das* musical instrument.

Musikkassette (*pl* -n) *die* cassette, tape.

musizieren *vi* to play an instrument.

Muskat *das* nutmeg.

Muskel (*pl* -n) *der* muscle.

Muskelkater *der* stiff muscles (*pl*).

Muskelzerrung (*pl* -en) *die* pulled muscle.

Muskulatur *die* muscles (*pl*).

muskulös *adj* muscular.

Müsli (*pl* -s) *das* muesli.

muss *präs* → müssen.

müssen (*präs* muss, *prät* musste, *pp* müssen ODER gemusst) *aux* (*pp müssen*) 1. (*gezwungen sein*) must ; etw tun ~ to have to do sthg ; du musst aufstehen you must get up ; sie musste lachen she had to laugh ; er hat niesen ~ he had to sneeze. 2. (*nötig sein*) : der Brief muss noch heute weg the letter has to go today ; das müsste geändert werden that should be changed, that ought to be changed ; muss das sein? is that really necessary? 3. (*wahrscheinlich sein*) : sie muss bald hier sein she should be here soon, she ought to be here soon ; das müsste alles sein that should be all.

◆ *vi* (*pp* gemusst) 1. (*gezwungen sein*) to have to. 2. (*an einen Ort*) : ich muss ins Büro I have to go to the office. 3. (*fam : zur Toilette*) : ich muss mal I need to go to the loo.

Muster (*pl* -) *das* (*auf Stoff, auf Teppich, Schema*) pattern ; (*Probe*) sample.

Mut *der* (*Furchtlosigkeit*) courage.

mutig *adj* brave.

Mutter[1] (*pl* Mütter) *die* (*Person*) mother.

Mutter[2] (*pl* -n) *die* (*für Schrauben*) nut.

Muttersprache (*pl* -n) *die* mother tongue.

Muttertag (*pl* -e) *der* Mother's Day.

Mütze (*pl* -n) *die* cap.

MwSt. (*abk für Mehrwertsteuer*) VAT (*Br*), sales tax (*Am*).

mysteriös *adj* mysterious.

Mythos (*pl* Mythen) *der* myth.

N

N (*abk für Nord*) N.

na *interj* so ; ~ und? so? ; ~ gut! all right! ; ~ also! finally! ; ~ ja, well then.

Nabe (*pl* -n) *die* hub.

Nabel (*pl* -) *der* navel.

nach präp (+D) 1. *(zur Angabe einer Richtung)* to ; ~ **oben** up ; *(in Haus)* upstairs ; ~ **unten** down ; *(in Haus)* downstairs ; ~ **links/rechts abbiegen** to turn left/right ; ~ **Frankfurt** to Frankfurt ; ~ **Süden** south, southwards. 2. *(zeitlich)* after ; ~ **dem Essen** after the meal ; **einer ~ dem anderen** one after another ; ~ **Ihnen!** after you! ; **fünf ~ drei** five past three *(Br)*, five after three *(Am)*. 3. *(entsprechend)* according to ; ~ **Angaben der Polizei** according to the police.

■ **nach und nach** adv little by little.

Nachbar, in *(mpl -n)* der, die neighbour.

Nachbarschaft die neighbourhood.

nach|bestellen vt *(Ware)* to reorder.

nachdem konj after ; **je ~** depending on.

nach|denken vi unr to think ; ~ **über** *(+A)* to think about.

nachdenklich adj thoughtful.

nacheinander adv one after the other.

nach|folgen vi ist *(+D)* *(folgen)* to follow.

nach|forschen vi to investigate.

Nachforschungsantrag *(pl -anträge)* der lost or damaged mail claim form.

Nachfrage die *(Kaufwunsch)* demand.

nach|fragen vi to ask.

nach|geben vi unr *(+D)* *(bei Streit)* to give in.

Nachgebühr *(pl -en)* die excess postage.

nach|gehen vi unr ist *(Uhr)* to be slow ; *(folgen)* to follow ; **etw** *(D)* ~ *(untersuchen)* to investigate sthg.

nach|helfen vi unr *(helfen)* to help.

nachher adv *(später)* afterwards ; **bis ~!** see you later!

Nachhilfe die *(SCHULE)* extra tuition.

nach|holen vt *(Versäumtes)* to catch up on.

nach|kommen intr ist to come along later.

nach|lassen vi unr *(Qualität)* to drop off ; *(Regen)* to ease off ; *(Schmerz)* to ease.

nachlässig adj careless. ◆ adv carelessly.

nach|lösen vt : **eine Fahrkarte** ~ to buy a ticket on the train.

nach|machen vt *(nachahmen)* to copy.

Nachmittag *(pl -e)* der afternoon ; **am** ~ in the afternoon ; **gestern/heute/morgen** ~ yesterday/this/tomorrow afternoon.

nachmittags adv in the afternoon.

Nachnahme die : **per** ~ cash on delivery.

Nachname *(pl -n)* der surname.

Nachporto *(pl -s)* das excess postage.

nach|prüfen vt to check.

nach|rechnen vt to work out.

Nachricht (pl -en) die (Mitteilung) message ; (Neuigkeit) (piece of) news ; eine ~ hinterlassen to leave a message.
◾ **Nachrichten** pl news (sg).

nach|sagen vt to repeat.

Nachsaison die : in der ~ out of season.

nach|schauen vt (prüfen) to check.

nach|schicken vt to forward.

nach|schlagen vt unr (in Wörterbuch) to look up.

Nachschlüssel (pl -) der duplicate key.

nach|sehen vt unr (prüfen) to check. ◆ vi unr (+D) (hinterhersehen) to watch.

Nachsendeantrag (pl -anträge) der application for redirection of mail.

nach|senden vt to forward.

nach|sitzen vi unr (SCHULE) to have detention.

Nachspeise (pl -n) die dessert.

nächste, r, s superl → nahe. ◆ adj next ; der Nächste, bitte! next, please! ; ~s Mal/Jahr next time/year ; wie heißt die ~ Haltestelle, bitte? what's the next stop, please?

nächstens adv soon.

Nacht (pl Nächte) die night ; gestern ~ last night ; heute ~ tonight ; gute ~! good night! ; über ~ overnight.

Nachtausgang (pl -gänge) der night exit.

Nachtbus (pl -se) der night bus.

Nachtcreme (pl -s) die night cream.

Nachteil (pl -e) der disadvantage.

Nachteingang (pl -gänge) der night entrance.

Nachtflug (pl -flüge) der night flight.

Nachtfrost der overnight frost.

Nachtglocke (pl -n) die (bei Apotheke) night bell.

Nachthemd (pl -en) das nightshirt.

Nachtisch (pl -e) der dessert.

Nachtklub (pl -s) der nightclub.

Nachtleben das nightlife.

Nachtportier (pl -s) der night porter.

nachtragend adj unforgiving.

nachträglich adv belatedly.

Nachtruhe die sleep.

nachts adv at night.

Nachtschalter (pl -) der night desk.

Nachtschicht (pl -en) die night shift.

Nachttarif (pl -e) der economy rate.

Nachtzug (pl -züge) der night train.

Nachwirkung (pl -en) die aftereffect.

nach|zahlen vt (Porto, Fahrgeld) to pay extra.

nach|zählen vt (Porto, Fahrgeld) to check.

Nacken (pl -) der neck.

nackt adj & adv naked.

Nacktbadestrand (pl -strände) der nudist beach.
Nadel (pl -n) die needle.
Nagel (pl Nägel) der nail.
Nagelbürste (pl -n) die nailbrush.
Nagelfeile (pl -n) die nailfile.
Nagellack (pl -e) der nail varnish.
Nagellackentferner der nail varnish remover.
nageln vt (mit Hammer) to nail.
Nagelschere (pl -n) die nail scissors (pl).
nah adj & nahe.
nahe (komp näher, superl am nächsten) adj near ; ~ bei jm/etw near (to) sb/sthg.
Nähe die nearness ; in der ~ nearby ; in der ~ von near (to) ; aus der ~ from close up ; in unserer ~ near us.
nahe liegend adj (Frage) obvious.
nähen vt (Stoff) to sew ; (Wunde) to stitch.
Naherholungsgebiet (pl -e) das area close to a town, with recreational facilities.
näher kommen vi unr ist (+D) : wir sind uns näher gekommen we've become closer.
nähern : sich nähern ref (+D) to approach.
nahe stehen vi unr (+D) : jm ~ to be close to sb.
nahezu adv almost.
nahm prät → nehmen.
Nähmaschine (pl -n) die sewing machine.
Nähnadel (pl -n) die (sewing) needle.

Nahrung die food.
Nahrungsmittel (pl -) das food.
Naht (pl Nähte) die (in Stoff) seam ; (Narbe) scar.
Nahverkehr der local traffic ; der öffentliche ~ local public transport.
Nahverkehrszug (pl -züge) der local train.
Nähzeug das sewing kit.
naiv adj naive.
Name (pl -n) der name ; mein ~ ist... my name is... ; auf den ~n Braun reservieren to make a reservation in the name of Braun.
Namenstag (pl -e) der name day.
nämlich adv (weil) because ; (und zwar) namely.
nanu interj well!
Narbe (pl -n) die scar.
Narkose (pl -n) die anaesthetic.
naschen vt & vi to nibble.
Nase (pl -n) die nose ; ich hab' die ~ voll I've had enough ; meine ~ läuft my nose is running.
Nasenbluten das nosebleed.
Nasenloch (pl -löcher) das nostril.
Nasentropfen pl nose drops.
nass adj wet ; ~ machen to wet.
Nässe die wet ; überfrierende ~ icy patches ; '80 km/h bei ~' 'speed limit 80 km/h in wet weather'.
Nation (pl -en) die nation.
national adj national.

Nationalfeiertag (*pl* -e) *der* national day.

Nationalhymne (*pl* -n) *die* national anthem.

Nationalität (*pl* -en) *die* nationality.

Nationalmannschaft (*pl* -en) *die* national team.

Nationalsozialismus *der* national socialism.

NATO *die* NATO.

Natur *die* nature ; **in der freien ~** in the countryside.

natürlich *adv* (*selbstverständlich*) of course ; (*nicht künstlich*) naturally. ◆ *adj* natural.

Naturpark (*pl* -s) *der* nature reserve.

naturrein *adj* (*Saft*) pure.

Naturschutz *der* conservation ; **unter ~ stehen** to be legally protected.

Naturschutzgebiet (*pl* -e) *das* nature reserve.

naturtrüb *adj* (*Saft*) naturally cloudy.

n. Chr. (*abk für nach Christus*) AD.

Nebel (*pl* -) *der* fog ; **dichter ~** dense fog.

Nebelscheinwerfer (*pl* -) *der* (AUTO) fog lamp.

Nebelschlussleuchte (*pl* -n) *die* (AUTO) rear fog lights (*pl*).

neben *präp* (+D) (*an der Seite von*) next to ; (*außer*) apart from, as well as. ◆ *präp* (+A) (*an die Seite von*) next to.

nebenan *adv* next door.

Nebenausgang (*pl* -gänge) *der* side exit.

nebenbei *adv* (*gleichzeitig*) at the same time ; **~ gesagt** by the way.

nebendran *adv* (*fam*) next door.

nebeneinander *adv* next to each other.

Nebeneingang (*pl* -eingänge) *der* side entrance.

Nebenfach (*pl* -fächer) *das* (SCHULE) subsidiary subject.

nebenher *adv* (*arbeiten*) on the side.

Nebenkosten *pl* additional costs (*pl*).

Nebensache (*pl* -n) *die* trivial matter.

nebensächlich *adj* trivial.

Nebenstraße (*pl* -n) *die* side street.

Nebenwirkung (*pl* -en) *die* (MED) side effect.

neblig *adj* foggy.

neblig-trüb *adj* dull and overcast.

Neffe (*pl* -n) *der* nephew.

negativ *adj* negative. ◆ *adv* negatively.

Negativ (*pl* -e) *das* (FOTO) negative.

Negerkuss (*pl* -küsse) *der* chocolate-covered marshmallow.

nehmen (*präs* **nimmt**, *prät* **nahm**, *pp* **genommen**) *vt* 1. (*greifen, holen*) to take ; **sich** (D) **etw ~** to help o.s. to sthg. 2. (*benützen*) to take ; **den Bus/ Zug ~** to take the bus/train. 3. (*annehmen*) to take ; **sie hat die Stelle genommen** she has taken the job. 4. (*kaufen*) to take ; **ich nehme**

diese Schuhe I'll take these shoes.

5. *(Medikament, Droge)* to take.

6. *(Gast, Kind)* : jn zu sich ~ *(auf Dauer)* to take sb in ; *(für begrenzte Zeit)* to have sb to stay.

7. *(Nahrung)* : etw zu sich ~ to take sthg, to consume sthg.

8. *(einschätzen, auffassen)* : jn/ etw ernst ~ to take sb/sthg seriously ; es leicht/schwer ~ to take it lightly/hard.

9. *(verlangen)* : für etw fünf Mark ~ to charge five marks for sthg.

neidisch *adj* jealous.

nein *adv* no ; ~ danke! no thank you ; zu etw Nein sagen to say no to sthg.

Nektarine *(pl -n)* die nectarine.

Nelke *(pl -n)* die *(Blume)* carnation ; *(Gewürz)* cloves *(pl)*.

nennen *(prät* nannte, *pp* genannt) *vt (mit Namen)* to call ; *(als Beispiel)* to name.

Neonlicht *(pl -er)* das neon light.

Nepp *der* rip-off.

Nerv *(pl -en)* der nerve. ■ **Nerven** *pl* nerves ; jm auf die ~en gehen to get on sb's nerves.

nervös *adj* nervous.

Nest *(pl -er)* das *(von Vögeln)* nest.

nett *adj* nice. ◆ *adv* nicely ; sei so ~... would you mind...

netto *adv* net.

Netz *(pl -e)* das net ; *(Tasche)* string bag.

Netzanschluss *(pl* -schlüsse) *der* electrical connection.

Netzkarte *(pl -n)* die *(für Bus, Bahn)* rover ticket.

Netzplan *(pl* -pläne) *der (von Bus, Bahn)* route map.

neu *adj* new ; *(frisch)* fresh ; von ~em again ; das Neueste the latest ; was gibt's Neues? what's new?

Neubau *(pl* -ten) *der* new building.

neuerdings *adv* recently.

Neueröffnung *(pl* -en) die *(Zeremonie)* opening ; *(Geschäft)* new business.

Neugier *die* curiosity.

neugierig *adj* inquisitive. ◆ *adv* inquisitively.

Neuheit *(pl* -en) die *(Ware)* latest thing.

Neuigkeit *(pl* -en) die news.

Neujahr *das* New Year ; prost ~! Happy New Year!

neulich *adv* recently.

Neumond *der* new moon.

neun *num* nine ; → sechs.

neunte *num* ninth ; → sechste.

neunzehn *num* nineteen ; ~hundertneunundneunzig nineteen ninety nine ; → sechs.

neunzig *num* ninety ; → sechs.

neureich *adj* nouveau riche.

neurotisch *adj* neurotic.

Neuseeland *nt* New Zealand.

neutral *adj* neutral.

neuwertig *adj* nearly new.

nicht *adv* not ; ist das ~ schön? isn't that nice? ; ~ nur..., sondern auch... not only... but also ; du wusstest es schon länger, ~ wahr? you've known for a while, haven't you?; **es ist wunderbar, ~ wahr?** it's wonderful, isn't it?; **noch ~** not yet; **gar ~** not at all; **warum ~?** why not?

Nichte (*pl* -n) *die* niece.

Nichtraucher (*pl* -) *der (Person)* non-smoker; *(Abteil)* no-smoking compartment.

Nichtraucherzone (*pl* -n) *die* no-smoking area.

nichts *pron* nothing; **gar ~** nothing at all; **~ mehr** nothing more; **~ als** nothing but; **das macht ~** that doesn't matter; **~ zu danken** don't mention it.

Nichtschwimmer (*pl* -) *der (Person)* non-swimmer; *(Becken)* beginners' pool.

Nichtschwimmerbecken (*pl* -) *das* beginners' pool.

nichts sagend *adj* meaningless.

Nichtzutreffende *das* : '~s bitte streichen' *(amt)* 'delete as applicable'.

nicken *vi* to nod.

Nickerchen (*pl* -) *das* nap; **ein ~ machen** to have a nap.

nie *adv* never; **noch ~** never; **~ mehr** ODER **wieder** never again.

Niederlage (*pl* -n) *die* defeat.

Niederlande *pl* : **die ~** the Netherlands.

Niederländer, in (*mpl* -) *der, die* Dutchman (Dutchwoman).

niederländisch *adj* Dutch.

Niederländisch(e) *das* Dutch.

Niederlassung (*pl* -en) *die (Filiale)* branch.

Niederösterreich *nt* Lower Austria.

Niedersachsen *nt* Lower Saxony.

Niederschlag (*pl* -schläge) *der* precipitation.

niedlich *adj* cute.

niedrig *adj* low.

niemals *adv* never.

niemand *pron* nobody, no one; **das kann ~ anders als Karl-Heinz gewesen sein** that can only have been Karl-Heinz.

Niere (*pl* -n) *die* kidney.

nieseln *vimp* to drizzle.

Nieselregen *der* drizzle.

niesen *vi* to sneeze.

Niete (*pl* -n) *die (Los)* blank; *(aus Metall)* stud.

Nikolaus *der* Santa Claus *(who brings presents on 6th December)*.

NIKOLAUS

Tradition dictates that in Germany, Santa Claus (St Nicholas) visits children on 6 December to reward those who have been good over the past year and to punish the bad ones. If the children have been well-behaved, then the shoes or plates they leave out the night before are filled with sweets and small presents. If they have been bad, they face punishment from Nikolaus' companion "Knecht Ruprecht" (sometimes also known as "Krampus") who will be waiting for them with his stick.

Nikolaustag (*pl -e*) *der 6th of December when children receive presents from Santa Claus.*

Nikotin *das* nicotine.

nimmt *präs* → **nehmen**.

nirgends *adv* nowhere.

nirgendwo *adv* nowhere.

nirgendwohin *adv* nowhere.

Nische (*pl -n*) *die (Ecke)* corner.

Niveau (*pl -s*) *das* level.

nobel *adj (kostspielig)* luxurious.

Nobelpreis (*pl -e*) *der* Nobel Prize.

noch *adv* 1. *(zum Ausdruck von Dauer)* still ; **wir haben ~ Zeit** we still have time ; **er hat ~ nichts gesagt** he still hasn't said anything ; **ich habe ihn ~ letzten Monat besucht** I visited him only last month ; **~ nicht** not yet.
2. *(vorher)* : **schafft ihr das ~ bis Freitag?** do you think you'll manage it by Friday? ; **das muss ~ heute gemacht werden** it has to be done today at the latest ; **er kann ~ kommen** he may still come.
3. *(zur Verstärkung)* even ; **~ schneller** even quicker ; **es kann ~ so regnen, ...** however much it rains ...
4. *(dazu)* : **~ einen Kaffee, bitte!** another coffee, please! ; **ich muss ~ ein paar Einkäufe machen** I have to buy a few more things ; **passt das ~ in den Kofferraum?** will it fit in the boot? ; **wer ~?** who else?
5. *(zur Nachfrage)* again ; **wie war ~ sein Name?** what was his name again?
◆ *konj* → **weder**.

▓ **noch einmal** *adv* again.

nochmal *adv* again.

Nominativ (*pl -e*) *der (GRAMM)* nominative.

nonstop *adj (Flug)* nonstop.

Nord *nt* north.

Nordamerika *nt* North America.

Norddeutschland *nt* Northern Germany.

Norden *der* north ; **im ~** in the north ; **nach ~** north.

Nordeuropa *nt* Northern Europe.

Nordhang (*pl -hänge*) *der* north-facing slope.

Nordirland *nt* Northern Ireland.

nördlich *adj* northern. ◆ *präp* : **~ von** to the north of.

Nordosten *der* northeast.

Nordrhein-Westfalen *nt* North Rhine-Westphalia.

Nordsee *die* : **die ~** the North Sea.

Nordwesten *der* northwest.

nörgeln *vi* to moan.

Norm (*pl -en*) *die* standard.

normal *adj* normal. ◆ *adv* normally.

Normal *das (AUTO)* regular.

Normalbenzin *das (AUTO)* regular petrol *(Br)*, regular gas *(Am)*.

normalerweise *adv* normally.

Normalnull *das* : **über/unter ~** above/below sea level.

Norwegen *nt* Norway.

Not *die* need ; **in ~** in need ; **zur ~** if needs be.

Notar, in (*mpl* -e) *der, die* notary.

Notarzt, ärztin (*mpl* -ärzte) *der, die* emergency doctor.

Notausgang (*pl* -gänge) *der* emergency exit.

Notausstieg (*pl* -e) *der* emergency exit.

Notbremse (*pl* -n) *die* emergency brake.

Notdienst (*pl* -e) *der* : **~ haben** to be on call.

Notdienstapotheke (*pl* -n) *die* emergency chemist's (*Br*), emergency drugstore (*Am*).

Note (*pl* -n) *die* (*MUS*) note ; (*Zensur*) mark (*Br*), grade (*Am*).

Notfall (*pl* -fälle) *der* emergency ; **in dringenden Notfällen** in an emergency.

notfalls *adv* if necessary.

Nothaltebucht (*pl* -en) *die* (*auf Straße*) escape lane.

notieren *vt* to note down ; **sich** (*D*) **etw ~** to make a note of sthg.

nötig *adj* necessary ; **~ sein** to be necessary ; **etw ~ haben** to need sthg ; **wenn ~** if needs be.

Notiz (*pl* -en) *die* (*persönlich*) note ; (*in Zeitung*) notice ; **sich ~en machen** to take notes ; **keine ~ von jm nehmen** to take no notice of sb.

Notizblock (*pl* -blöcke) *der* notepad.

Notizbuch (*pl* -bücher) *das* notebook.

Notlage (*pl* -n) *die* crisis.

Notlandung (*pl* -en) *die* emergency landing.

Notruf (*pl* -e) *der* emergency call.

Notrufsäule (*pl* -n) *die* emergency phone.

Notrutsche (*pl* -n) *die* (*im Flugzeug*) escape chute.

Notsignal (*pl* -e) *das* distress signal.

notwendig *adj* necessary.

Notwendigkeit (*pl* -en) *die* necessity.

Nougat *der* nougat.

November (*pl* -) *der* November ; → **September**.

Nr. (*abk für Nummer*) no.

NRW *abk* = **Nordrhein-Westfalen**.

Nu : **im Nu** *adv* in an instant.

nüchtern *adj* (*nicht betrunken*) sober ; (*Magen*) empty.

Nudeln *pl* noodles.

Nudelsalat *der* pasta salad.

Nudelsuppe (*pl* -n) *die* noodle soup.

null *num* zero ; → **sechs**.

Null (*pl* -en) *die* zero ; **über/unter ~** above/below zero.

Nummer (*pl* -n) *die* number ; (*Größe*) size.

nummerieren *vt* to number.

Nummernschild (*pl* -er) *das* (*AUTO*) numberplate (*Br*), license plate (*Am*).

ⓘ ▬▬ **NUMMERNSCHILD**

German car registration numbers comprise two groups of letters followed by a sequence of numbers. The first group of letters indicates the town in which the car was registered (e.g. M for Munich or B for Berlin), whilst the remaining letters and numbers are the registration number proper. German numberplates also carry a round badge which indicates that the car has been passed as roadworthy.

---

nun adv now ; ~, wie steht's? well, how are things? ; es ist ~ mal so it's like this ; was ~? what now?

nur adv only, just ; was meint er ~? what does he mean? ; der Putz bröckelt ~ so the plaster is crumbling really badly ; das sagt er ~ so he's just saying that ; ich habe ~ noch 20 Mark I've only got 20 marks left.

Nürnberg nt Nuremberg.

Nuss (pl Nüsse) die nut.

Nussknacker (pl -) der nutcracker.

Nutte (pl -n) die (fam) hooker.

nutzen vt to use. ◆ vi to be of use ; jm ~ to be of use to sb ; nichts ~ to be of no use.

nützen vi = nutzen.

nützlich adj useful.

nutzlos adj useless.

Nylonstrumpf (pl -strümpfe) der nylon stocking.

O

O (abk für Ost) E.

ob konj whether ; ~..., ~ whether... or ; ~... oder nicht whether... or not ; als ~ as if ; so

tun als ~ to pretend (that) ; und ~! you bet!

OB (pl -s) der (abk für Oberbürgermeister) mayor (of large city).

Obazter (pl Obazten) der (Süddt) soft camembert, mashed together with onions and pepper.

obdachlos adj homeless.

Obdachlose (pl -n) der, die homeless person.

oben adv (räumlich) at the top ; (im Text) above ; das fünfte Buch von ~ the fifth book down ; nach ~ up ; von ~ bis unten from top to bottom ; ~ ohne topless.

Ober (pl -) der waiter.

obere, r, s adj upper.

oberflächlich adj superficial.

oberhalb präp (+G) above.

Oberhemd (pl -en) das shirt.

Oberkörper (pl -) der upper body.

Oberschenkel (pl -) der thigh.

oberste, r, s adj top.

Oberstufe die (SCHULE) three final years of secondary education.

Oberteil (pl -e) das (von Kleidung) top.

Oberweite (pl -n) die bust (measurement).

Objekt (pl -e) das object ; (Immobilie) property.

objektiv adj objective. ◆ adv objectively.

Objektiv (pl -e) das lens.

obligatorisch adj obligatory.

Oboe (pl -n) die oboe.

Obst das fruit.

Obstkuchen (*pl* -) *der* fruit flan.

Obstsalat (*pl* -e) *der* fruit salad.

obszön *adj* obscene.

obwohl *konj* although.

Ochse (*pl* -n) *der* ox.

Ochsenschwanzsuppe (*pl* -n) *die* oxtail soup.

ocker *adj* ochre.

od. *abk* = **oder**.

oder *konj* or ; du kommst doch mit, ~? you're going to come, aren't you? ; ~ aber or ; ~ auch or ; ~ so or something like that, entweder.

Ofen (*pl* Öfen) *der* (*zum Backen*) oven ; (*zum Heizen*) stove.

Ofenheizung *die* stove heating.

offen *adj* open ; (*Knopf*) undone ; (*Rechnung*) outstanding ; (*Haare*) down ; (*Bein, Haut*) grazed. ◆ *adv* (*unverschlossen*) open ; (*erkennbar, sich verhalten*) openly ; das Geschäft hat bis 6 Uhr ~ the shop is open until 6 ; ~e Weine wine by the glass/carafe ; auf ~em Meer on the open sea ; ~ gesagt quite honestly ; Tag der ~en Tür open day.

offenbar *adv* obviously.

offenbleiben *vi unr ist* (*Fenster*) to stay open ; (*Frage*) to remain unresolved.

offen lassen *vt unr* to leave open.

offensichtlich *adv* obviously.

offen stehen *vi unr* to be open ; die Welt steht ihm offen the world's his oyster.

öffentlich *adj* public. ◆ *adv* publicly, in public.

Öffentlichkeit *die* public.

offiziell *adj* official.

öffnen *vt* to open. ■ **sich öffnen** *ref* to open.

Öffnungszeiten *pl* opening hours.

oft (*komp* öfter, *superl* am öftesten) *adv* often ; wie ~? how often?

öfters *adv* from time to time.

ohne *präp* (+A) *konj* without ; ~ mich! count me out! ; ~ weiteres without hesitation ; ~ dass without.

Ohnmacht *die* (*Bewusstlosigkeit*) unconsciousness ; in ~ fallen to faint.

ohnmächtig *adj* (*bewusstlos*) unconscious ; ~ werden to faint.

Ohr (*pl* -en) *das* ear.

Ohrentropfen *pl* ear drops.

ohrfeigen *vt* : jn ~ to slap sb's face.

Ohrklipp (*pl* -s) *der* clip-on earring.

Ohrring (*pl* -e) *der* earring.

okay *adv* okay, OK.

Ökoladen (*pl* -läden) *der* wholefood store.

ökologisch *adj* ecological.

ökonomisch *adj* economic.

Oktan *das* octane.

Oktober (*pl* -) *der* October ; der 3. ~ *German national holiday commemorating reunification on 3 October 1990* ; → **September**.

Oktoberfest (*pl* -e) *das Munich beer festival.*

OKTOBERFEST

The world-famous Munich beer festival began in 1811 and is held every year, starting in mid-September and continuing for 16 days. Huge beer tents are erected where the local Munich breweries serve their beers in 1-litre measures along with typical Bavarian food. There are also fairground attractions, such as merry-go-rounds, roller coasters and shooting galleries.

Öl (*pl* -e) *das* oil.

ölen *vt* to oil.

ölig *adj* oily.

Olive (*pl* -n) *die* olive.

Olivenöl *das* olive oil.

Ölstand *der* oil level ; **den ~ prüfen** to check the oil.

Ölverbrauch *der* oil consumption.

Ölwechsel (*pl* -) *der* oil change.

Olympische Spiele *pl* Olympic Games.

Oma (*pl* -s) *die* (*fam*) grandma.

Omelette (*pl* -s) *die* omelette.

Omnibus (*pl* -se) *der* (*Linienbus*) bus ; (*Reisebus*) coach.

Onkel (*pl* -) *der* uncle.

OP (*pl* -s) *der* operating theatre (*Br*), OR (*Am*).

Opa (*pl* -s) *der* (*fam*) grandpa, grandad.

Openair-Konzert (*pl* -e) *das* open-air concert.

Oper (*pl* -n) *die* opera ; (*Gebäude*) opera house ; **in die ~ gehen** to go to the opera.

Operation (*pl* -en) *die* operation.

Operette (*pl* -n) *die* operetta.

operieren *vt* to operate on ; **sich ~ lassen** to have an operation.

Opernfestspiele *pl* opera festival (*sg*).

Opernhaus (*pl* -häuser) *das* opera house.

Opfer (*pl* -) *das* sacrifice.

Opposition *die* opposition.

Optik *die* optics (*sg*).

Optiker, in (*mpl* -) *der, die* optician.

optimal *adj* optimal, optimum. ◆ *adv* optimally.

optimistisch *adj* optimistic.

orange *adj* orange.

Orange (*pl* -n) *die* (*Frucht*) orange.

Orangensaft (*pl* -säfte) *der* orange juice ; **frisch gepresster ~** freshly-squeezed orange juice.

Orchester (*pl* -) *das* orchestra.

ordentlich *adj* (*Raum, Person*) tidy ; (*Leben, Beruf*) respectable ; (*Mahlzeit, Arbeit*) proper. ◆ *adv* (*aufräumen*) tidily.

ordinär *adj* (*Person, Witz*) crude.

ordnen *vt* to put in order.

Ordner (*pl* -) *der* (*für Akten*) folder ; (*Person*) steward.

Ordnung *die* order ; **in ~!** sure! ; **~ machen** to tidy up ; **der Fernseher ist nicht in ~** there's something wrong with the television.

Ordnungswidrigkeit (*pl* -en) *die* (*amt*) minor offence.

Oregano *der* oregano.

Organ (*pl* -e) *das* (*Körperteil*) organ.

Organisation (*pl* -en) *die* organization.

Organisator (*pl* -toren) *der* organizer.

Organisatorin (*pl* -nen) *die* organizer.

organisieren *vt* to organize.

Organismus (*pl* -ismen) *der* organism.

Orgasmus (*pl* Orgasmen) *der* orgasm.

Orgel (*pl* -n) *die* organ.

orientieren : **sich orientieren** *ref* (*in Richtung*) to orientate o.s. ; **sich ~ über** (+A) (*informieren*) to inform o.s. about.

Orientierungssinn *der* sense of direction.

original *adj* original.

Original (*pl* -e) *das* original.

Orkan (*pl* -e) *der* hurricane.

Ort (*pl* -e) *der* place ; **an ~ und Stelle** on the spot ; '**andere ~e**' 'other routes'.

Orthopäde, **Orthopädin** (*mpl* -n) *der*, *die* orthopaedic surgeon.

orthopädisch *adj* orthopaedic.

örtlich *adj* local.

Ortschaft (*pl*-e n) *die* village ; **geschlossene ~** built-up area.

ortsgespräch (*pl* -e) *das* local call.

ortskundig *adj* ; **ein ~er** **Führer** a guide with local knowledge.

Ortsmitte *die* centre.

Ortsnetz (*pl*-e) *das* exchange.

Ortstarif (*pl* -e) *der* local rate.

Ortszeit (*pl* -en) *die* local time.

öS *abk* = **österreichischer Schilling**.

Ost *nt* east.

Ostdeutschland *nt* East Germany.

Osten *der* east ; **im ~** in the east ; **nach ~** east.

Osterei (*pl* -er) *das* Easter egg.

Osterhase (*pl* -n) *der* Easter bunny.

OSTERHASE

At Easter, Germans give each other not only chocolate Easter eggs, but also painted, boiled eggs. Tradition has it that these, together with chocolate rabbits and other sweets, are brought for children by the Easter bunny, who hides them in the garden, the barn, the park or anywhere around the house. On Easter day, the children must then hunt for their eggs.

Ostermontag (*pl*-e) *der* Easter Monday.

Ostern (*pl* -) *nt* Easter ; **zu ~** at Easter ; **frohe ~!** Happy Easter!

Österreich *nt* Austria.

Österreicher, **in** (*mpl* -) *der*, *die* Austrian.

österreichisch *adj* Austrian.

Ostersonntag (*pl* -e) *der* Easter Sunday.

Osteuropa *nt* Eastern Europe.

Ostküste (*pl* -n) *die* east coast.

östlich *adj* eastern. ◆ *präp* : ~ **von** to the east of.

Ostsee *die* : **die** ~ the Baltic (Sea).

oval *adj* oval.

Ozean (*pl* -e) *der* ocean.

Ozon *das* ozone.

Ozonloch *das* hole in the ozone layer.

P

paar *adj* few ; **ein** ~ a few.

Paar (*pl* -e) *das* (*zwei Personen*) couple ; (*zwei Dinge*) pair ; **ein** ~ **Socken** a pair of socks.

paarmal *adv* : **ein** ~ → **Mal**.

Pacht (*pl* -en) *die* (*Vertrag*) lease ; (*Geld*) rent.

Päckchen (*pl* -) *das* (*in Post*) small parcel ; (*Packung*) pack.

packen *vt* to pack ; (*fassen*) to seize.

Packpapier *das* brown paper.

Packung (*pl* -en) *die* (*für Waren*) packet ; (*Kosmetik*) beauty pack.

Packungsbeilage (*pl* -n) *die* (MED) enclosed information ; **'lesen Sie die** ~**'** 'please read the enclosed information'.

Packungsrückseite (*pl* -n) *die* back of the packet.

Pädagogik *die* education.

pädagogisch *adj* educational.

Paddel (*pl* -) *das* paddle.

Paddelboot (*pl* -e) *das* canoe.

paddeln *vi* to paddle.

Paket (*pl* -e) *das* (*Postpaket*) parcel ; (*Packung*) packet.

Paketannahme (*pl* -n) *die* (*Schalter*) counter dealing with parcels to be sent.

Paketausgabe (*pl* -n) *die* (*Schalter*) counter from which parcels may be collected.

Paketkarte (*pl* -n) *die* form showing sender and addressee, to be filled in when sending a parcel.

Pakistan *nt* Pakistan.

Palast (*pl* Paläste) *der* palace.

Palatschinken *der* stuffed pancakes.

Palme (*pl* -n) *die* palm.

Palmsonntag *der* Palm Sunday.

Pampelmuse (*pl* -n) *die* grapefruit.

Paniermehl *das* breadcrumbs (*pl*).

paniert *adj* in breadcrumbs, breaded.

Panik *die* panic.

panisch *adj* (*Reaktion*) panic-stricken ; ~**e Angst vor etw** (*D*) **haben** to be terrified of sthg.

Panne (*pl* -n) *die* (*mit Auto*) breakdown ; (*Fehler*) technical hitch ; **ich hatte eine** ~ **auf der Autobahn** my car broke down on the motorway.

Pannendienst (*pl* -e) *der* breakdown service.

Pannenhilfe *die* breakdown service.

Pantoffel (*pl* -n) *der* slipper.

Pantomime (*pl* -n) *die (Aufführung)* mime.

Panzer (*pl* -) *der (Fahrzeug)* tank ; *(von Tier)* shell.

Papa (*pl* -s) *der (fam)* dad.

Papagei (*pl* -en) *der* parrot.

Papier (*pl* -e) *das* paper. ■ **Papiere** *pl (Ausweise)* papers, documents.

Papiergeld *das* paper money.

Papierkorb (*pl* -körbe) *der* wastepaper basket *(Br)*, wastebasket *(Am)*.

Papiertaschentuch (*pl* -tücher) *das* paper handkerchief.

Papierwaren *pl* stationery *(sg)*.

Pappbecher (*pl* -) *der* paper cup.

Pappe (*pl* -n) *die* cardboard.

Pappkarton (*pl* -s) *der* cardboard box.

Paprika (*pl* -s) *der (Gemüse)* pepper ; *(Gewürz)* paprika.

Papst (*pl* Päpste) *der* pope.

Parade (*pl* -n) *die (Umzug)* parade.

Paradeiser (*pl* -) *der (Österr)* tomato.

paradiesisch *adj* heavenly.

Paragliding *das* paragliding.

Paragraf, Paragraph (*pl* -en) *der* paragraph.

parallel *adj* & *adv* parallel.

Paranuss (*pl* -nüsse) *die* brazil nut.

parat *adj* & *adv* ready.

Pärchen (*pl* -) *das (Liebespaar)* couple.

Pardon *interj* sorry.

Parfüm (*pl* -s) *das* perfume.

Parfümerie (*pl* -n) *die* perfumery.

parfümfrei *adj* unscented.

Pariser (*pl* -) *der (fam : Kondom)* rubber.

Park (*pl* -s) *der* park.

Parka (*pl* -s) *der, die* parka.

Park-and-Ride-System *das* park and ride system.

Parkanlage (*pl* -n) *die* park.

Parkdauer *die* : ~ 2 Stunden parking restricted to 2 hours.

Parkdeck (*pl* -s) *das* level *(of multi-storey car park)*.

parken *vt* & *vi* to park ; falsch ~ to park wrongly ; 'Parken verboten' 'no parking'.

Parkett (*pl* -s ODER -e) *das (Fußboden)* parquet ; *(in Zuschauerraum)* stalls *(Br)*, parquet *(Am)*.

Parkgebühr (*pl* -en) *die* parking fee.

Parkhaus (*pl* -häuser) *das* multi-storey car park.

Parkhöchstdauer *die* : ~ 1 Stunde maximum stay 1 hour.

Parklücke (*pl* -n) *die* parking space.

Parkmöglichkeit (*pl* -en) *die* parking space.

Parkplatz (*pl* -plätze) *der* car park *(Br)*, parking lot *(Am)*.

Parkscheibe (*pl* -n) *die* parking disc.

Parkschein (*pl* -e) *der* parking ticket.

Parkuhr (*pl* -en) *die* parking meter.

Parkverbot (*pl* -e) *das (Verbot)* parking ban ; *(Stelle)* no-parking zone.

Parlament (*pl* -e) *das* parliament.

Parmesan *der* parmesan (*cheese*).

Partei (*pl* -en) *die* party.

Parterre *das* ground floor; **im ~** on the ground floor.

Partie (*pl* -n) *die* (*Teil*) part; (*Spiel*) game.

Partner, in (*mpl* **Partner**) *der, die* partner.

Partnerschaft (*pl* -en) *die* (*zwischen Personen*) partnership; (*zwischen Städten*) twinning.

Partnerstadt (*pl* -städte) *die* twin town.

Party (*pl* -s) *die* party.

Pass (*pl* Pässe) *der* (*Dokument*) passport; (*Straße*) pass.

Passage (*pl* -n) *die* (*Einkaufspassage*) arcade; (*Textabschnitt, Reise*) passage.

Passagier (*pl* -e) *der* passenger; **blinder ~** stowaway.

Passagierschiff (*pl* -e) *das* passenger ship.

Passamt (*pl* -ämter) *das* passport office.

Passant, in (*mpl* -en) *der, die* passerby.

Passbild (*pl* -er) *das* passport photo.

passen *vi* (*Termin*) to be suitable; (*in Größe, Form*) to fit; (*bei Spiel*) to pass; **Freitag passt mir nicht** Friday doesn't suit me; **~ dir die Schuhe?** do the shoes fit you?; **zu etw ~** to go (well) with sthg; **zu jm ~** to be suited to sb; **das könnte dir so ~!** you'd like that, wouldn't you?

passend *adj* (*Farbe*) matching; **ein ~er Schlüssel** a key that fits; **haben Sie es ~?** do you have the right change?

Passfoto (*pl* -s) *das* passport photo.

passieren *vi ist* to happen; **mir ist was sehr Unangenehmes passiert** something very unpleasant happened to me; **ist etwas passiert?** (*bei Unfall*) did sb get hurt?; **was ist passiert?** what happened?

Passionsspiele *pl* : **die ~ von Oberammergau** the Oberammergau passion plays.

ⓘ **PASSIONSSPIELE**

The Oberammergau passion plays, in which the suffering and death of Christ is performed by amateur actors, are the most famous in the world. They started in 1633, during the plague, and take place every ten years, with over 1,000 locals taking part in the performances.

passiv *adj* passive.

Passkontrolle (*pl* -n) *die* passport control.

Paste (*pl* -n) *die* (*Masse*) paste.

Pastell (*pl* -e) *das* pastel.

Pastete (*pl* -n) *die* (*aus Teig*) pie; (*Aufstrich*) paste.

Pastor (*pl* -toren) *der* (*katholisch*) priest; (*evangelisch*) vicar.

Pastorin (*pl* -nen) *die* (*evangelisch*) vicar.

Pate (*pl* -n) *der* (*Patenonkel*) godfather.

Patient, in (*mpl* -en) *der, die* patient.

Patin (*pl* -nen) *die* godmother.

Patrone (*pl* -n) *die* cartridge.

Pauke (*pl* -n) *die* kettledrum.

pauschal *adj* (*Betrag, Preis*) total ; (*Kritik, Urteil*) general.

Pauschale (*pl* -n) *die* flat rate.

Pauschalpreis (*pl* -e) *der* all-inclusive price.

Pauschalreise (*pl* -n) *die* package holiday.

Pauschaltarif (*pl* -e) *der* flat rate.

Pause (*pl* -n) *die* break ; (*in Theater, Konzert*) interval.

pausenlos *adj* & *adv* non-stop.

Pavillon (*pl* -s) *der* (*in Park*) bandstand.

Pazifik *der* Pacific.

Pazifische Ozean *der* : **der ~** the Pacific Ocean.

PC (*pl* -s) *der* PC.

Pech *das* (*Unglück*) bad luck ; **~ haben** to be unlucky.

Pedal (*pl* -e) *das* pedal.

pedantisch *adj* (*Person*) pedantic. ◆ *adv* pedantically.

Peeling (*pl* -s) *das* (*Kosmetikartikel*) face pack.

peinlich *adj* (*unangenehm*) embarrassing ; **es war mir ~** I felt embarrassed.

Pellkartoffeln *pl* boiled unpeeled potatoes.

Pelz (*pl* -e) *der* fur.

Pelzmantel (*pl* -mäntel) *der* fur coat.

Pendelverkehr *der* commuter traffic.

Pendler, in (*mpl* -) *der, die* commuter.

penetrant *adj* (*Person*) insistent ; (*Geschmack, Geruch*) penetrating.

Penis (*pl* -se) *der* penis.

Penizillin *das* penicillin.

Pension (*pl* -en) *die* (*Hotel*) guesthouse ; (*Rente*) pension ; (*Ruhestand*) retirement ; **in ~ sein** to be retired.

PENSION

A "Pension" is a family guesthouse which usually has only a few rooms. Whilst the accommodation is often more basic than in a hotel, guests are normally welcomed into the host family, getting the opportunity to learn about the local culture.

pensionieren *vt* to pension off.

Pensionsgast (*pl* -gäste) *der* guest.

Peperoni (*pl* -) *die* chili pepper.

per *präp* (+A) by ; (*amt* : *pro*) per ; **~ Luftpost** (by) airmail.

perfekt *adj* perfect.

Pergamentpapier *das* greaseproof paper.

Periode (*pl* -n) *die* period.

Perle (*pl* -n) *die* (*aus Muschel*) pearl ; (*aus Holz, Glas*) bead.

Perlenkette (*pl* -n) *die* pearl necklace.

perplex *adj* stunned.

Person (*pl* -en) *die* person ; (*in Drama, Roman*) character.

Personal *das* staff.

Personalausweis *(pl -e) der* identity card.

Personalausweisnummer *(pl -n) die* identity card number.

Personalien *pl* personal details *(pl)*.

Personalpronomen *(pl -pronomina) das* personal pronoun.

Personenkraftwagen *(pl-)* *der (amt)* car *(Br)*, automobile *(Am)*.

Personenzug *(pl -züge) der (amt)* passenger train.

persönlich *adj* personal. ◆ *adv* personally.

Persönlichkeit *(pl -en) die* personality.

Perspektive *(pl -n) die (optisch)* perspective ; *(Möglichkeit)* prospect.

Perücke *(pl -n) die* wig.

pessimistisch *adj* pessimistic.

Petersilie *die* parsley.

Petroleum *das* paraffin *(Br)*, kerosene *(Am)*.

Pf. *abk* = Pfennig.

Pfad *(pl -e) der* path.

Pfadfinder, in *(mpl -) der, die* boy scout (girl guide).

Pfahl *(pl Pfähle) der* post.

Pfand *das (von Flaschen)* deposit.

Pfandflasche *(pl -n) die* returnable bottle.

Pfandleihhaus *(pl -häuser) das* pawnbroker's.

Pfandrückgabe *die* counter for returning bottles.

Pfanne *(pl -n) die (zum Braten)* frying pan ; **beschichtete ~** nonstick frying pan.

Pfannengericht *(pl -e) das* fried dish.

Pfannkuchen *(pl -) der* pancake.

Pfarrer *(pl -) der (katholisch)* priest ; *(evangelisch)* vicar.

Pfarrerin *(pl -n en) die (evangelisch)* vicar.

Pfeffer *der* pepper.

Pfefferkuchen *(pl -) der* gingerbread.

Pfefferminztee *der* peppermint tea.

pfeffern *vt (mit Pfeffer)* to season with pepper ; *(fam : werfen)* to fling.

Pfeife *(pl -n) die (zum Pfeifen)* whistle ; *(zum Rauchen)* pipe ; **~ rauchen** to smoke a pipe.

pfeifen *(prät pfiff, pp gepfiffen) vi* to whistle.

Pfeil *(pl -e) der* arrow ; **'folgen Sie dem gelben ~'** 'follow the yellow arrow'.

Pfeiler *(pl -) der* pillar.

Pfennig *(pl -e) der* pfennig.

Pferd *(pl -e) das (Tier)* horse.

Pferderennen *(pl -) das* horse race.

Pferdeschwanz *(pl-schwänze) der (Frisur)* ponytail.

Pferdesport *der* equestrian sport.

Pferdestärke *(pl -n) die (amt)* horsepower.

pfiff *prät* → pfeifen.

Pfiff *(pl -e) der (Ton)* whistle.

Pfifferling *(pl -e) der* chanterelle *(mushroom)*.

Pfingsten (*pl* -) *nt* Whit.

Pfingstmontag (*pl* -e) *der* Whit Monday.

Pfingstsonntag (*pl* -e) *der* Whit Sunday.

Pfirsich (*pl* -e) *der* peach.

Pflanze (*pl* -n) *die* plant.

pflanzen *vt* to plant.

pflanzlich *adj* vegetable.

Pflaster (*pl* -) *das* (*Verband*) plaster ; (*auf Straße*) road surface.

Pflaume (*pl* -n) *die* plum.

Pflaumenkuchen (*pl* -) *der* plum tart.

Pflaumenmus *das* plum jam.

Pflege *die* care ; (*von Kranken*) nursing.

pflegeleicht *adj* (*Material*) easycare.

pflegen *vt* to care for ; (*Kranke*) to nurse ; (*Garten*) to tend. ■ **sich pflegen** *ref* to take care with one's appearance.

Pflegepersonal *das* nursing staff.

Pfleger, in (*mpl* -) *der, die* (*in Krankenhaus*) nurse.

Pflicht (*pl* -en) *die* (*Aufgabe*) duty.

pflichtbewusst *adj* conscientious.

Pflichtversicherung (*pl* -en) *die* compulsory insurance.

pflücken *vt* to pick.

Pforte (*pl* -n) *die* gate.

Pförtner, in (*mpl* -) *der, die* porter.

Pfote (*pl* -n) *die* paw.

pfui *interj* yuck!

Pfund (*pl* -e) *das* pound ; (*Gewichtseinheit*) = 500 g, ≃ pound.

Pfütze (*pl* -n) *die* puddle.

Phantasie (*pl* -n) *die* → Fantasie.

phantastisch *adj* → fantastisch.

Phase (*pl* -n) *die* phase.

Philharmoniker *pl* (*Orchester*) philharmonic.

Philosoph, in (*mpl* -en) *der, die* philosopher.

Philosophie (*pl* -n) *die* philosophy.

Photo = Foto.

Phrase (*pl* -n) *die* (*abw*) cliché ; **leere ~n** empty words.

Physik *die* physics (*sg*).

physikalisch *adj* physical.

Physiker, in (*mpl* -) *der, die* physicist.

physisch *adj* physical.

Pianist, in (*mpl* -en) *der, die* pianist.

Pickel (*pl* -) *der* (*auf Haut*) spot ; (*Gerät*) pickaxe ; (*für Eis*) ice axe.

Picknick (*pl* -s) *das* picnic ; **ein ~ machen** to have a picnic.

Pik (*pl* -) *das* spades (*pl*).

pikant *adj* & *adv* spicy.

Pilger, in (*mpl* -) *der, die* pilgrim.

Pilgerfahrt (*pl* -en) *die* pilgrimage.

Pille (*pl* -n) *die* pill ; **die ~ nehmen** to be on the pill.

Pilot, in (*mpl* -en) *der, die* pilot.

Pils (*pl* -) *das* Pils (*lager*).

Pilz (pl -e) der (essbar) mushroom ; (giftig) toadstool ; (fam : Hauptpilz) fungal infection.

PIN (pl -s) (abk für persönliche Identifikationsnummer) die PIN (number).

pink adj pink.

pinkeln vi (fam) to pee.

Pinsel (pl -) der brush.

Pinzette (pl -n) die tweezers (pl).

Pistazie (pl -n) die pistachio.

Piste (pl -n) die (zum Skifahren) piste, run ; (Landebahn) runway.

Pistole (pl -n) die pistol.

Pizza (pl -s ODER Pizzen) die pizza.

Pizzaservice (pl -s) der pizza delivery service.

Pizzeria (pl -s) die pizzeria.

Pkw (pl -s) der = Personenkraftwagen.

Plakat (pl -e) das poster.

Plakette (pl -n) die sticker.

Plan (pl Pläne) der plan ; (Karte) map.

Plane (pl -n) die tarpaulin.

planen vt to plan.

Planet (pl -en) der planet.

Planetarium (pl -tarien) das planetarium.

planmäßig adj (Abfahrt) scheduled. ◆ adv (abfahren) on time.

Planschbecken (pl -) das paddling pool (Br), wading pool (Am).

planschen vi to splash about.

Planung (pl -en) die (Handlung) planning.

Plastik[1] das (Material) plastic.

Plastik[2] (pl -en) die (Skulptur) sculpture.

Plastiktüte (pl -n) die plastic bag.

Platin das platinum.

platt adj flat ; ~ sein (fam) to be gobsmacked ; einen Platten haben (fam) to have a flat.

Platt(deutsch) das Low German (dialect spoken in North Germany).

Platte (pl -n) die (zum Servieren) plate ; (aus Stein) slab ; (aus Metall, Glas) sheet ; (Schallplatte) record ; (von Herd) ring.

Plattenspieler (pl -) der record player.

Plattfüße pl flat feet.

Platz (pl Plätze) der (verfügbar) space, room ; (Stelle, Rang) place ; (Sitzplatz) seat ; (angelegt) square ; jm ~ machen to make room for sb ; nehmen Sie ~! sit down! ; viel ~ haben to have a lot of room ; auf die Plätze, fertig, los! on your marks, get set, go!

Platzanweiser, in (mpl -) der, die usher (usherette).

Plätzchen (pl -) das biscuit (Br), cookie (Am).

platzen vi ist (Reifen) to burst ; (fam : Termin) to fall through ; (Scheck) to bounce.

Platzkarte (pl -n) die (in Zug) seat reservation.

Platzreservierung (pl -en) die seat reservation.

Platzwunde (pl -n) die cut.

plaudern vi (sprechen) to chat.

pleite adj : ~ sein to be broke.

Plombe (*pl* -n) *die (in Zahn)* filling.

plombieren *vt (Zahn)* to fill.

plötzlich *adj* sudden. ◆ *adv* suddenly.

plump *adj (schwerfällig)* clumsy.

plumpsen *vi ist (fam)* to crash.

plus *konj* & *adv* plus ; **fünf Grad ~** plus five degrees.

PLZ *abk* = **Postleitzahl**.

Po (*pl* -s) *der (fam)* bottom.

Podest (*pl* -e) *das* pedestal.

Podium (*pl* **Podien**) *das* podium.

Podiumsdiskussion (*pl* -en) *die* panel discussion.

Poesie *die (Dichtung)* poetry.

Pointe (*pl* -n) *die* punchline.

Pokal (*pl* -e) *der (SPORT)* cup.

Poker *der* ODER *das* poker.

pokern *vi (Poker spielen)* to play poker.

Pol (*pl* -e) *der* pole.

Polen *nt* Poland.

Police (*pl* -n) *die* policy.

polieren *vt* to polish.

Politesse (*pl* -n) *die* traffic warden.

Politik *die (von Land, Stadt)* politics *(pl)* ; *(Taktik)* policy.

Politiker, in (*mpl* -) *der, die* politician.

politisch *adj* political.

Politur (*pl* -en) *die* polish.

Polizei *die* police *(pl)*.

Polizeibeamte (*pl* -n) *der* police officer.

Polizeibeamtin (*pl* -nen) *die* police officer.

polizeilich *adj* police ; **~es Kennzeichen** registration number *(Br)*, license number *(Am)*.

Polizeirevier (*pl* -e) *das* police station.

Polizeistunde (*pl* -n) *die* closing time.

Polizeiwache (*pl* -n) *die* police station.

Polizist, in (*mpl* -en) *der, die* police officer.

Pollen (*pl* -) *der* pollen.

Pollenflug (*pl* -flüge) *der* pollen count.

Polo *das* polo.

Polster (*pl* -) *das (zum Sitzen)* cushion ; *(Schulterpolster)* shoulder pad.

Polstermöbel *pl* upholstered furniture *(sg)*.

Polterabend (*pl* -e) *der* celebration usually held on evening before wedding, when crockery is broken to bring good luck.

Pommes *pl (fam)* chips *(Br)*, French fries *(Am)*.

Pommes frites *pl* chips *(Br)*, French fries *(Am)*.

Pony (*pl* -s) *das (Tier)* pony. ◆ *der (Frisur)* fringe *(Br)*, bangs *(pl) (Am)*.

Pool (*pl* -s) *der (Schwimmbecken)* pool.

Popmusik *die* pop music.

populär *adj (beliebt)* popular.

porös *adj* porous.

Porree *der* leek.

Portal (*pl* -e) *das* portal.

Portmonee, Portemonnaie (*pl* -s) *das* purse.

Portier (*pl* -s) *der* porter.

Portion (*pl* -en) *die* portion.

Porto (*pl* -s) *das* postage.

portofrei *adj* freepost.

Porträt (*pl* -s) *das* portrait.

Portugal *nt* Portugal.

Portugiese (*pl* -n) *der* Portugiese (man) ; **die ~n** the Portuguese.

Portugiesin (*pl* -nen) *die* Portuguese (woman).

portugiesisch *adj* Portuguese.

Portugiesisch(e) *das* Portuguese.

Portwein (*pl* -e) *der* port.

Porzellan (*pl* -e) *das* china.

Posaune (*pl* -n) *die* trombone.

Position (*pl* -en) *die* position.

positiv *adj* positive. ◆ *adv* positively.

Post *die* post ; *(Institution, Gebäude)* post office ; **etw mit der ~ schicken** to send sthg by post ; **zur ~ gehen** to go to the post office.

Postamt (*pl* -ämter) *das* post office.

Postanweisung (*pl* -en) *die* postal order *(Br)*, money order *(Am)*.

Postbote (*pl* -n) *der* postman *(Br)*, mailman *(Am)*.

Postbotin (*pl* -nen) *die* postwoman *(Br)*, mailwoman *(Am)*.

Posten (*pl* -) *der* (*beruflich*) post.

Poster (*pl* -) *das* poster.

Postf. *abk* = **Postfach**.

Postfach (*pl* -fächer) *das* PO box.

Postgiroamt (*pl* -ämter) *das* ≃ Girobank.

Postgirokonto (*pl* -konten) *das* ≃ Girobank account.

Postkarte (*pl* -n) *die* postcard.

postlagernd *adj* poste restante.

Postleitzahl (*pl* -en) *die* post code *(Br)*, zip code *(Am)*.

Postleitzahlenbuch (*pl* -bücher) *das* post code directory.

Postschalter (*pl* -) *der* post office counter.

Postscheck (*pl* -s) *der* giro cheque.

Postscheckamt (*pl* -ämter) *das* ≃ Girobank.

Postscheckkonto (*pl* -konten) *das* ≃ Girobank account.

Postsparkasse (*pl* -n) *die* Post Office Savings Bank.

Poststempel (*pl* -) *der* postmark.

Postüberweisung (*pl* -en) *die* Giro transfer.

Postvermerk (*pl* -e) *der* postmark.

Postweg *der* : **auf dem ~** by post.

Postwertzeichen (*pl* -) *das* (*amt*) postage stamp.

prächtig *adj* magnificent.

Prädikat (*pl* -e) *das* (*GRAMM*) predicate ; *(Note)* grade.

prahlen *vi* to boast.

Praktikant, in (*mpl* -en) *der, die* trainee.

Praktikum (*pl* Praktika) *das* work placement ; **ein ~ machen** to be on a work placement.

praktisch *adj* practical. ◆ *adv* practically.

Praline (*pl* -n) *die* chocolate.

prall *adj* bulging ; **in der ~en Sonne** in the blazing sun.

privat

Prämie (*pl* -n) *die (von Bank, Versicherung)* premium ; *(Belohnung)* bonus.

prämieren *vt* to award.

Präparat (*pl* -e) *das (Medikament)* preparation.

Präsens *das* present (tense).

präsentieren *vt* to present.

Präservativ (*pl* -e) *das* condom.

Präsident, in (*mpl* -en) *der, die* president.

Prater *der large park near Vienna.*

ⓘ **PRATER**

This huge national park is situated near Vienna, between the river Danube and the Danube canal. Besides its wide, open spaces and parkland, it boasts sports facilities such as a golf course, sports stadium and a trotting course for horses. It is also home to the "Wurstlprater", a permanent funfair which includes the 61 m high Ferris wheel that has become the symbol of Vienna.

Präteritum *das* imperfect (tense).

Praxis (*pl* Praxen) *die* practice ; **in der ~** *(Wirklichkeit)* in practice.

präzise *adj* precise.

predigen *vi* to preach.

Preis (*pl* -e) *der* price ; *(Belohnung)* prize ; **der ~ für** the price of ; **im ~ inbegriffen** included in the price.

Preisänderung (*pl* -en) *die* price change.

Preisausschreiben (*pl* -) *das* competition.

Preiselbeere (*pl* -n) *die* cranberry.

Preisermäßigung (*pl* -en) *die* reduction in price.

preisgünstig *adj* cheap.

Preislage (*pl* -n) *die* price range.

Preisliste (*pl* -n) *die* price list.

Preisschild (*pl* -er) *das* price tag.

Preisstufe (*pl* -n) *die (bei Bus)* fare stage.

preiswert *adj* cheap. ◆ *adv* cheaply.

prellen *vt* : **die Zeche ~** to leave without paying ; **sich** (*D*) **etw ~** *(verletzen)* to bruise sthg.

Prellung (*pl* -en) *die* bruise.

Premiere (*pl* -n) *die* premiere.

Premierminister, in (*mpl* -) *der, die* prime minister.

Presse (*pl* -n) *die* press.

pressen *vt* to press.

prickelnd *adj (Wein, Wasser)* sparkling.

Priester, in (*mpl* -) *der, die* priest.

prima *adj (fam)* brilliant.

primitiv *adj* primitive.

Prinz (*pl* -en) *der* prince.

Prinzessin (*pl* -nen) *die* princess.

Prinzip (*pl* -ien) *das* priciple ; **aus ~** on principle ; **im ~** in principle.

prinzipiell *adj* in principle.

Prise (*pl* -n) *die* pinch ; **eine ~ Salz** a pinch of salt.

priv. *abk* = **privat**.

privat *adj* private. ◆ *adv* privately.

Privatadresse (*pl* -n) *die* home address.

Privatbesitz *der* private ownership.

Privatfernsehen *das* commercial television.

Privatgespräch (*pl* -e) *das* private conversation.

Privatgrundstück (*pl* -e) *das* private property.

privatisieren *vt* to privatize.

Privatpatient, in (*mpl* -en) *der, die* private patient.

Privatquartier (*pl* -e) *das* private accommodation.

Privatsender (*pl* -) *der* commercial television channel.

Privatunterkunft (*pl* -künfte) *die* private accommodation.

Privatversicherung (*pl* -en) *die* private insurance.

Privatweg (*pl* -e) *der* private footpath.

pro *präp* (+A) per ; ~ Kopf ODER Person per person ; zweimal ~ Tag twice a day.

Probe (*pl* -n) *die* (*probieren, prüfen*) test ; (*Teil*) sample ; (*von Aufführung*) rehearsal.

Probefahrt (*pl* -en) *die* test drive.

Probezeit (*pl* -en) *die* trial period.

probieren *vt* (*Essen, Getränk*) to taste ; (*versuchen*) to try.

Problem (*pl* -e) *das* problem ; kein ~! (*fam*) no problem!

problematisch *adj* problematic.

problemlos *adj* problemfree.

Produkt (*pl* -e) *das* product.

Produktion (*pl* -en) *die* production.

Produzent, in (*mpl* -en) *der, die* (*von Ware*) manufacturer ; (*von Film*) producer.

produzieren *vt* to produce. ■ **sich produzieren** *ref* (*abw*) to show off.

Prof. *abk* = Professor.

professionell *adj* professional.

Professor (*pl* -ssoren) *der* professor.

Professorin (*pl* -nen) *die* professor.

Profi (*pl* -s) *der* pro.

Profil (*pl* -e) *das* (*von Reifen*) tread ; (*von Gesicht*) profile.

Profit (*pl* -e) *der* profit.

profitieren *vi* to profit.

Prognose (*pl* -n) *die* prognosis.

Programm (*pl* -e) *das* programme ; (*EDV*) program ; (*von Partei*) agenda.

Programmheft (*pl* -e) *das* programme.

Programmhinweis (*pl* -e) *der* trailer.

programmieren *vt* (*EDV*) to program.

Programmierer, in (*mpl* -) *der, die* programmer.

Programmkino (*pl* -s) *das* art house cinema.

Programmpunkt (*pl* -e) *der* item (*on agenda*).

Programmübersicht (*pl* -en) *die* programme preview.

Programmzeitschrift (*pl* -en) *die* TV guide.

progressiv *adj* progressive.

Projekt (*pl* -e) *das* project.

Projektor (*pl* -toren) *der* projector.

Promenade (*pl* -n) *die* promenade.

Promille (*pl* -) *das* (*von Alkohol*) alcohol level ; 1,5 ~ **haben** to have 1.5 grammes of alcohol in one's blood.

prominent *adj* prominent.

prompt *adv* promptly.

Propangas *das* propane.

prophylaktisch *adj* preventative.

prosit *interj* cheers!

Prospekt (*pl* -e) *der* brochure.

prost *interj* cheers!

Prostituierte (*pl* -n) *der, die* prostitute.

Protest (*pl* -e) *der* protest.

Protestant, in (*mpl* -en) *der, die* protestant.

protestantisch *adj* protestant.

protestieren *vi* to protest ; ~ **gegen** to protest against (*Br*), to protest (*Am*).

Prothese (*pl* -n) *die* artificial limb ; (*Zahnprothese*) dentures (*pl*).

Protokoll (*pl* -e) *das* (*Aufzeichnung*) record ; **etw zu ~ geben** to put sthg on the record.

protokollieren *vt* to record.

Proviant *der* provisions (*pl*).

Provinz (*pl* -en) *die* (*Landesteil*) province ; (*abw : Hinterland*) provinces (*pl*).

provinziell *adj* (*abw*) provincial.

Provision (*pl* -en) *die* commission.

provisorisch *adj* provisional.

provozieren *vt* to provoke.

Prozent (*pl* -e) *das* per cent. ▨ **Prozente** *pl* (*Preisnachlass*) discount (*sg*).

Prozess (*pl* -e) *der* (*vor Gericht*) trial ; (*Vorgang*) process.

Prozession (*pl* -en) *die* procession.

P+R-Parkplatz (*pl* -plätze) *der* park and ride car park.

prüfen *vt* (*Schüler, Qualität*) to test ; (*Rechnung, Maschine*) to check.

Prüfung (*pl* -en) *die* exam, examination ; **eine ~ bestehen** to pass an exam ; **eine ~ machen** to sit ODER take an exam.

Prügelei (*pl* -en) *die* fight.

prügeln *vt* to beat. ▨ **sich prügeln** *ref* to fight.

prunkvoll *adj* magnificent.

PS *das* (*abk für Pferdestärke*) HP ; (*abk für Postscriptum*) PS.

Pseudonym (*pl* -e) *das* pseudonym.

Psychiater, in (*mpl* -) *der, die* psychiatrist.

psychisch *adj* psychological. ◆ *adv* psychologically.

Psychologe (*pl* -n) *der* psychologist.

Psychologie *die* psychology.

Psychologin (*pl* -nen) *die* psychologist.

Psychotherapie *die* psychotherapy.

Pubertät *die* puberty.

Publikum *das* (*von Veranstaltung*) audience ; (*von Restaurant*) customers (*pl*).

Pudding (*pl* -s) *der* blancmange.

Puder (*pl* -) *der* powder.

Puderdose (*pl* -n) *die* (powder) compact.

pudern *vt* to powder. ▨ **sich pudern** *ref* to powder o.s.

Puderzucker *der* icing sugar.

Pulli (*pl* -s) *der* (*fam*) sweater, jumper (*Br*).

Pullover (*pl* -) *der* sweater, jumper (*Br*).

Puls (*pl* -e) *der* pulse.

Pulver (*pl* -) *das* powder.

Pulverkaffee *der* instant coffee.

Pulverschnee *der* powder snow.

Pumpe (*pl* -n) *die* (*Gerät*) pump.

pumpen *vt* & *vi* to pump ; jm etw ~ (*fam* : *leihen*) to lend sb sthg ; sich (*D*) etw ~ (*fam*) to borrow sthg.

Pumpernickel *das* pumpernickel (*dark hard bread made from rye flour*).

Pumps (*pl* -) *der* court shoe.

Punker, in (*mpl* -) *der*, *die* punk.

Punkt (*pl* -e) *der* point ; (*GRAMM*) full stop (*Br*), period (*Am*) ; (*auf Stoff*) dot ; ~ ein Uhr one o'clock on the dot.

pünktlich *adj* punctual. ◆ *adv* punctually.

Punsch (*pl* -e) *der* punch.

Puppe (*pl* -n) *die* (*Spielzeug*) doll.

pur *adj* pure.

Püree (*pl* -s) *das* puree.

Pute (*pl* -n) *die* turkey.

Putenschnitzel (*pl* -) *das* turkey escalope.

putzen *vt* & *vi* to clean ; sich (*D*) die Nase ~ to blow one's nose ; sich (*D*) die Zähne ~ to clean one's teeth. ▨ **sich putzen** *ref* (*Tier*) to wash o.s.

Putzfrau (*pl* -en) *die* cleaner.

Putzlappen (*pl* -) *der* cloth.

Putzmittel (*pl* -) *das* cleaning fluid.

Puzzle (*pl* -s) *das* jigsaw (puzzle).

Pyramide (*pl* -n) *die* pyramid.

Q

Quadrat (*pl* -e) *das* (*Form*) square.

quadratisch *adj* square.

Quadratmeter (*pl* -) *der* square metre.

quälen *vt* to torture. ▨ **sich quälen** *ref* to suffer.

Qualifikation (*pl* -en) *die* qualification.

Qualität (*pl* -en) *die* quality.

Qualle (*pl* -n) *die* jellyfish.

Qualm *der* thick smoke.

qualmen *vi* (*Feuer, Schornstein*) to smoke.

Quarantäne (*pl* -n) *die* quarantine.

Quark *der* soft cheese.

Quarktasche (*pl* -n) *die* pastry filled with soft cheese.

Quarktorte (*pl* -n) *die* cheesecake.

Quartett (*pl* -e) *das* (*MUS*) quartet ; (*Kartenspiel*) children's card game where players have to collect four of a kind.

Quartier (pl -e) das (Unterkunft) accommodation.

Quarzuhr (pl -en) die (Armband) quartz watch ; (an Wand) quartz clock.

quasi adv virtually.

Quatsch der (fam) rubbish.

quatschen vi (fam : reden) to chat ; (zu viel reden) to chatter.

Quelle (pl -n) die source ; (von Wasser) spring.

quellen (präs **quillt**, prät **quoll**, pp **gequollen**) vi (Flüssigkeit) to stream ; (Reis, Erbsen) to swell.

quer adv (diagonal) diagonally ; (rechtwinklig) at right angles.

querfeldein adv cross-country.

Querflöte (pl -n) die flute.

querschnittsgelähmt adj paraplegic.

Querstraße (pl -n) die : die nächste ~ rechts the next turning on the right.

quetschen vt (zerquetschen) to crush ; (verletzen) to squeeze ; ich hab' mir den Finger in der Tür gequetscht I caught my finger in the door. ■ sich **quetschen** ref (sich zwängen) to squeeze.

Quetschung (pl -en) die bruise.

quietschen vi to squeak.

quillt präs → quellen.

Quitte (pl -n) die quince.

quittieren vt (mit Unterschrift) to write a receipt for.

Quittung (pl -en) die (für Zahlung) receipt ; könnte ich bitte eine ~ bekommen? could I have a receipt please?

Quiz (pl -) das quiz.

quoll prät → quellen.

R

Rabatt (pl -e) der discount ; ~ bekommen/geben auf (+A) to get/give a discount on.

rabiat adj brutal.

Rache die revenge.

rächen vt to avenge. ■ sich **rächen** ref (Rache nehmen) to get one's revenge.

Rad (pl Räder) das wheel ; (Fahrrad) bike ; ~ fahren to cycle.

Radar der radar.

Radarkontrolle (pl -n) die speed trap.

radeln vi ist to cycle.

Radfahrer, in (mpl -) der, die cyclist.

Radfahrweg (pl -e) der cycle track.

Radi (pl -) der (Südent) radish.

radieren vi (mit Radiergummi) to erase. ◆ vt (Bild) to etch.

Radiergummi (pl -s) der rubber (Br), eraser (Am).

Radieschen (pl -) das radish.

radikal adj radical.

Radio (pl -s) das radio.

radioaktiv adj radioactive.

Radiologe (pl -n) der radiologist.

Radiologin (pl -nen) die radiologist.

Radiorekorder (pl -) der radio cassette player.

Radiosender (pl -) der radio station.

Radiosendung (pl -en) die radio programme.

Radiowecker (pl -) der radio alarm.

Radler, in (mpl -) der, die (fam : Radfahrer) cyclist.

Radrennen (pl -) das cycle race.

Radsport der cycling.

Radtour (pl -en) die cycling tour.

Radwechsel (pl -) der wheel change.

Radweg (pl -e) der cycle path.

raffiniert adj (schlau) cunning.

Ragout (pl -s) das stew.

Rahm der cream.

Rahmen (pl -) der frame ; (von Fahrzeug) chassis.

Rakete (pl -n) die rocket.

rammen vt (Auto, Bus) to ram.

Rampe (pl -n) die (Laderampe) ramp.

Rand (pl Ränder) der edge ; (von Gefäß) rim ; (auf Papier) margin.

randalieren vi to rampage.

Randstreifen (pl -) der (von Straße) verge (Br), berm (Am) ; (von Autobahn) hard shoulder (Br), shoulder (Am).

randvoll adj full to the brim.

rang prät → ringen.

Rang (pl Ränge) der rank ; (im Theater) circle ; der erste/zweite ~ dress/upper circle.

rangieren vt (Fahrzeug) to shunt. ◆ vi (Sportler) : **an dritter Stelle ~** to be in third place.

ranken vi ist (Pflanze) to climb. ■ **sich ranken** ref (Pflanze) to climb.

rann prät → rinnen.

rannte prät → rennen.

ranzig adj rancid.

Rappen (pl -) der (Münze) centime (one hundredth of a Swiss franc).

Rapsöl das rapeseed oil.

Rarität (pl -en) die (Gegenstand) rarity.

rasant adj (Tempo) rapid.

rasch adj quick.

rascheln vi (Blätter) to rustle.

rasen vi ist (fahren) to race.

Rasen der lawn ; (Gras) grass.

Rasenfläche (pl -n) die lawn.

Rasenmäher (pl -) der lawnmower.

Rasierapparat (pl -e) der shaver.

Rasiercreme (pl -s) die shaving cream.

rasieren vt to shave. ■ **sich rasieren** ref to shave ; **sich nass ~** to have a wet shave.

Rasierer (pl -) der shaver.

Rasierklinge (pl -n) die razor blade.

Rasiermesser (pl -) das razor.

Rasierpinsel (pl -) der shaving brush.

Rasierschaum der shaving foam.

Rasierseife (pl -n) die shaving soap.

Rasierwasser das aftershave.

Rasse (*pl* -n) *die (von Menschen)* race ; *(von Tieren)* breed.

Rassismus *der* racism.

Rast *die* rest ; ~ **machen** to have a rest.

rasten *vi* to rest.

Rasthof (*pl* -höfe) *der (an Autobahn)* services (*pl*) *(with accommodation)*.

Rastplatz (*pl* -plätze) *der (an Autobahn)* services (*pl*) ; *(an Wanderweg)* picnic area ; '~ **bitte sauber halten!**' 'please keep this picnic area tidy'.

Raststätte (*pl* -n) *die (an Autobahn)* services (*pl*).

Rasur (*pl* -en) *die* shave.

Rat (*pl* Räte) *der (Ausschuss)* council ; *(Ratschlag)* (piece of) advice ; **jm einen ~ geben** to advise sb ; **jn um ~ fragen** to ask sb for advice.

rät *präs* → **raten**.

Rate (*pl* -n) *die (Zahlung)* instalment.

raten (*präs* rät, *prät* riet, *pp* geraten) *vi* & *vt (erraten)* to guess ; **jm ~** *(Rat geben)* to advise sb.

Ratenzahlung (*pl* -en) *die* payment by instalments.

Ratgeber (*pl* -) *der (Buch, Heft)* guide.

Rathaus (*pl* -häuser) *das* town hall.

Ration (*pl* -en) *die* ration.

rational *adj* rational.

rationalisieren *vi* & *vt* to rationalize.

rationell *adj (wirksam)* efficient.

ratlos *adj* helpless.

ratsam *adj* advisable.

Ratschlag (*pl* -schläge) *der* piece of advice.

Ratschläge *pl* advice (*sg*).

Rätsel (*pl* -) *das* puzzle.

Ratskeller (*pl* -) *der* cellar bar underneath a town hall.

Ratte (*pl* -n) *die* rat.

rau *adj* rough ; *(Klima)* harsh.

Raub *der* robbery.

rauben *vt (Geld, Gegenstand)* to steal.

Raubüberfall (*pl* -fälle) *der* robbery.

Rauch *der* smoke.

rauchen *vi* & *vt* to smoke ; '**bitte nicht ~**' 'no smoking please' ; '**Rauchen verboten**' 'no smoking'.

Raucher, in (*mpl* -) *der, die (Person)* smoker.

Räucheraal (*pl* -e) *der* smoked eel.

Raucherabteil (*pl* -e) *das* smoking compartment.

Räucherlachs *der* smoked salmon.

räuchern *vt* to smoke.

Rauchfleisch *das* smoked meat.

rauchfrei *adj* : '~e **Zone**' *(in Restaurant)* 'no-smoking area'.

Rauchmelder (*pl* -) *der* smoke alarm.

Rauchverbot *das* ban on smoking.

rauf *adv (fam)* = **herauf**.

rauh *adj* → **rau**.

Rauhreif *der* → **Raureif**.

Raum (*pl* Räume) *der* room ; *(Dimension)* space ; *(Region)* area.

räumen vt to clear up; (Straße) to clear; (Wohnung, Haus) to vacate.

Raumfähre (pl -n) die space shuttle.

Raumfahrt die space travel.

Räumlichkeiten pl (Gebäude) premises.

Raumpfleger, in (mpl -) der, die cleaner.

Raumschiff (pl -e) das spaceship.

Raumtemperatur (pl -en) die room temperature.

Räumungsarbeiten pl clearance work (sg).

Räumungsverkauf (pl -käufe) der clearance sale.

Raupe (pl -n) die (Tier) caterpillar; (Karussell) funfair ride shaped like a caterpillar.

Raureif der frost.

raus adv (fam) = **heraus**; ~ hier! get out!

Rausch (pl Räusche) der (von Alkohol) intoxication; (Ekstase) ecstasy.

rauschen vi (Wasser) to roar; (Bäume) to rustle. ◆ vimp : es rauscht (in Telefon) it's a bad line.

Rauschgift (pl -e) das drug.

rauschgiftsüchtig adj addicted to drugs.

raus|fliegen vi unr ist (fam : aus Schule, Lokal) to be thrown out.

raus|halten : sich raushalten ref (fam) to stay out of it.

raus|kriegen vt unr (fam : Geheimnis) to find out.

räuspern : sich räuspern ref to clear one's throat.

raus|schmeißen vt unr (fam) to throw out.

reagieren vi to react.

Reaktion (pl -en) die reaction; allergische ~ allergic reaction.

real adj real.

realisieren vt to realize.

realistisch adj realistic.

Realität die reality.

Realschule (pl -n) die secondary school for pupils up to the age of 16.

Rebe (pl -n) die vine.

rebellieren vi to rebel.

Rebhuhn (pl -hühner) das partridge.

Rebstock (pl -stöcke) der vine.

rechnen vi (mit Zahlen) to calculate. ◆ vt (Aufgabe) to work out; ~ mit (erwarten) to expect; (sich verlassen auf) to count on; damit ~, etw zu tun to expect to do sthg.

Rechner (pl -) der (Computer) computer.

Rechnung (pl -en) die (Rechenaufgabe) calculation; (für Leistung, für Speisen) bill (Br), check (Am); auf js ~ at sb's expense; die ~, bitte! could I have the bill, please?

Rechnungsbetrag (pl -beträge) der total amount.

recht adj (richtig) right. ◆ adv (ziemlich) quite; ist Ihnen das ~? is that all right with you?

Recht (pl -e) das right; zu ~ rightly; jm ~ geben to agree with sb; ~ haben to be right.

rechte, r, s adj right; (politisch) right-wing.

Rechte[1] *die (politisch)* right wing.

Rechte[2] *das (das Richtige)* right thing.

Rechteck *(pl -e) das* rectangle.

rechteckig *adj* rectangular.

rechtfertigen *vt* to justify. ▦ **sich rechtfertigen** *ref* to justify o.s.

Rechtfertigung *(pl -en) die* justification.

rechthaberisch *adj* : er ist immer so ~ he always thinks he's right.

rechtlich *adj* legal.

rechts *adv (Seitenangabe)* on the right ; *(Richtungsangabe)* right ; ~ **sein** *(politisch)* to be right-wing ; **nach** ~ right ; ~ **von** jm/etw to the right of sb/sthg ; **von** ~ from the right.

Rechtsabbieger *(pl -) der* car turning right.

Rechtsanwalt, wältin *(mpl -wälte) der, die* lawyer.

Rechtschreibung *die* spelling.

rechtsherum *adv* to the right.

Rechtskurve *(pl -n) die* right-hand bend.

Rechtsradikale *(pl -n) der, die* right-wing extremist.

Rechtsverkehr *der* driving on the right.

Rechtsweg *der (amt)* legal action.

rechtswidrig *adj* illegal.

rechtzeitig *adj* timely. ◆ *adv* on time.

recyclen *vt* to recycle.

Recycling *das* recycling.

Recyclingpapier *das* recycled paper.

Redakteur, in *(mpl -e) der, die* editor.

Rede *(pl -n) die (Vortrag)* talk ; **eine** ~ **halten** to make a speech ; **direkte/indirekte** ~ *(GRAMM)* direct/indirect speech.

reden *vt & vi* to talk ; ~ **mit** to talk to ; ~ **über** *(+A)* to talk about.

Redewendung *(pl -en) die* idiom.

Redner, in *(mpl -) der, die* speaker.

reduzieren *vt (verringern)* to reduce. ▦ **sich reduzieren** *ref* to decrease.

reduziert *adj* : ~e **Ware** reduced goods.

Reederei *(pl -en) die* shipping company.

Reeperbahn *die street in Hamburg famous for its bars and nightclubs.*

ⓘ **REEPERBAHN**

The "Reeperbahn" is the main street in Hamburg's notorious St Pauli nightclub district. The area is home to several pubs, nightclubs, strip joints and amusement arcades and the name "Reeperbahn" has become synonymous with the city's red-light district.

reflektieren *vt (Licht)* to reflect.

Reflex *(pl -e) der (Reaktion)* reflex.

Reform *(pl -en) die* reform.

Reformationstag (pl -e) der Reformation Day, 31st October, day on which the Reformation is celebrated.

Reformhaus (pl -häuser) das health food shop.

 REFORMHAUS

In addition to health food, these shops, which are very common in Germany, sell natural health care and beauty products. Sometimes there is also a health food cafe on the premises.

reformieren vt to reform.

Reformkost die health food.

Regal (pl -e) das shelves (pl).

Regatta (pl -tten) die regatta.

rege adj (lebhaft) lively.

Regel (pl -n) die rule ; (Menstruation) period ; **in der ~** as a rule.

Regelblutung (pl -en) die period.

regelmäßig adj regular. ◆ adv regularly ; (fam : immer) always.

regeln vt to regulate ; (Verhältnisse) to settle ; **etw vertraglich ~** to stipulate sthg in a contract. ■ **sich regeln** ref to sort itself out.

Regelung (pl -en) die (Vorschrift) regulation.

Regen der rain ; **bei ~** if it rains ; **im ~** in the rain.

Regenbogen (pl -bögen) der rainbow.

Regenfälle pl rain (sg).

Regenjacke (pl -n) die raincoat.

Regenmantel (pl -mäntel) der raincoat.

Regenrinne (pl -n) die gutter.

Regenschauer (pl -) der shower.

Regenschirm (pl -e) der umbrella.

Regentropfen (pl -) der raindrop.

Regenwetter das rainy weather.

Regenwurm (pl -würmer) der earthworm.

Regie die direction.

regieren vt (Land) to govern. ◆ vi (König) to rule ; (Partei, Politiker) to be in power.

Regierung (pl -en) die government.

Regierungsbezirk (pl -e) der administrative division of a 'Land'.

Regierungssitz (pl -e) der seat of government.

Region (pl -en) die region.

regional adj regional. ◆ adv ~ **verschieden** different from region to region.

Regionalprogramm (pl -e) das regional channel.

Regisseur, in (mpl -e) der, die director.

registrieren vt (wahrnehmen) to note ; (eintragen) to register.

regnen vimp to rain ; **es regnet** it's raining.

regnerisch adj rainy.

regulär adj regular ; (fam : normal) normal.

regulieren vt to regulate.

Reh (*pl* -e) *das* (*Tier*) deer ; (*Fleisch*) venison.

Rehrücken (*pl* -) *der* saddle of venison.

Reibe (*pl* -n) *die* grater.

Reibekuchen (*pl* -) *der* potato waffle (*Br*), ≃ hash browns (*Am*).

reiben (*prät* **rieb**, *pp* **gerieben**) *vt* to rub ; (*Kartoffeln*) to grate. ◆ *vi* (*scheuern*) to rub ; **sich** (*D*) **die Augen/Hände ~** to rub one's eyes/hands.

Reiberdatschi (*pl* -) *der* (*Süddt*) potato waffle (*Br*), ≃ hash browns (*Am*).

reibungslos *adj* smooth.

reich *adj* rich ; (*Auswahl*) large ; **~ sein an** (+*D*) to be rich in.

Reich (*pl* -e) *das* (*Herrschaftsgebiet*) empire ; (*Bereich*) realm.

reichen *vi* (*genügen*) to be enough ; (*räumlich*) to reach. ◆ *vt* (*geh* : *geben*) to give, to pass ; **jm etw ~** to pass sthg to sb ; **der Wein reicht nicht** there isn't enough wine ; **jetzt reicht's mir!** (*fam*) I've had enough! ; **das reicht!** (*fam*) that's enough!

reichhaltig *adj* extensive ; **~es Essen** rich food.

reichlich *adj* (*groß*) large. ◆ *adv* (*viel*) plenty of ; (*ziemlich*) pretty.

Reichstag *der German parliament (1867-1945)*.

The Reichstag building in Berlin was built between 1884 and 1894, and the German Reichstag (parliament) met there until the building was burnt in suspicious circumstances on 27th February, 1933. The National Socialists (Nazis) used the opportunity to turn public feeling against the Communists, their political enemies. During the Second World War the building was almost completely destroyed and after its repair was only rarely used for sittings of the Bundestag (West German parliament). After reunification in 1990 the building was completely renovated, and a new glass cupola was added. In 1999 it once again became the regular site of German parliamentary meetings.

Reichtum *der* wealth.

reif *adj* (*Obst*) ripe ; (*Person*) mature.

Reif *der* (*Raureif*) frost.

reifen *vi ist* (*Obst*) to ripen.

Reifen (*pl* -) *der* (*von Auto, Fahrrad*) tyre ; (*Ring*) hoop ; **den ~ wechseln** to change the tyre.

Reifendruck *der* tyre pressure.

Reifenpanne (*pl* -n) *die* puncture.

Reifenwechsel (*pl* -) *der* tyre change.

Reihe (*pl* -n) *die* (*Linie*) line ; (*in Theater, Kino*) row ; (*in Fernsehen, Radio*) series ; **eine ~ von** (*Menge*) a number of ; **in einer ~** in a row ; **der ~ nach** in turn ; **Sie sind an der ~** it's your turn.

Reihenfolge *die* order.

Reihenhaus (*pl* -häuser) *das* terraced house.

rein *adj* (*sauber*) clean ; (*pur, ungemischt*) pure. ◆ *adv* (*ausnahmslos*) purely ; (*fam* : *überhaupt*) absolutely ; (*fam*) = **herein** ; **komm ~!** (*fam*) come in!

rein|fallen *vi unr ist* (*fam* : *hineinfallen*) to fall in ; (*fam* : *getäuscht werden*) to be taken for a ride ; **~ auf** (+*A*) (*fam*) to fall for.

reinigen *vt* to clean ; **chemisch ~** to dry-clean.

Reiniger (*pl* -) *der* cleaner.

Reinigung (*pl* -en) *die* (*Geschäft*) dry cleaner's ; (*Handlung*) cleaning.

Reinigungsmilch *die* cleansing milk.

Reinigungsmittel (*pl* -) *das* cleanser.

rein|legen *vt* (*fam* : *betrügen, ärgern*) to take for a ride ; (*hineinlegen*) to put in.

rein|reden *vi* : **jm ~** (*ins Wort fallen* : *fam*) to interrupt sb ; (*fam* : *beeinflussen*) to interfere with sb.

Reis *der* rice.

Reise (*pl* -n) *die* journey ; (*kurz*) trip ; **eine ~ machen** to go on a journey/trip ; **gute ~!** have a good journey/trip!

Reiseandenken (*pl* -) *das* souvenir.

Reiseapotheke (*pl* -n) *die* first-aid kit.

Reisebegleiter, in (*mpl* -) *der, die* travelling companion.

Reisebüro (*pl* -s) *das* travel agency.

Reisebus (*pl* -se) *der* coach.

Reiseführer (*pl* -) *der* (*Buch*) guide book ; (*Person*) guide, courier.

Reiseführerin (*pl* -nen) *die* guide, courier.

Reisegepäck *das* luggage.

Reisegesellschaft (*pl* -en) *die* (*Gruppe*) group of tourists ; (*Firma*) tour operator.

Reisegruppe (*pl* -n) *die* group of tourists.

reisekrank *adj* travelsick.

Reiseleiter, in (*mpl* -) *der, die* guide, courier.

reiselustig *adj* fond of travelling.

reisen *vi ist* to travel ; **~ nach** to go to.

Reisende (*pl* -n) *der, die* traveller ; **~ in Richtung Frankfurt** passengers travelling to Frankfurt.

Reisepass (*pl* -pässe) *der* passport.

Reiseproviant *der* food for the journey.

Reiseroute (*pl* -n) *die* route.

Reiseruf (*pl* -e) *der* emergency announcement broadcast over the radio.

Reisescheck (*pl* -s) *der* traveller's cheque.

Reisetasche (*pl* -n) *die* travel bag.

Reiseunternehmen (*pl* -) *das* tour operator.

Reiseveranstalter (*pl* -) *der* tour operator.

Reiseverkehr *der* holiday traffic.

Reiseversicherung (*pl* -en) *die* travel insurance.

Reisewetterbericht (*pl* -e) *der* holiday weather forecast.

Reisezeit (*pl* -en) *die* journey time.

Reiseziel (*pl* -e) *das* destination.

reißen (*prät* riss, *pp* gerissen) *vi ist (zerreißen)* to break. ◆ *vi hat (ziehen)* to pull. ◆ *vt hat (ziehen, wegziehen)* to pull ; *(zerreißen)* to tear ; **an etw** *(D)* ~ to pull sthg. ■ **sich reißen** *ref* : **sich** ~ **um** to scramble for.

Reißverschluss (*pl* -schlüsse) *der* zip *(Br)*, zipper *(Am)*.

Reißzwecke (*pl* -n) *die* drawing pin *(Br)*, thumbtack *(Am)*.

reiten (*prät* ritt, *pp* geritten) *vi ist & vt hat* to ride ; **auf einem Pferd** ~ to ride a horse.

Reiter, in (*mpl* -) *der, die* rider.

Reitpferd (*pl* -e) *das* horse *(for riding)*.

Reitsport *der* riding.

Reitstall (*pl* -ställe) *der* riding stable.

Reitweg (*pl* -e) *der* bridle path.

Reiz (*pl* -e) *der (physikalisch)* stimulus ; *(Schönheit)* attraction.

reizen *vt (verlocken)* to tempt ; *(provozieren)* to annoy ; *(Augen, Magen)* to irritate. ◆ *vi* : **es reizt zum Lachen** it makes you want to laugh.

reizend *adj* charming.

Reizung (*pl* -en) *die (von Schleimhaut, Magen)* irritation.

reizvoll *adj (schön)* attractive.

Reklamation (*pl* -en) *die* complaint.

Reklame *die* advertising.

reklamieren *vt (Ware, Service)* to complain about.

Rekord (*pl* -e) *der* record.

relativ *adj* relative. ◆ *adv* relatively.

relaxen *vi (fam)* to relax.

relevant *adj* relevant.

Religion (*pl* -en) *die* religion ; *(Schulfach)* religious education.

Relikt (*pl* -e) *das* relic.

Reling *die* rail.

remis *adv* : ~ **enden** to end in a draw.

Remoulade (*pl* -n) *die* remoulade, *sauce of eggs, oil and herbs*.

Renaissance *die* Renaissance.

Rendezvous (*pl* -) *das* rendezvous.

Rennbahn (*pl* -en) *die* racetrack.

rennen (*prät* rannte, *pp* gerannt) *vi ist (laufen)* to run ; *(fam : gehen)* to go.

Rennen (*pl* -) *das* racing ; *(Veranstaltung)* race.

Rennfahrer, in (*mpl* -) *der, die* racing driver.

Rennrad (*pl* -räder) *das* racing bike.

Rennsport *der* racing.

Rennwagen (*pl* -) *der* racing car.

renommiert *adj* famous.

renovieren *vt* to renovate.

Renovierung (*pl* -en) *die* renovation ; '**wegen** ~ **geschlossen**' 'closed for alterations'.

Rente (*pl* -n) *die (Pension)* pension.

Rentner, in (*mpl* -) *der, die* pensioner.

Reparatur (*pl* -en) *die* repair.

Reparaturdienst (*pl* -e) *der* repair service.

Reparaturkosten *pl* repair costs.

Reparaturwerkstatt (*pl* -stätten) *die* garage.

reparieren *vt* to repair.

Reportage (*pl* -n) *die* report.

Reporter, in (*mpl* -) *der, die* reporter.

repräsentativ *adj* representative ; *(Wagen, Villa)* imposing.

Republik (*pl* -en) *die* republic.

Reserve (*pl* -n) *die (Vorrat)* reserve ; *(SPORT)* reserves (*pl*) ; **etw in ~ haben** to have sthg in reserve.

Reservekanister (*pl* -) *der* spare can.

Reserverad (*pl* -räder) *das* spare wheel.

Reservereifen (*pl* -) *der* spare tyre.

Reservespieler, in (*mpl* -) *der, die* reserve.

reservieren *vt* to reserve.

reserviert *adj* reserved.

Reservierung (*pl* -en) *die* reservation.

resignieren *vi* to give up.

Respekt *der (Achtung)* respect ; *(Angst)* fear.

respektieren *vt* to respect.

Rest (*pl* -e) *der* rest.

Restaurant (*pl* -s) *das* restaurant.

Restbetrag (*pl* -träge) *der* balance.

Restgeld *das* : 'kein ~' 'no change' ; '~ **wird erstattet**' 'change given'.

restlich *adj* remaining.

restlos *adv* completely.

Resturlaub *der* remaining holidays (*pl*).

Resultat (*pl* -e) *das* result.

retten *vt* to save ; *(aus Gefahr)* to rescue. ■ **sich retten** *ref* to escape.

Retter, in (*mpl* -) *der, die* rescuer.

Rettich (*pl* -e) *der* radish.

Rettung (*pl* -en) *die (Handlung)* rescue.

Rettungsboot (*pl* -e) *das* lifeboat.

Rettungsdienst (*pl* -e) *der* emergency services (*pl*).

Rettungsring (*pl* -e) *der* life belt.

Rettungswagen (*pl* -) *der* ambulance.

Revier (*pl* -e) *das (Bezirk)* district.

Revolution (*pl* -en) *die* revolution.

Revolver (*pl* -) *der* revolver.

Revue (*pl* -n) *die* revue.

Rezept (*pl* -e) *das (für Gericht)* recipe ; *(für Medikament)* prescription ; **nur gegen ~** only on prescription.

rezeptfrei *adj* available without a prescription.

Rezeption (*pl* -en) *die (im Hotel)* reception.

rezeptpflichtig *adj* available only on prescription.

R-Gespräch (*pl* -e) *das* reverse charge call (*Br*), collect call (*Am*).

Rhabarber *der* rhubarb.

Rhein *der* : der ~ the Rhine.

rheinisch *adj* Rhenish.

Rheinland *das* Rhineland.

Rheinland-Pfalz *nt* Rhineland-Palatinate.

Rheinwein (*pl* -e) *der* Rhine wine, hock (*Br*).

rhetorisch *adj* rhetorical.

Rheuma *das* rheumatism.

Rhythmus (*pl* Rhythmen) *der* rhythm.

richten *vt* to direct. ◆ *vi* (*urteilen*) to judge. ▪ **sich richten** *ref* (*in Richtung*) to be directed ; **sich nach den Vorschriften ~** to go by the rules.

Richter, in (*mpl* -) *der*, *die* judge.

Richtgeschwindigkeit *die* recommended speed limit.

richtig *adj* right ; (*echt*) real. ◆ *adv* (*fam* : *wirklich*) really ; (*korrekt*) correctly ; **bin ich hier ~?** am I in the right place? ; **meine Uhr geht ~** my watch is right.

richtig stellen *vt* to correct.

Richtlinie (*pl* -n) *die* guideline.

Richtpreis (*pl* -e) *der* recommended price.

Richtung (*pl* -en) *die* direction ; **alle ~en** 'all routes' ; **in ~ Berlin fahren** to travel towards Berlin ; **in ~ Süden** southwards.

riechen (*prät* **roch**, *pp* **gerochen**) *vt* & *vi* to smell ; ~

nach to smell of ; **es riecht nach...** there is a smell of... ; **an etw** (*D*) ~ to smell sthg.

rief *prät* → **rufen**.

Riegel (*pl* -) *der* (*Verschluss*) bolt ; (*Süßigkeit*) bar.

Riemen (*pl* -) *der* (*Band*) strap.

rieseln *vi* ist (*Wasser*) to trickle ; (*Schnee*) to float down.

riesengroß *adj* enormous.

Riesenrad (*pl* -räder) *das* big wheel.

Riesenslalom *der* giant slalom.

riesig *adj* (*Person, Gegenstand*) enormous ; **ich hab ~en Hunger** (*fam*) I'm starving.

Riesling (*pl* -e) *der* Riesling (*white wine*).

riet *prät* → **raten**.

Riff (*pl* -e) *das* reef.

Rille (*pl* -n) *die* groove.

Rind (*pl* -er) *das* (*Tier*) cow ; (*Fleisch*) beef.

Rinde (*pl* -n) *die* (*von Brot*) crust ; (*von Käse*) rind ; (*von Bäumen*) bark.

Rinderbraten (*pl* -) *der* (*joint of*) roast beef.

Rindfleisch *das* beef.

Ring (*pl* -e) *der* the ring ; (*Straße*) ring road.

Ringbuch (*pl* -bücher) *das* ring binder.

ringen (*prät* **rang**, *pp* **gerungen**) *vi* to wrestle.

Ringer, in (*mpl* -) *der*, *die* wrestler.

Ringkampf (*pl* -kämpfe) *der* (*im Sport*) wrestling match.

ring : **ringsum** *präp* all around.

ringsherum *adv* all around.

Ringstraße (*pl* -n) *die* ring road.

ringsum *adv* all around.

rinnen (*prät* **rann**, *pp* **geronnen**) *vi ist* to run.

Rinnstein (*pl* -e) *der* gutter.

Rippchen (*pl* -) *das slightly smoked pork rib.*

Rippe (*pl* -n) *die* (*Knochen*) rib.

Rippenfellentzündung (*pl* -en) *die* pleurisy.

Risiko (*pl* -ken) *das* risk ; auf eigenes ~ at one's own risk ; 'zu Risiken und Nebenwirkungen' (*MED*) 'possible risks and side-effects'.

riskant *adj* risky.

riskieren *vt* to risk.

riss *prät* → **reißen**.

Riss (*pl* -e) *der* (*in Stoff*) tear ; (*in Holz, Wand*) crack.

rissig *adj* cracked.

ritt *prät* → **reiten**.

Ritt (*pl* -e) *der* ride.

Ritter (*pl* -) *der* knight.

ritzen *vt* (*gravieren*) to carve.

Rivale (*pl* -n) *der* rival.

Rivalin (*pl* -nen) *die* rival.

Roastbeef (*pl* -s) *das* roast beef.

Roboter (*pl* -) *der* robot.

robust *adj* robust.

roch *prät* → **riechen**.

Rock[1] (*pl* **Röcke**) *der* (*Kleidungsstück*) skirt.

Rock[2] *der* (*Musik*) rock.

Rockmusik *die* rock music.

Rodelbahn (*pl* -en) *die* toboggan run.

rodeln *vi ist* to toboggan.

Roggen *der* rye.

Roggenbrot (*pl* -e) *das* rye bread.

roh *adj* raw ; (*Person*) rough. ◆ *adv* (*behandeln*) roughly ; etw ~ essen to eat sthg raw.

Rohkost *die* raw fruit and vegetables (*pl*).

Rohr (*pl* -e) *das* (*für Wasser, Gas*) pipe ; (*Schilfrohr*) reed ; (*für Möbel, Körbe*) cane, wicker.

Rohrbruch (*pl* -brüche) *der* burst pipe.

Rohrzucker *der* cane sugar.

Rokoko *das* rococo.

Rollbahn (*pl* -en) *die* runway.

Rollbraten (*pl* -) *der* roast.

Rolle (*pl* -n) *die* roll ; (*Funktion, im Film, Theater*) role ; (*Rad*) castor ; es spielt keine ~ it doesn't matter.

rollen *vi ist* & *vt hat* to roll.

Roller (*pl* -) *der* scooter.

Rollerskates *pl* rollerskates.

Rollkragen (*pl* -) *der* polo neck.

Rollkragenpullover (*pl* -) *der* polo neck (jumper).

Rollladen (*pl* -läden) *der* (*vor Fenster*) shutters (*pl*).

Rollmops (*pl* -möpse) *der* rollmop, rolled-up pickled herring.

Rollo (*pl* -s) *das* roller blind.

Rollschuh (*pl* -e) *der* roller skate.

Rollschuhfahrer, in (*mpl* -) *der, die* roller-skater.

Rollsplit *der* loose chippings (*pl*).

Rollstuhl (*pl* -stühle) *der* wheelchair.

Rollstuhlfahrer, in (*mpl* -) *der, die* wheelchair user.

Rolltreppe (*pl* -n) *die* escalator.

Roman (*pl* -e) *der* novel.

romanisch *adj (Bauwerk, Kunst)* Romanesque ; *(Sprache)* Romance.

Romantik *die* Romanticism.

romantisch *adj* romantic ; *(Kunst)* Romantic.

römisch-katholisch *adj* Roman Catholic.

Rommé *das* rummy.

röntgen *vt* to X-ray.

Röntgenaufnahme (*pl* -n) *die* X-ray.

rosa *adj* pink.

Rose (*pl* -n) *die* rose.

Rosenkohl *der* (Brussels) sprouts *(pl)*.

Rosenmontag (*pl* -e) *der* day before Shrove Tuesday.

Roséwein (*pl* -e) *der* rosé (wine).

Rosine (*pl* -n) *die* raisin.

Rost (*pl* -e) *der (auf Metall)* rust ; *(Gitter)* grating.

Rostbratwurst (*pl* -würste) *die* : (Thüringer) ~ Thuringian grilled sausage.

rosten *vi hat & ist* to rust.

rösten *vt* to roast ; *(Brot)* to toast.

rostfrei *adj (Stahl)* stainless.

Rösti *pl (Schweiz)* fried potato pancake.

rostig *adj* rusty.

Rostschutzmittel (*pl* -) *das* rust-proofing agent.

rot (*komp* **röter** ODER **roter**, *superl* **am rötesten** ODER **am ro-** testen) *adj* red ; in den ~en Zahlen sein to be in the red.

Rot *das* red ; 'bei ~ hier halten' 'stop here when red light shows'.

Rote Kreuz *das* Red Cross.

Röteln *pl* German measles *(sg)*.

rothaarig *adj* red-haired.

rotieren *vi* to rotate ; *(fam : Person)* to be in a flap.

Rotkohl *der* red cabbage.

Rotkraut *das* red cabbage.

Rotlicht *das (rote Lampe)* red light.

Rotlichtviertel (*pl* -) *das* red light district.

Rotwein (*pl* -e) *der* red wine.

Rouge (*pl* -s) *das* blusher.

Roulade (*pl* -n) *die* ≃ beef olive.

Roulette (*pl* -s) *das* roulette.

Route (*pl* -n) *die* route.

Routine *die* experience ; *(Gewohnheit)* routine.

Rubbellos (*pl* -e) *das* lottery scratch card.

rubbeln *vi* to rub.

Rübe (*pl* -n) *die* turnip.

rüber *adv (fam)* = herüber.

Rubin (*pl* -e) *der* ruby.

Rubrik (*pl* -en) *die (Spalte)* column.

Rückantwort (*pl* -en) *die* reply.

Rückbank (*pl* -bänke) *die* back seat ; umklappbare ~ folding back seat.

rücken *vt hat & vi ist* to move ; nach links/rechts ~ to move to the left/right ; rück mal! move up!

Rücken (pl -) der back ; (von Buch) spine.

Rückenlage die : in ~ (lying) on one's back.

Rückenlehne (pl -n) die back (of chair).

Rückenschmerzen pl backache (sg).

Rückenschwimmen das backstroke.

Rückenwind der tailwind.

Rückerstattung (pl -en) die reimbursement.

Rückfahrkarte (pl -n) die return (ticket) (Br), round-trip (ticket) (Am).

Rückfahrt (pl -en) die return journey.

Rückfall (pl -fälle) der (Krankheit) relapse.

Rückflug (pl -flüge) der return flight.

Rückfrage (pl -n) die question.

Rückgabe die return ; gegen ~ on return.

Rückgabeknopf (pl -knöpfe) der coin return button.

Rückgaberecht das right to return goods if not satisfied.

rückgängig adv : etw ~ machen to cancel sthg.

Rückgrat (pl -e) das (Körperteil) spine.

Rückkehr die return.

rückläufig adj declining.

Rücklicht (pl -er) das rear light.

Rückporto das return postage.

Rückreise (pl -n) die return journey.

Rückreiseverkehr der homeward traffic.

Rückruf (pl -e) der (per Telefon) return call.

Rucksack (pl -säcke) der rucksack.

Rucksacktourist, in (mpl -en) der, die backpacker.

Rückschritt (pl -e) der step backwards.

Rückseite (pl -n) die back.

Rücksicht (pl -en) die consideration ; ~ nehmen auf (+A) to show consideration for.

rücksichtslos adj inconsiderate.

rücksichtsvoll adj considerate.

Rücksitz (pl -e) der back seat.

Rückspiegel (pl -) der rearview mirror.

Rückstand der (SPORT) : sie sind mit 16 Punkten im ~ they are 16 points behind.

Rückstau (pl -s) der tailback.

Rückstrahler (pl -) der reflector.

Rückvergütung (pl -en) die refund.

rückwärts adv backwards.

Rückwärtsgang der reverse (gear).

Rückweg (pl -e) der way back ; auf dem ~ on the way back.

rückwirkend adj retroactive.

Rückzahlung (pl -en) die repayment.

Rückzahlungsbetrag (pl -beträge) der repayment.

rüde adj rude.

Rüde (pl -n) der (male) dog.

Ruder (*pl* -) *das* (*zum Rudern*) oar ; (*zum Steuern*) rudder.

Ruderboot (*pl* -e) *das* rowing boat.

Ruderer (*pl* -) *der* rower.

Ruderin (*pl* -nen) *die* rower.

rudern *vi* ist (*mit Boot*) to row.

Ruf (*pl* -e) *der* (*Rufen*) call ; (*Image*) reputation.

rufen (*prät* rief, *pp* gerufen) *vt* & *vi* to call ; **um Hilfe ~** to call for help.

Rufname (*pl* -n) *der* first name.

Rufnummer (*pl* -n) *die* telephone number.

Ruhe *die* (*Stille*) silence ; (*von Person*) calm ; (*eines Ortes*) peacefulness ; **jn in ~ lassen** to leave sb in peace ; **~ bitte!** quiet, please!

ruhen *vi* to rest.

Ruhestand *der* retirement.

Ruhestörung (*pl* -en) *die* breach of the peace ; **nächtliche ~** breach of the peace at night.

Ruhetag (*pl* -e) *der* closing day ; '**montags ~**' 'closed on Mondays'.

ruhig *adj* quiet ; (*unbewegt*) still ; (*gelassen*) calm. ◆ *adv* quietly ; (*unbeweglich*) still ; (*gelassen*) calmly ; **mach das ~** (*fam*) do it, by all means.

Rührei (*pl* -er) *das* scrambled egg.

rühren *vt* (*mit Löffel*) to stir ; (*Person*) to move. ◆ *vi* : **~ von** to come from. ■ **sich rühren** *ref* (*sich bewegen*) to move.

Ruhrgebiet *nt* the Ruhr.

Rührteig (*pl* -e) *der* cake mixture.

Ruine (*pl* -n) *die* ruin.

ruinieren *vt* to ruin. ■ **sich ruinieren** *ref* to ruin o.s.

rülpsen *vi* to belch.

rum *adv* (*fam*) = herum.

Rum *der* rum.

rum|kriegen *vt* (*fam* : *Person*) to talk round ; (*Zeit*) to pass.

Rummel *der* (*fam* : *Theater*) fuss ; (*Trubel*) bustle.

Rummelplatz (*pl* -plätze) *der* fairground.

rumoren *vi* to rumble.

Rumpf (*pl* Rümpfe) *der* (*Körperteil*) trunk.

Rumpsteak (*pl* -s) *das* rump steak.

Rumtopf (*pl* -töpfe) *der* fruit soaked for a long time in rum.

rund *adj* round ; (*dick*) plump. ◆ *adv* (*ungefähr*) about ; (*im Kreis*) around ; **~ 500 Leute** about 500 people ; **~ um** around ; **~ um den Tisch** round the table.

Runde (*pl* -n) *die* (*Gang*) walk ; (*Rennen*) lap ; (*von Personen*) group ; **eine ~ ausgeben** to buy a round.

Rundfahrt (*pl* -en) *die* tour.

Rundflug (*pl* -flüge) *der* sightseeing flight.

Rundfunk *der* radio.

Rundfunkmeldung (*pl* -en) *die* radio report.

Rundfunkprogramm (*pl* -e) *das* radio programme.

Rundgang (*pl* -gänge) *der* (*Spaziergang*) walk.

rundherum *adv* (*ringsherum*) all around ; (*ganz*) completely.

Rundreise (*pl* -n) *die* tour.

Rundwanderweg (*pl* -e) *der* circular path.

runter *adv* (*fam*) = herunter.

Ruß *der* soot.

Russe (*pl* -n) *der* Russian.

Russin (*pl* -nen) *die* Russian.

russisch *adj* Russian.

Russisch(e) *das* Russian.

Russland *nt* Russia.

rustikal *adj* rustic.

Rüstung (*pl* -en) *die* (*für Militär*) arms (*pl*) ; (*von Rittern*) armour.

Rutsch *der* : guten ~! happy New Year!

Rutschbahn (*pl* -en) *die* slide.

rutschen *vi* ist (*ausrutschen*) to slip ; (*gleiten*) to slide ; (*fam* : *zur Seite rücken*) to move over ; (*Hose*) to slip down.

rutschfest *adj* non-slip.

rutschig *adj* slippery.

rütteln *vt* to shake.

S

s. *abk* = siehe.

S (*abk für Süd*) S.

S. (*abk für Seite*) p.

Saal (*pl* Säle) *der* hall.

Saarland *das* Saarland.

Säbel (*pl* -) *der* sabre.

sabotieren *vt* to sabotage.

Sachbearbeiter, in (*mpl* -) *der, die* employee in charge of a particular matter.

Sache (*pl* -n) *die* thing ; (*Angelegenheit*) matter ; das ist meine ~ that's my business ; bei der ~ bleiben to keep to the point ; zur ~ kommen to get to the point. ■ **Sachen** *pl* (*Kleidung*) things.

Sachertorte (*pl* -n) *die* chocolate cake.

sachkundig *adj* well-informed.

Sachlage *die* situation.

sachlich *adj* (*Person, Argument*) objective ; (*Gründe*) practical. ◆ *adv* (*argumentieren*) objectively.

sächlich *adj* (*GRAMM*) neuter.

Sachschaden (*pl* -schäden) *der* material damage.

Sachsen *nt* Saxony.

Sachsen-Anhalt *nt* Saxony-Anhalt.

sacht *adj* (*Berührung*) gentle.

Sachverständige (*pl* -n) *der, die* expert.

Sack (*pl* Säcke) *der* (*Verpackung*) sack.

Sackgasse (*pl* -n) *die* dead end.

Safe (*pl* -s) *der* safe.

Saft (*pl* Säfte) *der* juice.

saftig *adj* juicy.

Säge (*pl* -n) *die* saw.

sagen *vt* to say ; (*befehlen*) to tell ; (*bedeuten*) to mean ; jm etw ~ to tell sb sthg ; ~ zu to say to ; sag mal! tell me ; was sagst du dazu? what do you think about that? ; das kann man wohl ~! you can say that again! ; sag bloß! you don't say!

sägen *vt & vi* to saw.

sah *prät* → sehen.

Sahne *die* cream.

Sahnequark *der* cream curd cheese.

Sahnetorte (*pl* -n) *die* gâteau.

sahnig *adj* creamy.

Saison (*pl* -s) *die* season.

Sakko (*pl* -s) *das* jacket.

Salami (*pl* -s) *die* salami.

Salat (*pl* -e) *der* (*Pflanze*) lettuce ; (*Gericht*) salad ; **grüner ~** green salad.

Salatbar (*pl* -s) *die* salad bar.

Salatsoße (*pl* -n) *die* salad dressing.

Salatteller (*pl* -) *der* plate of salad.

Salbe (*pl* -n) *die* ointment.

Salmonellenvergiftung (*pl* -en) *die* salmonella (poisoning).

Salon (*pl* -s) *der* (*Geschäft*) salon.

Salz (*pl* -e) *das* salt.

Salzburg *nt* Salzburg.

Salzburger Festspiele *pl* *music and theatre festival held in Salzburg.*

ⓘ **SALZBURGER FESTSPIELE**

The Salzburg Festival was founded in 1920 and takes place every summer. It features a large number of concerts and operas, particularly the works of Mozart, although other composers such as Strauß and Verdi are also included. Another important component is drama, and traditionally every year there is a performance of the play "Jedermann" by Hugo von Hof-

mannsthal, who was one of the founders of the Festival.

Salzburger Nockerln *pl* (*Österr*) *hot dessert made from beaten egg whites and sugar.*

salzen (*pp* gesalzen) *vt* to salt.

Salzgurke (*pl* -n) *die* pickled gherkin.

salzig *adj* salty.

Salzkartoffeln *pl* boiled potatoes.

Salzstange (*pl* -n) *die* pretzel (stick).

Salzstreuer (*pl* -) *der* salt cellar.

Salzwasser *das* saltwater ; (*zum Kochen*) salted water.

Samen (*pl* -) *der* seed.

Sammelfahrschein (*pl* -e) *der* ≃ travelcard.

sammeln *vt* to collect ; (*Pilze, Kräuter*) to pick. ■ **sich sammeln** *ref* to gather.

Sammelstelle (*pl* -n) *die* collection point.

Sammler, in (*mpl* -) *der, die* collector.

Sammlung (*pl* -en) *die* collection.

Samstag (*pl* -e) *der* Saturday ; **am ~** on Saturday.

Samstagabend *der* Saturday evening ; (**am**) **~** Saturday evening.

Samstagmorgen *der* Saturday mornig ; (**am**) **~** Saturday morning.

Samstagnacht *adv* Saturday night.

samstags *adv* on Saturdays.

samt *präp* (+D) together with.

sämtlich adj all ; ~e Bücher all the books.

Sanatorium (pl -torien) das sanatorium.

Sand der sand.

Sandale (pl -n) die sandal.

sandig adj sandy.

Sandkasten (pl -kästen) der sandpit.

Sandpapier das sandpaper.

Sandstrand (pl -strände) der sandy beach.

sandte prät → senden.

sanft adj gentle ; (Musik) soft ; (Geburt) natural ; (Tourismus) sustainable. ◆ adv softly.

sang prät → singen.

Sänger, in (mpl -) der, die singer.

sanitär adj sanitary ; ~e Anlagen sanitation (sg).

Sanitäter, in (mpl -) der, die paramedic.

sank prät → sinken.

Sankt Gallen nt St. Gallen.

Sardelle (pl -n) die anchovy.

Sardine (pl -n) die sardine.

Sarg (pl Särge) der coffin.

saß prät → sitzen.

Satellit (pl -en) der satellite.

Satellitenfernsehen das satellite television.

Satellitenschüssel (pl -n) die satellite dish.

Satire (pl -n) die satire.

satt adj (nicht hungrig) full ; bist du ~? have you had enough? ; jn/etw ~ haben to be fed up with sb/sthg.

Sattel (pl Sättel) der saddle.

Satz (pl Sätze) der (GRAMM) sentence ; (Sprung) leap ; (SPORT) set ; (MUS) movement ; (Tarif) rate.

Satzzeichen (pl -) das punctuation mark.

sauber adj clean ; (gut, korrekt) neat.

sauber machen vt to clean.

säubern vt (sauber machen) to clean.

Sauce (pl -n) die sauce ; (Bratensoße) gravy.

Saudi-Arabien nt Saudi Arabia.

sauer adj sour ; (ärgerlich) annoyed. ◆ adv : ~ reagieren to be annoyed ; ~ sein auf (+A) to be annoyed with ; saurer Regen acid rain.

Sauerbraten (pl -) der braised beef marinated in vinegar, sauerbraten.

Sauerkirsche (pl -n) die sour cherry.

Sauerkraut das sauerkraut, pickled cabbage.

Sauerrahm der sour cream.

Sauerstoff der oxygen.

Sauerstoffmaske (pl -n) die oxygen mask.

Sauerteig der sour dough.

saufen (präs säuft, prät soff, pp gesoffen) vi (Tier) to drink ; (fam : Person) to booze.

säuft präs → saufen.

saugen[1] (prät sog, pp gesogen) vt & vi to suck.

saugen[2] vt (Teppich) to vacuum.

Säugling (pl -e) der baby.

Säule (pl -n) die (an Bauwerk) column, pillar.

Sauna (pl Saunen) die sauna.

Säure (*pl* -n) *die* (*chemisch*) acid.

Saxofon, Saxophon (*pl* -e) *das* saxophone.

SB *abk* → **Selbstbedienung**.

S-Bahn (*pl* -en) *die* suburban railway.

S-Bahn-Haltestelle (*pl* -n) *die* suburban railway stop.

S-Bahnhof (*pl* -höfe) *der* suburban railway station.

S-Bahn-Linie (*pl* -n) *die* suburban railway line.

Schach *das* (*Spiel*) chess.

Schachbrett (*pl* -er) *das* chessboard.

Schachfigur (*pl* -en) *die* chess piece.

Schachspiel (*pl* -e) *das* (*Spielen*) game of chess ; (*Brett und Figuren*) chess set.

Schachtel (*pl* -n) *die* (*aus Pappe*) box.

schade *adj* : es ist ~ it's a shame ; wie ~! what a shame!

schaden *vi* (+*D*) to damage ; (*Person*) to harm ; es kann nichts ~ it won't do any harm.

Schaden (*pl* Schäden) *der* damage ; (*Nachteil*) disadvantage.

Schadenersatz *der* compensation.

Schadenfreude *die* malicious pleasure.

schadenfroh *adj* gloating.

Schadensfall (*pl* -fälle) *der* : im ~ in the event of damage.

schadhaft *adj* damaged.

schädlich *adj* harmful.

Schadstoff (*pl* -e) *der* pollutant.

schadstoffarm *adj* low in pollutants.

Schaf (*pl* -e) *das* sheep.

Schäfer, in (*mpl* -) *der, die* shepherd (shepherdess).

Schäferhund (*pl* -e) *der* Alsatian.

schaffen[1] *vt* 1. (*zustande bringen, beenden*) to manage ; (*Prüfung*) to get through ; es ~, etw zu tun to manage to do sthg ; er hat nicht einmal das erste Semester geschafft he didn't even manage to finish the first semester ; geschafft! that's it! 2. (*fam : erschöpfen*) to wear out ; geschafft sein to be worn out. 3. (*transportieren*) to take. ◆ *vi* (*Süddt : arbeiten*) to work.

schaffen[2] (*präs* schafft, *prät* schuf, *pp* geschaffen) *vt* (*erschaffen*) to create.

Schaffner, in (*mpl* -) *der, die* (*im Zug*) ticket collector ; (*im Bus*) conductor.

Schafskäse *der* ewe's milk cheese.

schal *adj* (*Getränk*) flat.

Schal (*pl* -s) *der* scarf.

Schale (*pl* -n) *die* (*von Obst, Gemüse*) skin ; (*von Apfelsine, Apfel, Kartoffeln*) peel ; (*Schüssel*) bowl ; (*von Nuss, Ei*) shell.

schälen *vt* to peel. ▨ **sich schälen** *ref* to peel.

Schalldämpfer (*pl* -) *der* silencer.

Schallplatte (*pl* -n) *die* record.

schalt *prät* → **schelten**.

schalten *vi* (*im Auto*) to change gear ; aufs zweite Programm ~ to turn to channel two ; **in den vierten Gang ~** to change to fourth gear.

Schalter (pl -) der (Knopf) switch ; (bei Bank, Bahn) counter.

Schalterbeamte, beamtin (mpl -n) der, die counter clerk.

Schalterhalle (pl -n) die hall (at post office, station, etc).

Schalteröffnungszeiten pl opening hours.

Schalterschluss der closing time.

Schalthebel (pl -) der (im Auto) gear lever.

Schaltknüppel (pl -) der gear lever.

Schaltung (pl -en) die (Gangschaltung) gear change.

schämen : sich schämen ref to be ashamed.

Schanze (pl -n) die (SPORT) ski-jump.

scharf (komp schärfer, superl am schärfsten) adj sharp ; (Gericht) hot, spicy ; (fam : toll) great ; (fam : erotisch) sexy. ◆ adv (bremsen) hard ; (sehen, analysieren) closely ; ~ gewürzt hot, spicy ; ~ sein auf (+A) (fam) to be keen on.

Scharlach der (MED) scarlet fever.

Scharnier (pl -e) das hinge.

Schaschlik (pl -s) das (shish) kebab.

Schatten (pl -) der shadow ; **im ~** in the shade.

schattig adj shady.

Schatz (pl Schätze) der treasure ; (fam : Liebling) darling.

schätzen vt to estimate ; (glauben, meinen) to think ; (gern haben) to value.

schätzungsweise adv approximately.

Schau (pl -en) die show.

schauen vi to look ; ~ **nach** (sich kümmern) to look after ; **schau mal!** look!

Schauer (pl -) der (Regen) shower.

Schaufel (pl -n) die (zum Graben) shovel.

Schaufenster (pl -) das shop window.

Schaufensterbummel (pl -) der window-shopping trip.

Schaukel (pl -n) die (an Seilen) swing.

schaukeln vt & vi to rock.

Schaukelstuhl (pl -stühle) der rocking chair.

Schaulustige (pl -n) der, die onlooker.

Schaum der foam ; (von Seife) lather ; (von Bier) head.

Schaumbad (pl -bäder) das bubble bath.

Schaumfestiger (pl -) der (styling) mousse.

Schaumgummi der foam rubber.

Schaumkur (pl -en) die shampoo (for damaged hair).

Schaumwein (pl -e) der sparkling wine.

Schauspiel (pl -e) das play ; (fam : Spektakel) spectacle.

Schauspieler, in (mpl -) der, die actor (actress).

Schauspielhaus (pl -häuser) das theatre.

Scheck (*pl* -s) *der* cheque ; einen ~ einlösen to cash a cheque ; mit ~ bezahlen to pay by cheque ; '~s aller Art' 'all cheques welcome'.

Scheckgebühr (*pl* -en) *die* charge for cheques.

Scheckheft (*pl* -e) *das* chequebook.

Scheckkarte (*pl* -n) *die* cheque card.

Scheibe (*pl* -n) *die* (*von Brot, Käse*) slice ; (*Fensterscheibe*) window pane ; (*von Auto*) window.

Scheibenbremse (*pl* -n) *die* disc brake.

Scheibenwischer (*pl* -) *der* windscreen wiper.

Scheide (*pl* -n) *die* (*Vagina*) vagina.

scheiden (*prät* schied, *pp* geschieden) *vt* (*Ehe*) to dissolve ; sich ~ lassen to get a divorce.

Scheidung (*pl* -en) *die* divorce.

Schein (*pl* -e) *der* (*Formular, Bescheinigung*) certificate ; (*Geld*) note ; (*Anschein*) appearances (*pl*) ; (*Licht*) light.

scheinbar *adj* apparent. ◆ *adv* seemingly.

scheinen (*prät* schien, *pp* geschienen) *vi* (*Sonne*) to shine ; (*vermutlich*) to seem. ◆ *vimp* : es scheint it seems ; es scheint mir... it seems to me...

Scheinwerfer (*pl* -) *der* (AUTO) headlight ; (*in Halle, Stadion*) floodlight.

Scheinwerferlicht *das* (AUTO) headlights (*pl*) ; (*in Halle, Stadion*) floodlight.

Scheiße *die* (*vulg*) shit. ◆ *interj* (*vulg*) shit!

scheißen (*prät* schiss, *pp* geschissen) *vi* (*vulg*) to shit.

Scheitel (*pl* -) *der* (*Frisur*) parting (*Br*), part (*Am*).

Schelle (*pl* -n) *die* (*an Haustür*) doorbell.

schellen *vi* to ring ; es schellt the bell is ringing.

schelten (*präs* schilt, *prät* schalt, *pp* gescholten) *vt* (*geh* : *Kind*) to scold.

Schema (*pl* -ta) *das* (*Vorstellung*) scheme ; (*Abbildung*) diagram.

Schemel (*pl* -) *der* (*zum Sitzen*) stool.

Schenkel (*pl* -) *der* thigh.

schenken *vt* to give ; jm etw ~ (*Geschenk*) to give sb sthg (as a present) ; sich (*D*) etw ~ (*erlassen*) to give sthg a miss.

Scherbe (*pl* -n) *die* fragment.

Schere (*pl* -n) *die* (*zum Schneiden*) scissors (*pl*).

scheren : sich scheren (*prät* scherte, *pp* geschert) *ref* : sich nicht ~ um (*kümmern*) not to care about.

Scherz (*pl* -e) *der* joke.

scherzhaft *adj* joking.

scheu *adj* shy.

Scheuerlappen (*pl* -) *der* floorcloth.

scheuern *vt* (*putzen*) to scour. ◆ *vi* (*Sattel, Kleidung*) to rub ; jm eine ~ (*fam* : *Ohrfeige geben*) to clip sb round the ear.

Scheuerpulver *das* scouring powder.

Scheune (*pl* -n) *die* barn.

scheußlich *adj* terrible.

Schicht (*pl* -en) *die* layer ; *(in Gesellschaft)* class ; *(Arbeitszeit)* shift.

schick *adj* smart.

schicken *vt* to send ; jm etw ~ to send sb sthg ; ~ an *(+A)* to send to.

Schicksal (*pl* -e) *das* fate.

Schiebedach (*pl* -dächer) *das* sunroof.

schieben (*prät* schob, *pp* geschoben) *vt* to push ; die Schuld auf einen anderen ~ to put the blame on sb else. ■ **sich schieben** *ref* (*Person*) to push (one's way).

Schieber (*pl* -) *der* (*Gerät*) bar, bolt.

Schiebetür (*pl* -en) *die* sliding door.

schied *prät* → scheiden.

Schiedsrichter, in (*mpl* -) *der, die* (*in Fußball*) referee ; (*in Tennis*) umpire.

schief *adj* & *adv* crooked.

schief gehen *vi unr ist* (*fam*) to go wrong.

schielen *vi* to squint.

schien *prät* → scheinen.

Schienbein (*pl* -e) *das* shin.

Schiene (*pl* -n) *die* (*Gleis*) rail ; (*MED*) splint.

schießen (*prät* schoss, *pp* geschossen) *vi hat* & *ist* to shoot. ◆ *vt hat* to shoot ; (*Tor*) to score ; (*Foto*) to take ; (*Ball*) to kick.

Schiff (*pl* -e) *das* ship ; (*von Kirche*) nave ; mit dem ~ by ship.

Schifffahrt *die* shipping.

Schifffahrtsgesellschaft (*pl* -en) *die* shipping company.

Schiffskarte (*pl* -n) *die* (navigation) chart.

Schiffsreise (*pl* -n) *die* voyage.

Schiffsverbindung (*pl* -en) *die* connecting boat service.

Schiffsverkehr *der* shipping.

schikanieren *vt* (*abw*) to bully.

Schild (*pl* -er) *das* sign ; (*Etikett*) label ; (*Waffe*) shield.

Schilddrüse (*pl* -n) *die* thyroid gland.

schildern *vt* to describe.

Schildkröte (*pl* -n) *die* (*auf dem Land*) tortoise ; (*im Wasser*) turtle.

Schilf (*pl* -e) *das* (*Pflanze*) reed.

Schilling (*pl* -e) *der* schilling.

schilt *präs* → schelten.

Schimmel (*pl* -) *der* (*auf Obst, an Wand*) mould ; (*Pferd*) grey (horse).

schimmelig *adj* mouldy.

schimpfen *vi* to moan ; mit jm ~ to get angry with sb.

Schimpfwort (*pl* -e) *das* swearword.

Schinken (*pl* -) *der* (*Fleisch*) ham ; roher/gekochter/geräucherter ~ cured/cooked/smoked ham.

Schinkenspeck *der* bacon.

Schinkenwurst *die* ham sausage.

Schirm (*pl* -e) *der* (*Regenschirm*) umbrella.

schiss *prät* → scheißen.

Schlaf *der* sleep.

Schlafanzug (*pl* -anzüge) *der* pyjamas (*pl*).

schlafen (*präs* **schläft**, *prät* **schlief**, *pp* **geschlafen**) *vi* to sleep ; ~ **gehen** to go to bed ; ~ **mit** to sleep with ; **schlaf gut!** sleep well!

Schlafengehen *das* : **vor dem ~** before going to bed.

Schlafgelegenheit (*pl* -**en**) *die* place to sleep.

Schlaflosigkeit *die* insomnia.

Schlafmittel (*pl* -) *das* sleeping pill.

Schlafsaal (*pl* -**säle**) *der* dormitory.

Schlafsack (*pl* -**säcke**) *der* sleeping bag.

schläft *präs* → schlafen.

Schlaftablette (*pl* -**n**) *die* sleeping pill.

Schlafwagen (*pl*-) *der* sleeper.

Schlafwagenkarte (*pl* -**n**) *die* sleeper ticket.

Schlafwagenplatz(*pl*-**plätze**) *der* sleeper berth.

Schlafzimmer (*pl* -) *das* bedroom.

Schlag (*pl* **Schläge**) *der* blow ; (*elektrisch*) shock ; (*von Herz, Puls*) beat. ■ **Schläge** *pl* (*Prügel*) beating (*sg*).

Schlagader (*pl* -**n**) *die* artery.

Schlaganfall (*pl* -**anfälle**) *der* stroke.

schlagen (*präs* **schlägt**, *prät* **schlug**, *pp* **geschlagen**) *vt* (*verletzen*) to hit ; (*hämmern*) to bang ; (*besiegen, Eiweiß, Sahne*) to beat. ◆ *vi* (*mit Hand, Faust*) to hit ; (*Uhr*) to strike ; (*regelmäßig*) to beat ; **auf etw** (*A*) ~ (*aufprallen*) to hit sthg ; **jn eins**

zu null ~ to beat sb one-nil. ■ **sich schlagen** *ref* (*sich prügeln*) to fight.

Schlager (*pl* -) *der* (*Lied*) hit.

Schläger (*pl* -) *der* (*für Tennis, Badminton*) racquet ; (*für Tischtennis*) bat ; (*für Golf*) club ; (*für Hockey*) stick.

Schlagloch (*pl* -**löcher**) *das* pothole.

Schlagobers *das* (*Österr*) whipped cream.

Schlagsahne *die* whipped cream.

schlägt *präs* → schlagen.

Schlagzeile (*pl* -**n**) *die* headline.

Schlagzeug (*pl* -**e**) *das* (*in Band*) drums (*pl*) ; (*in Orchester*) percussion.

Schlamm *der* mud.

schlampig *adj* sloppy.

schlang *prät* → schlingen.

Schlange (*pl* -**n**) *die* (*Tier*) snake ; (*von Autos, Personen*) queue (*Br*), line (*Am*) ; ~ **stehen** to queue (*Br*), to stand in line (*Am*).

schlängeln : **sich schlängeln** *ref* (*Weg, Fluss*) to wind.

schlank *adj* slim ; ~ **werden** to slim.

schlapp *adj* (*müde, schwach*) tired out.

Schlauch (*pl* **Schläuche**) *der* (*für Wasser*) hose ; (*im Reifen*) tube.

schlau *adj* cunning ; **man wird nicht ~ aus ihm** I can't make him out.

Schlauchboot (*pl* -**e**) *das* rubber dinghy.

schlecht adj bad ; (Lebensmittel) off. ◆ adv badly ; (schmecken, riechen) bad ; (kaum) hardly ; ~ werden to go off ; mir wird ~ I feel ill ; das ist nicht ~ that's not bad.

schleichen (prät schlich, pp geschlichen) vi (Mensch, Tier) to creep ; (Verkehr, Auto) to crawl.

Schleife (pl -n) die (Band) bow ; (Kurve) bend.

schleifen[1] vt (zerren) to drag.

schleifen[2] (präs schleift, prät schliff, pp geschliffen) vt (Messer, Schere) to sharpen.

Schleim der (menschlich) mucus ; (von Schnecke) slime.

Schleimhaut (pl -häute) die mucous membrane.

Schlemmerlokal (pl -e) das gourmet restaurant.

schlendern vi ist to stroll.

schleppen vt to drag ; (Fahrzeug) to tow. ▧ **sich schleppen** ref to drag o.s.

Schlepplift (pl -e) der ski tow.

Schleswig-Holstein nt Schleswig-Holstein.

Schleuder (pl -n) die (für Wäsche) spin-dryer.

Schleudergefahr die : 'Vorsicht ~!' 'slippery road'.

schleudern vt hat to fling ; (Wäsche) to spin-dry. ◆ vi hat (Waschmaschine) to spin. ◆ vi ist (Auto, Fahrer) to skid ; ins Schleudern geraten ODER kommen to go into a skid.

Schleudersitz (pl -e) der ejector seat.

Schleuse (pl -n) die (an Kanal) lock.

schlich prät → schleichen.

schlicht adj simple.

schlief prät → schlafen.

schließen (prät schloss, pp geschlossen) vt to close ; (Betrieb, Lokal) to close down ; (schlussfolgern) to conclude. ◆ vi to close ; (Betrieb, Lokal) to close down. ▧ **sich schließen** ref (Tür, Vorhang) to close.

Schließfach (pl -fächer) das left-luggage locker (Br), baggage locker (Am).

schließlich adv (zuletzt) finally ; (nämlich) after all.

schliff prät → schleifen.

schlimm adj bad. ◆ adv badly ; halb so ~ not so bad.

schlingen (prät schlang, pp geschlungen) vt (Mahlzeit) to gobble down ; (Schnur) to tie.

Schlips (pl -e) der tie.

Schlitten (pl -) der (für Kinder) sledge.

Schlittschuh (pl -e) der ice skate ; ~ laufen to ice-skate.

Schlitz (pl -e) der (Spalt) slit ; (für Geld) slot.

schloss prät → schließen.

Schloss (pl Schlösser) das (Verschluss) lock ; (Gebäude) castle.

Schlosser, in (mpl -) der, die (Metallberuf) metalworker ; (Installateur) mechanic.

Schlosspark (pl -s) der castle grounds (pl).

Schlucht (pl -en) die ravine.

schluchzen vi to sob.

Schluck (pl -e) der (Schlucken) gulp, swallow ; (Menge) drop.

Schluckauf *der* hiccups *(pl)*.

schlucken *vi & vt* to swallow.

Schluckimpfung *(pl* -en*) die* oral vaccination.

schlug *prät →* **schlagen**.

Schlüpfer *(pl* -*) der* knickers *(pl)*.

schlurfen *vi ist* to shuffle.

schlürfen *vt* to slurp.

Schluss *(pl* Schlüsse*) der* end ; *(von Roman, Film)* ending ; *(Folgerung)* conclusion ; **bis zum ~** to the end ; **~ machen mit** *(Person)* to break off with ; *(Sache)* to stop.

Schlüssel *(pl* -*) der (für Schloss)* key ; *(Schraubenschlüssel)* spanner.

Schlüsselbund *(pl* -e*) der* bunch of keys.

Schlüsseldienst *(pl* -e*) der* key-cutting service.

Schlüsselloch *(pl* -löcher*) das* keyhole.

Schlussfolgerung *(pl* -en*) die* conclusion.

Schlussleuchte *(pl* -n*) die (Lampe)* rear light.

Schlussverkauf *(pl* -verkäufe*) der* end-of-season sale.

schmal *adj* narrow ; *(Person)* thin.

Schmalfilm *(pl* -e*) der* cine-film *(Br)*, movie film *(Am)*.

Schmalz *das (zum Kochen)* lard ; *(zum Essen)* dripping.

Schmalznudel *(pl* -n*) die (Österr)* flat, round cake made from deep-fried dough.

Schmankerl *(pl*-n*) das (Süddt & Österr)* delicacy.

schmatzen *vi* to eat noisily.

schmecken *vi* to taste ; *(gut schmecken)* to taste good ; **~ nach** to taste of ; **das schmeckt mir nicht** I don't like it ; **gut/ schlecht ~** to taste good/bad ; **hat es Ihnen geschmeckt?** did you enjoy your meal? ; **lass es dir ~!** enjoy your meal!

schmeißen *(prät* schmiss, *pp* geschmissen*) vt (fam : werfen)* to chuck.

schmelzen *(präs* schmilzt, *prät* schmolz, *pp* geschmolzen*) vi ist & vt hat* to melt.

Schmerz *(pl* -en*) der* pain.

schmerzen *vi* to hurt.

Schmerzensgeld *das* compensation.

schmerzlos *adj* painless.

Schmerzmittel *(pl* -*) das* painkiller.

schmerzstillend *adj* painkilling.

Schmerztablette *(pl* -n*) die* painkiller.

Schmetterling *(pl* -e*) der* butterfly.

Schmied *(pl* -e*) der* blacksmith.

schmieren *vt (Türangel, Maschine)* to oil ; *(Butterbrot)* to spread ; *(fam : bestechen)* to bribe.

Schmierkäse *der* cheese spread.

Schmiermittel *(pl* -*) das* lubricant.

Schmierseife *die* soft soap.

schmilzt *präs →* **schmelzen**.

Schminke *die* make-up.

schminken *vt* to make up.
■ **sich schminken** *ref* to put on one's make-up.

Schmirgelpapier das sand-paper.

schmiss prät → schmeißen.

schmollen vi to sulk.

schmolz prät → schmelzen.

Schmorbraten (pl -) der pot roast.

schmoren vt (zubereiten) to braise.

Schmuck der (für Person) jew-ellery ; (für Raum, Tannen-baum) decoration.

schmücken vt to decorate.

schmuggeln vt to smuggle.

schmunzeln vi to smile.

schmusen vi to cuddle.

Schmutz der dirt.

schmutzig adj dirty ; sich ~ machen to get dirty.

Schnalle (pl -n) die buckle.

schnappen vt to catch ; (fam : packen, nehmen) to grab. ◆ vi (Tier) to snap.

Schnappschuss (pl -schüsse) der snapshot.

Schnaps (pl Schnäpse) der schnapps.

Schnapsglas (pl -gläser) das shot glass.

schnarchen vi to snore.

Schnauze (pl -n) die (von Tier) muzzle ; (vulg : von Mensch) gob.

Schnecke (pl -n) die (Tier) snail ; (Gebäck) ≃ Chelsea bun.

Schnee der snow ; es liegt ~ there's snow on the ground.

Schneeball (pl -bälle) der snowball.

schneebedeckt adj snow-covered.

Schneebrille (pl -n) die snow-goggles (pl).

Schneefall der snowfall.

Schneeflocke (pl -n) die snowflake.

schneefrei adj free of snow.

Schneegestöber (pl -) das snowstorm.

Schneeglätte die packed snow.

Schneegrenze (pl -n) die snow-line.

Schneekette (pl -n) die snow-chain.

Schneemann (pl -männer) der snowman.

Schneepflug (pl -pflüge) der snowplough.

Schneeregen der sleet.

Schneeschmelze die thaw.

Schneesturm (pl -stürme) der snowstorm.

Schneetreiben (pl -) das driving snow.

Schneewehe (pl -n) die snowdrift.

schneiden (prät schnitt, pp geschnitten) vt to cut ; (ignorie-ren) to ignore ; (beim Überholen) to cut in on. ◆ vi to cut ; etw in Würfel ~ to cut sthg into cubes ; sich (D) in den Finger ~ to cut one's finger. ■ sich schnei-den ref (sich verletzen) to cut o.s. ; (sich kreuzen) to cross.

Schneider, in (mpl -) der, die (Beruf) tailor.

Schneiderei (pl -en) die (Ge-schäft) tailor's (shop).

schneien vimp : es schneit it's snowing.

schnell adj quick, fast. ◆ adv quickly, fast ; ~ **machen** to hurry up.

Schnellhefter (pl -) der loose-leaf folder.

Schnelligkeit die speed.

Schnellimbiss (pl -e) der snack bar.

Schnellreinigung (pl -en) die express cleaning.

Schnellstraße (pl -n) die expressway.

Schnellzug (pl -züge) der express train.

schnitt prät → schneiden.

Schnitt (pl -e) der cut ; (Schnittmuster) pattern.

Schnittblumen pl cut flowers.

Schnitte (pl -n) die (Brotscheibe) slice ; (belegtes Brot) open sandwich.

Schnittkäse der sliced cheese.

Schnittlauch der chives (pl).

Schnittwunde (pl -n) die cut.

Schnitzel (pl -) das : Wiener ~ escalope of veal.

Schnorchel (pl -) der snorkel.

schnorcheln vi to snorkel.

Schnuller (pl -) der dummy (Br), pacifier (Am).

Schnulze (pl -n) die (Lied) sentimental song.

Schnupfen der cold ; ~ **haben/bekommen** to have/get a cold.

Schnupftabak (pl -e) der snuff.

Schnur (pl Schnüre) die (zum Binden) string, cord ; (Kabel) lead.

Schnurrbart (pl -bärte) der moustache.

Schnürsenkel (pl -) der shoelace.

schob prät → schieben.

Schock (pl -s) der shock ; unter ~ **stehen** to be in shock.

schockieren vt to shock.

Schokolade (pl -n) die chocolate ; (Getränk) hot chocolate.

Scholle (pl -n) die (Fisch) plaice.

schon adv 1. (relativ früh, spät) already ; **wir essen heute ~ um elf Uhr** we're eating earlier today, at eleven o'clock ; **es ist ~ lange so** it has been like that for a long time ; ~ **jetzt** already. 2. (bis jetzt) yet ; **warst du ~ bei der Post?** have you been to the post office yet? ; **warst du ~ mal in Kanada?** have you ever been to Canada? ; **ich war ~ mal im Ausland** I've been abroad before ; **ich bereite das ~ mal vor** I'll get that ready now. 3. (relativ viel) already ; ~ **wieder** again. 4. (endlich) : **komm ~!** come on! 5. (zur Beruhigung) : **das schaffst du ~** don't worry, I'm sure you'll manage it ; ~ **gut!** all right! 6. (allein) just ; ~ **der Gedanke daran macht mich nervös** just thinking about it makes me nervous.

schön adj nice ; (Frau) beautiful ; (Mann) handsome ; (beträchtlich) considerable. ◆ adv well ; **ganz ~** really ; **na ~** all right.

schonen

schonen *vt (Person)* to go
easy on ; *(Gegenstand)* to look
after. ▪ **sich schonen** *ref* to
take it easy.

Schönheit *(pl* -en) *die*
beauty.

Schönheitssalon *(pl* -s) *der*
beauty salon.

Schonkost *die* light diet.

schön machen : **sich schön
machen** *ref (fam)* to get ready,
to do o.s. up.

Schönwetterlage *die* spell
of fine weather.

Schöpfkelle *(pl* -n) *die* ladle.

Schoppen *(pl* -) *der* large
glass of wine.

Schorf *der* scab.

Schorle *(pl* -) *die (mit Apfelsaft)* apple juice with mineral water ; *(mit Wein)* spritzer.

Schornstein *(pl* -e) *der* chimney.

schoss *prät* → **schießen**.

Schoß *(pl* Schöße) *der (Körperteil)* lap ; **bei jm auf dem ~ sitzen**
to sit on sb's lap.

Schotte *(pl* -n) *der* Scotsman ;
die ~n the Scots.

Schottin *(pl* -nen) *die* Scotswoman.

schottisch *adj* Scottish.

Schottland *nt* Scotland.

schräg *adj (schief)* sloping ;
(Linie) diagonal.

Schramme *(pl* -n) *die* scratch.

Schrank *(pl* Schränke) *der (mit
Fächern)* cupboard ; *(zum Aufhängen)* wardrobe.

Schranke *(pl* -n) *die (Gegenstand)* barrier.

Schrankwand *(pl* -wände)
die wall unit.

Schraube *(pl* -n) *die (aus Metall)* screw.

schrauben *vt* to screw.

Schraubenschlüssel *(pl* -)
der spanner *(Br)*, wrench *(Am)*.

Schraubenzieher *(pl* -) *der*
screwdriver.

Schrebergarten *(pl*-gärten)
der allotment.

Schreck *der* fright ; **einen ~
kriegen** to get a fright.

schreckhaft *adj* easily
scared.

schrecklich *adj* terrible.

Schrei *(pl* -e) *der (Geräusch)*
shout, cry.

schreiben *(prät* **schrieb**, *pp*
geschrieben) *vt (gen)* to write ;
**etw groß/klein ~ → großschrei-
ben → kleinschreiben** ; **wie
schreibt man das?** how do you
spell that?
◆ *vi* to write ; **an etw (D) ~** *(Roman)* to be writing sthg ; **über
etw (A) ~** to write about sthg.
▪ **sich schreiben** *ref* to be
spelt.

Schreiben *(pl* -) *das (amt)* letter.

Schreibheft *(pl* -e) *das* exercise book.

Schreibmaschine *(pl* -n) *die*
typewriter.

Schreibpapier *das* writing
paper.

Schreibtisch *(pl* -e) *der* desk.

Schreibwaren *pl* stationery
(sg).

Schreibwarengeschäft
(pl -e) *das* stationery shop.

schreien *(prät* **schrie**, *pp* **geschrien)** *vi* & *vt* to shout ; **~ nach**
to shout at.

Schreiner, in *(mpl -)* der, die joiner.

schreiten *(prät* schritt, *pp* geschritten) *vi* ist *(geh* : *gehen)* to stride.

schrie *prät →* schreien.

schrieb *prät →* schreiben.

Schrift *(pl -en)* die *(Handschrift)* handwriting ; *(Schriftbild)* type ; *(Aufschrift, Text)* writing ; *(lateinische, arabische)* script ; **die Heilige ~** the Scriptures *(pl).*

schriftlich *adj* written. ◆ *adv* in writing.

Schriftsteller, in *(mpl -)* der, die writer.

schritt *prät →* schreiten.

Schritt *(pl -e)* der step ; **'~ fahren''** 'dead slow'.

Schritttempo das walking speed.

Schrott der *(Metall)* scrap metal ; *(fam* : *Plunder)* rubbish.

Schrottplatz *(pl -plätze)* der scrapyard.

schrubben *vt & vi* to scrub.

Schrubber *(pl -)* der scrubbing brush.

Schubkarre *(pl -n)* die wheelbarrow.

Schublade *(pl -n)* die drawer.

schubsen *vt* to shove.

schüchtern *adj* shy.

schuf *prät →* schaffen.

Schüfeli das *(Schweiz)* smoked pork.

Schuh *(pl -e)* der shoe.

Schuhanzieher *(pl -)* der shoehorn.

Schuhbürste *(pl -n)* die shoe brush.

Schuhcreme *(pl -s)* die shoe polish.

Schuhgeschäft *(pl -e)* das shoe shop.

Schuhgröße *(pl -n)* die shoe size.

Schuhlöffel *(pl -)* der shoehorn.

Schuhmacher, in *(mpl -)* der, die shoemaker.

Schuhputzmittel *(pl -)* das shoe polish.

Schuhsohle *(pl -n)* die (shoe) sole.

Schulabschluss *(pl -abschlüsse)* der school-leaving qualification.

Schulbeginn der beginning of term.

schuld *adj* : **~ sein an** *(+D)* to be to blame for ; **du bist ~ daran** it's your fault.

Schuld die *(Verantwortung)* blame ; *(Unrecht)* guilt ; **~ haben an** *(+D)* to be to blame for. ■ **Schulden** *pl* debts ; **~en haben** to be in debt ; **~en machen** to run up debts.

schuldig *adj* guilty ; **jm etw ~ sein** to owe sb sthg.

Schuldschein *(pl -e)* der IOU.

Schule *(pl -n)* die school ; **zur** ODER **in die ~ gehen** to go to school ; **in der ~** at school.

schulen *vt* to train.

Schüler, in *(mpl -)* der, die pupil.

Schüleraustausch der (student) exchange.

Schülerausweis *(pl -e)* der *pupil's ID card entitling him/her to concessions etc.*

Schülerkarte (*pl* -n) *die (Fahrkarte)* school season ticket.

Schulferien *pl* school holidays.

schulfrei *adj* : morgen haben wir ~ we don't have to go to school tomorrow.

Schulfreund, in (*mpl* -e) *der, die* schoolfriend.

Schuljahr (*pl* -e) *das* school year.

Schulklasse (*pl* -n) *die* class.

Schulter (*pl* -n) *die* shoulder.

Schultüte *die large cone of sweets.*

SCHULTÜTE

A "Schultüte" is a large brightly-coloured paper cone full of sweets and small gifts which parents give to their children on their first day at school to try to make the day a little easier for them. The children may only open the cone once they have arrived at school.

Schulung (*pl* -en) *die* training.

Schulzeit *die* schooldays (*pl*).

Schuppe (*pl* -n) *die (von Fisch)* scale. ▪ **Schuppen** *pl (auf Kopf)* dandruff (*sg*).

Schürfwunde (*pl* -n) *die* graze.

Schurwolle *die* pure new wool.

Schürze (*pl* -n) *die* apron.

Schuss (*pl* Schüsse) *der* shot ; gut in ~ sein to be in good shape ; ein ~ Whisky a dash of whisky.

Schüssel (*pl* -n) *die* bowl.

Schuster, in (*mpl* -) *der, die* shoemaker.

Schutt *der* rubble ; '~ abladen verboten' 'no dumping'.

Schüttelfrost *der* shivering fit.

schütteln *vt* to shake ; den Kopf ~ to shake one's head ; vor Gebrauch ~ shake before use. ▪ **sich schütteln** *ref* to shake.

schütten *vt* to pour. ◆ *vimp* : es schüttet it's pouring (with rain).

Schutz *der* protection ; (*vor Regen, Wind*) shelter ; jn in ~ nehmen to stand up for sb.

Schutzblech (*pl* -e) *das* mudguard.

Schutzbrief (*pl* -e) *der* travel insurance certificate.

Schutzbrille (*pl* -n) *die* goggles (*pl*).

schützen *vt* to protect. ◆ *vi* (*Dach*) to give shelter ; (*Versicherung*) to give cover ; jn vor etw (D) ~ to protect sb against sthg. ▪ **sich schützen** *ref* to protect o.s.

Schützenfest (*pl* -e) *das shooting festival.*

SCHÜTZENFEST

The "Schützenfest" is a shooting festival held mainly in rural communities. It is organized by the local rifle club which is the centre of communal life in many of these rural areas. A competition is held to find the best shot, who is then crowned

"Schützenkönig" (king of the shooting festival). There are also beer tents and fairground attractions, including shooting galleries.

Schutzgebiet (*pl* -e) *das (von Wasser)* protected area.

Schutzhütte (*pl* -n) *die* shelter.

Schutzimpfung (*pl* -en) *die* vaccination.

Schutzumschlag (*pl* -umschläge) *der* dust jacket.

schwach (*komp* schwächer, *superl* am schwächsten) *adj* weak ; *(schlecht)* poor.

Schwäche (*pl* -n) *die* weakness.

schwachsinnig *adj (unsinnig)* nonsensical.

Schwachstrom *der* low-voltage current.

Schwager (*pl* -) *der* brother-in-law.

Schwägerin (*pl* -nen) *die* sister-in-law.

Schwalbe (*pl* -n) *die* swallow.

schwamm *prät* → schwimmen.

Schwamm (*pl* Schwämme) *der* sponge.

Schwammtuch (*pl* -tücher) *das* cloth.

Schwan (*pl* Schwäne) *der* swan.

schwang *prät* → schwingen.

schwanger *adj* pregnant.

Schwangerschaft (*pl* -en) *die* pregnancy.

Schwangerschaftstest (*pl* -s) *der* pregnancy test.

schwanken *vi* ist to sway ; *(gedanklich)* to waver ; *(Kurs, Preise)* to fluctuate.

Schwanz (*pl* Schwänze) *der* tail ; *(vulg : von Mann)* cock.

Schwarm (*pl* Schwärme) *der* *(von Tieren)* swarm.

schwarz *adj* black. ◆ *adv (illegal)* on the black market ; **der ~e Markt** the black market ; **in den ~en Zahlen** in the black.

Schwarz *das* black.

Schwarzarbeit *die* moonlighting.

Schwarzbrot (*pl* -e) *das* black bread.

Schwarze (*pl* -n) *der, die (Farbiger)* black ; *(Konservativer)* conservative.

schwarz|fahren *vi unr* ist to travel without a ticket.

Schwarzfahrer, in (*mpl* -) *der, die* fare dodger.

Schwarzmarkt *der* black market.

Schwarzwald *der* Black Forest.

Schwarzwälder Kirschtorte (*pl* -n) *die* black forest gateau.

schwarzweiß *adj* black and white.

Schwarzweißfilm (*pl* -e) *der* black and white film.

Schwarzwurzel (*pl* -n) *die* oyster plant.

Schwebebahn (*pl* -en) *die* cable railway.

schweben *vi (fliegen)* to float.

Schwede (*pl* -n) *der* Swede.

Schweden *nt* Sweden.

Schwedin (*pl* -nen) *die* Swede.

schwedisch adj Swedish.

Schwedisch(e) das Swedish.

Schwefel der sulphur.

schweigen (prät schwieg, pp geschwiegen) vi (Person) to be silent.

Schweigepflicht die confidentiality.

Schwein (pl -e) das pig; (Fleisch) pork.

Schweinebraten (pl -) der roast pork.

Schweinefleisch das pork.

Schweinerei (pl -en) die (fam : schlimme Sache) scandal; (fam : Schmutz) mess.

Schweinshaxe (pl -n) die (Süddt) fried knuckle of pork.

Schweiß der sweat.

schweißen vt to weld.

Schweiz die Switzerland.

Schweizer (pl -) der Swiss.

Schweizerin (pl -nen) die Swiss.

schwellen (präs schwillt, prät schwoll, pp geschwollen) vi (dick werden) to swell.

Schwellung (pl -en) die swelling.

schwer adj heavy; (stark) serious; (schwierig) difficult. ◆ adv (fam : sehr) really; (verletzt) seriously; (arbeiten) hard; das ist nur ~ möglich that won't be easy; zehn Kilo ~ sein to weigh ten kilos; es ~ haben mit to have a hard time with.

Schwerbehinderte (pl -n) der, die severely handicapped person.

schwerhörig adj hard of hearing.

schwer krank adj seriously ill.

schwer verletzt adj seriously injured.

Schwester (pl -n) die sister; (Krankenschwester) nurse.

schwieg prät → schweigen.

Schwiegereltern pl parents-in-law.

Schwiegermutter (pl -mütter) die mother-in-law.

Schwiegersohn (pl -söhne) der son-in-law.

Schwiegertochter (pl -töchter) die daughter-in-law.

Schwiegervater (pl -väter) der father-in-law.

schwierig adj difficult.

Schwierigkeit (pl -en) die (Problem) difficulty; in ~en geraten/stecken to get into difficulty/be having difficulties.

schwillt präs → schwellen.

Schwimmbad (pl -bäder) das swimming pool.

Schwimmbecken (pl -) das swimming pool.

schwimmen (prät schwamm, pp geschwommen) vi ist to swim; (Gegenstand) to float. ◆ vt ist (Strecke) to swim.

Schwimmer, in (mpl -) der, die swimmer.

Schwimmerbecken (pl -) das swimmers' pool.

Schwimmflosse (pl -n) die flipper (Br), fin (Am).

Schwimmflügel (pl -) der armband.

Schwimmhalle (pl -n) die indoor swimming pool.

Schwimmreifen (pl -) der rubber ring.

Schwimmweste (*pl* -n) *die* life jacket.

schwindelig *adj* dizzy ; **mir ist/wird ~** I am/am getting dizzy.

schwingen (*prät* schwang, *pp* geschwungen) *vi* to swing. ◆ *vt* (*Fahne*) to wave ; (*Peitsche*) to brandish. ■ **sich schwingen** *ref* (aufs Pferd, ins Auto) to jump.

Schwips (*pl* -e) *der* (*fam*) : einen ~ haben to be tipsy.

schwitzen *vi* to sweat.

schwoll *prät* → schwellen.

schwor *prät* → schwören.

schwören (*prät* schwor, *pp* geschworen) *vt* to swear.

schwul *adj* (*fam*) gay.

schwül *adj* (*Wetter*) muggy, close.

Schwung *der* (*Bewegung*) swing ; (*Elan*) zest ; **mit ~** with zest.

Schwur (*pl* Schwüre) *der* oath.

sechs *num & pron* six ; **fünf vor/nach ~** five to/past six ; **~ Uhr fünfundvierzig** six forty-five ; **um ~** (*Uhr*) at six (o'clock) ; **sie ist ~** (Jahre alt) she is six (years old) ; **wir waren ~** there were six of us.

sechshundert *num* six hundred.

sechsmal *adv* six times.

sechste, r, s *adj* sixth ; **der ~ Juni** the sixth of June, June the sixth.

Sechstel (*pl* -) *das* sixth.

sechzehn *num* sixteen ; → **sechs.**

sechzig *num* sixty ; → **sechs.**

See[1] (*pl* -n) *der* (*Teich*) lake.

See[2] *die* (*Meer*) sea ; **an die ~ fahren** to go to the seaside ; **an der ~** at the seaside.

Seebad (*pl* -bäder) *das* seaside resort.

Seegang *der* : **leichter/hoher ~** calm/rough seas (*pl*).

Seeigel (*pl* -) *der* sea urchin.

seekrank *adj* seasick.

Seele (*pl* -n) *die* soul.

Seeleute *pl* sailors.

seelisch *adj* mental.

Seelsorger, in (*mpl* -) *der, die* (*Priester*) pastor.

Seeluft *die* sea air.

Seemeile (*pl* -n) *die* nautical mile.

Seenot *die* distress.

Seereise (*pl* -n) *die* voyage.

Seeweg *der* : **auf dem ~** by sea.

Segel (*pl* -) *das* sail.

Segelboot (*pl* -e) *das* sailing boat.

Segelfliegen *das* gliding.

Segelflugzeug (*pl* -e) *das* glider.

segeln *vi* (mit Boot) to sail.

Segelschiff (*pl* -e) *das* sailing ship.

sehbehindert *adj* partially sighted.

sehen (*präs* sieht, *prät* sah, *pp* gesehen) *vt & vi* to see ; **gut/schlecht ~** to have good/bad eyesight ; **jm ähnlich ~** to look like sb ; **sieh mal!** look! ; **mal ~!** we'll see! ; **siehste** ODER **siehst du!** (*fam*) you see ; **nach jm ~** (*aufpassen*) to look after sb. ■ **sich sehen** *ref* (sich treffen) to see each other.

Sehne (*pl* -n) *die* (*von Muskeln*) tendon.

sehnen : **sich sehnen** *ref* : **sich ~ nach** to long for.

Sehnenscheidenentzündung (*pl* -en) *die* tendonitis.

Sehnsucht *die* longing.

sehr *adv* very ; **bitte ~!** you're welcome! ; **das gefällt mir ~** I like that a lot ; **danke ~!** thank you very much ; **~ viel Geld** an awful lot of money ; **zu ~** too much.

seid *präs* → **sein**[1].

Seide (*pl* -n) *die* silk.

Seife (*pl* -n) *die* soap.

Seifenlauge (*pl* -n) *die* soap suds (*pl*).

Seil (*pl* -e) *das* rope.

Seilbahn (*pl* -en) *die* cable railway.

sein[1] (*präs* **ist**, *prät* **war**, *pp* **gewesen**) *aux* 1. (*im Perfekt*) to have ; **sie ist gegangen** she has gone.
2. (*im Konjunktiv*) : **sie wäre gegangen** she would have gone.
◆ *vi* 1. (*Angabe von Eigenschaft, Zustand, Identität*) to be ; **mir ist schlecht/kalt** I'm ill/cold ; **Lehrer ~** to be a teacher.
2. (*Angabe von Position*) to be ; **das Hemd ist im Koffer** the shirt is in the suitcase.
3. (*Angabe der Zeit*) to be ; **das Konzert ist heute** the concert is today.
4. (*Angabe der Herkunft*) : **aus Indien/Zürich ~** to be from India/Zürich.
5. (*Angabe der Zusammensetzung*) : **aus etw ~** to be made of sthg.

6. (*Angabe der Meinung*) : **für etw ~** to be in favour of sthg ; **gegen etw ~** to be against sthg.
7. (*Angabe von Zwang*) : **mein Befehl ist sofort auszuführen** my order is to be carried out immediately.
8. (*Angabe von Möglichkeit*) : **das ist nicht zu ändern** there's nothing that can be done about it ; **dieses Spiel ist noch zu gewinnen** this game can still be won.
9. (*Angabe von Tätigkeit*) : **dabei ~, etw zu tun** to be doing sthg.
10. (*Angabe von Teilnahme*) : **dabei ~** to be there.
11. (*fam* : *Angabe von Reihenfolge*) : **ich bin dran** it's my turn ; **Sie sind als Nächste dran!** you're next!
◆ *vimp* : **es ist zwölf Uhr** it's twelve o'clock ; **es ist dunkel** it's dark ; **wie wäre es mit...?** how about...? ; **was ist?** what's up? ; **das wär's** that's all ; **es sei denn, dass...** unless...

sein[2], **e** *det* his.

seine, **r**, **s** ODER **seins** *pron* (*von Person*) his ; (*von Tier, Ding*) its.

sein lassen *vt unr* (*fam*) : **lass das sein!** stop that!

seit *konj* & *präp* (+D) since ; **ich wohne hier ~ drei Jahren** I've lived here for three years ; **~ langem** for a long time ; **~ wann** since when.

seitdem *adv* since then. ◆ *konj* since.

Seite (*pl* -n) *die* side ; (*von Buch, Heft*) page ; **auf der rechten/linken ~** on the right-

Semmel

hand/left-hand side ; zur ~ ge-hen ODER **treten** to step aside.
Seiteneingang (*pl* -gänge) *der* side entrance.
Seitensprung (*pl* -sprünge) *der* affair ; **einen ~ machen** to have an affair.
Seitenstechen *das* stitch.
Seitenstraße (*pl* -n) *die* side street.
Seitenstreifen (*pl* -) *der* hard shoulder (*Br*), shoulder (*Am*) ; **'~ nicht befahrbar'** 'soft verges'.
Seitenwind *der* : **'Vorsicht, ~!'** 'caution crosswind!'
seither *adv* since then.
Sekretär (*pl* -e) *der* secretary ; (*Möbelstück*) bureau.
Sekretärin (*pl* -nen) *die* secretary.
Sekt (*pl* -e) *der* German sparkling wine similar to champagne.
Sekte (*pl* -n) *die* sect.
Sektglas (*pl* -gläser) *das* champagne glass.
Sekunde (*pl* -n) *die* second.
Sekundenkleber (*pl* -) *der* superglue.
sekundenlang *adj* momentary.
selber *pron* (*fam*) = **selbst**.
selbst *adv* (*sogar*) even. ◆ *pron* (*er selbst*) himself ; (*sie selbst*) herself, themselves (*pl*) ; (*ich selbst*) myself ; (*wir selbst*) ourselves ; (*Sie selbst*) yourself, yourselves (*pl*) ; **von ~** (*automatisch*) automatically, by itself.
Selbstauslöser (*pl* -) *der* delayed-action shutter release.
Selbstbedienung *die* self-service.

Selbstbedienungsres-taurant (*pl* -s) *das* self-service restaurant.
Selbstbeteiligung *die* excess.
selbstbewusst *adj* self-confident.
Selbstbräuner (*pl* -) *der* artificial tanning cream.
selbst gemacht *adj* home-made.
Selbstkostenpreis (*pl* -e) *der* cost price.
Selbstmord (*pl* -e) *der* suicide.
selbstsicher *adj* self-confident.
selbstständig *adj* independent ; (*Unternehmer*) self-employed. ◆ *adv* independently.
Selbstversorger (*pl* -) *der* (*im Urlaub*) self-caterer.
selbstverständlich *adj* natural. ◆ *adv* naturally.
Selbstverteidigung *die* self-defence.
Selbstwählverkehr *der* direct dialling.
Sellerie *der* celery.
selten *adj* rare. ◆ *adv* rarely.
Selters (*pl* -) *die* ODER *das* sparkling mineral water.
seltsam *adj* strange.
Semester (*pl* -) *das* semester.
Semesterferien *pl* (university) vacation (*sg*).
Semikolon (*pl* -s) *das* semicolon.
Seminar (*pl* -e) *das* seminar ; (*Institut*) department.
Semmel (*pl* -n) *die* (bread) roll.

Semmelknödel (pl -) der bread dumpling.

senden[1] (prät **sandte**, pp **gesandt**) vt (Brief, Glückwünsche) to send; **jm etw ~** to send sb sthg.

senden[2] vt (Film, Konzert) to broadcast.

Sender (pl -) der (Station) station.

Sendung (pl -en) die (in Fernsehen, in Radio) programme; (Brief) letter; (Paket) parcel.

Senf (pl -e) der mustard.

Senior, in (mpl -en) der, die (in Firma) senior colleague. ■ **Senioren** pl (Alte) senior citizens; (SPORT) senior team (sg).

Seniorenpass (pl -pässe) der senior citizen's travel pass.

senken vt to lower.

senkrecht adj vertical. ◆ adv vertically.

Sensation (pl -en) die sensation.

sensibel adj (Mensch) sensitive.

separat adj separate.

September der September; **am ersten ~** on the first of September; **Anfang/Ende ~** at the beginning/end of September; **Mitte ~** in mid-September; **Berlin, den 12. ~ 2000** Berlin, 12 September 2000; **im ~** in September.

Serie (pl -n) die series; (von Produkten) line.

serienmäßig adj standard. ◆ adv in series.

seriös adj respectable.

Serpentine (pl -n) die (Straße) steep and winding road.

Service[1] der (von Firma, Hotel) service.

Service[2] (pl -s) das (von Essgeschirr) (dinner) service.

servieren vt to serve.

Serviette (pl -n) die serviette.

Servolenkung (pl -en) die power steering.

Servus interj (Süddt) hello.

Sesam der sesame.

Sessel (pl -) der armchair.

Sessellift (pl -e) der chairlift.

setzen vt hat (Person) to sit; (Gegenstand) to put; (festlegen, Text) to set; (Geld) to bet. ◆ vi (bei Wette, Roulette) to bet; **~ auf** (+A) to bet on. ■ **sich setzen** ref (Person, Tier) to sit (down); **sich ~ zu** to sit with.

Seuche (pl -n) die (Krankheit) epidemic.

seufzen vi to sigh.

Sex der sex.

sexuell adj sexual.

sfr. (abk für Schweizer Franken) Swiss francs.

Shampoo (pl -s) das shampoo.

Sherry (pl -s) der sherry.

Shorts pl shorts.

Show (pl -s) die show.

Shuttlebus (pl -se) der shuttle bus.

sich pron (Reflexivpronomen: unbestimmt) oneself; (Person) himself (herself), themselves (pl); (Ding, Tier) itself, themselves (pl); (bei Höflichkeitsform) yourself, yourselves (pl); **~ auf etw** (A) **freuen** to look forward to sthg ; ~ *(D)* etw kaufen to buy sthg (for o.s.).

sicher *adj (ungefährdet)* safe ; *(zuverlässig)* reliable. ◆ *adv (ungefährdet)* safely ; *(zuverlässig)* reliably ; *(sicherlich)* certainly, definitely ; **aber ~!** of course ; **bist du ~?** are you sure? ; **etw ~ wissen** to know sthg for sure ; **sich** *(D)* **~ sein** to be sure.

Sicherheit *(pl* -en) *die (Schutz)* safety ; *(Zuverlässigkeit)* certainty ; *(Selbstsicherheit)* confidence ; *(finanziell)* security.

Sicherheitsdienst *(pl* -e) *der* security service.

Sicherheitsgurt *(pl* -e) *der* safety belt.

Sicherheitsnadel *(pl* -n) *die* safety pin.

Sicherheitsschloss *(pl* -schlösser) *das* safety lock.

sicherlich *adv* certainly.

sichern *vt (Ort)* to secure.

Sicherung *(pl* -en) *die (elektrisch)* fuse ; *(Schutz)* safeguarding.

Sicht *die* view ; **gute ~** good visibility ; **in ~ sein** to be in sight.

sichtbar *adj* visible.

Sichtvermerk *(pl* -e) *der* visa.

Sichtweite *die* visibility ; **außer/in ~** out of/in sight.

sie *pron (Singular : Nominativ)* she ; *(Akkusativ)* her ; *(Tier, Gegenstand)* it ; *(Plural : Nominativ)* they ; *(Akkusativ)* them.

Sie *pron (Singular, Plural)* you.

Sieb *(pl* -e) *das* sieve.

sieben *num* seven ; → **sechs**. ◆ *vt (Sand, Tee)* to sieve.

siebenhundert *num* seven hundred.

siebenmal *adv* seven times.

siebte, r, s *adj* seventh ; → **sechste**.

siebzehn *num* seventeen ; → **sechs**.

siebzig *num* seventy ; → **sechs**.

siedend *adj* boiling.

Siedlung *(pl* -en) *die (Niederlassung)* settlement ; *(am Stadtrand)* (housing) estate.

Sieg *(pl* -e) *der* victory.

siegen *vi* to win ; **~ gegen** ODER **über** *(+A)* to beat.

Sieger, in *(mpl* -) *der, die* winner.

Siegerehrung *(pl* -en) *die (SPORT)* medals ceremony.

siehe *Imperativ* → **sehen** ; **~ oben/unten** see above/below.

sieht *präs* → **sehen**.

siezen *vt* : **jn ~** to use the 'Sie' form of address to sb.

Signal *(pl* -e) *das* signal.

Silbe *(pl* -n) *die* syllable.

Silber *das* silver.

Silberhochzeit *(pl* -en) *die* silver wedding (anniversary).

Silvester *(pl* -) *das* New Year's Eve.

ⓘ   **SILVESTER**

In Germany, the traditional way of seeing in the New Year is by letting off fireworks when midnight chimes. Another custom associated with New Year's Eve involves pouring molten lead into a bowl of water and trying to tell the future from the shapes into which the lead solidifies.

simultan *adj* simultaneous.

sind *präs* → **sein**[1].

Sinfonie (*pl* -n) *die* symphony.

Sinfonieorchester (*pl* -) *das* symphony orchestra.

singen (*prät* sang, *pp* gesungen) *vt & vi* to sing.

sinken (*prät* sank, *pp* gesunken) *vi ist* to sink ; (*Preis, Besucherzahlen*) to fall.

Sinn (*pl* -e) *der* (*körperlich*) sense ; (*Bedeutung*) meaning ; (*Zweck*) point ; **es hat keinen ~** there's no point.

sinnlos *adj* (*unsinnig*) pointless.

sinnvoll *adj* (*Arbeit*) meaningful ; (*vernünftig*) sensible.

Sirene (*pl* -n) *die* (*Gerät*) siren.

Sitte (*pl* -n) *die* (*Gepflogenheit*) custom. ▪ **Sitten** *pl* (*Benehmen*) manners.

Situation (*pl* -en) *die* situation.

Sitz (*pl* -e) *der* seat.

sitzen (*prät* saß, *pp* gesessen) *vi* to sit ; **~ auf** (+*D*) to be sitting on ; **gut ~** (*Kleidung*) to be a good fit.

sitzen lassen *vt unr* (*fam* : *Partner*) to dump ; (*bei Verabredung*) to stand up.

Sitzgelegenheit (*pl* -en) *die* seating, place to sit.

Sitzplatz (*pl* -plätze) *der* seat.

Sitzung (*pl* -en) *die* (*Konferenz*) meeting.

Skandal (*pl* -e) *der* scandal.

Skat *der* skat, *card game for three players*.

Skateboard (*pl* -s) *das* skateboard.

Skelett (*pl* -e) *das* skeleton.

Ski (*pl* -er) *der* ski ; **~ fahren** ODER **laufen** to ski.

Skianzug (*pl* -züge) *der* ski suit.

Skiausrüstung (*pl* -en) *die* skiing equipment.

Skigebiet (*pl* -e) *das* skiing area.

Skihose (*pl* -n) *die* ski pants (*pl*).

Skikurs (*pl* -e) *der* skiing course.

Skiläufer, in (*mpl* -) *der, die* skier.

Skilehrer, in (*mpl* -) *der, die* ski instructor.

Skilift (*pl* -e) *der* ski lift.

Skipiste (*pl* -n) *die* ski-run.

Skistiefel (*pl* -) *der* ski boot.

Skistock (*pl* -stöcke) *der* ski stick.

Skiurlaub (*pl* -e) *der* skiing holiday.

Skiwachs *das* ski wax.

Skizze (*pl* -n) *die* sketch.

Skorpion (*pl* -e) *der* (*Tier*) scorpion ; (*Sternzeichen*) Scorpio.

Skulptur (*pl* -en) *die* sculpture.

S-Kurve (*pl* -n) *die* S-bend.

Slalom (*pl* -s) *der* (*im Sport*) slalom.

Slip (*pl* -s) *der* briefs (*pl*).

Slipeinlage (*pl* -n) *die* panty liner.

Slowakei *die* Slovakia.

Smog *der* smog.

Smoking (*pl* -s) *der* dinner jacket.

Snowboard (*pl* -s) *das* snowboard ; snowboard fahren to go snowboarding.

so *adv* **1.** *(auf diese Art)* like this ; *(auf jene Art)* like that ; ~ was *(fam)* something like that ; gut ~! good!

2. *(dermaßen)* so ; ich bin ~ froh, dass du gekommen bist I'm so glad you came ; ~..., dass so... that ; ~ ein such a ; ~ ein Pech! what bad luck!

3. *(fam : circa)* about ; oder ~ or so.

4. *(mit Geste)* this ; es war ~ groß it was this big.

5. *(fam : ohne etwas)* as it is ; *(umsonst)* for free ; ich trinke den Tee lieber ~ I'd rather have the tea as it is ; ich bin ~ ins Kino reingekommen I got into the cinema for free.

6. *(fam : im Allgemeinen)* : was hast du sonst noch ~ gemacht? what else did you do, then?

7. *(vergleichend)* : ~ ... wie as... as ; das Loch war ~ breit wie tief the hole was as wide as it was deep.

◆ *konj* **1.** *(Ausdruck des Vergleichs)* as ; laufen, ~ schnell man kann to run as fast as one can.

2. *(Ausdruck der Folge)* : ~ daß → **sodass**.

◆ *interj* : ~, das war's so, that's it ; ~, glaubst du das? so, you believe that, do you?

▦ **so oder so** *adv* anyway.

s. o. *abk* = **siehe oben**.

sobald *konj* as soon as.

Söckchen (*pl* -) *das* ankle sock.

Socke (*pl* -n) *die* sock.

sodass *konj* so that.

Sodbrennen *das* heartburn.

Sofa (*pl* -s) *das* sofa.

soff *prät* → **saufen**.

sofort *adv* immediately ; *(gleich)* in a moment.

Sofortbildkamera (*pl* -s) *die* instant camera.

sog *prät* → **saugen**.

sogar *adv* even.

so genannt *adj* *(abw : angeblich)* so-called.

Sohle (*pl* -n) *die* sole.

Sohn (*pl* Söhne) *der* son.

Soja *die* soya bean.

solange *konj* as long as.

Solarium (*pl* -rien) *das* solarium.

solch *det* such ; ~ nette Leute such nice people.

solche, r, s *det* such ; ein ~r Mann such a man ; das Thema als ~s the topic as such.

Soldat (*pl* -en) *der* soldier.

solidarisch *adj* : sich ~ zeigen to show solidarity.

solide *adj* *(Material)* solid.

Solist, in (*mpl* -en) *der, die* soloist.

Soll *das* *(Schulden)* debit.

sollen[1] (*pp* sollen) *aux* to be supposed to ; ich soll um 10 Uhr dort sein I'm supposed ODER meant to be there at 10 ; wir hätten nicht kommen ~ we shouldn't have come ; soll ich das Fenster aufmachen? shall I open the window? ; sollte sie noch kommen, sag ihr... if she should turn up, tell her...

sollen[2] *(pp gesollt) vi* : die Waren ~ nach München the goods are meant to go to Munich ; **was soll das?** *(fam)* what's all this? ; **was soll's?** *(fam)* what the hell?

solo *adv (MUS)* solo ; *(fam : allein)* alone.

Sommer *(pl -) der* summer ; **im ~** in (the) summer.

Sommerfahrplan *(pl -pläne) der* summer timetable.

Sommerferien *pl* summer holidays.

sommerlich *adj* summery.

Sommerpause *(pl -n) die* summer break.

Sommerreifen *(pl -) der* summer tyre.

Sommerschlussverkauf *(pl -käufe) der* summer sale.

Sommersprosse *(pl -n) die* freckle.

Sommerzeit *die* summertime.

Sonate *(pl -n) die* sonata.

Sonderangebot *(pl -e) das* special offer.

Sonderausstattung *(pl -en) die* : **ein Auto mit ~** a car with optional extras.

sonderbar *adj* strange.

Sonderfahrplan *(pl -pläne) der* special timetable.

Sonderfahrt *(pl -en) die* *(Zugfahrt)* special train ; *(Busfahrt)* special bus.

Sondergenehmigung *(pl -en) die* special permit.

Sonderleistungen *pl* special benefits.

Sondermarke *(pl -n) die* special issue stamp.

Sondermaschine *(pl -n) die* special plane.

Sondermüll *der* hazardous waste.

sondern *konj* but.

Sonderpreis *(pl -e) der* special price.

Sonderschule *(pl -n) die* special school.

Sonderzug *(pl -züge) der* special train.

Sonnabend *(pl -e) der* Saturday ; → **Samstag**.

sonnabends *adv* on Saturdays.

Sonne *die* sun ; **die ~ scheint** the sun is shining ; **in der prallen ~** in the blazing sun.

sonnen : **sich sonnen** *ref (in Sonne)* to sun o.s.

Sonnenaufgang *(pl -gänge) der* sunrise.

Sonnenbad *(pl -bäder) das* : **ein ~ nehmen** to sunbathe.

Sonnenbank *(pl -bänke) die* sunbed.

Sonnenblume *(pl -n) die* sunflower.

Sonnenblumenbrot *(pl -e) das* sunflower seed bread.

Sonnenblumenkern *(pl -e) der* sunflower seed.

Sonnenblumenöl *das* sunflower oil.

Sonnenbrand *der* sunburn.

Sonnenbrille *(pl -n) die* sunglasses *(pl)*.

Sonnencreme *(pl -s) die* sun cream.

Sonnendach *(pl -dächer) das* *(für Auto)* sunroof.

Sonnendeck *(pl -s) das* sun deck.

Sonnenmilch *die* suntan lotion.

Sonnenöl (*pl* -e) *das* suntan oil.

Sonnenschein *der* sunshine.

Sonnenschirm (*pl* -e) *der* sunshade.

Sonnenschutzfaktor *der* protection factor.

Sonnenseite *die* (*von Gebäude*) sunny side.

Sonnenstich *der* sunstroke.

Sonnenstudio (*pl* -s) *das* tanning studio.

Sonnenuntergang (*pl* -gänge) *der* sunset.

sonnig *adj* sunny.

Sonntag (*pl* -e) *der* Sunday ; → Samstag.

sonntags *adv* on Sundays.

Sonntagsverkauf *der* Sunday trading.

sonn- und feiertags *adv* on Sundays and public holidays.

sonst *adv* (*außerdem*) else ; (*normalerweise*) usually ; (*abgesehen davon*) otherwise. ◆ *konj* (*andernfalls*) or ; ~ habe ich nichts I've got nothing else ; ~ nichts nothing else ; was ~? (*fam*) what else?

sonstig *adj* other.

sooft *konj* whenever.

Sopran (*pl* -e) *der* soprano.

Sorge (*pl* -n) *die* worry ; sich (*D*) ~n machen um to worry about ; keine ~! (*fam*) don't worry!

sorgen *vi* : ~ für (*beschaffen*) to see to ; (*sich kümmern um*) to

look after. ▪ **sich sorgen** *ref* to worry.

sorgfältig *adj* careful.

Sorte (*pl* -n) *die* (*von Dingen*) sort, type.

sortieren *vt* to sort.

Sortiment (*pl* -e) *das* assortment.

Soße (*pl* -n) *die* sauce.

Souvenir (*pl* -s) *das* souvenir.

souverän *adj* (*Person*) superior ; (*Staat*) sovereign.

soviel *konj* : ~ ich weiß as far as I know ; iss, ~ du willst eat as much as you like.

so viel *adv* as much ; doppelt ~ wie twice as much as.

so weit *adv* (*im Allgemeinen*) on the whole. ◆ *konj* as far as. ◆ *adj* : ~ sein to be ready.

sowie *konj* (*und*) as well as, and.

sowieso *adv* anyway.

sowohl *konj* : ~... als auch... as well as...

sozial *adj* social. ◆ *adv* socially.

Sozialarbeiter, in (*mpl* -) *der, die* social worker.

Sozialdemokrat, in (*mpl* -en) *der, die* social democrat.

sozialdemokratisch *adj* social-democratic.

Sozialhilfe *die* ≃ income support (*Br*), ≃ welfare (*Am*).

sozialistisch *adj* socialist.

Sozialversicherung (*pl*-en) *die* social security.

Sozialwohnung (*pl* -en) *die* council flat (*Br*).

Soziologie *die* sociology.

sozusagen *adv* so to speak.

Spachtel (*pl* -) *der* spatula.

Spaghetti, Spagetti *pl* spaghetti *(sg)*.

Spalte *(pl -n)* die *(in Fels, Holz)* crack ; *(von Text)* column.

Spanferkel *(pl -)* das *(Fleisch)* suckling pig.

Spange *(pl -n)* die *(im Haar)* hair slide *(Br)*, barrette *(Am)*.

Spanien *nt* Spain.

Spanier, in *(mpl -)* der, die Spaniard ; **die ~** the Spanish.

spanisch *adj* Spanish.

Spanisch(e) *das* Spanish.

spann *prät* → spinnen.

spannend *adj* exciting.

Spannung *(pl -en)* die tension ; *(elektrisch)* voltage.
■ **Spannungen** *pl (Krise)* tension *(sg)*.

Sparbuch *(pl -bücher)* das savings book.

Sparbüchse *(pl -n)* die piggy bank.

sparen *vt* & *vi* to save ; **~ für** ODER **auf (+A)** to save up for.

Spargel *der* asparagus.

Spargelsuppe *(pl -n)* die asparagus soup.

Sparkasse *(pl -n)* die savings bank.

Sparkonto *(pl -konten)* das savings account.

Sparpreis *(pl -e)* der economy price.

sparsam *adj* economical.

Sparschwein *(pl -e)* das piggy bank.

Spaß *(pl Späße)* der *(Vergnügen)* fun ; *(Scherz)* joke ; **~ machen** to joke ; **Sprachenlernen macht mir ~** I enjoy learning languages ; **~ haben** to have fun ; **viel ~!** have fun! ; **zum ~**

for fun ; **er versteht keinen ~** he has no sense of humour.

Spaß|bad *das* swimming pool with flumes, sauna etc.

spät *adj* & *adv* late ; **sie kam mal wieder zu ~** she was late again ; **wie ~ ist es?** what's the time?

Spaten *(pl -)* der spade.

später *adj* & *adv (dann)* later ; **bis ~!** see you later!

spätestens *adv* at the latest.

Spätlese *(pl -n)* die *(Wein)* late vintage.

Spätnachmittag *(pl -e)* der late afternoon.

Spätschicht *(pl -en)* die late shift.

Spätsommer *der* late summer.

Spätvorstellung *(pl -en)* die late show.

Spatz *(pl -en)* der *(Vogel)* sparrow.

Spätzli *pl (Schweiz)* small round noodles, similar to macaroni.

spazieren gehen *vi unr ist* to go for a walk.

Spaziergang *(pl -gänge)* der walk ; **einen ~ machen** to go for a walk.

Speck *der (geräuchert)* bacon ; *(Fett)* fat.

Spedition *(pl -en)* die *(für Umzug)* removal firm.

Speiche *(pl -n)* die *(am Rad)* spoke.

Speichel *der* saliva.

Speicher *(pl -)* der *(unterm Dach)* loft ; *(EDV)* memory.

speichern *vt (EDV)* to save.

Speise *(pl -n)* die *(geh : Nahrung)* food ; *(Gericht)* meal.

Speiseeis *das* ice cream.

Speisekarte (*pl* -n) *die* menu.

Speiseröhre (*pl* -n) *die* gullet.

Speisesaal (*pl* -säle) *der* dining room.

Speisewagen (*pl* -) *der* dining car.

Spende (*pl* -n) *die* donation.

spenden *vt* to donate.

spendieren *vt* : jm etw ~ to buy sb sthg (for a treat).

Sperre (*pl* -n) *die* (*auf Straße*) barrier.

sperren *vt* (*Straße*) to close ; (*Konto*) to freeze ; jn in ein Zimmer ~ to shut sb in a room.

Sperrgebiet (*pl* -e) *das* : militärisches ~ military range.

Sperrmüll *der* large items of rubbish (*pl*).

Sperrstunde (*pl* -n) *die* closing time.

Sperrung (*pl* -en) *die* (*von Straße*) closing ; (*von Konto*) freezing.

Spesen *pl* expenses.

Spezi® (*pl* -s) *das* (*Getränk*) Coke® and lemonade.

Spezialgebiet (*pl* -e) *das* specialist field.

Spezialist, in (*mpl* -en) *der, die* specialist.

Spezialität (*pl* -en) *die* speciality.

Spezialitätenrestaurant (*pl* -s) *das* speciality restaurant.

Spiegel (*pl* -) *der* mirror.

Spiegelei (*pl* -er) *das* fried egg.

spiegelglatt *adj* slippery.

Spiegelreflexkamera(*pl*-s) *das* reflex camera.

Spiel (*pl* -e) *das* game ; (*Karten*) deck, pack.

Spielautomat (*pl* -en) *der* fruit machine.

spielen *vt* to play. ◆ *vi* to play ; (*Roman, Film*) to be set ; (*um Geld*) to gamble ; (*Schauspieler*) to act ; ~ gegen to play against ; ~ um to play for ; Karten ~ to play cards ; Klavier ~ to play the piano ; Tennis ~ to play tennis.

Spieler, in (*mpl* -) *der, die* player.

Spielfilm (*pl* -e) *der* (feature) film.

Spielhalle (*pl* -n) *die* amusement arcade.

Spielkasino (*pl* -s) *das* casino.

Spielplan (*pl* -pläne) *der* (*von Theater*) programme.

Spielplatz (*pl* -plätze) *der* playground.

Spielregel (*pl* -n) *die* rule.

Spielsachen *pl* toys.

Spielwaren *pl* toys.

Spielzeug *das* toy.

Spieß (*pl* -e) *der* (*für Fleisch*) spit ; am ~ spit-roasted.

Spießchen (*pl* -) *das* skewer.

Spinat *der* spinach.

Spinne (*pl* -n) *die* spider.

spinnen (*prät* spann, *pp* gesponnen) *vt* (*Wolle*) to spin. ◆ *vi* (*fam* : verrückt sein) to be crazy ; du spinnst! you're joking!

spionieren *vi* to spy.

Spirale (*pl* -n) *die* spiral ; (*MED*) coil.

Spirituosen *pl* spirits.

Spiritus *der* spirit.

Spirituskocher (*pl* -) *der* spirit stove.

spitz *adj* pointed.

Spitze (*pl* -n) *die (von Messer, Nadel)* point ; *(von Berg)* peak ; *(von Kolonne, Gruppe)* head.

Spitzer (*pl* -) *der* pencil sharpener.

Spitzname (*pl* -n) *der* nickname.

Splitter (*pl* -) *der* splinter.

spontan *adj* spontaneous.

Sport *der* sport ; ~ **treiben** to do sport.

Sportanlage (*pl* -n) *die* sports complex.

Sportartikel (*pl* -) *der* piece of sports equipment.

Sportgerät (*pl* -e) *das* piece of sports equipment.

Sportgeschäft (*pl* -e) *das* sports shop.

Sporthalle (*pl* -n) *die* sports hall.

Sporthotel (*pl* -s) *das* hotel with sports facilities.

Sportkleidung *die* sportswear.

Sportler, in (*mpl* -) *der, die* sportsman (sportswoman).

sportlich *adj (Leistung)* sporting ; *(Person, Kleidung)* sporty.

Sportplatz (*pl* -plätze) *der* playing field.

Sportverein (*pl* -e) *der* sports club.

Sportwagen (*pl* -) *der* sports car.

spotten *vi* to mock.

sprach *prät* → **sprechen**.

Sprache (*pl* -n) *die* language ; **zur ~ kommen** to come up.

Sprachenschule (*pl* -n) *die* language school.

Sprachführer (*pl* -) *der* phrasebook.

Sprachkenntnisse *pl* knowledge *(sg) of* languages.

sprachlich *adj* linguistic.

Sprachreise (*pl* -n) *die* journey to a country to learn the language.

Sprachunterricht *der* language teaching.

sprang *prät* → **springen**.

Spray (*pl* -s) *das* spray.

Sprechanlage (*pl* -n) *die* intercom.

sprechen (*prät* sprach, *pp* gesprochen) *vi* 1. *(reden)* to talk, to speak ; **mit jm ~** to talk to sb ; **über jn/etw ~** to talk about sb/sthg ; **von jm/etw ~** to talk about sb/sthg.
2. *(am Telefon)* to speak ; **wer spricht da, bitte?** who's speaking?
3. *(urteilend)* : **was spricht dagegen, jetzt Urlaub zu nehmen?** why shouldn't we go on holiday now? ; **es spricht für ihn, dass...** it's in his favour that...
♦ *vt* 1. *(Sprache)* to speak ; **Deutsch ~** to speak German.
2. *(Person)* to speak to.
3. *(Gebet)* to say.
■ **sich sprechen** *ref* to talk.

Sprecher, in (*mpl* -) *der, die (im Radio, Fernsehen)* newsreader ; *(von Gruppe)* spokesperson.

Sprechstunde (*pl* -n) *die (beim Arzt)* surgery.

Sprechzimmer (*pl -*) *das* consulting room.

Sprengarbeiten *pl* :'Sprengarbeiten' *sign indicating that explosives are being used for excavation*.

Sprengstoff (*pl -e*) *der* explosive.

spricht *prät* → **sprechen**.

Sprichwort (*pl -wörter*) *das* proverb.

sprießen (*prät* spross, *pp* gesprossen) *vi ist* (*Blätter*) to shoot.

Springbrunnen (*pl -*) *der* fountain.

springen (*prät* sprang, *pp* gesprungen) *vi* (*Person, Tier*) to jump ; (*Glas*) to break.

Springflut (*pl -en*) *die* spring tide.

Sprint (*pl -s*) *der* sprint.

Spritze (*pl -n*) *die* (*Injektion*) injection ; (*Nadel, für Sahne*) syringe.

spritzen *vt* (*Injektion*) to inject ; (*Wasser, Gift, Auto*) to spray. ◆ *vi* to splash. ◆ *vimp* (*Fett*) to spit.

spröde *adj* (*Material*) brittle.

Sprudel (*pl -*) *der* (*Mineralwasser*) sparkling mineral water.

Sprudelwasser (*pl -*) *das* (*Mineralwasser*) sparkling mineral water.

sprühen *vt* (*Wasser*) to spray.

Sprühregen *der* drizzle.

Sprung (*pl* Sprünge) *der* (*Springen*) jump ; (*Riss*) crack.

Sprungbrett (*pl -er*) *das* springboard.

Sprungschanze (*pl -n*) *die* ski jump.

Spucke *die* (*fam*) spittle.

spucken *vi* (*ausspucken*) to spit.

Spüle (*pl -n*) *die* sink.

spülen *vt* to rinse. ◆ *vi* (*an Spüle*) to wash up ; (*in Toilette*) to flush ; Geschirr ~ to wash the dishes.

Spülmaschine (*pl -n*) *die* dishwasher.

Spülmittel (*pl -*) *das* washing-up liquid.

Spülung (*pl -en*) *die* (*von Toilette*) flush.

Spur (*pl -en*) *die* (*von Füßen, Dieb*) track ; (*kleine Menge*) touch ; (*Fahrspur*) lane ; **die ~ wechseln** to change lanes.

spüren *vt* to feel.

Spurrillen *pl* (*auf Straße*) : 'Spurrillen' 'temporary road surface'.

Squash *das* squash.

SSV *abk* = Sommerschlussverkauf

St. (*abk für Sankt*) St.

Staat (*pl -en*) *der* state ; (*Land*) country.

staatlich *adj* state. ◆ *adv* : **~ anerkannt** government-approved ; **~ geprüft** government-certified.

Staatsangehörigkeit (*pl -en*) *die* nationality.

Staatsbürger, in (*mpl -*) *der, die* citizen.

Staatsbürgerschaft (*pl -en*) *die* nationality.

Staatsexamen (*pl -*) *das* final exam taken by law and arts students at university.

Stäbchen (pl -) das (zum Essen) chopstick.

Stabhochsprung der pole vault.

stabil adj stable ; (Möbel, Bau) solid.

stach prät → stechen.

Stachel (pl -n) der (von Insekten) sting ; (von Pflanzen) thorn.

Stachelbeere (pl -n) die gooseberry.

Stacheldraht (pl -drähte) der barbed wire.

Stadion (pl Stadien) das stadium.

Stadium (pl Stadien) das stage.

Stadt (pl Städte) die town ; (sehr groß) city ; (Verwaltung) town council ; **in die ~ fahren** to go to town.

Stadtautobahn (pl -en) die urban motorway (Br), freeway (Am).

Stadtbahn (pl -en) die suburban railway.

Stadtbummel (pl -) der (fam) stroll through town.

Städtepartnerschaft (pl -en) die town twinning.

Stadtführung (pl -en) die city sightseeing tour.

Stadtgebiet (pl -e) das town area.

Stadthalle (pl -n) die civic hall.

städtisch adj (Kindergarten, Verwaltung) municipal ; (Bevölkerung) urban.

Stadtkern (pl -e) der town/city centre.

Stadtmauer (pl -n) die city wall.

Stadtmitte die town/city centre.

Stadtpark (pl -s) der municipal park.

Stadtplan (pl -pläne) der street map.

Stadtrand (pl -ränder) der outskirts (pl) ; **am ~** on the outskirts.

Stadtrat (pl -räte) der (Organ) town council ; (Person) town councillor.

Stadträtin (pl -nen) die town councillor.

Stadtrundfahrt (pl -en) die city tour.

Stadtstaat (pl -en) der city state.

Stadtteil (pl -e) der district, quarter.

Stadttor (pl -e) das city gate.

Stadtviertel (pl -) das district, quarter.

Stadtzentrum (pl -zentren) das town/city centre.

stahl prät → stehlen.

Stahl der steel.

Stall (pl Ställe) der stable.

Stamm (pl Stämme) der (von Baum) trunk ; (GRAMM) stem ; (Gruppe) tribe.

stammen vi : **~ aus/von** to come from.

Stammgast (pl -gäste) der regular.

Stammkunde, kundin (mpl -n) der, die regular customer.

Stammtisch (pl -e) der regulars' table at a pub.

ⓘ **STAMMTISCH**

The word "Stammtisch" can refer both to the table in a pub reserved for the regulars and to the group of regulars who always sit there. The "Stammtisch" is where the regulars play cards and talk, with politics, especially local politics, being a favourite topic for debate.

stand *prät* → stehen.

Stand (*pl* Stände) *der (auf Markt, Messe)* stand ; *(in Entwicklung)* state ; im ~e → imstande.

Stand-by (*pl* -s) *der* stand-by flight.

Ständer (*pl* -) *der* stand.

ständig *adj* constant. ◆ *adv* constantly.

Standlicht *das* sidelights (*pl*).

Standort (*pl* -e) *der (von Person)* position ; *(von Firma)* location.

Standpunkt (*pl* -e) *der* point of view.

Standspur (*pl* -en) *die* hard shoulder.

Stange (*pl* -n) *die (aus Holz)* pole ; *(aus Metall)* rod, bar ; eine ~ Zigaretten a carton of 200 cigarettes.

Stangenbrot (*pl* -e) *das* French stick.

stank *prät* → stinken.

Stapel (*pl* -) *der (Haufen)* pile.

Star[1] (*pl* -e) *der (Vogel)* starling.

Star[2] (*pl* -s) *der (Person)* star.

starb *prät* → sterben.

stark (*komp* stärker, *superl* am stärksten) *adj* strong ; *(Verkehr, Regen)* heavy ; *(Husten)* bad ; *(fam : toll)* great. ◆ *adv (intensiv)* heavily ; *(fam : toll)* brilliantly.

Stärke (*pl* -n) *die* strength ; *(in Nahrung, für Wäsche)* starch ; *(Dicke)* thickness.

stärken *vt (körperlich)* to strengthen ; *(Wäsche)* to starch. ■ **sich stärken** *ref* to fortify o.s.

Starkstrom *der* heavy current.

Stärkung (*pl* -en) *die (Nahrung, Getränk)* refreshment.

starren *vi (sehen)* : auf etw (A) ~ to stare at sthg.

Start (*pl* -s) *der (von Flugzeug)* takeoff ; *(von Rennen)* start.

Startautomatik *die* automatic choke.

Startbahn (*pl* -en) *die* runway.

starten *vt* to start. ◆ *vi (Läufer)* to start ; *(Flugzeug)* to take off.

Starthilfe *die (für Auto)* jump start ; jm ~ geben to give sb a jump start.

Starthilfekabel (*pl* -) *das* jump lead.

Station (*pl* -en) *die (von Bus, Zug, U-Bahn)* station ; *(von Reise)* stop ; *(im Krankenhaus)* ward.

stationär *adj (Behandlung)* in-patient *(vor Subst)*.

Statistik (*pl* -en) *die* statistics *(sg)*.

Stativ (*pl* -e) *das* tripod.

statt *präp* (+G) instead of.

stattdessen *konj* instead.

statt|finden *vi unr* to take place.

Statue (*pl* -n) *die* statue.

Stau (*pl* -s) *der* (*im Verkehr*) traffic jam ; **im ~ stehen** to be stuck in a traffic jam ; **ein 5 km langer ~** a 5 km tailback.

Staub *der* dust.

stauben *vi* to be dusty. ◆ *vimp* : **es staubt** it's dusty.

staubig *adj* dusty.

Staubsauger (*pl* -) *der* vacuum cleaner.

Staudamm (*pl* -dämme) *der* dam.

Staugefahr *die* : **es besteht ~** delays are possible.

staunen *vi* to be amazed.

Stausee (*pl* -n) *der* reservoir.

Stauwarnung (*pl* -en) *die* traffic report.

Std. (*abk für Stunde*) hr.

Steak (*pl* -s) *das* steak.

Steakhaus (*pl* -häuser) *das* steakhouse.

stechen (*präs* sticht, *prät* stach, *pp* gestochen) *vt* (*mit Nadel, Stachel*) to prick ; (*mit Messer*) to stab ; (*subj : Insekt*) to sting. ■ **sich stechen** *ref* to prick o.s.

Stechmücke (*pl* -n) *die* mosquito.

Steckdose (*pl* -n) *die* socket.

stecken *vt* (*einstecken*) to put. ◆ *vi* (*Gegenstand*) to be ; **wo habt ihr gesteckt?** (*fam*) where were you?

stecken lassen *vt unr* : **ich habe den Schlüssel ~** I left the key in the lock.

Stecker (*pl* -) *der* plug.

Stecknadel (*pl* -n) *die* pin.

Steg (*pl* -e) *der* (*Brücke*) footbridge.

Stehcafé (*pl* -s) *das* café where customers drink coffee standing at a counter.

stehen (*prät* stand, *pp* gestanden) *vi* 1. (*Person, Tier*) to stand. 2. (*Gegenstand, Pflanze*) to be ; **die Vase steht auf dem Tisch** the vase is on the table ; **in der Zeitung steht, dass...** it says in the paper that... 3. (*Uhr, Motor*) to have stopped. 4. (*unterstützend*) : **zu jm/etw ~** to stand by sb/sthg. 5. (*Kleidung, Frisur*) : **jm ~** to suit sb ; **jm gut/nicht ~** to suit/not to suit sb. 6. (*fam : mögen*) : **auf etw (A) ~** to be into sthg ; **auf jn ~** to fancy sb. ◆ *vimp* 1. (*im Sport*) : **es steht 1 : 0** the score is 1-0. 2. (*gesundheitlich*) : **wie steht es um den Patienten?** how is the patient? ; **es steht schlecht um ihn** he is not doing very well.

stehen bleiben *vi unr* ist to stop.

stehen lassen *vt unr* to leave.

stehlen (*präs* stiehlt, *prät* stahl, *pp* gestohlen) *vt* to steal.

Stehplatz (*pl* -plätze) *der* standing place.

steif *adj* stiff.

Steiermark *nt* Styria.

steigen (*prät* stieg, *pp* gestiegen) *vi* ist (*klettern*) to climb ; (*in die Luft, ansteigen*) to rise ; **in**

etw *(A)* aus etw ~ to get on/out of sthg ; **auf einen Berg** ~ to climb (up) a mountain.

steigern *vt* to raise ; *(GRAMM)* to form the comparative/superlative of.

Steigung *(pl* -en) *die (von Straße)* gradient.

steil *adj* steep.

Steilhang *(pl* -hänge) *der* steep slope.

Steilküste *(pl* -n) *die* cliffs *(pl)*.

Stein *(pl* -e) *der* stone ; *(zum Bauen)* brick ; *(zum Spielen)* piece.

Steinbock *(pl* -böcke) *der (Tier)* ibex ; *(Sternzeichen)* Capricorn.

Steinbutt *(pl* -e) *der* turbot.

Steingut *das (Material)* earthsenware.

Steinpilz *(pl* -e) *der* cep, *type of large wild mushroom with a rich flavour.*

Steinschlag *der* : 'Achtung ~' 'danger - falling rocks'.

Stelle *(pl* -n) *die (Platz, Rang)* place ; *(Fleck)* patch ; *(Arbeitsplatz)* job ; *(im Text)* passage ; **an zweiter** ~ **liegen** to be in second place ; **an deiner** ~ if I were you ; **auf der** ~ on the spot ; **an** ~ → **anstelle**.

stellen *vt* 1. *(hinstellen)* to put ; **eine Vase auf den Tisch** ~ to put a vase on the table. 2. *(halten)* : **etw kalt** ~ to chill sthg ; **etw warm** ~ to keep sthg warm.

3. *(einstellen)* to set ; **den Fernseher leiser** ~ to turn the television down.

4. *(Diagnose, Prognose)* to make.

5. *(Frage)* to ask ; *(Bedingung)* to set.

■ **sich stellen** *ref* 1. *(sich hinstellen)* : **sich ans Fenster** ~ to walk to the window. 2. *(nicht ausweichen)* : **sich etw** *(D)* ~ to face sthg. 3. *(sich verstellen)* : **sich krank** ~ to pretend to be ill ; **sich dumm** ~ to pretend not to understand.

Stellenangebot *(pl* -e) *das* job offer.

stellenweise *adv* in places.

Stellung *(pl* -en) *die* position ; ~ **zu etw nehmen** to comment on sthg.

Stellvertreter, in *(mpl* -) *der, die* representative.

Stempel *(pl* -) *der* stamp.

stempeln *vt* to stamp.

Steppdecke *(pl* -n) *die* quilt.

sterben *(präs* **stirbt**, *prät* **starb**, *pp* **gestorben**) *vi* ist to die ; ~ **an** *(+D)* to die of.

Stereoanlage *(pl* -n) *die* stereo system.

steril *adj* sterile.

sterilisieren *vt* to sterilize.

Stern *(pl* -e) *der* star.

Sternbild *(pl* -er) *das* constellation.

Sternschnuppe *(pl* -n) *die* shooting star.

Sternwarte *(pl* -n) *die* observatory.

Sternzeichen *(pl* -) *das* sign of the zodiac.

stets *adv (geh)* always.

Steuer[1] *(pl* -n) *die (Abgabe)* tax.

Steuer² (*pl* -) *das* (*von Auto*) steering wheel.

Steuerbord *das* starboard.

steuerfrei *adj* tax-free.

steuern *vt* to steer.

steuerpflichtig *adj* taxable.

Steuerrad (*pl* -räder) *das* steering wheel.

Steuerung (*pl* -en) *die* (*Gerät*) controls (*pl*).

Steward (*pl* -s) *der* steward.

Stewardess (*pl* -en) *die* stewardess.

Stich (*pl* -e) *der* (*Stechen*) stab; (*von Insekt*) sting; (*beim Nähen*) stitch; (*Schmerz*) stabbing pain; (*Bild*) engraving; **jn/etw im ~ lassen** to leave sb/sthg in the lurch.

sticht *präs* → **stechen**.

sticken *vi* to embroider.

Sticker (*pl* -) *der* sticker.

Stiefbruder (*pl* -brüder) *der* stepbrother.

Stiefel (*pl* -) *der* (*Schuh*) boot.

Stiefmutter (*pl* -mütter) *die* stepmother.

Stiefschwester (*pl* -n) *die* stepsister.

Stiefvater (*pl* -väter) *der* stepfather.

stieg *prät* → **steigen**.

Stiel (*pl* -e) *der* (*von Blumen*) stem; (*von Besen, Pfanne*) handle.

Stier (*pl* -e) *der* (*Tier*) bull; (*Sternzeichen*) Taurus.

stieß *prät* → **stoßen**.

Stift (*pl* -e) *der* (*zum Schreiben*) pencil; (*aus Metall*) tack.

Stiftung (*pl* -en) *die* (*Institution*) foundation; (*Schenkung*) donation.

Stil (*pl* -e) *der* style.

stilistisch *adj* stylistic.

still *adj* quiet; (*bewegungslos*) still. ◆ *adv* (*geräuschlos*) quietly; (*bewegungslos*) still; **sei bitte ~!** please be quiet!

stillen *vt* (*Baby*) to breastfeed; (*Schmerz*) to relieve.

stillhalten *vt unr* (*sich nicht bewegen*) to keep still.

Stimme (*pl* -n) *die* (*zum Sprechen*) voice; (*bei Wahl*) vote.

stimmen *vi* (*richtig sein*) to be right; (*bei Wahl*) to vote. ◆ *vt* (*Instrument*) to tune; **~ für/gegen** to vote for/against; **das stimmt nicht!** that's not true!; **stimmt!** that's right!; **stimmt so!** keep the change!

Stimmrecht *das* right to vote.

Stimmung (*pl* -en) *die* (*Laune*) mood; (*Atmosphäre*) atmosphere.

stinken (*prät* stank, *pp* gestunken) *vi* (*schlecht riechen*) to stink; **das stinkt mir** (*fam*) I'm fed up with it.

Stipendium (*pl* -dien) *das* grant.

stirbt *präs* → **sterben**.

Stirn (*pl* -en) *die* forehead.

Stock (*pl* Stöcke) *der* (*aus Holz*) stick; (*Etage*) floor, storey; **am ~ gehen** to walk with a stick; **im ersten ~** on the first floor.

Stockung (*pl* -en) *die* (*im Verkehr*) hold-up.

Stockwerk (*pl* -e) *das* floor, storey.

Stoff (*pl* -e) *der* (*Tuch*) material; (*Substanz*) substance.

stöhnen vi to groan.

Stollen (pl -) der (Kuchen) stollen, sweet bread made with dried fruit and nuts, eaten at Christmas.

stolpern vi ist (beim Gehen) to stumble.

stolz adj (Person) proud.

stopfen vt (Socken) to darn; (hineinstecken) to stuff. ◆ vi (fam : Nahrung) to cause constipation.

stopp interj stop!

Stopp (pl -s) der (Anhalten) stop.

stoppen vt & vi (anhalten) to stop.

Stoppschild (pl -er) das stop sign.

Stoppuhr (pl -en) die stopwatch.

Stöpsel (pl -) der plug.

Storch (pl Störche) das stork.

stören vt (beeinträchtigen) to disturb; (missfallen) to annoy. ◆ vi (missfallen) to be annoying; störe ich? am I disturbing you?; 'bitte nicht ~!' 'do not disturb!'

stornieren vt to cancel.

Stornogebühr (pl -en) die cancellation charge.

Störung (pl -en) die (Belästigung) disturbance; (im Fernsehen, Radio) interference; entschuldigen Sie die ~ sorry to bother you.

Störungsstelle (pl -n) die faults service.

Stoß (pl Stöße) der (Schlag) punch; (Stapel) pile.

Stoßdämpfer (pl -) der shock absorber.

stoßen (präs stößt, prät stieß, pp gestoßen) vt hat (schubsen) to push. ◆ vi ist : ~ an (+A) to hit; ~ auf (+A) to come across; ~ gegen to bump into. ■ sich stoßen ref to bang o.s.

Stoßstange (pl -n) die bumper.

stößt präs → stoßen.

Stoßzeit (pl -en) die rush hour.

stottern vi to stutter.

Str. (abk für Straße) St.

strafbar adj punishable.

Strafe (pl -n) die (Bestrafung) punishment; (Geldbuße) fine; zur ~ as a punishment; ~ zahlen to pay a fine.

Strafmandat (pl -e) das (Zettel) ticket.

Straftat (pl -en) die criminal offence.

Strafzettel (pl -) der (fam) ticket.

Strahl (pl -en) der (von Wasser) jet; (von Licht) ray. ■ **Strahlen** pl (von Energie) rays.

strahlen vi (Licht) to shine; (Person) to beam; (radioaktiv) to radiate.

Strähne (pl -n) die strand.

stramm adj (Band, Seil) taut.

strampeln vi (Säugling) to kick about.

Strand (pl Strände) der beach.

Strandkorb (pl -körbe) der wicker beach chair.

Strandpromenade (pl -n) die promenade.

strapazieren vt (Material) to wear away; (Person) to strain.

Straße (pl -n) die (in einer Stadt) street; das Zimmer liegt

zur ~ the room looks out onto the street.

Straßenarbeiten *pl* road-works.

Straßenbahn (*pl* -en) *die* tram (*Br*), streetcar (*Am*).

Straßenbahnlinie (*pl* -n) *die* tram route.

Straßencafé (*pl* -s) *das* street café.

Straßenfest (*pl* -e) *das* street party.

Straßenglätte *die* slippery road ; 'mit ~ muss gerechnet werden' 'slippery road surface ahead'.

Straßenkarte (*pl* -n) *die* road map.

Straßenlage *die* (von Auto) road holding.

Straßenschäden *pl* : 'Achtung ~' 'uneven road surface'.

Straßenschild (*pl* -er) *das* street sign.

Straßensperre (*pl* -n) *die* roadblock.

Straßenverhältnisse *pl* road conditions.

Straßenverkehr *der* traffic.

Straßenverkehrsordnung *die* Road Traffic Act.

Straßenzustandsbericht (*pl* -e) *der* report on road conditions.

Strategie (*pl* -n) *die* strategy.

Strauch (*pl* Sträucher) *der* bush.

Strauß[1] (*pl* Sträuße) *der* (Blumen) bunch of flowers.

Strauß[2] (*pl* -e) *der* (Vogel) ostrich.

Strecke (*pl* -n) *die* (Entfernung) distance ; (Weg) route ; **die ~**

strecken *vt* (Körperteil) to stretch. ■ **sich strecken** *ref* (sich recken) to stretch.

streckenweise *adv* in places.

streicheln *vt* to stroke.

streichen (*prät* strich, *pp* gestrichen) *vt* (mit Farbe) to paint ; (Butter) to spread ; (durchstreichen) to cross out ; (annullieren) to cancel. ◆ *vi* (mit der Hand) : jm übers Haar ~ to stroke sb's hair.

Streichholz (*pl* -hölzer) *das* match.

Streichholzschachtel (*pl* -n) *die* matchbox.

Streichkäse *der* cheese spread.

Streifen (*pl* -) *der* (Muster) stripe ; (Stück) strip.

Streifenkarte (*pl* -n) *die* economy ticket for several bus or metro journeys.

Streifenwagen (*pl* -) *der* patrol car.

Streik (*pl* -s) *der* strike.

streiken *vi* (Arbeiter) to strike ; (fam : Gerät) to be on the blink.

Streit *der* argument ; ~ **haben mit** to argue with.

streiten (*prät* stritt, *pp* gestritten) *vi* (zanken) to argue ; ~ **über** (+A) (sich auseinander setzen) to argue about. ■ **sich streiten** *ref* (sich zanken) to argue.

streng *adj* strict. ◆ *adv* strictly.

Stress *der* stress.

streuen *vt (Salz, Kräuter)* to sprinkle. ◆ *vi (gegen Eis)* to grit.

Streuselkuchen *(pl -) der* cake with crumble topping.

strich *prät* → **streichen**.

Strich *(pl -e) der (Linie)* line ; *(fam : Prostitution)* prostitution.

strichweise *adv* : ~ Regen patchy rain.

Strick *(pl -e) der* the rope.

stricken *vt* to knit.

Strickjacke *(pl -n) die* cardigan.

Strickleiter *(pl -n) die* rope ladder.

Stricknadel *(pl -n) die* knitting needle.

Strickwaren *pl* knitwear *(pl)*.

Strickzeug *das* knitting.

Striptease *der* striptease.

stritt *prät* → **streiten**.

Stroh *das* straw.

Strohhalm *(pl -e) der* straw.

Strom *(pl Ströme) der (elektrisch)* electricity ; *(Fluss)* river ; *(Menge)* stream ; **es regnet in Strömen** it's pouring (with rain).

Stromanschluss *(pl -anschlüsse) der* connection to the mains.

Stromausfall *(pl -ausfälle) der* power failure.

strömen *vi ist* to stream.

Stromstärke *(pl -n) die* strength of electric current.

Strömung *(pl -en) die (von Fluss, Meer)* current.

Stromverbrauch *der* electricity consumption.

Stromzähler *(pl -) der* electricity meter.

Strophe *(pl -n) die* verse.

Strudel[1] *(pl -) der (im Wasser)* whirlpool.

Strudel[2] *(pl -) der (Gebäck)* strudel.

Struktur *(pl -en) die (Aufbau)* structure.

Strumpf *(pl Strümpfe) der* stocking.

Strumpfhose *(pl -n) die* tights *(pl) (Br)*, pantyhose *(pl) (Am)*.

Stube *(pl -n) die (Raum)* room.

Stück *(pl -e) das (Teil)* piece ; *(von Zucker)* lump ; *(Theaterstück)* play ; **wie viele Brötchen? - 10 ~, bitte** how many rolls? - 10 please ; **am ~** unsliced.

Stückzahl *(pl -en) die* number of pieces.

Student, in *(mpl -en) der, die* student.

Studentenausweis *(pl -e) der* student card.

Studienfahrt *(pl -en) die* study trip.

studieren *vt & vi* to study.

Studium *(pl Studien) das* study.

Stufe *(pl -n) die (von Treppe)* step ; **'Vorsicht ~!'** 'mind the step!'

Stuhl *(pl Stühle) der (zum Sitzen)* chair ; *(Kot)* stool.

Stuhlgang *der* bowel movement.

stumm *adj (behindert)* dumb ; *(still)* silent.

stumpf *adj* blunt ; *(glanzlos)* dull ; *(abgestumpft)* apathetic.

Stumpfsinn der (Monotonie) monotony.

Stunde (pl -n) die hour ; (Unterrichtsstunde) lesson.

Stundenkilometer pl kilometres per hour.

stundenlang adj for hours.

Stundenlohn (pl -löhne) der hourly wage.

stündlich adj & adv hourly.

Sturm (pl Stürme) der (Wetter) storm ; (SPORT) forward line ; (Andrang) : ein ~ auf a run on.

stürmen vt hat (überrennen) to storm. ◆ vi ist (laufen) to rush. ◆ vi hat (SPORT) to attack. ◆ vimp hat : es stürmt it's blowing a gale.

Sturmflut (pl -en) die storm tide.

stürmisch adj (Wetter) stormy ; (Person, Begrüßung) passionate ; es ist ~ it's blowing a gale.

Sturmwarnung (pl -en) die gale warning.

Sturz (pl Stürze) der (Fallen) fall.

stürzen vt hat (stoßen) to push ; (Regierung) to bring down. ◆ vi ist (fallen) to fall ; (laufen) to rush. ▨ sich stürzen ref (springen) to jump.

Sturzhelm (pl -e) der crash helmet.

Stute (pl -n) die mare.

Stuten (pl -) der loaf of white bread with raisins and almonds.

stützen vt to support. ▨ sich stützen ref (Person) to lean.

Subjekt (pl -e) das subject.

subjektiv adj subjective.

Substanz (pl -en) die substance.

subtrahieren vt to subtract.

Suche die search ; auf der ~ nach in search of.

suchen vt to look for. ◆ vi : ~ nach to look for.

süchtig adj addicted.

Süd der south.

Südafrika nt South Africa.

Südamerika nt South America.

Süddeutschland nt South Germany.

Süden der south ; im ~ in the south ; nach ~ south.

Südeuropa nt Southern Europe.

Südfrucht (pl -früchte) die tropical fruit.

Südhang (pl -hänge) der south-facing slope.

südlich adj (Gegend) southern ; (Richtung) southerly. ◆ präp : ~ von south of.

Südosten der (Gegend) south-east ; (Richtung) south-easterly.

Südwesten der (Gegend) south-west ; (Richtung) south-westerly.

Sultanine (pl -n) die sultana.

Sülze (pl -n) die brawn (Br), headcheese (Am).

Summe (pl -n) die sum, total.

Sumpf (pl Sümpfe) der marsh.

super adj & interj (fam) great.

Super das (Benzin) four-star petrol ; ~verbleit four-star leaded petrol.

Superlativ (*pl* -e) *der (GRAMM)* superlative.

Supermarkt (*pl* -märkte) *der* supermarket.

Suppe (*pl* -n) *die* soup.

Suppengrün *das* parsley, leeks, celery and carrots, used for making soup.

Suppenlöffel (*pl* -) *der* soup spoon.

Suppentasse (*pl* -n) *die* soup bowl.

Suppenteller (*pl* -) *der* soup plate.

Surfbrett (*pl* -er) *das (mit Segel)* sailboard ; *(ohne Segel)* surfboard.

surfen *vi* ist/hat *(mit Segel)* to windsurf ; *(ohne Segel)* to surf.

Surfer, in (*mpl* -) *der, die (mit Segel)* windsurfer ; *(ohne Segel)* surfer.

Surrealismus *der* surrealism.

süß *adj* sweet.

süßen *vt* to sweeten.

Süßigkeit (*pl* -en) *die* sweet *(Br)*, candy *(Am)*.

süßsauer *adj (Geschmack)* sweet and sour.

Süßspeise (*pl* -n) *die* dessert.

Süßstoff (*pl* -e) *der* sweetener.

Süßwaren *pl* sweets *(Br)*, candy *(sg) (Am)*.

Süßwasser *das* fresh water.

Süßwasserfisch (*pl* -e) *der* freshwater fish.

Swimmingpool (*pl* -s) *der* swimming pool.

Sylt *nt* Sylt.

SYLT

The island of Sylt is the largest of the North Frisian Islands and lies off the coast of Schleswig-Holstein and Denmark. It is a very popular holiday and health resort, with beautiful sandy beaches, moorland, cliffs and bird sanctuaries. The exclusive resort of Westerland is the favourite haunt of the rich and famous during the summer months.

Symbol (*pl* -e) *das* symbol.

Symmetrie (*pl* -n) *die* symmetry.

symmetrisch *adj* symmetrical.

sympathisch *adj* nice. ◆ *adv* : er wirkt sehr ~ he seems very nice.

Symphonie (*pl* -n) *die* = Sinfonie.

Symptom (*pl* -e) *das (von Krankheit)* symptom.

Synagoge (*pl* -n) *die* synagogue.

synthetisch *adj* synthetic.

System (*pl* -e) *das* system.

Szene (*pl* -n) *die* scene.

T

Tabak (*pl* -e) *der* tobacco.

Tabakladen (*pl* -läden) *der* tobacconist's.

Tabakwaren *pl* tobacco *(sg)*.

Tabelle (*pl* -n) *die (Liste)* table.

Tablett (*pl* -s) *das* tray.

Tablette (*pl* -n) *die* tablet.

Tachometer (*pl* -) *der* speedometer.

Tafel (*pl* -n) *die (in Schule)* blackboard ; *(geh : Tisch)* table ; eine ~ Schokolade a bar of chocolate.

tafelfertig *adj* ready to eat.

Tafelwasser (*pl* -wässer) *das* mineral water.

Tafelwein (*pl* -e) *der* table wine.

Tag (*pl* -e) *der* day ; eines ~es one day ; guten ~! hello! ; jeden ~ every day ; ~ für ~ day after day. ■ **Tage** *pl (Menstruation)* : sie hat/bekommt ihre ~e she's got her period.

Tag der Deutschen Einheit *der* Day of German Unity.

ⓘ **TAG DER DEUTSCHEN EINHEIT**

This day, 3 October, is a public holiday in Germany, commemorating the anniversary of German reunification in 1990, when the GDR officially ceased to exist. It replaces the previous "Tag der Deutschen Einheit" which before 1990 was celebrated in West Germany on 17 June to mark the crushing of the political uprising in the GDR in 1953 by Soviet troops.

Tagebuch (*pl* -bücher) *das* diary.

tagelang *adv* for days.

Tagesanbruch *der* dawn.

Tagesausflug (*pl* -ausflüge) *der* day trip.

Tagescreme (*pl* -s) *die* day cream.

Tagesfahrkarte (*pl* -n) *die* day ticket.

Tagesfahrt (*pl* -en) *die* day trip.

Tagesgericht (*pl* -e) *das (in Restaurant)* : 'Tagesgericht' 'today's special'.

Tageskarte (*pl* -n) *die (Speisekarte)* today's menu ; *(Fahrkarte)* day ticket.

Tageslicht *das* daylight.

Tagesordnung (*pl* -en) *die* agenda.

Tagesrückfahrkarte (*pl* -n) *die* day return (ticket).

Tagesschau *die* news.

Tagessuppe (*pl* -n) *die* soup of the day.

Tagestour (*pl* -en) *die* day trip.

Tageszeit (*pl* -en) *die* time of day.

Tageszeitung (*pl* -en) *die* daily newspaper.

täglich *adj* & *adv* daily ; dreimal ~ three times a day.

tagsüber *adv* during the day.

Tagung (*pl* -en) *die* conference.

Taille (*pl* -n) *die* waist.

tailliert *adj* fitted.

Takt (*pl* -e) *der (musikalische Einheit)* bar ; *(Rhythmus)* time ; *(Feingefühl)* tact.

Taktik (*pl* -en) *die* tactics (*pl*).

Tal (*pl* Täler) *das* valley.

talentiert *adj* talented.

Talkshow (*pl* -s) *die* talk show.

Talsperre (*pl* -n) die dam.

Tampon (*pl* -s) der (*für Menstruation*) tampon.

Tandem (*pl* -s) das tandem.

Tang der seaweed.

Tank (*pl* -s) der tank.

Tankanzeige (*pl* -n) die fuel gauge.

Tankdeckel (*pl* -) der petrol cap.

tanken *vi* to fill up. ◆ *vt* : Benzin ~ to get some petrol (*Br*), to get some gas (*Am*).

Tankschloss (*pl* -schlösser) das petrol cap lock.

Tankstelle (*pl* -n) die petrol station (*Br*), gas station (*Am*).

Tankwart, in (*mpl* -e) der, die petrol station attendant (*Br*), gas station attendant (*Am*).

Tanne (*pl* -n) die fir (tree).

Tante (*pl* -n) die aunt.

Tanz (*pl* Tänze) der dance.

tanzen *vi* & *vt* to dance.

Tänzer, in (*mpl* -) der, die dancer.

Tapete (*pl* -n) die wallpaper.

tapezieren *vt* to paper.

tapfer *adj* brave.

Tarif (*pl* -e) der (*Preis*) charge ; (*von Lohn*) rate.

Tarifzone (*pl* -n) die fare zone.

Tasche (*pl* -n) die (*zum Tragen*) bag ; (*in Kleidung*) pocket.

Taschenbuch (*pl* -bücher) das paperback.

Taschendieb, in (*mpl* -e) der, die pickpocket ; 'vor ~en wird gewarnt' 'beware of pickpockets'.

Taschenformat (*pl* -e) das pocket size.

Taschenkalender (*pl* -) der pocket diary.

Taschenlampe (*pl* -n) die torch (*Br*), flashlight (*Am*).

Taschenmesser (*pl* -) das penknife.

Taschenrechner (*pl* -) der pocket calculator.

Taschenschirm (*pl* -e) der collapsible umbrella.

Taschentuch (*pl* -tücher) das handkerchief.

Taschenuhr (*pl* -en) die pocket watch.

Tasse (*pl* -n) die cup.

Taste (*pl* -n) die key.

tasten *vi* to feel.

Tastendruck der : auf ~ at the touch of a button.

Tastentelefon (*pl* -e) das push-button telephone.

tat *prät* → tun.

Tat (*pl* -en) die (*Handlung*) action ; (*Straftat*) crime.

Tatar das steak tartare.

Täter, in (*mpl* -) der, die culprit.

Tätigkeit (*pl* -en) die (*beruflich*) job ; (*Aktivität*) activity.

Tätowierung (*pl* -en) die tattoo.

Tatsache (*pl* -n) die fact.

tatsächlich *adj* actual. ◆ *adv* actually.

Tau[1] der (*Niederschlag*) dew.

Tau[2] (*pl* -e) das (*Seil*) rope.

taub *adj* (*Person*) deaf ; (*Hände, Gefühl*) numb.

Taube (*pl* -n) der, die (*Person*) deaf person. ◆ die (*Vogel*) pigeon.

taubstumm *adj* deaf and dumb.

tauchen *vi hat/ist* to dive. ◆ *vt hat (eintauchen)* to dip.

Taucher, in *(mpl -) der, die* diver.

Taucherausrüstung *(pl -en) die* diving equipment.

Taucherbrille *(pl -n) die* diving goggles *(pl)*.

Tauchkurs *(pl -e) der* diving course.

Tauchsieder *(pl -) der* portable water heater.

tauen *vi ist (Eis)* to melt. ◆ *vimp hat :* es taut it's thawing.

taufen *vt (Kind, Person)* to baptize.

tauschen *vt & vi* to swap.

täuschen *vt (Person)* to deceive. ◆ *vi (Eindruck)* to be deceptive. ■ **sich täuschen** *ref* to be wrong.

tausend *num* a ODER one thousand.

Tausend *(pl - ODER -e) das* thousand.

Tausender *(pl -) der (Geldschein)* thousand mark note.

Tauwetter *das* thaw.

Taxi *(pl -s) das* taxi.

Taxifahrer, in *(mpl -) der, die* taxi driver.

Taxirufsäule *(pl -n) die* public telephone exclusively for ordering taxis.

Taxistand *(pl -stände) der* taxi rank.

Team *(pl -s) das* team.

Technik *(pl -en) die* technology ; *(Methode)* technique.

Techniker, in *(mpl -) der, die* engineer ; *(im Sport, in Musik)* technician.

technisch *adj* technological ; *(methodisch)* technical. ◆ *adv* technologically ; *(methodisch)* technically ; ~e Daten specifications.

Teddy *(pl -s) der* teddy bear.

Tee *(pl -s) der* tea ; schwarzer ~ *(Getränk)* black tea.

Teebeutel *(pl -) der* tea bag.

Tee-Ei *(pl -er) das* tea infuser.

Teekanne *(pl -n) die* teapot.

Teelöffel *(pl -) der* teaspoon.

Teesieb *(pl -e) das* tea strainer.

Teich *(pl -e) der* pond.

Teig *(pl -e) der* dough.

Teigwaren *pl* pasta *(sg)*.

Teil *(pl -e) der (Teilmenge, Teilstück)* part ; *(Anteil)* share. ◆ *das (Einzelteil)* part ; zum ~ partly.

teilen *vt* to divide ; *(übereinstimmen)* to share. ◆ *vi (aufteilen)* to share ; *(dividieren)* to divide ; sich *(D)* etw ~ to share sthg. ■ **sich teilen** *ref (Gruppe)* to split up ; *(Straße)* to fork.

Teilkaskoversicherung *(pl -en) die* third party insurance.

teilmöbliert *adj* partially furnished.

Teilnahme *die (an Veranstaltung)* participation.

teilnehmen *vi unr* to take part.

Teilnehmer, in *(mpl -) der, die* participant.

teils *adv* partly. ◆ *konj :* ~... ~ *(sowohl... als auch)* both... and...

Teilstück *(pl -e) das* part.

Teilsumme (*pl* -n) *die* subtotal.

teilweise *adv* (*zu gewissen Teilen*) partly ; (*zeitweise*) sometimes.

Teilzahlung (*pl* -en) *die* payment by instalments.

Tel. (*abk für Telefon*) tel.

Telefax (*pl* -e) *das* fax.

Telefon (*pl* -e) *das* telephone ; **bleiben Sie bitte am ~** please hold the line.

Telefonanruf (*pl* -e) *der* telephone call.

Telefonansage (*pl* -n) *die* telephone information service.

Telefonanschluss (*pl* -anschlüsse) *der* telephone line.

Telefonat (*pl* -e) *das* telephone call.

Telefonbuch (*pl* -bücher) *das* telephone book.

Telefongespräch (*pl* -e) *das* telephone conversation.

telefonieren *vi* to make a telephone call ; **mit jm** ~ to talk to sb on the telephone ; **~ ohne Münzen** to use a phonecard.

telefonisch *adj* (*Abmachung, Verbindung*) telephone (*vor Subst*).

Telefonkarte (*pl* -n) *die* phonecard.

Telefonnummer (*pl* -n) *die* telephone number.

Telefonverbindung (*pl* -en) *die* telephone line.

Telefonzelle (*pl* -n) *die* telephone box.

Telefonzentrale (*pl* -n) *die* switchboard.

telegrafieren *vt* to telegraph.

Telegramm (*pl* -e) *das* telegram.

Telekom *die* German partly state-owned telecommunications organization.

Teleobjektiv (*pl* -e) *das* telephoto lens.

Teller (*pl* -) *der* plate.

Tellerfleisch *das* (*Süddt*) roast beef served with horseradish and boiled potatoes.

Tempel (*pl* -) *der* temple.

Temperament *das* (*Wesen*) temperament ; (*Energie*) liveliness.

temperamentvoll *adj* lively.

Temperatur (*pl* -en) *die* temperature ; **~ haben** to have a temperature.

Temperaturanzeige (*pl* -n) *die* temperature gauge.

Tempo[1] (*pl* -s) *das* (*fam : Papiertaschentuch*) tissue.

Tempo[2] (*pl* -s) *das* (*Geschwindigkeit*) speed.

Tempo[3] (*pl* Tempi) *das* (*von Musik*) tempo.

Tempolimit (*pl* -s) *das* speed limit.

Tempotaschentuch® (*pl* -tücher) *das* tissue.

Tendenz (*pl* -en) *die* tendency.

Tennis *das* tennis.

Tennishalle (*pl* -n) *die* tennis centre.

Tennisplatz (*pl* -plätze) *der* tennis court.

Tennisschläger (*pl* -) *der* tennis racquet.

Tennisspieler, in (*mpl -*)
der, die tennis player.

Tenor (*pl* Tenöre) *der* tenor.

Teppich (*pl -e*) *der* (*Einzelstück*) rug ; (*Teppichboden*) carpet.

Teppichboden (*pl -böden*)
der carpet.

Termin (*pl -e*) *der* (*Zeitpunkt*)
date ; (*Vereinbarung*) appointment ; **einen ~ haben** to have an
appointment.

Terminal (*pl -s*) *der* (*Gebäude*) terminal.

Terminkalender (*pl -*) *der*
diary.

Terpentin *das* turpentine.

Terrasse (*pl -n*) *die* (*am Haus*)
patio.

Terror *der* terror ; (*Terrorismus*) terrorism.

terrorisieren *vt* to terrorize.

Tesafilm® *der* Sellotape®
(*Br*), Scotch® tape (*Am*).

Tessin *das* Ticino (*canton in
south-east Switzerland*).

Test (*pl -s*) *der* test.

Testament (*pl -e*) *das* will ;
das Alte/Neue ~ the Old/New
Testament.

Tetanus *der* tetanus.

teuer *adj* expensive. ◆ *adv* at
a high price ; **das haben wir uns ~
erkauft** we paid dearly for it.

Teufel (*pl -*) *der* devil.

Text (*pl -e*) *der* text.

Textilien *pl* textiles.

Textmarker (*pl -*) *der* marker
pen.

Textverarbeitung *die* (*EDV*)
word processing.

Theater (*pl -*) *das* (*Gebäude*)
theatre ; (*fam : Ärger*) trouble ;

(*fam : Vortäuschung*) act ; **ins ~
gehen** to go to the theatre.

Theateraufführung (*pl
-en*) *die* performance.

Theaterkarte (*pl -n*) *die* theatre ticket.

Theaterkasse (*pl -n*) *die* theatre box office.

Theaterstück (*pl -e*) *das*
play.

Theatervorstellung(*pl-en*)
die performance.

Theke (*pl -n*) *die* (*Bar*) bar ; (*im
Geschäft*) counter.

Thema (*pl* Themen) *das* (*von
Text, Gespräch*) subject ; (*musikalisch*) theme.

Themse *die* : **die ~** the
Thames.

theoretisch *adj* theoretical.

Theorie (*pl -n*) *die* theory.

Therapeut, in (*mpl -en*) *der,
die* therapist.

Therapie (*pl -n*) *die* (*medizinisch*) treatment ; (*Psychotherapie*) therapy.

Thermalbad (*pl -bäder*) *das*
(*Schwimmbad*) thermal bath.

Thermometer (*pl -*) *das* thermometer.

Thermosflasche (*pl -n*) *die*
thermos (flask).

Thermoskanne (*pl -n*) *die*
thermos (flask).

Thermostat (*pl -e*) *das* thermostat.

These (*pl -n*) *die* thesis.

Thron (*pl -e*) *der* throne.

Thunfisch, Tunfisch (*pl -e*)
der tuna.

Thüringen *nt* Thuringia.

Ticket (*pl -s*) *das* ticket.

tief *adj* deep ; *(Fall)* long ; *(niedrig)* low. ◆ *adv* deep ; *(unten)* low ; *(atmen)* deeply ; ~ schlafen to be in a deep sleep.

Tief *(pl -s)* das *(Wetter)* depression.

Tiefdruckgebiet *(pl -e)* das area of low pressure.

Tiefe *(pl -n)* die depth.

Tiefebene *(pl -n)* die *(lowland)* plain.

Tiefgarage *(pl -n)* die underground car park.

tiefgefroren *adj* frozen.

tiefgekühlt *adj* frozen.

Tiefkühlfach *(pl -fächer)* das freezer compartment.

Tiefkühlkost die frozen food.

Tiefkühltruhe *(pl -n)* die freezer.

Tier *(pl -e)* das animal.

Tierarzt, -ärztin *(mpl -ärzte)* der, die vet.

Tiergarten *(pl -gärten)* der zoo.

Tierhandlung *(pl -en)* die pet shop.

Tierheim *(pl -e)* das animal home.

tierisch *adj (Erzeugnis, Fett)* animal *(vor Subst)* ; *(fam : stark)* great.

Tierkreiszeichen *(pl -)* das sign of the zodiac.

Tiernahrung die animal food.

Tierpark *(pl -s)* der zoo.

Tierschutz der protection of animals.

Tiger *(pl -)* der tiger.

Tilsiter *(pl -)* der *strong firm cheese with holes in it.*

Tinktur *(pl -en)* die tincture.

Tinte *(pl -n)* die ink.

Tintenfisch *(pl -e)* der *(mit acht Armen)* octopus ; *(Kalmar)* squid.

Tipp *(pl -s)* der the tip ; jm einen ~ geben to give sb a tip.

tippen *vt (mit Schreibmaschine)* to type. ◆ *vi (vorhersagen)* to bet ; *(fam : bei Lotto, Wette)* to bet ; an etw *(A)* ~ to tap sthg.

Tirol *nt* the Tyrol.

Tisch *(pl -e)* der table ; den ~ decken to set the table.

Tischdecke *(pl -n)* die tablecloth.

Tischler, -in *(mpl -)* der, die carpenter.

Tischtennis das table tennis.

Tischtuch *(pl -tücher)* das tablecloth.

Titel *(pl -)* der title.

Toast *(pl -s)* der *(Brotscheibe)* (slice of) toast.

Toastbrot *(pl -e)* das sliced white bread.

toasten *vt* to toast.

Toaster *(pl -)* der toaster.

toben *vi hat (Sturm)* to rage ; *(Person)* to go crazy. ◆ *vi ist (rennen)* to charge about.

Tochter *(pl Töchter)* die *(Verwandte)* daughter.

Tod *(pl -e)* der death.

Todesopfer *(pl -)* das casualty.

todkrank *adj* terminally ill.

tödlich *adj* fatal.

todmüde *adj (fam)* dead tired.

todsicher *adj (fam)* dead certain.

Tofu der tofu.

Toilette (pl -n) die (Klo) toilet ; zur ~ gehen to go to the toilet.

Toilettenartikel pl toiletries.

Toilettenpapier das toilet paper.

tolerant adj tolerant.

toll adj (fam : wunderbar) brilliant. ◆ adv (fam : wunderbar) brilliantly.

Tollwut die rabies.

Tollwutgebiet (pl -e) das rabies-infected area.

Tomate (pl -n) die tomato.

Tomatenmark das tomato puree.

Tomatensaft (pl -säfte) der tomato juice.

Tombola (pl -s) die tombola.

Ton¹ (pl Töne) der (bei Fernsehen, Radio) sound ; (in Tonleiter) note ; (Tonfall, von Farbe) tone.

Ton² (pl -e) der (Lehm) clay.

Tonausfall (pl -fälle) der loss of sound.

Tonband (pl -bänder) das (Band) tape ; (Gerät) tape recorder.

tönen vt (Haare) to tint.

Tonne (pl -n) die (Behälter) barrel ; (Gewichtseinheit) tonne.

Tönung (pl -en) die tint.

Top (pl -s) das top.

Topf (pl Töpfe) der (Kochtopf) pan ; (Blumentopf) pot.

Topfen der (Süddt & Österr) curd cheese.

Topfenstrudel (pl -) der (Süddt & Österr) curd cheese strudel.

Töpfer, in (mpl -) der, die potter.

Töpferei (pl -en) die pottery.

Topfpflanze (pl -n) die potted plant.

Tor (pl -e) das (Tür) gate ; (von Scheune, Garage) door ; (bei Fußball) goal ; ein ~ schießen to score a goal.

Toreinfahrt (pl -en) die entrance gate.

Torf der peat.

Torte (pl -n) die gâteau.

Tortelett (pl -s) das tartlet.

Torwart (pl -e) der goalkeeper.

tot adj & adv dead ; ~ umfallen to drop dead.

total adj total. ◆ adv totally.

Totalschaden (pl -schäden) der write-off.

Tote (pl -n) der, die dead person.

töten vt to kill.

Totensonntag (pl -e) der day for commemoration of the dead, Sunday before Advent.

totlachen : sich totlachen ref (fam) to kill o.s. laughing.

Toto das football pools (pl).

Toupet (pl -s) das toupee.

toupieren vt to backcomb.

Tour (pl -en) die (Ausflug) trip ; (fam : Verhalten) way.

Tourenski (pl -er) der cross-country ski.

Tourismus der tourism.

Tourist, in (mpl -en) der, die tourist.

Tourjstenklasse *die* tourist class.

Tourjstenort *(pl -e) der* tourist resort.

tourjstisch *adj* tourist.

Tournee *(pl -n) die* tour.

traben *vi ist (Pferd)* to trot.

Trabrennen *(pl -) das* trotting.

Tracht *(pl -en) die (Kleidung)* traditional costume ; **eine ~ Prügel** *(fam : Schläge)* a beating.

Trachtenfest *(pl -e) das event at which traditional costumes are worn.*

Trachtenverein *(pl -e) der society for the preservation of regional customs.*

Tradition *(pl -en) die* tradition.

traditionell *adj* traditional.

traf *prät →* treffen.

Trafik *die (Österr)* tobacconist's.

 TRAFIK

A "Trafik" is a small shop found in Austria where all sorts of useful items can be bought, such as stamps, postcards, tickets for local transport services, magazines, cigarettes and tobacco.

Tragbahre *(pl -n) die* stretcher.

tragbar *adj (Gerät)* portable ; *(akzeptabel)* acceptable.

träge *adj (Person, Bewegung)* lazy.

tragen *(präs* **trägt**, *prät* **trug**, *pp* **getragen**) *vt (transportieren)* to carry ; *(Kleidung, Frisur)* to wear ; *(abstützen)* to support ; *(ertragen, Kosten)* to bear ; *(Risiko, Konsequenzen)* to accept. ◆ *vi (Eis, Wände)* to hold ; *(Tier)* to be pregnant. ■ **sich tragen** *ref (finanziell)* to be self-supporting.

Träger *(pl -) der (Beruf)* porter ; *(Geldgeber)* sponsor ; *(von Kleid)* strap ; *(Hosenträger)* braces *(pl) (Br)*, suspenders *(pl) (Am)* ; *(aus Eisen)* girder.

Trägerin *(pl -nen) die (Beruf)* porter ; *(Geldgeberin)* sponsor.

Tragetasche *(pl -n) die* carrier bag.

tragisch *adj* tragic.

Tragödie *(pl -n) die* tragedy.

trägt *präs →* tragen.

Trainer, in *(mpl -) der, die* trainer.

trainieren *vi & vt* to train.

Training *(pl -s) das* training.

Trainingsanzug *(pl -züge) der* tracksuit.

Traktor *(pl -toren) der* tractor.

Trambahn *(pl -en) die (Süddt)* tram *(Br)*, streetcar *(Am)*.

trampen *vi hat/ist* to hitchhike.

Tramper, in *(mpl -) der, die* hitchhiker.

Träne *(pl -n) die* tear.

tränen *vi* to water.

Tränengas *das* tear gas.

trank *prät →* trinken.

Transfusion *(pl -en) die* transfusion.

Transitverkehr *der* transit traffic.

Transitvisum (*pl* -visa) *das* transit visa.

Transport (*pl* -e) *der* transport.

transportabel *adj* (*Fernseher*) portable.

transportieren *vt* (*befördern*) to transport ; (*Film*) to wind on. ◆ *vi* (*Kamera*) to wind on.

Transportmittel (*pl* -) *das* means of transport.

Transportunternehmen (*pl* -) *das* haulier.

Transvestit (*pl* -en) *der* transvestite.

trat *prät* → treten.

Traube (*pl* -n) *die* (*Frucht*) grape.

Traubensaft (*pl* -säfte) *der* grape juice.

Traubenzucker *der* glucose.

trauen *vt* (*Brautpaar*) to marry. ◆ *vi* (+D) (*vertrauen*) to trust. ▦ **sich trauen** *ref* (*wagen*) to dare.

Trauer *die* mourning.

Traum (*pl* Träume) *der* dream.

träumen *vi* to dream ; (*abwesend sein*) to daydream.

traumhaft *adj* fantastic.

traurig *adj* sad. ◆ *adv* sadly.

Trauung (*pl* -en) *die* wedding ; **kirchliche/standesamtliche ~** church/registry office wedding.

Travellerscheck (*pl* -s) *der* traveller's cheque.

treffen (*präs* trifft, *prät* traf, *pp* getroffen) *vt* hat (*begegnen*) to meet ; (*Ziel*) to hit ; (*Verabredung, Entscheidung*) to make ; (*traurig machen*) to affect. ◆ *vi*

hat (*ins Ziel*) to score. ▦ **sich treffen** *ref* to meet ; **sich mit jm ~** to meet sb ; **wo sollen wir uns ~?** where should we meet?

Treffen (*pl* -) *das* meeting.

Treffer (*pl* -) *der* (SPORT) goal ; (*Schuss*) hit.

Treffpunkt (*pl* -e) *der* meeting place.

treiben (*prät* trieb, *pp* getrieben) *vt* hat to drive ; (*machen, tun*) to do. ◆ *vi* ist (*im Wasser*) to drift ; **was treibst du denn so in deiner Freizeit?** what do you do in your spare time?

Treibstoff (*pl* -e) *der* fuel.

Trend (*pl* -s) *der* trend.

trennen *vt* to separate ; (*unterscheiden*) to distinguish. ▦ **sich trennen** *ref* to separate.

Trennung (*pl* -en) *die* (*von Beziehung*) separation ; (GRAMM) division.

Treppe (*pl* -n) *die* stairs (*pl*).

Treppengeländer (*pl* -) *das* banisters (*pl*).

Treppenhaus (*pl* -häuser) *das* stairwell.

Tresen (*pl* -) *der* (*Norddt*) counter.

Tretboot (*pl* -e) *das* pedal boat.

treten (*präs* tritt, *prät* trat, *pp* getreten) *vt* & *vi* hat to kick. ◆ *vi* ist (*gehen*) to step ; **auf die Bremse ~** to brake.

treu *adj* faithful.

Triathlon (*pl* -s) *der* triathlon.

Tribüne (*pl* -n) *die* stand.

Trichter (*pl* -) *der* (*Gerät*) funnel.

Trick (*pl* -s) *der* trick.

Trickfilm (*pl* -e) *der* cartoon.

trieb *prät* → treiben.

triefen (*prät* troff ODER **trief**te, *pp* **getrieft**) *vi ist* & *vt hat* to drip.

trifft *präs* → treffen.

Trikot (*pl* -s) *das* jersey.

Trillerpfeife (*pl* -n) *die* whistle.

Trimester (*pl* -) *das* term.

Trimm-dich-Pfad (*pl* -e) *der* fitness trail.

trinkbar *adj* drinkable.

trinken (*prät* trank, *pp* getrunken) *vt* & *vi* to drink ; einen ~ gehen (*fam*) to go for a drink.

Trinkgeld (*pl* -er) *das* tip.

Trinkhalle (*pl* -n) *die* drinks stall.

Trinkhalm (*pl* -e) *der* (drinking) straw.

Trinkschokolade (*pl* -n) *die* drinking chocolate.

Trinkwasser *das* drinking water.

Trio (*pl* -s) *das* trio.

tritt *präs* → treten.

Tritt (*pl* -e) *der* (*Stoß*) kick ; (*Schritt*) step.

triumphieren *vi* to triumph.

trivial *adj* trivial.

trocken *adj* dry ; '~ aufbewahren' 'keep in a dry place'.

Trockenhaube (*pl* -n) *die* hair dryer.

Trockenheit *die* dryness ; (*Wassermangel*) drought.

trocken|legen *vt* (*Sumpf*) to drain ; (*Baby*) to change.

trocknen *vt hat* & *vi ist* to dry.

Trockner (*pl* -) *der* dryer.

Trödel *der* (*Gegenstände*) junk ; (*fam* : Trödelmarkt) flea market.

Trödelmarkt (*pl* -märkte) *der* flea market.

trödeln *vi hat/ist* (*fam* : langsam sein) to dawdle.

troff *prät* → triefen.

trog *prät* → trügen.

Trommel (*pl* -n) *die* (*Instrument*) drum.

Trommelfell (*pl* -e) *das* eardrum.

Trompete (*pl* -n) *die* trumpet.

Tropen *pl* tropics.

Tropf (*pl* -e) *der* (*Gerät*) drip.

tropfen *vi* & *vt* to drip.

Tropfen (*pl* -) *der* drop.

tropfnass *adv* : ~ aufhängen to drip-dry.

Tropfsteinhöhle (*pl* -n) *die* cave with stalactites and stalagmites.

trösten *vt* to console. ■ **sich trösten** *ref* to find consolation.

Trostpreis (*pl* -e) *der* consolation prize.

Trottoir (*pl* -e) *das* (*Süddt*) pavement (*Br*), sidewalk (*Am*).

trotz *präp* (+G) despite, in spite of.

trotzdem *adv* nevertheless.

trotzig *adj* stubborn.

trüb *adj* (*nicht klar*) cloudy.

Trüffel (*pl* -) *der* truffle.

trug *prät* → tragen.

trügen (*prät* trog, *pp* getrogen) *vi* to be deceptive.

Truhe (*pl* -n) *die* chest.

Trümmer *pl* (*eines Gebäudes*) ruins ; (*eines Fahrzeugs*) wreckage (*sg*).

Trumpf (*pl* Trümpfe) *der (bei Kartenspiel)* trumps (*pl*).

Trunkenheit *die (amt)* inebriation.

Truthahn (*pl* -hähne) *der* turkey.

Tschechien *nt* Czech Republic.

tschüs *interj* bye!

Tsd. *abk* = Tausend.

T-Shirt (*pl* -s) *das* T-shirt.

Tube (*pl* -n) *die* tube.

Tuberkulose *die* tuberculosis.

Tuch[1] (*pl* Tücher) *das (Halstuch)* scarf ; *(zum Putzen, Abtrocknen)* cloth.

Tuch[2] (*pl* -e) *das (Stoff)* cloth.

tüchtig *adj (geschickt)* competent ; *(fam : groß)* big. ◆ *adv (fam : viel)* : ~ essen to tuck in.

Tulpe (*pl* -n) *die* tulip.

Tümpel (*pl* -) *der* pond.

tun (*präs* tut, *prät* tat, *pp* getan) *vt* 1. *(machen)* to do ; was kann ich für Sie ~? what can I do for you? ; ich habe noch nichts für die Prüfung getan I haven't done any work for the exam yet.

2. *(fam : stellen, legen)* to put.

3. *(schaden, antun)* : jm/sich etwas ~ to do something to sb/o.s.

4. *(fam : funktionieren, ausreichen)* : ich denke, das tut es I think that will do ; das Auto tut es noch/nicht mehr the car still works/has had it.

◆ *vi* 1. *(spielen, vortäuschen)* : so ~, als ob to act as if ; er tut nur so he's only pretending.

2. *(Ausdruck von Gefühl, Wirkung)* : der Bettler tut mir Leid I feel sorry for the beggar ; jm gut ~ to do sb good.

3. *(Ausdruck einer Beziehung)* : zu ~ haben mit to be linked to ; nichts zu ~ haben mit to have nothing to do with.

◆ *vimp* : es tut sich etwas something is going on.

Tunfisch *der* → Thunfisch.

tunken *vt* to dunk.

Tunnel (*pl* -) *der* tunnel.

tupfen *vt* to dab.

Tür (*pl* -en) *die* door ; die ~ aufmachen/zumachen to open/close the door ; ~ zu! shut the door!

Türke (*pl* -n) *der* Turk.

Türkei *die* Turkey.

Türkin (*pl* -nen) *die* Turk.

türkisch *adj* Turkish.

Türkisch(e) *das* Turkish.

Türklinke (*pl* -n) *die* door handle.

Turm (*pl* Türme) *der (Gebäude)* tower.

turnen *vi (SPORT)* to do gymnastics.

Turner, in (*mpl* -) *der, die* gymnast.

Turnhalle (*pl* -n) *die* gym.

Turnhose (*pl* -n) *die* shorts (*pl*).

Turnier (*pl* -e) *das (SPORT)* tournament.

Turnschuh (*pl* -e) *der* gymshoe (*Br*), sneaker (*Am*).

Türschloss (*pl* -schlösser) *das* lock.

tuscheln *vi* to whisper.

tut *präs* → tun.

Tüte (*pl* -n) *die* bag.

TÜV *der* ≃ MOT *(Br), regular official test of car's roadworthiness.*

TV *das (abk für Television)* TV.

Typ *(pl -en) der (Art, Charakter)* type ; *(Modell)* model ; *(fam : Mann)* guy.

Typhus *der* typhoid.

typisch *adj* typical.

tyrannisieren *vt* to tyrannize.

U

u. *abk* = **und**.

u. a. *abk* = **unter anderem**.

u. a. m. *(abk für und anderes mehr)* etc.

UB *(pl -s) die (abk für Universitätsbibliothek)* university library.

U-Bahn *(pl -en) die* underground *(Br),* subway *(Am).*

U-Bahn-Haltestelle *(pl -n) die* underground station *(Br),* subway station *(Am).*

U-Bahn-Linie *(pl -n) die* underground line *(Br),* subway line *(Am).*

U-Bahn-Netz *(pl -e) das* underground system *(Br),* subway system *(Am).*

übel *(komp* übler, *superl* am übelsten) *adj* bad ; mir ist/wird ~ I am/feel sick ; nicht ~ *(fam)* not bad.

Übelkeit *(pl -en) die* nausea.

übel nehmen *vt unr* to take badly.

üben *vt* & *vi* to practise *(Br),* practice *(Am).*

über *präp (+A)* 1. *(höher als)* over, above ; das Flugzeug flog ~ das Tal the plane flew over the valley.
2. *(quer)* over ; ~ die Straße gehen to cross (over) the road.
3. *(Angabe der Route)* via.
4. *(Angabe des Themas)* about ; ein Buch ~ Mozart a book about Mozart.
5. *(Angabe des Betrages)* for ; eine Rechnung ~ 30 DM a bill for 30 marks.
6. *(mehr als)* over ; ~ eine Stunde over an hour ; ~ Null above zero ; Kinder ~ zehn Jahre children over ten (years of age).
7. *(zeitlich)* over ; ~ Nacht overnight.
◆ *präp (+D)* 1. *(räumlich : höher)* above, over ; die Lampe hängt ~ dem Tisch the lamp hangs above ODER over the table ; er wohnt ~ uns he lives above us.
2. *(mehr als)* above ; ~ dem Durchschnitt liegen to be above average.
◆ *adv* 1. *(zeitlich)* : den Sommer ~ bleiben wir hier we're staying here all summer.
2. *(fam : übrig)* left(over).
■ **über und über** *adv* all over.

überall *adv* everywhere.

überallhin *adv* everywhere.

überanstrengen *vt* to overstrain. ■ **sich überanstrengen** *ref* to overdo it.

überarbeiten *vt* to revise. ■ **sich überarbeiten** *ref* to overwork.

überbacken (*präs* überbackt ODER überbäckt, *prät* überbackte, *pp* überbacken) *vt* to bake or grill with a cheese topping.

überbelichtet *adj* overexposed.

Überblick (*pl* -e) der (*Übersicht*) summary.

überblicken *vt* (*einschätzen*) to grasp ; (*sehen*) to overlook.

überbrücken *vt* (*Zeit*) to fill in.

überbucht *adj* overbooked.

überdurchschnittlich *adj* above average.

übereinander *adv* on top of each other ; ~ sprechen/denken to talk/think about each other.

überein|stimmen *vi* (*Personen, Meinungen*) to agree.

überfahren (*präs* überfährt, *prät* überfuhr, *pp* überfahren) *vt* (*Tier, Person*) to run over.

Überfahrt (*pl* -en) die crossing.

Überfall (*pl* -fälle) der (*Angriff*) attack.

überfallen (*präs* überfällt, *prät* überfiel, *pp* überfallen) *vt* (*angreifen*) to attack.

überfällig *adj* (*Zug*) late ; (*Rechnung*) outstanding.

Überfluss der surplus.

überflüssig *adj* superfluous.

überfordert *adj* : damit bin ich ~ that's asking too much of me.

Überführung (*pl* -en) die (*Brücke*) bridge ; (*Transport*) transfer.

überfüllt *adj* overcrowded.

Übergabe die (*von Dingen*) handing over.

Übergang (*pl* -gänge) der (*Phase*) transition.

übergeben (*präs* übergibt, *prät* übergab, *pp* übergeben) *vt* (*Gegenstand*) to hand over.
■ **sich übergeben** *ref* to vomit.

übergehen[1] (*prät* überging, *pp* übergangen) *vt* (*ignorieren*) to ignore.

über|gehen[2] *vi unr* ist (*wechseln*) : in etw (A) ~ to change into sthg.

Übergewicht das overweight ; ~ haben to be overweight.

Übergröße (*pl* -n) die (*von Kleidung*) outsize.

überhand nehmen *vi unr* to get out of hand.

überhaupt *adv* (*Ausdruck von Zweifel*) at all ; (*allgemein, eigentlich*) really ; ich habe ~ kein Geld mehr (*gar kein*) I've got no money left at all ; ~ nicht (*gar nicht*) not at all.

überholen *vt* to overtake.

Überholspur (*pl* -en) die overtaking lane.

Überholverbot (*pl* -e) das ban on overtaking.

überhören *vt* (*nicht hören*) not to hear.

überlassen (*präs* überlässt, *prät* überließ, *pp* überlassen) *vt* (*leihen*) to lend.

überlastet *adj* (*Person*) overworked.

über|laufen[1] *vi unr* ist (*Topf, Wasser*) to overflow.

überlaufen[2] *adj* overcrowded.

überleben *vt* & *vi* to survive.

überlegen[1] *vt (nachdenken)* to consider. ◆ *vi (nachdenken)* to think ; **sich** *(D)* **etw ~** to think sthg over.

überlegen[2] *adj* superior. ◆ *adv (siegen)* convincingly ; *(arrogant)* patronizingly.

Überlegung *(pl -en) die* consideration.

übermorgen *adv* the day after tomorrow.

übermüdet *adj* overtired.

übernächste, r, s *adj* next... but one ; **die ~ Haltestelle** not this stop but the next one ; **die ~ Woche** the week after next.

übernachten *vi* to stay (the night).

übernächtigt *adj* worn out.

Übernachtung *(pl -en) die* overnight stay ; **~ mit Frühstück** bed and breakfast.

Übernachtungsmöglichkeit *(pl -en) die* overnight accommodation.

übernehmen *(präs* **übernimmt,** *prät* **übernahm,** *pp* **übernommen)** *vt (Kosten)* to pay ; *(kopieren)* to adopt ; *(Mitarbeiter)* to take on. ▨ **sich übernehmen** *ref* to overdo it.

überprüfen *vt* to check.

überqueren *vt* to cross.

überraschen *vi* to come as a surprise. ◆ *vt* to surprise ; **ich lasse mich ~** I'll wait and see.

Überraschung *(pl -en) die* surprise.

überreden *vt* to persuade.

überreichen *vt* to present.

Überrest *(pl -e) der* remains *(pl)*.

übers *präp (fam)* = **über + das.**

überschlagen *(präs* **überschlägt,** *prät* **überschlug,** *pp* **überschlagen)** *vt (Anzahl, Summe)* to estimate. ▨ **sich überschlagen** *ref (Auto)* to turn over ; *(Skifahrer)* to crash.

überschneiden : **sich überschneiden** *(prät* **überschnitt,** *pp* **überschnitten)** *ref (zeitlich)* to overlap.

Überschrift *(pl -en) die* heading.

Überschwemmung *(pl -en) die* flood.

Übersee *nt* : **aus ~** from overseas ; **nach ~** abroad.

übersehen *(präs* **übersieht,** *prät* **übersah,** *pp* **übersehen)** *vt (nicht sehen)* to overlook.

übersetzen[1] *vt* to translate.

über|setzen[2] *vt hat (befördern)* to take across. ◆ *vi ist (überqueren)* to cross.

Übersetzer, in *(mpl -) der, die* translator.

Übersetzung *(pl -en) die* translation.

Übersicht *(pl -en) die (Zusammenfassung)* outline.

übersichtlich *adj (Gebiet)* open ; *(Tabelle)* clear.

Übersichtskarte *(pl -n) die* general map.

überspielen *vt (kopieren)* to record ; *(löschen)* to record over.

Überspielkabel *(pl -) das* connecting lead.

überstehen[1] *(prät* **überstand,** *pp* **überstanden)** *vt (Ereignis)* to survive.

über|stehen² *vi unr (vorstehen)* to jut out.

Überstunde *(pl -n) die* overtime.

übertragbar *adj (Fahrkarte)* transferable ; *(Krankheit)* infectious.

übertragen *(präs* überträgt, *prät* übertrug, *pp* übertragen) *vt (Krankheit)* to pass on ; *(Sendung)* to broadcast ; *(Blut)* to transfuse ; *(anwenden)* to apply. ▪ **sich übertragen** *ref (Stimmung)* to be infectious ; *(Krankheit)* to be passed on.

Übertragung *(pl -en) die (von Sendung)* broadcast ; *(von Krankheit)* passing on ; *(von Blut)* transfusion.

übertreffen *(präs* übertrifft, *prät* übertraf, *pp* übertroffen) *vt (besser sein)* to surpass.

übertreiben *(prät* übertrieb, *pp* übertrieben) *vt (bei Darstellung)* to exaggerate ; *(Handlung)* to overdo. ◆ *vi (darstellen)* to exaggerate.

übertreten *(präs* übertritt, *prät* übertrat, *pp* übertreten) *vt (Gesetz)* to break.

übertrieben *pp → übertreiben.* ◆ *adj (Darstellung)* exaggerated ; *(Vorsicht, Eifer)* excessive.

überwachen *vt* to monitor.

überweisen *(prät* überwies, *pp* überwiesen) *vt (Geld)* to transfer ; *(Patienten)* to refer ; **jn ins Krankenhaus ~** to have sb admitted to hospital.

Überweisung *(pl -en) die (von Geld)* transfer ; *(von Patienten)* referral.

Überweisungsauftrag *(pl -träge) der* money transfer order.

überwinden *(prät* überwand, *pp* überwunden) *vt (Angst, Ekel)* to overcome ; *(Hindernis)* to get over. ▪ **sich überwinden** *ref* to force o.s.

Überzelt *(pl -e) das* flysheet.

überzeugen *vt* to convince. ▪ **sich überzeugen** *ref* to convince o.s.

überzeugt *adj* convinced ; **~ sein von** to be convinced of.

Überzeugung *(pl -en) die* conviction.

überziehen¹ *(prät* überzog, *pp* überzogen) *vt (Konto)* to overdraw ; **die Betten frisch ~** to put clean sheets on the beds.

über|ziehen² *vt unr (Jacke, Pullover)* to pull on.

Überziehungskredit *(pl -e) der* overdraft facility.

üblich *adj* usual.

übrig *adj* remaining ; **~ sein** to be left over.

übrig bleiben *vi unr ist* to be left over.

übrigens *adv* by the way.

Übung *(pl -en) die* exercise.

Ufer *(pl -) das (von Fluss)* bank ; *(von See)* shore ; **am ~** *(von Fluss)* on the bank ; *(von See)* on the shore.

Uferstraße *(pl -n) die* road which runs alongside a lake or river.

Uhr *(pl -en) die (am Arm)* watch ; *(an der Wand)* clock ; *(Zeit)* : **es ist 3 ~** it's 3 o'clock ; **um 3 ~** at 3 o'clock ; **um wie viel**

~? what time? ; **wie viel ~ ist es?** what time is it?

Uhrzeit (*pl* -en) *die* time.

UKW *die* FM.

Ultraschall *der* ultrasound.

um *präp* (+A) **1.** (*räumlich*) around ; **~ etw herum** around sthg.

2. (*Angabe der Uhrzeit*) at ; **~ drei Uhr** at three o'clock.

3. (*Angabe von Ansteigen, Sinken*) by ; **die Preise steigen ~ 15%** prices are rising by 15%.

4. (*Angabe von Grund*) for ; **~ etw kämpfen** to fight for sthg ; **~ ein Spielzeug streiten** to quarrel over a toy.

5. (*ungefähr*) around ; **es kostet ~ die 300 DM** it costs around 300 Marks ; **so ~ Ostern herum** some time around Easter ; → **um sein.**

◆ *konj* : **~ zu** (in order) to.

um|adressieren *vt* to re-address.

umarmen *vt* to hug.

Umbau (*pl* -ten) *der* renovation.

um|bauen *vt* to renovate.

um|binden *vt unr* to tie ; **sich** (*D*) **eine Schürze ~** to put on an apron.

um|blättern *vt* to turn over.

um|bringen *vt unr* to kill.

um|buchen *vt* : **eine Reise ~** to change one's booking for a trip.

um|drehen *vt hat* (*Schlüssel, Pfannkuchen*) to turn. ◆ *vi ist/hat* (*wenden, umkehren*) to turn back. ▇ **sich umdrehen** *ref* (*Person*) to turn round.

um|fahren[1] *vt unr* (*fam* : *überfahren*) to knock down.

umfahren[2] (*präs* **umfährt**, *prät* **umfuhr**, *pp* **umfahren**) *vt* (*ausweichen*) to avoid.

um|fallen *vi unr ist* (*umkippen*) to fall down.

Umfang (*pl* -fänge) *der* (*von Bauch, Tonne*) circumference.

Umfrage (*pl* -n) *die* survey.

um|füllen *vt* to transfer.

Umgangssprache *die* slang.

Umgebung (*pl* -en) *die* (*Gebiet*) surroundings (*pl*) ; (*Umfeld*) environment.

um|gehen[1] *vi unr ist* **1.** (*Erkältung*) to go around. **2.** (*mit Person, Sache*) : **~ mit** (+D) to handle.

umgehen[2] (*prät* **umging**, *pp* **umgangen**) *vt* (*Problem*) to avoid.

Umgehungsstraße (*pl* -n) *die* bypass.

umgekehrt *adj* opposite. ◆ *adv* the other way round ; **in ~er Richtung** in the opposite direction.

Umhang (*pl* -hänge) *der* cloak.

umher *adv* around.

um|kehren *vi ist* (*zurückgehen, zurückfahren*) to turn back.

um|kippen *vi ist* (*Person, Vase*) to fall over. ◆ *vt hat* (*Lampe, Vase*) to knock over.

Umkleidekabine (*pl* -n) *die* changing room.

Umkleideraum (*pl* -räume) *der* changing room.

Umkreis der (Gebiet) surrounding area ; im ~ von 50 km within a 50 km radius.

Umlaut (pl -e) der umlaut.

um|leiten vt to divert.

Umleitung (pl -en) die diversion.

umrandet adj : rot ~ circled in red.

um|rechnen vt to convert.

Umrechnungskurs (pl -e) der conversion table.

um|rühren vt & vi to stir.

ums präp = um + das.

Umsatz (pl -sätze) der turnover.

um|schalten vt (Programm, Fernseher) to turn over. ◆ vi (auf Programm) to turn over.

Umschlag (pl -schläge) der (für Briefe) envelope ; (von Buch) dust jacket ; (MED) compress.

um|schlagen vi unr ist (Wetter, Laune) to change. ◆ vt unr hat (umdrehen) to turn over.

um|sehen : sich umsehen ref unr to look round ; sich ~ nach (suchen) to look around for.

um sein vi unr ist (fam) to be over ; die zehn Minuten sind um the ten minutes are up.

umso konj : je schneller, ~ besser the quicker the better ; ~ besser (fam : als Antwort) so much the better.

umsonst adv (erfolglos) in vain ; (gratis) for free. ◆ adj : ~ sein (erfolglos) to be in vain ; (gratis) to be for free.

umständlich adj (Methode) laborious ; (Person) awkward.

Umstandsmoden pl maternity wear (sg).

Umsteigebahnhof (pl -höfe) der station where passengers may change to a different line.

um|steigen vi unr ist (beim Reisen) to change ; (wechseln) to switch ; in Köln ~ to change in Cologne.

Umstellung (pl -en) die (Anpassung) adjustment ; (Änderung) switch.

Umtausch der exchange ; 'vom ~ ausgeschlossen' 'no refunds or exchanges'.

um|tauschen vt (Ware) to exchange ; (Geld) to change ; Mark in Pfund ~ to change marks into pounds.

Umverpackung (pl -en) die repackaging.

Umweg (pl -e) der detour.

Umwelt die environment.

Umweltbewusstsein das environmental awareness.

 **UMWELTBEWUSSTSEIN**

Protection of the environment is a major concern amongst Germans, who see themselves as world leaders in environmental issues and the fight against pollution, having introduced the catalytic converter and large-scale recycling programmes. The need to protect the environment and conserve natural resources is now recognized by all sectors of society.

umweltfreundlich adj environmentally friendly.

Umweltpapier das recycled paper.

umweltschädlich adj damaging to the environment.

Umweltschutz der environmental protection.

Umweltverschmutzung die pollution.

um|werfen vt unr (umstürzen) to knock over ; sich (D) einen Mantel ~ to put a coat around one's shoulders.

um|ziehen vi unr ist to move. ◆ vt unr hat to change. ▧ **sich umziehen** ref to get changed.

Umzug (pl -züge) der (Wohnungswechsel) move ; (Parade) parade.

unabhängig adj independent. ◆ adv independently.

Unabhängigkeit die independence.

unabsichtlich adj unintentional. ◆ adv unintentionally.

unangenehm adj (Geschmack, Person) unpleasant ; (peinlich) embarrassing. ◆ adv : ich war ~ berührt I was embarrassed.

unauffällig adj inconspicuous.

unbeabsichtigt adj unintentional.

unbedingt adv (auf jeden Fall) really ; du musst ~ mitkommen! you really must come!

unbefriedigend adj (schlecht) unsatisfactory. ◆ adv (schlecht) unsatisfactorily.

unbefristet adj for an unlimited period.

unbefugt adj unauthorized.

Unbefugte (pl -n) der, die unauthorized person ; 'für ~ Zutritt verboten!' 'authorized personnel only'.

unbegrenzt adj unlimited.

unbekannt adj unknown.

unbeliebt adj unpopular.

unbemerkt adv unnoticed.

unbenutzt adj unused.

unbequem adj (Stuhl, Kleidung) uncomfortable. ◆ adv (sitzen, fahren) uncomfortably.

unberechtigt adj unjustified. ◆ adv without authorization ; ~ parkende Fahrzeuge illegally parked vehicles.

unbeständig adj (Wetter) changeable.

unbeteiligt adj (nicht interessiert) uninterested ; (nicht verwickelt) uninvolved.

unbewacht adj unattended.

unbewusst adj unconscious. ◆ adv unconsciously.

unbrauchbar adj useless.

und konj 1. (gen) and ; drei drei ist sechs three and three makes six ; ~ so (fam) and so on ; ~ so weiter and so on ; ~ wie! (fam) not half!

2. (Ausdruck eines Widerspruchs) : ~ wenn even if.

3. (ironisch) : ich ~ Motorrad fahren? Nie! me ride a motor bike? Never!

◆ interj (fam) : na ~! so what?

undankbar adj (Person) ungrateful.

undeutlich adj unclear.

undicht adj leaky.

undurchlässig adj impermeable.

uneben adj uneven ; '~e Fahrbahn' 'uneven road surface'.

unecht adj (Schmuck, Stein) fake.

unendlich adj endless.

unentbehrlich adj indispensable.

unentgeltlich adj free.

unentschieden adj (Ergebnis) undecided ; **das Spiel endete ~** the game was a draw.

unerlässlich adj essential.

unerlaubt adj unauthorized.

unerträglich adj unbearable.

unerwartet adj unexpected.

unerwünscht adj unwelcome.

unfähig adj incapable ; **~ sein, etw zu tun** to be incapable of doing sthg.

unfair adj unfair.

Unfall (pl -fälle) der accident ; **einen ~ haben/verursachen** to have/cause an accident.

Unfallflucht die failure to stop after an accident.

Unfallhergang der : **den ~ beschreiben** to give details of the accident.

Unfallschaden der damage.

Unfallstation (pl -en) die casualty (Br), emergency ward (Am).

Unfallstelle (pl -n) die scene of the accident.

Unfallversicherung (pl -en) die accident insurance.

unfreundlich adj (Person, Verhalten) unfriendly. ◆ adv (sich verhalten) coldly ; **~ sein zu** to be unfriendly to.

Unfug der nonsense.

Ungarn nt Hungary.

ungeduldig adj impatient.

ungeeignet adj unsuitable.

ungefähr adv about, approximately. ◆ adj rough.

ungefährlich adj safe.

ungehorsam adj disobedient.

ungemütlich adj (Raum, Kleidung) uncomfortable.

ungenau adj inaccurate. ◆ adv inaccurately.

ungenießbar adj inedible ; (fam : Person) unbearable.

ungenügend adj (schlecht) insufficient ; (Schulnote) unsatisfactory. ◆ adv (schlecht) badly.

ungerecht adj unjust.

ungern adv reluctantly.

ungeschickt adj (Mensch, Bewegung) clumsy ; (Verhalten, Reaktion) undiplomatic.

ungesund adj unhealthy. ◆ adv : **sie leben sehr ~** they lead a very unhealthy life.

ungewiss adj uncertain.

ungewöhnlich adj unusual.

ungewohnt adj unfamiliar.

Ungeziefer das pests (pl).

unglaublich adj unbelievable. ◆ adv unbelievably.

Unglück (pl -e) das (Unfall) accident ; (Leid) unhappiness ; (Pech) bad luck.

unglücklich adj (Person) unhappy ; (unklug) unfortunate.

ungültig adj invalid.

unheimlich adj (gruselig) sinister ; (fam : riesig) incredible. ◆ adv (fam : sehr) incredibly.

unhöflich adj impolite.

Uni (pl -s) die (fam) uni.

Uniform (*pl* -en) *die* uniform.

Universität (*pl* -en) *die* university.

Universitätsstadt (*pl* -städte) *die* university town.

 UNIVERSITÄTSSTADT

The most famous German university towns include Heidelberg, Marburg, Göttingen and Freiburg. The large, old universities attract large numbers of students, giving the towns a particularly lively atmosphere and cultural life.

Unkosten *pl* expenses.

Unkostenbeitrag (*pl* -beiträge) *der* contribution towards expenses.

Unkraut *das* weed.

unlogisch *adj* illogical.

Unmenge (*pl* -n) *die* (*fam*) masses (*pl*); **eine ~ Leute** masses of people.

unmittelbar *adj* immediate. ◆ *adv* immediately; **in ~er Nähe** in the immediate vicinity.

unmöbliert *adj* unfurnished.

unmöglich *adj* impossible. ◆ *adv*: **ich kann ~ um 3 Uhr kommen** I can't possibly come at 3 o'clock; **jm ~ sein** (*nicht möglich*) to be impossible for sb.

unnötig *adj* unnecessary.

unnütz *adj* useless.

UNO *die*: **die ~** the UN.

Unordnung *die* chaos.

unpassierbar *adj* impassable.

unpersönlich *adj* impersonal.

unpraktisch *adj* (*Kleidung, Möbel*) impractical; (*Person*) unpractical.

unpünktlich *adj* unpunctual; **~ sein** to be late.

Unrecht *das* wrong; **im ~ sein** to be wrong.

unregelmäßig *adj* irregular. ◆ *adv* irregularly.

unreif *adj* (*Obst*) unripe.

Unruhe (*pl* -n) *die* (*Gefühl*) unease; (*Bewegung*) noise. ■ **Unruhen** *pl* riots.

unruhig *adj* (*besorgt*) restless.

uns *pron* (*Personalpronomen*) us; (*Reflexivpronomen*) ourselves.

unschädlich *adj* harmless.

unscharf *adj* (*Aufnahme*) blurred.

unschuldig *adj* innocent.

unselbstständig *adj* dependent.

unser, e *ODER* **unsre** *det* our.

unsere, r, s *pron* ours. ◆ *det* → **unser**.

unsicher *adj* (*Person*) insecure; (*Zukunft*) uncertain; (*Gegend, Weg*) unsafe; **da bin ich mir ~** I'm not sure about that.

Unsinn *der* nonsense.

Unsumme (*pl* -n) *die* enormous amount of money.

unsympathisch *adj* (*Mensch*) unpleasant.

unten *adv* at the bottom; (*südlich*) down; (*in Haus*) downstairs; **nach ~** down; **von ~** from below; **siehe ~** see below; **die sind bei uns ~ durch**

(fam) we're finished with them.

unter *präp (+D)* **1.** *(räumlich)* under ; ~ **dem Tisch liegen** to lie under the table. **2.** *(weniger als)* under ; ~ **Null** below zero ; **Kinder ~ 12 Jahren** children under the age of 12. **3.** *(zwischen Dingen, Personen)* among ; ~ **anderem** among other things. **4.** *(Angabe von Umständen)* under ; ~ **Stress arbeiten** to work under stress. **5.** *(Angabe von Hierarchie)* under ; ~ **der Leitung von...** under the supervision of...
◆ *präp (+A)* **1.** *(räumlich)* under ; ~ **den Tisch kriechen** to crawl under the table. **2.** *(weniger als)* below. **3.** *(zwischen)* : **etw ~ etw mischen** to mix sthg into sthg. **4.** *(Angabe von Hierarchie)* under.
◆ *adj* **1.** *(räumlich)* lower ; *(Etage)* bottom. **2.** *(in Rangfolge)* lower.

unterbelichtet *adj (Foto, Film)* underexposed.

Unterbewusstsein *das* subconscious.

unterbrechen *(präs* unterbricht, *prät* unterbrach, *pp* unterbrochen) *vt & vi* to interrupt.

Unterbrecherkontakt *(pl -e) der* contact breaker.

Unterbrechung *(pl -en) die* interruption.

unter|bringen *vt unr (Gäste)* to put up ; *(Gegenstand)* to put.

Unterbringung *die* accommodation.

unterdessen *adv (geh)* meanwhile.

unterdrücken *vt (Person, Volk, Widerstand)* to suppress.

untereinander *adv (unter sich)* among ourselves/themselves ; *(unter das andere)* one under the other.

Unterführung *(pl -en) die* subway *(Br)*, underpass *(Am)*.

Untergang *(pl -gänge) der (von Schiff)* sinking ; *(von Volk, Kultur)* decline ; *(von Sonne, Mond)* setting.

unter|gehen *vi unr - ist (Sonne, Mond)* to go down ; *(Schiff, Person)* to sink ; *(Volk, Kultur)* to decline.

Untergeschoss *(pl -e) das* basement.

Untergewicht *das* : ~ **haben** to be underweight.

Untergrund *der (Boden)* subsoil.

Untergrundbahn *(pl -en) die* underground *(Br)*, subway *(Am)*.

unterhalb *adv & präp (+G)* below.

unterhalten *(präs* unterhält, *prät* unterhielt, *pp* unterhalten) *vt (amüsieren)* to entertain ; *(Familie)* to support. ▪ **sich unterhalten** *ref (reden)* to talk ; *(sich amüsieren)* to have fun ; **sich ~ mit** *(sprechen)* to talk with.

Unterhaltung *(pl -en) die (Gespräch)* conversation ; *(Amüsement)* entertainment.

Unterhemd *(pl -en) das* vest.

Unterhose (*pl* -n) *die* underpants (*pl*).

Unterkunft (*pl* -künfte) *die* accommodation.

unterlassen (*präs* unterlässt, *prät* unterließ, *pp* unterlassen) *vt* to refrain from.

Unterleib (*pl* -e) *der* abdomen.

unternehmen (*präs* unternimmt, *prät* unternahm, *pp* unternommen) *vt* (*Ausflug, Reise*) to make ; etwas/nichts ~ to do something/nothing.

Unternehmer, in (*mpl* -) *der, die* entrepreneur.

unternehmungslustig *adj* enterprising.

Unterricht *der* lessons (*pl*) ; jm ~ geben to teach sb.

unterrichten *vt* (*Schüler, Schulfach*) to teach ; (*mitteilen*) to inform.

Unterrock (*pl* -röcke) *der* slip.

untersagt *adj* prohibited.

unterscheiden (*prät* unterschied, *pp* unterschieden) *vt* to distinguish. ◆ *vi* : ~ zwischen to differentiate between ; etw ~ von to distinguish sthg from. ▣ **sich unterscheiden** *ref* to be different.

Unterschied (*pl* -e) *der* difference.

unterschiedlich *adj* different.

unterschreiben (*prät* unterschrieb, *pp* unterschrieben) *vt* & *vi* to sign ; hier ~ sign here.

Unterschrift (*pl* -en) *die* signature ; Datum und ~ date and signature.

Unterseeboot (*pl* -e) *das* submarine.

Untersetzer (*pl* -) *der* coaster.

unter|stellen[1] *vt* to store. ▣ **sich unterstellen** *ref* to shelter.

unterstellen[2] *vt* (*Boshaftigkeit, Gemeinheit*) to imply.

unterstreichen (*prät* unterstrich, *pp* unterstrichen) *vt* (*mit Strich*) to underline.

unterstützen *vt* to support.

Unterstützung *die* support.

untersuchen *vt* to examine ; (*absuchen*) to investigate.

Untersuchung (*pl* -en) *die* examination ; (*von Justiz, Polizei*) investigation.

Untertasse (*pl* -n) *die* saucer.

Unterteil (*pl* -e) *das* bottom half.

Untertitel (*pl* -) *der* subtitle.

Unterwäsche *die* underwear.

unterwegs *adv* on the way. ◆ *adj* : ~ sein to be on the way ; ~ nach... ~ sein to be on the way to...

unterzeichnen *vt* to sign.

unüberlegt *adj* rash. ◆ *adv* rashly.

ununterbrochen *adj* uninterrupted. ◆ *adv* nonstop.

unverbindlich *adj* (*ohne Verpflichtung*) not binding.

unverbleit *adj* lead-free.

unverheiratet *adj* unmarried.

unverkäuflich *adj* not for sale.

unvermeidlich *adj* unavoidable.

ụnvernünftig adj irresponsible.

ụnverschämt adj (taktlos) impertinent.

ụnverständlich adj incomprehensible.

ụnverträglich adj (Nahrung) indigestible.

ụnvollständig adj incomplete.

ụnvorsichtig adj careless.

ụnwahrscheinlich adj (Geschichte) improbable ; (fam : Glück) incredible.

Ụnwetter (pl -) das storm.

ụnwichtig adj unimportant.

unwiderstehlich adj irresistible.

ụnwohl adj unwell ; sich ~ fühlen (körperlich) to feel unwell ; (psychisch) to feel uneasy.

unzerbrẹchlich adj unbreakable.

ụnzufrieden adj dissatisfied ; ~ mit dissatisfied with.

ụnzugänglich adv : 'für Kinder ~ aufbewahren' 'keep out of reach of children'.

ụnzulässig adj (nicht erlaubt) forbidden.

ụ̈ppig adj (Essen) sumptuous ; (Person) curvaceous.

ụralt adj ancient.

Ụraufführung (pl -en) die premiere.

Ụrenkel, in (mpl -) der, die great-grandchild.

Ụrgroßeltern pl great-grandparents.

Ụrin der urine.

Ụrkunde (pl -n) die certificate.

Urlaub (pl -e) der holiday (Br), vacation (Am) ; im ~ sein to be on holiday (Br), to be on vacation (Am) ; in ~ fahren to go on holiday (Br), to go on vacation (Am) ; ~ machen to have a holiday (Br), to vacation (Am).

Urlauber, in (mpl -) der, die holidaymaker (Br), vacationer (Am).

Urlaubsanschrift (pl -en) die holiday address.

Urlaubsort (pl -e) der holiday resort.

Urlaubszeit (pl -en) die holiday season (Br), vacation season (Am).

Ụrsache (pl -n) die cause ; keine ~! don't mention it!

Ụrsprung (pl -sprünge) der origin.

ụrsprünglich adj (Idee, Meinung) original.

Ụrsprungsland (pl -länder) das country of origin.

Ụrteil (pl -e) das (vor Gericht) verdict ; (Bewertung) judgement.

Ụrwald (pl -wälder) der jungle.

usw. (abk für und so weiter) etc.

Utensilien pl utensils.

Utopie (pl -n) die utopia.

V

vage adj vague.

Vagina (pl -ginen) die vagina.

vakuumverpackt adj vacuum-packed.

Vanille *die* vanilla.

Vanilleeis *das* vanilla ice cream.

Vanillezucker *der* vanilla sugar.

Varietee, Varieté (*pl* -s) *das* variety show.

variieren *vt* & *vi* to vary.

Vase (*pl* -n) *die* vase.

Vaseline *die* Vaseline®.

Vater (*pl* Väter) *der* father.

Vatertag (*pl* -e) *der* Father's Day.

V-Ausschnitt (*pl* -e) *der* V-neck.

v. Chr. *(abk für vor Christus)* BC.

Vegetarier, in (*mpl* -) *der, die* vegetarian.

vegetarisch *adj* vegetarian.

Vene (*pl* -n) *die* vein.

Ventil (*pl* -e) *das* (TECH) valve.

Ventilator (*pl* -toren) *der* fan.

verabreden *vt* to arrange. ■ **sich verabreden** *ref* to arrange to meet ; **sich mit jm ~** to arrange to meet sb.

verabredet *adj* : sie ist mit Karla ~ she has arranged to meet Karla ; ich bin schon ~ I have something else on.

Verabredung (*pl* -en) *die* (*Treffen*) appointment ; (*mit Freund*) date.

verabscheuen *vt* to detest.

verabschieden *vt* (*Gast*) to say goodbye to. ■ **sich verabschieden** *ref* to say goodbye.

Veranda (*pl* -den) *die* veranda.

verändern *vt* to change. ■ **sich verändern** *ref* (*anders werden*) to change.

Veränderung (*pl* -en) *die* change.

veranlassen *vt* : jn ~, etw zu tun to cause sb to do sthg ; etw ~ to arrange for sthg.

veranstalten *vt* (*organisieren*) to organize.

Veranstalter, in (*mpl* -) *der, die* organizer.

Veranstaltung (*pl* -en) *die* (*Ereignis*) event ; (*Organisation*) organization.

Veranstaltungskalender (*pl* -) *der* calendar of events.

Veranstaltungsprogramm (*pl* -e) *das* programme of events.

verantwortlich *adj* responsible.

Verantwortung *die* responsibility.

verarbeiten *vt* (*Material*) to process ; (*fig : Ereignis*) to come to terms with.

Verb (*pl* -en) *das* verb ; starkes/ schwaches ~ strong/weak verb.

Verband (*pl* -bände) *der* (*Organisation*) association ; (*für Wunde*) bandage ; einen ~ anlegen to apply a bandage.

Verbandskasten (*pl* -kästen) *der* first-aid box.

Verbandzeug *das* first-aid kit.

verbergen (*präs* verbirgt, *prät* verbarg, *pp* verborgen) *vt* to hide. ■ **sich verbergen** *ref* to hide.

verbessern *vt* (*besser machen*) to improve ; (*Fehler*) to correct. ■ **sich verbessern** *ref* (*besser werden*) to improve ; (*sich korrigieren*) to correct o.s.

Verbesserung (*pl* -en) *die*
(von Fehlern, Text) correction ;
(von Anlage, Angebot) improvement.

verbieten (*prät* verbat, *pp*
verboten) *vt* to forbid.

verbilligt *adj* reduced.

verbinden (*prät* verband, *pp*
verbunden) *vt* to connect ;
(Wunde) to bandage ; *(am Telefon)* to put through. ◆ *vi (am
Telefon)* : einen Moment, ich ver-
binde one moment please, I'll
put you through ; falsch verbund-
en! wrong number!

Verbindung (*pl* -en) *die* connection ; *(chemisch)* compound ; sich in ~ setzen mit to
contact.

verbleit *adj (Benzin)* leaded ;
Super ~ super leaded.

verborgen *pp* → verbergen.

Verbot (*pl* -e) *das* ban.

verboten *pp* → verbieten.
◆ *adj* forbidden ; streng ~!
strictly forbidden!

Verbotsschild (*pl* -er) *das*
sign indicating a restriction, eg no
parking, no entry etc.

verbrannt *pp* → verbrennen. ◆ *adj* burnt.

Verbrauch *der* consumption.

verbrauchen *vt* to consume.

Verbraucher, in (*mpl* -) *der,
die* consumer.

Verbraucherberatung (*pl*
-en) *die (Institution)* consumer
advice agency.

Verbrechen (*pl* -) *das* crime.

Verbrecher, in (*mpl* -) *der,
die* criminal.

verbrennen (*prät* verbrann-
te, *pp* verbrannt) *vt* hat & ist
to burn. ▓ **sich verbrennen**
ref : er hat sich verbrannt he
burned himself ; er hat sich *(D)*
die Finger verbrannt he burnt his
fingers.

Verbrennung (*pl* -en) *die
(Verletzung)* burn ; *(Verbrennen)* burning.

verbringen (*prät* verbrachte,
pp verbracht) *vt* to spend.

verbrühen : **sich verbrühen** *ref* to scald o.s.

Verdacht *der* suspicion.

verdammt *adj* & *adv* (*fam*)
damn.

verdarb *prät* → verderben.

verdaulich *adj* : leicht/schwer
~ easy/difficult to digest.

Verdauung *die* digestion.

Verdeck (*pl* -e) *das (von Auto)*
soft top ; *(von Kinderwagen)*
hood.

verderben (*präs* verdirbt,
prät verdarb, *pp* verdorben) *vt*
hat to ruin. ◆ *vi ist (Nahrung)* to
go off.

verderblich *adj* perishable.

verdienen *vt* to earn.

Verdienst (*pl* -e) *der (Gehalt)*
salary. ◆ *das (Leistung)* achieve-
ment.

verdirbt *präs* → verderben.

verdoppeln *vt* to double.
▓ **sich verdoppeln** *ref* to
double.

verdorben *pp* → verderben.
◆ *adj (Lebensmittel)* off.

verdünnen *vt* to dilute.

verehren *vt (anbeten)* to worship.

Verehrer, in (*mpl* -) *der, die
(Bewunderer)* admirer.

Verein (*pl* -e) *der* association, society ; **eingetragener ~** registered society ; **wohltätiger ~** charity.

 VEREIN

More than half the population of Germany belongs to one of the country's 300,000 clubs and societies, making them one of the most popular ways in which people spend their leisure time. The most popular types of club are sports clubs, bowling clubs, rifle clubs, music societies and pet breeding clubs.

vereinbaren *vt* (*Termin, Treffen*) to arrange.

Vereinbarung (*pl* -en) *die* arrangement.

vereinen *vt* to unite. ▓ **sich vereinen** *ref* to unite.

vereinheitlichen *vt* to standardize.

Vereinigte Staaten *pl* United States.

Vereinigung (*pl* -en) *die* (*Gruppe*) organization ; (*Vorgang*) unification.

Vereinte Nationen *pl* United Nations.

vereist *adj* (*Straße*) icy.

Verf. *abk* = **Verfasser**.

verfahren (*präs* **verfährt**, *prät* **verfuhr**, *pp* **verfahren**) *vi ist* (*umgehen, handeln*) to proceed.
◆ *vt hat* (*Benzin*) to use up. ▓ **sich verfahren** *ref* to get lost.

verfallen (*präs* **verfällt**, *prät* **verfiel**, *pp* **verfallen**) *vi ist* (*Fahrkarte, Garantie*) to expire ; (*Gutschein*) to be no longer valid ; (*Haus*) to decay.

Verfallsdatum (*pl* -daten) *das* (*von Lebensmittel*) sell-by date.

verfärben : **sich verfärben** *ref* to change colour ; **der Himmel verfärbte sich rot** the sky turned red.

Verfasser, in (*mpl* -) *der, die* author.

Verfassung (*pl* -en) *die* (*Gesetz*) constitution ; (*Zustand*) condition.

verfaulen *vi ist* to rot.

verfeinern *vt* to refine.

Verfilmung (*pl* -en) *die* film version.

verfolgen *vt* (*jagen*) to pursue ; (*beobachten*) to follow ; (*unterdrücken*) to persecute.

verfügen *vi* : **~ über** (+A) (*besitzen*) to have ; (*benutzen*) to make use of ; (*bestimmen*) to be in charge of.

Verfügung (*pl* -en) *die* (*Gebrauch, Bestimmung*) : **etw zur ~ haben** to have sthg at one's disposal ; **zur ~ stehen** to be available.

verführerisch *adj* (*anziehend*) attractive ; (*erotisch*) seductive.

vergangen *adj* (*letzte*) last ; **~e Woche** last week.

Vergangenheit *die* past ; (*GRAMM*) past tense.

Vergaser (*pl* -) *der* carburettor.

vergaß *prät* → **vergessen**.

vergeben (*präs* **vergibt**, *prät* **vergab**, *pp* **vergeben**) *vt* (*verzei-*

hen) to forgive ; *(Zimmer)* to allocate ; *(Preis)* to award.

vergeblich *adj* in vain.

vergessen *(präs* vergisst, *prät* vergaß, *pp* vergessen) *vt* to forget.

vergesslich *adj* forgetful.

vergewaltigen *vt* to rape.

Vergewaltigung *(pl* -en) *die* rape.

Vergiftung *(pl* -en) *die* poisoning.

vergisst *präs* → vergessen.

Vergleich *(pl* -e) *der* comparison ; im ~ zu compared to.

vergleichen *(prät* verglich, *pp* verglichen) *vt* to compare ; verglichen mit compared with.

Vergnügen *das* pleasure ; mit ~ with pleasure ; viel ~! have fun!

Vergnügungsdampfer *(pl* -) *der* pleasure steamer.

Vergnügungspark *(pl* -s) *der* fun fair.

Vergnügungsviertel *(pl* -) *das* area of a town where most bars, nightclubs, cinemas, etc are situated.

vergoldet *adj* gilded.

vergriffen *adj (Buch)* out of print.

vergrößern *vt* to enlarge. ◆ *vi (Mikroskop)* to magnify. ▪ **sich vergrößern** *ref* to expand.

Vergrößerung *(pl* -en) *die* enlargement.

Vergünstigung *(pl* -en) *die* reduction.

vergüten *vt (bezahlen)* to pay.

verhaften *vt* to arrest.

verhalten : **sich verhalten** *(präs* verhält, *prät* verhielt, *pp* verhalten) *ref (sich benehmen)* to behave.

Verhalten *das* behaviour.

Verhältnis *(pl* -se) *das* relationship ; *(von Größe, Anzahl)* ratio.

verhältnismäßig *adv* relatively.

verhandeln *vi* to negotiate. ◆ *vt (vor Gericht)* to hear ; ~ über etw (A) to negotiate sthg.

Verhandlung *(pl* -en) *die (Beratung)* negotiation ; *(vor Gericht)* hearing.

verheilen *vi ist* to heal.

verheimlichen *vt* to keep secret.

verheiratet *adj* married.

verhindern *vt* to prevent.

Verhör *(pl* -e) *das* interrogation.

verhüten *vi (beim Sex)* to take precautions. ◆ *vt* to prevent.

Verhütungsmittel *(pl* -) *das* contraceptive.

verirren : **sich verirren** *ref* to get lost.

verk. *abk* = verkaufen.

Verkauf *der* sale.

verkaufen *vt & vi* to sell ; etw an jn ~ to sell sb sthg, to sell sthg to sb ; zu ~ for sale.

Verkäufer, in *(mpl* -) *der, die (in Geschäft)* sales assistant *(Br)*, sales clerk *(Am)* ; *(juristisch)* trader.

verkäuflich *adj (zum Verkauf bestimmt)* for sale.

verkaufsoffen *adj* : ~er Samstag first Saturday in the

month, on which shops are open till 6pm.

Verkaufsstelle (*pl* -n) *die* point of sale.

Verkaufsveranstaltung (*pl* -en) *die* event organized to sell a product.

verkauft *adj* sold.

Verkehr *der* (*Straßenverkehr*) traffic ; (*amt : Sex*) intercourse.

verkehren *vi* (*amt : Zug, Bus*) to run ; **in einem Lokal ~** to frequent a bar ; '**verkehrt nicht täglich**' 'does not run daily'.

Verkehrsampel (*pl* -n) *die* traffic light.

Verkehrsaufkommen *das* : **hohes/dichtes ~** heavy traffic.

Verkehrsberuhigung *die* traffic calming.

Verkehrsführung (*pl* -en) *die* : '**~ beachten**' 'follow road signs'.

Verkehrsfunk *der* traffic bulletin service.

Verkehrsmeldung (*pl* -en) *die* traffic bulletin.

Verkehrsmittel (*pl* -) *das* means of transport ; **öffentliche ~** public transport.

Verkehrsnachrichten *pl* traffic news.

Verkehrspolizist, in (*mpl* -en) *der, die* traffic policeman (traffic policewoman).

Verkehrsregel (*pl* -n) *die* traffic regulation.

Verkehrsschild (*pl* -er) *das* road sign.

Verkehrsunfall (*pl* -unfälle) *der* road accident.

Verkehrsverbindung (*pl* -en) *die* connection.

Verkehrsverein (*pl* -e) *der* tourist information office.

Verkehrszeichen (*pl* -) *das* road sign.

verkehrt *adj* wrong. ◆ *adv* wrongly ; **~ herum** inside out.

verklagen *vt* to prosecute.

Verkleidung (*pl* -en) *die* (*Kostüm*) costume ; (*von Wand, Fassade*) covering.

Verkleinerung (*pl* -en) *die* reduction.

verkommen (*prät* **verkam**, *pp* **verkommen**) *vi* ist (*Lebensmittel*) to go off ; (*Haus, Wohnung*) to become run-down. ◆ *adj* (*Haus, Wohnung*) run-down.

verkraften *vt* to cope with.

verkratzt *adj* scratched.

verkürzen *vt* to shorten.

verladen (*präs* **verlädt**, *prät* **verlud**, *pp* **verladen**) *vt* to load.

Verlag (*pl* -e) *der* publishing house.

verlangen *vt* (*fordern*) to demand ; (*im Geschäft, Lokal*) to ask for ; (*erfordern*) to call for ; **jn am Telefon ~** to ask to speak to sb on the phone.

Verlangen *das* (*Wunsch*) desire ; (*Forderung*) request ; **auf ~** on demand.

verlängern *vt* to extend ; (*Rock*) to lengthen ; (*Pass, Erlaubnis*) to renew. ◆ **sich verlängern** *ref* (*Frist, Vertrag*) to be extended.

Verlängerung (*pl* -en) *die* extension ; (*von Rock*) lengthening ; (*von Pass, Erlaub-*

nis) renewal ; *(SPORT)* extra time.

Verlängerungskabel (*pl* -) *das* extension lead.

verlassen (*präs* verlässt, *prät* verließ, *pp* verlassen) *vt* to leave. ■ **sich verlassen** *ref* : sich ~ auf (+A) to rely on.

verlaufen (*präs* verläuft, *prät* verlief, *pp* verlaufen) *vi ist* (*Weg, Strecke, Farbe*) to run ; (*Operation, Prüfung*) to go. ■ **sich verlaufen** *ref (sich verirren)* to get lost.

verlegen *vt* (*Brille, Portmonee*) to mislay ; (*Veranstaltung, Besuch*) to postpone ; (*Standort*) to move ; (*Kabel, Teppichboden*) to lay ; (*Buch*) to publish. ◆ *adj* embarrassed.

Verleger, in (*mpl* -) *der, die* publisher.

Verleih (*pl* -e) *der* rental shop.

verleihen (*prät* verlieh, *pp* verliehen) *vt* (*leihen*) to lend ; (*vermieten*) to hire (Br), to rent ; (*Preis, Auszeichnung*) to award.

verlernen *vt* to forget.

verletzen *vt* to injure ; (*Gefühl*) to hurt. ■ **sich verletzen** *ref* to hurt o.s.

verletzt *adj* injured ; (*psychisch*) hurt.

Verletzte (*pl* -n) *der, die* injured person.

Verletzung (*pl* -en) *die* injury.

verlieben : **sich verlieben** *ref* to fall in love.

verlieren (*prät* verlor, *pp* verloren) *vt & vi* to lose. ■ **sich verlieren** *ref (Personen)* to lose each other.

Verlierer, in (*mpl* -) *der, die* loser.

verlobt *adj* engaged.

Verlobung (*pl* -en) *die* engagement.

verlor *prät* → **verlieren**.

verloren *pp* → **verlieren**. ◆ *adj* lost.

verloren gehen *vi unr ist* (*Kind, Brille*) to go missing ; (*Geschmack, Qualität*) to disappear.

Verlosung (*pl* -en) *die* prize draw.

Verlust (*pl* -e) *der* loss ; einen ~ melden to report a loss.

verm. *abk* = **vermieten**.

vermeiden (*prät* vermied, *pp* vermieden) *vt* to avoid.

Vermerk (*pl* -e) *der* note.

vermerken *vt* to make a note of.

vermieten *vt & vi* to rent out ; 'zu ~!' 'for rent'.

Vermieter, in (*mpl* -) *der, die* landlord (landlady).

vermischen *vt* (*Farben, Zutaten*) to mix.

vermissen *vt* to miss ; er vermisst seine Uhr his watch is missing.

vermisst *adj* missing.

vermitteln *vt* (*Ehe, Treffen*) to arrange ; (*Wissen, Erfahrung*) to impart. ◆ *vi* (*bei Streit, Verhandlung*) to arbitrate ; jm eine Arbeitsstelle/einen Babysitter ~ to find a job/babysitter for sb.

Vermittlung (pl -en) die (Telefonzentrale) telephone exchange ; (von Arbeit, Mitarbeitern) finding ; (von Ehe, Treffen) arranging ; (bei Streit, Verhandlung) arbitration ; (von Erfahrung, Kenntnissen) imparting ; (Büro) agency.

Vermittlungsgebühr (pl -en) die commission.

Vermögen (pl -) das (Besitz) fortune.

vermuten vt to suspect.

vermutlich adv probably.

vernehmen (präs vernimmt, prät vernahm, pp vernommen) vt (befragen) to question.

verneinen vt : eine Frage ~ to say no (to a question).

vernichten vt to destroy.

Vernissage (pl -n) die preview.

Vernunft die reason.

vernünftig adj (klug) sensible.

veröffentlichen vt to publish.

verordnen vt (Medikament) to prescribe.

Verordnung (pl -en) die (medizinisch) prescription ; (amtlich) decree.

verpacken vt (Produkt) to pack ; (Geschenk) to wrap up.

Verpackung (pl -en) die packaging.

verpassen vt (Person, Film, Chance) to miss ; (fam : geben) to give ; den Bus/Zug ~ to miss the bus/train.

Verpflegung die (Essen) food.

verpflichtet adj & adv obliged.

verprügeln vt to beat up.

verraten (präs verrät, prät verriet, pp verraten) vt (Geheimnis, Land) to betray ; (sagen) to let slip. ■ **sich verraten** ref to give o.s. away.

verrechnen vt to offset. ■ **sich verrechnen** ref (falsch rechnen) to miscalculate ; sich um 3 Mark ~ to be 3 marks out.

Verrechnung die miscalculation.

Verrechnungsscheck (pl -s) der crossed cheque.

verregnet adj : ~ sein to be a wash-out.

verreisen vi ist to go away.

Verrenkung (pl -en) die dislocation.

verrosten vi ist to rust.

verrückt adj (geistesgestört) mad ; (ausgefallen) crazy ; ~ sein nach to be mad about ; wie ~ like mad.

versagen vi to fail ; 'bei Versagen Knopf drücken' 'in the event of failure, press button'.

versalzen vt (Essen) to put too much salt in. ◆ adj (Essen) too salty.

versammeln vt to assemble. ■ **sich versammeln** ref to assemble.

Versammlung (pl -en) die meeting.

Versand der (Schicken) dispatch ; (Abteilung) dispatch department.

Versandhaus (pl -häuser) das mail order firm.

versäumen vt (verpassen) to miss.

verschaffen vt (besorgen) to get.

verschenken vt (Geschenk) to give away; zu ~ to give away.

verscheuchen vt (Hund, Wespe) to shoo away.

verschicken vt (per Post) to send out.

verschieben (prät verschob, pp verschoben) vt (Termin, Urlaub) to postpone; (Bett, Kommode) to move. ■ sich verschieben ref to be postponed.

verschieden adj different. ◆ adv differently; ~ groß of different sizes.

verschiedene adj (einige) several.

verschimmelt adj mouldy.

verschlafen (präs verschläft, prät verschlief, pp verschlafen) vi to oversleep. ◆ vt (Morgen) to sleep through. ■ sich verschlafen ref to oversleep.

verschlechtern vt to make worse. ■ sich verschlechtern ref to deteriorate.

Verschlechterung (pl -en) die (von Zustand) deterioration.

Verschleiß der (von Material) wear.

verschleißen (prät verschliss, pp verschlissen) vi ist to become worn.

verschließen (prät verschloss, pp verschlossen) vt (Haus, Tür, Schrank) to lock; (Dose, Flasche) to seal. ■ sich

verschließen ref (Person) to shut o.s. off.

verschlimmern vt to make worse. ■ sich verschlimmern ref to get worse.

verschlingen (prät verschlang, pp verschlungen) vt (Mahlzeit) to wolf down.

verschlossen pp → verschließen. ◆ adj (Person) reticent; (Tür, Safe) locked; (Dose, Briefumschlag) sealed.

verschlucken vt (schlucken) to swallow. ■ sich verschlucken ref to choke.

Verschluss (pl Verschlüsse) der (von Kette, Tasche) fastener; (von Flaschen) top.

Verschmutzung (pl -en) die pollution.

verschneit adj snow-covered.

verschreiben (prät verschrieb, pp verschrieben) vt (Medikamente) to prescribe. ■ sich verschreiben ref (falsch schreiben): ich habe mich verschrieben I've written it down wrongly.

verschreibungspflichtig adj available on prescription only.

verschrotten vt to scrap.

verschulden vt (Unfall, Verlust) to be to blame for.

verschweigen (prät verschwieg, pp verschwiegen) vt to hide.

verschwenden vt to waste.

verschwinden (prät verschwand, pp verschwunden) vi ist to disappear.

Versehen *(pl -)* das oversight ; **aus ~** accidentally.

versehentlich *adv* accidentally.

versenden *(prät* versandte, *pp* versendet) *vt* to send.

versichern *vt (bei Versicherung)* to insure ; *(sagen)* to assure. ■ **sich versichern** *ref (bei Versicherung)* to insure o.s. ; *(prüfen)* to assure o.s.

versichert *adj* insured.

Versicherte *(pl -n)* der, die insured party.

Versicherung *(pl -en)* die *(Firma)* insurance company ; *(Vertrag)* insurance.

Versicherungsbedingungen *pl* terms of insurance.

Versicherungskarte *(pl -n)* die insurance card ; **grüne ~** green card *(Br)*, insurance card *required if taking a vehicle abroad.*

versilbert *adj* silver-plated.

versöhnen *vt* to reconcile. ■ **sich versöhnen** *ref* to make up.

versorgen *vt (mit Lebensmitteln, Nachrichten)* to supply ; *(Patienten, Tier)* to look after.

Versorgung die *(mit Lebensmitteln, Nachrichten)* supply ; *(von Patienten, Tier)* care.

verspäten : **sich verspäten** *ref* to be late.

Verspätung *(pl -en)* die delay ; **mit ~** late ; **~ haben** to be delayed ; **5 Minuten ~ haben** to be 5 minutes late.

versprechen *(präs* verspricht, *prät* versprach, *pp* ver-

sprochen) *vt* to promise ; **jm etw ~** to promise sb sthg. ■ **sich versprechen** *ref* to make a mistake.

Versprechen *(pl -)* das promise.

verstaatlichen *vt* to nationalize.

Verstand der *(Denkvermögen)* reason.

verständigen *vt (informieren)* to notify. ■ **sich verständigen** *ref (kommunizieren)* to make o.s. understood.

Verständigung die *(Kommunikation)* communication ; *(Information)* notification.

verständlich *adj (Stimme)* audible ; *(Text)* comprehensible ; *(Handlung, Reaktion)* understandable ; **sich ~ machen** to make o.s. understood.

Verständnis das understanding.

verständnisvoll *adj* understanding.

Verstärker *(pl)* der amplifier.

verstauchen *vt :* **sich *(D)* etw ~** to sprain sthg.

Verstauchung *(pl -en)* die sprain.

Versteck *(pl -e)* das hiding place ; **~ spielen** to play hide-and-seek.

verstecken *vt* to hide. ■ **sich verstecken** *ref* to hide.

verstehen *(prät* verstand, *pp* verstanden) *vt* to understand ; **etwas/nichts ~ von** to know a bit/nothing about. ■ **sich verstehen** *ref (Personen)* to get on ; **sich gut ~ mit** to get on well

with ; es versteht sich von selbst
it goes without saying.

Versteigerung (pl -en) die
auction.

verstellbar adj adjustable.

verstellen vt (Hebel, Wecker)
to reset ; (Weg, Tür) to block ;
(Stimme) to disguise. ◼ **sich
verstellen** ref (Person) to disguise o.s.

Verstopfung die constipation.

Verstoß (pl Verstöße) der
breach.

Versuch (pl -e) der (Handlung)
attempt ; (wissenschaftlich) experiment.

versuchen vt & vi to try.

vertauschen vt to mix up.

verteidigen vt to defend.
◼ **sich verteidigen** ref to defend o.s.

verteilen vt to distribute.
◼ **sich verteilen** ref (sich ausbreiten) to spread out.

Vertrag (pl Verträge) der contract.

vertragen (präs verträgt,
prät vertrug, pp vertragen) vt
(Hitze, Kaffee) to stand, to
bear. ◼ **sich vertragen** ref
(Personen) to get on.

Vertragshändler (pl -) der
authorized dealer.

Vertragswerkstatt (pl
-werkstätten) die authorized
workshop.

vertrauen vi (+D) to trust.

Vertrauen das confidence,
trust ; ~ **haben zu** to have confidence in.

vertreten (präs vertritt, prät
vertrat, pp vertreten) vt (bei Urlaub, Krankheit) to stand in for ;
(Interessen) to represent. ◆ adj
represented ; sich (D) den Fuß ~
to trip and hurt one's foot.

Vertreter, in (mpl Vertreter)
der, die (bei Urlaub, Krankheit)
stand-in ; (Repräsentant) representative ; (Beruf) rep.

Vertretung (pl -en) die (Lehrer) supply teacher ; (Arzt) locum ; (Delegation) representa-
tives (pl) ; (bei Urlaub, Krankheit) : die ~ für jn übernehmen to
stand in for sb.

vertrocknen vi ist to dry out.

vertun (prät vertat, pp vertan)
vt (verschwenden) to waste.
◼ **sich vertun** ref (fam : sich irren) to get it wrong.

verunglücken vi ist (bei Unfall) to have a nasty accident.

verursachen vt to cause.

Verurteilung (pl -en) die (vor
Gericht) sentence.

verwackelt adj blurred.

verwählen : sich verwählen ref to dial the wrong number.

verwahren vt (aufbewahren)
to put away.

verwalten vt to adminis-
trate.

Verwalter, in (mpl -) der, die
administrator.

Verwaltung (pl -en) die administration.

verwandt pp → verwenden.
◆ adj (Personen) related ; ~ sein
mit to be related to.

Verwandte (*pl* -n) *der, die* relative.

Verwandtschaft (*pl* -en) *die* family.

Verwarnung (*pl* -en) *die* caution ; gebührenpflichtige ~ fine.

verwechseln *vt* to mix up ; jn mit jm ~ to mistake sb for sb.

verweigern *vt* to refuse.

verwendbar *adj* usable.

verwenden (*prät* verwandte ODER verwendete, *pp* verwandt ODER verwendet) *vt* to use.

Verwendung *die* use.

verwirklichen *vt* (*Traum, Wunsch*) to come true. ■ **sich verwirklichen** *ref* (*Person*) to fulfil o.s.

verwirrt *adj* confused.

verwitwet *adj* widowed.

verwöhnen *vt* to spoil.

Verwundete (*pl* -n) *der, die* wounded person.

verzählen : sich verzählen *ref* to miscount.

Verzehr *der* (*geh*) consumption.

verzehren *vt* (*geh* : *essen*) to consume.

Verzeichnis (*pl* -se) *das* catalogue ; alphabetisches ~ index.

verzeihen (*prät* verzieh, *pp* verziehen) *vt* to forgive ; ~ Sie bitte! excuse me, please!

Verzeihung *die* forgiveness ; ~! sorry!

verzichten *vi* : ~ auf (+A) to do without.

verzögern *vt* (*verschieben*) to delay. ■ **sich verzögern** *ref* (*sich verspäten*) to be delayed.

Verzögerung (*pl* -en) *die* (*Verspätung*) delay.

verzollen *vt* to declare ; haben Sie etwas zu ~? have you anything to declare?

verzweifeln *vi* ist to despair.

verzweifelt *adj* desperate.

Vesper (*pl* -n) *die* (*Süddt* : *Mahlzeit*) afternoon snack.

Veterinär, in (*mpl* -e) *der, die* (*amt*) veterinary surgeon.

Vetter (*pl* -n) *der* cousin.

vgl. (*abk für vergleiche*) cf.

vibrieren *vi* to vibrate.

Video (*pl* -s) *das* video.

Videofilm (*pl* -e) *der* video.

Videogerät (*pl* -e) *das* video (*Br*), VCR (*Am*).

Videokamera (*pl* -s) *die* video camera.

Videokassette (*pl* -n) *die* video (tape).

Videokonsole (*pl* -n) *die* video console.

Videorekorder (*pl* -) *der* video (recorder) (*Br*), VCR (*Am*).

Videospiel (*pl* -e) *das* video game.

Videothek (*pl* -en) *die* video store.

Vieh *das* (*Tiere*) cattle.

viel (*kompar* mehr, *superl* am meisten) *det* 1. (*Menge, Anzahl*) a lot of ; ~ Tee a lot of tea ; ~e Bücher a lot of books ; ~e Leute many people.
2. (*in Floskeln*) : ~en Dank!

thank you very much! ; **~ Spaß!** have fun!

◆ *adv* 1. *(intensiv, oft)* a lot ; **~ arbeiten** to work a lot.

2. *(zum Ausdruck der Verstärkung)* much ; **~ mehr** much more ; **~ zu...** much too... ; **es dauert ~ zu lange** it's far too long ; **~ zu ~ much** too much ; **~ zu ~** much too much.

◆ *pron* a lot.

◆ *adj* : **das ~e Geld** all the money ; **das Kleid mit den ~en Knöpfen** the dress with all the buttons.

viele *det* → **viel**. ◆ *pron* lots.

vielfach *adj* multiple.

Vielfalt *die* variety.

vielleicht *adv* perhaps ; *(fam : etwa, sehr)* really.

vielmals *adv* : **danke ~** thank you very much.

vielseitig *adj (Person)* versatile.

vier *num* four ; → **sechs**.

Viereck *(pl -e) das* rectangle.

viereckig *adj* rectangular.

vierhundert *num* four hundred.

viermal *adv* four times.

vierspurig *adj* four-lane.

vierte, r, s *adj* fourth ; → **sechste**.

Viertel *(pl Viertel) das* quarter ; **~ vor sechs** a quarter to six ; **~ nach sechs** a quarter past six *(Br)*, a quarter after six *(Am)*.

Viertelstunde *(pl -n) die* quarter of an hour.

Vierwaldstätter See *der* Lake Lucerne.

vierzehn *num* fourteen ; **~ Tage** a fortnight ; → **sechs**.

vierzig *num* forty ; → **sechs**.

Villa *(pl Villen) die* villa.

violett *adj* purple.

Violine *(pl -n) die* violin.

Virus *(pl Viren) der* virus.

Virusinfektion *(pl -en) die* viral infection.

Visite *(pl -n) die (MED)* rounds *(pl)*.

Visitenkarte *(pl -n) die* visiting card.

Visum *(pl Visa) das* visa.

Vitamin *(pl -e) das* vitamin.

Vogel *(pl Vögel) der* bird.

Vokabel *(pl -n) die* vocabulary.

Vokal *(pl -e) der* vowel.

Volk *(pl Völker) das* people.

Völkerkunde *die* anthropology.

Volksfest *(pl -e) das* festival.

Volkshochschule *(pl -n) die* ≃ college of adult education.

Volkslied *(pl -er) das* folk song.

Volkstanz *(pl -tänze) der* folk dance.

Volkswagen® *(pl -) der* Volkswagen®.

voll *adj* full. ◆ *adv (ganz)* fully ; *(fam : total, absolut)* totally ; **~ mit** ODER **von** full of ; **halb ~** half full ; **~ sein** *(fam : betrunken)* to be plastered.

vollendet *adj (perfekt)* perfect ; *(fertig)* completed. ◆ *adv (perfekt)* perfectly ; **mit ~em 18. Lebensjahr** at 18 years of age.

Volleyball (*pl* -bälle) *der* volleyball.

Vollgas *das* full throttle.

völlig *adj* total. ◆ *adv* totally.

volljährig *adj* of age.

Vollkaskoversicherung (*pl* -en) *die* comprehensive insurance.

vollklimatisiert *adj* fully air-conditioned.

vollkommen *adj* (*perfekt*) perfect; (*vollständig, total*) total. ◆ *adv* (*perfekt*) perfectly; (*vollständig*) totally.

Vollkornbrot (*pl* -e) *das* wholemeal bread.

voll machen *vt* (*Behälter*) to fill up. ▓ **sich voll machen** *ref* (*fam* : *sich beschmutzen*) to get dirty.

Vollmacht (*pl* -en) *die* (*Befugnis*) authority; (*Dokument*) authorization.

Vollmilch *die* full-fat milk.

Vollmilchschokolade *die* milk chocolate.

Vollmond *der* full moon.

Vollpension *die* full board.

vollständig *adj* (*Sammlung*) complete.

voll tanken *vi* to fill up.

Vollwaschmittel (*pl* -) *das* detergent.

vollwertig *adj* (*Ernährung*) wholefood; (*gleichwertig*) equal.

Vollwertkost *die* wholefood.

vollzählig *adj* entire.

Volt (*pl* Volt) *das* volt.

Volumen (*pl* -) *das* volume.

vom *präp* = **von dem**.

von *präp* (+D) **1.** (*räumlich*) from; ~ hier an from here; ~ hier aus from here; ~ Köln bis Paris from Cologne to Paris; ~ der Straße her from the street; ~... nach from... to. **2.** (*zeitlich*) of; die Zeitung ~ gestern yesterday's paper; ~ heute an from today; ~ Montag bis Freitag from Monday to Friday. **3.** (*in Passivsätzen*) by; ~ einem Hund gebissen werden to be bitten by a dog; das war dumm ~ dir that was stupid of you. **4.** (*Angabe von Besitz*) : ist das Buch ~ dir? is the book yours? **5.** (*Angabe von Zusammengehörigkeit*) of; der Bürgermeister ~ Frankfurt the mayor of Frankfurt; ein Verwandter ~ mir a relation of mine. **6.** (*Angabe der Herkunft*) from; ich bin ~ hier (*fam*) I'm from round here; ein Brief ~ meiner Schwester a letter from my sister. **7.** (*Angabe der Ursache*) from; mir aus (*fam*) as far as I'm concerned; ~ wegen! (*fam*) no way! **8.** (*Angabe des Maßes*) of; ein Sack ~ 25 kg a 25 kg bag.

voneinander *adv* from each other.

vor *präp* (+D) **1.** (*räumlich*) in front of; ~ dem Haus stehen to stand in front of the house. **2.** (*zeitlich*) before; fünf ~ zwölf five to twelve (*Br*), five before twelve (*Am*); fünf ~ halb neun twenty-five past eight (*Br*),

twenty-five after eight *(Am)*; ~ **kurzem** recently; ~ **(fünf) Jahren** (five) years ago.
3. *(Angabe des Grunds)* with; ~ **Freude** in die Luft springen to jump for joy; ~ **allem** *(hauptsächlich)* above all.
◆ *präp (+A)* in front of.
◆ *adv* forwards.

Voralberg *nt* Voralberg.

voran *adv (vorne)* at the front; **mach ~!** *(fam)* hurry up!

voraus *adv* : **im Voraus** in advance.

vorausgesetzt *adj* provided (that).

Voraussetzung *(pl -en)* die *(Bedingung)* condition; *(Annahme)* assumption.

voraussichtlich *adj* expected. ◆ *adv* probably.

vorbei *adj* : ~ **sein** *(zeitlich)* to be over; *(räumlich)* to be past.

vorbei|fahren *vi unr ist (an Stadt, Haus)* to drive past; *(fam : bei Person)* to drop in.

vorbei|gehen *vi unr ist* to pass; *(fam : Besuch)* to drop in.

vorbei|kommen *vi unr ist (an Stadt, Haus)* to go past; *(fam : bei Person)* to call round; *(an Hindernis)* to get past.

vorbei|lassen *vt unr* to let past.

vor|bereiten *vt* to prepare. ■ **sich vorbereiten** *ref* to prepare o.s.; **sich ~ auf** *(+A)* to prepare for.

Vorbereitung *(pl -en)* die preparation; ~ **für etw treffen** make preparations for sth.

vor|bestellen *vt* to order in advance.

Vorbestellung *(pl -en)* die advance booking.

vor|beugen *vi (+D)* to prevent. ■ **sich vorbeugen** *ref* to lean forwards.

Vorbild *(pl -er)* das *(Idol)* example.

Vorderachse *(pl -n)* die front axle.

vordere, r, s *adj* front.

Vordergrund der foreground.

Vorderrad *(pl -räder)* das front wheel.

Vorderradantrieb *(pl -e)* der front-wheel drive.

Vorderseite *(pl -n)* die front.

Vordersitz *(pl -e)* der front seat.

vor|drängen : **sich vordrängen** *ref (räumlich)* to push one's way forward.

Vordruck *(pl -e)* der form.

vor|fahren *vi unr ist (nach vorn)* to drive up.

Vorfahrt die right of way; '~ **gewähren**' 'give way'; '~ **geändert**' 'altered right of way'.

Vorfahrtsstraße *(pl -n)* die major road.

Vorfall *(pl -fälle)* der *(Ereignis)* occurrence.

Vorführung *(pl -en)* die *(im Theater, Kino)* performance; *(von Auto, Maschine)* demonstration.

Vorgänger, in *(mpl -)* der, die predecessor.

vor|gehen *vi unr ist (passieren)* to go on; *(handeln)* to proceed ; *(Uhr)* to be fast ; *(nach vorn)* to go forward ; *(fam : voraus)* to go on ahead.

vorgekocht *adj* precooked.

vorgesehen *adj* intended.

Vorgesetzte *(pl -n) der, die* superior.

vorgestern *adv (vor zwei Tagen)* the day before yesterday.

vor|haben *vt unr :* etw ~ to have sthg planned.

vorhanden *adj* available.

Vorhang *(pl -hänge) der* curtain.

Vorhängeschloss *(pl -schlösser) das* padlock.

vorher *adv* beforehand.

Vorhersage *(pl -n) die (für Wetter)* forecast.

vorhin *adv* just now.

vorige *adj* last.

Vorkenntnisse *pl* prior knowledge *(sg).*

vor|kommen *vi unr ist (passieren)* to occur ; *(existieren)* to exist. ◆ *vi (+D) (scheinen)* to seem ; *(fam : nach vorne)* to come forwards.

Vorkommnis *(pl -se) das (amt)* incident.

vor|lassen *vt unr :* jn ~ to let sb go first.

vorläufig *adj* provisional. ◆ *adv* provisionally.

vor|lesen *vt unr* to read out.

Vorlesung *(pl -en) die* lecture.

vorletzte *(m -r, nt -s) adj* last but one.

vorm. *(abk für vormittags)* am.

vor|machen *vt (vortäuschen)* to fool ; *(zeigen) :* jm etw ~ to show sb how to do sthg.

vor|merken *vt (Termin)* to pencil in.

Vormittag *(pl -e) der* morning ; heute/gestern/morgen ~ this/yesterday/tomorrow morning.

vormittags *adv* in the morning.

vorn *adv* at the front ; da ~ over there ; nach ~ *(zeitlich)* forwards ; von ~ from the beginning.

Vorname *(pl -n) der* first name.

vorne *adv* = vorn.

vornehm *adj* elegant.

vor|nehmen *vt (ausführen)* to undertake ; sich (D) etw ~ *(planen)* to plan to do sthg.

Vorort *(pl -e) der* suburb.

vorrangig *adj* principal.

Vorrat *(pl -räte) der* store ; auf ~ in stock ; solange der ~ reicht while stocks last.

vorrätig *adj* in stock.

Vorsaison *die* pre-season.

Vorsatz *(pl -sätze) der* resolution.

Vorschau *(pl -en) die* preview.

Vorschlag *(pl -schläge) der* suggestion.

vor|schlagen *vt unr* to suggest ; jm etw ~ to suggest sthg to sb.

vor|schreiben *vt unr (befehlen)* to dictate.

Vorschrift *(pl -en) die* regulation.

Vorschuss (*pl* -schüsse) *der* advance.

Vorsicht *die* care.; ~! look out!

vorsichtig *adj* careful. ◆ *adv* carefully.

Vorsilbe (*pl* -n) *die* prefix.

Vorspeise (*pl* -n) starter.

Vorsprung (*pl* -sprünge) *der* (*Abstand*) lead ; (*an Mauer*) projection.

vor|stellen *vt* (*Person, Projekt*) to introduce ; (*Uhr*) to put forward ; sich (*D*) etw ~ (*ausdenken*) to imagine sthg. ■ sich vorstellen *ref* (*bekannt machen*) to introduce o.s.

Vorstellung (*pl* -en) *die* (*in Kino, Theater*) performance ; (*von Bekannten*) introduction ; (*Idee*) idea ; (*bei Firma*) interview.

vor|strecken *vt* (*Geld*) to advance.

Vorteil (*pl* -e) *der* advantage.

Vortrag (*pl* -träge) *der* (*Rede*) talk ; einen ~ halten to give a talk.

vorüber *adj* : ~ sein to be over.

vorüber|gehen *vi unr ist* (*vorbeigehen*) to pass by ; (*zu Ende gehen*) to come to an end.

vorübergehend *adj* temporary. ◆ *adv* temporarily ; ~ geschlossen temporarily closed.

Vor- und Zuname (*pl* -n) *der* first name and surname.

Vorurteil (*pl* -e) *das* prejudice.

Vorverkauf *der* advance booking.

Vorverkaufskasse (*pl* -n) *die* advance booking desk.

Vorverkaufsstelle (*pl* -n) *die* advance booking office.

Vorwahl (*pl* -en) *die* (*Telefonnummer*) dialling code (*Br*), area code (*Am*).

Vorwahlnummer (*pl* -n) *die* dialling code (*Br*), area code (*Am*).

vorwärts *adv* (*nach vorn*) forwards.

vorwärts kommen *vi unr ist* to make progress.

vor|werfen *vt unr* (*Fehler*) jm etw ~ to accuse sb of sthg.

Vorwort (*pl* -e) *das* preface.

Vorwurf (*pl* -würfe) *der* accusation.

vor|zeigen *vt* to show.

vor|ziehen *vt unr* (*lieber mögen*) to prefer ; (*Vorhang*) to draw ; (*nach vorn ziehen*) to pull up.

vorzüglich *adj* excellent.

Vorzugspreis (*pl* -e) *der* special price.

vulgär *adj* vulgar.

Vulkan (*pl* -e) *der* volcano.

W

W (*abk für West*) W.

Waadt *die* Vaud (*Swiss canton*).

Waage (*pl* -n) *die* (*Gerät*) scales (*pl*) ; (*Sternzeichen*) Libra.

waagerecht *adj* horizontal.

wach adj (nicht schlafend) : ~ sein to be awake ; ~ werden to wake up.

Wache (pl -n) die (Wächter) guard ; (Polizeidienststelle) police station.

Wacholder der (Gewürz) juniper.

Wachs das wax.

wachsen[1] (präs wächst, prät wuchs, pp gewachsen) vi ist to grow.

wachsen[2] vt (Skier) to wax.

Wachsfigurenkabinett (pl -e) das waxworks (pl).

Wachsmalstift (pl -e) der wax crayon.

wächst präs → wachsen.

Wachstum das growth.

Wachtel (pl -n) die quail.

Wächter, in (mpl -) der, die guard.

wackelig adj (Möbel) wobbly.

Wackelkontakt (pl -e) der loose contact.

wackeln vi (Möbel) to be wobbly ; (bewegen) to shake.

Wackelpeter der jelly.

Wade (pl -n) die calf.

Waffe (pl -n) die weapon.

Waffel (pl -n) die waffle.

Waffeleisen (pl -) das waffle iron.

wagen vt (riskieren) to risk. ▓ **sich wagen** ref (sich trauen) to dare.

Wagen (pl -) der (Auto) car ; (von Zug, U-Bahn) carriage (Br), car (Am) ; (Pferdewagen) carriage ; '~ hält' 'bus stopping'.

Wagenheber (pl -) der jack.

Wagenpapiere pl vehicle documents.

Wagentyp (pl -en) der make of car.

Wagenwäsche (pl -n) die car wash.

Waggon (pl -s) der carriage (Br), car (Am).

Wahl (pl -en) die (Auswahl) choice ; (Abstimmung) election ; erste ~ top quality.

wählen vt (aussuchen) to choose ; (Telefonnummer) to dial ; (Kandidaten) to elect. ◆ vi (aussuchen) to choose ; (am Telefon) to dial ; (abstimmen) to vote.

Wählscheibe (pl -n) die dial.

wahlweise adv : ~ in Rot, Grün oder Blau in either red, green or blue ; ~ mit Reis oder Gemüse with a choice of rice or vegetables.

Wahnsinn der madness ; ~! brilliant!

wahnsinnig adj (unvernünftig) mad. ◆ adv (fam : groß, stark) incredibly.

wahr adj true.

während konj (zeitlich) while. ◆ präp (+G) during.

währenddessen adv in the meantime.

Wahrheit (pl -en) die truth ; in ~ in reality.

wahr|nehmen vt unr (bemerken) to notice.

Wahrsager, in (mpl -) der, die fortune-teller.

wahrscheinlich adj probable. ◆ adv probably.

Währung (*pl* -en) *die* currency.

Wahrzeichen (*pl* -) *das* symbol.

Waise (*pl* -n) *die* orphan.

Wald (*pl* Wälder) *der* wood ; (*groß*) forest.

Waldbrand (*pl* -brände) *der* forest fire.

Wäldchen (*pl* -) *das* copse.

Waldgebiet (*pl*-e) *das* wooded area.

waldig *adj* wooded.

Waldlauf (*pl* -läufe) *der* cross-country run.

Waldlehrpfad (*pl*-e) *der* nature trail.

Waldmeister *der* (*Pflanze*) woodruff.

Waldorfsalat (*pl* -e) *der* Waldorf salad.

Waldpilz (*pl* -e) *der* wild mushroom.

Waldsterben *das* forest dieback.

 WALDSTERBEN

This is the German term used to refer to the damage caused to trees by environmental pollution. It was in Germany that public attention was first drawn to this phenomenon during the 1970s. The characteristic symptoms whereby needles, leaves and entire treetops turn yellow and die initially affected only coniferous trees, but have now spread to deciduous trees as well. Forest dieback is attributed to acid rain, the hole in the ozone layer and general chemical pollution, and two-thirds of German forests now suffer from its effects.

Waldweg (*pl* -e) *der* forest track.

Wales *nt* Wales.

Waliser (*pl* -n) *der* Welshman ; **die ~n** the Welsh.

Waliserin (*pl* -nen) *die* Welshwoman.

walisisch *adj* Welsh.

Walkie-Talkie (*pl* -s) *das* walkie-talkie.

Walkman® (*pl* -men) *der* Walkman®.

Wallfahrt (*pl* -en) *die* pilgrimage.

Wallfahrtsort (*pl* -e) *der* place of pilgrimage.

Wallis *das* Valais (*Swiss canton*).

Walnuss (*pl* -nüsse) *die* walnut.

Walzer (*pl* -) *der* waltz.

wand *prät* → winden.

Wand (*pl* Wände) *die* (*von Häusern, Räumen*) wall.

wandeln : **sich wandeln** *ref* to change.

Wanderer (*pl* -) *der* rambler.

Wanderkarte (*pl* -n) *die* walking map.

wandern *vi ist* to go walking.

Wanderschuh (*pl* -e) *der* walking boot.

Wanderweg (*pl* -e) *der* trail.

Wandmalerei (*pl* -en) *die* mural.

Wandschrank (*pl* -schränke) *der* built-in cupboard.

wandte *prät* → wenden.

Wandteppich *(pl -e)* er tapestry.

Wange *(pl -n) die (geh)* cheek.

wann *adv* when; bis ~? till when?; seit ~ lebst du schon hier? how long have you been living here?

Wanne *(pl -n) die (Badewanne)* bath; *(Gefäß)* tank.

Wappen *(pl -)* das coat of arms.

war *prät* → sein[1].

warb *prät* → werben.

Ware *(pl -n) die* product; ~n goods.

Warenhaus *(pl -häuser) das* department store.

Warenlager *(pl -)* das warehouse.

Warenmuster *(pl -)* das sample.

Warensendung *(pl -en) die* sample sent by post.

Warenzeichen *(pl -)* das trademark.

warf *prät* → werfen.

warm *(komp* wärmer, *superl* am wärmsten) adj warm. ◆ adv warmly; ~ essen to have a hot meal; sich ~ anziehen to put on warm clothes; es ist ~ it's warm; ist dir nicht zu ~? aren't you too hot?; ~e Getränke hot drinks.

Wärme *die* warmth.

wärmen *vt* to warm. ▓ **sich wärmen** *ref* to warm o.s.

Wärmflasche *(pl -n) die* hot-water bottle.

Warmfront *(pl -en) die* warm front.

warm laufen *vi unr ist (Motor)* to warm up. ▓ **sich warm laufen** *ref (Person)* to warm up.

Warmmiete *(pl -n) die* rent including heating bills.

Warmwasser *das* hot water.

Warnblinkanlage *(pl -n) die* hazard lights *(pl)*.

Warndreieck *(pl -e) das* warning triangle.

warnen *vt* to warn; 'vor... wird gewarnt' 'beware of...'

Warnschild *(pl -er) das* warning sign.

Warnung *(pl -en) die* warning.

Warteliste *(pl -n) die* waiting list.

warten *vi* to wait. ◆ *vt (TECH)* to service; ~ auf *(+A)* to wait for; 'hier ~' 'wait here'.

Wartenummer *(pl -n) die* number assigned to someone to indicate their position in a waiting system.

Wärter, in *(mpl -) der, die* attendant.

Wartesaal *(pl -säle) der* waiting room.

Wartezimmer *(pl -)* das waiting room.

Wartung *(pl -en) die* servicing.

warum *adv* why; ~ nicht? why not?

Warze *(pl -n) die* wart.

was *pron* what; *(Relativpronomen)* which; *(fam :etwas)* something; *(fam : nicht wahr)*: da freust du dich, ~? you're pleased, aren't you? ; ~ für what kind of ; na so ~! well!

Waschanlage (*pl* -n) *die* car wash.

waschbar *adj* washable.

Waschbecken (*pl* -) *das* washbasin.

Wäsche (*pl* -n) *die* washing ; *(Unterwäsche)* underwear ; schmutzige ~ dirty washing.

waschecht *adj (Kleidung)* colourfast.

Wäscheklammer (*pl* -n) *die* clothes peg *(Br)*, clothespin *(Am)*.

Wäscheleine (*pl* -n) *die* washing line.

waschen (*präs* wäscht, *prät* wusch, *pp* gewaschen) *vt* to wash. ■ **sich waschen** *ref* to have a wash ; sich *(D)* die Hände ~ to wash one's hands ; Waschen und Legen shampoo and set.

Wäscherei (*pl* -en) *die* laundrette.

Wäscheschleuder (*pl* -n) *die* spin-dryer.

Wäscheständer (*pl* -) *der* clotheshorse.

Wäschestärke *die* starch.

Wäschetrockner (*pl* -) *der* *(Maschine)* tumble-dryer.

Waschgelegenheit (*pl* -en) *die* washing facilities.

Waschlappen (*pl* -) *der (zum Waschen)* face cloth.

Waschmaschine (*pl* -n) *die* washing machine.

Waschmittel (*pl* -) *das* detergent.

Waschpulver (*pl* -) *das* washing powder.

Waschraum (*pl* -räume) *der* washroom.

Waschsalon (*pl* -s) *der* laundrette.

Waschstraße (*pl* -n) *die* car wash.

wäscht *präs* → waschen.

Wasser (*pl* Wässer ODER Wasser) *das* water ; am ~ next to the water ; im ~ in the water ; destilliertes ~ distilled water.

Wasseranschluss (*pl* -anschlüsse) *der* water mains.

wasserdicht *adj* waterproof.

Wasserfall (*pl* -fälle) *der* waterfall.

Wasserfarbe (*pl* -n) *die* watercolour.

Wassergraben (*pl* -gräben) *der* ditch.

Wasserhahn (*pl* -hähne) *der* tap *(Br)*, faucet *(Am)*.

Wasserleitung (*pl* -en) *die* *(Rohr)* water pipe ; *(Anlage)* plumbing.

wasserlöslich *adj* soluble *(in water)*.

Wassermangel *der* drought.

Wassermann *der (Sternzeichen)* Aquarius.

Wassermelone (*pl* -n) *die* watermelon.

wasserscheu *adj* scared of water.

Wasserschutzpolizei *die* river police.

Wasserski (*pl* -e r) *der (Gerät)* water ski. ◆ *das (Sportart)* water skiing.

Wasserspiegel (*pl* -) *der (Wasserstand)* water level.

Wassersport *der* water sport.

Wasserspülung (*pl* -en) *die* flush.

Wasserstand (*pl* -stände) *der* water level.

wasserundurchlässig *adj* waterproof.

Wasserversorgung *die* water supply.

Wasserwerk (*pl* -e) *das* waterworks (*sg*).

Watt¹ (*pl* -en) *das (Küstengebiet)* mudflats (*pl*).

Watt² (*pl* -) *das (Maßeinheit)* watt.

Watte *die* cotton wool.

Wattenmeer (*pl* -e) *das* mudflats (*pl*).

ⓘ WATTENMEER

This is the name given to an area of mud flats on the North Sea coast, characterized by "Priele" (occasionally very deep water channels). At high tide the area is covered by the sea, but at low tide a unique natural landscape is revealed, making it a very popular place for visitors to go on walks.

Wattestäbchen (*pl* -) *das* cotton bud.

wattiert *adj* padded.

WC (*pl* -s) *das* WC.

WC-Reiniger (*pl* -) *der* lavatory cleaner.

weben (*prät* **webte** ODER **wob**, *pp* **gewebt** ODER **gewoben**) *vt (Teppich, Stoff)* to weave.

Wechsel (*pl* -) *der (Austausch, Änderung)* change ; *(von Devisen)* exchange.

Wechselbad (*pl* -bäder) *das (in Wasser)* bath in alternating hot and then cold water.

Wechselgeld *das* change.

wechselhaft *adj* changeable.

Wechseljahre *pl* menopause (*sg*).

Wechselkurs (*pl* -e) *der* exchange rate.

wechseln *vt* & *vi* to change ; **Mark in Pfund ~** to change marks into pounds.

Wechselrahmen (*pl* -) *der* clip frame.

Wechselstrom *der* alternating current.

Wechselstube (*pl* -n) *die* bureau de change.

Weckdienst (*pl* -e) *der* morning call.

wecken *vt (Person, Tier)* to wake.

Wecker (*pl* -) *der* alarm clock.

weder *konj* neither ; **~... noch** neither... nor.

weg *adv* away ; **weit ~** far away ; **Frau Miller ist schon ~** Frau Miller has already gone.

Weg (*pl* -e) *der (Pfad)* path ; *(Strecke, Methode)* way ; **der ~ nach** the way to ; **dem ausgeschilderten ~ folgen** follow the signposted path ; **im ~ sein** to be in the way.

weg|bringen vt unr to take away.

wegen präp (+G or D) because of.

weg|fahren vi unr ist to leave. ◆ vt unr hat to drive away.

weg|gehen vi unr ist (Person) to go away ; (Fleck) to come off.

weg|kommen vi unr ist (fam : fortgehen können) to get away ; (verschwinden) to disappear.

weg|lassen vt unr (fam : Textstelle) to leave out ; (Gäste) to let go.

weg|laufen vi unr ist to run away.

weg|legen vt to put down.

weg|machen vt (fam) to get off.

weg|müssen vi unr (fam) to have to go.

weg|nehmen vt unr to take away.

weg|räumen vt to clear away.

weg|schicken vt (Brief, Packet) to send ; (Person) to send away.

weg|sehen vi unr (nicht hinsehen) to look away.

weg|tun vt unr (fam : weglegen) to put away ; (wegwerfen) to throw away.

Wegweiser (pl -) der signpost.

weg|werfen vt unr to throw away.

weg|wischen vt to wipe away.

weh adj : **~ tun** (schmerzen) to hurt ; **jm ~ tun** (verletzen) to hurt sb.

Wehe (pl -n) die contraction.

wehen vi (Wind) to blow.

Wehrdienst der military service.

wehren : **sich wehren** ref to defend o.s.

weiblich adj female ; (GRAMM) feminine.

weich adj soft. ◆ adv (sitzen, liegen) comfortably.

weich gekocht adj soft-boiled.

Weichkäse der soft cheese.

Weichspüler (pl -) der fabric conditioner.

Weide (pl -n) die (mit Gras) meadow.

weigern : **sich weigern** ref to refuse.

Weigerung (pl -en) die refusal.

Weihnachten (pl -) Christmas ; **frohe ~!** Merry Christmas!

ⓘ WEIHNACHTEN

German Christmas traditions differ somewhat from those in the English-speaking world. Presents are exchanged on Christmas Eve rather than on Christmas Day and before going to Midnight Mass it is customary to light the candles with which the Christmas tree is decorated. "Weihnachtsplätzchen" are plates of typical Christmas biscuits and cakes such as "Lebkuchen", and mulled wine is the traditional drink. In addition to Christmas Day, 26 December is also a public holiday.

Weihnachtsabend (*pl* -e) *der* Christmas Eve.

Weihnachtsbaum (*pl* -bäume) *der* Christmas tree.

Weihnachtsferien *pl* Christmas holidays (*Br*), Christmas vacation (*sg*)(*Am*).

Weihnachtsgeschäft *das* Christmas trade.

Weihnachtsgeschenk (*pl* -e) *das* Christmas present.

Weihnachtslied (*pl* -er) *das* Christmas carol.

Weihnachtsmann (*pl* -männer) *der* Father Christmas.

Weihnachtsmarkt (*pl* -märkte) *der* Christmas market.

ⓘ **WEIHNACHTSMARKT**

During the Christmas period, many German towns have a "Weihnachtsmarkt" or Christmas market, usually on the main square, where you can buy Christmas decorations, handmade goods, gift items, Christmas biscuits and cakes, etc. There are also several stalls selling mulled wine and the local culinary specialities. The Nuremberg "Christkindlmarkt" and the Dresden

Christmas market are the best-known.

Weihnachtstag (*pl* -e) *der* Christmas Day ; **erster** ~ Christmas Day ; **zweiter** ~ Boxing Day.

Weihnachtszeit *die* Christmas.

weil *konj* because.

Wein (*pl* -e) *der* (*Getränk*) wine ; (*Pflanze*) vine.

  WEIN

Almost 90% of the wine produced in Germany is white wine. The main wine-producing areas are the Rhineland, the Mosel-Saar-Ruwer region, Nahe, Baden, Württemberg, Franconia, the Elbe valley and Saale-Unstrut. Franconian wine is bottled in characteristic wide, round bottles called "Bocksbeutel". After the grape harvest, many areas hold wine festivals where the local wines may be sampled. "Federweißer" is a young, cloudy, sweet wine which is especially popular in the autumn, whilst on special occasions Germans drink "Sekt", a champagne-style wine that must contain a specific percentage of German grapes.

Weinberg (*pl* -e) *der* vineyard.

Weinbergschnecke (*pl* -n) *die* snail.

Weinbrand (*pl* -brände) *der* brandy.

weinen *vi* to cry.

Weinflasche (*pl* -n) *die* wine bottle.

Weinglas (*pl* -gläser) *das* wine glass.

Weinkarte (*pl* -n) *die* wine list.

Weinkeller (*pl* -) *der* wine cellar.

Weinlese (*pl* -n) *die* grape harvest.

Weinprobe (*pl* -n) *die* wine tasting.

Weinstube (*pl* -n) *die* wine bar.

Weintraube (*pl* -n) *die* grape.

weisen (*prät* **wies**, *pp* **gewiesen**) *vt* (*zeigen*) to show. ◆ *vi* (*zeigen*) to point.

Weisheit *die* (*Klugheit*) wisdom.

weiß *präs* → **wissen**. ◆ *adj* white.

Weiß *das* white.

Weißbier (*pl* -e) *das* fizzy lager beer made from wheat.

Weißbrot (*pl* -e) *das* white bread.

Weiße[1] (*pl* -n) *der, die* (*Mensch*) white person.

Weiße[2] (*pl*-) *die* (*fam*) = **Weißbier** ; Berliner ~ *type of fizzy lager often drunk with raspberry syrup.*

Weißkohl *der* white cabbage.

Weißwein (*pl* -e) *der* white wine.

Weißwurst (*pl* **Weißwürste**) *die* white sausage.

weit *adj* wide ; (*Reise, Fahrt*) long. ◆ *adv* (*wesentlich*) far ; (*gehen, fahren, fallen*) a long way ; **bei ~em** by far ; **von ~em** from a distance ; **~ weg** far away ; **wie ~ ist es bis...?** how far is it to...? ; **so ~ sein** (*fam*) to be ready ; **zu ~ gehen** to go too far.

weiter *adv* (*fortgesetzt*) further ; (*sonst*) else ; **immer ~** on and on ; **nicht ~** (*nicht weiter fort*) no further ; **nichts ~** nothing more ; **und so ~** and so on.

weiter|arbeiten *vi* to carry on working.

weitere *adj* further ; **ohne ~s** (*problemlos*) with no problem at all.

weiter|empfehlen *vt unr* to recommend.

weiter|fahren *vi unr ist* to drive on.

Weiterfahrt *die* : **zur ~ in Richtung Hausen bitte hier umsteigen** passengers for Hausen, please change here.

weiter|geben *vt unr* to pass on.

weiter|gehen *vi unr ist* to go on.

weiter|helfen *vi unr* (+D) to help.

weiter|machen *vi* to carry on.

weitsichtig *adj* farsighted ; (*MED*) longsighted (*Br*), farsighted (*Am*).

Weitsprung *der* long jump.

Weitwinkelobjektiv (*pl*-e) *das* wide-angle lens.

Weizen *der* wheat.

Weizenbier (*pl* -e) *das fizzy lager beer made from wheat.*

welche, r, s *det* (*zur Einleitung einer Frage*) which. ◆ *pron* (*Relativpronomen*) which, that ; (*Indefinitpronomen*) any ; (*Interrogativpronomen*) which (one) ; hast du ~? have you got any?

welk *adj* wilted.

Welle (*pl* -n) *die* wave.

Wellenbad (*pl* -bäder) *das swimming pool with wave machine.*

Wellengang *der* swell.

Wellenreiten *das* surfing.

wellig *adj* (*Haar*) wavy ; (*Landschaft*) undulating.

Welt (*pl* -en) *die* world ; auf der ~ in the world.

Weltall *das* universe.

weltberühmt *adj* world-famous.

Weltkrieg (*pl* -e) *der* : der Erste/Zweite ~ the First/Second World War.

Weltmeister, in (*mpl* -) *der, die* world champion.

Weltmeisterschaft (*pl* -en) *die* world championship.

Weltreise (*pl* -n) *die* round-the-world trip.

Weltrekord (*pl* -e) *der* world record.

Weltstadt (*pl* -städte) *die* cosmopolitan city.

weltweit *adj* & *adv* worldwide.

wem *pron* (to) who.

wen *pron* who.

Wendefläche (*pl* -n) *die* turning area.

Wendekreis (*pl* -e) *der* (*von Fahrzeug*) turning circle.

Wendemöglichkeit (*pl* -en) *die* turning ; keine ~ no turning.

wenden[1] *vt* & *vi* to turn.

wenden[2] ■ **sich wenden** (*prät* wandte, *pp* gewandt) *ref* : sich an jn ~ to consult sb.

wenig *det* (*Geld, Interesse*) little ; (*Tage, Leute*) a few. ◆ *pron* (*Geld, Kaffee*) a little ; (*Leute*) a few. ◆ *adv* a little ; ein ~ a little ; zu ~ too little.

weniger *adv* (*minus*) minus.

wenigste, r, s *adj* least ; am ~n least.

wenigstens *adv* at least.

wenn *konj* (*zeitlich*) when ; (*falls*) if.

wer *pron* who.

Werbefernsehen *das* television advertising.

Werbegeschenk (*pl* -e) *das* free sample.

werben (*präs* wirbt, *prät* warb, *pp* geworben) *vi* (*Firma, Produzent*) to advertise. ◆ *vt* (*Mitglieder*) to recruit ; (*Kunden*) to attract.

Werbung *die* (*in Zeitung, Fernsehen*) advertising.

werden (*präs* wird, *prät* wurde, *pp* ist geworden ODER worden) *aux* 1. (*im Futur*) will ; sie wird kommen she will come ; sie wird nicht kommen she won't come.

2. (*im Konjunktiv*) would ; würden Sie das machen? would you do this? ; ich würde gern gehen I would like to go ; ich würde lie-

ber noch bleiben I would prefer to stay a bit longer.

3. *(im Passiv : pp worden)* to be ; **sie wurde kritisiert** she was criticized.

4. *(Ausdruck der Möglichkeit)* : **sie wird es wohl vergessen haben** she has probably forgotten.

◆ *vi (pp geworden)* to become ; **Vater ~** to become a father ; **er will Lehrer ~** he wants to be a teacher ; **ich werde morgen 25** I'll be 25 tomorrow ; **das Kind wird groß** the child's getting bigger ; **alt ~** to grow old, to get old ; **rot ~** to go red, to turn red ; **zu Stein ~** to turn to stone ; **schlecht ~** to go off ; **mir wird schlecht** I feel sick.

◆ *vimp (pp geworden)* : **es wird langsam spät** it's getting late ; **es wird bald Sommer** it will soon be summer.

werfen *(präs* **wirft**, *prät* **warf**, *pp* **geworfen)** *vt & vi* to throw.

Werft *(pl* -en) *die* shipyard.

Werk *(pl* -e) *das (Arbeit)* work ; *(Fabrik)* works *(pl)*.

Werkstatt *(pl* -stätten) *die* workshop.

Werktag *(pl* -e) *der* working day.

werktags *adv* on working days.

Werkzeug *(pl* -e) *das* tool.

Werkzeugkasten *(pl* -kästen) *der* tool box.

Wermut *(pl* -s) *der (Getränk)* vermouth.

wert *adj* : **~ sein** to be worth.

Wert *(pl* -e) *der* value ; **im ~ steigen/fallen** to increase/decrease in value.

Wertangabe *(pl* -n) *die* registered value ; **Sendung mit ~** registered mail.

Wertbrief *(pl* -e) *der* registered letter.

Wertgegenstand *(pl* -gegenstände) *der* valuable object.

wertlos *adj* worthless.

Wertmarke *(pl* -n) *die* token.

Wertpapier *(pl* -e) *das* bond.

Wertsachen *pl* valuables ; **'bitte achten Sie auf Ihre ~!'** 'please take care of your valuables'.

wertvoll *adj* valuable.

Wertzeichen *(pl* -) *das* stamp.

Wesen *(pl* -) *das (Charakter)* nature ; *(Lebewesen)* creature.

wesentlich *adj (wichtig)* essential. ◆ *adv (viel)* considerably.

weshalb *adv* why.

Wespe *(pl* -n) *die* wasp.

wessen *pron* whose.

West *der* West.

Westdeutschland *das (westliche Teil)* western Germany ; *(frühere BRD)* West Germany.

Weste *(pl* -n) *die* waistcoat.

Westen *der* west ; **im ~** in the west ; **nach ~** *(Richtung)* west.

Westeuropa *nt* Western Europe.

Westküste *(pl* -n) *die* west coast.

westlich adj western. ◆ präp : ~ **von** west of.

weswegen adv why.

Wettbewerb (pl -e) der (Veranstaltung) competition.

Wettbüro (pl -s) das betting office.

Wette (pl -n) die bet.

wetten vi & vt to bet ; ich wette mit dir um 10 DM I bet you 10 marks.

Wetter das weather ; bei gutem/schlechtem ~ if the weather is good/bad.

Wetteraussichten pl weather prospects.

Wetterbericht (pl -e) der weather report.

wetterfest adj weatherproof.

Wetterkarte (pl -n) die weather map.

Wetterlage (pl -n) die general weather situation.

Wettervorhersage (pl -n) die weather forecast.

Wettkampf (pl -kämpfe) der contest.

Wettlauf (pl -läufe) der race.

Wettrennen (pl -) das race.

WG abk = **Wohngemeinschaft**.

Whg. abk = **Wohnung**.

Whirlpool der whirlpool, jacuzzi.

Whiskey (pl -s) der whisky.

wichtig adj & adv important.

wickeln vt (Schnur, Papier) to wind ; (Baby) : **ein Kind ~** to change a child's nappy (Br), to change a child's diaper (Am).

Wickelraum (pl -räume) der baby changing room.

Widder der (Sternzeichen) Aries.

widerlich adj disgusting.

widerrechtlich adj illegal. ◆ adv : ~ **abgestellte Fahrzeuge** illegally parked cars.

Widerruf (pl -e) der retraction.

widerrufen (prät widerrief, pp widerrufen) vt (Aussage) to retract.

widersprechen (präs widerspricht, prät widersprach, pp widersprochen) vi (+D) to contradict ; **sich** (D) ~ to contradict o.s.

Widerspruch (pl -sprüche) der contradiction ; (Protest) objection.

Widerstand (pl -stände) der (Abwehr) resistance.

widerstandsfähig adj resilient.

Widmung (pl -en) die dedication.

wie adv 1. (in Fragesätzen) how ; ~ **heißen Sie?** what's your name? ; ~ **war das Wetter?** what was the weather like? ; ~ **spät ist es?** what is the time? ; ~ **bitte?** sorry? ; ~ **oft?** how often? ; ~ **wäre es, wenn...?** how about if...? ; **sie fragte ihn, ~ alt er sei** she asked him how old he was.
2. (als Ausruf) how ; ~ **nett von dir!** how kind of you!
◆ konj 1. (zum Vergleich) like ; **so... ~ as...** as ; ~ **ich schon sagte** as I was saying.

2. *(Maßangabe, Qualitätsangabe)* as ; **so viel, ~ möglich** as much as possible ; **und ~!** not half!

wieder *adv* again ; **immer ~** again and again ; **nie ~** never again.

wieder|bekommen *vt unr* to get back.

wieder erkennen *vt unr* to recognize.

wieder finden *vt unr* to find.

wieder|geben *vt unr (zurückgeben)* to give back.

wiederholen *vt (noch einmal)* to repeat ; *(lernen)* to revise. ▪ **sich wiederholen** *ref (Person)* to repeat o.s. ; *(Ereignis)* to recur ; **~ Sie bitte!** could you repeat that please?

Wiederholung *(pl -en) die (von Lernstoff)* revision ; *(von Test, Klasse)* repeat ; *(von Satz)* repetition.

Wiederhören *das* : **auf ~!** *(am Telefon)* bye!

wieder|kommen *vi unr ist (zurückkommen)* to come back ; *(noch einmal kommen)* to come again.

Wiedersehen *(pl -) das* reunion ; **auf ~!** goodbye!

wieder treffen *vt unr* to meet up again.

Wiedervereinigung *(pl -en) die* reunification.

Wiederverwendung *die* reuse.

wiegen *(prät wog, pp gewogen) vi* to weigh. ▪ **sich wie-**

gen *ref (auf Waage)* to weigh o.s.

Wien *nt* Vienna.

Wiener Schnitzel *(pl -) das* Wiener schnitzel *(escalope of veal coated with breadcrumbs)*.

wies *prät* → **weisen**.

Wiese *(pl -n) die* meadow.

wieso *pron* why.

wie viel *pron* how much ; **~ Uhr ist es?** what time is it?

wievielte, r, s *adj* : **das ~ Glas ist das?** how many glasses is that? ; **der Wievielte ist heute?** what's today's date?

wild *adj* wild ; *(heftig)* frenzied. ◆ *adv (unkultiviert)* wild ; *(heftig)* furiously ; *(parken, zelten)* illegally.

Wild *das* game.

Wildbret *das* game.

Wildleder *das* suede.

Wildpark *(pl -s) der* game reserve.

Wildschwein *(pl -e) das* wild boar.

Wildwasser *(pl -) das* white water.

will *präs* → **wollen**.

Wille *der (Absicht)* wishes *(pl)* ; *(Fähigkeit)* will ; **seinen eigenen ~n haben** to have a mind of one's own.

willkommen *adj* welcome ; **herzlich ~!** welcome!

Willkommen *das* welcome.

Wimper *(pl -n) die* eyelash.

Wimperntusche *(pl -n) die* mascara.

Wind (*pl* -e) *der* wind ; starker/
schwacher/böiger ~ strong/
mild/gusty wind.

Windbeutel (*pl* -) *der* ≃
éclair.

Windel (*pl* -n) *die* nappy *(Br)*,
diaper *(Am)*.

winden : sich winden (*prät*
wand, *pp* gewunden) *ref (Weg,
Linie)* to wind.

windgeschützt *adj* sheltered.

windig *adj (Tag, Wetter)*
windy ; es ist ~ it's windy.

Windjacke (*pl* -n) *die* wind-
cheater.

Windmühle (*pl* -n) *die* windmill.

Windpocken *pl* chickenpox
(sg).

Windrichtung (*pl* -en) *die*
wind direction.

Windschutzscheibe (*pl* -n)
die windscreen *(Br)*, windshield *(Am)*.

Windstärke (*pl* -n) *die* force
(of wind).

windstill *adj* still.

Windsurfen *das* windsurfing.

Winkel (*pl* -) *der (von Linien)*
angle ; *(Platz)* corner.

winken (*pp* gewinkt ODER
gewunken) *vi (+D)* to wave ; jm
~ to wave to sb.

Winter (*pl* Winter) *der* winter ; im ~ in winter.

Winterausrüstung (*pl* -en)
die (zum Skifahren) skiing
equipment.

Winterfahrplan (*pl* -pläne)
der winter timetable.

Wintermantel (*pl* -mäntel)
der winter coat.

Winterreifen (*pl* -) *der* winter tyre.

Winterschlussverkauf (*pl*
-verkäufe) *der* January sale.

Wintersport *der* winter
sport.

Winzer, in (*mpl* -) *der, die*
wine grower.

winzig *adj* tiny.

wir *pron* we.

Wirbel (*pl* -) *der (Knochen)*
vertebra ; *(in Wasser)* whirlpool.

Wirbelsäule (*pl* -n) *die* spine.

wirbt *präs* → **werben**.

wird *präs* → **werden**.

wirft *präs* → **werfen**.

wirken *vi (erscheinen)* to
seem ; *(Mittel)* to have an effect ; ~ gegen to counteract.

wirklich *adj* real. ◆ *adv*
really.

Wirklichkeit *die* reality.

wirksam *adj* effective.

Wirkstoff (*pl* -e) *der* active
substance.

Wirkung (*pl* -en) *die (von Mittel)* effect.

Wirsing *der* savoy cabbage.

Wirt, in (*mpl* -e) *der, die (Gastwirt)* landlord (landlady).

Wirtschaft (*pl* -en) *die (Öko-
nomie)* economy ; *(Lokal)* pub.

wirtschaftlich *adj (ökonomisch)* economic.

Wirtschaftspolitik *die* economic policy.

Wirtshaus (*pl* -häuser) *das*
pub, often with accommodation.

Wirtsleute *pl (von Lokal)* landlord and landlady.

Wirtsstube *(pl -n) die* bar.

Wischblatt *(pl -blätter) das* wiper blade.

wischen *vt (Boden, Mund)* to wipe ; *(Schmutz)* to wipe away. ◆ *vi (putzen)* to clean.

wissen *(präs* **weiß**, *prät* **wusste**, *pp* **gewusst**) *vt* to know. ◆ *vi* : **von etw ~** to know about sthg ; **etw ~ über** *(+A)* to know sthg about ; **ich weiß!** I know! ; **weißt du was?** you know what?

Wissenschaft *(pl -en) die* science.

Wissenschaftler, in *(mpl -)* *der, die* scientist.

Witterung *die (Wetter)* weather.

Witwe *(pl -n) die* widow.

Witwer *(pl -) der* widower.

Witz *(pl -e) der* joke.

WM *abk* = **Weltmeisterschaft**.

wo *adv & pron* where ; **von ~ kam das Geräusch?** where did that noise come from?

woanders *adv* somewhere else.

woandershin *adv* somewhere else.

wob *prät* → **weben**.

wobei *pron (als Frage)* : **~ ist er erwischt worden?** what was he caught doing?

Woche *(pl -n) die* week ; **diese/ letzte/nächste ~** this/last/next week.

Wochenende *(pl -n) das* weekend ; **schönes ~!** have a good weekend!

Wochenendtarif *(pl -e) der* weekend rate.

Wochenkarte *(pl -n) die* weekly season ticket.

wochenlang *adj & adv* for weeks.

Wochenmarkt *(pl -märkte) der* weekly market.

Wochentag *(pl -e) der* weekday.

wochentags *adv* on weekdays.

wöchentlich *adj & adv* weekly.

Wodka *(pl -s) der* vodka.

wodurch *pron (als Frage)* : **~ unterscheiden sich die beiden?** what is the difference between the two?

wofür *pron (als Frage)* for what ; **~ hast du das Geld ausgegeben?** what did you spend the money on? ; **~ brauchst du das?** what do you need that for?

wog *prät* → **wiegen**.

Woge *(pl -n) die (im Wasser)* breaker.

wogegen *pron (als Frage)* against what.

woher *pron* from where ; **~ kommen Sie?** where do you come from?

wohin *pron* where.

wohl *(komp* **wohler** ODER **besser**, *superl* **am wohlsten** ODER **am besten**) *adv* well ; *(wahrscheinlich)* probably ; **sich ~ fühlen** *(gesund)* to feel well ; *(angenehm)* to feel at home.

Wohl *das* : **auf Ihr ~!** your good health! ; **zum ~!** cheers!

Wohlstand *der* affluence.

wohl tuend *adj* pleasant.

Wohnanlage (*pl* -n) *die* housing estate.

Wohnblock (*pl* -blöcke) *der* block of flats (*Br*), apartment house (*Am*).

wohnen *vi* (*dauerhaft*) to live; (*vorübergehend*) to stay; **wo ~ Sie?** (*dauerhaft*) where do you live?; (*vorübergehend*) where are you staying?

Wohngemeinschaft (*pl* -en) *die*: **in einer ~ leben** to share a flat/house.

wohnhaft *adj* (*amt*): **~ in...** resident at...

Wohnhaus (*pl* -häuser) *das* house.

Wohnmobil (*pl* -e) *das* camper (van) (*Br*), RV (*Am*).

Wohnort (*pl* -e) *der* place of residence.

Wohnsitz (*pl* -e) *der* (*amt*) place of residence.

Wohnung (*pl* -en) *die* flat (*Br*), apartment (*Am*).

Wohnwagen (*pl* -) *der* caravan (*Br*), trailer (*Am*).

Wohnzimmer (*pl* -) *das* living room.

Wolf (*pl* Wölfe) *der* (*Tier*) wolf.

Wolke (*pl* -n) *die* cloud.

Wolkenbruch (*pl* -brüche) *der* cloudburst.

Wolkenkratzer (*pl* -) *der* skyscraper.

wolkenlos *adj* cloudless.

wolkig *adj* cloudy.

Wolldecke (*pl* -n) *die* blanket.

Wolle *die* wool.

wollen (*präs* will, *prät* wollte, *pp* gewollt ODER wollen) *aux* (*pp* wollen) (*Ausdruck einer Absicht*): **er will anrufen** he wants to make a call; **ich wollte gerade gehen** I was just about to go; **ich wollte, das wäre schon vorbei!** I wish it was over!; **diese Entscheidung will überlegt sein** this decision needs to be thought about.

◆ *vi* (*pp* gewollt) **1.** (*Ausdruck einer Absicht*): **wie du willst!** as you like!; **das Kind will nicht** the child doesn't want to.

2. (*an einen Ort*) to want to go; **sie will nach Hause** she wants to go home.

◆ *vt* (*pp* gewollt) (*haben wollen*) to want; **ich will ein Eis** I want an ice cream; **ich will, dass du gehst** I want you to go.

Wollstoff (*pl* -e) *der* wool.

Wollwaschmittel (*pl* -) *das* detergent for woollens.

womit *pron* (*als Frage*) with what; **~ habe ich das verdient?** what did I do to deserve that?

wonach *pron* (*als Frage*) for what; **~ suchst du?** what are you looking for?

woran *pron* (*als Frage*) on what; **~ denkst du?** what are you thinking about?

worauf *pron* (*als Frage*) on what; **~ wartest du?** what are you waiting for?

woraus *pron* (*als Frage*) from what; **~ ist das?** what is it made of?

worin pron (als Frage) in what ; ~ besteht der Unterschied? what's the difference?

Workshop (pl -s) der workshop.

World Wide Web das (ohne pl) (EDV) World Wide Web ; im ~ on the (World Wide) Web.

Wort[1] (pl Wörter) das (sprachliche Einheit) word.

Wort[2] (pl -e) das (Äußerung, Zusage) word.

Wörterbuch (pl -bücher) das dictionary.

wörtlich adj (Wiederholung) word-for-word ; ~e Rede direct speech.

wortlos adj silent.

worüber pron (als Frage) about what ; ~ lachst du? what are you laughing about?

worum pron (als Frage) about what ; ~ geht es? what's it about?

worunter pron (als Frage) under what ; ~ hast du es eingeordnet? what did you file it under?

wovon pron (als Frage) from what ; ~ hast du geträumt? what did you dream about?

wovor pron (als Frage) of what ; ~ hast du Angst? what are you frightened of?

wozu pron (als Frage) why.

WSV abk = Winterschlussverkauf.

Wucherpreis (pl -e) der extortionate price.

wuchs prät → wachsen.

wühlen vi to rummage.

Wühltisch (pl -e) der bargain counter.

wund adj sore.

Wunde (pl -n) die wound.

wunderbar adj wonderful.

wundern vt to amaze ; es wundert mich I'm amazed. ◼ sich wundern ref to be amazed.

wunderschön adj beautiful.

Wundstarrkrampf der tetanus.

Wunsch (pl Wünsche) der wish ; auf ~ on request ; nach ~ as desired. mit den besten Wünschen von with best wishes from.

wünschen vt to wish ; jm etw ~ to wish sb sthg ; sich (D) etw ~ to want sthg ; was ~ Sie? can I help you?

wünschenswert adj desirable.

wurde prät → werden.

Wurf (pl Würfe) der (Werfen) throw.

Würfel (pl -) der (zum Spielen) dice ; (Form) cube.

würfeln vt (Fleisch, Brot) to dice ; (Zahl) to throw. ◆ vi (beim Spielen) to throw the dice.

Würfelspiel (pl -e) das dice game.

Würfelzucker der sugar cubes (pl).

Wurm (pl Würmer) der (Tier) worm.

Wurst (pl Würste) die sausage.

WURST

Sausages are extremely popular in Germany and there is a wide variety, with every region having its own speciality. Some sausages are always eaten hot - they may be fried, grilled or boiled. These include "Bratwurst", "Bockwurst", "Wiener" and "Frankfurter". Others, such as "Leberwurst" (liver sausage) and "Blutwurst" (black pudding) can be served hot or cold. Cold meats such as salami are also popular and are eaten with bread for supper or even for breakfast.

Wurstbraterei (*pl* -en) *die* hot dog stand.

Würstchen (*pl* -) *das* sausage.

Wurstwaren *pl* sausages and cold meats.

Würze (*pl* -n) *die* (*Gewürz*) spice.

Wurzel (*pl* -n) *die* root.

würzen *vt* (*Speisen*) to season.

würzig *adj* spicy.

Würzmischung (*pl* -en) *die* spice mix.

wusch *prät* → **waschen**.

wusste *prät* → **wissen**.

wüst *adj* (*chaotisch*) chaotic ; (*wild*) wild.

Wüste (*pl* -n) *die* desert.

Wut *die* rage.

wütend *adj* (*Person*) furious ; ~ **sein auf** (+A) to be furious with ; ~ **sein über** (+A) to be furious about.

X

x-beliebig *adj* (*fam*) any (old).

x-mal *adv* (*fam*) countless times.

Y

Yacht (*pl* -en) *die* yacht.

Yachthafen (*pl* -häfen) *der* marina.

Yoga *das* yoga.

Z

zäh *adj* tough. ◆ *adv* : ~ **fließender Verkehr** slow-moving traffic.

Zahl (*pl* -en) *die* number ; (*Ziffer*) figure ; **in den roten/schwarzen ~en sein** to be in the red/black.

zahlbar *adj* payable.

zahlen *vt & vi* to pay ; **ich zahle den Wein** I'll pay for the wine ; ~, **bitte!** the bill please! (*Br*), the check, please! (*Am*).

zählen *vt & vi* to count ; ~ **zu** (*gehören*) to be among.

Zähler (*pl* -) *der* (*Gerät*) meter.

Zahlgrenze (*pl* -n) *die* fare stage.

Zahlkarte (*pl* -n) *die* money transfer form.

zahlreich adj numerous.

Zahlschein (pl -e) der payment slip.

Zahlung (pl -en) die payment.

Zählung (pl -en) die census.

Zahlungsanweisung (pl -en) die money transfer order.

zahm adj (Tier) tame.

Zahn (pl Zähne) der tooth ; sich (D) die Zähne putzen to clean one's teeth ; die dritten Zähne (Gebiss) false teeth.

Zahnarzt, ärztin (mpl -ärzte) der, die dentist.

Zahnbürste (pl -n) die toothbrush.

Zahncreme (pl -s) die toothpaste.

Zahnersatz der false teeth (pl).

Zahnfleisch das gums (pl).

Zahnfleischbluten das bleeding gums (pl).

Zahnfüllung (pl -en) die filling.

Zahnklammer (pl -n) die brace.

Zahnpasta (pl -pasten) die toothpaste.

Zahnradbahn (pl -en) die cog railway.

Zahnschmerzen pl toothache (sg).

Zahnseide (pl -n) die dental floss.

Zahnspange (pl -n) die brace.

Zahnstocher (pl -) der toothpick.

Zange (pl -n) die (Werkzeug) pliers (pl).

zanken vi (fam) to quarrel.
■ **sich zanken** ref (fam) to have a row.

Zäpfchen (pl -) das (Medikament) suppository.

zapfen vt to draw.

Zapfsäule (pl -n) die petrol pump.

zart adj (Fleisch, Gemüse) tender ; (Haut) smooth.

zartbitter adj (Schokolade) dark.

zärtlich adj (Berührung) affectionate.

Zauberer (pl -) der (Zauberkünstler) magician.

zauberhaft adj (sehr schön) enchanting. ◆ adv enchantingly.

Zauberin (pl -nen) die (Zauberkünstlerin) magician.

Zauberkünstler, in (mpl -) der, die magician.

zaubern vi (Zauberer) to do magic.

Zaun (pl Zäune) der fence.

z. B. (abk für zum Beispiel) e.g.

Zebrastreifen (pl -) der zebra crossing (Br), crosswalk (Am).

Zeche (pl -n) die (Bergwerk) pit ; (fam : Rechnung) tab.

Zechtour (pl -en) die (fam) pub crawl.

Zecke (pl -n) die tick.

Zeh (pl -en) der toe.

Zehe (pl -n) die (Zeh) toe ; (von Knoblauch) clove.

Zehennagel (*pl* -nägel) *der* toe nail.

zehn *num* ten ; → **sechs**.

Zehner (*pl* -) *der* (*fam* : *Geldschein*) ten mark note.

Zehnerkarte (*pl* -n) *die* book of ten tickets.

zehnmal *adv* ten times.

Zehnmarkschein (*pl* -e) *der* ten mark note.

zehntausend *num* ten thousand.

zehnte, r, s *adj* tenth ; → sechste.

Zehntel (*pl* -) *das* tenth.

Zehntelsekunde (*pl* -n) *die* tenth of a second.

Zeichen (*pl* -) *das* sign ; jm ein ~ geben to give sb a signal.

Zeichenblock (*pl* -blöcke) *der* drawing pad.

Zeichenerklärung (*pl* -en) *die* key.

Zeichensetzung *die* punctuation.

Zeichensprache (*pl* -n) *die* sign language.

Zeichentrickfilm (*pl* -e) *der* cartoon.

zeichnen *vt* & *vi* to draw.

Zeichnung (*pl* -en) *die* (*Bild*) drawing.

zeigen *vt* to show ; (*vorführen*) to demonstrate. ◆ *vi* : ~ **auf** (+A) to point at ; jm etw ~ to show sb sthg. ■ **sich zeigen** *ref* (*sich herausstellen*) to emerge ; (*erscheinen*) to show o.s.

Zeiger (*pl* -) *der* hand.

Zeile (*pl* -n) *die* (*von Text*) line.

Zeit (*pl* -en) *die* time ; (GRAMM) tense ; sich (D) ~ **lassen** to take one's time ; ~ **haben** to be free ; **zur** ~ at the moment ; **von** ~ **zu** from time to time.

Zeitansage (*pl* -n) *die* speaking clock.

Zeitarbeit *die* temporary work.

Zeitgeist *der* spirit of the times.

zeitig *adj* & *adv* early.

zeitlich *adj* (*Reihenfolge*) chronological.

Zeitlupe *die* slow motion.

Zeitplan (*pl* -pläne) *der* timetable.

Zeitpunkt (*pl* -e) *der* point in time.

Zeitraum (*pl* -räume) *der* period.

Zeitschrift (*pl* -en) *die* (*illustriert*) magazine ; (*literaturwissenschaftlich*) periodical.

Zeitung (*pl* -en) *die* newspaper.

Zeitungsannonce (*pl* -n) *die* newspaper advertisement.

Zeitungsartikel (*pl* -) *der* newspaper article.

Zeitungskiosk (*pl* -e) *der* newspaper kiosk.

Zeitunterschied (*pl* -e) *der* time difference.

Zeitverschiebung (*pl* -en) *die* (*Unterschied*) time difference.

zeitweise *adv* (*gelegentlich*) occasionally ; (*vorübergehend*) temporarily.

Zeitzone (*pl* -n) *die* time zone.

Zelle (*pl* -n) *die (biologisch)* cell.

Zellophan *das* cellophane®.

Zellstoff *der* cellulose.

Zelt (*pl* -e) *das* tent.

zelten *vi* to camp.

Zeltlager (*pl* -) *das* campsite.

Zeltplane (*pl* -n) *die* tarpaulin.

Zeltplatz (*pl* -plätze) *der* campsite.

Zeltstange (*pl* -n) *die* tent pole.

Zentimeter (*pl* -) *der* centimetre.

Zentimetermaß (*pl* -e) *das* tape measure.

Zentner (*pl* -) *der* unit of measurement, equivalent to 50 kg in Germany and 100 kg in Austria and Switzerland.

zentral *adj* central.

Zentrale (*pl* -n) *die (Telefonzentrale)* switchboard ; *(übergeordnete Stelle)* headquarters (*pl*).

Zentralheizung (*pl* -en) *die* central heating.

Zentralverriegelung (*pl* -en) *die* central locking.

Zentrum (*pl* Zentren) *das* centre.

zerbrechen (*präs* zerbricht, *prät* zerbrach, *pp* zerbrochen) *vi* ist & *vt* hat to smash.

zerbrechlich *adj (Gegenstand)* fragile.

Zeremonie (*pl* -en) *die* ceremony.

zerkleinern *vt* to cut up.

zerknautscht *adj* scrunched up.

zerkratzen *vt* to scratch.

zerlassen *adj (Butter)* to melt.

zerlegen *vt (Möbel)* to take apart ; *(Braten)* to carve.

zerreißen (*prät* zerriss, *pp* zerrissen) *vt* hat *(Brief, Stoff)* to tear up. ◆ *vi* ist to tear.

zerren *vt (ziehen)* to drag.

Zerrung (*pl* -en) *die* pulled muscle.

zerschneiden (*prät* zerschnitt, *pp* zerschnitten) *vt (in Stücke)* to cut up.

Zerstäuber (*pl* -) *der* atomizer.

zerstören *vt* to destroy.

Zerstörung (*pl* -en) *die* destruction.

zerstreut *adj* distracted.

zerteilen *vt* to cut up.

Zertifikat (*pl* -e) *das* certificate.

Zettel (*pl* -) *der* note.

Zeug *das (fam : Sachen)* stuff ; *(Kleidung)* gear ; dummes ~ *(fam)* rubbish.

Zeuge (*pl* -n) *der* witness.

Zeugin (*pl* -nen) *die* witness.

Zeugnis (*pl* -se) *das (von Schüler)* report ; *(von Prüfung)* certificate ; *(von Arbeitgeber)* reference.

Zickzack *der* : im ~ fahren to zigzag.

Ziege (*pl* -n) *die (Tier)* goat.

Ziegenkäse *der* goat's cheese.

Ziegenleder *das* goatskin.

ziehen (prät **zog**, pp **gezogen**) vt hat (bewegen, betätigen) to pull ; (herausziehen) to pull out ; (auslosen) to draw. ◆ vi ist (umziehen) to move. ◆ vi hat (bewegen) to pull ; (Tee) to brew. ◆ vimp : **es zieht** there's a draught ; ~ **an** (+D) (bewegen) to pull. ▮ **sich ziehen** ref (fam : zeitlich) to drag on.

Ziehung (pl -**en**) die draw.

Ziel (pl -**e**) das destination ; (SPORT) finish ; (Zweck) goal.

Zielbahnhof (pl -**bahnhöfe**) der destination.

zielen vi (mit Waffe, Ball) to aim.

Zielscheibe (pl -**n**) die target.

ziemlich adv (relativ) quite ; (fast) almost ; ~ **viel** quite a lot.

zierlich adj (Person) petite.

Ziffer (pl -**n**) die (Zahlensymbol) figure.

Zifferblatt (pl -**blätter**) das face.

zig num (fam) umpteen.

Zigarette (pl -**n**) die cigarette.

Zigarettenautomat (pl -**en**) der cigarette machine.

Zigarettenpapier das cigarette paper.

Zigarettenschachtel (pl -**n**) die cigarette packet.

Zigarettentabak (pl -**e**) der tobacco.

Zigarillo (pl -**s**) der cigarillo.

Zigarre (pl -**n**) die cigar.

Zigeuner, in (mpl -) der, die gypsy.

Zimmer (pl -) das room ; '~ frei' 'vacancies' ; ~ **mit Bad** room with en suite bathroom ; ~ **mit Frühstück** bed and breakfast.

Zimmerkellner (pl -) der room-service waiter.

Zimmermädchen (pl -) das chambermaid.

Zimmernachweis (pl -**e**) der accommodation service.

Zimmerpflanze (pl -**n**) die house plant.

Zimmerschlüssel (pl -) der room key.

Zimmerservice der room service.

Zimt der cinnamon.

Zinn das (Metall) tin.

Zins (pl -**en**) der interest.

zinslos adj interest-free.

Zinssatz (pl -**sätze**) der interest rate.

zirka adv circa.

Zirkel (pl -) der (Gerät) compasses (pl).

Zirkus (pl -**se**) der (Betrieb) circus ; (fam : Aufregung) palaver.

zischen vi (Geräusch) to hiss.

Zitat (pl -**e**) das quote.

zitieren vt & vi to quote.

Zitronat das candied lemon peel.

Zitrone (pl -**n**) die lemon.

Zitronensaft (pl -**säfte**) der lemon juice.

Zitruspresse (pl -**n**) die lemon squeezer.

zittern vi (vibrieren) to tremble.

zivil adj (nicht militärisch) civil.

Zivildienst der community work undertaken by men who choose not to do military service.

Zivilisation (pl -en) die civilization.

ZOB (abk für Zentraler Omnibusbahnhof) central bus station.

zog prät → ziehen.

zögern vi to hesitate.

Zoll (pl Zölle) der (Abgabe) duty ; (Behörde) customs (pl).

Zollabfertigung die customs clearance.

Zollamt (pl -ämter) das customs office.

Zollbeamte (pl -n) der customs officer.

Zollbeamtin (pl -nen) die customs officer.

Zollerklärung (pl -en) die customs declaration.

zollfrei adj duty-free.

Zollgebühren pl duty (sg).

Zollkontrolle (pl -n) die customs check.

Zöllner, in (mpl -) der, die customs officer.

zollpflichtig adj liable for duty.

Zollschranke (pl -n) die customs barrier.

Zollstock (pl -stöcke) der ruler.

Zone (pl -n) die (Gebiet) zone.

Zoo (pl -s) der zoo.

zoologische Garten (pl -n Gärten) der zoo.

Zopf (pl Zöpfe) der plait (Br), braid (Am).

Zopfspange (pl -n) die hair slide (Br), barrette (Am).

Zorn der anger.

zornig adj angry. ◆ adv angrily.

zu präp (+D) 1. (an einen Ort) to ; ~r Post gehen to go to the post office ; ~m Friseur gehen to go to the hairdresser's ; ~ Hause home.
2. (Angabe des Mittels) : ~ Fuß on foot ; ~ Fuß gehen to walk.
3. (zeitlich) at ; ~ Ostern/Weihnachten at Easter/Christmas.
4. (mit) with ; weiße Socken ~m Anzug tragen to wear white socks with a suit.
5. (Angabe des Grunds) for ; ~m Spaß for fun ; alles Gute ~m Geburtstag! best wishes on your birthday!
6. (Mengenangabe) : Säcke ~ 50 kg 50 kg bags.
7. (Angabe des Produkts) into ; ~ Eis werden to turn into ice.
8. (SPORT) : eins ~ null one-nil.
◆ adv 1. (mit Adjektiv) too ; ~ viel too many.
2. (fam : zumachen) : Tür ~! shut the door! → zu sein.
◆ konj (mit Infinitiv) to ; es fängt an ~ schneien it's starting to snow ; ~ verkaufen for sale.

Zubehör (pl -e) das accessories (pl).

zubereiten vt to prepare.

Zubereitung (pl -en) die preparation.

zubinden vt unr to fasten.

Zubringer (pl -) der (Straße) slip road (Br), ramp (Am).

Zucchini (pl -s) die courgette (Br), zucchini (Am).

züchten vt to breed.

Züchter, in (mpl -) der, die breeder.

zucken *vi (Person, Muskel)* to twitch.

Zucker *der* sugar.

Zuckerdose *(pl -n) die* sugar bowl.

zuckerkrank *adj* diabetic.

zuckern *vt* to sweeten.

Zuckerwatte *die* candyfloss.

Zuckerzusatz *der* : ohne ~ no added sugar.

zu|decken *vt (Person)* to cover up ; *(Gegenstand)* to cover. ■ **sich zudecken** *ref* to cover o.s. up.

zu|drehen *vt (Wasserhahn)* to turn off.

zueinander *adv (sprechen)* to each other ; **sie passen gut ~** they go well together.

zuerst *adv (als Erster)* first ; *(am Anfang)* at first.

Zufahrt *(pl -en) die* access.

Zufahrtsstraße *(pl -n) die* access road.

Zufall *(pl Zufälle) der* coincidence.

zufällig *adj* chance. ◆ *adv* by chance.

zufrieden *adj* satisfied ; ~ **sein mit** to be satisfied with.

zufrieden stellend *adj* satisfactory.

Zug *(pl Züge) der (Eisenbahn)* train ; *(Menschenmenge)* procession ; *(Zugluft)* draught ; *(mit Spielfigur)* move ; *(Geste)* gesture ; **mit dem ~ fahren** to go by train.

Zugabe *(pl -n) die (bei Konzert)* encore.

Zugabteil *(pl -e) das* compartment.

Zugang *(pl -gänge) der* access.

Zugauskunft *(pl -auskünfte) die* train information.

Zugbegleiter *(pl -) der (Fahrplanauszug)* timetable.

Zugbrücke *(pl -n) die* drawbridge.

zu|geben *vi unr (gestehen)* to admit ; *(hinzutun)* to add.

zu|gehen *vi unr ist (sich schließen)* to close ; ~ **auf** *(+A) (gehen)* to approach.

Zügel *(pl -) der* reins *(pl).*

Zuger Kirschtorte *(pl -n) die (Schweiz)* buttercream cake with a middle layer of sponge soaked in kirsch and a top and bottom layer of nut meringue.

Zugführer, in *(mpl -) der, die* senior conductor.

zugig *adj* draughty.

zügig *adj* rapid. ◆ *adv* rapidly.

Zugluft *die* draught.

Zugpersonal *das* train crew.

zu|greifen *vi unr* : **greifen Sie zu!** help yourself!

Zugrestaurant *(pl -s) das* restaurant car.

zugrunde *adv* : ~ **gehen** to perish.

Zugschaffner, in *(mpl -) der, die* ticket inspector.

Zugunglück *(pl -e) das* train crash.

zugunsten *präp (+G)* in favour of.

Zugverbindung *(pl -en) die* (train) connection.

zu|haben *vi unr (fam)* to be shut.

Zuhause *das* home.

zu|hören *vi (+D)* to listen ; jm ~ to listen to sb.

Zuhörer, in *(mpl -) der, die* listener.

zu|kleben *vt (Loch)* to glue ; *(Brief)* to seal.

zu|kommen *vi unr ist* : ~ auf *(+A) (Person, Fahrzeug)* to approach.

zu|kriegen *vt (fam)* : ich krieg' die Tür nicht zu the door won't shut.

Zukunft *die* future.

zu|lassen *vt unr (erlauben)* to allow ; *(Auto)* to license ; *(fam : nicht öffnen)* : lass das Paket bis Weihnachten zu! don't open the parcel till Christmas!

zulässig *adj* permissable ; ~e Höchstgeschwindigkeit maximum speed limit ; ~es Gesamtgewicht maximum weight limit.

Zulassung *(pl -en) die* authorization.

zu|laufen *vi unr ist (Tier)* : der Hund ist uns zugelaufen the dog adopted us ; ~ auf *(+A) (Person)* to run towards.

zuletzt *adv (als Letzter)* lastly ; *(am Ende)* in the end, finally ; *(fam : das letzte Mal)* : ~ war ich vor 3 Jahren hier I was last here three years ago.

zuliebe *präp (+D)* : ihr ~ for her sake.

zum *präp* = zu + dem.

zu|machen *vt & vi* to close.

zu|muten *vt* : jm etw ~ to expect sthg of sb.

zunächst *adv (als Erster)* first ; *(am Anfang)* at first.

Zuname *(pl -n) der* surname.

zünden *vi (Motor)* to fire.

Zündholz *(pl -hölzer) das* match.

Zündkerze *(pl -n) die* spark plug.

Zündschloss *(pl -schlösser) das* ignition.

Zündschlüssel *(pl -) der* ignition key.

Zündung *(pl -en) die (AUTO)* ignition.

zu|nehmen *vi unr* to increase ; *(dicker werden)* to put on weight.

Zunge *(pl -n) die* tongue.

zupfen *vi (ziehen)* to tug. ◆ *vt (herausziehen)* to pick ; *(Augenbrauen)* to pluck.

zur *präp* = zu + der.

Zürich *nt* Zürich.

zurück *adv* back.

zurück|bekommen *vt unr* to get back.

zurück|bringen *vt unr* to bring back.

zurück|erstatten *vt* to refund.

zurück|fahren *vi unr ist & vt unr hat (an Ausgangspunkt)* to drive back ; *(rückwärts)* to back away.

zurück|führen *vt (begründen)* to attribute. ◆ *vi (Weg, Straße)* to lead back.

zurück|geben vt unr to give back ; jm etw ~ to give sb sthg back.

zurück|gehen vi unr ist (zum Ausgangspunkt) to go back ; (rückwärts) to retreat ; (Anzahl, Häufigkeit) to fall.

zurück|halten vt unr (festhalten) to hold back. ■ **sich zurückhalten** ref to restrain o.s.

zurück|holen vt to bring back.

zurück|kommen vi unr ist to come back.

zurück|lassen vt unr to leave behind.

zurück|legen vt (wieder hinlegen) to put back ; (reservieren) to put aside ; (Strecke) to cover ; (Kopf) to lay back ; etw ~ lassen (reservieren) to have sthg put aside. ■ **sich zurücklegen** ref to lie back.

zurück|nehmen vt unr to take back.

zurück|rufen vt unr & vi to call back.

zurück|schicken vt to send back.

zurück|stellen vt to put back.

zurück|treten vi unr ist (rückwärts) to step back ; (Präsident, Vorstand) to resign ; bitte ~! stand back, please!

zurück|verlangen vt to demand back.

zurück|zahlen vt (Geld) to pay back.

Zusage (pl -n) die (auf Einladung, Bewerbung) acceptance.

zu|sagen vt (bei Einladung) to accept.

zusammen adv together ; (insgesamt) altogether.

Zusammenarbeit die collaboration.

zusammen|brechen vi unr ist (Person) to collapse ; (psychisch, Verkehr) to break down.

zusammen|fassen vt (Text) to summarize.

Zusammenfassung (pl -en) die summary.

zusammen|gehören vt to belong together.

zusammen|halten vi unr (Personen) to stick together.

Zusammenhang (pl -hänge) der context.

zusammenhängend adj (Text) coherent.

zusammenhanglos adj incoherent.

zusammenklappbar adj collapsible.

zusammen|knüllen vt to scrunch up.

Zusammenkunft (pl -künfte) die gathering.

zusammen|legen vt (Gruppen, Termine) to group together ; (falten) to fold up. ◆ vi (bezahlen) to club together.

zusammen|nehmen : sich zusammennehmen ref unr to pull o.s. together.

zusammen|passen vi (Personen) to be well suited ; (Einzelteile) to fit together.

zusammen|rechnen vt to add up.

Zusammensetzung *(pl* -en*)*
die composition.

Zusammenstoß *(pl* -stöße*)*
der crash.

zusammen|stoßen *vi unr*
ist (Fahrzeuge) to crash.

zusammen|zählen *vt* to
add up.

zusammen|ziehen *vt unr*
hat (addieren) to add up. ◆ *vi unr*
ist (in Wohnung) to move in together.

zusammen|zucken *vi ist* to
jump.

Zusatz *(pl* Zusätze*) der (Subs-*
tanz) additive.

Zusatzgerät *(pl* -e*) das* attachment.

zusätzlich *adj* extra. ◆ *adv* in
addition.

Zusatzzahl *(pl* -en*) die* bonus
number.

zu|schauen *vi* to watch.

Zuschauer, in *(mpl* -*) der, die*
(von Fernsehen) viewer ; *(von*
Sport) spectator.

Zuschauertribüne *(pl* -n*)*
die stands *(pl)*.

zu|schicken *vt* to send.

Zuschlag *(pl* Zuschläge*) der*
supplement ; ~ erforderlich supplement required.

zuschlagpflichtig *adj* subject to a supplement.

zu|schließen *vt unr* to lock.

Zuschuss *(pl* Zuschüsse*) der*
grant.

zu|sehen *vi unr (zuschauen)* to
watch.

zu|sein *vi unr ist* to be closed.

zu|sichern *vt* to assure.

Zustand *(pl* Zustände*) der*
state, condition. ▓ **Zustände**
pl situation *(sg)*.

zuständig *adj* responsible ; ~
sein für to be responsible for.

zu|steigen *vi unr ist* to get on ;
noch jemand zugestiegen? tickets, please.

Zustellung *(pl* -en*) die (von*
Post) delivery.

zu|stimmen *vi (+D)* to agree ;
er stimmte dem Plan zu he agreed
to the plan.

Zustimmung *die* agreement.

zu|stoßen *vi unr ist* : was ist
ihm zugestoßen? what happened to him?

Zutat *(pl* -en*) die* ingredient.

zu|teilen *vt (Ration)* to allo-
cate.

zu|trauen *vt* : jm etw ~ to think
sb capable of sthg.

zu|treffen *vi unr* to apply ; 'Zu-
treffendes bitte ankreuzen' 'tick
as applicable'.

Zutritt *der* entry.

zuverlässig *adj* reliable.

zu viel *pron* too much.

Zuwachs *der* growth.

zu|weisen *vt unr* to allocate.

zu wenig *pron* too little.

zu|winken *vi (+D)* : jm ~ to
wave to sb.

zu|zahlen *vt* : 5 Mark ~ to pay
another 5 marks.

zuzüglich *präp (+G or D)* plus.

zwang *prät* → zwingen.

Zwang *(pl* Zwänge*) der* force.

zwanglos *adj* relaxed.

zwanzig *num* twenty ; →
sechs.

Zwanziger (*pl* -) *der* (*Person*) someone in their twenties ; (*Geld*) twenty mark note.

Zwanzigmarkschein (*pl* -e) *der* twenty mark note.

zwanzigste, r, s *adj* twentieth ; das ~ Jahrhundert the twentieth century.

zwar *adv* : und ~ (*genauer*) to be exact ; das ist ~ schön, aber viel zu teuer it is nice but far too expensive.

Zweck (*pl* -e) *der* purpose ; es hat keinen ~ there's no point.

zwecklos *adj* pointless.

zweckmäßig *adj* practical.

zwei *num* two ; → sechs.

Zweibettabteil (*pl* -e) *das* compartment with two beds.

Zweibettkabine (*pl* -n) *die* cabin with two beds.

Zweibettzimmer (*pl* -) *das* twin room.

zweifach *adj* twice.

Zweifel (*pl* -) *der* doubt ; ohne ~ without doubt ; ~ haben an (+D) to doubt.

zweifellos *adv* doubtless.

zweifeln *vi* to doubt ; an etw (D) ~ to doubt sthg.

Zweig (*pl* -e) *der* branch.

Zweigstelle (*pl* -n) *die* branch.

zweihundert *num* two hundred.

Zweihundertmarkschein (*pl* -e) *der* two hundred mark note.

zweimal *adv* twice.

Zweimarkstück (*pl* -stücke) *das* two mark coin.

Zweirad (*pl* -räder) *das* two-wheeled vehicle.

zweisprachig *adj* bilingual.

zweispurig *adj* two-lane.

zweit *adv* : sie waren nur zu ~ there were only two of them.

Zweitakter (*pl* -) *der* two-stroke engine.

Zweitakter-Gemisch *das* two-stroke mixture.

zweitbeste, r, s *adj* second best.

zweite, r, s *adj* second ; → sechs.

zweiteilig *adj* two-part.

zweitens *adv* secondly.

Zwerchfell (*pl* -e) *das* diaphragm.

Zwerg (*pl* -e) *der* dwarf.

Zwetschge (*pl* -n) *die* (*Frucht*) plum.

Zwetschgendatschi (*pl* -) *der* (*Süddt*) plum slice.

Zwieback (*pl* -bäcke) *der* rusk.

Zwiebel (*pl* -n) *die* (*Gemüse*) onion.

Zwiebelsuppe (*pl* -n) *die* onion soup.

Zwilling (*pl* -e) *der* (*Geschwister*) twin ; (*Sternzeichen*) Gemini.

zwingen (*prät* zwang, *pp* gezwungen) *vt* to force. ■ **sich zwingen** *ref* to force o.s.

zwinkern *vi* to wink.

Zwirn *der* thread.

zwischen *präp* (+A,D) between ; (*in Menge*) among.

zwischendurch *adv* (*zeitlich*) every now and then.

Zwischenfall (*pl* -fälle) *der* incident.

Zwischenlandung (*pl* -en) *die* short stopover.

Zwischenraum (*pl* -räume) *der* gap.

Zwischenstecker (*pl* -) *der* adapter.

Zwischenstopp (*pl* -s) *der* stop.

Zwischensumme (*pl* -n) *die* subtotal.

Zwischenzeit *die* : in der ~ in the meantime.

zwölf *num* twelve ; →**sechs**.

zynisch *adj* cynical.